8.3 Why might an appliance retailer instruct its clerks to hammer dents into the sides of its stoves and refrigerators?
9.1 Why are cartel agreements notoriously unstable?
9.2 How did Congress unwittingly solve the television advertising dilemma confronting cigarette producers?
9.3 Why do people shout at parties?
9.4 Why do we often see convenience stores on adjacent street corners?
10.1 What is the purpose of free speech laws?
10.2 Why does the government subsidize private property owners to plant trees on their hillsides?
10.3 Why do blackberries in public parks get picked too soon?
10.4 Why are shared milkshakes consumed too quickly?
10.5 Why do football players take anabolic steroids?
11.1 Why is a patient with a sore knee more likely to receive an MRI exam if he has conventional health insurance than if he belongs to a health maintenance organization?
11.2 In the richest country on Earth, why do so many people lack basic health insurance?
12.1 Why has female participation in the labor market increased by so much?
12.2 Can nominal and real GDP ever move in different directions?
12.3 Why do people work fewer hours today than their great-grandparents did?
12.4 Why do far fewer children complete high school in poor countries than in rich countries?
15.1 Why did medieval China stagnate economically?
15.2 Why do almost all countries provide free public education?
16.1 Why has investment in computers increased so much in recent decades?
17.1 Why did the U.S. stock market rise sharply in the 1990s, then fall in the new millennium?
18.1 Why did the Coca-Cola Company test a vending machine that "knows" when the weather is hot?
19.1 Why did Japan build roads that nobody wanted to use?
20.1 Why does news of inflation hurt the stock market?
20.2 Why does the average Argentine hold more U.S. dollars than the average U.S. citizen?

PRINCIPLES OF ECONOMICS

Brief Edition

THE McGRAW-HILL SERIES IN ECONOMICS

Essentials of Economics

Brue, McConnell, and Flynn
Essentials of Economics
Second Edition

Mandel
Economics: The Basics
First Edition

Schiller
Essentials of Economics
Seventh Edition

Principles of Economics

Colander
Economics, Microeconomics, and Macroeconomics
Seventh Edition

Frank and Bernanke
Principles of Economics, Principles of Microeconomics, Principles of Macroeconomics
Fourth Edition

Frank and Bernanke
Brief Editions: Principles of Economics, Principles of Microeconomics, Principles of Macroeconomics
First Edition

McConnell, Brue, and Flynn
Economics, Microeconomics, and Macroeconomics
Eighteenth Edition

McConnell, Brue, and Flynn
Brief Editions: Economics, Microeconomics, Macroeconomics
First Edition

Miller
Principles of Microeconomics
First Edition

Samuelson and Nordhaus
Economics, Microeconomics, and Macroeconomics
Eighteenth Edition

Schiller
The Economy Today, The Micro Economy Today, and The Macro Economy Today
Eleventh Edition

Slavin
Economics, Microeconomics, and Macroeconomics
Ninth Edition

Economics of Social Issues

Guell
Issues in Economics Today
Fourth Edition

Sharp, Register, and Grimes
Economics of Social Issues
Eighteenth Edition

Econometrics

Gujarati and Porter
Basic Econometrics
Fifth Edition

Gujarati and Porter
Essentials of Econometrics
Fourth Edition

Managerial Economics

Baye
Managerial Economics and Business Strategy
Sixth Edition

Brickley, Smith, and Zimmerman
Managerial Economics and Organizational Architecture
Fifth Edition

Thomas and Maurice
Managerial Economics
Ninth Edition

Intermediate Economics

Bernheim and Whinston
Microeconomics
First Edition

Dornbusch, Fischer, and Startz
Macroeconomics
Tenth Edition

Frank
Microeconomics and Behavior
Seventh Edition

Advanced Economics

Romer
Advanced Macroeconomics
Third Edition

Money and Banking

Cecchetti
Money, Banking, and Financial Markets
Second Edition

Urban Economics

O'Sullivan
Urban Economics
Seventh Edition

Labor Economics

Borjas
Labor Economics
Fourth Edition

McConnell, Brue, and Macpherson
Contemporary Labor Economics
Eighth Edition

Public Finance

Rosen and Gayer
Public Finance
Eighth Edition

Seidman
Public Finance
First Edition

Environmental Economics

Field and Field
Environmental Economics: An Introduction
Fifth Edition

International Economics

Appleyard, Field, and Cobb
International Economics
Sixth Edition

King and King
International Economics, Globalization, and Policy: A Reader
Fifth Edition

Pugel
International Economics
Fourteenth Edition

PRINCIPLES OF ECONOMICS

Brief Edition

ROBERT H. FRANK
Cornell University

BEN S. BERNANKE
Princeton University [affiliated]
Chairman, Board of Governors of the Federal Reserve System

with special contribution by

LOUIS D. JOHNSTON
College of Saint Benedict | Saint John's University

McGraw-Hill Irwin

Boston Burr Ridge, IL Dubuque, IA New York San Francisco St. Louis
Bangkok Bogotá Caracas Kuala Lumpur Lisbon London Madrid Mexico City
Milan Montreal New Delhi Santiago Seoul Singapore Sydney Taipei Toronto

McGraw-Hill Irwin

PRINCIPLES OF ECONOMICS BRIEF EDITION

Published by McGraw-Hill/Irwin, a business unit of The McGraw-Hill Companies, Inc., 1221 Avenue of the Americas, New York, NY, 10020.

This book is printed on acid-free paper.

1 2 3 4 5 6 7 8 9 0 QPD/QPD 0 9 8

ISBN 978-0-07-337587-8
MHID 0-07-337587-X

Design of book: The images in the design of this book are based on elements of the architecture of Frank Lloyd Wright, specifically from the leaded glass windows seen in many of his houses. Wright's design was rooted in nature and based on simplicity and harmony. His windows use elemental geometry to abstract natural forms, complementing and framing the natural world outside. This concept of seeing the world through an elegantly structured framework ties in nicely to the idea of framing one's view of the world through the window of economics.

The typeface used for some of the elements was taken from the Arts and Crafts movement. The typeface, as well as the color palette, brings in the feeling of that movement in a way that complements the geometric elements of Wright's windows. The Economic Naturalist icon is visually set apart from the more geometric elements but is a representation of the inspirational force behind all of Wright's work.

Editor-in-chief: *Brent Gordon*
Publisher: *Douglas Reiner*
Developmental editor: *Angela Cimarolli*
Senior marketing manager: *Melissa Larmon*
Senior project manager: *Susanne Riedell*
Production supervisor: *Gina Hangos*
Lead designer: *Matthew Baldwin*
Senior photo research coordinator: *Jeremy Cheshareck*
Photo researcher: *Robin Sand*
Senior media project manager: *Cathy Tepper*
Cover design: *Matt Diamond*
Cover image: © *Jill Braaten*
Typeface: *10/12 Sabon Roman*
Compositor: *Aptara®, Inc.*
Printer: *Quebecor World Dubuque Inc.*

Library of Congress Cataloging-in-Publication Data

Frank, Robert H.
Principles of economics / Robert H. Frank, Ben S. Bernanke; with special contribution by Louis D. Johnston.—Brief ed.
p. cm.—(The McGraw-Hill series in economics)
Includes index.
ISBN-13: 978-0-07-337587-8 (alk. paper)
ISBN-10: 0-07-337587-X (alk. paper)
1. Economics. I. Bernanke, Ben S. II. Johnston, Louis (Louis Dorrance) III. Title.
HB171.5.F7343 2009
330—dc22

2008034339

DEDICATION

For Ellen

R. H. F.

For Anna

B. S. B.

ABOUT THE AUTHORS

ROBERT H. FRANK

Professor Frank is the Henrietta Johnson Louis Professor of Management and Professor of Economics at the Johnson Graduate School of Management at Cornell University, where he has taught since 1972. His "Economic View" column appears regularly in *The New York Times*. After receiving his B.S. from Georgia Tech in 1966, he taught math and science for two years as a Peace Corps Volunteer in rural Nepal. He received his M.A. in statistics in 1971 and his Ph.D. in economics in 1972 from The University of California at Berkeley. During leaves of absence from Cornell, he has served as chief economist for the Civil Aeronautics Board (1978–1980), a Fellow at the Center for Advanced Study in the Behavioral Sciences (1992–93), and Professor of American Civilization at l'École des Hautes Études en Sciences Sociales in Paris (2000–01).

Professor Frank is the author of a best-selling intermediate economics textbook—*Microeconomics and Behavior*, Seventh Edition (Irwin/McGraw-Hill, 2008). He has published on a variety of subjects, including price and wage discrimination, public utility pricing, the measurement of unemployment spell lengths, and the distributional consequences of direct foreign investment. His research has focused on rivalry and cooperation in economic and social behavior. His books on these themes, which include *Choosing the Right Pond* (Oxford, 1995), *Passions Within Reason* (W. W. Norton, 1988), *What Price the Moral High Ground?* (Princeton, 2004), *The Economic Naturalist* (Basic Books, 2007), and *Falling Behind* (University of California Press, 2007), have been translated into 15 languages. *The Winner-Take-All Society* (The Free Press, 1995), co-authored with Philip Cook, received a Critic's Choice Award, was named a Notable Book of the Year by *The New York Times*, and was included in *BusinessWeek*'s list of the 10 best books of 1995. *Luxury Fever* (The Free Press, 1999) was named to the *Knight-Ridder* Best Books list for 1999.

Professor Frank has been awarded an Andrew W. Mellon Professorship (1987–1990), a Kenan Enterprise Award (1993), and a Merrill Scholars Program Outstanding Educator Citation (1991). He is a co-recipient of the 2004 Leontief Prize for Advancing the Frontiers of Economic Thought. He was awarded the Johnson School's Stephen Russell Distinguished Teaching Award in 2004 and the School's Apple Distinguished Teaching Award in 2005. His introductory microeconomics course has graduated more than 7,000 enthusiastic economic naturalists over the years.

BEN S. BERNANKE

Professor Bernanke received his B.A. in economics from Harvard University in 1975 and his Ph.D. in economics from MIT in 1979. He taught at the Stanford Graduate School of Business from 1979 to 1985 and moved to Princeton University in 1985, where he was named the Howard Harrison and Gabrielle Snyder Beck Professor of Economics and Public Affairs, and where he served as Chairman of the Economics Department.

Professor Bernanke was sworn in on February 1, 2006, as Chairman and a member of the Board of Governors of the Federal Reserve System. Professor Bernanke also serves as Chairman of the Federal Open Market Committee, the System's principal monetary policymaking body. He was appointed as a member of the Board to a full 14-year term, which expires January 31, 2020, and to a four-year term as Chairman, which expires January 31, 2010. Before his appointment as Chairman, Professor Bernanke was Chairman of the President's Council of Economic Advisers, from June 2005 to January 2006.

Professor Bernanke's intermediate textbook, with Andrew Abel, *Macroeconomics*, Sixth Edition (Addison-Wesley, 2008), is a best seller in its field. He has authored more than 50 scholarly publications in macroeconomics, macroeconomic history, and finance. He has done significant research on the causes of the Great Depression, the role of financial markets and institutions in the business cycle, and measuring the effects of monetary policy on the economy.

Professor Bernanke has held a Guggenheim Fellowship and a Sloan Fellowship, and he is a Fellow of the Econometric Society and of the American Academy of Arts and Sciences. He served as the Director of the Monetary Economics Program of the National Bureau of Economic Research (NBER) and as a member of the NBER's Business Cycle Dating Committee. In July 2001, he was appointed editor of the *American Economic Review*. Professor Bernanke's work with civic and professional groups includes having served two terms as a member of the Montgomery Township (N.J.) Board of Education.

PREFACE

Although many millions of dollars are spent each year on introductory economics instruction in American colleges and universities, the return on this investment has been disturbingly low. Studies have shown, for example, that several months after having taken a principles of economics course, former students are no better able to answer simple economic questions than others who never even took the course. Most students, it seems, leave our introductory courses without having learned even the most important basic economic principles.

The problem, in our view, is that these courses almost always try to teach students far too much. In the process, really important ideas get little more coverage than minor ones, and everything ends up going by in a blur. Many instructors ask themselves, "How much can I cover today?" when instead they should be asking, "How much can my students absorb?"

Our textbook grew out of our conviction that students will learn far more if we attempt to cover much less, and this Brief Edition only further supports our goal. Our basic premise is that a small number of basic principles do most of the heavy lifting in economics, and that if we focus narrowly and repeatedly on those principles, students can actually master them in just a single semester.

The enthusiastic reactions of users of the first four editions of the full principles books we authored affirm the validity of this premise. We have constructed *Principles of Economics,* Brief Edition to support a concise approach to teaching economics by focusing on the most imperative information. Avoiding excessive reliance on formal mathematical derivations, we present concepts intuitively through examples drawn from familiar contexts. We rely throughout on a well-articulated list of seven core principles, which we reinforce repeatedly by illustrating and applying each principle in numerous contexts. We ask students periodically to apply these principles themselves to answer related questions, exercises, and problems.

Throughout this process, we encourage students to become "economic naturalists," people who employ basic economic principles to understand and explain what they observe in the world around them. An economic naturalist understands, for example, that infant safety seats are required in cars but not in airplanes because the marginal cost of space to accommodate these seats is typically zero in cars but often hundreds of dollars in airplanes. Scores of such examples are sprinkled throughout the book. Each one, we believe, poses a question that should make any normal, curious person eager to learn the answer. These examples stimulate interest while teaching students to see each feature of their economic landscape as the reflection of one or more of the core principles. Students talk about these examples with their friends and families. Learning economics is like learning a language. In each case, there is no substitute for actually speaking. By inducing students to speak economics, the economic naturalist examples serve this purpose.

For those who would like to learn more about the role of examples in learning economics, Bob Frank's lecture on this topic is posted on YouTube's "Authors @ Google" series (**http://www.youtube.com/watch? v=QalNVxeIKEE** or search "Authors @ Google Robert Frank").

FEATURES OF THE BRIEF EDITION

- **An emphasis on seven core principles:** As noted, a few core principles do most of the work in economics. By focusing almost exclusively on these principles, the text assures that students leave the course with a deep mastery of them. In contrast, traditional encyclopedic texts so overwhelm students with detail that they often leave the course with little useful working knowledge at all.

Scarcity

1 **The Scarcity Principle:** Having more of one good thing usually means having less of another.

Cost-Benefit

2 **The Cost-Benefit Principle:** Take no action unless its marginal benefit is at least as great as its marginal cost.

Incentive

3 **The Incentive Principle:** Cost-benefit comparisons are relevant not only for identifying the decisions that rational people should make, but also for predicting the actual decisions they do make.

Comparative Advantage

4 **The Principle of Comparative Advantage:** Everyone does best when each concentrates on the activity for which he or she is relatively most productive.

Increasing Opportunity Cost

5 **The Principle of Increasing Opportunity Cost:** Use the resources with the lowest opportunity cost before turning to those with higher opportunity costs.

Efficiency

6 **The Efficiency Principle:** Efficiency is an important social goal because when the economic pie grows larger, everyone can have a larger slice.

Equilibrium

7 **The Equilibrium Principle:** A market in equilibrium leaves no unexploited opportunities for individuals but may not exploit all gains achievable through collective action.

- **Economic naturalism:** Our ultimate goal is to produce economic naturalists—people who see each human action as the result of an implicit or explicit cost-benefit calculation. The economic naturalist sees mundane details of ordinary existence in a new light and becomes actively engaged in the attempt to understand them. Some representative examples:

In Micro:

- Why are whales and elephants, but not chickens, threatened with extinction?
- Why do we often see convenience stores located on adjacent street corners?
- Why do supermarket checkout lines all tend to be roughly the same length?

In Macro:

- Why has investment in computers increased so much in recent decades?
- Why does news of inflation hurt the stock market?
- Why did Japan build roads that nobody wants to use?

- **Active learning stressed:** The only way to learn to hit an overhead smash in tennis is through repeated practice. The same is true for learning economics. Accordingly, we consistently introduce new ideas in the context of simple examples and then follow them with applications showing how they work in familiar settings. At frequent intervals, we pose exercises that both test and reinforce the understanding of these ideas. The end-of-chapter questions and problems are carefully crafted to help students internalize and extend core concepts. Experience with our first three editions confirms that this approach really does prepare students to apply basic economic principles to solve economic puzzles drawn from the real world.

- **Modern Microeconomics:** *Economic surplus,* introduced in Chapter 1 and employed repeatedly thereafter, is more fully developed here than in any other text. This concept underlies the argument for economic efficiency as an important social goal. Rather than speak of trade-offs between efficiency and other goals, we stress that maximizing economic surplus facilitates the achievement of *all* goals. *Common decision pitfalls* identified by 2002 Nobel Laureate Daniel Kahneman and others—such as the tendency to ignore implicit costs, the tendency not to ignore sunk costs, and the tendency to confuse average and marginal costs and benefits—are introduced early in Chapter 1 and invoked repeatedly in subsequent chapters.

  There is perhaps no more exciting toolkit for the economic naturalist than a few *principles of elementary game theory.* In Chapter 9, we show how these principles enable students to answer a variety of strategic questions that arise in the marketplace and everyday life. We believe that the insights of the Nobel Laureate Ronald Coase are indispensable for understanding a host of familiar laws, customs, and social norms. In Chapter 10 we show how such devices function to minimize misallocations that result from externalities. A few simple principles from the *economics of information* form another exciting addition to the economic naturalist's toolkit. In Chapter 11 we show how the insights that earned the 2001 Nobel Prize in economics for George Akerlof, Joseph Stiglitz, and Michael Spence can be employed to answer a variety of questions from everyday experience.

- **Modern Macroeconomics:** Recent developments have renewed interest in cyclical fluctuations without challenging the importance of such long-run issues as growth, productivity, the evolution of real wages, and capital formation. Our treatment of these issues is organized as follows:

  - A three-chapter treatment of long-run issues, followed by a modern treatment of short-term fluctuations and stabilization policy, emphasizing the important distinction between short- and long-run behavior of the economy.
  - Consistent with both media reporting and recent research on monetary policy rules, we treat the interest rate rather than the money supply as the primary instrument of Fed policy.
  - The analysis of aggregate demand and aggregate supply relates output to inflation, rather than to the price level, sidestepping the necessity of a separate derivation of the link between the output gap and inflation.
  - This book places a heavy emphasis on globalization, starting with an analysis of its effects on real wage inequality and progressing to such issues as the benefits of trade, the causes and effects of protectionism, the role of capital flows in domestic capital formation, and the links between exchange rates and monetary policy.

STRENGTHS OF THE BRIEF EDITION

IN MICROECONOMICS

- **More and clearer emphasis on the core principles:** If we asked a thousand economists to provide their own versions of the most important economic principles, we'd get a thousand different lists. Yet to dwell on their differences would be to miss their essential similarities. It is less important to have exactly the best short list of principles than it is to use some well-thought-out list of this sort.

- Outsourcing discussion supports comparative advantage material in Chapter 2. Students will see a full-spectrum view of production possibilities and the realities economies face considering outsourcing decisions.
- Chapter 7 makes strong connections among market equilibrium and efficiency, the cost of preventing price adjustments, economic profit, and the Invisible Hand theory.
- Chapter 11 features important policy decisions and uses economics to sort out the best options. Health care, environmental regulation, international trade, and income redistribution are all discussed in this relevant and interesting chapter.

IN MACROECONOMICS

- **Flexible, modular presentation:** Part 5, "Macroeconomics: Data and Issues," is a self-contained group of chapters that covers measurement issues. This allows instructors to proceed to either the long run (Part 6, "The Economy in the Long Run") or the short run (Part 7, "The Economy in the Short Run) first with no loss of continuity.
- **Thorough discussion of labor markets:** Labor market trends in employment, wages, and unemployment are covered together in Chapter 14 to help students fully understand the connections between all three topics.
- **Strong connection drawn between financial markets and money:** Chapter 17 brings together information on financial intermediaries, bond and stock markets, and money so that students can make the connections among stock markets, bond markets, commercial banks, and money.
- **Clear discussion of output gaps and Okun's Law:** The output gap is written as $Y - Y^*$ so that when actual output is below potential output, the output gap is a negative number. This allows us to develop Okun's Law as a negative relationship between the output gap and cyclical unemployment.
- **The simple Keynesian model:** We present the simple Keynesian model through examples that are developed both graphically and numerically.
- **Monetary Policy coverage organization:** The institutional details of the Federal Reserve are discussed at the beginning of Chapter 20, followed by the effects of Federal Reserve policy on planned aggregate expenditure. The money market is also discussed, but instructors who wish to skip this material can easily do so. In addition, the effects of monetary policy are summarized using logic chains that students can easily understand. Finally, the relationship between output gaps and monetary policy that we discuss using the simple Keynesian model is used to motivate the Fed's monetary policy rule.
- **The presentation of Aggregate Demand and Aggregate Supply:** Chapter 21 gives students a thorough understanding of both the theory and application of the AD-AS model. We develop carefully the reasoning behind the *AD* curve and the *AS* curve. In particular:

- We develop the *AD* curve by tracing the effects of the Fed's monetary policy rule on short-run spending and output.
- The *AS* curve is an upward-sloping curve with inflation on the vertical axis. This provides the advantage of placing inflationary expectations at the center of the story of how the economy's self-correcting mechanism works and how Federal Reserve credibility affects short-run and long-run equilibrium.
- We provide students with a series of examples that show how the *AD* curve and the *AS* curve work together to determine short-run equilibrium and how the economy adjusts to long-run equilibrium.

We also apply the AD-AS model to macroeconomic policy. Specifically, we examine monetary policy with a focus on whether or not the Fed should accommodate spending shocks and inflation shocks and discuss supply-side effects of fiscal policy with a focus on how changes in marginal tax rates can affect labor supply and hence potential output. Finally, we use what students have learned to address important current topics such as anchored inflationary expectations, central bank independence, and inflation targeting.

- **Flexible coverage of international economics:** Chapter 22 is a self-contained discussion of exchange rates that can be used whenever an instructor thinks it best to introduce this important subject. This chapter also integrates the discussion of trade and capital flows so that students see that the balance of trade and net capital inflows are two sides of the same issue.

ORGANIZED LEARNING IN THE BRIEF EDITION

- **Chapter learning objectives:** Students and professors can be confident that the organization of each chapter surrounds common themes outlined by five to seven learning objectives listed on the first page of each chapter. These objectives, along with AASCB and Bloom's Taxonomy Learning Categories, are connected to all Test Bank questions and end-of-chapter material to offer a comprehensive, thorough teaching and learning experience.
- **Assurance of learning ready:** Many educational institutions today are focused on the notion of assurance of learning, an important element of some accreditation standards. *Principles of Economics*, Brief Edition is designed specifically to support your assurance of learning initiatives with a simple, yet powerful, solution.

  You can use our test bank software, EZTest, to easily query for Learning Objectives that directly relate to the objectives for your course. You can then use the reporting features of EZTest to aggregate student results in a similar fashion, making the collection and presentation of assurance of learning data simple and easy.

SUPPLEMENTS FOR THE INSTRUCTOR

McGraw-Hill's HOMEWORK MANAGER®

McGraw-Hill's Homework Manager Plus™: McGraw-Hill's Homework Manager Plus is a complete, Web-based solution that includes and expands upon the actual problem sets found at the end of each chapter. It features enhanced technology that provides a varied supply of auto-graded assignments and graphing exercises, tied to the learning objectives in the book.

McGraw-Hill's Homework Manager can be used for student practice, graded homework assignments, and formal examinations; the results are easily integrated with your course management system, including WebCT and Blackboard.

Instructor's Manual: Prepared by Louis D. Johnston of the College of Saint Benedict | Saint John's University, this expanded manual will be extremely useful for all teachers. In addition to such general topics as Using the Web Site, Economic Education Resources, and Innovative Ideas, there will be for each chapter: An Overview, Core Principles, Important Concepts Covered, Teaching Objectives, Teaching Tips/Student Stumbling Blocks, More Economic Naturalists, In-Class and Web Activities, Annotated Chapter Outline, Answers to Textbook Problems, Sample Homework, and a Sample Reading Quiz.

Test Banks: Prepared by Kate Krause of the University of New Mexico [micro] and William J. Brennan of the University of Minnesota–Mankato [macro], each manual contains nearly 4,000 questions categorized by chapter learning objectives, AACSB learning categories, and Bloom's Taxonomy objectives. The test banks are available in the latest EZTest test-generating software—micro and macro—ensuring maximum flexibility in test preparation.

PowerPoints: Prepared by Carol Swartz of the University of North Carolina–Charlotte, these slides contain a detailed, chapter-by-chapter review of the important ideas presented in the textbook, accompanied by animated graphs and slide notes.

Customizable Micro Lecture Notes and PowerPoints: One of the biggest hurdles to an instructor considering changing textbooks is the prospect of having to prepare new lecture notes and slides. For the microeconomics chapters, this hurdle no longer exists. A full set of lecture notes for principles of microeconomics, prepared by Bob Frank for his award-winning introductory microeconomics course at Cornell University, is available as Microsoft Word files that instructors are welcome to customize as they see fit. The challenge for any instructor is to reinforce the lessons of the text in lectures without generating student unrest by merely repeating what's in the book. These lecture notes address that challenge by constructing examples that run parallel to those presented in the book, yet are different from them in interesting contextual ways. Also available is a complete set of richly illustrated PowerPoint files to accompany these lecture notes. Instructors are also welcome to customize these files as they wish.

Instructor's CD-ROM: This remarkable Windows software program contains the complete Instructor's Manual with solutions to end-of-chapter problems, Solman Videos, Computerized Test Banks, PowerPoints, and the complete collection of art from the text.

Online Learning Center (www.mhhe.com/fbbrief1e): The contents of the IRCD are also available online at the textbook's Web site for quick download and convenient access for professors.

SUPPLEMENTS FOR THE STUDENT

Study Guide: Revised by Louis D. Johnson of the College of Saint Benedict | Saint John's University, this book contains for each chapter a pre-test; a "Key Point Review" that integrates the learning objectives with the chapter content; a self-test with matching and multiple-choice problems; short-answer problems; and an Economic Naturalist case study that helps students apply what they learned.

Online Learning Center (www.mhhe.com/fbbrief1e): For students there are such useful features as the Glossary from the textbook, Graphing Exercises, a set of study PowerPoints, and practice quizzes.

EN 2

Premium Content: The Online Learning Center now offers students the opportunity to purchase premium content. Like an electronic study guide, the OLC Premium Content enables students to take self-grading quizzes for each chapter as well as to download Frank and Bernanke exclusive iPod content including podcasts by the authors, narrated lecture slides, and Paul Solman videos—all accessible through the student's MP3 device. In the chapter, when you see an iPod icon, there is a podcast that correlates to that material. The label EN stands for Economic Naturalist, and the number represents the chapter number.

A NOTE ON THE WRITING OF THIS EDITION

Ben Bernanke was sworn in on February 1, 2006, as Chairman and a member of the Board of Governors of the Federal Reserve System. From June 2005 until January 2006, he served as chairman of the President's Council of Economic Advisers. These positions have allowed him to play an active role in making U.S. economic policy, but the rules of government service have restricted his ability to participate in the preparation of the Brief Edition.

Fortunately, we were able to enlist the aid of Louis D. Johnston of the College of Saint Benedict | Saint John's University to take the lead in creating the macro portion of the Brief Edition. Ben Bernanke and Robert Frank express their deep gratitude to Louis for the energy and creativity he has brought to his work on the book. He has created a great tool for students and professors in this Brief Edition.

ACKNOWLEDGMENTS

Our thanks first and foremost go to our publisher, Douglas Reiner, and our development editor, Angela Cimarolli. Douglas encouraged us to think deeply about how to improve the book and helped us transform our ideas into concrete changes. Angie shepherded us through the revision process in person, on the telephone, through the mail, and via e-mail with intelligence, sound advice, and good humor. We are grateful as well to the production team, whose professionalism (and patience) was outstanding: Susanne Riedell, senior project manager; Matthew Baldwin, designer; Debra Sylvester, senior production supervisor; Jeremy Cheshareck, senior photo research coordinator; and all of those who worked on the production team to turn our manuscript into the book you hold in your hands. Finally, we also thank Melissa Larmon, senior marketing manager, for getting our message into the wider world.

Finally, our sincere thanks to the following teachers and colleagues, whose thorough reviews and thoughtful suggestions led to innumerable substantive improvements to the Fourth Edition and, therefore, this Brief Edition of *Principles of Economics*.

Adel Abadeer, *Calvin College*

Cynthia Abadie, *Southwest Tennessee Community College*

Hesham Abdel-Rahman, *University of New Orleans*

Teshome Abebe, *Eastern Illinois University*

Roger L. Adkins, *Marshall University*

Richard Agesa, *Marshall University*

Frank Albritton, *Seminole Community College*

Rashid Al-Hmoud, *Texas Tech University*

Farhad Ameen, *SUNY - Westchester Community College*

Mauro C. Amor, *Northwood University*

Nejat Anbarci, *Florida International University*

Giuliana Campanelli Andreopoulos, *William Paterson University*

Michael Applegate, *Oklahoma State University*

Becca Arnold, *Mesa College*

Mohsen Bahmani-Oskooee, *University of Wisconsin–Milwaukee*

Sudeshna Bandyopadhyay, *West Virginia University*

Gyanendra Baral, *Oklahoma City Community College*

James Bartkus, *Xavier University*

Hamid Bastin, *Shippensburg University*

John H. Beck, *Gonzaga University*

Klaus Becker, *Texas Tech University*

Doris Bennett, *Jacksonville State University*

Derek Berry, *Calhoun Community College*

Tom Beveridge, *Durham Technical Community College*

Okmyung Bin, *East Carolina University*

Robert G. Bise, *Orange Coast College*

John Bishop, *East Carolina University*

John L. Brassel, *Southwest Tennessee Community College*

William J. Brennan, *Minnesota State University at Mankato*

Jozell Brister, *Abilene Christian University*

Taggert Brooks, *University of Wisconsin–La Crosse*

Christopher Burkart, *University of West Florida*

Joseph Calhoun, *Florida State University*

Colleen Callahan, *American University*

Denis G. Carter, *University of North Carolina, Wilmington*

Shawn Carter, *Jacksonville State University*

Peter Cashel-Cordo, *University of Southern Indiana*

Andrew Cassey, *University of Minnesota*

Rebecca Chakraborty, *Northwood University*

Joni S. Charles, *Texas State University–San Marcos*

Adhip Chaudhuri, *Georgetown University*

Richard Cherrin, *Delaware Technical & Community College*

Eric P. Chiang, *Florida Atlantic University*

Unk Christiadi, *University of the Pacific, Stockton*

James Cobbe, *Florida State University*

Howard Cochran, *Belmont University*

Jeffrey P. Cohen, *University of Hartford*

Barbara Connolly, *Westchester Community College*

Jim Couch, *University of North Alabama*

Elizabeth Crowell, *University of Michigan–Dearborn*

William Dawes, *SUNY at Stony Brook*

Matthew Dawson, *Charleston Southern University*

Marcelin W. Diagne, *Towson University*

Vernon J. Dobis, *Minnesota State University, Moorhead*

Amrik Singh Dua, *Mt. San Antonio College*

Tran Dung, *Wright State University*

Faruk Eray Duzenli, *Bowling Green State University*

Angela Dzata, *Alabama State University*

Dennis S. Edwards, *Coastal Carolina University*

Ishita Edwards, *Oxnard College*

Ceyhun Elgin, *University of Minnesota*

Paul Emberton, *Texas State University*

Jim Fain, *Oklahoma State University*

Nick Feltovich, *University of Houston*

William J. Field, *DePauw University*

Harold Steven Floyd, *Manatee Community College*

Charles Fraley, *Cincinnati State Technical and Community College*

Johanna Francis, *Fordham University*

Dan Friesner, *Gonzaga University*

Marc Fusaro, *East Carolina University*

Mary N. Gade, *Oklahoma State University*

S. N. Gajanan, *University of Pittsburgh*

Alejandro Gallegos, *Winona State University*

Subrahmanyam Ganti, *University at Buffalo*

Suman Ghosh, *Florida Atlantic University*

George M. Greenlee, *St. Petersburg College*

Sandra Grigg, *East Carolina University*

Sunil Gulati, *Columbia University*

Barnali Gupta, *Miami University*

Richard L. Hannah, *Middle Tennessee State University*

Mehdi Haririan, *Bloomsburg University of Pennsylvania*

Robert Harris, *Indiana University-Purdue University Indianapolis*

Tina J. Harvell, *Blinn College*

Joe Haslag, *University of Missouri*

Philip S. Heap, *James Madison University*

George Heitmann, *Muhlenberg College*

John Hejkal, *University of Iowa*

Mickey Hepner, *University of Central Oklahoma*

Michael J. Hilmer, *San Diego State University*

George E. Hoffer, *Virginia Commonwealth University*

Carol Hogan, *University of Michigan–Dearborn*

James Holcomb, *University of Texas at El Paso*

Lora Holcombe, *Florida State University*

Calvin Hoy, *County College of Morris*

Yu Hsing, *Southeastern Louisiana University*

Eric Isenberg, *DePauw University*

David E. Kalist, *Shippensburg University*

Lillian Kamal, *Northwestern University*

Brad Kamp, *University of South Florida*

Tim D. Kane, *University of Texas at Tyler*

Janis Y. F. Kea, *West Valley College*

Brian Kench, *University of Tampa*

Kamau Kinuthia, *American River College–Sacramento*

Mary Knudson, *University of Iowa*

Janet Koscianski, *Shippensburg University*

Stephan Kroll, *California State University, Sacramento*

Patricia Kuzyk, *Washington State University*

Felix Kwan, *Maryville University*

Katherine Lande, *University of Minnesota*

Gary F. Langer, *Roosevelt University*

Fritz Laux, *Northeastern State University, Oklahoma*

Sang H. Lee, *Southeastern Louisiana University*

Hui Li, *Eastern Illinois University*

Yan Li, *University of Iowa*

Clifford A. Lipscomb, *Valdosta State University*

Donald Liu, *University of Minnesota, Twin Cities*

Teresa Long, *Marymount University*

Alina Luca, *Drexel University*

Brian M. Lynch, *Lake Land College*

Karla Lynch, *North Central Texas College*

Alyson Ma, *University of San Diego*

Rita Madarass, *Westminster College*

Y. Lal Mahajan, *Monmouth University*

John G. Marcis, *Coastal Carolina University*

Dale Matcheck, *Northwood University*

Mike McIlhon, *Metropolitan State University*

Russell McKenzie, *Southeastern Louisiana University*

Matthew McPherson, *Gonzaga University*

Kimberly D. Mencken, *Baylor University*

Lewis E. Metcalf, *Parkland College*

Arthur W. Meyer, *Lincoln Land Community College*

Douglas Miller, *University of Missouri–Columbia*

Norman C. Miller, *Miami University–Oxford*

Ed Miseta, *Penn State University–Erie*

David Mitch, *University of Maryland Baltimore County*

Amlan Mitra, *Purdue University at Calumet*

Robert Moden, *Central Virginia Community College*

James A. Moreno, *Blinn College*

Thaddeaus Mounkurai, *Daytona Beach Community College*

Sudesh Mujumdar, *University of Southern Indiana*

David C. Murphy, *Boston College*

Christopher Mushrush, *Illinois State University*

Annette Najjar, *Lindenwood University*

Helen Naughton, *University of Oregon*

Charles Newton, *Houston Community College*

Daniel Nguyen, *Purdue University*

James Nguyen, *Southeastern Louisiana University*

Sung C. No, *Southern University and A&M College*

Richard Numrich, *Community College of Southern Nevada*

Norman P. Obst, *Michigan State University*

Thomas A. Odegaard, *Baylor University*

Babatunde Odusami, *Southeastern Louisiana University*

Sebastien Oleas, *University of Minnesota Duluth*

Maria P. Olivero, *Drexel University*

Una Okonkwo Osili, *Indiana University-Purdue University Indianapolis*

Stephanie Owings, *Fort Lewis College*

Debashis Pal, *University of Cincinnati*

Michel-Ange Pantal, *University of Missouri*

James M. Payne, *Calhoun Community College*

Richard Peck, *University of Illinois at Chicago*

Robert L. Pennington, *University of Central Florida*

Martin M. Perline, *Wichita State University*

Genevieve Peters, *University of California–San Diego*

Josh Pickrell, *South Plains College*

Rex Pjesky, *Northeastern State University*

Linnea Polgreen, *University of Iowa*

Robert C. Posatko, *Shippensburg University*

Edgar Preugschat, *University of Minnesota*

William Pritchard, *Metropolitan State University*

Farhad Rassekh, *University of Hartford*

Mitchell Redlo, *Monroe Community College*

Jong C. Rhim, *University of Southern Indiana*

Terry L. Riddle, *Central Virginia Community College*

Richard M. Romano, *SUNY/Broome Community College*

Brian Rosario, *University of California–Davis*

Thomas Rossi, *Broome Community College*

Sara Saderion, *Houston Community College–Southwest*

George E. Samuels, *Sam Houston State University*

Jonathan Sandy, *University of San Diego*

George Santopietro, *Radford University*

Samuel Sarri, *University & Community College System of Nevada*

Eric Schansberg, *Indiana University Southeast*

Gerald Scott, *Florida Atlantic University*

Mourad Sebti, *Central Texas College*

Ousmane Seck, *California State University at Fullerton*

Anirban Sengupta, *Texas A&M University*

Luis Guillermo Serpa, *University of Illinois at Chicago*

Dennis Shannon, *Southwestern Illinois College*

Rimma Shiptosva, *Utah State University*

Noel S. Smith, *Palm Beach Community College*

Stephen Smith, *Bakersfield College*

Nick Spangenberg, *Ozarks Technical Community College*

Vera Tabakova, *East Carolina University*

Henry S. Terrell, *University of Maryland College Park*

Charles Thompson, *Troy University*

Wendine R. Thompson-Dawson, *University of Utah*

Steve Thorpe, *Phoenix College*

Derek Tittle, *Georgia Institute of Technology*

Elwin Tobing, *California State University at Fullerton*

Brian M. Trinque, *The University of Texas at Austin*

Boone A. Turchi, *University of North Carolina at Chapel Hill*

Markland Tuttle, *Sam Houston State University*

Jesus M. Valencia, *Slippery Rock University*

James Walker, *Indiana University, Bloomington*

Elizabeth Wark, *Worcester State College*

James Wetzel, *Virginia Commonwealth University*

Jennifer Wissink, *Cornell University*

Kristen Wolfe, *St. Johns River Community College*

James Woods, *Portland State University*

J. Christopher Wreh, *North Central Texas College*

Mickey Wu, *Coe College*

Steven Yamarik, *California State University at Long Beach*

Tao Chen Yeh, *University of Alabama*

Andrew M. Yuengert, *Pepperdine University*

Reviewers for previous editions

Ugur Aker, *Hiram College*

Ercument Aksoy, *Los Angeles Valley College*

Rashid Al-Hmoud, *Texas Tech University*

Richard Anderson, *Texas A&M University*

Sudeshna Bandyopadhay, *West Virginia University*

Michael Bar, *University of Minnesota*

Klaus Becker, *Texas Tech University*

Ariel Belason, *Binghamton University*

Daniel Berkowitz, *University of Pittsburgh*

Guatam Bhattacharya, *University of Kansas*

Scott Bierman, *Carleton College*

Calvin Blackwell, *College of Charleston*

Bruce Blonigen, *University of Oregon*

Beth Bogan, *Princeton University*

George Borts, *Brown University*

Nancy Brooks, *University of Vermont*

Clair Brown, *University of California–Berkeley*

Douglas Brown, *Georgetown University*

Andrew Buck, *Temple University*

Marie Bussings-Burk, *Southern Indiana University*

James Butikofer, *Washington University in St. Louis*

Randy Campbell, *Mississippi State University*

Lon Carlson, *Illinois State University*

David Carr, *University of Colorado*

Nevin Cavusoglu, *University of New Hampshire*

Jack Chambless, *Valencia Community College*

Xia Chen, *Tulane University*

Nan-Ting Chou, *University of Louisville*

James Cover, *University of Alabama*

Eleanor Craig, *University of Delaware*

Ward Curran, *Trinity College*

Donald Dale, *Muhlenberg College*

Carl Davidson, *Michigan State University*

Fred Derrick, *Loyola University, Maryland*

Lynn Pierson, *Doti Chapman College*

Donald Dutkowsky, *Syracuse University*

Linda Dynan, *Northern Kentucky University*

Michael Enz, *Western New England College*

Belton Fleisher, *The Ohio State University*

Robert Florence, *St. Bonaventure University*

Kent Ford, *Onondaga Community College*

Nancy Fox, *Saint Joseph's College*

Joseph Friedman, *Temple University*

Ynon Gablinger, *City University of New York–Hunter College*

Rob Garnett, *Texas Christian University*

Jonah Gelbach, *University of Maryland*

Linda Ghent, *East Carolina University*

Kirk Gifford, *Ricks College*

Robert Gillette, *University of Kentucky*

Stephen Gohman, *University of Louisville*

Gregory Green, *Idaho State University*

Sunil Gulati, *Columbia University*

Alan Gummerson, *Florida International University*

Refet Gurkaynak, *Princeton University*

Paul Hamilton, *DePauw University*

Mehdi Haririan, *Bloomsburg University of Pennsylvania*

Joe Haslag, *University of Missouri–Columbia*

Jeff Hefel, *Saint Mary's University*

Barry Hirsch, *Trinity University, Texas*

Mary Jean, *Horney Furman University*

Nancy Jianakoplos, *Colorado State University*

Robert Johnson, *University of San Diego*

Brett Katzman, *Kennesaw State University*

Brendan Kennelly, *National University of Ireland*

Herbert Kiesling, *Indiana University*

Bruce Kingma, *State University of New York–Albany*

Frederick Kolb, *University of Wisconsin–Eau Claire*

Stephan Kroll, *California State University–Sacramento*

Christopher Laincz, *Drexel University*

Leonard Lardaro, *University of Rhode Island*

Tom Lehman, *Indiana Wesleyan*

Anthony Lima, *California State University–Hayward*

Patricia Lindsey, *Butte College*

Tom Love, *North Central University*

Alina Luca, *Drexel University*

Jeffrey Macher, *Georgetown University*

Steven McCafferty, *The Ohio State University*

Edward McNertney, *Texas Christian University*

William Merrill, *Iowa State University*

Norman Miller, *Miami University, Ohio*

Christopher Mushrush, *Illinois State University*

Paul Nelson, *Northeast Louisiana State University*

Wilhelm Neuefeind, *Washington University in St. Louis*

Neil Niman, *University of New Hampshire*

Norman Obst, *Michigan State University*

Frank O'Connor, *Eastern Kentucky University*

Thomas Odegaard, *Baylor University*

Charles Okeke, *Community College of Southern Nevada*

Ronald Olive, *University of Massachusetts–Lowell*

Terry Olson, *Truman State University*

Duane Oyen, *University of Wisconsin–Eau Claire*

Theodore Palivos, *Louisiana State University*

Santiago Pinto, *West Virginia University*

Michael Potepan, *San Francisco State University*

Robert Rebelein, *Vassar College*

Steve Robinson, *University of North Carolina–Wilmington*

Michael Rolleigh, *University of Minnesota*

Christina Romer, *University of California–Berkeley*

David Romer, *University of California–Berkeley*

Greg Rose, *Sacramento City College*

Robert Rossana, *Wayne State University*

Dan Rubenson, *Southern Oregon University*

Richard Salvucci, *Trinity University*

Edward Scahill, *University of Scranton*

Pamela Schmitt, *Indiana University*

Esther-Mirjam Sent, *University of Notre Dame*

John Solow, *University of Iowa*

Sumati Srinivas, *Radford University*

Dennis Starleaf, *Iowa State University*

Petia Stoytcheva, *Louisiana State University*

Helen Tauchen, *University of North Carolina–Chapel Hill*

Marie Truesdell, *Marian College, Indiana*

Nora Underwood, *Central Florida University*

Kay Unger, *University of Montana*

Norman Van Cott, *Ball State University*

Kristin Van Gaasbeck, *California State University–Sacramento*

Stephan Weiler, *Colorado State University*

Jeffrey Weiss, *City University of New York–Baruch College*

William Welch, *Saginaw Valley State University*

Richard Winkelman, *Arizona State University*

Mark Wohar, *University of Nebraska–Omaha*

Louise Wolitz, *University of Texas–Austin*

Paula Worthington, *University of Chicago*

Micky Wu, *Coe College*

Zhenhui Xu, *Georgia College and State University*

Darrel Young, *University of Texas–Austin*

Zenon Zygmont, *Western Oregon University*

AACSB STATEMENT

McGraw-Hill Companies is a proud corporate member of AACSB International. Recognizing the importance and value of AACSB accreditation, the author of *Principles of Economics, Brief Edition* has sought to recognize the curricula guidelines detailed in AACSB standards for business accreditation by connecting questions in the test bank and end-of-chapter material to the general knowledge and skill guidelines found in the AACSB standards. It is important to note that the statements contained in *Principles of Economics, Brief Edition* are provided only as a guide for the users of this text.

BRIEF CONTENTS

CONTENTS

PART 3 Market Imperfections

SEVEN CORE PRINCIPLES

Scarcity

CORE PRINCIPLE 1
The Scarcity Principle (also called "The No-Free-Lunch Principle")
Although we have boundless needs and wants, the resources available to us are limited. So having more of one good thing usually means having less of another.

Cost-Benefit

CORE PRINCIPLE 2
The Cost-Benefit Principle
An individual (or a firm or a society) should take an action if, and only if, the extra benefits from taking the action are at least as great as the extra costs.

Incentive

CORE PRINCIPLE 3
The Incentive Principle
A person (or a firm or a society) is more likely to take an action if the benefit rises and less likely to take it if the cost rises.

Comparative Advantage

CORE PRINCIPLE 4
The Principle of Comparative Advantage
Everyone does best when each person (or each country) concentrates on the activities for which his or her opportunity cost is lowest.

Increasing Opportunity Cost

CORE PRINCIPLE 5
The Principle of Increasing Opportunity Cost (also called "The Low-Hanging-Fruit Principle")
In expanding the production of any good, first employ those resources with the lowest opportunity cost, and only afterward turn to resources with higher opportunity costs.

Efficiency

CORE PRINCIPLE 6
The Efficiency Principle
Efficiency is an important social goal because when the economic pie grows larger, everyone can have a larger slice.

Equilibrium

CORE PRINCIPLE 7
The Equilibrium Principle (also called "The No-Cash-on-the-Table Principle")
A market in equilibrium leaves no unexploited opportunities for individuals but may not exploit all gains achievable through collective action.

PART I

INTRODUCTION

As you begin the study of economics, perhaps the most important thing to realize is that economics is not a collection of settled facts, to be copied down and memorized. Mark Twain said that nothing is older than yesterday's newspaper, and the same can be said of yesterday's economic statistics. Indeed, the only prediction about the economy that can be made with confidence is that there will continue to be large, and largely unpredictable, changes.

If economics is not a set of durable facts, then what is it? Fundamentally, it is a way of thinking about the world. Over many years economists have developed some simple but widely applicable principles that are useful for understanding almost any economic situation, from the relatively simple economic decisions that individuals make every day to the workings of highly complex markets such as international financial markets. The principal objective of this book, and of this course, is to help you learn these principles and how to apply them to a variety of economic questions and issues.

The three chapters in Part I lay out the Core Principles that will be used throughout the book. All seven Core Principles are listed on the previous page and on the back of the book for easy reference.

Chapter 1 introduces and illustrates three Core Principles, the first of which is the *Scarcity Principle*—the unavoidable fact that, although our needs and wants are boundless, the resources available to satisfy them are limited. The chapter goes on to show that the *Cost-Benefit Principle,* deciding whether to take an action by comparing the cost and benefit of the action, is a useful approach for dealing with the inevitable trade-offs that scarcity creates. After discussing several important decision pitfalls, the chapter concludes by describing the *Incentive Principle* and introducing the concept of economic naturalism.

Chapter 2 goes beyond individual decision making to consider trade among both individuals and countries. An important reason for trade is the *Principle of Comparative Advantage:* by specializing in the production of particular goods and services, people and countries enhance their productivity and raise standards of living. Further, people and countries expand their production of the goods or services by applying the *Principle of Increasing Opportunity Cost*—first employing those resources with the lowest opportunity cost and only afterward turning to resources with higher opportunity costs.

Chapter 3 presents an overview of the concepts of supply and demand, perhaps the most basic and familiar tools used by economists. These tools are used to show the final two Core Principles: the *Efficiency Principle* (efficiency is an important social goal because when the economics pie grows larger, everyone can have a larger slice) and the *Equilibrium Principle* (a market in equilibrium leaves no unexploited opportunities for individuals but may not exploit all gains achievable through collective action).

CHAPTER

1

Thinking Like an Economist

LEARNING OBJECTIVES

In this chapter, we'll introduce three simple principles that will help you understand and explain patterns of behavior you observe in the world around you. These principles also will help you avoid three pitfalls that plague decision makers in everyday life. The principles and pitfalls you'll learn about are

1. The Scarcity Principle, which says that having more of any good thing necessarily requires having less of something else.
2. The Cost-Benefit Principle, which says that an action should be taken if, but only if, its benefit is at least as great as its cost.
3. The Incentive Principle, which says that if you want to predict people's behavior, a good place to start is by examining their incentives.
4. The pitfall of measuring costs and benefits as proportions rather than as absolute dollar amounts.
5. The pitfall of ignoring implicit costs.
6. The pitfall of failing to weigh costs and benefits at the margin.

How many students are in your introductory economics class? Some classes have just 20 or so; others average 35, 100, or 200 students. At some schools, introductory economics classes may have as many as 2,000 students. What size is best?

If cost were no object, the best size for an introductory economics course—or any other course, for that matter—might be a single student. Think about it: the whole course, all term long, with just you and your professor! Everything could be custom-tailored to your own background and ability, allowing you to cover the material at just the right pace. The tutorial format also would promote

Are small classes "better" than large ones?

close communication and personal trust between you and your professor. And your grade would depend more heavily on what you actually learned than on your luck when taking multiple-choice exams. We may even suppose, for the sake of discussion, that studies by educational psychologists prove definitively that students learn best in the tutorial format.

Why, then, do so many universities continue to schedule introductory classes with hundreds of students? The simple reason is that costs *do* matter. They matter not just to the university administrators who must build classrooms and pay faculty salaries, but also to *you*. The direct cost of providing you with your own personal introductory economics course—most notably, the professor's salary and the expense of providing a classroom in which to meet—might easily top $50,000. *Someone* has to pay these costs. In private universities, a large share of the cost would be recovered directly from higher tuition payments; in state universities, the burden would be split between higher tuition payments and higher tax payments. But, in either case, the course would be unaffordable for many, if not most, students.

With a larger class size, of course, the cost per student goes down. For example, in a class of 300 students, the cost of an introductory economics course might come to as little as $200 per student. But a class that large would surely compromise the quality of the learning environment. Compared to the custom tutorial format, however, it would be dramatically more affordable.

In choosing what size introductory economics course to offer, then, university administrators confront a classic economic trade-off. In making the class larger, they lower the quality of instruction—a bad thing—but, at the same time, they reduce costs, and hence the tuition students must pay—a good thing.

ECONOMICS: STUDYING CHOICE IN A WORLD OF SCARCITY

Even in rich societies like the United States, *scarcity* is a fundamental fact of life. There is never enough time, money, or energy to do everything we want to do or have everything we would like to have. **Economics** is the study of how people make choices under conditions of scarcity and of the results of those choices for society.

economics the study of how people make choices under conditions of scarcity and of the results of those choices for society

In the class-size example just discussed, a motivated economics student might definitely prefer to be in a class of 20 rather than a class of 100, everything else being equal. But other things, of course, are not equal. Students can enjoy the benefits of having smaller classes, but only at the price of having less money for other activities. The student's choice inevitably will come down to the relative importance of competing activities.

That such trade-offs are widespread and important is one of the core principles of economics. We call it the **scarcity principle** because the simple fact of scarcity makes trade-offs necessary. Another name for the scarcity principle is the **no-free-lunch principle** (which comes from the observation that even lunches that are given to you are never really free—somebody, somehow, always has to pay for them).

Scarcity

The Scarcity Principle (also called the No-Free-Lunch Principle): Although we have boundless needs and wants, the resources available to us are limited. So having more of one good thing usually means having less of another.

Inherent in the idea of a trade-off is the fact that choice involves compromise between competing interests. Economists resolve such trade-offs by using *cost-benefit analysis*, which is based on the disarmingly simple principle that an action should be taken if, and only if, its benefits exceed its costs. We call this statement the **cost-benefit principle,** and it, too, is one of the core principles of economics:

The Cost-Benefit Principle: An individual (or a firm or a society) should take an action if, and only if, the extra benefits from taking the action are at least as great as the extra costs.

Cost-Benefit

With the Cost-Benefit Principle in mind, let's think about our class-size question again. Imagine that classrooms come in only two sizes—100-seat lecture halls and 20-seat classrooms—and that your university currently offers introductory economics courses to classes of 100 students. Question: Should administrators reduce the class size to 20 students? Answer: Reduce if, and only if, the value of the improvement in instruction outweighs its additional cost.

This rule sounds simple, but to apply it we need some way to measure the relevant costs and benefits—a task that is often difficult in practice. If we make a few simplifying assumptions, however, we can see how the analysis might work. On the cost side, the primary expense of reducing class size from 100 to 20 is that we will now need five professors instead of just one. We'll also need five smaller classrooms rather than a single big one, and this too may add slightly to the expense of the move. For the sake of discussion, suppose that the cost with a class size of 20 turns out to be $1,000 per student more than the cost per student when the class size is 100. Should administrators switch to the smaller class size? If they apply the Cost-Benefit Principle, they will realize that *the reduction in class size makes sense only if the value of attending the smaller class is at least $1,000 per student greater than the value of attending the larger class.*

Cost-Benefit

Would you (or your family) be willing to pay an extra $1,000 for a smaller economics class? If not, and if other students feel the same way, then sticking with the larger class size makes sense. But if you and others would be willing to pay the extra tuition, then reducing the class size to 20 makes good economic sense.

Notice that the "best" class size, from an economic point of view, will generally not be the same as the "best" size from the point of view of an educational psychologist. The difference arises because the economic definition of "best" takes into account both the benefits *and* the costs of different class sizes. The psychologist ignores costs and looks only at the learning benefits of different class sizes.

In practice, of course, different people will feel differently about the value of smaller classes. People with high incomes, for example, tend to be willing to pay more for the advantage, which helps to explain why average class size is smaller, and tuition higher, at private schools whose students come predominantly from high-income families.

The cost-benefit framework for thinking about the class-size problem also suggests a possible reason for the gradual increase in average class size that has been taking place in American colleges and universities. During the last 20 years, professors' salaries have risen sharply, making smaller classes more costly. During the same period, median family income—and hence the willingness to pay for smaller classes—has remained roughly constant. When the cost of offering smaller classes goes up but willingness to pay for smaller classes does not, universities shift to larger class sizes.

Scarcity and the trade-offs that result also apply to resources other than money. Bill Gates is one of the richest men on Earth. His wealth was once estimated at over $100 billion—more than the combined wealth of the poorest 40 percent of Americans. Gates has enough money to buy more houses, cars, vacations, and other consumer goods than he could possibly use. Yet Gates, like the rest of us, has only 24 hours each day and a limited amount of energy. So even he confronts trade-offs, in that any activity he pursues—whether it be building his business empire or redecorating his mansion—uses up time and energy that he could otherwise spend on other things. Indeed, someone once calculated that the value of Gates's time is so great that pausing to pick up a $100 bill from the sidewalk simply wouldn't be worth his while.

If Bill Gates saw a $100 bill lying on the sidewalk, would it be worth his time to pick it up?

APPLYING THE COST-BENEFIT PRINCIPLE

rational person someone with well-defined goals who tries to fulfill those goals as best he or she can

In studying choice under scarcity, we'll usually begin with the premise that people are **rational,** which means they have well-defined goals and try to fulfill them as best they can. The cost-benefit principle illustrated in the class-size example is a fundamental tool for the study of how rational people make choices.

As in the class-size example, often the only real difficulty in applying the cost-benefit rule is to come up with reasonable measures of the relevant benefits and costs. Only in rare instances will exact dollar measures be conveniently available. But the cost-benefit framework can lend structure to your thinking even when no relevant market data are available.

To illustrate how we proceed in such cases, the following example asks you to decide whether to perform an action whose cost is described only in vague, qualitative terms.

Should you walk downtown to save $10 on a $25 computer game?

Imagine you are about to buy a $25 computer game at the nearby campus store when a friend tells you that the same game is on sale at a downtown store for only $15. If the downtown store is a 30-minute walk away, where should you buy the game?

Cost-Benefit

The Cost-Benefit Principle tells us that you should buy it downtown if the benefit of doing so exceeds the cost. The benefit of taking any action is the dollar value of everything you gain by taking it. Here, the benefit of buying downtown is exactly $10, since that is the amount you will save on the purchase price of the game. The cost of taking any action is the dollar value of everything you give up by taking it. Here, the cost of buying downtown is the dollar value you assign to the time and trouble it takes to make the trip. But how do we estimate that dollar value?

One way is to perform the following hypothetical auction. Imagine that a stranger has offered to pay you to do an errand that involves the same walk downtown (perhaps to drop off a letter for her at the post office). If she offered you a payment of, say, $1,000, would you accept? If so, we know that your cost of walking downtown and back must be less than $1,000. Now imagine her offer being reduced in small increments until you finally refuse the last offer. For example, if you would agree to walk downtown and back for $9.00 but not for $8.99, then your cost of making the trip is $9.00. In this case, you should buy the game downtown because the $10 you'll save (your benefit) is greater than your $9.00 cost of making the trip.

But suppose, alternatively, that your cost of making the trip had been greater than $10. In that case, your best bet would have been to buy the game from the nearby campus store. Confronted with this choice, different people may choose differently, depending on how costly they think it is to make the trip downtown. But although there is no uniquely correct choice, most people who are asked what they would do in this situation say they would buy the game downtown. ◆

ECONOMIC SURPLUS

economic surplus the economic surplus from taking any action is the benefit of taking that action minus its cost

Suppose again that in the preceding example your "cost" of making the trip downtown was $9. Compared to the alternative of buying the game at the campus store, buying it downtown resulted in an **economic surplus** of $1, the difference between the benefit of making the trip and its cost. In general, your goal as an economic decision maker is to choose those actions that generate the largest possible economic surplus. This means taking all actions that yield a positive total economic surplus, which is just another way of restating the Cost-Benefit Principle.

Cost-Benefit

Note that the fact that your best choice was to buy the game downtown doesn't imply that you *enjoy* making the trip, any more than choosing a large class means that you prefer large classes to small ones. It simply means that the trip is less unpleasant than the prospect of paying $10 extra for the game. Once again, you've faced a trade-off—in this case, the choice between a cheaper game and the free time gained by avoiding the trip.

OPPORTUNITY COST

Of course, your mental auction could have produced a different outcome. Suppose, for example, that the time required for the trip is the only time you have left to study for a difficult test the next day. Or suppose you are watching one of your favorite movies on cable, or that you are tired and would love a short nap. In such cases, we say that the **opportunity cost** of making the trip—that is, the value of what you must sacrifice to walk downtown and back—is high and you are more likely to decide against making the trip.

opportunity cost the opportunity cost of an activity is the value of what must be forgone in order to undertake the activity

Strictly speaking, your opportunity cost of engaging in an activity is the value of everything you must sacrifice to engage in it. For instance, if seeing a movie requires not only that you buy a $10 ticket but also that you give up a $20 babysitting job that you would have been willing to do for free, then the opportunity cost of seeing the film is $30.

Under this definition, *all* costs—both implicit and explicit—are opportunity costs. Unless otherwise stated, we will adhere to this strict definition.

We must warn you, however, that some economists use the term *opportunity cost* to refer only to the implicit value of opportunities forgone. Thus, in the example just discussed, these economists would not include the $10 ticket price when calculating the opportunity cost of seeing the film. But virtually all economists would agree that your opportunity cost of not doing the babysitting job is $20.

In the previous example, if watching the last hour of the cable TV movie is the most valuable opportunity that conflicts with the trip downtown, the opportunity cost of making the trip is the dollar value you place on pursuing that opportunity—that is, the largest amount you'd be willing to pay to avoid missing the end of the movie. Note that the opportunity cost of making the trip is not the combined value of *all* possible activities you could have pursued, but only the value of your *best* alternative—the one you would have chosen had you not made the trip.

Throughout the text we will pose exercises like the one that follows. You'll find that pausing to answer them will help you to master key concepts in economics. Because doing these exercises isn't very costly (indeed, many students report that they are actually fun), the Cost-Benefit Principle indicates that it's well worth your while to do them.

Cost-Benefit

EXERCISE 1.1

You would again save $10 by buying the game downtown rather than at the campus store, but your cost of making the trip is now $12, not $9. How much economic surplus would you get from buying the game downtown? Where should you buy it?

THE ROLE OF ECONOMIC MODELS

Economists use the cost-benefit principle as an abstract model of how an idealized rational individual would choose among competing alternatives. (By "abstract model" we mean a simplified description that captures the essential elements of a situation and allows us to analyze them in a logical way.) A computer model of a complex phenomenon like climate change, which must ignore many details and includes only the major forces at work, is an example of an abstract model.

Noneconomists are sometimes harshly critical of the economist's cost-benefit model on the grounds that people in the real world never conduct hypothetical mental auctions before deciding whether to make trips downtown. But this criticism betrays a fundamental misunderstanding of how abstract models can help to explain and predict human behavior. Economists know perfectly well that people don't conduct hypothetical mental auctions when they make simple decisions. All the cost-benefit principle really says is that a rational decision is one that is explicitly or implicitly based on a weighing of costs and benefits.

Most of us make sensible decisions most of the time, without being consciously aware that we are weighing costs and benefits, just as most people ride a bike without being consciously aware of what keeps them from falling. Through trial and error, we gradually learn what kinds of choices tend to work best in different contexts, just as bicycle riders internalize the relevant laws of physics, usually without being conscious of them.

Even so, learning the explicit principles of cost-benefit analysis can help us make better decisions, just as knowing about physics can help in learning to ride a bicycle. For instance, when a young economist was teaching his oldest son to ride a bike, he followed the time-honored tradition of running alongside the bike and holding onto his son, then giving him a push and hoping for the best. After several hours and painfully skinned elbows and knees, his son finally got it. A year later, someone pointed out that the trick to riding a bike is to turn slightly in whichever direction the bike is leaning. Of course! The economist passed this information along to his second son, who learned to ride almost instantly. Just as knowing a little physics can help you learn to ride a bike, knowing a little economics can help you make better decisions.

RECAP	COST-BENEFIT ANALYSIS

Scarcity is a basic fact of economic life. Because of it, having more of one good thing almost always means having less of another (the Scarcity Principle). The Cost-Benefit Principle holds that an individual (or a firm or a society) should take an action if, and only if, the extra benefit from taking the action is at least as great as the extra cost. The benefit of taking any action minus the cost of taking the action is called the *economic surplus* from that action. Hence, the Cost-Benefit Principle suggests that we take only those actions that create additional economic surplus.

THREE IMPORTANT DECISION PITFALLS*

Rational people will apply the Cost-Benefit Principle most of the time, although probably in an intuitive and approximate way, rather than through explicit and precise calculation. Knowing that rational people tend to compare costs and benefits enables economists to predict their likely behavior. As noted earlier, for example, we can predict that students from wealthy families are more likely than others to attend colleges that offer small classes. (Again, while the cost of small classes is the same for all families, the benefit of small classes, as measured by what people are willing to pay for them, tends to be higher for wealthier families.)

Yet researchers have identified situations in which people tend to apply the cost-benefit principle inconsistently. In these situations, the cost-benefit principle may not predict behavior accurately, but it proves helpful in another way, by identifying specific strategies for avoiding bad decisions.

*The examples in this section are inspired by the pioneering research of Daniel Kahneman and the late Amos Tversky. Kahneman was awarded the 2002 Nobel Prize in economics for his efforts to integrate insights from psychology into economics.

PITFALL 1: MEASURING COSTS AND BENEFITS AS PROPORTIONS RATHER THAN ABSOLUTE DOLLAR AMOUNTS

As the next example makes clear, even people who seem to know they should weigh the pros and cons of the actions they are contemplating sometimes don't have a clear sense of how to measure the relevant costs and benefits.

Should you walk downtown to save $10 on a $2,020 laptop computer?

You are about to buy a $2,020 laptop computer at the nearby campus store when a friend tells you that the same computer is on sale at a downtown store for only $2,010. If the downtown store is half an hour's walk away, where should you buy the computer?

Assuming that the laptop is light enough to carry without effort, the structure of this example is exactly the same as that of the earlier example about where to buy the computer game—the only difference being that the price of the laptop is dramatically higher than the price of the computer game. As before, the benefit of buying downtown is the dollar amount you'll save, namely, $10. And since it's exactly the same trip, its cost also must be the same as before. So if you are perfectly rational, you should make the same decision in both cases. Yet when real people are asked what they would do in these situations, the overwhelming majority say they would walk downtown to buy the game but would buy the laptop at the campus store. When asked to explain, most of them say something like "The trip was worth it for the game because you save 40 percent, but not worth it for the laptop because you save only $10 out of $2,020."

This is faulty reasoning. The benefit of the trip downtown is not the *proportion* you save on the original price. Rather, it is the *absolute dollar amount* you save. Since the benefit of walking downtown to buy the laptop is $10—exactly the same as for the computer game—and since the cost of the trip must also be the same in both cases, the economic surplus from making both trips must be exactly the same. And that means that a rational decision maker would make the same decision in both cases. Yet, as noted, most people choose differently. ◆

EXERCISE 1.2

Which is more valuable: saving $100 on a $2,000 plane ticket to Tokyo or saving $90 on a $200 plane ticket to Chicago?

The pattern of faulty reasoning in the decision just discussed is one of several decision pitfalls to which people are often prone. In the discussion that follows, we will identify two additional decision pitfalls. In some cases, people ignore costs or benefits that they ought to take into account, while on other occasions they are influenced by costs or benefits that are irrelevant.

PITFALL 2: IGNORING IMPLICIT COSTS

Sherlock Holmes, Arthur Conan Doyle's legendary detective, was successful because he saw details that most others overlooked. In *Silver Blaze,* Holmes is called on to investigate the theft of an expensive racehorse from its stable. A Scotland Yard inspector assigned to the case asks Holmes whether some particular aspect of the crime requires further study. "Yes," Holmes replies, and describes "the curious incident of the dog in the nighttime." "The dog did nothing in the nighttime," responds the puzzled inspector. But as Holmes realized, that was precisely the problem.

Implicit costs are like dogs that fail to bark in the night.

The watchdog's failure to bark when Silver Blaze was stolen meant that the watchdog knew the thief. This clue ultimately proved the key to unraveling the mystery.

Just as we often don't notice when a dog fails to bark, many of us tend to overlook the implicit value of activities that fail to happen. As discussed earlier, however, intelligent decisions require taking the value of forgone opportunities properly into account.

The opportunity cost of an activity, once again, is the value of all that must be forgone in order to engage in that activity. If buying a computer game downtown means not watching the last hour of a movie, then the value to you of watching the end of that movie is an implicit cost of the trip. Many people make bad decisions because they tend to ignore the value of such forgone opportunities. To avoid overlooking implicit costs, economists often translate questions like "Should I walk downtown?" into ones like "Should I walk downtown or watch the end of the movie?"

Should you use your frequent-flyer coupon to fly to Fort Lauderdale for spring break?

With spring break only a week away, you are still undecided about whether to go to Fort Lauderdale with a group of classmates at the University of Iowa. The round-trip airfare from Cedar Rapids is $500, but you have a frequent-flyer coupon you could use to pay for the trip. All other relevant costs for the vacation week at the beach total exactly $1,000. The most you would be willing to pay for the Fort Lauderdale vacation is $1,350. That amount is your benefit of taking the vacation. Your only alternative use for your frequent-flyer coupon is for your plane trip to Boston the weekend after spring break to attend your brother's wedding. (Your coupon expires shortly thereafter.) If the Cedar Rapids–Boston round-trip airfare is $400, should you use your frequent-flyer coupon to fly to Fort Lauderdale for spring break?

Cost-Benefit

The Cost-Benefit Principle tells us that you should go to Fort Lauderdale if the benefits of the trip exceed its costs. If not for the complication of the frequent-flyer coupon, solving this problem would be a straightforward matter of comparing your benefit from the week at the beach to the sum of all relevant costs. And since your airfare and other costs would add up to $1,500, or $150 more than your benefit from the trip, you would not go to Fort Lauderdale.

© Jeff Greenberg/Alamy

Is your flight to Fort Lauderdale "free" if you travel on a frequent-flyer coupon?

But what about the possibility of using your frequent-flyer coupon to make the trip? Using it for that purpose might make the flight to Fort Lauderdale seem free, suggesting you would reap an economic surplus of $350 by making the trip. But doing so also would mean you would have to fork over $400 for your airfare to Boston. So the implicit cost of using your coupon to go to Fort Lauderdale is really $400. If you use it for that purpose, the trip still ends up being a loser because the cost of the vacation, $1,400, exceeds the benefit by $50. In cases like these, you are much more likely to decide sensibly if you ask yourself, "Should I use my frequent-flyer coupon for this trip or save it for an upcoming trip?" ◆

We cannot emphasize strongly enough that the key to using the Cost-Benefit Principle correctly lies in recognizing precisely what taking a given action prevents us from doing. The following exercise illustrates this point by modifying the details of the previous example slightly.

EXERCISE 1.3

Same as the previous example, except that now your frequent-flyer coupon expires in a week, so your only chance to use it will be for the Fort Lauderdale trip. Should you use your coupon?

PITFALL 3: FAILURE TO THINK AT THE MARGIN

When deciding whether to take an action, the only costs and benefits that are relevant are those that would occur as a result of taking the action. Sometimes people are influenced by costs they ought to ignore while other times they compare the wrong costs and benefits. *The only costs that should influence a decision about whether to take an action are those that we can avoid by not taking the action. Similarly, the only benefits we should consider are those that would not occur unless the action were taken.* As a practical matter, however, many decision makers appear to be influenced by costs or benefits that would have occurred independently of whether the action was taken. Thus, people are often influenced by **sunk costs**—costs that are beyond recovery at the moment a decision is made. For example, money spent on a nontransferable, nonrefundable airline ticket is a sunk cost.

sunk cost a cost that is beyond recovery at the moment a decision must be made

As the following example illustrates, sunk costs must be borne *whether or not an action is taken,* so they are irrelevant to the decision of whether to take the action.

How much should you eat at an all-you-can-eat restaurant?

Sangam, an Indian restaurant in Philadelphia, offers an all-you-can-eat lunch buffet for $5. Customers pay $5 at the door, and no matter how many times they refill their plates, there is no additional charge. One day, as a goodwill gesture, the owner of the restaurant tells 20 randomly selected guests that their lunch is on the house. The remaining guests pay the usual price. If all diners are rational, will there be any difference in the average quantity of food consumed by people in these two groups?

Having eaten their first helping, diners in each group confront the following question: "Should I go back for another helping?" For rational diners, if the benefit of doing so exceeds the cost, the answer is yes; otherwise it is no. Note that at the moment of decision about a second helping, the $5 charge for the lunch is a sunk cost. Those who paid it have no way to recover it. Thus, for both groups, the (extra) cost of another helping is exactly zero. And since the people who received the free lunch were chosen at random, there is no reason to suppose that their appetites or incomes are different from those of other diners. The benefit of another helping thus should be the same, on average, for people in both groups. And since their respective costs and benefits of an additional helping are the same, the two groups should eat the same number of helpings, on average.

Psychologists and economists have experimental evidence, however, that people in such groups do *not* eat similar amounts.[1] In particular, those for whom the luncheon charge is not waived tend to eat substantially more than those for whom the charge is waived. People in the former group seem somehow determined to "get their money's worth." Their implicit goal is apparently to minimize the average cost per bite of the food they eat. Yet minimizing average cost is not a particularly sensible objective. It brings to mind the man who drove his car on the highway at night, even though he had nowhere to go, because he wanted to boost his average fuel economy. The irony is that diners who are determined to get their money's worth usually end up eating too much, as evidenced later by their regrets about having gone back for their last helpings. ◆

The fact that the cost-benefit criterion failed the test of prediction in this example does nothing to invalidate its advice about what people *should* do. If you are letting sunk costs influence your decisions, you can do better by changing your behavior. In addition to paying attention to costs and benefits that should be ignored, people often use incorrect measures of the relevant costs and benefits. This error often occurs when we must choose the *extent* to which an activity should be pursued

[1]See, for example, Richard Thaler, "Toward a Positive Theory of Consumer Choice," *Journal of Economic Behavior and Organization* 1, no. 1 (1980).

(as opposed to choosing whether to pursue it at all). We can apply the Cost-Benefit Principle in such situations by repeatedly asking the question "Should I increase the level at which I am currently pursuing the activity?"

In attempting to answer this question, the focus should always be on the benefit and cost of an *additional* unit of activity. To emphasize this focus, economists refer to the cost of an additional unit of activity as the **marginal cost** of the activity. Similarly, the benefit of an additional unit of the activity is the **marginal benefit** of the activity.

marginal cost the increase in total cost that results from carrying out one additional unit of an activity

marginal benefit the increase in total benefit that results from carrying out one additional unit of an activity

When the problem is to discover the proper level at which to pursue an activity, the cost-benefit rule is to keep increasing the level as long as the marginal benefit of the activity exceeds its marginal cost. As the following example illustrates, however, people often fail to apply this rule correctly.

Should NASA expand the space shuttle program from four launches per year to five?

Professor Kösten Banifoot, a prominent supporter of the National Aeronautics and Space Administration's (NASA) space shuttle program, estimated that the gains from the program are currently $24 billion per year (an average of $6 billion per launch) and that its costs are currently $20 billion per year (an average of $5 billion per launch). On the basis of these estimates, Professor Banifoot testified before Congress that NASA should definitely expand the space shuttle program. Should Congress follow his advice?

To discover whether expanding the program makes economic sense, we must compare the marginal cost of a launch to its marginal benefit. The professor's estimates, however, tell us only the **average cost** and **average benefit** of the program—which are, respectively, the total cost of the program divided by the number of launches and the total benefit divided by the number of launches. Knowing the average benefit and average cost per launch for all shuttles launched thus far is simply not useful for deciding whether to expand the program. Of course, the average cost of the launches undertaken so far *might* be the same as the cost of adding another launch. But it also might be either higher or lower than the marginal cost of a launch. The same statement holds true regarding average and marginal benefits.

average cost the total cost of undertaking *n* units of an activity divided by *n*

average benefit the total benefit of undertaking *n* units of an activity divided by *n*

Suppose, for the sake of discussion, that the benefit of an additional launch is in fact the same as the average benefit per launch thus far, $6 billion. Should NASA add another launch? Not if the cost of adding the fifth launch would be more than $6 billion. And the fact that the average cost per launch is only $5 billion simply does not tell us anything about the marginal cost of the fifth launch.

Suppose, for example, that the relationship between the number of shuttles launched and the total cost of the program is as described in Table 1.1. The average

TABLE 1.1
How Total Cost Varies with the Number of Launches

Number of launches	Total cost ($ billions)	Average cost ($ billion/launch)
0	0	0
1	3	3
2	7	3.5
3	12	4
4	20	5
5	32	6.4

cost per launch (third column) when there are four launches would then be \$20 billion/4 = \$5 billion per launch, just as Professor Banifoot testified. But note in the second column of the table that adding a fifth launch would raise costs from \$20 billion to \$32 billion, making the marginal cost of the fifth launch \$12 billion. So if the benefit of an additional launch is \$6 billion, increasing the number of launches from four to five would make absolutely no economic sense. ◆

The following example illustrates how to apply the Cost-Benefit Principle correctly in this case.

How many space shuttles should NASA launch?

NASA must decide how many space shuttles to launch. The benefit of each launch is estimated to be \$6 billion and the total cost of the program again depends on the number of launches in the manner shown in Table 1.1. How many shuttles should NASA launch?

NASA should continue to launch shuttles as long as the marginal benefit of the program exceeds its marginal cost. In this example, the marginal benefit is constant at \$6 billion per launch, regardless of the number of shuttles launched. NASA should thus keep launching shuttles as long as the marginal cost per launch is less than or equal to \$6 billion.

Applying the definition of marginal cost to the total cost entries in the second column of Table 1.1 yields the marginal cost values in the third column of Table 1.2. (Because marginal cost is the change in total cost that results when we change the number of launches by one, we place each marginal cost entry midway between the rows showing the corresponding total cost entries.) Thus, for example, the marginal cost of increasing the number of launches from one to two is \$4 billion, the difference between the \$7 billion total cost of two launches and the \$3 billion total cost of one launch.

TABLE 1.2
How Marginal Cost Varies with the Number of Launches

Number of launches	Total cost (\$ billion)	Marginal cost (\$ billion/launch)
0	0	
		3
1	3	
		4
2	7	
		5
3	12	
		8
4	20	
		12
5	32	

As we see from a comparison of the \$6 billion marginal benefit per launch with the marginal cost entries in the third column of Table 1.2, the first three launches satisfy the cost-benefit test, but the fourth and fifth launches do not. NASA should thus launch three space shuttles. ◆

EXERCISE 1.4

If the marginal benefit of each launch had been not \$6 billion but \$9 billion, how many shuttles should NASA have launched?

The cost-benefit framework emphasizes that the only relevant costs and benefits in deciding whether to pursue an activity further are *marginal* costs and benefits—measures that correspond to the *increment* of activity under consideration. In many contexts, however, people seem more inclined to compare the *average* cost and benefit of the activity. As the first shuttle launch example made clear, increasing the level of an activity may not be justified, even though its average benefit at the current level is significantly greater than its average cost.

Here's an exercise that further illustrates the importance of thinking at the margin.

EXERCISE 1.5

Should a basketball team's best player take all the team's shots?

A professional basketball team has a new assistant coach. The assistant notices that one player scores on a higher percentage of his shots than other players. Based on this information, the assistant suggests to the head coach that the star player should take *all* the shots. That way, the assistant reasons, the team will score more points and win more games.

On hearing this suggestion, the head coach fires his assistant for incompetence. What was wrong with the assistant's idea?

RECAP | THREE IMPORTANT DECISION PITFALLS

1. **The pitfall of measuring costs or benefits proportionally.** Many decision makers treat a change in cost or benefit as insignificant if it constitutes only a small proportion of the original amount. Absolute dollar amounts, not proportions, should be employed to measure costs and benefits.

2. **The pitfall of ignoring implicit costs.** When performing a cost-benefit analysis of an action, it is important to account for all relevant costs, including the implicit value of alternatives that must be forgone in order to carry out the action. A resource (such as a frequent-flyer coupon) may have a high implicit cost, even if you originally got it "for free," if its best alternative use has high value. The identical resource may have a low implicit cost, however, if it has no good alternative uses.

3. **The pitfall of failing to think at the margin.** When deciding whether to perform an action, the only costs and benefits that are relevant are those that would result from taking the action. It is important to ignore sunk costs—those costs that cannot be avoided even if the action is not taken. Even though a ticket to a concert may have cost you $100, if you have already bought it and cannot sell it to anyone else, the $100 is a sunk cost and should not influence your decision about whether to go to the concert. It is also important not to confuse average costs and benefits with marginal costs and benefits. Decision makers often have ready information about the total cost and benefit of an activity, and from these it is simple to compute the activity's average cost and benefit. A common mistake is to conclude that an activity should be increased if its average benefit exceeds its average cost. The Cost-Benefit Principle tells us that the level of an activity should be increased if, and only if, its *marginal* benefit exceeds its *marginal* cost.

Some costs and benefits, especially marginal costs and benefits and implicit costs, are important for decision making, while others, like sunk costs and average costs and benefits, are essentially irrelevant. This conclusion is implicit in our original statement of the Cost-Benefit Principle (an action should be taken if, and only if, the extra benefits of taking it exceed the extra costs). When we encounter additional examples of decision pitfalls, we will flag them by inserting the icon for the Cost-Benefit Principle in the margin.

Cost-Benefit

NORMATIVE ECONOMICS VERSUS POSITIVE ECONOMICS

The examples discussed in the preceding section make the point that people *sometimes* choose irrationally. We must stress that our purpose in discussing these examples was not to suggest that people *generally* make irrational choices. On the contrary, most people appear to choose sensibly most of the time, especially when their decisions are important or familiar ones. The economist's focus on rational choice thus offers not only useful advice about making better decisions, but also a basis for predicting and explaining human behavior. We used the cost-benefit approach in this way when discussing how rising faculty salaries have led to larger class sizes. And as we will see, similar reasoning helps to explain human behavior in virtually every other domain.

The Cost-Benefit Principle is an example of a **normative economic principle,** one that provides guidance about how we *should* behave. For example, according to the Cost-Benefit Principle, we should ignore sunk costs when making decisions about the future. As our discussion of the various decision pitfalls makes clear, however, the Cost-Benefit Principle is not always a **positive,** or descriptive, **economic principle,** one that describes how we actually *will* behave. As we saw, the Cost-Benefit Principle can be tricky to implement, and people sometimes fail to heed its prescriptions.

normative economic principle one that says how people should behave

positive economic principle one that predicts how people will behave

That said, we stress that knowing the relevant costs and benefits surely does enable us to predict how people will behave much of the time. If the benefit of an action goes up, it is generally reasonable to predict that people will be more likely to take that action. And conversely, if the cost of an action goes up, the safest prediction will be that people will be less likely to take that action. This point is so important that we designate it as the **Incentive Principle.**

The Incentive Principle: A person (or a firm or a society) is more likely to take an action if its benefit rises, and less likely to take it if its cost rises. In short, incentives matter.

Incentive

The Incentive Principle is a positive economic principle. It stresses that the relevant costs and benefits usually help us predict behavior, but at the same time does not insist that people will behave rationally in each instance. For example, if the price of heating oil were to rise sharply, we would invoke the Cost-Benefit Principle to say that people *should* turn their thermostats down, and invoke the Incentive Principle to predict that average thermostat settings *will* in fact go down in most cases.

ECONOMICS: MICRO AND MACRO

By convention, we use the term **microeconomics** to describe the study of individual choices and of group behavior in individual markets. **Macroeconomics,** by contrast, is the study of the performance of national economies and of the policies that governments use to try to improve that performance. Macroeconomics tries to understand the determinants of such things as the national unemployment rate, the overall price level, and the total value of national output.

microeconomics the study of individual choice under scarcity and its implications for the behavior of prices and quantities in individual markets

macroeconomics the study of the performance of national economies and the policies that governments use to try to improve that performance

Our focus in this chapter is on issues that confront the individual decision maker, whether that individual confronts a personal decision, a family decision, a business decision, a government policy decision, or indeed any other type of decision. Further on, we'll consider economic models of groups of individuals such as all buyers or all sellers in a specific market. Later still we will turn to broader economic issues and measures.

No matter which of these levels is our focus, however, our thinking will be shaped by the fact that although economic needs and wants are effectively unlimited, the material and human resources that can be used to satisfy them are finite. Clear thinking about economic problems must therefore always take into account the idea of trade-offs—the idea that having more of one good thing usually means having less of another. Our economy and our society are shaped to a substantial degree by the choices people have made when faced with trade-offs.

THE APPROACH OF THIS TEXT

Scarcity

Choosing the number of students to register in each class is just one of many important decisions in planning an introductory economics course. Another decision, to which the Scarcity Principle applies just as strongly, concerns which of many different topics to include on the course syllabus. There is a virtually inexhaustible set of topics and issues that might be covered in an introductory course, but only limited time in which to cover them. There is no free lunch. Covering some topics inevitably means omitting others.

All textbook authors are necessarily forced to pick and choose. A textbook that covered *all* the issues ever written about in economics would take up more than a whole floor of your campus library. It is our firm view that most introductory textbooks try to cover far too much. One reason that each of us was drawn to the study of economics was that a relatively short list of the discipline's core ideas can explain a great deal of the behavior and events we see in the world around us. So rather than cover a large number of ideas at a superficial level, our strategy is to focus on this short list of core ideas, returning to each entry again and again, in many different contexts. This strategy will enable you to internalize these ideas remarkably well in the brief span of a single course. And the benefit of learning a small number of important ideas well will far outweigh the cost of having to ignore a host of other, less important ideas.

So far, we've already encountered three core ideas: the Scarcity Principle, the Cost-Benefit Principle, and the Incentive Principle. As these core ideas reemerge in the course of our discussions, we'll call your attention to them. And shortly after a *new* core idea appears, we'll highlight it by formally restating it.

A second important element in the philosophy of this text is our belief in the importance of active learning. In the same way that you can learn Spanish only by speaking and writing it, or tennis only by playing the game, you can learn economics only by *doing* economics. And because we want you to learn how to do economics, rather than just to read or listen passively as the authors or your instructor does economics, we will make every effort to encourage you to stay actively involved.

For example, instead of just telling you about an idea, we will usually first motivate the idea by showing you how it works in the context of a specific example. Often, these examples will be followed by exercises for you to try, as well as applications that show the relevance of the idea to real life. Try working the exercises *before* looking up the answers (which are at the back of the corresponding chapter).

Think critically about the applications: Do you see how they illustrate the point being made? Do they give you new insight into the issue? Work the problems at the end of the chapters and take extra care with those relating to points that you do not fully understand. Apply economic principles to the world around you. (We'll say more about this when we discuss economic naturalism below.) Finally, when you come across an idea or example that you find interesting, tell a friend about it. You'll be surprised to discover how much the mere act of explaining it helps you understand and remember the underlying principle. The more actively you can become engaged in the learning process, the more effective your learning will be.

ECONOMIC NATURALISM

With the rudiments of the cost-benefit framework under your belt, you are now in a position to become an "economic naturalist," someone who uses insights from economics to help make sense of observations from everyday life. People who have studied biology are able to observe and marvel at many details of nature that would otherwise have escaped their notice. For example, on a walk in the woods in early April, the novice may see only trees whereas the biology student notices many different species of trees and understands why some are already into leaf while others still lie dormant. Likewise, the novice may notice that in some animal species males are much larger than females, but the biology student knows that pattern occurs only in species in which males take several mates. Natural selection favors larger males in those species because their greater size helps them prevail in the often bloody contests among males for access to females. By contrast, males tend to be roughly the same size as females in monogamous species, in which there is much less fighting for mates.

In similar fashion, learning a few simple economic principles enables us to see the mundane details of ordinary human existence in a new light. Whereas the uninitiated often fail even to notice these details, the economic naturalist not only sees them, but becomes actively engaged in the attempt to understand them. Let's consider a few examples of questions economic naturalists might pose for themselves.

Example 1.1
THE ECONOMIC NATURALIST

Why do many hardware manufacturers include more than $1,000 worth of "free" software with a computer selling for only slightly more than that?

The software industry is different from many others in the sense that its customers care a great deal about product compatibility. When you and your classmates are working on a project together, for example, your task will be much simpler if you all use the same word-processing program. Likewise, an executive's life will be easier at tax time if her financial software is the same as her accountant's.

The implication is that the benefit of owning and using any given software program increases with the number of other people who use that same product. This unusual relationship gives the producers of the most popular programs an enormous advantage and often makes it hard for new programs to break into the market.

Recognizing this pattern, the Intuit Corporation offered computer makers free copies of *Quicken*, its personal financial-management software. Computer makers, for their part, were only too happy to include the program, since it made their new computers more attractive to buyers. *Quicken* soon became the standard for personal financial-management programs. By giving away free copies of the program, Intuit "primed the pump," creating an enormous demand for upgrades of *Quicken* and for more advanced versions of related software. Thus, *TurboTax* and *Macintax,* Intuit's personal income-tax software, have become the standards for tax-preparation programs. ●

Inspired by this success story, other software developers have jumped onto the bandwagon. Most hardware now comes bundled with a host of free software programs. Some software developers are even rumored to *pay* computer makers to include their programs!

The free-software example illustrates a case in which the *benefit* of a product depends on the number of other people who own that product. As the next example demonstrates, the *cost* of a product may also depend on the number of others who own it.

Example 1.2
THE ECONOMIC NATURALIST

Why don't auto manufacturers make cars without heaters?

Virtually every new car sold in the United States today has a heater. But not every car has a CD player. Why this difference?

One might be tempted to answer that although everyone *needs* a heater, people can get along without CD players. Yet heaters are of little use in places like Hawaii and southern California. What is more, cars produced as recently as the 1950s did *not* all have heaters. (The classified ad that led one young economic naturalist to his first car, a 1955 Pontiac, boasted that the vehicle had a radio, heater, and whitewall tires.)

Although heaters cost extra money to manufacture and are not useful in all parts of the country, they do not cost *much* money and are useful on at least a few days each year in most parts of the country. As time passed and people's incomes grew, manufacturers found that people were ordering fewer and fewer cars without heaters. At some point it actually became cheaper to put heaters in *all* cars, rather than bear the administrative expense of making some cars with heaters and others without. No doubt a few buyers would still order a car without a heater if they could save some money in the process, but catering to these customers is just no longer worth it.

Similar reasoning explains why certain cars today cannot be purchased without a CD player. Buyers of the 2009 BMW 750i, for example, got a CD player whether they wanted one or not. Most buyers of this car, which sells for more than $75,000, have high incomes, so the overwhelming majority of them would have chosen to order a CD player had it been sold as an option. Because of the savings made possible when all cars are produced with the same equipment, it would have actually cost BMW more to supply cars for the few who would want them without CD players.

Buyers of the least-expensive makes of car have much lower incomes on average than BMW 750i buyers. Accordingly, most of them have more pressing alternative uses for their money than to buy CD players for their cars, and this explains why some inexpensive makes continue to offer CD players only as options. But as incomes continue to grow, new cars without CD players will eventually disappear. ●

EN 1

The insights afforded by the preceding example suggest an answer to the following strange question:

Example 1.3
THE ECONOMIC NATURALIST

Why do the keypad buttons on drive-up automatic teller machines have Braille dots?

Braille dots on elevator buttons and on the keypads of walk-up automatic teller machines enable blind people to participate more fully in the normal flow of daily activity. But even though blind people can do many remarkable things, they cannot drive automobiles on public roads. Why, then, do the manufacturers of automatic teller machines install Braille dots on the machines at drive-up locations?

The answer to this riddle is that once the keypad molds have been manufactured, the cost of producing buttons with Braille dots is no higher than the cost of producing smooth buttons. Making both would require separate sets of molds and two different types of inventory. If the patrons of drive-up machines found buttons with Braille dots harder to use, there might be a reason to incur these extra costs. But since the dots pose no difficulty for sighted users, the best and cheapest solution is to produce only keypads with dots. ●

Why do the keypad buttons on drive-up automatic teller machines have Braille dots?

The preceding example was suggested by Cornell student Bill Tjoa, in response to the following assignment:

EXERCISE 1.6

In 500 words or less, use cost-benefit analysis to explain some pattern of events or behavior you have observed in your own environment.

There is probably no more useful step you can take in your study of economics than to perform several versions of the assignment in Exercise 1.6. Students who do so almost invariably become lifelong economic naturalists. Their mastery of economic concepts not only does not decay with the passage of time; it actually grows stronger. We urge you, in the strongest possible terms, to make this investment!

▪ SUMMARY ▪

- Economics is the study of how people make choices under conditions of scarcity and of the results of those choices for society. Economic analysis of human behavior begins with the assumption that people are rational—that they have well-defined goals and try to achieve them as best they can. In trying to achieve their goals, people normally face trade-offs: Because material and human resources are limited, having more of one good thing means making do with less of some other good thing. **LO1**

- Our focus in this chapter has been on how rational people make choices among alternative courses of action. Our basic tool for analyzing these decisions is cost-benefit analysis. The Cost-Benefit Principle says that a person should take an action if, and only if, the benefit of that action is at least as great as its cost. The benefit of an action is defined as the largest dollar amount the person would be willing to pay in order to take the action. The cost of an action is defined as the dollar value of everything the person must give up in order to take the action. **LO2**

- Often the question is not whether to pursue an activity but rather how many units of it to pursue. In these cases, the rational person pursues additional units as long as the marginal benefit of the activity (the benefit from pursuing an additional unit of it) exceeds its marginal cost (the cost of pursuing an additional unit of it). **LO2**

- In using the cost-benefit framework, we need not presume that people choose rationally all the time. Indeed, we identified three common pitfalls that plague decision makers in all walks of life: a tendency to treat small proportional changes as insignificant, a tendency to ignore implicit costs, and a tendency to fail to think at the margin—for example, by failing to ignore sunk costs or by failing to compare marginal costs and benefits. **LO4, LO5, LO6**

- Microeconomics is the study of individual choices and of group behavior in individual markets, while macroeconomics is the study of the performance of national economics and of the policies that governments use to try to improve economic performance.

CORE PRINCIPLES

Scarcity

The Scarcity Principle (also called the No-Free-Lunch Principle)
Although we have boundless needs and wants, the resources available to us are limited. So having more of one good thing usually means having less of another.

Cost-Benefit

The Cost-Benefit Principle
An individual (or a firm or a society) should take an action if, and only if, the extra benefits from taking the action are at least as great as the extra costs.

Incentive

The Incentive Principle
A person (or a firm or a society) is more likely to take an action if its benefit rises, and less likely to take it if its cost rises.

KEY TERMS

average benefit (12)
average cost (12)
economic surplus (16)
economics (4)
macroeconomics (15)
marginal benefit (12)
marginal cost (12)
microeconomics (15)
normative economic principle (15)
opportunity cost (7)
positive economic principle (15)
rational person (6)
sunk cost (11)

REVIEW QUESTIONS

1. A friend of yours on the tennis team says, "Private tennis lessons are definitely better than group lessons." Explain what you think he means by this statement. Then use the Cost-Benefit Principle to explain why private lessons are not necessarily the best choice for everyone. **LO2**
2. True or false: Your willingness to drive downtown to save $30 on a new appliance should depend on what fraction of the total selling price $30 is. Explain. **LO4**
3. Why might someone who is trying to decide whether to see a movie be more likely to focus on the $10 ticket price than on the $20 she would fail to earn by not babysitting? **LO5**
4. Many people think of their air travel as being free when they use frequent-flyer coupons. Explain why these people are likely to make wasteful travel decisions. **LO5**
5. Is the nonrefundable tuition payment you made to your university this semester a sunk cost? How would your answer differ if your university were to offer a full tuition refund to any student who dropped out of school during the first two months of the semester? **LO6**

PROBLEMS

McGraw-Hill's HOMEWORK MANAGER®

1. The most you would be willing to pay for having a freshly washed car before going out on a date is $6. The smallest amount for which you would be willing to wash someone else's car is $3.50. You are going out this evening and your car is dirty. How much economic surplus would you receive from washing it? **LO2**
2. To earn extra money in the summer, you grow tomatoes and sell them at the farmers' market for 30 cents per pound. By adding compost to your garden, you can increase your yield as shown in the table below. If compost costs 50 cents per pound and your goal is to make as much money as possible, how many pounds of compost should you add? **LO2**

Pounds of compost	Pounds of tomatoes
0	100
1	120
2	125
3	128
4	130
5	131
6	131.5

3. Residents of your city are charged a fixed weekly fee of $6 for garbage collection. They are allowed to put out as many cans as they wish. The average household disposes of three cans of garbage per week under this plan. Now suppose that your city changes to a "tag" system. Each can of refuse to be collected must have a tag affixed to it. The tags cost $2 each and are not reusable. What effect do you think the introduction of the tag system will have on the total quantity of garbage collected in your city? Explain briefly. **LO2**
4. Once a week, Smith purchases a six-pack of cola and puts it in his refrigerator for his two children. He invariably discovers that all six cans are gone on the first day. Jones also purchases a six-pack of cola once a week for his two children, but unlike Smith, he tells them that each may drink no more than three cans. If the children use cost-benefit analysis each time they decide whether to drink a can of cola, explain why the cola lasts much longer at Jones's house than at Smith's. **LO2**
5. Tom is a mushroom farmer. He invests all his spare cash in additional mushrooms, which grow on otherwise useless land behind his barn. The mushrooms double in weight during their first year, after which time they are harvested and sold at a constant price per pound. Tom's friend Dick asks Tom for a loan of $200, which he promises to repay after 1 year. How much interest will Dick have to pay Tom in order for Tom to recover his opportunity cost of making the loan? Explain briefly. **LO2**
6. Suppose that in the last few seconds you devoted to question 1 on your physics exam you earned 4 extra points, while in the last few seconds you devoted to question 2 you earned 10 extra points. You earned a total of 48 and 12 points, respectively, on the two questions and the total time you spent on each was the same. If you could take the exam again, how—if at all—should you reallocate your time between these questions? **LO2**
7. Martha and Sarah have the same preferences and incomes. Just as Martha arrived at the theater to see a play, she discovered that she had lost the $10 ticket she had purchased earlier. Sarah also just arrived at the theater planning to buy a ticket to see the same play when she discovered that she had lost a $10 bill from her wallet. If both Martha and Sarah are rational and both still have enough money to pay for a ticket, is one of them more likely than the other to go ahead and see the play anyway? **LO2**
8.* You and your friend Joe have identical tastes. At 2 p.m., you go to the local Ticketmaster outlet and buy a $30 ticket to a basketball game to be played that night in Syracuse, 50 miles north of your home in Ithaca. Joe plans to attend the same game, but because he cannot get to the Ticketmaster outlet, he plans to buy his ticket at the game. Tickets sold at the game cost only $25 because they carry no Ticketmaster surcharge. (Many people nonetheless pay the higher

*Problems marked with an asterisk (*) are more difficult.

price at Ticketmaster, to be sure of getting good seats.) At 4 p.m., an unexpected snowstorm begins, making the prospect of the drive to Syracuse much less attractive than before (but assuring the availability of good seats). If both you and Joe are rational, is one of you more likely to attend the game than the other? **LO2**

9.* For each long-distance call anywhere in the continental United States, a new phone service will charge users 30 cents per minute for the first 2 minutes and 2 cents per minute for additional minutes in each call. Tom's current phone service charges 10 cents per minute for all calls, and his calls are never shorter than 7 minutes. If Tom's dorm switches to the new phone service, what will happen to the average length of his calls? **LO3**

10.* The meal plan at university A lets students eat as much as they like for a fixed fee of $500 per semester. The average student there eats 250 pounds of food per semester. University B charges $500 for a book of meal tickets that entitles the student to eat 250 pounds of food per semester. If the student eats more than 250 pounds, he or she pays $2 for each additional pound; if the student eats less, he or she gets a $2 per pound refund. If students are rational, at which university will average food consumption be higher? Explain briefly. **LO3**

ANSWERS TO IN-CHAPTER EXERCISES

1.1 The benefit of buying the game downtown is again $10 but the cost is now $12, so your economic surplus from buying it downtown would be $10 − $12 = −$2. Since your economic surplus from making the trip would be negative, you should buy at the campus store. **LO2**

1.2 Saving $100 is $10 more valuable than saving $90, even though the percentage saved is much greater in the case of the Chicago ticket. **LO4**

1.3 Since you now have no alternative use for your coupon, the opportunity cost of using it to pay for the Fort Lauderdale trip is zero. That means your economic surplus from the trip will be $1,350 − $1,000 = $350 > 0, so you should use your coupon and go to Fort Lauderdale. **LO2**

1.4 The marginal benefit of the fourth launch is $9 billion, which exceeds its marginal cost of $8 billion, so the fourth launch should be added. But the fifth launch should not, since its marginal cost ($12 billion) exceeds its marginal benefit ($9 billion). **LO2**

1.5 If the star player takes one more shot, some other player must take one less. The fact that the star player's *average* success rate is higher than the other players' does not mean that the probability of making his *next* shot (the marginal benefit of having him shoot once more) is higher than the probability of another player making his next shot. Indeed, if the best player took all his team's shots, the other team would focus its defensive effort entirely on him, in which case letting others shoot would definitely pay. **LO6**

*Problems marked with an asterisk (*) are more difficult.

APPENDIX

Working with Equations, Graphs, and Tables

Although many of the examples and most of the end-of-chapter problems in this book are quantitative, none requires mathematical skills beyond rudimentary high school algebra and geometry. In this brief appendix, we review some of the skills you'll need for dealing with these examples and problems.

One important skill is to be able to read simple verbal descriptions and translate the information they provide into the relevant equations or graphs. You'll also need to be able to translate information given in tabular form into an equation or graph, and sometimes you'll need to translate graphical information into a table or equation. Finally, you'll need to be able to solve simple systems with two equations and two unknowns. The following examples illustrate all the tools you'll need.

USING A VERBAL DESCRIPTION TO CONSTRUCT AN EQUATION

We begin with an example that shows how to construct a long-distance telephone billing equation from a verbal description of the billing plan.

Your long-distance telephone plan charges you $5 per month plus 10 cents per minute for long-distance calls. Write an equation that describes your monthly telephone bill.

equation a mathematical expression that describes the relationship between two or more variables

variable a quantity that is free to take a range of different values

dependent variable a variable in an equation whose value is determined by the value taken by another variable in the equation

independent variable a variable in an equation whose value determines the value taken by another variable in the equation

constant (or parameter) a quantity that is fixed in value

An **equation** is a simple mathematical expression that describes the relationship between two or more **variables**, or quantities that are free to assume different values in some range. The most common type of equation we'll work with contains two types of variables: **dependent variables** and **independent variables.** In this example, the dependent variable is the dollar amount of your monthly telephone bill and the independent variable is the variable on which your bill depends, namely, the volume of long-distance calls you make during the month. Your bill also depends on the $5 monthly fee and the 10 cents per minute charge. But, in this example, those amounts are **constants,** not variables. A constant, also called a **parameter,** is a quantity in an equation that is fixed in value, not free to vary. As the terms suggest, the dependent variable describes an outcome that depends on the value taken by the independent variable.

Once you've identified the dependent variable and the independent variable, choose simple symbols to represent them. In algebra courses, X is typically used to represent the independent variable and Y the dependent variable. Many people find it easier to remember what the variables stand for, however, if they choose symbols that are linked in some straightforward way to the quantities that the variables represent. Thus, in this example, we might use B to represent your monthly *bill* in dollars and T to represent the total *time* in minutes you spent during the month on long-distance calls.

Having identified the relevant variables and chosen symbols to represent them, you are now in a position to write the equation that links them:

$$B = 5 + 0.10T, \tag{1A.1}$$

where B is your monthly long-distance bill in dollars and T is your monthly total long-distance calling time in minutes. The fixed monthly fee (5) and the charge per minute (0.10) are parameters in this equation. Note the importance of being clear about the units of measure. Because B represents the monthly bill in dollars, we must also express the fixed monthly fee and the per-minute charge in dollars, which is why the latter number appears in Equation 1A.1 as 0.10 rather than 10. Equation 1A.1 follows the normal convention in which the dependent variable appears by itself on the left-hand side while the independent variable or variables and constants appear on the right-hand side.

Once we have the equation for the monthly bill, we can use it to calculate how much you'll owe as a function of your monthly volume of long-distance calls. For example, if you make 32 minutes of calls, you can calculate your monthly bill by simply substituting 32 minutes for T in Equation 1A.1:

$$B = 5 + 0.10(32) = 8.20. \tag{1A.2}$$

Your monthly bill when you make 32 minutes of calls is thus equal to $8.20. ◆

EXERCISE 1A.1

Under the monthly billing plan described in the example above, how much would you owe for a month during which you made 45 minutes of long-distance calls?

GRAPHING THE EQUATION OF A STRAIGHT LINE

The next example shows how to portray the billing plan described in the preceding example as a graph.

Construct a graph that portrays the monthly long-distance telephone billing plan described in the preceding example, putting your telephone charges, in dollars per month, on the vertical axis and your total volume of calls, in minutes per month, on the horizontal axis.

The first step in responding to this instruction is the one we just took, namely, to translate the verbal description of the billing plan into an equation. When graphing an equation, the normal convention is to use the vertical axis to represent the dependent variable and the horizontal axis to represent the independent variable. In Figure 1A.1, we therefore put B on the vertical axis and T on the horizontal axis. One way to construct the graph shown in the figure is to begin by plotting the monthly bill values that correspond to several different total amounts of long-distance calls. For example, someone who makes 10 minutes of calls during the month would have a bill of $B = 5 + 0.10(10) = \$6$. Thus, in Figure 1A.1 the value of 10 minutes per month on the horizontal axis corresponds to a bill of \$6 per month on the vertical axis (point A). Someone who makes 30 minutes of long-distance calls during the month will have a monthly bill of $B = 5 + 0.10(30) = \$8$, so the value of 30 minutes per month on the horizontal axis corresponds to \$8 per month on the vertical axis (point C). Similarly, someone who makes 70 minutes of long-distance calls during the month will have a monthly bill of $B = 5 + 0.10(70) = \$12$, so the value of 70 minutes on the horizontal axis corresponds to \$12 on the vertical axis (point D). The line joining these points is the graph of the monthly billing Equation 1A.1.

As shown in Figure 1A.1, the graph of the equation $B = 5 + 0.10T$ is a straight line. The parameter 5 is the **vertical intercept** of the line—the value of B when $T = 0$, or the point at which the line intersects the vertical axis. The parameter 0.10 is the **slope** of the line, which is the ratio of the **rise** of the line to the corresponding **run.** The ratio rise/run is simply the vertical distance between any two points on the line divided by the horizontal distance between those points. For example, if we choose points A and C in Figure 1A.1, the rise is $8 - 6 = 2$ and the corresponding run is $30 - 10 = 20$, so rise/run $= 2/20 = 0.10$. More generally, for the graph of any equation $Y = a + bX$, the parameter a is the vertical intercept and the parameter b is the slope. ◆

vertical intercept in a straight line, the value taken by the dependent variable when the independent variable equals zero

slope in a straight line, the ratio of the vertical distance the straight line travels between any two points ***(rise)*** to the corresponding horizontal distance ***(run)***

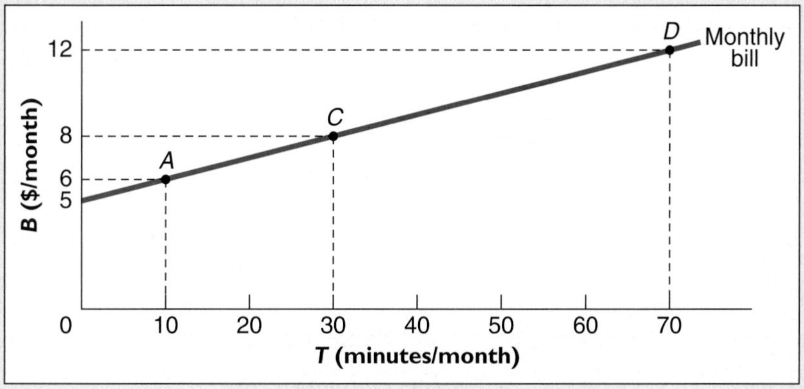

FIGURE 1A.1
The Monthly Telephone Bill in Example 1A.1.
The graph of the equation $B = 5 + 0.10T$ is the straight line shown. Its vertical intercept is 5 and its slope is 0.10.

DERIVING THE EQUATION OF A STRAIGHT LINE FROM ITS GRAPH

The next example shows how to derive the equation for a straight line from a graph of the line.

Figure 1A.2 shows the graph of the monthly billing plan for a new long-distance plan. What is the equation for this graph? How much is the fixed monthly fee under this plan? How much is the charge per minute?

FIGURE 1A.2
Another Monthly Long-Distance Plan.
The vertical distance between points A and C is $12 - 8 = 4$ units, and the horizontal distance between points A and C is $40 - 20 = 20$, so the slope of the line is $4/20 = 1/5 = 0.20$. The vertical intercept (the value of B when $T = 0$) is 4. So the equation for the billing plan shown is $B = 4 + 0.20T$.

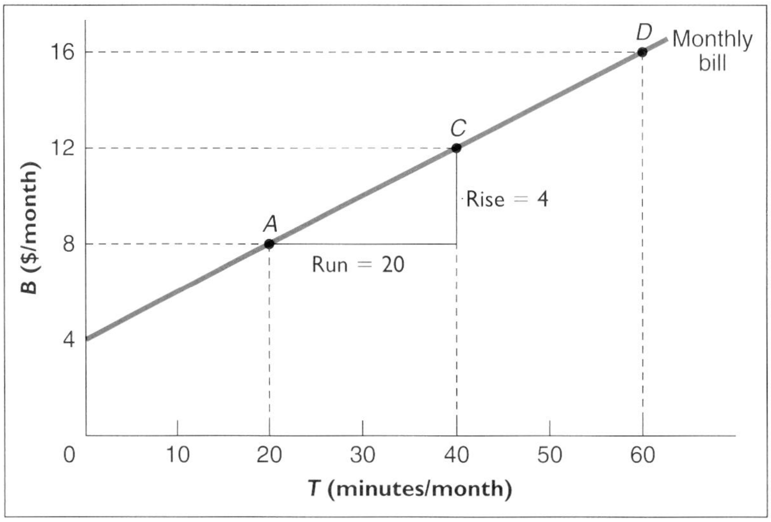

The slope of the line shown is the rise between any two points divided by the corresponding run. For points A and C, rise $= 12 - 8 = 4$ and run $= 40 - 20 = 20$, so the slope equals rise/run $= 4/20 = 1/15 = 0.20$. And since the horizontal intercept of the line is 4, its equation must be given by

$$B = 4 + 0.20T. \tag{1A.3}$$

Under this plan, the fixed monthly fee is the value of the bill when $T = 0$, which is \$4. The charge per minute is the slope of the billing line, 0.20, or 20 cents per minute. ◆

EXERCISE 1A.2

Write the equation for the billing plan shown in the accompanying graph. How much is its fixed monthly fee? Its charge per minute?

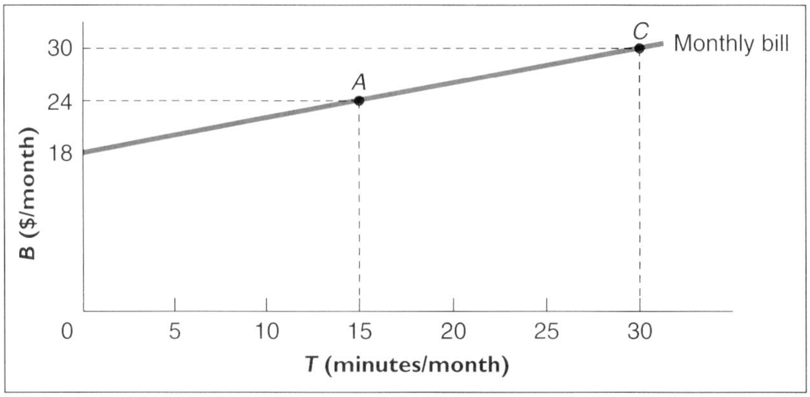

CHANGES IN THE VERTICAL INTERCEPT AND SLOPE

The next two examples and exercises provide practice in seeing how a line shifts with a change in its vertical intercept or slope.

Show how the billing plan whose graph is in Figure 1A.2 would change if the monthly fixed fee were increased from \$4 to \$8.

An increase in the monthly fixed fee from \$4 to \$8 would increase the vertical intercept of the billing plan by \$4 but would leave its slope unchanged. An increase in the fixed fee thus leads to a parallel upward shift in the billing plan by \$4, as shown in Figure 1A.3. For any given number of minutes of long-distance calls, the monthly charge on the new bill will be \$4 higher than on the old bill. Thus 20 minutes of calls per month costs \$8 under the original plan (point *A*) but \$12 under the new plan (point *A′*). And 40 minutes costs \$12 under the original plan (point C), \$16 under the new plan (point C′); and 60 minutes costs \$16 under the original plan (point *D*), \$20 under the new plan (point *D′*). ◆

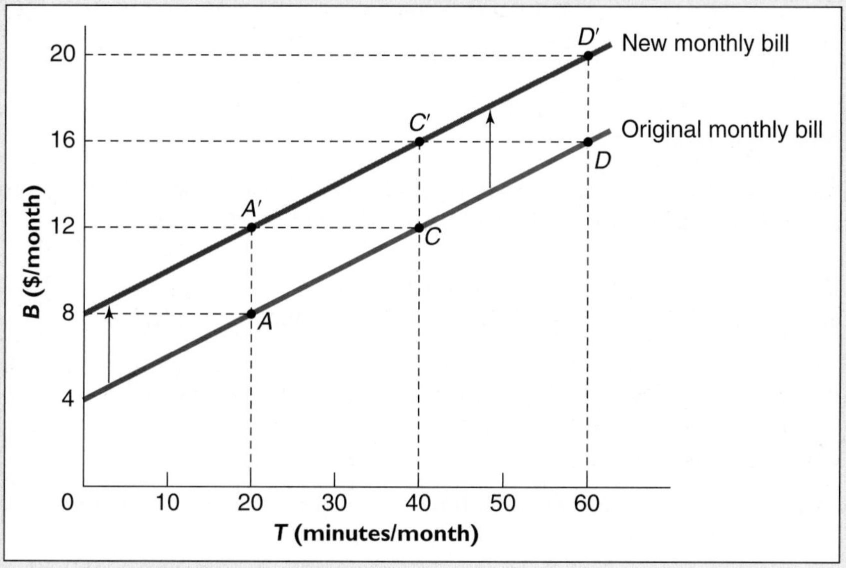

FIGURE 1A.3
The Effect of an Increase in the Vertical Intercept.
An increase in the vertical intercept of a straight line produces an upward parallel shift in the line.

EXERCISE 1A.3

Show how the billing plan whose graph is in Figure 1A.2 would change if the monthly fixed fee were reduced from \$4 to \$2.

Show how the billing plan whose graph is in Figure 1A.2 would change if the charge per minute were increased from 20 cents to 40 cents.

Because the monthly fixed fee is unchanged, the vertical intercept of the new billing plan continues to be 4. But the slope of the new plan, shown in Figure 1A.4, is 0.40, or twice the slope of the original plan. More generally, in the equation $Y = a + bX$, an increase in b makes the slope of the graph of the equation steeper.

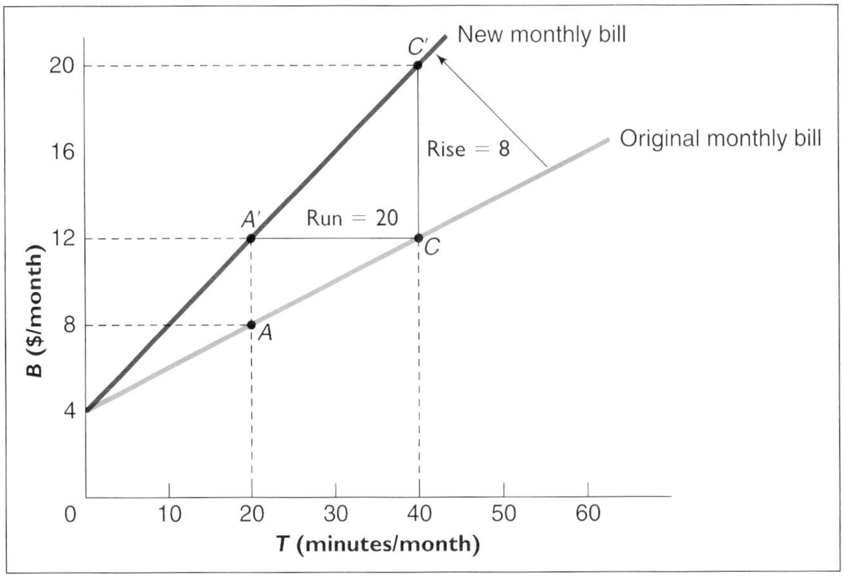

FIGURE 1A.4
The Effect of an Increase in the Charge per Minute.
Because the fixed monthly fee continues to be $4, the vertical intercept of the new plan is the same as that of the original plan. With the new charge per minute of 40 cents, the slope of the billing plan rises from 0.20 to 0.40.

◆

EXERCISE 1A.4

Show how the billing plan whose graph is in Figure 1A.2 would change if the charge per minute were reduced from 20 cents to 10 cents.

Exercise 1A.4 illustrates the general rule that in an equation $Y = a + bX$, a reduction in b makes the slope of the graph of the equation less steep.

CONSTRUCTING EQUATIONS AND GRAPHS FROM TABLES

The next example and exercise show how to transform tabular information into an equation or graph.

Table 1A.1 shows four points from a monthly long-distance telephone billing equation. If all points on this billing equation lie on a straight line, find the vertical intercept of the equation and graph it. What is the monthly fixed fee? What is the charge per minute? Calculate the total bill for a month with 1 hour of long-distance calls.

TABLE 1A.1
Points on a Long-Distance Billing Plan

Long-distance bill ($/month)	Total long-distance calls (minutes/month)
10.50	10
11.00	20
11.50	30
12.00	40

One approach to this problem is simply to plot any two points from the table on a graph. Since we are told that the billing equation is a straight line, that line must be

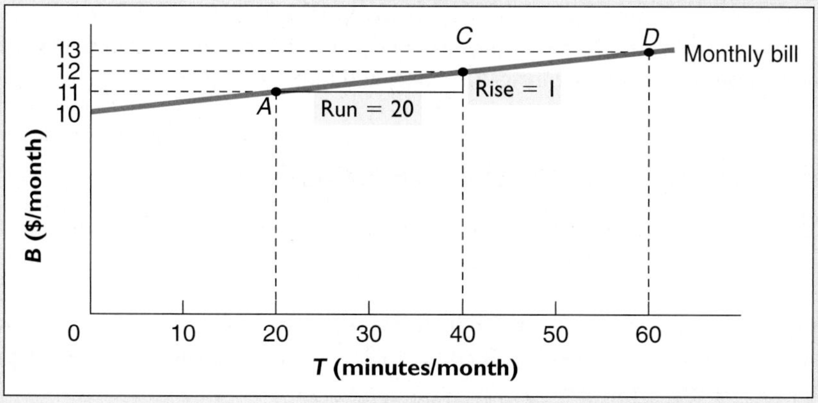

FIGURE 1A.5
Plotting the Monthly Billing Equation from a Sample of Points.
Point *A* is taken from row 2, Table 1A.1, and point *C* from row 4. The monthly billing plan is the straight line that passes through these points.

the one that passes through any two of its points. Thus, in Figure 1A.5 we use *A* to denote the point from Table 1A.1 for which a monthly bill of $11 corresponds to 20 minutes per month of calls (second row) and *C* to denote the point for which a monthly bill of $12 corresponds to 40 minutes per month of calls (fourth row). The straight line passing through these points is the graph of the billing equation.

Unless you have a steady hand, however, or use extremely large graph paper, the method of extending a line between two points on the billing plan is unlikely to be very accurate. An alternative approach is to calculate the equation for the billing plan directly. Since the equation is a straight line, we know that it takes the general form $B = f + sT$, where f is the fixed monthly fee and s is the slope. Our goal is to calculate the vertical intercept f and the slope s. From the same two points we plotted earlier, *A* and *C*, we can calculate the slope of the billing plan as $s = \text{rise/run} = 1/20 = 0.05$.

So all that remains is to calculate f, the fixed monthly fee. At point *C* on the billing plan, the total monthly bill is $12 for 40 minutes, so we can substitute $B = 12$, $s = 0.05$, and $T = 40$ into the general equation $B = f + sT$ to obtain

$$12 = f + 0.05(40), \tag{1A.4}$$

or

$$12 = f + 2, \tag{1A.5}$$

which solves for $f = 10$. So the monthly billing equation must be

$$B = 10 + 0.05T. \tag{1A.6}$$

For this billing equation, the fixed fee is $10 per month, the calling charge is 5 cents per minute ($0.05/minute), and the total bill for a month with 1 hour of long-distance calls is $B = 10 + 0.05(60) = \$13$, just as shown in Figure 1A.5. ◆

EXERCISE 1A.5

The following table shows four points from a monthly long-distance telephone billing plan.

Long-distance bill ($/month)	Total long-distance calls (minutes/month)
20.00	10
30.00	20
40.00	30
50.00	40

If all points on this billing plan lie on a straight line, find the vertical intercept of the corresponding equation without graphing it. What is the monthly fixed fee? What is the charge per minute? How much would the charges be for 1 hour of long-distance calls per month?

SOLVING SIMULTANEOUS EQUATIONS

The next example and exercise demonstrate how to proceed when you need to solve two equations with two unknowns.

Suppose you are trying to choose between two rate plans for your long-distance telephone service. If you choose Plan 1, your charges will be computed according to the equation

$$B = 10 + 0.04T, \quad (1A.7)$$

where *B* is again your monthly bill in dollars and *T* is your monthly volume of long-distance calls in minutes. If you choose Plan 2, your monthly bill will be computed according to the equation

$$B = 20 + 0.02T. \quad (1A.8)$$

How many minutes of long-distance calls would you have to make each month, on average, to make Plan 2 cheaper?

Plan 1 has the attractive feature of a relatively low monthly fixed fee, but also the unattractive feature of a relatively high rate per minute. In contrast, Plan 2 has a relatively high fixed fee but a relatively low rate per minute. Someone who made an extremely low volume of calls (for example, 10 minutes per month) would do better under Plan 1 (monthly bill = \$10.40) than under Plan 2 (monthly bill = \$20.20) because the low fixed fee of Plan 1 would more than compensate for its higher rate per minute. Conversely, someone who made an extremely high volume of calls (say, 10,000 minutes per month) would do better under Plan 2 (monthly bill = \$220) than under Plan 1 (monthly bill = \$410) because Plan 2's lower rate per minute would more than compensate for its higher fixed fee.

Our task here is to find the *break-even calling volume,* which is the monthly calling volume for which the monthly bill is the same under the two plans. One way to answer this question is to graph the two billing plans and see where they cross. At that crossing point, the two equations are satisfied simultaneously, which means that the monthly call volumes will be the same under both plans, as will the monthly bills.

In Figure 1A.6, we see that the graphs of the two plans cross at *A*, where both yield a monthly bill of \$30 for 500 minutes of calls per month. The break-even calling volume for these plans is thus 500 minutes per month. If your calling volume is higher than that, on average, you will save money by choosing Plan 2. For example, if you average 700 minutes, your monthly bill under Plan 2 (\$34) will be \$4 cheaper than under Plan 1 (\$38). Conversely, if you average fewer than 500 minutes each month, you will do better under Plan 1. For example, if you average only 200 minutes, your monthly bill under Plan 1 (\$18) will be \$6 cheaper than under Plan 2 (\$24). At 500 minutes per month, the two plans cost exactly the same (\$30).

The question posed here also may be answered algebraically. As in the graphical approach just discussed, our goal is to find the point (T, B) that satisfies both billing equations simultaneously. As a first step, we rewrite the two billing equations, one on top of the other, as follows:

$$B = 10 + 0.04T. \qquad \text{(Plan 1)}$$

$$B = 20 + 0.02T. \qquad \text{(Plan 2)}$$

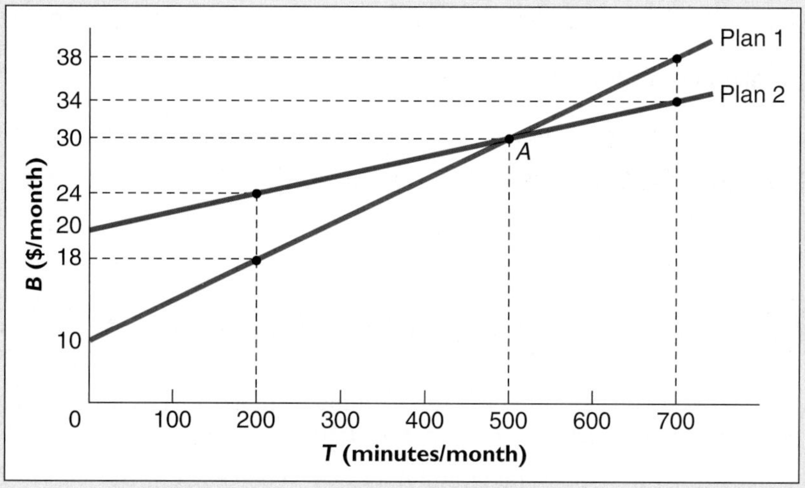

FIGURE 1A.6
The Break-Even Volume of Long-Distance Calls.
When your volume of long-distance calls is 500 minutes per month, your monthly bill will be the same under both plans. For higher calling volumes, Plan 2 is cheaper; Plan 1 is cheaper for lower volumes.

As you'll recall from high school algebra, if we subtract the terms from each side of one equation from the corresponding terms of the other equation, the resulting differences must be equal. So if we subtract the terms on each side of the Plan 2 equation from the corresponding terms in the Plan 1 equation, we get

$$B = 10 + 0.04T \qquad \text{(Plan 1)}$$

$$-B = -20 - 0.02T \qquad \text{(−Plan 2)}$$

$$0 = -10 + 0.02T \qquad \text{(Plan 1 − Plan 2).}$$

Finally, we solve the last equation (Plan 1 − Plan 2) to get $T = 500$.

Plugging $T = 500$ into either plan's equation, we then find $B = 30$. For example, Plan 1's equation yields $10 + 0.04(500) = 30$, as does Plan 2's: $20 + 0.2(500) = 30$.

Because, the point $(T, B) = (500, 30)$ lies on the equations for both plans simultaneously, the algebraic approach just described is often called *the method of simultaneous equations.* ◆

EXERCISE 1A.6

Suppose you are trying to choose between two rate plans for your long-distance telephone service. If you choose Plan 1, your monthly bill will be computed according to the equation

$$B = 10 + 0.10T \qquad \textbf{(Plan 1),}$$

where *B* is again your monthly bill in dollars and *T* is your monthly volume of long-distance calls in minutes. If you choose Plan 2, your monthly bill will be computed according to the equation

$$B = 100 + 0.01T \qquad \textbf{(Plan 2).}$$

Use the algebraic approach described in the preceding example to find the break-even level of monthly call volume for these plans.

KEY TERMS

constant (24)
dependent variable (24)
equation (24)
independent variable (24)
parameter (24)
rise (25)
run (25)
slope (25)
variable (24)
vertical intercept (25)

ANSWERS TO IN-APPENDIX EXERCISES

1A.1 To calculate your monthly bill for 45 minutes of calls, substitute 45 minutes for T in equation 1A.1 to get $B = 5 + 0.10(45) = \$9.50$.

1A.2 Calculating the slope using points A and C, we have rise $= 30 - 24 = 6$ and run $= 30 - 15 = 15$, so rise/run $= 6/15 = 2/5 = 0.40$. And since the horizontal intercept of the line is 18, its equation is $B = 18 + 0.40T$. Under this plan, the fixed monthly fee is \$18 and the charge per minute is the slope of the billing line, 0.40, or 40 cents per minute.

1A.3 A \$2 reduction in the monthly fixed fee would produce a downward parallel shift in the billing plan by \$2.

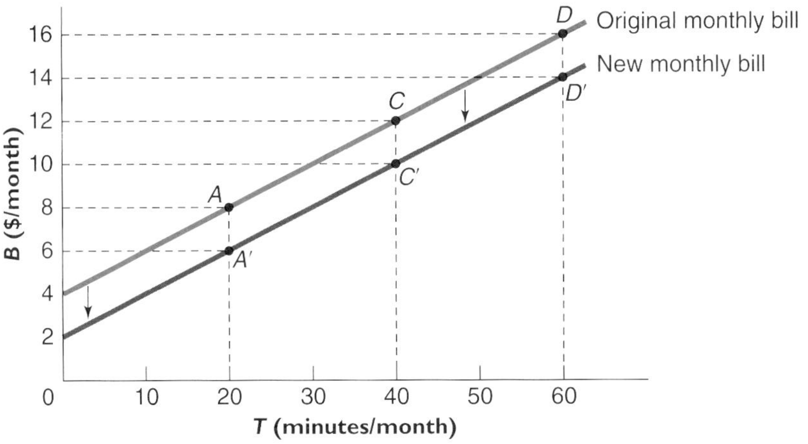

1A.4 With an unchanged monthly fixed fee, the vertical intercept of the new billing plan continues to be 4. The slope of the new plan is 0.10, half the slope of the original plan.

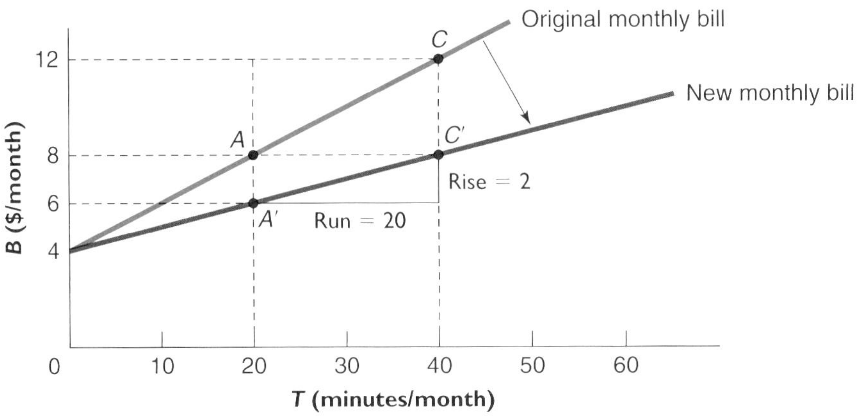

1A.5 Let the billing equation be $B = f + sT$, where f is the fixed monthly fee and s is the slope. From the first two points in the table, calculate the slope s = rise/run = 10/10 = 1.0. To calculate f, we can use the information in row 1 of the table to write the billing equation as $20 = f + 1.0(10)$ and solve for $f = 10$. So the monthly billing equation must be $B = 10 + 1.0T$. For this billing equation, the fixed fee is \$10 per month, the calling charge is \$1 per minute, and the total bill for a month with 1 hour of long-distance calls is $B = 10 + 1.0(60) = \$70$.

1A.6 Subtracting the Plan 2 equation from the Plan 1 equation yields the equation

$$0 = -90 + 0.09T \qquad \text{(Plan 1 − Plan 2)},$$

which solves for $T = 1{,}000$. So if you average more than 1,000 minutes of long-distance calls each month, you'll do better on Plan 2.

CHAPTER 2

Comparative Advantage

LEARNING OBJECTIVES

In this chapter, you'll master ideas that help explain observed patterns of exchange in the marketplace. These ideas include

1. The principle of comparative advantage
2. The principle of increasing opportunity cost (also called the low-hanging fruit principle)
3. Factors that shift the menu of production possibilities.
4. The role of comparative advantage in international trade.
5. Why some jobs are more vulnerable to outsourcing than others.

During a stint as a Peace Corps volunteer in rural Nepal, a young economic naturalist employed a cook named Birkhaman, who came from a remote Himalayan village in neighboring Bhutan. Although Birkhaman had virtually no formal education, he was spectacularly resourceful. His primary duties, to prepare food and maintain the kitchen, he performed extremely well. But he also had other skills. He could thatch a roof, butcher a goat, and repair shoes. An able tinsmith and a good carpenter, he could sew and fix a broken alarm clock, as well as plaster walls. And he was a local authority on home remedies.

Birkhaman's range of skills was broad even in Nepal, where the least-skilled villager could perform a wide range of services that most Americans hire others to perform. Why this difference in skills and employment?

One might be tempted to answer that the Nepalese are simply too poor to hire others to perform these services. Nepal is indeed a poor country, whose income per person is less than one one-fortieth that of the United States. Few Nepalese have spare cash to spend on outside services. But as reasonable as this poverty explanation may seem, the reverse is actually the case. The Nepalese do not perform their own services because they are poor; rather, they are poor largely *because* they perform their own services.

The alternative to a system in which everyone is a jack of all trades is one in which people *specialize* in particular goods and services, then satisfy their needs by trading among themselves. Economic systems based on specialization and the

Photo Courtesy of Robert H. Frank

Did this man perform most of his own services because he was poor, or was he poor because he performed most of his own services?

exchange of goods and services are generally far more productive than those with less specialization. Our task in this chapter is to investigate why this is so. In doing so, we will explore why people choose to exchange goods and services in the first place, rather than having each person produce his or her own food, cars, clothing, shelter, and the like.

As this chapter will show, the reason that specialization is so productive is the existence of what economists call *comparative advantage*. Roughly, a person has a comparative advantage at producing a particular good or service, say, haircuts, if that person is *relatively* more efficient at producing haircuts than at producing other goods or services. We will see that we can all have more of *every* good and service if each of us specializes in the activities at which we have a comparative advantage.

This chapter also will introduce the *production possibilities curve*, which is a graphical method of describing the combinations of goods and services that an economy can produce. The development of this tool will allow us to see much more precisely how specialization enhances the productive capacity of even the simplest economy.

EXCHANGE AND OPPORTUNITY COST

Scarcity

The Scarcity Principle (see Chapter 1) reminds us that the opportunity cost of spending more time on any one activity is having less time available to spend on others. As the following example makes clear, this principle helps explain why everyone can do better by concentrating on those activities at which he or she performs best relative to others.

Should Joe Jamail write his own will?

Courtesy of Joe Jamail

Should a Joe Jamail prepare his own will?

Joe Jamail, known in the legal profession as "The King of Torts," is the most renowned trial lawyer in American history. And at number 317 on the Forbes list of the 400 richest Americans, he is also one of the wealthiest, with net assets totaling more than $1 billion.

But although Mr. Jamail devotes virtually all of his working hours to high-profile litigation, he is also competent to perform a much broader range of legal services. Suppose, for example, that he could prepare his own will in two hours, only half as long as it would take any other attorney. Does that mean that Jamail should prepare his own will?

On the strength of his talent as a litigator, Jamail earns many millions of dollars a year, which means that the opportunity cost of any time he spends preparing his will would be several thousand dollars per hour. Attorneys who specialize in property law typically earn far less than that amount. Jamail would have little difficulty engaging a competent property lawyer who could prepare his will for him for less than $800. So even though Jamail's considerable skills would enable him to perform this task more quickly than another attorney, it would not be in his interest to prepare his own will. ◆

absolute advantage one person has an absolute advantage over another if he or she takes fewer hours to perform a task than the other person

comparative advantage one person has a comparative advantage over another if his or her opportunity cost of performing a task is lower than the other person's opportunity cost

In the preceding example, economists would say that Jamail has an **absolute advantage** at preparing his will but a **comparative advantage** at trial work. He has an absolute advantage at preparing his will because he can perform that task in less time than a property lawyer could. Even so, the property lawyer has a comparative advantage at preparing wills because his opportunity cost of performing that task is lower than Jamail's.

The point of the preceding example is not that people whose time is valuable should never perform their own services. That example made the implicit assumption that Jamail would have been equally happy to spend an hour preparing his will or preparing for a trial. But suppose he was tired of trial preparation and felt it might be enjoyable to refresh his knowledge of property law. Preparing his own will might then have made perfect sense! But unless he expected to gain special satisfaction from performing that task, he would almost certainly do better to hire a property lawyer. The property lawyer would also benefit, or else she wouldn't have offered to prepare wills for the stated price.

THE PRINCIPLE OF COMPARATIVE ADVANTAGE

One of the most important insights of modern economics is that when two people (or two nations) have different opportunity costs of performing various tasks, they can always increase the total value of available goods and services by trading with one another. The following simple example captures the logic behind this insight.

Should Paula update her own Web page?

Consider a small community in which Paula is the only professional bicycle mechanic and Beth is the only professional HTML programmer. Paula also happens to be an even better HTML programmer than Beth. If the amount of time each of them takes to perform these tasks is as shown in Table 2.1, and if each regards the two tasks as equally pleasant (or unpleasant), does the fact that Paula can program faster than Beth imply that Paula should update her own Web page?

The entries in the table show that Paula has an absolute advantage over Beth in both activities. While Paula, the mechanic, needs only 20 minutes to update a Web page, Beth, the programmer, needs 30 minutes. Paula's advantage over Beth is even greater when the task is fixing bikes: She can complete a repair in only 10 minutes, compared to Beth's 30 minutes.

TABLE 2.1
Productivity Information for Paula and Beth

	Time to update a Web page	Time to complete a bicycle repair
Paula	20 minutes	10 minutes
Beth	30 minutes	30 minutes

But the fact that Paula is a better programmer than Beth does *not* imply that Paula should update her own Web page. As with the lawyer who litigates instead of preparing his own will, Beth has a comparative advantage over Paula at programming: She is *relatively* more productive at programming than Paula. Similarly, Paula has a comparative advantage in bicycle repair. (Remember that a person has a comparative advantage at a given task if his or her opportunity cost of performing that task is lower than another person's.)

What is Beth's opportunity cost of updating a Web page? Since she takes 30 minutes to update each page—the same amount of time she takes to fix a bicycle—her opportunity cost of updating a Web page is one bicycle repair. In other words, by taking the time to update a Web page, Beth is effectively giving up the opportunity to do one bicycle repair. Paula, in contrast, can complete two bicycle repairs in the time she takes to update a single Web page. For her, the opportunity cost of updating a Web page is two bicycle repairs. Paula's opportunity cost of programming, measured in terms of bicycle repairs forgone, is twice as high as Beth's. Thus, Beth has a comparative advantage at programming.

TABLE 2.2
Opportunity Costs for Paula and Beth

	Opportunity cost of updating a Web page	Opportunity cost of a bicycle repair
Paula	2 bicycle repairs	0.5 Web page update
Beth	1 bicycle repair	1 Web page update

The interesting and important implication of the opportunity cost comparison summarized in Table 2.2 is that the total number of bicycle repairs and Web updates accomplished if Paula and Beth both spend part of their time at each activity will always be smaller than the number accomplished if each specializes in the activity in which she has a comparative advantage. Suppose, for example, that people in their community demand a total of 16 Web page updates per day. If Paula spent half her time updating Web pages and the other half repairing bicycles, an eight-hour workday would yield 12 Web page updates and 24 bicycle repairs. To complete the remaining 4 updates, Beth would have to spend two hours programming, which would leave her six hours to repair bicycles. And since she takes 30 minutes to do each repair, she would have time to complete 12 of them. So when the two women try to be jacks-of-all-trades, they end up completing a total of 16 Web page updates and 36 bicycle repairs.

Consider what would have happened had each woman specialized in her activity of comparative advantage. Beth could have updated 16 Web pages on her own and Paula could have performed 48 bicycle repairs. Specialization would have created an additional 12 bicycle repairs out of thin air. ◆

"We're a natural, Rachel. I handle intellectual property, and you're a content-provider."

When computing the opportunity cost of one good in terms of another, we must pay close attention to the form in which the productivity information is presented. In the preceding example, we were told how many minutes each person needed to perform each task. Alternatively, we might be told how many units of each task each person can perform in an hour. Work through the following exercise to see how to proceed when information is presented in this alternative format.

EXERCISE 2.1

Should Barb update her own Web page?

Consider a small community in which Barb is the only professional bicycle mechanic and Pat is the only professional HTML programmer. If their productivity rates at the two tasks are as shown in the table, and if each regards the two tasks as equally pleasant (or unpleasant), does the fact that Barb can program faster than Pat imply that Barb should update her own Web page?

	Productivity in programming	Productivity in bicycle repair
Pat	2 Web page updates per hour	1 repair per hour
Barb	3 Web page updates per hour	3 repairs per hour

The principle illustrated by the preceding examples is so important that we state it formally as one of the core principles of the course:

Comparative Advantage

The Principle of Comparative Advantage: Everyone does best when each person (or each country) concentrates on the activities for which his or her opportunity cost is lowest.

Indeed, the gains made possible from specialization based on comparative advantage constitute the rationale for market exchange. They explain why each person does not devote 10 percent of his or her time to producing cars, 5 percent to growing food, 25 percent to building housing, 0.0001 percent to performing brain surgery, and so on. By concentrating on those tasks at which we are relatively most productive, together we can produce vastly more than if we all tried to be self-sufficient.

This insight brings us back to Birkhaman the cook. Though Birkhaman's versatility was marvelous, he was neither as good a doctor as someone who has been trained in medical school, nor as good a repairman as someone who spends each day fixing things. If a number of people with Birkhaman's native talents had joined together, each of them specializing in one or two tasks, together they would have enjoyed more and better goods and services than each could possibly have produced independently. Although there is much to admire in the resourcefulness of people who have learned through necessity to rely on their own skills, that path is no route to economic prosperity.

Specialization and its effects provide ample grist for the economic naturalist. Here's an example from the world of sports.

Example 2.1

THE ECONOMIC NATURALIST

Where have all the .400 hitters gone?

In baseball, a .400 hitter is a player who averages at least four hits every 10 times he comes to bat. Though never common in professional baseball, .400 hitters used to appear relatively frequently. Early in the twentieth century, for example, a player known as Wee Willie Keeler batted .432, meaning that he got a hit in over 43 percent of his times at bat. But since Ted Williams of the Boston Red Sox batted .406 in 1941, there has not been a single .400 hitter in the major leagues. Why not?

Some baseball buffs argue that the disappearance of the .400 hitter means today's baseball players are not as good as yesterday's. But that claim does not withstand close

© Bettmann/CORBIS

Why has no major league baseball player batted .400 since Ted Williams did it more than half a century ago?

examination. We can document, for example, that today's players are bigger, stronger, and faster than those of Willie Keeler's day. (Wee Willie himself was just a little over 5 feet, 4 inches, and he weighed only 140 pounds.)

Bill James, a leading analyst of baseball history, argues that the .400 hitter has disappeared because the quality of play in the major leagues has *improved,* not declined. In particular, pitching and fielding standards are higher, which makes batting .400 more difficult.

Why has the quality of play in baseball improved? Although there are many reasons, including better nutrition, training, and equipment, specialization also has played an important role.[1] At one time, pitchers were expected to pitch for the entire game. Now pitching staffs include pitchers who specialize in starting the game ("starters"), others who specialize in pitching two or three innings in the middle of the game ("middle relievers"), and still others who specialize in pitching only the last inning ("closers"). Each of these roles requires different skills and tactics. Pitchers also may specialize in facing left-handed or right-handed batters, in striking batters out, or in getting batters to hit balls on the ground. Similarly, few fielders today play multiple defensive positions; most specialize in only one. Some players specialize in defense (to the detriment of their hitting skills); these "defensive specialists" can be brought in late in the game to protect a lead. Even in managing and coaching, specialization has increased markedly. Relief pitchers now have their own coaches, and statistical specialists use computers to discover the weaknesses of opposing hitters. The net result of these increases in specialization is that even the weakest of today's teams play highly competent defensive baseball. With no "weaklings" to pick on, hitting .400 over an entire season has become a near-impossible task. ●

SOURCES OF COMPARATIVE ADVANTAGE

At the individual level, comparative advantage often appears to be the result of inborn talent. For instance, some people seem to be naturally gifted at programming computers while others seem to have a special knack for fixing bikes. But comparative advantage is more often the result of education, training, or experience. Thus, we usually leave the design of kitchens to people with architectural training, the drafting of contracts to people who have studied law, and the teaching of physics to people with advanced degrees in that field.

At the national level, comparative advantage may derive from differences in natural resources or from differences in society or culture. The United States, which has a disproportionate share of the world's leading research universities, has a comparative advantage in the design of electronic computing hardware and software. Canada, which has one of the world's highest per-capita endowments of farm and forest land, has a comparative advantage in the production of agricultural products. Topography and climate explain why Colorado specializes in the skiing industry while Hawaii specializes as an ocean resort.

Seemingly noneconomic factors also can give rise to comparative advantage. For instance, the emergence of English as the de facto world language gives English-speaking countries a comparative advantage over non–English-speaking nations in the production of books, movies, and popular music. Even a country's institutions may affect the likelihood that it will achieve comparative advantage in a particular pursuit. For example, cultures that encourage entrepreneurship will tend to have a comparative advantage in the introduction of new products, whereas those that promote high standards of care and craftsmanship will tend to have a comparative advantage in the production of high-quality variants of established products.

[1] For an interesting discussion of specialization and the decline of the.400 hitter from the perspective of an evolutionary biologist, see Stephen Jay Gould, *Full House* (New York: Three Rivers Press, 1996), Part 3.

Example 2.2
THE ECONOMIC NATURALIST

Televisions and videocassette recorders were developed and first produced in the United States, but today the United States accounts for only a minuscule share of the total world production of these products. Why did the United States fail to retain its lead in these markets?

That televisions and VCRs were developed in the United States is explained in part by the country's comparative advantage in technological research, which in turn was supported by the country's outstanding system of higher education. Other contributing factors were high expenditures on the development of electronic components for the military and a culture that actively encourages entrepreneurship. As for the production of these products, America enjoyed an early advantage partly because the product designs were themselves evolving rapidly at first, which favored production facilities located in close proximity to the product designers. Early production techniques also relied intensively on skilled labor, which is abundant in the United States. In time, however, product designs stabilized and many of the more complex manufacturing operations were automated. Both of these changes gradually led to greater reliance on relatively less-skilled production workers. And at that point, factories located in high-wage countries like the United States could no longer compete with those located in low-wage areas overseas. ●

Why was the United States unable to remain competitive as a manufacturer of televisions and other electronic equipment?

RECAP	EXCHANGE AND OPPORTUNITY COST

Gains from exchange are possible if trading partners have comparative advantages in producing different goods and services. You have a comparative advantage in producing, say, Web pages if your opportunity cost of producing a Web page—measured in terms of other production opportunities forgone—is smaller than the corresponding opportunity costs of your trading partners. Maximum production is achieved if each person specializes in producing the good or service in which he or she has the lowest opportunity cost (the Principle of Comparative Advantage). Comparative advantage makes specialization worthwhile even if one trading partner is more productive than others, in absolute terms, in every activity.

COMPARATIVE ADVANTAGE AND PRODUCTION POSSIBILITIES

Comparative advantage and specialization allow an economy to produce more than if each person tries to produce a little of everything. In this section, we gain further insight into the advantages of specialization by introducing a graph that can be used to describe the various combinations of goods and services that an economy can produce.

THE PRODUCTION POSSIBILITIES CURVE

We begin with a hypothetical economy in which only two goods are produced: coffee and pine nuts. It is a small island economy and "production" consists either of picking coffee beans that grow on small bushes on the island's central valley floor or of gathering pine nuts that fall from trees on the steep hillsides overlooking the valley. The more time workers spend picking coffee, the less time they have available for gathering nuts. So if people want to drink more coffee, they must make do with a smaller amount of nuts.

If we know how productive workers are at each activity, we can summarize the various combinations of coffee and nuts they can produce each day. This menu of possibilities is known as the **production possibilities curve.**

production possibilities curve a graph that describes the maximum amount of one good that can be produced for every possible level of production of the other good

To keep matters simple, we begin with an example in which the economy has only a single worker who can divide her time between the two activities.

What is the production possibilities curve for an economy in which Susan is the only worker?

Consider a society consisting only of Susan, who allocates her production time between coffee and nuts. She has nimble fingers, a quality that makes her more productive at picking coffee than at gathering nuts. She can gather 2 pounds of nuts or pick 4 pounds of coffee in an hour. If she works a total of 6 hours per day, describe her production possibilities curve—the graph that displays, for each level of nut production, the maximum amount of coffee that Susan can pick.

The vertical axis in Figure 2.1 shows Susan's daily production of coffee and the horizontal axis shows her daily production of nuts. Let's begin by looking at two extreme allocations of her time. First, suppose she employs her entire workday (6 hours) picking coffee. In that case, since she can pick 4 pounds of coffee per hour, she would pick 24 pounds per day of coffee and gather zero pounds of nuts. That combination of coffee and nut production is represented by point *A* in Figure 2.1. It is the vertical intercept of Susan's production possibilities curve.

Now suppose, instead, that Susan devotes all her time to gathering nuts. Since she can gather 2 pounds of nuts per hour, her total daily production would be 12 pounds of nuts. That combination is represented by point *D* in Figure 2.1, the horizontal intercept of Susan's production possibilities curve. Because Susan's production of each good is exactly proportional to the amount of time she devotes to that good, the remaining points along her production possibilities curve will lie on the straight line that joins *A* and *D*.

For example, suppose that Susan devotes 4 hours each day to picking coffee and 2 hours to gathering nuts. She will then end up with (4 hours/day) × (4 pounds/hour) = 16 pounds of coffee per day and (2 hours/day) × (2 pounds/hour) = 4 pounds of nuts. This is the point labeled *B* in Figure 2.1. Alternatively, if she devotes 2 hours to coffee and 4 to nuts, she will get (2 hours/day) × (4 pounds/hour) = 8 pounds of coffee per day and (4 hours/day) × (2 pounds/hour) = 8 pounds of nuts. This alternative combination is represented by point *C* in Figure 2.1.

FIGURE 2.1
Susan's Production Possibilities.
For the production relationships given, the production possibilities curve is a straight line.

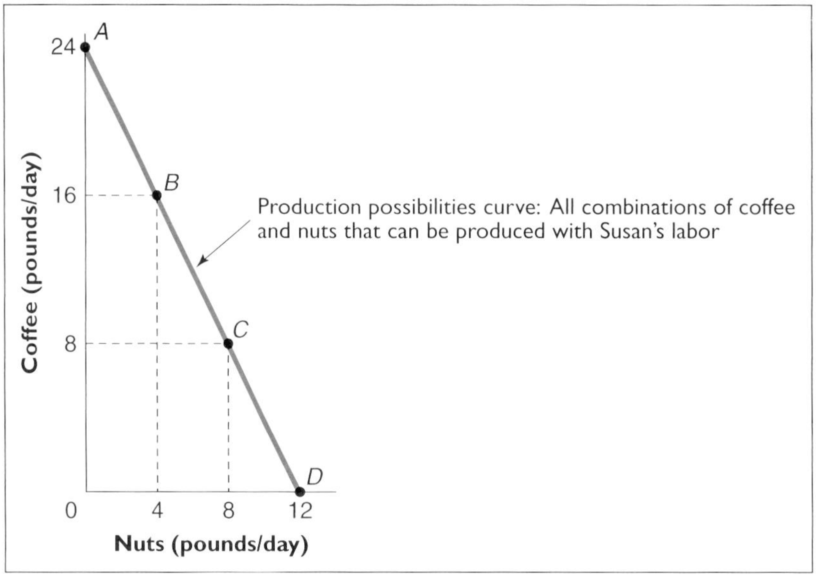

Since Susan's production possibilities curve (PPC) is a straight line, its slope is constant. The absolute value of the slope of Susan's PPC is the ratio of its vertical intercept to its horizontal intercept: (24 pounds of coffee/day)/(12 pounds of nuts/day) = (2 pounds of coffee)/(1 pound of nuts). (Be sure to keep track of the units of measure on each axis when computing this ratio.) *This ratio means that Susan's opportunity cost of an additional pound of nuts is 2 pounds of coffee.*

Note that Susan's opportunity cost (*OC*) of nuts can also be expressed as the following simple formula:

$$OC_{\text{nuts}} = \frac{\text{loss in coffee}}{\text{gain in nuts}}, \tag{2.1}$$

where "loss in coffee" means the amount of coffee given up and "gain in nuts" means the corresponding increase in nuts. Likewise, Susan's opportunity cost of coffee is expressed by this formula:

$$OC_{\text{coffee}} = \frac{\text{loss in nuts}}{\text{gain in coffee}}. \tag{2.2}$$

To say that Susan's opportunity cost of an additional pound of nuts is 2 pounds of coffee is thus equivalent to saying that her opportunity cost of a pound of coffee is ½ pound of nuts. ◆

The downward slope of the production possibilities curve shown in Figure 2.1 illustrates the Scarcity Principle—the idea that because our resources are limited, having more of one good thing generally means having to settle for less of another (see Chapter 1). Susan can have an additional pound of coffee if she wishes, but only if she is willing to give up half a pound of nuts. If Susan is the only person in the economy, her opportunity cost of producing a good becomes, in effect, its price. Thus, the price she has to pay for an additional pound of coffee is half a pound of nuts; or the price she has to pay for an additional pound of nuts is 2 pounds of coffee.

Scarcity

Any point that lies either along the production possibilities curve or within it is said to be an **attainable point,** meaning that it can be produced with currently available resources. In Figure 2.2, for example, points *A, B, C, D,* and *E* are attainable

attainable point any combination of goods that can be produced using currently available resources

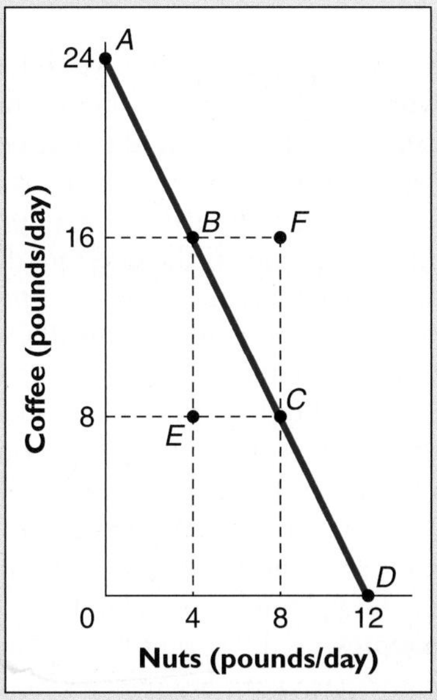

FIGURE 2.2
Attainable and Efficient Points on Susan's Production Possibilities Curve.
Points that lie either along the production possibilities curve (for example, *A, B, C,* and *D*) or within it (for example, *E*) are said to be attainable. Points that lie outside the production possibilities curve (for example, *F*) are unattainable. Points that lie along the curve are said to be efficient, while those that lie within the curve are said to be inefficient.

unattainable point any combination of goods that cannot be produced using currently available resources

inefficient point any combination of goods for which currently available resources enable an increase in the production of one good without a reduction in the production of the other

efficient point any combination of goods for which currently available resources do not allow an increase in the production of one good without a reduction in the production of the other

points. Points that lie outside the production possibilities curve are said to be **unattainable**, meaning that they cannot be produced using currently available resources. In Figure 2.2, *F* is an unattainable point because Susan cannot pick 16 pounds of coffee per day *and* gather 8 pounds of nuts. Points that lie within the curve are said to be **inefficient**, in the sense that existing resources would allow for production of more of at least one good without sacrificing the production of any other good. At *E*, for example, Susan is picking only 8 pounds of coffee per day and gathering 4 pounds of nuts, which means that she could increase her coffee harvest by 8 pounds per day without giving up any nuts (by moving from *E* to *B*). Alternatively, Susan could gather as many as 4 additional pounds of nuts each day without giving up any coffee (by moving from *E* to *C*). An **efficient** point is one that lies along the production possibilities curve. At any such point, more of one good can be produced only by producing less of the other.

EXERCISE 2.2

For the PPC shown in Figure 2.2, state whether the following points are attainable and/or efficient:

a. **20 pounds per day of coffee, 4 pounds per day of nuts.**

b. **12 pounds per day of coffee, 6 pounds per day of nuts.**

c. **4 pounds per day of coffee, 8 pounds per day of nuts.**

HOW INDIVIDUAL PRODUCTIVITY AFFECTS THE SLOPE AND POSITION OF THE PPC

To see how the slope and position of the production possibilities curve depend on an individual's productivity, let's compare Susan's PPC to that of Tom, who is less productive at picking coffee but more productive at gathering nuts.

How do changes in productivity affect the opportunity cost of nuts?

Tom is short and has keen eyesight, qualities that make him especially well-suited for gathering nuts that fall beneath trees on the hillsides. He can gather 4 pounds of nuts or pick 2 pounds of coffee per hour. If Tom were the only person in the economy, describe the economy's production possibilities curve.

We can construct Tom's PPC the same way we did Susan's. Note first that if Tom devotes an entire workday (6 hours) to coffee picking, he ends up with (6 hours/day) × (2 pounds/hour) = 12 pounds of coffee per day and zero pounds of nuts. So the vertical intercept of Tom's PPC is *A* in Figure 2.3. If instead he devotes all his time to gathering nuts, he gets (6 hours/day) × (4 pounds/hour) = 24 pounds of nuts per day and no coffee. That means the horizontal intercept of his PPC is *D* in Figure 2.3. Because Tom's production of each good is proportional to the amount of time he devotes to it, the remaining points on his PPC will lie along the straight line that joins these two extreme points.

For example, if he devotes 4 hours each day to picking coffee and 2 hours to gathering nuts, he will end up with (4 hours/day) × (2 pounds/hour) = 8 pounds of coffee per day and (2 hours/day) × (4 pounds/hour) = 8 pounds of nuts per day. This is the point labeled *B* in Figure 2.3. Alternatively, if he devotes 2 hours to coffee and 4 to nuts, he will get (2 hours/day) × (2 pounds/hour) = 4 pounds of coffee per day and (4 hours/day) × (4 pounds/hour) = 16 pounds of nuts. This alternative combination is represented by point *C* in Figure 2.3.

How does Tom's PPC compare with Susan's? Note in Figure 2.4 that because Tom is absolutely less productive than Susan at picking coffee, the vertical intercept

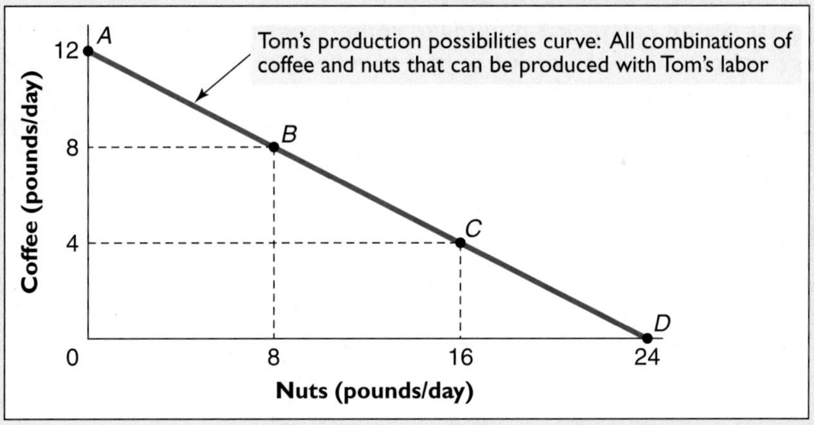

FIGURE 2.3
Tom's Production Possibilities Curve.
Tom's opportunity cost of producing one pound of nuts is only half a pound of coffee.

of his PPC lies closer to the origin than Susan's. By the same token, because Susan is absolutely less productive than Tom at gathering nuts, the horizontal intercept of her PPC lies closer to the origin than Tom's. For Tom, the opportunity cost of an additional pound of nuts is ½ pound of coffee, which is one-fourth Susan's opportunity cost of nuts. This difference in opportunity costs shows up as a difference in the slopes of their PPCs: the absolute value of the slope of Tom's PPC is ½, whereas Susan's is 2.

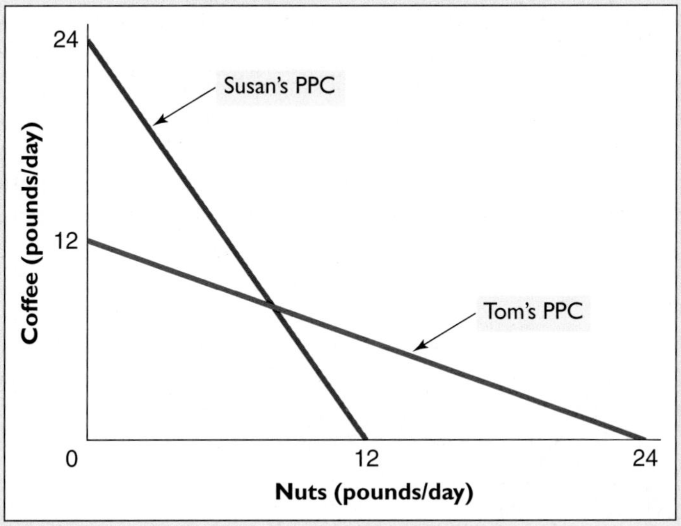

FIGURE 2.4
Individual Production Possibilities Curves Compared.
Tom is less productive in coffee than Susan, but more productive in nuts.

In this example, Tom has both an absolute advantage and a comparative advantage over Susan in gathering nuts. Susan, for her part, has both an absolute advantage and a comparative advantage over Tom in picking coffee. ◆

We cannot emphasize strongly enough that the principle of comparative advantage is a relative concept—one that makes sense only when the productivities of two or more people (or countries) are being compared. To cement this idea, work through the following exercise.

EXERCISE 2.3

Suppose Susan can pick 2 pounds of coffee per hour or gather 4 pounds of nuts per hour; Tom can pick 1 pound of coffee per hour and gather 1 pound of nuts per hour. What is Susan's opportunity cost of gathering a pound of nuts? What is Tom's opportunity cost of gathering a pound of nuts? Where does Susan's comparative advantage now lie?

THE GAINS FROM SPECIALIZATION AND EXCHANGE

Earlier we saw that a comparative advantage arising from disparities in individual opportunity costs creates gains for everyone (see the first two examples in this chapter). The following example shows how the same point can be illustrated using production possibility curves.

How costly is failure to specialize?

Suppose that in the preceding example Susan and Tom had divided their time so that each person's output consisted of half nuts and half coffee. How much of each good would Tom and Susan have been able to consume? How much could they have consumed if each had specialized in the activity for which he or she enjoyed a comparative advantage?

Since Tom can produce twice as many pounds of nuts in an hour as pounds of coffee, to produce equal quantities of each, he must spend 2 hours picking coffee for every hour he devotes to gathering nuts. And since he works a 6-hour day, that means spending 2 hours gathering nuts and 4 hours picking coffee. Dividing his time in this way, he will end up with 8 pounds of coffee per day and 8 pounds of nuts. Similarly, since Susan can produce twice as many pounds of coffee in an hour as pounds of nuts, to pick equal quantities of each, she must spend 2 hours gathering nuts for every hour she devotes to picking coffee. And since she too works a 6-hour day, that means spending 2 hours picking coffee and 4 hours gathering nuts. So, like Tom, she will end up with 8 pounds of coffee per day and 8 pounds of nuts. (See Figure 2.5.) Their combined daily production will thus be 16 pounds of each good. By contrast, had they each specialized in their respective activities of comparative advantage, their combined daily production would have been 24 pounds of each good.

FIGURE 2.5
Production without Specialization.
When Tom and Susan divide their time so that each produces the same number of pounds of coffee and nuts, they can consume a total of 16 pounds of coffee and 16 pounds of nuts each day.

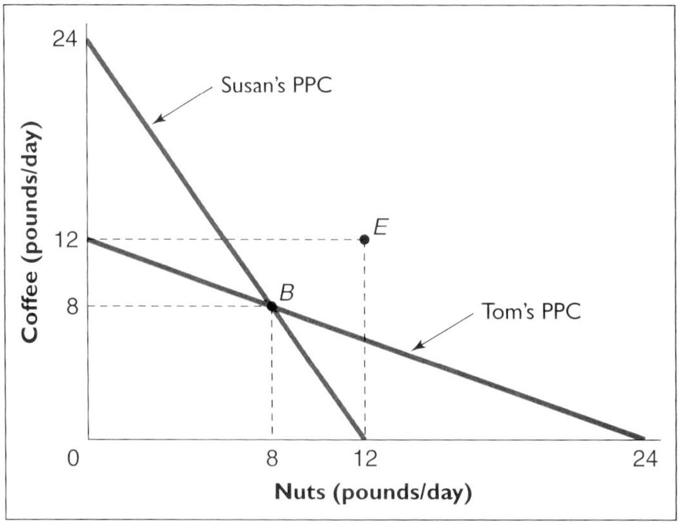

If they exchange coffee and nuts with one another, each can consume a combination of the two goods that would have been unattainable if exchange had not been possible. For example, Susan can give Tom 12 pounds of coffee in exchange for 12 pounds of nuts, enabling each to consume 4 pounds per day more of each good than when each produced and consumed alone. Note that point *E* in Figure 2.5, which has 12 pounds per day of each good, lies beyond each person's PPC, yet is easily attainable with specialization and exchange. ◆

As the following exercise illustrates, the gains from specialization grow larger as the difference in opportunity costs increases.

EXERCISE 2.4

How do differences in opportunity cost affect the gains from specialization?

Susan can pick 5 pounds of coffee or gather 1 pound of nuts in an hour. Tom can pick 1 pound of coffee or gather 5 pounds of nuts in an hour. Assuming they again work 6-hour days and want to consume coffee and nuts in equal quantities, by how much will specialization increase their consumption compared to the alternative in which each produced only for his or her own consumption?

Although the gains from specialization and exchange grow with increases in the differences in opportunity costs among trading partners, these differences alone still seem insufficient to account for the enormous differences in living standards between rich and poor countries. Average income in the 20 richest countries in the year 2000, for example, was over $27,000 per person, compared to only $211 per person in the 20 poorest countries.[2] Although we will say more later about specialization's role in explaining these differences, we first discuss how to construct the PPC for an entire economy and examine how factors other than specialization might cause it to shift outward over time.

A PRODUCTION POSSIBILITIES CURVE FOR A MANY-PERSON ECONOMY

Although most actual economies consist of millions of workers, the process of constructing a production possibilities curve for an economy of that size is really no different from the process for a one-person economy. Consider again an economy in which the only two goods are coffee and nuts, with coffee again on the vertical axis and nuts on the horizontal axis. The vertical intercept of the economy's PPC is the total amount of coffee that could be picked if all available workers worked full-time picking coffee. Thus, the maximum attainable amount of coffee production is shown for the hypothetical economy in Figure 2.6 as 100,000 pounds per day (an amount chosen arbitrarily, for illustrative purposes). The horizontal intercept of the PPC is the amount of nuts that could be gathered if all available workers worked full-time gathering nuts, shown for this same economy as 80,000 pounds per day (also an amount chosen arbitrarily). But note that the PPC shown in the diagram is not a straight line—as in the earlier examples involving only a single worker—but rather a curve that is bowed out from the origin.

[2]High-income countries: Australia, Austria, Belgium, Canada, China, Hong Kong, Denmark, Finland, France, Germany, Iceland, Ireland, Japan, Luxembourg, Netherlands, Norway, Singapore, Sweden, Switzerland, United Kingdom, and United States. Low-income countries: Burkina Faso, Burundi, Central African Republic, Chad, Ethiopia, Ghana, Guinea-Bisau, Kenya, Madagascar, Malawi, Mali, Mozambique, Myanmar, Nepal, Niger, Nigeria, Rwanda, Sierra Leone, Tanzania, and Uganda. (Source: Global Policy Forum, http://www.globalpolicy.org/).

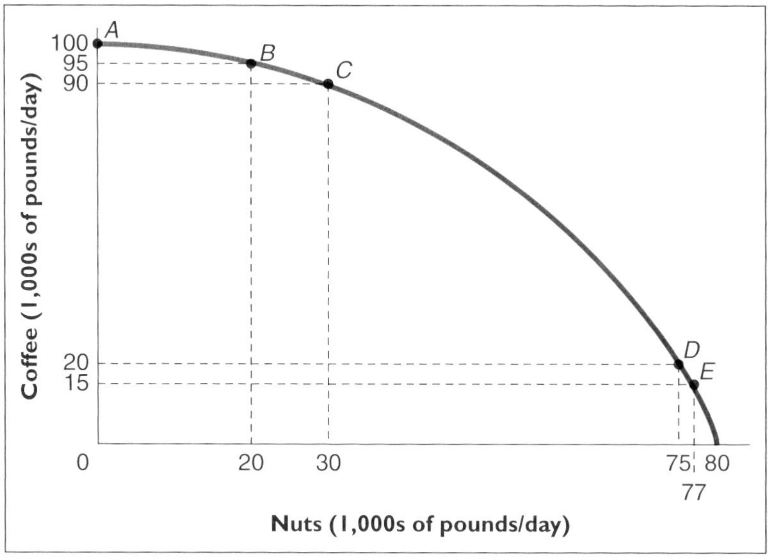

FIGURE 2.6
Production Possibilities Curve for a Large Economy.
For an economy with millions of workers, the PPC typically has a gentle outward bow shape.

We'll say more in a moment about the reasons for this shape. But first note that a bow-shaped PPC means that the opportunity cost of producing nuts increases as the economy produces more of them. Notice, for example, that when the economy moves from *A*, where it is producing only coffee, to *B*, it gets 20,000 pounds of nuts per day by giving up only 5,000 pounds per day of coffee. When nut production is increased still further, however—for example, by moving from *B* to *C*—the economy again gives up 5,000 pounds per day of coffee, yet this time gets only 10,000 additional pounds of nuts. This pattern of increasing opportunity cost persists over the entire length of the PPC. For example, note that in moving from *D* to *E*, the economy again gives up 5,000 pounds per day of coffee but now gains only 2,000 pounds a day of nuts. Note, finally, that the same pattern of increasing opportunity cost applies to coffee. Thus, as more coffee is produced, the opportunity cost of producing additional coffee—as measured by the amount of nuts that must be sacrificed—also rises.

Why is the PPC for the multiperson economy bow-shaped? The answer lies in the fact that some resources are relatively well-suited for gathering nuts while others are relatively well-suited for picking coffee. If the economy is initially producing only coffee and wants to begin producing some nuts, which workers will it reassign? Recall Susan and Tom, the two workers discussed in the preceding example, in which Tom's comparative advantage was gathering nuts and Susan's comparative advantage was picking coffee. If both workers were currently picking coffee and you wanted to reassign one of them to gather nuts instead, whom would you send? Tom would be the clear choice, because his departure would cost the economy only half as much coffee as Susan's and would augment nut production by twice as much.

The principle is the same in any large multiperson economy, except that the range of opportunity cost differences across workers is even greater than in the earlier two-worker example. As we keep reassigning workers from coffee production to nut production, sooner or later we must withdraw even coffee specialists like Susan from coffee production. Indeed, we must eventually reassign others whose opportunity cost of producing nuts is far higher than hers.

The shape of the production possibilities curve shown in Figure 2.6 illustrates the general principle that when resources have different opportunity costs, we should always exploit the resource with the lowest opportunity cost first. We call this the *low-hanging-fruit principle,* in honor of the fruit picker's rule of picking the most accessible fruit first:

The Principle of Increasing Opportunity Cost (also called "The Low-Hanging-Fruit Principle"): In expanding the production of any good, first employ those resources with the lowest opportunity cost, and only afterward turn to resources with higher opportunity costs.

Increasing Opportunity Cost

A Note on the Logic of the Fruit Picker's Rule

Why should a fruit picker harvest the low-hanging fruit first? This rule makes sense for several reasons. For one, the low-hanging fruit is easier (and hence cheaper) to pick, and if he planned on picking only a limited amount of fruit to begin with, he would clearly come out ahead by avoiding the less-accessible fruit on the higher branches. But even if he planned on picking all the fruit on the tree, he would do better to start with the lower branches first because this would enable him to enjoy the revenue from the sale of the fruit sooner.

The fruit picker's job can be likened to the task confronting a new CEO who has been hired to reform an inefficient, ailing company. The CEO has limited time and attention, so it makes sense to focus first on problems that are relatively easy to correct and whose elimination will provide the biggest improvements in performance—the low-hanging fruit. Later on, the CEO can worry about the many smaller improvements needed to raise the company from very good to excellent.

Again, the important message of the low-hanging-fruit principle is to be sure to take advantage of your most favorable opportunities first.

RECAP	COMPARATIVE ADVANTAGE AND PRODUCTION POSSIBILITIES

For an economy that produces two goods, the production possibilities curve describes the maximum amount of one good that can be produced for every possible level of production of the other good. Attainable points are those that lie on or within the curve and efficient points are those that lie along the curve. The slope of the production possibilities curve tells us the opportunity cost of producing an additional unit of the good measured along the horizontal axis. The Principle of Increasing Opportunity Cost, or the Low-Hanging-Fruit Principle, tells us that the slope of the production possibilities curve becomes steeper as we move downward to the right. The greater the differences among individual opportunity costs, the more bow-shaped the production possibilities curve will be and the more bow-shaped the production possibilities curve, the greater will be the potential gains from specialization.

FACTORS THAT SHIFT THE ECONOMY'S PRODUCTION POSSIBILITIES CURVE

As its name implies, the production possibilities curve provides a summary of the production options open to any society. At any given moment, the PPC confronts society with a trade-off. The only way people can produce and consume more nuts is to produce and consume less coffee. In the long run, however, it is often possible to increase production of all goods. This is what is meant when people speak of economic growth. As shown in Figure 2.7, economic growth is an outward shift in the economy's production possibilities curve. It can result from increases in the amount of productive resources available or from improvements in knowledge or technology that render existing resources more productive.

FIGURE 2.7
Economic Growth: An Outward Shift in the Economy's PPC.
Increases in productive resources (such as labor and capital equipment) or improvements in knowledge and technology cause the PPC to shift outward. They are the main factors that drive economic growth.

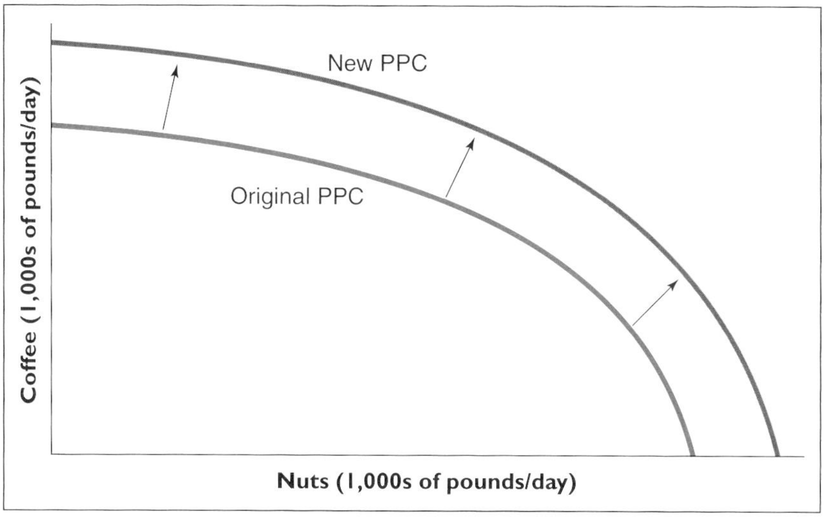

What causes the quantity of productive resources to grow in an economy? One factor is investment in new factories and equipment. When workers have more and better equipment to work with, their productivity increases, often dramatically. This is surely an important factor behind the differences in living standards between rich and poor countries. According to one study, for example, the value of capital investment per worker in the United States is about \$30,000, while in Nepal the corresponding figure is less than \$1,000.[3]

Such large differences in capital per worker don't occur all at once. They are a consequence of decades, even centuries, of differences in rates of savings and investment. Over time, even small differences in rates of investment can translate into extremely large differences in the amount of capital equipment available to each worker. Differences of this sort are often self-reinforcing: Not only do higher rates of saving and investment cause incomes to grow, but the resulting higher income levels also make it easier to devote additional resources to savings and investment. Over time, then, even small initial productivity advantages from specialization can translate into very large income gaps.

Population growth also causes an economy's PPC curve to shift outward and thus is often listed as one of the sources of economic growth. But because population growth also generates more mouths to feed, it cannot by itself raise a country's standard of living. Indeed it may even cause a decline in the standard of living if existing population densities have already begun to put pressure on available land, water, and other scarce resources.

Perhaps the most important source of economic growth is improvements in knowledge and technology. As economists have long recognized, such improvements often lead to higher output through increased specialization. Improvements in technology often occur spontaneously, but more frequently they are directly or indirectly the result of increases in education.

Earlier we discussed a two-person example in which individual differences in opportunity cost led to a threefold gain from specialization (Exercise 2.4). Real-world gains from specialization often are far more spectacular than those in the example. One reason is that specialization not only capitalizes on preexisting differences in individual skills but also deepens those skills through practice and experience. Moreover, it eliminates many of the switching and start-up costs people incur when they move back and forth among numerous tasks. These gains apply

[3]Alan Heston and Robert Summers, "The Penn World Table (Mark 5): An Expanded Set of International Comparisons, 1950–1988," *Quarterly Journal of Economics*, May 1991, pp. 327–68.

not only to people but also to the tools and equipment they use. Breaking a task down into simple steps, each of which can be performed by a different machine, greatly multiplies the productivity of individual workers.

Even in simple settings, these factors can combine to increase productivity hundreds- or even thousands-fold. Adam Smith, the Scottish philosopher who is remembered today as the founder of modern economics, was the first to recognize the enormity of the gains made possible by the division and specialization of labor. Consider, for instance, his description of work in an eighteenth-century Scottish pin factory:

> One man draws out the wire, another straightens it, a third cuts it, a fourth points it, a fifth grinds it at the top for receiving the head; to make the head requires two or three distinct operations ... I have seen a small manufactory of this kind where only ten men were employed ... [who] could, when they exerted themselves, make among them about twelve pounds of pins in a day. There are in a pound upwards of four thousand pins of middling size. Those ten persons, therefore, could make among them upwards of forty-eight thousand pins in a day. Each person, therefore, making a tenth part of forty-eight thousand pins, might be considered as making four thousand eight hundred pins in a day. But if they had all wrought separately and independently, and without any of them having been educated to this peculiar business, they certainly could not each of them have made twenty, perhaps not one pin in a day.[4]

The gains in productivity that result from specialization are indeed often prodigious. They constitute the single most important explanation for why societies that don't rely heavily on specialization and exchange are rapidly becoming relics.

WHY HAVE SOME COUNTRIES BEEN SLOW TO SPECIALIZE?

You may be asking yourself, "If specialization is such a great thing, why don't people in poor countries like Nepal just specialize?" If so, you are in good company. Adam Smith spent many years attempting to answer precisely the same question. In the end, his explanation was that population density is an important precondition for specialization. Smith, ever the economic naturalist, observed that work tended to be far more specialized in the large cities of England in the eighteenth century than in the rural highlands of Scotland:

> In the lone houses and very small villages which are scattered about in so desert a country as the Highlands of Scotland, every farmer must be butcher, baker and brewer for his own family. . . . A country carpenter . . . is not only a carpenter, but a joiner, a cabinet maker, and even a carver in wood, as well as a wheelwright, a ploughwright, a cart and waggon maker.[5]

In contrast, each of these same tasks was performed by a different specialist in the large English and Scottish cities of Smith's day. Scottish highlanders also would have specialized had they been able to, but the markets in which they participated were simply too small and fragmented. Of course, high population density by itself provides no guarantee that specialization will result in rapid economic growth. But especially before the arrival of modern shipping and electronic communications technology, low population density was a definite obstacle to gains from specialization.

Nepal remains one of the most remote and isolated countries on the planet. As recently as the mid-1960s, its average population density was less than 30 people per square mile (as compared, for example, to more than 1,000 people per square

[4] Adam Smith, *The Wealth of Nations* (New York: Everyman's Library, 1910 (1776)), book 1.
[5] *Id.*, chapter 3.

Drawing by Gini Kennedy

Can specialization proceed too far?

mile in New Jersey). Specialization was further limited by Nepal's rugged terrain. Exchanging goods and services with residents of other villages was difficult, because the nearest village in most cases could be reached only after trekking several hours, or even days, over treacherous Himalayan trails. More than any other factor, this extreme isolation accounts for Nepal's longstanding failure to benefit from widespread specialization.

Population density is by no means the only important factor that influences the degree of specialization. Specialization may be severely impeded, for example, by laws and customs that limit people's freedom to transact freely with one another. The communist governments of North Korea and the former East Germany restricted exchange severely, which helps explain why those countries achieved far less specialization than South Korea and the former West Germany, whose governments were far more supportive of exchange.

CAN WE HAVE TOO MUCH SPECIALIZATION?

Of course, the mere fact that specialization boosts productivity does not mean that more specialization is always better than less, for specialization also entails costs. For example, most people appear to enjoy variety in the work they do, yet variety tends to be one of the first casualties as workplace tasks become ever more narrowly specialized.

Indeed, one of Karl Marx's central themes was that the fragmentation of workplace tasks often exacts a heavy psychological toll on workers. Thus, he wrote,

> All means for the development of production . . . mutilate the laborer into a fragment of a man, degrade him to the level of an appendage of a machine, destroy every remnant of charm in his work and turn it into hated toil.[6]

Charlie Chaplin's 1936 film *Modern Times* paints a vivid portrait of the psychological costs of repetitive factory work. As an assembly worker, Chaplin's only task, all day every day, is to tighten the nuts on two bolts as they pass before him on the assembly line. Finally, he snaps and staggers from the factory, wrenches in hand, tightening every nutlike protuberance he encounters.

[6]Karl Marx, *Das Kapital* (New York: Modern Library), pp. 708, 709.

Do the extra goods made possible by specialization simply come at too high a price? We must certainly acknowledge at least the *potential* for specialization to proceed too far. Yet specialization need not entail rigidly segmented, mind-numbingly repetitive work. And it is important to recognize that *failure* to specialize entails costs as well. Those who don't specialize must accept low wages or work extremely long hours.

When all is said and done, we can expect to meet life's financial obligations in the shortest time—thereby freeing up more time to do whatever else we wish—if we concentrate at least a significant proportion of our efforts on those tasks for which we have a comparative advantage.

COMPARATIVE ADVANTAGE AND INTERNATIONAL TRADE

The same logic that leads the individuals in an economy to specialize and exchange goods with one another also leads nations to specialize and trade among themselves. As with individuals, each nation can benefit from exchange, even though one may be generally more productive than the other in absolute terms.

Example 2.3

THE ECONOMIC NATURALIST

If trade between nations is so beneficial, why are free-trade agreements so controversial?

One of the most heated issues in the 1996 presidential campaign was President Clinton's support for the North American Free Trade Agreement (NAFTA), a treaty to sharply reduce trade barriers between the United States and its immediate neighbors north and south. The treaty attracted fierce opposition from third-party candidate Ross Perot, who insisted that it would mean unemployment for millions of American workers. If exchange is so beneficial, why does anyone oppose it?

If free trade is so great, why do so many people oppose it?

The answer is that while reducing barriers to international trade increases the total value of all goods and services produced in each nation, it does not guarantee that each individual citizen will do better. One specific concern regarding NAFTA was that it would help Mexico to exploit a comparative advantage in the production of goods made by unskilled labor. Although U.S. consumers would benefit from reduced prices for such goods, many Americans feared that unskilled workers in the United States would lose their jobs to workers in Mexico.

In the end, NAFTA was enacted over the vociferous opposition of American labor unions. So far, however, studies have failed to detect significant overall job losses among unskilled workers in the United States, although there have been some losses in specific industries. ●

OUTSOURCING

An issue very much in the news in recent years has been the **outsourcing** of U.S. service jobs. Although the term once primarily meant having services performed by subcontractors anywhere outside the confines of the firm, increasingly it connotes the act of replacing relatively expensive American service workers with much cheaper service workers in overseas locations.

outsourcing a term increasingly used to connote having services performed by low-wage workers overseas

A case in point is the transcription of medical records. In an effort to maintain accurate records, many physicians dictate their case notes for later transcription after examining their patients. In the past, transcription was often performed by the physician's secretary in spare moments. But secretaries also must attend to a variety of other tasks that disrupt concentration. They must answer phones, serve as receptionists, prepare correspondence, and so on. As insurance disputes and malpractice litigation became more frequent during the 1980s and 1990s, errors in medical records became much more costly to physicians. In response, many turned to independent companies that offered transcription services by full-time, dedicated specialists.

These companies typically served physicians whose practices were located in the same community. But while many of the companies that manage transcription services are still located in the United States, an increasing fraction of the actual work itself is now performed outside the United States. For example, Eight Crossings, a company headquartered in northern California, enables physicians to upload voice dictation files securely to the internet, whereupon they are transmitted to transcribers who perform the work in India. The finished documents are then transmitted back, in electronic form, to physicians, who may edit and even sign them online. The advantage for physicians, of course, is that the fee for this service is much lower than for the same service performed domestically because wage rates in India are much lower than in the United States.

In China, Korea, Indonesia, India, and elsewhere, even highly skilled professionals still earn just a small fraction of what their counterparts in the United States are paid. Accordingly, companies face powerful competitive pressure to import not just low-cost goods from overseas suppliers, but also a growing array of professional services. As Microsoft chairman Bill Gates put it in a 1999 interview,

> As a business manager, you need to take a hard look at your core competencies. Revisit the areas of your company that aren't directly involved in those competencies, and consider whether Web technologies can enable you to spin off those tasks. Let another company take over the management responsibilities for that work, and use modern communication technology to work closely with the people—now partners instead of employees are doing the work. In the Web work style, employees can push the freedom the Web provides to its limits.

EN 2

In economic terms, the outsourcing of services to low-wage foreign workers is exactly analogous to the importation of goods manufactured by low-wage foreign workers. In both cases, the resulting cost savings benefit consumers in the United States. And in both cases, jobs in the United States may be put in jeopardy, at least temporarily. An American manufacturing worker's job is at risk if it is possible to import the good he produces from another country at lower cost. By the same token, an American service worker's job is at risk if a lower-paid worker can perform that same service somewhere else.

Example 2.4

THE ECONOMIC NATURALIST

Is PBS economics reporter Paul Solman's job a likely candidate for outsourcing?

Paul Solman and his associate Lee Koromvokis produce video segments that provide in-depth analysis of current economic issues for the PBS evening news program *The NewsHour with Jim Lehrer.* Is it likely that his job will someday be outsourced to a low-wage reporter from Hyderabad?

In a recent book, the economists Frank Levy and Richard Murnane attempt to identify the characteristics of a job that make it a likely candidate for outsourcing.[7] In their view, any job that is amenable to computerization is also vulnerable to outsourcing. To computerize a task means to break it down into units that can be managed with simple rules. ATM machines, for example, were able to replace many of the tasks that bank tellers once performed because it was straightforward to reduce these tasks to a simple series of questions that a machine could answer. By the same token, the workers in offshore call centers who increasingly book our airline and hotel reservations are basically following simple scripts much like computer programs.

[7]Frank Levy and Richard Murnane, *The New Division of Labor: How Computers Are Creating the Next Job Market* (Princeton, NJ: Princeton University Press, 2004).

So the less rules-based a job is, the less vulnerable it is to outsourcing. Safest of all are those that Levy and Murnane describe as "face-to-face" jobs. Unlike most rules-based jobs, these jobs tend to involve complex face-to-face communication with other people, precisely the kind of communication that dominates Mr. Solman's economics reporting.

In an interview for the *NewsHour*, Mr. Solman asked Mr. Levy what he meant, exactly, by "complex communication."

> "Suppose I say the word *bill*," Levy responded, "and you hear that. And the question is what does that mean? . . . Am I talking about a piece of currency? Am I talking about a piece of legislation, the front end of a duck? The only way you're going to answer that is to think about the whole context of the conversation. But that's very complicated work to break down into some kind of software."[8]

Courtesy MacNeil/Lehrer Productions.

Is a low-wage foreign economics reporter likely to replace Paul Solman?

Levy and Murnane describe a second category of tasks that are less vulnerable to outsourcing—namely, those that for one reason or another require the worker to be physically present. For example, it is difficult to see how someone in China or India could build an addition to someone's house in a Chicago suburb or repair a blown head gasket on someone's Chevrolet Corvette in Atlanta or fill a cavity in someone's tooth in Los Angeles.

So on both counts, Paul Solman's job appears safe for the time being. Because it involves face-to-face, complex communication, and because many of his interviews can be conducted only in the United States, it is difficult to see how a reporter from Hyderabad could displace him. ●

Of course, the fact that a job is relatively safe does not mean that it is completely sheltered. For example, although most dentists continue to think themselves immune from outsourcing, it is now possible for someone requiring extensive dental work to have the work done in New Delhi and still save enough to cover his airfare and a two-week vacation in India.

There are more than 135 million Americans in the labor force. Every three months or so, approximately 7 million of them lose their jobs and 7 million find new ones. At various points in your life, you are likely to be among this group in transition. In the long run, the greatest security available to you or any other worker is the ability to adapt quickly to new circumstances. Having a good education provides no guarantee against losing your job, but it should enable you to develop a comparative advantage at the kinds of tasks that require more than just executing a simple set of rules.

RECAP **COMPARATIVE ADVANTAGE AND INTERNATIONAL TRADE**

Nations, like individuals, can benefit from exchange, even though one trading partner may be more productive than the other in absolute terms. The greater the difference between domestic opportunity costs and world opportunity costs, the more a nation benefits from exchange with other nations. But expansions of exchange do not guarantee that each individual citizen will do better. In particular, unskilled workers in high-wage countries may be hurt in the short run by the reduction of barriers to trade with low-wage nations.

[8] http://www.pbs.org/newshour/bb/economy/july-dec04/jobs_8-16.html.

SUMMARY

- One person has an *absolute* advantage over another in the production of a good if she can produce more of that good than the other person. One person has a *comparative* advantage over another in the production of a good if she is relatively more efficient than the other person at producing that good, meaning that her opportunity cost of producing it is lower than her counterpart's. Specialization based on comparative advantage is the basis for economic exchange. When each person specializes in the task at which he or she is relatively most efficient, the economic pie is maximized, making possible the largest slice for everyone. **LO1**
- At the individual level, comparative advantage may spring from differences in talent or ability or from differences in education, training, and experience. At the national level, sources of comparative advantage include these innate and learned differences, as well as differences in language, culture, institutions, climate, natural resources, and a host of other factors. **LO1**
- The production possibilities curve is a simple device for summarizing the possible combinations of output that a society can produce if it employs its resources efficiently. In a simple economy that produces only coffee and nuts, the PPC shows the maximum quantity of coffee production (vertical axis) possible at each level of nut production (horizontal axis). The slope of the PPC at any point represents the opportunity cost of nuts at that point, expressed in pounds of coffee. **LO3**
- All production possibilities curves slope downward because of the Scarcity Principle, which states that the only way a consumer can get more of one good is to settle for less of another. In economies whose workers have different opportunity costs of producing each good, the slope of the PPC becomes steeper as consumers move downward along the curve. This change in slope illustrates the Principle of Increasing Opportunity Cost (or the Low-Hanging-Fruit Principle), which states that in expanding the production of any good, a society should first employ those resources that are relatively efficient at producing that good, only afterward turning to those that are less efficient. **LO2**
- Factors that cause a country's PPC to shift outward over time include investment in new factories and equipment, population growth, and improvements in knowledge and technology. **LO3**
- The same logic that prompts individuals to specialize in their production and exchange goods with one another also leads nations to specialize and trade with one another. On both levels, each trading partner can benefit from an exchange, even though one may be more productive than the other, in absolute terms, for each good. For both individuals and nations, the benefits of exchange tend to be larger the larger are the differences between the trading partners' opportunity costs. **LO4**

CORE PRINCIPLES

Comparative Advantage

The Principle of Comparative Advantage
Everyone does best when each person (or each country) concentrates on the activities for which his or her opportunity cost is lowest.

Increasing Opportunity Cost

The Principle of Increasing Opportunity Cost (also called "The Low-Hanging-Fruit Principle")
In expanding the production of any good, first employ those resources with the lowest opportunity cost, and only afterward turn to resources with higher opportunity costs.

KEY TERMS

absolute advantage (36)
attainable point (43)
comparative advantage (36)
efficient point (44)
inefficient point (44)
outsourcing (53)
production possibilities curve (41)
unattainable point (44)

REVIEW QUESTIONS

1. Explain what "having a comparative advantage" at producing a particular good or service means. What does "having an absolute advantage" at producing a good or service mean? **LO1**
2. How will a reduction in the number of hours worked each day affect an economy's production possibilities curve? **LO3**
3. How will technological innovations that boost labor productivity affect an economy's production possibilities curve? **LO3**
4. Why does saying that people are poor because they do not specialize make more sense than saying that people perform their own services because they are poor? **LO1**
5. What factors have helped the United States to become the world's leading exporter of movies, books, and popular music? **LO4**

PROBLEMS

1. Ted can wax 4 cars per day or wash 12 cars. Tom can wax 3 cars per day or wash 6. What is each man's opportunity cost of washing a car? Who has a comparative advantage in washing cars? **LO1**
2. Ted can wax a car in 20 minutes or wash a car in 60 minutes. Tom can wax a car in 15 minutes or wash a car in 30 minutes. What is each man's opportunity cost of washing a car? Who has a comparative advantage in washing cars? **LO1**
3. Toby can produce 5 gallons of apple cider or 2.5 ounces of feta cheese per hour. Kyle can produce 3 gallons of apple cider or 1.5 ounces of feta cheese per hour. Can Toby and Kyle benefit from specialization and trade? Explain. **LO1**
4. Nancy and Bill are auto mechanics. Nancy takes 4 hours to replace a clutch and 2 hours to replace a set of brakes. Bill takes 6 hours to replace a clutch and 2 hours to replace a set of brakes. State whether anyone has an absolute advantage at either task and, for each task, identify who has a comparative advantage. **LO1**
5. Consider a society consisting only of Helen, who allocates her time between sewing dresses and baking bread. Each hour she devotes to sewing dresses yields 4 dresses and each hour she devotes to baking bread yields 8 loaves of bread. If Helen works a total of 8 hours per day, graph her production possibilities curve. **LO3**
6. Refer to the preceding question. Which of the points listed below is efficient? Which is attainable? **LO3**
   a. 28 dresses per day, 16 loaves per day.
   b. 16 dresses per day, 32 loaves per day.
   c. 18 dresses per day, 24 loaves per day.
7. Suppose that in Problem 5 a sewing machine is introduced that enables Helen to sew 8 dresses per hour rather than only 4. Show how this development shifts her production possibilities curve. **LO3**
8. Refer to the preceding question to explain what is meant by the following statement: "An increase in productivity with respect to any one good increases our options for producing and consuming all other goods." **LO3**
9. Susan can pick 4 pounds of coffee in an hour or gather 2 pounds of nuts. Tom can pick 2 pounds of coffee in an hour or gather 4 pounds of nuts. Each works 6 hours per day. **LO2**
   a. What is the maximum number of pounds of coffee the two can pick in a day?
   b. What is the maximum number of pounds of nuts the two can gather in a day?

c. If Susan and Tom were picking the maximum number of pounds of coffee when they decided that they would like to begin gathering 4 pounds of nuts per day, who would gather the nuts, and how many pounds of coffee would they still be able to pick?
d. Now suppose Susan and Tom were gathering the maximum number of pounds of nuts when they decided that they would like to begin picking 8 pounds of coffee per day. Who would pick the coffee, and how many pounds of nuts would they still be able to gather?
e. Would it be possible for Susan and Tom in total to gather 26 pounds of nuts and pick 20 pounds of coffee each day? If so, how much of each good should each person pick?

10.* Refer to the two-person economy described in the preceding problem. **LO1**
a. Is the point (30 pounds of coffee per day, 12 pounds of nuts per day) an attainable point? Is it an efficient point? What about the point (24 pounds of coffee per day, 24 pounds of nuts per day)?
b. On a graph with pounds of coffee per day on the vertical axis and pounds of nuts per day on the horizontal axis, show all the points you identified in Problem 9, parts a–e, and Problem 10a. Connect these points with straight lines. Is the result the PPC for the economy consisting of Susan and Tom?
c. Suppose that Susan and Tom could buy or sell coffee and nuts in the world market at a price of $2 per pound for coffee and $2 per pound for nuts. If each person specialized completely in the good for which he or she had a comparative advantage, how much could they earn by selling all their produce?
d. At the prices just described, what is the maximum amount of coffee Susan and Tom could buy in the world market? The maximum amount of nuts? Would it be possible for them to consume 40 pounds of nuts and 8 pounds of coffee each day?
e. In light of their ability to buy and sell in world markets at the stated prices, show on the same graph all combinations of the two goods it would be possible for them to consume.

ANSWERS TO IN-CHAPTER EXERCISES

2.1

	Productivity in programming	Productivity in bicycle repair
Pat	2 Web page updates per hour	1 repair per hour
Barb	3 Web page updates per hour	3 repairs per hour

The entries in the table tell us that Barb has an absolute advantage over Pat in both activities. While Barb, the mechanic, can update 3 Web pages per hour, Pat, the programmer, can update only 2. Barb's absolute advantage over Pat is even greater in the task of fixing bikes—3 repairs per hour versus Pat's 1.

But as in second example in this chapter, the fact that Barb is a better programmer than Pat does not imply that Barb should update her own Web page. Barb's opportunity cost of updating a Web page is 1 bicycle repair, whereas Pat must give up only half a repair to update a Web page. Pat has a comparative advantage over Barb at programming and Barb has a comparative advantage over Pat at bicycle repair. **LO1**

*Problems marked with an asterisk (*) are more difficult.

2.2 In the accompanying graph, *A* (20 pounds per day of coffee, 4 pounds per day of nuts) is unattainable; *B* (12 pounds per day of coffee, 6 pounds per day of nuts) is both attainable and efficient; and *C* (4 pounds per day of coffee, 8 pounds per day of nuts) is both attainable and inefficient. **LO3**

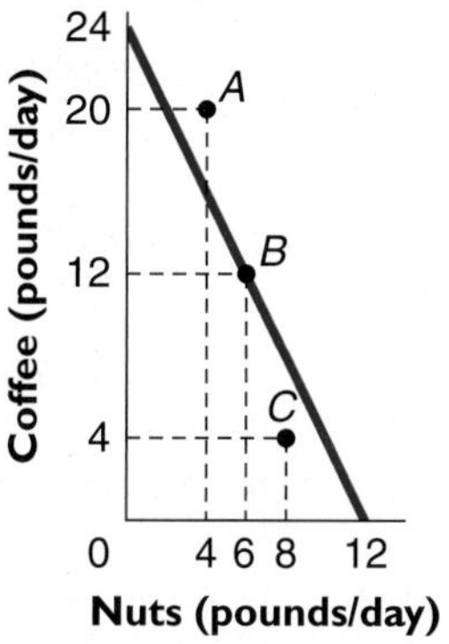

2.3 Susan's opportunity cost of gathering a pound of nuts is now ½ pound of coffee and Tom's opportunity cost of gathering a pound of nuts is now only 1 pound of coffee. So Tom has a comparative advantage at picking coffee and Susan has a comparative advantage at gathering nuts. **LO3**

2.4 Since Tom can produce five times as many pounds of nuts in an hour as pounds of coffee, to produce equal quantities of each, he must spend 5 hours picking coffee for every hour he devotes to gathering nuts. And since he works a 6-hour day, that means spending 5 hours picking coffee and 1 hour gathering nuts. Dividing his time in this way, he will end up with 5 pounds of each good. Similarly, if she is to produce equal quantities of each good, Susan must spend 5 hours gathering nuts and 1 hour picking coffee. So she too produces 5 pounds of each good if she divides her 6-hour day in this way. Their combined daily production will thus be 10 pounds of each good. By working together and specializing, however, they can produce and consume a total of 30 pounds per day of each good. **LO1**

CHAPTER 3

Supply and Demand

LEARNING OBJECTIVES

In this chapter, we will take up the basic supply and demand model. In the process, you will learn

1. How the demand curve summarizes the behavior of buyers in the marketplace.
2. How the supply curve summarizes the behavior of sellers in the marketplace.
3. How the supply and demand curves interact to determine the equilibrium price and quantity.
4. How shifts in supply and demand curves cause prices and quantities to change.
5. The Efficiency Principle, which says that efficiency is an important social goal because, when the economic pie grows larger, it is always possible for everyone to have a larger slice than before.
6. The Equilibrium Principle (also called the No-Cash-on-the-Table Principle), which says that a market in equilibrium leaves no unexploited opportunities for individuals.

The stock of foodstuffs on hand at any moment in New York City's grocery stores, restaurants, and private kitchens is sufficient to feed the area's 10 million residents for at most a week or so. Since most of these residents have nutritionally adequate and highly varied diets, and since almost no food is produced within the city proper, provisioning New York requires that millions of pounds of food and drink be delivered to locations throughout the city each day.

No doubt many New Yorkers, buying groceries at their favorite local markets or eating at their favorite Italian restaurants, give little or no thought to the nearly miraculous coordination of people and resources that is required to feed city residents on a daily basis. But near-miraculous it is, nevertheless. Even if the supplying of New York City consisted only of transporting a fixed collection of foods to a given list of destinations each day, it would be quite an impressive operation, requiring at least a small (and well-managed) army to carry out.

Yet the entire process is astonishingly more complex than that. For example, the system must somehow ensure that not only *enough* food is delivered to satisfy New Yorkers' discriminating palates, but also the *right kinds* of food. There mustn't be too much pheasant and not enough smoked eel; or too much bacon and not enough eggs; or too much caviar and not enough canned tuna; and so on. Similar judgments must be made *within* each category of food and drink: There must be the right amount of Swiss cheese and the right amounts of provolone, gorgonzola, and feta.

But even this doesn't begin to describe the complexity of the decisions and actions required to provide our nation's largest city with its daily bread. Someone has to decide where each particular type of food gets produced, and how, and by whom. Someone must decide how much of each type of food gets delivered to *each* of the tens of thousands of restaurants and grocery stores in the city. Someone must determine whether the deliveries should be made in big trucks or small ones, arrange that the trucks be in the right place at the right time, and ensure that gasoline and qualified drivers be available.

Thousands of individuals must decide what role, if any, they will play in this collective effort. Some people—just the right number—must choose to drive food-delivery trucks rather than trucks that deliver lumber. Others must become the mechanics who fix these trucks rather than carpenters who build houses. Others must become farmers rather than architects or bricklayers. Still others must become chefs in upscale restaurants, or flip burgers at McDonald's, instead of becoming plumbers or electricians.

Yet despite the almost incomprehensible number and complexity of the tasks involved, somehow the supplying of New York City manages to get done remarkably smoothly. Oh, a grocery store will occasionally run out of flank steak or a diner will sometimes be told that someone else has just ordered the last serving of roast duck. But if episodes like these stick in memory, it is only because they are rare. For the most part, New York's food delivery system—like that of every other city in the country—functions so seamlessly that it attracts virtually no notice.

The situation is strikingly different in New York City's rental housing market. According to one recent estimate, the city needs between 20,000 and 40,000 new housing units each year merely to keep up with population growth and to replace existing housing that is deteriorated beyond repair. The actual rate of new construction in the city, however, is only 6,000 units per year. As a result, America's most densely populated city has been experiencing a protracted housing shortage. Yet, paradoxically, in the midst of this shortage, apartment houses are being demolished; and in the vacant lots left behind, people from the neighborhoods are planting flower gardens!

© Robert Brenner/Photo Edit

New York City is experiencing not only a growing shortage of rental housing, but also chronically strained relations between landlords and tenants. In one all-too-typical case, for example, a photographer living in a loft on the Lower East Side waged an eight-year court battle with his landlord that generated literally thousands of pages of legal documents. "Once we put up a doorbell for ourselves," the photographer recalled, "and [the landlord] pulled it out, so we pulled out the wires to his doorbell."[1] The landlord, for his part, accused the photographer of obstructing his efforts to renovate the apartment. According to the landlord, the tenant preferred for the apartment to remain in substandard condition since that gave him an excuse to withhold rent payments.

© Joseph Sohm/Visions of America/Corbis

Why does New York City's food distribution system work so much better than its housing market?

Same city, two strikingly different patterns: In the food industry, goods and services are available in wide variety and people (at least those with adequate income) are generally satisfied with what they receive and the choices available to them. In contrast, in the rental housing industry, chronic shortages and chronic dissatisfaction are rife among both buyers and sellers. Why this difference?

[1] Quoted by John Tierney, "The Rentocracy: At the Intersection of Supply and Demand," *New York Times Magazine*, May 4, 1997, p. 39.

The brief answer is that New York City relies on a complex system of administrative rent regulations to allocate housing units but leaves the allocation of food essentially in the hands of market forces—the forces of supply and demand. Although intuition might suggest otherwise, both theory and experience suggest that the seemingly chaotic and unplanned outcomes of market forces, in most cases, can do a better job of allocating economic resources than can (for example) a government agency, even if the agency has the best of intentions.

In this chapter we'll explore how markets allocate food, housing, and other goods and services, usually with remarkable efficiency despite the complexity of the tasks. To be sure, markets are by no means perfect, and our stress on their virtues is to some extent an attempt to counteract what most economists view as an underappreciation by the general public of their remarkable strengths. But, in the course of our discussion, we'll see why markets function so smoothly most of the time and why bureaucratic rules and regulations rarely work as well in solving complex economic problems.

To convey an understanding of how markets work is a major goal of this course, and in this chapter we provide only a brief introduction and overview. As the course proceeds, we will discuss the economic role of markets in considerably more detail, paying attention to some of the problems of markets as well as their strengths.

WHAT, HOW, AND FOR WHOM? CENTRAL PLANNING VERSUS THE MARKET

No city, state, or society—regardless of how it is organized—can escape the need to answer certain basic economic questions. For example, how much of our limited time and other resources should we devote to building housing, how much to the production of food, and how much to providing other goods and services? What techniques should we use to produce each good? Who should be assigned to each specific task? And how should the resulting goods and services be distributed among people?

In the thousands of different societies for which records are available, issues like these have been decided in essentially one of two ways. One approach is for all economic decisions to be made centrally, by an individual or small number of individuals on behalf of a larger group. For example, in many agrarian societies throughout history, families or other small groups consumed only those goods and services that they produced for themselves and a single clan or family leader made most important production and distribution decisions. On an immensely larger scale, the economic organization of the former Soviet Union (and other communist countries) was also largely centralized. In so-called centrally planned communist nations, a central bureaucratic committee established production targets for the country's farms and factories, developed a master plan for how to achieve the targets (including detailed instructions concerning who was to produce what), and set up guidelines for the distribution and use of the goods and services produced.

Neither form of centralized economic organization is much in evidence today. When implemented on a small scale, as in a self-sufficient family enterprise, centralized decision making is certainly feasible. For the reasons discussed in the preceding chapter, however, the jack-of-all-trades approach was doomed once it became clear how dramatically people could improve their living standards by specialization—that is, by having each individual focus his or her efforts on a relatively narrow range of tasks. And with the fall of the Soviet Union and its satellite nations in the late 1980s, there are now only three communist economies left in the world: Cuba, North Korea, and China. The first two of these appear to be on their last legs, economically speaking, and China has by now largely abandoned any attempt to control production and distribution decisions from the center. The major remaining examples of centralized allocation and control now reside in the bureaucratic agencies that administer programs like New York City's rent controls—programs that are themselves becoming increasingly rare.

At the beginning of the twenty-first century, we are therefore left, for the most part, with the second major form of economic system, one in which production and distribution decisions are left to individuals interacting in private markets. In the so-called capitalist, or free-market, economies, people decide for themselves which careers to pursue and which products to produce or buy. In fact, there are no *pure* free-market economies today. Modern industrial countries are more properly described as "mixed economies," meaning that goods and services are allocated by a combination of free markets, regulation, and other forms of collective control. Still, it makes sense to refer to such systems as free-market economies because people are for the most part free to start businesses, to shut them down, or to sell them. And within broad limits, the distribution of goods and services is determined by individual preferences backed by individual purchasing power, which in most cases comes from the income people earn in the labor market.

In country after country, markets have replaced centralized control for the simple reason that they tend to assign production tasks and consumption benefits much more effectively. The popular press, and the conventional wisdom, often asserts that economists disagree about important issues. (As someone once quipped, "If you lay all the economists in the world end to end, they still wouldn't reach a conclusion.") The fact is, however, that there is overwhelming agreement among economists about a broad range of issues, with the great majority accepting the efficacy of markets as means for allocating society's scarce resources. For example, a recent survey found that more than 90 percent of American professional economists believe that rent regulations like the ones implemented by New York City do more harm than good. That the stated aim of these regulations—to make rental housing more affordable for middle- and low-income families—is clearly benign was not enough to prevent them from wreaking havoc on New York City's housing market. To see why, we must explore how goods and services are allocated in private markets, and why nonmarket means of allocating goods and services often do not produce the expected results.

BUYERS AND SELLERS IN MARKETS

Why do Pablo Picasso's paintings sell for so much more than Jackson Pollock's?

market the market for any good consists of all buyers or sellers of that good

Beginning with some simple concepts and definitions, we will explore how the interactions among buyers and sellers in markets determine the prices and quantities of the various goods and services traded in those markets. We begin by defining a market: The **market** for any good consists of all the buyers and sellers of that good. So, for example, the market for pizza on a given day in a given place is just the set of people (or other economic actors such as firms) potentially able to buy or sell pizza at that time and location.

In the market for pizza, sellers comprise the individuals and companies that either do sell—or might, under the right circumstances, sell—pizza. Similarly, buyers in this market include all individuals who buy—or might buy—pizza.

In most parts of the country, a decent pizza—or some other life-sustaining meal—can still be had for less than $10. Where does the market price of pizza come from? Looking beyond pizza to the vast array of other goods that are bought and sold every day, we may ask, "Why are some goods cheap and others expensive?" Aristotle had no idea. Nor did Plato, or Copernicus, or Newton. On reflection, it is astonishing that, for almost the entire span of human history, not even the most intelligent and creative minds on Earth had any real inkling of how to answer that seemingly simple question. Even Adam Smith, the Scottish moral philosopher whose *Wealth of Nations* launched the discipline of economics in 1776, suffered confusion on this issue.

Smith and other early economists (including Karl Marx) thought that the market price of a good was determined by its cost of production. But although costs surely do affect prices, they cannot explain why one of Pablo Picasso's paintings sells for so much more than one of Jackson Pollock's.

Stanley Jevons and other nineteenth-century economists tried to explain price by focusing on the value people derived from consuming different goods and services. It certainly seems plausible that people will pay a lot for a good they value highly. Yet willingness to pay cannot be the whole story, either. Deprive a person in the desert of water, for example, and he will be dead in a matter of hours, and yet water sells for less than a penny a gallon. By contrast, human beings can get along perfectly well without gold, and yet gold sells for more than $800 an ounce.

Cost of production? Value to the user? Which is it? The answer, which seems obvious to today's economists, is that both matter. Writing in the late nineteenth century, the British economist Alfred Marshall was among the first to show clearly how costs and value interact to determine both the prevailing market price for a good and the amount of it that is bought and sold. Our task in the pages ahead will be to explore Marshall's insights and gain some practice in applying them. As a first step, we introduce the two main components of Marshall's pathbreaking analysis: the demand curve and the supply curve.

THE DEMAND CURVE

In the market for pizza, the **demand curve** for pizza is a simple schedule or graph that tells us how many slices people would be willing to buy at different prices. By convention, economists usually put price on the vertical axis of the demand curve and quantity on the horizontal axis.

demand curve a schedule or graph showing the quantity of a good that buyers wish to buy at each price

A fundamental property of the demand curve is that it is downward-sloping with respect to price. For example, the demand curve for pizza tells us that as the price of pizza falls, buyers will buy more slices. Thus, the daily demand curve for pizza in Chicago on a given day might look like the curve seen in Figure 3.1. (Although economists usually refer to demand and supply "curves," we often draw them as straight lines in examples.)

The demand curve in Figure 3.1 tells us that when the price of pizza is low—say $2 per slice—buyers will want to buy 16,000 slices per day, whereas they will want to buy only 12,000 slices at a price of $3 and only 8,000 at a price of $4. The demand curve for pizza—as for any other good—slopes downward for multiple reasons. Some of these reasons have to do with the individual consumer's reactions to price changes. Thus, as pizza becomes more expensive, a consumer may switch to chicken sandwiches, hamburgers, or other foods that substitute for pizza. This is called the **substitution effect** of a price change. In addition, a price increase reduces the quantity demanded because it reduces purchasing power: A consumer simply can't afford to buy as many slices of pizza at higher prices as at lower prices. This is called the **income effect** of a price change.

substitution effect the change in the quantity demanded of a good that results because buyers switch to or from substitutes when the price of the good changes

income effect the change in the quantity demanded of a good that results because a change in the price of a good changes the buyer's purchasing power

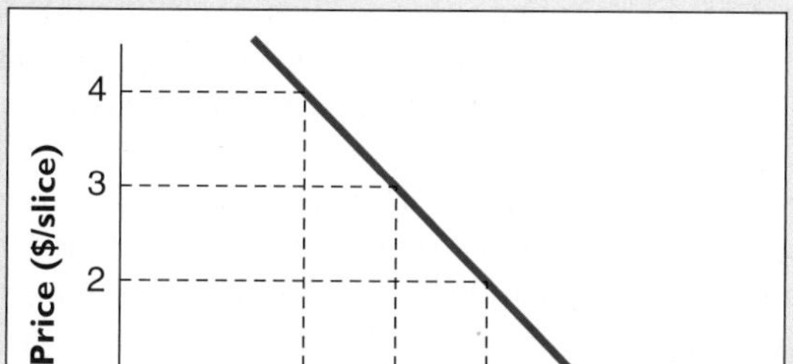

FIGURE 3.1
The Daily Demand Curve for Pizza in Chicago.
The demand curve for any good is a downward-sloping function of its price.

Cost-Benefit

buyer's reservation price the largest dollar amount the buyer would be willing to pay for a good

Another reason that the demand curve slopes downward is that consumers differ in terms of how much they are willing to pay for the good. The Cost-Benefit Principle tells us that a given person will buy the good if the benefit he expects to receive from it exceeds its cost. The benefit is the **buyer's reservation price,** the highest dollar amount he would be willing to pay for the good. The cost of the good is the actual amount that the buyer actually must pay for it, which is the market price of the good. In most markets, different buyers have different reservation prices. Thus, when the good sells for a high price, it will satisfy the cost-benefit test for fewer buyers than when it sells for a lower price.

To put this same point another way, the fact that the demand curve for a good is downward-sloping reflects the fact that the reservation price of the marginal buyer declines as the quantity of the good bought increases. Here the marginal buyer is the person who purchases the last unit of the good that is sold. If buyers are currently purchasing 12,000 slices of pizza a day in Figure 3.1, for example, the reservation price for the buyer of the 12,000th slice must be \$3. (If someone had been willing to pay more than that, the quantity demanded at a price of \$3 would have been more than 12,000 to begin with.) By similar reasoning, when the quantity sold is 16,000 slices per day, the marginal buyer's reservation price must be only \$2.

We defined the demand curve for any good as a schedule telling how much of it consumers wish to purchase at various prices. This is called the *horizontal interpretation* of the demand curve. Using the horizontal interpretation, we start with price on the vertical axis and read the corresponding quantity demanded on the horizontal axis. Thus, at a price of \$4 per slice, the demand curve in Figure 3.1 tells us that the quantity of pizza demanded will be 8,000 slices per day.

The demand curve also can be interpreted in a second way, which is to start with quantity on the horizontal axis and then read the marginal buyer's reservation price on the vertical axis. Thus, when the quantity of pizza sold is 8,000 slices per day, the demand curve in Figure 3.1 tells us that the marginal buyer's reservation price is \$4 per slice. This second way of reading the demand curve is called the *vertical interpretation.*

EXERCISE 3.1

In Figure 3.1, what is the marginal buyer's reservation price when the quantity of pizza sold is 10,000 slices per day? For the same demand curve, what will be the quantity of pizza demanded at a price of \$2.50 per slice?

THE SUPPLY CURVE

supply curve a graph or schedule showing the quantity of a good that sellers wish to sell at each price

In the market for pizza, the **supply curve** is a simple schedule or graph that tells us, for each possible price, the total number of slices that all pizza vendors would be willing to sell at that price. What does the supply curve of pizza look like? The answer to this question is based on the logical assumption that suppliers should be willing to sell additional slices as long as the price they receive is sufficient to cover their opportunity costs of supplying them. Thus, if what someone could earn by selling a slice of pizza is insufficient to compensate her for what she could have earned if she had spent her time and invested her money in some other way, she will not sell that slice. Otherwise, she will.

Just as buyers differ with respect to the amounts they are willing to pay for pizza, sellers also differ with respect to their opportunity costs of supplying pizza. For those with limited education and work experience, the opportunity cost of selling pizza is relatively low (because such individuals typically do not have a lot of high-paying alternatives). For others, the opportunity cost of selling pizza is of moderate value, and for still others—like rock stars and professional athletes—it is prohibitively high. In part because of these differences in opportunity cost among people, the daily supply curve of pizza will be *upward-sloping* with respect to price. As an illustration, see Figure 3.2, which shows a hypothetical supply curve for pizza in the Chicago market on a given day.

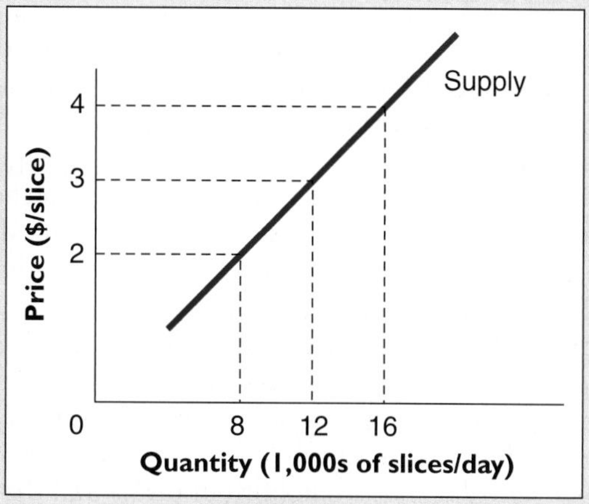

FIGURE 3.2
The Daily Supply Curve of Pizza in Chicago.
At higher prices, sellers generally offer more units for sale.

The fact that the supply curve slopes upward may be seen as a consequence of the Low-Hanging-Fruit Principle, discussed in the preceding chapter. This principle tells us that as we expand the production of pizza, we turn first to those whose opportunity costs of producing pizza are lowest, and only then to others with higher opportunity costs.

Increasing Opportunity Cost

Like the demand curve, the supply curve can be interpreted either horizontally or vertically. Under the horizontal interpretation, we begin with a price, then go over to the supply curve to read the quantity that sellers wish to sell at that price on the horizontal axis. For instance, at a price of $2 per slice, sellers in Figure 3.2 wish to sell 8,000 slices per day.

Under the vertical interpretation, we begin with a quantity, then go up to the supply curve to read the corresponding marginal cost on the vertical axis. Thus, if sellers in Figure 3.2 are currently supplying 12,000 slices per day, the opportunity cost of the marginal seller is $3 per slice. In other words, the supply curve tells us that the marginal cost of producing the 12,000th slice of pizza is $3. (If someone could produce a 12,001st slice for less than $3, she would have an incentive to supply it, so the quantity of pizza supplied at $3 per slice would not have been 12,000 slices per day to begin with.) By similar reasoning, when the quantity of pizza supplied is 16,000 slices per day, the marginal cost of producing another slice must be $4. The **seller's reservation price** for selling an additional unit of a good is her marginal cost of producing that good. It is the smallest dollar amount for which she would not be worse off if she sold an additional unit.

seller's reservation price the smallest dollar amount for which a seller would be willing to sell an additional unit, generally equal to marginal cost

EXERCISE 3.2

In Figure 3.2, what is the marginal cost of a slice of pizza when the quantity of pizza sold is 10,000 slices per day? For the same supply curve, what will be the quantity of pizza supplied at a price of $3.50 per slice?

RECAP	DEMAND AND SUPPLY CURVES

The *market* for a good consists of the actual and potential buyers and sellers of that good. For any given price, the *demand curve* shows the quantity that demanders would be willing to buy and the *supply curve* shows the quantity that suppliers of the good would be willing to sell. Suppliers are willing to sell more at higher prices (supply curves slope upward) and demanders are willing to buy less at higher prices (demand curves slope downward).

MARKET EQUILIBRIUM

equilibrium a system is in equilibrium when there is no tendency for it to change

The concept of **equilibrium** is employed in both the physical and social sciences, and it is of central importance in economic analysis. In general, a system is in equilibrium when all forces at work within the system are canceled by others, resulting in a balanced or unchanging situation. In physics, for example, a ball hanging from a spring is said to be in equilibrium when the spring has stretched sufficiently that the upward force it exerts on the ball is exactly counterbalanced by the downward force of gravity. In economics, a market is said to be in equilibrium when no participant in the market has any reason to alter his or her behavior, so that there is no tendency for production or prices in that market to change.

equilibrium price and *equilibrium quantity* the values of price and quantity for which quantity supplied and quantity demanded are equal

If we want to determine the final position of a ball hanging from a spring, we need to find the point at which the forces of gravity and spring tension are balanced and the system is in equilibrium. Similarly, if we want to find the price at which a good will sell (which we will call the **equilibrium price**) and the quantity of it that will be sold (the **equilibrium quantity**), we need to find the equilibrium in the market for that good. The basic tools for finding the equilibrium in a market for a good are the supply and demand curves for that good. For reasons that we will explain, the equilibrium price and equilibrium quantity of a good are the price and quantity at which the supply and demand curves for the good intersect. For the hypothetical supply and demand curves shown earlier for the pizza market in Chicago, the equilibrium price will therefore be $3 per slice, and the equilibrium quantity of pizza sold will be 12,000 slices per day, as shown in Figure 3.3.

In Figure 3.3, note that at the equilibrium price of $3 per slice, both sellers and buyers are "satisfied" in the following sense: Buyers are buying exactly the quantity of pizza they wish to buy at that price (12,000 slices per day) and sellers are selling exactly the quantity of pizza they wish to sell (also 12,000 slices per day). And since they are satisfied in this sense, neither buyers nor sellers face any incentives to change their behavior.

market equilibrium occurs in a market when all buyers and sellers are satisfied with their respective quantities at the market price

Note the limited sense of the term "satisfied" in the definition of **market equilibrium**. It doesn't mean that sellers would not be pleased to receive a price higher than the equilibrium price. Rather, it means only that they're able to sell all they wish to sell at that price. Similarly, to say that buyers are satisfied at the equilibrium price doesn't mean that they would not be happy to pay less than the equilibrium price. Rather, it means only that they're able to buy exactly as many units of the good as they wish to at the equilibrium price.

Note also that if the price of pizza in our Chicago market were anything other than $3 per slice, either buyers or sellers would be frustrated. Suppose, for example, that the price of pizza were $4 per slice, as shown in Figure 3.4. At that price, buyers wish to buy only 8,000 slices per day, but sellers wish to sell 16,000. And since no one can force someone to buy a slice of pizza against her wishes, this means that

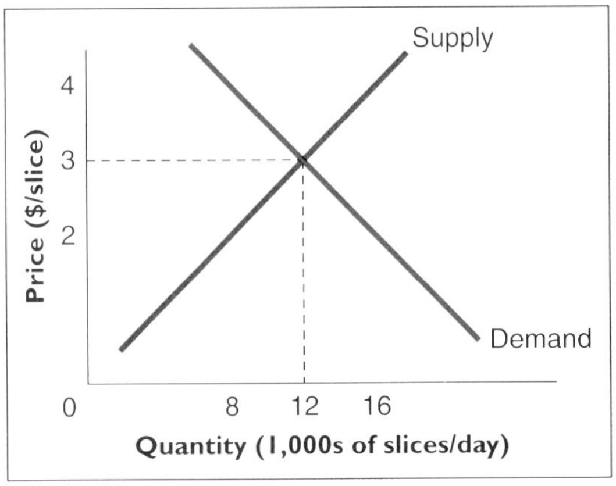

FIGURE 3.3
The Equilibrium Price and Quantity of Pizza in Chicago.
The equilibrium quantity and price of a product are the values that correspond to the intersection of the supply and demand curves for that product.

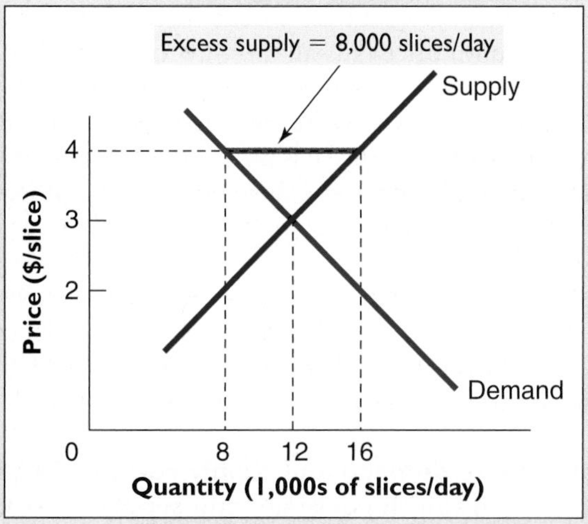

FIGURE 3.4
Excess Supply.
When price exceeds the equilibrium price, there is excess supply, or surplus, the difference between quantity supplied and quantity demanded.

buyers will buy only the 8,000 slices they wish to buy. So when the price exceeds the equilibrium price, it is sellers who end up being frustrated. At a price of $4 in this example, they are left with an **excess supply** of 8,000 slices per day.

excess supply the amount by which quantity supplied exceeds quantity demanded when the price of a good exceeds the equilibrium price

Conversely, suppose that the price of pizza in our Chicago market were less than the equilibrium price—say, $2 per slice. As shown in Figure 3.5, buyers want to buy 16,000 slices per day at that price, whereas sellers want to sell only 8,000. And since sellers cannot be forced to sell pizza against their wishes, this time it is the buyers who end up being frustrated. At a price of $2 per slice in this example, they experience an **excess demand** of 8,000 slices per day.

excess demand the amount by which quantity demanded exceeds quantity supplied when the price of a good lies below the equilibrium price

An extraordinary feature of private markets for goods and services is their automatic tendency to gravitate toward their respective equilibrium prices and quantities. This tendency is a simple consequence of the Incentive Principle. The mechanisms by which the adjustment happens are implicit in our definitions of excess supply and excess demand. Suppose, for example, that the price of pizza in our hypothetical market was $4 per slice, leading to excess supply as shown in Figure 3.4. Because sellers are frustrated in the sense of wanting to sell more pizza than buyers wish to buy, sellers have an incentive to take whatever steps they can to increase their sales. The simplest strategy available to them is to cut their price slightly. Thus, if one seller reduced his price from $4 to, say, $3.95 per slice, he would attract many of the buyers who had been paying $4 per slice for pizza supplied by other sellers. Those sellers, in order to recover their lost business, would then have an incentive to match the price cut. But notice that if all sellers lowered

Incentive

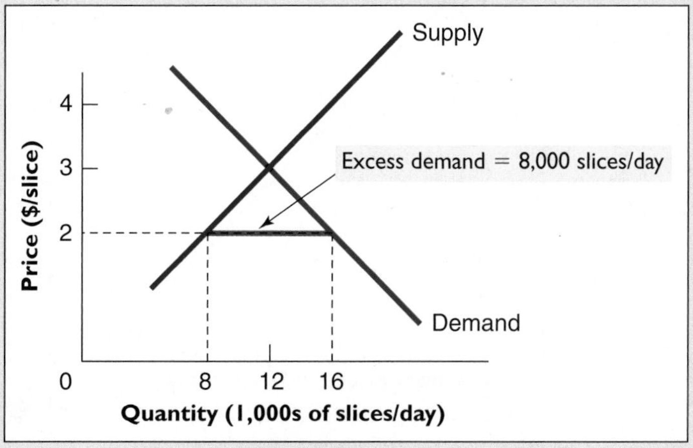

FIGURE 3.5
Excess Demand.
When price lies below the equilibrium price, there is excess demand, the difference between quantity demanded and quantity supplied.

their prices to \$3.95 per slice, there would still be considerable excess supply. So sellers would face continuing incentives to cut their prices. This pressure to cut prices will not go away until price falls all the way to \$3 per slice.

Conversely, suppose that price starts out less than the equilibrium price—say, \$2 per slice. This time it is buyers who are frustrated. A person who can't get all the pizza he wants at a price of \$2 per slice has an incentive to offer a higher price, hoping to obtain pizza that would otherwise have been sold to other buyers. And sellers, for their part, will be only too happy to post higher prices as long as queues of frustrated buyers remain.

The upshot is that price has a tendency to gravitate to its equilibrium level under conditions of either excess supply or excess demand. And when price reaches its equilibrium level, both buyers and sellers are satisfied in the technical sense of being able to buy or sell precisely the amounts of their choosing.

Samples of points on the demand and supply curves of a pizza market are provided in Table 3.1. Graph the demand and supply curves for this market and find its equilibrium price and quantity.

TABLE 3.1
Points along the Demand and Supply Curves of a Pizza Market

Demand for Pizza		Supply of Pizza	
Price (\$/slice)	Quantity demanded (1,000s of slices/day)	Price (\$/slice)	Quantity supplied (1,000s of slices/day)
1	8	1	2
2	6	2	4
3	4	3	6
4	2	4	8

The points in the table are plotted in Figure 3.6 and then joined to indicate the supply and demand curves for this market. These curves intersect to yield an equilibrium price of \$2.50 per slice and an equilibrium quantity of 5,000 slices per day.

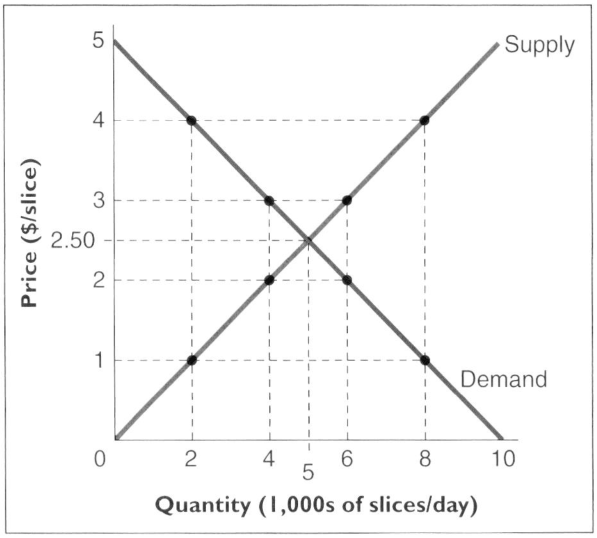

FIGURE 3.6
Graphing Supply and Demand and Finding the Equilibrium Price and Quantity.
To graph the demand and supply curves, plot the relevant points given in the table and then join them with a line. The equilibrium price and quantity occur at the intersection of these curves.

We emphasize that market equilibrium does not necessarily produce an ideal outcome for all market participants. Thus, in the example just considered, market participants are satisfied with the amount of pizza they buy and sell at a price of \$2.50 per slice, but for a poor buyer this may signify little more than that he *can't* buy additional pizza without sacrificing other more highly valued purchases.

Indeed, buyers with extremely low incomes often have difficulty purchasing even basic goods and services, which has prompted governments in almost every society to attempt to ease the burdens of the poor. Yet the laws of supply and demand cannot simply be repealed by an act of the legislature. In the next section, we will see that when legislators attempt to prevent markets from reaching their equilibrium prices and quantities, they often do more harm than good.

RENT CONTROLS RECONSIDERED

Consider again the market for rental housing units in New York City and suppose that the demand and supply curves for one-bedroom apartments are as shown in Figure 3.7. This market, left alone, would reach an equilibrium monthly rent of \$1,600, at which 2 million one-bedroom apartments would be rented. Both landlords and tenants would be satisfied, in the sense that they would not wish to rent either more or fewer units at that price.

This would not necessarily mean, of course, that all is well and good. Many potential tenants, for example, might simply be unable to afford a rent of \$1,600 per month and thus be forced to remain homeless (or to move out of the city to a cheaper location). Suppose that, acting purely out of benign motives, legislators made it unlawful for landlords to charge more than \$800 per month for one-bedroom apartments. Their stated aim in enacting this law was that no person should have to remain homeless because decent housing was unaffordable.

But note in Figure 3.8 that when rents for one-bedroom apartments are prevented from rising above \$800 per month, landlords are willing to supply only 1 million apartments per month, 1 million fewer than at the equilibrium monthly rent of \$1,600. Note also that at the controlled rent of \$800 per month, tenants want to rent 3 million one-bedroom apartments per month. (For example, many people who would have decided to live in New Jersey rather than pay \$1,600 a month in New York will now choose to live in the city.) So when rents are prevented from rising above \$800 per month, we see an excess demand for one-bedroom apartments of 2 million units each month. Put another way, the rent controls result in a housing shortage of 2 million units each month. What is more, the number of apartments actually available *declines* by 1 million units per month.

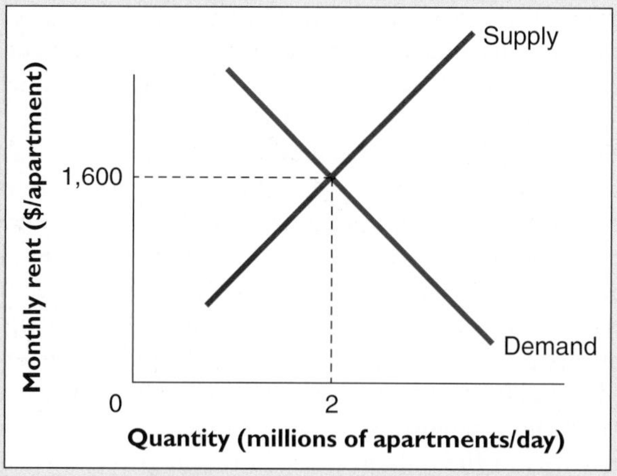

FIGURE 3.7
An Unregulated Housing Market.
For the supply and demand curves shown, the equilibrium monthly rent is \$1,600 and 2 million apartments will be rented at that price.

FIGURE 3.8
Rent Controls.
When rents are prohibited from rising to the equilibrium level, the result is excess demand in the housing market.

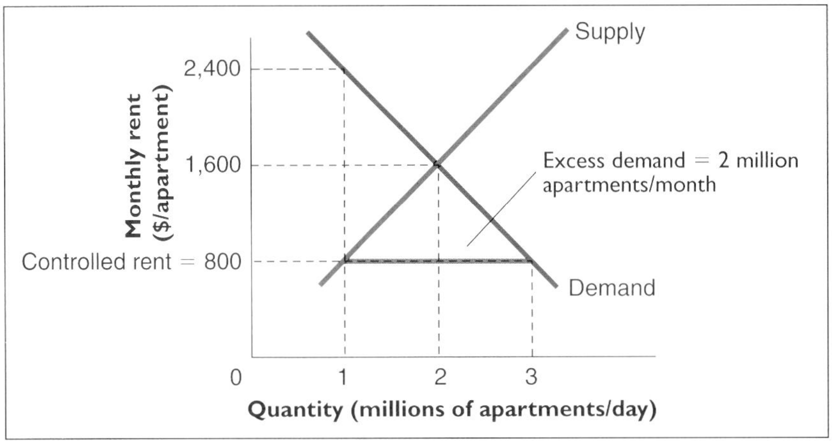

If the housing market were completely unregulated, the immediate response to such a high level of excess demand would be for rents to rise sharply. But here the law prevents them from rising above $800. Many other ways exist, however, in which the pressures of excess demand can make themselves felt. For instance, owners will quickly learn that they are free to spend less on maintaining the quality of their rental units. After all, if there are scores of renters knocking at the door of each vacant apartment, a landlord has considerable room to maneuver. Leaking pipes, peeling paint, broken furnaces, and other problems are less likely to receive prompt attention—or, indeed, any attention at all—when rents are set well below market-clearing levels.

Nor are reduced availability of apartments and poorer maintenance of existing apartments the only difficulties. With an offering of only 1 million apartments per month, we see in Figure 3.8 that there are renters who would be willing to pay as much as $2,400 per month for an apartment. As the Incentive Principle suggests, this pressure will almost always find ways, legal or illegal, of expressing itself. In New York City, for example, it is not uncommon to see "finder's fees" or "key deposits" as high as several thousand dollars. Owners who cannot charge a market-clearing rent for their apartments also have the option of converting them to condominiums or co-ops, which enables them to sell their assets for prices much closer to their true economic value.

Incentive

Even when rent-controlled apartment owners do not hike their prices in these various ways, serious misallocations result. For instance, ill-suited roommates often remain together despite their constant bickering because each is reluctant to reenter the housing market. Or a widow might steadfastly remain in her seven-room apartment even after her children have left home because it is much cheaper than alternative dwellings not covered by rent control. It would be much better for all concerned if she relinquished that space to a larger family that valued it more highly. But under rent controls, she has no economic incentive to do so.

There is also another more insidious cost of rent controls. In markets without rent controls, landlords cannot discriminate against potential tenants on the basis of race, religion, sexual orientation, physical disability, or national origin without suffering an economic penalty. Refusal to rent to members of specific groups would reduce the demand for their apartments, which would mean having to accept lower rents. When rents are artificially pegged below their equilibrium level, however, the resulting excess demand for apartments enables landlords to engage in discrimination with no further economic penalty.

Rent controls are not the only instance in which governments have attempted to repeal the law of supply and demand in the interest of helping the poor. During the late 1970s, for example, the federal government tried to hold the price of gasoline below its equilibrium level out of concern that high gasoline prices imposed unacceptable hardships on low-income drivers. As with controls in the rental housing market, unintended consequences of price controls in the gasoline market made the policy an extremely costly way of trying to aid the poor. For example, gasoline shortages resulted in long lines at the pumps, a waste not only of valuable time, but also of gasoline as cars sat idling for extended periods.

In their opposition to rent controls and similar measures, are economists revealing a total lack of concern for the poor? Although this claim is sometimes made by those who don't understand the issues, or who stand to benefit in some way from government regulations, there is little justification for it. *Economists simply realize that there are much more effective ways to help poor people than to try to give them apartments and other goods at artificially low prices.*

One straightforward approach would be to give the poor additional income and let them decide for themselves how to spend it. True, there are also practical difficulties involved in transferring additional purchasing power into the hands of the poor—most importantly, the difficulty of targeting cash to the genuinely needy without weakening others' incentives to fend for themselves. But there are practical ways to overcome this difficulty. For example, for far less than the waste caused by price controls, the government could afford generous subsidies to the wages of the working poor and could sponsor public-service employment for those who are unable to find jobs in the private sector.

Regulations that peg prices below equilibrium levels have far-reaching effects on market outcomes. The following exercise asks you to consider what happens when a price control is established at a level above the equilibrium price.

EXERCISE 3.3

In the rental housing market whose demand and supply curves are shown below, what will be the effect of a law that prevents rents from rising above $1,200 per month?

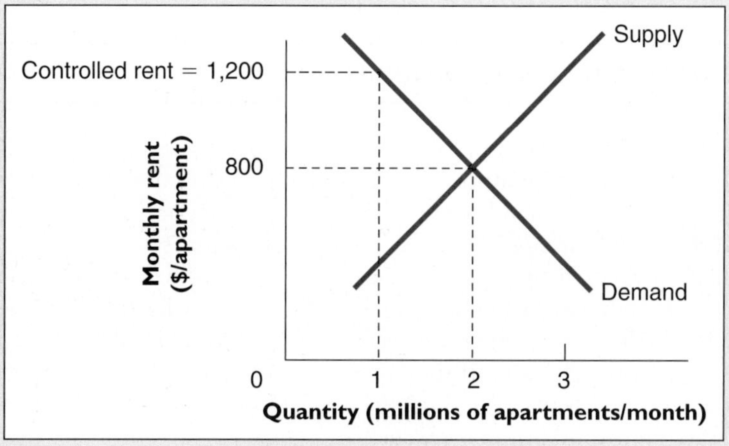

PIZZA PRICE CONTROLS?

The sources of the contrast between the rent-controlled housing market and the largely unregulated food markets in New York City can be seen more vividly by trying to imagine what would happen if concern for the poor led the city's leaders to implement price controls on pizza. Suppose, for example, that the supply and

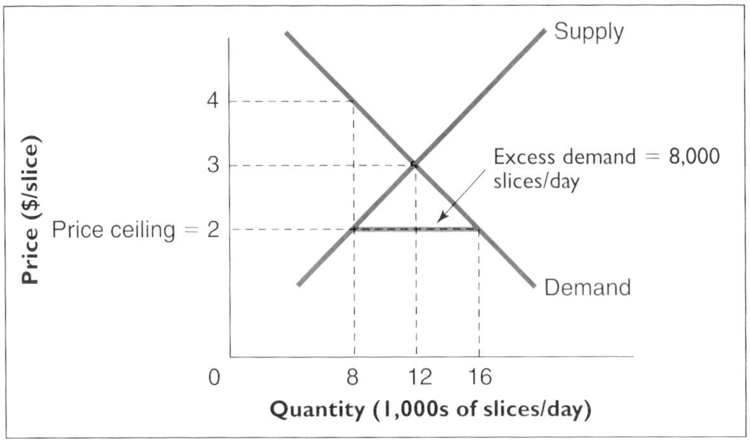

FIGURE 3.9
Price Controls in the Pizza Market.
A price ceiling below the equilibrium price of pizza would result in excess demand for pizza.

price ceiling a maximum allowable price, specified by law

demand curves for pizza are as shown in Figure 3.9 and that the city imposes a **price ceiling** of $2 per slice, making it unlawful to charge more than that amount. At $2 per slice, buyers want to buy 16,000 slices per day, but sellers want to sell only 8,000.

At a price of $2 per slice, every pizza restaurant in the city will have long queues of buyers trying unsuccessfully to purchase pizza. Frustrated buyers will behave rudely to clerks, who will respond in kind. Friends of restaurant managers will begin to get preferential treatment. Devious pricing strategies will begin to emerge (such as the $2 slice of pizza sold in combination with a $5 cup of Coke). Pizza will be made from poorer-quality ingredients. Rumors will begin to circulate about sources of black-market pizza. And so on.

The very idea of not being able to buy a pizza seems absurd, yet precisely such things happen routinely in markets in which prices are held below the equilibrium levels. For example, prior to the collapse of communist governments, it was considered normal in those countries for people to stand in line for hours to buy basic goods, while the politically connected had first choice of those goods that were available.

EN 3

RECAP	MARKET EQUILIBRIUM

Market equilibrium, the situation in which all buyers and sellers are satisfied with their respective quantities at the market price, occurs at the intersection of the supply and demand curves. The corresponding price and quantity are called the *equilibrium price* and the *equilibrium quantity.*

Unless prevented by regulation, prices and quantities are driven toward their equilibrium values by the actions of buyers and sellers. If the price is initially too high, so that there is excess supply, frustrated sellers will cut their price in order to sell more. If the price is initially too low, so that there is excess demand, competition among buyers drives the price upward. This process continues until equilibrium is reached.

PREDICTING AND EXPLAINING CHANGES IN PRICES AND QUANTITIES

If we know how the factors that govern supply and demand curves are changing, we can make informed predictions about how prices and the corresponding quantities will change. But when describing changing circumstances in the marketplace,

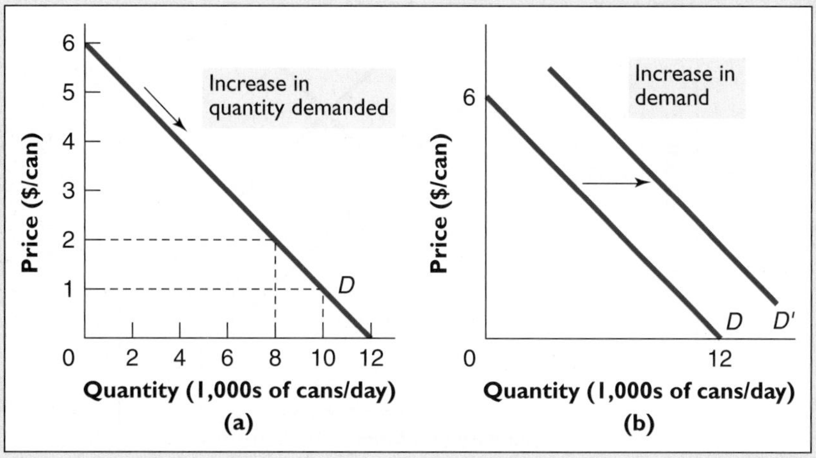

FIGURE 3.10
An Increase in the Quantity Demanded versus an Increase in Demand.
(a) An increase in quantity demanded describes a downward movement along the demand curve as price falls. (b) An increase in demand describes an outward shift of the demand curve.

we must take care to recognize some important terminological distinctions. For example, we must distinguish between the meanings of the seemingly similar expressions **change in the quantity demanded** and **change in demand.** When we speak of a "change in the quantity demanded," this means the change in the quantity that people wish to buy that occurs in response to a change in price. For instance, Figure 3.10(a) depicts an increase in the quantity demanded that occurs in response to a reduction in the price of tuna. When the price falls from \$2 to \$1 per can, the quantity demanded rises from 8,000 to 10,000 cans per day. By contrast, when we speak of a "change in demand," this means a *shift in the entire demand curve.* For example, Figure 3.10(b) depicts an increase in demand, meaning that at every price the quantity demanded is higher than before. In summary, a "change in the quantity demanded" refers to a movement *along* the demand curve and a "change in demand" means a *shift* of the entire curve.

change in the quantity demanded a movement along the demand curve that occurs in response to a change in price

change in demand a shift of the entire demand curve

A similar terminological distinction applies on the supply side of the market. A **change in supply** means a shift in the entire supply curve, whereas a **change in the quantity supplied** refers to a movement along the supply curve.

change in supply a shift of the entire supply curve

change in the quantity supplied a movement along the supply curve that occurs in response to a change in price

Alfred Marshall's supply and demand model is one of the most useful tools of the economic naturalist. Once we understand the forces that govern the placements of supply and demand curves, we are suddenly in a position to make sense of a host of interesting observations in the world around us.

SHIFTS IN DEMAND

To get a better feel for how the supply and demand model enables us to predict and explain price and quantity movements, it is helpful to begin with a few simple examples. The first one illustrates a shift in demand that results from events outside the particular market itself.

What will happen to the equilibrium price and quantity of tennis balls if court rental fees decline?

Let the initial supply and demand curves for tennis balls be as shown by the curves *S* and *D* in Figure 3.11, where the resulting equilibrium price and quantity are \$1 per ball and 40 million balls per month, respectively. Tennis courts and tennis balls are what economists call **complements,** goods that are more valuable when used in combination than when used alone. Tennis balls, for example, would be of little value if there were no tennis courts on which to play. (Tennis balls would still have *some* value even without courts—for example, to the parents who pitch them to their children for batting practice.) As tennis courts become cheaper to use, people

complements two goods are complements in consumption if an increase in the price of one causes a leftward shift in the demand curve for the other (or if a decrease causes a rightward shift)

FIGURE 3.11
The Effect on the Market for Tennis Balls of a Decline in Court-Rental Fees.
When the price of a complement falls, demand shifts right, causing equilibrium price and quantity to rise.

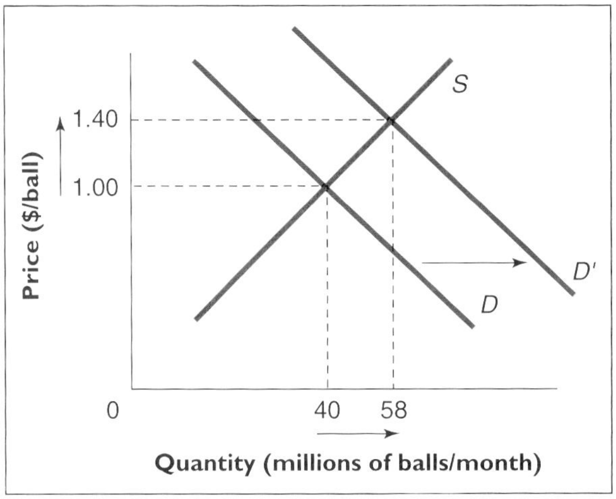

will respond by playing more tennis, and this will increase their demand for tennis balls. A decline in court-rental fees will thus shift the demand curve for tennis balls rightward to *D'*. (A "rightward shift" of a demand curve also can be described as an "upward shift." These distinctions correspond, respectively, to the horizontal and vertical interpretations of the demand curve.)

Note in Figure 3.11 that for the illustrative demand shift shown, the new equilibrium price of tennis balls, $1.40, is higher than the original price and the new equilibrium quantity, 58 million balls per month, is higher than the original quantity. ◆

What will happen to the equilibrium price and quantity of overnight letter delivery service as the price of internet access falls?

substitutes two goods are substitutes in consumption if an increase in the price of one causes a rightward shift in the demand curve for the other (or if a decrease causes a leftward shift).

Suppose the initial supply and demand curves for overnight letter deliveries are as shown by the curves *S* and *D* in Figure 3.12 and that the resulting equilibrium price and quantity are denoted *P* and *Q*. E-mail messages and overnight letters are examples of what economists call **substitutes**, meaning that, in many applications at least, the two serve similar functions for people. (Many noneconomists would call them substitutes, too. Economists don't *always* choose obscure terms for important concepts!) When two goods or services are substitutes, a decrease in the price of one will cause a leftward shift in the demand curve for the other. (A "leftward shift" in

FIGURE 3.12
The Effect on the Market for Overnight Letter Delivery of a Decline in the Price of Internet Access.
When the price of a substitute falls, demand shifts left, causing equilibrium price and quantity to fall.

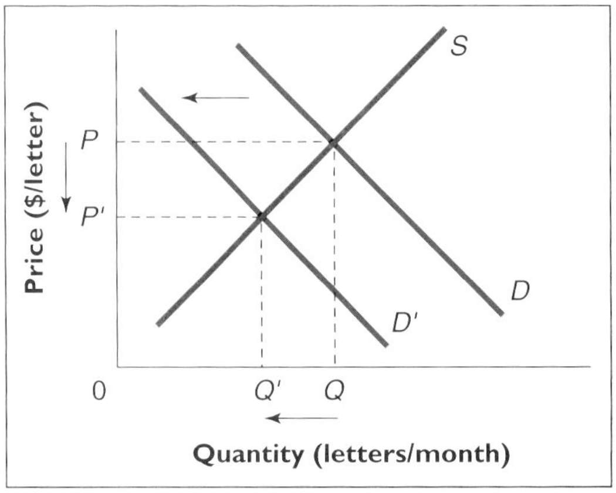

a demand curve can also be described as a "downward shift.") Diagrammatically, the demand curve for overnight delivery service shifts from *D* to *D′* in Figure 3.12.

As the figure shows, both the new equilibrium price, *P′*, and the new equilibrium quantity, *Q′*, are lower than the initial values, *P* and *Q*. Cheaper internet access probably won't put Federal Express and UPS out of business, but it will definitely cost them many customers. ◆

To summarize, economists define goods as substitutes if an increase in the price of one causes a rightward shift in the demand curve for the other. By contrast, goods are complements if an increase in the price of one causes a leftward shift in the demand curve for the other.

The concepts of substitutes and complements enable you to answer questions like the one posed in the following exercise.

EXERCISE 3.4

How will a decline in airfares affect intercity bus fares and the price of hotel rooms in resort communities?

Demand curves are shifted not just by changes in the prices of substitutes and complements but also by other factors that change the amounts that people are willing to pay for a given good or service. One of the most important such factors is income.

Example 3.1

THE ECONOMIC NATURALIST

When the federal government implements a large pay increase for its employees, why do rents for apartments located near Washington Metro stations go up relative to rents for apartments located far away from Metro stations?

For the citizens of Washington, D.C., a substantial proportion of whom are government employees, it is more convenient to live in an apartment located one block from the nearest subway station than to live in one that is 20 blocks away. Conveniently located apartments thus command relatively high rents. Suppose the initial demand and supply curves for such apartments are as shown in Figure 3.13. Following a federal pay raise, some government employees who live in less convenient apartments will be willing and able to use part of their extra income to bid for more conveniently located apartments, and those who already live in such apartments will be willing and able to pay more to keep them. The effect of the pay raise is thus to shift the demand curve for conveniently located apartments to the right, as indicated by the demand curve labeled *D′* in Figure 3.13. As a result, both the equilibrium price and quantity of such apartments, *P′* and *Q′*, will be higher than before.

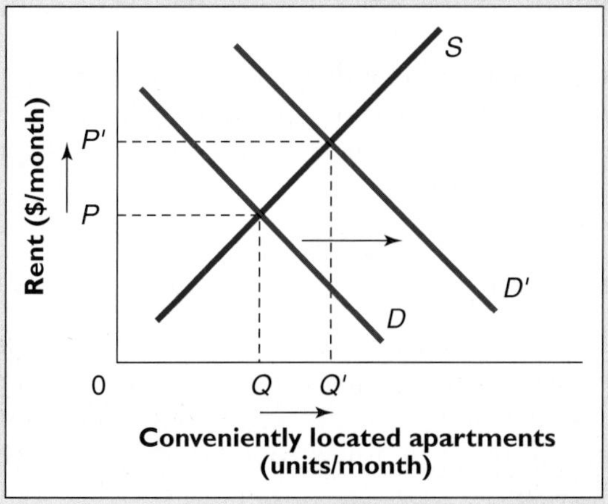

FIGURE 3.13
The Effect of a Federal Pay Raise on the Rent for Conveniently Located Apartments in Washington, D.C.
An increase in income shifts demand for a normal good to the right, causing equilibrium price and quantity to rise.

Who gets to live in the most conveniently located apartments?

Incentive

It might seem natural to ask how there could be an increase in the number of conveniently located apartments, which might appear to be fixed by the constraints of geography. But the Incentive Principle reminds us never to underestimate the ingenuity of sellers when they confront an opportunity to make money by supplying more of something that people want. For example, if rents rose sufficiently, some landlords might respond by converting warehouse space to residential use. Or perhaps people with cars who do not place high value on living near a subway station might sell their apartments to landlords, thereby freeing them for people eager to rent them. (Note that these responses constitute movements along the supply curve of conveniently located apartments, as opposed to shifts in that supply curve.)

When incomes increase, the demand curves for most goods will behave like the demand curve for conveniently located apartments, and in recognition of that fact, economists have chosen to call such goods **normal goods**.

normal good one whose demand curve shifts rightward when the incomes of buyers increase and leftward when the incomes of buyers decrease

inferior good one whose demand curve shifts leftward when the incomes of buyers increase and rightward when the incomes of buyers decrease

Not all goods are normal goods, however. In fact, the demand curves for some goods actually shift leftward when income goes up; such goods are called **inferior goods**.

When would having more money tend to make you want to buy less of something? In general, this will happen in the case of goods for which there exist attractive substitutes that sell for only slightly higher prices. Apartments in an unsafe, inconveniently located neighborhood are an example. Most residents would choose to move out of such neighborhoods as soon as they could afford to, which means that an increase in income would cause the demand for such apartments to shift leftward.

EXERCISE 3.5

How will a large pay increase for federal employees affect the rents for apartments located far away from Washington Metro stations?

Ground beef with high fat content is another example of an inferior good. For health reasons, most people prefer grades of meat with low fat content, and when they do buy high-fat meats it is usually a sign of budgetary pressure. When people in this situation receive higher incomes, they usually switch quickly to leaner grades of meat.

Cost-Benefit

Preferences, or tastes, are another important factor that determines whether the purchase of a given good will satisfy the Cost-Benefit Principle. Steven Spielberg's film *Jurassic Park* appeared to kindle a powerful, if previously latent, preference among children for toy dinosaurs. When this film was first released, the demand for such toys shifted sharply to the right. And the same children who couldn't find enough dinosaur toys suddenly seemed to lose interest in toy designs involving horses and other present-day animals, whose respective demand curves shifted sharply to the left.

Expectations about the future are another factor that may cause demand curves to shift. If Apple Macintosh users hear a credible rumor, for example, that a cheaper or significantly upgraded model will be introduced next month, the demand curve for the current model is likely to shift leftward.

SHIFTS IN THE SUPPLY CURVE

The preceding examples involved changes that gave rise to shifts in demand curves. Next, we'll look at what happens when supply curves shift. Because the supply curve is based on costs of production, anything that changes production costs will shift the supply curve, and hence will result in a new equilibrium quantity and price.

What will happen to the equilibrium price and quantity of skateboards if the price of fiberglass, a substance used for making skateboards, rises?

Suppose the initial supply and demand curves for skateboards are as shown by the curves *S* and *D* in Figure 3.14, resulting in an equilibrium price and quantity of

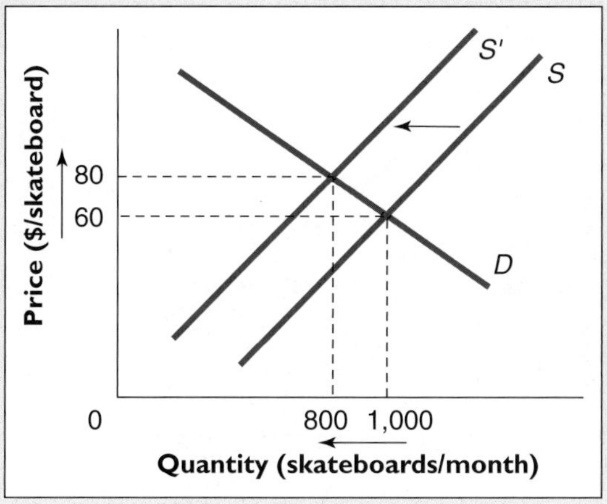

FIGURE 3.14
The Effect on the Skateboard Market of an Increase in the Price of Fiberglass.
When input prices rise, supply shifts left, causing equilibrium price to rise and equilibrium quantity to fall.

$60 per skateboard and 1,000 skateboards per month, respectively. Since fiberglass is one of the ingredients used to produce skateboards, the effect of an increase in the price of fiberglass is to raise the marginal cost of producing skateboards. How will this affect the supply curve of skateboards? Recall that the supply curve is upward-sloping because when the price of skateboards is low, only those potential sellers whose marginal cost of making skateboards is low can sell boards profitably, whereas at higher prices, those with higher marginal costs also can enter the market profitably (again, the Low-Hanging-Fruit Principle). So if the cost of one of the ingredients used to produce skateboards rises, the number of potential sellers who can profitably sell skateboards at any given price will fall. And this, in turn, implies a leftward shift in the supply curve for skateboards. Note that a "leftward shift" in a supply curve also can be viewed as an "upward shift" in the same curve. The first corresponds to the horizontal interpretation of the supply curve, while the second corresponds to the vertical interpretation. We will use these expressions to mean exactly the same thing. The new supply curve (after the price of fiberglass rises) is the curve labeled *S′* in Figure 3.14.

Increasing Opportunity Cost

Does an increase in the cost of fiberglass have any effect on the demand curve for skateboards? The demand curve tells us how many skateboards buyers wish to purchase at each price. Any given buyer is willing to purchase a skateboard if his reservation price for it exceeds its market price. And since each buyer's reservation price, which is based on the benefits of owning a skateboard, does not depend on the price of fiberglass, there should be no shift in the demand curve for skateboards.

In Figure 3.14, we can now see what happens when the supply curve shifts leftward and the demand curve remains unchanged. For the illustrative supply curve shown, the new equilibrium price of skateboards, $80, is higher than the original price and the new equilibrium quantity, 800 per month, is lower than the original quantity. (These new equilibrium values are merely illustrative. There is insufficient information provided in the example to determine their exact values.) People who don't place a value of at least $80 on owning a skateboard will choose to spend their money on something else. ◆

The effects on equilibrium price and quantity run in the opposite direction whenever marginal costs of production decline, as illustrated in the next example.

What will happen to the equilibrium price and quantity of new houses if the wage rate of carpenters falls?

Suppose the initial supply and demand curves for new houses are as shown by the curves *S* and *D* in Figure 3.15, resulting in an equilibrium price of $120,000 per house and an equilibrium quantity of 40 houses per month. A decline in the wage rate of carpenters reduces the marginal cost of making new houses, and this means that, for any given price of houses, more builders can profitably serve the market than before. Diagrammatically, this means a rightward shift in the supply curve of houses, from *S* to *S′*. (A "rightward shift" in the supply curve also can be described as a "downward shift.")

FIGURE 3.15
The Effect on the Market for New Houses of a Decline in Carpenters' Wage Rates.
When input prices fall, supply shifts right, causing equilibrium price to fall and equilibrium quantity to rise.

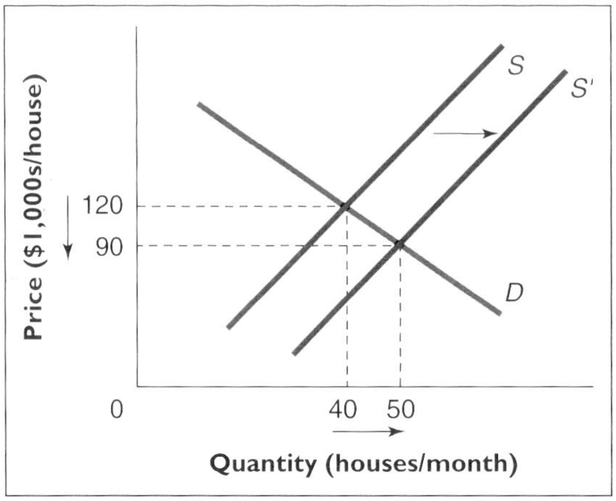

Does a decrease in the wage rate of carpenters have any effect on the demand curve for houses? The demand curve tells us how many houses buyers wish to purchase at each price. Because carpenters are now earning less than before, the maximum amount that they are willing to pay for houses may fall, which would imply a leftward shift in the demand curve for houses. But because carpenters make up only a tiny fraction of all potential home buyers, we may assume that this shift is negligible. Thus, a reduction in carpenters' wages produces a significant rightward shift in the supply curve of houses, but no appreciable shift in the demand curve.

We see from Figure 3.15 that the new equilibrium price, $90,000 per house, is lower than the original price and the new equilibrium quantity, 50 houses per month, is higher than the original quantity. ◆

Both of the preceding examples involved changes in the cost of an ingredient, or input, in the production of the good in question—fiberglass in the production of skateboards and carpenters' labor in the production of houses. As the following example illustrates, supply curves also shift when technology changes.

Example 3.2
THE ECONOMIC NATURALIST

Why do major term papers go through so many more revisions today than in the 1970s?

Students in the dark days before word processors were in widespread use could not make even minor revisions in their term papers without having to retype their entire manuscripts from scratch. The availability of word-processing technology has, of course, radically changed the picture. Instead of having to retype the entire draft, now only the changes need be entered.

In Figure 3.16, the curves labeled S and D depict the supply and demand curves for revisions in the days before word processing, and the curve S' depicts the supply curve for revisions today. As the diagram shows, the result is not only a sharp decline in the price per revision, but also a corresponding increase in the equilibrium number of revisions.

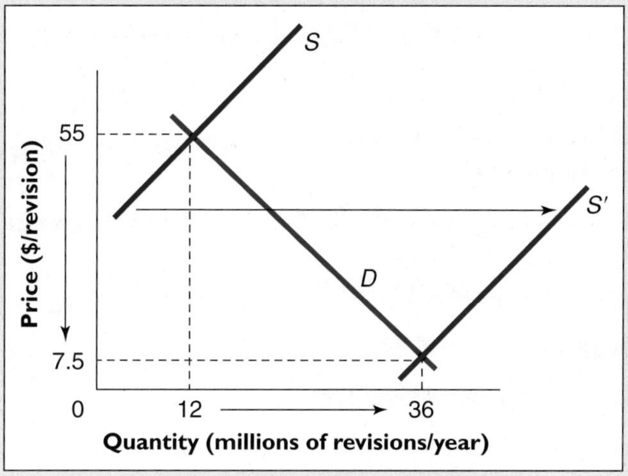

FIGURE 3.16
The Effect of Technical Change on the Market for Term-Paper Revisions.
When a new technology reduces the cost of production, supply shifts right, causing equilibrium price to fall and equilibrium quantity to rise.

Why does written work go through so many more revisions now than in the 1970s?

Note that in the preceding discussion we implicitly assumed that students purchased typing services in a market. In fact, however, many students type their own term papers. Does that make a difference? Even if no money actually changes hands, students pay a price when they revise their term papers—namely, the opportunity cost of the time it takes to perform that task. Because technology has radically reduced that cost, we would expect to see a large increase in the number of term-paper revisions even if most students type their own work.

Changes in input prices and technology are two of the most important factors that give rise to shifts in supply curves. In the case of agricultural commodities, weather may be another important factor, with favorable conditions shifting the supply curves of such products to the right and unfavorable conditions shifting them to the left. (Weather also may affect the supply curves of nonagricultural products through its effects on the national transportation system.) Expectations of future price changes also may shift current supply curves, as when the expectation of poor crops from a current drought causes suppliers to withhold supplies from existing stocks in the hope of selling at higher prices in the future. Changes in the number of sellers in the market also can cause supply curves to shift.

FOUR SIMPLE RULES

For supply and demand curves that have the conventional slopes (upward-sloping for supply curves, downward-sloping for demand curves), the preceding examples illustrate the four basic rules that govern how shifts in supply and demand affect equilibrium prices and quantities. These rules are summarized in Figure 3.17.

RECAP	FACTORS THAT SHIFT SUPPLY AND DEMAND

Factors that cause an increase (rightward or upward shift) in demand:

1. A decrease in the price of complements to the good or service.
2. An increase in the price of substitutes for the good or service.

3. An increase in income (for a normal good).
4. An increased preference by demanders for the good or service.
5. An increase in the population of potential buyers.
6. An expectation of higher prices in the future.

When these factors move in the opposite direction, demand will shift left.

Factors that cause an **increase** (rightward or downward shift) in **supply**:

1. A decrease in the cost of materials, labor, or other inputs used in the production of the good or service.
2. An improvement in technology that reduces the cost of producing the good or service.
3. An improvement in the weather (especially for agricultural products).
4. An increase in the number of suppliers.
5. An expectation of lower prices in the future.

When these factors move in the opposite direction, supply will shift left.

FIGURE 3.17
Four Rules Governing the Effects of Supply and Demand Shifts.

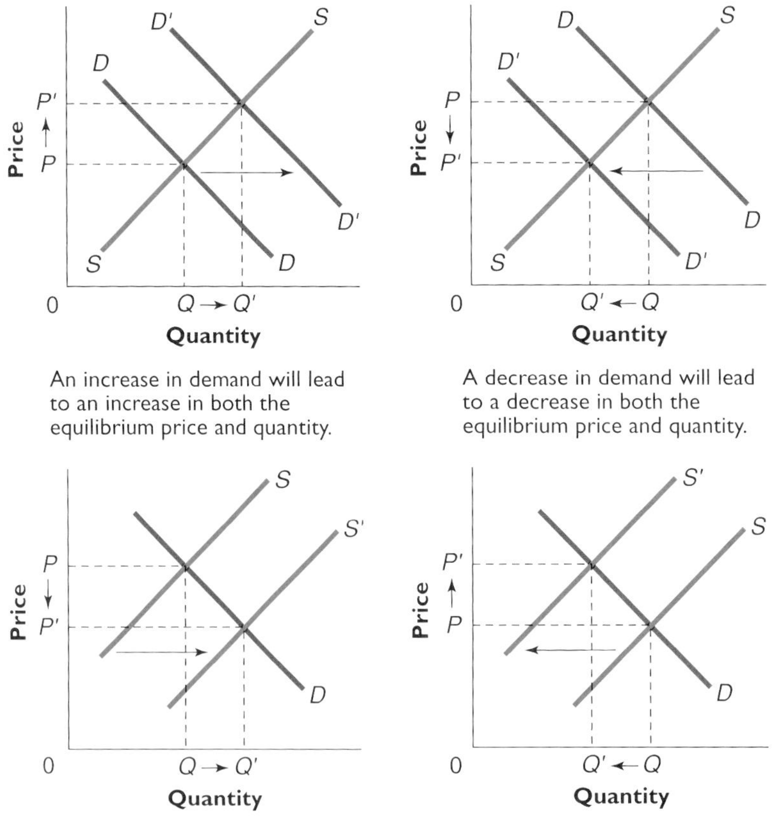

An increase in demand will lead to an increase in both the equilibrium price and quantity.

A decrease in demand will lead to a decrease in both the equilibrium price and quantity.

An increase in supply will lead to a decrease in the equilibrium price and an increase in the equilibrium quantity.

A decrease in supply will lead to an increase in the equilibrium price and a decrease in the equilibrium quantity.

The qualitative rules summarized in Figure 3.17 hold for supply or demand shifts of any magnitude, provided the curves have their conventional slopes. But as the next example demonstrates, when both supply and demand curves shift at the same time, the direction in which equilibrium price or quantity changes will depend on the relative magnitudes of the shifts.

How do shifts in *both* demand and supply affect equilibrium quantities and prices?

What will happen to the equilibrium price and quantity in the corn tortilla chip market if both of the following events occur: (1) researchers prove that the oils in which tortilla chips are fried are harmful to human health and (2) the price of corn harvesting equipment falls?

The conclusion regarding the health effects of the oils will shift the demand for tortilla chips to the left because many people who once bought chips in the belief that they were healthful will now switch to other foods. The decline in the price of harvesting equipment will shift the supply of chips to the right because additional farmers will now find it profitable to enter the corn market. In Figures 3.18(a) and 3.18(b), the original supply and demand curves are denoted by *S* and *D*, while the new curves are denoted by *S*′ and *D*′. Note that in both panels, the shifts lead to a decline in the equilibrium price of chips.

But note also that the effect of the shifts on equilibrium quantity cannot be determined without knowing their relative magnitudes. Taken separately, the demand shift causes a decline in equilibrium quantity, whereas the supply shift causes an increase in equilibrium quantity. The net effect of the two shifts thus depends on which of the individual effects is larger. In Figure 3.18(a), the demand shift dominates, so equilibrium quantity declines. In Figure 3.18(b), the supply shift dominates, so equilibrium quantity goes up.

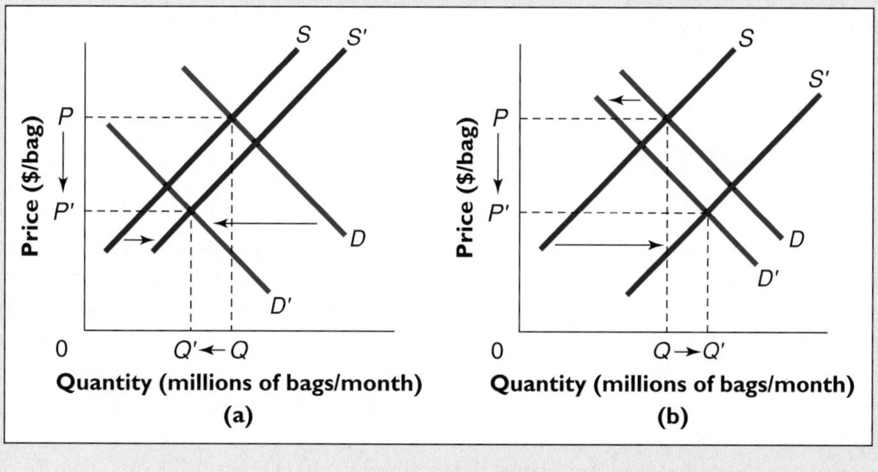

FIGURE 3.18
The Effects of Simultaneous Shifts in Supply and Demand.
When demand shifts left and supply shifts right, equilibrium price falls, but equilibrium quantity may either rise (b) or fall (a).

◆

The following exercise asks you to consider a simple variation on the problem posed in the previous example.

EXERCISE 3.6

What will happen to the equilibrium price and quantity in the corn tortilla chip market if both of the following events occur: (1) researchers discover that a vitamin found in corn helps protect against cancer and heart disease and (2) a swarm of locusts destroys part of the corn crop?

Example 3.3
THE ECONOMIC NATURALIST

Why do the prices of some goods, like airline tickets to Europe, go up during the months of heaviest consumption, while others, like sweet corn, go down?

Seasonal price movements for airline tickets are primarily the result of seasonal variations in demand. Thus, ticket prices to Europe are highest during the summer months because the demand for tickets is highest during those months, as shown in Figure 3.19(a), where the *w* and *s* subscripts denote winter and summer values, respectively.

Why are some goods cheapest during the months of heaviest consumption, while others are most expensive during those months?

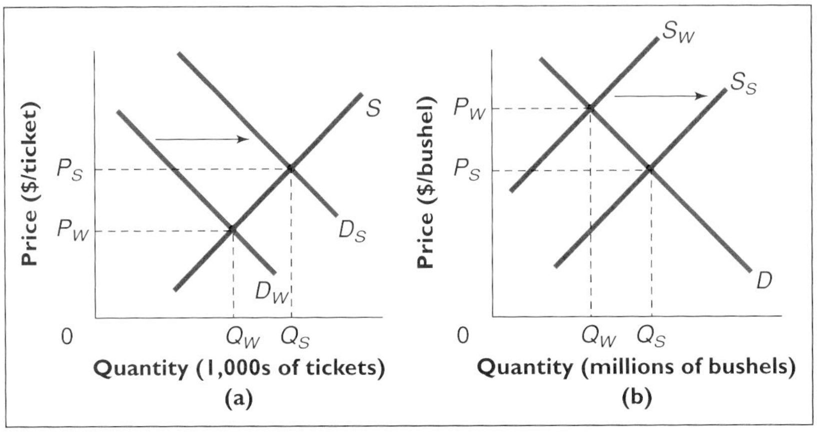

FIGURE 3.19
Seasonal Variation in the Air Travel and Corn Markets.
(a) Prices are highest during the period of heaviest consumption when heavy consumption is the result of high demand. (b) Prices are lowest during the period of heaviest consumption when heavy consumption is the result of high supply.

By contrast, seasonal price movements for sweet corn are primarily the result of seasonal variations in supply. The price of sweet corn is lowest in the summer months because its supply is highest during those months, as seen in Figure 3.19(b). ●

EFFICIENCY AND EQUILIBRIUM

Markets represent a highly effective system of allocating resources. When a market for a good is in equilibrium, the equilibrium price conveys important information to potential suppliers about the value that potential demanders place on that good. At the same time, the equilibrium price informs potential demanders about the opportunity cost of supplying the good. This rapid, two-way transmission of information is the reason that markets can coordinate an activity as complex as supplying New York City with food and drink, even though no one person or organization oversees the process.

But are the prices and quantities determined in market equilibrium socially optimal, in the sense of maximizing total economic surplus? That is, does equilibrium in unregulated markets always maximize the difference between the total benefits and total costs experienced by market participants? As we will see, the answer is "it depends": A market that is out of equilibrium, such as the rent-controlled New York housing market, always creates opportunities for individuals to arrange transactions that will increase their individual economic surplus. As we will see, however, a market for a good that is in equilibrium makes the largest possible contribution to total economic surplus only when its supply and demand curves fully reflect all costs and benefits associated with the production and consumption of that good.

CASH ON THE TABLE

In economics we assume that all exchange is purely voluntary. This means that a transaction cannot take place unless the buyer's reservation price for the good exceeds the seller's reservation price. When that condition is met and a transaction takes place, both parties receive an economic surplus. The **buyer's surplus** from the transaction is the difference between his reservation price and the price he actually pays. The **seller's surplus** is the difference between the price she receives and her reservation price. The **total surplus** from the transaction is the sum of the buyer's surplus and the seller's surplus. It is also equal to the difference between the buyer's reservation price and the seller's reservation price.

buyer's surplus the difference between the buyer's reservation price and the price he or she actually pays

seller's surplus the difference between the price received by the seller and his or her reservation price

total surplus the difference between the buyer's reservation price and the seller's reservation price

Suppose there is a potential buyer whose reservation price for an additional slice of pizza is \$4 and a potential seller whose reservation price is only \$2. If this buyer purchases a slice of pizza from this seller for \$3, the total surplus generated by this exchange is \$4 − \$2 = \$2, of which \$4 − \$3 = \$1 is the buyer's surplus and \$3 − \$2 = \$1 is the seller's surplus.

A regulation that prevents the price of a good from reaching its equilibrium level unnecessarily prevents exchanges of this sort from taking place, and in the process reduces total economic surplus. Consider again the effect of price controls imposed in the market for pizza. The demand curve in Figure 3.20 tells us that if a price ceiling of \$2 per slice were imposed, only 8,000 slices of pizza per day would be sold. At that quantity, the vertical interpretations of the supply and demand curves tell us that a buyer would be willing to pay as much as \$4 for an additional slice and that a seller would be willing to sell one for as little as \$2. The difference—\$2 per slice—is the additional economic surplus that would result if an additional slice were produced and sold. As noted earlier, an extra slice sold at a price of \$3 would result in an additional \$1 of economic surplus for both buyer and seller.

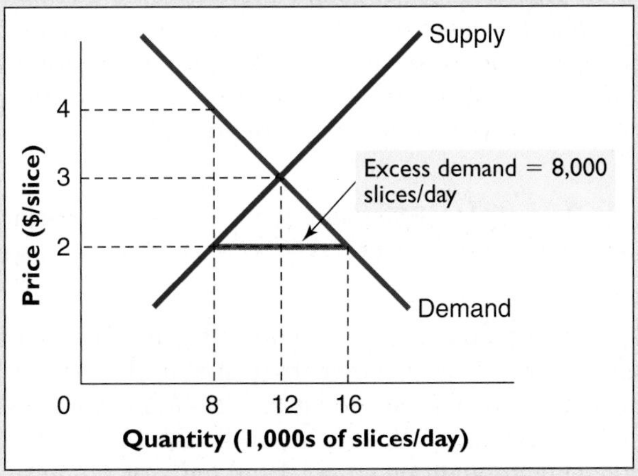

FIGURE 3.20
Price Controls in the Pizza Market.
A price ceiling below the equilibrium price of pizza would result in excess demand for pizza.

When a market is out of equilibrium, it is always possible to identify mutually beneficial exchanges of this sort. When people have failed to take advantage of all mutually beneficial exchanges, we often say that there is **"cash on the table"**—the economist's metaphor for unexploited opportunities. When the price in a market is below the equilibrium price, there is cash on the table because the reservation price of sellers (marginal cost) will always be lower than the reservation price of buyers. In the absence of a law preventing buyers paying more than \$2 per slice, restaurant owners would quickly raise their prices and expand their production until the equilibrium price of \$3 per slice was reached. At that price, buyers would be able to get precisely the 12,000 slices of pizza they want to buy each day. All mutually beneficial opportunities for exchange would have been exploited, leaving no more cash on the table.

cash on the table economic metaphor for unexploited gains from exchange

Incentive

With the Incentive Principle in mind, it should be no surprise that buyers and sellers in the marketplace have an uncanny ability to detect the presence of cash on the table. It is almost as if unexploited opportunities gave off some exotic scent triggering neurochemical explosions in the olfactory centers of their brains. The desire to scrape cash off the table and into their pockets is what drives sellers in each of New York City's thousands of individual food markets to work diligently to meet their customers' demands. That they succeed to a far higher degree than participants in the city's rent-controlled housing market is plainly evident. Whatever flaws it might have, the market system moves with considerably greater speed and agility than any centralized allocation mechanisms yet devised. But as we emphasize in the following section, this does not mean that markets *always* lead to the greatest good for all.

SMART FOR ONE, DUMB FOR ALL

The **socially optimal quantity** of any good is the quantity that maximizes the total economic surplus that results from producing and consuming the good. From the Cost-Benefit Principle, we know that we should keep expanding production of the good as long as its marginal benefit is at least as great as its marginal cost. This means that the socially optimal quantity is that level for which the marginal cost and marginal benefit of the good are the same.

Cost-Benefit

socially optimal quantity the quantity of a good that results in the maximum possible economic surplus from producing and consuming the good

efficiency (also called ***economic efficiency***) occurs when all goods and services are produced and consumed at their respective socially optimal levels

When the quantity of a good is less than the socially optimal quantity, boosting its production will increase total economic surplus. By the same token, when the quantity of a good exceeds the socially optimal quantity, reducing its production will increase total economic surplus. **Economic efficiency**, or **efficiency**, occurs when all goods and services in the economy are produced and consumed at their respective socially optimal levels.

Efficiency is an important social goal. Failure to achieve efficiency means that total economic surplus is smaller than it could have been. Movements toward efficiency make the total economic pie larger, making it possible for everyone to have a larger slice. The importance of efficiency will be a recurring theme as we move forward, and we state it here as one of the core principles:

Efficiency

The Efficiency Principle: Efficiency is an important social goal because when the economic pie grows larger, everyone can have a larger slice.

Is the market equilibrium quantity of a good efficient? That is, does it maximize the total economic surplus received by participants in the market for that good? When the private market for a given good is in equilibrium, we can say that the cost *to the seller* of producing an additional unit of the good is the same as the benefit *to the buyer* of having an additional unit. If all costs of producing the good are borne directly by sellers, and if all benefits from the good accrue directly to buyers, it follows that the market equilibrium quantity of the good will equate the marginal cost and marginal benefit of the good. And this means that the equilibrium quantity also maximizes total economic surplus.

But sometimes the production of a good entails costs that fall on people other than those who sell the good. This will be true, for instance, for goods whose production generates significant levels of environmental pollution. As extra units of these goods are produced, the extra pollution harms other people besides sellers. In the market equilibrium for such goods, the benefit *to buyers* of the last good produced is, as before, equal to the cost incurred by sellers to produce that good. But since producing that good also imposed pollution costs on others, we know that the *full* marginal cost of the last unit produced—the seller's private marginal cost plus the marginal pollution cost borne by others—must be higher than the benefit of the last unit produced. So in this case the market equilibrium quantity of the good will be larger than the socially optimal quantity. Total economic surplus would be higher if output of the good were lower. Yet neither sellers nor buyers have any incentive to alter their behavior.

Another possibility is that people other than those who buy a good may receive significant benefits from it. For instance, when someone purchases a vaccination against measles from her doctor, she not only protects herself against measles, but she also makes it less likely that others will catch this disease. From the perspective of society as a whole, we should keep increasing the number of vaccinations until their marginal cost equals their marginal benefit. The marginal benefit of a vaccination is the value of the protection it provides the person vaccinated *plus* the value of the protection it provides all others. Private consumers, however, will choose to be vaccinated only if the marginal benefit *to them* exceeds the price of the vaccination. In this case, then, the market equilibrium quantity of vaccinations will be smaller than the quantity that maximizes total economic surplus. Again, however, individuals would have no incentive to alter their behavior.

Situations like the ones just discussed provide examples of behaviors that we may call "smart for one but dumb for all." In each case, the individual actors are behaving rationally. They are pursuing their goals as best they can, and yet there remain unexploited opportunities for gain from the point of view of the whole society. The difficulty is that these opportunities cannot be exploited by individuals acting alone. In subsequent chapters, we will see how people can often organize collectively to exploit such opportunities. For now, we simply summarize this discussion in the form of the following core principle:

The Equilibrium Principle (also called the "No-Cash-on-the-Table" Principle): A market in equilibrium leaves no unexploited opportunities for individuals but may not exploit all gains achievable through collective action.

Equilibrium

RECAP	MARKETS AND SOCIAL WELFARE

When the supply and demand curves for a good reflect all significant costs and benefits associated with the production and consumption of that good, the market equilibrium will result in the largest possible economic surplus. But if people other than buyers benefit from the good, or if people other than sellers bear costs because of it, market equilibrium need not result in the largest possible economic surplus.

SUMMARY

- Eighteenth-century economists tried to explain differences in the prices of goods by focusing on differences in their cost of production. But this approach cannot explain why a conveniently located house sells for more than one that is less conveniently located. Early nineteenth-century economists tried to explain price differences by focusing on differences in what buyers were willing to pay. But this approach cannot explain why the price of a lifesaving appendectomy is less than that of a surgical facelift. **LO3**
- Alfred Marshall's model of supply and demand explains why neither cost of production nor value to the purchaser (as measured by willingness to pay) is, by itself, sufficient to explain why some goods are cheap and others are expensive. To explain variations in price, we must examine the interaction of cost and willingness to pay. As we've seen in this chapter, goods differ in price because of differences in their respective supply and demand curves. **LO3**
- The demand curve is a downward-sloping line that tells what quantity buyers will demand at any given price. The supply curve is an upward-sloping line that tells what quantity sellers will offer at any given price. Market equilibrium occurs when the quantity buyers

demand at the market price is exactly the same as the quantity that sellers offer. The equilibrium price-quantity pair is the one at which the demand and supply curves intersect. In equilibrium, market price measures both the value of the last unit sold to buyers and the cost of the resources required to produce it. **LO1, LO2**

- When the price of a good lies above its equilibrium value, there is an excess supply of that good. Excess supply motivates sellers to cut their prices and price continues to fall until the equilibrium price is reached. When price lies below its equilibrium value, there is excess demand. With excess demand, frustrated buyers are motivated to offer higher prices and the upward pressure on prices persists until equilibrium is reached. A remarkable feature of the market system is that, relying only on the tendency of people to respond in self-interested ways to market price signals, it somehow manages to coordinate the actions of literally billions of buyers and sellers worldwide. When excess demand or excess supply occurs, it tends to be small and brief, except in markets where regulations prevent full adjustment of prices. **LO3**

- The efficiency of markets in allocating resources does not eliminate social concerns about how goods and services are distributed among different people. For example, we often lament the fact many buyers enter the market with too little income to buy even the most basic goods and services. Concern for the well-being of the poor has motivated many governments to intervene in a variety of ways to alter the outcomes of market forces. Sometimes these interventions take the form of laws that peg prices below their equilibrium levels. Such laws almost invariably generate harmful, if unintended, consequences. Programs like rent-control laws, for example, lead to severe housing shortages, black marketeering, and a rapid deterioration of the relationship between landlords and tenants. **LO5**

- If the difficulty is that the poor have too little money, the best solution is to discover ways of boosting their incomes directly. The law of supply and demand cannot be repealed by the legislature. But legislatures do have the capacity to alter the underlying forces that govern the shape and position of supply and demand schedules. **LO5**

- The basic supply and demand model is a primary tool of the economic naturalist. Changes in the equilibrium price of a good, and in the amount of it traded in the marketplace, can be predicted on the basis of shifts in its supply or demand curves. The following four rules hold for any good with a downward-sloping demand curve and an upward-sloping supply curve:
  - An increase in demand will lead to an increase in equilibrium price and quantity.
  - A reduction in demand will lead to a reduction in equilibrium price and quantity.
  - An increase in supply will lead to a reduction in equilibrium price and an increase in equilibrium quantity.
  - A decrease in supply will lead to an increase in equilibrium price and a reduction in equilibrium quantity. **LO4**

- Incomes, tastes, population, expectations, and the prices of substitutes and complements are among the factors that shift demand schedules. Supply schedules, in turn, are primarily governed by such factors as technology, input prices, expectations, the number of sellers, and, especially for agricultural products, the weather. **LO4**

- When the supply and demand curves for a good reflect all significant costs and benefits associated with the production and consumption of that good, the market equilibrium price will guide people to produce and consume the quantity of the good that results in the largest possible economic surplus. This conclusion, however, does not apply if others, besides buyers, benefit from the good (as when someone benefits from his neighbor's purchase of a vaccination against measles) or if others besides sellers bear costs because of the good (as when its production generates pollution). In such cases, market equilibrium does not result in the greatest gain for all. **LO6**

■ CORE PRINCIPLES ■

Efficiency

The Efficiency Principle
Efficiency is an important social goal because when the economic pie grows larger, everyone can have a larger slice.

Equilibrium

The Equilibrium Principle (also called the "No-Cash-on-the-Table" Principle)
A market in equilibrium leaves no unexploited opportunities for individuals but may not exploit all gains achievable through collective action.

KEY TERMS

buyer's reservation price (66)
buyer's surplus (85)
cash on the table (85)
change in demand (75)
change in the quantity demanded (75)
change in the quantity supplied (75)
change in supply (75)
complements (75)
demand curve (65)
economic efficiency (86)
efficiency (86)
equilibrium (68)
equilibrium price (68)
equilibrium quantity (68)
excess demand (69)
excess supply (69)
income effect (65)
inferior good (78)
market (64)
market equilibrium (68)
normal good (78)
price ceiling (74)
seller's reservation price (67)
seller's surplus (85)
socially optimal quantity (86)
substitutes (76)
substitution effect (65)
supply curve (66)
total surplus (85)

REVIEW QUESTIONS

1. Why isn't knowing the cost of producing a good sufficient to predict its market price? **LO3**
2. Distinguish between the meaning of the expressions "change in demand" and "change in the quantity demanded." **LO4**
3. Last year a government official proposed that gasoline price controls be imposed to protect the poor from rising gasoline prices. What evidence could you consult to discover whether this proposal was enacted? **LO3**
4. Explain the distinction between the horizontal and vertical interpretations of the demand curve. **LO1**
5. Give an example of behavior you have observed that could be described as "smart for one but dumb for all." **LO6**

PROBLEMS

1. State whether the following pairs of goods are complements or substitutes. (If you think a pair is ambiguous in this respect, explain why.) **LO1**
   a. Tennis courts and squash courts.
   b. Squash racquets and squash balls.
   c. Ice cream and chocolate.
   d. Cloth diapers and paper diapers.
2. How would each of the following affect the U.S. market supply curve for corn? **LO2**
   a. A new and improved crop rotation technique is discovered.
   b. The price of fertilizer falls.
   c. The government offers new tax breaks to farmers.
   d. A tornado sweeps through Iowa.
3. Indicate how you think each of the following would shift demand in the indicated market: **LO1**
   a. Incomes of buyers in the market for Adirondack vacations increase.
   b. Buyers in the market for pizza read a study linking hamburger consumption to heart disease.
   c. Buyers in the market for CDs learn of an increase in the price of audiocassettes (a substitute for CDs).
   d. Buyers in the market for CDs learn of an increase in the price of CDs.
4. An Arizona student claims to have spotted a UFO over the desert outside of Tucson. How will his claim affect the *supply* (not the quantity supplied) of binoculars in Tucson stores? **LO2**
5. What will happen to the equilibrium price and quantity of oranges if the wage paid to orange pickers rises? **LO4**

6. How will an increase in the birth rate affect the equilibrium price of land? **LO4**
7. What will happen to the equilibrium price and quantity of fish if fish oils are found to help prevent heart disease? **LO4**
8. What will happen to the equilibrium price and quantity of beef if the price of chickenfeed increases? **LO4**
9. Use supply and demand analysis to explain why hotel room rental rates near your campus during parents' weekend and graduation weekend might differ from the rates charged during the rest of the year. **LO4**
10. How will a new law mandating an increase in required levels of automobile insurance affect the equilibrium price and quantity in the market for new automobiles? **LO4**
11. Suppose the current issue of the *New York Times* reports an outbreak of mad cow disease in Nebraska, as well as the discovery of a new breed of chicken that gains more weight than existing breeds that consume the same amount of food. How will these developments affect the equilibrium price and quantity of chickens sold in the United States? **LO4**
12. What will happen to the equilibrium quantity and price of potatoes if population increases and a new, higher-yielding variety of potato plant is developed? **LO4**
13. What will happen to the equilibrium price and quantity of apples if apples are discovered to help prevent colds and a fungus kills 10 percent of existing apple trees? **LO4**
14. What will happen to the equilibrium quantity and price of corn if the price of butter (a complement) increases and the price of fertilizer decreases? **LO4**
15. Twenty-five years ago, tofu was available only from small businesses operating in predominantly Asian sections of large cities. Today tofu has become popular as a high-protein health food and is widely available in supermarkets throughout the United States. At the same time, tofu production has evolved to become factory-based using modern food-processing technologies. Draw a diagram with demand and supply curves depicting the market for tofu 25 years ago and the market for tofu today. Given the information above, what does the demand-supply model predict about changes in the volume of tofu sold in the United States between then and now? What does it predict about changes in the price of tofu? **LO4**

ANSWERS TO IN-CHAPTER EXERCISES

3.1 At a quantity of 10,000 slices per day, the marginal buyer's reservation price is \$3.50 per slice. At a price of \$2.50 per slice, the quantity demanded will be 14,000 slices per day. **LO1**

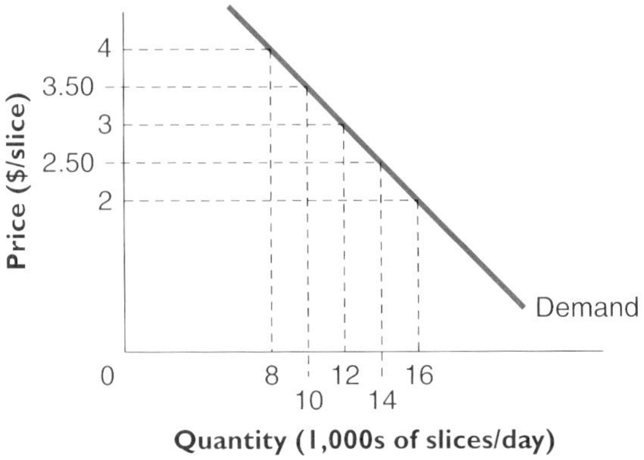

3.2 At a quantity of 10,000 slices per day, the marginal cost of pizza is \$2.50 per slice. At a price of \$3.50 per slice, the quantity supplied will be 14,000 slices per day. **LO2**

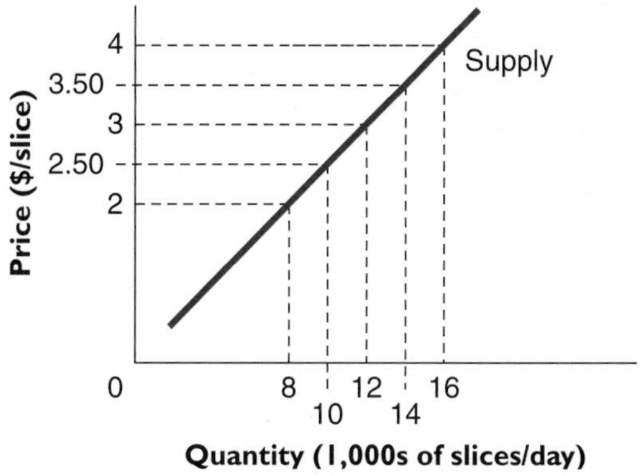

3.3 Since landlords are permitted to charge less than the maximum rent established by rent-control laws, a law that sets the maximum rent at \$1,200 will have no effect on the rents actually charged in this market, which will settle at the equilibrium value of \$800 per month. **LO3**

3.4 Travel by air and travel by intercity bus are substitutes, so a decline in airfares will shift the demand for bus travel to the left, resulting in lower bus fares and fewer bus trips taken. Travel by air and the use of resort hotels are complements, so a decline in airfares will shift the demand for resort hotel rooms to the right, resulting in higher hotel rates and an increase in the number of rooms rented. **LO4**

3.5 Apartments located far from Washington Metro stations are an inferior good. A pay increase for federal workers will thus shift the demand curve for such apartments downward, which will lead to a reduction in their equilibrium rent. **LO4**

3.6 The vitamin discovery shifts the demand for chips to the right and the crop losses shift the supply of chips to the left. Both shifts result in an increase in the equilibrium price of chips. But depending on the relative magnitude of the shifts, the equilibrium quantity of chips may either rise (left panel) or fall (right panel). **LO4**

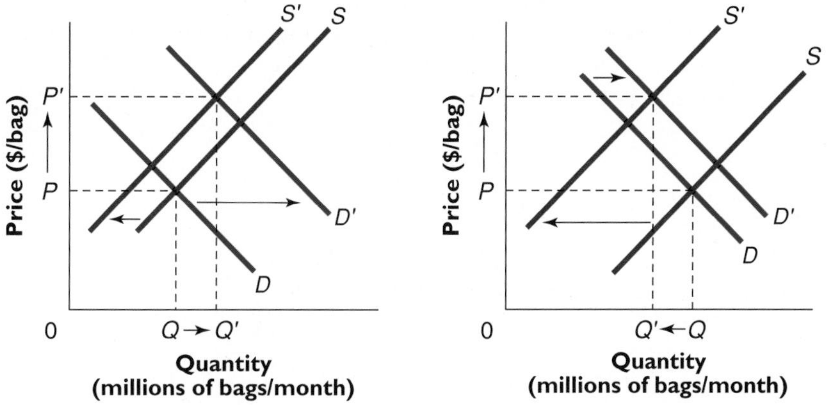

APPENDIX

The Algebra of Supply and Demand

In the text of this chapter, we developed supply and demand analysis in a geometric framework. The advantage of this framework is that many find it an easier one within which to visualize how shifts in either curve affect equilibrium price and quantity.

It is a straightforward extension to translate supply and demand analysis into algebraic terms. In this brief appendix, we show how this is done. The advantage of the algebraic framework is that it greatly simplifies computing the numerical values of equilibrium prices and quantities.

Consider, for example, the supply and demand curves in Figure 3A.1, where P denotes the price of the good and Q denotes its quantity. What are the equations of these curves?

Recall from the appendix to Chapter 1 that the equation of a straight-line demand curve must take the general form $P = a + b\,Q^d$, where P is the price of the product (as measured on the vertical axis), Q^d is the quantity demanded at that price (as measured on the horizontal axis), a is the vertical intercept of the demand curve, and b is its slope. For the demand curve shown in Figure 3A.1, the vertical intercept is 16 and the slope is -2. So the equation for this demand curve is

$$P = 16 - 2Q^d. \qquad (3A.1)$$

Similarly, the equation of a straight-line supply curve must take the general form $P = c + dQ^s$, where P is again the price of the product, Q^s is the quantity supplied at that price, c is the vertical intercept of the supply curve, and d is its slope. For the supply curve shown in Figure 3A.1, the vertical intercept is 4 and the slope is also 4. So the equation for this supply curve is

$$P = 4 + 4Q^s. \qquad (3A.2)$$

If we know the equations for the supply and demand curves in any market, it is a simple matter to solve them for the equilibrium price and quantity using the method of simultaneous equations described in the appendix to Chapter 1. The following example illustrates how to apply this method.

FIGURE 3A.1
Supply and Demand Curves

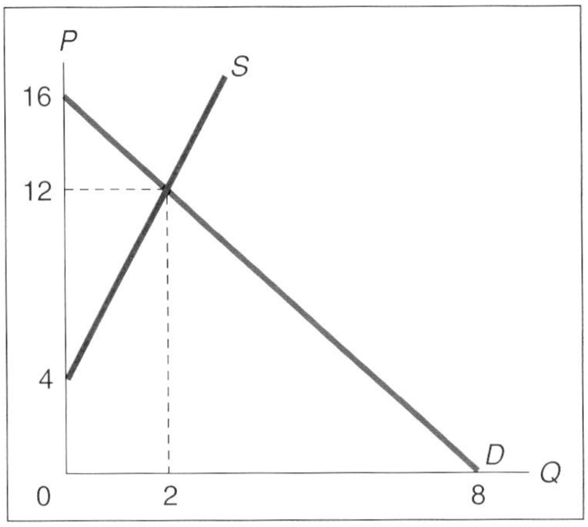

If the supply and demand curves for a market are given by $P = 4 + 4Q^s$ and $P = 16 - 2Q^d$, respectively, find the equilibrium price and quantity for this market.

In equilibrium, we know that $Q^s = Q^d$. Denoting this common value as Q^*, we may then equate the right-hand sides of Equations 3A.1 and 3A.2 and solve:

$$4 + 4Q^* = 16 - 2Q^*, \tag{3A.3}$$

which yields $Q^* = 2$. Substituting $Q^* = 2$ back into either the supply or demand equation gives the equilibrium price $P^* = 12$. ◆

Of course, having already begun with the graphs of Equations 3A.1 and 3A.2 in hand, we could have identified the equilibrium price and quantity by a simple glance at Figure 3A.1. (That is why it seems natural to say that the graphical approach helps us visualize the equilibrium outcome.) As the following exercise illustrates, the advantage of the algebraic approach to finding the equilibrium price and quantity is that it is much less painstaking than having to produce accurate drawings of the supply and demand schedules.

EXERCISE 3A.1

Find the equilibrium price and quantity in a market whose supply and demand curves are given by $P = 2Q^s$ and $P = 8 - 2Q^d$, respectively.

■ ANSWER TO IN-APPENDIX EXERCISE ■

3A.1 Let Q^* denote the equilibrium quantity. Since the equilibrium price and quantity lie on both the supply and demand curves, we equate the right-hand sides of the supply and demand equations to obtain

$$2Q^* = 8 - 2Q^*,$$

which solves for $Q^* = 2$. Substituting $Q^* = 2$ back into either the supply or demand equation gives the equilibrium price $P^* = 4$.

PART

2

COMPETITION AND THE INVISIBLE HAND

Having grasped the basic core principles of economics, you are now in a position to sharpen your understanding of how consumers and firms behave. In Part 2 our focus will be on how things work in an idealized, perfectly competitive economy in which consumers are perfectly informed and no firm has market power.

We begin in Chapter 4 by exploring the concept of elasticity, which describes the sensitivity of demand and supply to variations in prices, incomes, and other economic factors. In our discussion of supply and demand in Part 1, we asked you simply to assume the law of demand, which says that demand curves are downward-sloping. In Chapter 5 we will see that this law is a simple consequence of the fact that people spend their limited incomes in rational ways. In Chapter 6 our focus will shift to the seller's side of the market, where our task will be to see why upward-sloping supply curves are a consequence of production decisions taken by firms whose goal is to maximize profit.

Our agenda in Chapter 7 is to investigate the economic forces by which the invisible hand of the marketplace guides profit-seeking firms and satisfaction-seeking consumers in ways that, to a surprising degree, serve society's ends. These forces encourage aggressive cost cutting by firms, even though the resulting gains will eventually take the form of lower prices rather than higher profits. We will also develop more carefully the concept of economic surplus introduced in Part 1 and investigate the conditions under which unregulated markets generate the largest possible surplus. We will also explore why attempts to interfere with market outcomes sometimes lead to unintended and undesired outcomes.

CHAPTER

4

Elasticity

LEARNING OBJECTIVES

After reading this chapter, you should be able to:

1. Define the price elasticity of demand and explain its determinants.
2. Calculate the price elasticity of demand using information from a demand curve.
3. Understand the relationship between price elasticity of demand and total expenditure.
4. Define the cross-price elasticity of demand and the income elasticity of demand.
5. Define the price elasticity of supply and explain its determinants.

Many illicit drug users commit crimes to finance their addiction. The connection between drugs and crime has led to calls for more vigorous efforts to stop the smuggling of illicit drugs. But can such efforts reduce the likelihood that your iPod or laptop computer will be stolen in the next month? If attempts to reduce the supply of illicit drugs are successful, our basic supply and demand analysis tells us that the supply curve for drugs will shift to the left and the market price of drugs will increase. Given that demand curves are downward-sloping, drug users will respond by consuming a smaller quantity of drugs. But the amount of crime drug users commit depends not on the *quantity* of drugs they consume, but rather on their *total expenditure* on drugs. Depending on the specific characteristics of the demand curve for illicit drugs, a price increase might reduce total expenditure on drugs, but it also could raise total expenditure.

Suppose, for example, that extra border patrols shift the supply curve in the market for illicit drugs to the left, as shown in Figure 4.1. As a result, the equilibrium quantity of drugs would fall from 50,000 to 40,000 ounces per day and the price of drugs would rise from \$50 to \$80 per ounce. The total amount spent on drugs, which was \$2,500,000 per day (50,000 ounces/day × \$50/ounce),

FIGURE 4.1
The Effect of Extra Border Patrols on the Market for Illicit Drugs.
Extra patrols shift supply leftward and reduce the quantity demanded, but they may actually increase the total amount spent on drugs.

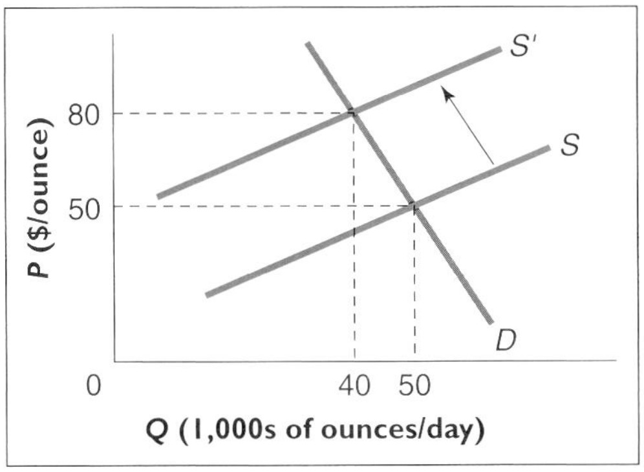

Could reducing the supply of illegal drugs cause an increase in drug-related burglaries?

would rise to $3,200,000 per day (40,000 ounces/day × $80/ounce). In this case, then, efforts to stem the supply of drugs would actually increase the likelihood of your laptop being stolen.

Other benefits from stemming the flow of illicit drugs might still outweigh the resulting increase in crime. But knowing that the policy might increase drug-related crime would clearly be useful to law-enforcement authorities.

Our task in this chapter will be to introduce the concept of elasticity, a measure of the extent to which quantity demanded and quantity supplied respond to variations in price, income, and other factors. In the preceding chapter, we saw how shifts in supply and demand curves enabled us to predict the direction of change in the equilibrium values of price and quantity. An understanding of price elasticity will enable us to make even more precise statements about the effects of such changes. In the illicit-drug example just considered, the decrease in supply led to an increase in total spending. In many other cases, a decrease in supply will lead to a reduction in total spending. Why this difference? The underlying phenomenon that explains this pattern, we will see, is price elasticity of demand. We will explore why some goods have higher price elasticity of demand than others and the implications of that fact for how total spending responds to changes in prices. We also will discuss price elasticity of supply and examine the factors that explain why it takes different values for different goods.

PRICE ELASTICITY OF DEMAND

When the price of a good or service rises, the quantity demanded falls. But to predict the effect of the price increase on total expenditure, we also must know by how much quantity falls. The quantity demanded of some goods such as salt is not very sensitive to changes in price. Indeed, even if the price of salt were to double, or to fall by half, most people would hardly alter their consumption of it. For other goods, however, the quantity demanded is extremely responsive to changes in price. For example, when a luxury tax was imposed on yachts in the early 1990s, purchases of yachts plummeted sharply.

PRICE ELASTICITY DEFINED

price elasticity of demand percentage change in quantity demanded that results from a 1 percent change in price

The **price elasticity of demand** for a good is a measure of the responsiveness of the quantity demanded of that good to changes in its price. Formally, the price elasticity of demand for a good is defined as the percentage change in the quantity demanded that results from a 1 percent change in its price. For example, if the price of beef falls by 1 percent and the quantity demanded rises by 2 percent, then the price elasticity of demand for beef has a value of −2.

Although the definition just given refers to the response of quantity demanded to a 1 percent change in price, it also can be adapted to other variations in price, provided they are relatively small. In such cases, we calculate the price elasticity of demand as the percentage change in quantity demanded divided by the corresponding percentage change in price. Thus, if a 2 percent reduction in the price of pork led to a 6 percent increase in the quantity of pork demanded, the price elasticity of demand for pork would be

$$\frac{\text{Percentage change in quantity demanded}}{\text{Percentage change in price}} = \frac{6 \text{ percent}}{-2 \text{ percent}} = -3. \quad (4.1)$$

elastic demand is elastic with respect to price if price elasticity of demand is greater than 1

Strictly speaking, the price elasticity of demand will always be negative (or zero) because price changes are always in the opposite direction from changes in quantity demanded. So for convenience, we drop the negative sign and speak of price elasticities in terms of absolute value. The demand for a good is said to be **elastic** with respect to price if the absolute value of its price elasticity is greater than 1. It is said to be **inelastic** if the absolute value of its price elasticity is less than 1. Finally, demand is said to be **unit elastic** if the absolute value of its price elasticity is equal to 1. (See Figure 4.2.)

inelastic demand is inelastic with respect to price if price elasticity of demand is less than 1

unit elastic demand is unit elastic with respect to price if price elasticity of demand equals 1

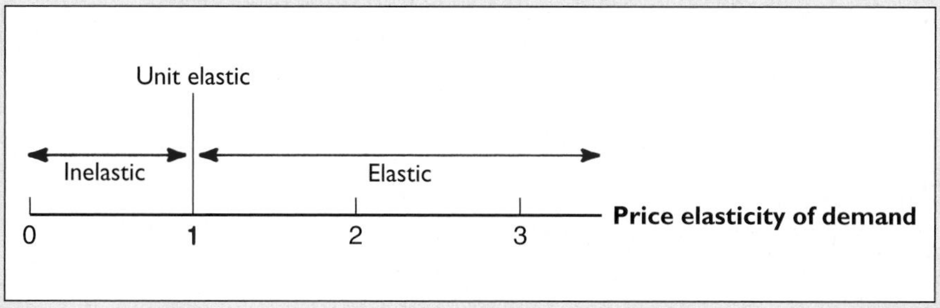

FIGURE 4.2
Elastic and Inelastic Demand.
Demand for a good is called elastic, unit elastic, or inelastic with respect to price if the price elasticity is greater than 1, equal to 1, or less than 1, respectively.

What is the elasticity of demand for pizza?

When the price of pizza is $1 per slice, buyers wish to purchase 400 slices per day, but when price falls to $0.97 per slice, the quantity demanded rises to 404 slices per day. At the original price, what is the price elasticity of demand for pizza? Is the demand for pizza elastic with respect to price?

The fall in price from $1 to $0.97 is a decrease of 3 percent. The rise in quantity demanded from 400 slices to 404 slices is an increase of 1 percent. The price elasticity of demand for pizza is thus (1 percent)/(3 percent) = 1/3. So when the initial price of pizza is $1, the demand for pizza is not elastic with respect to price; it is inelastic. ◆

EXERCISE 4.1

What is the elasticity of demand for season ski passes?

When the price of a season ski pass is $400, buyers wish to purchase 10,000 passes per year, but when price falls to $380, the quantity demanded rises to 12,000 passes per year. At the original price, what is the price elasticity of demand for ski passes? Is the demand for ski passes elastic with respect to price?

DETERMINANTS OF PRICE ELASTICITY OF DEMAND

Cost-Benefit

What factors determine the price elasticity of demand for a good or service? To answer this question, recall that before a rational consumer buys any product, the purchase decision must first satisfy the Cost-Benefit Principle. For instance, consider a good (such as a dorm refrigerator) that you buy only one unit of (if you buy it at all). Suppose that, at the current price, you have decided to buy it. Now imagine that the price goes up by 10 percent. Will a price increase of this magnitude be likely to make you change your mind? The answer will depend on factors like the following.

Substitution Possibilities

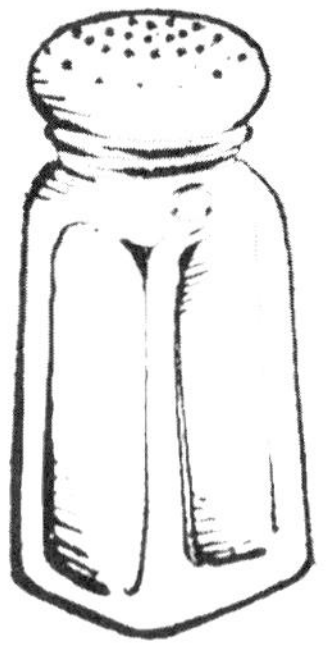

If the price of salt were to double, would you use less of it?

When the price of a product you want to buy goes up significantly, you are likely to ask yourself, "Is there some other good that can do roughly the same job, but for less money?" If the answer is yes, then you can escape the effect of the price increase by simply switching to the substitute product. But if the answer is no, you are more likely to stick with your current purchase.

These observations suggest that demand will tend to be more elastic with respect to price for products for which close substitutes are readily available. Salt, for example, has no close substitutes, which is one reason that the demand for it is highly inelastic. Note, however, that while the quantity of salt people demand is highly insensitive to price, the same cannot be said of the demand for any *specific brand* of salt. After all, despite what salt manufacturers say about the special advantages of their own labels, consumers tend to regard one brand of salt as a virtually perfect substitute for another. Thus, if Morton were to raise the price of its salt significantly, many people would simply switch to some other brand.

The vaccine against rabies is another product for which there are essentially no attractive substitutes. A person who is bitten by a rabid animal and does not take the vaccine faces a certain and painful death. Most people in that position would pay any price they could afford rather than do without the vaccine.

Budget Share

Suppose the price of key rings suddenly were to double. How would that affect the number of key rings you buy? If you're like most people, it would have no effect at all. Think about it—a doubling of the price of a $1 item that you buy only every few years is simply nothing to worry about. By contrast, if the price of the new car you were about to buy suddenly doubled, you would definitely want to check out possible substitutes such as a used car or a smaller new model. You also might consider holding on to your current car a little longer. The larger the share of your budget an item accounts for, the greater is your incentive to look for substitutes when the price of the item rises. Big-ticket items, therefore, tend to have higher price elasticities of demand.

Time

Home appliances come in a variety of models, some more energy-efficient than others. As a general rule, the more efficient an appliance is, the higher its price. Suppose that you were about to buy a new air conditioner and electric rates suddenly rose sharply. It would probably be in your interest to buy a more efficient machine than you had originally planned. However, what if you had already bought a new air conditioner before you learned of the rate increase? You would not think it worthwhile to discard the machine right away and replace it with a more efficient model. Rather, you would wait until the machine wore out, or until you moved, before making the switch.

As this example illustrates, substitution of one product or service for another takes time. Some substitutions occur in the immediate aftermath of a price increase, but many others take place years or even decades later. For this reason, the price elasticity of demand for any good or service will be higher in the long run than in the short run.

RECAP	FACTORS THAT INFLUENCE PRICE ELASTICITY

The price elasticity of demand for a good or service tends to be larger when substitutes for the good are more readily available, when the good's share in the consumer's budget is larger, and when consumers have more time to adjust to a change in price.

SOME REPRESENTATIVE ELASTICITY ESTIMATES

The entries in Table 4.1 show that the price elasticities of demand for different products often differ substantially—in this sample, ranging from a high of 2.8 for green peas to a low of 0.18 for theater and opera tickets. This variability is explained in part by the determinants of elasticity just discussed. Patrons of theater and opera, for example, tend to have high incomes, implying that the shares of their budgets devoted to these items are likely to be small. What is more, theater and opera patrons are often highly knowledgeable and enthusiastic about these art forms; for many of them, there are simply no acceptable substitute forms of entertainment.

TABLE 4.1
Historical Price Elasticity of Demand Estimates for Selected Products

Good or service	Price elasticity of demand
Green peas	2.80
Restaurant meals	1.63
Automobiles	1.35
Electricity	1.20
Beer	1.19
Movies	0.87
Air travel (foreign)	0.77
Shoes	0.70
Coffee	0.25
Theater, opera	0.18

SOURCE: These short-run elasticity estimates are taken from the following sources: Ronald Fisher, *State and Local Public Finance,* Chicago: Irwin, 1996; H. S. Houthakker and Lester Taylor, *Consumer Demand in the United States: Analyses and Projections,* 2nd ed., Cambridge, MA: Harvard University Press, 1970; L. Taylor, "The Demand for Electricity: A Survey," *Bell Journal of Economics,* Spring 1975; K. Elzinga, "The Beer Industry," in *The Structure of American Industry,* Walter Adams, ed., New York: Macmillan, 1977.

Why is the price elasticity of demand more than 14 times larger for green peas than for theater and opera performances? The answer cannot be that income effects loom larger for green peas than for theater tickets. Even though the average consumer of green peas earns much less than the average theater or opera patron, the share of a typical family's budget devoted to green peas is surely very small. What differentiates green peas from theater and opera performances is that there are so many more close substitutes for peas than for opera and theater. The lowly green pea, which is mostly found in the canned goods or frozen foods sections of supermarkets, does not seem to have inspired a loyal consumer following.

USING PRICE ELASTICITY OF DEMAND

An understanding of the factors that govern price elasticity of demand is necessary not only to make sense of consumer behavior, but also to design effective public policy. Consider, for example, the debate about how taxes affect smoking among teenagers.

Example 4.1

THE ECONOMIC NATURALIST

Will a higher tax on cigarettes curb teenage smoking?

Consultants hired by the tobacco industry have testified in Congress against higher cigarette taxes aimed at curbing teenage smoking. The main reason teenagers smoke is that their friends smoke, these consultants testified, and they concluded that higher taxes would have little effect. Does the consultants' testimony make economic sense?

Do high cigarette prices discourage teen smoking?

The consultants are almost certainly right that peer influence is the most important determinant of teen smoking. But that does not imply that a higher tax on cigarettes would have little impact on adolescent smoking rates. Because most teenagers have little money to spend at their own discretion, cigarettes constitute a significant share of a typical teenage smoker's budget. The price elasticity of demand is thus likely to be far from negligible. For at least some teenage smokers, a higher tax would make smoking unaffordable. And even among those who could afford the higher prices, at least some others would choose to spend their money on other things rather than pay the higher prices.

Given that the tax would affect at least *some* teenage smokers, the consultants' argument begins to unravel. If the tax deters even a small number of smokers directly through its effect on the price of cigarettes, it will also deter others indirectly, by reducing the number of peer role models who smoke. And those who refrain because of these indirect effects will in turn no longer influence others to smoke, and so on. So even if the direct effect of higher cigarette taxes on teen smoking is small, the cumulative effects may be extremely large. The mere fact that peer pressure may be the primary determinant of teen smoking therefore does not imply that higher cigarette taxes will have no significant impact on the number of teens who smoke. ●

Example 4.2

THE ECONOMIC NATURALIST

Why was the luxury tax on yachts such a disaster?

In 1990, Congress imposed a luxury tax on yachts costing more than $100,000, along with similar taxes on a handful of other luxury goods. Before these taxes were imposed, the Joint Committee on Taxation estimated that they would yield more than $31 million in revenue in 1991. However, the tax actually generated a bit more than half that amount, $16.6 million.[1] Several years later, the Joint Economic Committee estimated that the tax on yachts had led to a loss of 7,600 jobs in the U.S. boating industry. Taking account of lost income taxes and increased unemployment benefits, the U.S. government actually came out $7.6 million behind in fiscal 1991 as a result of its luxury taxes—almost $39 million worse than the initial projection. What went wrong?

Why did the luxury tax on yachts backfire?

The 1990 law imposed no luxury taxes on yachts built and purchased outside the United States. What Congress failed to consider was that foreign-built yachts are almost perfect substitutes for yachts built and purchased in the United States. And, no surprise, when prices on domestic yachts went up because of the tax, yacht buyers switched in droves to foreign models. A tax imposed on a good with a high price elasticity of demand stimulates large rearrangements of consumption but yields little revenue. Had Congress done the economic analysis properly, it would have predicted that this particular tax would be a big loser. Facing angry protests from unemployed New England shipbuilders, Congress repealed the luxury tax on yachts in 1993. ●

[1]For an alternative view, see Dennis Zimmerman, "The Effect of the Luxury Excise Tax on the Sale of Luxury Boats," Congressional Research Service, February 10, 1992.

A GRAPHICAL INTERPRETATION OF PRICE ELASTICITY

For small changes in price, price elasticity of demand is the proportion by which quantity demanded changes divided by the corresponding proportion by which price changes. This formulation enables us to construct a simple expression for the price elasticity of demand for a good using only minimal information about its demand curve.

Look at Figure 4.3. P represents the current price of a good and Q the quantity demanded at that price. ΔP represents a small change in the current price and the resulting change in quantity demanded is given by ΔQ. The expression $\Delta P/P$ will

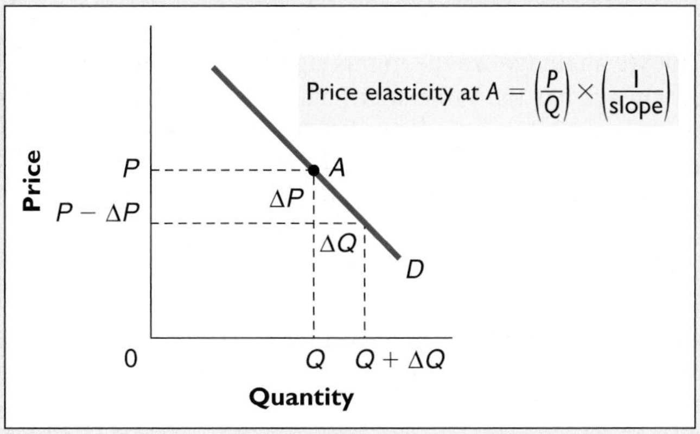

FIGURE 4.3
A Graphical Interpretation of Price Elasticity of Demand.
Price elasticity of demand at any point along a straight-line demand curve is the ratio of price to quantity at that point times the reciprocal of the slope of the demand curve.

then stand for the proportion by which price changes and $\Delta Q/Q$ will stand for the corresponding proportion by which quantity changes. These two expressions, along with our definition of the price elasticity of demand (Equation 4.1), give us the formula for price elasticity:

$$\text{Price elasticity} = \epsilon = \frac{\Delta Q/Q}{\Delta P/P}. \tag{4.2}$$

Suppose, for example, that 20 units were sold at the original price of 100 and that when price rose to 105, quantity demanded fell to 15 units. Neglecting the negative sign of the quantity change, we would then have $\Delta Q/Q = 5/20$ and $\Delta P/P = 5/100$, which yields $\epsilon = (5/20)/(5/100) = 5$.

One attractive feature of this formula is that it has a straightforward graphical interpretation. Thus, if we want to calculate the price elasticity of demand at point A on the demand curve shown in Figure 4.3, we can begin by rewriting the right-hand side of Equation 4.2 as $(P/Q) \times (\Delta Q/\Delta P)$. And since the slope of the demand curve is equal to $\Delta P/\Delta Q$, $\Delta Q/\Delta P$ is the reciprocal of that slope: $\Delta Q/\Delta P = 1/\text{slope}$. The price elasticity of demand at point A, denoted ϵ_A, therefore has the following simple formula:

$$\epsilon_A = \frac{P}{Q} \times \frac{1}{\text{slope}}. \tag{4.3}$$

To demonstrate how convenient this graphical interpretation of elasticity can be, suppose we want to find the price elasticity of demand at point A on the demand curve in Figure 4.4. The slope of this demand curve is the ratio of its vertical intercept to its horizontal intercept: $20/5 = 4$. So $1/\text{slope} = 1/4$. (Actually, the

FIGURE 4.4
Calculating Price Elasticity of Demand.
The price elasticity of demand at A is given by $(P/Q) \times (1/\text{slope}) = (8/3) \times (1/4) = 2/3$.

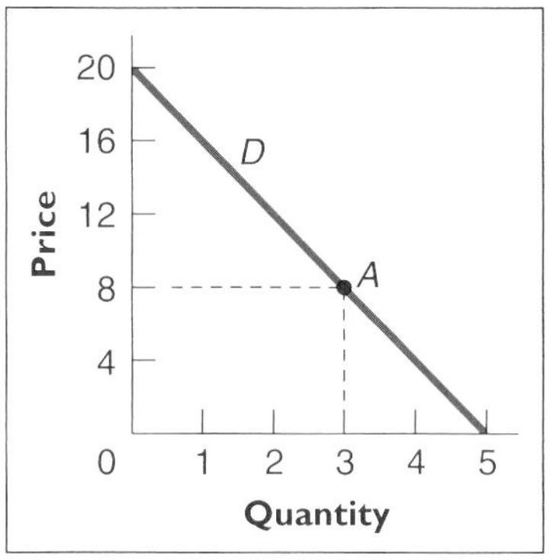

slope is -4, but we again ignore the minus sign for convenience, since price elasticity of demand always has the same sign.) The ratio P/Q at point A is $8/3$, so the price elasticity at point A is equal to $(P/Q) \times (1/\text{slope}) = (8/3) \times (1/4) = 2/3$. This means that when the price of the good is 8, a 3 percent reduction in price will lead to a 2 percent increase in quantity demanded.

EXERCISE 4.2

What is the price elasticity of demand when $P = 4$ on the demand curve in Figure 4.4?

For the demand curves D_1 and D_2 shown in Figure 4.5, calculate the price elasticity of demand when $P = 4$. What is the price elasticity of demand on D_2 when $P = 1$?

FIGURE 4.5
Price Elasticity and the Steepness of the Demand Curve.
When price and quantity are the same, price elasticity of demand is always greater for the less steep of two demand curves.

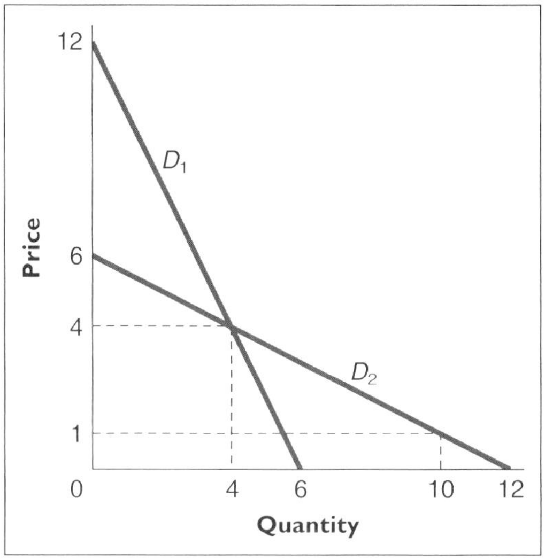

These elasticities can be calculated easily using the formula $\epsilon = (P/Q) \times (1/\text{slope})$. The slope of D_1 is the ratio of its vertical intercept to its horizontal intercept: $12/6 = 2$. So $(1/\text{slope})$ is $1/2$ for D_1. Similarly, the slope of D_2 is the ratio of its vertical intercept to its horizontal intercept: $6/12 = 1/2$. So the reciprocal of the slope of D_2 is 2. For both demand curves, $Q = 4$ when $P = 4$, so $(P/Q) = 4/4 = 1$ for each. Thus the price elasticity of demand when $P = 4$ is $(1) \times (1/2) = 1/2$ for D_1

and (1) × (2) = 2 for D_2. When $P = 1$, $Q = 10$ on D_2, so $(P/Q) = 1/10$. Thus price elasticity of demand = (1/10) × (2) = 1/5 when $P = 1$ on D_2. ◆

This example illustrates a general rule: if two demand curves have a point in common, the steeper curve must be the less price elastic of the two with respect to price at that point. However, this does not mean that the steeper curve is less elastic at *every* point. Thus, we saw that at $P = 1$, price elasticity of demand on D_2 was only 1/5, or less than half the corresponding elasticity on the steeper D_1 at $P = 4$.

PRICE ELASTICITY CHANGES ALONG A STRAIGHT-LINE DEMAND CURVE

As a glance at our elasticity formula makes clear, price elasticity has a different value at every point along a straight-line demand curve. The slope of a straight-line demand curve is constant, which means that 1/slope is also constant. But the price-quantity ratio, P/Q, declines as we move down the demand curve. The elasticity of demand thus declines steadily as we move downward along a straight-line demand curve.

Since price elasticity is the percentage change in quantity demanded divided by the corresponding percentage change in price, this pattern makes sense. After all, a price movement of a given absolute size is small in percentage terms when it occurs near the top of the demand curve, where price is high, but large in percentage terms when it occurs near the bottom of the demand curve, where price is low. Likewise, a quantity movement of a given absolute value is large in percentage terms when it occurs near the top of the demand curve, where quantity is low, and small in percentage terms when it occurs near the bottom of the curve, where quantity is high.

The graphical interpretation of elasticity also makes it easy to see why the price elasticity of demand at the midpoint of any straight-line demand curve must always be 1. Consider, for example, the price elasticity of demand at point A on the demand curve D shown in Figure 4.6. At that point, the ratio P/Q is equal to $6/3 = 2$. The slope of this demand curve is the ratio of its vertical intercept to its horizontal intercept, $12/6 = 2$. So $(1/\text{slope}) = 1/2$ (again, we neglect the negative sign for simplicity). Inserting these values into the graphical elasticity formula yields $\epsilon_A = (P/Q) \times (1/\text{slope}) = (2) \times (1/2) = 1$.

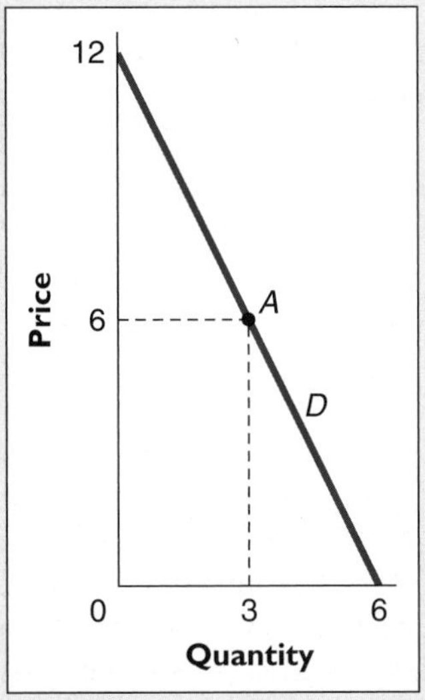

FIGURE 4.6
Elasticity at the Midpoint of a Straight-Line Demand Curve.
The price elasticity of demand at the midpoint of any straight-line demand curve always takes the value 1.

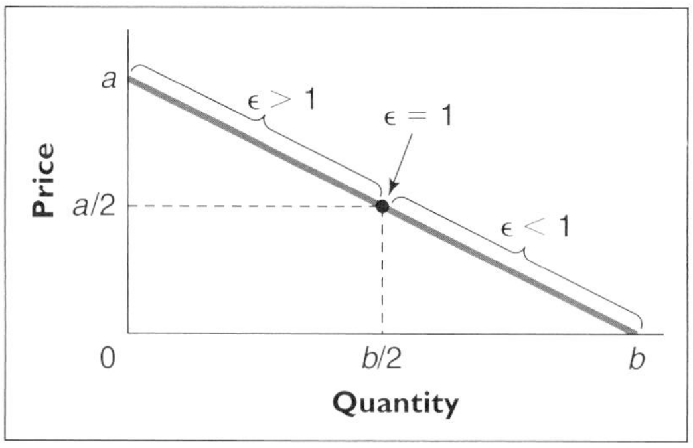

FIGURE 4.7
Price Elasticity Regions along a Straight-Line Demand Curve.
Demand is elastic on the top half, unit elastic at the midpoint, and inelastic on the bottom half of a straight-line demand curve.

This result holds not just for Figure 4.6, but also for any other straight-line demand curve.[2] A glance at the formula also tells us that since P/Q declines as we move downward along a straight-line demand curve, price elasticity of demand must be less than 1 at any point below the midpoint. By the same token, price elasticity must be greater than 1 for any point above the midpoint. Figure 4.7 summarizes these findings by denoting the elastic, inelastic, and unit elastic portions of any straight-line demand curve.

TWO SPECIAL CASES

There are actually two important exceptions to the general rule that elasticity declines along straight-line demand curves. First, the horizontal demand curve in Figure 4.8(a) has a slope of zero, which means that the reciprocal of its slope is infinite. Price elasticity of demand is thus infinite at every point along a horizontal demand curve. Such demand curves are said to be **perfectly elastic.**

perfectly elastic demand
demand is perfectly elastic with respect to price if price elasticity of demand is infinite

Second, the demand curve in Figure 4.8(b) is vertical, which means that its slope is infinite. The reciprocal of its slope is thus equal to zero. Price elasticity of

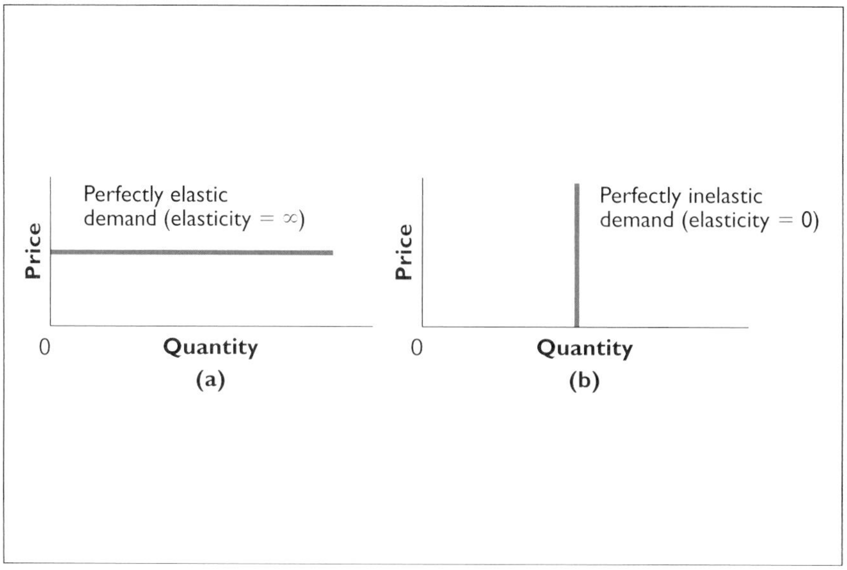

FIGURE 4.8
Perfectly Elastic and Perfectly Inelastic Demand Curves.
The horizontal demand curve (a) is perfectly elastic, or infinitely elastic, at every point. Even the slightest increase in price leads consumers to desert the product in favor of substitutes. The vertical demand curve (b) is perfectly inelastic at every point. Consumers do not, or cannot, switch to substitutes even in the face of large increases in price.

[2] To see why, note that at the midpoint of any such curve, P is exactly half the vertical intercept of the demand curve and Q is exactly half the horizontal intercept. Since the ratio of the vertical intercept to the horizontal intercept is the slope of the demand curve, the ratio (P/Q) must also be equal to the slope of the demand curve. And this means that (1/slope) will always be equal to (Q/P). Thus, the product $(P/Q) \times (1/\text{slope}) = (P/Q) \times (Q/P)$ will always be exactly 1 at the midpoint of any straight-line demand curve.

demand is thus exactly zero at every point along the curve. For this reason, vertical demand curves are said to be **perfectly inelastic.**

perfectly inelastic demand demand is perfectly inelastic with respect to price if price elasticity of demand is zero

RECAP	CALCULATING PRICE ELASTICITY OF DEMAND

The price elasticity of demand for a good is the percentage change in the quantity demanded that results from a 1 percent change in its price. Mathematically, the elasticity of demand at a point along a demand curve is equal to $(P/Q) \times (1/\text{slope})$, where P and Q represent price and quantity and (1/slope) is the reciprocal of the slope of the demand curve at that point. Demand is elastic with respect to price if the absolute value of its price elasticity exceeds 1; inelastic if price elasticity is less than 1; and unit elastic if price elasticity is equal to 1.

ELASTICITY AND TOTAL EXPENDITURE

Sellers of goods and services have a strong interest in being able to answer questions like "Will consumers spend more on my product if I sell more units at a lower price or fewer units at a higher price?" As it turns out, the answer to this question depends critically on the price elasticity of demand. To see why, let us first examine how the total amount spent on a good varies with the price of the good.

The total daily expenditure on a good is simply the daily number of units bought times the price for which it sells. The market demand curve for a good tells us the quantity that will be sold at each price. We can thus use the information on the demand curve to show how the total amount spent on a good will vary with its price.

To illustrate, let's calculate how much moviegoers will spend on tickets each day if the demand curve is as shown in Figure 4.9 and the price is \$2 per ticket (a). The demand curve tells us that at a price of \$2 per ticket, 500 tickets per day will be sold, so total expenditure at that price will be \$1,000 per day. If tickets sell not for \$2 but for \$4 apiece, 400 tickets will be sold each day (b), so total expenditure at the higher price will be \$1,600 per day.

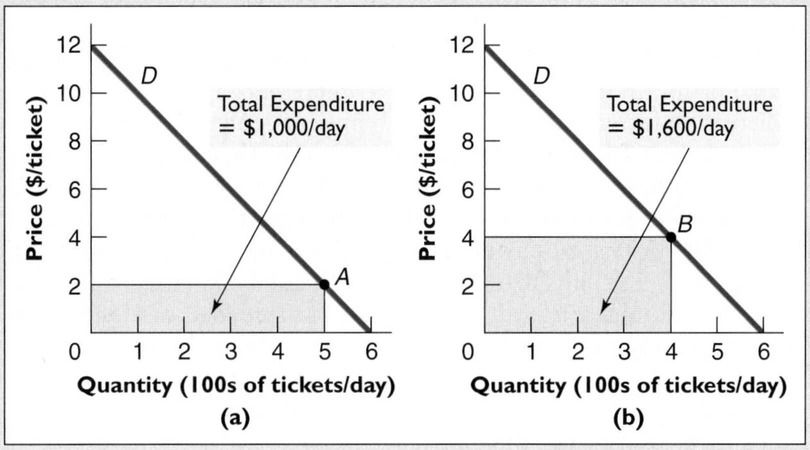

FIGURE 4.9
The Demand Curve for Movie Tickets.
An increase in price from \$2 to \$4 per ticket increases total expenditure on tickets.

Note that the total amount consumers spend on a product each day must equal the total amount sellers of the product receive. That is to say, the terms **total expenditure** and **total revenue** are simply two sides of the same coin:

> **Total Expenditure = Total Revenue:** The dollar amount that consumers spend on a product ($P \times Q$) is equal to the dollar amount that sellers receive.

It might seem that an increase in the market price of a product should always result in an increase in the total revenue received by sellers. Although that happened in the case we just saw, it needn't always be so. The law of demand tells us that when the price of a good rises, people will buy less of it. The two factors that govern total revenue—price and quantity—will thus always move in opposite directions as we move along a demand curve. When price goes up and quantity goes down, the product of the two may go either up or down.

Note, for example, that for the demand curve shown in Figure 4.10 (which is the same as the one in Figure 4.9), a rise in price from $8 per ticket (a) to $10 per ticket (b) will cause total expenditure on tickets to go down. Thus people will spend $1,600 per day on tickets at a price of $8, but only $1,000 per day at a price of $10.

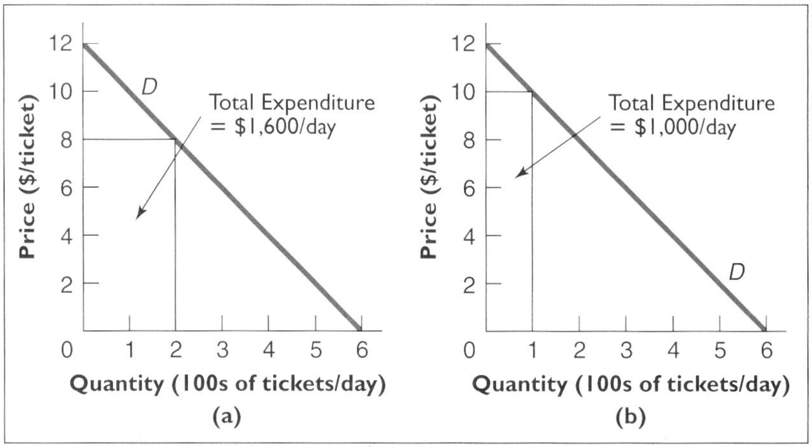

FIGURE 4.10
The Demand Curve for Movie Tickets.
An increase in price from $8 to $10 per ticket results in a fall in total expenditure on tickets.

The general rule illustrated by Figures 4.9 and 4.10 is that a price increase will produce an increase in total revenue whenever it is greater, in percentage terms, than the corresponding percentage reduction in quantity demanded. Although the two price increases (from $2 to $4 and from $8 to $10) were of the same absolute value—$2 in each case—they are much different when expressed as a percentage of the original price. An increase from $2 to $4 represents a 100 percent increase in price, whereas an increase from $8 to $10 represents only a 25 percent increase in price. And although the quantity reductions caused by the two price increases were also equal in absolute terms, they too are very different when expressed as percentages of the quantities originally sold. Thus, although the decline in quantity demanded was 100 tickets per day in each case, it was just a 20 percent reduction in the first case (from 500 units to 400 in Figure 4.9) but a 50 percent reduction in the second (from 200 units to 100 in Figure 4.10). In the second case, the negative effect on total expenditure of the 50 percent quantity reduction outweighed the positive effect of the 25 percent price increase. The reverse happened in the first case: the 100 percent increase in price (from $2 to $4) outweighed the 20 percent reduction in quantity (from 5 units to 4 units).

The following example provides further insight into the relationship between total revenue and price.

For the demand curve shown in Figure 4.11, draw a separate graph showing how total expenditure varies with the price of movie tickets.

The first step in constructing this graph is to calculate total expenditure for each price shown in the graph and record the results, as in Table 4.2. The next step is to

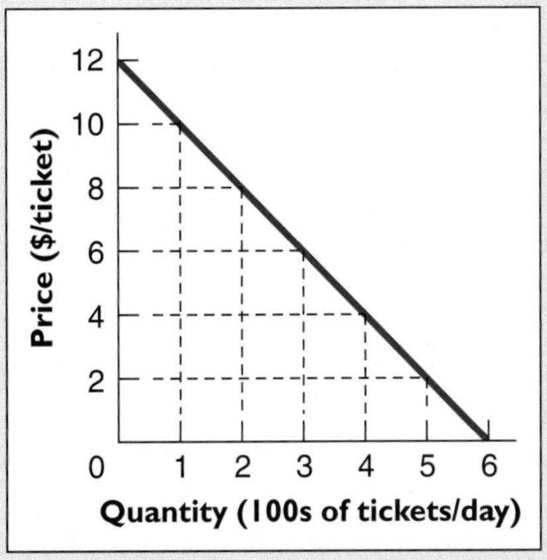

FIGURE 4.11
The Demand Curve for Movie Tickets.

plot total expenditure at each of the price points on a graph, as in Figure 4.12. Finally, sketch the curve by joining these points. (If greater accuracy is required, you can use a larger sample of points than the one shown in Table 4.2.)

TABLE 4.2
Total Expenditure as a Function of Price

Price ($/ticket)	Total expenditure ($/day)
12	0
10	1,000
8	1,600
6	1,800
4	1,600
2	1,000
0	0

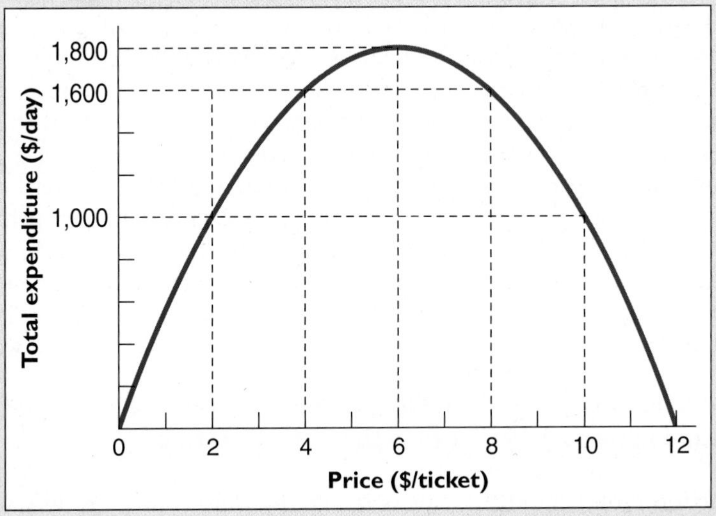

FIGURE 4.12
Total Expenditure as a Function of Price.
For a good whose demand curve is a straight line, total expenditure reaches a maximum at the price corresponding to the midpoint of the demand curve.

Note in Figure 4.12 that as the price per ticket increases from 0 to \$6, total expenditure increases. But as the price rises from \$6 to \$12, total expenditure decreases. Total expenditure reaches a maximum of \$1,800 per day at a price of \$6. ◆

The pattern observed in the preceding example holds true in general. For a straight-line demand curve, total expenditure is highest at the price that lies on the midpoint of the demand curve.

Bearing in mind these observations about how expenditure varies with price, let's return to the question of how the effect of a price change on total expenditure depends on the price elasticity of demand. Suppose, for example, that the business manager of a rock band knows he can sell 5,000 tickets to the band's weekly summer concerts if he sets the price at \$20 per ticket. If the elasticity of demand for tickets is equal to 3, will total ticket revenue go up or down in response to a 10 percent increase in the price of tickets?

Total revenue from tickets sold is currently (\$20/ticket) × (5,000 tickets/week) = \$100,000 per week. The fact that the price elasticity of demand for tickets is 3 implies that a 10 percent increase in price will produce a 30 percent reduction in the number of tickets sold, which means that quantity will fall to 3,500 tickets per week. Total expenditure on tickets will therefore fall to (3,500 tickets/week) × (\$22/ticket) = \$77,000 per week, which is significantly less than the current spending total.

What would have happened to total expenditure if the band manager had *reduced* ticket prices by 10 percent, from \$20 to \$18? Again assuming a price elasticity of 3, the result would have been a 30 percent increase in tickets sold—from 5,000 per week to 6,500 per week. The resulting total expenditure would have been (\$18/ticket) × (6,500 tickets/week) = \$117,000 per week, significantly more than the current total.

These examples illustrate the following important rule about how price changes affect total expenditure for an elastically demanded good:

When price elasticity of demand is greater than 1, changes in price and changes in total expenditure always move in opposite directions.

Let's look at the intuition behind this rule. Total expenditure is the product of price and quantity. For an elastically demanded product, the percentage change in quantity will be larger than the corresponding percentage change in price. Thus the change in quantity will more than offset the change in revenue per unit sold.

Now let's see how total spending responds to a price increase when demand is *inelastic* with respect to price. Consider a case like the one just considered except that the elasticity of demand for tickets is not 3 but 0.5. How will total expenditure respond to a 10 percent increase in ticket prices? This time the number of tickets sold will fall by only 5 percent to 4,750 tickets per week, which means that total expenditure on tickets will rise to (4,750 tickets/week) × (\$22/ticket) = \$104,500 per week, or \$4,500 per week more than the current expenditure level.

In contrast, a 10 percent price reduction (from \$20 to \$18 per ticket) when price elasticity is 0.5 would cause the number of tickets sold to grow by only 5 percent, from 5,000 per week to 5,250 per week, resulting in total expenditure of (\$18/ticket) × (5,250 tickets/week) = \$94,500 per week, significantly less than the current total.

As these examples illustrate, the effect of price changes on total expenditure when demand is inelastic is precisely the opposite of what it was when demand was elastic:

When price elasticity of demand is less than 1, changes in price and changes in total expenditure always move in the same direction.

Again, the intuition behind this rule is straightforward. For a product whose demand is inelastic with respect to price, the percentage change in quantity demanded will be smaller than the corresponding percentage change in price. The change in revenue per unit sold (price) will thus more than offset the change in the number of units sold.

The relationship between elasticity and the effect of a price change on total revenue is summarized in Table 4.3, where the symbol ϵ is used to denote elasticity.

TABLE 4.3
Elasticity and the Effect of a Price Change on Total Expenditure

If demand is...	A price increase will...	A price reduction will...
elastic ($\epsilon > 1$)	reduce total expenditure P × Q = PQ	increase total expenditure P × Q = PQ
Inelastic ($\epsilon < 1$)	increase total expenditure P × Q = PQ	reduce total expenditure P × Q = PQ

Recall that in the example with which we began this chapter, an increase in the price of drugs led to an increase in the total amount spent on drugs. That will happen whenever the demand for drugs is inelastic with respect to price, as it was in that example. Had the demand for drugs instead been elastic with respect to price, the drug supply interruption would have led to a reduction in total expenditure on drugs.

INCOME ELASTICITY AND CROSS-PRICE ELASTICITY OF DEMAND

The elasticity of demand for a good can be defined not only with respect to its own price but also with respect to the prices of substitutes or complements, or even to income. For example, the elasticity of demand for peanuts with respect to the price of cashews—also known as the **cross-price elasticity of demand** for peanuts with respect to cashew prices—is the percentage by which the quantity of peanuts demanded changes in response to a 1 percent change in the price of cashews. The **income elasticity of demand** for peanuts is the percentage by which the quantity demanded of peanuts changes in response to a 1 percent change in income.

Unlike the elasticity of demand for a good with respect to its own price, these other elasticities may be either positive or negative, so it is important to note their algebraic signs carefully. The income elasticity of demand for inferior goods, for example, is negative, whereas the income elasticity of demand for normal goods is positive. When the cross-price elasticity of demand for two goods is positive—as in the peanuts/cashews example—the two goods are substitutes. When it is negative, the two goods are complements. The elasticity of demand for tennis racquets with respect to court rental fees, for example, is less than zero.

cross-price elasticity of demand the percentage by which quantity demanded of the first good changes in response to a 1 percent change in the price of the second

income elasticity of demand the percentage by which quantity demanded changes in response to a 1 percent change in income

EXERCISE 4.3

If a 10 percent increase in income causes the number of students who choose to attend private universities to go up by 5 percent, what is the income elasticity of demand for private universities?

RECAP	CROSS-PRICE AND INCOME ELASTICITIES

When the cross-price elasticity of demand for one good with respect to the price of another good is positive, the two goods are substitutes; when the cross-price elasticity of demand is negative, the two goods are complements. A normal good has positive income elasticity of demand and an inferior good has negative income elasticity of demand.

THE PRICE ELASTICITY OF SUPPLY

price elasticity of supply the percentage change in quantity supplied that occurs in response to a 1 percent change in price

On the buyer's side of the market, we use price elasticity of demand to measure the responsiveness of quantity demanded to changes in price. On the seller's side of the market, the analogous measure is **price elasticity of supply**. It is defined as the percentage change in quantity supplied that occurs in response to a 1 percent change in price. For example, if a 1 percent increase in the price of peanuts leads to a 2 percent increase in the quantity supplied, the price elasticity of supply of peanuts would be 2.

The mathematical formula for price elasticity of supply at any point is the same as the corresponding expression for price elasticity of demand:

$$\text{Price elasticity of supply} = \frac{\Delta Q/Q}{\Delta P/P}, \tag{4.4}$$

where P and Q are the price and quantity at that point, ΔP is a small change in the initial price, and ΔQ the resulting change in quantity.

As with the corresponding expression for price elasticity of demand, Equation 4.4 can be rewritten as $(P/Q) \times (\Delta Q/\Delta P)$. And since $(\Delta Q/\Delta P)$ is the reciprocal of the slope of the supply curve, the right-hand side of Equation 4.4 is equal to $(P/Q) \times (1/\text{slope})$—the same expression we saw in Equation 4.3 for price elasticity of demand. Price and quantity are always positive, as is the slope of the typical supply curve, so price elasticity of supply will be a positive number at every point.

Consider the supply curve shown in Figure 4.13. The slope of this supply curve is 2, so the reciprocal of this slope is 1/2. Using the formula, this means that the price elasticity of supply at A is $(8/2) \times (1/2) = 2$. The corresponding expression at B is $(10/3) \times (1/2) = 5/3$, a slightly smaller value.

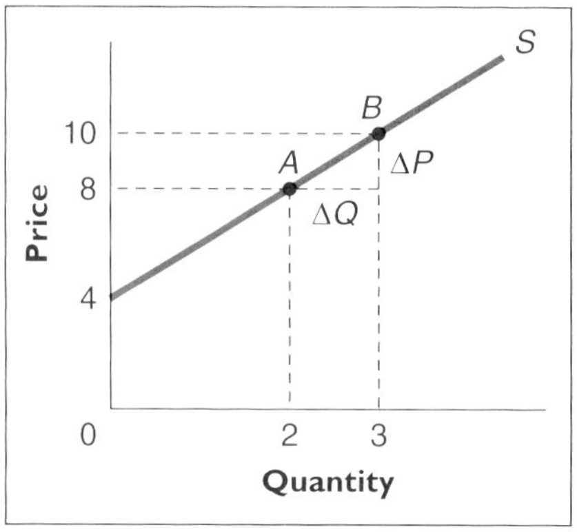

FIGURE 4.13
A Supply Curve for Which Price Elasticity Declines as Quantity Rises.
For the supply curve shown, (1/slope) is the same at every point, but the ratio P/Q declines as Q increases. So elasticity = $(P/Q) \times (1/\text{slope})$ declines as quantity increases.

EXERCISE 4.4

For the supply curve shown in Figure 4.13, calculate the elasticity of supply when $P = 6$.

Not all supply curves, however, have the property that price elasticity declines as quantity rises. Consider, for example, the supply curve shown in Figure 4.14. Because the ratio P/Q is the same at every point along this supply curve, and because the slope of the supply curve is also constant, price elasticity of supply will take exactly the same value at every point along this curve. At A, for example, price elasticity of supply $= (P/Q) \times (1/\text{slope}) = (4/12) \times (12/4) = 1$. Similarly, at B price elasticity of supply $= (4/12) \times (12/4) = 1$ again.

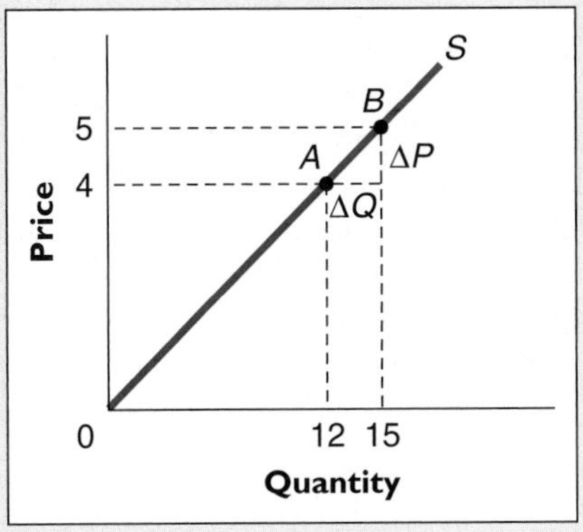

FIGURE 4.14
Calculating the Price Elasticity of Supply Graphically.
Price elasticity of supply is $(P/Q) \times (1/\text{slope})$, which at A is $(4/12) \times (12/4) = 1$, exactly the same as at B. The price elasticity of supply is equal to 1 at any point along a straight-line supply curve that passes through the origin.

Indeed, the price elasticity of supply will always be equal to 1 at any point along a straight-line supply curve that passes through the origin. The reason is that for movements along any such line, both price and quantity always change in exactly the same proportion.

On the buyer's side of the market, two important polar cases were demand curves with infinite price elasticity and zero price elasticity. As the next two examples illustrate, analogous polar cases exist on the seller's side of the market.

What is the elasticity of supply of land within the borough limits of Manhattan?

Land in Manhattan sells in the market for a price, just like aluminum or corn or automobiles or any other product. And the demand for land in Manhattan is a downward-sloping function of its price. For all practical purposes, however, its supply is completely fixed. No matter whether its price is high or low, the same amount of it is available in the market. The supply curve of such a good is vertical, and its price elasticity is zero at every price. Supply curves like the one shown in Figure 4.15 are said to be **perfectly inelastic**.

perfectly inelastic supply supply is perfectly inelastic with respect to price if elasticity is zero

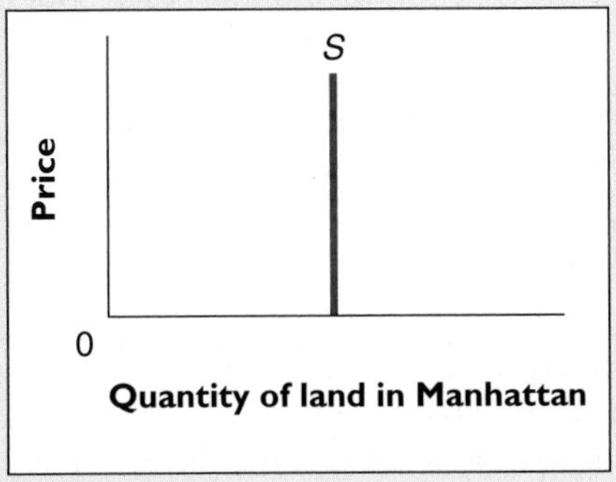

FIGURE 4.15
A Perfectly Inelastic Supply Curve.
Price elasticity of supply is zero at every point along a vertical supply curve.

◆

What is the elasticity of supply of lemonade?

Suppose that the ingredients required to bring a cup of lemonade to market and their respective costs are as follows:

Paper cup	2.0 cents
Lemon	3.8 cents
Sugar	2.0 cents
Water	0.2 cent
Ice	1.0 cent
Labor (30 seconds @ $6/hour)	5.0 cents

If these proportions remain the same no matter how many cups of lemonade are made, and the inputs can be purchased in any quantities at the stated prices, draw the supply curve of lemonade and compute its price elasticity.

Since each cup of lemonade costs exactly 14¢ to make, no matter how many cups are made, the marginal cost of lemonade is constant at 14¢ per cup. And since each point on a supply curve is equal to marginal cost (see Chapter 3), this means that the supply curve of lemonade is not upward-sloping but is instead a horizontal line at 14¢ per cup (Figure 4.16). The price elasticity of supply of lemonade is infinite.

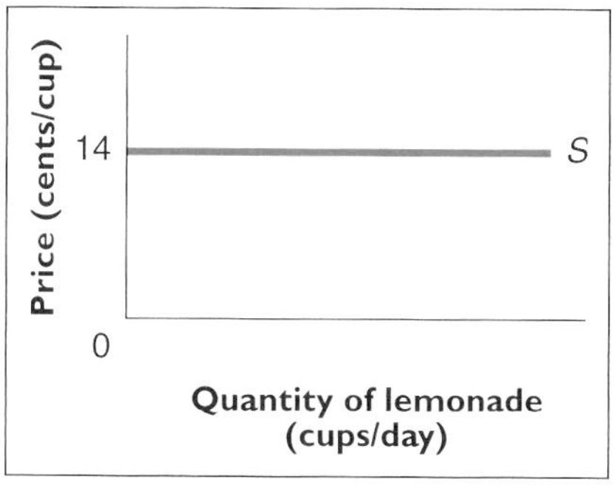

FIGURE 4.16
A Perfectly Elastic Supply Curve.
The elasticity of supply is infinite at every point along a horizontal supply curve.

perfectly elastic supply supply is perfectly elastic with respect to price if elasticity of supply is infinite

Whenever additional units of a good can be produced by using the same combination of inputs, purchased at the same prices, as have been used so far, the supply curve of that good will be horizontal. Such supply curves are said to be **perfectly elastic.** ◆

DETERMINANTS OF SUPPLY ELASTICITY

The two preceding examples suggest some of the factors that govern the elasticity of supply of a good or service. The lemonade case was one whose production process was essentially like a cooking recipe. For such cases, we can exactly double our output by doubling each ingredient. If the price of each ingredient remains fixed, the marginal cost of production for such goods will be constant—and hence their horizontal supply curves.

The Manhattan land example is a contrast in the extreme. The inputs that were used to produce land in Manhattan—even if we knew what they were—could not be duplicated at any price.

The key to predicting how elastic the supply of a good will be with respect to price is to know the terms on which additional units of the inputs involved in producing that good can be acquired. In general, the more easily additional units of these inputs can be acquired, the higher price elasticity of supply will be. The following factors (among others) govern the ease with which additional inputs can be acquired by a producer.

Flexibility of Inputs

To the extent that production of a good requires inputs that are also useful for the production of other goods, it is relatively easy to lure additional inputs away from their current uses, making supply of that good relatively elastic with respect to price. Thus the fact that lemonade production requires labor with only minimal skills means that a large pool of workers could shift from other activities to lemonade production if a profitable opportunity arose. Brain surgery, by contrast, requires elaborately trained and specialized labor, which means that even a large price increase would not increase available supplies, except in the very long run.

Mobility of Inputs

If inputs can be easily transported from one site to another, an increase in the price of a product in one market will enable a producer in that market to summon inputs from other markets. For example, the supply of agricultural products is made more elastic with respect to price by the fact that thousands of farm workers are willing to migrate northward during the growing season. The supply of entertainment is similarly made more elastic by the willingness of entertainers to hit the road. Circus performers, lounge singers, comedians, and even exotic dancers often spend a substantial fraction of their time away from home. For instance, according to a 1996 *New York Times* article, the top exotic dancers "basically follow the action, so the same entertainers who worked the Indianapolis 500 now head to Atlanta for the Olympics."

For most goods, the price elasticity of supply increases each time a new highway is built, or when the telecommunications network improves, or indeed when any other development makes it easier to find and transport inputs from one place to another.

Ability to Produce Substitute Inputs

The inputs required to produce finished diamond gemstones include raw diamond crystal, skilled labor, and elaborate cutting and polishing machinery. In time, the number of people with the requisite skills can be increased, as can the amount of specialized machinery. The number of raw diamond crystals buried in the earth is probably fixed in the same way that Manhattan land is fixed, but unlike Manhattan land, rising prices will encourage miners to spend the effort required to find a larger proportion of those crystals. Still, the supply of natural gemstone diamonds tends to be relatively inelastic because of the difficulty of augmenting the number of diamond crystals.

The day is close at hand, however, when gemstone makers will be able to produce synthetic diamond crystals that are indistinguishable from real ones. Indeed, there are already synthetic crystals that fool even highly experienced jewelers. The introduction of a perfect synthetic substitute for natural diamond crystals would increase the price elasticity of supply of diamonds (or, at any rate, the price elasticity of supply of gemstones that look and feel just like diamonds).

Time

Because it takes time for producers to switch from one activity to another, and because it takes time to build new machines and factories and train additional skilled workers, the price elasticity of supply will be higher for most goods in the long run than in the short run. In the short run, a manufacturer's inability to augment existing stocks of equipment and skilled labor may make it impossible to expand output beyond a certain limit. But if a shortage of managers was the bottleneck, new MBAs can be trained in only two years. Or if a shortage of legal staff is the problem, new lawyers can be trained in three years. In the long run, firms can always buy new equipment, build new factories, and hire additional skilled workers.

The conditions that gave rise to the perfectly elastic supply curve for lemonade in the example we discussed earlier are satisfied for many other products in the long run. If a product can be copied (in the sense that any company can acquire the design and other technological information required to produce it), and if the inputs needed for its production are used in roughly fixed proportions and are available at fixed market prices, then the long-run supply curve for that product will be horizontal. But many products do not satisfy these conditions, and their supply curves remain steeply upward-sloping, even in the very long run.

Example 4.3

THE ECONOMIC NATURALIST

EN 4

Why are gasoline prices so much more volatile than car prices?

Automobile price changes in the United States usually occur just once a year, when manufacturers announce an increase of only a few percentage points. In contrast, gasoline prices often fluctuate wildly from day to day. As shown in Figure 4.17, for example, the highest daily gasoline prices in California's two largest cities were three times higher than the lowest daily prices in 2001 and early 2002. Why this enormous difference in volatility?

With respect to price volatility, at least two important features distinguish the gasoline market from the market for cars. One is that the short-run price elasticity of demand for gasoline is much smaller than the corresponding elasticity for cars. The other is that

FIGURE 4.17
Gasoline Prices in Two California Cities.

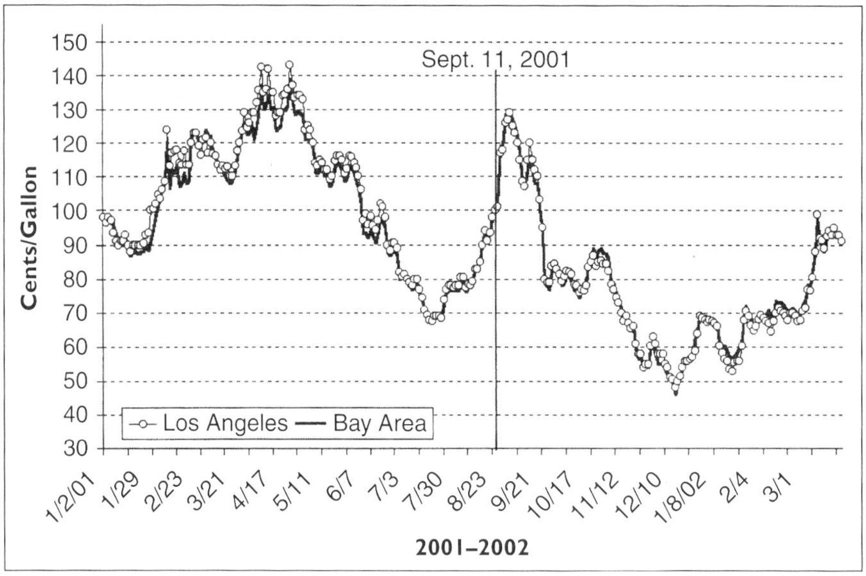

SOURCE: Oil Price Information Service (http://www.opisnet.com).

supply shifts are much more pronounced and frequent in the gasoline market than in the car market. (See Figure 4.18.)

Why are the two markets different in these ways? Consider first the difference in price elasticities of demand. The quantity of gasoline we demand depends largely on the kinds of cars we own and the amounts we drive them. In the short run, car ownership and commuting patterns are almost completely fixed, so even if the price of gasoline were to change sharply, the quantity we demand would not change by much. In contrast, if there were a sudden dramatic change in the price of cars, we could always postpone or accelerate our next car purchases.

To see why the supply curve in the gasoline market experiences larger and more frequent shifts than the supply curve in the car market, we need only examine the relative

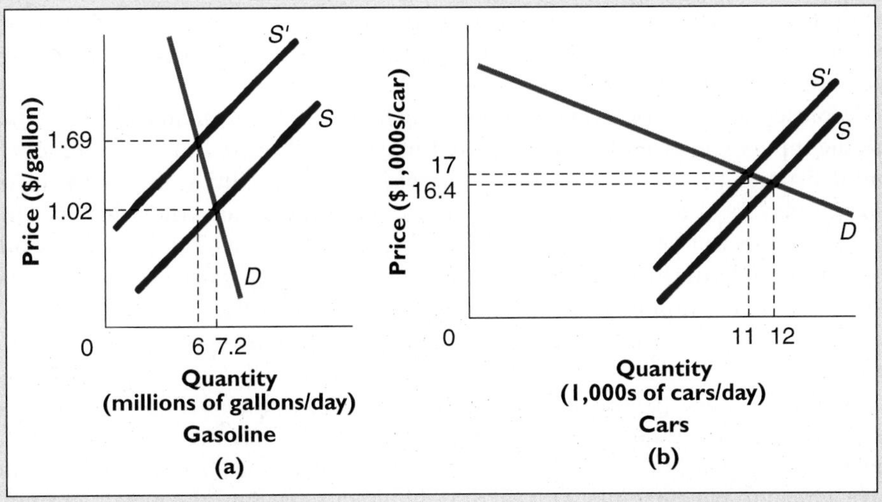

FIGURE 4.18
Greater Volatility in Gasoline Prices Than in Car Prices.
Gasoline prices are more volatile prices because supply shifts are larger and more frequent in the gasoline market (a) than in the car market (b), and also because supply and demand are less elastic in the short run in the gasoline market.

stability of the inputs employed by sellers in these two markets. Most of the inputs used in producing cars—steel, glass, rubber, plastics, electronic components, labor, and others—are reliably available to car makers. In contrast, the key input used in making gasoline—crude oil—is subject to profound and unpredictable supply interruptions.

This is so in part because much of the world's supply of crude oil is controlled by OPEC, a group of oil-exporting countries that has sharply curtailed its oil shipments to the United States on several previous occasions. Even in the absence of formal OPEC action, however, large supply curtailments often occur in the oil market—for example, whenever producers fear that political instability might engulf the major oil-producing countries of the Middle East.

Note in Figure 4.17 the sharp spike in gasoline prices that occurred just after the terrorist attacks on the World Trade Center and Pentagon on September 11, 2001. Because many believed that the aim of these attacks was to provoke large-scale war between Muslim societies and the West, fears of an impending oil supply interruption were perfectly rational. Such fears alone can trigger a temporary supply interruption, even if war is avoided. The prospect of war creates the expectation of oil supply cutbacks that would cause higher prices in the future, which leads producers to withdraw some of their oil from current markets (in order to sell it at higher prices later). But once the fear of war recedes, the supply curve of gasoline reverts with equal speed to its earlier position. Given the low short-run price elasticity of demand for gasoline, that's all it takes to generate the considerable price volatility we see in this market. ●

Why are gasoline prices so much less stable than automobile prices?

Price volatility is also common in markets in which demand curves fluctuate sharply and supply curves are highly inelastic. One such market was California's unregulated market for wholesale electricity during the summer of 2000. The supply of electrical generating capacity was essentially fixed in the short run. And because air conditioning accounts for a large share of demand, several spells of unusually warm weather caused demand to shift sharply to the right. Price at one point reached more than four times its highest level from the previous summer.

UNIQUE AND ESSENTIAL INPUTS: THE ULTIMATE SUPPLY BOTTLENECK

Fans of professional basketball are an enthusiastic bunch. Directly through their purchases of tickets and indirectly through their support of television advertisers, they spend literally billions of dollars each year on the sport. But these dollars are not distributed evenly across all teams. A disproportionate share of all revenues and product endorsement fees accrue to the people associated with consistently winning teams, and at the top of this pyramid generally stands the National Basketball Association's championship team.

Consider the task of trying to produce a championship team in the NBA. What are the inputs you would need? Talented players, a shrewd and dedicated coach and assistants, trainers, physicians, an arena, practice facilities, means for transporting players to away games, a marketing staff, and so on. And whereas some of these inputs can be acquired at reasonable prices in the marketplace, many others cannot. Indeed, the most important input of all—highly talented players—is in extremely limited supply. *This is so because the very definition of talented player is inescapably relative—simply put, such a player is one who is better than most others.*

Given the huge payoff that accrues to the NBA championship team, it is no surprise that the bidding for the most talented players has become so intense. If there were a long list of 7-foot, 1-inch, 325-pound centers, the Phoenix Suns wouldn't have agreed to pay Shaquille O'Neal $20 million a year. But, of course, the supply of such players is extremely limited. There are many hungry organizations that would like nothing better than to claim the NBA championship each year, yet no matter how much each is willing to spend, only one can succeed. The supply of NBA championship teams is perfectly inelastic with respect to price even in the very long run.

Sports champions are by no means the only important product whose supply elasticity is constrained by the inability to reproduce unique and essential inputs. In the movie industry, for example, although the supply of movies starring Jim Carrey is not perfectly inelastic, there are only so many films he can make each year. Because his films consistently generate huge box office revenues, scores of film producers want to sign him for their projects. But because there isn't enough of him to go around, his salary per film is more than $20 million.

In the long run, unique and essential inputs are the only truly significant supply bottleneck. If it were not for the inability to duplicate the services of such inputs, most goods and services would have extremely high price elasticities of supply in the long run.

■ SUMMARY ■

- The price elasticity of demand is a measure of how strongly buyers respond to changes in price. It is the percentage change in quantity demanded that occurs in response to a 1 percent change in price. The demand for a good is called elastic with respect to price if the absolute value of its price elasticity is more than 1, inelastic if its price elasticity is less than 1, and unit elastic if its price elasticity is equal to 1. **LO1**
- Goods such as salt, which occupy only a small share of the typical consumer's budget and have few or no good substitutes, tend to have low price elasticity of demand. Goods like new cars of a particular make and model, which occupy large budget shares and have many attractive substitutes, tend to have high price elasticity of demand. Price elasticity of demand is higher in the long run than in the short run because people often need time to adjust to price changes. **LO1**
- The price elasticity of demand at a point along a demand curve also can be expressed as the formula $\epsilon = (\Delta Q/Q)/(\Delta P/P)$. Here, P and Q represent price and quantity at that point and ΔQ and ΔP represent small changes in price and quantity. For straight-line demand curves, this formula can also be expressed as $\epsilon = (P/Q) \times (1/\text{slope})$. These formulations tell us that price elasticity declines in absolute terms as we move down a straight-line demand curve. **LO2**
- A cut in price will increase total spending on a good if demand is elastic but reduce it if demand is inelastic. An increase in price will increase total spending on a good if demand is inelastic but reduce it if demand is elastic. Total expenditure on a good reaches a maximum when price elasticity of demand is equal to 1. **LO3**

- Analogous formulas are used to define the elasticity of demand for a good with respect to income and the prices of other goods. In each case, elasticity is the percentage change in quantity demanded divided by the corresponding percentage change in income or price. **LO4**

- Price elasticity of supply is defined as the percentage change in quantity supplied that occurs in response to a 1 percent change in price. The mathematical formula for the price elasticity of supply at any point is $(\Delta Q/Q)/(\Delta P/P)$, where P and Q are the price and quantity at that point, ΔP is a small change in the initial price, and ΔQ is the resulting change in quantity. This formula also can be expressed as $(P/Q) \times (1/\text{slope})$ where $(1/\text{slope})$ is the reciprocal of the slope of the supply curve. **LO5**

- The price elasticity of supply of a good depends on how difficult or costly it is to acquire additional units of the inputs involved in producing that good. In general, the more easily additional units of these inputs can be acquired, the higher price elasticity of supply will be. It is easier to expand production of a product if the inputs used to produce that product are similar to inputs used to produce other products, if inputs are relatively mobile, or if an acceptable substitute for existing inputs can be developed. And like the price elasticity of demand, the price elasticity of supply is greater in the long run than in the short run. **LO5**

■ KEY TERMS ■

cross-price elasticity of demand (111)
elastic (99)
income elasticity of demand (111)
inelastic (99)
perfectly elastic demand (106)
perfectly elastic supply (114)
perfectly inelastic demand (107)
perfectly inelastic supply (113)
price elasticity of demand (98)
price elasticity of supply (112)
total expenditure (107)
total revenue (107)
unit elastic (99)

■ REVIEW QUESTIONS ■

1. Why does a consumer's price elasticity of demand for a good depend on the fraction of the consumer's income spent on that good? **LO1**
2. Why does the price elasticity of demand for a good decline as we move down along a straight-line demand curve? **LO2**
3. Under what conditions will an increase in the price of a product lead to a reduction in total spending for that product? **LO3**
4. Why do economists pay little attention to the algebraic sign of the elasticity of demand for a good with respect to its own price, yet pay careful attention to the algebraic sign of the elasticity of demand for a good with respect to another good's price? **LO4**
5. Why is supply elasticity higher in the long run than in the short run? **LO5**

■ PROBLEMS ■

1. Calculate the price elasticity of demand at points A, B, C, D, and E on the demand curve below. **LO3**

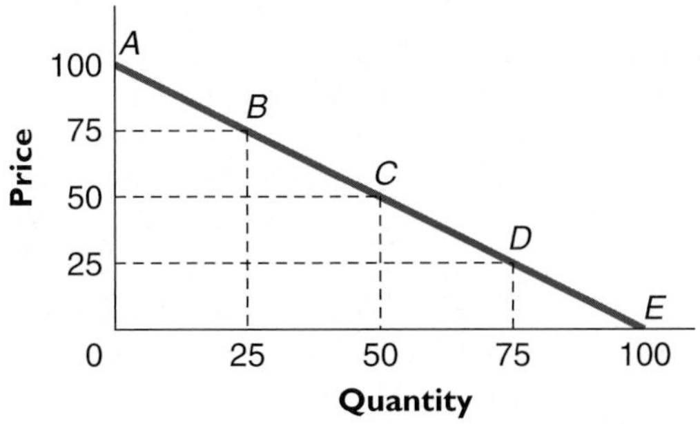

2. The schedule below shows the number of packs of bagels bought in Davis, California, each day at a variety of prices. **LO2, LO3**

Price of bagels ($/pack)	Number of packs purchased per day
6	0
5	3,000
4	6,000
3	9,000
2	12,000
1	15,000
0	18,000

a. Graph the daily demand curve for packs of bagels in Davis.
b. Calculate the price elasticity of demand at the point on the demand curve at which the price of bagels is $3 per pack.
c. If all bagel shops increased the price of bagels from $3 per pack to $4 per pack, what would happen to total revenues?
d. Calculate the price elasticity of demand at a point on the demand curve where the price of bagels is $2 per pack.
e. If bagel shops increased the price of bagels from $2 per pack to $3 per pack, what would happen to total revenues?

3. Suppose, while rummaging through your uncle's closet, you found the original painting of *Dogs Playing Poker*, a valuable piece of art. You decide to set up a display in your uncle's garage. The demand curve to see this valuable piece of art is as shown in the diagram. What price should you charge if your goal is to maximize your revenues from tickets sold? On a graph, show the inelastic and elastic regions of the demand curve. **LO3**

4. Is the demand for a particular brand of car, like a Chevrolet, likely to be more or less price-elastic than the demand for all cars? Explain. **LO1**

5. Among the following groups—senior executives, junior executives, and students—which is likely to have the most and which is likely to have the least price-elastic demand for membership in the Association of Business Professionals? **LO1**

6. A 2 percent increase in the price of milk causes a 4 percent reduction in the quantity demanded of chocolate syrup. What is the cross-price elasticity of demand for chocolate syrup with respect to the price of milk? Are the two goods complements or substitutes? **LO4**

7. What are the respective price elasticities of supply at *A* and *B* on the supply curve shown in the accompanying figure? **LO5**

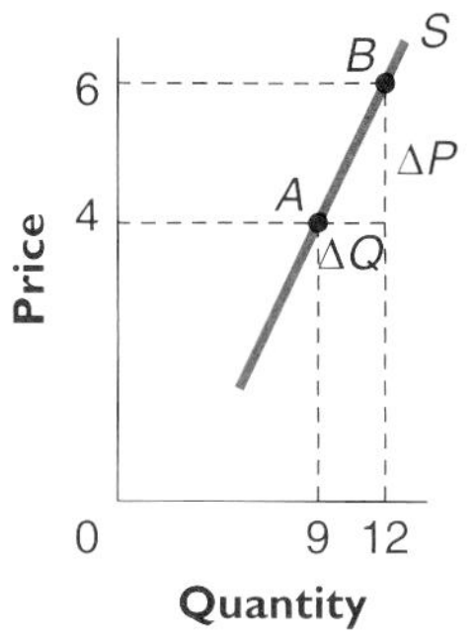

8. Suppose that the ingredients required to bring a slice of pizza to market and their respective costs are as listed in the table:

Paper plate	2 cents
Flour	8 cents
Tomato sauce	20 cents
Cheese	30 cents
Labor (3 minutes @ $12/hour)	60 cents

If these proportions remain the same no matter how many slices are made, and the inputs can be purchased in any quantities at the stated prices, draw the supply curve of pizza slices and compute its price elasticity. **LO5**

9.* At point *A* on the demand curve shown, by what percentage will a 1 percent increase in the price of the product affect total expenditure on the product? **LO2, LO3**

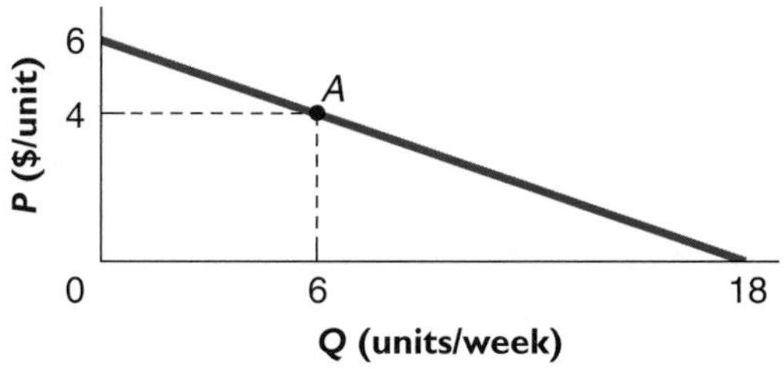

10.* Suppose that, in an attempt to induce citizens to conserve energy, the government enacted regulations requiring that all air conditioners be more efficient in their use of electricity. After this regulation was implemented, government officials were then surprised to discover that people used even more electricity than before. Using the concept of price elasticity, explain how this increase might have occurred. **LO3**

*Problems marked with an asterisk (*) are more difficult.

■ ANSWERS TO IN-CHAPTER EXERCISES ■

4.1 In response to a 5 percent reduction in the price of ski passes, the quantity demanded increased by 20 percent. The price elasticity of demand for ski passes is thus (20 percent)/(5 percent) = 4, and that means that at the initial price of $400, the demand for ski passes is elastic with respect to price. **LO2**

4.2 At point *A* in the accompanying diagram, $P/Q = 4/4 = 1$. The slope of this demand curve is $20/5 = 4$, so $\epsilon = 1 \times (1/\text{slope}) = 1/4$. **LO2**

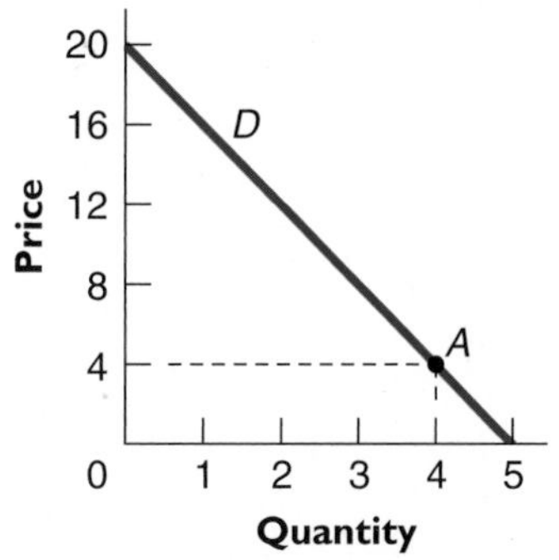

4.3 Income elasticity = percentage change in quantity demanded/percentage change in income = 5 percent/10 percent = 0.5. **LO4**

4.4 For the supply curve below, $Q = 1$ when $P = 6$, so elasticity of supply = $(P/Q) \times (1/\text{slope}) = (6) \times (1/2) = 3$. **LO5**

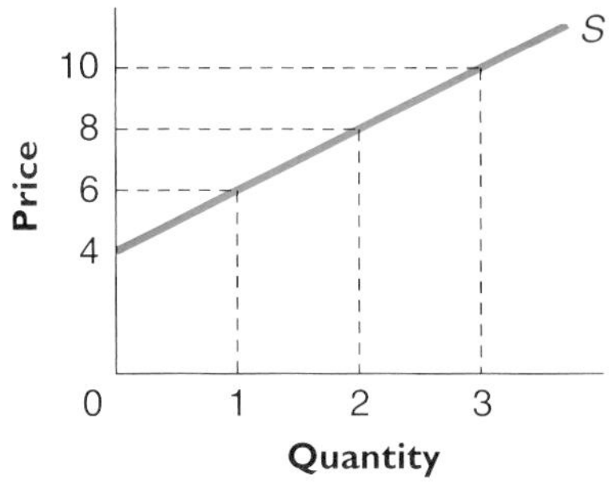

CHAPTER

5

Demand

LEARNING OBJECTIVES

After reading this chapter, you should be able to:

1. Discuss the law of diminishing marginal utility, which underlies individual demand.
2. Show how the Rational Spending Rule is related to substitution and income effects.
3. Discuss the relationship between individual demand curves and the market demand curve.
4. Define and calculate consumer surplus.

On the northern border of a large university in the East, a creek widens to form a picturesque lake, fondly remembered by generations of alumni as a popular recreation spot. Over the years, the lake had gradually silted in, and by the late 1980s, even paddling a canoe across it had become impossible. A generous alumnus then sponsored an effort to restore the lake. Heavy dredging equipment hauled out load after load of mud, and months later the lake was silt-free.

To mark the occasion, the university held a ceremony. Bands played, the president spoke, a chorus sang, and distinguished visitors applauded the donor's generosity. Hundreds of faculty and students turned out for the festivities. Spotting a good opportunity to promote their product, the proprietors of a local ice cream store set up a temporary stand at the water's edge, with a large sign: "Free Ice Cream."

Word spread. Soon scores of people were lined up waiting to try Vanilla Almond Delight, Hazelnut Cream, and Fudge Faire. The ice cream was plentiful, and because it was free, everyone could obviously afford it—or so it seemed. In fact, many people who wanted ice cream that day never got any. The reason, of course, was that they found waiting in a long line too steep a price to pay for ice cream.

When a good or service is scarce, it must somehow be rationed among competing users. In most markets, monetary prices perform that task. But in the case of a stand offering free ice cream, waiting time becomes the effective rationing device. Having to stand in line is a cost, no less so than having to part with some money.

This example drives home the point that although the demand curve is usually described as a relationship between the quantity demanded of a good and its monetary price, the relationship is really a much more general one. At bottom, the demand curve is a relationship between the quantity demanded and *all* costs—monetary and nonmonetary—associated with acquiring a good.

Our task in this chapter will be to explore the demand side of the market in greater depth than was possible in Chapter 3. There we merely asked you to accept as an intuitively plausible claim that the quantity demanded of a good or service declines as its price rises. This relationship is known as the Law of Demand, and we will see how it emerges as a simple consequence of the assumption that people spend their limited incomes in rational ways. In the process, we will see more clearly the dual roles of income and substitution as factors that account for the Law of Demand. We also will see how to generate market demand curves by adding the demand curves for individual buyers horizontally. Finally, we will see how to use the demand curve to generate a measure of the total benefit that buyers reap from their participation in a market.

THE LAW OF DEMAND

With our discussion of the free ice cream offer in mind, let us restate the law of demand as follows:

Law of Demand: People do less of what they want to do as the cost of doing it rises.

By stating the law of demand this way, we can see it as a direct consequence of the Cost-Benefit Principle, which says that an activity should be pursued if (and only if) its benefits are at least as great as its costs. Recall that we measure the benefit of an activity by the highest price we'd be willing to pay to pursue it—namely, our reservation price for the activity. When the cost of an activity rises, it is more likely to exceed our reservation price, and we are therefore less likely to pursue that activity.

Cost-Benefit

The law of demand applies to BMWs, cheap key rings, and "free" ice cream, not to mention compact discs, manicures, medical care, and acid-free rain. It stresses that a "cost" is the sum of *all* the sacrifices—monetary and nonmonetary, implicit and explicit—we must make to engage in an activity.

THE ORIGINS OF DEMAND

How much are you willing to pay for the latest Amy Winehouse CD? The answer will clearly depend on how you feel about her music. To her diehard fans, buying the new release might seem absolutely essential; they'd pay a steep price indeed. But those who don't like her music may be unwilling to buy it at any price.

Wants (also called "preferences" or "tastes") are clearly an important determinant of a consumer's reservation price for a good. But that begs the question of where wants come from. Many tastes—such as the taste for water on a hot day or for a comfortable place to sleep at night—are largely biological in origin. But many others are heavily shaped by culture, and even basic cravings may be socially molded. For example, people raised in southern India develop a taste for hot curry dishes, while those raised in England generally prefer milder foods.

Tastes for some items may remain stable for many years, but tastes for others may be highly volatile. Although books about the *Titanic* disaster have been continuously available since the vessel sank in the spring of 1912, not until the appearance of James Cameron's blockbuster film did these books begin to sell in large quantities. In the spring of 1998, five of the 15 books on the *New York Times* paperback bestseller list were about the *Titanic* itself or one of the actors in the film. Yet none of these books, or any other book about the *Titanic,* has made the bestseller list in the years since then. Still, echoes of the film continued to reverberate in the marketplace. In the years since its release, for example, demand for ocean cruises has grown sharply and several television networks have introduced shows set on cruise ships.

Peer influence provides another example of how social forces often influence demand. Indeed, it is often the most important single determinant of demand. For instance, if our goal is to predict whether a young man will purchase an illegal recreational drug, knowing how much income he has is not very helpful. Knowing the prices of whiskey and other legal substitutes for illicit drugs also tells us little. Although these factors do influence purchase decisions, by themselves they are weak predictors. But if we know that most of the young man's best friends are heavy drug users, there is a reasonably good chance that he will use drugs as well.

EN 5

Another important way in which social forces shape demand is in the relatively common desire to consume goods and services that are recognized as the best of their kind. For instance, many people want to hear Placido Domingo sing, not just because of the quality of his voice, but because he is widely regarded as the world's best—or at least the world's best known—living tenor.

Consider, too, the decision of how much to spend on an interview suit. Employment counselors never tire of reminding us that making a good first impression is extremely important when you go for a job interview. At the very least, that means showing up in a suit that looks good. But looking good is a relative concept. If everyone else shows up in a \$200 suit, you'll look good if you show up in a \$300 suit. But you won't look as good in that same \$300 suit if everyone else shows up in suits costing \$1,000. The amount you'll choose to spend on an interview suit, then, clearly depends on how much others in your circle are spending.

NEEDS VERSUS WANTS

In everyday language, we distinguish between goods and services people need and those they merely want. For example, we might say that someone wants a ski vacation in Utah, but what he really needs is a few days off from his daily routine; or that someone wants a house with a view, but what she really needs is shelter from the elements. Likewise, since people need protein to survive, we might say that a severely malnourished person needs more protein. But it would strike us as odd to say that anyone—even a malnourished person—needs more prime filet of beef, since health can be restored by consuming far less expensive sources of protein.

Economists like to emphasize that once we have achieved bare subsistence levels of consumption—the amount of food, shelter, and clothing required to maintain our health—we can abandon all reference to needs and speak only in terms of wants. This linguistic distinction helps us to think more clearly about the true nature of our choices.

For instance, someone who says, "Californians don't have nearly as much water as they need" will tend to think differently about water shortages than someone who says, "Californians don't have nearly as much water as they want when the price of water is low." The first person is likely to focus on regulations to prevent people from watering their lawns, or on projects to capture additional runoff from the Sierra Nevada mountains. The second person is more likely to focus on the artificially low price of water in California. Whereas remedies of the first sort are often costly and extremely difficult to implement, raising the price of water is both simple and effective.

Example 5.1
THE ECONOMIC NATURALIST

Why do farmers grow water-intensive crops like rice in an arid state like California?

Why does California experience chronic water shortages?

Some might respond that the state must serve the needs of a large population with a relatively low average annual rainfall. Yet other states, like New Mexico, have even less rainfall per person and do not experience water shortages nearly as often as California. California's problem exists because local governments sell water at extremely low prices, which encourages Californians to use water in ways that make no sense for a state with low rainfall. For instance, rice, which is well suited for conditions in high-rainfall states like South Carolina, requires extensive irrigation in California. But because California farmers can obtain water so cheaply, they plant and flood hundreds of thousands of acres of rice paddies each spring in the Central Valley. Two thousand tons of water are needed to produce one ton of rice, but many other grains can be produced with only half that amount. If the price of California water were higher, farmers would simply switch to other grains.

Likewise, cheap water encourages homeowners in Los Angeles and San Diego to plant water-intensive lawns and shrubs, like the ones common in the East and Midwest. By contrast, residents of cities like Santa Fe, New Mexico, where water prices are high, choose native plantings that require little or no watering. ●

TRANSLATING WANTS INTO DEMAND

It's a simple fact of life that although our resources are finite, our appetites for good things are boundless. Even if we had unlimited bank accounts, we'd quickly run out of the time and energy needed to do all the things we wanted to do. Our challenge is to use our limited resources to fulfill our desires to the greatest possible degree. That leaves us with a practical question: How should we allocate our incomes among the various goods and services that are available? To answer this question, it's helpful to begin by recognizing that the goods and services we buy are not ends in themselves, but rather means for satisfying our desires.

MEASURING WANTS: THE CONCEPT OF UTILITY

Economists use the concept of *utility* to represent the satisfaction people derive from their consumption activities. The assumption is that people try to allocate their incomes so as to maximize their satisfaction, a goal that is referred to as *utility maximization*.

Early economists imagined that the utility associated with different activities might someday be subject to precise measurement. The nineteenth-century British economist Jeremy Bentham, for example, wrote of a "utilometer," a device that could be used to measure the amount of utility provided by different consumption activities. Although no such device existed in Bentham's day, contemporary neuropsychologists now have equipment that can generate at least crude measures of satisfaction.

Figure 5.1, for example, shows a subject who is connected to an apparatus that measures the intensity of electrical waves emanating from his brain. University of Wisconsin psychologist Richard Davidson and his colleagues documented that subjects with relatively heavy brain-wave measures emanating from the left prefrontal cortex tend to be happier (as assessed by a variety of other measures) than subjects with relatively heavy brain-wave measures emanating from the right prefrontal cortex.

Jeremy Bentham would have been thrilled to learn that a device like the one pictured in Figure 5.1 might exist some day. His ideal utilometer would measure utility in utils, much as a thermometer measures temperature in degrees Fahrenheit or Celsius. It would assign a numerical utility value to every activity—watching a movie, eating a cheeseburger, and so on. Unfortunately, even sophisticated devices like the one shown in Figure 5.1 are far from capable of such fine-grained assessments.

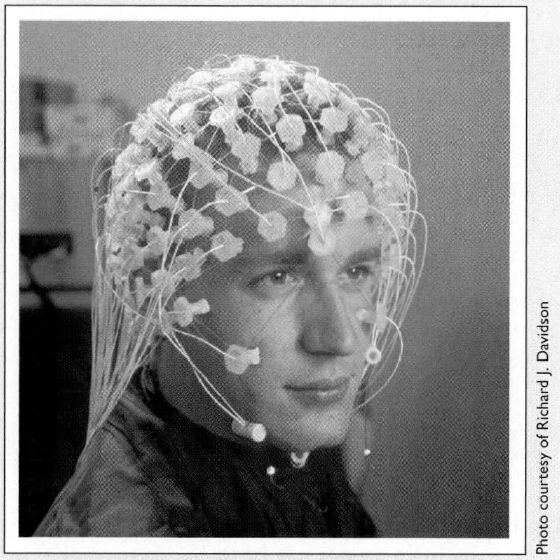

FIGURE 5.1
Can Utility Be Measured Electronically?
Scientists have shown that higher levels of electrical activity on the brain's left side are strongly associated with higher levels of satisfaction.

For Bentham's intellectual enterprise, however, the absence of a real utilometer was of no practical significance. Even without such a machine, he could continue to envision the consumer as someone whose goal was to maximize the total utility she obtained from the goods she consumed. Bentham's "utility maximization model," we will see, affords important insights about how a rational consumer ought to spend her income.

To explore how the model works, we begin with a very simple problem, the one facing a consumer who reaches the front of the line at a free ice cream stand. How many cones of ice cream should this person, whom we'll call Sarah, ask for? Table 5.1 shows the relationship between the total number of ice cream cones Sarah eats per hour and the total utility, measured in utils per hour, she derives from them. Note that the measurements in the table are stated in terms of cones per hour and utils per hour. Why "per hour"? Because without an explicit time dimension, we would have no idea whether a given quantity was a lot or a little. Five ice cream cones in a lifetime isn't much, but five in an hour would be more than most of us would care to eat.

As the entries in Table 5.1 show, Sarah's total utility increases with each cone she eats, up to the fifth cone. Eating five cones per hour makes her happier than eating four, which makes her happier than eating three, and so on. But beyond five cones per hour, consuming more ice cream actually makes Sarah less happy. Thus, the sixth cone reduces her total utility from 150 utils per hour to 140 utils per hour.

TABLE 5.1
Sarah's Total Utility from Ice Cream Consumption

Cone quantity (cones/hour)	Total utility (utils/hour)
0	0
1	50
2	90
3	120
4	140
5	150
6	140

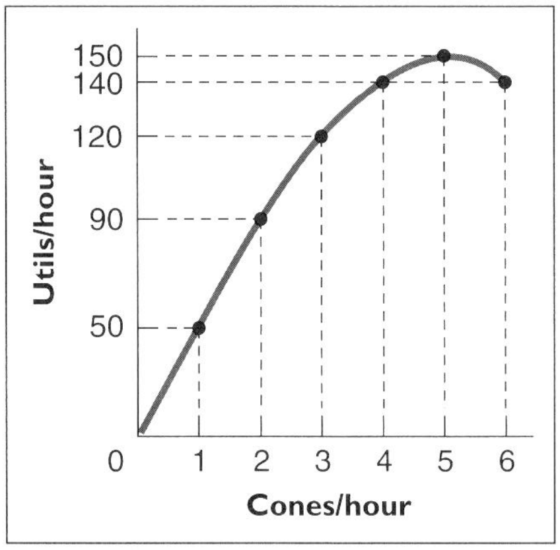

FIGURE 5.2
Sarah's Total Utility from Ice Cream Consumption.
For most goods, utility rises at a diminishing rate with additional consumption.

We can display the utility information in Table 5.1 graphically, as in Figure 5.2. Note in the graph that the more cones per hour Sarah eats, the more utils she gets—but again only up to the fifth cone. Once she moves beyond five, her total utility begins to decline. Sarah's happiness reaches a maximum of 150 utils when she eats five cones per hour. At that point she has no incentive to eat the sixth cone, even though it's absolutely free. Eating it would actually make her worse off.

Table 5.1 and Figure 5.2 illustrate another important aspect of the relationship between utility and consumption—namely, that the additional utility from additional units of consumption declines as total consumption increases. Thus, whereas one cone per hour is a *lot* better—by 50 utils—than zero, five cones per hour is just a *little* better than four (just 10 utils' worth).

marginal utility the additional utility gained from consuming an additional unit of a good

The term **marginal utility** denotes the amount by which total utility changes when consumption changes by one unit. In Table 5.2, the third column shows the marginal utility values that correspond to changes in Sarah's level of ice cream consumption. For example, the second entry in that column represents the increase in

TABLE 5.2
Sarah's Total and Marginal Utility from Ice Cream Consumption

Cone quantity (cones/hour)	Total utility (utils/hour)	Marginal utility (utils/cone)
0	0	
		50
1	50	
		40
2	90	
		30
3	120	
		20
4	140	
		10
5	150	
		−10
6	140	

Marginal utility

$$= \frac{\text{change in utility}}{\text{change in consumption}}$$

$$= \frac{90 \text{ utils} - 50 \text{ utils}}{2 \text{ cones} - 1 \text{ cone}}$$

$$= 40 \text{ utils/cone}$$

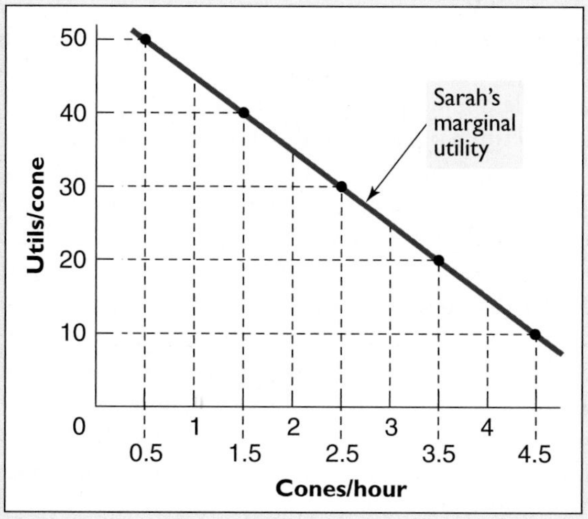

FIGURE 5.3
Diminishing Marginal Utility.
The more cones Sarah consumes each hour, the smaller her marginal utility will be. For Sarah, consumption of ice cream cones satisfies the law of diminishing marginal utility.

total utility (measured in utils per cone) when Sarah's consumption rises from one cone per hour to two. Note that the marginal utility entries in the third column are placed midway between the rows of the preceding columns. We do this to indicate that marginal utility corresponds to the movement from one consumption quantity to the next. Thus, we would say that the marginal utility of moving from one to two cones per hour is 40 utils per cone.

Because marginal utility is the change in utility that occurs as we move from one quantity to another, when we graph marginal utility, we normally adopt the convention of plotting each specific marginal utility value halfway between the two quantities to which it corresponds. Thus, in Figure 5.3, we plot the marginal utility value of 40 utils per cone midway between one cone per hour and two cones per hour, and so on. (In this example, the marginal utility graph is a downward-sloping straight line for the region shown, but this need not always be the case.)

The tendency for marginal utility to decline as consumption increases beyond some point is called the **law of diminishing marginal utility**. It holds not just for Sarah's consumption of ice cream in this illustration, but also for most other goods for most consumers. If we have one brownie or one Ferrari, we're happier than we are with none; if we have two, we'll be even happier—but not twice as happy—and so on. Though this pattern is called a law, there are exceptions. Indeed, some consumption activities even seem to exhibit *increasing* marginal utility. For example, an unfamiliar song may seem irritating the first time you hear it, then gradually become more tolerable the next few times you hear it. Before long, you may discover that you *like* the song, and you may even find yourself singing it in the shower. Notwithstanding such exceptions, the law of diminishing marginal utility is a plausible characterization of the relationship between utility and consumption for many goods. Unless otherwise stated, we'll assume that it holds for the various goods we discuss.

law of diminishing marginal utility the tendency for the additional utility gained from consuming an additional unit of a good to diminish as consumption increases beyond some point

What will Sarah do when she gets to the front of the line? At that point, the opportunity cost of the time she spent waiting is a sunk cost and is hence irrelevant to her decision about how many cones to order. And since there is no monetary charge for the cones, the cost of ordering an additional one is zero. According to the Cost-Benefit Principle, Sarah should therefore continue to order cones as long as the marginal benefit (here, the marginal utility she gets from an additional cone) is greater than or equal to zero. As we can see from the entries in Table 5.2, marginal utility is positive up to and including the fifth cone but becomes negative after five cones. Thus, as noted earlier, Sarah should order five cones.

Cost-Benefit

ALLOCATING A FIXED INCOME BETWEEN TWO GOODS

Most of the time we face considerably more complex purchase decisions than the one Sarah faced. For one thing, we generally must make decisions about many goods, not just a single one like ice cream. Another complication is that the cost of consuming additional units of each good will rarely be zero.

To see how to proceed in more complex cases, let's suppose Sarah must decide how to spend a fixed sum of money on two different goods, each with a positive price. Should she spend all of it on one of the goods or part of it on each? The law of diminishing marginal utility suggests that spending it all on a single good isn't a good strategy. Rather than devote more and more money to the purchase of a good we already consume in large quantities (and whose marginal utility is therefore relatively low), we generally do better to spend that money on other goods we don't have much of, whose marginal utility will likely be higher.

The simplest way to illustrate how economists think about the spending decisions of a utility-maximizing consumer is to work through a series of examples, beginning with the following:

Is Sarah maximizing her utility from consuming chocolate and vanilla ice cream (I)?

Chocolate ice cream sells for \$2 per pint and vanilla sells for \$1. Sarah has a budget of \$400 per year to spend on ice cream and her marginal utility from consuming each type varies with the amount consumed, as shown in Figure 5.4. If she is currently buying 200 pints of vanilla and 100 pints of chocolate each year, is she maximizing her utility?

FIGURE 5.4

Marginal Utility Curves for Two Flavors of Ice Cream (I).

At Sarah's current consumption levels, her marginal utility of chocolate ice cream is 25 percent higher than her marginal utility of vanilla. But chocolate is twice as expensive as vanilla.

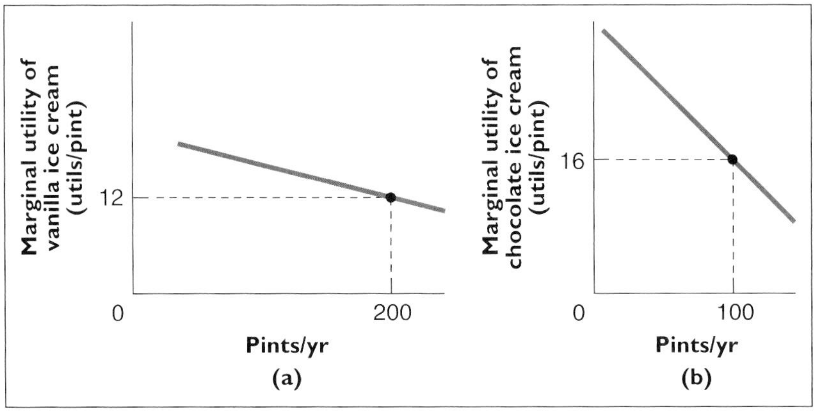

Note first that with 200 pints per year of vanilla and 100 pints of chocolate, Sarah is spending \$200 per year on each type of ice cream, for a total expenditure of \$400 per year on ice cream, exactly the amount in her budget. By spending her money in this fashion, is she getting as much utility as possible? Note in Figure 5.4(b) that her marginal utility from chocolate ice cream is 16 utils per pint. Since chocolate costs \$2 per pint, her current spending on chocolate is yielding additional utility at the rate of (16 utils/pint)/(\$2/pint) = 8 utils per dollar. Similarly, note in Figure 5.4(a) that Sarah's marginal utility for vanilla is 12 utils per pint. And since vanilla costs only \$1 per pint, her current spending on vanilla is yielding (12 utils/pint)/(\$1/pint) = 12 utils per dollar. In other words, at her current rates of consumption of the two flavors, her spending yields higher marginal utility per dollar for vanilla than for chocolate. And this means that Sarah cannot possibly be maximizing her total utility.

To see why, note that if she spent \$2 less on chocolate (that is, if she bought one pint less than before), she would lose about 16 utils;[1] but with the same \$2, she could buy two additional pints of vanilla, which would boost her utility by about 24 utils,[2] for a net gain of about 8 utils. Under Sarah's current budget allocation, she is thus spending too little on vanilla and too much on chocolate. ◆

In the next example, we'll see what happens if Sarah spends \$100 per year less on chocolate and \$100 per year more on vanilla.

Is Sarah maximizing her utility from consuming chocolate and vanilla ice cream (II)?

Sarah's total ice cream budget and the prices of the two flavors are the same as in the earlier example. If her marginal utility from consuming each type varies with the amount consumed, as shown in Figure 5.5, and if she is currently buying 300 pints of vanilla and 50 pints of chocolate each year, is she maximizing her utility?

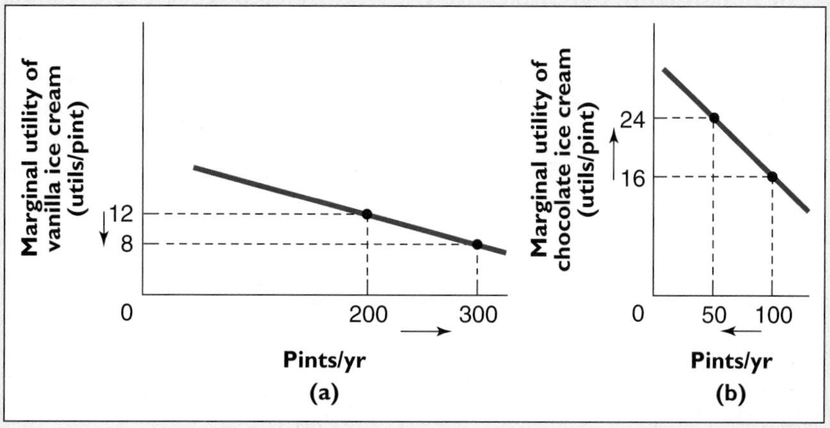

FIGURE 5.5
Marginal Utility Curves for Two Flavors of Ice Cream (II).
When Sarah increases her consumption of vanilla (a), her marginal utility of vanilla falls. Conversely, when she reduces her consumption of chocolate (b), her marginal utility of chocolate rises.

Note first that the direction of Sarah's rearrangement of her spending makes sense in light of the original example, in which we saw that she was spending too much on chocolate and too little on vanilla. Spending \$100 less on chocolate ice cream causes her marginal utility from that flavor to rise from 16 to 24 utils per pint [Figure 5.5(b)]. By the same token, spending \$100 more on vanilla ice cream causes her marginal utility from that flavor to fall from 12 to 8 utils per pint [Figure 5.5(a)]. Both movements are a simple consequence of the law of diminishing marginal utility.

Since chocolate still costs \$2 per pint, her spending on chocolate now yields additional utility at the rate of (24 utils/pint)/(\$2/pint) = 12 utils per dollar. Similarly, since vanilla still costs \$1 per pint, her spending on vanilla now yields additional utility at the rate of only (8 utils/pint)/(\$1/pint) = 8 utils per dollar. So at her new rates of consumption of the two flavors, her spending yields higher marginal utility per dollar for chocolate than for vanilla—precisely the opposite of the ordering we saw in the original example.

Sarah has thus made too big an adjustment in her effort to remedy her original consumption imbalance. Starting from the new combination of flavors (300 pints per year of vanilla and 50 pints per year of chocolate), for example, if she then

[1]The actual reduction would be slightly larger than 16 utils because her marginal utility of chocolate rises slightly as she consumes less of it.
[2]The actual increase will be slightly smaller than 24 utils because her marginal utility of vanilla falls slightly as she buys more of it.

bought two fewer pints of vanilla (which would reduce her utility by about 16 utils) and used the $2 she saved to buy an additional pint of chocolate (which would boost her utility by about 24 utils), she would experience a net gain of about 8 utils. So again, her current combination of the two flavors fails to maximize her total utility. This time, she is spending too little on chocolate and too much on vanilla. ◆

EXERCISE 5.1

In the preceding examples, verify that the stated combination of flavors costs exactly the amount that Sarah has budgeted for ice cream.

optimal combination of goods the affordable combination that yields the highest total utility

What is Sarah's **optimal combination** of the two flavors? In other words, among all the combinations of vanilla and chocolate ice cream that Sarah can afford, which one provides the maximum possible total utility? The following example illustrates the condition that this optimal combination must satisfy.

Is Sarah maximizing her utility from consuming chocolate and vanilla ice cream (III)?

Sarah's total ice cream budget and the prices of the two flavors are the same as in the previous examples. If her marginal utility from consuming each type varies with the amounts consumed, as shown in Figure 5.6, and if she is currently buying 250 pints of vanilla and 75 pints of chocolate each year, is she maximizing her utility?

FIGURE 5.6
Marginal Utility Curves for Two Flavors of Ice Cream (III).
At her current consumption levels, marginal utility per dollar is exactly the same for each flavor.

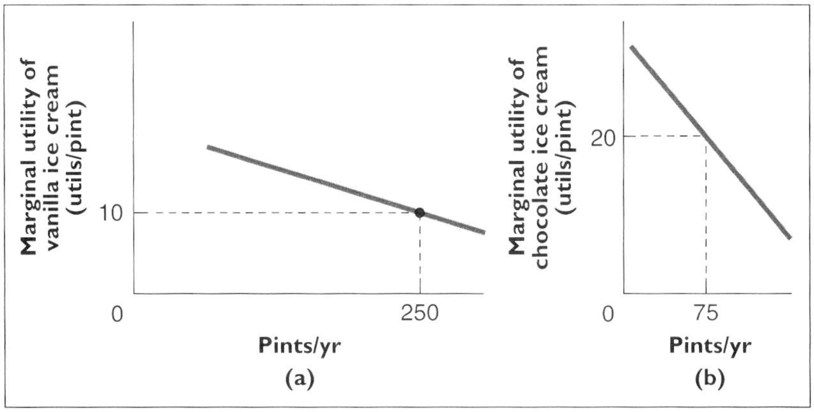

As you can easily verify, the combination of 250 pints per year of vanilla and 75 pints per year of chocolate again costs a total of $400, exactly the amount of Sarah's ice cream budget. Her marginal utility from chocolate is now 20 utils per pint [Figure 5.6(b)], and since chocolate still costs $2 per pint, her spending on chocolate now yields additional utility at the rate of (20 utils/pint)/($2/pint) = 10 utils per dollar. Sarah's marginal utility for vanilla is now 10 utils per pint [Figure 5.6(a)], and since vanilla still costs $1 per pint, her last dollar spent on vanilla now also yields (10 utils/pint)/($1/pint) = 10 utils per dollar. So at her new rates of consumption of the two flavors, her spending yields precisely the same marginal utility per dollar for each flavor. Thus, if she spent a little less on chocolate and a little more on vanilla (or vice versa), her total utility would not change at all. For example, if she bought two more pints of vanilla (which would increase her utility by 20 utils) and one fewer pint of chocolate (which would reduce her utility by 20 utils), both her total expenditure on ice cream and her total utility would remain the same as before. *When her marginal utility per dollar is the same for each flavor, it is impossible for Sarah to rearrange her spending to increase total utility.* Therefore, 250 pints of vanilla and 75 pints of chocolate per year form the optimal combination of the two flavors. ◆

THE RATIONAL SPENDING RULE

The examples we have worked through illustrate the **Rational Spending Rule** for solving the problem of how to allocate a fixed budget across different goods. The optimal, or utility-maximizing, combination must satisfy this rule.

The Rational Spending Rule: Spending should be allocated across goods so that the marginal utility per dollar is the same for each good.

The rational spending rule can be expressed in the form of a simple formula. If we use MU_C to denote marginal utility from chocolate ice cream consumption (again measured in utils per pint) and P_C to denote the price of chocolate (measured in dollars per pint), then the ratio MU_C/P_C will represent the marginal utility per dollar spent on chocolate, measured in utils per dollar. Similarly, if we use MU_V to denote the marginal utility from vanilla ice cream consumption and P_V to denote the price of vanilla, then MU_V/P_V will represent the marginal utility per dollar spent on vanilla. The marginal utility per dollar will be exactly the same for the two types—and hence total utility will be maximized—when the following simple equation for the rational spending rule for two goods is satisfied:

$$MU_C/P_C = MU_V/P_V.$$

The rational spending rule is easily generalized to apply to spending decisions regarding large numbers of goods. In its most general form, it says that the ratio of marginal utility to price must be the same for each good the consumer buys. If the ratio were higher for one good than for another, the consumer could always increase her total utility by buying more of the first good and less of the second.

Strictly speaking, the rational spending rule applies to goods that are perfectly divisible, such as milk or gasoline. Many other goods, such as bus rides and television sets, can be consumed only in whole-number amounts. In such cases, it may not be possible to satisfy the rational spending rule exactly. For example, when you buy one television set, your marginal utility per dollar spent on televisions may be somewhat higher than the corresponding ratio for other goods, yet if you bought a second set, the reverse might well be true. Your best alternative in such cases is to allocate each additional dollar you spend to the good for which your marginal utility per dollar is highest.[3]

Notice that we have not chosen to classify the rational spending rule as one of the core principles of economics. We omit it from this list not because the rule is unimportant, but because it follows directly from the Cost-Benefit Principle. As we noted earlier, there is considerable advantage in keeping the list of core principles as small as possible.

Cost-Benefit

INCOME AND SUBSTITUTION EFFECTS REVISITED

In Chapter 3, we saw that the quantity of a good that consumers wish to purchase depends on its own price, on the prices of substitutes and complements, and on consumer incomes. We also saw that when the price of a good changes, the quantity of

[3]See Problems 6 and 10 at the end of the chapter for examples.

it demanded changes for two reasons: the substitution effect and the income effect. The substitution effect refers to the fact that when the price of a good goes up, substitutes for that good become relatively more attractive, causing some consumers to abandon the good for its substitutes.

The income effect refers to the fact that a price change makes the consumer either poorer or richer in real terms. Consider, for instance, the effect of a change in the price of one of the ice cream flavors in the preceding examples. At the original prices ($2 per pint for chocolate, $1 per pint for vanilla), Sarah's $400 annual ice cream budget enabled her to buy at most 200 pints per year of chocolate or 400 pints per year of vanilla. If the price of vanilla rose to $2 per pint, that would reduce not only the maximum amount of vanilla she could afford (from 400 to 200 pints per year) but also the maximum amount of chocolate she could afford in combination with any given amount of vanilla. For example, at the original price of $1 per pint for vanilla, Sarah could afford to buy 150 pints of chocolate while buying 100 pints of vanilla; but when the price of vanilla rises to $2, she can buy only 100 pints of chocolate while buying 100 pints of vanilla. As noted in Chapter 3, a reduction in real income shifts the demand curves for normal goods to the left.

The rational spending rule helps us see more clearly why a change in the price of one good affects demands for other goods. The rule requires that the ratio of marginal utility to price be the same for all goods. This means that if the price of one good goes up, the ratio of its current marginal utility to its new price will be lower than for other goods. Consumers can then increase their total utility by devoting smaller proportions of their incomes to that good and larger proportions to others.

How should Sarah respond to a reduction in the price of chocolate ice cream?

Suppose that Sarah's total ice cream budget is still $400 per year and the prices of the two flavors are again $2 per pint for chocolate and $1 per pint for vanilla. Her marginal utility from consuming each type varies with the amounts consumed, as shown in Figure 5.7. As we showed in the previous examples, she is currently buying 250 pints of vanilla and 75 pints of chocolate each year, which is the optimal combination for her at these prices. How should she reallocate her spending among the two flavors if the price of chocolate ice cream falls to $1 per pint?

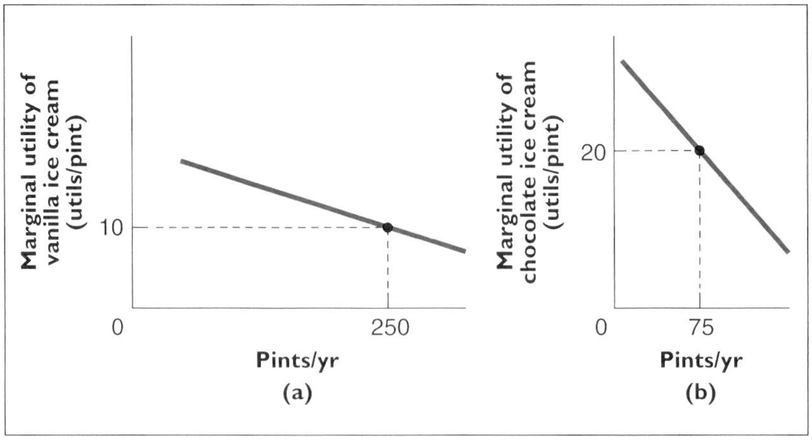

FIGURE 5.7
Marginal Utility Curves for Two Flavors of Ice Cream (IV).
At the current combination of flavors, marginal utility per dollar is the same for each flavor. When the price of chocolate falls, marginal utility per dollar becomes higher for chocolate than for vanilla. To redress this imbalance, Sarah should buy more chocolate and less vanilla.

Because the quantities shown in Figure 5.7 constitute the optimal combination of the two flavors for Sarah at the original prices, they must exactly satisfy the rational spending rule:

$$MU_C/P_C = (20 \text{ utils/pint})/(\$2\text{/pint}) = 10 \text{ utils/dollar}$$
$$= MU_V/P_V = (10 \text{ utils/pint})/(\$1\text{/pint}).$$

When the price of chocolate falls to $1 per pint, the original quantities will no longer satisfy the rational spending rule because the marginal utility per dollar for chocolate will suddenly be twice what it was before:

$$MU_C/P_C = (20 \text{ utils/pint})/(\$1/\text{pint}) = 20 \text{ utils/dollar} > MU_V/P_V = 10 \text{ utils/dollar.}$$

To redress this imbalance, Sarah must rearrange her spending on the two flavors in such a way as to increase the marginal utility per dollar for vanilla relative to the marginal utility per dollar for chocolate. And as we see in Figure 5.7, that will happen if she buys a larger quantity than before of chocolate and a smaller quantity than before of vanilla. ◆

EXERCISE 5.2

John spends all of his income on two goods: food and shelter. The price of food is $5 per pound and the price of shelter is $10 per square yard. At his current consumption levels, his marginal utilities for the two goods are 20 utils per pound and 30 utils per square yard, respectively. Is John maximizing his utility? If not, how should he reallocate his spending?

In Chapter 1 we saw that people often make bad decisions because they fail to appreciate the distinction between average and marginal costs and benefits. As the following example illustrates, this pitfall also arises when people attempt to apply the economist's model of utility maximization.

Should Eric consume more apples?

Eric gets a total of 1,000 utils per week from his consumption of apples and a total of 400 utils per week from his consumption of oranges. The price of apples is $2 each, the price of oranges is $1 each, and he consumes 50 apples and 50 oranges each week. True or false: Eric should consume more apples and fewer oranges.

Eric spends $100 per week on apples and $50 on oranges. He thus averages (1,000 utils/week)/($100/week) = 10 utils per dollar from his consumption of apples and (400 utils/week)/($50/week) = 8 utils per dollar from his consumption of oranges. Many might be tempted to respond that because Eric's average utility per dollar for apples is higher than for oranges, he should consume more apples. But knowing only his *average* utility per dollar for each good does not enable us to say whether his current combination is optimal. To make that determination, we need to compare Eric's *marginal* utility per dollar for each good. The information given simply doesn't permit us to make that comparison. ◆

RECAP	TRANSLATING WANTS INTO DEMAND

The Scarcity Principle challenges us to allocate our incomes among the various goods that are available so as to fulfill our desires to the greatest possible degree. The optimal combination of goods is the affordable combination that yields the highest total utility. For goods that are perfectly divisible, the rational spending rule tells us that the optimal combination is one for which the marginal utility per dollar is the same for each good. If this condition were not satisfied, the consumer could increase her utility by spending less on goods for which the marginal utility per dollar was lower and more on goods for which her marginal utility was higher.

Scarcity

APPLYING THE RATIONAL SPENDING RULE

The real payoff from learning the law of demand and the rational spending rule lies in using these abstract concepts to make sense of the world around you. To encourage you in your efforts to become an economic naturalist, we turn now to a sequence of examples in this vein.

SUBSTITUTION AT WORK

In the first of these examples, we focus on the role of substitution. When the price of a good or service goes up, rational consumers generally turn to less expensive substitutes. Can't meet the payments on a new car? Then buy a used one, or rent an apartment on a bus or subway line. French restaurants too pricey? Then go out for Chinese, or eat at home more often. National Football League tickets too high? Watch the game on television, or read a book. Can't afford a book? Check one out of the library, or download some reading matter from the internet. Once you begin to see substitution at work, you will be amazed by the number and richness of the examples that confront you every day.

Example 5.2
THE ECONOMIC NATURALIST

Why do the wealthy in Manhattan live in smaller houses than the wealthy in Seattle?

Microsoft cofounder Bill Gates lives in a 45,000-square-foot house in Seattle, Washington. His house is large even by the standards of Seattle, many of whose wealthy residents live in houses with more than 10,000 square feet of floor space. By contrast, persons of similar wealth in Manhattan rarely live in houses larger than 5,000 square feet. Why this difference?

For people trying to decide how large a house to buy, the most obvious difference between Manhattan and Seattle is the huge difference in housing prices. The cost of land alone is several times higher in Manhattan than in Seattle, and construction costs are also much higher. Although plenty of New Yorkers could *afford* to build a 45,000-square-foot mansion, Manhattan housing prices are so high that they simply choose to live in smaller houses and spend what they save in other ways—on lavish summer homes in eastern Long Island, for instance. New Yorkers also eat out and go to the theater more often than their wealthy counterparts in other U.S. cities. ●

Would Bill Gates build a 45,000-square-foot house if he lived in Manhattan?

An especially vivid illustration of substitution occurred during the late 1970s, when fuel shortages brought on by interruptions in the supply of oil from the Middle East led to sharp increases in the price of gasoline and other fuels. In a variety of ways—some straightforward, others remarkably ingenious—consumers changed their behavior to economize on the use of energy. They formed car pools; switched to public transportation; bought four-cylinder cars; moved closer to work; took fewer trips; turned down their thermostats; installed insulation, storm windows, and solar heaters; and bought more efficient appliances. Many people even moved farther south to escape high winter heating bills.

As the next example points out, consumers not only abandon a good in favor of substitutes when it gets more expensive, but they also return to that good when prices return to their original levels.

Example 5.3
THE ECONOMIC NATURALIST

Why did people turn to four-cylinder cars in the 1970s, only to shift back to six- and eight-cylinder cars in the 1990s?

In 1973, the price of gasoline was 38 cents per gallon. The following year the price shot up to 52 cents per gallon in the wake of a major disruption of oil supplies. A second disruption in 1979 drove the 1980 price to $1.19 per gallon. These sharp increases in the price of gasoline led to big increases in the demand for cars with four-cylinder engines, which delivered much better fuel economy than the six- and eight-cylinder cars most people had owned. After 1980, however, fuel supplies stabilized, and prices rose only slowly, reaching $1.40 per gallon by 1999. Yet despite the continued rise in the price of gasoline, the switch to smaller engines did not continue. By the late 1980s, the proportion of cars sold with six- and eight-cylinder engines began rising again. Why this reversal?

The key to explaining these patterns is to focus on changes in the **real price** of gasoline. When someone decides how big an automobile engine to choose, what matters is not the **nominal price** of gasoline, but the price of gasoline *relative* to all other goods. After all, for a consumer faced with a decision of whether to spend $1.40 for a gallon of gasoline, the important question is how much utility she could get from other things she could purchase with the same money. Even though the price of gasoline continued to rise slowly in nominal, or dollar, terms through the 1980s and 1990s, it declined sharply relative to the price of other goods. Indeed, in terms of real purchasing power, the 1999 price was actually slightly lower than the 1973 price. (That is, in 1999 $1.40 bought slightly fewer goods and services than 38 cents bought in 1973.) It is this decline in the real price of gasoline that accounts for the reversal of the trend toward smaller engines. ●

real price the dollar price of a good relative to the average dollar price of all other goods

nominal price the absolute price of a good in dollar terms

A sharp decline in the real price of gasoline also helps account for the explosive growth in sport utility vehicles in the 1990s. Almost 4 million SUVs were sold in the United States in 2001, up from only 750,000 in 1990. Some of them—like the Ford Excursion—weigh more than 7,500 pounds (three times as much as a Honda Civic) and get less than 10 miles per gallon on city streets. Vehicles like these would have been dismal failures during the 1970s, but they were by far the hottest sellers in the cheap-energy environment of 2001.

"We motored over to say hi!"

In 2004, gasoline prices yet again began to rise sharply in real terms, and by the summer of 2008 had reached almost $4 per gallon in some parts of the country. Just as expected, the patterns of vehicle purchases began to shift almost immediately. Large SUVs, in high demand just months earlier, began selling at deep discounts. And with long waiting lists for fuel-efficient hybrids such as the Toyota Prius, buyers not only seldom received discounts, they frequently paid even more than the sticker price.

Here's another closely related example of the influence of price on spending decisions.

Example 5.4
THE ECONOMIC NATURALIST

Does the quantity of horsepower demanded depend on gasoline prices?

Why are automobile engines smaller in England than in the United States?

In England, the most popular model of BMW's 5-series car is the 516i, whereas in the United States it is the 530i. The engine in the 516i is almost 50 percent smaller than the engine in the 530i. Why this difference?

In both countries, BMWs appeal to professionals with roughly similar incomes, so the difference cannot be explained by differences in purchasing power. Rather, it is the direct result of the heavy tax the British levy on gasoline. With tax, a gallon of gasoline sells for more than $8 in England—about two times the price in the United States. This difference encourages the British to choose smaller, more fuel-efficient engines. ●

THE IMPORTANCE OF INCOME DIFFERENCES

The most obvious difference between the rich and the poor is that the rich have higher incomes. To explain why the wealthy generally buy larger houses than the poor, we need not assume that the wealthy feel more strongly about housing than the poor. A much simpler explanation is that the total utility from housing, as with most other goods, increases with the amount that one consumes.

As the next example illustrates, income influences the demand not only for housing and other goods, but also for quality of service.

Example 5.5
THE ECONOMIC NATURALIST

Why are lines longer in low-income neighborhoods?

Why are waiting lines longer in poorer neighborhoods?

As part of a recent promotional campaign, a Baskin-Robbins retailer offered free ice cream at two of its franchise stores. The first was located in a high-income neighborhood, the second in a low-income neighborhood. Why was the queue for free ice cream longer in the low-income neighborhood?

Residents of both neighborhoods must decide whether to stand in line for free ice cream or go to some other store and avoid the line by paying the usual price. If we make the plausible assumption that people with higher incomes are more willing than others to pay to avoid standing in line, we should expect to see shorter lines in the high-income neighborhood. ●

Similar reasoning helps explain why lines are shorter in grocery stores that cater to high-income consumers. Keeping lines short at *any* grocery store means hiring more clerks, which means charging higher prices. High-income consumers are more likely than others to be willing to pay for shorter lines.

RECAP	APPLYING THE RATIONAL SPENDING RULE

Application of the rational spending rule highlights the important roles of income and substitution in explaining differences in consumption patterns—among individuals, among communities, and across time. The rule also highlights the fact that real, as opposed to nominal, prices and income are what matter. The demand for a good falls when the real price of a substitute falls or the real price of a complement rises.

INDIVIDUAL AND MARKET DEMAND CURVES

If we know what each individual's demand curve for a good looks like, how can we use that information to construct the market demand curve for the good? We must add the individual demand curves together, a process that is straightforward but requires care.

HORIZONTAL ADDITION

Suppose that there are only two buyers—Smith and Jones—in the market for canned tuna and that their demand curves are as shown in Figure 5.8(a) and (b). To construct the market demand curve for canned tuna, we simply announce a sequence of prices and then add the quantity demanded by each buyer at each price. For example, at a price of 40 cents per can, Smith demands six cans per week (a) and Jones demands two cans per week (b), for a market demand of eight cans per week (c).

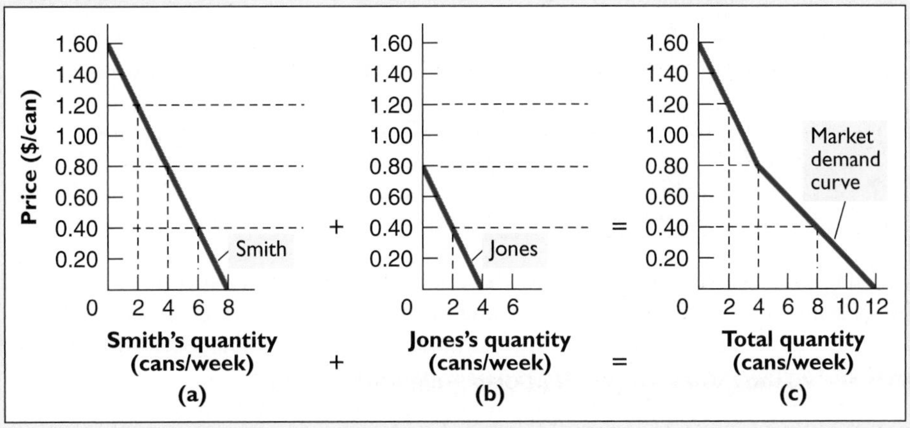

FIGURE 5.8
Individual and Market Demand Curves for Canned Tuna.
The quantity demanded at any price on the market demand curve (c) is the sum of the individual quantities demanded at that price, (a) and (b).

The process of adding individual demand curves to get the market demand curve is known as *horizontal addition,* a term used to emphasize that we are adding quantities, which are measured on the horizontal axes of individual demand curves.

EXERCISE 5.3

The buyers' side of the market for movie tickets consists of two consumers whose demands are as shown in the diagram below. Graph the market demand curve for this market.

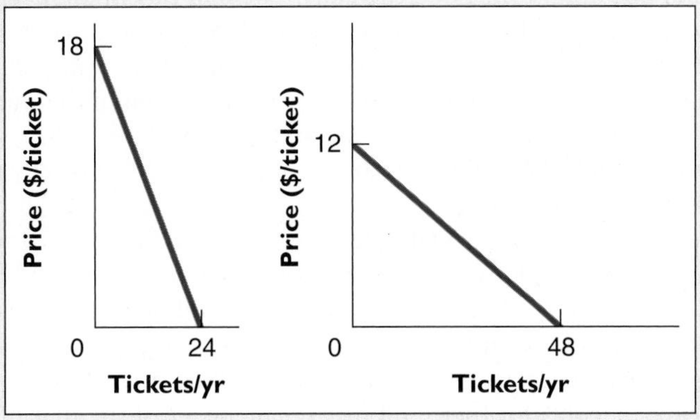

Figure 5.9 illustrates the special case in which each of 1,000 consumers in the market has the same demand curve (a). To get the market demand curve (b) in this case, we simply multiply each quantity on the representative individual demand curve by 1,000.

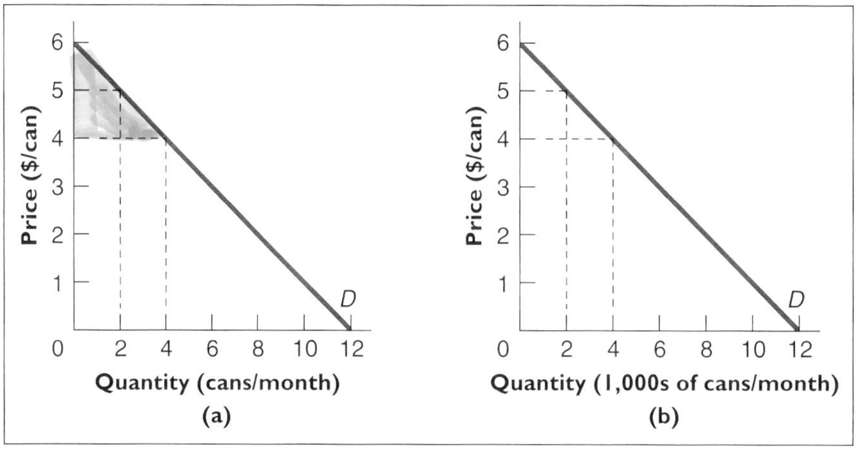

FIGURE 5.9
The Individual and Market Demand Curves When All Buyers Have Identical Demand Curves. When individual demand curves are identical, we get the market demand curve (b) by multiplying each quantity on the individual demand curve (a) by the number of consumers in the market.

DEMAND AND CONSUMER SURPLUS

In Chapter 1 we first encountered the concept of economic surplus, which in a buyer's case is the difference between the most she would have been willing to pay for a product and the amount she actually pays for it. The economic surplus received by buyers is often referred to as **consumer surplus**.

consumer surplus the difference between a buyer's reservation price for a product and the price actually paid

The term *consumer surplus* sometimes refers to the surplus received by a single buyer in a transaction. On other occasions, it is used to denote the total surplus received by all buyers in a market or collection of markets.

CALCULATING CONSUMER SURPLUS

For performing cost-benefit analysis, it is often important to be able to measure the total consumer surplus received by all buyers who participate in a given market. For example, a road linking a mountain village and a port city would create a new market for fresh fish in the mountain village; in deciding whether the road should be built, analysts would want to count as one of its benefits the gains that would be reaped by buyers in this new market.

To illustrate how economists actually measure consumer surplus, we'll consider a hypothetical market for a good with 11 potential buyers, each of whom can buy a maximum of one unit of the good each day. The first potential buyer's reservation price for the product is $11; the second buyer's reservation price is $10; the third buyer's reservation price is $9; and so on. The demand curve for this market will have the staircase shape shown in Figure 5.10. We can think of this curve as the digital counterpart of traditional analog demand curves. (If the units shown on the horizontal axis were fine enough, this digital curve would be visually indistinguishable from its analog counterparts.)

Suppose the good whose demand curve is shown in Figure 5.10 were available at a price of $6 per unit. How much total consumer surplus would buyers in this market reap? At a price of $6, six units per day would be sold in this market. The buyer of the sixth unit would receive no economic surplus since his reservation price for that unit was exactly $6, the same as its selling price. But the first five buyers would reap a surplus for their purchases. The buyer of the first unit, for example, would have been willing to pay as much as $11 for it, but since she would pay only $6, she would receive a surplus of exactly $5. The buyer of the second unit, who would have been willing to pay as much as $10, would receive a surplus of $4. The surplus would be $3 for the buyer of the third unit, $2 for the buyer of the fourth unit, and $1 for the buyer of the fifth unit.

If we add all the buyers' surpluses together, we get a total of $15 of consumer surplus each day. That surplus corresponds to the shaded area shown in Figure 5.11.

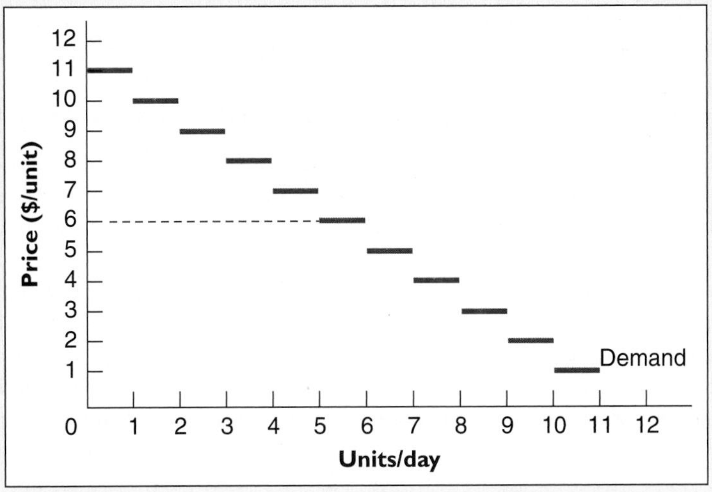

FIGURE 5.10
A Market with a "Digital" Demand Curve.
When a product can be sold only in whole-number amounts, its demand curve has the stair-step shape shown.

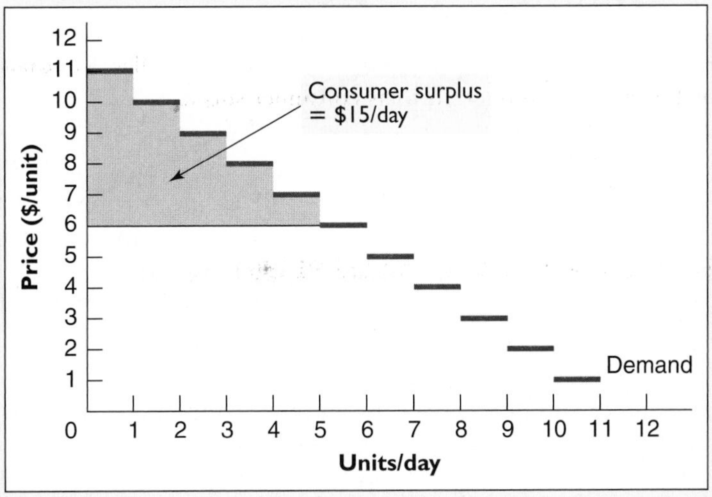

FIGURE 5.11
Consumer Surplus.
Consumer surplus (shaded region) is the cumulative difference between the most that buyers are willing to pay for each unit and the price they actually pay.

EXERCISE 5.4

Calculate consumer surplus for a demand curve like the one just described except that the buyers' reservation prices for each unit are $2 higher than before.

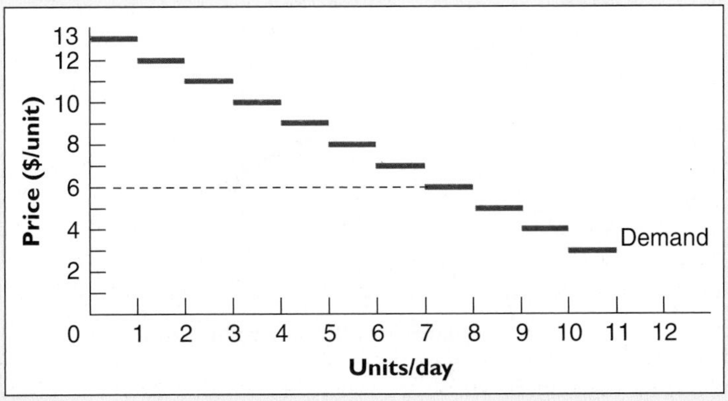

Now suppose we want to calculate consumer surplus in a market with a conventional straight-line demand curve. As the following example illustrates, this task is a simple extension of the method used for digital demand curves.

How much do buyers benefit from their participation in the market for milk?

Consider the market for milk whose demand and supply curves are shown in Figure 5.12, which has an equilibrium price of $2 per gallon and an equilibrium quantity of 4,000 gallons per day. How much consumer surplus do the buyers in this market reap?

In Figure 5.12, note first that, as in Figure 5.11, the last unit exchanged each day generates no consumer surplus at all. Note also that for all milk sold up to 4,000 gallons per day, buyers receive consumer surplus, just as in Figure 5.11. For these buyers, consumer surplus is the cumulative difference between the most they would be willing to pay for milk (as measured on the demand curve) and the price they actually pay.

FIGURE 5.12
Supply and Demand in the Market for Milk.
For the supply and demand curves shown, the equilibrium price of milk is $2 per gallon and the equilibrium quantity is 4,000 gallons per day.

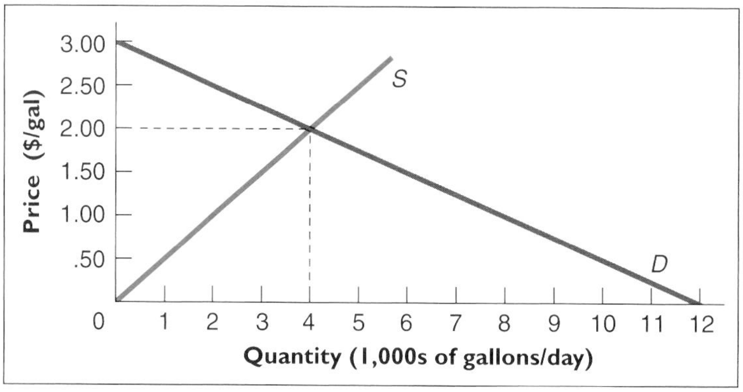

Total consumer surplus received by buyers in the milk market is thus the shaded triangle between the demand curve and the market price in Figure 5.13. Note that this area is a right triangle whose vertical arm is h = $1/gallon and whose horizontal arm is b = 4,000 gallons/day. And since the area of any triangle is equal to $(1/2)bh$, consumer surplus in this market is equal to

(1/2)(4,000 gallons/day)($1/gallon) = $2,000/day.

FIGURE 5.13
Consumer Surplus in the Market for Milk.
Consumer surplus is the area of the shaded triangle ($2,000/day).

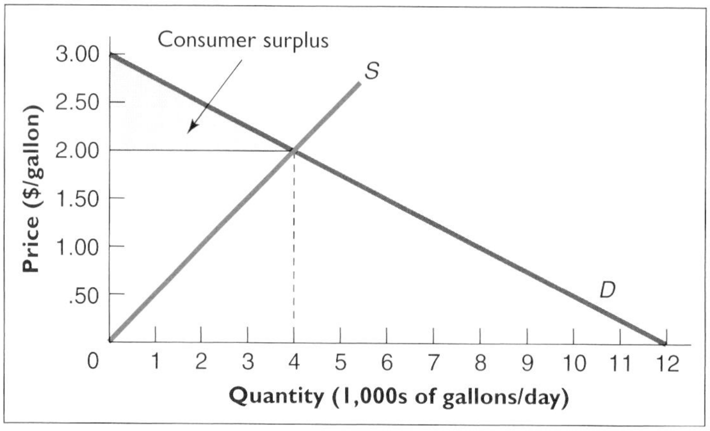

A useful way of thinking about consumer surplus is to ask what is the highest price consumers would pay, in the aggregate, for the right to continue participating in this milk market. The answer is $2,000 per day, since that is the amount by which their combined benefits exceed their combined costs. ◆

As discussed in Chapter 3, the demand curve for a good can be interpreted either horizontally or vertically. The horizontal interpretation tells us, for each price, the total quantity that consumers wish to buy at that price. The vertical interpretation tells us, for each quantity, the most a buyer would be willing to pay for the good at that quantity. For the purpose of computing consumer surplus, we rely on the vertical interpretation of the demand curve. The value on the vertical axis that corresponds to each point along the demand curve corresponds to the marginal buyer's reservation price for the good. Consumer surplus is the cumulative sum of the differences between these reservation prices and the market price. It is the area bounded above by the demand curve and bounded below by the market price.

SUMMARY

- The rational consumer allocates income among different goods so that the marginal utility gained from the last dollar spent on each good is the same. This rational spending rule gives rise to the law of demand, which states that people do less of what they want to do as the cost of doing it rises. Here, "cost" refers to the sum of all monetary and nonmonetary sacrifices—explicit and implicit—that must be made in order to engage in the activity. **LO1, LO2**
- The ability to substitute one good for another is an important factor behind the law of demand. Because virtually every good or service has at least some substitutes, economists prefer to speak in terms of wants rather than needs. We face choices, and describing our demands as needs is misleading because it suggests we have no options. **LO2**
- For normal goods, the income effect is a second important reason that demand curves slope downward. When the price of such a good falls, not only does it become more attractive relative to its substitutes, but the consumer also acquires more real purchasing power, and this, too, augments the quantity demanded. **LO2**
- The demand curve is a schedule that shows the amounts of a good people want to buy at various prices. Demand curves can be used to summarize the price–quantity relationship for a single individual, but more commonly we employ them to summarize that relationship for an entire market. At any quantity along a demand curve, the corresponding price represents the amount by which the consumer (or consumers) would benefit from having an additional unit of the product. For this reason, the demand curve is sometimes described as a summary of the benefit side of the market. **LO3**
- Consumer surplus is a quantitative measure of the amount by which buyers benefit as a result of their ability to purchase goods at the market price. It is the area between the demand curve and the market price. **LO4**

KEY TERMS

consumer surplus (140)
law of demand (124)
law of diminishing marginal utility (129)
marginal utility (128)
nominal price (137)
optimal combination of goods (132)
rational spending rule (133)
real price (137)

REVIEW QUESTIONS

1. Why do economists prefer to speak of demands arising out of "wants" rather than "needs"? **LO1**
2. Explain why economists consider the concept of utility useful, even if psychologists cannot measure it precisely. **LO1**

3. Why does the law of diminishing marginal utility encourage people to spread their spending across many different types of goods? **LO2**
4. Explain why a good or service that is offered at a monetary price of zero is unlikely to be a truly "free" good from an economic perspective. **LO2**
5. Give an example of a good that you have consumed for which your marginal utility increased with the amount of it you consumed. **LO1**

PROBLEMS

1. In which type of restaurant do you expect the service to be more prompt and courteous: an expensive gourmet restaurant or an inexpensive diner? Explain. **LO2**
2. You are having lunch at an all-you-can-eat buffet. If you are rational, what should be your marginal utility from the last morsel of food you swallow? **LO2**
3. Martha's current marginal utility from consuming orange juice is 75 utils per ounce and her marginal utility from consuming coffee is 50 utils per ounce. If orange juice costs 25 cents per ounce and coffee costs 20 cents per ounce, is Martha maximizing her total utility from the two beverages? If so, explain how you know. If not, how should she rearrange her spending? **LO2**
4. Toby's current marginal utility from consuming peanuts is 100 utils per ounce and his marginal utility from consuming cashews is 200 utils per ounce. If peanuts cost 10 cents per ounce and cashews cost 25 cents per ounce, is Toby maximizing his total utility from the kinds of nuts? If so, explain how you know. If not, how should he rearrange his spending? **LO2**
5. Sue gets a total of 20 utils per week from her consumption of pizza and a total of 40 utils per week from her consumption of yogurt. The price of pizza is \$1 per slice, the price of yogurt is \$1 per cup, and she consumes 10 slices of pizza and 20 cups of yogurt each week. True or false: Sue is consuming the optimal combination of pizza and yogurt. **LO2**
6. Ann lives in Princeton, New Jersey, and commutes by train each day to her job in New York City (20 round trips per month). When the price of a round trip goes up from \$10 to \$20, she responds by consuming exactly the same number of trips as before, while spending \$200 per month less on restaurant meals. **LO2**
   a. Does the fact that her quantity of train travel is completely unresponsive to the price increase imply that Ann is not a rational consumer?
   b. Explain why an increase in train travel might affect the amount she spends on restaurant meals.
7. For the demand curve shown, find the total amount of consumer surplus that results in the gasoline market if gasoline sells for \$2 per gallon. **LO4**

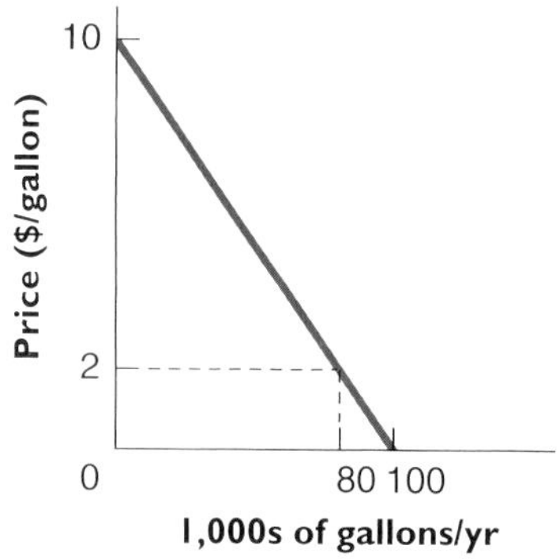

8. Tom has a weekly allowance of \$24, all of which he spends on pizza and movie rentals, whose prices are \$6 per slice and \$3 per rental, respectively. If slices of pizza and movie rentals are available only in whole-number amounts, list all possible combinations of the two goods that Tom can purchase each week with his allowance. **LO2**

9.* Refer to problem 8. Tom's total utility is the sum of the utility he derives from pizza and movie rentals. If these utilities vary with the amounts consumed as shown in the table, and pizzas and movie rentals are again consumable only in whole-number amounts, how many pizzas and how many movie rentals should Tom consume each week? **LO2**

Pizzas/week	Utils/week from pizza	Movie rentals/ week	Utils/week from rentals
0	0	0	0
1	20	1	40
2	38	2	46
3	54	3	50
4	68	4	54
5	80	5	56
6	90	6	57
7	98	7	57
8	104	8	57

10.* The buyers' side of the market for amusement park tickets consists of two consumers whose demands are as shown in the diagram below. **LO3**

a. Graph the market demand curve for this market.

b. Calculate the total consumer surplus in the amusement park market if tickets sell for \$12 each.

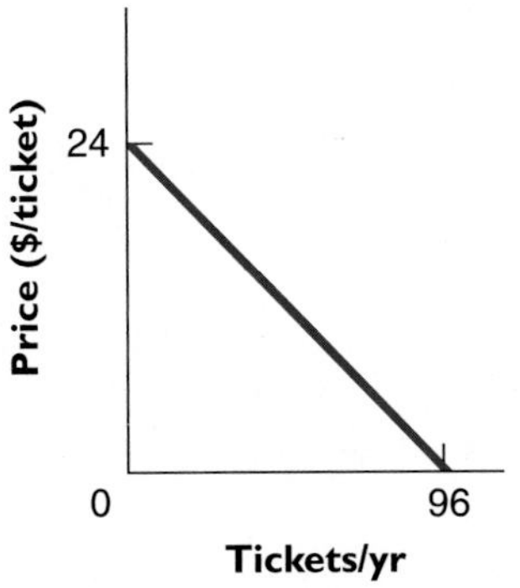

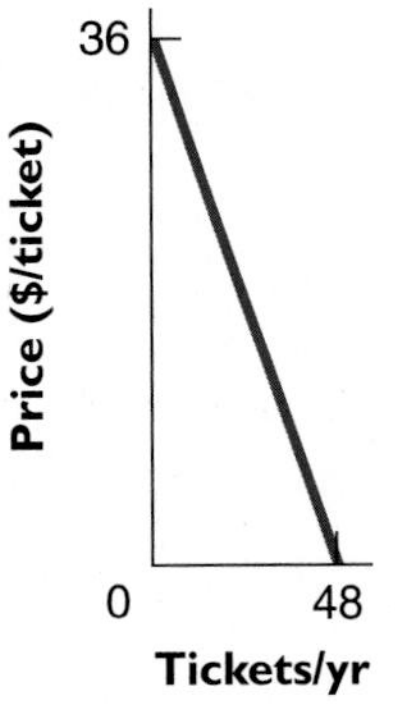

*Problems marked with an asterisk (*) are more difficult.

ANSWERS TO IN-CHAPTER EXERCISES

5.1 The combination of 300 pints per year of vanilla (\$300) and 50 pints of chocolate (\$100) costs a total of \$400, which is exactly equal to Sarah's ice cream budget. **LO2**

5.2 The rational spending rule requires $MU_F/P_F = MU_S/P_S$ where MU_F and MU_S are John's marginal utilities from food and shelter and P_F and P_S are the prices of food and shelter, respectively. At John's original combination,

$MU_F/P_F = 4$ utils per dollar and $MU_S/P_S = 3$ utils per dollar. John should thus spend more of his income on food and less on shelter. **LO2**

5.3 Adding the two individual demand curves, (a) and (b), horizontally yields the market demand curve (c): **LO3**

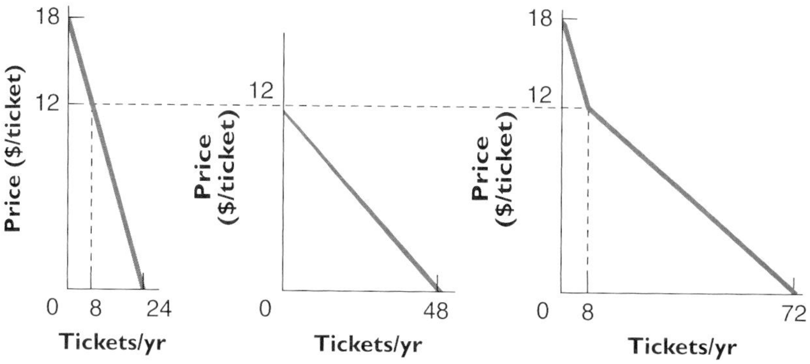

5.4 Consumer surplus is now the new shaded area, \$28 per day. **LO4**

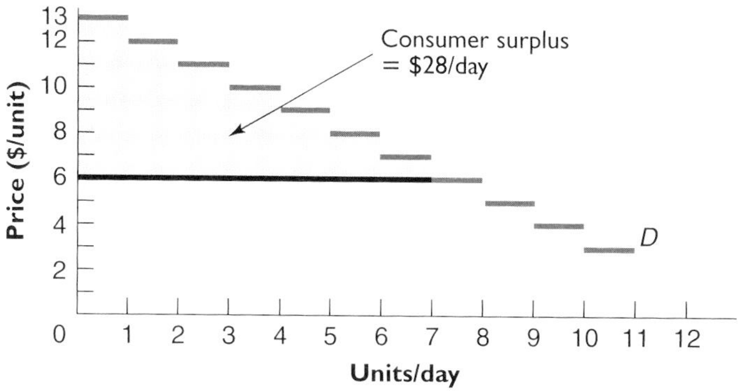

CHAPTER

6

Perfectly Competitive Supply

LEARNING OBJECTIVES

After reading this chapter, you should be able to:

1. Identify the firm's demand curve, and explain its derivation.
2. Discuss the different types of costs that underlie the firm's production decisions.
3. Determine why price equals marginal cost at the profit-maximizing output level.
4. Construct the industry supply curve from the supply curves of individual firms.
5. Define and calculate producer surplus.

Cars that took more than 50 hours to assemble in the 1970s are now built in less than 8 hours. Similar productivity growth has occurred in many other manufacturing industries. Yet in many service industries, productivity has grown only slowly, if at all. For example, the London Philharmonic Orchestra performs Beethoven's Fifth Symphony with no fewer musicians today than it did in 1850. And it still takes a barber about half an hour to cut someone's hair, just as it always has.

Given the spectacular growth in manufacturing workers' productivity, it is no surprise that their real wages have risen more than fivefold during the last century. But why have real wages for service workers risen just as much? If barbers and musicians are no more productive than they were at the turn of the century, why are they now paid five times as much?

An answer is suggested by the observation that the opportunity cost of pursuing any given occupation is the most one could have earned in some other occupation. Most people who become barbers or musicians could instead have chosen jobs in manufacturing. If workers in service industries were not paid roughly as much as they could have earned in other occupations, many of them would not have been willing to work in service industries in the first place.

The trajectories of wages in manufacturing and service industries illustrate the intimate link between the prices at which goods and services are offered for sale in the market and the opportunity cost of the resources required to produce them.

In the previous chapter, we saw that the demand curve is a schedule that tells how many units buyers wish to purchase at different prices. Our task here is to gain insight into the factors that shape the supply curve, the schedule that tells how many units suppliers wish to sell at different prices.

Cost-Benefit

Although the demand side and the supply side of the market are different in several ways, many of these differences are superficial. Indeed, the behavior of both buyers and sellers is, in an important sense, fundamentally the same. After all, the two groups confront essentially similar questions—in the buyer's case, "Should I buy another unit?" and in the seller's, "Should I sell another unit?" What is more, buyers and sellers use the same criterion for answering these questions. Thus, a rational consumer will buy another unit if its benefit exceeds its cost and a rational seller will sell another unit if the cost of making it is less than the extra revenue he can get from selling it (the familiar Cost-Benefit Principle again).

THINKING ABOUT SUPPLY: THE IMPORTANCE OF OPPORTUNITY COST

Do you live in a state that requires refundable soft drink container deposits? If so, you've probably noticed that some people always redeem their own containers while other people pass up this opportunity, leaving their used containers to be recycled by others. Recycling used containers is a service and its production obeys the same logic that applies to the production of other goods and services. The following sequence of recycling examples shows how the supply curve for a good or service is rooted in the individual's choice of whether to produce it.

Why are barbers paid five times as much now as in 1900, even though they can't cut hair any faster than they could then?

How much time should Harry spend recycling soft drink containers?

Harry is trying to decide how to divide his time between his job as a dishwasher in the dining hall, which pays $6 an hour for as many hours as he chooses to work, and gathering soft drink containers to redeem for deposit, in which case his pay depends on both the deposit per container and the number of containers he finds. Earnings aside, Harry is indifferent between the two tasks, and the number of containers he will find depends, as shown in the table below, on the number of hours per day he searches:

Search time (hours/day)	Total number of containers found	Additional number of containers found
0	0	
		600
1	600	
		400
2	1,000	
		300
3	1,300	
		200
4	1,500	
		100
5	1,600	

If the containers may be redeemed for 2 cents each, how many hours should Harry spend searching for containers?

For each additional hour Harry spends searching for soft drink containers, he loses the $6 he could have earned as a dishwasher. This is his hourly opportunity cost of searching for soft drink containers. His benefit from each hour spent searching for containers is the number of additional containers he finds (shown in column 3 of the table) times the deposit he collects per container. Since he can redeem each container for 2 cents, his first hour spent collecting containers will yield earnings of 600($0.02) = $12, or $6 more than he could have earned as a dishwasher.

By the Cost-Benefit Principle, then, Harry should spend his first hour of work each day searching for soft drink containers rather than washing dishes. A second hour searching for containers will yield 400 additional containers, for additional earnings of $8, so it too satisfies the cost-benefit test. A third hour spent searching yields 300 additional containers, for 300($0.02) = $6 of additional earnings. Since this is exactly what Harry could have earned washing dishes, he is indifferent between spending his third hour of work each day on one task or the other. For the sake of discussion, however, we'll assume that he resolves ties in favor of searching for containers, in which case he will spend three hours each day searching for containers. ◆

Cost-Benefit

What is the lowest redemption price that would induce Harry to spend at least one hour per day recycling? Since he will find 600 containers in his first hour of search, a one-cent deposit on each container would enable him to match his $6 per hour opportunity cost. More generally, if the redemption price is p, and the next hour spent searching yields ΔQ additional containers, then Harry's additional earnings from searching the additional hour will be $p(\Delta Q)$. This means that the smallest redemption price that will lead Harry to search another hour must satisfy the equation

$$p(\Delta Q) = \$6. \tag{6.1}$$

How high would the redemption price of containers have to be to induce Harry to search for a second hour? Since he can find $\Delta Q = 400$ additional containers if he searches for a second hour, the smallest redemption price that will lead him to do so must satisfy $p(400) = \$6$, which solves for $p = 1.5$ cents.

EXERCISE 6.1

In the example above, calculate the lowest container redemption prices that will lead Harry to search a third, fourth, and fifth hour.

By searching for soft drink containers, Harry becomes, in effect, a supplier of container-recycling services. In Exercise 6.1, we saw that Harry's reservation prices for his third, fourth, and fifth hours of container search are 2, 3, and 6 cents, respectively. Having calculated these reservation prices, we can now plot his supply curve of container-recycling services. This curve, which plots the redemption price per container on the vertical axis and the number of containers recycled each day on the horizontal axis, is shown in Figure 6.1. Harry's individual supply curve of

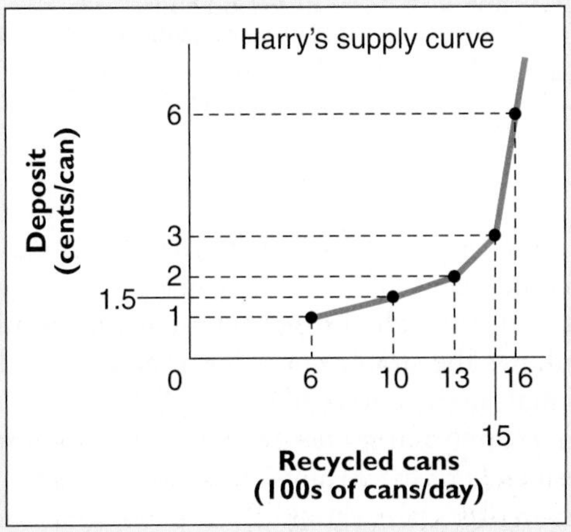

FIGURE 6.1
An Individual Supply Curve for Recycling Services.
When the deposit price increases, it becomes attractive to abandon alternative pursuits to spend more time searching for soft drink containers.

container-recycling services tells us the number of containers he is willing to recycle at various redemption prices.

The supply curve shown in Figure 6.1 is upward-sloping, just like those we saw in Chapter 3. There are exceptions to this general rule, but sellers of most goods will offer higher quantities at higher prices.

INDIVIDUAL AND MARKET SUPPLY CURVES

The relationship between the individual and market supply curves for a product is analogous to the relationship between the individual and market demand curves. The quantity that corresponds to a given price on the market demand curve is the sum of the quantities demanded at that price by all individual buyers in the market. Likewise, the quantity that corresponds to any given price on the market supply curve is the sum of the quantities supplied at that price by all individual sellers in the market.

Suppose, for example, that the supply side of the recycling-services market consists only of Harry and his identical twin, Barry, whose individual supply curve is the same as Harry's. To generate the market supply curve, we first put the individual supply curves side by side, as shown in Figure 6.2(a) and (b). We then announce a price, and for that price add the individual quantities supplied to obtain the total quantity supplied in the market. Thus, at a price of 3 cents per container, both Harry and Barry wish to recycle 1,500 cans per day, so the total market supply at that price is 3,000 cans per day. Proceeding in like manner for a sequence of prices, we generate the market supply curve for recycling services shown in Figure 6.2(c). This is the same process of horizontal summation by which we generated market demand curves from individual demand curves in the previous chapter.

FIGURE 6.2
The Market Supply Curve for Recycling Services.
To generate the market supply curve (c) from the individual supply curves (a) and (b), we add the individual supply curves horizontally.

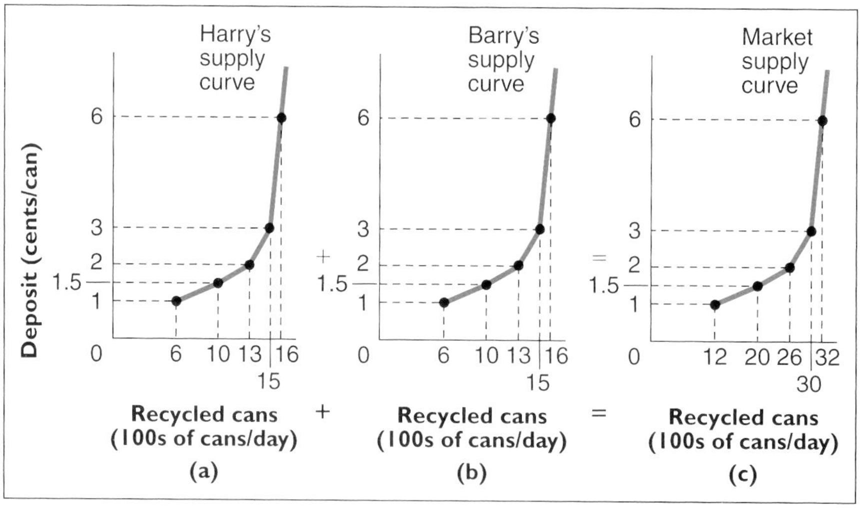

Alternatively, if there were many suppliers with individual supply curves identical to Harry's, we could generate the market supply curve by simply multiplying each quantity value on the individual supply curve by the number of suppliers. For instance, Figure 6.3 shows the supply curve for a market in which there are 1,000 suppliers with individual supply curves like Harry's.

Increasing Opportunity Cost

Why do individual supply curves tend to be upward-sloping? One explanation is suggested by the Principle of Increasing Opportunity Cost, or the Low-Hanging-Fruit Principle. Container recyclers should always look first for the containers that

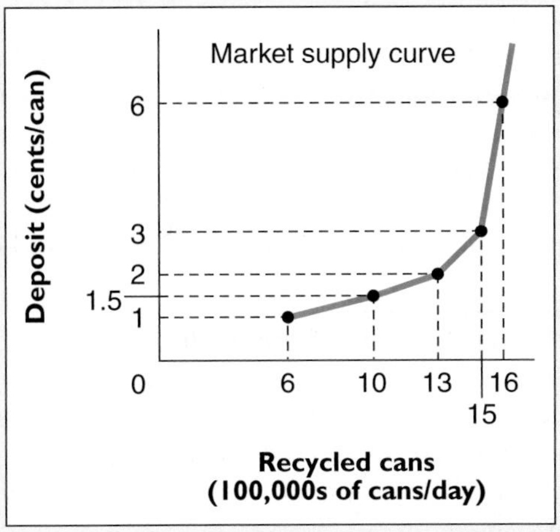

FIGURE 6.3
The Market Supply Curve with 1,000 Identical Sellers.
To generate the market supply curve for a market with 1,000 identical sellers, we simply multiply each quantity value on the individual supply curve by 1,000.

are easiest to find—such as those in plain view in readily accessible locations. As the redemption price rises, it will pay to incur the additional cost of searching farther from the beaten path.

If all individuals have identical upward-sloping supply curves, the market supply curve will be upward-sloping as well. But there is an important additional reason for the positive slope of market supply curves: Individual suppliers generally differ with respect to their opportunity costs of supplying the product. (The Principle of Increasing Opportunity Cost applies not only to each individual searcher, but also *across* individuals.) Thus, whereas people facing unattractive employment opportunities in other occupations may be willing to recycle soft drink containers even when the redemption price is low, those with more attractive options will recycle only if the redemption price is relatively high.

Increasing Opportunity Cost

In summary, then, the upward slope of the supply curve reflects the fact that costs tend to rise at the margin when producers expand production, partly because each individual exploits her most attractive opportunities first, but also because different potential sellers face different opportunity costs.

PROFIT-MAXIMIZING FIRMS IN PERFECTLY COMPETITIVE MARKETS

To explore the nature of the supply curve of a product more fully, we must say more about the goals of the organizations that supply the product and the kind of economic environment in which they operate. In virtually every economy, goods and services are produced by a variety of organizations that pursue a host of different motives. The Red Cross supplies blood because its organizers and donors want to help people in need; the local government fixes potholes because the mayor was elected on a promise to do so; karaoke singers perform because they like public attention; and car-wash employees are driven primarily by the hope of making enough money to pay their rent.

PROFIT MAXIMIZATION

Notwithstanding this rich variety of motives, *most* goods and services that are offered for sale in a market economy are sold by private firms whose main reason for existing is to earn **profit** for their owners. A firm's profit is the difference between the total revenue it receives from the sale of its product and all costs it incurs in producing it.

profit the total revenue a firm receives from the sale of its product minus all costs—explicit and implicit—incurred in producing it *profit-maximizing firm* a firm whose primary goal is to maximize the difference between its total revenues and total costs

perfectly competitive market a market in which no individual supplier has significant influence on the market price of the product

price taker a firm that has no influence over the price at which it sells its product

A **profit-maximizing firm** is one whose primary goal is to maximize the amount of profit it earns. The supply curves that economists use in standard supply and demand theory are based on the assumption that goods are sold by profit-maximizing firms in **perfectly competitive markets**, which are markets in which individual firms have no influence over the market prices of the products they sell. Because of their inability to influence market price, perfectly competitive firms are often described as **price takers**.

The following four conditions are characteristic of markets that are perfectly competitive:

1. *All firms sell the same standardized product.* Although this condition is almost never literally satisfied, it holds as a rough approximation for many markets. Thus, the markets for concrete building blocks of a given size, or for apples of a given variety, may be described in this way. This condition implies that buyers are willing to switch from one seller to another if by so doing they can obtain a lower price.

2. *The market has many buyers and sellers, each of which buys or sells only a small fraction of the total quantity exchanged.* This condition implies that individual buyers and sellers will be price takers, regarding the market price of the product as a fixed number beyond their control. For example, a single farmer's decision to plant fewer acres of wheat would have no appreciable impact on the market price of wheat, just as an individual consumer's decision to become a vegetarian would have no perceptible effect on the price of beef.

3. *Productive resources are mobile.* This condition implies that if a potential seller identifies a profitable business opportunity in a market, he or she will be able to obtain the labor, capital, and other productive resources necessary to enter that market. By the same token, sellers who are dissatisfied with the opportunities they confront in a given market are free to leave that market and employ their resources elsewhere.

4. *Buyers and sellers are well informed.* This condition implies that buyers and sellers are aware of the relevant opportunities available to them. If that were not so, buyers would be unable to seek out sellers who charge the lowest prices, and sellers would have no means of deploying their resources in the markets in which they would earn the most profit.

The market for wheat closely approximates a perfectly competitive market. The market for operating systems for desktop computers, however, does not. More than 90 percent of desktop operating systems are sold by Microsoft, giving the company enough influence in that market to have significant control over the price it charges. For example, if it were to raise the price of its latest edition of Windows by, say, 20 percent, some consumers might switch to Macintosh or Linux, and others might postpone their next upgrade; but many—perhaps even most—would continue with their plans to buy Windows.

By contrast, if an individual wheat farmer were to charge even a few cents more than the current market price for a bushel of wheat, he wouldn't be able to sell any of his wheat at all. And since he can sell as much wheat as he wishes at the market price, he has no motive to charge less.

THE DEMAND CURVE FACING A PERFECTLY COMPETITIVE FIRM

From the perspective of an individual firm in a perfectly competitive market, what does the demand curve for its product look like? Since it can sell as much or as little as it wishes at the prevailing market price, the demand curve for its product is

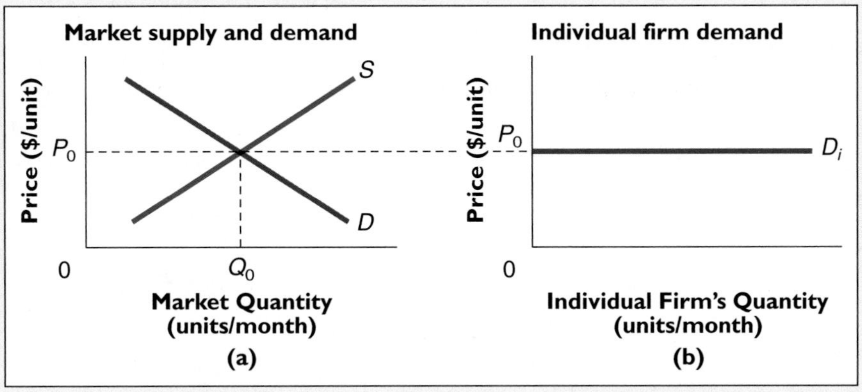

FIGURE 6.4
The Demand Curve Facing a Perfectly Competitive Firm.
The market demand and supply curves intersect to determine the market price of the product (a). The individual firm's demand curve, D_i (b), is a horizontal line at the market price.

perfectly elastic at the market price. Figure 6.4(a) shows the market demand and supply curves intersecting to determine a market price of P_0. Figure 6.4(b) shows the product demand curve, D_i, as seen by any individual firm in this market, a horizontal line at the market price level P_0.

Many of the conclusions of the standard supply and demand model also hold for **imperfectly competitive firms**—those firms, like Microsoft, that have at least some ability to vary their own prices. But certain other conclusions do not, as we shall see when we examine the behavior of such firms more closely in Chapter 8.

imperfectly competitive firm a firm that has at least some control over the market price of its product

Since a perfectly competitive firm has no control over the market price of its product, it needn't worry about choosing the level at which to set that price. As we've seen, the equilibrium market price in a competitive market comes from the intersection of the industry supply and demand curves. The challenge confronting the perfectly competitive firm is to choose its output level so that it makes as much profit as it can at that price. As we investigate how the competitive firm responds to this challenge, we'll see that some costs are more important than others.

PRODUCTION IN THE SHORT RUN

To gain a deeper understanding of the origins of the supply curve, it is helpful to consider a perfectly competitive firm confronting the decision of how much to produce. The firm in question is a small company that makes glass bottles. To keep things simple, suppose that the silica required for making bottles is available free of charge from a nearby desert and that the only costs incurred by the firm are the wages it pays its employees and the lease payment on its bottle-making machine. The employees and the machine are the firm's only two **factors of production**—inputs used to produce goods and services. In more complex examples, factors of production also might include land, structures, entrepreneurship, and possibly others, but for the moment we consider only labor and capital.

factor of production an input used in the production of a good or service

When we refer to the **short run**, we mean a period of time during which at least some of the firm's factors of production cannot be varied. For our bottle maker, we will assume that the number of employees can be varied on short notice but that the capacity of its bottle-making machine can be altered only with significant delay. For this firm, then, the short run is simply that period of time during which the firm cannot alter the capacity of its bottle-making machine. By contrast, when we speak of the **long run**, we refer to a time period of sufficient length that all the firm's factors of production are variable.

short run a period of time sufficiently short that at least some of the firm's factors of production are fixed

long run a period of time of sufficient length that all the firm's factors of production are variable

Table 6.1 shows how the company's bottle production depends on the number of hours its employees spend on the job each day. The output–employment relationship described in Table 6.1 exhibits a pattern that is common to many such

TABLE 6.1
Employment and Output for a Glass Bottle Maker

Total number of employees per day	Total number of bottles per day
0	0
1	80
2	200
3	260
4	300
5	330
6	350
7	362

law of diminishing returns a property of the relationship between the amount of a good or service produced and the amount of a variable factor required to produce it; it says that when some factors of production are fixed, increased production of the good eventually requires ever-larger increases in the variable factor

fixed factor of production an input whose quantity cannot be altered in the short run

variable factor of production an input whose quantity can be altered in the short run

fixed cost the sum of all payments made to the firm's fixed factors of production

variable cost the sum of all payments made to the firm's variable factors of production

total cost the sum of all payments made to the firm's fixed and variable factors of production

marginal cost as output changes from one level to another, the change in total cost divided by the corresponding change in output

relationships. Each time we add an additional unit of labor, output grows, but beyond some point the additional output that results from each additional unit of labor begins to diminish. Note in the right column, for example, that output gains begin to diminish with the third employee. Economists refer to this pattern as the **law of diminishing returns,** and it always refers to situations in which at least some factors of production are fixed. Here, the **fixed factor** is the bottle-making machine, and the **variable factor** is labor. In the context of this example, the law of diminishing returns says simply that successive increases in the labor input eventually yield smaller and smaller increments in bottle output. (Strictly speaking, the law ought to be called the law of *eventually* diminishing returns because output may initially grow at an increasing rate with additional units of the variable factor.)

Typically, returns from additional units of the variable input eventually diminish because of some form of congestion. For instance, in an office with three secretaries and only a single desktop computer, we would not expect to get three times as many letters typed per hour as in an office with only one secretary because only one person can use a computer at a time.

SOME IMPORTANT COST CONCEPTS

For the bottle-making firm described in Table 6.1, suppose the lease payment for the company's bottle-making machine is \$40 per day, which must be paid whether the company makes any bottles or not. This payment is both a **fixed cost** (since it does not depend on the number of bottles per day the firm makes) and, for the duration of the lease, a sunk cost. The first two columns of Table 6.2 reproduce the employment and output entries from Table 6.1, and the firm's fixed cost appears in column 3.

The company's payment to its employees is called **variable cost** because, unlike fixed cost, it varies with the number of bottles the company produces. The variable cost of producing 200 bottles per day, for example, is shown in column 4 of Table 6.2 as \$24 per day. Column 5 shows the firm's **total cost,** which is the sum of its fixed and variable costs. Column 6, finally, shows the firm's **marginal cost,** a measure of how its total cost changes when its output changes. Specifically, marginal cost is defined as the change in total cost divided by the corresponding change in output. Note, for example, that when the firm expands production from 80 to 200 bottles per day, its total cost goes up by \$12, which gives rise to the marginal cost entry of (\$12/day)/(120 bottles/day) = \$0.10 per bottle. To emphasize that marginal cost refers to the change in total cost when quantity changes, we place the marginal cost entries between the corresponding quantity rows of the table.

TABLE 6.2
Fixed, Variable, and Total Costs of Bottle Production

Employees per day	Bottles per day	Fixed cost ($/day)	Variable cost ($/day)	Total cost ($/day)	Marginal cost ($/bottle)
0	0	40	0	40	
					0.15
1	80	40	12	52	
					0.10
2	200	40	24	64	
					0.20
3	260	40	36	76	
					0.30
4	300	40	48	88	
					0.40
5	330	40	60	100	
					0.60
6	350	40	72	112	
					1.00
7	362	40	84	124	

CHOOSING OUTPUT TO MAXIMIZE PROFIT

In the following examples and exercises, we'll explore how the company's decision about how many bottles to produce depends on the price of bottles, the wage, and the cost of capital. Again, our starting assumption is that the firm's basic goal is to maximize the amount of profit it earns from the production and sale of bottles, where profit is the difference between its total revenue and its total cost.

$$\begin{aligned}\text{Profit} &= \text{Total revenue} - \text{Total cost}\\ &= \text{Total revenue} - \text{Variable cost} - \text{Fixed cost}\end{aligned} \tag{6.2}$$

If bottles sell for 35 cents each, how many bottles should the company described in Table 6.2 produce each day?

Cost-Benefit

To answer this question, we need simply apply the Cost-Benefit Principle to the question "Should the firm expand its level of output?" If its goal is to maximize its profit, the answer to this question will be to expand as long as the marginal benefit from expanding is at least as great as the marginal cost. Since the perfectly competitive firm can sell as many bottles as it wishes at the market price of $0.35 per bottle, its marginal benefit from selling an additional bottle is $0.35. If we compare this marginal benefit with the marginal cost entries shown in column 6 of Table 6.2, we see that the firm should keep expanding until it reaches 300 bottles per day (four employees per day). To expand beyond that level, it would have to hire a fifth employee, and the resulting marginal cost ($0.40 per bottle) would exceed the marginal benefit.

To confirm that the Cost-Benefit Principle thus applied identifies the profit-maximizing number of bottles to produce, we can calculate profit levels directly, as in Table 6.3. Column 3 of this table reports the firm's revenue from the sale of bottles, which is calculated as the product of the number of bottles produced per day and the price of $0.35 per bottle. Note, for example, that in the third row of that column, total revenue is (200 bottles/day)($0.35/bottle) = $70 per day. Column 5 reports the firm's total daily profit, which is just the difference between its total revenue (column 3) and its total cost (column 4). Note that the largest profit entry in column 5, $17 per day, occurs at an output of 300 bottles per day, just as suggested by our earlier application of the Cost-Benefit Principle.

TABLE 6.3

Output, Revenue, Costs, and Profit

Employees per day	Output (bottles/day)	Total revenue ($/day)	Total cost ($/day)	Profit ($/day)
0	0	0	40	−40
1	80	28	52	−24
2	200	70	64	6
3	260	91	76	15
4	300	105	88	17
5	330	115.50	100	15.50
6	350	122.50	112	10.50
7	362	126.70	124	2.70

◆

As the following exercise demonstrates, an increase in the price of the product gives rise to an increase in the profit-maximizing level of output.

EXERCISE 6.2

How would the profit-maximizing level of bottle production change in the example above if bottles sell for 62 cents each?

The following exercise illustrates that a fall in the wage rate leads to a decline in marginal cost, which also causes an increase in the profit-maximizing level of output.

EXERCISE 6.3

How would the profit-maximizing level of bottle production change in the example above if bottles sell for 35 cents each, but wages fall to $6 per day?

Suppose that in the example the firm's fixed cost had been not $40 per day but $45 per day. How, if at all, would that have affected the firm's profit-maximizing level of output? The answer is "not at all." Each entry in the profit column of Table 6.3 would have been $5 per day smaller than before, but the maximum profit entry still would have been 300 bottles per day.

Cost-Benefit

The observation that the profit-maximizing quantity does not depend on fixed costs is not an idiosyncrasy of this example. That it holds true in general is an immediate consequence of the Cost-Benefit Principle, which says that a firm should increase its output if, and only if, the *marginal* benefit exceeds the *marginal* cost. Neither the marginal benefit of expanding (which is the market price of bottles) nor the marginal cost of expanding is affected by a change in the firm's fixed cost.

When the law of diminishing returns applies (that is, when some factors of production are fixed), marginal cost goes up as the firm expands production beyond some point. Under these circumstances, the firm's best option is to keep expanding output as long as marginal cost is less than price.

Note that if the bottle company's fixed cost had been any more than $57 per day, it would have made a loss at *every* possible level of output. As long as it still had to pay its fixed cost, however, its best bet would have been to continue producing 300 bottles per day. It is better, after all, to experience a smaller loss than a larger one. If a firm in that situation expected conditions to remain the same, though, it would want to get out of the bottle business as soon as its equipment lease expired.

A NOTE ON THE FIRM'S SHUTDOWN CONDITION

It might seem that a firm that can sell as much output as it wishes at a constant market price would *always* do best in the short run by producing and selling the output level for which price equals marginal cost. But there are exceptions to this rule. Suppose, for example, that the market price of the firm's product falls so low that its revenue from sales is smaller than its variable cost at all possible levels of output. The firm should then cease production for the time being. By shutting down, it will suffer a loss equal to its fixed costs. But by remaining open, it would suffer an even larger loss.

More formally, if P denotes the market price of the product and Q denotes the number of units produced and sold, then $P \times Q$ is the firm's total revenue from sales, and if we use VC to denote the firm's variable cost, the rule is that the firm should shut down in the short run if $P \times Q$ is less than VC for every level of Q:

Short-run shutdown condition: $P \times Q < VC$ for all levels of Q. (6.3)

EXERCISE 6.4

Using the bottle company example, suppose bottles sold not for \$0.35 but only \$0.10. Calculate the profit corresponding to each level of output, as in Table 6.3, and verify that the firm's best option is to cease operations in the short run.

AVERAGE VARIABLE COST AND AVERAGE TOTAL COST

Suppose that the firm is unable to cover its variable cost at any level of output—that is, suppose that $P \times Q < VC$ for all levels of Q. It must then also be true that $P < VC/Q$ for all levels of Q, since we obtain the second inequality by simply dividing both sides of the first one by Q. VC/Q is the firm's **average variable cost**—its variable cost divided by its output. The firm's short-run shutdown condition may thus be restated a second way: Discontinue operations in the short run if the product price is less than the minimum value of its average variable cost (AVC). Thus

average variable cost (AVC) variable cost divided by total output

Short-run shutdown condition (alternate version): $P <$ minimum value of AVC. (6.4)

As we'll see in the next section, this version of the shutdown condition often enables us to tell at a glance whether the firm should continue operations.

A related cost concept that facilitates assessment of the firm's profitability is **average total cost** (ATC), which is total cost (TC) divided by output (Q): $ATC = TC/Q$. The firm's profit, again, is the difference between its total revenue ($P \times Q$) and its total cost. And since total cost is equal to average total cost times quantity, the firm's profit is also equal to $(P \times Q) - (ATC \times Q)$. A firm is said to be **profitable** if its revenue ($P \times Q$) exceeds its total cost ($ATC \times Q$). A firm can thus be profitable only if the price of its product price (P) exceeds its ATC for some level of output.

average total cost (ATC) total cost divided by total output

profitable firm a firm whose total revenue exceeds its total cost

Keeping track of all these cost concepts may seem tedious. In the next section, however, we will see that the payoff from doing so is that they enable us to recast the profit-maximization decision in a simple graphical framework.

A GRAPHICAL APPROACH TO PROFIT MAXIMIZATION

For the bottle-making firm we have been discussing, average variable cost and average total cost values are shown in columns 4 and 6 of Table 6.4. Using the entries in this table, we plot the firm's average total cost, average variable cost, and marginal cost curves in Figure 6.5. (Because marginal cost corresponds to the change in total cost as we move between two output levels, each marginal cost value in Table 6.4 is plotted at an output level midway between those in the adjacent rows.)

TABLE 6.4
Average Variable Cost and Average Total Cost of Bottle Production

Employees per day	Bottles per day	Variable cost ($/day)	Average variable cost ($/unit of output)	Total cost ($/day)	Average total cost ($/unit of output)	Marginal cost ($/bottle)
0	0	0		40		
						0.15
1	80	12	0.15	52	0.65	
						0.10
2	200	24	0.12	64	0.32	
						0.20
3	260	36	0.138	76	0.292	
						0.30
4	300	48	0.16	88	0.293	
						0.40
5	330	60	0.182	100	0.303	
						0.60
6	350	72	0.206	112	0.32	
						1.00
7	362	84	0.232	124	0.343	

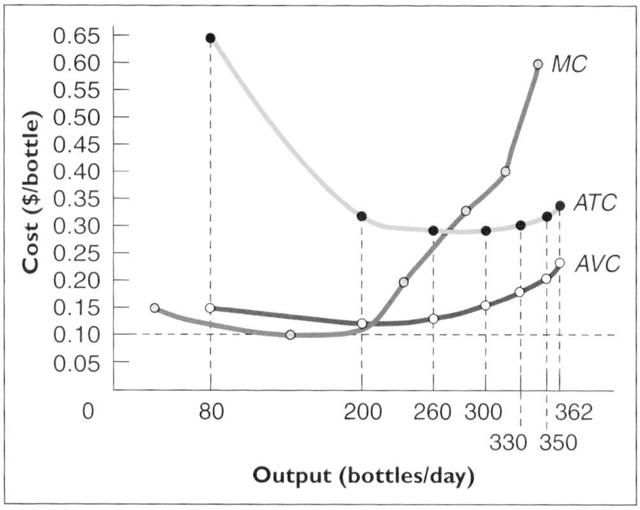

FIGURE 6.5
The Marginal, Average Variable, and Average Total Cost Curves for a Bottle Manufacturer.
The *MC* curve cuts both the *AVC* and *ATC* curves at their minimum points. The upward-sloping portion of the marginal cost curve corresponds to the region of diminishing returns.

We call your attention to several features of the cost curves in Figure 6.5. Note, for example, that the upward-sloping portion of the marginal cost curve (*MC*) corresponds to the region of diminishing returns discussed earlier. Thus, as the firm moves beyond two employees per day (200 bottles per day), the increments to total output become smaller with each additional employee, which means that the cost of producing additional bottles (*MC*) must be increasing in this region.

Note also that the definition of marginal cost implies that the marginal cost curve must intersect both the average variable cost curve (*AVC*) and the average total cost curve (*ATC*) at their respective minimum points. To see why, consider the logic that explains what happens to the average weight of children in a third-grade class when a new student joins the class. If the new (marginal) student is lighter than the previous average weight for the class, average weight will fall, but if the new student is heavier than the previous average, average weight will rise. By the same token, when marginal cost is below average total cost or average variable cost, the corresponding average cost must be falling, and vice versa. And this ensures that the marginal cost curve must pass through the minimum points of both average cost curves.

Seeing the bottle maker's *AVC* curve displayed graphically makes the question posed in Exercise 6.4 much easier to answer. The question, recall, was whether the firm should shut down in the short run if the price per bottle was only \$0.10. A glance at Figure 6.5 reveals that the firm should indeed shut down because this price lies below the minimum value of its *AVC* curve, making it impossible for the firm to cover its variable costs at any output level.

PRICE = MARGINAL COST: THE MAXIMUM-PROFIT CONDITION

So far, we have implicitly assumed that the bottle maker could employ workers only in whole-number amounts. Under these conditions, we saw that the profit-maximizing output level was one for which marginal cost was somewhat less than price (because adding yet another employee would have pushed marginal cost higher than price). In the next example, we will see that when output and employment can be varied continuously, the maximum-profit condition is that price be equal to marginal cost.

For the bottle maker whose cost curves are shown in Figure 6.6, find the profit-maximizing output level if bottles sell for \$0.20 each. How much profit will this firm earn? What is the lowest price at which this firm would continue to operate in the short run?

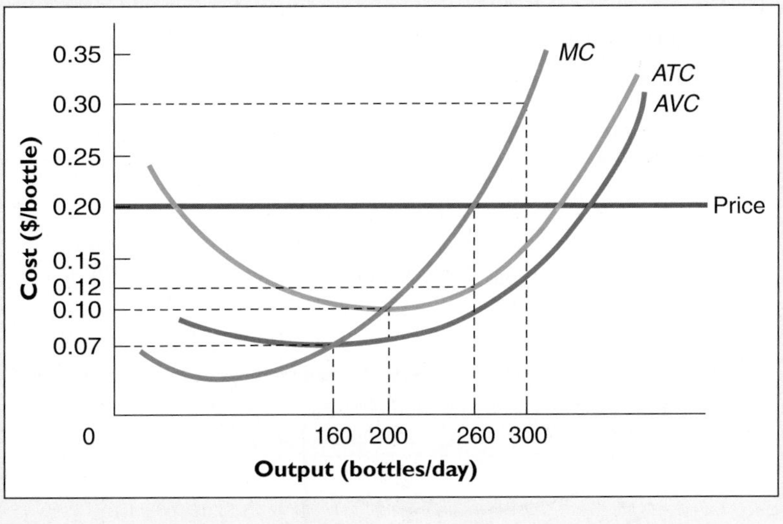

FIGURE 6.6
Price = Marginal Cost: The Perfectly Competitive Firm's Profit-Maximizing Supply Rule.
If price is greater than marginal cost, the firm can increase its profit by expanding production and sales. If price is less than marginal cost, the firm can increase its profit by producing and selling less output.

Cost-Benefit

The Cost-Benefit Principle tells us that this firm should continue to expand as long as price is at least as great as marginal cost. In Figure 6.6 we see that if the firm follows this rule, it will produce 260 bottles per day, the quantity at which price and marginal cost are equal. To gain further confidence that 260 must be the profit-maximizing quantity when the price is \$0.20 per bottle, first suppose that the firm had sold some amount less than that—say, only 200 bottles per day. Its benefit from expanding output by one bottle would then be the bottle's market price, here 20 cents. The cost of expanding output by one bottle is equal (by definition) to the firm's marginal cost, which at 200 bottles per day is only 10 cents (see Figure 6.6). So by selling the 201st bottle for 20 cents and producing it for an extra cost of only 10 cents, the firm will increase its profit by 20 − 10 = 10 cents per day. In a similar way, we can show that for *any* quantity less than the level at which price equals marginal cost, the seller can boost profit by expanding production.

Conversely, suppose that the firm was currently selling more than 260 bottles per day—say, 300—at a price of 20 cents each. In Figure 6.6 we see that marginal cost at an output of 300 is 30 cents per bottle. If the firm then contracted its output by one bottle per day, it would cut its costs by 30 cents while losing only 20 cents in revenue. As a result, its profit would grow by 10 cents per day. The same argument can be made regarding any quantity larger than 260, so if the firm is currently selling an output at which price is less than marginal cost, it can always do better by producing and selling fewer bottles.

We have thus established that if the firm sold fewer than 260 bottles per day, it could earn more profit by expanding; and if it sold more than 260, it could earn more by contracting. It follows that at a market price of 20 cents per bottle, the seller maximizes its profit by selling 260 units per day, the quantity for which price and marginal cost are exactly the same.

At that quantity the firm will collect total revenue of $P \times Q$ = (\$0.20/bottle)(260 bottles/day) = \$52 per day. Note in Figure 6.6 that at 260 bottles per day the firm's average total cost is ATC = \$0.12 per bottle, which means that its total cost is $ATC \times Q$ = (\$0.12/bottle)(260 bottles/day) = \$31.20 per day. The firm's profit is the difference between its total revenue and its total cost, or \$20.80 per day. Note, finally, that the minimum value of the firm's AVC curve is \$0.07. So if the price of bottles fell below 7 cents each, the firm would shut down in the short run. ◆

Another attractive feature of the graphical method of finding the profit-maximizing output level is that it permits us to calculate the firm's profit graphically. Thus, for the firm in the preceding example, daily profit is simply the difference between price and ATC times the number of units sold: (\$0.20/bottle − \$0.12/bottle)(260 bottles/day) = \$20.80 per day, which is the area of the shaded rectangle in Figure 6.7.

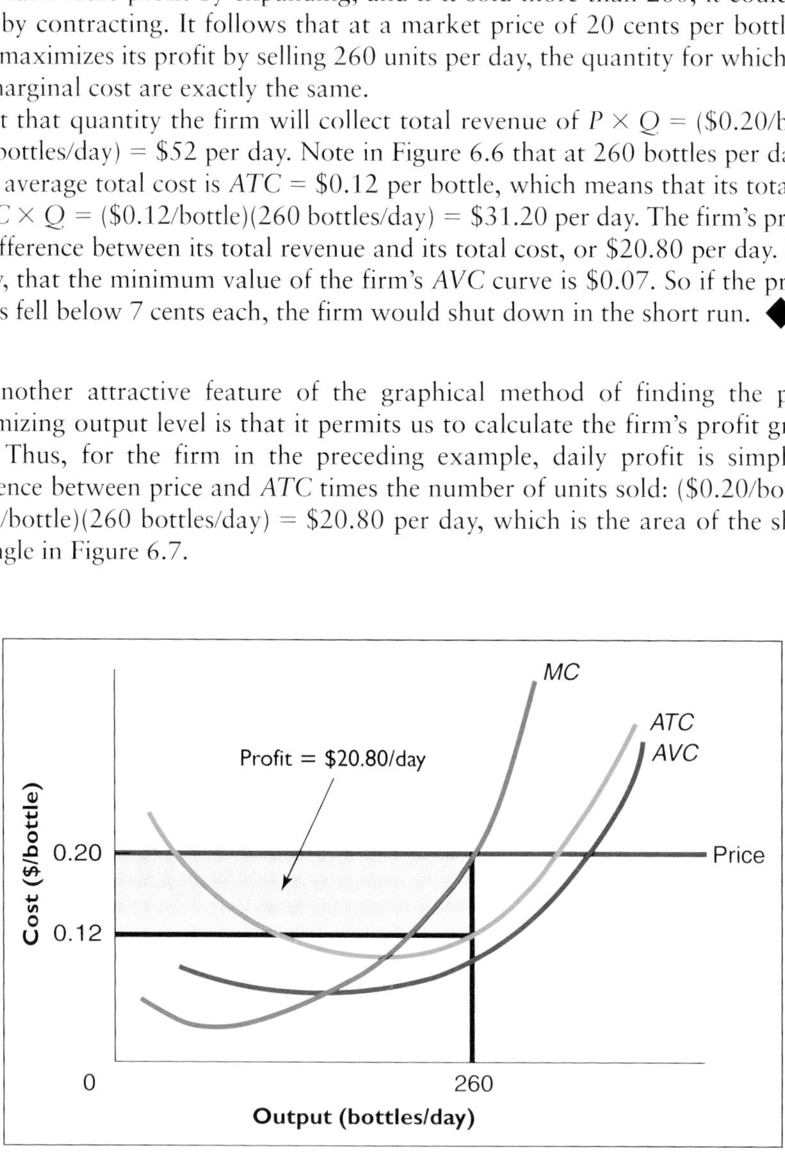

FIGURE 6.7
Measuring Profit Graphically.
Profit is equal to ($P - ATC$) × Q, which is equal to the area of the shaded rectangle.

Not all firms are as fortunate as the one shown in Figure 6.7. Suppose, for example, that the price of bottles had been not 20 cents but only 8 cents. Since that price is greater than the minimum value of AVC (see Figure 6.8), the firm should continue to operate in the short run by producing the level of output for which price equals marginal cost (180 bottles per day). But because price is less than ATC at that level of output, the firm will now experience a loss, or negative profit, on

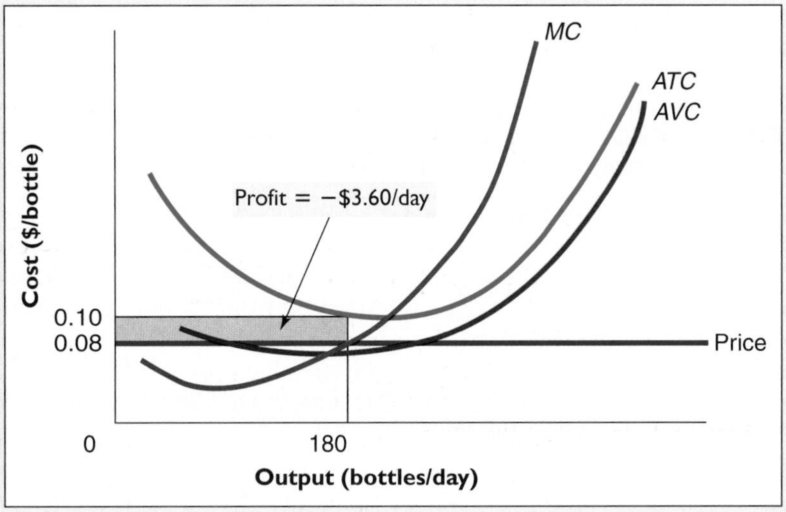

FIGURE 6.8
A Negative Profit.
When price is less than *ATC* at the profit-maximizing quantity, the firm experiences a loss, which is equal to the area of the shaded rectangle.

its operations. This profit is calculated as $(P - ATC) \times Q = (\$0.08/\text{bottle} - \$0.10/\text{bottle}) \times (180\ \text{bottles/day}) = -\$3.60$ per day, which is equal to the area of the shaded rectangle in Figure 6.8.

In Chapter 7, we will see how firms move resources from one market to another in response to the incentives implicit in profits and losses. But such movements occur in the long run, and our focus here is on production decisions in the short run.

THE "LAW" OF SUPPLY

The law of demand tells us that consumers buy less of a product when its price rises. If there were an analogous law of supply, it would say that producers offer more of a product for sale when its price rises. Is there such a law? We know that supply curves are essentially marginal cost curves and that because of the law of diminishing returns, marginal cost curves are upward-sloping in the short run. And so there is indeed a law of supply that applies as stated in the short run.

In the long run, however, the law of diminishing returns does not apply. (Recall that it holds only if at least some factors of production are fixed.) Because firms can vary the amounts of *all* factors of production they use in the long run, they can often double their production by simply doubling the amount of each input they use. In such cases, costs would be exactly proportional to output and the firm's marginal cost curve in the long run would be horizontal, not upward-sloping. So for now we'll say only that the "law" of supply holds as stated in the short run but not necessarily in the long run. For both the long run and the short run, however, *the perfectly competitive firm's supply curve is its marginal cost curve.*[1]

Every quantity of output along the market supply curve represents the summation of all the quantities individual sellers offer at the corresponding price. So the correspondence between price and marginal cost exists for the market supply curve as well as for the individual supply curves that lie behind it. That is, *for every price–quantity pair along the market supply curve, price will be equal to each seller's marginal cost of production.*

This is why we sometimes say that the supply curve represents the cost side of the market, whereas the demand curve represents the benefit side of the market. At every point along a market demand curve, price represents what buyers would be willing to pay for an additional unit of the product—and this, in turn, is how we

[1]Again, this rule holds subject to the provision that total revenue exceed variable production cost at the output level for which price equals marginal cost.

measure the amount by which they would benefit by having an additional unit of the product. Likewise, at every point along a market supply curve, price measures what it would cost producers to expand production by one unit.

RECAP	PROFIT-MAXIMIZING FIRMS IN PERFECTLY COMPETITIVE MARKETS

The perfectly competitive firm faces a horizontal demand curve for its product, meaning that it can sell any quantity it wishes at the market price. In the short run, the firm's goal is to choose the level of output that maximizes its profits. It will accomplish this by choosing the output level for which its marginal cost is equal to the market price of its product, provided that price exceeds average variable cost. The perfectly competitive firm's supply curve is the portion of its marginal cost curve that lies above its average variable cost curve. At the profit-maximizing quantity, the firm's profit is the product of that quantity and the difference between price and average total cost.

DETERMINANTS OF SUPPLY REVISITED

What factors give rise to changes in supply? (Again, remember that a "change in supply" refers to a shift in the entire supply curve, as opposed to a movement along the curve, which we call a "change in the quantity supplied.") A seller will offer more units if the benefit of selling extra output goes up relative to the cost of producing it. And since the benefit of selling output in a perfectly competitive market is a fixed market price that is beyond the seller's control, our search for factors that influence supply naturally focuses on the cost side of the calculation. The preceding examples suggest why the following factors, among others, will affect the likelihood that a product will satisfy the cost-benefit test for a given supplier.

TECHNOLOGY

Perhaps the most important determinant of production cost is technology. Improvements in technology make it possible to produce additional units of output at lower cost. This shifts each individual supply curve downward (or, equivalently, to the right) and hence shifts the market supply curve downward as well. Over time, the introduction of more sophisticated machinery has resulted in dramatic increases in the number of goods produced per hour of effort expended. Every such development gives rise to an rightward shift in the market supply curve.

But how do we know technological change will reduce the cost of producing goods and services? Might not new equipment be so expensive that producers who used it would have higher costs than those who relied on earlier designs? If so, then rational producers simply would not use the new equipment. The only technological changes that rational producers will adopt are those that will reduce their cost of production.

INPUT PRICES

Whereas technological change generally (although not always) leads to gradual shifts in supply, changes in the prices of important inputs can give rise to large supply shifts literally overnight. As discussed in Chapter 4, for example, the price of crude oil, which is the most important input in the production of gasoline, often fluctuates sharply, and the resulting shifts in supply cause gasoline prices to exhibit corresponding fluctuations.

Similarly, when wage rates rise, the marginal cost of any business that employs labor also rises, shifting supply curves to the left (or, equivalently, upward). When interest rates fall, the opportunity cost of capital equipment also falls, causing supply to shift to the right.

THE NUMBER OF SUPPLIERS

Just as demand curves shift to the right when population grows, supply curves also shift to the right as the number of individual suppliers grows. For example, if container recyclers die or retire at a higher rate than new recyclers enter the industry, the supply curve for recycling services will shift to the left. Conversely, if a rise in the unemployment rate leads more people to recycle soft drink containers (by reducing the opportunity cost of time spent recycling), the supply curve of recycling services will shift to the right.

EXPECTATIONS

Expectations about future price movements can affect how much sellers choose to offer in the current market. Suppose, for example, that recyclers expect the future price of aluminum to be much higher than the current price because of growing use of aluminum components in cars. The rational recycler would then have an incentive to withhold aluminum from the market at today's lower price, thereby to have more available to sell at the higher future price. Conversely, if recyclers expected next year's price of aluminum to be lower than this year's, their incentive would be to offer more aluminum for sale in today's market.

CHANGES IN PRICES OF OTHER PRODUCTS

Apart from technological change, perhaps the most important determinant of supply is variation in the prices of other goods and services that sellers might produce. Prospectors, for example, search for those precious metals for which the surplus of benefits over costs is greatest. When the price of silver rises, many stop looking for gold and start looking for silver. Conversely, when the price of platinum falls, many platinum prospectors shift their attention to gold.

RECAP	THE DETERMINANTS OF SUPPLY

Among the relevant factors causing supply curves to shift are new technologies, changes in input prices, changes in the number of sellers, expectations of future price changes, and changes in the prices of other products that firms might produce.

APPLYING THE THEORY OF SUPPLY

Whether the activity is producing new soft drink containers or recycling used ones, or indeed any other production activity at all, the same logic governs all supply decisions in perfectly competitive markets (and in any other setting in which sellers can sell as much as they wish to at a constant price): Keep expanding output until marginal cost is equal to the price of the product. This logic helps us understand why recycling efforts are more intensive for some products than others.

Example 6.1
THE ECONOMIC NATURALIST

When recycling is left to private market forces, why are many more aluminum beverage containers recycled than glass ones?

In both cases, recyclers gather containers until their marginal costs are equal to the containers' respective redemption prices. When recycling is left to market forces, the redemption price for a container is based on what companies can sell it (or the materials in it) for. Aluminum containers can be easily processed into scrap aluminum, which commands a high price, and this leads profit-seeking companies to offer a high redemption price for aluminum cans. By contrast, the glass from which glass containers are made has only limited resale value, primarily because the raw materials required to make new glass containers are so cheap. This difference leads profit-seeking companies to offer much lower redemption prices for glass containers than for aluminum ones.

The high redemption prices for aluminum cans induce many people to track these cans down, whereas the low redemption prices for glass containers leads most people to ignore them. If recycling is left completely to market forces, then, we would expect to see aluminum soft drink containers quickly recycled, whereas glass containers would increasingly litter the landscape. This is in fact the pattern we do see in states without recycling laws. (More on how these laws work in a moment.) This pattern is a simple consequence of the fact that the supply curves of container-recycling services are upward-sloping. ●

In states that don't have beverage container deposit laws, why are aluminum cans more likely to be recycled than glass bottles?

The acquisition of valuable raw materials is only one of two important benefits from recycling. The second is that, by removing litter, recycling makes the environment more pleasant for everyone. As the next example suggests, this second benefit might easily justify the cost of recycling substantial numbers of glass containers.

What is the socially optimal amount of recycling of glass containers?

EN 6

Suppose that the 60,000 citizens of Burlington, Vermont, would collectively be willing to pay 6 cents for each glass container removed from their local environment. If the local market supply curve of glass container recycling services is as shown in Figure 6.9, what is the socially optimal level of glass container recycling?

FIGURE 6.9
The Supply Curve of Container Recycling Services for Burlington, Vermont.

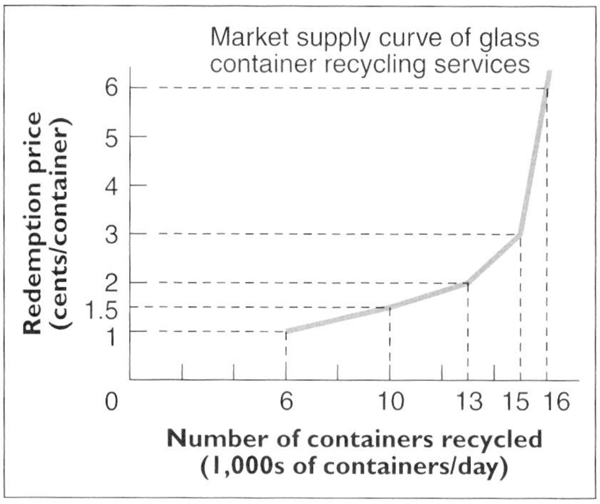

Suppose the citizens of Burlington authorize their city government to collect tax money to finance litter removal. If the benefit of each glass container removed, as measured by what residents are collectively willing to pay, is 6 cents, the government should offer to pay 6 cents for each glass container recycled. To maximize the total economic surplus from recycling, we should recycle that number of containers for which the marginal cost of recycling is equal to the 6-cent marginal benefit. Given the market supply curve shown, the optimal quantity is 16,000 containers per day, and that is how many will be redeemed when the government offers 6 cents per container. ◆

Although 16,000 containers per day will be removed from the environment in the preceding example, others will remain. After all, some are discarded in remote locations, and a redemption price of 6 cents per container is simply not high enough to induce people to track them all down.

So why not offer an even higher price and get rid of *all* glass container litter? For the example given, the reason is that the marginal cost of removing the 16,001st glass container each day is greater than the benefit of removing it. Total economic surplus is largest when we remove litter only up to the point that the marginal benefit of litter removal is equal to its marginal cost, which occurs when 16,000 containers per day are recycled. To proceed past that point is actually wasteful.

Many people become upset when they hear economists say that the socially optimal amount of litter is greater than zero. In the minds of these people, the optimal amount of litter is *exactly* zero. But this position completely ignores the Scarcity Principle. Granted, there would be benefits from reducing litter further, but there also would be costs. Spending more on litter removal therefore means spending less on other useful things. No one would insist that the optimal amount of dirt in his own home is zero. (If someone does make this claim, ask him why he doesn't stay home all day vacuuming the dust that is accumulating in his absence.) If it doesn't pay to remove all the dust from your house, it doesn't pay to remove all the bottles from the environment. Precisely the same logic applies in each case.

Scarcity

© PhotoAlto

Is the socially optimal quantity of litter zero?

If 16,000 containers per day is the optimal amount of litter removal, can we expect the individual spending decisions of private citizens to result in that amount of litter removal? Unfortunately we cannot. The problem is that anyone who paid for litter removal individually would bear the full cost of those services while reaping only a tiny fraction of the benefit. In the previous example, the 60,000 citizens of Burlington reaped a total benefit of 6 cents per container removed, which means a benefit of only (6/60,000) = 0.0001 cent per person! Someone who paid 6 cents for someone else to remove a container would thus be incurring a cost 60,000 times greater than his share of the resulting benefit.

Note that the incentive problem here is similar to the one discussed in Chapter 3 for the person deciding whether to be vaccinated against an illness. The problem was that the incentive to be vaccinated was too weak because, even though the patient bears the full cost of the vaccination, many of the resulting benefits accrue to others. Thus, an important part of the extra benefit from any one person being vaccinated is that others also become less likely to contract the illness.

The case of glass container litter is an example in which private market forces do not produce the best attainable outcome for society as a whole. Even people who carelessly toss containers on the ground, rather than recycle them, are often offended by the unsightly landscape to which their own actions contribute. Indeed, this is why they often support laws mandating adequate redemption prices for glass containers.

Equilibrium

Activities that generate litter are a good illustration of the Equilibrium Principle described in Chapter 3. People who litter do so not because they don't care about the environment, but because their private incentives make littering misleadingly attractive. Recycling requires some effort, after all, yet no individual's recycling efforts have a noticeable effect on the quality of the environment. The soft-drink-container deposit laws enacted by numerous states were a simple way to bring individual interests more closely into balance with the interests of society as a whole. The vast majority of container litter disappeared almost literally overnight in states that enacted these laws.

EXERCISE 6.5

If the supply curve of glass container recycling services is as shown in the diagram, and each of the city's 60,000 citizens would be willing to pay 0.00005 cent for each glass container removed from the landscape, at what level should the city government set the redemption price for glass containers, and how many will be recycled each day?

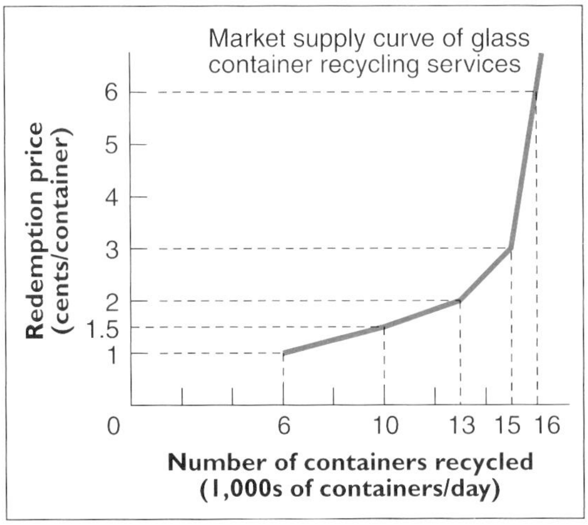

SUPPLY AND PRODUCER SURPLUS

producer surplus the amount by which price exceeds the seller's reservation price

The economic surplus received by a buyer is called *consumer surplus*. The analogous construct for a seller is **producer surplus**, the difference between the price a seller actually receives for the product and the lowest price for which she would have been willing to sell it (her reservation price, which in general will be her marginal cost).

As in the case of consumer surplus, the term *producer surplus* sometimes refers to the surplus received by a single seller in a transaction, while on other occasions it describes the total surplus received by all sellers in a market or collection of markets.

CALCULATING PRODUCER SURPLUS

In the preceding chapter, we saw that consumer surplus in a market is the area bounded above by the demand curve and bounded below by the market price. Producer surplus in a market is calculated in an analogous way. As the following example illustrates, it is the area bounded above by the market price and bounded below by the market supply curve.

How much do sellers benefit from their participation in the market for milk?

Consider the market for milk, whose demand and supply curves are shown in Figure 6.10, which has an equilibrium price of $2 per gallon and an equilibrium quantity of 4,000 gallons per day. How much producer surplus do the sellers in this market reap?

In Figure 6.10, note first that for all milk sold up to 4,000 gallons per day, sellers receive a surplus equal to the difference between the market price of $2 per gallon and

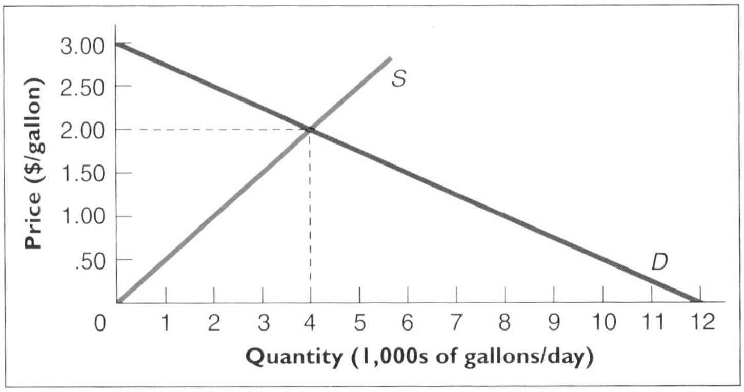

FIGURE 6.10
Supply and Demand in the Market for Milk.
For the supply and demand curves shown, the equilibrium price of milk is $2 per gallon and the equilibrium quantity is 4,000 gallons per day.

their reservation price as given by the supply curve. Total producer surplus received by buyers in the milk market is thus the shaded triangle between the supply curve and the market price in Figure 6.11. Note that this area is a right triangle whose vertical arm is h = \$2/gallon and whose horizontal arm is b = 4,000 gallons/day. And since the area of any triangle is equal to (1/2)bh, producer surplus in this market is equal to

$$(1/2)(4{,}000 \text{ gallons/day})(\$2/\text{gallon}) = \$4{,}000/\text{day}.$$

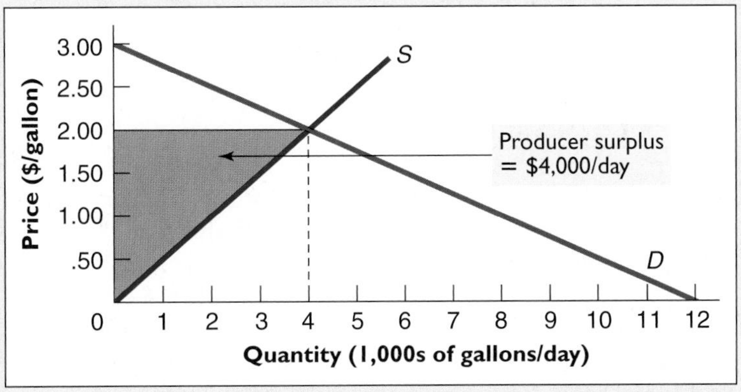

FIGURE 6.11
Producer Surplus in the Market for Milk.
Producer surplus is the area of the shaded triangle (\$4,000/day).

Producer surplus in this example may be thought of as the highest price sellers would pay, in the aggregate, for the right to continue participating in the milk market. It is \$4,000 per day, since that is the amount by which their combined benefits exceed their combined costs. ◆

As discussed in Chapter 3, the supply curve for a good can be interpreted either horizontally or vertically. The horizontal interpretation tells us, for each price, the total quantity that producers wish to sell at that price. The vertical interpretation tells us, for each quantity, the smallest amount a seller would be willing to accept for the good. For the purpose of computing producer surplus, we rely on the vertical interpretation of the supply curve. The value on the vertical axis that corresponds to each point along the supply curve corresponds to the marginal seller's reservation price for the good, which is the marginal cost of producing it. Producer surplus is the cumulative sum of the differences between the market price and these reservation prices. It is the area bounded above by market price and bounded below by the supply curve.

■ SUMMARY ■

- The demand curve facing a perfectly competitive firm is a horizontal line at the price for which industry supply and demand intersect. **LO1**
- The supply curve for a good or service is a schedule that, for any price, tells us the quantity that sellers wish to supply at that price. The prices at which goods and services are offered for sale in the market depend, in turn, on the opportunity cost of the resources required to produce them. **LO2**
- Supply curves tend to be upward-sloping, at least in the short run, in part because of the Increasing Opportunity Cost Principle. In general, rational producers will always take advantage of their best opportunities first, moving on to more difficult or costly opportunities only after their best ones have been exhausted. Reinforcing this tendency is the law of diminishing returns, which says that when some factors of production are held fixed, the amount of additional variable factors required to produce successive increments in output grows larger. **LO2**
- For perfectly competitive markets—or, more generally, for markets in which individual sellers can sell whatever quantity they wish at constant price—the seller's best option is to sell that quantity of output for which price equals marginal cost, provided price exceeds the minimum value of average variable cost.

The supply curve for the seller thus coincides with the portion of his marginal cost curve that exceeds average variable cost. This is why we sometimes say the supply curve represents the cost side of the market (in contrast to the demand curve, which represents the benefit side of the market). **LO3**

- The industry supply curve is the horizontal summation of the supply curves of individual firms in the industry. **LO4**
- Producer surplus is a measure of the economic surplus reaped by a seller or sellers in a market. It is the cumulative sum of the differences between the market price and their reservation prices, which is the area bounded above by market price and bounded below by the supply curve. **LO5**

KEY TERMS

average total cost (*ATC*) (157)
average variable cost (*AVC*) (157)
factor of production (153)
fixed cost (154)
fixed factor of production (154)
imperfectly competitive firm (153)
law of diminishing returns (154)
long run (153)
marginal cost (154)
perfectly competitive market (152)
price taker (152)
producer surplus (166)
profit (151)
profit-maximizing firm (152)
profitable firm (157)
short run (153)
total cost (154)
variable cost (154)
variable factor of production (154)

REVIEW QUESTIONS

1. Explain why you would expect supply curves to slope upward on the basis of the Principle of Increasing Opportunity Cost. **LO3**
2. Which do you think is more likely to be a fixed factor of production for an ice cream producer during the next two months: its factory building or its workers who operate the machines? Explain. **LO2**
3. Economists often stress that congestion helps account for the law of diminishing returns. With this in mind, explain why it would be impossible to feed all the people on Earth with food grown in a single flowerpot, even if unlimited water, labor, seed, fertilizer, sunlight, and other inputs were available. **LO2**
4. True or false: The perfectly competitive firm should *always* produce the output level for which price equals marginal cost. **LO5**
5. Why do we use the vertical interpretation of the supply curve when we measure producer surplus? **LO5**

PROBLEMS

1. Zoe is trying to decide how to divide her time between her job as a wedding photographer, which pays $27 per hour for as many hours as she chooses to work, and as a fossil collector, in which her pay depends on both the price of fossils and the number of them she finds. Earnings aside, Zoe is indifferent between the two tasks, and the number of fossils she can find depends on the number of hours a day she searches, as shown in the table below: **LO3**

Hours per day	Total fossils per day
1	5
2	9
3	12
4	14
5	15

a. Derive a table with price in dollar increments from \$0 to \$30 in the first column and the quantity of fossils Zoe is willing to supply per day at that price in the second.
b. Plot these points in a graph with price on the vertical axis and quantity per day on the horizontal. What is this curve called?

2. A price-taking firm makes air conditioners. The market price of one of their new air conditioners is \$120. Its total cost information is given in the table below:

Air conditioners per day	Total cost (\$ per day)
1	100
2	150
3	220
4	310
5	405
6	510
7	650
8	800

How many air conditioners should the firm produce per day if its goal is to maximize its profit? **LO3**

3. The Paducah Slugger Company makes baseball bats out of lumber supplied to it by Acme Sporting Goods, which pays Paducah \$10 for each finished bat. Paducah's only factors of production are lathe operators and a small building with a lathe. The number of bats per day it produces depends on the number of employee-hours per day, as shown in the table below. **LO2, LO3**

Number of bats per day	Number of employee-hours per day
0	0
5	1
10	2
15	4
20	7
25	11
30	16
35	22

a. If the wage is \$15 per hour and Paducah's daily fixed cost for the lathe and building is \$60, what is the profit-maximizing quantity of bats?
b. What would be the profit-maximizing number of bats if the firm's fixed cost were not \$60 per day but only \$30?

4. In the preceding question, how would Paducah's profit-maximizing level of output be affected if the government imposed a tax of \$10 per day on the company? (Hint: Think of this tax as equivalent to a \$10 increase in fixed cost.) What would Paducah's profit-maximizing level of output be if the government imposed a tax of \$2 per bat? (Hint: Think of this tax as a \$2-per-bat increase in the firm's marginal cost.) Why do these two taxes have such different effects? **LO2, LO3**

5. The supply curves for the only two firms in a competitive industry are given by $P = 2Q_1$ and $P = 2 + Q_2$, where Q_1 is the output of firm 1 and Q_2 is the output of firm 2. What is the market supply curve for this industry? (Hint: Graph the two curves side by side, then add their respective quantities at a sample of different prices.) **LO4**

6. Calculate daily producer surplus for the market for pizza whose demand and supply curves are shown in the graph. **LO5**

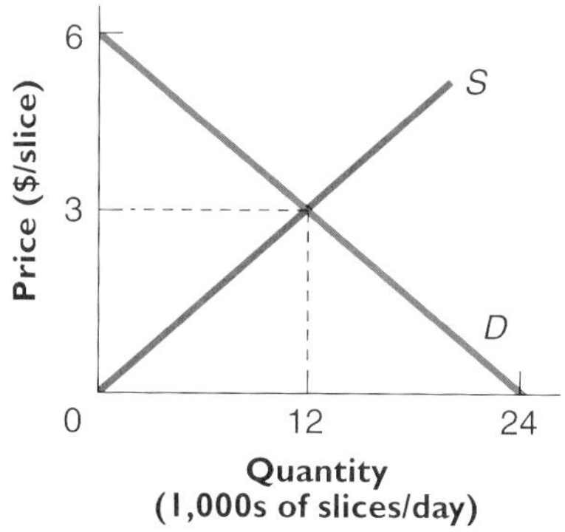

7. For the pizza seller whose marginal, average variable, and average total cost curves are shown in the accompanying diagram, what is the profit-maximizing level of output and how much profit will this producer earn if the price of pizza is $2.50 per slice? **LO2, LO3**

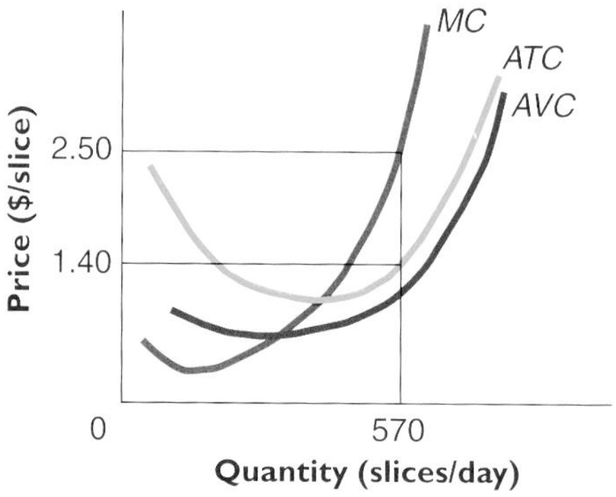

8. For the pizza seller whose marginal, average variable, and average total cost curves are shown in the accompanying diagram, what is the profit-maximizing level of output and how much profit will this producer earn if the price of pizza is $0.80 per slice? **LO2, LO3**

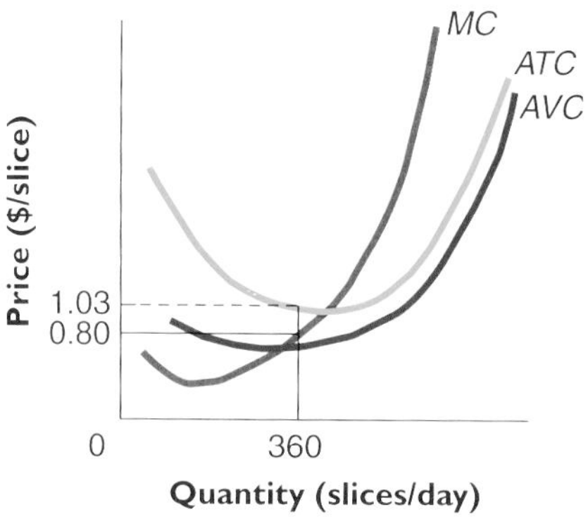

9.* For the pizza seller whose marginal, average variable, and average total cost curves are shown in the accompanying diagram, what is the profit-maximizing level of output and how much profit will this producer earn if the price of pizza is \$0.50 per slice? **LO2, LO3**

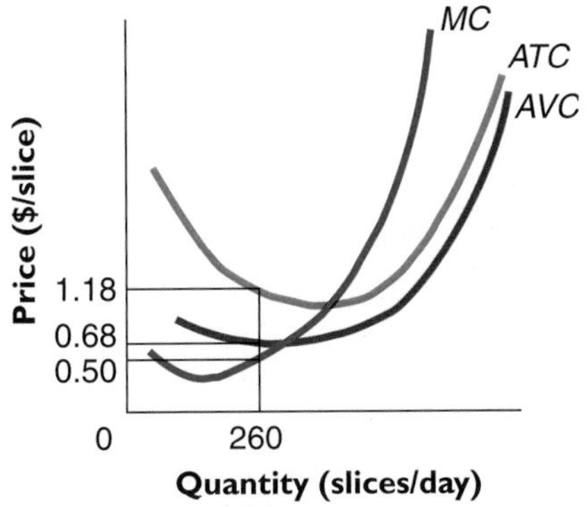

10.* For the pizza seller whose marginal, average variable, and average total cost curves are shown in the accompanying diagram (who is the same seller as in problem 9), what is the profit-maximizing level of output and how much profit will this producer earn if the price of pizza is \$1.18 per slice? **LO2, LO3**

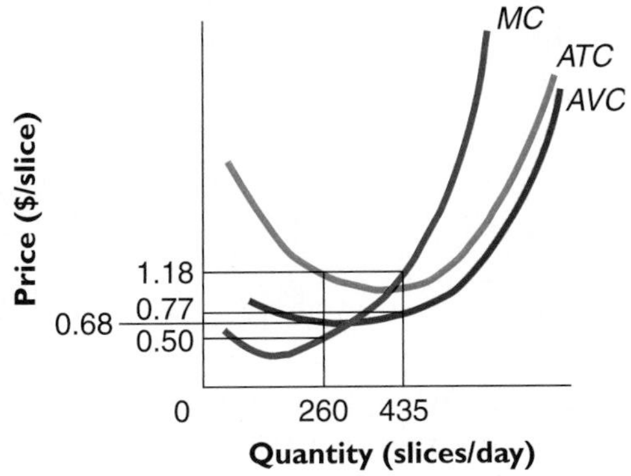

ANSWERS TO IN-CHAPTER EXERCISES

6.1 Since Harry will find 300 containers if he searches a third hour, we find his reservation price for searching a third hour by solving $p(300) = \$6$ for $p = 2$ cents. His reservation prices for additional hours of search are calculated in an analogous way. **LO3**

Fourth hour: $p(200) = \$6$, so $p = 3$ cents.
Fifth hour: $p(100) = \$6$, so $p = 6$ cents.

6.2 If bottles sell for 62 cents each, the firm should continue to expand up to and including the sixth employee (350 bottles per day). **LO3**

6.3 The relevant costs are now as shown in the table on the next page. With each variable and marginal cost entry half what it was in the original example, the firm should now hire six employees and produce 350 bottles per day. **LO2, LO3**

*Problems marked with an asterisk (*) are more difficult.

Employees per day	Bottles per day	Fixed cost ($/day)	Variable cost ($/day)	Total cost ($/day)	Marginal cost ($/bottle)
0	0	40	0	40	
1	80	40	6	46	0.075
2	200	40	12	52	0.05
3	260	40	18	58	0.10
4	300	40	24	64	0.167
5	330	40	30	70	0.20
6	350	40	36	76	0.30
7	362	40	42	82	0.50

6.4 Because the firm makes its smallest loss when it hires zero employees, it should shut down in the short run. **LO2, LO3**

Employees per day	Output (bottles/day)	Total revenue ($/day)	Total cost ($/day)	Profit ($/day)
0	0	0	40	−40
1	80	8	52	−44
2	200	20	64	−44
3	260	26	76	−50
4	300	30	88	−58
5	330	33	100	−67
6	350	35	112	−77
7	362	36.20	124	−87.80

6.5 The fact that each of the city's 60,000 residents is willing to pay 0.00005 cent for each bottle removed means that the collective benefit of each bottle removed is (60,000)(0.00005) = 3 cents. So the city should set the redemption price at 3 cents, and from the supply curve we see that 15,000 bottles per day will be recycled at that price. **LO3**

CHAPTER 7

Efficiency, Exchange, and the Invisible Hand in Action

LEARNING OBJECTIVES

After reading this chapter, you should be able to:

1. Define and explain the differences between accounting profit, economic profit, and normal profit.
2. Understand why the quest for economic profit drives firms to enter some industries and leave others.
3. Explain why economic profit, unlike economic rent, tends toward zero in the long run.
4. Explain why no opportunities for gain remain open to individuals when a market is in equilibrium.
5. Determine if the market equilibrium is socially efficient based on certain conditions.
6. Calculate total economic surplus and explain how it is affected by policies that prevent markets from reaching equilibrium.

The market for ethnic cuisine in Ithaca, New York, offered few choices in the early 1970s: the city had one Japanese, two Greek, four Italian, and three Chinese restaurants. Today, more than 30 years later and with essentially the same population, Ithaca has one Sri Lankan, two Indian, one French, one Spanish, six Thai, two Korean, two Vietnamese, four Mexican, three Greek, seven Italian, two Caribbean, two Japanese, and nine Chinese restaurants. In some of the city's other markets, however, the range of available choices has narrowed.

Why do most American cities now have more tattoo parlors and fewer watch repair shops than in 1972?

For example, several companies provided telephone answering service in 1972, but only one does so today.

Rare indeed is the marketplace in which the identities of the buyers and sellers remain static for extended periods. New businesses enter, established ones leave. There are more body-piercing studios in Ithaca now and fewer watch-repair shops; more marketing consultants and fewer intercity bus companies; and more appliances in stainless steel or black finishes, fewer in avocado or coppertone.

Driving these changes is the businessowner's quest for profit. Businesses migrate to industries and locations in which profit opportunities abound and desert those whose prospects appear bleak. In perhaps the most widely quoted passage from his landmark treatise, *The Wealth of Nations*, Adam Smith wrote,

> It is not from the benevolence of the butcher, the brewer, or the baker that we expect our dinner, but from their regard of their own interest. We address ourselves not to their humanity, but to their self-love, and never talk to them of our necessities, but of their advantage.

Smith went on to argue that although the entrepreneur "intends only his own gain," he is "led by an invisible hand to promote an end which was no part of his intention." As Smith saw it, even though self-interest is the prime mover of economic activity, the end result is an allocation of goods and services that serves society's collective interests remarkably well. If producers are offering "too much" of one product and "not enough" of another, profit opportunities alert entrepreneurs to that fact and provide incentives for them to take remedial action. All the while, the system exerts relentless pressure on producers to hold the price of each good close to its cost of production, and indeed to reduce that cost in any ways possible. The invisible hand, in short, is about all the good things that can happen because of the Incentive Principle.

Incentive

Our task in this chapter is to gain deeper insight into the nature of the forces that guide the invisible hand. What exactly does "profit" mean? How is it measured, and how does the quest for it serve society's ends? And if competition holds price close to the cost of production, why do so many entrepreneurs become fabulously wealthy? We will also discuss cases in which misunderstanding of Smith's theory results in costly errors, both in everyday decision making and in the realm of government policy.

THE CENTRAL ROLE OF ECONOMIC PROFIT

The economic theory of business behavior is built on the assumption that the firm's goal is to maximize its profit. So we must be clear at the outset about what, exactly, profit means.

THREE TYPES OF PROFIT

explicit costs the actual payments a firm makes to its factors of production and other suppliers

accounting profit the difference between a firm's total revenue and its explicit costs

The economist's understanding of profit is different from the accountant's, and the distinction between the two is important to understanding how the invisible hand works. Accountants define the annual profit of a business as the difference between the revenue it takes in and its **explicit costs** for the year, which are the actual payments the firm makes to its factors of production and other suppliers. Profit thus defined is called **accounting profit**.

$$\text{Accounting profit} = \text{total revenue} - \text{explicit costs}.$$

Accounting profit is the most familiar profit concept in everyday discourse. It is the one that companies use, for example, when they provide statements about their profits in press releases or annual reports.[1]

Economists, by contrast, define profit as the difference between the firm's total revenue and not just its explicit costs, but also its **implicit costs**, which are the opportunity costs of all the resources supplied by the firm's owners. Profit thus defined is called **economic profit**, or **excess profit**.

implicit costs the opportunity costs of the resources supplied by the firm's owners

economic profit (or excess profit) the difference between a firm's total revenue and the sum of its explicit and implicit costs

Economic profit = total revenue − explicit costs − implicit costs.

To illustrate the difference between accounting profit and economic profit, consider a firm with $400,000 in total annual revenue whose only explicit costs are workers' salaries, totaling $250,000 per year. The owners of this firm have supplied machines and other capital equipment with a total resale value of $1 million. This firm's accounting profit then is $150,000, or the difference between its total revenue of $400,000 per year and its explicit costs of $250,000 per year.

To calculate the firm's economic profit, we must first calculate the opportunity cost of the resources supplied by the firm's owners. Suppose the current annual interest rate on savings accounts is 10 percent. Had owners not invested in capital equipment, they could have earned an additional $100,000 per year interest by depositing their $1 million in a savings account. So the firm's economic profit is $400,000 per year − $250,000 per year − $100,000 per year = $50,000 per year.

Note that this economic profit is smaller than the accounting profit by exactly the amount of the firm's implicit costs—the $100,000 per year opportunity cost of the resources supplied by the firm's owners. This difference between a business's accounting profit and its economic profit is called its **normal profit**. Normal profit is simply the opportunity cost of the resources supplied to a business by its owners.

normal profit the opportunity cost of the resources supplied by a firm's owners, equal to accounting profit minus economic profit

Figure 7.1 illustrates the difference between accounting and economic profit. Figure 7.1(a) represents a firm's total revenues, while (b) and (c) show how these revenues are apportioned among the various cost and profit categories.

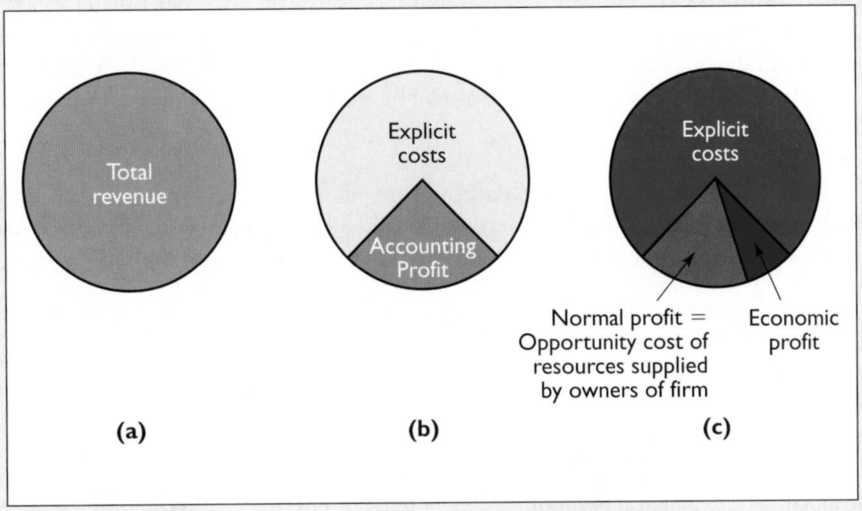

FIGURE 7.1
The Difference between Accounting Profit and Economic Profit.
Accounting profit (b) is the difference between total revenue and explicit costs. Normal profit (c) is the opportunity cost of all resources supplied by a firm's owners. Economic profit (c) is the difference between total revenue and all costs, explicit and implicit (also equal to the difference between accounting profit and normal profit).

[1]For simplicity, this discussion ignores any costs associated with depreciation of the firm's capital equipment. Because the buildings and machines owned by a firm tend to wear out over time, the government allows the firm to consider a fraction of their value each year as a current cost of doing business. For example, a firm that employs a $1,000 machine with a 10-year lifespan might allowed to record $100 as a current cost of doing business each year.

"All I know, Harrison, is that I've been on the board forty years and have yet to see an excess profit."

The following examples illustrate why the distinction between accounting and economic profit is so important.

Should Pudge Buffet stay in the farming business?

Pudge Buffet is a corn farmer who lives near Lincoln, Nebraska. His payments for land and equipment rental and for other supplies come to $10,000 per year. The only input he supplies is his own labor, and he considers farming just as attractive as his only other employment opportunity, managing a retail store at a salary of $11,000 per year. Apart from the matter of pay, Pudge is indifferent between farming and being a manager. Corn sells for a constant price per bushel in an international market too large to be affected by changes in one farmer's corn production. Pudge's revenue from corn sales is $22,000 per year. What is his accounting profit? His economic profit? His normal profit? Should he remain a corn farmer?

As shown in Table 7.1, Pudge's accounting profit is $12,000 per year, the difference between his $22,000 annual revenue and his $10,000 yearly payment for land, equipment, and supplies. His economic profit is that amount less the opportunity

TABLE 7.1
Revenue, Cost, and Profit Summary

Total revenue ($/year)	Explicit costs ($/year)	Implicit costs ($/year)	Accounting profit (= total revenue − explicit costs) ($/year)	Economic profit (= total revenue − explicit costs − implicit costs) ($/year)	Normal profit (= implicit costs) ($/year)
22,000	10,000	11,000	12,000	1,000	11,000

cost of his labor. Since the latter is the $11,000 per year he could have earned as a store manager, he is making an economic profit of $1,000 per year. Finally, his normal profit is the $11,000 opportunity cost of the only resource he supplies, namely, his labor. Since Pudge likes the two jobs equally well, he will be better off by $1,000 per year if he remains in farming.

EXERCISE 7.1

In the example above, how will Pudge's economic profit change if his annual revenue from corn production is not $22,000, but $20,000? Should he continue to farm?

When revenue falls from $22,000 to $20,000, Pudge has an economic profit of −$1,000 per year. A negative economic profit is also called an **economic loss.** If Pudge expects to sustain an economic loss indefinitely, his best bet would be to abandon farming in favor of managing a retail store.

economic loss an economic profit that is less than zero

You might think that if Pudge could just save enough money to buy his own land and equipment, his best option would be to remain a farmer. But as the following example illustrates, that impression is based on a failure to perceive the difference between accounting profit and economic profit.

Does owning one's own land make a difference?

Let's build on the previous example. Suppose Pudge's Uncle Warren, who owns the farmland Pudge has been renting, dies and leaves Pudge that parcel of land. If the land could be rented to some other farmer for $6,000 per year, should Pudge remain in farming?

TABLE 7.2
Revenue, Cost, and Profit Summary

Total revenue ($/year)	Explicit costs ($/year)	Implicit costs ($/year)	Accounting profit (= total revenue − explicit costs) ($/year)	Economic profit (= total revenue − explicit costs − implicit costs) ($/year)	Normal profit (= implicit costs) ($/year)
20,000	4,000	17,000	16,000	−1,000	17,000

As shown in Table 7.2, if Pudge continues to farm his own land, his accounting profit will be $16,000 per year, or $6,000 more than in Exercise 7.1. But his economic profit will still be the same as before—that is, −$1,000 per year—because Pudge must deduct the $6,000 per year opportunity cost of farming his own land, even though he no longer must make an explicit payment to his uncle for it. The normal profit from owning and operating his farm will be $17,000 per year—the opportunity cost of the land and labor he provides. But since Pudge earns an accounting profit of only $16,000, he will again do better to abandon farming for the managerial job. ◆

Pudge obviously would be wealthier as an owner than he was as a renter. But the question of whether to remain a farmer is answered the same way whether Pudge rents his farmland or owns it. He should stay in farming only if that is the option that yields the highest economic profit.

RECAP	THE CENTRAL ROLE OF ECONOMIC PROFIT

A firm's accounting profit is the difference between its revenue and the sum of all explicit costs it incurs. Economic profit is the difference between the firm's revenue and *all* costs it incurs—both explicit and implicit. Normal profit is the opportunity cost of the resources supplied by the owners of the firm. When a firm's accounting profit is exactly equal to the opportunity cost of the inputs supplied by the firm's owners, the firm's economic profit is zero. For a firm to remain in business in the long run, it must earn an economic profit greater than or equal to zero.

THE INVISIBLE HAND THEORY

TWO FUNCTIONS OF PRICE

rationing function of price to distribute scarce goods to those consumers who value them most highly

allocative function of price to direct resources away from overcrowded markets and toward markets that are underserved

invisible hand theory Adam Smith's theory that the actions of independent, self-interested buyers and sellers will often result in the most efficient allocation of resources

In the free enterprise system, market prices serve two important and distinct functions. The first, the **rationing function of price**, is to distribute scarce goods among potential claimants, ensuring that those who get them are the ones who value them most. Thus, if three people want the only antique clock for sale at an auction, the clock goes home with the person who bids the most for it. The second function, the **allocative function of price**, is to direct productive resources to different sectors of the economy. Resources leave markets in which price cannot cover the cost of production and enter those in which price exceeds the cost of production.

Both the allocative and rationing functions of price underlie Adam Smith's celebrated theory of the **invisible hand** of the market. Recall that Smith thought the market system channels the selfish interests of individual buyers and sellers so as to promote the greatest good for society. The carrot of economic profit and the stick of economic loss, he argued, were the only forces necessary to ensure that existing supplies in any market would be allocated efficiently and that resources would be allocated across markets to produce the most efficient possible mix of goods and services.

RESPONSES TO PROFITS AND LOSSES

To get a feel for how the invisible hand works, we begin by looking at how firms respond to economic profits and losses. If a firm is to remain in business in the long run, it must cover all its costs, both explicit and implicit. A firm's normal profit is just a cost of doing business. Thus, the owner of a firm that earns no more than a normal profit has managed only to recover the opportunity cost of the resources invested in the firm. By contrast, the owner of a firm that makes a positive economic profit earns more than the opportunity cost of the invested resources; she earns a normal profit and then some.

Naturally, everyone would be delighted to earn more than a normal profit, and no one wants to earn less. The result is that those markets in which firms are earning an economic profit tend to attract additional resources, whereas markets in which firms are experiencing economic losses tend to lose resources.

To see how this happens, we'll examine the workings of the market for corn, whose short-run supply and demand curves are shown in Figure 7.2(a). Figure 7.2(b) depicts the marginal and average total cost curves for a representative farm. The equilibrium price of $2 per bushel is determined by the supply–demand intersection in (a). The representative farm whose MC and ATC curves are shown in (b) then maximizes its profit by producing the quantity for which price equals marginal cost, 130,000 bushels of corn per year.

Recall from Chapter 6 that average total cost at any output level is the sum of all costs, explicit and implicit, divided by output. The difference between price and

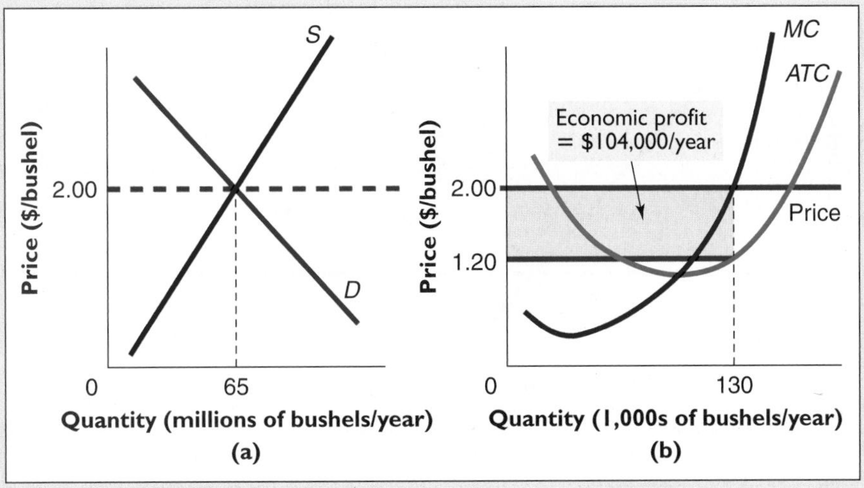

FIGURE 7.2
Economic Profit in the Short Run in the Corn Market.
At an equilibrium price of $2 per bushel (a), the typical farm earns an economic profit of $104,000 per year (b).

ATC is thus equal to the average amount of economic profit earned per unit sold. In Figure 7.2(b), that difference is $0.80 per unit. With 130,000 bushels per year sold, the representative farm earns an economic profit of $104,000 per year.

The existence of positive economic profit in the corn market means that producers in that market are earning more than their opportunity cost of farming. For simplicity, we assume that the inputs required to enter the corn market—land, labor, equipment, and the like—are available at constant prices and that anyone is free to enter this market if he or she chooses. The key point is that since price exceeds the opportunity cost of the resources required to enter the market, others *will* want to enter. And as they add their corn production to the amount already on offer, supply shifts to the right, causing the market equilibrium price to fall, as shown in Figure 7.3(a). At the new price of $1.50 per bushel, the representative farm now earns much less economic profit than before, only $50,400 per year [Figure 7.3(b)].

For simplicity, we assume that all farms employ the same standard production method, so that their *ATC* curves are identical. Entry will then continue until price falls all the way to the minimum value of *ATC*. (At any price higher than that, economic profit would still be positive, and entry would continue, driving price still lower.) Recall from Chapter 6 that the short-run marginal cost curve intersects the

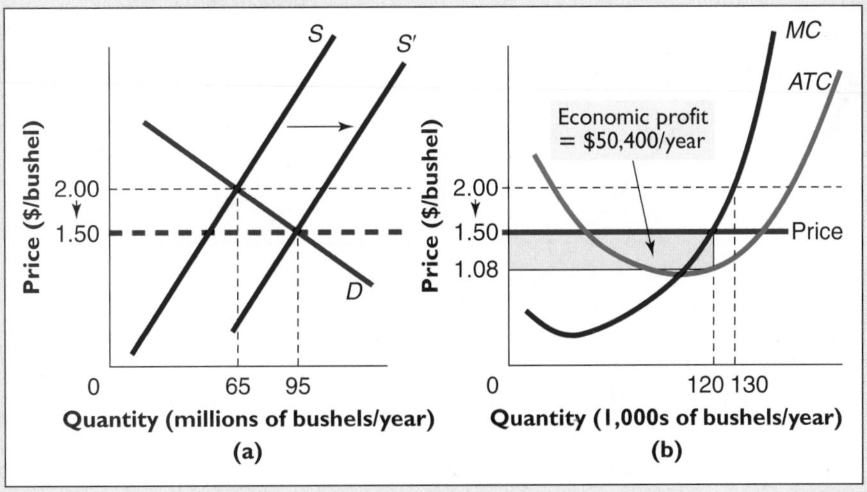

FIGURE 7.3
The Effect of Entry on Price and Economic Profit.
At the original price of $2 per bushel, existing farmers earned economic profit, prompting new farmers to enter. With entry, supply shifts right [from *S* to *S′* in (a)] and equilibrium price falls, as does economic profit (b).

FIGURE 7.4

Equilibrium when Entry Ceases.

Further entry ceases once price falls to the minimum value of *ATC*. At that point, all firms earn a normal economic profit. Equivalently, each earns an economic profit of zero.

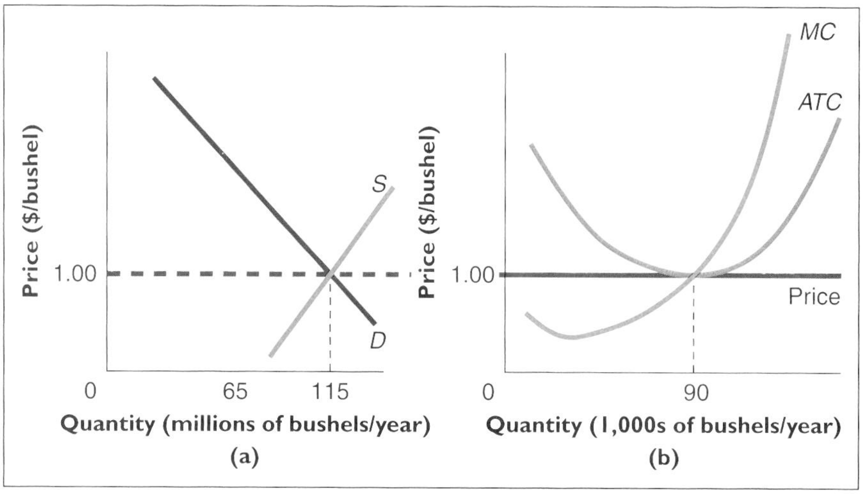

ATC curve at the minimum point of the *ATC* curve. This means that once price reaches the minimum value of *ATC*, the profit-maximizing rule of setting price equal to marginal cost results in a quantity for which price and *ATC* are the same. And when that happens, economic profit for the representative farm will be exactly zero, as shown in Figure 7.4(b).

In the adjustment process just considered, the initial equilibrium price was above the minimum value of *ATC*, giving rise to positive economic profits. Suppose instead that the market demand curve for corn had intersected the short-run supply curve at a price below the minimum value of each firm's *ATC* curve, as shown in Figure 7.5(a). As long as this price is above the minimum value of average variable cost,[2] each farm will supply that quantity of corn for which price equals marginal cost, shown as 70,000 bushels per year in Figure 7.5(b). Note, however, that at that quantity, the farm's average total cost is $1.05 per bushel, or $0.30 more than the price for which it sells each bushel. As shown in (b), the farm thus sustains an economic loss of $21,000 per year.

FIGURE 7.5

A Short-Run Economic Loss in the Corn Market.

When price is below the minimum value of *ATC* (a), each farm sustains an economic loss (b).

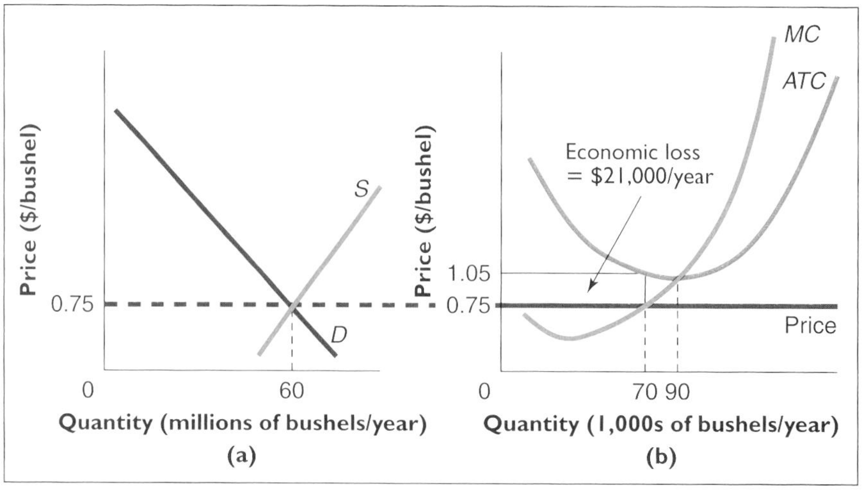

[2]This qualification refers to the firm's shutdown condition, discussed in Chapter 6.

If the demand curve that led to the low price and resulting economic losses in Figure 7.5 is expected to persist, farmers will begin to abandon farming for other activities that promise better returns. This means that the supply curve for corn will shift to the left, resulting in higher prices and smaller losses. Exit from corn farming will continue, in fact, until price has again risen to $1 per bushel, at which point there will be no incentive for further exit. Once again we see a stable equilibrium in which price is $1 per bushel, as shown in Figure 7.6.

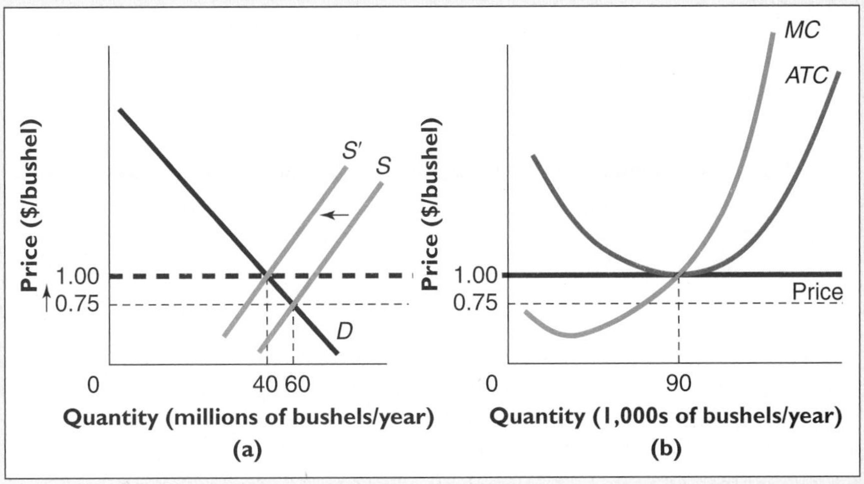

FIGURE 7.6
Equilibrium when Exit Ceases.
Further exit ceases once price rises to the minimum value of *ATC*. At that point, all firms earn a normal economic profit. Equivalently, each earns an economic profit of zero.

Given our simplifying assumptions that all corn farms employ a standardized production method and that inputs can be purchased in any quantities at fixed prices, the price of corn cannot remain above $1 per bushel (the minimum point on the *ATC* curve) in the long run. Any higher price would stimulate additional entry until price again fell to that level. Further, the price of corn cannot remain below $1 per bushel in the long run because any lower price would stimulate exit until the price of corn again rose to $1 per bushel.

The fact that firms are free to enter or leave an industry at any time ensures that, in the long run, all firms in the industry will tend to earn zero economic profit. Their *goal* is not to earn zero profit. Rather, the zero-profit tendency is a consequence of the price movements associated with entry and exit. As the Equilibrium Principle—also called the No-Cash-on-the-Table Principle (see Chapter 2)—predicts, when people confront an opportunity for gain, they are almost always quick to exploit it.

Equilibrium

What does the long-run supply curve look like in the corn market just discussed? This question is equivalent to asking, "What is the marginal cost of producing additional bushels of corn in the long run?" In general, adjustment in the long run may entail not just entry and exit of standardized firms, but also the ability of firms to alter the mix of capital equipment and other fixed inputs they employ. Explicit consideration of this additional step would complicate the analysis considerably but would not alter the basic logic of the simpler account we present here, which assumes that all firms operate with the same standard mix of fixed inputs in the short run. Under this assumption, the long-run adjustment process consists exclusively of the entry and exit of firms that use a single standardized production method.

The fact that a new firm could enter or leave this corn market at any time means that corn production can always be augmented or reduced in the long run at a cost of $1 per bushel. And this, in turn, means that the long-run supply curve of corn will be a horizontal line at a price equal to the minimum value of the *ATC* curve, $1 per bushel. Since the long-run marginal cost (*LMC*) of producing corn is constant, so is the long-run average cost (*LAC*) and it, too, is $1 per bushel,

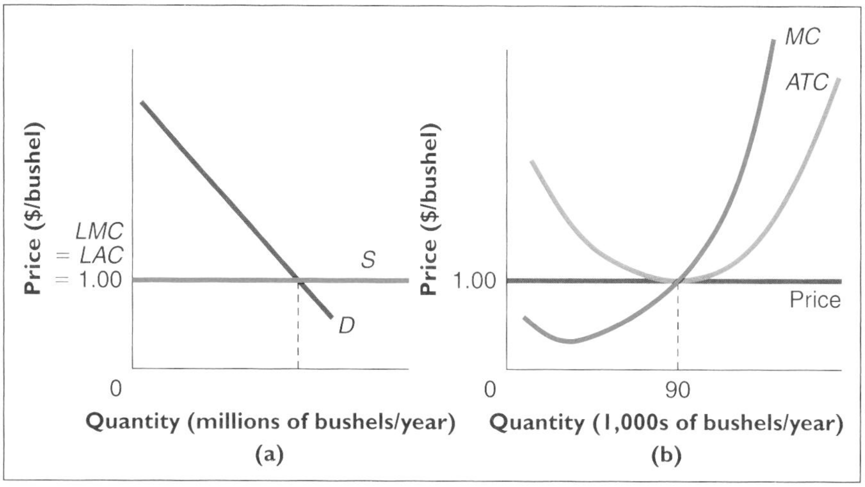

FIGURE 7.7
Long-Run Equilibrium in a Corn Market with Constant Long-Run Average Cost.
When each producer has the same *ATC* curve, the industry can supply as much or as little output as buyers wish to buy at a price equal to the minimum value of *ATC* (a). At that price, the representative producer (b) earns zero economic profit.

as shown in Figure 7.7(a). Figure 7.7(b) shows the *MC* and *ATC* curves of a representative corn farm. At a price of $1 per bushel, this corn market is said to be in long-run equilibrium. The representative farm produces 90,000 bushels of corn each year, the quantity for which price equals its marginal cost. And since price is exactly equal to *ATC*, this farm also earns an economic profit of zero.

These observations call attention to two attractive features of the invisible hand theory. One is that the market outcome is efficient in the long run. Note, for example, that when the corn market is in long-run equilibrium, the value to buyers of the last unit of corn sold is $1 per bushel, which is exactly the same as the long-run marginal cost of producing it. Thus, there is no possible rearrangement of resources that would make some participants in this market better off without causing harm to some others. If farmers were to expand production, for example, the added costs incurred would exceed the added benefits; and if they were to contract production, the cost savings would be less than the benefits forgone.

A second attractive feature of long-run competitive equilibrium is the market outcome can be described as fair, in the sense that the price buyers must pay is no higher than the cost incurred by suppliers. That cost includes a normal profit, the opportunity cost of the resources supplied by owners of the firm.

We must emphasize that Smith's invisible hand theory does not mean that market allocation of resources is optimal in every way. It simply means that markets are efficient in the limited technical sense discussed in the preceding chapter. Thus, if the current allocation differs from the market-equilibrium allocation, the invisible hand theory implies that we can reallocate resources in a way that makes some people better off without harming others.

The following example affords additional insight into how Smith's invisible hand works in practice.

What happens in a city with "too many" hair stylists and "too few" aerobics instructors?

At the initial equilibrium quantities and prices in the markets for haircuts and aerobics classes shown in Figure 7.8, all suppliers are currently earning zero economic profit. Now suppose that styles suddenly change in favor of longer hair and increased physical fitness. If the long-run marginal cost of altering current production levels is constant in both markets, describe how prices and quantities will change in each market, in both the short run and the long run. Are the new equilibrium quantities socially optimal?

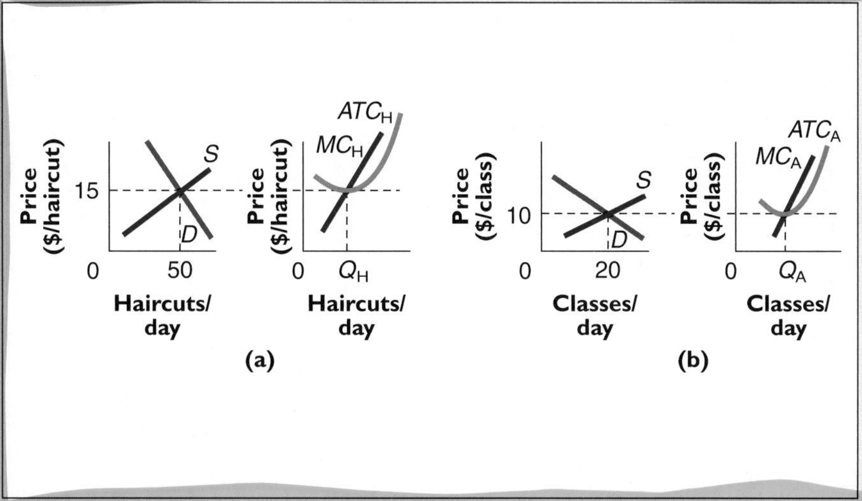

FIGURE 7.8
Initial Equilibrium in the Markets for (a) Haircuts and (b) Aerobics Classes.
MC_H and ATC_H are the marginal cost and average total cost curves for a representative hair stylist and MC_A and ATC_A are the marginal cost and average total cost curves for a representative aerobics instructor. Both markets are initially in long-run equilibrium, with sellers in each market earning zero economic profit.

The shift to longer hair styles means a leftward shift in the demand for haircuts, while the increased emphasis on physical fitness implies a rightward shift in the demand curve for aerobics classes, as seen in Figure 7.9. As a result of these demand shifts, the new short-run equilibrium prices change. For the sake of illustration, these new prices are shown as \$12 per haircut and \$15 per aerobics class.

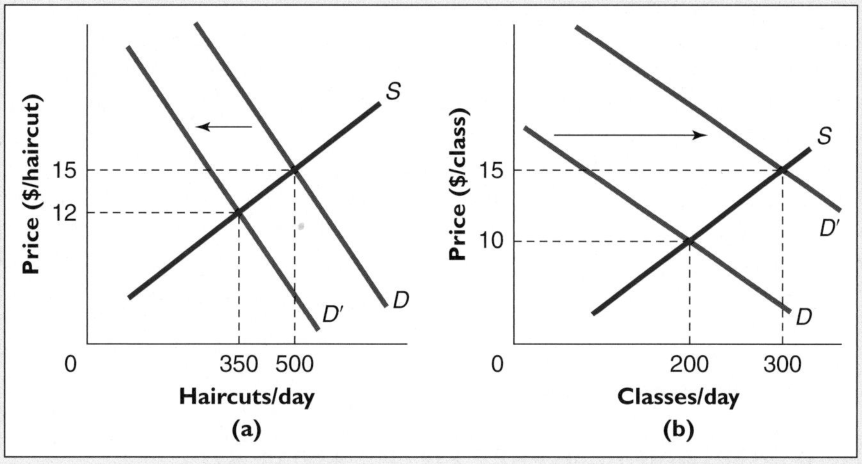

FIGURE 7.9
The Short-Run Effect of Demand Shifts in Two Markets.
(a) The decline in demand for haircuts causes the price of haircuts to fall from \$15 to \$12 in the short run.
(b) The increase in demand for aerobics classes causes the price of classes to rise from \$10 to \$15 in the short run.

Because each producer was earning zero economic profit at the original equilibrium prices, hair stylists will experience economic losses and aerobics instructors will experience economic profits at the new prices, as seen in Figure 7.10.

Because the short-run equilibrium price of haircuts results in economic losses for hair stylists, some hair stylists will begin to leave that market in search of more favorable opportunities elsewhere. As a result, the short-run supply curve of haircuts will shift leftward, resulting in a higher equilibrium price. Exit of hair stylists will continue until the price of haircuts rises sufficiently to cover the long-run opportunity cost of providing them, which by assumption is \$15.

By the same token, because the short-run equilibrium price of aerobics classes results in economic profits for instructors, outsiders will begin to enter that market,

FIGURE 7.10
Economic Profit and Loss in the Short Run.
The assumed demand shifts result in an economic loss for the representative hair stylist (a) and an economic profit for the representative aerobics instructor (b).

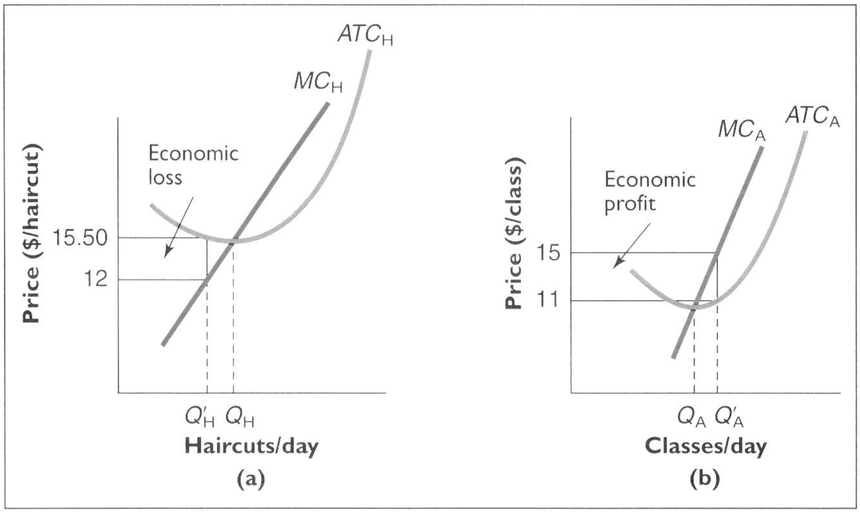

causing the short-run supply curve of classes to shift rightward. New instructors will continue to enter until the price of classes falls to the long-run opportunity cost of providing them. By assumption, that cost is $10. Once all adjustments have taken place, there will be fewer haircuts and more aerobics classes than before. But because marginal costs in both markets were assumed constant in the long run, the prices of the two goods will again be at their original levels.

It bears mention that those stylists who leave the hair-cutting market will not necessarily be the same people who enter the aerobics teaching market. Indeed, given the sheer number of occupations a former hair stylist might choose to pursue, the likelihood of such a switch is low. Movements of resources will typically involve several indirect steps. Thus, a former hair stylist might become a secretary, and a former postal worker might become an aerobics instructor.

We also note that the invisible hand theory says nothing about how long these adjustments might take. In some markets, especially labor markets, the required movements might take months or even years. But if the supply and demand curves remain stable, the markets will eventually reach equilibrium prices and quantities. And the new prices and quantities will be socially optimal in the same sense as before. Because the value to buyers of the last unit sold will be the same as the marginal cost of producing it, no additional transactions will be possible that benefit some without harming others. ◆

THE IMPORTANCE OF FREE ENTRY AND EXIT

The allocative function of price cannot operate unless firms can enter new markets and leave existing ones at will. If new firms could not enter a market in which existing firms were making a large economic profit, economic profit would not tend to fall to zero over time, and price would not tend to gravitate toward the marginal cost of production.

barrier to entry any force that prevents firms from entering a new market

Forces that inhibit firms from entering new markets are called **barriers to entry.** In the book publishing market, for example, the publisher of a book enjoys copyright protection granted by the government. Copyright law forbids other publishers from producing and selling their own editions of protected works. This barrier allows the price of a popular book to remain significantly above its cost of production for an extended period, all the while generating an economic profit for its publisher. (A copyright provides no *guarantee* of a profit, and indeed most new books actually generate an economic loss for their publishers.)

Barriers to entry may result from practical as well as legal constraints. Some economists, for example, have argued that the compelling advantages of product compatibility have created barriers to entry in the computer software market. Since more than 90 percent of new desktop computers come with Microsoft's Windows software already installed, rival companies have difficulty selling other operating systems that may prevent users from exchanging files with friends and colleagues. This fact, more than any other, explains Microsoft's spectacular profit history.

No less important than the freedom to enter a market is the freedom to leave. When the airline industry was regulated by the federal government, air carriers were often required to serve specific markets, even though they were losing money in them. When firms discover that a market, once entered, is difficult or impossible to leave, they become reluctant to enter new markets. Barriers to exit thus become barriers to entry. Without reasonably free entry and exit, then, the implications of Adam Smith's invisible hand theory cannot be expected to hold.

All things considered, producers enjoy a high degree of freedom of entry in most U.S. markets. Because free entry is one of the defining characteristics of perfectly competitive markets, unless otherwise stated, we'll assume its existence.

RECAP | THE INVISIBLE HAND THEORY

In market economies, the allocative and rationing functions of prices guide resources to their most highly valued uses. Prices influence how much of each type of good gets produced (the allocative function). Firms enter industries in which prices are sufficiently high to sustain an economic profit and leave those in which low prices result in an economic loss. Prices also direct existing supplies of goods to the buyers who value them most (the rationing function).

Industries in which firms earn a positive economic profit tend to attract new firms, shifting industry supply to the right. Firms tend to leave industries in which they sustain an economic loss, shifting supply curves to the left. In each case, the supply movements continue until economic profit reaches zero. In long-run equilibrium, the value of the last unit produced to buyers is equal to its marginal cost of production, leaving no possibility for additional mutually beneficial transactions.

ECONOMIC RENT VERSUS ECONOMIC PROFIT

Microsoft chairman Bill Gates is the wealthiest man on the planet, largely because the problem of compatibility prevents rival suppliers from competing effectively in the many software markets dominated by his company. Yet numerous people have become fabulously rich even in markets with no conspicuous barriers to entry. If market forces push economic profit toward zero, how can that happen?

The answer to this question hinges on the distinction between economic profit and **economic rent**. Most people think of rent as the payment they make to a landlord or the supplier of a dorm refrigerator, but the term *economic rent* has a different meaning. Economic rent is that portion of the payment for an input that is above the supplier's reservation price for that input. Suppose, for example, that a landowner's reservation price for an acre of land is $100 per year. That is, suppose he would be willing to lease it to a farmer as long as he received an annual payment of at least $100, but for less than that amount he would rather leave it fallow. If a farmer gives him an annual payment not of $100 but of $1,000, the landowner's economic rent from that payment will be $900 per year.

economic rent that part of the payment for a factor of production that exceeds the owner's reservation price

Economic profit is like economic rent in that it, too, may be seen as the difference between what someone is paid (the businessowner's total revenue) and her reservation price for remaining in business (the sum of all her costs, explicit and implicit). But whereas competition pushes economic profit toward zero, it has no such effect on the economic rent for inputs that cannot be replicated easily. For example, although the lease payments for land may remain substantially above the landowner's reservation price, year in and year out, new land cannot come onto the market to reduce or eliminate the economic rent through competition. There is, after all, only so much land to be had.

As the following example illustrates, economic rent can accrue to people as well as land.

How much economic rent will a talented chef get?

EN 7

A community has 100 restaurants, 99 of which employ chefs of normal ability at a salary of \$30,000 per year, the same as the amount they could earn in other occupations that are equally attractive to them. But the 100th restaurant has an unusually talented chef. Because of her reputation, diners are willing to pay 50 percent more for the meals she cooks than for those prepared by ordinary chefs. Owners of the 99 restaurants with ordinary chefs each collects \$300,000 per year in revenue, which is just enough to ensure that each earns exactly a normal profit. If the talented chef's opportunities outside the restaurant industry are the same as those of ordinary chefs, how much will she be paid by her employer at equilibrium? How much of her pay will be economic rent? How much economic profit will her employer earn?

Because diners are willing to pay 50 percent more for meals cooked by the talented chef, the owner who hires her will take in total receipts not of \$300,000 per year but of \$450,000. In the long run, competition should assure that the talented chef's total pay each year will be \$180,000 per year, the sum of the \$30,000 that ordinary chefs get and the \$150,000 in extra revenues for which she is solely responsible. Since the talented chef's reservation price is the amount she could earn outside the restaurant industry—by assumption, \$30,000 per year, the same as for ordinary chefs—her economic rent is \$150,000 per year. The economic profit of the owner who hires her will be exactly zero. ◆

Since the talented chef's opportunities outside the restaurant industry are no better than an ordinary chef's, why is it necessary to pay the talented chef so much? Suppose her employer were to pay her only \$60,000, which they both would consider a generous salary since it is twice what ordinary chefs earn. The employer would then earn an economic profit of \$120,000 per year since his annual revenue would be \$150,000 more than that of ordinary restaurants, but his costs would be only \$30,000 more.

But this economic profit would create an opportunity for the owner of some other restaurant to bid the talented chef away. For example, if the owner of a competing restaurant were to hire the talented chef at a salary of \$70,000, the chef would be \$10,000 per year better off and the rival owner would earn an economic profit of \$110,000 per year, rather than his current economic profit of zero. Furthermore, if the talented chef is the sole reason that a restaurant earns a positive economic profit, the bidding for that chef should continue as long as any economic profit remains. Some other owner will pay her \$80,000, still another \$90,000, and so on. Equilibrium will be reached only when the talented chef's salary has been bid up to the point that no further economic profit remains—in our example, at an annual paycheck of \$180,000.

This bidding process assumes, of course, that the reason for the chef's superior performance is that she possesses some personal talent that cannot be copied. If instead it were the result of, say, training at a culinary institute in France, then her privileged position would erode over time, as other chefs sought similar training.

RECAP	ECONOMIC RENT VERSUS ECONOMIC PROFIT

Economic rent is the amount by which the payment to a factor of production exceeds the supplier's reservation price. Unlike economic profit, which is driven toward zero by competition, economic rent may persist for extended periods, especially in the case of factors with special talents that cannot easily be duplicated.

THE INVISIBLE HAND IN ACTION

To help develop your intuition about how the invisible hand works, we will examine how it helps us gain insight into patterns we observe in a wide variety of different contexts. In each case, the key idea we want you to focus on is that opportunities for private gain seldom remain unexploited for very long. Perhaps more than any other, this idea encapsulates the essence of that distinctive mindset known as "thinking like an economist."

THE INVISIBLE HAND AT THE SUPERMARKET AND ON THE FREEWAY

As the following example illustrates, the No-Cash-on-the-Table Principle refers not just to opportunities to earn economic profits in cash, but also to any other opportunity to achieve a more desirable outcome.

Equilibrium

Example 7.1

THE ECONOMIC NATURALIST

Why do supermarket checkout lines all tend to be roughly the same length?

Pay careful attention the next few times you go grocery shopping and you'll notice that the lines at all the checkout stations tend to be roughly the same length. Suppose you saw one line that was significantly shorter than the others as you wheeled your cart toward the checkout area. Which line would you choose? The shorter one, of course; and because most shoppers would do the same, the short line seldom remains shorter for long. ●

EXERCISE 7.2

Use the No-Cash-on-the-Table Principle to explain why all lanes on a crowded, multilane freeway move at about the same speed.

Equilibrium

Why do you seldom see one supermarket checkout line that is substantially shorter than all the others?

THE INVISIBLE HAND AND COST-SAVING INNOVATIONS

When economists speak of perfectly competitive firms, they have in mind businesses whose contribution to total market output is too small to have a perceptible impact on market price. As explained in Chapter 6, such firms are often called price takers: They take the market price of their product as given and then produce that quantity of output for which marginal cost equals that price.

This characterization of the competitive firm gives the impression that the firm is essentially a passive actor in the marketplace. Yet for most firms, that is anything but the case. As the next example illustrates, even those firms that cannot hope to influence the market prices of their products have very powerful incentives to develop and introduce cost-saving innovations.

How do cost-saving innovations affect economic profit in the short run? In the long run?

Forty merchant marine companies operate supertankers that carry oil from the Middle East to the United States. The cost per trip, including a normal profit, is $500,000. An engineer at one of these companies develops a more efficient propeller design that results in fuel savings of $20,000 per trip. How will this innovation affect the company's accounting and economic profits? Will these changes persist in the long run?

In the short run, the reduction in a single firm's costs will have no impact on the market price of transoceanic shipping services. The firm with the more efficient propeller will thus earn an economic profit of $20,000 per trip (since its total revenue will be the same as before, while its total cost will now be $20,000 per trip lower). As other firms learn about the new design, however, they will begin to adopt it, causing their individual supply curves to shift downward (since the marginal cost per trip at these firms will drop by $20,000). The shift in these individual supply curves will cause the market supply curve to shift, which in turn will result in a lower market price for shipping and a decline in economic profit at the firm where the innovation originated. When all firms have adopted the new, efficient design, the long-run supply curve for the industry will have shifted downward by $20,000 per trip and each company will again be earning only a normal profit. At that point, any firm that did *not* adopt the new propeller design would suffer an economic loss of $20,000 per trip. ◆

The incentive to come up with cost-saving innovations in order to reap economic profit is one of the most powerful forces on the economic landscape. Its beauty, in terms of the invisible hand theory, is that competition among firms ensures that the resulting cost savings will be passed along to consumers in the long run.

THE DISTINCTION BETWEEN AN EQUILIBRIUM AND A SOCIAL OPTIMUM

Equilibrium

The Equilibrium, or No-Cash-on-the-Table, Principle tells us that when a market reaches equilibrium, no further opportunities for gain are available to individuals. This principle implies that the market prices of resources that people own will eventually reflect their economic value. (As we will see in later chapters, the same cannot be said of resources that are not owned by anyone, such as fish in international waters.)

The No-Cash-on-the-Table Principle is sometimes misunderstood to mean that there are *never* any valuable opportunities to exploit. For example, the story is told of two economists on their way to lunch when they spot what appears to be a $100 bill lying on the sidewalk. When the younger economist stoops to pick up the bill, his older colleague restrains him, saying, "That can't be a $100 bill." "Why not?" asks the younger colleague. "If it were, someone would have picked it up by now," the older economist replies.

Equilibrium

The No-Cash-on-the-Table Principle means not that there *never* are any unexploited opportunities, but that there are none when the market is *in equilibrium*. Occasionally a $100 bill does lie on the sidewalk, and the person who first spots it and picks it up gains a windfall. Likewise, when a company's earnings prospects improve, *somebody* must be the first to recognize the opportunity, and that person can make a lot of money by purchasing the stock quickly.

Still, the No-Cash-on-the-Table Principle is important. It tells us, in effect, that there are only three ways to earn a big payoff: to work especially hard; to have some unusual skill, talent, or training; or simply to be lucky. The person who finds a big bill on the sidewalk is lucky, as are many of the investors whose stocks perform better than average. Other investors whose stocks do well achieve their gains through hard work or special talent. For example, the legendary investor Warren Buffett, whose portfolio has grown in value at almost three times the stock market average for the last 40 years, spends long hours studying annual financial reports and has a remarkably keen eye for the telling detail. Thousands of others work just as hard yet fail to beat the market averages.

It is important to stress, however, that a market being in equilibrium implies only that no additional opportunities are available *to individuals*. It does not imply that the resulting allocation is necessarily best from the point of view of society as a whole.

SMART FOR ONE, DUMB FOR ALL

Adam Smith's profound insight was that the individual pursuit of self-interest often promotes the broader interests of society. But unlike some of his modern disciples, Smith was under no illusion that this is *always* the case. Note, for example, Smith's elaboration on his description of the entrepreneur led by the invisible hand "to promote an end which was no part of his intention":

> Nor is it *always* the worse for society that it was no part of it. By pursuing his own interest he *frequently* promotes that of society more effectively than when he really intends to promote it. (Emphasis added.)

Smith was well aware that the individual pursuit of self-interest often does not coincide with society's interest. In Chapter 3 we cited activities that generate environmental pollution as an example of conflicting economic interests, noting that behavior in those circumstances may be described as smart for one but dumb for all. As the following example suggests, extremely high levels of investment in earnings forecasts also can be smart for one, dumb for all.

Example 7.2

THE ECONOMIC NATURALIST

Are there "too many" smart people working as corporate earnings forecasters?

Stock analysts use complex mathematical models to forecast corporate earnings. The more analysts invest in the development of these models, the more accurate the models become. Thus, the analyst whose model produces a reliable forecast sooner than others can reap a windfall by buying stocks whose prices are about to rise. Given the speed with which stock prices respond to new information, however, the results of even the second-fastest forecasting model may come too late to be of much use. Individual stock analysts thus face a powerful incentive to invest more and more money in their models, in the hope of generating the fastest forecast. Does this incentive result in the socially optimal level of investment in forecast models?

"Hi, Dad. Investment banking wasn't that great after all."

Beyond some point, increased speed of forecasting is of little benefit to society as a whole, whose interests suffer little when the price of a stock moves to its proper level a few hours more slowly. If *all* stock analysts spent less money on their forecasting models, *someone's* model would still produce the winning forecast, and the resources that might otherwise be devoted to fine-tuning the models could be put to more valued uses. Yet if any one individual spends less, he can be sure the winning forecast will not be his.

The invisible hand went awry in the situation just described because the benefit of an investment to the individual who made it was larger than the benefit of that investment to society as a whole. In later chapters we will discuss a broad class of investments with this property. In general, the efficacy of the invisible hand depends on the extent to which the individual costs and benefits of actions taken in the marketplace coincide with the respective costs and benefits of those actions to society. These exceptions notwithstanding, some of the most powerful forces at work in competitive markets clearly promote society's interests. ●

RECAP	EQUILIBRIUM VERSUS SOCIAL OPTIMUM

A market in equilibrium is one in which no additional opportunities for gain remain available to individual buyers or sellers. The No-Cash-on-the-Table Principle describes powerful forces that help push markets toward equilibrium. But even if all markets are in equilibrium, the resulting allocation of resources need not be socially optimal. Equilibrium will not be socially optimal when the costs or benefits to individual participants in the market differ from those experienced by society as a whole.

MARKET EQUILIBRIUM AND EFFICIENCY

Private markets cannot by themselves guarantee an income distribution that most people regard as fair. Nor can they ensure clean air, uncongested highways, or safe neighborhoods for all.

In virtually all successful societies, markets are supplemented by active political coordination in at least some instances. We will almost always achieve our goals more effectively if we know what tasks private markets can do well, and then allow them to perform those tasks. Unfortunately, the discovery that markets cannot solve *every* problem seems to have led some critics to conclude that markets cannot solve *any* problems. This misperception is a dangerous one because it has prompted attempts to prevent markets from doing even those tasks for which they are ideally suited.

Our task in this section will be to explore why many tasks are best left to the market. We will explore the conditions under which unregulated markets generate the largest possible economic surplus. We also will discuss why attempts to interfere with market outcomes often lead to unintended and undesired consequences.

As noted in Chapter 3, the mere fact that markets coordinate the production of a large and complex list of goods and services is reason enough to marvel at them. But in the absence of pollution and other externalities like the ones discussed in the preceding section, economists make an even stronger claim—namely, that markets not only produce these goods, but also produce them as efficiently as possible.

***efficient* (or *Pareto efficient*)** a situation is efficient if no change is possible that will help some people without harming others

The term **efficient**, as economists use it, has a narrow technical meaning. When we say that market equilibrium is efficient, we mean simply this: *If price and quantity take anything other than their equilibrium values, a transaction that will make at least some people better off without harming others can always be found.* This conception of efficiency is also known as **Pareto efficiency**, after Vilfredo Pareto, the nineteenth-century Italian economist who introduced it.

Why is market equilibrium efficient in this sense? The answer is that it is always possible to construct an exchange that helps some without harming others whenever a market is out of equilibrium. Suppose, for example, that the supply and demand curves for milk are as shown in Figure 7.11 and that the current price of milk is $1 per gallon. At that price, sellers offer only 2,000 gallons of milk a day. At that quantity, the marginal buyer values an extra gallon of milk at $2. This is the price that corresponds to 2,000 gallons a day on the demand curve, which represents what the marginal buyer is willing to pay for an additional gallon (another application of the vertical interpretation of the demand curve). We also know that the cost of producing an extra gallon of milk is only $1. This is the price that corresponds to 2,000 gallons a day on the supply curve, which equals marginal cost (another application of the vertical interpretation of the supply curve).

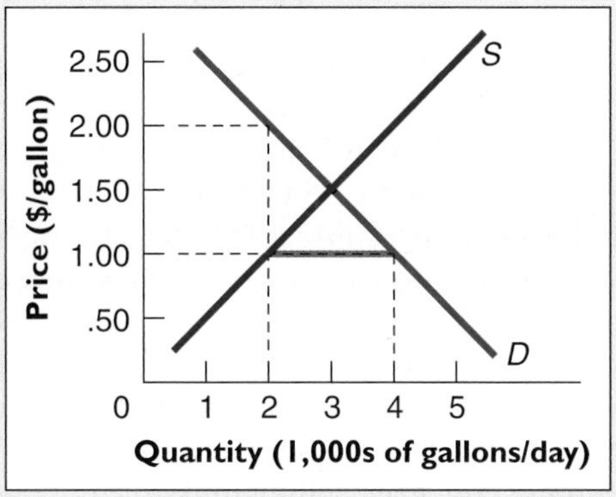

FIGURE 7.11
A Market in Which Price Is Below the Equilibrium Level.
In this market, milk is currently selling for $1 per gallon, $0.50 below the equilibrium price of $1.50 per gallon.

Furthermore, a price of $1 per gallon leads to excess demand of 2,000 gallons per day, which means that many frustrated buyers cannot buy as much milk as they want at the going price. Now suppose a supplier sells an extra gallon of milk to the most eager of these buyers for $1.25, as in Figure 7.12. Since the extra gallon cost only $1 to produce, the seller is $0.25 better off than before. And since the most eager buyer values the extra gallon at $2, that buyer is $0.75 better off than before. In sum, the transaction creates an extra $1 of economic surplus out of thin air!

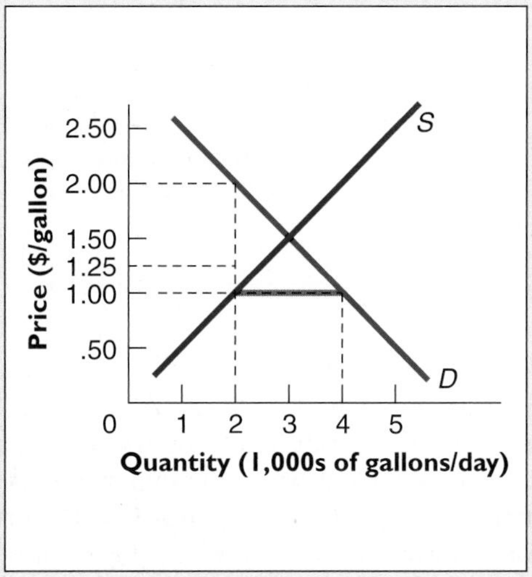

FIGURE 7.12
How Excess Demand Creates an Opportunity for a Surplus-Enhancing Transaction.
At a market price of $1 per gallon, the most intensely dissatisfied buyer is willing to pay $2 for an additional gallon, which a seller can produce at a cost of only $1. If this buyer pays the seller $1.25 for the extra gallon, the buyer gains an economic surplus of $0.75 and the seller gains an economic surplus of $0.25.

Note that none of the other buyers or sellers is harmed by this transaction. Thus, milk selling for only $1 per gallon cannot be efficient. As the following exercise illustrates, there was nothing special about the price of $1 per gallon. Indeed, if milk sells for *any* price below $1.50 per gallon (the market equilibrium price), we can design a similar transaction, which means that selling milk for any price less than $1.50 per gallon cannot be efficient.

EXERCISE 7.3

In Figure 7.11, suppose that milk initially sells for 50 cents per gallon. Describe a transaction that will create additional economic surplus for both buyer and seller without causing harm to anyone else.

What is more, it is always possible to describe a transaction that will create additional surplus for both buyer and seller whenever the price lies above the market equilibrium level. Suppose, for example, that the current price is \$2 per gallon in the milk market shown in Figure 7.11. At that price, we have excess supply of 2,000 gallons per day (see Figure 7.13). Suppose the most dissatisfied producer sells a gallon of milk for \$1.75 to the buyer who values it most highly. This buyer, who would have been willing to pay \$2, will be \$0.25 better off than before. Likewise the producer, who would have been willing to sell milk for as little as \$1 per gallon (the marginal cost of production at 2,000 gallons per day), will be \$0.75 better off than before. As when the price was \$1 per gallon, the new transaction creates \$1 of additional economic surplus without harming any other buyer or seller. Since we could design a similar surplus-enhancing transaction at any price above the equilibrium level, selling milk for more than \$1.50 per gallon cannot be efficient.

FIGURE 7.13
How Excess Supply Creates an Opportunity for a Surplus-Enhancing Transaction.
At a market price of \$2 per gallon, dissatisfied sellers can produce an additional gallon of milk at a cost of only \$1, which is \$1 less than a buyer would be willing to pay for it. If the buyer pays the seller \$1.75 for an extra gallon, the buyer gains an economic surplus of \$0.25 and the seller gains an economic surplus of \$0.75.

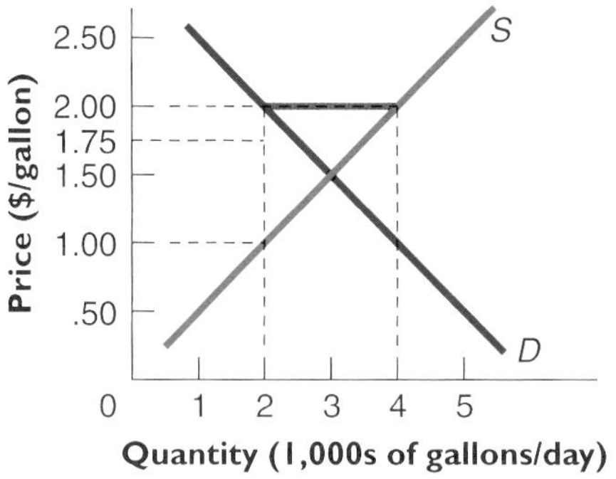

The vertical interpretations of the supply and demand curves thus make it clear why only the equilibrium price in a market can be efficient. When the price is either higher or lower than the equilibrium price, the quantity exchanged in the market will always be lower than the equilibrium quantity. If the price is below equilibrium, the quantity sold will be the amount that sellers offer. If the price is above equilibrium, the quantity sold will be the amount that buyers wish to buy. In either case, the vertical value on the demand curve at the quantity exchanged, which is the value of an extra unit to buyers, must be larger than the vertical value on the supply curve, which is the marginal cost of producing that unit.

So the market equilibrium price is the *only* price at which buyers and sellers cannot design a surplus-enhancing transaction. The market equilibrium price leads, in other words, to the largest possible total economic surplus. In this specific, limited sense, free markets are said to produce and distribute goods and services efficiently.

Actually, to claim that market equilibrium is always efficient even in this limited sense is an overstatement. The claim holds only if buyers and sellers are well informed, if markets are perfectly competitive, and if the demand and supply curves satisfy certain other restrictions. For example, market equilibrium will not be efficient if the individual marginal cost curves that add up to the market supply curve fail to include all relevant costs of producing the product. Thus, as we saw in Chapter 3, the true cost of expanding output will be higher than indicated by the market supply curve if production generates pollution that harms others. The equilibrium output will then be inefficiently large and the equilibrium price inefficiently low.

Likewise, market equilibrium will not be efficient if the individual demand curves that make up the market demand curve do not capture all the relevant benefits of buying additional units of the product. For instance, if a homeowner's willingness to pay for ornamental shrubs is based only on the enjoyment she herself gains from them, and not on any benefits that may accrue to her neighbors, the market demand curve for shrubs will understate their value to the neighborhood. The equilibrium quantity of ornamental shrubs will be inefficiently small and the market price for shrubs will be inefficiently low.

We will take up such market imperfections in greater detail in later chapters. For now, we will confine our attention to perfectly competitive markets whose demand curves capture all relevant benefits and whose supply curves capture all relevant costs. For such goods, market equilibrium will always be efficient in the limited sense described earlier.

EFFICIENCY IS NOT THE ONLY GOAL

The fact that market equilibrium maximizes economic surplus is an attractive feature, to be sure. Bear in mind, however, that "efficient" does not mean the same thing as "good." For example, the market for milk may be in equilibrium at a price of $1.50 per gallon, yet many poor families may be unable to afford milk for their children at that price. Still others may not even have a place for their children to sleep.

Efficiency is a concept that is based on predetermined attributes of buyers and sellers—their incomes, tastes, abilities, knowledge, and so on. Through the combined effects of individual cost-benefit decisions, these attributes give rise to the supply and demand curves for each good produced in an economy. If we are concerned about inequality in the distribution of attributes like income, we should not be surprised to discover that markets do not always yield outcomes we like.

Most of us could agree, for example, that the world would be a better one if all people had enough income to feed their families adequately. The claim that equilibrium in the market for milk is efficient means simply that *taking people's incomes as given,* the resulting allocation of milk cannot be altered so as to help some people without at the same time harming others.

To this a critic of the market system might respond: So what? As such critics rightly point out, imposing costs on others may be justified if doing so will help those with sufficiently important unmet demands. For example, most people would prefer to fund homeless shelters with their tax dollars rather than let the homeless freeze to death. Arguing in these terms, American policymakers responded to rapid increases in the price of oil in the late 1970s by imposing price controls on home heating oil. Many of us might agree that if the alternative had been to take no action at all, price controls might have been justified in the name of social justice.

The economist's concept of market efficiency makes clear that there *must* be a better alternative policy. Price controls on oil prevent the market from reaching equilibrium, and as we've seen, that means forgoing transactions that would benefit some people without harming others.

WHY EFFICIENCY SHOULD BE THE FIRST GOAL

Efficiency is important not because it is a desirable end in itself, but because it enables us to achieve all our other goals to the fullest possible extent. It is always

RECAP	EQUILIBRIUM AND EFFICIENCY

A market in equilibrium is said to be efficient, or Pareto efficient, meaning that no reallocation is possible that will benefit some people without harming others.

When a market is not in equilibrium—because price is either above the equilibrium level or below it—the quantity exchanged is always less than the equilibrium level. At such a quantity, a transaction can always be made in which both buyer and seller benefit from the exchange of an additional unit of output.

Total economic surplus in a market is maximized when exchange occurs at the equilibrium price. But the fact that equilibrium is "efficient" in this sense does not mean that it is "good." All markets can be in equilibrium, yet many people may lack sufficient income to buy even basic goods and services. Still, permitting markets to reach equilibrium is important because, when economic surplus is maximized, it is possible to pursue every goal more fully.

possible to generate additional economic surplus when a market is out of equilibrium. To gain additional economic surplus is to gain more of the resources we need to do the things we want to do.

THE COST OF PREVENTING PRICE ADJUSTMENTS

PRICE CEILINGS

During 1979, an interruption in oil supplies from the Middle East caused the price of home heating oil to rise by more than 100 percent. Concern about the hardship this sudden price increase would impose on poor families in northern states led the government to impose a price ceiling in the market for home heating oil. This price ceiling prohibited sellers from charging more than a specified amount for heating oil.

The following example illustrates why imposing a price ceiling on heating oil, though well intended, was a bad idea.

How much waste does a price ceiling on heating oil cause?

Suppose the demand and supply curves for home heating oil are as shown in Figure 7.14, in which the equilibrium price is \$1.40 per gallon. Suppose that at that price, many poor families cannot heat their homes adequately. Out of concern for the poor, legislators pass a law setting the maximum price at \$1 per gallon. How much lost economic surplus does this policy cost society?

First, let's calculate total economic surplus without price controls. If this market is not regulated, 3,000 gallons per day will be sold at a price of \$1.40 per gallon. In Figure 7.14, the economic surplus received by buyers is the area of the upper shaded triangle. Since the height of this triangle is \$0.60 per gallon and its base is 3,000 gallons per day, its area is equal to (1/2)(3,000 gallons/day)(\$0.60/gallon) = \$900 per day. The economic surplus received by producers is the area of the lower shaded triangle. Since this triangle also has an area of \$900 per day, total economic surplus in this market will be \$1,800 per day.

If the price of heating oil is prevented from rising above \$1 per gallon, only 1,000 gallons per day will be sold and the total economic surplus will be reduced

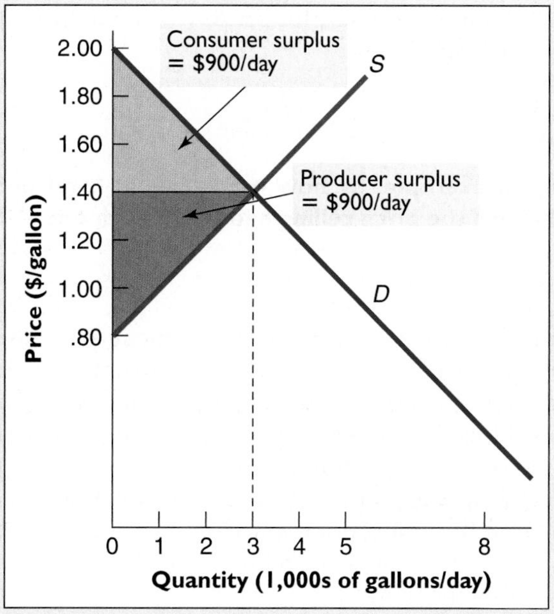

FIGURE 7.14
Economic Surplus in an Unregulated Market for Home Heating Oil.
For the supply and demand curves shown, the equilibrium price of home heating oil is $1.40 per gallon and the equilibrium quantity is 3,000 gallons per day. Consumer surplus is the area of the upper shaded triangle ($900 per day). Producer surplus is the area of the lower shaded triangle (also $900 per day).

by the area of the lined triangle shown in Figure 7.15. Since the height of this triangle is $0.80 per gallon and its base is 2,000 gallons per day, its area is (1/2)(2,000 gallons/day)($0.80/gallon) = $800 per day. Producer surplus falls from $900 per day in the unregulated market to the area of the lower shaded triangle, or (1/2)(1,000 gallons/day)($0.20/gallon) = $100 per day, which is a loss of $800 per day. Thus, the loss in total economic surplus is equal to the loss in producer surplus, which means that the new consumer surplus must be the same as the original consumer surplus. To verify this, note that consumer surplus with the price ceiling is the area of the upper shaded figure, which is again $900 per day. (Hint: To compute this area, first split the figure into a rectangle and a triangle.)

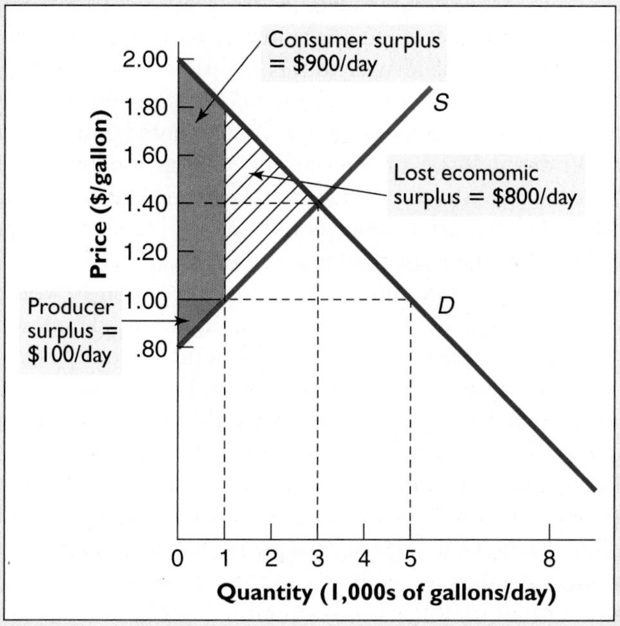

FIGURE 7.15
The Waste Caused by Price Controls.
By limiting output in the home heating oil market to 1,000 gallons per day, price controls cause a loss in economic surplus of $800 per day (area of the lined triangle).

By preventing the home heating oil market from reaching equilibrium, price controls waste \$800 of producer surplus per day without creating any additional surplus for consumers! ◆

EXERCISE 7.4

In the heating oil example, by how much would total economic surplus have been reduced if the price ceiling had been set not at \$1 but at \$1.20 per gallon?

For several reasons, the reduction in total economic surplus shown in Figure 7.15 is a conservative estimate of the waste caused by attempts to hold price below its equilibrium level. For one thing, the analysis assumes that each of the 1,000 gallons per day that are sold in this market will end up in the hands of the consumers who value them most—in the diagram, those whose reservation prices are above \$1.80 per gallon. But since any buyer whose reservation price is above \$1 per gallon will want to buy at the ceiling price, much of the oil actually sold is likely to go to buyers whose reservation prices are below \$1.80. Suppose, for example, that a buyer whose reservation price was \$1.50 per gallon made it into the line outside a heating oil supplier just ahead of a buyer whose reservation price was \$1.90 per gallon. If each buyer had a 20-gallon tank to fill, and if the first buyer got the last of the day's available oil, then total surplus would be smaller by \$8 that day than if the oil had gone to the second buyer.

A second reason that the reduction in surplus shown in Figure 7.15 is likely to be an underestimate is that shortages typically prompt buyers to take costly actions to enhance their chances of being served. For example, if the heating oil distributor begins selling its available supplies at 6:00 a.m., many buyers may arrive several hours early to ensure a place near the front of the line. Yet when all buyers incur the cost of arriving earlier, no one gets any more oil than before.

Notwithstanding the fact that price ceilings reduce total economic surplus, their defenders might argue that controls are justified because they enable at least some low-income families to buy heating oil at affordable prices. Yes, but the same objective could have been accomplished in a much less costly way—namely, by giving the poor more income with which to buy heating oil.

It may seem natural to wonder whether the poor, who have limited political power, can really hope to receive income transfers that would enable them to heat their homes. On reflection, the answer to this question would seem to be yes, *if the alternative is to impose price controls that would be even more costly than the income transfers*. After all, the price ceiling as implemented ends up costing heating oil sellers \$800 per day in lost economic surplus. So they ought to be willing to pay some amount less than \$800 a day in additional taxes in order to escape the burden of controls. The additional tax revenue could finance income transfers that would be far more beneficial to the poor than price controls.

This point is so important, and so often misunderstood by voters and policymakers, that we will emphasize it by putting it another way. Think of the economic surplus from a market as a pie to be divided among the various market participants. Figure 7.16(a) represents the \$1,000 per day of total economic surplus available to participants in the home heating oil market when the government limits the price of oil to \$1 per gallon. We divided this pie into two slices, labeled *R* and *P*, to denote the surpluses received by rich and poor participants. Figure 7.16(b) represents the \$1,800 per day of total economic surplus available when the price of home heating oil is free to reach its equilibrium level. This pie is divided among rich and poor participants in the same proportion as the pie in the left panel.

The important point to notice is this: *Because the pie on the right side is larger, both rich and poor participants in the home heating oil market can get a bigger slice*

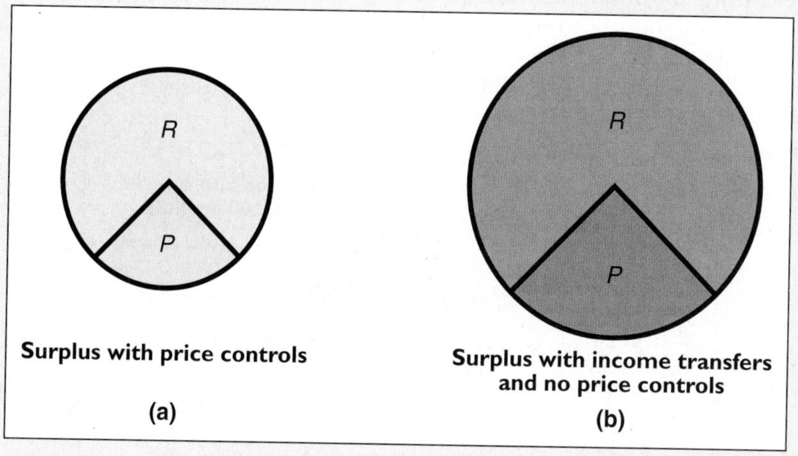

FIGURE 7.16
When the Pie Is Larger, Everyone Can Have a Bigger Slice.
Any policy that reduces total economic surplus is a missed opportunity to make everyone better off.

of the pie than they would have had under price controls. Rather than tinker with the market price of oil, it is in everyone's interest to simply transfer additional income to the poor.

Incentive

With the Incentive Principle in mind, supporters of price controls may object that income transfers to the poor might weaken people's incentive to work, and thus might prove extremely costly in the long run. Difficult issues do indeed arise in the design of programs for transferring income to the poor—issues we will consider in some detail in later chapters. But for now, suffice it to say that ways exist to transfer income without undermining work incentives significantly. One such method is the Earned Income Tax Credit, a program that supplements the wages of low-income workers. Given such programs, transferring income to the poor will always be more efficient than trying to boost their living standard through price controls.

PRICE SUBSIDIES

Sometimes governments try to assist low-income consumers by subsidizing the prices of "essential" goods and services. France and Russia, for example, have taken this approach at various points by subsidizing the price of bread. As the following example illustrates, such subsidies are like price ceilings in that they reduce total economic surplus.

By how much do subsidies reduce total economic surplus in the market for bread?

A small island nation imports bread for its population at the world price of \$2 per loaf. If the domestic demand curve for bread is as shown in Figure 7.17, by how much will total economic surplus decline in this market if the government provides a \$1 per loaf subsidy?

With no subsidy, the equilibrium price of bread in this market would be the world price of \$2 per loaf and the equilibrium quantity would be 4,000,000 loaves per month. The shaded triangle in Figure 7.17 represents consumer economic surplus for buyers in the domestic bread market. The height of this triangle is \$2 per loaf, and its base is 4,000,000 loaves per month, so its area is equal to (1/2)(4,000,000 loaves/month)(\$2/loaf) = \$4,000,000 per month. Because the country can import as much bread as it wishes at the world price of \$2 per loaf, supply is perfectly elastic in this market. Because the marginal cost of each loaf of bread to sellers is exactly the same as the price buyers pay, producer surplus in this market is zero. So total economic surplus is exactly equal to consumer surplus, which, again, is \$4,000,000 per month.

FIGURE 7.17
Economic Surplus in a Bread Market without Subsidy.
For the demand curve shown, consumer surplus (area of the shaded triangle) is $4,000,000 per month. This amount is equal to total economic surplus in the domestic bread market, since no bread is produced domestically.

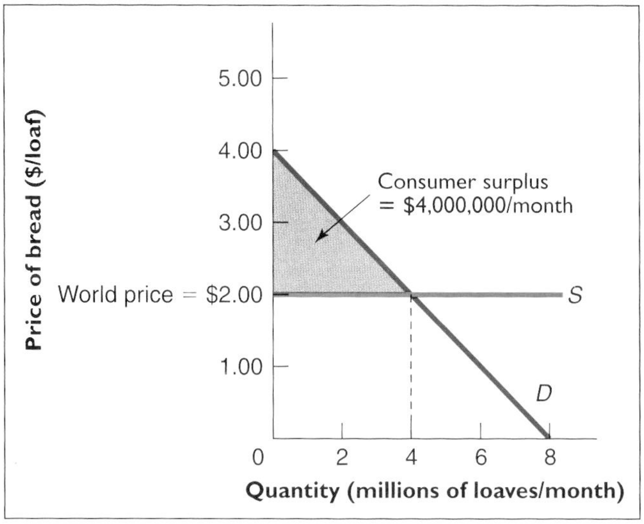

Now suppose that the government administers its $1 per loaf subsidy program by purchasing bread in the world market at $2 per loaf and reselling it in the domestic market for only $1 per loaf. At the new lower price, buyers will now consume not 4,000,000 loaves per month but 6,000,000. Consumer surplus for buyers in the bread market is now the area of the larger shaded triangle in Figure 7.18: (1/2)($3/loaf)(6,000,000 loaves/month) = $9,000,000 per month, or $5,000,000 per month more than before. The catch is that the subsidy wasn't free. Its cost, which must be borne by taxpayers, is ($1/loaf)(6,000,000 loaves/month) = $6,000,000 per month. So even though consumer surplus in the bread market is larger than before, the net effect of the subsidy program is actually to reduce total economic surplus by $1,000,000 per month.

Another way to see why the subsidy reduces total economic surplus by that amount is to note that total economic surplus is maximized at 4,000,000 loaves per month, the quantity for which the marginal buyer's reservation price is equal to marginal cost, and that the subsidy induces additional consumption of 2,000,000

FIGURE 7.18
The Reduction in Economic Surplus from a Subsidy.
Since the marginal cost of bread is $2 per loaf, total economic surplus is maximized at 4,000,000 loaves per month, the quantity for which the marginal buyer's reservation price is equal to marginal cost. The reduction in economic surplus from consuming an additional 2,000,000 loaves per month is $1,000,000 per month, the area of the smaller shaded triangle.

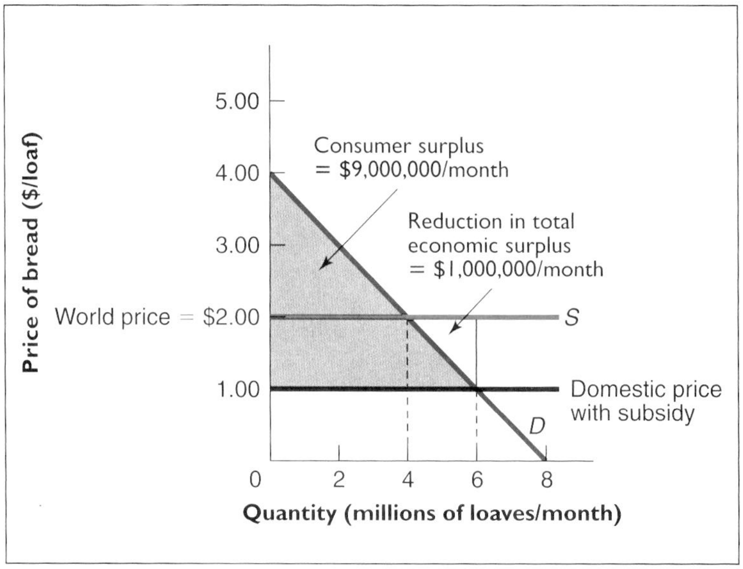

loaves per month. Each additional loaf has a marginal cost of $2 but is worth less than that to the buyer (as indicated by the fact that the vertical coordinate of the demand curve lies below $2 for consumption beyond 4,000,000). As monthly consumption expands from 4,000,000 to 6,000,000 loaves per month, the cumulative difference between the marginal cost of bread and its value to buyers is the area of the smaller shaded triangle in Figure 7.18, which is $1,000,000 per month.

This reduction in economic surplus constitutes pure waste—no different, from the perspective of participants in this market, than if someone had siphoned that much cash out of their bank accounts each month and thrown it into a bonfire. ◆

EXERCISE 7.5

How much total economic surplus would have been lost if the bread subsidy had been set at $0.50 per loaf instead of $1.00?

Compared to a bread subsidy, a much better policy would be to give low-income people some additional income and then let them buy bread on the open market. Subsidy advocates who complain that taxpayers would be unwilling to give low-income people income transfers must be asked to explain why people would be willing to tolerate subsidies, which are *more* costly than income transfers. Logically, if voters are willing to support subsidies, they should be even more eager to support income transfers to low-income persons.

This is not to say that the poor reap no benefit at all from bread subsidies. Since they get to buy bread at lower prices and since the subsidy program is financed by taxes collected primarily from middle- and upper-income families, poor families probably come out ahead on balance. *The point is that for the same expense, we could do much more to help the poor.* Their problem is that they have too little income. The simplest and best solution is not to try to peg the prices of the goods they and others buy below equilibrium levels, but rather to give them some additional money.

■ SUMMARY ■

- Accounting profit is the difference between a firm's revenue and its explicit expenses. It differs from economic profit, which is the difference between revenue and the sum of the firm's explicit and implicit costs. Normal profit is the difference between accounting profit and economic profit. It is the opportunity cost of the resources supplied to a business by its owners. **LO1**

- The quest for economic profit is the invisible hand that drives resource allocation in market economies. Markets in which businesses earn an economic profit tend to attract additional resources, whereas markets in which businesses experience an economic loss tend to lose resources. If new firms enter a market with economic profits, that market's supply curve shifts to the right, causing a reduction in the price of the product. Prices will continue to fall until economic profits are eliminated. By contrast, the departure of firms from markets with economic losses causes the supply curve in such markets to shift left, increasing the price of the product. Prices will continue to rise until economic losses are eliminated. In the long run, market forces drive economic profits and losses toward zero. **LO2, LO3**

- When market supply and demand curves reflect the underlying costs and benefits to society of the production of a good or service, the quest for economic profit ensures not only that existing supplies are allocated efficiently among individual buyers, but also that resources are allocated across markets in the most efficient way possible. In any allocation other than the one generated by the market, resources could be rearranged to benefit some people without harming others. **LO4**

- Economic rent is the portion of the payment for an input that exceeds the reservation price for that input. If a professional baseball player who is willing to play for as little as $100,000 per year is paid $15 million, he earns an economic rent of $14,900,000 per year. Whereas the invisible hand drives economic profit toward zero over the long run, economic rent can persist indefinitely because replicating the services of players like Derek Jeter is impossible. Talented individuals who are responsible for the superior performance of a business will tend to capture the resulting financial gains as economic rents. **LO3**

- The No-Cash-on-the-Table Principle implies that if someone owns a valuable resource, the market price of that resource will fully reflect its economic value. The implication of this principle is not that lucrative opportunities never exist, but rather that such opportunities cannot exist when markets are in equilibrium. **LO4**
- The benefit of an investment to an individual sometimes differs from its benefit to society as a whole. Such conflicting incentives may give rise to behavior that is smart for one but dumb for all. Despite such exceptions, the invisible hand of the market works remarkably well much of the time. One of the market system's most important contributions to social well-being is the pressure it creates to adopt cost-saving innovations. Competition among firms ensures that the resulting cost savings get passed along to consumers in the long run. **LO5**
- When the supply and demand curves for a product capture all the relevant costs and benefits of producing that product, then market equilibrium for that product will be efficient. In such a market, if price and quantity do not equal their equilibrium values, a transaction can be found that will make at least some people better off without harming others. **LO5**
- Total economic surplus is a measure of the amount by which participants in a market benefit by participating in it. It is the sum of total consumer surplus and total producer surplus in the market. One of the attractive properties of market equilibrium is that it maximizes the value of total economic surplus. **LO6**
- Efficiency should not be equated with social justice. If we believe that the distribution of income among people is unjust, we won't like the results produced by the intersection of the supply and demand curves based on that income distribution, even though those results are efficient. **LO6**
- Even so, we should always strive for efficiency because it enables us to achieve all our other goals to the fullest possible extent. Whenever a market is out of equilibrium, the economic pie can be made larger. And with a larger pie, everyone can have a larger slice. **LO6**
- Regulations or policies that prevent markets from reaching equilibrium—such as price ceilings and price subsidies—are often defended on the grounds that they help the poor. But such schemes reduce economic surplus, meaning that we can find alternatives under which both rich and poor would be better off. The main difficulty of the poor is that they have too little income. Rather than trying to control the prices of the goods they buy, we could do better by enacting policies that raise the incomes of the poor and then letting prices seek their equilibrium levels. Those who complain that the poor lack the political power to obtain such income transfers must explain why the poor have the power to impose regulations that are far more costly than income transfers. **LO6**

KEY TERMS

accounting profit (174)
allocative function of price (178)
barrier to entry (184)
economic loss (177)
economic profit (175)
economic rent (185)
efficient (or Pareto efficient) (190)
explicit costs (174)
implicit costs (175)
invisible hand theory (178)
normal profit (175)
rationing function of price (178)

REVIEW QUESTIONS

1. Why do most cities in the United States now have more radios but fewer radio repair shops than they did in 1960? **LO2**
2. How can a businessowner who earns $10 million per year from his business credibly claim to earn zero economic profit? **LO1**
3. Why do market forces drive economic profit but not economic rent toward zero? **LO3**
4. Why do economists emphasize efficiency as an important goal of public policy? **LO6**
5. You are a senator considering how to vote on a policy that would increase the economic surplus of workers by $100 million per year but reduce the economic surplus of retirees by $1 million per year. What additional measure might you combine with the policy to ensure that the overall result is a better outcome for everyone? **LO6**

■ PROBLEMS ■

McGraw-Hill's HOMEWORK MANAGER®

1. True or False: Explain why the following statements are true or false: **LO1, LO5**
   a. The economic maxim "There's no cash on the table" means that there are never any unexploited economic opportunities.
   b. Firms in competitive environments make no accounting profit when the market is in long-run equilibrium.
   c. Firms that can introduce cost-saving innovations can make an economic profit in the short run.

2. John Jones owns and manages a café in Collegetown whose annual revenue is $5,000. Annual expenses are as follows: **LO1, LO2**

Labor	$2,000
Food and drink	500
Electricity	100
Vehicle lease	150
Rent	500
Interest on loan for equipment	1,000

   a. Calculate John's annual accounting profit.
   b. John could earn $1,000 per year as a recycler of aluminum cans. However, he prefers to run the café. In fact, he would be willing to pay up to $275 per year to run the café rather than to recycle. Is the café making an economic profit? Should John stay in the café business? Explain.

3. Refer to the preceding question. **LO1, LO2**
   a. Suppose the café's revenues and expenses remain the same, but recyclers' earnings rise to $1,100 per year. Is the café still making an economic profit? Explain.
   b. Suppose John had not had to get a $10,000 loan at an annual interest rate of 10 percent to buy equipment, but instead had invested $10,000 of his own money in equipment. How would your answer to 2a and 2b change?
   c. If John can earn $1,000 a year as a recycler, and he likes recycling just as well as running the café, how much additional revenue would the café have to collect each year to earn a normal profit?

4. The city of New Orleans has 200 advertising companies, 199 of which employ designers of normal ability at a salary of $100,000 a year. Paying this salary, each of the 199 firms makes a normal profit on $500,000 in revenue. However, the 200th company employs Janus Jacobs, an unusually talented designer. This company collects $1,000,000 in revenues because of Jacobs's talent. **LO3**
   a. How much will Jacobs earn? What proportion of his annual salary will be economic rent?
   b. Why won't the advertising company for which Jacobs works be able to earn an economic profit?

5. Explain carefully why, in the absence of a patent, a technical innovation invented and pioneered in one tofu factory will cause the supply curve for the entire tofu industry to shift to the right. What will finally halt the rightward shift? **LO3**

6. Unskilled workers in a poor cotton-growing region must choose between working in a factory for $6,000 a year and being a tenant cotton farmer. One farmer

can work a 120-acre farm, which rents for \$10,000 a year. Such farms yield \$20,000 worth of cotton each year. The total nonlabor cost of producing and marketing the cotton is \$4,000 a year. A local politician whose motto is "working people come first" has promised that if he is elected, his administration will fund a fertilizer, irrigation, and marketing scheme that will triple cotton yields on tenant farms at no charge to tenant farmers. **LO3**

a. If the market price of cotton would be unaffected by this policy and no new jobs would be created in the cotton-growing industry, how would the project affect the incomes of tenant farmers in the short run? In the long run?
b. Who would reap the benefit of the scheme in the long run? How much would they gain each year?

7. Suppose the weekly demand and supply curves for used DVDs in Lincoln, Nebraska, are as shown in the diagram. Calculate **LO6**
   a. The weekly consumer surplus.
   b. The weekly producer surplus.
   c. The maximum weekly amount that producers and consumers in Lincoln would be willing to pay to be able to buy and sell used DVDs in any given week.

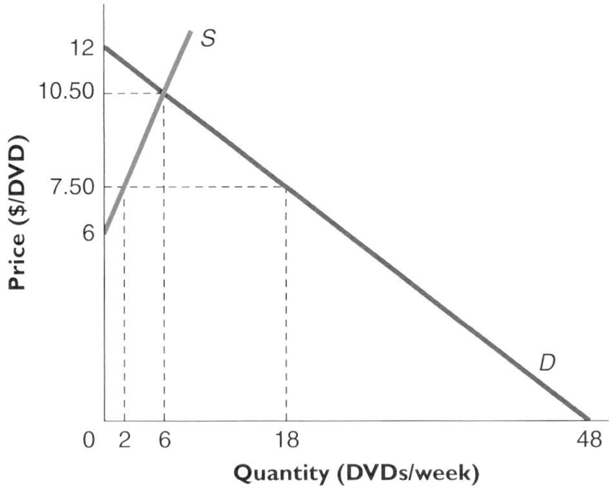

8. Refer to problem 7. Suppose a coalition of students from Lincoln High School succeeds in persuading the local government to impose a price ceiling of \$7.50 on used DVDs, on the grounds that local suppliers are taking advantage of teenagers by charging exorbitant prices. **LO6**
   a. Calculate the weekly shortage of used DVDs that will result from this policy.
   b. Calculate the total economic surplus lost every week as a result of the price ceiling.

9.* The government of Islandia, a small island nation, imports heating oil at a price of \$2 per gallon and makes it available to citizens at a price of \$1 per gallon. If Islandians' demand curve for heating oil is given by $P = 6 - Q$, where P is the price per gallon in dollars and Q is the quantity in millions of gallons per year, how much economic surplus is lost as a result of the government's policy? **LO6**

10.* Refer to problem 9. Suppose each of the 1 million Islandian households has the same demand curve for heating oil. **LO6**
   a. What is the household demand curve?
   b. How much consumer surplus would each household lose if it had to pay \$2 per gallon instead of \$1 per gallon for heating oil, assuming there were no other changes in the household budget?

*Problems marked with an asterisk (*) are more difficult.

c. With the money saved by not subsidizing oil, by how much could the Islandian government afford to cut each family's annual taxes?
d. If the government abandoned its oil subsidy and implemented the tax cut, by how much would each family be better off?
e. How does the resulting total gain for the 1 million families compare with your calculation of the lost surplus in problem 9?

ANSWERS TO IN-CHAPTER EXERCISES

7.1 As shown in the table below, Pudge's accounting profit is now \$10,000, the difference between his \$20,000 annual revenue and his \$10,000-per-year payment for land, equipment, and supplies. His economic profit is that amount minus the opportunity cost of his labor—again, the \$11,000 per year he could have earned as a store manager. So Pudge is now earning a negative economic profit, −\$1,000 per year. As before, his normal profit is the \$11,000-per-year opportunity cost of his labor. Although an accountant would say Pudge is making an annual profit of \$10,000, that amount is less than a normal profit for his activity. An economist would therefore say that he is making an economic loss of \$1,000 per year. Since Pudge likes the two jobs equally well, he will be better off by \$1,000 per year if he leaves farming to become a manager. **LOI**

Total revenue (\$/year)	Explicit costs (\$/year)	Implicit costs (\$/year)	Accounting profit (= total revenue − explicit costs) (\$/year)	Economic profit (= total revenue − explicit costs− implicit costs) (\$/year)	Normal profit (= implicit costs) (\$/year)
20,000	10,000	11,000	10,000	−1,000	11,000

7.2 If each lane did not move at about the same pace, any driver in a slower lane could reduce his travel time by simply switching to a faster one. People will exploit these opportunities until each lane moves at about the same pace. **LO3**

7.3 At a price of 50 cents per gallon, there is excess demand of 4,000 gallons per day. Suppose a seller produces an extra gallon of milk (marginal cost = 50 cents) and sells it to the buyer who values it most (reservation price = \$2.50) for \$1.50. Both buyer and seller will gain additional economic surplus of \$1, and no other buyers or sellers will be hurt by the transaction. **LO4**

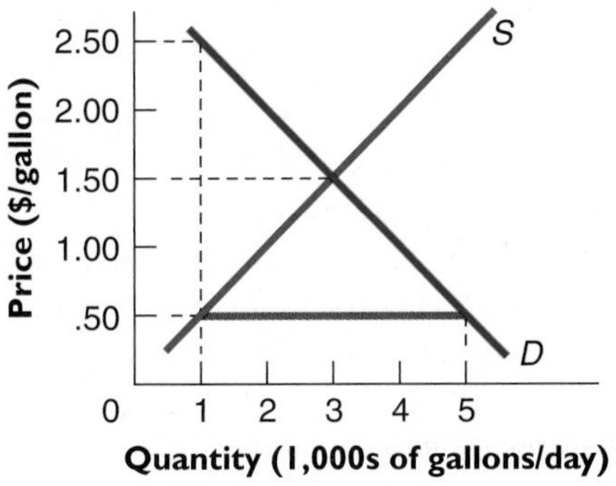

7.4 As shown in the accompanying diagram, the new loss in total economic surplus is $200 per day. **LO6**

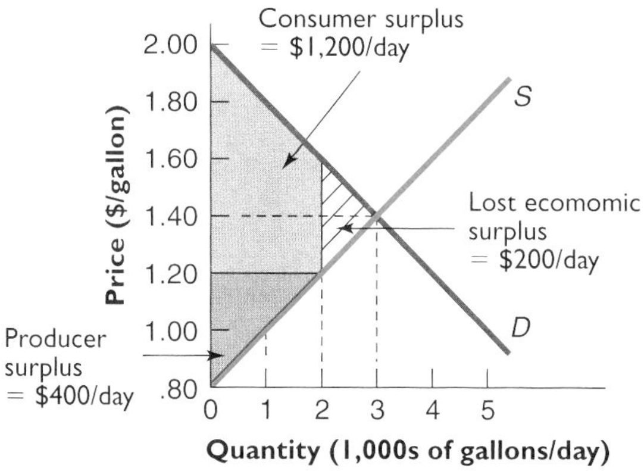

7.5 With a $0.50 per loaf subsidy, the new domestic price becomes $1.50 per loaf. The new lost surplus is the area of the small shaded triangle in the diagram: (1/2)($0.50/loaf)(1,000,000 loaves/month) = $250,000 per month. **LO6**

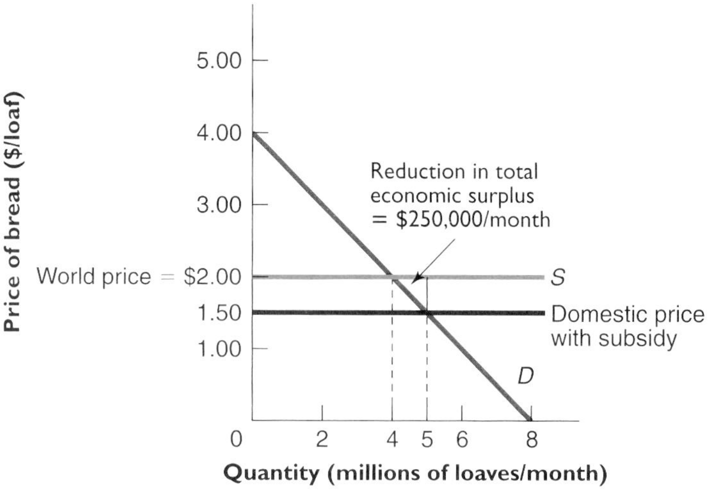

PART 3

MARKET IMPERFECTIONS

We now abandon Adam Smith's frictionless world to investigate what happens when people and firms interact in markets plagued by a variety of imperfections. Not surprisingly, the invisible hand that served society so well in the perfectly competitive world often goes astray in this new environment.

Our focus in Chapter 8 will be on how markets served by only one or a small number of firms differ from those served by perfectly competitive firms. We will see that although monopolies often escape the pressures that constrain the profits of their perfectly competitive counterparts, the two types of firms have many important similarities.

In Chapters 1 to 7 economic decision makers confronted an environment that was essentially fixed. In Chapter 9, however, we will discuss cases in which people expect their actions to alter the behavior of others, as when a firm's decision to advertise or launch a new product induces a rival to follow suit. Interdependencies of this sort are the rule rather than the exception, and we will explore how to take them into account using simple theories of games.

In Chapter 10 we will investigate how the allocation of resources is affected when activities generate costs or benefits that accrue to people not directly involved in those activities. We will see that if parties cannot easily negotiate with one another, the self-serving actions of individuals will not lead to efficient outcomes.

CHAPTER

8

Monopoly, Oligopoly, and Monopolistic Competition

LEARNING OBJECTIVES

After reading this chapter, you should be able to:

1. Distinguish among three types of imperfectly competitive industries: monopoly, oligopoly, and monopolistic competition.
2. Define imperfect competition and describe how it differs from perfect competition.
3. Understand why economies of scale are the most enduring of the various sources of monopoly power.
4. Understand the concepts of marginal cost and marginal revenue to find the output level and price that maximize a monopolist's profit.
5. Explain why the profit-maximizing output level for a monopolist is too small from society's perspective.
6. Discuss why firms often offer discounts to buyers who are willing to jump some form of hurdle.

Some years ago, schoolchildren around the country became obsessed with the game of Magic. To play, you need a deck of Magic Cards, available only from the creators of the game. But unlike ordinary playing cards, which can be bought in most stores for only a dollar or two, a deck of Magic Cards sells for upward of $10. And since Magic Cards cost no more to manufacture than ordinary playing cards, their producer earns an enormous economic profit.

In a perfectly competitive market, entrepreneurs would see this economic profit as cash on the table. It would entice them to offer Magic Cards at slightly lower prices so that eventually the cards would sell for roughly their cost of production, just as ordinary playing cards do. But Magic Cards have been on the market for years now, and that hasn't happened. The reason is that the cards are

Why do Magic Cards sell for 10 times as much as ordinary playing cards, even though they cost no more to produce?

copyrighted, which means the government has granted the creators of the game an exclusive license to sell them.

The holder of a copyright is an example of an **imperfectly competitive firm,** or **price setter,** that is, a firm with at least some latitude to set its own price. The competitive firm, by contrast, is a price taker, a firm with no influence over the price of its product.

imperfectly competitive firm or price setter a firm with at least some latitude to set its own price

Our focus in this chapter will be on the ways in which markets served by imperfectly competitive firms differ from those served by perfectly competitive firms. One salient difference is the imperfectly competitive firm's ability, under certain circumstances, to charge more than its cost of production. But if the producer of Magic Cards could charge any price it wished, why does it charge only $10? Why not $100, or even $1,000? We'll see that even though such a company may be the only seller of its product, its pricing freedom is far from absolute. We'll also see how some imperfectly competitive firms manage to earn an economic profit, even in the long run, and even without government protections like copyright. And we'll explore why Adam Smith's invisible hand is less in evidence in a world served by imperfectly competitive firms.

IMPERFECT COMPETITION

The perfectly competitive market is an ideal; the actual markets we encounter in everyday life differ from the ideal in varying degrees. Economics texts usually distinguish among three types of imperfectly competitive market structures. The classifications are somewhat arbitrary, but they are quite useful in analyzing real-world markets.

DIFFERENT FORMS OF IMPERFECT COMPETITION

Farthest from the perfectly competitive ideal is the **pure monopoly,** a market in which a single firm is the lone seller of a unique product. The producer of Magic Cards is a pure monopolist, as are many providers of electric power. If the residents of Miami don't buy their electricity from the Florida Power and Light Company, they simply do without. In between these two extremes are many different types of imperfect competition. We focus on two of them here: monopolistic competition and oligopoly.

pure monopoly the only supplier of a unique product with no close substitutes

Monopolistic Competition

Recall from the chapter on perfectly competitive supply that in a perfectly competitive industry, a large number of firms typically sell products that are essentially perfect substitutes for one another. In contrast, **monopolistic competition** is an industry structure in which a large number of rival firms sell products that are close, but not quite perfect, substitutes. Rival products may be highly similar in many respects, but there are always at least some features that differentiate one product from another in the eyes of some consumers. Monopolistic competition has in common with perfect competition the feature that there are no significant barriers preventing firms from entering or leaving the market.

monopolistic competition an industry structure in which a large number of firms produce slightly differentiated products that are reasonably close substitutes for one another

Local gasoline retailing is an example of a monopolistically competitive industry. The gas sold by different stations may be nearly identical in chemical terms, but a station's particular location is a feature that matters for many consumers. Convenience stores are another example. Although most of the products found on any given store's shelves are also carried by most other stores, the product lists of different stores are not identical. Some offer small stocks of rental DVDs, for example, while others do not. And even more so than in the case of gasoline retailing, location is an important differentiating feature of convenience stores.

Recall that if a perfectly competitive firm were to charge even just slightly more than the prevailing market price for its product, it would not sell any output at all. Things are different for the monopolistically competitive firm. The fact that its offering is not a perfect substitute for those of its rivals means that it can charge a slightly higher price than they do and not lose all its customers.

But that does not mean that monopolistically competitive firms can expect to earn positive economic profits in the long run. On the contrary, because new firms are able to enter freely, a monopolistically competitive industry is essentially the same as a perfectly competitive industry in this respect. If existing monopolistically competitive firms were earning positive economic profits at prevailing prices, new firms would have an incentive to enter the industry. Downward pressure on prices would then result as the larger number of firms competed for a limited pool of potential customers.[1] As long as positive economic profits remained, entry would continue and prices would be driven ever lower. Conversely, if firms in a monopolistically competitive industry were initially suffering economic losses, some firms would begin leaving the industry. As long as economic losses remained, exit and the resulting upward pressure on prices would continue. So in long-run equilibrium, monopolistically competitive firms are in this respect essentially like perfectly competitive firms: All expect to earn zero economic profit.

Although monopolistically competitive firms have some latitude to vary the prices of their product in the short run, pricing is not the most important strategic decision they confront. A far more important issue is how to differentiate their products from those of existing rivals. Should a product be made to resemble a rival's product as closely as possible? Or should the aim be to make it as different as possible? Or should the firm strive for something in between? We will consider these questions in the next chapter, where we will focus on this type of strategic decision making.

Oligopoly

Further along the continuum between perfect competition and pure monopoly lies **oligopoly**, a structure in which the entire market is supplied by a small number of large firms. Cost advantages associated with large size are one of the primary reasons for pure monopoly, as we will discuss presently. Oligopoly is also typically a consequence of cost advantages that prevent small firms from being able to compete effectively.

oligopoly an industry structure in which a small number of large firms produce products that are either close or perfect substitutes

In some cases, oligopolists sell undifferentiated products. In the market for wireless phone service, for example, the offerings of AT&T, Verizon, and Sprint are essentially identical. The cement industry is another example of an oligopoly selling an essentially undifferentiated product. The most important strategic decisions facing firms in such cases are more likely to involve pricing and advertising than specific features of their product. Here, too, we postpone more detailed discussion of such decisions until the next chapter.

In other cases, such as the automobile and tobacco industries, oligopolists are more like monopolistic competitors than pure monopolists, in the sense that differences in their product features have significant effects on consumer demand. Many long-time Ford buyers, for example, would not even consider buying a Chevrolet, and very few smokers ever switch from Camels to Marlboros. As with oligopolists who produce undifferentiated products, pricing and advertising are important strategic decisions for firms in these industries, but so, too, are those related to specific product features.

Because cost advantages associated with large size are usually so important in oligopolies, there is no presumption that entry and exit will push economic profit

[1]See Edward Chamberlin, *The Theory of Monopolistic Competition* (Cambridge, MA: Harvard University Press, first edition 1933, 8th edition 1962), and Joan Robinson, *The Economics of Imperfect Competition* (London: Macmillan, first edition 1933, second edition 1969).

to zero. Consider, for example, an oligopoly served by two firms, each of which currently earns an economic profit. Should a new firm enter this market? Possibly, but it also might be that a third firm large enough to achieve the cost advantages of the two incumbents would effectively flood the market, driving price so low that all three firms would suffer economic losses. There is no guarantee, however, that an oligopolist will earn a positive economic profit.

As we'll see in the next section, the essential characteristic that differentiates imperfectly competitive firms from perfectly competitive firms is the same in each of the three cases. So for the duration of this chapter, we'll use the term *monopolist* to refer to any of the three types of imperfectly competitive firms. In the next chapter, we will consider the strategic decisions confronting oligopolists and monopolistically competitive firms in greater detail.

RECAP	MONOPOLISTIC COMPETITION AND OLIGOPOLY

Monopolistic competition is the industry structure in which a large number of small firms offer products that are similar in many respects, yet not perfect substitutes in the eyes of at least some consumers. Monopolistically competitive industries resemble perfectly competitive industries in that entry and exit cause economic profits to tend toward zero in the long run.

Oligopoly is the industry structure in which a small number of large firms supply the entire market. Cost advantages associated with large-scale operations tend to be important. Oligopolists may produce either standardized products or differentiated products.

THE ESSENTIAL DIFFERENCE BETWEEN PERFECTLY AND IMPERFECTLY COMPETITIVE FIRMS

In advanced economics courses, professors generally devote much attention to the analysis of subtle differences in the behavior of different types of imperfectly competitive firms. Far more important for our purposes, however, will be to focus on the single, common feature that differentiates all imperfectly competitive firms from their perfectly competitive counterparts—namely, that *whereas the perfectly competitive firm faces a perfectly elastic demand curve for its product, the imperfectly competitive firm faces a downward-sloping demand curve.*

In the perfectly competitive industry, the supply and demand curves intersect to determine an equilibrium market price. At that price, the perfectly competitive firm can sell as many units as it wishes. It has no incentive to charge more than the market price because it won't sell anything if it does so. Nor does it have any incentive to charge less than the market price because it can sell as many units as it wants to at the market price. The perfectly competitive firm's demand curve is thus a horizontal line at the market price, as we saw in the previous chapters.

If the Sunoco station at State and Meadow Streets raised its gasoline prices by 3 cents per gallon, would all its customers shop elsewhere?

By contrast, if a local gasoline retailer—an imperfect competitor—charges a few pennies more than its rivals for a gallon of gas, some of its customers may desert it. But others will remain, perhaps because they are willing to pay a little extra to continue stopping at their most convenient location. An imperfectly competitive firm thus faces a negatively sloped demand curve. Figure 8.1 summarizes this contrast between the demand curves facing perfectly competitive and imperfectly competitive firms.

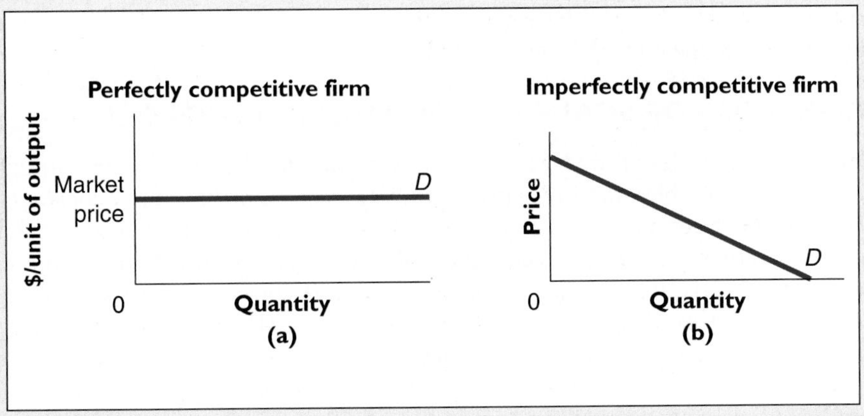

FIGURE 8.1
The Demand Curves Facing Perfectly and Imperfectly Competitive Firms.
(a) The demand curve confronting a perfectly competitive firm is perfectly elastic at the market price.
(b) The demand curve confronting an imperfectly competitive firm is downward-sloping.

FIVE SOURCES OF MARKET POWER

Firms that confront downward-sloping demand curves are said to enjoy **market power,** a term that refers to their ability to set the prices of their products. A common misconception is that a firm with market power can sell any quantity at any price it wishes. It cannot. All it can do is pick a price–quantity combination on its demand curve. If the firm chooses to raise its price, it must settle for reduced sales.

market power a firm's ability to raise the price of a good without losing all its sales

Why do some firms have market power while others do not? Since market power often carries with it the ability to charge a price above the cost of production, such power tends to arise from factors that limit competition. In practice, the following five factors often confer such power: exclusive control over inputs, patents and copyrights, government licenses or franchises, economies of scale, and network economies.

EXCLUSIVE CONTROL OVER IMPORTANT INPUTS

If a single firm controls an input essential to the production of a given product, that firm will have market power. For example, to the extent that some tenants are willing to pay a premium for office space in the country's tallest building, the Sears Tower, the owner of that building has market power.

PATENTS AND COPYRIGHTS

Patents give the inventors or developers of new products the exclusive right to sell those products for a specified period of time. By insulating sellers from competition for an interval, patents enable innovators to charge higher prices to recoup their product's development costs. Pharmaceutical companies, for example, spend millions of dollars on research in the hope of discovering new drug therapies for serious illnesses. The drugs they discover are insulated from competition for an interval—currently 20 years in the United States—by government patents. For the life of the patent, only the patent holder may legally sell the drug. This protection enables the patent holder to set a price above the marginal cost of production to recoup the cost of the research on the drug. In the same way, copyrights protect the authors of movies, software, music, books, and other published works.

GOVERNMENT LICENSES OR FRANCHISES

The Yosemite Concession Services Corporation has an exclusive license from the U.S. government to run the lodging and concession operations at Yosemite National Park. One of the government's goals in granting this monopoly was to preserve the wilderness character of the area to the greatest degree possible. And indeed, the inns

constant returns to scale a production process is said to have constant returns to scale if, when all inputs are changed by a given proportion, output changes by the same proportion

increasing returns to scale a production process is said to have increasing returns to scale if, when all inputs are changed by a given proportion, output changes by more than that proportion; also called ***economies of scale***

natural monopoly a monopoly that results from economies of scale

and cabins offered by the Yosemite Concession Services Company blend nicely with the valley's scenery. No garish neon signs mar the national park as they do in places where rivals compete for the tourist's dollars.

ECONOMIES OF SCALE AND NATURAL MONOPOLIES

When a firm doubles all its factors of production, what happens to its output? If output exactly doubles, the firm's production process is said to exhibit **constant returns to scale.** If output more than doubles, the production process is said to exhibit **increasing returns to scale,** or **economies of scale.** When production is subject to economies of scale, the average cost of production declines as the number of units produced increases. For example, in the generation of electricity, the use of larger generators lowers the unit cost of production. The markets for such products tend to be served by a single seller, or perhaps only a few sellers, because having a large number of sellers would result in significantly higher costs. A monopoly that results from economies of scale is called a **natural monopoly.**

NETWORK ECONOMIES

Although most of us don't care what brand of dental floss others use, many products do become much more valuable to us as more people use them. In the case of home videotape recorders, for instance, the VHS format's defeat of the competing Beta format was explained not by its superior picture quality—indeed, on most important technical dimensions, Beta was regarded by experts as superior to VHS. Rather, VHS won simply because it managed to gain a slight sales edge on the initial version of Beta, which could not record programs longer than one hour. Although Beta later corrected this deficiency, the VHS lead proved insuperable. Once the fraction of consumers owning VHS passed a critical threshold, the reasons for choosing it became compelling—variety and availability of tape rental, access to repair facilities, the capability to exchange tapes with friends, and so on.

A similar network economy helps to account for the dominant position of Microsoft's Windows operating system, which, as noted earlier, is currently installed in more than 90 percent of all personal computers. Because Microsoft's initial sales advantage gave software developers a strong incentive to write for the Windows format, the inventory of available software in the Windows format is now vastly larger than that for any competing operating system. And although general-purpose software such as word processors and spreadsheets continues to be available for multiple operating systems, specialized professional software and games usually appear first—and often only—in the Windows format. This software gap and the desire to achieve compatibility for file sharing gave people a good reason for choosing Windows, even if, as in the case of many Apple Macintosh users, they believed a competing system was otherwise superior.

By far the most important and enduring of these sources of market power are economies of scale and network economies. Lured by economic profit, firms almost always find substitutes for exclusive inputs. Thus, real estate developer Donald Trump has proposed a building taller than the Sears Tower, to be built in Chicago. Likewise, firms can often evade patent laws by making slight changes in design of products. Patent protection is only temporary, in any case. Finally, governments grant very few franchises each year. But economies of scale are both widespread and enduring.

Firmly entrenched network economies can be as persistent a source of natural monopoly as economies of scale. Indeed, network economies are essentially similar to economies of scale. When network economies are of value to the consumer, a product's quality increases as the number of users increases, so we can say that any given quality level can be produced at lower cost as sales volume increases. Thus network economies may be viewed as just another form of economies of scale in production, and that's how we'll treat them here.

RECAP	FIVE SOURCES OF MARKET POWER

A firm's power to raise its price without losing its entire market stems from exclusive control of important inputs, patents and copyrights, government licenses, economies of scale, or network economies. By far the most important and enduring of these are economies of scale and network economies.

ECONOMIES OF SCALE AND THE IMPORTANCE OF START-UP COSTS

As we saw in a previous chapter, variable costs are those that vary with the level of output produced, while fixed costs are independent of output. Strictly speaking, there are no fixed costs in the long run because all inputs can be varied. But as a practical matter, start-up costs often loom large for the duration of a product's useful life. Most of the costs involved in the production of computer software, for example, are start-up costs of this sort, one-time costs incurred in writing and testing the software. Once those tasks are done, additional copies of the software can be produced at a very low marginal cost. A good such as software, whose production entails large fixed start-up costs and low variable costs, will be subject to significant economies of scale. Because by definition fixed costs don't increase as output increases, the average total cost of production for such goods will decline sharply as output increases.

To illustrate, consider a production process for which total cost is given by the equation $TC = F + M^*Q$, where F is fixed cost, M is marginal cost (assumed constant in this illustration), and Q is the level of output produced. For the production process with this simple total cost function, variable cost is simply M^*Q, the product of marginal cost and quantity. Average total cost, TC/Q, is equal to $F/Q + M$. As Q increases, average cost declines steadily because the fixed costs are spread out over more and more units of output.

Figure 8.2 shows the total production cost [part (a)] and average total cost [part (b)] for a firm with the total cost curve $TC = F + M^*Q$ and the corresponding average total cost curve $ATC = F/Q + M$. The average total cost curve [part (b)] shows the decline in per-unit cost as output grows. Though average total cost is always higher than marginal cost for this firm, the difference between the two diminishes as

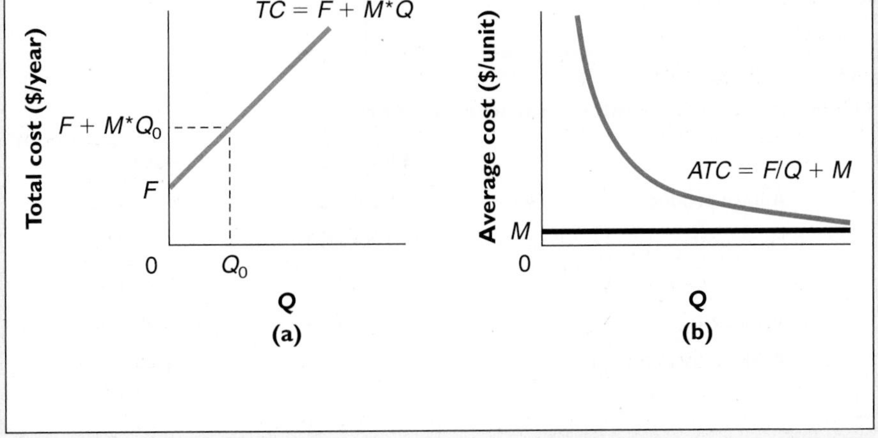

FIGURE 8.2
Total and Average Total Costs for a Production Process with Economies of Scale.
For a firm whose total cost curve of producing Q units of output per year is $TC = F + M^*Q$, total cost (a) rises at a constant rate as output grows, while average total cost (b) declines. Average total cost is always higher than marginal cost for this firm, but the difference becomes less significant at high output levels.

output grows. At extremely high levels of output, average total cost becomes very close to marginal cost (*M*). Because the firm is spreading out its fixed cost over an extremely large volume of output, fixed cost per unit becomes almost insignificant.

As the following examples illustrate, the importance of economies of scale depends on how large fixed cost is in relation to marginal cost.

Two video game producers, Nintendo and Playstation, each have fixed costs of $200,000 and marginal costs of $0.80 per game. If Nintendo produces 1 million units per year and Playstation produces 1.2 million, how much lower will Playstation's average total production cost be?

Table 8.1 summarizes the relevant cost categories for the two firms. Note in the bottom row that Playstation enjoys only a 3-cent average cost advantage over Nintendo. Even though Nintendo produces 20 percent fewer copies of its video game than Playstation, it does not suffer a significant cost disadvantage because fixed cost is a relatively small part of total production cost.

TABLE 8.1
Costs for Two Computer Game Producers (1)

	Nintendo	Playstation
Annual production	1,000,000	1,200,000
Fixed cost	$200,000	$200,000
Variable cost	$800,000	$960,000
Total cost	$1,000,000	$1,160,000
Average total cost per game	$1.00	$0.97

◆

In the next example, note how the picture changes when fixed cost looms large relative to marginal cost.

Two video game producers, Nintendo and Playstation, each have fixed costs of $10,000,000 and marginal costs of $0.20 per video game. If Nintendo produces 1 million units per year and Playstation produces 1.2 million, how much lower will Playstation's average total cost be?

The relevant cost categories for the two firms are now summarized in Table 8.2. The bottom row shows that Playstation enjoys a $1.67 average total cost advantage over Nintendo, substantially larger than in the previous example.

TABLE 8.2
Costs for Two Computer Game Producers (2)

	Nintendo	Playstation
Annual production	1,000,000	1,200,000
Fixed cost	$10,000,000	$10,000,000
Variable cost	$200,000	$240,000
Total cost	$10,200,000	$10,240,000
Average total cost per game	$10.20	$8.53

TABLE 8.3
Costs for Two Computer Game Producers (3)

	Nintendo	Playstation
Annual production	500,000	1,700,000
Fixed cost	$10,000,000	$10,000,000
Variable cost	$100,000	$340,000
Total cost	$10,100,000	$10,340,000
Average total cost per game	$20.20	$6.08

If the video games the two firms produce are essentially similar, the fact that Playstation can charge significantly lower prices and still cover its costs should enable it to attract customers away from Nintendo. As more and more of the market goes to Playstation, its cost advantage will become self-reinforcing. Table 8.3 shows how a shift of 500,000 units from Nintendo to Playstation would cause Nintendo's average total cost to rise to $20.20 per unit, while Playstation's average total cost would fall to $6.08 per unit. The fact that a firm cannot long survive at such a severe disadvantage explains why the video game market is served now by only a small number of firms. ◆

EXERCISE 8.1

How big will Playstation's unit cost advantage be if it sells 2,000,000 units per year, while Nintendo sells only 200,000?

An important worldwide economic trend during recent decades is that an increasing share of the value embodied in the goods and services we buy stems from fixed investment in research and development. For example, in 1984 some 80 percent of the cost of a computer was in its hardware (which has relatively high marginal cost); the remaining 20 percent was in its software. But by 1990 those proportions were reversed. Fixed cost now accounts for about 85 percent of total costs in the computer software industry, whose products are included in a growing share of ordinary manufactured goods.

Example 8.1

THE ECONOMIC NATURALIST

Why does Intel sell the overwhelming majority of all microprocessors used in personal computers?

The fixed investment required to produce a new leading-edge microprocessor such as the Intel Pentium chip currently runs upward of $2 billion. But once the chip has been designed and the manufacturing facility built, the marginal cost of producing each chip is only pennies. This cost pattern explains why Intel currently sells more than 80 percent of all microprocessors. ●

Why are most personal computers equipped with Intel microprocessors?

As fixed cost becomes more and more important, the perfectly competitive pattern of many small firms, each producing only a small share of its industry's total output, becomes less common. For this reason, we must develop a clear sense of how the behavior of firms with market power differs from that of the perfectly competitive firm.

RECAP	ECONOMIES OF SCALE AND THE IMPORTANCE OF START-UP COSTS

Research, design, engineering, and other fixed costs account for an increasingly large share of all costs required to bring products successfully to market. For products with large fixed costs, marginal cost is lower, often substantially, than average total cost, and average total cost declines, often sharply, as output grows. This cost pattern explains why many industries are dominated by either a single firm or a small number of firms.

PROFIT MAXIMIZATION FOR THE MONOPOLIST

Cost-Benefit

Regardless of whether a firm is a price taker or a price setter, economists assume that its basic goal is to maximize its profit. In both cases, the firm expands output as long as the benefit of doing so exceeds the cost. Further, the calculation of marginal cost is also the same for the monopolist as for the perfectly competitive firm.

The profit-maximizing decision for a monopolist differs from that of a perfectly competitive firm when we look at the benefits of expanding output. For both the perfectly competitive firm and the monopolist, the marginal benefit of expanding output is the additional revenue the firm will receive if it sells one additional unit of output. In both cases, this marginal benefit is called the firm's **marginal revenue.** For the perfectly competitive firm, marginal revenue is exactly equal to the market price of the product. If that price is $6, for example, then the marginal benefit of selling an extra unit is exactly $6.

marginal revenue the change in a firm's total revenue that results from a one-unit change in output

MARGINAL REVENUE FOR THE MONOPOLIST

The situation is different for a monopolist. *To a monopolist, the marginal benefit of selling an additional unit is strictly less than the market price.* As the following discussion will make clear, the reason is that while the perfectly competitive firm can

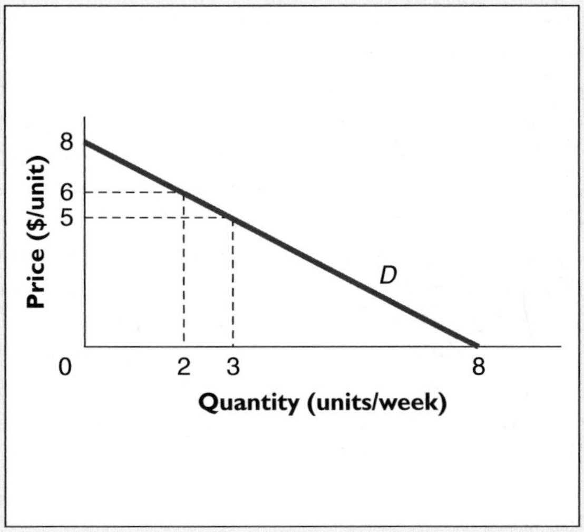

FIGURE 8.3
The Monopolist's Benefit from Selling an Additional Unit.
The monopolist shown receives $12 per week in total revenue by selling 2 units per week at a price of $6 each. This monopolist could earn $15 per week by selling 3 units per week at a price of $5 each. In that case, the benefit from selling the third unit would be $15 − $12 = $3, less than its selling price of $5.

sell as many units as it wishes at the market price, the monopolist can sell an additional unit only if it cuts the price—and it must do so not just for the additional unit but for the units it is currently selling.

Suppose, for example, that a monopolist with the demand curve shown in Figure 8.3 is currently selling 2 units of output at a price of $6 per unit. What would be its marginal revenue from selling an additional unit?

This monopolist's total revenue from the sale of 2 units per week is ($6 per unit)(2 units per week) = $12 per week. Its total revenue from the sale of 3 units per week would be $15 per week. The difference—$3 per week—is the marginal revenue from the sale of the third unit each week. Note that this amount is not only smaller than the original price ($6) but smaller than the new price ($5) as well.

EXERCISE 8.2

Calculate marginal revenue for the monopolist in Figure 8.3 as it expands output from 3 to 4 units per week, and then from 4 to 5 units per week.

For the monopolist whose demand curve is shown in Figure 8.3, a sequence of increases in output—from 2 to 3, from 3 to 4, and from 4 to 5—will yield marginal revenue of $3, $1, and −$1, respectively. We display these results in tabular form in Table 8.4.

TABLE 8.4
Marginal Revenue for a Monopolist ($ per unit)

Quantity	Marginal revenue
2	
	3
3	
	1
4	
	−1
5	

Note in the table that the marginal revenue values are displayed between the two quantity figures to which they correspond. For example, when the firm expanded its output from 2 units per week to 3, its marginal revenue was \$3 per unit. Strictly speaking, this marginal revenue corresponds to neither quantity but to the movement between those quantities, hence its placement in the table. Likewise, in moving from 3 to 4 units per week, the firm earned marginal revenue of \$1 per unit, so that figure is placed midway between the quantities of 3 and 4, and so on.

To graph marginal revenue as a function of quantity, we would plot the marginal revenue for the movement from 2 to 3 units of output per week (\$3) at a quantity value of 2.5, because 2.5 lies midway between 2 and 3. Similarly, we would plot the marginal revenue for the movement from 3 to 4 units per week (\$1) at a quantity of 3.5 units per week, and the marginal revenue for the movement from 4 to 5 units per week (−\$1) at a quantity of 4.5. The resulting marginal revenue curve, *MR*, is shown in Figure 8.4.

FIGURE 8.4
Marginal Revenue in Graphical Form.
Because a monopolist must cut price to sell an extra unit, not only for the extra unit sold but also for all existing units, marginal revenue from the sale of the extra unit is less than its selling price.

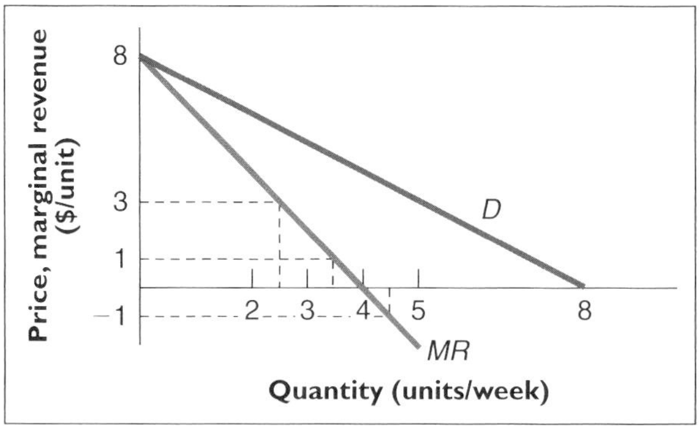

More generally, consider a monopolist with a straight-line demand curve whose vertical intercept is a and whose horizontal intercept is Q_0, as shown in Figure 8.5. This monopolist's marginal revenue curve also will have a vertical intercept of a, and it will be twice as steep as the demand curve. Thus, its horizontal intercept will be not Q_0, but $Q_0/2$, as shown in Figure 8.5.

Marginal revenue curves also can be expressed algebraically. If the formula for the monopolist's demand curve is $P = a - bQ$, then the formula for its marginal revenue curve will be $MR = a - 2bQ$. If you have had calculus, this relationship is easy to derive,[2] but even without calculus you can verify it by working through a few numerical examples. First, translate the formula for the demand curve into a diagram, and then construct the corresponding marginal revenue curve graphically. Reading from the graph, write the formula for that marginal revenue curve.

THE MONOPOLIST'S PROFIT-MAXIMIZING DECISION RULE

Cost-Benefit

Having derived the monopolist's marginal revenue curve, we are now in a position to describe how the monopolist chooses the output level that maximizes profit. As in the case of the perfectly competitive firm, the Cost-Benefit Principle says that the monopolist should continue to expand output as long as the gain from doing so exceeds the cost. At the current level of output, the benefit from expanding output is the

[2]For those who have had an introductory course in calculus, marginal revenue can be expressed as the derivative of total revenue with respect to output. If $P = a - bQ$, then total revenue will be given by $TR = PQ = aQ - bQ^2$, which means that $MR = dTR/dQ = a - 2bQ$.

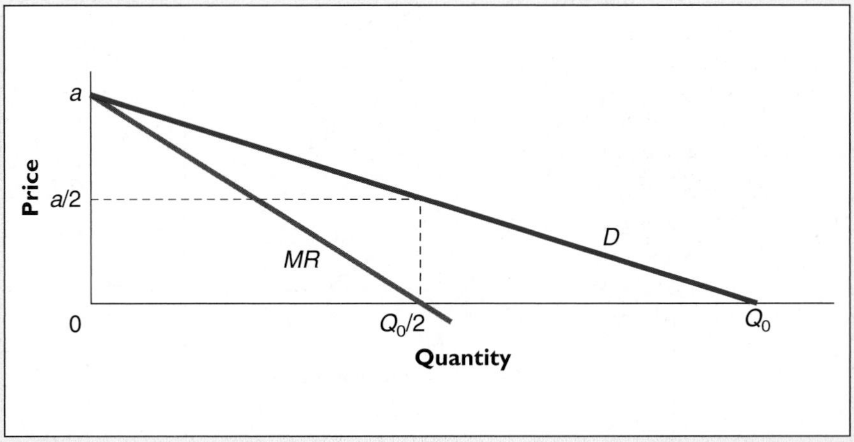

FIGURE 8.5
The Marginal Revenue Curve for a Monopolist with a Straight-Line Demand Curve.
For a monopolist with the demand curve shown, the corresponding marginal revenue curve has the same vertical intercept as the demand curve, and a horizontal intercept only half as large as that of the demand curve.

marginal revenue value that corresponds to that output level. The cost of expanding output is the marginal cost at that level of output. Whenever marginal revenue exceeds marginal cost, the firm should expand. Conversely, whenever marginal revenue falls short of marginal cost, the firm should reduce its output. *Profit is maximized at the level of output for which marginal revenue precisely equals marginal cost.*

When the monopolist's profit-maximizing rule is stated in this way, we can see that the perfectly competitive firm's rule is actually a special case of the monopolist's rule. When the perfectly competitive firm expands output by one unit, its marginal revenue exactly equals the product's market price (because the perfectly competitive firm can expand sales by a unit without having to cut the price of existing units). So when the perfectly competitive firm equates price with marginal cost, it is also equating marginal revenue with marginal cost. *Thus, the only significant difference between the two cases concerns the calculation of marginal revenue.*

What is the monopolist's profit-maximizing output level?

Consider a monopolist with the demand and marginal cost curves shown in Figure 8.6. If this firm is currently producing 12 units per week, should it expand or contract production? What is the profit-maximizing level of output?

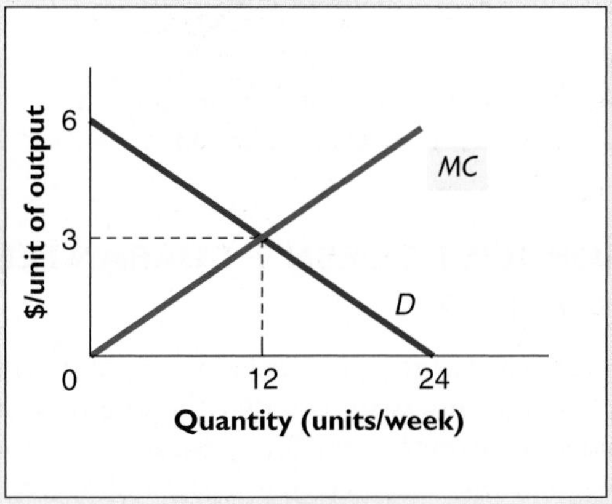

FIGURE 8.6
The Demand and Marginal Cost Curves for a Monopolist.
At the current output level of 12 units per week, price equals marginal cost. Since the monopolist's price is always greater than marginal revenue, marginal revenue must be less than marginal cost, which means this monopolist should produce less.

In Figure 8.7, we begin by constructing the marginal revenue curve that corresponds to the monopolist's demand curve. It has the same vertical intercept as the demand curve, and its horizontal intercept is half as large. Note that the monopolist's marginal revenue at 12 units per week is zero, which is clearly less than its marginal

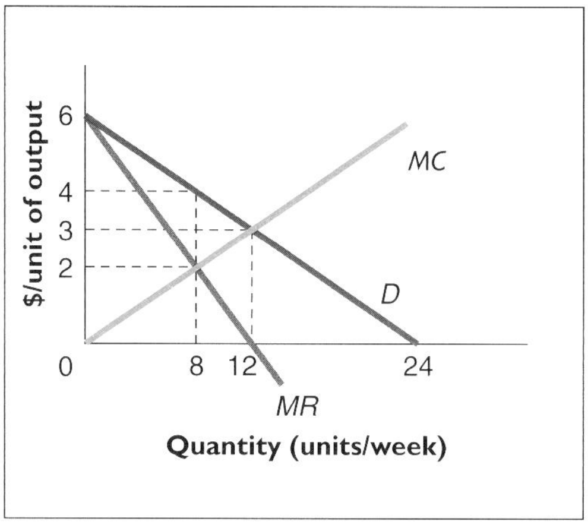

FIGURE 8.7
The Monopolist's Profit-Maximizing Output Level.
This monopolist maximizes profit by selling 8 units per week, the output level at which marginal revenue equals marginal cost. The profit-maximizing price is $4 per unit, the price that corresponds to the profit-maximizing quantity on the demand curve.

cost of $3 per unit. This monopolist will therefore earn a higher profit by contracting production until marginal revenue equals marginal cost, which occurs at an output level of 8 units per week. At this profit-maximizing output level, the firm will charge $4 per unit, the price that corresponds to 8 units per week on the demand curve. ◆

EXERCISE 8.3

For the monopolist with the demand and marginal cost curves shown, find the profit-maximizing price and level of output.

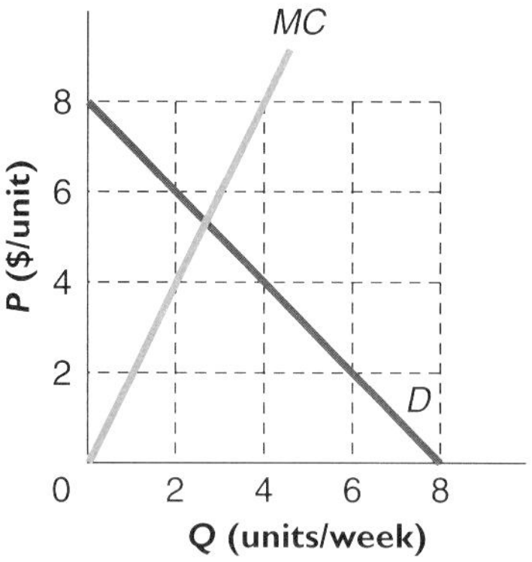

BEING A MONOPOLIST DOESN'T GUARANTEE AN ECONOMIC PROFIT

The fact that the profit-maximizing price for a monopolist will always be greater than marginal cost provides no assurance that the monopolist will earn an economic profit. Consider, for example, the long-distance telephone service provider whose demand, marginal revenue, marginal cost, and average total cost curves are shown in Figure 8.8(a). This monopolist maximizes its daily profit by selling 20 million minutes per day of calls at a price of $0.10 per minute. At that quantity, $MR = MC$, yet price is $0.02 per minute less than the company's average total cost of $0.12 per minute. As a result, the company sustains an economic loss of $0.02 per minute on all calls provided, or a total loss of ($0.02 per minute)(20,000,000 minutes per day) = $400,000 per day.

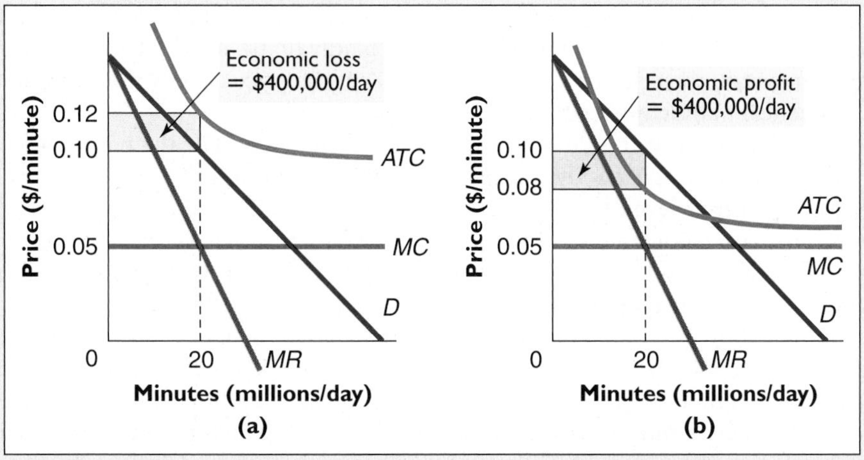

FIGURE 8.8
Even a Monopolist May Suffer an Economic Loss.
The monopolist in (a) maximizes its profit by selling 20 million minutes per day of calls but suffers an economic loss of $400,000 per day in the process. Because the profit-maximizing price of the monopolist in (b) exceeds *ATC*, this monopolist earns an economic profit.

The monopolist in Figure 8.8(a) suffered a loss because its profit-maximizing price was lower than its *ATC*. If the monopolist's profit-maximizing price exceeds its average total cost, however, the company will, of course, earn an economic profit. Consider, for example, the long-distance provider shown in Figure 8.8(b). This firm has the same demand, marginal revenue, and marginal cost curves as the firm shown in Figure 8.8(a). But because the firm in part (b) has lower fixed costs, its *ATC* curve is lower at every level of output than the *ATC* curve in (a). At the profit-maximizing price of $0.10 per minute, the firm in Figure 8.8(b) earns an economic profit of $0.02 per minute, for a total economic profit of $400,000 per day.

RECAP | PROFIT MAXIMIZATION FOR THE MONOPOLIST

Both the perfectly competitive firm and the monopolist maximize profit by choosing the output level at which marginal revenue equals marginal cost. But whereas marginal revenue equals the market price for the perfectly competitive firm, it is always less than the market price for the monopolist. A monopolist will earn an economic profit only if price exceeds average total cost at the profit-maximizing level of output.

WHY THE INVISIBLE HAND BREAKS DOWN UNDER MONOPOLY

In our discussion of equilibrium in perfectly competitive markets in Chapter 7, we saw conditions under which the self-serving pursuits of consumers and firms were consistent with the broader interests of society as a whole. Let's explore whether the same conclusion holds true for the case of imperfectly competitive firms.

Consider the monopolist in Figures 8.6 and 8.7. Is this firm's profit-maximizing output level efficient from society's point of view? For any given level of output, the corresponding price on the demand curve indicates the amount buyers would be willing to pay for an additional unit of output. When the monopolist is producing 8 units per week, the marginal benefit to society of an additional unit of output is thus $4 (see Figure 8.7). And since the marginal cost of an additional unit at that output level is only $2 (again, see Figure 8.7), society would gain a net benefit of $2 per unit if the monopolist were to expand production by one unit above the profit-maximizing level. Because this economic surplus is not realized, the profit-maximizing monopolist is socially inefficient.

Recall that the existence of inefficiency means that the economic pie is smaller than it might be. If that is so, why doesn't the monopolist simply expand production? The answer is that the monopolist would gladly do so, if only there were some way to maintain the price of existing units and cut the price of only the extra units. As a practical matter, however, that is not always possible.

Now, let's look at this situation from a different angle. For the market served by this monopolist, what *is* the socially efficient level of output?

At any output level, the cost to society of an additional unit of output is the same as the cost to the monopolist, namely, the amount shown on the monopolist's marginal cost curve. The marginal benefit *to society* (not to the monopolist) of an extra unit of output is simply the amount people are willing to pay for it, which is the amount shown on the monopolist's demand curve. To achieve social efficiency, the monopolist should expand production until the marginal benefit to society equals the marginal cost, which in this case occurs at a level of 12 units per week. Social efficiency is thus achieved at the output level at which the market demand curve intersects the monopolist's marginal cost curve.

The fact that marginal revenue is less than price for the monopolist results in a deadweight loss. For the monopolist just discussed, the size of this deadweight loss is equal to the area of the pale blue triangle in Figure 8.9, which is (½)($2 per unit)(4 units per week) = $4 per week. That is the amount by which total economic surplus is reduced because the monopolist produces too little.

FIGURE 8.9
The Deadweight Loss from Monopoly.
A loss in economic surplus results because the profit-maximizing level of output (8 units per week) is less than the socially optimal level of output (12 units per week). This deadweight loss is the area of the pale blue triangle, $4 per week.

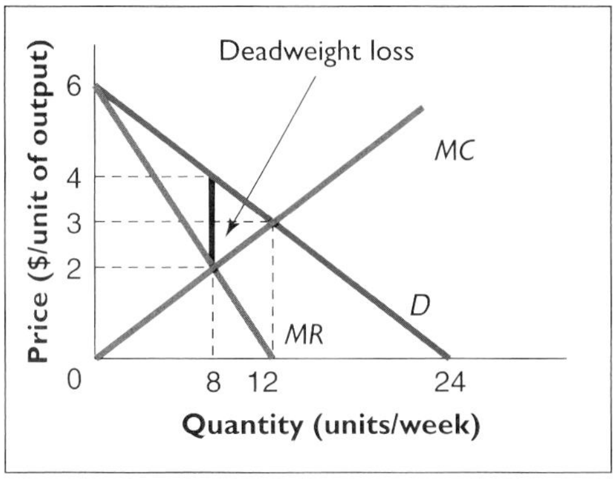

For a monopolist, profit maximization occurs when marginal cost equals marginal revenue. Since the monopolist's marginal revenue is always less than price, the monopolist's profit-maximizing output level is always below the socially efficient level. Under perfect competition, by contrast, profit maximization occurs when marginal cost equals the market price—the same criterion that must be satisfied for social efficiency. This difference explains why the invisible hand of the market is less evident in monopoly markets than in perfectly competitive markets.

If perfect competition is socially efficient and monopoly is not, why isn't monopoly against the law? Congress has, in fact, tried to limit the extent of monopoly through the antitrust laws. But even the most enthusiastic proponents of those laws recognize the limited usefulness of the legislative approach since the alternatives to monopoly often entail problems of their own.

Suppose, for example, that a monopoly results from a patent that prevents all but one firm from manufacturing some highly valued product. Would society be better off without patents? Probably not because eliminating such protection would discourage innovation. Virtually all successful industrial nations grant some form of patent protection, which gives firms a chance to recover the research and development costs without which new products would seldom reach the market.

Or suppose that the market in question is a natural monopoly—one that, because of economies of scale, is most cheaply served by a single firm. Would society do better to require this market to be served by many small firms, each with significantly higher average costs of production? Such a requirement would merely replace one form of inefficiency with another.

In short, we live in an imperfect world. Monopoly is socially inefficient, and that, needless to say, is bad. But the alternatives to monopoly aren't perfect either.

RECAP	WHY THE INVISIBLE HAND BREAKS DOWN UNDER MONOPOLY

The monopolist maximizes profit at the output level for which marginal revenue equals marginal cost. Because its profit-maximizing price exceeds marginal revenue, and hence also marginal cost, the benefit to society of the last unit produced (the market price) must be greater than the cost of the last unit produced (the marginal cost). So the output level for an industry served by a profit-maximizing monopolist is smaller than the socially optimal level of output.

USING DISCOUNTS TO EXPAND THE MARKET

The source of inefficiency in monopoly markets is the fact that the benefit to the monopolist of expanding output is less than the corresponding benefit to society. From the monopolist's point of view, the price reduction the firm must grant existing buyers to expand output is a loss. But from the point of view of those buyers, each dollar of price reduction is a gain—one dollar more in their pockets.

Note the tension in this situation, which is similar to the tension that exists in all other situations in which the economic pie is smaller than it might otherwise be. As the Efficiency Principle reminds us, when the economic pie grows larger, everyone can have a larger slice. To say that monopoly is inefficient means that steps could be taken to make some people better off without harming others. If people have a healthy regard for their own self-interest, why doesn't someone take those steps? Why, for example, doesn't the monopolist from the earlier examples sell 8 units of output at a price of \$4, and then once those buyers are out the door, cut the price for more price-sensitive buyers?

Efficiency

PRICE DISCRIMINATION DEFINED

Sometimes the monopolist does precisely that. Charging different buyers different prices for the same good or service is a practice known as **price discrimination.** Examples of price discrimination include senior citizens' and children's discounts on movie tickets, supersaver discounts on air travel, and rebate coupons on retail merchandise.

price discrimination the practice of charging different buyers different prices for essentially the same good or service

Attempts at price discrimination seem to work effectively in some markets, but not in others. Buyers are not stupid, after all; if the monopolist periodically offered a 50 percent discount on the \$8 list price, those who were paying \$8 might anticipate the next price cut and postpone their purchases to take advantage of it. In some markets, however, buyers may not know, or simply may not take the trouble to find out, how the price they pay compares to the prices paid by other buyers. Alternatively, the monopolist may be in a position to prevent some groups from buying at the discount prices made available to others. In such cases, the monopolist can price-discriminate effectively.

Example 8.2

THE ECONOMIC NATURALIST

Why do students pay lower ticket prices at many movie theaters?

Why do many movie theaters offer discount tickets to students?

Whenever a firm offers a discount, the goal is to target that discount to buyers who would not purchase the product without it. People with low incomes generally have lower reservation prices for movie tickets than people with high incomes. Because students generally have lower disposable incomes than working adults, theater owners can expand their audiences by charging lower prices to students than to adults. Student discounts are one practical way of doing so. Offering student discounts also entails no risk of some people buying the product at a low price and then reselling it to others at a higher price. ●

HOW PRICE DISCRIMINATION AFFECTS OUTPUT

In the following examples, we will see how the ability to price-discriminate affects the monopolist's profit-maximizing level of output. First we will consider a baseline case in which the monopolist must charge the same price to every buyer.

How many manuscripts should Carla edit?

Carla supplements her income as a teaching assistant by editing term papers for undergraduates. There are eight students per week for whom she might edit, each with a reservation price as given in the following table.

Student	Reservation price
A	$40
B	38
C	36
D	34
E	32
F	30
G	28
H	26

Carla is a profit maximizer. If the opportunity cost of her time to edit each paper is $29 and she must charge the same price to each student, how many papers should she edit? How much economic profit will she make? How much accounting profit?

Table 8.5 summarizes Carla's total and marginal revenue at various output levels. To generate the amounts in the total revenue column, we simply multiplied the corresponding reservation price by the number of students whose reservation prices were at least that high. For example, to edit 4 papers per week (for students *A*, *B*, *C*, and *D*), Carla must charge a price no higher than *D*'s reservation price ($34). So her total revenue when she edits 4 papers per week is (4)($34) = $136 per week. Carla should keep expanding the number of students she serves as long as her marginal revenue exceeds the opportunity cost of her time. Marginal revenue, or the difference in total revenue that results from adding another student, is shown in the last column of Table 8.5.

Note that if Carla were editing 2 papers per week, her marginal revenue from editing a third paper would be $32. Since that amount exceeds her $29 opportunity cost, she should take on the third paper. But since the marginal revenue of taking on a fourth paper would be only $28, Carla should stop at 3 papers per week. The total opportunity cost of the time required to edit the 3 papers is (3)($29) = $87, so

TABLE 8.5
Total and Marginal Revenue from Editing

Student	Reservation price ($ per paper)	Total revenue ($ per week)	Marginal revenue ($ per paper)
			40
A	40	40	
			36
B	38	76	
			32
C	36	108	
			28
D	34	136	
			24
E	32	160	
			20
F	30	180	
			16
G	28	196	
			12
H	26	208	

Carla's economic profit is $108 − $87 = $21 per week. Since Carla incurs no explicit costs, her accounting profit will be $108 per week. ◆

What is the socially efficient number of papers for Carla to edit?

Again, suppose that Carla's opportunity cost of editing is $29 per paper and that she could edit as many as 8 papers per week for students whose reservation prices are again as listed in the following table.

Student	Reservation price
A	$40
B	38
C	36
D	34
E	32
F	30
G	28
H	26

What is the socially efficient number of papers for Carla to edit? If she must charge the same price to each student, what will her economic and accounting profits be if she edits the socially efficient number of papers?

Students *A* to *F* are willing to pay more than Carla's opportunity cost, so serving these students is socially efficient. But students *G* and *H* are unwilling to pay at least $29 for Carla's services. The socially efficient outcome, therefore, is for Carla to edit 6 papers per week. To attract that number, she must charge a price no higher than $30 per paper. Her total revenue will be (6)($30) = $180 per week, slightly more than her total opportunity cost of (6)($29) = $174 per week. Her economic profit will thus be only $6 per week. Again, because Carla incurs no explicit costs, her accounting profit will be the same as her total revenue, $180 per week. ◆

If Carla can price-discriminate, how many papers should she edit?

Suppose Carla is a shrewd judge of human nature. After a moment's conversation with a student, she can discern that student's reservation price. The reservation prices of her potential customers are again as given in the following table. If Carla confronts the same market as before, but can charge students their respective reservation prices, how many papers should she edit, and how much economic and accounting profit will she make?

Student	Reservation price
A	$40
B	38
C	36
D	34
E	32
F	30
G	28
H	26

Carla will edit papers for students *A* to *F* and charge each exactly his or her reservation price. Because students *G* and *H* have reservation prices below $29, Carla will not edit their papers. Carla's total revenue will be $40 + $38 + $36 + $34 + $32 + $30 = $210 per week, which is also her accounting profit. Her total opportunity cost of editing 6 papers is (6)($29) = $174 per week, so her economic profit will be $210 − $174 = $36 per week, $30 per week more than when she edited six papers but was constrained to charge each customer the same price. ◆

perfectly discriminating monopolist a firm that charges each buyer exactly his or her reservation price

A monopolist who can charge each buyer exactly his or her reservation price is called a **perfectly discriminating monopolist.** Notice that when Carla was discriminating among customers in this way, her profit-maximizing level of output was exactly the same as the socially efficient level of output: 6 papers per week. With a perfectly discriminating monopoly, there is no loss of efficiency. All buyers who are willing to pay a price high enough to cover marginal cost will be served.

Note that although total economic surplus is maximized by a perfectly discriminating monopolist, consumers would have little reason to celebrate if they found themselves dealing with such a firm. After all, consumer surplus is exactly zero for the perfectly discriminating monopolist. In this instance, total economic surplus and producer surplus are one and the same.

In practice, of course, perfect price discrimination can never occur because no seller knows each and every buyer's precise reservation price. But even if some sellers did know, practical difficulties would stand in the way of their charging a separate price to each buyer. For example, in many markets the seller could not prevent buyers who bought at low prices from reselling to other buyers at higher prices, capturing some of the seller's business in the process. Despite these difficulties, price discrimination is widespread. But it is generally *imperfect price discrimination*, that is, price discrimination in which at least some buyers are charged less than their reservation prices.

THE HURDLE METHOD OF PRICE DISCRIMINATION

The profit-maximizing seller's goal is to charge each buyer the highest price that buyer is willing to pay. Two primary obstacles prevent sellers from achieving this goal. First, sellers don't know exactly how much each buyer is willing to pay. And second, they need some means of excluding those who are willing to pay a high price from buying at a low price. These are formidable problems, which no seller can hope to solve completely.

One common method by which sellers achieve a crude solution to both problems is to require buyers to overcome some obstacle to be eligible for a discount price. This method is called the **hurdle method of price discrimination.** For example, the seller might sell a product at a standard list price and offer a rebate to any buyer who takes the trouble to mail in a rebate coupon.

hurdle method of price discrimination the practice by which a seller offers a discount to all buyers who overcome some obstacle

The hurdle method solves both of the seller's problems, provided that buyers with low reservation prices are more willing than others to jump the hurdle. Because a decision to jump the hurdle must satisfy the Cost-Benefit Principle, such a link seems to exist. As noted earlier, buyers with low incomes are more likely than others to have low reservation prices (at least in the case of normal goods). Because of the low opportunity cost of their time, they are more likely than others to take the trouble to send in rebate coupons. Rebate coupons thus target a discount toward those buyers whose reservation prices are low and who therefore might not buy the product otherwise.

Cost-Benefit

A **perfect hurdle** is one that separates buyers precisely according to their reservation prices, and in the process imposes no cost on those who jump the hurdle. With a perfect hurdle, the highest reservation price among buyers who jump the hurdle will be lower than the lowest reservation price among buyers who choose not to jump the hurdle. In practice, perfect hurdles do not exist. Some buyers will always jump the hurdle, even though their reservation prices are high. And hurdles will always exclude at least some buyers with low reservation prices. Even so, many commonly used hurdles do a remarkably good job of targeting discounts to buyers with low reservation prices. In the examples that follow, we will assume for convenience that the seller is using a perfect hurdle.

perfect hurdle a threshold that completely segregates buyers whose reservation prices lie above it from others whose reservation prices lie below it, imposing no cost on those who jump the hurdle

How much should Carla charge for editing if she uses a perfect hurdle?

Suppose Carla again has the opportunity to edit as many as 8 papers per week for the students whose reservation prices are as given in the following table. This time she can offer a rebate coupon that gives a discount to any student who takes the trouble to mail it back to her. Suppose further that students whose reservation prices are at least $36 never mail in the rebate coupons, while those whose reservation prices are below $36 always do so.

Student	Reservation price
A	$40
B	38
C	36
D	34
E	32
F	30
G	28
H	26

If Carla's opportunity cost of editing each paper is again $29, what should her list price be, and what amount should she offer as a rebate? Will her economic profit be larger or smaller than when she lacked the discount option?

The rebate coupon allows Carla to divide her original market into two submarkets in which she can charge two different prices. The first submarket consists of students *A*, *B*, and *C*, whose reservation prices are at least $36 and who therefore will not bother to mail in a rebate coupon. The second submarket consists of students *D* to *H*, whose lower reservation prices indicate a willingness to use rebate coupons.

In each submarket, Carla must charge the same price to every buyer, just like an ordinary monopolist. She should therefore keep expanding output in each submarket as long as marginal revenue in that market exceeds her marginal cost. The relevant data for the two submarkets are displayed in Table 8.6.

TABLE 8.6
Price Discrimination with a Perfect Hurdle

Student	Reservation price ($ per paper)	Total revenue ($ per week)	Marginal revenue ($ per paper)
		List Price Submarket	
			40
A	40	40	
			36
B	38	76	
			32
C	36	108	
		Discount Price Submarket	
			34
D	34	34	
			30
E	32	64	
			26
F	30	90	
			22
G	28	112	
			18
H	26	130	

On the basis of the entries in the marginal revenue column for the list price submarket, we see that Carla should serve all three students (*A*, *B*, and *C*) since marginal revenue for each exceeds $29. Her profit-maximizing price in the list price submarket is $36, the highest price she can charge in that market and still sell her services to students *A*, *B*, and *C*. For the discount price submarket, marginal revenue exceeds $29 only for the first two students (*D* and *E*). So the profit-maximizing price in this submarket is $32, the highest price Carla can charge and still sell her services to *D* and *E*. (A discount price of $32 means that students who mail in the coupon will receive a rebate of $4 on the $36 list price.)

Note that the rebate offer enables Carla to serve a total of five students per week, compared to only three without the offer. Carla's combined total revenue for the two markets is (3)($36) + 2($32) = $172 per week. Since her opportunity cost is $29 per paper, or a total of (5)($29) = $145 per week, her economic profit is $172 per week − $145 per week = $27 per week, $6 more than when she edited three papers and did not offer the rebate. ◆

EXERCISE 8.4

In the previous example, how much should Carla charge in each submarket if she knows that only those students whose reservation prices are below $34 will use rebate coupons?

IS PRICE DISCRIMINATION A BAD THING?

We are so conditioned to think of discrimination as bad that we may be tempted to conclude that price discrimination must run counter to the public interest. In the example above, however, both consumer and producer surplus were actually enhanced by the monopolist's use of the hurdle method of price discrimination. To show this, let's compare consumer and producer surplus when Carla employs the hurdle method to the corresponding values when she charges the same price to all buyers.

When Carla had to charge the same price to every customer, she edited only the papers of students *A*, *B*, and *C*, each of whom paid a price of \$36. We can tell at a glance that the total surplus must be larger under the hurdle method because not only are students *A*, *B*, and *C* served at the same price (\$36), but also students *D* and *E* are now served at a price of \$32.

To confirm this intuition, we can calculate the exact amount of the surplus. For any student who hires Carla to edit her paper, consumer surplus is the difference between her reservation price and the price actually paid. In both the single price and discount price examples, student *A*'s consumer surplus is thus \$40 − \$36 = \$4; student *B*'s consumer surplus is \$38 − \$36 = \$2; and student *C*'s consumer surplus is \$36 − \$36 = 0. Total consumer surplus in the list price submarket is thus \$4 + \$2 = \$6 per week, which is the same as total consumer surplus in the original situation. But now the discount price submarket generates additional consumer surplus. Specifically, student *D* receives \$2 per week of consumer surplus since this student's reservation price of \$34 is \$2 more than the discount price of \$32. So total consumer surplus is now \$6 + \$2 = \$8 per week, or \$2 per week more than before.

Carla's producer surplus also increases under the hurdle method. For each paper she edits, her producer surplus is the price she charges minus her reservation price (\$29). In the single-price case, Carla's surplus was (3)(\$36 − \$29) = \$21 per week. When she offers a rebate coupon, she earns the same producer surplus as before from students *A*, *B*, and *C* and additional (2)(\$32 − \$29) = \$6 per week from students *D* and *E*. Total producer surplus with the discount is thus \$21 + \$6 = \$27 per week. Adding that amount to the total consumer surplus of \$8 per week, we get a total economic surplus of \$35 per week with the rebate coupons, \$8 per week more than without the rebate.

Note, however, that even with the rebate, the final outcome is not socially efficient because Carla does not serve student *F*, even though this student's reservation price of \$30 exceeds her opportunity cost of \$29. But though the hurdle method is not perfectly efficient, it is still more efficient than charging a single price to all buyers.

EXAMPLES OF PRICE DISCRIMINATION

Once you grasp the principle behind the hurdle method of price discrimination, you will begin to see examples of it all around you. Next time you visit a grocery, hardware, or appliance store, for instance, notice how many different product promotions include cash rebates. Temporary sales are another illustration of the hurdle method. Most of the time, stores sell most of their merchandise at the "regular" price but periodically offer special sales at a significant discount. The hurdle in this instance is taking the trouble to find out when and where the sales occur and then going to the store during that period. This technique works because buyers who care most about price (mainly, those with low reservation prices) are more likely to monitor advertisements carefully and buy only during sale periods.

To give another example, book publishers typically launch a new book in hardcover at a price from \$20 to \$30, and a year later they bring out a paperback edition priced between \$5 and \$15. In this instance, the hurdle involves having to wait the extra year and accepting a slight reduction in the quality of the finished product.

People who are strongly concerned about price end up waiting for the paperback edition, while those with high reservation prices usually spring for the hardback.

Or take the example of automobile producers, who typically offer several different models with different trim and accessories. Although GM's actual cost of producing a Cadillac may be only $2,000 more than its cost of producing a Chevrolet, the Cadillac's selling price may be $10,000 to $15,000 higher than the Chevrolet's. Buyers with low reservation prices purchase the Chevrolet, while those with high reservation prices are more likely to choose the Cadillac.

Commercial air carriers have perfected the hurdle method to an extent matched by almost no other seller. Their supersaver fares are often less than half their regular coach fares. To be eligible for these discounts, travelers must purchase their tickets 7 to 21 days in advance and their journey must include a Saturday night stayover. Vacation travelers can more easily satisfy these restrictions than business travelers, whose schedules often change at the last moment and whose trips seldom involve Saturday stayovers. And—no surprise—the business traveler's reservation price tends to be much higher than the vacation traveler's.

Many sellers employ not just one hurdle but several by offering deeper discounts to buyers who jump successively more difficult hurdles. For example, movie producers release their major films to first-run theaters at premium prices, then several months later to neighborhood theaters at a few dollars less. Still later they make the films available on pay-per-view cable channels, then release them on DVD, and finally permit them to be shown on network television. Each successive hurdle involves waiting a little longer, and in the case of the televised versions, accepting lower quality. These hurdles are remarkably effective in segregating moviegoers according to their reservation prices.

Recall that the efficiency loss from single-price monopoly occurs because to the monopolist, the benefit of expanding output is smaller than the benefit to society as a whole. The hurdle method of price discrimination reduces this loss by giving the monopolist a practical means of cutting prices for price-sensitive buyers only. In general, the more finely the monopolist can partition a market using the hurdle method, the smaller the efficiency loss. Hurdles are not perfect, however, and some degree of efficiency will inevitably be lost.

EN 8

Example 8.3
THE ECONOMIC NATURALIST

Why might an appliance retailer instruct its clerks to hammer dents into the sides of its stoves and refrigerators?

The Sears "Scratch 'n' Dent Sale" is another example of how retailers use quality differentials to segregate buyers according to their reservation prices. Many Sears stores hold an annual sale in which they display appliances with minor scratches and blemishes in the parking lot at deep discounts. People who don't care much about price are unlikely to turn out for these events, but those with very low reservation prices often get up early to be first in line. Indeed, these sales have proven so popular that it might even be in a retailer's interest to put dents in some of its sale items deliberately. ●

Would a profit-maximizing appliance retailer ever deliberately damage its own merchandise?

RECAP	USING DISCOUNTS TO EXPAND THE MARKET

A price-discriminating monopolist is one who charges different prices to different buyers for essentially the same good or service. A common method of price discrimination is the hurdle method, which involves granting a discount to buyers who jump over a hurdle such as mailing in a rebate coupon. An effective hurdle is one that is more easily cleared by buyers with low reservation prices than by buyers with high reservation prices. Such a hurdle enables the monopolist to expand output and thereby reduce the deadweight loss from monopoly pricing.

SUMMARY

- Our concern in this chapter was the conduct and performance of the imperfectly competitive firm, a firm that has at least some latitude to set its own price. Economists often distinguish among three different types of imperfectly competitive firms: the pure monopolist, the lone seller of a product in a given market; the oligopolist, one of only a few sellers of a given product; and the monopolistic competitor, one of a relatively large number of firms that sell similar though slightly differentiated products. **LO1**

- Although advanced courses in economics devote much attention to differences in behavior among these three types of firms, our focus was on the common feature that differentiates them from perfectly competitive firms. Whereas the perfectly competitive firm faces an infinitely elastic demand curve for its product, the imperfectly competitive firm faces a downward-sloping demand curve. For convenience, we use the term *monopolist* to refer to any of the three types of imperfectly competitive firms. **LO2**

- Monopolists are sometimes said to enjoy market power, a term that refers to their power to set the price of their product. Market power stems from exclusive control over important inputs, from economies of scale, from patents and government licenses or franchises, and from network economies. The most important and enduring of these five sources of market power are economies of scale and network economies. **LO3**

- Research, design, engineering, and other fixed costs account for an increasingly large share of all costs required to bring products successfully to market. For products with large fixed costs, marginal cost is lower, often substantially, than average total cost and average total cost declines, often sharply, as output grows. This cost pattern explains why many industries are dominated by either a single firm or a small number of firms. **LO3**

- Unlike the perfectly competitive firm, for which marginal revenue exactly equals market price, the monopolist realizes a marginal revenue that is always less than its price. This shortfall reflects the fact that to sell more output, the monopolist must cut the price not only to additional buyers but to existing buyers as well. For the monopolist with a straight-line demand curve, the marginal revenue curve has the same vertical intercept and a horizontal intercept that is half as large as the intercept for the demand curve. **LO2**

- Whereas the perfectly competitive firm maximizes profit by producing at the level at which marginal cost equals the market price, the monopolist maximizes profit by equating marginal cost with marginal revenue, which is significantly lower than the market price. The result is an output level that is best for the monopolist but smaller than the level that would be best for society as a whole. At the profit-maximizing level of output, the benefit of an extra unit of output (the market price) is greater than its cost (the marginal cost). At the socially efficient level of output, where the monopolist's marginal cost curve intersects the demand curve, the benefit and cost of an extra unit are the same. **LO4**

- Both the monopolist and its potential customers can do better if the monopolist can grant discounts to price-sensitive buyers. The extreme example is the perfectly discriminating monopolist, who charges each buyer exactly his or her reservation price. Such producers are socially efficient because they sell to every buyer whose reservation price is at least as high as the marginal cost. **LO5**

KEY TERMS

constant returns to scale (212)
economies of scale (212)
hurdle method of price discrimination (227)
imperfectly competitive firm (208)
increasing returns to scale (212)
marginal revenue (216)
market power (211)
monopolistic competition (208)
natural monopoly (212)
oligopoly (209)
perfect hurdle (227)
perfectly discriminating monopolist (226)
price discrimination (223)
price setter (208)
pure monopoly (208)

REVIEW QUESTIONS

1. What important characteristic do all three types of imperfectly competitive firms share? **LO2**
2. True or false: A firm with market power can sell whatever quantity it wishes at whatever price it chooses. **LO2**
3. Why do most successful industrial societies offer patents and copyright protection, even though these protections enable sellers to charge higher prices? **LO3**
4. Why is marginal revenue always less than price for a monopolist but equal to price for a perfectly competitive firm? **LO2**
5. True or false: Because a natural monopolist charges a price greater than marginal cost, it necessarily earns a positive economic profit. **LO4**

PROBLEMS

McGraw-Hill's HOMEWORK MANAGER®

1. Two car manufacturers, Saab and Volvo, have fixed costs of \$1 billion and marginal costs of \$10,000 per car. If Saab produces 50,000 cars per year and Volvo produces 200,000, calculate the average production cost for each company. On the basis of these costs, which company's market share do you think will grow in relative terms? **LO3**
2. State whether the following statements are true or false, and explain why. **LO2, LO3**
   a. In a perfectly competitive industry, the industry demand curve is horizontal, whereas for a monopoly it is downward-sloping.
   b. Perfectly competitive firms have no control over the price they charge for their product.
   c. For a natural monopoly, average cost declines as the number of units produced increases over the relevant output range.
3. A single-price, profit-maximizing monopolist: **LO4**
   a. Causes excess demand, or shortages, by selling too few units of a good or service.
   b. Chooses the output level at which marginal revenue begins to increase.
   c. Always charges a price above the marginal cost of production.
   d. Also maximizes marginal revenue.
   e. None of the above statements is true.
4. If a monopolist could perfectly price-discriminate: **LO2, LO5**
   a. The marginal revenue curve and the demand curve would coincide.
   b. The marginal revenue curve and the marginal cost curve would coincide.
   c. Every consumer would pay a different price.
   d. Marginal revenue would become negative at some output level.
   e. The resulting pattern of exchange would still be socially inefficient.
5. Explain why price discrimination and the existence of slightly different variants of the same product tend to go hand in hand. Give an example from your own experience. **LO6**
6. What is the socially desirable price for a natural monopoly to charge? Why will a natural monopoly that attempts to charge the socially desirable price invariably suffer an economic loss? **LO5**
7. TotsPoses, Inc., a profit-maximizing business, is the only photography business in town that specializes in portraits of small children. George, who owns and runs TotsPoses, expects to encounter an average of eight customers per day, each with a reservation price shown in the following table. **LO4, LO6**

Customer	Reservation price ($ per photo)
A	50
B	46
C	42
D	38
E	34
F	30
G	26
H	22

a. If the total cost of each photo portrait is $12, how much should George charge if he must charge a single price to all customers? At this price, how many portraits will George produce each day? What will be his economic profit?
b. How much consumer surplus is generated each day at this price?
c. What is the socially efficient number of portraits?
d. George is very experienced in the business and knows the reservation price of each of his customers. If he is allowed to charge any price he likes to any consumer, how many portraits will he produce each day and what will his economic profit be?
e. In this case, how much consumer surplus is generated each day?
f. Suppose George is permitted to charge two prices. He knows that customers with a reservation price above $30 never bother with coupons, whereas those with a reservation price of $30 or less always use them. At what level should George set the list price of a portrait? At what level should he set the discount price? How many photo portraits will he sell at each price?
g. In this case, what is George's economic profit and how much consumer surplus is generated each day?

8. Serena is a single-price, profit-maximizing monopolist in the sale of her own patented perfume, whose demand and marginal cost curves are as shown. Relative to the consumer surplus that would result at the socially optimal quantity and price, how much consumer surplus is lost from her selling at the monopolist's profit-maximizing quantity and price? **LO5**

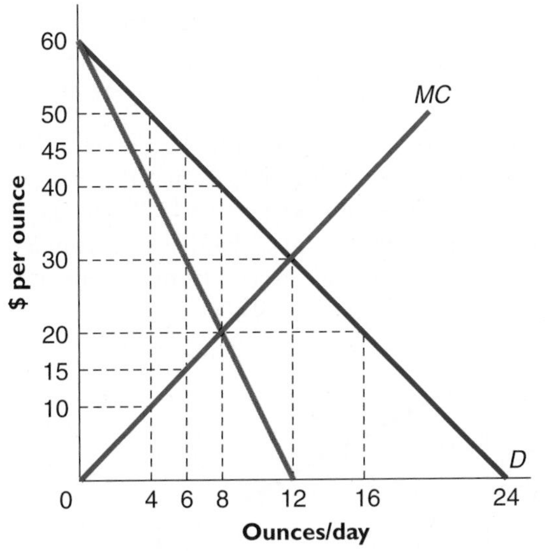

9. In the preceding question, how much total surplus would result if Serena could act as a perfectly price-discriminating monopolist? **LO6**

10. Beth is a second-grader who sells lemonade on a street corner in your neighborhood. Each cup of lemonade costs Beth 20 cents to produce; she has no fixed costs. The reservation prices for the 10 people who walk by Beth's lemonade stand each day are listed in the following table.

Person	*A*	*B*	*C*	*D*	*E*	*F*	*G*	*H*	*I*	*J*
Reservation price	$1.00	$0.90	$0.80	$0.70	$0.60	$0.50	$0.40	$0.30	$0.20	$0.10

Beth knows the distribution of reservation prices (that is, she knows that one person is willing to pay $1, another $0.90, and so on), but she does not know any specific individual's reservation price. **LO4, LO6**

a. Calculate the marginal revenue of selling an additional cup of lemonade. (Start by figuring out the price Beth would charge if she produced only one cup of lemonade, and calculate the total revenue; then find the price Beth would charge if she sold two cups of lemonade; and so on.)
b. What is Beth's profit-maximizing price?
c. At that price, what are Beth's economic profit and total consumer surplus?
d. What price should Beth charge if she wants to maximize total economic surplus?
e. Now suppose Beth can tell the reservation price of each person. What price would she charge each person if she wanted to maximize profit? Compare her profit to the total surplus calculated in part *d*.

ANSWERS TO IN-CHAPTER EXERCISES

8.1 The relevant cost figures are as shown in the following table, which shows that the Playstation's unit-cost advantage is now $50.20 − $5.20 = $45.00. **LO3**

	Nintendo	**Playstation**
Annual production	200,000	2,000,000
Fixed cost	$10,000,000	$10,000,000
Variable cost	$40,000	$400,000
Total cost	$10,040,000	$10,400,000
Average total cost per game	$50.20	$5.20

8.2 When the monopolist expands from 3 to 4 units per week, total revenue rises from $15 to $16 per week, which means that the marginal revenue from the sale of the fourth unit is only $1 per week. When the monopolist expands from 4 to 5 units per week, total revenue drops from $16 to $15 per week, which means that the marginal revenue from the sale of the fifth unit is actually negative, or −$1 per week. **LO2**

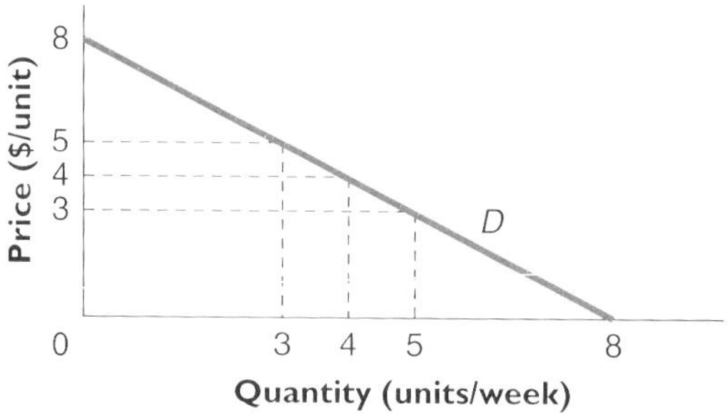

8.3 The profit-maximizing price and quantity are $P^* = \$6$/unit and $Q^* = 2$ units/week. **LO4**

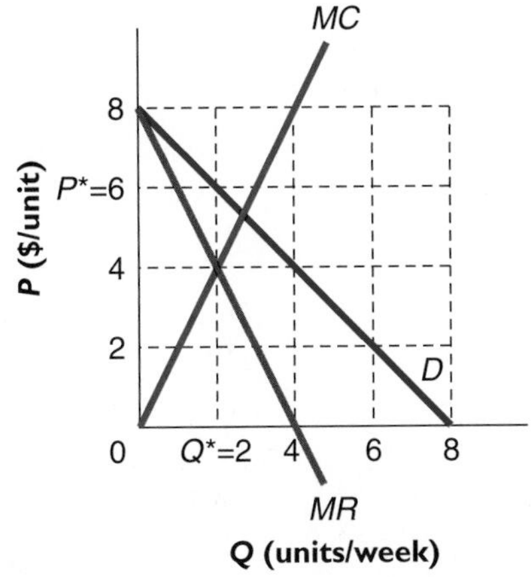

8.4 As the marginal revenue column in the following table shows, Carla should again serve students *A*, *B*, and *C* in the list price submarket (at a price of \$36) and only student *E* in the discount submarket (at a price of \$32). **LO4, LO6**

Student	Reservation price ($ per paper)	Total revenue ($ per week)	Marginal revenue ($ per paper)
		List Price Submarket	
			40
A	40	40	
			36
B	38	76	
			32
C	36	108	
			28
D	34	136	
		Discount Price Submarket	
			32
E	32	32	
			28
F	30	60	
			24
G	28	84	
			20
H	26	104	

APPENDIX

The Algebra of Monopoly Profit Maximization

In the text of this chapter, we developed the profit-maximization analysis for monopoly in a geometric framework. In this brief appendix, we show how this analysis can be done in an algebraic framework. The advantage of the algebraic framework is that it greatly simplifies computing the numerical values of the profit-maximizing prices and quantities.

Find the profit-maximizing price and quantity for a monopolist with the demand curve $P = 15 - 2Q$ and the marginal cost curve $MC = Q$, where P is the product price in dollars per unit and Q is the quantity in units of output per week.

The first step is to find the equation for the marginal revenue curve associated with the monopolist's demand curve. Recall that in the case of a straight-line demand curve, the associated marginal revenue curve has the same vertical intercept as the demand curve and twice the slope of the demand curve. So the equation for this monopolist's marginal revenue curve is $MR = 15 - 4Q$. Letting Q^* denote the profit-maximizing output level, setting $MR = MC$ then yields

$$15 - 4Q^* = Q^*,$$

which solves for $Q^* = 3$. The profit-maximizing price, P^*, is then found by substituting $Q^* = 3$ into the demand equation:

$$P^* = 15 - 2Q^* = 15 - 6 = 9.$$

Thus, the profit-maximizing price and quantity are \$9 per unit and 3 units per week, respectively. ◆

EXERCISE 8A.1

Find the profit-maximizing price and level of output for a monopolist with the demand curve $P = 12 - Q$ and the marginal cost curve $MC = 2Q$, where P is the price of the product in dollars per unit and Q is output in units per week.

▪ PROBLEMS ▪

1. Suppose that the University of Michigan Cinema is a local monopoly whose demand curve for adult tickets on Saturday night is $P = 12 - 2Q$, where P is the price of a ticket in dollars and Q is the number of tickets sold in hundreds. The demand for children's tickets on Sunday afternoon is $P = 8 - 3Q$, and for adult tickets on Sunday afternoon, $P = 10 - 4Q$. On both Saturday night and Sunday afternoon, the marginal cost of an additional patron, child or adult, is \$2. **LO4**
   a. What is the marginal revenue curve in each of the three submarkets?
   b. What price should the cinema charge in each of the three markets if its goal is to maximize profit?
2. Suppose you are a monopolist in the market for a specific video game. Your demand curve is given by $P = 80 - Q/2$; your marginal cost curve is $MC = Q$. Your fixed costs equal \$400. **LO4, LO5**
   a. Graph the demand and marginal cost curves.
   b. Derive and graph the marginal revenue curve.
   c. Calculate and indicate on the graph the equilibrium price and quantity.
   d. What is your profit?
   e. What is the level of consumer surplus?

▪ ANSWER TO IN-APPENDIX EXERCISES ▪

8A.1 For the demand curve $P = 12 - Q$, the corresponding marginal revenue curve is $MR = 12 - 2Q$. Equating MR and MC, we solve the equation $12 - 2Q = 2Q$ for $Q = 3$. Substituting $Q = 3$ into the demand equation, we solve for the profit-maximizing price, $P = 12 - 3 = 9$. **LO4**

CHAPTER

9

Games and Strategic Behavior

LEARNING OBJECTIVES

After reading this chapter, you should be able to:

1. Describe the three basic elements of a game.
2. Recognize and discuss the effects of dominant strategy choices and dominated strategy choices.
3. Define and explain the Prisoner's Dilemma and how it applies to real-world situations.
4. Explain games in which the timing of players' choices matters.
5. Discuss strategies that enable players to reap gains through cooperation.

At a Christmas Eve dinner party in 1997, actor Robert DeNiro pulled singer Tony Bennett aside for a moment. "Hey, Tony—there's a film I want you in," DeNiro said. He was referring to the project that became the 1999 Warner Brothers hit comedy *Analyze This,* in which the troubled head of a crime family, played by DeNiro, seeks the counsel of a psychotherapist, played by Billy Crystal. In the script, both the mob boss and his therapist are big fans of Bennett's music.

Bennett heard nothing further about the project for almost a year. Then his son and financial manager, Danny Bennett, got a phone call from Warner Brothers, in which the studio offered Tony $15,000 to sing "Got the World on a String" in the movie's final scene. As Danny described the conversation, ". . . they made a fatal mistake. They told me they had already shot the film. So I'm like: 'Hey, they shot the whole film around Tony being the end gag and they're offering me $15,000?'"[1]

[1]As quoted by Geraldine Fabrikant, "Talking Money with Tony Bennett," *The New York Times,* May 2, 1999, Money & Business, p. 1.

Warner Brothers wound up paying $200,000 for Bennett's performance.

In business negotiations, as in life, timing can be everything. If executives at Warner Brothers had thought the problem through carefully, they would have negotiated with Bennett *before* shooting the movie. At that point, Bennett would have realized that the script could be rewritten if he asked too high a fee. By waiting, studio executives left themselves with no attractive option other than to pay Bennett's price.

The payoff to many actions depends not only on the actions themselves, but also on when they are taken and how they relate to actions taken by others. In previous chapters, economic decision makers confronted an environment that was essentially fixed. This chapter will focus on cases in which people must consider the effect of their behavior on others. For example, an imperfectly competitive firm will want to weigh the likely responses of rivals when deciding whether to cut prices or to increase its advertising budget. Interdependencies of this sort are the rule rather than the exception in economic and social life. To make sense of the world we live in, then, we must take these interdependencies into account.

Our focus in Chapter 8 was on the pure monopolist. In this chapter, we will explore how a few simple principles from the theory of games can help us better understand the behavior of oligopolists and monopolistic competitors—the two types of imperfectly competitive firms for which strategic interdependencies are most important. Along the way, we also will see how the same principles enable us to answer a variety of interesting questions drawn from everyday social interaction.

USING GAME THEORY TO ANALYZE STRATEGIC DECISIONS

In chess, tennis, or any other game, the payoff to a given move depends on what your opponent does in response. In choosing your move, therefore, you must anticipate your opponent's responses, how you might respond, and what further moves your own response might elicit. Economists and other behavioral scientists have devised the theory of games to analyze situations in which the payoffs to different actors depend on the actions their opponents take.

THE THREE ELEMENTS OF A GAME

basic elements of a game the players, the strategies available to each player, and the payoffs each player receives for each possible combination of strategies

A game has three **basic elements:** the players, the list of possible actions (or strategies) available to each player, and the payoffs the players receive for each possible combination of strategies. We will use a series of examples to illustrate how these elements combine to form the basis of a theory of behavior.

The first example focuses on an important strategic decision confronting two oligopolists who produce an undifferentiated product and must decide how much to spend on advertising.

Should United Airlines spend more money on advertising?

Suppose that United Airlines and American Airlines are the only air carriers that serve the Chicago–St. Louis market. Each currently earns an economic profit of $6,000 per flight on this route. If United increases its advertising spending in this market by $1,000 per flight, and American spends no more on advertising than it does now, United's profit will rise to $8,000 per flight and American's will fall to $2,000. If both spend $1,000 more on advertising, each will earn an economic profit of $5,500 per flight. These payoffs are symmetric, so that if United stands pat while American increases its spending by $1,000, United's economic profit will fall to $2,000 per flight and American's will rise to $8,000. The payoff structure is also common knowledge—that is, each company knows what the relevant payoffs will be for both parties under each of the possible combinations of choices. If each must decide independently whether to increase spending on advertising, what should United do?

Think of this situation as a game. What are its three elements? The players are the two airlines. Each airline must choose one of two strategies: to raise ad spending by $1,000 or leave it the same. The payoffs are the economic profits that correspond to the four possible scenarios resulting from their choices. One way to summarize the relevant information about this game is to display the players, strategies, and payoffs in the form of a simple table called a **payoff matrix** (see Table 9.1).

payoff matrix a table that describes the payoffs in a game for each possible combination of strategies

Confronted with the payoff matrix in Table 9.1, what should United Airlines do? The essence of strategic thinking is to begin by looking at the situation from the other party's point of view. Suppose United assumes that American will raise its spending on advertising (the left column in Table 9.1). In that case, United's best bet would be to follow suit (the top row in Table 9.1). Why is the top row United's best response when American chooses the left column? United's economic profits, given in the upper-left cell of Table 9.1, will be $5,500, compared to only $2,000 if it keeps spending the same (see the lower-left cell).

Alternatively, suppose United assumes that American will keep ad spending the same (that is, that American will choose the right column in Table 9.1). In that case, United would still do better to increase spending because it would earn $8,000 (the upper-right cell), compared to only $6,000 if it keeps spending the same (the lower-right cell). In this particular game, no matter which strategy American chooses, United will earn a higher economic profit by increasing its spending on advertising. And since this game is perfectly symmetric, a similar conclusion holds for American: No matter which strategy United chooses, American will do better by increasing its spending on ads.

When one player has a strategy that yields a higher payoff no matter which choice the other player makes, that player is said to have a **dominant strategy.** Not all games involve dominant strategies, but both players in this game have one, and that is to increase spending on ads. For both players, to leave ad spending the same

dominant strategy one that yields a higher payoff no matter what the other players in a game choose

TABLE 9.1
The Payoff Matrix for an Advertising Game

United's Choices		American's Choices: Raise ad spending	American's Choices: Leave ad spending the same
	Raise ad spending	$5,500 for United $5,500 for American	$8,000 for United $2,000 for American
	Leave ad spending the same	$2,000 for United $8,000 for American	$6,000 for United $6,000 for American

Both airlines do better if both leave ad spending the same than if both raise spending. Yet if one holds spending the same, the other always does better to raise spending.

dominated strategy any other strategy available to a player who has a dominant strategy

is a **dominated strategy**—one that leads to a lower payoff than an alternative choice, regardless of the other player's choice.

Notice, however, that when each player chooses the dominant strategy, the resulting payoffs are smaller than if each had left spending unchanged. When United and American increase their spending on ads, each earns only $5,500 in economic profits, compared to the $6,000 each would have earned without the increase. ◆

NASH EQUILIBRIUM

Nash equilibrium any combination of strategies in which each player's strategy is his or her best choice, given the other players' choices

A game is said to be in equilibrium if each player's strategy is the best he or she can choose, given the other players' choices. This definition of equilibrium is sometimes called a **Nash equilibrium,** after the mathematician John Nash, who developed the concept in the early 1950s. Nash was awarded the Nobel Prize in Economics in 1994 for his contributions to game theory.[2] When a game is in equilibrium, no player has any incentive to deviate from his current strategy.

If each player in a game has a dominant strategy, as in the advertising example, equilibrium occurs when each player follows that strategy. But even in games in which not every player has a dominant strategy, we can often identify an equilibrium outcome. Consider, for instance, the following variation on the advertising game.

Should American spend more money on advertising?

Suppose United Airlines and American are the only carriers that serve the Chicago–St. Louis market. Their payoff matrix for advertising decisions is shown in Table 9.2. Does United have a dominant strategy? Does American? If each firm does the best it can, given the incentives facing the other, what will be the outcome of this game?

In this game, no matter what United does, American will do better to raise its ad spending, so raising the advertising budget is a dominant strategy for American. United, however, does not have a dominant strategy. If American raises its spending, United will do better to stand pat; if American stands pat, however, United will do

TABLE 9.2
Equilibrium When One Player Lacks a Dominant Strategy

United's Choices	American's Choices: Raise ad spending	American's Choices: Leave ad spending the same
Raise ad spending	$3,000 for United $4,000 for American	$8,000 for United $3,000 for American
Leave ad spending the same	$4,000 for United $5,000 for American	$5,000 for United $2,000 for American

In this game, United lacks a dominant strategy, but American's dominant strategy is to raise its ad spending. Because United can predict that American will choose the left column, United will do best to leave its ad spending the same. Equilibrium occurs in the lower-left cell.

[2]Nash was awarded the Nobel Prize in Economics in 1994 for his contributions to game theory. His life was also the subject of the Academy Award–winning film *A Beautiful Mind*.

better to spend more. Even though United does not have a dominant strategy, we can employ the Incentive Principle to predict what is likely to happen in this game. United's managers are assumed to know what the payoff matrix is, so they can predict that American will spend more on ads since that is American's dominant strategy. Thus the best strategy for United, given the prediction that American will spend more on ads, is to keep its own spending unchanged. If both players do the best they can, taking account of the incentives each faces, this game will end in the lower-left cell of the payoff matrix: American will raise its spending on ads and United will not. ◆

Incentive

Note that the choices corresponding to the lower-left cell in Table 9.2 satisfy the definition of a Nash equilibrium. If United found itself in that cell, its alternative would be to raise its ad spending, a move that would reduce its payoff from $4,000 to $3,000. So United has no incentive to abandon the lower-left cell. Similarly, if American found itself in the lower-left cell of Table 9.2, its alternative would be to leave ad spending the same, a move that would reduce its payoff from $5,000 to $2,000. So American also has no incentive to abandon the lower-left cell. The lower left cell of Table 9.2 is a Nash equilibrium—a combination of strategies for which each player's choice is the best available option, given the choice made by the other player.

EXERCISE 9.1

What should United and American do if their payoff matrix is modified as follows?

		American: Raise ad spending	American: Leave spending the same
United	Raise ad spending	$3,000 for United $8,000 for American	$4,000 for United $5,000 for American
United	Leave spending the same	$8,000 for United $4,000 for American	$5,000 for United $2,000 for American

RECAP	USING GAME THEORY TO ANALYZE STRATEGIC DECISIONS

The three elements of any game are the players, the list of strategies from which they can choose, and the payoffs to each combination of strategies. This information can be summarized in a payoff matrix.

Equilibrium in a game occurs when each player's strategy choice yields the highest payoff available, given the strategies chosen by other players. Such a combination of strategies is called a Nash equilibrium.

THE PRISONER'S DILEMMA

prisoner's dilemma a game in which each player has a dominant strategy, and when each plays it, the resulting payoffs are smaller than if each had played a dominated strategy

The first advertising example we discussed above belongs to an important class of games called the **prisoner's dilemma.** In the prisoner's dilemma, when each player chooses his dominant strategy, the result is unattractive to the group of players as a whole.

THE ORIGINAL PRISONER'S DILEMMA

The next example recounts the original scenario from which the prisoner's dilemma drew its name.

Should the prisoners confess?

Two prisoners, Horace and Jasper, are being held in separate cells for a serious crime that they did in fact commit. The prosecutor, however, has only enough hard evidence to convict them of a minor offense, for which the penalty is a year in jail. Each prisoner is told that if one confesses while the other remains silent, the confessor will go scot-free, and the other will spend 20 years in prison. If both confess, they will get an intermediate sentence of five years. These payoffs are summarized in Table 9.3. The two prisoners are not allowed to communicate with one another. Do they have a dominant strategy? If so, what is it?

In this game, the dominant strategy for each prisoner is to confess. No matter what Jasper does, Horace will get a lighter sentence by speaking out. If Jasper confesses, Horace will get five years (upper-left cell) instead of 20 (lower-left cell). If Jasper remains silent, Horace will go free (upper-right cell) instead of spending a year in jail (lower-right cell). Because the payoffs are perfectly symmetric, Jasper will also do better to confess, no matter what Horace does. The difficulty is that when each follows his dominant strategy and confesses, both will do worse than if each had shown restraint. When both confess, they each get five years (upper-left cell), instead of the one year they would have gotten by remaining silent (lower-right cell). Hence the name of this game, the prisoner's dilemma. ◆

TABLE 9.3
The Payoff Matrix for a Prisoner's Dilemma

		Jasper	
		Confess	Remain Silent
Horace	Confess	5 years for each	0 years for Horace 20 years for Jasper
	Remain Silent	20 years for Horace 0 years for Jasper	1 year for each

The payoffs describe the lengths of prison sentences the two will receive under different combinations of choices.

EXERCISE 9.2

GM and Chrysler must both decide whether to invest in a new process. Games 1 and 2 below show how their profits depend on the decisions they might make. Which of these games is a prisoner's dilemma?

Game 1

GM \ Chrysler	Don't invest	Invest
Don't invest	10 for each	4 for GM 12 for Chrysler
Invest	12 for GM 4 for Chrysler	5 for each

Game 2

GM \ Chrysler	Don't invest	Invest
Don't invest	4 for GM 12 for Chrysler	5 for each
Invest	10 for each	12 for GM 4 for Chrysler

The prisoner's dilemma is one of the most powerful metaphors in all of human behavioral science. Countless social and economic interactions have payoff structures analogous to the one confronted by the two prisoners. Some of those interactions occur between only two players, as in the examples just discussed; many others involve larger groups. Games of the latter sort are called *multiplayer prisoner's dilemmas*. But regardless of the number of players involved, the common thread is one of conflict between the narrow self-interest of individuals and the broader interests of larger communities.

THE ECONOMICS OF CARTELS

A **cartel** is any coalition of firms that conspires to restrict production for the purpose of earning an economic profit. As we will see in the next example, the problem confronting oligopolists who are trying to form a cartel is a classic illustration of the prisoner's dilemma.

cartel a coalition of firms that agree to restrict output for the purpose of earning an economic profit

Example 9.1

THE ECONOMIC NATURALIST

Why are cartel agreements notoriously unstable?

Consider a market for bottled water served by two oligopolists, Aquapure and Mountain Spring. Each firm can draw water free of charge from a mineral spring located on its own land. Customers supply their own bottles. Rather than compete with one another, the two firms decide to collude by selling water at the price a profit-maximizing pure monopolist would charge. Under their agreement (which constitutes a cartel), each firm would produce and sell half the quantity of water demanded by the market at the monopoly price (see Figure 9.1). The agreement is not legally enforceable, however, which means that each firm has the option of charging less than the agreed price. If one firm sells water for less than the other firm, it will capture the entire quantity demanded by the market at the lower price.

Why is this agreement likely to collapse?

Since the marginal cost of mineral water is zero, the profit-maximizing quantity for a monopolist with the demand curve shown in Figure 9.1 is 1,000 bottles per day, the

FIGURE 9.1
The Market Demand for Mineral Water.
Faced with the demand curve shown, a monopolist with zero marginal cost would produce 1,000 bottles per day (the quantity at which marginal revenue equals zero) and sell them at a price of $1.00 per bottle.

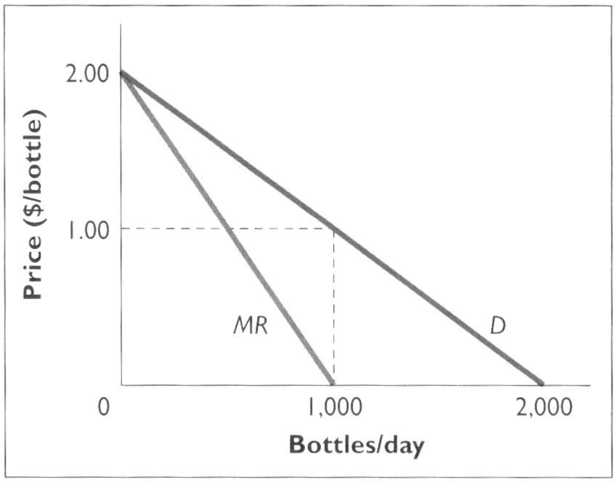

Why is it so difficult for companies to enforce agreements against price cutting?

quantity for which marginal revenue equals marginal cost. At that quantity, the monopoly price is $1 per bottle. If the firms abide by their agreement, each will sell half the market total, or 500 bottles per day, at a price of $1 per bottle, for an economic profit of $500 per day.

But suppose Aquapure reduced its price to 90 cents per bottle. By underselling Mountain Spring, it would capture the entire quantity demanded by the market, which, as shown in Figure 9.2, is 1,100 bottles per day. Aquapure's economic profit would rise from $500 per day to ($0.90 per bottle)(1,100 bottles per day) = $990 per day—almost twice as much as before. In the process, Mountain Spring's economic profit would fall from $500 per day to zero. Rather than see its economic profit disappear, Mountain Spring would match Aquapure's price cut, recapturing its original 50-percent share of the market. But when each firm charges $0.90 per bottle and sells 550 bottles per day, each earns an economic profit of ($.90 per bottle)(550 bottles per day) = $495 per day, or $5 less per day than before.

Suppose we view the cartel agreement as an economic game in which the two available strategies are to sell for $1 per bottle or to sell for $0.90 per bottle. The payoffs are the economic profits that result from these strategies. Table 9.4 shows the payoff matrix for this game. Each firm's dominant strategy is to sell at the lower price, yet in following that strategy, each earns a lower profit than if each had sold at the higher price.

The game does not end with both firms charging $0.90 per bottle. Each firm knows that if it cuts the price a little further, it can recapture the entire market, and in the process earn a substantially higher economic profit. At every step, the rival firm

FIGURE 9.2
The Temptation to Violate a Cartel Agreement.
By cutting its price from $1 per bottle to 90 cents per bottle, Aquapure can sell the entire market quantity demanded at that price, 1,100 bottles per day, rather than half the monopoly quantity of 1,000 bottles per day.

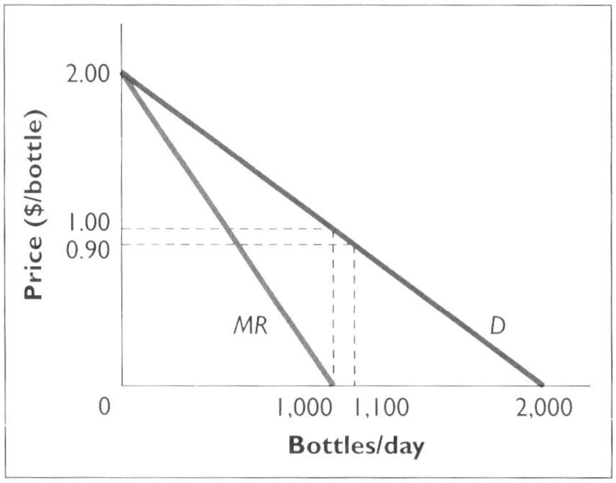

TABLE 9.4
The Payoff Matrix for a Cartel Agreement

		Mountain Spring: Charge $1/bottle	Mountain Spring: Charge $0.90/bottle
Aquapure	Charge $1/bottle	$500/day for each	$0 for Aquapure; $990/day for Mt. Spring
Aquapure	Charge $0.90/bottle	$990/day Aquapure; 0 for Mt. Spring	$495/day for each

The dominant strategy for each firm is to charge $0.90 per bottle, or 10 cents per bottle less than called for by the cartel agreement. Hence the notorious instability of cartel agreements.

will match any price cut, until the price falls all the way to the marginal cost—in this example, zero.

Cartel agreements confront participants with the economic incentives inherent in the prisoner's dilemma, which explains why such agreements have historically been so unstable. Usually a cartel involves not just two firms, but several, an arrangement that can make retaliation against price cutters extremely difficult. In many cases, discovering which parties have broken the agreement is difficult. For example, the Organization of Petroleum Exporting Countries (OPEC), a cartel of oil producers formed in the 1970s to restrict oil production, has no practical way to prevent member countries from secretly pumping oil offshore in the dead of night. ●

TIT-FOR-TAT AND THE REPEATED PRISONER'S DILEMMA

When all players cooperate in a prisoner's dilemma, each gets a higher payoff than when all defect. So people who confront prisoner's dilemmas will be on the lookout for ways to create incentives for mutual cooperation. What they need is some way to penalize players who defect. When players interact with one another only once, this turns out to be difficult. But when they expect to interact repeatedly, new possibilities emerge.

A **repeated prisoner's dilemma** is a standard prisoner's dilemma that confronts the same players not just once but many times. Experimental research on repeated prisoner's dilemmas in the 1960s identified a simple strategy that proves remarkably effective at limiting defection. The strategy is called **tit-for-tat,** and here is how it works: The first time you interact with someone, you cooperate. In each subsequent interaction, you simply do what that person did in the previous interaction. Thus, if your partner defected on your first interaction, you would then defect on your next interaction with her. If she then cooperates, your move next time will be to cooperate as well.

repeated prisoner's dilemma a standard prisoner's dilemma that confronts the same players repeatedly

tit-for-tat a strategy for the repeated prisoner's dilemma in which players cooperate on the first move, then mimic their partner's last move on each successive move

On the basis of elaborate computer simulations, University of Michigan political scientist Robert Axelrod showed that tit-for-tat was a remarkably effective strategy, even when pitted against a host of ingenious counterstrategies that had been designed for the explicit purpose of trying to exploit it. The success of tit-for-tat requires a reasonably stable set of players, each of whom can remember what other players have done in previous interactions. It also requires that players have a significant stake in what happens in the future, for it is the fear of retaliation that deters people from defecting.

Since rival firms in the same industry interact with one another repeatedly, it might seem that the tit-for-tat strategy would assure widespread collusion to raise prices. And yet, as noted earlier, cartel agreements are notoriously unsuccessful. One difficulty is that tit-for-tat's effectiveness depends on there being only two players in the game. In competitive and monopolistically competitive industries, there are generally many firms, and even in oligopolies there are often several. When there are more than two firms, and one defects now, how do the cooperators selectively punish the defector later? By cutting price? That will penalize everyone, not just the defector. Even if there are only two firms in an industry, these firms realize that other firms may enter their industry. So the would-be cartel members have to worry not only about each other, but also about the entire list of firms that might decide to compete with them. Each firm may see this as a hopeless task and decide to defect now, hoping to reap at least some economic profit in the short run. What seems clear, in any event, is that the practical problems involved in implementing tit-for-tat have made it difficult to hold cartel agreements together for long.

Example 9.2

THE ECONOMIC NATURALIST

How did Congress unwittingly solve the television advertising dilemma confronting cigarette producers?

Why were cigarette manufacturers happy when Congress made it illegal for them to advertise on television?

In 1970, Congress enacted a law making cigarette advertising on television illegal after January 1, 1971. As evidenced by the steadily declining proportion of Americans who smoke, this law seems to have achieved its stated purpose of protecting citizens against a proven health hazard. But the law also had an unintended effect, which was to increase the economic profit of cigarette makers, at least in the short run. In the year before the law's passage, manufacturers spent more than $300 million on advertising—about $60 million more than they spent during the year after the law was enacted. Much of the saving in advertising expenditures in 1971 was reflected in higher cigarette profits at year end. But if eliminating television advertising made companies more profitable, why didn't the manufacturers eliminate the ads on their own?

When an imperfectly competitive firm advertises its product, its demand curve shifts rightward, for two reasons. First, people who have never used that type of product learn about it, and some buy it. Second, people who consume a different brand of the product may switch brands. The first effect boosts sales industrywide; the second merely redistributes existing sales among brands.

Although advertising produces both effects in the cigarette industry, its primary effect is brand switching. Thus, the decision of whether to advertise confronts the individual firm with a prisoner's dilemma. Table 9.5 shows the payoffs facing a pair of cigarette producers trying to decide whether to advertise. If both firms advertise on TV (upper-left cell), each earns a profit of only $10 million per year, compared to a profit of $20 million per year for each if neither advertises (lower-right cell). Clearly, both will benefit if neither advertises.

Yet note the powerful incentive that confronts each firm. RJR sees that if Philip Morris doesn't advertise, RJR can earn higher profits by advertising ($35 million per year) than by not advertising ($20 million per year). RJR also sees that if Philip Morris does advertise, RJR will again earn more by advertising ($10 million per year) than by not advertising ($5 million per year). Thus, RJR's dominant strategy is to advertise. And because the payoffs are symmetric, Philip Morris's dominant strategy is also to advertise. So when each firm behaves rationally from its own point of view, the two together do worse than if they had both shown restraint. The congressional ad ban forced cigarette manufacturers to do what they could not have accomplished on their own. ●

As the following example makes clear, understanding the prisoner's dilemma can help the economic naturalist to make sense of human behavior not only in the world of business, but also in other domains of life as well.

TABLE 9.5
Cigarette Advertising as a Prisoner's Dilemma

		Philip Morris	
		Advertise on TV	Don't advertise on TV
RJR	Advertise on TV	$10 million/yr for each	$35 million/yr for RJR $5 million/yr for Philip Morris
	Don't advertise on TV	$5 million/yr for RJR $35 million/yr for Philip Morris	$20 million/yr for each

In many industries, the primary effect of advertising is to encourage consumers to switch brands. In such industries, the dominant strategy is to advertise heavily (upper-left cell), even though firms as a group would do better by not advertising (lower-right cell).

Example 9.3

THE ECONOMIC NATURALIST

Why do people shout at parties?

Whenever large numbers of people gather for conversation in a closed space, the ambient noise level rises sharply. After attending such gatherings, people often complain of sore throats and hoarse voices. If everyone spoke at a normal volume at parties, the overall noise level would be lower, and people would hear just as well. So why do people shout?

The problem involves the difference between individual incentives and group incentives. Suppose everyone starts by speaking at a normal level. But because of the crowded conditions, conversation partners have difficulty hearing one another, even when no one is shouting. The natural solution, from the point of the individual, is to simply raise one's voice a bit. But that is also the natural solution for everyone else. And when everyone speaks more loudly, the ambient noise level rises, so that no one hears any better than before.

No matter what others do, the individual will do better by speaking more loudly. Doing so is a dominant strategy for everyone, in fact. Yet when everyone follows the dominant strategy, the result is worse (no one can hear well) than if everyone had continued to speak normally. While shouting is wasteful, individuals acting alone have no better option. If anyone were to speak softly while others shout, that person wouldn't be heard. No one wants to go home with raw vocal cords, but people apparently prefer that cost to the alternative of not being heard at all. ●

Why do people often have to shout to be heard at parties?

EN 9

RECAP	THE PRISONER'S DILEMMA

The prisoner's dilemma is a game in which each player has a dominant strategy, and in which the payoff to each player when each chooses that strategy is smaller than if each had chosen a dominated strategy. Incentives analogous to those found in the prisoner's dilemma help to explain a broad range of behavior in business and everyday life—among them excessive spending on advertising and cartel instability. The tit-for-tat strategy can help sustain cooperation in two-player repeated prisoner's dilemmas but tends to be ineffective in multiplayer repeated prisoner's dilemmas.

GAMES IN WHICH TIMING MATTERS

In the games discussed so far, players were assumed to choose their strategies simultaneously, and which player moved first didn't matter. For example, in the prisoner's dilemma, self-interested players would follow their dominant strategies even if they knew in advance what strategies their opponents had chosen. But in other situations, such as the negotiations between Warner Brothers and Tony Bennett described at the beginning of this chapter, timing is of the essence.

We begin with an example of a game whose outcome cannot be predicted if both players move simultaneously, but whose outcome is clear if one player has the opportunity to move before the other.

Should Dodge build a hybrid Viper?

The Dodge Viper and the Chevrolet Corvette compete for a limited pool of domestic sports car enthusiasts. Each company knows that the other is considering whether to bring out a hybrid version of its car. If both companies bring out hybrids, each will earn $60 million in profit. If neither brings out a hybrid, each company will earn $50 million. If Chevrolet introduces a hybrid and Dodge does not, Chevrolet will earn $80 million and Dodge will earn $70 million. If Dodge brings out a hybrid and Chevrolet does not, Dodge will earn $80 million and Chevrolet will earn $70 million. Does either firm have a dominant strategy in this situation? What will happen in this game if Dodge gets to choose first, with Chevrolet choosing after having seen Dodge's choice?

When both companies must make their decisions simultaneously, the payoff matrix for the example looks like Table 9.6.

TABLE 9.6
The Advantage of Being Different

	Dodge Viper: Offer hybrid	Dodge Viper: Don't offer hybrid
Offer hybrid	$60 million for Dodge	$70 million for Dodge
Don't offer hybrid	$80 million for Dodge	$50 million for Dodge

Profits are higher when each company offers a different type of car than the other (upper-right and lower-left cells). Customers generally prefer hybrid cars (upper-left cell) to nonhybrids (lower-right cell).

The logic of the profit figures in Table 9.6 is that although consumers generally like the idea of a hybrid sports car (hence the higher profits when both companies bring out hybrids than when neither does), the companies will have to compete more heavily with one another if both offer the same type of car (and hence the lower profits when both offer the same type of car than when each offers a different type).

In the payoff matrix in Table 9.6, neither company has a dominant strategy. The best outcome for Dodge is to offer a hybrid Viper while Chevrolet does not offer a hybrid Corvette (lower-left cell). The best outcome for Chevrolet is to offer a hybrid Corvette while Dodge does not offer a hybrid Viper (upper-right cell). Both the lower-left and upper-right cells are Nash equilibria of this game because if the companies found themselves in either of these cells, neither would unilaterally want to change its position. Thus, in the upper-right cell, Chevrolet wouldn't want to change (that cell is, after all, the best possible outcome for Chevrolet), and neither would Dodge (since switching to a hybrid would reduce its profit from $70 million to $60 million). But without being told more, we simply cannot predict where the two companies will end up.

If one side can move before the other, however, the incentives for action become instantly clearer. For games in which timing matters, a **decision tree,** or **game tree,** is a more useful way of representing the payoffs than a traditional payoff matrix. This type of diagram describes the possible moves in the sequence in which they may occur, and lists the final payoffs for each possible combination of moves.

decision tree *(also called a* ***game tree)*** a diagram that describes the possible moves in a game in sequence and lists the payoffs that correspond to each possible combination of moves

If Dodge has the first move, the decision tree for the game is shown in Figure 9.3. At *A,* Dodge begins the game by deciding whether to offer a hybrid. If it chooses to offer one, Chevrolet must then make its own choice at *B*. If Dodge does not offer a hybrid, Chevrolet will make its choice at C. In either case, once Chevrolet makes its choice, the game is over.

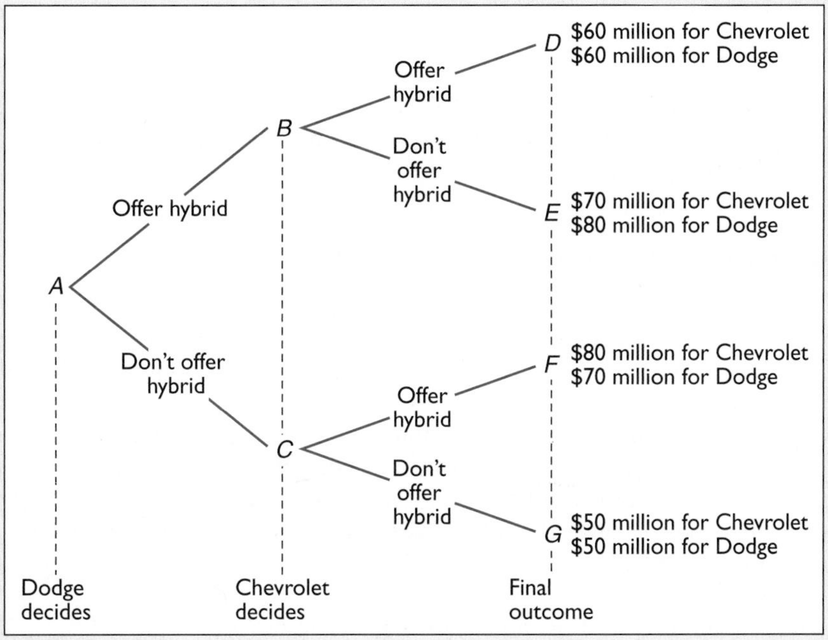

FIGURE 9.3
Decision Tree for Hybrid Example.
This decision tree shows the possible moves and payoffs for the game in the hybrid example, in the sequence in which they may occur.

In thinking strategically about this game, the key for Dodge is to put itself in Chevrolet's shoes and imagine how Chevrolet would react to the various choices it might confront. In general, it will make sense for Dodge to assume that Chevrolet will respond in a self-interested way—that is, by choosing the available option that offers the highest profit for Chevrolet. Dodge knows that if it chooses to offer a hybrid, Chevy's best option at *B* will be not to offer a hybrid (since Chevy's profit is $10 million higher at *E* than at *D*). Dodge also knows that if it chooses not to offer a hybrid, Chevy's best option at C will be to offer one (since Chevy's profit is $30 million higher at F than at G). Dodge thus knows that if it offers a hybrid, it will end up at E, where it will earn \$80 million, whereas if it does not offer a hybrid, it will end up at F, where it will earn only \$70 million. So when Dodge has the first move in this game, its best strategy is to offer a hybrid. And Chevrolet then follows by choosing not to offer one. ◆

CREDIBLE THREATS AND PROMISES

credible threat a threat to take an action that is in the threatener's interest to carry out

Incentive

Could Chevrolet have deterred Dodge from offering a hybrid by threatening to offer a hybrid of its own, no matter what Dodge did? The problem with this strategy is such a threat would not have been credible. In the language of game theory, a **credible threat** is one that will be in the threatener's interest to carry out when the time comes to act. As the Incentive Principle suggests, people are likely to be skeptical of any threat if they know there will be no incentive to follow through when the time comes. The problem here is that Dodge knows that it would not be in Chevrolet's interest to carry out its threat in the event that Dodge offered a hybrid. After all, once Dodge has already offered the hybrid, Chevy's best option is to offer a nonhybrid.

The concept of a credible threat figured prominently in the negotiations between Warner Brothers' managers and Tony Bennett over the matter of Mr. Bennett's fee for performing in *Analyze This*. Once most of the film had been shot, managers knew they couldn't threaten credibly to refuse Mr. Bennett's salary demand because at that point adapting the film to another singer would have been extremely costly. In contrast, a similar threat made before production of the movie had begun would have been credible.

credible promise a promise to take an action that is in the promiser's interest to keep

Just as in some games credible threats are impossible to make, in others **credible promises** are impossible. A credible promise is one that is in the interests of the promiser to keep when the time comes to act. In the following example, both players suffer because of the inability to make a credible promise.

Should the business owner open a remote office?

The owner of a thriving business wants to start up an office in a distant city. If she hires someone to manage the new office, she can afford to pay a weekly salary of \$1,000—a premium of \$500 over what the manager would otherwise be able to earn—and still earn a weekly economic profit of \$1,000 for herself. The owner's concern is that she will not be able to monitor the manager's behavior. The owner knows that by managing the remote office dishonestly, the manager can boost his take-home pay to \$1,500 while causing the owner an economic loss of \$500 per week. If the owner believes that all managers are selfish income-maximizers, will she open the new office?

The decision tree for the remote-office game is shown in Figure 9.4. At A, the managerial candidate promises to manage honestly, which brings the owner to B, where she must decide whether to open the new office. If she opens it, they reach C, where the manager must decide whether to manage honestly. If the manager's only goal is to make as much money as he can, he will manage dishonestly (bottom branch at C) since that way he will earn \$500 more than by managing honestly (top branch at C).

So if the owner opens the new office, she will end up with an economic loss of \$500. If she had not opened the office (bottom branch at B), she would have realized an economic profit of zero. Since zero is better than −\$500, the owner will choose not to open the remote office. In the end, the opportunity cost of the manager's inability to make a credible promise is \$1,500: the manager's forgone \$500 salary premium and the owner's forgone \$1,000 return.

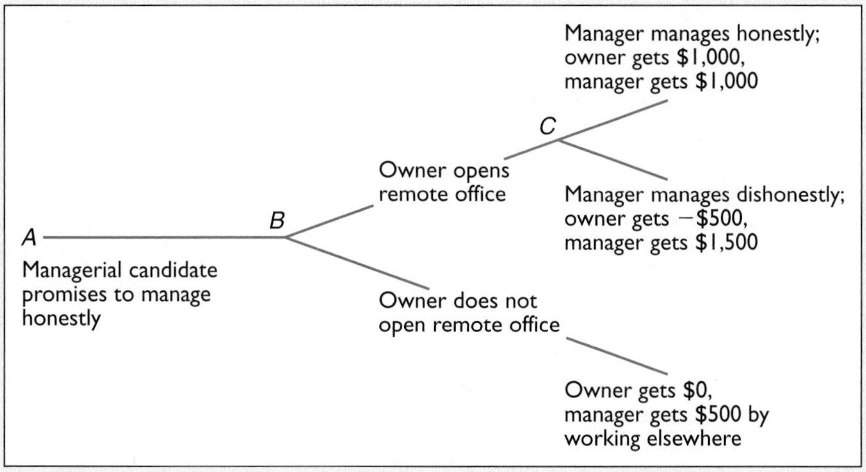

FIGURE 9.4
Decision Tree for the Remote Office Game.
The best outcome is for the manager to open the office at *B* and for the manager to manage the office honestly at *C*. But if the manager is purely self-interested and the owner knows it, this path will not be an equilibrium outcome.

◆

EXERCISE 9.3

Smith and Jones are playing a game in which Smith has the first move at *A* in the decision tree shown below. Once Smith has chosen either the top or bottom branch at *A*, Jones, who can see what Smith has chosen, must choose the top or bottom branch at *B* or *C*. If the payoffs at the end of each branch are as shown, what is the equilibrium outcome of this game? If before Smith chose, Jones could make a credible commitment to choose either the top or bottom branch when his turn came, what would he do?

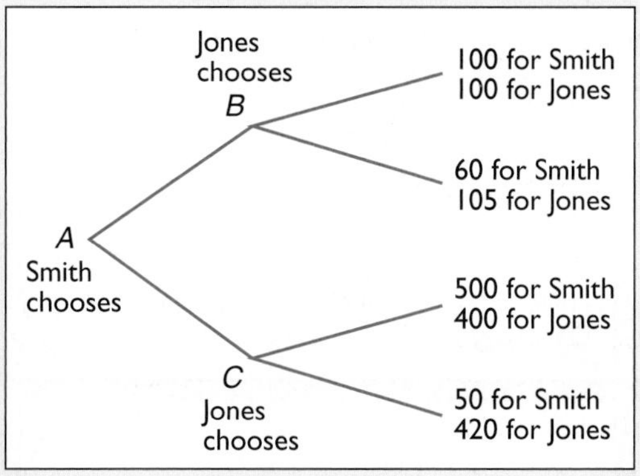

MONOPOLISTIC COMPETITION WHEN LOCATION MATTERS

In many sequential games, the player who gets to move first enjoys a strategic advantage. That was the case, for instance, in the decision of whether to produce a hybrid sports car. In that example, the first mover did better because he was able to exploit the knowledge that both firms do better if each one's product is different from the other's rather than similar to it. But that won't always be true. When the feature that differentiates one seller's product from another's is temporal or spatial location, the firm with the last move in a game sometimes enjoys the upper hand, as Example 9.4 illustrates.

Example 9.4

THE ECONOMIC NATURALIST

Why do we often see convenience stores located on adjacent street corners?

In many cities, it is common to see convenience stores located in clusters, followed by long stretches with no stores at all. If the stores were more spread out, almost all consumers would enjoy a shorter walk to the nearest convenience store. Why do stores tend to cluster in this fashion?

Why do retail merchants tend to locate in clusters?

In Figure 9.5, suppose that when the convenience store located at *A* first opened, it was the closest store for the 1,200 shoppers who live in identical apartment houses evenly distributed along the road between *A* and the freeway one mile to the east.[3] Those who live to the east of the freeway shop elsewhere because they cannot cross the freeway. Those who live to the west of the store at *A* shop either at *A* or at some other store still further to the west, whichever is closer. In this setting, why might a profit-maximizing entrepreneur planning to open a new store between *A* and the freeway choose to locate at *B* rather than at some intermediate location such as *C*?

It turns out that a store located at *C* would in fact minimize the distance that shoppers living between *A* and the freeway would have to walk to reach the nearest store. If there were a store at *C*, no shopper on this stretch of road would have to walk more than ⅓ of a mile to reach the nearest store. The 800 people who live between point *D* (which is halfway between *A* and *C*) and the freeway would shop at *C*, while the 400 who live between *D* and *A* would shop at *A*.

Despite the fact that *C* is the most attractive location for a new store from the perspective of consumers, it is not the most advantageous for the store's owner. The reason is that the owner's profit depends on how many people choose to shop at his store, not on how far they have to walk to get there. Given that consumers shop at the store closest to where they live, the best option from the entrepreneur's perspective is to locate his store at *B*, on the street corner just east of *A*. That way, his store will be closer to all 1,200 people who live between *A* and the freeway. It is this logic that helps explain the clustering of convenience stores, gas stations, and other monopolistically competitive firms whose most important differentiating feature is geographic location.

FIGURE 9.5
The Curious Tendency of Monopolistic Competitors to Cluster.
As a group, consumers would enjoy a shorter walk if the store at *B* were instead located at *C*, or even at *D*. But a second store will attract more customers by locating at *B*.

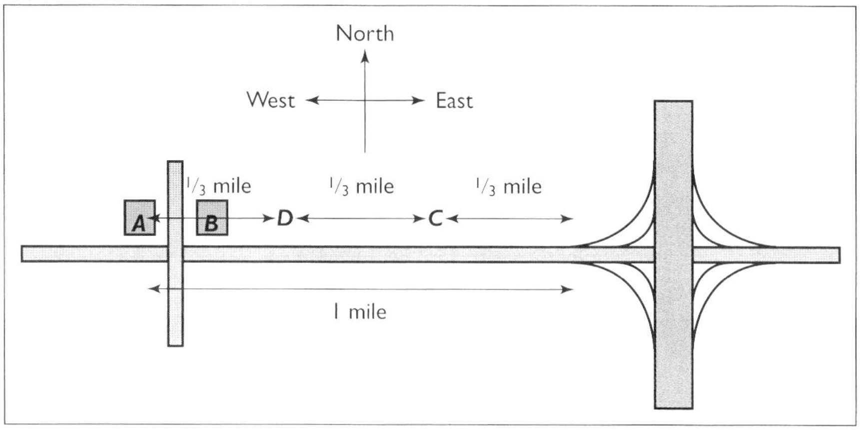

●

The insight that helped answer the question posed in Example 9.4 is due to the economist Harold Hotelling.[4] Hotelling employed this insight to explain why two

[3]"Evenly distributed" means that the number of shoppers who live on any segment of the road between *A* and the freeway is exactly proportional to the length of that segment. For example, the number who live along a segment one-tenth of a mile in length would be $\frac{1}{10} \times 1{,}200 = 120$.

[4]Harold Hotelling, "Stability and Competition," *Economic Journal* 39, no. 1 (1929), pp. 41–57.

hot dog vendors on a stretch of beach almost invariably locate next to one another midway between the endpoints of the beach.

For many oligopolistic or monopolistically competitive firms, an important dimension of product differentiation is location in time rather than in physical space. The timing of flight departures for different airlines in the New York–Los Angeles market is one example. The timing of film showings by different local movie theaters is another. In these cases, too, we often see product clustering. Thus, in the New York–Los Angeles market, both United and American have flights throughout the afternoon departing exactly on the hour. And in many local movie markets, the first evening showing starts at 7:15 p.m. in dozens of different theaters.

In other examples, the differentiating features that matter most might be said to describe the product's location in a more abstract "product space." With soft drinks, for example, we might array different products according to their degrees of sweetness or carbonation. Here, too, it is common to see rival products that lie very close to one another such as Coca-Cola and Pepsi. Clustering occurs in these cases for the reasons analogous to those discussed by Hotelling in his classic paper.

RECAP	GAMES IN WHICH TIMING MATTERS

The outcomes in many games depend on the timing of each player's move. For such games, the payoffs are best summarized by a decision tree rather than a payoff matrix. Sometimes the second mover does best to offer a product that differs markedly from existing products. Other times the second mover does best to mimic existing products closely.

COMMITMENT PROBLEMS

Games like the one in Exercise 9.3, as well as the prisoner's dilemma, the cartel game, and the remote-office game, confront players with a **commitment problem**—a situation in which they have difficulty achieving the desired outcome because they cannot make credible threats or promises. If both players in the original prisoner's dilemma could make a binding promise to remain silent, both would be assured of a shorter sentence, hence the logic of the underworld code of *Omerta,* under which the family of anyone who provides evidence against a fellow mob member is killed. A similar logic explains the adoption of military-arms-control agreements, in which opponents sign an enforceable pledge to curtail weapons spending.

commitment problem a situation in which people cannot achieve their goals because of an inability to make credible threats or promises

The commitment problem in the remote office game could be solved if the managerial candidate could find some way of committing himself to manage honestly if hired. The candidate needs a **commitment device**—something that provides the candidate with an incentive to keep his promise.

commitment device a way of changing incentives so as to make otherwise empty threats or promises credible

Business owners are well aware of commitment problems in the workplace and have adopted a variety of commitment devices to solve them. Consider, for example, the problem confronting the owner of a restaurant. She wants her table staff to provide good service so that customers will enjoy their meals and come back in the future. Since good service is valuable to her, she would be willing to pay waiters extra for it. For their part, waiters would be willing to provide good service in return for the extra pay. The problem is that the owner cannot always monitor whether the waiters do provide good service. Her concern is that, having been paid extra for it, the waiters may slack off when she isn't looking. Unless the owner can find some way to solve this problem, she will not pay extra, the waiters will not provide good service, and she, they, and the diners will suffer. A better outcome for all concerned would be for the waiters to find some way to commit themselves to good service.

Restaurateurs in many countries have tried to solve this commitment problem by encouraging diners to leave tips at the end of their meals. The attraction of this solution is that the diner is *always* in a good position to monitor service quality. The diner should be happy to reward good service with a generous tip since doing so will help to assure good service in the future. And the waiter has a strong incentive to provide good service because he knows that the size of his tip may depend on it.

The various commitment devices just discussed—the underworld code of *Omerta*, military-arms-control agreements, the tip for the waiter—all work because they change the incentives facing the decision makers. But as the next example illustrates, changing incentives in precisely the desired way is not always practical.

Will leaving a tip at an out-of-town restaurant affect the quality of service you receive?

Will Sylvester leave a tip when dining on the road?

Sylvester has just finished a $100 steak dinner at a restaurant that is 500 miles from where he lives. The waiter provided good service. If Sylvester cares only about himself, will he leave a tip?

Once the waiter has provided good service, there is no way for him to take it back if the diner fails to leave a tip. In restaurants patronized by local diners, failure to tip is not a problem because the waiter can simply provide poor service the next time a nontipper comes in. But the waiter lacks that leverage with out-of-town diners. Having already received good service, Sylvester must choose between paying $100 and paying $115 for his meal. If he is an essentially selfish person, the former choice may be a compelling one. ◆

EXERCISE 9.4

A traveler dines at a restaurant far from home. Both he and the waiter who serves him are rational and self-interested in the narrow sense. The waiter must first choose between providing good service and bad service, whereupon the diner must choose whether or not to leave a tip. The payoffs for their interaction are as summarized on the accompanying game tree. What is the most the diner would be willing to pay for the right to make a binding commitment (visible to the waiter) to leave a tip at the end of the meal in the event of having received good service?

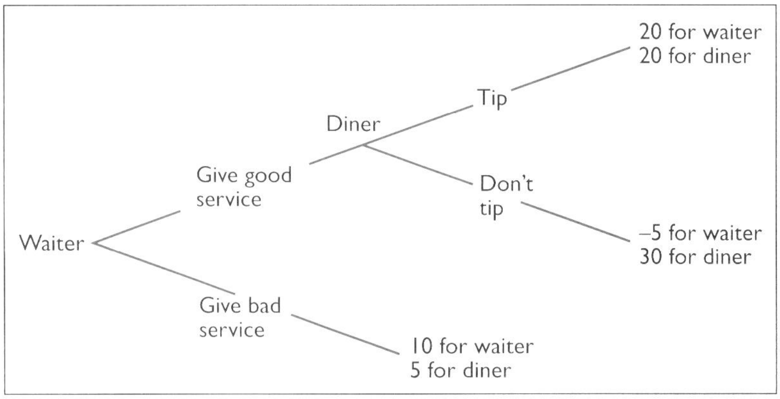

RECAP	COMMITMENT PROBLEMS

Commitment problems arise when the inability to make credible threats and promises prevents people from achieving desired outcomes. Such problems can sometimes be solved by employing commitment devices—ways of changing incentives to facilitate making credible threats or promises.

THE STRATEGIC ROLE OF PREFERENCES

In all the games we have discussed so far, players were assumed to care only about obtaining the best possible outcome for themselves. Thus, each player's goal was to get the highest monetary payoff, the shortest jail sentence, the best chance to be heard, and so on. The irony, in most of these games, is that players do not attain the best outcomes. Better outcomes can sometimes be achieved by altering the material incentives selfish players face, but not always.

If altering the relevant material incentives is not possible, commitment problems can sometimes be solved by altering people's psychological incentives. As the next example illustrates, in a society in which people are strongly conditioned to develop moral sentiments—feelings of guilt when they harm others, feelings of sympathy for their trading partners, feelings of outrage when they are treated unjustly—commitment problems arise less often than in more narrowly self-interested societies.

In a moral society, will the business owner open a remote office?

Consider again the owner of the thriving business who is trying to decide whether to open an office in a distant city. Suppose the society in which she lives is one in which all citizens have been strongly conditioned to behave honestly. Will she open the remote office?

Suppose, for instance, that the managerial candidate would suffer guilt pangs if he embezzled money from the owner. Most people would be reluctant to assign a monetary value to guilty feelings. But for the sake of discussion, let's suppose that those feelings are so unpleasant, the manager would be willing to pay at least \$10,000 to avoid them. On this assumption, the manager's payoff if he manages dishonestly will be not \$1,500, but \$1,500 − \$10,000 = −\$8,500. The new decision tree is shown in Figure 9.6.

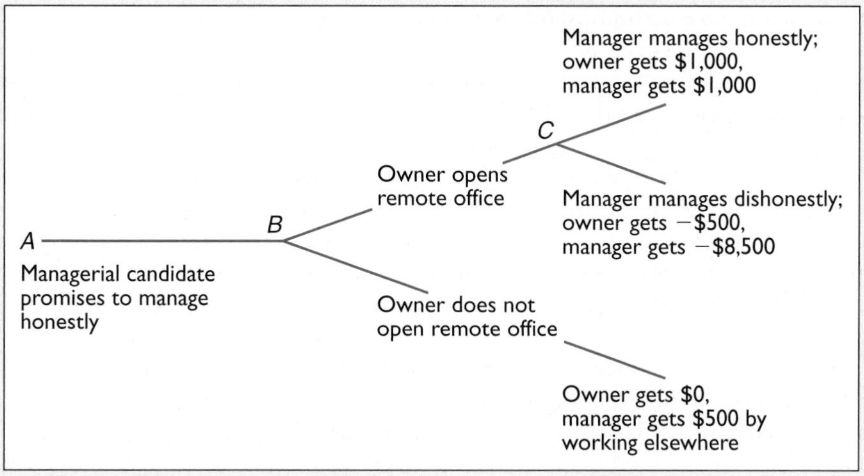

FIGURE 9.6
The Remote Office Game with an Honest Manager.
If the owner can identify a managerial candidate who would choose to manage honestly at *C*, she will hire that candidate at *B* and open the remote office.

In this case, the best choice for the owner at *B* will be to open the remote office because she knows that at *C* the manager's best choice will be to manage honestly. The irony, of course, is that the honest manager in this example ends up richer than the selfish manager in the previous example, who earned only a normal salary. ◆

ARE PEOPLE FUNDAMENTALLY SELFISH?

As the preceding example suggests, the assumption that people are self-interested in the narrow sense of the term does not always capture the full range of motives that govern choice in strategic settings. Think, for example, about the last time you had a meal at an out-of-town restaurant. Did you leave a tip? If so, your behavior was quite normal. Researchers have found that tipping rates in restaurants patronized mostly by out-of-town diners are essentially the same as in restaurants patronized mostly by local diners.

Indeed, there are many exceptions to the outcomes predicted on the basis of the assumption that people are self-interested in the most narrow sense of the term. People who have been treated unjustly often seek revenge even at ruinous cost to themselves. Every day, people walk away from profitable transactions whose terms they believe to be "unfair." In these and countless other ways, people do not seem to be pursuing self-interest narrowly defined. And if motives beyond narrow self-interest are significant, we must take them into account in attempting to predict and explain human behavior.

PREFERENCES AS SOLUTIONS TO COMMITMENT PROBLEMS

Economists tend to view preferences as ends in themselves. Taking them as given, they calculate what actions will best serve those preferences. This approach to the study of behavior is widely used by other social scientists, and by game theorists, military strategists, philosophers, and others. In its standard form, it assumes purely self-interested preferences for present and future consumption goods of various sorts, leisure pursuits, and so on. Concerns about fairness, guilt, honor, sympathy, and the like typically play no role.

Yet such concerns clearly affect the choices people make in strategic interactions. Sympathy for one's trading partner can make a businessperson trustworthy even when material incentives favor cheating. A sense of justice can prompt a person to incur the costs of retaliation, even when incurring those costs will not undo the original injury.

Preferences can clearly shape behavior in these ways; however, this alone does not solve commitment problems. The solution to such problems requires not only that a person *have* certain preferences, but also that others have some way of *discerning* them. Unless the business owner can identify the trustworthy employee, that employee cannot land a job whose pay is predicated on trust. And unless the predator can identify a potential victim whose character will motivate retaliation, that person is likely to become a victim.

From among those with whom we might engage in ventures requiring trust, can we identify reliable partners? If people could make *perfectly* accurate character judgments, they could always steer clear of dishonest persons. That people continue to be victimized at least occasionally by dishonest persons suggests that perfectly reliable character judgments are either impossible to make or prohibitively expensive.

Vigilance in the choice of trading partners is an essential element in solving (or avoiding) commitment problems, for if there is an advantage in being honest and being perceived as such, there is an even greater advantage in only *appearing* to be honest. After all, a liar who appears trustworthy will have better opportunities than one who glances about furtively, sweats profusely, and has difficulty making eye contact. Indeed, he will have the same opportunities as an honest person but will get higher payoffs because he will exploit them to the fullest.

In the end, the question of whether people can make reasonably accurate character judgments is an empirical one. Experimental studies have shown that even on the basis of brief encounters involving strangers, subjects are adept at predicting who will cooperate and who will defect in prisoner's dilemma games. For example, in one experiment in which only 26 percent of subjects defected, the accuracy rate of predicted defections was more than 56 percent. One might expect that predictions regarding those we know well would be even more accurate.

Do you know someone who would return an envelope containing $1,000 in cash to you if you lost it at a crowded concert? If so, then you accept the claim that personal character can help people to solve commitment problems. As long as honest individuals can identify at least some others who are honest, and can interact selectively with them, honest individuals can prosper in a competitive environment.

RECAP	THE STRATEGIC ROLE OF PREFERENCES

Most applications of the theory of games assume that players are self-interested in the narrow sense of the term. In practice, however, many choices—such as leaving tips in out-of-town restaurants—appear inconsistent with this assumption.

The fact that people seem driven by a more complex range of motives makes behavior more difficult to predict, but also creates new ways of solving commitment problems. Psychological incentives often can serve as commitment devices when changing players' material incentives is impractical. For example, people who are able to identify honest trading partners, and interact selectively with them, are able to solve commitment problems that arise from lack of trust.

▪ SUMMARY ▪

- Economists use the theory of games to analyze situations in which the payoffs of one's actions depend on the actions taken by others. Games have three basic elements: the players; the list of possible actions, or strategies, from which each player can choose; and the payoffs the players receive for those strategies. The payoff matrix is the most useful way to summarize this information in games in which the timing of the players' moves is not decisive. In games in which timing matters, a decision tree provides a much more useful summary of the information. **LO1, LO4**
- Equilibrium in a game occurs when each player's strategy choice yields the highest payoff available, given the strategies chosen by the other. **LO2**
- A dominant strategy is one that yields a higher payoff regardless of the strategy chosen by the other player. In some games such as the prisoner's dilemma, each player has a dominant strategy. The equilibrium occurs in such games when each player chooses his or her dominant strategy. In other games, not all players have a dominant strategy. **LO2, LO3**
- Equilibrium outcomes are often unattractive from the perspective of players as a group. The prisoner's dilemma has this feature because it is each prisoner's dominant strategy to confess, yet each spends more time in jail if both confess than if both remain silent. The incentive structure of this game helps explain such disparate social dilemmas as excessive advertising, military arms races, and failure to reap the potential benefits of interactions requiring trust. **LO3**
- Individuals often can resolve these dilemmas if they can make binding commitments to behave in certain ways. Some commitments—such as those involved in military-arms-control agreements—are achieved by altering the material incentives confronting the players. Other commitments can be achieved by relying

on psychological incentives to counteract material payoffs. Moral sentiments such as guilt, sympathy, and a sense of justice often foster better outcomes than can be achieved by narrowly self-interested players. For this type of commitment to work, the relevant moral sentiments must be discernible by one's potential trading partners. **LO5**

KEY TERMS

basic elements of a game (240)
cartel (245)
commitment device (255)
commitment problem (255)
credible promise (252)
credible threat (252)
decision tree (251)
dominant strategy (241)
dominated strategy (242)
game tree (251)
Nash equilibrium (242)
payoff matrix (241)
prisoner's dilemma (244)
repeated prisoner's dilemma (247)
tit-for-tat (247)

REVIEW QUESTIONS

1. Explain why a military arms race is an example of a prisoner's dilemma. **LO3**
2. Why did Warner Brothers make a mistake by waiting until the filming of *Analyze This* was almost finished before negotiating with Tony Bennett to perform in the final scene? **LO4**
3. Suppose General Motors is trying to hire a small firm to manufacture the door handles for Pontiac sedans. The task requires an investment in expensive capital equipment that cannot be used for any other purpose. Why might the president of the small firm refuse to undertake this venture without a long-term contract fixing the price of the door handles? **LO4**
4. How is your incentive to defect in a prisoner's dilemma altered if you learn that you will play the game not just once but rather indefinitely many times with the same partner? **LO3**
5. Describe the commitment problem that narrowly self-interested diners and waiters would confront at restaurants located on interstate highways. Given that in such restaurants tipping does seem to assure reasonably good service, do you think people are always selfish in the narrowest sense? **LO3**

PROBLEMS

1. In studying for his economics final, Sam is concerned about only two things: his grade and the amount of time he spends studying. A good grade will give him a benefit of 20; an average grade, a benefit of 5; and a poor grade, a benefit of 0. By studying a lot, Sam will incur a cost of 10; by studying a little, a cost of 6. Moreover, if Sam studies a lot and all other students study a little, he will get a good grade and they will get poor ones. But if they study a lot and he studies a little, they will get good grades and he will get a poor one. Finally, if he and all other students study the same amount of time, everyone will get average grades. Other students share Sam's preferences regarding grades and study time. **LO3**
   a. Model this situation as a two-person prisoner's dilemma in which the strategies are to study a little and to study a lot, and the players are Sam and all other students. Include the payoffs in the matrix.
   b. What is the equilibrium outcome in this game? From the students' perspective, is it the best outcome?
2. Consider the following "dating game," which has two players, A and B, and two strategies, to buy a movie ticket or a baseball ticket. The payoffs, given in points, are as shown in the matrix below. Note that the highest payoffs occur when both A and B attend the same event.

		B: Buy movie ticket	B: Buy baseball ticket
A	Buy movie ticket	2 for A 3 for B	0 for A 0 for B
A	Buy baseball ticket	1 for A 1 for B	3 for A 2 for B

Assume that players A and B buy their tickets separately and simultaneously. Each must decide what to do knowing the available choices and payoffs but not what the other has actually chosen. Each player believes the other to be rational and self-interested. **LO2, LO3**

a. Does either player have a dominant strategy?
b. How many potential equilibria are there? (Hint: To see whether a given combination of strategies is an equilibrium, ask whether either player could get a higher payoff by changing his or her strategy.)
c. Is this game a prisoner's dilemma? Explain.
d. Suppose player A gets to buy his or her ticket first. Player B does not observe A's choice but knows that A chose first. Player A knows that player B knows he or she chose first. What is the equilibrium outcome?
e. Suppose the situation is similar to part d, except that player B chooses first. What is the equilibrium outcome?

3. Blackadder and Baldrick are rational, self-interested criminals imprisoned in separate cells in a dark medieval dungeon. They face the prisoner's dilemma displayed in the matrix.

		Blackadder: Confess	Blackadder: Deny
Baldrick	Confess	5 years for each	0 for Baldrick 20 years for Blackadder
Baldrick	Deny	20 years for Baldrick 0 for Blackadder	1 year for each

Assume that Blackadder is willing to pay $1,000 for each year by which he can reduce his sentence below 20 years. A corrupt jailer tells Blackadder that before he decides whether to confess or deny the crime, she can tell him Baldrick's decision. How much is this information worth to Blackadder? **LO3**

4. The owner of a thriving business wants to open a new office in a distant city. If he can hire someone who will manage the new office honestly, he can afford to pay that person a weekly salary of \$2,000 (\$1,000 more than the manager would be able to earn elsewhere) and still earn an economic profit of \$800. The owner's concern is that he will not be able to monitor the manager's behavior and that the manager would therefore be in a position to embezzle money from the business. The owner knows that if the remote office is managed dishonestly, the manager can earn \$3,100, while causing the owner an economic loss of \$600 per week. **LO4**
   a. If the owner believes that all managers are narrowly self-interested income maximizers, will he open the new office?
   b. Suppose the owner knows that a managerial candidate is a devoutly religious person who condemns dishonest behavior, and who would be willing to pay up to \$15,000 to avoid the guilt she would feel if she were dishonest. Will the owner open the remote office?

5. Imagine yourself sitting in your car in a campus parking lot that is currently full, waiting for someone to pull out so that you can park your car. Somebody pulls out, but at the same moment a driver who has just arrived overtakes you in an obvious attempt to park in the vacated spot before you can. Suppose this driver would be willing to pay up to \$10 to park in that spot and up to \$30 to avoid getting into an argument with you. (That is, the benefit of parking is \$10 and the cost of an argument is \$30.) At the same time he guesses, accurately, that you too would be willing to pay up to \$30 to avoid a confrontation and up to \$10 to park in the vacant spot. **LO4**
   a. Model this situation as a two-stage decision tree in which his bid to take the space is the opening move and your strategies are (1) to protest and (2) not to protest. If you protest (initiate an argument), the rules of the game specify that he has to let you take the space. Show the payoffs at the end of each branch of the tree.
   b. What is the equilibrium outcome?
   c. What would be the advantage of being able to communicate credibly to the other driver that your *failure* to protest would be a significant psychological cost to you?

6. Newfoundland's fishing industry has recently declined sharply due to overfishing, even though fishing companies were supposedly bound by a quota agreement. If all fishermen had abided by the agreement, yields could have been maintained at high levels. **LO3**
   a. Model this situation as a prisoner's dilemma in which the players are Company A and Company B and the strategies are to keep the quota and break the quota. Include appropriate payoffs in the matrix. Explain why overfishing is inevitable in the absence of effective enforcement of the quota agreement.
   b. Provide another environmental example of a prisoner's dilemma.
   c. In many potential prisoner's dilemmas, a way out of the dilemma for a would-be cooperator is to make reliable character judgments about the trustworthiness of potential partners. Explain why this solution is not available in many situations involving degradation of the environment.

7. Consider the following game, called matching pennies, which you are playing with a friend. Each of you has a penny hidden in your hand, facing either heads up or tails up (you know which way the one in your hand is facing). On the count of "three," you simultaneously show your pennies to each other. If the face-up side of your coin matches the face-up side of your friend's coin, you get to keep the two pennies. If the faces do not match, your friend gets to keep the pennies. **LO2**
   a. Who are the players in this game? What are each player's strategies? Construct a payoff matrix for the game.

b. Is there a dominant strategy? If so, what?
c. Is there an equilibrium? If so, what?

8. Consider the following game. Harry has four quarters. He can offer Sally from one to four of them. If she accepts his offer, she keeps the quarters Harry offered her and Harry keeps the others. If Sally declines Harry's offer, they both get nothing ($0). They play the game only once, and each cares only about the amount of money he or she ends up with. **LO2**
   a. Who are the players? What are each player's strategies? Construct a decision tree for this game.
   b. Given their goal, what is the optimal choice for each player?

9. Two airplane manufacturers are considering the production of a new product, a 150-passenger jet. Both are deciding whether to enter the market and produce the new planes. The payoff matrix is as follows (payoff values are in millions of dollars):

		Airbus	
		Produce	Don't produce
Boeing	Produce	–5 for each	100 for Boeing 0 for Airbus
	Don't produce	0 for Boeing 100 for Airbus	0 for each

   The implication of these payoffs is that the market demand is large enough to support only one manufacturer. If both firms enter, both will sustain a loss. **LO3**
   a. Identify two possible equilibrium outcomes in this game.
   b. Consider the effect of a subsidy. Suppose the European Union decides to subsidize the European producer, Airbus, with a check for $25 million if it enters the market. Revise the payoff matrix to account for this subsidy. What is the new equilibrium outcome?
   c. Compare the two outcomes (pre- and post-subsidy). What qualitative effect does the subsidy have?

10. Jill and Jack both have two pails that can be used to carry water down from a hill. Each makes only one trip down the hill, and each pail of water can be sold for $5. Carrying the pails of water down requires considerable effort. Both Jill and Jack would be willing to pay $2 each to avoid carrying one bucket down the hill, and an additional $3 to avoid carrying a second bucket down the hill. **LO3**
   a. Given market prices, how many pails of water will each child fetch from the top of the hill?
   b. Jill and Jack's parents are worried that the two children don't cooperate enough with one another. Suppose they make Jill and Jack share equally their revenues from selling the water. Given that both are self-interested, construct the payoff matrix for the decisions Jill and Jack face regarding the number of pails of water each should carry. What is the equilibrium outcome?

ANSWERS TO IN-CHAPTER EXERCISES

9.1 No matter what American does, United will do better to leave ad spending the same. No matter what United does, American will do better to raise ad spending. So each player will play its dominant strategy: American will raise its ad spending and United will leave its ad spending the same. **LO2**

United's Choice	American's Choice: Raise ad spending	American's Choice: Leave ad spending the same
Raise ad spending	United gets \$3,000 American gets \$8,000	United gets \$4,000 American gets \$5,000
Leave ad spending the same	United gets \$8,000 American gets \$4,000	United gets \$5,000 American gets \$2,000

9.2 In game 1, no matter what Chrysler does, GM will do better to invest, and no matter what GM does, Chrysler will do better to invest. Each has a dominant strategy, but in following it, each does worse than if it had not invested. So game 1 is a prisoner's dilemma. In game 2, no matter what Chrysler does, GM again will do better to invest; but no matter what GM does, Chrysler will do better *not* to invest. Each has a dominant strategy, and in following it, each gets a payoff of 10—5 more than if each had played its dominated strategy. So game 2 is not a prisoner's dilemma. **LO3**

9.3 Smith assumes that Jones will choose the branch that maximizes his payoff, which is the bottom branch at either *B* or *C*. So Jones will choose the bottom branch when his turn comes, no matter what Smith chooses. Since Smith will do better (60) on the bottom branch at *B* than on the bottom branch at *C* (50), Smith will choose the top branch at *A*. So equilibrium in this game is for Smith to choose the top branch at *A* and Jones to choose the bottom branch at *B*. Smith gets 60 and Jones gets 105. **LO5**

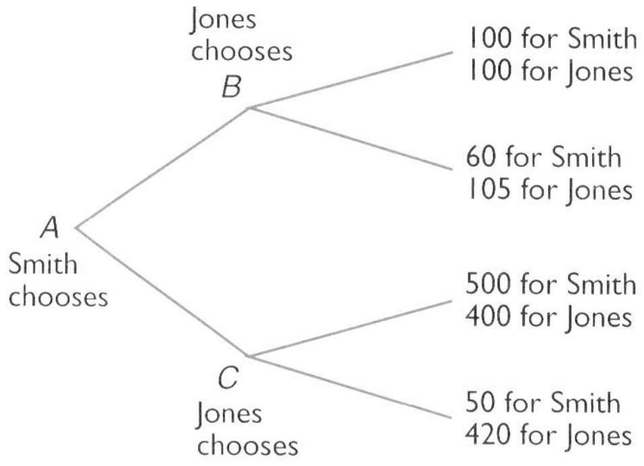

If Jones could make a credible commitment to choose the top branch no matter what, both would do better. Smith would choose the bottom branch at *A* and Jones would choose the top branch at *C*, giving Smith 500 and Jones 400.

9.4 The equilibrium of this game in the absence of a commitment to tip is that the waiter will give bad service because if he provides good service, he knows that the diner's best option will be not to tip, which leaves the waiter worse off than if he had provided good service. Since the diner gets an outcome of 20 if he can commit to leaving a tip (15 more than he would get in the absence of such a commitment), he would be willing to pay up to 15 for the right to commit. **LO4**

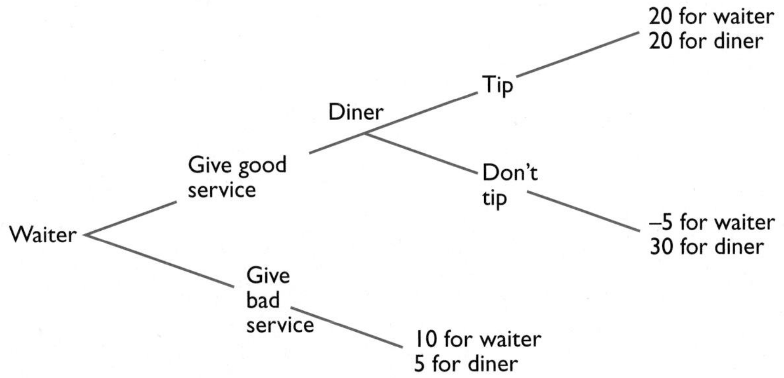

CHAPTER

10

Externalities and Property Rights

LEARNING OBJECTIVES

After reading this chapter, you should be able to:

1. Define negative and positive externalities and analyze their effect on resource allocation.
2. Explain and discuss the Coase Theorem.
3. Explain how the effects of externalities can be remedied.
4. Discuss why the optimal amount of an externality is almost never zero.
5. Characterize the tragedy of the commons, and show how private ownership is a way of preventing it.
6. Define positional externalities and their effects and show how they can be remedied.

A droll television ad for a British brand of pipe tobacco opens with a distinguished-looking gentleman sitting quietly on a park bench, smoking his pipe and reading a book of poetry. Before him lies a pond, unrippled except for a mother duck swimming peacefully with her ducklings. Suddenly a raucous group of teenage boys bursts onto the scene with a remote-controlled toy warship. Yelling and chortling, they launch their boat and maneuver it in aggressive pursuit of the terrified ducks.

Interrupted from his reverie, the gentleman looks up from his book and draws calmly on his pipe as he surveys the scene before him. He then reaches into his bag, pulls out a remote control of his own, and begins manipulating the joystick. The scene shifts underwater, where a miniature submarine rises from the depths of the pond. Once the boys' boat is in the sub's sights, the gentleman pushes a button on his remote control. Seconds later, the boat is blown to smithereens by a torpedo. The scene fades to a close-up of the tobacco company's label.

EXTERNAL COSTS AND BENEFITS

external cost (or negative externality) a cost of an activity that falls on people other than those who pursue the activity

external benefit (or positive externality) a benefit of an activity received by people other than those who pursue the activity

externality an external cost or benefit of an activity

External costs and **benefits—externalities**, for short—are activities that generate costs or benefits that accrue to people not directly involved in those activities. These effects are generally unintended. From the pipe smoker's point of view, the noise generated by the marauding boys was an external cost. Had others been disturbed by the boys' rowdiness, they may well have regarded the pipe smoker's retaliatory gesture as an external benefit.

This chapter focuses on how externalities affect the allocation of resources. Adam Smith's theory of the invisible hand applies to an ideal marketplace in which externalities do not exist. In such situations, Smith argued, the self-interested actions of individuals would lead to socially efficient outcomes. We will see that when the parties affected by externalities can easily negotiate with one another, the invisible hand will still produce an efficient outcome.

But in many cases, such as the scene depicted in the tobacco ad, negotiation is impractical. In those cases, the self-serving actions of individuals will not lead to efficient outcomes. The need to deal with externalities is one of the most important rationales for the existence of government along with a variety of other forms of collective action.

HOW EXTERNALITIES AFFECT RESOURCE ALLOCATION

The following examples illustrate the ways in which externalities distort the allocation of resources.

Does the honeybee keeper face the right incentives? (Part 1)

Phoebe earns her living as a keeper of honeybees. Her neighbors on all sides grow apples. Because bees pollinate apple trees as they forage for nectar, the more hives Phoebe keeps, the larger the harvests will be in the surrounding orchards. If Phoebe takes only her own costs and benefits into account in deciding how many hives to keep, will she keep the socially optimal number of hives?

Phoebe's hives constitute an external benefit, or a positive externality, for the orchard owners. If she takes only her own personal costs and benefits into account, she will add hives only until the added revenue she gets from the last hive just equals the cost of adding it. But since the orchard owners also benefit from additional hives, the total benefit of adding another hive at that point will be greater than its cost. Phoebe, then, will keep too few hives. ◆

As we will discuss later in the chapter, problems like the one just discussed have several possible solutions. One is for orchard owners to pay beekeepers for keeping additional hives. But such solutions often require complex negotiations between the affected parties. For the moment, we assume that such negotiations are not practical.

Does the honeybee keeper face the right incentives? (Part 2)

As in the previous example, Phoebe earns her living as a keeper of honeybees. But now her neighbors are not apple growers but an elementary school and a nursing home. The more hives Phoebe keeps, the more students and nursing home residents will be stung by bees. If Phoebe takes only her own costs and benefits into account in deciding how many hives to keep, will she keep the socially optimal number of hives?

For the students and nursing home residents, Phoebe's hives constitute an external cost, or a negative externality. If she considers only her own costs and benefits in deciding how many hives to keep, she will continue to add hives until the added revenue from the last hive is just enough to cover its cost. But since Phoebe's neighbors also incur costs when she adds a hive, the benefit of the last hive at that point will be smaller than its cost. Phoebe, in other words, will keep too many hives. ◆

Every activity involves costs and benefits. When all the relevant costs and benefits of an activity accrue directly to the person who carries it out—that is, when the activity generates no externalities—the level of the activity that is best for the individual will be best for society as a whole. But when an activity generates externalities, be they positive or negative, individual self-interest does not produce the best allocation of resources. Individuals who consider only their own costs and benefits will tend to engage too much in activities that generate negative externalities and too little in activities that generate positive externalities. When an activity generates both positive and negative externalities, private and social interests will coincide only in the unlikely event that the opposing effects offset one another exactly.

HOW DO EXTERNALITIES AFFECT SUPPLY AND DEMAND?

The effects of externalities on resource allocation can be shown in a supply and demand diagram. Consider first the case of negative externalities. Figure 10.1(a) depicts the supply (Private *MC*) and demand curves for a product whose production involves no external costs or benefits. Imagine, say, that the energy that powers the factories in this market comes from nonpolluting hydroelectric generators. The resulting equilibrium price and quantity in the market for this product will then be socially optimal, for the reasons discussed in Chapters 3 and 7: The value to buyers of the last unit of the product consumed (as measured on the demand curve) will be exactly equal to the marginal cost of producing it (as measured on the supply curve), leaving no further possible gains from exchange.

But now suppose that a protracted drought has eliminated hydroelectric power generation, forcing factories to rely instead on electric power produced by coal-burning generators. Now each unit of output produced is accompanied by an external pollution cost of *XC*, as shown in Figure 10.1(b). Since the external pollution cost falls not on firm owners but on others who live downwind from their factories, Private *MC* is still the supply curve for this product, and its demand curve is again

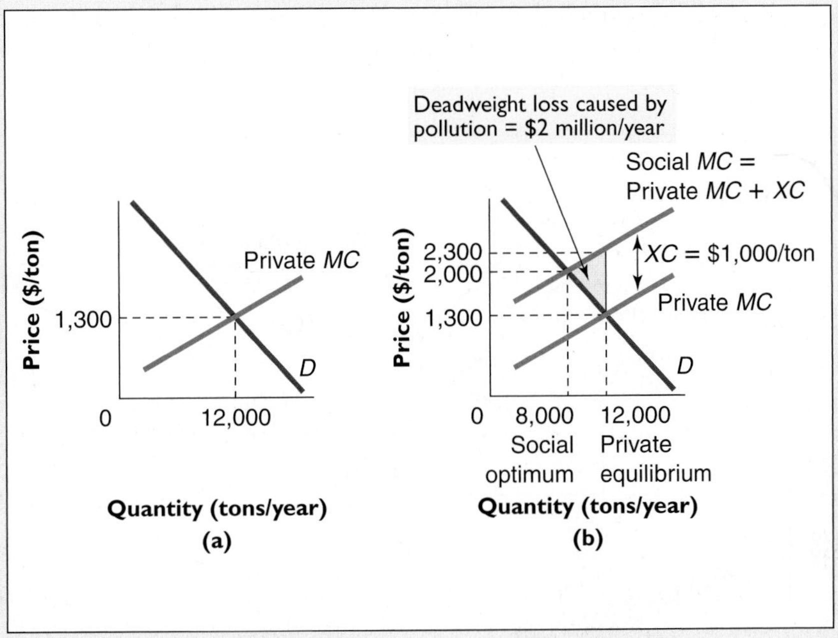

FIGURE 10.1
How External Costs Affect Resource Allocation.
(a) When a market has no external costs or benefits, the resulting equilibrium quantity and price are socially optimal. (b) By contrast, when production of a good is accompanied by an external cost, the market equilibrium price ($1,300 per ton) is too low and the market equilibrium quantity (12,000 tons per year) is too high. The deadweight loss from the negative externality is the area of the blue-shaded triangle, $2 million per year.

as before, so the equilibrium price and quantity will be exactly the same as in Figure 10.1(a). But this time the private market equilibrium is not socially optimal. As before, the market equilibrium level of output is 12,000 tons per year, the output level at which the demand curve (*D*) intersects Private *MC*. Note, however, that at that output level, the value to consumers of the last unit of output produced is only \$1,300 per ton, while the true cost of producing that last unit (including the external cost) is \$2,300 per ton.

This means that society could gain additional economic surplus by producing fewer units of the product. Indeed, the same conclusion will continue to hold whenever the current output exceeds 8,000 tons per year, the output level at which the demand curve intersects Social *MC*. Social *MC*, which includes all relevant marginal costs of producing the product, is constructed by adding the external pollution cost, *XC*, to every value along Private *MC*. The socially optimal level of output of the good occurs where Social *MC* intersects the demand curve. As shown in Figure 10.1(b), it is 8,000 tons per year. This is the level of output that exhausts all possibilities from exchange. At that quantity, the marginal benefit of the product, as measured by what buyers are willing to pay for it, is exactly equal to the marginal cost of producing it, which is the private marginal cost *MC* plus the marginal pollution cost *XC*. The market equilibrium quantity thus will be higher than the socially optimal quantity for a good whose production generates external costs.

By how much does the presence of pollution reduce total economic surplus from its maximum value, which occurs at an output level of 8,000 tons per year in Figure 10.1(b)? Note in the diagram that as output expands past 8,000, the marginal cost of each successive unit (as measured on the Social *MC* curve) is greater than the marginal benefit of that unit (as measured on the demand curve). Expanding output from 8,000 tons per year to the private equilibrium level, 12,000 tons per year, thus entails a cumulative reduction in total economic surplus equal to the area of the blue-shaded triangle in Figure 10.1(b), or \$2 million per year. The deadweight loss from pollution is \$2 million per year in this market.

What about a good whose production generates external benefits? In Figure 10.2, Private demand is the demand curve for a product whose production generates an external benefit of *XB* per unit. The market equilibrium quantity of this good, Q_{pvt}, is the output level at which Private demand intersects the supply curve of the product (*MC*). This time, market equilibrium quantity is smaller than the socially optimal level of output, denoted Q_{soc}. Q_{soc} is the output level at which *MC* intersects the socially optimal demand curve (the curve labeled Social demand in Figure 10.2), which is constructed by adding the external benefit, *XB*, to every

FIGURE 10.2
A Good Whose Production Generates a Positive Externality for Consumers.
For such goods, the market equilibrium quantity, Q_{pvt}, is smaller than the socially optimal quantity, Q_{soc}, because individual buyers are willing to pay only for the benefits they reap from directly consuming the product. The deadweight loss from the positive externality is the area of the blue-shaded triangle.

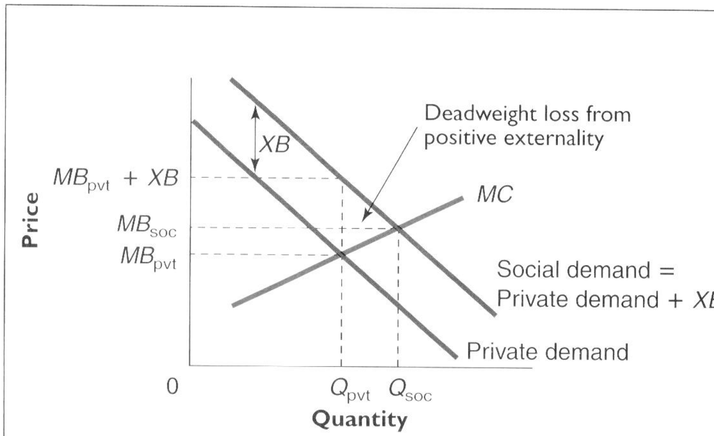

value along Private demand. Note that the private market equilibrium again fails to exhaust all possible gains from exchange. Thus, at Q_{pvt}, the marginal cost of producing an additional unit of output is only MB_{pvt}, which is smaller than the marginal benefit of an additional unit by the amount XB. The market equilibrium quantity thus will be lower than the socially optimal quantity for a good whose production generates external benefits.

In comparison with the maximum attainable total economic surplus in this market, how much does the total economic surplus associated with the private equilibrium fall short? In Figure 10.2, note that at Q_{pvt}, the marginal benefit of the product (as measured on the curve labeled Social demand) is XB units larger than its marginal cost (as measured on MC). Total economic surplus will continue to increase by successively smaller increments as output grows from Q_{pvt} to Q_{soc}, the socially optimal quantity. The total deadweight loss associated with the positive externality is thus the area of the blue-shaded triangle in Figure 10.2.

If the production of a product generates a positive externality, why do we say that this product causes a reduction in total economic surplus? To say that there is a deadweight loss in this market does not mean that the positive externality causes harm. Rather, it means that failure to take the positive externality into account makes the economic surplus associated with private equilibrium smaller than it could have been. Failure to reap an economic benefit is the same thing as sustaining an economic loss.

To summarize, whether externalities are positive or negative, they distort the allocation of resources in otherwise efficient markets. When externalities are present, the individual pursuit of self-interest will not result in the largest possible economic surplus. This outcome is thus inefficient by definition.

THE COASE THEOREM

To say that a situation is inefficient means that it can be rearranged in a way that would make at least some people better off without harming others. Such situations, we have seen, are a source of creative tension. The existence of inefficiency, after all, means that there is cash on the table, which usually triggers a race to see who can capture it. For example, we saw that because monopoly pricing results in an inefficiently low output level, the potential for gain gave monopolists an incentive to make discounts available to price-sensitive buyers. As the next examples illustrate, the inefficiencies that result from externalities create similar incentives for remedial action.

Equilibrium

Will Abercrombie dump toxins in the river? (Part I)

Abercrombie's factory produces a toxic waste by-product. If Abercrombie dumps it in the river, he causes damage to Fitch, a fisherman located downstream. The toxins are short-lived and cause no damage to anyone other than Fitch. At a cost, Abercrombie can filter out the toxins, in which case Fitch will suffer no damage at all. The relevant gains and losses for the two individuals are listed in Table 10.1.

TABLE 10.1
Costs and Benefits of Eliminating Toxic Waste (Part I)

	With filter	Without filter
Gains to Abercrombie	$100/day	$130/day
Gains to Fitch	$100/day	$50/day

If the law does not penalize Abercrombie for dumping toxins in the river, and if Abercrombie and Fitch cannot communicate with one another, will Abercrombie operate with or without a filter? Is that choice socially efficient?

Abercrombie has an incentive to operate without a filter since he earns \$30 per day more than if he operates with a filter. But the outcome when he does so is socially inefficient. Thus, when Abercrombie operates without a filter, the total daily gain to both parties is only \$130 + \$50 = \$180, compared to \$100 + \$100 = \$200 if Abercrombie had operated with a filter. The daily cost of the filter to Abercrombie is only \$130 − \$100 = \$30, which is smaller than its daily benefit to Fitch of \$100 − \$50 = \$50. The fact that Abercrombie does not install the filter implies a squandered daily surplus of \$20. ◆

Will Abercrombie dump toxins in the river? (Part 2)

Suppose the costs and benefits of using the filter are as in the previous example except that Abercrombie and Fitch can now communicate with one another at no cost. Even though the law does not require him to do so, will Abercrombie use a filter?

Efficiency

This time, Abercrombie will use a filter. Recall from Chapter 7 the observation that when the economic pie grows larger, everyone can have a larger slice (the Efficiency Principle). Because use of a filter would result in the largest possible economic surplus, it would enable both Abercrombie and Fitch to have a larger net gain than before. Fitch thus has an incentive to *pay* Abercrombie to use a filter. Suppose, for instance, that Fitch offers Abercrombie \$40 per day to compensate him for operating with a filter. Both Abercrombie and Fitch will then be exactly \$10 per day better off than before, for a total daily net gain of \$20. ◆

EXERCISE 10.1

In the example above, what is the largest whole-dollar amount by which Fitch could compensate Abercrombie for operating with a filter and still be better off than before?

Coase theorem if at no cost people can negotiate the purchase and sale of the right to perform activities that cause externalities, they can always arrive at efficient solutions to the problems caused by externalities

Ronald Coase, a professor at the University of Chicago Law School, was the first to see clearly that if people can negotiate with one another at no cost over the right to perform activities that cause externalities, they will always arrive at an efficient solution. This insight, which is often called the **Coase theorem**, is a profoundly important idea, for which Coase (rhymes with "dose") was awarded the 1991 Nobel Prize in Economics.

Why, you might ask, should Fitch pay Abercrombie to filter out toxins that would not be there in the first place if not for Abercrombie's factory? The rhetorical force of this question is undeniable. Yet Coase points out that externalities are reciprocal in nature. The toxins do harm Fitch, to be sure, but preventing Abercrombie from emitting them would penalize Abercrombie, by exactly \$30 per day. Why should Fitch necessarily have the right to harm Abercrombie? Indeed, as the next example illustrates, even if Fitch had that right, he would exercise it only if filtering the toxins proved the most efficient outcome.

Will Abercrombie dump toxins in the river? (Part 3)

Suppose the law says that Abercrombie may *not* dump toxins in the river unless he has Fitch's permission. If the relevant costs and benefits of filtering the toxins are as shown in Table 10.2, and if Abercrombie and Fitch can negotiate with one another at no cost, will Abercrombie filter the toxins?

TABLE 10.2
Costs and Benefits of Eliminating Toxic Waste (Part 3)

	With filter	Without filter
Gains to Abercrombie	$100/day	$150/day
Gains to Fitch	$100/day	$70/day

Note that this time the most efficient outcome is for Abercrombie to operate without a filter, for the total daily surplus in that case will be $220 as compared to only $200 with a filter. Under the law, however, Fitch has the right to insist that Abercrombie use a filter. We might expect him to exercise that right since his own gain would rise from $70 to $100 per day if he did so. But because this outcome would be socially inefficient, we know that each party can do better.

Suppose, for example, that Abercrombie gives Fitch $40 per day in return for Fitch's permission to operate without a filter. Each would then have a net daily gain of $110, which is $10 better for each of them than if Fitch had insisted that Abercrombie use a filter. Abercrombie's pollution harms Fitch, sure enough. But failure to allow the pollution would have caused even greater harm to Abercrombie. ◆

The Coase theorem tells us that regardless of whether the law holds polluters liable for damages, the affected parties will achieve efficient solutions to externalities if they can negotiate costlessly with one another. Note carefully that this does not imply that affected parties will be indifferent about whether the law holds polluters responsible for damages. If polluters are liable, they will end up with lower incomes and those who are injured by pollutants will end up with higher incomes than if the law does not hold polluters liable—even though the same efficient production methods are adopted in each case. When polluters are held liable, they must remove the pollution at their own expense. When they are not held liable, those who are injured by pollution must pay polluters to cut back.

Externalities are hardly rare and isolated occurrences. On the contrary, finding examples of actions that are altogether free of them is difficult. And because externalities can distort the allocation of resources, it is important to recognize them and deal intelligently with them. Consider the following example of an externality that arises because of shared living arrangements.

Will Ann and Betty share an apartment?

Ann and Betty can live together in a two-bedroom apartment for $600 per month, or separately in 2 one-bedroom apartments, each for $400 per month. If the rent paid were the same for both alternatives, the two women would be indifferent between living together or separately, except for one problem: Ann talks constantly on the telephone. Ann would pay up to $250 per month for this privilege. Betty, for her part, would pay up to $150 per month to have better access to the phone. If the two cannot install a second phone line, should they live together or separately?

Ann and Betty should live together only if the benefit of doing so exceeds the cost. The benefit of living together is the reduction in their rent. Since 2 one-bedroom apartments would cost a total of $800 per month, compared to $600 for a two-bedroom unit, their benefit from living together is $200 per month. Their cost of living together is the least costly accommodation they can make to Ann's objectionable telephone habits. Since Ann would be willing to pay up to $250 per month to avoid changing her behavior, the $200 rent saving is too small to persuade her to change. But Betty is willing to put up with Ann's behavior for a compensation payment of only $150 per month. Since that amount is smaller than the total saving in rent, the least costly solution to the problem is for Betty to live with Ann and simply put up with her behavior.

Cost-Benefit

Table 10.3 summarizes the relevant costs and benefits of this shared living arrangement. The Cost-Benefit Principle tells us that Ann and Betty should live together if and only if the benefit of living together exceeds the cost. The cost of the shared living arrangement is not the sum of all possible costs but the least costly accommodation to the problem (or problems) of shared living. Since the $200 per month saving in rent exceeds the least costly accommodation to the phone problem, Ann and Betty can reap a total gain in economic surplus of $50 per month by sharing their living quarters.

TABLE 10.3
The Gain in Surplus from Shared Living Arrangements

Benefits of Shared Living		
Total cost of separate apartments	**Total cost of shared apartment**	**Rent savings from sharing**
(2)($400/month) $800/month	$600/month	$200/month

Costs of Shared Living			
Problem	**Ann's cost of solving problem**	**Betty's cost of solving problem**	**Least costly solution to the problem**
Ann's phone usage	Curtailed phone usage: $250/month	Tolerate phone usage: $150/month	Betty tolerates Ann's phone usage: $150/month

Gain in Surplus from Shared Living				
Rent savings ($200/month)	−	Least costly accommodation to shared living problems ($150/month)	=	Gain in surplus: ($50/month)

◆

Some people might conclude that Ann and Betty should not live together because if the two share the rent equally, Betty will end up paying $300 per month—which when added to the $150 cost of putting up with Ann's phone behavior comes to $50 more than the cost of living alone. As persuasive as that argument may sound, however, it is mistaken. The source of the error, as the following example illustrates, is the assumption that the two must share the rent equally.

What is the highest rent Betty would be willing to pay for the two-bedroom apartment?

In the previous example, Betty's alternative is to live alone, which would mean paying $400 per month, her reservation price for a living arrangement with no phone problem. Since the most she would be willing to pay to avoid the phone problem is $150 per month, the highest monthly rent she would be willing to pay for the shared apartment is $400 − $150 = $250. If she pays that amount, Ann will have to pay the difference, namely, $350 per month, which is clearly a better alternative for Ann than paying $400 to live alone. ◆

How much should Ann and Betty pay if they agree to split their economic surplus equally?

As we saw in Table 10.3, the total rent saving from the shared apartment is $200, and since the least costly solution to the phone problem is $150, the monthly gain in economic surplus is $50. We know from the previous example that Ann's reservation price for living together is $400 per month and Betty's is $250. So if the two women want to split the $50 monthly surplus equally, each should pay $25 less than her reservation price. Ann's monthly rent will thus be $375 and Betty's, $225. The result is that each is $25 per month better off than if she had lived alone. ◆

EXERCISE 10.2

As in the preceding examples, Ann and Betty can live together in a two-bedroom apartment for $600 per month or separately in 2 one-bedroom apartments, each for $400 per month. Ann would pay up to $250 per month rather than moderate her telephone habits, and Betty would pay up to $150 per month to achieve reasonable access to the telephone. Now, suppose Betty would also be willing to pay up to $60 per month to avoid the loss of privacy that comes with shared living space. Should the two women live together?

LEGAL REMEDIES FOR EXTERNALITIES

We have seen that efficient solutions to externalities can be found whenever the affected parties can negotiate with one another at no cost. But negotiation is not always practical. A motorist with a noisy muffler imposes costs on others, yet they cannot flag him down and offer him a compensation payment to fix his muffler. In recognition of this difficulty, most governments simply require that cars have working mufflers. Indeed, the explicit or implicit purpose of a large share—perhaps the lion's share—of laws is to solve problems caused by externalities. The goal of such laws is to help people achieve the solutions they might have reached had they been able to negotiate with one another.

When negotiation is costless, the task of adjustment generally falls on the party who can accomplish it at the lowest cost. For instance, in our examples, Betty put up with Ann's annoying phone habits because doing so was less costly than asking Ann to change her habits. Many municipal noise ordinances also place the burden of adjustment on those who can accomplish it at the lowest cost. Consider, for example, the restrictions on loud party music, which often take effect at a later hour on weekends than on weekdays. This pattern reflects both the fact that the gains from loud music tend to be larger on weekends and the fact that such music is more likely to disturb people on weekdays. By setting the noise curfew at different hours on different days of the week, the law places the burden on partygoers during the week and on sleepers during the weekend. Similar logic explains why noise ordinances allow motorists to honk their horns in most neighborhoods, but not in the immediate vicinity of a hospital.

The list of laws and regulations that may be fruitfully viewed as solutions to externalities is a long one. When a motorist drives his car at high speed, he endangers not just his own life and property, but also the lives and property of others. Speed limits, no-passing zones, right-of-way rules, and a host of other traffic laws may be seen as reasoned attempts to limit the harm one party inflicts on another. Many jurisdictions even have laws requiring that motorists install snow tires on their cars by the first of November. These laws promote not just safety, but also the smooth flow of traffic: if one motorist can't get up a snow-covered hill, he delays not only himself, but also the motorists behind him.

Similar reasoning helps us understand the logic of zoning laws that restrict the kinds of activities that take place in various parts of cities. Because many residents place a high value on living in an uncongested neighborhood, some cities have enacted zoning laws specifying minimum lot sizes. In places like Manhattan, where a shortage of land encourages developers to build very large and tall buildings, zoning laws limit both a building's height and the proportion of a lot it may occupy. Such restrictions recognize that the taller a building is, and the greater the proportion of its lot that it occupies, the more it blocks sunlight from reaching surrounding properties. The desire to control external costs also helps to explain why many cities establish separate zones for business and residential activity. Even within business districts, many cities limit certain kinds of commercial activity. For example, in an effort to revitalize the Times Square neighborhood, New York City enacted a zoning law banning adult bookstores and pornographic movie theaters from the area.

Limitations on the discharge of pollutants into the environment are perhaps the clearest examples of laws aimed at solving problems caused by externalities. The details of these laws reflect the principle of placing the burden of adjustment on those who can accomplish it at least costs. The discharge of toxic wastes into rivers, for example, tends to be most strictly regulated on those waterways whose commercial fishing or recreational uses are most highly valued. On other waterways, the burden of adjustment is likely to fall more heavily on fishermen, recreational boaters, and swimmers. Similarly, air-quality regulations tend to be strictest in the most heavily populated regions of the country, where the marginal benefit of pollution reduction is the greatest.

The following examples suggest additional ways in which Coase's insights about how societies deal with externalities provide rich fodder for the economic naturalist.

Example 10.1
THE ECONOMIC NATURALIST

Why does the U.S. Constitution protect the right of free speech?

What is the purpose of free speech laws?

The First Amendment's protection of free speech and the pattern of exceptions to that protection are another illustration of how legal remedies are used to solve the problems caused by externalities. The First Amendment acknowledges the decisive value of open communication, as well as the practical difficulty of identifying and regulating acts of speech that cause more harm than good. Yet there are some important exceptions. The Supreme Court has ruled, for instance, that the First Amendment does not allow someone to yell "fire" in a crowded theater if there is no fire, nor does it allow someone to advocate the violent overthrow of the government. In those instances, the external benefits of free speech are far too small to justify the external costs. ●

Example 10.2
THE ECONOMIC NATURALIST

Why does the government subsidize scientific research?

Why does government subsidize private property owners to plant trees on their hillsides?

Societies use laws not only to discourage activities that generate negative externalities, but also to encourage activities that generate positive externalities. The planting of trees on hillsides, for example, benefits not just the landowner, but also his neighbors by limiting the danger of flooding. In recognition of this fact, many jurisdictions subsidize the planting of trees. Similarly, Congress budgets millions of dollars each year in support of basic research—an implicit acknowledgment of the positive externalities associated with the generation of new knowledge. ●

THE OPTIMAL AMOUNT OF NEGATIVE EXTERNALITIES IS NOT ZERO

Curbing pollution and other negative externalities entails both costs and benefits. As we saw in Chapter 6, when we analyzed how many cans should be recycled, the best policy is to curtail pollution until the cost of further abatement just equals the marginal benefit. In general, the marginal cost of abatement rises with the amount of pollution eliminated. (Following the Low-Hanging-Fruit Principle, polluters use the cheapest cleanup methods first and then turn to more expensive ones.) And the law of diminishing marginal utility suggests that beyond some point, the marginal benefit of pollution reduction tends to fall as more pollution is removed. As a result, the marginal cost and marginal benefit curves almost always intersect at less than the maximum amount of pollution reduction.

Increasing Opportunity Cost

The intersection of the two curves marks the socially optimal level of pollution reduction. If pollution is curtailed by any less than that amount, society will gain more than it will lose by pushing the cleanup effort a little further. But if regulators push beyond the point at which the marginal cost and benefit curves intersect, society will incur costs that exceed the benefits. The existence of a socially optimal level of pollution reduction implies the existence of a socially optimal level of pollution, and that level will almost always be greater than zero.

We saw in Chapter 6 that because people have been conditioned to think of pollution as bad, many cringe when they hear the phrase "socially optimal level of pollution." How can any positive level of pollution be socially optimal? *But to speak of a socially optimal level of pollution is not the same as saying that pollution is good.* It is merely to recognize that society has an interest in cleaning up the environment, but only up to a certain point. The underlying idea is no different from the idea of an optimal level of dirt in an apartment. After all, even if you spent the whole day, every day, vacuuming your apartment, there would be *some* dirt left in it. And because you have better things to do than vacuum all day, you probably tolerate substantially more than the minimal amount of dirt. A dirty apartment is not good, nor is pollution in the air you breathe. But in both cases, the cleanup effort should be expanded only until the marginal benefit equals the marginal cost.

COMPENSATORY TAXES AND SUBSIDIES

As noted, when transaction costs prohibit negotiation among affected parties, negative externalities lead to excessive output levels because activities that produce negative externalities are misleadingly attractive to those who engage in them. One solution to this problem, proposed by the British economist A. C. Pigou, is to make such activities less attractive by taxing them. Figure 10.3(a) reproduces Figure 10.1's portrayal of a market in which each unit of output generates an external cost of XC equal to \$1,000 per ton. Because producers fail to take this external cost into account, the private equilibrium is 12,000 tons per year, or 4,000 tons per year more than the socially optimal level of 8,000 tons per year.

Figure 10.3(b) portrays that same market after the imposition of a tax of \$1,000 per unit of output. This tax has the effect of raising each producer's marginal cost curve by \$1,000, so the industry supply curve shifts upward by \$1,000 at every quantity. Note that the resulting private equilibrium output, 8,000 tons per year, is now exactly equal to the socially optimal output. Although many critics insist that taxes always reduce economic efficiency, here we have an example of a tax that actually makes the economy *more* efficient. The tax has that effect because it forces producers to take explicit account of the fact that each additional unit of output they produce imposes an external cost of \$1,000 on the rest of society.

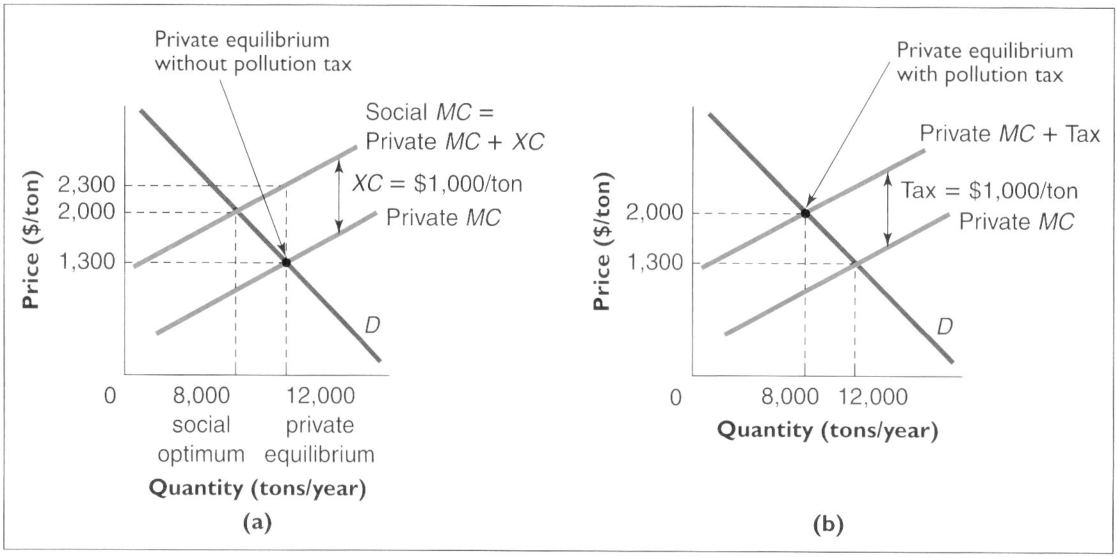

FIGURE 10.3
Taxing a Negative Externality.
(a) Negative externalities lead to an equilibrium with more than the socially optimal level of output. (b) Imposing a tax equal to the external cost leads to an equilibrium in which the output level is socially optimal. The tax makes the economy more efficient because it leads producers to take account of a relevant cost that they would otherwise ignore.

Similar reasoning suggests that a subsidy to producers can serve to counteract misallocations that result from positive externalities. Figure 10.4(a) portrays a market in which each unit of output generates an external benefit XB = $6 per ton. In this market, the socially optimal output level occurs at the intersection of the supply curve (MC) and the Social demand curve, which is constructed by adding XB = $6 per ton to the height of Private demand at each level of output. The

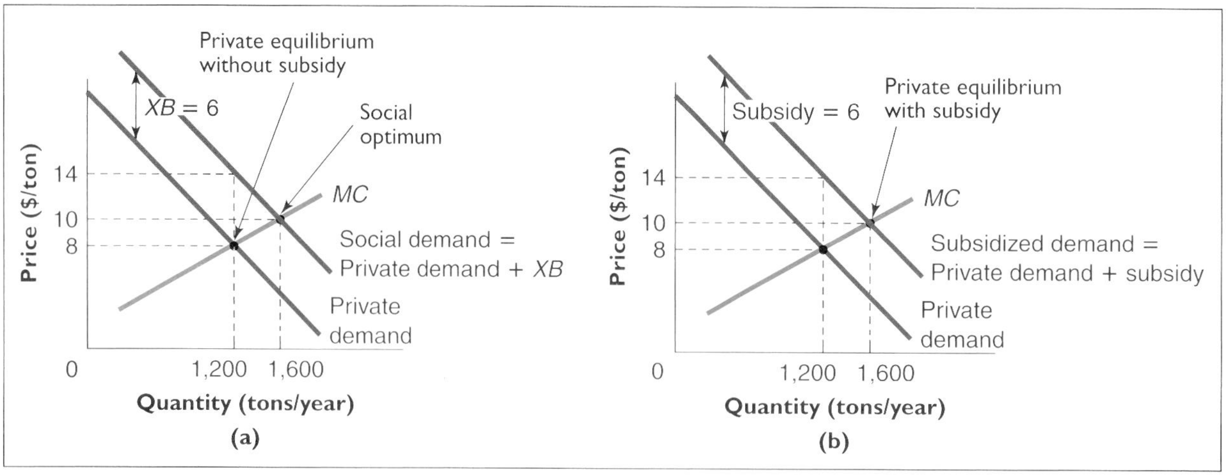

FIGURE 10.4
Subsidizing a Positive Externality.
(a) Positive externalities lead to an equilibrium with less than the socially optimal level of output. (b) Paying producers a subsidy equal to the external benefit of the activity leads to an equilibrium in which the output level is socially optimal. The subsidy makes the economy more efficient because it leads producers to take account of a relevant benefit that they would otherwise ignore.

socially optimal level of output is thus 1,600 tons per year. But private equilibrium in this market will occur at the intersection of Private demand and *MC*, which means that the equilibrium output, 1,200 tons per year, falls short of the social optimum by 400 tons per year.

Figure 10.4(b) shows the effect of paying a subsidy to producers of $6 per ton, the amount of the external benefit. In the presence of this subsidy, the new private equilibrium is 1,600 tons per year, exactly the socially optimal level. The subsidy makes the economy more efficient because it induces producers to take account of a relevant benefit that they otherwise would have ignored.

RECAP	EXTERNAL COSTS AND BENEFITS

Externalities occur when the costs or benefits of an activity accrue to people other than those directly involved in the activity. The Coase theorem says that when affected parties can negotiate with one another without cost, activities will be pursued at efficient levels, even in the presence of positive or negative externalities. But when negotiation is prohibitively costly, inefficient behavior generally results. Activities that generate negative externalities are pursued to excess, while those that generate positive externalities are pursued too little. Laws and regulations, including taxes and subsidies, are often adopted in an effort to alter inefficient behavior that results from externalities.

PROPERTY RIGHTS AND THE TRAGEDY OF THE COMMONS

People who grow up in industrialized nations tend to take the institution of private property for granted. Our intuitive sense is that people have the right to own any property they acquire by lawful means and to do with that property as they see fit. In reality, however, property laws are considerably more complex in terms of the rights they confer and the obligations they impose.

THE PROBLEM OF UNPRICED RESOURCES

To understand the laws that govern the use of property, let's begin by asking why societies created the institution of private property in the first place. The following examples, which show what happens to property that nobody owns, suggest an answer.

How many steers will villagers send onto the commons?

A village has five residents, each of whom has accumulated savings of $100. Each villager can use the money to buy a government bond that pays 13 percent interest per year or to buy a year-old steer, send it onto the commons to graze, and sell it after 1 year. The price the villager will get for the 2-year-old steer depends on the amount of weight it gains while grazing on the commons, which in turn depends on the number of steers sent onto the commons, as shown in Table 10.4.

The price of a 2-year-old steer declines with the number of steers grazing on the commons because the more steers, the less grass available to each. The villagers make their investment decisions one at a time, and the results are public. If each villager decides how to invest individually, how many steers will be sent onto the commons, and what will be the village's total income?

TABLE 10.4
The Relationship between Herd Size and Steer Price

Number of steers on the commons	Price per 2-year-old steer ($)	Income per steer ($/year)
1	126	26
2	119	19
3	116	16
4	113	13
5	111	11

If a villager buys a $100 government bond, he will earn $13 of interest income at the end of 1 year. Thus, he should send a steer onto the commons if and only if that steer will command a price of at least $113 as a 2-year-old. When each villager chooses in this self-interested way, we can expect four villagers to send a steer onto the commons. (Actually, the fourth villager would be indifferent between investing in a steer or buying a bond since he would earn $13 either way. For the sake of discussion, we'll assume that in the case of a tie, people choose to be cattlemen.) The fifth villager, seeing that he would earn only $11 by sending a fifth steer onto the commons, will choose instead to buy a government bond. As a result of these decisions, the total village income will be $65 per year—$13 for the one bondholder and 4($13) = $52 for the four cattlemen. ◆

Has Adam Smith's invisible hand produced the most efficient allocation of these villagers' resources? We can tell at a glance that it has not since their total village income is only $65—precisely the same as it would have been had the possibility of cattle raising not existed. The source of the difficulty will become evident in the following example.

What is the socially optimal number of steers to send onto the commons?

Suppose the five villagers in the previous example confront the same investment opportunities as before, except that this time they are free to make their decisions as a group rather than individually. How many steers will they send onto the commons, and what will be their total village income?

This time the villagers' goal is to maximize the income received by the group as a whole. When decisions are made from this perspective, the criterion is to send a steer onto the commons only if its marginal contribution to village income is at least $13, the amount that could be earned from a government bond. As the entries in the last column of Table 10.5 indicate, the first steer clearly meets this criterion since it contributes $26 to total village income. But the second steer does not. Sending that steer onto the commons raises the village's income from cattle raising from $26 to $38, a gain of just $12. The $100 required to buy the second steer would thus have been better invested in a government bond. Worse, the collective return from sending a third steer is only $10; from a fourth, only $4; and from a fifth, only $3.

In sum, when investment decisions are made with the goal of maximizing total village income, the best choice is to buy four government bonds and send only a single steer onto the commons. The resulting village income will be $78: $26 from sending the single steer and $52 from the four government bonds. That amount is $13 more than the total income that resulted when villagers made their investment

TABLE 10.5
Marginal Income and the Socially Optimal Herd Size

Number of steers on the commons	Price per 2-year-old steer ($)	Income per steer ($/year)	Total cattle income ($/year)	Marginal income ($/year)
1	126	26	26	26
2	119	19	38	12
3	116	16	48	10
4	113	13	52	4
5	111	11	55	3

decisions individually. Once again, the reward from moving from an inefficient allocation to an efficient one is that the economic pie grows larger. And when the pie grows larger, everyone can get a larger slice. For instance, if the villagers agree to pool their income and share it equally, each will get $15.60, or $2.60 more than before. ◆

EXERCISE 10.3

How would your answers to the grazing examples change if the interest rate was 11 percent per year rather than 13 percent?

Why do the villagers in these examples do better when they make their investment decisions collectively? The answer is that when individuals decide alone, they ignore the fact that sending another steer onto the commons will cause existing steers to gain less weight. Their failure to consider this effect makes the return from sending another steer seem misleadingly high to them.

The grazing land on the commons is a valuable economic resource. When no one owns it, no one has any incentive to take the opportunity cost of using it into account. And when that happens, people will tend to use it until its marginal benefit is zero. This problem, and others similar to it, are known as the **tragedy of the commons.** The essential cause of the tragedy of the commons is the fact that one person's use of commonly held property imposes an external cost on others by making the property less valuable. The tragedy of the commons also provides a vivid illustration of the Equilibrium Principle. Each individual villager behaves rationally by sending an additional steer onto the commons, yet the overall outcome falls far short of the attainable ideal.

tragedy of the commons the tendency for a resource that has no price to be used until its marginal benefit falls to zero

Equilibrium

THE EFFECT OF PRIVATE OWNERSHIP

As the following examples illustrate, one solution to the tragedy of the commons is to place the village grazing land under private ownership.

How much will the right to control the village commons sell for?

Suppose the five villagers face the same investment opportunities as before, except that this time they decide to auction off the right to use the commons to the highest bidder. Assuming that villagers can borrow as well as lend at an annual interest rate of 13 percent, what price will the right to use the commons fetch? How will the owner of that property right use it, and what will be the resulting village income?

To answer these questions, simply ask yourself what you would do if you had complete control over how the grazing land were used. As we saw earlier, the most profitable way to use this land is to send only a single steer to graze on it. If you do so, you will earn a total of \$26 per year. Since the opportunity cost of the \$100 you spent on the single yearling steer is the \$13 in interest you could have earned from a bond, your economic profit from sending a single steer onto the commons will be \$13 per year, provided you can use the land for free. But you cannot; to finance your purchase of the property right, you must borrow money (since you used your \$100 savings to buy a year-old steer).

What is the most you would be willing to pay for the right to use the commons? Since its use generates an income of \$26 per year, or \$13 more than the opportunity cost of your investment in the steer, the most you would pay is \$100 (because that amount used to purchase a bond that pays 13 percent interest would also generate income of \$13 per year). If the land were sold at auction, \$100 is precisely the amount you would have to pay. Your annual earnings from the land would be exactly enough to pay the \$13 interest on your loan and cover the opportunity cost of not having put your savings into a bond.

Note that when the right to use the land is auctioned to the highest bidder, the village achieves a more efficient allocation of its resources because the owner has a strong incentive to take the opportunity cost of more intensive grazing fully into account. Total village income in this case will again be \$78. If the annual interest on the \$100 proceeds from selling the land rights is shared equally among the five villagers, each will again have an annual investment income of \$15.60. ◆

The logic of economic surplus maximization helps to explain why the most economically successful nations have all been ones with well-developed private property laws. Property that belongs to everyone belongs, in effect, to no one. Not only is its potential economic value never fully realized; it usually ends up being of no value at all.

Bear in mind, however, that in most countries the owners of private property are not free to do *precisely* as they wish with it. For example, local zoning laws may give the owner of a residential building lot the right to build a three-story house but not a six-story house. Here, too, the logic of economic surplus maximization applies, for a fully informed and rational legislature would define property rights so as to create the largest possible total economic surplus. In practice, of course, such ideal legislatures never really exist. Yet the essence of politics is the cutting of deals that make people better off. If a legislator could propose a change in the property laws that would enlarge the total economic surplus, she could also propose a scheme that would give each of her constituents a larger slice, thus enhancing her chances for reelection.

As an economic naturalist, challenge yourself to use this framework when thinking about the various restrictions you encounter in private property laws: zoning laws that constrain what you can build and what types of activities you can conduct on your land; traffic laws that constrain what you can do with your car; employment and environmental laws that constrain how you can operate your business. Your understanding of these and countless other laws will be enhanced by the insight that everyone can gain when the private property laws are defined so as to create the largest total economic surplus.

WHEN PRIVATE OWNERSHIP IS IMPRACTICAL

Do not be misled into thinking that the law provides an *ideal* resolution of all problems associated with externalities and the tragedy of the commons. Defining and enforcing efficient property rights entails costs, after all, and sometimes, as in the following examples, the costs outweigh the gains.

Example 10.3
THE ECONOMIC NATURALIST

Why do blackberries in public parks get picked too soon?

Wild blackberries grow profusely at the edge of a wooded area in a crowded city park. The blackberries will taste best if left to ripen fully, but they still taste reasonably good if picked and eaten a few days early. Will the blackberries be left to ripen fully?

Obviously, the costs of defining and enforcing the property rights to blackberries growing in a public park are larger than the potential gains, so the blackberries will remain common property. That means that whoever picks them first gets them. Even though everyone would benefit if people waited until the berries were fully ripe, everyone knows that those who wait are likely to end up with no berries at all. And that means that the berries will be eaten too soon. ●

Why does fruit that grows in public places get picked too soon?

Example 10.4
THE ECONOMIC NATURALIST

Why are shared milkshakes consumed too quickly?

Sara and Susan are identical twins who have been given a chocolate milkshake to share. If each has a straw and each knows that the other is self-interested, will the twins consume the milkshake at an optimal rate?

Because drinking a milkshake too quickly chills the taste buds, the twins will enjoy their shake more if they drink it slowly. Yet each knows that the other will drink any part of the milkshake she doesn't finish herself. The result is that each will consume the shake at a faster rate than she would if she had half a shake all to herself. ●

Why are shared milkshakes drunk too quickly?

Here are some further examples in which the tragedy of the commons is not easily solved by defining private ownership rights.

Harvesting timber on remote public land On remote public lands, enforcing restrictions against cutting down trees may be impractical. Each tree cutter knows that a tree that is not harvested this year will be bigger, and hence more valuable, next year. But he also knows that if he doesn't cut the tree down this year, someone else might do so. In contrast, private companies that grow trees on their own land have no incentive to harvest timber prematurely and a strong incentive to prevent outsiders from doing so.

Harvesting whales in international waters Each individual whaler knows that harvesting an extra whale reduces the breeding population, and hence the size of the future whale population. But the whaler also knows that any whale that is not harvested today may be taken by some other whaler. The solution would be to define and enforce property rights to whales. But the oceans are vast, and the behavior of whalers is hard to monitor. And even if their behavior could be monitored, the concept of national sovereignty would make the international enforcement of property rights problematic.

More generally, the animal species that are most severely threatened with extinction tend to be those that are economically valuable to humans but that are not privately owned by anyone. This is the situation confronting whales as well as elephants. Contrast this with the situation confronting chickens, which are also economically valuable to humans but which, unlike whales, are governed by traditional laws of private property. This difference explains why no one worries that Colonel Sanders might threaten the extinction of chickens.

Controlling multinational environmental pollution Each individual polluter may know that if he and all others pollute, the damage to the environment will be greater than the cost of not polluting. But if the environment is common property into which all are free to dump, each has a powerful incentive to pollute. Enforcing laws and regulations that limit the discharge of pollution may be practical if all polluters live under the jurisdiction of a single government. But if polluters come from many different countries, solutions are much more difficult to implement. Thus, the Mediterranean Sea has long suffered serious pollution since none of the many nations that border it has an economic incentive to consider the effects of its discharges on other countries.

As the world's population continues to grow, the absence of an effective system of international property rights will become an economic problem of increasing significance.

RECAP	PROPERTY RIGHTS AND THE TRAGEDY OF THE COMMONS

When a valuable resource has a price of zero, people will continue to exploit it as long as its marginal benefit remains positive. The tragedy of the commons describes situations in which valuable resources are squandered because users are not charged for them. In many cases, an efficient remedy is to define and enforce rights to the use of valuable property. But this solution is difficult to implement for resources such as the oceans and the atmosphere because no single government has the authority to enforce property rights for these resources.

POSITIONAL EXTERNALITIES

Former tennis champion Steffi Graf received more than $1.6 million in tournament winnings in 1992; her endorsement and exhibition earnings totaled several times that amount. By any reasonable measure, the quality of her play was outstanding, yet she consistently lost to archrival Monica Seles. But in April of 1993, Seles was stabbed in the back by a deranged fan and forced to withdraw from the tour. In the ensuing months, Graf's tournament winnings accumulated at almost double her 1992 pace, despite little change in the quality of her play.

PAYOFFS THAT DEPEND ON RELATIVE PERFORMANCE

In professional tennis and a host of other competitive situations, the rewards people receive typically depend not only on how they perform in absolute terms but also on how they perform relative to their closest rivals. In these situations, competitors have an incentive to take actions that will increase their odds of winning. For example, tennis players can increase their chances of winning by hiring personal fitness trainers and sports psychologists to travel with them on the tour. Yet the simple mathematics of competition tells us that the sum of all individual payoffs from such investments will be larger than the collective payoff. In any tennis match, for example, each contestant will get a sizable payoff from money spent on fitness trainers and sports psychologists, yet each match will have exactly one winner and one loser, no matter how much players spend. The overall gain to tennis spectators is likely to be small, and the overall gain to players as a group must be zero. To the extent that each contestant's payoff depends on his or her relative performance, then, the incentive to undertake such investments will be excessive, from a collective point of view.

Consider the following example.

Example 10.5
THE ECONOMIC NATURALIST

Why do so many football players take steroids?

EN 10

Why do football players take anabolic steroids?

The offensive linemen of many National Football League teams currently average more than 330 pounds. In the 1970s, by contrast, offensive linemen in the league averaged barely 280 pounds, and the all-decade linemen of the 1940s averaged only 229 pounds. One reason that today's players are so much heavier is that players' salaries have escalated sharply over the last two decades, which has intensified competition for the positions. Size and strength are the two cardinal virtues of an offensive lineman, and other things being equal, the job will go to the larger and stronger of two rivals.

Size and strength, in turn, can be enhanced by the consumption of anabolic steroids. But if all players consume these substances, the rank ordering of players by size and strength—and hence the question of who lands the jobs—will be largely unaffected. And since the consumption of anabolic steroids entails potentially serious long-term health consequences, as a group football players are clearly worse off if they consume these drugs. So why do football players take steroids?

The problem here is that contestants for starting berths on the offensive line confront a prisoner's dilemma, like the ones analyzed in the preceding chapter. Consider two closely matched rivals—Smith and Jones—who are competing for a single position. If neither takes steroids, each has a 50 percent chance of winning the job and a starting salary of $1 million per year. If both take steroids, each again has a 50 percent chance of winning the job. But if one takes steroids and the other doesn't, the first is sure to win the job. The loser ends up selling insurance for $60,000 per year. Neither likes the fact that the drugs may have adverse health consequences, but each would be willing to take that risk in return for a shot at the big salary. Given these choices, the two competitors face a payoff matrix like the one shown in Table 10.6.

TABLE 10.6
Payoff Matrix for Steroid Consumption

		Jones: Don't take steroids	Jones: Take steroids
Smith	Don't take steroids	Second best for each	Best for Jones Worst for Smith
	Take steroids	Best for Smith Worst for Jones	Third best for each

Clearly, the dominant strategy for both Smith and Jones is to take steroids. Yet when they do, each gets only the third-best outcome, whereas they could have gotten the second-best outcome by not taking the drugs—hence the attraction of rules that forbid the consumption of anabolic steroids. ●

POSITIONAL ARMS RACES AND POSITIONAL ARMS CONTROL AGREEMENTS

positional externality occurs when an increase in one person's performance reduces the expected reward of another in situations in which reward depends on relative performance

The steroid problem is an example of a **positional externality.** Whenever the payoffs to one contestant depend at least in part on how he or she performs relative to a rival, any step that improves one side's relative position must necessarily worsen the other's. The shouting-at-parties example discussed in Chapter 9 is another instance of a positional externality. Just as the invisible hand of the market is weakened by the presence of standard externalities, it is also weakened by positional externalities.

We have seen that positional externalities often lead contestants to engage in an escalating series of mutually offsetting investments in performance enhancement. We call such spending patterns **positional arms races.**

positional arms race a series of mutually offsetting investments in performance enhancement that is stimulated by a positional externality

positional arms control agreement an agreement in which contestants attempt to limit mutually offsetting investments in performance enhancement

Because positional arms races produce inefficient outcomes, people have an incentive to curtail them. Steps taken to reduce positional arms races such as blue laws and rules against anabolic steroids may therefore be thought of as **positional arms control agreements.**

Once you become aware of positional arms races, you will begin to see them almost everywhere. You can hone your skills as an economic naturalist by asking these questions about every competitive situation you observe: What form do the investments in performance enhancement take? What steps have contestants taken to limit these investments? Sometimes positional arms control agreements are achieved by the imposition of formal rules or by the signing of legal contracts. Some examples of this type of agreement follow.

Campaign spending limits In the United States, presidential candidates routinely spend more than $100 million on advertising. Yet if both candidates double their spending on ads, each one's odds of winning will remain essentially the same. Recognition of this pattern led Congress to adopt strict spending limits for presidential candidates. (That those regulations have proved difficult to enforce does not call into question the logic behind the legislation.)

Roster limits Major League Baseball permits franchises to have only 25 players on the roster during the regular season. The National Football League sets its roster limit at 53; the National Basketball Association at 12. Why these limits? In their absence, any team could increase its chance of winning by simply adding players. Inevitably, other teams would follow suit. On the plausible assumption that, beyond some point, larger rosters do not add much to the entertainment value for fans, roster limits are a sensible way to deliver sports entertainment at a more reasonable cost.

Arbitration agreements In the business world, contracting parties often sign a binding agreement that commits them to arbitration in the event of a dispute. By doing so, they sacrifice the option of pursuing their interests as fully as they might wish to later, but they also insulate themselves from costly legal battles. Other parties in the legal system may sometimes take steps to limit spending on litigation. For example, a federal judge in South Dakota announced—presumably to the approval of litigants—that he would read only the first 15 pages of any brief submitted to his court.

Mandatory starting dates for kindergarten A child who is a year or so older than most of her kindergarten classmates is likely to perform better, in relative terms, than if she had entered school with children her own age. And since most parents are aware that admission to prestigious universities and eligibility for top jobs upon graduation depend largely on *relative* academic performance, many are tempted to keep their children out of kindergarten a year longer than necessary. Yet there is no social advantage in holding *all* children back an extra year since their relative performance would essentially be unaffected. In most jurisdictions, therefore, the law requires children who reach their fifth birthday before December 1 of a given year to start kindergarten the same year.

SOCIAL NORMS AS POSITIONAL ARMS CONTROL AGREEMENTS

In some cases, social norms may take the place of formal agreements to curtail positional arms races. Some familiar examples follow.

Nerd norms Some students care more—in the short run, at least—about the grades they get than how much they actually learn. When such students are graded on the curve—that is, on the basis of their performance relative to other students—a positional arms race ensues because if all students were to double the amount of time they studied, the distribution of grades would remain essentially the same. Students who find themselves in this situation are often quick to embrace "nerd norms," which brand as social misfits those who "study too hard."

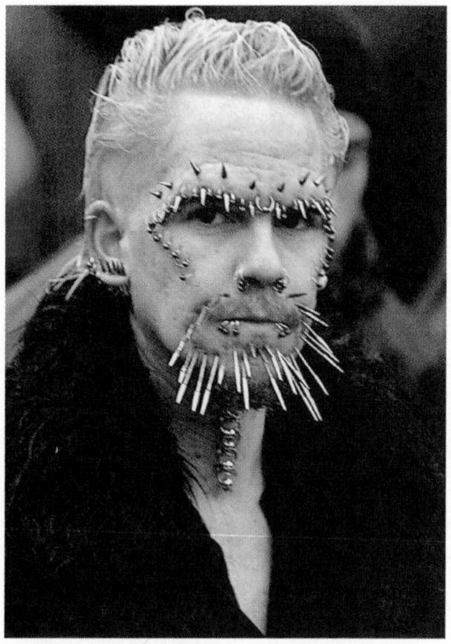

Is being on fashion's cutting edge more valuable now than in the 1950s?

Fashion norms Social norms regarding dress and fashion often change quickly because of positional competitions. Consider, for instance, the person who wishes to be on the cutting edge of fashion. In some American social circles during the 1950s, that goal could be accomplished by having pierced ears. But as more and more people adopted the practice, it ceased to communicate avant-garde status. At the same time, those who wanted to make a conservative fashion statement gradually became freer to have their ears pierced.

For a period during the 1960s and 1970s, one could be on fashion's cutting edge by wearing two earrings in one earlobe. But by the 1990s multiple ear piercings had lost much of their social significance, the threshold of cutting-edge status having been raised to upward of a dozen piercings of each ear, or a smaller number of piercings of the nose, eyebrows, or other body parts. A similar escalation has taken place in the number, size, and placement of tattoos.

The increase in the required number of tattoos or body piercings has not changed the value of avant-garde fashion status to those who desire it. Being on the outer limits of fashion has much the same meaning now as it once did. To the extent that there are costs associated with body piercings, tattoos, and other steps required to achieve avant-garde status, the current fashions are wasteful compared to earlier ones. In this sense, the erosion of social norms against tattoos and body piercings has produced a social loss. Of course, the costs associated with this loss are small in most cases. Yet since each body piercing entails a small risk of infection, the costs will continue to rise with the number of piercings. And once those costs reach a certain threshold, support may mobilize on behalf of social norms that discourage body mutilation.

Norms of taste Similar cycles occur with respect to behaviors considered to be in bad taste. In the 1950s, for example, prevailing norms prevented major national magazines from accepting ads that featured nude photographs. Naturally, advertisers had a powerful incentive to chip away at such norms in an effort to capture the reader's limited attention. And indeed, taboos against nude photographs have eroded in the same way as taboos against body mutilation.

Consider, for instance, the evolution of perfume ads. First came the nude silhouette; then, increasingly well-lighted and detailed nude photographs; and more recently, photographs of what appear to be group sex acts. Each innovation achieved just the desired effect: capturing the reader's instant and rapt attention. Inevitably, however, other advertisers followed suit, causing a shift in our sense of what is considered attention-grabbing. Photographs that once would have shocked readers now often draw little more than a bored glance.

Opinions differ, of course, about whether this change is an improvement. Many believe that the earlier, stricter norms were ill-advised, the legacy of a more prudish and repressive era. Yet even people who take that view are likely to believe that *some* kinds of photographic material ought not to be used in magazine advertisements. Obviously, what is acceptable will differ from person to person, and each person's threshold of discomfort will depend in part on current standards. But as advertisers continue to break new ground in their struggle to capture attention, the point may come when people begin to mobilize in favor of stricter standards of

"We're looking for the kind of bad taste that will grab—but not appall."

"public decency." Such a campaign would provide yet another case of a positional arms control agreement.

Norms against vanity Cosmetic and reconstructive surgery has produced dramatic benefits for many people, enabling badly disfigured accident victims to recover a normal appearance. It also has eliminated the extreme self-consciousness felt by people born with strikingly unusual features. Such surgery, however, is by no means confined to the conspicuously disfigured. Increasingly, "normal" people are seeking surgical improvements to their appearance. Some 2 million cosmetic "procedures" were done in 1991—six times the number just a decade earlier[1]—and demand has continued to grow steadily in the years since. Once a carefully guarded secret, these procedures are now offered as prizes in southern California charity raffles.

In individual cases, cosmetic surgery may be just as beneficial as reconstructive surgery is for accident victims. Buoyed by the confidence of having a straight nose or a wrinkle-free complexion, patients sometimes go on to achieve much more than they ever thought possible. But the growing use of cosmetic surgery also has had an unintended side effect: It has altered the standards of normal appearance. A nose that once would have seemed only slightly larger than average may now seem jarringly big. The same person who once would have looked like an average 55-year-old may now look nearly 70. And someone who once would have tolerated slightly thinning hair or an average amount of cellulite may now feel compelled to undergo hair transplantation or liposuction. Because such procedures shift people's frame of

[1]*The Economist*, January 11, 1992, p. 25.

reference, their payoffs to individuals are misleadingly large. From a social perspective, therefore, reliance on them is likely to be excessive.

Legal sanctions against cosmetic surgery are difficult to imagine. But some communities have embraced powerful social norms against cosmetic surgery, heaping scorn and ridicule on the consumers of face-lifts and tummy tucks. In individual cases, such norms may seem cruel. Yet without them, many more people might feel compelled to bear the risk and expense of cosmetic surgery.

RECAP	POSITIONAL EXTERNALITIES

Positional externalities occur when an increase in one person's performance reduces the expected reward of another person in situations in which reward depends on relative performance. Positional arms races are a series of mutually offsetting investments in performance enhancement that are stimulated by a positional externality. Positional arms control agreements are sometimes enacted in an attempt to limit positional arms races. In some cases, social norms can act as positional arms control agreements.

SUMMARY

- Externalities are the costs and benefits of activities that accrue to people who are not directly involved in those activities. When all parties affected by externalities can negotiate with one another at no cost, the invisible hand of the market will produce an efficient allocation of resources. According to the Coase theorem, the allocation of resources is efficient in such cases because the parties affected by externalities can compensate others for taking remedial action. **LO1, LO2**
- Negotiation over externalities is often impractical, however. In these cases, the self-serving actions of individuals typically will not lead to an efficient outcome. The attempt to forge solutions to the problems caused by externalities is one of the most important rationales for collective action. Sometimes collective action takes the form of laws and government regulations that alter the incentives facing those who generate, or are affected by, externalities. Such remedies work best when they place the burden of accommodation on the parties who can accomplish it at the lowest cost. Traffic laws, zoning laws, environmental protection laws, and free speech laws are examples. **LO3**
- Curbing pollution and other negative externalities entails costs as well as benefits. The optimal amount of pollution reduction is the amount for which the marginal benefit of further reduction just equals the marginal cost. In general, this formula implies that the socially optimal level of pollution, or of any other negative externality, is greater than zero. **LO4**
- When grazing land and other valuable resources are owned in common, no one has an incentive to take into account the opportunity cost of using those resources. This problem is known as the tragedy of the commons. Defining and enforcing private rights governing the use of valuable resources is often an effective solution to the tragedy of the commons. Not surprisingly, most economically successful nations have well-developed institutions of private property. Property that belongs to everyone belongs, in effect, to no one. Not only is its potential economic value never fully realized; it usually ends up having no value at all. **LO6**
- The difficulty of enforcing property rights in certain situations explains a variety of inefficient outcomes such as the excessive harvest of whales in international waters and the premature harvest of timber on remote public lands. The excessive pollution of seas that are bordered by many countries also results from a lack of enforceable property rights. **LO5**
- Situations in which people's rewards depend on how well they perform in relation to their rivals give rise to positional externalities. In these situations, any step that improves one side's relative position necessarily worsens the other's. Positional externalities tend to spawn positional arms races—escalating patterns of mutually offsetting investments in performance enhancement. Collective measures to curb positional arms races are known as positional arms control agreements. These collective actions may

take the form of formal regulations or rules such as rules against anabolic steroids in sports, campaign spending limits, and binding arbitration agreements. Informal social norms can also curtail positional arms races. **LO6**

■ KEY TERMS ■

Coase theorem (272)
external benefit (268)
external cost (268)
externality (268)
negative externality (268)
positional arms control agreement (286)
positional arms race (286)
positional externality (286)
positive externality (268)
tragedy of the commons (281)

■ REVIEW QUESTIONS ■

1. What incentive problem explains why the freeways in cities like Los Angeles suffer from excessive congestion? **LO3**
2. How would you explain to a friend why the optimal amount of freeway congestion is not zero? **LO4**
3. If Congress could declare any activity that imposes external costs on others illegal, would such legislation be advisable? **LO2**
4. Why does the Great Salt Lake, which is located wholly within the state of Utah, suffer lower levels of pollution than Lake Erie, which is bordered by several states and Canada? **LO3**
5. Explain why the wearing of high-heeled shoes might be viewed as the result of a positional externality. **LO6**

■ PROBLEMS ■

McGraw-Hill's HOMEWORK MANAGER®

1. Determine whether the following statements are true or false, and briefly explain why: **LO3**
   a. A given total emission reduction in a polluting industry will be achieved at the lowest possible total cost when the cost of the last unit of pollution curbed is equal for each firm in the industry.
   b. In an attempt to lower their costs of production, firms sometimes succeed merely in shifting costs to outsiders.
2. Phoebe keeps a bee farm next door to an apple orchard. She chooses her optimal number of beehives by selecting the honey output level at which her private marginal benefit from beekeeping equals her private marginal cost. **LO3**
   a. Assume that Phoebe's private marginal benefit and marginal cost curves from beekeeping are normally shaped. Draw a diagram of them.
   b. Phoebe's bees help to pollinate the blossoms in the apple orchard, increasing the fruit yield. Show the social marginal benefit from Phoebe's beekeeping in your diagram.
   c. Phoebe's bees are Africanized killer bees that aggressively sting anyone who steps into their flight path. Phoebe, fortunately, is naturally immune to the bees' venom. Show the social marginal cost curve from Phoebe's beekeeping in your diagram.
   d. Indicate the socially optimal quantity of beehives on your diagram. Is it higher or lower than the privately optimal quantity? Explain.
3. Suppose the supply curve of boom box rentals in Golden Gate Park is given by $P = 5 + 0.1Q$, where P is the daily rent per unit in dollars and Q is the volume of units rented in hundreds per day. The demand curve for boom boxes is $20 - 0.2Q$. If each boom box imposes \$3 per day in noise costs on others, by

how much will the equilibrium number of boom boxes rented exceed the socially optimal number? **LO3**

4. Refer to problem 3. How would the imposition of a tax of $3 per unit on each daily boom box rental affect efficiency in this market? **LO4**

5. Suppose the law says that Jones may *not* emit smoke from his factory unless he gets permission from Smith, who lives downwind. If the relevant costs and benefits of filtering the smoke from Jones's production process are as shown in the following table, and if Jones and Smith can negotiate with one another at no cost, will Jones emit smoke? **LO2**

	Jones emits smoke	Jones does not emit smoke
Surplus for Jones	$200	$160
Surplus for Smith	$400	$420

6. John and Karl can live together in a two-bedroom apartment for $500 per month, or each can rent a single-bedroom apartment for $350 per month. Aside from the rent, the two would be indifferent between living together and living separately, except for one problem: John leaves dirty dishes in the sink every night. Karl would be willing to pay up to $175 per month to avoid John's dirty dishes. John, for his part, would be willing to pay up to $225 to be able to continue his sloppiness. Should John and Karl live together? If they do, will there be dirty dishes in the sink? Explain. **LO2**

7. How, if at all, would your answer to problem 6 differ if John would be willing to pay up to $30 per month to avoid giving up his privacy by sharing quarters with Karl? **LO2**

8. Barton and Statler are neighbors in an apartment complex in downtown Manhattan. Barton is a concert pianist, and Statler is a poet working on an epic poem. Barton rehearses his concert pieces on the baby grand piano in his front room, which is directly above Statler's study. The following matrix shows the monthly payoffs to Barton and Statler when Barton's front room is and is not soundproofed. The soundproofing will be effective only if it is installed in Barton's apartment. **LO2**

	Soundproofed	Not soundproofed
Gains to Barton	$100/month	$150/month
Gains to Statler	$120/month	$80/month

   a. If Barton has the legal right to make any amount of noise he wants and he and Statler can negotiate with one another at no cost, will Barton install and maintain soundproofing? Explain. Is his choice socially efficient?
   b. If Statler has the legal right to peace and quiet and can negotiate with Barton at no cost, will Barton install and maintain soundproofing? Explain. Is his choice socially efficient?
   c. Does the attainment of an efficient outcome depend on whether Barton has the legal right to make noise, or Statler the legal right to peace and quiet?

9. Refer to problem 8. Barton decides to buy a full-sized grand piano. The new payoff matrix is as follows: **LO2**

	Soundproofed	Not soundproofed
Gains to Barton	$100/month	$150/month
Gains to Statler	$120/month	$60/month

a. If Statler has the legal right to peace and quiet and Barton and Statler can negotiate at no cost, will Barton install and maintain soundproofing? Explain. Is this outcome socially efficient?
b. Suppose that Barton has the legal right to make as much noise as he likes and that negotiating an agreement with Barton costs $15 per month. Will Barton install and maintain soundproofing? Explain. Is this outcome socially efficient?
c. Suppose Statler has the legal right to peace and quiet, and it costs $15 per month for Statler and Barton to negotiate any agreement. (Compensation for noise damage can be paid without incurring negotiation cost.) Will Barton install and maintain soundproofing? Is this outcome socially efficient?
d. Why does the attainment of a socially efficient outcome now depend on whether Barton has the legal right to make noise?

10.* A village has six residents, each of whom has accumulated savings of $100. Each villager can use this money either to buy a government bond that pays 15 percent interest per year or to buy a year-old llama, send it onto the commons to graze, and sell it after 1 year. The price the villager gets for the 2-year-old llama depends on the quality of the fleece it grows while grazing on the commons. That in turn depends on the animal's access to grazing, which depends on the number of llamas sent to the commons, as shown in the following table:

Number of llamas on the commons	Price per 2-year-old llama ($)
1	122
2	118
3	116
4	114
5	112
6	109

The villagers make their investment decisions one after another, and their decisions are public. **LO5**
a. If each villager decides individually how to invest, how many llamas will be sent onto the commons, and what will be the resulting net village income?
b. What is the socially optimal number of llamas for this village? Why is that different from the actual number? What would net village income be if the socially optimal number of llamas were sent onto the commons?
c. The village committee votes to auction the right to graze llamas on the commons to the highest bidder. Assuming villagers can both borrow and lend at 15 percent annual interest, how much will the right sell for at auction? How will the new owner use the right, and what will be the resulting village income?

*Problems marked with an asterisk (*) are more difficult.

ANSWERS TO IN-CHAPTER EXERCISES

10.1 Since Fitch gains $50 per day when Abercrombie operates with a filter, he could pay Abercrombie as much as $49 per day and still come out ahead. **LO2**

10.2 If the two were to live together, the most efficient way to resolve the telephone problem would be as before, for Betty to give up reasonable access to the phone. But on top of that cost, which is $150, Betty would also bear a $60 cost from the loss of her privacy. The total cost of their living together would thus be $210 per month. Since that amount is greater than the $200 saving in rent, the two should live separately. **LO2**

10.3 The income figures from the different levels of investment in cattle would remain as before, as shown in the table. What is different is the opportunity cost of investing in each steer, which is now $11 per year instead of $13. The last column of the table shows that the socially optimal number of steers is now 2 instead of 1. And if individuals still favor holding cattle, all other things being equal, they will now send 5 steers onto the commons instead of 4, as shown in the middle column. **LO5**

Number of steers on the commons	Price per 2-year-old steer ($)	Income per steer ($/year)	Total village income ($/year)	Marginal income ($/year)
				26
1	126	26	26	
				12
2	119	19	38	
				10
3	116	16	48	
				4
4	113	13	52	
				3
5	111	11	55	

PART 4

ECONOMICS OF PUBLIC POLICY

The fundamental economic problem implicit in every choice is that while human desires are boundless, the resources necessary to satisfy them are limited. The upshot is that we confront tradeoffs at every turn. Having more of one good thing always requires making do with less of others.

A recurrent theme in this book has been that failure to think intelligently about these tradeoffs results in waste. Popular economic discourse has conditioned us to think of efficiency and equity as competing goals. This tradition has led many to believe that a certain measure of waste must be tolerated in the name of fairness. But we have argued in this book for the opposite claim—that efficiency is always and everywhere the best way to promote equity.

In one sense, this claim is true by definition. After all, any step that makes the economic pie larger necessarily makes it possible for everyone to have a larger slice than before. Of course, there is no guarantee that everyone will automatically get a bigger slice. Redistribution is often necessary.

Distributional objections are more difficult to address in some domains than in others. But it is almost always an error to regard them as insurmountable. The important point is that waste makes fewer resources available to meet important human needs. And because many important human needs remain unmet, that's always a bad thing.

Our aim in this final segment of the book will be to explore how careful economic reasoning can improve the design of public policy. Specific areas of focus will be health care delivery, environmental regulation, and international trade. In each domain, we will see how intelligent application of core economic principles can both expand the economic pie and make everyone's slice larger.

CHAPTER 11

Using Economics to Make Better Policy Choices

LEARNING OBJECTIVES

After reading this chapter, you should be able to:

1. Understand how the Scarcity Principle applies even to choices involving health.
2. Explain using the Incentive Principle, why health care costs have been rising so rapidly.
3. Discuss pollution taxes and effluent permits as a means to helping reduce the cost of improved air quality.
4. Determine why free trade is often politically controversial, even though it promises to increase total income.
5. Weigh the economic pros and cons of various components of the social safety net.

In 1979, in the wake of the second major oil supply interruption in a decade, officials in the Carter administration met to discuss policies for reducing the risks to domestic security inherent in U.S. dependence on foreign oil. The proposal they ultimately put forward was a gasoline tax of 50 cents per gallon. Anticipating objections that the tax would impose an unacceptable hardship on the poor, policymakers proposed to return the revenues from the tax to the citizenry by reducing the payroll tax—the tax on wages that supports the Social Security system.

Proponents of the gasoline tax argued that in addition to reducing the nation's dependence on foreign oil, the tax would reduce air pollution and ease highway congestion. But critics ridiculed the proposal, charging that if the revenues from the tax were returned to the people, the quantity of gasoline demanded would remain essentially the same. Their argument tipped the debate, and officials never managed to implement the proposal.

Whatever the ultimate merits of the administration's proposal, there was no merit at all in the argument the critics used to attack it. True, the proposed tax rebate meant that people *could* have bought just as much gasoline as before the tax. Yet the tax would have given them a powerful incentive not to do so. As we saw in Chapter 5, consumers can change their behavior to escape the effects of a steep rise in the after-tax price of gasoline—by switching to cars with smaller, more fuel-efficient engines; forming carpools; and so on. Such changes free up money to spend on other goods and services, which become relatively more attractive because they are not taxed.

No society can hope to formulate and implement intelligent economic policies unless its citizens and leaders share an understanding of basic economic principles. Our aim in this chapter is to explore how careful application of these principles can help us design policies that both expand the economic pie and make everyone's slice larger. We will explore the economics of health care delivery, environmental regulation, and public health and safety regulation. The unifying thread running through these issues is the problem of scarcity. In each case, we will explore how the Cost-Benefit Principle can help to resolve the resulting trade-offs.

Scarcity

Cost-Benefit

THE ECONOMICS OF HEALTH CARE

Political leaders are often reluctant to discuss expenditures on public health programs in cost-benefit terms. But because we live in a world of scarcity, we cannot escape the fact that spending more on health means spending less on other things of value.

Illnesses, like accidents, are costly to prevent. The socially optimal expenditure on a health measure that reduces a specific illness is that amount for which the marginal benefit to society of the measure exactly equals its marginal cost. For example, in deciding how much to spend on vaccinating against measles, a rational public health policy would expand the proportion of the population vaccinated until the marginal cost of an additional vaccination was exactly equal to the marginal value of the illnesses thus prevented.

As we explain in the following section, however, the decision of whether to become vaccinated looks very different from each individual's perspective.

THE CASE FOR MANDATORY IMMUNIZATION LAWS

Being vaccinated against a childhood illness entails a small but potentially serious risk. The vaccine against pertussis (whooping cough), for example, is believed to cause some form of permanent brain damage in one out of every 110,000 children vaccinated. Contracting the disease itself also poses serious health risks, and in an environment in which infections were sufficiently likely to occur, individuals would have a compelling reason to bear the risk of being vaccinated in order to reduce the even larger risk from infection. The problem is that in an environment in which most children were vaccinated, infection rates would be low, making the risk of vaccination loom relatively large in the eyes of individual families.

The ideal situation from the perspective of any individual family would be to remain unvaccinated in an environment in which all other families were vaccinated. But as more and more families decided to forgo vaccination, infection rates would mount. Eventually the vaccination rate would stabilize at the point at which the additional risk to the individual family of becoming vaccinated would be exactly equal to the risk from remaining unvaccinated. But this calculation ignores the fact that a decision to remain unvaccinated poses risk not just to the individual decision maker, but also to others who have decided to become vaccinated (since no vaccine affords 100 percent protection against infection).

Relegating the vaccination decision to individuals thus results in a suboptimally low vaccination rate because individual decision makers fail to take adequate account of the cost that their becoming infected will impose on others. It is for this reason that most states require vaccinations against specific childhood illnesses. Proof of immunization against diphtheria, measles, poliomyelitis, and rubella, for example, is now universally required for entry into American public schools. Most states also require immunization against tetanus (49 states), pertussis (44 states), mumps (43 states), and hepatitis B (26 states).

EN 11

Even these laws, however, allow parents to apply for exemptions on religious or philosophical grounds. Communities vary in the extent to which parents avail themselves of these exemptions. In Colorado, for instance, Boulder County heads the list of parents who opt to exempt their children from taking the pertussis vaccine (with an exemption rate of 8.4 percent, more than four times the rate statewide). Not surprisingly, the incidence of whooping cough is much higher in Boulder (34.7 cases per year per 100,000 people) than in the state as a whole (9.4 cases per year per 100,000 people).[1]

EXPLAINING RISING HEALTH CARE COSTS

In the United States, real health care expenditures per capita have grown more rapidly than real income per capita for as long as the relevant data have been available. As a share of national income, health care costs have risen from only 4 percent in 1940 to roughly 16 percent today. Part of this increase is the result of costly new health care technologies and procedures. Diagnostic tests have grown more expensive and sophisticated, and procedures like coronary bypass surgery and organ transplantation have grown far more common. Yet a great deal of medical expenditure inflation has nothing to do with these high-tech developments. Rather, it is the result of fundamental changes in the way we pay for medical services.

The most important change has been the emergence of the so-called third-party payment system. Earlier in this century, many people insured themselves against catastrophic illness but purchased routine medical care out of their own pockets, just as they did food, clothing, and other consumer goods. Starting after World War II, and increasingly since the mid-1960s, people have come to depend on insurance for even routine medical services. Some of this insurance is provided privately by employers; some, by the government. In the latter category, Medicaid covers the medical expenses of the poor and Medicare, those of the elderly and disabled.

The spread of medical insurance, especially government-financed medical insurance, owes much to the belief that an inability to pay should not prevent people from receiving medical care they need. Indeed, medical insurance has surely done much to shelter people from financial hardship. The difficulty is that in its most common form, it also has spawned literally hundreds of billions of dollars of waste each year.

To understand the nature of this waste, we must recognize that although medical services differ from other services in many ways, they are in one fundamental respect the same: The cost-benefit test is the only sensible criterion for deciding which services ought to be performed. The fact that a medical procedure has *some* benefit does not, by itself, imply that the procedure should be performed. Rather, it should be performed only if its marginal benefit, broadly construed, exceeds its marginal cost.

Cost-Benefit

The costs of medical procedures are relatively easy to measure, using the same methods applied to other goods and services. But the usual measure of the benefit of a good or service, a person's willingness to pay, may not be acceptable in the case of many medical services. For example, most of us would not conclude that a

[1]http://www.cdphe.state.co.us.de/Epidemiology/vaccinepreventable2000.pdf.

lifesaving appendectomy that costs $2,000 is unjustified merely because one person who needs it can afford to pay only $1,000. When someone lacks the resources to pay for what most of us would consider an essential medical service, society has at least some responsibility to help. Hence the proliferation of government-sponsored medical insurance.

Cost-Benefit

Many other medical expenditures are not as pressing as an emergency appendectomy, however. Following such surgery, for example, the patient requires a period of recuperation in the hospital. How long should that period last—2 days? 5? 10? The Cost-Benefit Principle is critically important to thinking intelligently about such questions. But as the following example illustrates, the third-party payment system has virtually eliminated cost-benefit thinking from the medical domain.

How long should David stay in the hospital?

To eliminate recurrent sore throats, David plans to have his tonsils removed. His surgeon tells him that the average hospital stay after this procedure is two days (some people stay only one day, while others stay three, four, or even five days). Hospital rooms cost $300 per day. If David's demand curve for days in the hospital is as shown in Figure 11.1, how many days will he stay if he must pay for his hospital room himself? How many days will he stay if his medical insurance fully covers the cost of his hospital room?

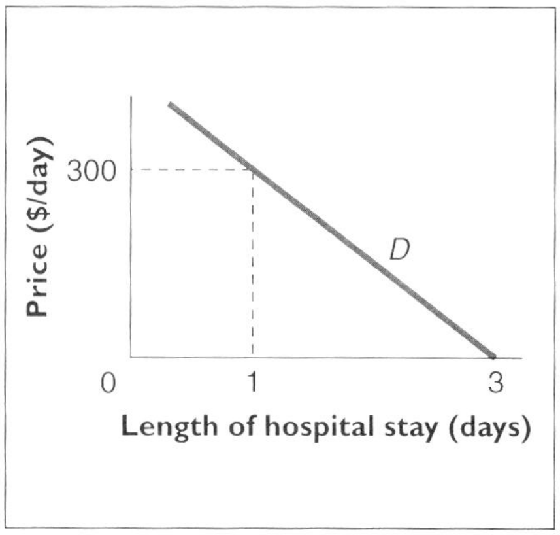

FIGURE 11.1
The Demand for Hospital Care.
The demand curve for postoperative hospital care is downward-sloping, just like any other demand curve. At higher prices, people choose shorter hospital stays, not because there is no benefit to a longer stay, but because they prefer to spend their money in other ways.

If David must pay for his hospital room himself, his best option will be to stay for just one day. But if the cost of his hospital room is completely covered by insurance, the marginal cost *to him* will be zero. In that case, he will stay for three days. ◆

EXERCISE 11.1

In the preceding example above, how long would David choose to stay in the hospital if his health insurance covered 50 percent of the cost of his hospital room?

Cost-Benefit

Should we be concerned that people choose longer hospital stays when their expenses are fully insured? The Cost-Benefit Principle tells us that a hospital stay should be extended another day only if the benefit of doing so would be at least as great as the cost of the resources required to extend the stay. But when hospital costs are fully covered by insurance, the decision maker sees a marginal cost of zero, when in fact the marginal cost is several hundred dollars. According to the Cost-Benefit Principle, then, full insurance coverage leads to wastefully long hospital stays. That is not to say that the additional days in the hospital do no good at all. Rather, their benefit is less than their cost. As the next example illustrates, a shorter hospital stay would increase total economic surplus.

How much waste does full insurance coverage cause?

Using the demand and cost information from the hospital stay example, calculate how much waste results from full insurance coverage of David's hospital room.

If the marginal cost of an additional day in the hospital is \$300, the supply curve of hospital room days in an open market would be horizontal at \$300. If David had to pay that price, he would choose a one-day stay, which would result in the largest possible economic surplus. If he extends his stay past one day, cost continues to accumulate at the rate of \$300 per day, but the benefit of additional care—as measured by his demand curve—falls below \$300. If he stays three days, as he will if he has full insurance coverage, the two extra days cost society \$600 but benefit David by only \$300 (the area of the lower shaded triangle under David's demand curve in Figure 11.2). The amount by which the extra cost exceeds the extra benefit will thus be \$300 (the area of the upper shaded triangle).

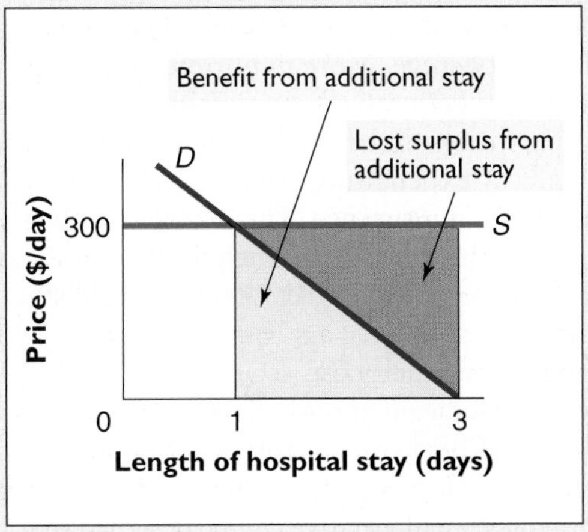

FIGURE 11.2
The Waste That Results from Full Insurance Coverage.
The area of the lower shaded triangle (\$300) represents the benefit of extending the hospital stay from one day to three days. Since the cost of the extra two days is \$600, the area of the upper shaded triangle (\$300) represents the loss in economic surplus that results from the longer stay. ◆

EXERCISE 11.2

In the last example, how much waste would be caused by an insurance policy that reimbursed hospital room expenses at the rate of \$150 per day?

DESIGNING A SOLUTION

In circumstances in which economic surplus has not been maximized, a transaction can always be found that will make both the patient *and* the insurance company better off. Suppose, for instance, that the insurance company in the previous example gives David a cash payment of \$700 toward hospital expenses and lets him decide for himself how long to stay in the hospital. Confronted with a price of \$300 per day, David would choose to stay only a single day. The \$400 cash he would have left after paying his hospital bill is \$100 more than enough to compensate him for the benefit he would lose by not staying an extra two days. (Again, that benefit is \$300, the area of the lower shaded triangle in Figure 11.2.) A \$700 cash payment also would leave his insurance company better off by \$200 than if it had provided unlimited hospital coverage at no extra charge (since David would have stayed three days in that case, at a cost of \$900 to his insurance company). And since no one else is harmed by this transaction, it represents a *Pareto improvement* over unlimited coverage, meaning a change that makes some people better off without harming others.

The amount of waste caused by full insurance coverage depends on the price elasticity of demand for medical services—the more elastic the demand, the greater the waste. Proponents of full coverage believe that the demand for medical services is almost completely inelastic with respect to price and that the resulting waste is therefore negligible. Critics of full coverage argue that the demand for medical services is actually quite sensitive to price and that the resulting waste is significant.

Who is right? One way to determine this is to examine whether people who lack full insurance coverage spend significantly less than those who have it. The economist W. G. Manning and several co-authors did so by performing an experiment in which they assigned subjects randomly to one of two different kinds of medical insurance policy.[2] The first group of subjects received **first-dollar coverage**, meaning that 100 percent of their medical expenses was covered by insurance. The second group got "$1,000-deductible" coverage, meaning that only expenses beyond the first $1,000 a year were covered. (For example, someone with $1,200 of medical bills would receive $1,200 from his insurance company if he belonged to the first group, but only $200 if he belonged to the second.) In effect, since most people incur less than $1,000 a year in medical expenses, most subjects in the second group effectively paid full price for their medical services, while subjects in the first group paid nothing. Manning and his colleagues found that *people with $1,000-deductible policies spent between 40 and 50 percent less on health care than subjects with first-dollar coverage. More important, there were no measurable differences in health outcomes between the two groups.*

first-dollar insurance coverage insurance that pays all expenses generated by the insured activity

Taken at face value, the results of the Manning study suggest that a large share of the inflation in medical expenditures since World War II has been caused by growth in first-dollar medical insurance. The problem with first-dollar coverage is that it completely ignores the Incentive Principle. Why not simply abandon first-dollar coverage in favor of high deductibles? People would still be protected against financial catastrophe but would have a strong incentive to avoid medical services whose benefit does not exceed their cost.

Incentive

Some would say that Medicaid and Medicare should not carry high deductibles because the resulting out-of-pocket payments would impose too great a burden on poor families. But as in other instances in which concern for the poor is offered in defense of an inefficient policy, an alternative can be designed that is better for rich and poor alike. For example, all health insurance could be written to include high deductibles, and the poor could be given an annual stipend to defray the initial medical expenses not covered by insurance. At year's end, any unspent stipend would be theirs to keep. Here again, concern for the well-being of the poor is no reason for not adopting the most efficient policy. As the Efficiency Principle reminds us, when the economic pie grows larger, it is possible for everyone to have a larger slice.

Efficiency

THE HMO REVOLUTION

During the 1990s, the high cost of conventional health insurance led many people to switch to **health maintenance organizations** (HMOs). An HMO is a group of physicians that provides its patients with medical services in return for a fixed annual fee. As the next example illustrates, the incentive to provide any given medical service is weaker under the standard HMO contract than under conventional health insurance.

health maintenance organization (HMO) a group of physicians that provides health services to individuals and families for a fixed annual fee

Example 11.1

THE ECONOMIC NATURALIST

Why is a patient with a sore knee more likely to receive an MRI exam if he has conventional health insurance than if he belongs to a Health Maintenance Organization?

[2]W. G. Manning, J. P. Newhouse, E. B. Keeler, A. Liebowitz, and M. S. Marquis, "Health Insurance and the Demand for Medical Care," *American Economic Review* 77 (June 1987), pp. 251–77.

When a patient visits his physician complaining of a sore knee, the physician has several options. After hearing the patient describe his symptoms and examining the knee manually, the physician may prescribe anti-inflammatory drugs and advise the patient to abstain from vigorous physical activity for a period; or she may advise the patient to undergo a magnetic resonance imaging (MRI) exam, a costly diagnostic procedure that generates images of the inner workings of the injured joint. The physician in an HMO receives no additional revenue if she orders the MRI because all services are covered by the patient's fixed annual fee. Under conventional health insurance, in contrast, the physician will be reimbursed at a fixed rate, usually well above her marginal cost, for each additional service performed.

"Well, Bob, it looks like a paper cut, but just to be sure let's do lots of tests."

In many instances, the most prudent course of treatment is unambiguous, and in such cases physicians will make the same recommendation despite this striking difference in incentives. But in many other cases, it may not be obvious which decision is best. And in these cases, HMO physicians are less likely to order expensive tests. ●

People who switch to HMOs pay less for their health plans than those who stick with conventional health insurance since the HMO contract provides a strong incentive for doctors not to prescribe nonessential services. Many people fear, however, that the very same incentive may sometimes result in their not receiving valuable care. These concerns have led to proposed legislation granting patients rights of appeal when they are denied care by an HMO.

PAYING FOR HEALTH INSURANCE

It is troubling but perhaps not surprising that access to medical care is extremely limited in many of the world's poorest nations. After all, citizens of those nations lack enough income to buy adequate food, shelter, and many other basic goods and services. What *is* surprising, however, is that despite the movement to less expensive HMO plans, some 47 million Americans had no health coverage of any kind in 2007. Politicians in both parties agree that something must be done to expand health coverage. But before an intelligent solution to this problem can be implemented, we must first understand why so many are without coverage in the first place.

Example 11.2
THE ECONOMIC NATURALIST

In the richest country on Earth, why do so many people lack basic health insurance?

Why do 47 million Americans have no health insurance?

As noted earlier, the rise of employer-provided health insurance took place during the decades following World War II, a time when large corporations were far more insulated from international competition than they are now. Workers during that era also tended to remain with the same employer for much longer periods than they do today. In addition, health care costs have risen sharply during recent decades. The combined effect of these changes has been to threaten the economic viability of employer-provided health insurance.

By appealing to employees who are optimistic about the likelihood that they will remain healthy, some companies have succeeded in cutting costs by offering jobs that pay slightly higher wages but do not offer health coverage. To the extent that the workers who are attracted to these jobs are right in their predictions about their health, one consequence is that workers who remain in jobs offering health insurance tend to be less healthy, on average, than others. As a result, costs go up even further for companies that continue to offer health coverage, and that provides an even greater incentive for the healthiest workers to accept jobs that don't offer coverage. Some health economists have argued that this phenomenon, known as *adverse selection,* has pushed the American system of employer-provided health-insurance system into a long-term downward spiral. And as more people become uninsured, the problem will get worse because the costs borne by those who remain insured will continue to escalate.●

Government could eliminate the downward spiral by simply reimbursing each family up to $5,000 a year for health insurance. Government bureaucrats would not need to prescribe which doctors we see or micromanage any of the other details. They would simply process insurance receipts and send out reimbursement checks. This plan sounds expensive but would actually be less costly than the current system. The principal savings would come from delivering more cost-effective care to those who are now uninsured.

As it stands now, the untreated minor illnesses of the uninsured often develop into major illnesses, which are far more costly to treat. And when such illnesses befall the uninsured, we almost always treat them, often in costly emergency rooms. The resulting burden on hospitals leads to higher fees and increased government support—both of which now come largely out of the pockets of high-income taxpayers with health insurance.

The total budget needed to finance a $5,000 health insurance reimbursement for every American family—some $350 billion a year—would obviously require higher taxes. But for those whose employers currently provide health insurance, these taxes would be offset by an increase in salaries. After all, companies offer insurance not because they are charitable, but because they find doing so an effective way to compete for workers. Any company that did not offer higher salaries to previously insured workers would risk losing them to a company that did.

A universal reimbursement program would impose no net burden on taxpayers because of both salary adjustments and reductions in the high cost of care for the uninsured. And by providing a powerful incentive for all families to buy insurance, it would reverse the current downward spiral.

Critics of health care reform may say that if some people want to save money by going without health insurance, that's their problem or their choice. Perhaps, but it's a problem for the rest of society as well, one that if left untended will grow steadily worse.

RECAP	THE ECONOMICS OF HEALTH CARE DELIVERY

The rapid escalation in medical expenditures since World War II is attributable in large part to the spread of first-dollar insurance coverage, which encourages people to behave as if medical services were free of charge. Total economic surplus would be larger if we switched to insurance coverage with high deductibles because such policies provide an incentive to use only those services whose benefit exceeds their cost.

The switch to HMOs addresses this problem because the standard HMO contract provides a strong incentive for physicians not to prescribe nonessential services. Some voice concern, however, that HMO contracts may lead physicians to withhold services that satisfy the cost-benefit test.

Mounting insurance premiums have caused many people in good health to do without health coverage, resulting in higher premiums for those who remain insured. Government reimbursement for health coverage is one way to stop the downward spiral in health coverage.

USING PRICE INCENTIVES IN ENVIRONMENTAL REGULATION

As we saw in Chapter 10, goods whose production generates negative externalities, such as atmospheric pollution, tend to be overproduced whenever negotiation among private parties is costly. Suppose we decide, as a society, that the best attainable outcome would be to have half as much pollution as would occur under completely unregulated conditions. In that case, how should the cleanup effort be distributed among those firms that currently discharge pollution into the environment?

The most efficient—and hence best—distribution of effort is the one for which each polluter's marginal cost of abatement is exactly the same. To see why, imagine that under current arrangements, the cost to one firm of removing a ton of pollution from the air is larger than the cost to another firm. Society could then achieve the same total reduction in pollution at lower cost by having the first firm discharge 1 ton more into the air and the second firm 1 ton less.

Unfortunately, government regulators seldom have detailed information on how the cost of reducing pollution varies from one firm to another. Many pollution laws therefore require all polluters simply to cut back their emissions by the same proportion or to meet the same absolute emissions standards. If different polluters have different marginal costs of pollution abatement, however, these approaches will not be efficient.

TAXING POLLUTION

Fortunately, alternative policies can distribute the cleanup more efficiently, even if the government lacks detailed information about how much it costs different firms to curtail pollution. One method is to tax pollution and allow firms to decide for themselves how much pollution to emit. The following example illustrates the logic of this approach.

What is the least costly way to cut pollution by half?

Two firms, Sludge Oil and Northwest Lumber, each has access to five production processes, each of which has a different cost and produces a different amount of pollution. The daily costs of the processes and the number of tons of smoke emitted are as shown in Table 11.1. Pollution is currently unregulated, and negotiation

TABLE 11.1
Costs and Emissions for Different Production Processes

Process (smoke)	A (4 tons/day)	B (3 tons/day)	C (2 tons/day)	D (1 ton/day)	E (0 tons/day)
Cost to Sludge Oil ($/day)	100	200	600	1,300	2,300
Cost to Northwest Lumber ($/day)	300	320	380	480	700

between the firms and those who are harmed by pollution is impossible, which means that each firm uses process *A*, the least costly of the five. Each firm emits 4 tons of pollution per day, for a total of 8 tons of pollution per day.

The government is considering two options for reducing total emissions by half. One is to require each firm to curtail its emissions by half. The other is to set a tax of $\$T$ per ton of smoke emitted each day. How large must T be to curtail emissions by half? What would be the total cost to society under each alternative?

If each firm is required to cut pollution by half, each must switch from process *A* to process *C*. The result will be 2 tons per day of pollution for each firm. The cost of the switch for Sludge Oil will be \$600 per day − \$100 per day = \$500 per day. The cost to Northwest Lumber will be \$380 per day − \$300 per day = \$80 per day, for a total cost of \$580 per day.

Consider now how each firm would react to a tax of $\$T$ per ton of pollution. If a firm can cut pollution by 1 ton per day, it will save $\$T$ per day in tax payments. Whenever the cost of cutting a ton of pollution is less than $\$T$, then, each firm has an incentive to switch to a cleaner process. For example, if the tax were set at \$40 per ton, Sludge Oil would stick with process *A* because switching to process *B* would cost \$100 per day extra but would save only \$40 per day in taxes. Northwest Lumber, however, would switch to process *B* because the \$40 saving in taxes would be more than enough to cover the \$20 cost of switching.

The problem is that a \$40 per day tax on each ton of pollution results in a reduction of only 1 ton per day, 3 short of the 4-ton target. Suppose instead that the government imposed a tax of \$101 per ton. Sludge Oil would then adopt process *B* because the \$100 extra daily cost of doing so would be less than the \$101 saved in taxes. Northwest Lumber would adopt process *D* because, for every process up to and including *C*, the cost of switching to the next process would be less than the resulting tax saving.

Overall, then, a tax of \$101 per ton would result in the desired pollution reduction of 4 tons per day. The total cost of the reduction would be only \$280 per day (\$100 per day for Sludge Oil and \$180 per day for Northwest Lumber), or \$300 per day less than when each firm was required to cut its pollution by half. (The taxes paid by the firms do not constitute a cost of pollution reduction because the money can be used to reduce whatever taxes would otherwise need to be levied on citizens.) ◆

EXERCISE 11.3

In the example above, if the tax were \$61 per ton of pollution emitted each day, which production processes would the two firms adopt?

The advantage of the tax approach is that it concentrates pollution reduction in the hands of the firms that can accomplish it at least cost. Requiring each firm to cut emissions by the same proportion ignores the fact that some firms can reduce pollution much more cheaply than others. Note that under the tax approach, the cost of the last ton of smoke removed is the same for each firm, so the efficiency condition is satisfied.

One problem with the tax approach is that unless the government has detailed knowledge about each firm's cost of reducing pollution, it cannot know how high to set the pollution tax. A tax that is too low will result in too much pollution, while a tax that is too high will result in too little. Of course, the government could start by setting a low tax rate and gradually increase the rate until pollution is reduced to the target level. But because firms often incur substantial sunk costs when they switch from one process to another, that approach might be even more wasteful than requiring all firms to cut their emissions by the same proportion.

AUCTIONING POLLUTION PERMITS

Another alternative is to establish a target level for pollution and then auction off permits to emit that level. The virtues of this approach are illustrated in the following example.

How much will pollution permits sell for?

Two firms, Sludge Oil and Northwest Lumber, again have access to the production processes described earlier (which are reproduced in Table 11.2). The government's goal is to cut the current level of pollution, 8 tons per day, by half. To do so, the government auctions off four permits, each of which entitles the bearer to emit 1 ton of smoke per day. No smoke may be emitted without a permit. What price will the pollution permits fetch at auction, how many permits will each firm buy, and what will be the total cost of the resulting pollution reduction?

TABLE 11.2
Costs and Emissions for Different Production Processes

Process (smoke)	A (4 tons/day)	B (3 tons/day)	C (2 tons/day)	D (1 ton/day)	E (0 tons/day)
Cost to Sludge Oil ($/day)	100	200	600	1,300	2,300
Cost to Northwest Lumber ($/day)	300	320	380	480	700

If Sludge Oil has no permits, it must use process *E*, which costs $2,300 per day to operate. If it had one permit, it could use process *D*, which would save it $1,000 per day. Thus, the most Sludge Oil would be willing to pay for a single 1-ton pollution permit is $1,000 per day. With a second permit, Sludge Oil could switch to process *C* and save another $700 per day; with a third permit, it could switch to process *B* and save another $400; and with a fourth permit, it could switch to process *A* and save another $100. Using similar reasoning, we can see that Northwest Lumber would pay up to $220 for one permit, up to $100 for a second, up to $60 for a third, and up to $20 for a fourth.

Suppose the government starts the auction at a price of $90. Sludge Oil will then demand four permits and Northwest Lumber will demand two, for a total demand of six permits. Since the government wishes to sell only four permits, it will keep raising the price until the two firms together demand a total of only four permits. Once the price reaches $101, Sludge Oil will demand three permits and Northwest Lumber will demand only one, for a total quantity demanded of four permits. Compared to the unregulated alternative, in which each firm used process *A*, the daily cost of the auction solution is $280: Sludge Oil spends $100 switching from process *A* to process *B*, and Northwest Lumber spends $180 switching from *A* to *D*. This total is $300 less than the cost of requiring each firm to reduce its emissions by half. (Again, the permit fees paid by the firms do not constitute a cost of cleanup because the money can be used to reduce taxes that would otherwise have to be collected.) ◆

The auction method has the same virtue as the tax method: It concentrates pollution reduction in the hands of those firms that can accomplish it at the lowest cost. But the auction method has other attractive features that the tax approach does not. First, it does not induce firms to commit themselves to costly investments that they will have to abandon if the cleanup falls short of the target level. And second, it allows private citizens a direct voice in determining where the emission level will be set. For example, any group that believes the pollution target is too lenient could raise money to buy permits at auction. By keeping those permits locked away in a safe, the group could ensure that they will not be used to emit pollution.

Several decades ago, when economists first proposed the auctioning of pollution permits, reactions of outrage were widely reported in the press. Most of those reactions amounted to the charge that the proposal would "permit rich firms to pollute to their hearts' content." Such an assertion betrays a total misunderstanding of the forces that generate pollution. Firms pollute not because they *want* to pollute but because dirty production processes are cheaper than clean ones. Society's only real interest is in keeping the total amount of pollution from becoming excessive, not in *who* actually does the polluting. And in any event, the firms that do most of the polluting under an auction system will not be rich firms, but those for whom pollution reduction is most costly.

Economists have argued patiently against these misinformed objections to the auction system, and their efforts have finally borne fruit. The sale of pollution permits is now common in several parts of the United States, and there is growing interest in the approach in other countries.

RECAP	USING PRICE INCENTIVES IN ENVIRONMENTAL REGULATION

An efficient program for reducing pollution is one for which the marginal cost of abatement is the same for all polluters. Taxing pollution has this desirable property, as does the auction of pollution permits. The auction method has the advantage that regulators can achieve a desired abatement target without having detailed knowledge of the abatement technologies available to polluters.

OVERCOMING OPPOSITION TO INTERNATIONAL TRADE

On April 13, 1861, Southern troops fired on Fort Sumter in Charleston harbor, initiating the American Civil War. Less than a week later, on April 19, President Lincoln proclaimed a naval blockade of the South. Code-named the Anaconda Plan (after the snake that squeezes its prey to death), the blockade required the Union navy to patrol the southern coastline, stopping and boarding ships that were attempting to land or depart. The object of the blockade was to prevent the Confederacy from shipping cotton to Europe, where it could be traded for military equipment, clothing, foodstuffs, and other supplies.

Historians are divided on the effectiveness of the Union blockade in choking off Confederate trade. In the early years of the war, the North had too few ships to cover the 3,600-mile southern coastline, so "running" the blockade was not difficult. But in the latter part of the war the number of Union ships enforcing the blockade increased from about 90 to over 600, and sailing ships were replaced with faster, more lethal ironclad vessels. Still, private blockade-runners—like the fictitious Rhett Butler in Margaret Mitchell's novel *Gone with the Wind*—attempted to elude the Union navy in small, fast ships. Because the price of raw cotton in Great Britain was between 10 and 20 times what it was in the Confederacy (a differential that indicated disruption in the normal flow of trade), blockade-runners enjoyed huge profits when they were successful. But despite their efforts, by 1864 the southern war effort was seriously hampered by a lack of military equipment and supplies, at least in part as a result of the blockade.

The Everest Collection

"He appreciated the economic benefits of trade."

The use of a naval blockade as a weapon of war highlights a paradox in contemporary attitudes toward trade between nations. Presumably, an attempt by a foreign power to blockade U.S. ports would today be considered a hostile act that would elicit a strong response from the U.S. government. Yet one often hears politicians and others arguing that trade with other nations is harmful to the United States and should be restricted—in effect, that the United States should blockade its own ports! Despite support from President Clinton and virtually all professional economists, for example, many politicians opposed the 1993 signing of the North American Free Trade Agreement (NAFTA), which was intended to increase U.S. trade with Mexico and Canada, on the grounds that it might cost American jobs. Opponents of increased trade routinely attempt to disrupt meetings of the World Trade Organization, an international body set up to promote trade and enforce trade agreements. So is trade a good thing or not? And if it is, why does it sometimes face determined and even violent opposition?

Opposition is rooted in the fact that although free trade benefits the economy as a whole, specific groups may suffer losses from it. If groups who are hurt by trade have sufficient political influence, they may be able to persuade politicians to enact policies that restrict the free flow of goods and services across borders.

To illustrate, suppose that Brazil has a comparative advantage in the production of coffee and the United States has a comparative advantage in the production of computers. When Brazil opens its computer market to international competition, Brazilian consumers enjoy a larger quantity of computers at a lower price. Clearly, Brazilian computer users benefit from the free trade in computers. In general, *domestic consumers of imported goods benefit from free trade.* However, Brazilian computer producers will not be so happy about opening their market to international competition. The fall in computer prices to the international level implies that less efficient domestic producers will go out of business, and that those who remain will earn lower profits. Unemployment in the Brazilian computer industry will rise and may persist over time, particularly if displaced computer workers cannot easily move to a new industry.[3] In general *domestic producers of imported goods are hurt by free trade.*

Consumers are helped, and producers hurt, when imports increase. The opposite conclusions apply for an increase in exports. In the example of Brazil, an opening of the coffee market raises the domestic price of coffee to the world price and creates the opportunity for Brazil to export coffee. Domestic producers of coffee benefit from the increased market (they can now sell coffee abroad as well as at home) and from the higher price of their product. In short, *domestic producers of exported goods benefit from free trade.* Brazilian coffee drinkers will be less enthusiastic, however, since they must now have to pay the higher world price of coffee, and can therefore consume less. *Thus, domestic consumers of exported goods are hurt by free trade.*

[3]The wages paid to Brazilian computer workers also will fall, reflecting the lower relative price of computers.

It is an iron law of politics that the losers from any policy change cry much louder than the winners sing. So even though proposals to open domestic markets to international trade promise to make the overall economic pie larger, it is no mystery that these proposals often attract fierce opposition.

The view that free trade is injurious and should be restricted is known as **protectionism.** Supporters of this view believe the government should attempt to "protect" domestic markets by raising legal barriers to imports. (Interestingly, protectionists rarely attempt to restrict exports, even though they hurt consumers of the exported good.) Two of the most common types of such barriers are *tariffs* and *quotas*. A **tariff** is a tax imposed on an imported good. A **quota** is a legal limit on the quantity of a good that may be imported.

protectionism the view that free trade is injurious and should be restricted

tariff a tax imposed on an imported good

quota a legal limit on the quantity of a good that may be imported

But the important point to remember is that although there are winners and losers from trade, the overall effect of trade is to make the total economic pie larger than before. And as the Efficiency Principle reminds us, when the economic pie grows larger, it is always possible for everyone to get a larger slice than before. In general, policies to assist those who are harmed by trade, such as assistance and retraining for workers idled by imports, are preferable to trade restrictions.

Efficiency

Competition from abroad is by no means the only reason that some groups of workers confront economic hardships. In the next section, we consider broader steps a country might take to promote economic security for all its citizens, even those who fare poorly in the marketplace.

RECAP | WINNERS AND LOSERS FROM TRADE

When countries open their borders to international trade, the expected result is an increase in the overall value of goods and services produced in every country. But the overall gains are not distributed equally across people in each country. The general pattern is that the consumers of imported goods and the producers of exported goods are most likely to be the biggest winners, while the domestic consumers of exported goods and the domestic producers of imported goods are most likely to suffer losses. Rather than protecting losers by using tariffs and quotas to restrict trade, it is generally better to permit trade and use part of the gains to compensate losers.

METHODS OF INCOME REDISTRIBUTION

The challenge is to find ways to raise the living standard of low-income people, without at the same time undermining their incentive to work, and without using scarce resources to subsidize those who are not poor. Of course, some people simply cannot work, or cannot find work that pays enough to live on. In a world of perfect information, the government could make generous cash payments to those people, and withhold support from those who can fend for themselves. In practice, however, the two groups are often hard to distinguish from each other. And so we must choose among imperfect alternative measures.

WELFARE PAYMENTS AND IN-KIND TRANSFERS

Cash transfers and in-kind transfers are at the forefront of antipoverty efforts around the globe. **In-kind transfers** are direct transfers of goods or services to low-income individuals or families, such as food stamps, public housing, subsidized school lunches, and Medicaid.

in-kind transfer a payment made not in the form of cash, but in the form of a good or service

From the mid-1960s until 1996, the most important federal program of cash transfers was Aid to Families with Dependent Children (AFDC), which in most cases provided cash payments to poor single-parent households. Critics of this program charged that the program ignored the Incentive Principle. AFDC created incentives that undermined family stability because a poor mother was ineligible for AFDC payments in many states if her husband or other able-bodied adult male lived with her and her children. This provision confronted many long-term unemployed fathers with an agonizing choice. They could leave their families, making them eligible for public assistance; or they could remain, making them ineligible. Even many who deeply loved their families understandably chose to leave.

Incentive

Concern about work incentives led Congress to pass the **Personal Responsibility Act** in 1996, abolishing the federal government's commitment to provide cash assistance to low-income families. The new law requires the federal government to make lump-sum cash grants to the states, which are then free to spend it on AFDC benefits or other income-support programs of their own design. For each welfare recipient, the new law also sets a five-year lifetime limit on receipt of benefits under the AFDC program.

Personal Responsibility Act the 1996 federal law that transferred responsibility for welfare programs from the federal level to the state level and placed a five-year lifetime limit on payment of AFDC benefits to any given recipient

Supporters of the Personal Responsibility Act argue that it has reduced the nation's welfare rolls substantially and that it will encourage greater self-reliance over the long run. Skeptics fear that denial of benefits may eventually impose severe hardships on poor children if overall economic conditions deteriorate even temporarily. Debate continues about the extent to which the observed rise in homelessness and malnutrition among the nation's poorest families during the economic downturn of 2001 and 2008 was attributable to the Personal Responsibility Act. What is clear, however, is that abolition of a direct federal role in the nation's antipoverty effort does not eliminate the need to discover efficient ways of providing assistance to people in need.

MEANS-TESTED BENEFIT PROGRAMS

Many welfare programs, including AFDC, are **means-tested,** which means that the more income a family has, the smaller are the benefits it receives under these programs. The purpose of means testing is to avoid paying benefits to those who don't really need them. But because of the way welfare programs are administered, means testing often has a pernicious effect on work incentives.

means-tested a benefit program whose benefit level declines as the recipient earns additional income

Consider, for example, an unemployed participant in four welfare programs: food stamps, rent stamps, energy stamps, and day care stamps. Each program gives him $100 worth of stamps per month, which he is then free to spend on food, rent, energy, and day care. If he gets a job, his benefits in each program are reduced by 50 cents for each dollar he earns. Thus, if he accepts a job that pays $50 per week, he will lose $25 in weekly benefits from each of the four welfare programs, for a total benefit reduction of $100 per week. Taking the job thus leaves him $50 per week worse off than before. Low-income persons need no formal training in economics to realize that seeking gainful employment does not pay under these circumstances.

What is more, means-tested programs of cash and in-kind transfers are extremely costly to administer. If the government were to eliminate all existing welfare and social service agencies that are involved in these programs, the resulting savings would be enough to lift every poor person out of poverty. One proposal to do precisely this is the negative income tax.

THE NEGATIVE INCOME TAX

Under the **negative income tax** (NIT), every man, woman, and child—rich or poor—would receive a substantial income tax credit, say $4,500 per year. A person who earns no income would receive this credit in cash. People who earn income would receive the same initial credit, and their income would continue to be taxed at some rate less than 100 percent.

negative income tax (NIT) a system under which the government would grant every citizen a cash payment each year, financed by an additional tax on earned income

The negative income tax would do much less than current programs to weaken work incentives because, unlike current programs, it would ensure that someone who earned an extra dollar would keep at least a portion of it. And because the program would be administered by the existing Internal Revenue Service, administrative costs would be far lower than under the current welfare system.

Despite these advantages, however, the negative income tax is by no means a perfect solution to the income-transfer problem. Although the incentive problem under the program would be less severe than under current welfare programs, it would remain a serious difficulty. To see why, note that if the negative income tax were the *sole* means of insulating people against poverty, the payment to people with no earned income would need to be at least as large as the government's official **poverty threshold.**

poverty threshold the level of income below which the federal government classifies a family as poor

The poverty threshold is the annual income level below which a family is officially classified as "poor" by the government. The threshold is based on government estimates of the cost of the so-called economy food plan, the least costly of four nutritionally adequate food plans designed by the Department of Agriculture. The department's 1955 Household Food Consumption Survey found that families of three or more people spent approximately one-third of their after-tax income on food, so the government pegs the poverty threshold at three times the cost of the economy food plan. In 2007, that threshold was approximately $20,600 for a family of four.

For a family of four living in a city, $20,600 a year is scarcely enough to make ends meet. But suppose a group of, say, eight families were to pool their negative tax payments and move to the mountains of northern New Mexico. With a total of $144,000 per year to spend, plus the fruits of their efforts at gardening and animal husbandry, such a group could live very nicely indeed.

Once a small number of experimental groups demonstrated the feasibility of quitting their jobs and living well on the negative income tax, others would surely follow suit. Two practical difficulties would ensue. First, as more and more people left their jobs to live at government expense, the program would eventually become prohibitively costly. And second, the political cost of the program would almost surely force supporters to abandon it long before that point. Reports of people living lives of leisure at taxpayers' expense would be sure to appear on the nightly news. People who work hard at their jobs all day long would wonder why their tax dollars were being used to support those who are capable of holding paying jobs, yet choose not to work. If the resulting political backlash did not completely eliminate the negative income tax program, it would force policymakers to cut back the payment so that members of rural communes could no longer afford to live comfortably. And that would mean the payment would no longer support an urban family. This difficulty has led policymakers to focus on other ways to increase the incomes of the working poor.

MINIMUM WAGES

The United States and many other industrialized countries have sought to ease the burden of low-wage workers by enacting minimum wage legislation—laws that prohibit employers from paying workers less than a specified hourly wage. The federal minimum wage in the United States is currently set at $5.85 per hour and slated to rise to $7.25 per hour by 2009.

At one point, economists were almost unanimous in their opposition to minimum wage laws, arguing that those laws reduce total economic surplus, as do other regulations that prevent markets from reaching equilibrium. In recent years, however, some economists have softened their opposition to minimum wage laws, citing studies that have failed to show significant reductions in employment following increases in minimum wage levels. These studies may well imply that, as a group, low-income workers are better off with minimum wage laws than without them. But as we saw in Chapter 7, any policy that prevents a market from reaching equilibrium causes a reduction in total economic surplus—which means society ought to be able to find a more effective policy for helping low-wage workers.

THE EARNED-INCOME TAX CREDIT

One such policy is the **earned-income tax credit** (EITC), which gives low-wage workers a credit on their federal income tax each year. The EITC was enacted into law in 1975, and in the years since has drawn praise from both liberals and conservatives. The program is essentially a wage subsidy in the form of a credit against the amount a family owes in federal income taxes. For example, a family of four with total earned income of $16,500 in 2006 would have received an annual tax credit of approximately $4,500 under this program. That is, the program would have reduced the annual federal income tax payment of this family by roughly that amount. Families who earned more would have received a smaller tax credit, with no credit at all for families earning more than $38,000. Families whose tax credit exceeds the amount of tax owed actually receive a check from the government for the difference. The EITC is thus essentially the same as a negative income tax, except that eligibility for the program is confined to people who work.

earned-income tax credit (EITC) a policy under which low-income workers receive credits on their federal income tax

Like both the negative income tax and the minimum wage, the EITC puts extra income into the hands of workers who are employed at low wage levels. But unlike the minimum wage, the earned-income tax credit creates no incentive for employers to lay off low-wage workers.

PUBLIC EMPLOYMENT FOR THE POOR

The main shortcoming of the EITC is that it does nothing for the unemployed poor. The negative income tax lacks that shortcoming but may substantially weaken work incentives. There is yet another method of transferring income to the poor that avoids both shortcomings. Government-sponsored jobs could pay wages to the unemployed poor for useful work. With public service employment, the specter of people living lives of leisure at public expense simply does not arise.

But public service employment has difficulties of its own. Evidence shows that if government jobs pay the same wages as private jobs, many people will leave their private jobs in favor of government jobs, apparently because they view government jobs as being more secure. Such a migration would make public service employment extremely expensive. Other worrisome possibilities are that such jobs might involve make-work tasks, and that they would prompt an expansion in government bureaucracy.

Acting alone, government-sponsored jobs for the poor, the EITC, or the negative income tax cannot solve the income-transfer problem. But a combination of these programs might do so.

A COMBINATION OF METHODS

Consider a negative income tax whose cash grant is far too small for anyone to live on, but that is supplemented if necessary by a public service job at below minimum wage. Keeping the wage in public service jobs well below the minimum wage would eliminate the risk of a large-scale exodus from private jobs. And while living well on either the negative income tax or the public service wage would be impossible, the two programs together could lift people out of poverty (see Figure 11.3).

To prevent an expansion of the bureaucracy, the government could solicit bids from private management companies to oversee the public service employment program. The fear that this program would inevitably become a make-work project is

Can unskilled workers perform useful public service jobs?

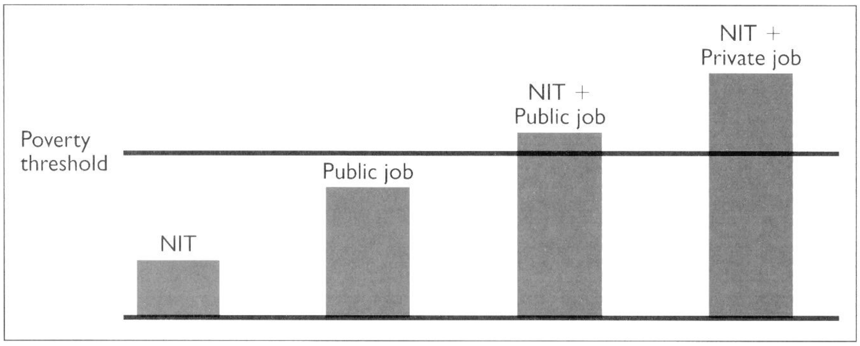

FIGURE 11.3
Income by Source in a Combination NIT–Jobs Program.
Together, a small negative income tax and a public job at below minimum wage would provide a family enough income to escape poverty, without weakening work incentives significantly.

allayed by evidence that unskilled workers can, with proper supervision, perform many valuable tasks that would not otherwise be performed in the private sector. They can, for example, do landscaping and maintenance in public parks; provide transportation for the elderly and those with disabilities; fill potholes in city streets and replace burned-out street lamps; transplant seedlings in erosion control projects; remove graffiti from public places and paint government buildings; recycle newspapers and containers; staff day care centers; and so on.

This combination of a small negative income tax payment and public service employment at a subminimum wage would not be cheap. But the direct costs of existing welfare programs are also large, and the indirect costs, in the form of perverse work incentives and misguided attempts to control prices, are even larger. In economic terms, dealing intelligently with the income-transfer problem may in fact prove relatively inexpensive, once society recognizes the enormous opportunity cost of failing to deal intelligently with it.

RECAP | METHODS OF INCOME REDISTRIBUTION

Minimum wage laws reduce total economic surplus by contracting employment. The earned-income tax credit boosts the incomes of the working poor without that drawback, but neither policy provides benefits for those who are not employed.

Other instruments in the battle against poverty include in-kind transfers such as food stamps, subsidized school lunches, Medicaid, and public housing as well as cash transfers such as Aid to Families with Dependent Children. Because benefits under most of these programs are means-tested, beneficiaries often experience a net decline in income when they accept paid employment.

SUMMARY

- Our aim in this chapter has been to apply basic microeconomic principles to a variety of government policy questions. These principles help to show how different methods of paying for health care affect the efficiency with which medical services are delivered. In the case of health care, the gains from marginal cost pricing can often be achieved through insurance policies with large deductibles. **LO1, LO2**
- An understanding of the forces that give rise to environmental pollution can help to identify those policy measures that will achieve a desired reduction in pollution at the lowest possible cost. Both the taxing of pollution and the sale of transferable pollution rights promote this goal. Each distributes the cost of the environmental cleanup effort so that the marginal cost of pollution abatement is the same for all polluters. **LO3**

- Although free trade is beneficial to the economy as a whole, some groups—such as domestic producers of imported goods—are hurt by free trade. Because free trade is efficient, the winners from free trade should be able to compensate the losers so that everyone becomes better off. Thus, policies to assist those who are harmed by trade, such as assistance and retraining for workers idled by imports, are usually preferable to trade restrictions. **LO4**

- Policies and programs for reducing poverty include minimum wage laws, the earned-income tax credit, food stamps, subsidized school lunches, Medicaid, public housing, and Aid to Families with Dependent Children. Of these, all but the earned-income tax credit fail to maximize total economic surplus, either by interfering with work incentives or by preventing markets from reaching equilibrium. **LO5**

- The negative income tax works much like the earned-income tax credit, except that it includes those who are not employed. A combination of a small negative income tax and access to public service jobs at subminimum wages could ensure adequate living standards for the poor without significantly undermining work incentives. **LO5**

KEY TERMS

earned-income tax credit (EITC) (313)
first-dollar insurance coverage (302)
health maintenance organization (HMO) (302)
in-kind transfer (310)
means-tested (311)
negative income tax (NIT) (311)
Personal Responsibility Act (311)
poverty threshold (312)
protectionism (310)
quota (310)
tariff (310)

REVIEW QUESTIONS

1. Why is vaccination against many childhood illnesses a legal requirement for entry into public schools? **LO1**
2. Why do economists believe that pollution taxes and effluent permits are a more efficient way to curb pollution than laws mandating across-the-board cutbacks? **LO3**
3. Why is first-dollar health care coverage inefficient? **LO2**
4. Suppose France has a comparative advantage in cheese production and England has a comparative advantage in bicycle manufacturing. How would you expect French bicycle manufactures and British dairy farmers to react to a proposal to reduce trade barriers between Britain and France? **LO4**
5. Why is a negative income tax, by itself, unlikely to be successful policy for maintaining the living standards of the poor? **LO5**

PROBLEMS

1. In the event he requires an appendectomy, David's demand for hospital accommodations is as shown in the diagram. David's current insurance policy fully covers the cost of hospital stays. The marginal cost of providing a hospital room is $150 per day. If David's only illness this year results in an appendectomy, how many days will he choose to stay in the hospital? **LO2**

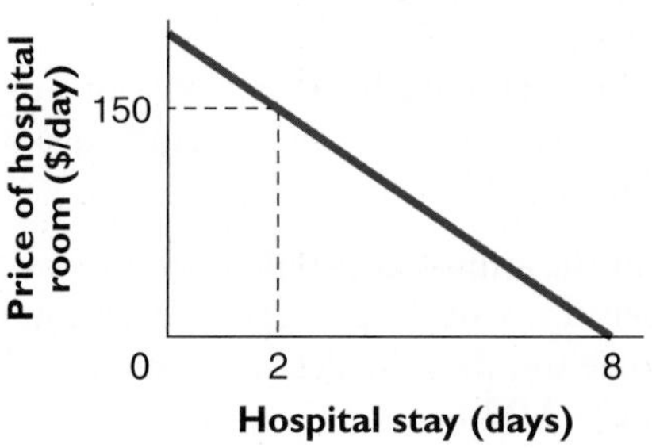

2. Refer to problem 1. By how much would total economic surplus have been higher this year if David's hospital insurance covered only the cost of hospital stays that exceed $1,000 per illness? **LO2**

3. Refer to problems 1 and 2. Suppose David's employer adopts a new health care plan that pays 50 percent of all medical expenses up to $1,000 per illness, with full coverage thereafter. How will economic surplus under this plan compare with economic surplus with the policy in problem 2? **LO2**

4. In Los Angeles, the demand for Botox injections (a procedure that removes wrinkles and smooths the skin) is as shown in the diagram. The marginal cost of a Botox injection is $1,000 and the procedure is not currently covered by health insurance. By how much will total economic surplus change if the city council passes a law requiring employers to include full reimbursement for Botox injections in their employees' health coverage? **LO2**

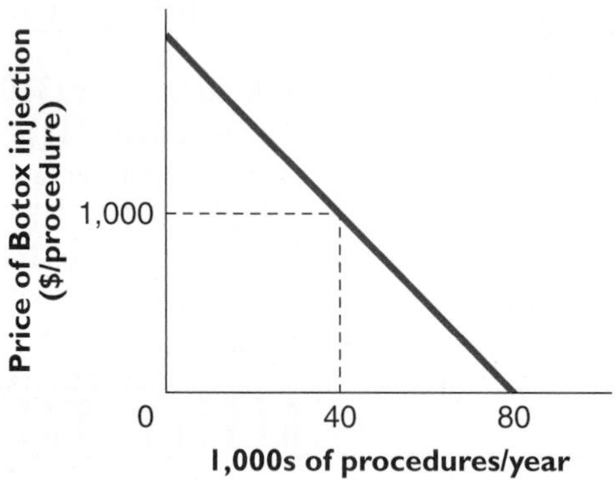

5. Refer to problem 4. How would the change in total economic surplus be affected if the law instead required health insurance to pay only $500 per procedure? **LO2**

6. Two firms, Sludge Oil and Northwest Lumber, have access to five production processes, each one of which has a different cost and gives off a different amount of pollution. The daily costs of the processes and the corresponding number of tons of smoke emitted are as shown in the following table: **LO6**

Process (smoke)	***A* (4 tons/day)**	***B* (3 tons/day)**	***C* (2 tons/day)**	***D* (1 ton/day)**	***E* (0 tons/day)**
Cost to Sludge Oil ($/day)	50	70	120	200	500
Cost to Northwest Lumber ($/day)	100	180	500	1,000	2,000

a. If pollution is unregulated, which process will each firm use, and what will be the daily smoke emission?

b. The City Council wants to curb smoke emissions by 50 percent. To accomplish this, it requires each firm to curb its emissions by 50 percent. What will be the total cost to society of this policy?

7. The City Council in the previous problem again wants to curb emissions by half. This time, it sets a tax of $\$T$ per day on each ton of smoke emitted. How large will T have to be to effect the desired reduction? What is the total cost to society of this policy? **LO3**

8. Refer to problem 7. Instead of taxing pollution, the city council decides to auction off four permits, each of which entitles the bearer to emit 1 ton of smoke per day. No smoke may be emitted without a permit. Suppose the government conducts the auction by starting at $1 and asking how many permits each firm wants to buy at that price. If the total is more than four, it then raises the price by $1 and asks again, and so on, until the total quantity of demanded permits falls to four. How much will each permit sell for in this auction? How many permits will each firm buy? What will be the total cost to society of this reduction in pollution? **LO3**

9. You are the president of Islandia, a small island nation that enjoys a comparative advantage in tourism. Trade representatives from the United States, which enjoys a comparative advantage in manufactured goods, have proposed a free trade agreement between the two countries. Manufacturing workers have opposed the agreement, arguing that Islandia should maintain its steep tariff on American manufactured goods. In an election, the union representing these workers has more enough votes to prevail over the union representing tourism workers. If you are determined to keep your job, how should you respond to the American proposal? **LO4**

ANSWERS TO IN-CHAPTER EXERCISES

11.1 With 50 percent coverage, David would have to pay $150 for each additional day in the hospital, so he would choose to stay for two days. **LO2**

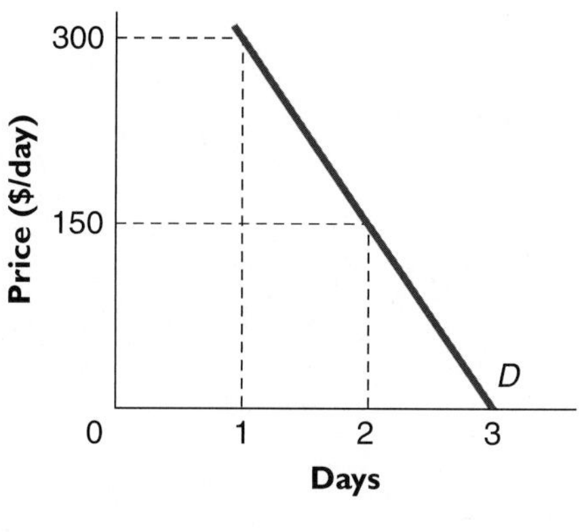

11.2 The optimal stay is still one day. If insurance reimburses $150 per day, then the marginal charge seen by David will be the remaining $150 per day, so he will stay two days. The cost to society of the additional day is $300 and the benefit to David of the extra day is only $225 (the area of the lower shaded figure). The loss in surplus from the additional day's stay is thus $75. **LO2**

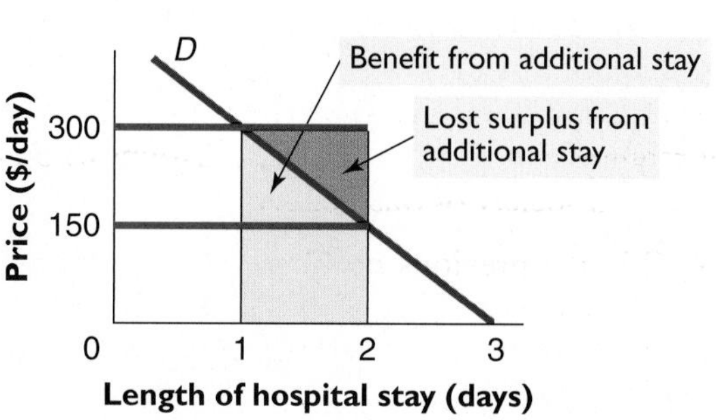

11.3 With a tax of $61 per ton each day, Sludge Oil would adopt process *A* and Northwest Lumber would adopt process *C*. **LO3**

Process (smoke)	*A* (4 tons/day)	*B* (3 tons/day)	*C* (2 tons/day)	*D* (1 ton/day)	*E* (0 tons/day)
Cost to Sludge Oil ($/day)	100	200	600	1,300	2,300
Cost to Northwest Lumber ($/day)	300	320	380	480	700

PART 5

MACROECONOMICS: DATA AND ISSUES

Physical scientists study the world at many different scales, ranging from the inner workings of the atom to the vast dimensions of the cosmos, and may apply different tools depending on the level of analysis. Similarly, an economic naturalist finds it very useful to be able to move back and forth between the small-scale, or "micro-" level, and the large-scale, or "macro-" level.

In Chapter 1, we discussed the differences between microeconomics, which is the study of individual choices and of group behavior in individual markets, and macroeconomics, which is the study of the performance of national economies and the policies that governments use to try to improve that performance. The chapters in this section begin our discussion of macroeconomics by introducing you to the central concepts and measurements used in the field. We begin in Chapter 12 with a discussion of gross domestic product (GDP), probably the most well-known but often misunderstood concept in macroeconomics. In addition to describing how GDP is constructed, we examine how U.S. GDP has grown over time and the ways in which it is (or is not) related to the economic well-being of the typical person.

Chapter 13 explains how economists measure the general level of prices in an economy, what we call the price level, and inflation. We also discuss the costs imposed on an economy by inflation, including the effects of inflation on interest rates. Chapter 14 studies long-term trends in the labor market from two perspectives. First, we analyze five significant labor market trends in real wages and employment opportunities around the world. Second, we carefully work through how economists measure employment and unemployment in real-world economies.

Throughout this section and those that follow, we will connect the concepts and measurements we develop with some key macroeconomic issues and questions. These include the search for the factors that cause productivity to improve and living standards to rise over long periods of time in many countries while stagnating and even declining in others. Macroeconomists also study shorter-term fluctuations in the economy (called recessions and expansions), the causes of unemployment and inflation, and the consequences of economic interdependence among nations, among other topics. Finally, we will begin to consider macroeconomic policies—government actions to improve the performance of the economy—since these are of particular concern to macroeconomists. As you will learn in the sections to come, the quality of macroeconomic policymaking is an important determinant of a nation's economic health.

CHAPTER 12

Spending, Income, and GDP

LEARNING OBJECTIVES

After reading this chapter, you should be able to:

1. Explain how economists define and measure an economy's output.
2. Use the expenditure method for measuring GDP to analyze economic activity.
3. Define and compute nominal GDP and real GDP.
4. Discuss the relationships between real GDP and economic well-being.

"Nonfarm payrolls grew at a 2 percent rate in the third quarter . . ."

"The Dow Jones Industrial Average closed up 93 points yesterday in moderate trading . . ."

"Inflation appears subdued as the consumer price index registered an increase of only 0.2 percent last month . . ."

"The unemployment rate last month rose to 5.8 percent, its highest level since . . ."

News reports like these fill the airwaves—some TV and radio stations carry nothing else. In fact, all kinds of people are interested in economic data. The average person hopes to learn something that will be useful in a business decision, a financial investment, or a career move. The professional economist depends on economic data in much the same way that a doctor depends on a patient's vital signs—pulse, blood pressure, and temperature—to make an accurate diagnosis. To understand economic developments and to be able to give useful advice to policymakers, businesspeople, and financial investors, an economist simply must have up-to-date, accurate data. Political leaders and policymakers also need economic data to help them in their decisions and planning.

Interest in measuring the economy, and attempts to do so, date back as far as the mid-seventeenth century, when Sir William Petty (1623–1687) conducted a detailed survey of the land and wealth of Ireland. Not until the twentieth century, though, did economic measurement come into its own. World War II was an important catalyst for the development of accurate economic statistics since its very outcome was thought to depend on the mobilization of economic resources. Two economists—Simon Kuznets in the United States and Richard Stone in the United Kingdom—developed comprehensive systems for measuring a nation's output of goods and services, which were of great help to Allied leaders in their wartime planning. Kuznets and Stone each received a Nobel Prize in economics for their work, which became the basis for the economic accounts used today by almost all the world's countries. The governments of the United States and many other countries now collect and publish a wealth of statistics covering all aspects of their economies.

Beginning with this chapter, we will discuss how economists measure three basic macroeconomic variables that arise frequently in analyses of the state of the economy: *gross domestic product,* or *GDP;* the *rate of inflation;* and the *rate of unemployment.* The focus of this chapter is on GDP, which measures the overall level of economic activity in a country. The next two chapters spotlight inflation and unemployment, respectively.

Measuring economic activity might sound like a straightforward and uncontroversial task, but that is not the case. Indeed, GDP has been criticized on many grounds. Some critics have complained that GDP does not adequately reflect factors such as the effect of economic growth on the environment or the rate of resource depletion. Because of problems like these, they charge, policies based on GDP statistics are likely to be flawed. By the end of this chapter, you will understand how official measures of output are constructed and used and will have gained some insight into these debates over their accuracy. Understanding the strengths and limitations of economic data is the first critical step toward becoming an intelligent user of economic statistics, as well as a necessary background for the economic analysis in the chapters to come.

GROSS DOMESTIC PRODUCT: MEASURING THE NATION'S OUTPUT

The most frequently used measure of an economy's output is called the *gross domestic product,* or *GDP.* GDP is intended to measure how much an economy produces in a given period, such as a quarter (three months) or a year. More precisely, **gross domestic product (GDP)** is the market value of the final goods and services produced in a country during a given period. To understand this definition, let's take it apart and examine each of its parts separately. The first key phrase in the definition is "market value."

gross domestic product (GDP) the market value of the final goods and services produced in a country during a given period

MARKET VALUE

A modern economy produces many different goods and services, from dental floss (a good) to acupuncture (a service). Macroeconomists are not interested in this kind of detail, however; rather, their goal is to understand the behavior of the economy as a whole. For example, a macroeconomist might ask, Has the overall capacity of the economy to produce goods and services increased over time? If so, by how much?

To be able to talk about concepts like the "total output" or "total production"—as opposed to the production of specific items like dental floss—economists need to *aggregate* the quantities of the many different goods and services into a single number. They do so by adding up the *market values* of the different goods and services the economy produces. A simple example will illustrate the process. In the imaginary economy of Orchardia, total production is 4 apples and 6 bananas. To find the total output of Orchardia, we could add the number of apples to the number of bananas and conclude that total output is 10 pieces of fruit. But what if this economy also produced 3 pairs of shoes? There really is no sensible way to add apples and bananas to shoes.

Suppose, though, that we know that apples sell for \$0.25 each, bananas for \$0.50 each, and shoes for \$20.00 a pair. Then the market value of this economy's production, or its GDP, is equal to

$$(4 \text{ apples} \times \$0.25/\text{apple}) + (6 \text{ bananas} \times \$0.50/\text{banana}) + (3 \text{ pairs of shoes} \times \$20.00/\text{pair}) = \$64.00.$$

Notice that when we calculate total output this way, the more expensive items (the shoes) receive a higher weighting than the cheaper items (the apples and bananas). In general, the amount people are willing to pay for an item is an indication of the economic benefit they expect to receive from it (see Chapter 3). For this reason, higher-priced items should count for more in a measure of aggregate output.

Orchardia's GDP

Suppose Orchardia were to produce 3 apples, 3 bananas, and 4 pairs of shoes at the same prices as in the preceding text. What is its GDP now?

Now the Orchardian GDP is equal to

$$(3 \text{ apples} \times \$0.25/\text{apple}) + (3 \text{ bananas} \times \$0.50/\text{banana}) + (4 \text{ pairs of shoes} \times \$20.00/\text{pair}) = \$82.25.$$

Notice that Orchardian GDP is higher in this case even though two of the three goods (apples and bananas) are being produced in smaller quantities than before. The reason is that the good whose production has increased (shoes) is much more valuable than the goods whose production has decreased (apples and bananas). ◆

EXERCISE 12.1

Suppose Orchardia produces the original quantities of the three goods at the same prices as above. In addition, it produces 5 oranges at \$0.30 each. What is the GDP of Orchardia now?

EXERCISE 12.2

Following are data for May 2008 on U.S. sales of passenger cars and other light vehicles (a category that includes minivans, light trucks, and sports utility vehicles). The data are broken down into two categories: U.S. auto producers (GM, Ford, and Chrysler) and foreign-owned plants (such as Honda, Toyota, and BMW). Suppose the average selling price is \$25,000 for passenger cars and \$30,000 for other light vehicles.

	Passenger cars	Other light vehicles
U.S. producers	247,269	365,400
Foreign-owned plants	270,130	115,347

Compare the output of U.S. producers to that of foreign-owned plants in terms of both the total number of vehicles produced and their market values (contribution to GDP). Explain why the two measures give different impressions of the relative importance of production by U.S.-owned and foreign-owned plants.

Market values provide a convenient way to add together, or aggregate, the many different goods and services produced in a modern economy. A drawback of using market values, however, is that not all economically valuable goods and services are bought and sold in markets. For example, the unpaid work of a homemaker, although it is of economic value, is not sold in markets and so isn't counted in GDP. But paid housekeeping and child care services, which are sold in markets, do count. This distinction can create some pitfalls, as the next example illustrates.

Women's labor force participation and GDP measurement

The percentage of adult American women working outside the home has increased dramatically in the past four decades, from less than 40 percent in 1960 to about 60 percent today (see Figure 12.1). This trend has led to a substantial increase in the demand for paid day care and housekeeping services, as working wives and mothers require more help at home. How have these changes affected measured GDP?

FIGURE 12.1
Percentages of American Men and Women over Age 16 Working Outside the Home, 1960–2006.
The fraction of American women working outside the home has risen by about 20 percentage points since 1960, while the fraction of men working outside the home has declined slightly.

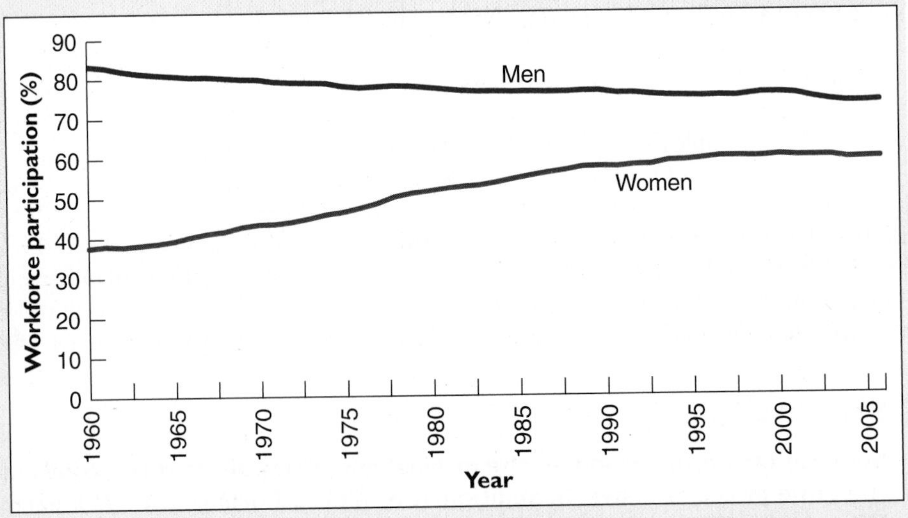

SOURCE: *Economic Report of the President*, February 2007, Table B-39 (http://www.gpoaccess.gov/eop/).

The entry of many women into the labor market has raised measured GDP in two ways. First, the goods and services that women produce in their new jobs have contributed directly to increasing GDP. Second, the fact that paid workers took over previously unpaid housework and child care duties has increased measured GDP by the amount paid to those workers. The first of these two changes represents a genuine increase in economic activity, but the second reflects a transfer of existing economic activities from the unpaid sector to the market sector. Overall, then, the increase in measured GDP associated with increased participation in the labor force by women probably overstates the actual increase in economic activity. ◆

Example 12.1
THE ECONOMIC NATURALIST

Why has female participation in the labor market increased by so much? What explains the trends illustrated in Figure 12.1?

In a world governed only by economic principles—without social conventions, customs, or traditions—homemaking tasks like cleaning, cooking, and child rearing would be jobs like any other. As such, they would be subject to the principle of comparative advantage: Those people (either men or women) whose comparative advantage lay in performing homemaking tasks would specialize in them, freeing people whose comparative advantage lies elsewhere to work outside the home. In other words, homemaking tasks would be done by those with the lowest opportunity cost in those tasks. In such a world, to see a woman with a medical degree doing housework would be very unusual—her opportunity cost of doing housework would be too high.

But, of course, we don't live in a world driven only by economic considerations. Traditionally, social custom has severely limited the economic opportunities of women (and in some societies still does). However, social restrictions on women have weakened considerably over the past century, particularly in the industrialized countries, as a result of the increased educational attainment of women, the rise of the feminist movement, and other factors. As traditional social restraints on women have loosened, domestic arrangements have moved in the direction dictated by comparative advantage—to an increasing degree, homemaking tasks are now performed by paid specialists, while the majority of women (and men) work outside the home. ●

Comparative Advantage

Why is the female labor force participation rate now more than 50 percent greater than in the 1960s?

Although homemaking activities are excluded from measured GDP, in a few cases goods and services that are not sold in markets are included in GDP. By far the most important are the goods and services provided by federal, state, and local governments. The protection provided by the army and navy, the transportation convenience of the interstate highway system, and the education provided by public school systems are examples of publicly provided goods and services that are not sold in markets. As market prices for publicly provided goods and services do not exist, economic statisticians add to the GDP the *costs* of providing those goods and services as rough measures of their economic value. For instance, to include public education in the GDP, the statisticians add to GDP the salaries of teachers and administrators, the costs of textbooks and supplies, and the like. Similarly, the economic value of the national defense establishment is approximated, for the purposes of measuring GDP, by the *costs* of defense: the pay earned by soldiers and sailors, the costs of acquiring and maintaining weapons, and so on.

With a few exceptions, like publicly provided goods and services, GDP is calculated by adding up market values. However, not all goods and services that have a market value are counted in GDP. As we will see next, GDP includes only those goods and services that are the end products of the production process, called *final goods and services.* Goods and services that are used up in the production process are not counted in GDP.

FINAL GOODS AND SERVICES

Many goods are used in the production process. Before a baker can produce a loaf of bread, grain must be grown and harvested, then the grain must be ground into flour, and, together with other ingredients, baked into bread. Of the three major goods that are produced during this process—the grain, the flour, and the bread—only the bread is used by consumers. Because producing the bread is the ultimate purpose of the process, the bread is called a *final good.* In general, a **final good or service** is the end product of a process, the product or service that consumers actually use. The goods or services produced on the way toward making the final product—here, the grain and the flour—are called **intermediate goods or services.**

final goods or services goods or services consumed by the ultimate user; because they are the end products of the production process, they are counted as part of GDP

intermediate goods or services goods or services used up in the production of final goods and services and therefore not counted as part of GDP

Since we are interested in measuring only those items that are of direct economic value, *only final goods and services are included in GDP.* Intermediate goods and services are *not* included. To illustrate, suppose that the grain from the previous example has a market value of $0.50 (the price the milling company paid for the grain). The grain is then ground into flour, which has a market value of $1.20 (the price the baker paid for the flour). Finally, the flour is made into a loaf of fine French bread, worth $2.00 at the local store. In calculating the contribution of these activities to GDP, would we want to add together the values of the grain, the flour, and the bread? No. This would incorrectly measure GDP as \$.50 + \$1.20 + \$2.00 = \$3.70. The value of the grain would then be counted three times: once as grain, then as part of the value of the flour, and finally as part of the value of the bread. The grain and flour are valuable only because they are intermediate goods that can be used to make bread. Since their value is included in the \$2.00 value of the final product, the loaf of bread, the total contribution to GDP is \$2.00.

The following example illustrates the same distinction but this time with a focus on services.

The barber and his assistant

Your barber charges \$10 for a haircut. In turn, the barber pays his assistant \$2 per haircut in return for sharpening the scissors, sweeping the floor, and other chores. For each haircut given, what is the total contribution of the barber and his assistant, taken together, to GDP?

The answer to this problem is \$10, the price, or market value, of the haircut. The haircut is counted in GDP because it is the final service, the one that actually has value to the final user. The services provided by the assistant have value only because they contribute to the production of the haircut. Their \$2 value is included in the \$10 price of the haircut. ◆

Our next example demonstrates that the same good can be either intermediate or final, depending on how it is used.

A good that can be either intermediate or final

Farmer Brown produces \$100 worth of milk. He sells \$40 worth of milk to his neighbors and uses the rest to feed his pigs, which he sells to his neighbors for \$120. What is Farmer Brown's contribution to the GDP?

The final goods in this example are the \$40 worth of milk and the \$120 worth of pigs sold to the neighbors. Adding \$40 and \$120, we get \$160, which is Farmer Brown's contribution to the GDP. Note that part of the milk Farmer Brown produced serves as an intermediate good and part as a final good. The \$60 worth of milk that is fed to the pigs is an intermediate good, and so it is not counted in GDP. The \$40 worth of milk sold to the neighbors is a final good, and so it is counted. ◆

capital good a long-lived good that is used in the production of other goods and services

A special type of good that is difficult to classify as intermediate or final is a capital good. A **capital good** is a long-lived good that is used in the production of other goods or services. Factories and machines are examples of capital goods. Houses and apartment buildings, which produce dwelling services, are also a form of capital good. Capital goods do not fit the definition of final goods since their purpose is to produce other goods. On the other hand, they are not used up during the production process, except over a very long period, so they are not exactly intermediate goods either. For purposes of measuring GDP, economists have agreed to classify newly produced capital goods as final goods even though they are not consumed by the ultimate user. Otherwise, a country that invested in its future by building modern factories and buying new machines would be counted as having a lower GDP than a country that devoted all its resources to producing consumer goods.

We have established the rule that only final goods and services (including newly produced capital goods) are counted in GDP. Intermediate goods and services, which are used up in the production of final goods and services, are not counted. In practice, however, this rule is not easy to apply because the production process often stretches over several periods. To illustrate, recall the earlier example of the grain that was milled into flour, which in turn was baked into a loaf of French bread. The contribution of the whole process to GDP is $2, the value of the bread (the final product). Suppose, though, that the grain and the flour were produced near the end of the year 2008 and the bread was baked early the next year in 2009. In this case, should we attribute the $2 value of the bread to the GDP for the year 2008 or to the GDP for the year 2009?

Neither choice seems quite right since part of the bread's production process occurred in each year. Part of the value of the bread should probably be counted in the year 2008 GDP and part in the year 2009 GDP. But how should we make the split? To deal with this problem, economists determine the market value of final goods and services indirectly, by adding up the *value added* by each firm in the production process. The **value added** by any firm equals the market value of its product or service minus the cost of inputs purchased from other firms. As we'll see, summing the value added by all firms (including producers of both intermediate and final goods and services) gives the same answer as simply adding together the value of final goods and services. But the value-added method eliminates the problem of dividing the value of a final good or service between two periods.

value added for any firm, the market value of its product or service minus the cost of inputs purchased from other firms

To illustrate this method, let's revisit the example of the French bread, which is the result of multiple stages of production. We have already determined that the total contribution of this production process to GDP is $2, the value of the bread. Let's show now that we can get the same answer by summing value added. Suppose that the bread is the ultimate product of three corporations: ABC Grain Company, Inc., produces grain; General Flour produces flour; and Hot'n'Fresh Baking produces the bread. If we make the same assumptions as before about the market value of the grain, the flour, and the bread, what is the value added by each of these three companies?

ABC Grain Company produces $0.50 worth of grain, with no inputs from other companies, so ABC's value added is $0.50. General Flour uses $0.50 worth of grain from ABC to produce $1.20 worth of flour. The value added by General Flour is thus the value of its product ($1.20) less the cost of purchased inputs ($0.50), or $0.70. Finally, Hot'n'Fresh Baking buys $1.20 worth of flour from General Flour and uses it to produce $2.00 worth of bread. So the value added by Hot'n'Fresh is $0.80. These calculations are summarized in Table 12.1.

You can see that summing the value added by each company gives the same contribution to GDP, $2.00, as the method based on counting final goods and services only. Basically, the value added by each firm represents the portion of the value of the final good or service that the firm creates in its stage of production. Summing the value added by all firms in the economy yields the total value of final goods and services, or GDP.

TABLE 12.1
Value Added in Bread Production

Company	Revenues	− Cost of purchased inputs	= Value added
ABC Grain	$0.50	$0.00	$0.50
General Flour	$1.20	$0.50	$0.70
Hot'n'Fresh	$2.00	$1.20	$0.80
Total			$2.00

You also can see now how the value-added method solves the problem of production processes that bridge two or more periods. Suppose that the grain and flour are produced during the year 2008, but the bread is not baked until 2009. Using the value-added method, the contribution of this production process to the year 2008 GDP is the value added by the grain company plus the value added by the flour company, or \$1.20. The contribution of the production process to the year 2009 GDP is the value added by the baker, which is \$0.80. Thus, part of the value of the final product, the bread, is counted in the GDP for each year, reflecting the fact that part of the production of the bread took place in each year.

EXERCISE 12.3

Amy's card shop receives a shipment of Valentine's Day cards in December 2008. Amy pays the wholesale distributor of the cards a total of \$500. In February 2009 she sells the cards for a total of \$700. What are the contributions of these transactions to GDP in the years 2008 and 2009?

We have now established that GDP is equal to the market value of final goods and services. Let's look at the last part of the definition, "produced within a country during a given period."

PRODUCED WITHIN A COUNTRY DURING A GIVEN PERIOD

The word *domestic* in the term *gross domestic product* tells us that GDP is a measure of economic activity within a given country. Thus, only production that takes place within the country's borders is counted. For example, the GDP of the United States includes the market value of *all* cars produced within U.S. borders, even if they are made in foreign-owned plants (recall Exercise 12.2). However, cars produced in Mexico by a U.S.-based company like General Motors are *not* counted.

We have seen that GDP is intended to measure the amount of production that occurs during a given period such as the calendar year. For this reason, only goods and services that are actually produced during a particular year are included in the GDP for that year. The example and exercise below demonstrate this point.

The sale of a house and GDP

A 20-year-old house is sold to a young family for \$200,000. The family pays the real estate agent a 6 percent commission, or \$12,000. What is the contribution of this transaction to GDP?

Because the house was not produced during the current year, its value is *not* counted in this year's GDP. (The value of the house was included in the GDP 20 years earlier, the year the house was built.) In general, purchases and sales of existing assets such as old houses or used cars do not contribute to the current year's GDP. However, the \$12,000 fee paid to the real estate agent represents the market value of the agent's services in helping the family find the house and make the purchase. Since those services were provided during the current year, the agent's fee *is* counted in current-year GDP. ◆

EXERCISE 12.4

Lotta Doe sells 100 shares of stock in Benson Buggywhip for \$50 per share. She pays her broker a 2 percent commission for executing the sale. How does Lotta's transaction affect the current-year GDP?

RECAP	MEASURING GDP

Gross domestic product (GDP) equals

the market value

GDP is an aggregate of the market values of the many goods and services produced in the economy.

Goods and services that are not sold in markets, such as unpaid housework, are not counted in GDP. An important exception is goods and services provided by the government, which are included in GDP at the government's cost of providing them.

of final goods and services

Final goods and services—goods and services consumed by the ultimate user—are counted in GDP. By convention, newly produced capital goods, such as factories and machines, also are treated as final goods and are counted in GDP. Intermediate goods and services, which are used up in the production of final goods and services, are not counted.

In practice, the value of final goods and services is determined by the value-added method. The value added by any firm equals the firm's revenue from selling its product minus the cost of inputs purchased from other firms. Summing the value added by all firms in the production process yields the value of the final good or service.

produced within a country during a given period.

Only goods and services produced within a nation's borders are included in GDP.

Only goods and services produced during the current year (or the portion of the value produced during the current year) are counted as part of the current-year GDP.

THE EXPENDITURE METHOD FOR MEASURING GDP

GDP is a measure of the quantity of goods and services *produced* by an economy. But any good or service that is produced also will be *purchased* and used by some economic agent—a consumer buying Christmas gifts or a firm investing in new machinery, for example. For many purposes, knowing not only how much is produced, but who uses it and how, is important.

Economic statisticians divide the users of the final goods and services that make up the GDP for any given year into four categories: *households, firms, governments,* and the *foreign sector* (that is, foreign purchasers of domestic products). They assume that all the final goods and services that are produced in a country in a given year will be purchased and used by members of one or more of these four groups. Furthermore, the amounts that purchasers spend on various goods and services should be equal to the market values of those goods and services. As a result, GDP can be measured with equal accuracy by either of two methods: (1) adding up the market values of all the final goods and services that are produced domestically or (2) adding up the total amount spent by each of the four groups on final goods and services and subtracting spending on imported goods and services. The values obtained by the two methods will be the same.

Corresponding to the four groups of final users are four components of expenditure: consumption, investment, government purchases, and net exports. That is,

TABLE 12.2
Expenditure Components of U.S. GDP, 2007 (billions of dollars)

Consumption		**9,732.0**
Durable goods	1,079.6	
Nondurable goods	2,833.0	
Services	5,819.4	
Investment		**2,132.3**
Business fixed investment	1,483.2	
Residential investment	641.5	
Inventory investment	7.6	
Government purchases		**2,691.4**
Net exports		**−712.7**
Exports	1,640.3	
Imports	2,353.0	
Total: Gross domestic product		**13,843.0**

SOURCE: http://www.bea.gov.

households consume, firms invest, governments make government purchases, and the foreign sector buys the nation's exports. Table 12.2 gives the dollar values for each of these components for the U.S. economy in 2007. As the table shows, GDP for the United States in 2007 was about $13.8 trillion, roughly $45,000 per person. Detailed definitions of the components of expenditure, and their principal subcomponents, follow. As you read through them, refer to Table 12.2 to get a sense of the relative importance of each type of spending.

consumption expenditure, or consumption spending by households on goods and services such as food, clothing, and entertainment

Consumption expenditure, or simply **consumption,** is spending by households on goods and services such as food, clothing, and entertainment. Consumption expenditure is subdivided into three subcategories:

- *Consumer durables* are long-lived consumer goods such as cars and furniture. Note that new houses are not treated as consumer durables but as part of investment.
- *Consumer nondurables* are shorter-lived goods like food and clothing.
- *Services,* the largest single component of consumer spending, include everything from haircuts and taxi rides to legal, financial, and educational services.

investment spending by firms on final goods and services, primarily capital goods

Investment is spending by firms on final goods and services, primarily capital goods. Investment is divided into three subcategories:

- *Business fixed investment* is the purchase by firms of new capital goods such as machinery, factories, and office buildings. (Remember that for the purposes of calculating GDP, long-lived capital goods are treated as final goods rather than as intermediate goods.) Firms buy capital goods to increase their capacity to produce.
- *Residential investment* is construction of new homes and apartment buildings. Recall that homes and apartment buildings, sometimes called residential capital, are also capital goods. For GDP accounting purposes, residential investment is treated as an investment by the business sector, which then sells the homes to households.

- *Inventory investment* is the addition of unsold goods to company inventories. In other words, the goods that a firm produces but doesn't sell during the current period are treated, for accounting purposes, as if the firm had bought those goods from itself. (This convention guarantees that production equals expenditure.) Inventory investment can be positive or negative, depending on whether the value of inventories rises or falls over the course of the year.

People often refer to purchases of financial assets, such as stocks or bonds, as "investments." That use of the term is different from the definition we give here. A person who buys a share of a company's stock acquires partial ownership of the *existing* physical and financial assets controlled by the company. A stock purchase does not usually correspond to the creation of *new* physical capital, however, and so is not investment in the sense we are using the term in this chapter. We will generally refer to purchases of financial assets, such as stocks and bonds, as "financial investments," to distinguish them from a firm's investment in new capital goods such as factories and machines.

Government purchases are purchases by federal, state, and local governments of final goods, such as fighter planes, and services, such as teaching in public schools. Government purchases do *not* include *transfer payments,* which are payments made by the government in return for which no current goods or services are received. Examples of transfer payments (which, again, are *not* included in government purchases) are Social Security benefits, unemployment benefits, pensions paid to government workers, and welfare payments. Interest paid on the government debt is also excluded from government purchases.

government purchases purchases by federal, state, and local governments of final goods and services; government purchases do *not* include *transfer payments,* which are payments made by the government in return for which no current goods or services are received, nor do they include interest paid on the government debt

Net exports equal exports minus imports.

net exports exports minus imports

- *Exports* are domestically produced final goods and services that are sold abroad.
- *Imports* are purchases by domestic buyers of goods and services that were produced abroad. Since imports are included in consumption, investment, and government purchases but do not represent spending on domestic production, they must be subtracted. A shorthand way of adding exports and subtracting imports is to add net exports, which equal exports minus imports.

"My parents sent back all my stuff that came from China."

A country's net exports reflect the net demand by the rest of the world for its goods and services. Net exports can be negative, since imports can exceed exports in any given year. As Table 12.2 shows, the United States had significantly greater imports than exports in 2007.

The relationship between GDP and expenditures on goods and services can be summarized by an equation. Let

$$Y \equiv \text{gross domestic product, or output}$$
$$C \equiv \text{consumption expenditure}$$
$$I \equiv \text{investment}$$
$$G \equiv \text{government purchases}$$
$$NX \equiv \text{net exports.}$$

Using these symbols, we can write that GDP equals the sum of the four types of expenditure algebraically as

$$Y = C + I + G + NX.$$

Measuring GDP by production and by expenditure

An economy produces 1,000,000 automobiles valued at $15,000 each. Of these, 700,000 are sold to consumers, 200,000 are sold to businesses, 50,000 are sold to the government, and 25,000 are sold abroad. No automobiles are imported. The automobiles left unsold at the end of the year are held in inventory by the auto producers.

The market value of the production of final goods and services in this economy is 1,000,000 autos times $15,000 per auto, or $15 billion.

To measure GDP in terms of expenditure, we must add spending on consumption, investment, government purchases, and net exports. Consumption is 700,000 autos times $15,000, or $10.5 billion. Government purchases are 50,000 autos times $15,000, or $0.75 billion. Net exports are equal to exports (25,000 autos at $15,000, or $0.375 billion) minus imports (zero), so net exports are $0.375 billion.

But what about investment? Here we must be careful. The 200,000 autos that are sold to businesses, worth $3 billion, count as investment. But notice too that the auto companies produced 1,000,000 automobiles but sold only 975,000 (700,000 + 200,000 + 50,000 + 25,000). Hence, 25,000 autos were unsold at the end of the year and were added to the automobile producers' inventories. This addition to producer inventories (25,000 autos at $15,000, or $0.375 billion) counts as inventory investment, which is part of total investment. Thus, total investment spending equals the $3 billion worth of autos sold to businesses plus the $0.375 billion in inventory investment, or $3.375 billion.

Recapitulating, in this economy, consumption is $10.5 billion, investment (including inventory investment) is $3.375 billion, government purchases equal $0.75 billion, and net exports are $0.375 billion. Summing these four components of expenditure yields $15 billion—the same value for GDP that we got by calculating the market value of production. ◆

EXERCISE 12.5

Extending the previous example, suppose that 25,000 of the automobiles purchased by households are imported rather than domestically produced. Domestic production remains at 1,000,000 autos valued at $15,000 each. Once again, find GDP in terms of (a) the market value of production and (b) the components of expenditure.

RECAP	EXPENDITURE COMPONENTS OF GDP

GDP can be expressed as the sum of expenditures on domestically produced final goods and services. The four types of expenditure that are counted in the GDP, and the economic groups that make each type of expenditure, are as follows:

Type of expenditure?	Who makes the expenditure?	Examples
Consumption	Households	Food, clothes, haircuts, new cars
Investment	Business firms	New factories and equipment, new houses, increases in inventory stocks
Government purchases	Government	New school buildings, new military hardware, salaries of soldiers and government officials
Net exports, or exports minus imports	Foreign sector	Exported manufactured goods, legal or financial services provided by domestic residents to foreigners

GDP AND THE INCOMES OF CAPITAL AND LABOR

GDP can be thought of equally well as a measure of total production or as a measure of total expenditure—either method of calculating GDP gives the same final answer. There is yet a third way to think of GDP, which is as the *incomes of capital and labor.*

Whenever a good or service is produced or sold, the revenue from the sale is distributed to the workers and the owners of the capital involved in the production of the good or service. Thus, except for some technical adjustments that we will ignore, GDP also equals labor income plus capital income. *Labor income* (equal to about two-thirds of GDP) comprises wages, salaries, and the incomes of the self-employed. *Capital income* (about one-third of GDP) is made up of payments to owners of physical capital (such as factories, machines, and office buildings) and intangible capital (such as copyrights and patents). The components of capital income include items such as profits earned by businessowners, the rents paid to owners of land or buildings, interest received by bondholders, and the royalties received by the holders of copyrights or patents. Both labor income and capital income are to be understood as measured prior to payment of taxes; ultimately, of course, a portion of both types of income is captured by the government in the form of tax collections.

Figure 12.2 may help you visualize the three equivalent ways of thinking about GDP: the market value of production, the total value of expenditure, and the sum of labor income and capital income. The figure also roughly captures the relative importance of the expenditure and income components. About 70 percent of expenditure is consumption spending, about 20 percent is government purchases, and the rest is investment spending and net exports. (Actually, as Table 12.2 shows, net exports have been negative in recent years, reflecting the U.S. trade deficit.) As we mentioned, labor income is about two-thirds of total income, with capital income making up the rest.

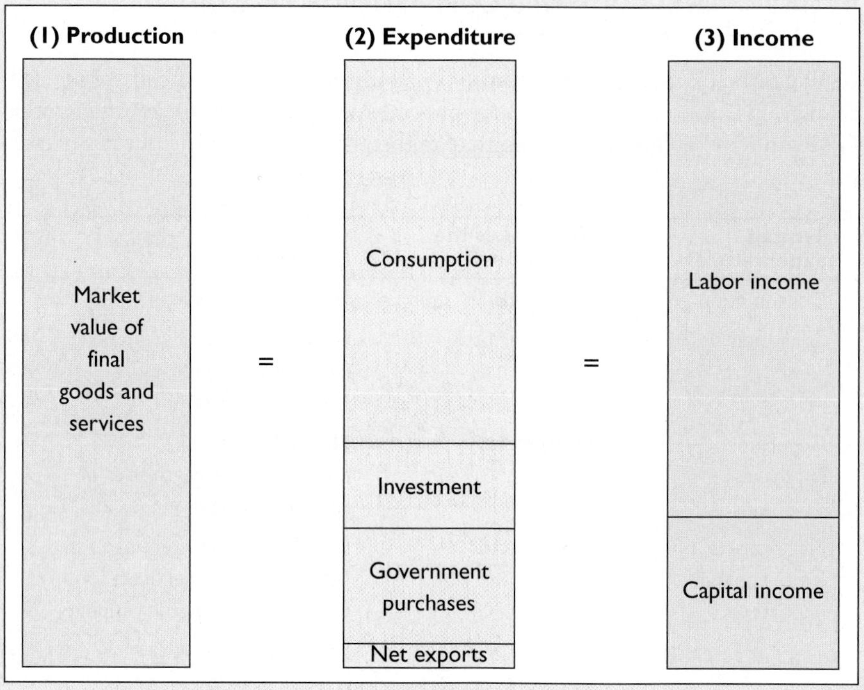

FIGURE 12.2
The Three Faces of GDP. The GDP can be expressed equally well as (1) the market value of production, (2) total expenditure (consumption, investment, government purchases, net exports), or (3) total income (labor income and capital income).

NOMINAL GDP VERSUS REAL GDP

As a measure of the total production of an economy over a given period, such as a particular year, GDP is useful in comparisons of economic activity in different places. For example, GDP data for the year 2007, broken down state by state, could be used to compare aggregate production in New York and California during that year. However, economists are interested in comparing levels of economic activity not only in different *locations* but *over time* as well. For instance, a president who is running for reelection on the basis of successful economic policies might want to know by how much output in the U.S. economy had increased during his term.

Using GDP to compare economic activity at two different points in time may give misleading answers, however, as the following example shows. Suppose, for the sake of illustration, that the economy produces only pizzas and calzones. The prices and quantities of the two goods in the years 2009 and 2013, the beginning and end of the president's term, are shown in Table 12.3. If we calculate GDP in each year as the market value of production, we find that the GDP for 2009 is (10 pizzas × \$10/pizza) + (15 calzones × \$5/calzone) = \$175. The GDP for 2013 is (20 pizzas × \$12/pizza) + (30 calzones × \$6/calzone) = \$420. Comparing the GDP for the year 2009 to the GDP for the year 2013, we might conclude that it is 2.4 times greater (\$420/\$175).

TABLE 12.3
Prices and Quantities in 2009 and 2013

	Quantity of pizzas	Price of pizzas	Quantity of calzones	Price of calzones
2009	10	\$10	15	\$5
2013	20	\$12	30	\$6

But look more closely at the data given in Table 12.3. Can you see what is wrong with this conclusion? The quantities of both pizzas and calzones produced in the year 2013 are exactly twice the quantities produced in the year 2009. If economic activity, as measured by actual production of both goods, exactly doubled over the four years, why do the calculated values of GDP show a greater increase?

The answer, as you also can see from the table, is that prices as well as quantities rose between 2009 and 2013. Because of the increase in prices, the *market value* of production grew more over those four years than the *physical volume* of production. So in this case, GDP is a misleading gauge of economic growth during the president's term, since the physical quantities of the goods and services produced in any given year, not the dollar values, are what determine people's economic well-being. Indeed, if the prices of pizzas and calzones had risen 2.4 times between 2009 and 2013 with no changes in the quantities and calzones produced, GDP would have risen 2.4 times as well, with no increase in physical production! In that case, the claim that the economy's (physical) output had more than doubled during the president's term would obviously be wrong.

As this example shows, if we want to use GDP to compare economic activity at different points in time, we need some method of excluding the effects of price changes. In other words, we need to adjust for inflation. To do so, economists use a common set of prices to value quantities produced in different years. The standard approach is to pick a particular year, called the *base year,* and use the prices from that year to calculate the market value of output. There is no particular rule about which year to choose as the base year, but it is usually some recent year. When GDP is calculated using the prices from a base year, rather than the current year's prices, it is called **real GDP,** to indicate that it is a measure of real physical production. Real GDP is GDP adjusted for inflation. To distinguish real GDP, in which quantities produced are valued at base-year prices, from GDP valued at current-year prices, economists refer to the latter measure as **nominal GDP.**

real GDP a measure of GDP in which the quantities produced are valued at the prices in a base year rather than at current prices; real GDP measures the actual *physical volume* of production

nominal GDP a measure of GDP in which the quantities produced are valued at current-year prices; nominal GDP measures the *current dollar value* of production

Calculating the change in real GDP over the president's term

Using data from Table 12.3 and assuming that 2009 is the base year, find real GDP for the years 2013 and 2009. By how much did real output grow between 2009 and 2013?

To find real GDP for the year 2013, we must value the quantities produced that year using the prices in the base year, 2009. Using the data in Table 12.3:

Year 2013 real GDP = (year 2013 quantity of pizzas × year 2009 price of pizzas) + (year 2013 quantity of calzones × year 2009 price of calzones)
= (20 × \$10) + (30 × \$5)
= \$350.

The real GDP of this economy in the year 2013 is \$350. What is the real GDP for 2009?

By definition, the real GDP for 2009 equals 2009 quantities valued at base-year prices. The base year in this example happens to be 2009, so real GDP for 2009 equals 2009 quantities valued at 2009 prices, which is the same as nominal GDP for 2009. In general, in the base year, real GDP and nominal GDP are the same. We already found nominal GDP for 2009, \$175, so that is also the real GDP for 2009.

We can now determine how much real production has actually grown over the four-year period. Since real GDP was \$175 in 2009 and \$350 in 2013, the physical volume of production doubled between 2009 and 2013. This conclusion makes good sense, since Table 12.3 shows that the production of both pizzas and calzones exactly doubled over the period. By using real GDP, we have eliminated the effects of price changes and obtained a reasonable measure of the actual change in physical production over the four-year span. ◆

Of course, the production of all goods will not necessarily grow in equal proportion, as in the previous example. Exercise 12.6 asks you to find real GDP when pizza and calzone production grow at different rates.

EXERCISE 12.6

Suppose production and prices of pizza and calzones in 2009 and 2013 are as follows:

	Quantity of pizzas	Price of pizzas	Quantity of calzones	Price of calzones
2009	10	$10	15	$5
2013	30	$12	30	$6

These data are the same as those in Table 12.3, except that pizza production has tripled rather than doubled between 2009 and 2013. Find real GDP in 2013 and 2009, and calculate the growth in real output over the four-year period. (Continue to assume that 2009 is the base year.)

If you complete Exercise 12.6, you will find that the growth in real GDP between 2009 and 2013 reflects a sort of average of the growth in physical production of pizzas and calzones. Real GDP therefore remains a useful measure of overall physical production, even when the production of different goods and services grows at different rates.

The method of calculating real GDP just described was followed for many decades by the Bureau of Economic Analysis (BEA), the U.S. government agency responsible for GDP statistics. However, in recent years the BEA has adopted a more complicated procedure of determining real GDP, called *chain weighting*. The new procedure makes the official real GDP data less sensitive to the particular base year chosen. However, the chain-weighting and traditional approaches share the basic idea of valuing output in terms of base-year prices, and the results obtained by the two methods are generally similar. Box 12.1 discusses chain weighting in more detail.

Example 12.2
THE ECONOMIC NATURALIST

Can nominal and real GDP ever move in different directions?

In most countries, both nominal and real GDP increase in almost every year. It is quite possible, however, for them to move in opposite directions. The last time this happened in the United States was 1990–1991. In that period real GDP using the year 2000 as a base year *fell* by 0.2 percent, from $7,113 billion to $7,101 billion. This reflected an overall reduction in the physical quantities of goods and services produced. Nominal GDP, however, rose by 3.3 percent, from $5,803 billion to $5,996 billion, during the same period because prices rose by more than quantities fell.

The preceding example also illustrates the fact that nominal GDP will be *less* than real GDP if prices during the current year are less than prices during the base year. This will generally be the case when the current year is earlier than the base year.

Could real GDP ever rise during a year in which nominal GDP fell? Once again, the answer is yes. This may occur in some (but not all) instances in which a country is experiencing economic growth and deflation (falling prices) at the same time. If the rate at which prices are falling (indicating deflation) is greater than the rate at which the production of physical quantities is rising, real GDP will rise and nominal GDP will decrease. This actually happened in Japan during several years in the 1990s. ●

BOX 12.1: CHAIN WEIGHTING

Students who are comfortable with square roots may find it interesting to see how *chain weighting* actually works. As the name implies, annual data are "linked" with data from adjacent years using what is called a geometric average. The ratio of real GDP in 2008 relative to real GDP in 2007 is calculated using prices from both 2007 and 2008 as follows:

Ratio of real GDP in 2008 relative to real GDP in 2007

$$= \sqrt{(\text{Ratio of real GDPs using 2007 prices})}\ \sqrt{(\text{Ratio of real GDPs using 2008 prices})}.$$

The first term, the ratio of real GDPs using 2007 prices, is equal to

$$\frac{\text{Year 2008 real GDP using 2007 prices}}{\text{Year 2007 real GDP using 2007 prices}}.$$

Recall that this calculation would first use 2007 prices to value the quantities produced in 2008. It would then divide this sum by the value of the quantities produced in 2007 using 2007 prices once again. (This, of course, also will equal nominal GDP in year 2007.) Suppose this ratio were 1.06.

The ratio of real GDPs using 2008 prices, on the other hand, is equal to

$$\frac{\text{Year 2008 real GDP using 2008 prices}}{\text{Year 2007 real GDP using 2008 prices}}.$$

This second calculation would first use 2008 prices to value the quantities produced in 2008. (This would also equal nominal GDP in 2008.) It would then divide this sum by the value of the quantities produced in 2007 using 2008 prices. Suppose this ratio were 1.03.

The chain-weighted ratio of real GDP between 2008 and 2007 would then equal the geometric average of these two ratios. In our example, this would equal

$$\sqrt{1.06}\sqrt{1.03} = 1.0449.$$

This would imply that real GDP grew by 4.49 percent between 2007 and 2008. (Note that this is very close to the simple arithmetic average of 4.5 percent.)

Recall that real GDP in the base year is equal to nominal GDP in that same year. Consequently, we can use the chain-weighted growth rates of real GDP in each successive year to compute the level of real GDP in each year.

RECAP **NOMINAL GDP VERSUS REAL GDP**

Real GDP is calculated using the prices of goods and services that prevailed in a base year rather than in the current year. Nominal GDP is calculated using current-year prices. Real GDP is GDP adjusted for inflation; it may be thought of as measuring the physical volume of production. Comparisons of economic activity at different times should always be done using real GDP, not nominal GDP.

REAL GDP IS NOT THE SAME AS ECONOMIC WELL-BEING

Figure 12.3 shows the level of real GDP in the United States from 1900 to 2007. Government policymakers pay close attention to these data, often behaving as if the higher the real GDP, the better. At best, it is an imperfect measure of economic well-being because, for the most part, it captures only those goods and services that are priced and sold in markets. Many factors that contribute to people's economic well-being are not priced and sold in markets and thus are largely or even entirely omitted from GDP. Maximizing real GDP is not, therefore, always the right goal for government policymakers. Whether or not policies that increase GDP will also make people better off has to be determined on a case-by-case basis.

FIGURE 12.3
Output of the U.S. Economy, 1900–2007.
The output of the U.S. economy has increased by more than 33 times since 1900 and by more than 6 times since 1950.

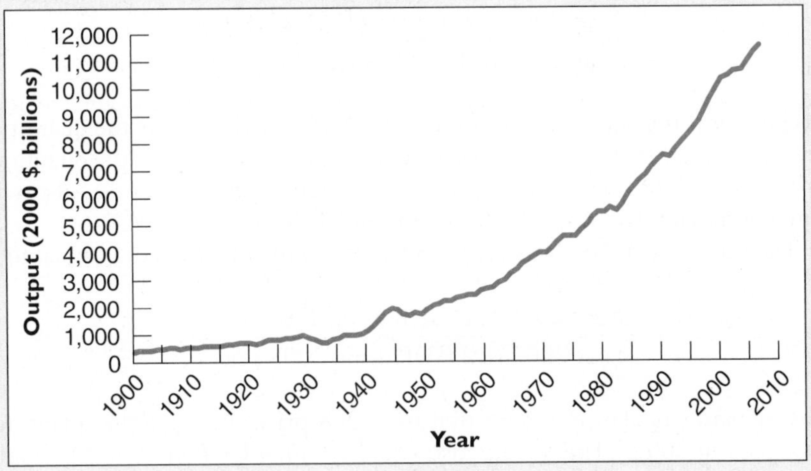

To understand why an increase in real GDP does not always promote economic well-being, let's look at some factors that are not included in GDP but do affect whether people are better off.

LEISURE TIME

Most Americans (and most people in other industrialized countries as well) work many fewer hours than their great-grandparents did 100 years ago. Early in the twentieth century, some industrial workers—steelworkers, for example—worked as many as 12 hours a day, 7 days a week. Today, the 40-hour workweek is typical. Today, Americans also tend to start working later in life (after college or graduate school), and, in many cases, they are able to retire earlier. The increased leisure time available to workers in the United States and other industrialized countries—which allows them to pursue many worthwhile activities, including being with family and friends, participating in sports and hobbies, and pursuing cultural and educational activities—is a major benefit of living in a wealthy society. These extra hours of leisure are not priced in markets, however, and therefore are not reflected in GDP.

Example 12.3
THE ECONOMIC NATURALIST

Why do people work fewer hours today than their great-grandparents did?

Americans start work later in life, retire earlier, and in many cases work fewer hours per week than people of 50 or 100 years ago.

The *opportunity cost* of working less—retiring earlier, for example, or working fewer hours per week—is the earnings you forgo by not working. If you can, say, make $400 per week at a summer job in a department store, then leaving the job two weeks early to take a trip with some friends has an opportunity cost of $800. The fact that people are working fewer hours today suggests that their opportunity cost of forgone earnings is lower than their grandparents' and great-grandparents' opportunity cost. Why this difference?

We can use the Cost-Benefit Principle to help us understand this phenomenon. Over the past century, rapid economic growth in the United States and other industrialized countries has greatly increased the purchasing power of the average worker's wages (see Chapter 14 for data on real wages). In other words, the typical worker today can buy more goods and services with his or her hourly earnings than ever before. This fact would seem to suggest that the opportunity cost of forgone earnings (measured in terms of what those earnings can buy) is greater, not smaller, today than in earlier times. But because the buying power of wages is so much higher today than in the past, Americans can achieve a reasonable standard of living by working fewer hours than they did in the past. Thus, while your grandparents may have had to work long hours to pay the rent or put food on the table, today the extra income from working long hours is more likely to buy relative luxuries, like nicer clothes or a fancier car. Because such discretionary purchases are easier to give up than basic food and shelter, the true opportunity cost of forgone earnings is lower today than it was 50 years ago. As the opportunity cost of leisure has fallen, Americans have chosen to enjoy more of it. ●

Cost-Benefit

EN 12

NONMARKET ECONOMIC ACTIVITIES

Not all economically important activities are bought and sold in markets; with a few exceptions, such as government services, nonmarket economic activities are omitted from GDP. We mentioned earlier the example of unpaid housekeeping services. Another example is volunteer services, such as the volunteer fire and rescue squads that serve many small towns. The fact that these unpaid services are left out of GDP does *not* mean that they are unimportant. The problem is that, because there are no market prices and quantities for unpaid services, estimating their market values is very difficult.

How far do economists go wrong by leaving nonmarket economic activities out of GDP? The answer depends on the type of economy being studied. Although nonmarket economic activities exist in all economies, they are particularly important in poor economies. For example, in rural villages of developing countries, people commonly trade services with each other or cooperate on various tasks without exchanging any money. Families in these communities also tend to be relatively self-sufficient, growing their own food and providing many of their own basic services (recall the many skills of the Nepalese cook Birkhaman, described in Chapter 2). Because such nonmarket economic activities are not counted in official statistics, GDP data may substantially understate the true amount of economic activity in the poorest countries. In 2005, according to the World Bank,[1] the official GDP per person in Nepal was about $340, an amount that seems impossibly low. Part of the explanation for this figure is that because the Nepalese seldom use formal markets, many economic activities that would ordinarily be included in GDP are excluded from it in Nepal.

Closely related to nonmarket activities is what is called the *underground economy,* which includes transactions that are never reported to government officials and data collectors. The underground economy encompasses both legal and illegal activities, from informal babysitting jobs to organized crime. For instance, some people pay temporary or part-time workers like housecleaners and painters in cash, which allows these workers to avoid paying taxes on their income. Economists who have tried to estimate the value of such services by studying how much cash the public holds have concluded that these sorts of transactions make up an important share of overall economic activity, even in advanced industrial economies.

[1]http://siteresources.worldbank.org/ICPINT/Resources/summary-tables.pdf.

ENVIRONMENTAL QUALITY AND RESOURCE DEPLETION

China has recently experienced tremendous growth in real GDP. But in expanding its manufacturing base, it also has suffered a severe decline in air and water quality. Increased pollution certainly detracts from the quality of life, but because air and water quality are not bought and sold in markets, the Chinese GDP does not reflect this downside of their economic growth.

The exploitation of finite natural resources also tends to be overlooked in GDP. When an oil company pumps and sells a barrel of oil, GDP increases by the value of the oil. But the fact that there is one less barrel of oil in the ground, waiting to be pumped sometime in the future, is not reflected in GDP.

A number of efforts have been made to incorporate factors like air quality and resource depletion into a comprehensive measure of GDP. Doing so is difficult, since it often involves placing a dollar value on intangibles, like having a clean river to swim in instead of a dirty one. But the fact that the benefits of environmental quality and resource conservation are hard to measure in dollars and cents does not mean that they are unimportant.

QUALITY OF LIFE

What makes a particular town or city an attractive place to live? Some desirable features you might think of are reflected in GDP: spacious, well-constructed homes, good restaurants and stores; a variety of entertainment; and high-quality medical services. However, other indicators of the good life are not sold in markets and so may be omitted from GDP. Examples include a low crime rate, minimal traffic congestion, active civic organizations, and open space. Thus, while some citizens of a community may oppose the construction of a new Wal-Mart because they believe it may have a negative effect on the quality of life, others may support it because Wal-Mart sells goods at lower prices and may increase local GDP.

POVERTY AND ECONOMIC INEQUALITY

GDP measures the *total* quantity of goods and services produced and sold in an economy, but it conveys no information about who gets to enjoy those goods and services. Two countries may have identical GDPs but differ radically in the distribution of economic welfare across the population. Suppose, for example, that in one country—call it Equalia—most people have a comfortable middle-class existence; both extreme poverty and extreme wealth are rare. But in another country, Inequalia—which has the same real GDP as Equalia—a few wealthy families control the economy, and the majority of the population lives in poverty. While most people would say that Equalia has a better economic situation overall, that judgment would not be reflected in the GDPs of the two countries, which are the same.

In the United States, absolute poverty has been declining. Today, many families whose income is below today's official "poverty line" (in 2008, $21,200 for a family of four) own a television, a car, and in some cases their own home. Some economists have argued that people who are considered poor today live as well as many middle-class people did in the 1950s.

But, though absolute poverty seems to be decreasing in the United States, inequality of income has generally been rising. The chief executive officer of a large U.S. corporation may earn hundreds of times what the typical worker in the same firm receives. Psychologists tell us that people's economic satisfaction depends not only on their absolute economic position—the quantity and quality of food, clothing, and shelter they have—but on what they have compared to what others have. If you own an old, beat-up car but are the only person in your neighborhood to have a car, you may feel privileged. But if everyone else in the neighborhood owns a luxury car, you are likely to be less satisfied. To the extent that such comparisons affect people's well-being, inequality matters as well as absolute poverty. Again, because GDP focuses on total production rather than on the distribution of output, it does not capture the effects of inequality.

BUT GDP IS RELATED TO ECONOMIC WELL-BEING

You might conclude from the list of important factors omitted from the official figures that GDP is useless as a measure of economic welfare. Indeed, numerous critics have made that claim. Clearly, in evaluating the effects of a proposed economic policy, considering only the likely effects on GDP is not sufficient. Planners must also ask whether the policy will affect aspects of economic well-being that are not captured in GDP. Environmental regulations may reduce production of steel, for example, which reduces the GDP. But that fact is not a sufficient basis on which to decide whether such regulations are good or bad. The right way to decide such questions is to apply the Cost-Benefit Principle: are the benefits of cleaner air worth more to people than the costs the regulations impose in terms of lost output and lost jobs? If so, then the regulations should be adopted; otherwise, they should not.

Cost-Benefit

Although looking at the effects of a proposed policy on real GDP is not the only basis on which to evaluate a policy, real GDP per person *does* tend to be positively associated with many things people value, including a high material standard of living, better health and life expectancies, and better education. We discuss next some of the ways in which a higher real GDP implies greater economic well-being.

AVAILABILITY OF GOODS AND SERVICES

Obviously, citizens of a country with a high GDP are likely to possess more and better goods and services (after all, that is what GDP measures). On average, people in high-GDP countries enjoy larger, better-constructed, and more comfortable homes; higher-quality food and clothing; a greater variety of entertainment and cultural opportunities; better access to transportation and travel; better communications and sanitation; and other advantages. While social commentators may question the value of material consumption—and we agree that riches do not necessarily bring happiness or peace of mind—the majority of people in the world place great importance on achieving material prosperity. Throughout history people have made tremendous sacrifices and taken great risks to secure a higher standard of living for themselves and their families. In fact, to a great extent the United States was built by people who were willing to leave their native lands, often at great personal hardship, in hopes of bettering their economic condition.

HEALTH AND EDUCATION

Beyond an abundance of consumer goods, a high GDP brings other more basic advantages. Table 12.4 shows the differences between rich and poor countries with regard to some important indicators of well-being, including life expectancy, infant and child mortality rates, number of doctors, measures of nutrition, and educational opportunity. Three groups of countries are compared: (1) developing countries as a group (total population, 5.2 billion); (2) the least developed countries (50 countries with a total population of about 765 million); and (3) the industrialized countries (24 countries, including the United States, Canada, the western European countries, and Japan, with a total population of about 930 million). As the first row of Table 12.4 shows, these three groups of countries have radically different levels of GDP per person. Most notably, GDP per person in the industrialized countries is more than 20 times that of the least developed countries.[2]

[2]The GDP data in Table 12.4 use U.S. prices to value goods and services in developing nations. Since basic goods and services tend to be cheaper in poor countries, this adjustment significantly increases measured GDP in those countries.

TABLE 12.4
GDP and Basic Indicators of Well-Being

Indicator	All developing countries	Least developed countries	Industrialized countries
GDP per person (U.S. dollars)	5,282	1,499	33,831
Life expectancy at birth (years)	66.1	54.5	79.4
Infant mortality rate (per 1,000 live births)	57	97	5
Under-5 mortality rate (per 1,000 live births)	83	153	6
Births attended by skilled health personnel (%)	60	35	99
Undernourished people (%)	17	35	Negligible
Combined gross enrollment rate for primary, secondary, and tertiary schools (%)	64.1	47.8	93.5
Adult literacy rate (%)	76.6	53.9	99
Total population in group of countries (millions)	5,215.0	765.7	931.5

SOURCE: United Nations, *Human Development Report 2007*, available at http://hdr.undp.org/. All data are for 2005, except births attended by skilled health personnel (1997–2005), undernourished people (average for 2002–2004), and adult literacy rate (1995–2005). Data for high-income OECD countries is used for all data in the "Industrialized countries" column. GDP data are adjusted to account for local differences in prices of basic commodities and services (i.e., they are adjusted for purchasing power parity).

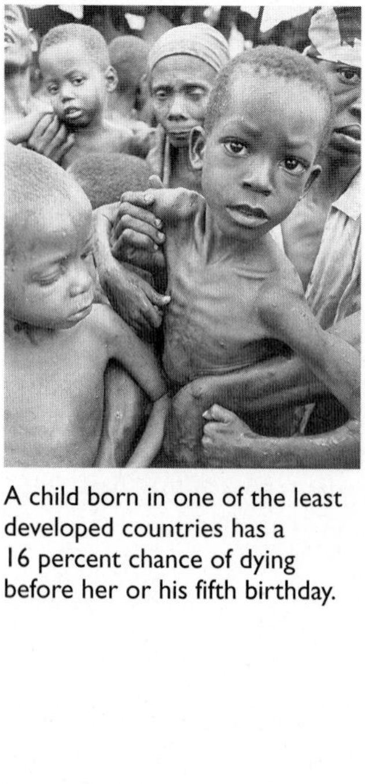

A child born in one of the least developed countries has a 16 percent chance of dying before her or his fifth birthday.

How do these large differences in GDP relate to other measures of well-being? Table 12.4 shows that on some of the most basic measures of human welfare, the developing countries fare much worse than the industrial countries. A child born in one of the least developed countries has roughly a 10 percent (97/1,000) chance of dying before her or his first birthday and about a 15 percent (153/1,000) chance of dying before her or his fifth birthday. The corresponding figures for the industrialized countries are 0.5 percent (5/1,000) and 0.6 percent (6/1,000), respectively. A child born in an industrialized country has a life expectancy of about 79 years, compared to about 55 years for a child born in one of the least developed countries. Superior nutrition, sanitation, and medical services in the richer countries account for these large discrepancies in basic welfare. Skilled health personnel assist in the delivery of 99 percent of births in industrialized countries but only 35 percent of births in the least developed countries.

On another important dimension of human well-being, literacy and education rates, high-GDP countries also have the advantage. Table 12.4 shows that in the industrialized countries, the percentage of adults who can read and write is virtually 100 percent, almost twice the percentage (54 percent) in the poorest developing countries. The percentage of children enrolled in primary, secondary, and tertiary schools is 93 percent in industrialized countries, compared to 48 percent in the least developed countries. Furthermore, enrollment rates do not capture important differences in the quality of education available in rich and poor countries, as measured by indicators such as the educational backgrounds of teachers and student–teacher ratios. Once again, the average person in an industrialized country seems to be better off than the average person in a poor developing country.

Example 12.4

THE ECONOMIC NATURALIST

Why do far fewer children complete high school in poor countries than in rich countries?

One possible explanation is that people in poor countries place a lower priority on getting an education than people in rich countries. But immigrants from poor countries often put a heavy emphasis on education—though it may be that people who emigrate from poor countries are unrepresentative of the population as a whole.

An economic naturalist's explanation for the lower schooling rates in poor countries would rely not on cultural differences but on differences in opportunity costs. In poor societies, most of which are heavily agricultural, children are an important source of labor. Beyond a certain age, sending children to school imposes a high opportunity cost on the family. Children who are in school are not available to help with planting, harvesting, and other tasks that must be done if the family is to survive. In addition, the cost of books and school supplies imposes a major hardship on poor families. The Cost-Benefit Principle thus implies that children will stay at home rather than go to school. In rich, nonagricultural countries, school-age children have few work opportunities, and their potential earnings are small relative to other sources of family income. The low opportunity cost of sending children to school in rich countries is an important reason for the higher enrollment rates in those countries. ●

Cost-Benefit

In Chapter 15, we will discuss the costs and benefits of economic growth—which in practice means growth in real GDP per person—in greater depth. In that context we will return to the question of whether a growing real GDP is necessarily equated with greater economic well-being.

RECAP | REAL GDP AND ECONOMIC WELL-BEING

Real GDP is at best an imperfect measure of economic well-being. Among the factors affecting well-being omitted from real GDP are the availability of leisure time, nonmarket services such as unpaid homemaking and volunteer services, environmental quality and resource conservation, and quality-of-life indicators such as a low crime rate. The GDP also does not reflect the degree of economic inequality in a country. Because real GDP is not the same as economic well-being, proposed policies should not be evaluated strictly in terms of whether or not they increase the GDP.

Although GDP is not the same as economic well-being, it is positively associated with many things that people value, including a higher material standard of living, better health, longer life expectancies, and higher rates of literacy and educational attainment. This relationship between real GDP and economic well-being has led many people to emigrate from poor nations in search of a better life and has motivated policymakers in developing countries to try to increase their nations' rates of economic growth.

SUMMARY

- The basic measure of an economy's output is *gross domestic product (GDP)*, the market value of the final goods and services produced in a country during a given period. Expressing output in terms of market values allows economists to aggregate the millions of goods and services produced in a modern economy. **LO1**

- Only *final goods and services* (which include *capital goods*) are counted in GDP, since they are the only goods and services that directly benefit final users. *Intermediate goods and services,* which are used up in the production of final goods and services, are not counted in GDP, nor are sales of existing assets. Summing the value added by each firm in the production process is a useful method of determining the value of final goods and services. **LO1**
- GDP also can be expressed as the sum of four types of expenditure: *consumption, investment, government purchases,* and *net exports.* These four types of expenditure correspond to the spending of households, firms, the government, and the foreign sector, respectively. **LO2**
- To compare levels of GDP over time, economists must eliminate the effects of inflation. They do so by measuring the market value of goods and services in terms of the prices in a base year. GDP measured in this way is called *real GDP,* while GDP measured in terms of current-year prices is called *nominal GDP.* Real GDP should always be used in making comparisons of economic activity over time. **LO3**
- Real GDP per person is an imperfect measure of economic well-being. With a few exceptions, notably government purchases of goods and services (which are included in GDP at their cost of production), GDP includes only those goods and services sold in markets. It excludes important factors that affect people's well-being, such as the amount of leisure time available to them, the value of unpaid or volunteer services, the quality of the environment, the quality of life indicators such as the crime rate, and the degree of economic inequality. **LO4**
- Real GDP is still a useful indicator of economic well-being, however. Countries with a high real GDP per person not only enjoy high average standards of living; they also tend to have higher life expectancies, low rates of infant and child mortality, and high rates of school enrollment and literacy. **LO4**

KEY TERMS

capital good (326)
consumption expenditure (330)
final goods or services (325)
government purchases (331)
gross domestic product (GDP) (322)
intermediate goods or services (325)
investment (330)
net exports (331)
nominal GDP (335)
real GDP (335)
value added (327)

REVIEW QUESTIONS

1. Why do economists use market values when calculating GDP? What is the economic rationale for giving high-value items more weight in GDP than low-value items? **LO1**
2. A large part of the agricultural sector in developing countries is subsistence farming, in which much of the food that is produced is consumed by the farmer and the farmer's family. Discuss the implications of this fact for the measurement of GDP in poor countries. **LO1**
3. Give examples of each of the four types of aggregate expenditure. Which of the four represents the largest share of GDP in the United States? Can an expenditure component be negative? Explain. **LO2**
4. Al's Shoeshine Stand shined 1,000 pairs of shoes last year and 1,200 pairs this year. He charged $4 for a shine last year and $5 this year. If last year is taken as the base year, find Al's contribution to both nominal GDP and real GDP in both years. Which measure would be better to use if you were trying to measure the change in Al's productivity over the past year? Why? **LO3**
5. Would you say that real GDP per person is a useful measure of economic well-being? Defend your answer. **LO4**

PROBLEMS

McGraw-Hill's HOMEWORK MANAGER®

1. George and John, stranded on an island, use clamshells for money. Last year George caught 300 fish and 5 wild boars. John grew 200 bunches of bananas. In the two-person economy that George and John set up, fish sell for 1

clamshell each, boars sell for 10 clamshells each, and bananas go for 5 clamshells a bunch. George paid John a total of 30 clamshells for helping him to dig bait for fishing, and he also purchased five of John's mature banana trees for 30 clamshells each. What is the GDP of George's and John's island in terms of clamshells? **LO1**

2. How would each of the following transactions affect the GDP of the United States? **LO1**
   a. The U.S. government pays $1 billion in salaries for government workers.
   b. The U.S. government pays $1 billion to Social Security recipients.
   c. The U.S. government pays a U.S. firm $1 billion for newly produced airplane parts.
   d. The U.S. government pays $1 billion in interest to holders of U.S. government bonds.
   e. The U.S. government pays $1 billion to Saudi Arabia for crude oil to add to U.S. government-owned oil reserves.
3. Intelligence Incorporated produces 100 computer chips and sells them for $200 each to Bell Computers. Using the chips and other labor and materials, Bell produces 100 personal computers. Bell sells the computers, bundled with software that Bell licenses from Macrosoft at $50 per computer, to PC Charlie's for $800 each. PC Charlie's sells the computers to the public for $1,000 each. Calculate the total contribution to GDP using the value-added method. Do you get the same answer by summing up the market values of final goods and services? **LO1**
4. MNLogs harvested logs (with no inputs from other companies) from their property in northern Minnesota. They sold these logs to MNLumber for $1,500 and MNLumber cut and planed the logs into lumber. MNLumber then sold the lumber for $4,000 to MNFurniture. MNFurniture used the lumber to produce 100 tables that they sold to customers for $70 each. **LO1**
   a. Complete the table below to calculate the value added by each firm.

Company	Revenues	Cost of purchased inputs	Value added
MNLogs			
MNLumber			
MNFurniture			

   b. Suppose that all of these transactions took place in 2007. By how much did GDP increase because of these transactions?
   c. Suppose that MNLogs harvested the logs in October 2007 and sold them to MNLumber in December 2007. MNLumber then sold the finished lumber to MNFurniture in April 2008 and MNFurniture sold all 100 tables during the rest of 2008. By how much did GDP increase in 2007 and 2008 because of these transactions?
5. For each of the following transactions, state the effect both on U.S. GDP and on the four components of aggregate expenditure. **LO2**
   a. Your mother buys a new car from a U.S. producer.
   b. Your mother buys a new car imported from Sweden.
   c. Your mother's car rental business buys a new car from a U.S. producer.
   d. Your mother's car rental business buys a new car imported from Sweden.
   e. The U.S. government buys a new, domestically produced car for the use of your mother, who has been appointed the ambassador to Sweden.
6. Here are some data for an economy. Find its GDP. Explain your calculation. **LO2**

Consumption expenditures	$600
Exports	75
Government purchases of goods and services	200
Construction of new homes and apartments	100
Sales of existing homes and apartments	200
Imports	50
Beginning-of-year inventory stocks	100
End-of-year inventory stocks	125
Business fixed investment	100
Government payments to retirees	100
Household purchases of durable goods	150

7. The nation of Potchatoonie produces hockey pucks, cases of root beer, and back rubs. Here are data on prices and quantities of the three goods in the years 2000 and 2007.

	Pucks		**Root beer**		**Back rubs**	
Year	**Quantity**	**Price**	**Quantity**	**Price**	**Quantity**	**Price**
2000	100	$5	300	$20	100	$20
2007	125	$7	250	$20	110	$25

Assume that 2000 is the base year. Find nominal GDP and real GDP for both years. **LO3**

8. Data on U.S. GDP is available from the Bureau of Economic Analysis (www.bea.gov). Download NIPA Table 1.1.6. (Real Gross Domestic Product, Chained Dollars) and do the following: **LO2**
   a. Make a table like Table 12.2 for the most recent year available.
   b. Discuss how, if at all, the sizes of consumption, investment, government purchases, and net exports relative to GDP have changed compared to the data in Table 12.2.
   c. Use the data you downloaded to make a graph of the shares of consumption, investment, government purchases, and next exports in GDP (i.e., each category's percentage of GDP) for 1929 to the present. Discuss the main points you see in this graph.
9. The government is considering a policy to reduce air pollution by restricting the use of "dirty" fuels by factories. In deciding whether to implement the policy, how, if at all, should the likely effects of the policy on real GDP be taken into account? Discuss. **LO4**
10. We discussed how the opportunity cost of sending children to school affects the level of school enrollment across countries. The United Nations *Human Development Report 2007* reports the following data for per capita income in 2005 (in the equivalent of U.S. dollars): **LO4**

Canada	33,375
Denmark	33,973
Greece	23,381
Lesotho	3,335
Ethiopia	1,055

a. Which country would you expect to have the highest school enrollment rate? The lowest rate?
b. Discuss what other factors besides GDP per capita a family might consider when applying the Cost-Benefit Principle to the decision of whether or not to send a child to school.

ANSWERS TO IN-CHAPTER EXERCISES

12.1 In the text, GDP was calculated to be \$64.00. If, in addition, Orchardia produces 5 oranges at \$0.30 each, GDP is increased by \$1.50 to \$65.50. **LO1**

12.2 Plants owned by U.S. companies produced a total of 612,669 vehicles, or 1.6 times the 385,477 vehicles produced by foreign-owned plants. In market value terms, with passenger cars valued at \$25,000 and other light vehicles at \$30,000, plants owned by U.S. companies produced (247,269 × \$25,000) + (365,400 × \$30,000) = \$17.14 billion worth of vehicles. Foreign-owned plants produced (270,130 × \$25,000) + (115,347 × \$30,000) = \$7.65 billion worth of vehicles. In market value terms, U.S.-owned plants outproduced the foreign-owned plants by a ratio of 1.68 to 1. The U.S. producers have a slight advantage when output is compared in market value terms instead of in terms of number of vehicles because the U.S. companies produce relatively more of the higher-value types of vehicles than the foreign companies do. **LO1**

12.3 The value added of the wholesale distributor together with the ultimate producers of the cards is \$500. Amy's value added—her revenue less her payments to other firms—is \$200. Since the cards were produced and purchased by Amy during the year 2005 (we assume), the \$500 counts toward year 2005 GDP. The \$200 in value added originating in Amy's card shop counts in year 2009 GDP since Amy actually sold the cards in that year. **LO1**

12.4 The sale of stock represents a transfer of ownership of part of the assets of Benson Buggywhip, not the production of new goods or services. Hence, the stock sale itself does not contribute to GDP. However, the broker's commission of \$100 (2 percent of the stock sale proceeds) represents payment for a current service and is counted in GDP. **LO1**

12.5 As in the original example, the market value of domestic production is 1,000,000 autos times \$15,000 per auto, or \$15 billion.

Also as in the original example, consumption is \$10.5 billion and government purchases are \$0.75 billion. However, because 25,000 of the autos that are purchased are imported rather than domestic, the domestic producers have unsold inventories at the end of the year of 50,000 (rather than 25,000 as in the original example). Thus, inventory investment is 50,000 autos times \$15,000, or \$0.75 billion, and total investment (autos purchased by businesses plus inventory investment) is \$3.75 billion. Since exports and imports are equal (both are 25,000 autos), net exports (equal to exports minus imports) are zero. Notice that since we subtract imports to get net exports, it is unnecessary also to subtract imports from consumption. Consumption is defined as total purchases by households, not just purchases of domestically produced goods.

Total expenditure is $C + I + G + NX =$ \$10.5 billion + \$3.75 billion + \$0.75 billion + 0 = \$15 billion, the same as the market value of production. **LO2**

12.6 Real GDP in the year 2013 equals the quantities of pizzas and calzones produced in the year 2013, valued at the market prices that prevailed in the base year 2009. So real GDP in 2013 = (30 pizzas × \$10/pizza) + (30 calzones × \$5/calzone) = \$450.

Real GDP in 2009 equals the quantities of pizzas and calzones produced in 2009, valued at 2009 prices, which is \$175. Notice that since 2009 is the base year, real GDP and nominal GDP are the same for that year.

The real GDP in the year 2013 is \$450/\$175, or about 2.6 times what it was in 2009. Hence the expansion of real GDP lies between the threefold increase in pizza production and the doubling in calzone production that occurred between 2009 and 2013. **LO3**

CHAPTER

13

Inflation and the Price Level

LEARNING OBJECTIVES

After reading this chapter, you should be able to:

1. Explain how the Consumer Price Index (CPI) is constructed and use it to calculate the inflation rate.
2. Show how the CPI is used to adjust economic data to eliminate the effects of inflation.
3. Discuss the two most important biases in the CPI.
4. Distinguish between inflation and relative price changes in order to find the true costs of inflation.
5. Understand the connections among inflation, nominal interest rates, and real interest rates.

In 1930 the great baseball player Babe Ruth earned a salary of $80,000. When it was pointed out to him that he had earned more than President Hoover, Ruth replied, with some justification, "I had a better year than he did." In 2001 Barry Bonds broke the major league home run record by hitting 73 home runs and earned $10.3 million. Which baseball player was better off? Was Barry Bonds able to buy more goods and services in 2001 with his $10.3 million or was Babe Ruth better off with his $80,000 in 1930? The answer is not obvious because the price of just about everything increased dramatically between 1930 and 2001, reflecting the inflation that occurred in the United States over that time period. The question then is whether the salaries of baseball stars "kept up" with the increases in prices.

Inflation can make a comparison of economic conditions at different points in time quite difficult. Your grandparents remember being able to buy both a comic book and a chocolate sundae for a quarter. Today the same two items might cost $4 or $5. You might conclude from this fact that kids were much better off in "the good old days," but were they really? Without more information, we can't tell, for though the prices of comic books and sundaes have gone up, so have allowances. The real question is whether young people's spending money has increased as much as or more than the prices of the things they want to buy. If so, then they are no worse off today than their grandparents were when they were young and candy bars cost a nickel.

Inflation also creates uncertainty when we try to look into the future, to ask questions such as, "How much should I plan to save for retirement?" The answer to this question depends on how much inflation is likely to occur before one retires (and thus how much heating oil, food, and clothing will cost). Inflation can pose similar problems for policymakers. For example, to plan long-term government spending programs, they must estimate how much the government's purchases will cost several years in the future.

An important benefit of studying macroeconomics is learning how to avoid the confusion inflation interjects into comparisons of economic conditions over time or projections for the future. In this chapter, we will see how both prices and inflation are measured and how dollar amounts, such as the price of a comic book, can be "adjusted" to eliminate the effects of inflation. Quantities that are measured in dollars (or other currency units) and then adjusted for inflation are called *real* quantities (recall, for example, the concept of real GDP in the last chapter). By working with real quantities, economists can compare the real incomes of Babe Ruth and Barry Bonds.

More important than the complications inflation creates for economic measurement are the costs that it imposes on the economy. In this chapter we will see why high inflation can significantly impair an economy's performance, to the extent that economic policymakers claim a low and stable rate of inflation as one of their chief objectives. We will conclude the chapter by showing how inflation is linked to another key economic variable, the rate of interest on financial assets.

THE CONSUMER PRICE INDEX: MEASURING THE PRICE LEVEL

consumer price index (CPI) for any period, measures the cost in that period of a standard basket of goods and services relative to the cost of the same basket of goods and services in a fixed year, called the *base year*

The basic tool economists use to measure the price level and inflation in the U.S. economy is the *consumer price index,* or CPI for short. The CPI is a measure of the "cost of living" during a particular period. Specifically, the **consumer price index (CPI)** for any period measures the cost in that period of a standard set, or basket, of goods and services *relative* to the cost of the same basket of goods and services in a fixed year, called the *base year.*

To illustrate how the CPI is constructed, suppose the government has designated 2000 as the base year. Assume for the sake of simplicity that in 2000 a typical American family's monthly household budget consisted of spending on just three items: rent on a two-bedroom apartment, hamburgers, and movie tickets. In reality, of course, families purchase hundreds of different items each month, but the basic principles of constructing the CPI are the same no matter how many items are included. Suppose too that the family's average monthly expenditures in 2000, the base year, were as shown in Table 13.1.

TABLE 13.1
Monthly Household Budget of the Typical Family in 2000 (Base Year)

Item	Cost (in 2000)
Rent, two-bedroom apartment	$500
Hamburgers (60 at $2.00 each)	120
Movie tickets (10 at $6.00 each)	60
Total expenditure	$680

Now let's fast-forward to the year 2008. Over that period, the prices of various goods and services are likely to have changed; some will have risen and some fallen. Let's suppose that by the year 2008 the rent that our family pays for their two-bedroom apartment has risen to \$630. Hamburgers now cost \$2.50 each, and the price of movie tickets has risen to \$7.00 each. So, in general, prices have been rising.

By how much did the family's cost of living increase between 2000 and 2008? Table 13.2 shows that if the typical family wanted to consume the *same basket of goods and services* in the year 2008 as they did in the year 2000, they would have to spend \$850 per month, or \$170 more than the \$680 per month they spent in 2000. In other words, to live the same way in the year 2008 as they did in the year 2000, the family would have to spend 25 percent more (\$170/\$680) each month. So, in this example, the cost of living for the typical family rose 25 percent between 2000 and 2008.

TABLE 13.2
Cost of Reproducing the 2000 (Base-Year) Basket of Goods and Services in Year 2008

Item	Cost (in 2008)	Cost (in 2000)
Rent, two-bedroom apartment	\$630	\$500
Hamburgers (60 at \$2.50 each)	150	120
Movie tickets (10 at \$7.00 each)	70	60
Total expenditure	\$850	\$680

The Bureau of Labor Statistics (BLS) calculates the official consumer price index (CPI) using essentially the same method. The first step in deriving the CPI is to pick a base year and determine the basket of goods and services that were consumed by the typical family during that year. In practice, the government learns how consumers allocate their spending through a detailed survey, called the Consumer Expenditure Survey, in which randomly selected families record every purchase they make and the price they paid over a given month. (Quite a task!) Let's call the basket of goods and services that results the *base-year basket.* Then, each month BLS employees visit thousands of stores and conduct numerous interviews to determine the current prices of the goods and services in the base-year basket.[1]

The CPI in any given year is computed using this formula:

$$\text{CPI} = \frac{\text{Cost of base-year basket of goods and services in current year}}{\text{Cost of base-year basket of goods and services in base year}}.$$

Returning to the example of the typical family that consumes three goods, we can calculate the CPI in the year 2008 as

$$\text{CPI in year 2008} = \frac{\$850}{\$680} = 1.25.$$

In other words, in this example, the cost of living in the year 2008 is 25 percent higher than it was in 2000, the base year. Notice that the base-year CPI is always equal to 1.00, since in that year the numerator and the denominator of the CPI formula are the same. The CPI for a given period (such as a month or year) measures the cost of living in that period *relative* to what it was in the base year.

The BLS multiplies the CPI by 100 to get rid of the decimal point. If we were to do that here, the year 2005 CPI would be expressed as 125 rather than 1.25, and the base-year CPI would be expressed as 100 rather than 1.00. However, many calculations are simplified if the CPI is stated in decimal form, so we will not adopt the convention of multiplying it by 100.

[1]More details on how the BLS constructs the CPI are available at www.bls.gov/cpi/cpifaq.htm.

Measuring the typical family's cost of living

Suppose that in addition to the three goods and services the typical family consumed in 2000 they also bought four sweaters at $30 each. In the year 2008 the same sweaters cost $50 each. The prices of the other goods and services in 2000 and 2008 were the same as in Table 13.2. With this additional item, what was the change in the family's cost of living between 2000 and 2008?

In the example in the text, the cost of the base-year (2000) basket was $680. Adding four sweaters at $30 each raises the cost of the base-year basket to $800. What does this same basket (including the four sweaters) cost in 2008? The cost of the apartment, the hamburgers, and the movie tickets is $850, as before. Adding the cost of the four sweaters at $50 each raises the total cost of the basket to $1,050. The CPI equals the cost of the basket in 2008 divided by the cost of the basket in 2000 (the base year), or $1,050/$800 = 1.31. We conclude that the family's cost of living rose 31 percent between 2000 and 2008. ◆

EXERCISE 13.1

Returning to the three-good example in Tables 13.1 and 13.2, find the year 2008 CPI if the rent on the apartment falls from $500 in 2000 to $400 in 2008. The prices for hamburgers and movie tickets in the two years remain the same as in the two tables.

The CPI is not itself the price of a specific good or service. Indeed, it has no units of measurement at all since the dollars in the numerator of the fraction cancel with the dollars in the denominator. Rather, the CPI is an *index*. The *value* of an index in a particular year has meaning only in comparison with the value of that index in another year. Thus, a **price index** measures the average price of a class of goods or services relative to the price of those same goods or services in a base year. The CPI is an especially well-known price index, one of many economists use to assess economic trends. For example, because manufacturers tend to pass on increases in the prices of raw materials to their customers, economists use indexes of raw materials' prices to try to forecast changes in the prices of manufactured goods. Other indexes are used to study the rate of price change in energy, food, health care, and other major sectors.

price index a measure of the average price of a given class of goods or services relative to the price of the same goods and services in a base year

EXERCISE 13.2

The consumer price index captures the cost of living for the "typical" or average family. Suppose you were to construct a personal price index to measure changes in your own cost of living over time. In general, how would you go about constructing such an index? Why might changes in your personal price index differ from changes in the CPI?

INFLATION

The CPI provides a measure of the average *level* of prices relative to prices in the base year. *Inflation,* in contrast, is a measure of how fast the average price level is *changing* over time. The **rate of inflation** is defined as the annual percentage rate of change in the price level, as measured, for example, by the CPI. Suppose, for example, that the CPI has a value of 1.25 in the year 2008 and a value of 1.30 in the year 2009. The rate of inflation between 2008 and 2009 is the percentage increase in the price level, or the increase in the price level (0.05) divided by the initial price level (1.25), which is equal to 4 percent.

rate of inflation the annual percentage rate of change in the price level, as measured, for example, by the CPI

Calculating inflation rates: 2003–2007

CPI values for the years 2003 through 2007 are shown below.

Year	CPI
2003	1.840
2004	1.889
2005	1.953
2006	2.016
2007	2.073

The inflation rate between 2003 and 2004 is the percentage increase in the price level between those years, or (1.889 − 1.840)/1.840 = 0.049/1.840 = 0.027 = 2.7 percent. Do the calculations on your own to confirm that inflation during each of the next three years was 3.4, 3.2, and 2.8 percent. ◆

EXERCISE 13.3

Below are CPI values for the years 1929 through 1933. Find the rates of inflation between 1929 and 1930, 1930 and 1931, 1931 and 1932, and 1932 and 1933.

Year	CPI
1929	0.171
1930	0.167
1931	0.152
1932	0.137
1933	0.130

How did inflation rates in the 1930s differ from those since 2003?

The results of the calculations for Exercise 13.3 include some examples of *negative* inflation rates. A situation in which the prices of most goods and services are falling over time so that inflation is negative is called **deflation.** The early 1930s was the last time the United States experienced significant deflation. Japan experienced relatively mild deflation during the past decade.

deflation a situation in which the prices of most goods and services are falling over time so that inflation is negative

Figure 13.1 puts the previous examples in context by showing the inflation rate in the United States for 1900 to 2007.

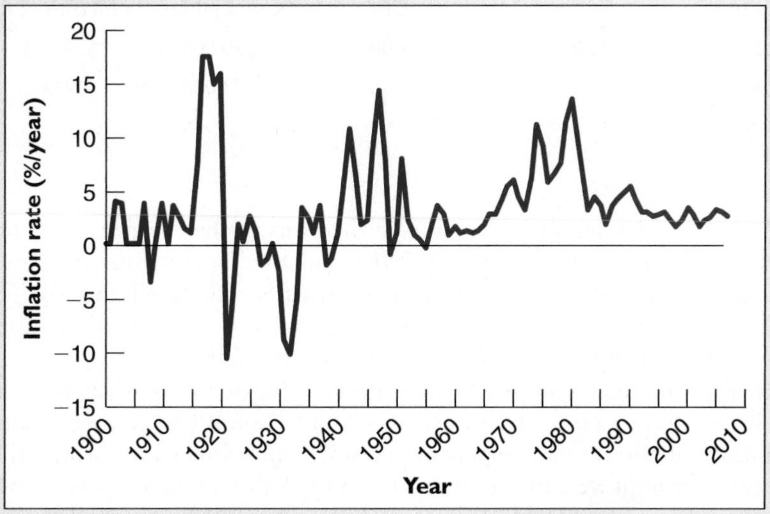

SOURCE: 1900–1959: www.measuringworth.com; 1960–2007: *Economic Report of the President*, February 2008, Table B-60 (http://www.gpoaccess.gov/eop/).

FIGURE 13.1
The U.S. Inflation Rate, 1900–2007.
The U.S. Inflation rate has fluctuated over time. Inflation was high in the 1970s but has been quite low recently.

ADJUSTING FOR INFLATION

The CPI is an extremely useful tool. Not only does it allow us to measure changes in the cost of living; it also can be used to adjust economic data to eliminate the effects of inflation. In this section we will see how the CPI can be used to convert quantities measured at current dollar values into real terms, a process called *deflating*. We also will see that the CPI can be used to convert real quantities into current-dollar terms, a procedure called *indexing*. Both procedures are useful not only to economists but to anyone who needs to adjust payments, accounting measures, or other economic quantities for the effects of inflation.

DEFLATING A NOMINAL QUANTITY

nominal quantity a quantity that is measured in terms of its current dollar value

An important use of the CPI is to adjust **nominal quantities**—quantities measured at their current dollar values—for the effects of inflation. To illustrate, suppose we know that the typical family in a certain metropolitan area had a total income of $20,000 in 2000 and $22,000 in the year 2008. Was this family economically better off in the year 2008 than in 2000?

Without any more information than this, we might be tempted to say yes. After all, their income rose by 10 percent over the eight-year period. But prices also might have been rising, as fast as or faster than the family's income. Suppose the prices of the goods and services the family consumes rose 25 percent over the same period. Since the family's income rose only 10 percent, we would have to conclude that the family is worse off, in terms of the goods and services they can afford to buy, despite the increase in their *nominal,* or current-dollar, income.

real quantity a quantity that is measured in physical terms—for example, in terms of quantities of goods and services

We can make a more precise comparison of the family's purchasing power in 2000 and 2008 by calculating their incomes in those years in *real* terms. In general, a **real quantity** is one that is measured in physical terms—for example, in terms of quantities of goods and services. To convert a nominal quantity into a real quantity, we must divide the nominal quantity by a price index for the period, as shown in Table 13.3. The calculations in the table show that in *real* or purchasing power terms, the family's income actually *decreased* by $2,400, or 12 percent of their initial real income of $20,000, between 2000 and 2008.

TABLE 13.3
Comparing the Real Values of a Family's Income in 2000 and 2008

Year	Nominal family income	CPI	Real family income = Nominal family income/CPI
2000	$20,000	1.00	$20,000/1.00 = $20,000
2008	$22,000	1.25	$22,000/1.25 = $17,600

deflating (a nominal quantity) the process of dividing a nominal quantity by a price index (such as the CPI) to express the quantity in real terms

The problem for this family is that though their income has been rising in nominal (dollar) terms, it has not kept up with inflation. Dividing a nominal quantity by a price index to express the quantity in real terms is called **deflating** the nominal quantity. (Be careful not to confuse the idea of deflating a nominal quantity with deflation, or negative inflation. The two concepts are different.)

Dividing a nominal quantity by the current value of a price index to measure it in real or purchasing power terms is a very useful tool. It can be used to eliminate the effects of inflation from comparisons of any nominal quantity—workers' wages, health care expenditures, the components of the federal budget—over time. Why does this method work? In general, if you know both how many dollars you have spent on a given item and the item's price, you can figure out how many of the item you bought (by dividing your expenditures by the price). For example, if you spent \$100 on hamburgers last month and hamburgers cost \$2.50 each, you can determine that you purchased 40 hamburgers. Similarly, if you divide a family's dollar income or expenditures by a price index, which is a measure of the average price of the goods and services they buy, you will obtain a measure of the real quantity of goods and services they purchased. Such real quantities are sometimes referred to as *inflation-adjusted* quantities.

Babe Ruth vs. Barry Bonds: who earned more?

Let's return to the question posed at the beginning of this chapter. When Barry Bonds earned \$10.3 million in 2001, was he better or worse off than Babe Ruth was in 1930 earning \$80,000?

To answer this question, we need to convert both men's earnings into real terms. The CPI (using the average of 1982–1984 as the base year since an extensive survey of consumer purchases was made in this period) was 0.167 in 1930 and 1.78 in 2001. Dividing Babe Ruth's salary by 0.167, we obtain approximately \$479,000, which is Ruth's salary "in 1982–1984 dollars." In other words someone would need \$479,000 in the 1982–1984 period to buy the same amount of goods and services as Babe Ruth could in 1930 with his \$80,000 salary. Dividing Barry Bonds' 2001 salary by the 2001 CPI, 1.78, yields a salary of \$5.79 million in 1982–1984 dollars. Thus, someone would need \$5.79 million in the 1982–1984 period to buy the same amount of goods and services as Barry Bonds could in 2001 with his \$10.3 million salary. We can now compare the real earnings of the two power hitters in 1982–1984 dollars: \$479,000 and \$5.79 million. Although adjusting for inflation brings the two figures closer together (since part of Bonds' higher salary compensates for the increase in prices between 1930 and 2001), in real terms Bonds still earned more than 12 times Ruth's salary. Incidentally, Bonds also earned about 25 times what President Bush earned in 2001. ◆

Clearly, in comparing wages or earnings at two different points in time, we must adjust for changes in the price level. Doing so yields the **real wage**—the wage measured in terms of real purchasing power. The real wage for any given period is calculated by dividing the nominal (dollar) wage by the CPI for that period.

real wage the wage paid to workers measured in terms of purchasing power; the real wage for any given period is calculated by dividing the nominal (dollar) wage by the CPI for that period

EXERCISE 13.4

In 2007 Alex Rodriguez of the New York Yankees earned \$22.7 million. In that year the CPI was 2.07. How did Rodriguez's 2007 real earnings compare to Bond's 2001 real earnings?

Real wages of U.S. production workers

Production workers are nonsupervisory workers, such as those who work on factory assembly lines. The average U.S. production worker earned \$3.40 per hour in 1970 and \$17.41 in 2007.[2] Compare the real wages for this group of workers in these years.

To find the real wage in 1970 and 2007, we need to know that the CPI was 0.388 in 1970 and 2.073 in 2007 (again using the 1982–1984 average as the base period). Dividing \$3.40 by 0.388, we find that the real wage in 1970 was \$8.76. Dividing \$17.41 by 2.073, we find that the real wage in 2007 was only \$8.40. In real or purchasing power terms, production workers' wages actually fell between 1970 and 2007, despite the fact that the nominal or dollar wage almost quintupled.

[2]Economic Report of the President, February 2008, Table B-47, www.gpoaccess.gov/eop/2008/B47.xls.

Figure 13.2 shows nominal wages and real wages for U.S. production workers for the period 1960–2007. Notice the dramatic difference between the two trends. Looking only at nominal wages, one might conclude that production-line workers were much better paid in 2007 than in 1960. But once wages are adjusted for inflation, we see that, in terms of buying power, production-line workers' wages have stagnated since the early 1970s. This example illustrates the crucial importance of adjusting for inflation when comparing dollar values over time.

FIGURE 13.2
Nominal and Real Wages for Production Workers, 1960–2007.
Though nominal wages of production workers have risen dramatically since 1960, real wages have stagnated.

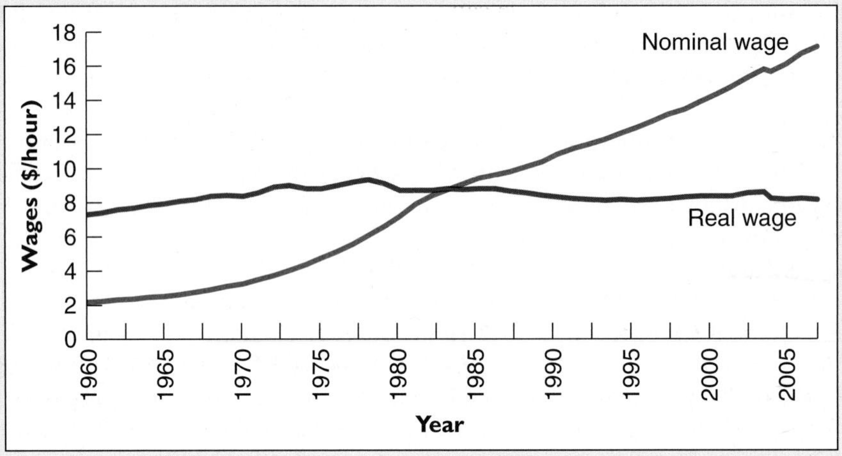

SOURCE: *Economic Report of the President*, February 2008, Table B-47 (http://www.gpoaccess.gov/eop/).

EXERCISE 13.5

In 1950 the minimum wage prescribed by federal law was $0.75 per hour. In 2007 it was $5.85 per hour. How does the real minimum wage in 2007 compare to that of 1950? The CPI was 0.241 in 1950 and 2.073 in 2007.

INDEXING TO MAINTAIN BUYING POWER

The consumer price index also can be used to convert real quantities to nominal quantities. Suppose, for example, that in the year 2000 the government paid certain Social Security recipients $1,000 per month in benefits. Let's assume that Congress would like the buying power of these benefits to remain constant over time so that the recipients' standard of living is unaffected by inflation. To achieve that goal, at what level should Congress set the monthly Social Security benefit in the year 2008?

The nominal, or dollar, benefit Congress should pay in the year 2008 to maintain the purchasing power of retired people depends on how much inflation has taken place between 2000 and 2008. Suppose that the CPI has risen 20 percent between 2000 and 2008. That is, on average the prices of the goods and services consumers buy have risen 20 percent over that period. For Social Security recipients to "keep up" with inflation, their benefit in the year 2008 must be $1,000 + .20($1,000) = $1,200 per month, or 20 percent more than it was in 2000. In general, to keep purchasing power constant, the dollar benefit must be increased each year by the percentage increase in the CPI.

indexing the practice of increasing a nominal quantity each period by an amount equal to the percentage increase in a specified price index. Indexing prevents the purchasing power of the nominal quantity from being eroded by inflation

The practice of increasing a nominal quantity according to changes in a price index to prevent inflation from eroding purchasing power is called **indexing.** In the case of Social Security, federal law provides for the automatic indexing of benefits. Each year, without any action by Congress, benefits increase by an amount equal to the percentage increase in the CPI. Some labor contracts are indexed as well so that wages are adjusted fully or partially for changes in inflation.

An indexed labor contract

A labor contract provides for a first-year wage of \$12.00 per hour and specifies that the real wage will rise by 2 percent in the second year of the contract and by another 2 percent in the third year. The CPI is 1.00 in the first year, 1.05 in the second year, and 1.10 in the third year. What are the dollar wages that must be paid in the second and third years of the contract?

Because the CPI is 1.00 in the first year, both the nominal wage and the real wage are \$12.00. Let W_2 stand for the nominal wage in the second year. Deflating by the CPI in the second year, we can express the real wage in the second year as $W_2/1.05$. The contract says that the second-year real wage must be 2 percent higher than the real wage in the first year, so $W_2/1.05 = \$12.00 \times 1.02 = \$12.24$. Multiplying through by 1.05 to solve for W_2, we get $W_2 = \$12.85$, the nominal wage required by the contract in the second year. In the third year the nominal wage W_3 must satisfy the equation $W_3/1.10 = \$12.24 \times 1.02 = \$12.48$. (Why?) Solving this equation for W_3 yields \$13.73 as the nominal wage that must be paid in the third year. ◆

EXERCISE 13.6

The minimum wage is not indexed to inflation, but suppose it had been starting in 1950. What would the nominal minimum wage have been in 2007? See Exercise 13.5 for the data necessary to answer this question.

Because the minimum wage is not indexed to inflation, its purchasing power falls as prices rise. Congress must therefore raise the nominal minimum wage periodically to keep the real value of the minimum wage from eroding. Ironically, despite the public's impression that Congress has raised the nominal minimum wage steeply over the years, the real minimum wage has fallen about one-third since 1970.

Why doesn't Congress index the minimum wage to the CPI and eliminate the need to reconsider it so often? Evidently, some members of Congress prefer to hold a highly publicized debate on the issue every few years—perhaps because it mobilizes both advocates and opponents of the minimum wage to make campaign donations to those members who represent their views.

RECAP	METHODS TO ADJUST FOR INFLATION

Deflating. To correct a nominal quantity, such as a family's dollar income, for changes in the price level, divide it by a price index such as the CPI. This process, called *deflating* the nominal quantity, expresses the nominal quantity in terms of real purchasing power. If nominal quantities from two different years are deflated by a price index with the same base year, the purchasing power of the two deflated quantities can be compared.

Indexing. To ensure that a nominal payment, such as a Social Security benefit, represents a constant level of real purchasing power, increase the nominal quantity each year by a percentage equal to the rate of inflation for that year (a procedure known as *indexing*).

DOES THE CPI MEASURE "TRUE" INFLATION?

You may have concluded that measuring inflation is straightforward, but as with GDP the issue is not free from controversy. Because the CPI is one of the most important U.S. economic statistics, the issue is far from academic. Policymakers pay close attention to the latest inflation numbers when deciding what actions to take. Furthermore, because of the widespread use of indexing, changes in the CPI directly impact the government's budget. For example, if the CPI rises by 3 percent during a given year, by law Social Security benefits—which are a significant part of the federal budget—increase automatically by 3 percent. Many other government payments and private contracts, such as union labor contracts, are indexed to the CPI as well.

When a 1996 report concluded that changes in the CPI are a poor measure of "true" inflation, therefore, a major controversy ensued. The report, prepared by a commission headed by Michael Boskin, formerly the chief economic adviser to President George H. W. Bush, concluded that the official CPI inflation rate *overstates* the true inflation rate by as much as one to two percentage points a year. In other words, if the official CPI inflation rate is reported to be 3 percent, the "true" inflation rate might be 2 percent, or even 1 percent.

If this assessment is in fact correct, the indexing of Social Security and other government benefits to the CPI could be costing the federal government billions of dollars more than necessary every year. In addition, an overstated rate of inflation would lead to an underestimation of the true improvement in living standards over time. If the typical family's nominal income increases by 3 percent per year, and inflation is reported to be 3 percent per year, economists would conclude that American families are experiencing no increase in their real income. But if the "true" inflation rate is really 2 percent per year, then the family's real income is actually rising by 1 percent per year (the 3 percent increase in nominal income minus 2 percent inflation).

The Boskin Commission gave a number of reasons why the official inflation rate, based on the CPI, may overestimate the true rate of inflation. Two are particularly important. First, in practice, government statisticians cannot always adjust adequately for changes in the *quality* of goods and services. Suppose a new personal computer has 20 percent more memory, computational speed, and data storage capacity than last year's model. Suppose too for the sake of illustration that its price is 20 percent higher. Has there been inflation in computer prices? Economists would say no; although consumers are paying 20 percent more for a computer, they are getting a 20 percent better machine. The situation is really no different from paying 20 percent more for a pizza that is 20 percent bigger. However, because quality change is difficult to measure precisely and because they have many thousands of goods and services to consider, government statisticians often miss or understate changes in quality. In general, whenever statisticians fail to adjust adequately for improvements in the quality of goods or services, they will tend to overstate inflation. This type of overstatement is called *quality adjustment bias*.[3]

EN 13

An extreme example of quality adjustment bias can occur whenever a totally new good becomes available. For instance, the introduction of the first effective AIDS drugs significantly increased the quality of medical care received by AIDS patients. In practice, however, quality improvements that arise from totally new products are likely to be poorly captured by the CPI, if at all. The problem is that since the new good was not produced in the base year, there is no base-year price with which to compare the current price of the good. Government statisticians use various approaches to correct for this problem, such as comparing the cost of the new drug to the cost of the next-best therapies. But such methods are necessarily imprecise and open to criticism.

The second problem emphasized by the Boskin Commission arises from the fact that the CPI is calculated for a fixed basket of goods and services. This procedure does not allow for the possibility that consumers can switch from products whose prices are rising to those whose prices are stable or falling. Ignoring the fact

[3]There are many hard-working employees at the Bureau of Labor Statistics trying to measure quality changes. Some improvements, such as increases in computer speeds and memory, are relatively easy to measure. But many others are much harder to quantify.

that consumers can switch from more expensive to less expensive goods leads statisticians to overestimate the true increase in the cost of living.

Suppose, for instance, that people like coffee and tea equally well and in the base year consumed equal amounts of each. But then a frost hits a major coffee-producing nation, causing the price of coffee to double. The increase in coffee prices encourages consumers to forgo coffee and drink tea instead—a switch that doesn't make them worse off, since they like coffee and tea equally well. However, the CPI, which measures the cost of buying the base-year basket of goods and services, will rise significantly when the price of coffee doubles. This rise in the CPI, which ignores the fact that people can substitute tea for coffee without being made worse off, exaggerates the true increase in the cost of living. This type of overstatement of inflation is called *substitution bias.*

Substitution bias

Suppose the CPI basket for 2000, the base year, is as follows:

Item	Expenditure
Coffee (50 cups at $1/cup)	$ 50.00
Tea (50 cups at $1/cup)	50.00
Scones (100 at $1 each)	100.00
Total	$200.00

Assume that consumers are equally happy to drink coffee or tea with their scones. In 2000, coffee and tea cost the same, and the average person drinks equal amounts of coffee and tea.

In the year 2008, coffee has doubled in price to $2 per cup. Tea remains at $1 per cup, and scones are $1.50 each. What has happened to the cost of living as measured by the CPI? How does this result compare to the true cost of living?

To calculate the value of the CPI for the year 2008, we must first find the cost of consuming the 2000 basket of goods in that year. At year 2008 prices, 50 cups each of coffee and tea and 100 scones cost $(50 \times \$2) + (50 \times \$1) + (100 \times \$1.50) =$ $300. Since consuming the same basket of goods cost $200 in 2000, the base year, the CPI in 2008 is $300/$200, or 1.50. This calculation leads us to conclude that the cost of living has increased 50 percent between 2000 and 2008.

However, we have overlooked the possibility that consumers can substitute a cheaper good (tea) for the more expensive one (coffee). Indeed, since consumers like coffee and tea equally well, when the price of coffee doubles they will shift entirely to tea. Their new consumption basket—100 cups of tea and 100 scones—is just as enjoyable to them as their original basket. If we allow for the substitution of less expensive goods, how much has the cost of living really increased? The cost of 100 cups of tea and 100 scones in the year 2008 is only $250, not $300. From the consumer's point of view, the true cost of living has risen by only $50, or 25 percent. The 50 percent increase in the CPI therefore overstates the increase in the cost of living as the result of substitution bias. ◆

The Boskin Commission's findings have been controversial. While quality adjustment bias and substitution bias undoubtedly distort the measurement of inflation, estimating precisely how much of an overstatement they create is difficult. (If economists knew exactly how big these biases were, they could simply correct the data.) But the Bureau of Labor Statistics has recently made significant efforts to improve the quality of its data as a result of the Commission's report.

THE COSTS OF INFLATION: NOT WHAT YOU THINK

In the late 1970s, when inflation was considerably higher than it is now, the public told poll takers that they viewed it as "public enemy number one"—that is, as the nation's most serious problem. Although U.S. inflation rates have not been very high in recent years, today many Americans remain concerned about inflation or the threat of inflation. Why do people worry so much about inflation? Detailed opinion surveys often find that many people are confused about the meaning of inflation and its economic effects. When people complain about inflation, they are often concerned primarily about relative price changes. Before describing the true economic costs of inflation, which are real and serious, let's examine this confusion people experience about inflation and its costs.

price level a measure of the overall level of prices at a particular point in time as measured by a price index such as the CPI

relative price the price of a specific good or service *in comparison to* the prices of other goods and services

We need first to distinguish between the *price level* and the *relative price* of a good or service. The **price level** is a measure of the overall level of prices at a particular point in time as measured by a price index such as the CPI. Recall that the inflation rate is the percentage change in the price level from year to year. In contrast, a **relative price** is the price of a specific good or service *in comparison to* the prices of other goods and services. For example, if the price of oil were to rise by 10 percent while the prices of other goods and services were rising on average by 3 percent, the relative price of oil would increase. But if oil prices rise by 3 percent while other prices rise by 10 percent, the relative price of oil would decrease. That is, oil would become cheaper relative to other goods and services, even though it has not become cheaper in absolute terms.

Public opinion surveys suggest that many people are confused about the distinction between inflation, which is an increase in the overall *price level,* and an increase in a specific *relative price.* Suppose that supply disruptions in the Middle East were to double the price of gas at the pump, leaving other prices unaffected. Appalled by the increase in gasoline prices, people might demand that the government do something about "this inflation." But while the increase in gas prices hurts consumers, is it an example of inflation? Gasoline is only one item in a consumer's budget, one of the thousands of goods and services that people buy every day. Thus, the increase in the price of gasoline might affect the overall price level, and hence the inflation rate, only slightly. In this example, inflation is not the real problem. What upsets consumers is the change in the *relative price* of oil, particularly compared to the price of labor (wages). By increasing the cost of using a car, the increase in the relative price of oil reduces the income people have left over to spend on other things.

Again, changes in relative prices do *not* necessarily imply a significant amount of inflation. For example, increases in the prices of some goods could well be counterbalanced by decreases in the prices of other goods, in which case the price level and the inflation rate would be largely unaffected. Conversely, inflation can be high without affecting relative prices. Imagine, for instance, that all prices in the economy, including wages and salaries, go up exactly 10 percent each year. The inflation rate is 10 percent, but relative prices are not changing. Indeed, because wages (the price of labor) are increasing by 10 percent per year, people's ability to buy goods and services is unaffected by the inflation.

These examples show that changes in the price level and changes in the relative prices of specific goods are two quite different issues. The public's tendency to confuse the two is important because the remedies for the two problems are different. To counteract changes in relative prices, the government would need to implement policies that affect the supply and demand for specific goods. In the case of an increase in oil prices, for example, the government could try to encourage the development of alternative sources of energy. To counteract inflation, however, the government must resort (as we will see) to changes in macroeconomic policies such as monetary or fiscal policies. If, in confusion, the public forces the government to adopt anti-inflationary policies when the real problem is a relative price change, the economy could actually be hurt by the effort. This is an important example of why economic literacy is important, to both policymakers and the general public.

The price level, relative prices, and inflation

Suppose the value of the CPI is 1.20 in the year 2006, 1.32 in 2007, and 1.40 in 2008. Assume also that the price of oil increases 8 percent between 2006 and 2007 and another 8 percent between 2007 and 2008. What is happening to the price level, the inflation rate, and the relative price of oil?

The price level can be measured by the CPI. Since the CPI is higher in 2007 than in 2006 and higher still in 2008 than in 2007, the price level is rising throughout the period. Since the CPI increases by 10 percent between 2006 and 2007, the inflation rate between those years is 10 percent. However, the CPI increases only about 6 percent between 2007 and 2008 ($1.40/1.32 \approx 1.06$), so the inflation rate decreases to about 6 percent between those years. The decline in the inflation rate implies that although the price level is still rising, it is doing so at a slower pace than the year before.

The price of oil rises 8 percent between 2006 and 2007. But because the general inflation over that period is 10 percent, the relative price of oil—that is, its price *relative to all other goods and services*—falls by about 2 percent ($8\% - 10\% = -2\%$). Between 2007 and 2008 the price of oil rises by another 8 percent, while the general inflation rate is about 6 percent. Hence the relative price of oil rises between 2007 and 2008 by about 2 percent ($8\% - 6\%$). ◆

EXERCISE 13.7

In April 1991, unleaded, regular gasoline cost \$1.08 per gallon and the CPI was 1.35. In April 2008, unleaded, regular gas cost \$3.46 per gallon and the CPI was 2.15. Did the price of gasoline relative to the other items in the CPI rise or fall between these two years?

EXERCISE 13.8

In 1980, when the CPI was 0.824, the average cost of attending a private university was \$5,013, including tuition, room, board, and fees. In 2006, when the CPI was 2.016, the average cost was \$27,317. By how much did the average cost rise relative to other items in the CPI?

THE TRUE COSTS OF INFLATION

Having dispelled the common confusion between inflation and relative price changes, we are now free to address the true economic costs of inflation. There are a variety of such costs, each of which tends to reduce the efficiency of the economy. Five of the most important are discussed here.

"NOISE" IN THE PRICE SYSTEM

In Chapter 3 we described the remarkable economic coordination that is necessary to provide the right amount and the right kinds of food to New Yorkers every day. This feat is not orchestrated by some Food Distribution Ministry staffed by bureaucrats. It is done much better than a Ministry ever could by the workings of free markets, operating without central guidance.

How do free markets transmit the enormous amounts of information necessary to accomplish complex tasks like the provisioning of New York City? The answer, as we saw in Chapter 3, is through the price system. When the owners of French restaurants in Manhattan cannot find sufficient quantities of chanterelles, a particularly rare and desirable mushroom, they bid up its market price. Specialty food suppliers notice the higher price for chanterelles and realize that they can make a profit by supplying more chanterelles to the market. At the same time, price-conscious diners will shift to cheaper, more available mushrooms. The market for chanterelles will reach equilibrium only when there are no more unexploited opportunities for profit, and both suppliers and demanders are satisfied at the market price (the Equilibrium Principle). Multiply this example a million times, and you will gain a sense of how the price system achieves a truly remarkable degree of economic coordination.

Equilibrium

When inflation is high, however, the subtle signals that are transmitted through the price system become more difficult to interpret, much in the way that static, or "noise," makes a radio message harder to interpret. In an economy with little or no inflation, the supplier of specialty foodstuffs will immediately recognize the increase in chanterelle prices as a signal to bring more to market. If inflation is high, however, the supplier must ask whether a price increase represents a true increase in the demand for chanterelles or is just a result of the general inflation, which causes all food prices to rise. If the price rise reflects only inflation, the price of chanterelles *relative to other goods and services* has not really changed. The supplier therefore should not change the quantity of mushrooms he brings to market.

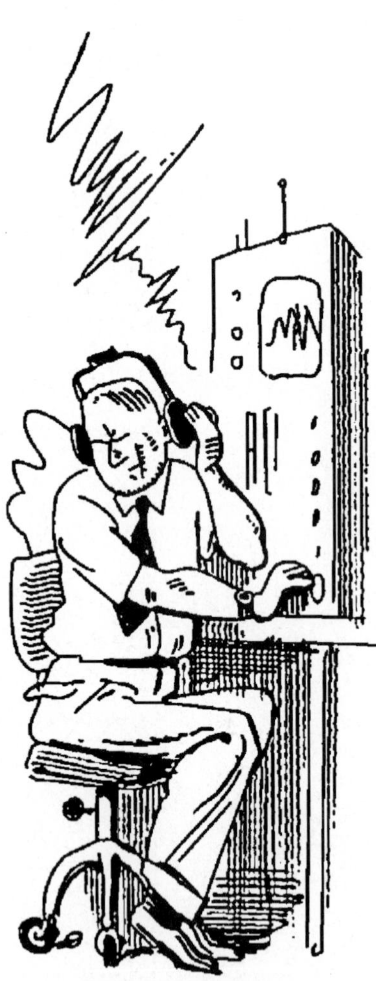

Inflation adds static to the information conveyed by changes in prices.

In an inflationary environment, to discern whether the increase in chanterelle prices is a true signal of increased demand, the supplier needs to know not only the price of chanterelles but also what is happening to the prices of other goods and services. Since this information takes time and effort to collect, the supplier's response to the change in chanterelle prices is likely to be slower and more tentative.

In summary, price changes are the market's way of communicating information to suppliers and demanders. An increase in the price of a good or service, for example, tells demanders to economize on their use of the good or service and suppliers to bring more of it to market. But in the presence of inflation, prices are affected not only by changes in the supply and demand for a product but by changes in the general price level. Inflation creates static, or "noise," in the price system, obscuring the information transmitted by prices and reducing the efficiency of the market system. This reduction in efficiency imposes real economic costs.

DISTORTIONS OF THE TAX SYSTEM

Just as some government expenditures, such as Social Security benefits, are indexed to inflation, many taxes are also indexed. In the United States, people with higher incomes pay a higher *percentage* of their income in taxes. Without indexing, an inflation that raises people's nominal incomes would force them to pay an increasing percentage of their income in taxes, even though their *real* incomes may not have increased. To avoid this phenomenon, which is known as *bracket creep,* Congress has indexed income tax brackets to the CPI. The effect of this indexation is that a family whose nominal income is rising at the same rate as inflation does not have to pay a higher percentage of income in taxes.

Although indexing has solved the problem of bracket creep, many provisions of the tax code have not been indexed, either because of lack of political support or because of the complexity of the task. As a result, inflation can produce unintended changes in the taxes people pay, which in turn may cause them to change their behavior in economically undesirable ways.

To illustrate, an important provision in the business tax code for which inflation poses problems is the *capital depreciation allowance,* which works as follows. Suppose a firm buys a machine for $1,000, expecting it to last for 10 years. Under

U.S. tax law, the firm can take one-tenth of the purchase price, or $100, as a deduction from its taxable profits in each of the 10 years. By deducting a fraction of the purchase price from its taxable profits, the firm reduces its taxes. The exact amount of the yearly tax reduction is the tax rate on corporate profits times $100.

The idea behind this provision of the tax code is that the wearing out of the machine is a cost of doing business that should be deducted from the firm's profit. Also, in giving firms a tax break for investing in new machinery, Congress intended to encourage firms to modernize their plants. Yet capital depreciation allowances are not indexed to inflation. Suppose that, at a time when the inflation rate is high, a firm is considering purchasing a $1,000 machine. The managers know that the purchase will allow them to deduct $100 per year from taxable profits for the next 10 years. But that $100 is a fixed amount that is not indexed to inflation. Looking forward, managers will recognize that 5, 6, or 10 years into the future, the real value of the $100 tax deduction will be much lower than at present because of inflation. They will have less incentive to buy the machine and may decide not to make the investment at all. Indeed, many studies have found that a high rate of inflation can significantly reduce the rate at which firms invest in new factories and equipment.

Because the complex U.S. tax code contains hundreds of provisions and tax rates that are not indexed, inflation can seriously distort the incentives provided by the tax system for people to work, save, and invest. The resulting adverse effects on economic efficiency and economic growth represent a real cost of inflation.

"SHOE-LEATHER" COSTS

As all shoppers know, cash is convenient. Unlike checks, which are not accepted everywhere, and credit cards, for which a minimum purchase is often required, cash can be used in almost any routine transaction. Businesses, too, find cash convenient to hold. Having plenty of cash on hand facilitates transactions with customers and reduces the need for frequent deposits and withdrawals from the bank.

Inflation raises the cost of holding cash to consumers and businesses. Consider a miser with $10,000 in $20 bills under his mattress. What happens to the buying power of his hoard over time? If inflation is zero so that on average the prices of goods and services are not changing, the buying power of the $10,000 does not change over time. At the end of a year, the miser's purchasing power is the same as it was at the beginning of the year. But suppose the inflation rate is 10 percent. In that case, the purchasing power of the miser's hoard will fall by 10 percent each year. After a year, he will have only $9,000 in purchasing power. In general, the higher the rate of inflation, the less people will want to hold cash because of the loss of purchasing power that they will suffer.

Technically, currency is a debt owed by the government to the currency holder. So when currency loses value, the losses to holders of cash are offset by gains to the government, which now owes less in real terms to currency holders. Thus, from the point of view of society as a whole, the loss of purchasing power is not in itself a cost of inflation because it does not involve wasted resources. (Indeed, no real goods or services were used up when the miser's currency hoard lost part of its value.) However, when faced with inflation, people are not likely to accept a loss in purchasing power but instead will take actions to try to "economize" on their cash holdings. For example, instead of drawing out enough cash for a month the next time they visit the bank, they will draw out only enough to last a week. The inconvenience of visiting the bank more often to minimize one's cash holdings is a real cost of inflation. Similarly, businesses will reduce their cash holdings by sending employees to the bank more frequently, or by installing computerized systems to monitor cash usage. To deal with the increase in bank transactions required by consumers and businesses trying to use less cash, banks will need to hire more employees and expand their operations.

The costs of more frequent trips to the bank, new cash management systems, and expanded employment in banks are real costs. They use up resources, including time and effort, that could be used for other purposes. Traditionally, the costs of economizing on cash have been called *shoe-leather costs*—the idea being that shoe leather is worn out during extra trips to the bank. Shoe-leather costs probably are not a significant problem in the United States today, where inflation is only 2 to 3 percent per year. But in economies with high rates of inflation, they can become quite significant.

Shoe-leather costs at Woodrow's Hardware

Woodrow's Hardware needs $5,000 cash per day for customer transactions. Woodrow has a choice between going to the bank first thing on Monday morning to withdraw $25,000—enough cash for the whole week—or going to the bank first thing every morning for $5,000 each time. Woodrow puts the cost of going to the bank, in terms of inconvenience and lost time, at $4 per trip. Assume that funds left in the bank earn precisely enough interest to keep their purchasing power unaffected by inflation.

If inflation is zero, how often will Woodrow go to the bank? If it is 10 percent? In this example, what are the shoe-leather costs of a 10 percent inflation rate?

If inflation is zero, there is no cost to holding cash. Woodrow will go to the bank only once a week, incurring a shoe-leather cost of $4 per week. But if inflation is 10 percent, Woodrow may need to change his banking habits. If he continues to go to the bank only on Monday mornings, withdrawing $25,000 for the week, what will be Woodrow's average cash holding over the week? At the beginning of each day, his cash holding will be as follows:

Monday	$25,000
Tuesday	20,000
Wednesday	15,000
Thursday	10,000
Friday	5,000

Averaging the holdings on those five days, we can calculate that Woodrow's average cash holding at the beginning of each day is $75,000/5 = $15,000. If inflation is 10 percent a year, over the course of a year the cost to Woodrow of holding an average of $15,000 in cash equals 10 percent of $15,000, or $1,500.

On the other hand, if Woodrow goes to the bank every day, his average cash holding at the beginning of the day will be only $5,000. In that case, his losses from inflation will be $500 (10 percent of $5,000) a year. Will Woodrow start going to the bank every day when inflation reaches 10 percent? The *benefit* of changing his banking behavior is a loss of only $500 per year to inflation, rather than $1,500, or $1,000 saved. The *cost* of going to the bank every day is $4 per trip. Assuming Woodrow's store is open 50 weeks a year, going to the bank 5 days a week instead of 1 day a week adds 200 trips per year, at a total cost of $800. Since the $800 cost is less than the $1,000 benefit, Woodrow will begin going to the bank more often.

Cost-Benefit

To repeat, the shoe-leather costs of a high inflation rate are the extra costs incurred to avoid holding cash. In this example, they are the additional $800 per year associated with Woodrow's daily trips to the bank. ◆

UNEXPECTED REDISTRIBUTION OF WEALTH

When inflation is unexpected, it may arbitrarily redistribute wealth from one group to another. Consider a group of union workers who signed a contract setting their wages for the next three years. If those wages are not indexed to inflation, then the workers will be vulnerable to upsurges in the price level. Suppose, for example, that inflation is much higher than expected over the three years of the contract. In that case, the buying power of the workers' wages—their real wages—will be less than anticipated when they signed the contract.

From society's point of view, is the buying power that workers lose to inflation really "lost"? The answer is no; the loss in their buying power is exactly matched by an unanticipated gain in the employer's buying power because the real cost of paying the workers is less than anticipated. In other words, the effect of the inflation is not to *destroy* purchasing power but to *redistribute* it, in this case from the workers to the employer. If inflation had been *lower* than expected, the workers would have enjoyed greater purchasing power than they anticipated and the employer would have been the loser.

Another example of the redistribution caused by inflation takes place between borrowers (debtors) and lenders (creditors). Suppose one of the authors of this book wants to buy a house on a lake and borrows $150,000 from the bank to pay for it. Shortly after signing the mortgage agreement, he learns that inflation is likely to be much higher than expected. How should he react to the news? Perhaps as a public-spirited macroeconomist, the author should be saddened to hear that inflation is rising, but as a consumer he should be pleased. In real terms, the dollars with which he will repay his loan in the future will be worth much less than expected. The loan officer should be distraught because the dollars the bank will receive from the author will be worth less, in purchasing power terms, than expected at contract signing. Once again, no real wealth is "lost" to the inflation; rather, the borrower's gain is just offset by the lender's loss. *In general, unexpectedly high inflation rates help borrowers at the expense of lenders* because borrowers are able to repay their loans in less-valuable dollars. Unexpectedly low inflation rates, in contrast, help lenders and hurt borrowers by forcing borrowers to repay in dollars that are worth more than expected when the loan was made.

Although redistributions caused by inflation do not directly destroy wealth, but only transfer it from one group to another, they are still bad for the economy. Our economic system is based on incentives. For it to work well, people must know that if they work hard, save some of their income, and make wise financial investments, they will be rewarded in the long run with greater real wealth and a better standard of living. Some observers have compared a high-inflation economy to a casino, in which wealth is distributed largely by luck—that is, by random fluctuations in the inflation rate. In the long run, a "casino economy" is likely to perform poorly, as its unpredictability discourages people from working and saving. (Why bother if inflation can take away your savings overnight?) Rather, a high-inflation economy encourages people to use up resources in trying to anticipate inflation and protect themselves against it.

INTERFERENCE WITH LONG-RUN PLANNING

The fifth and final cost of inflation we will examine is its tendency to interfere with the long-run planning of households and firms. Many economic decisions take place within a long time horizon. Planning for retirement, for example, may begin when workers are in their twenties or thirties. And firms develop long-run investment and business strategies that look decades into the future.

Clearly, high and erratic inflation can make long-term planning difficult. Suppose, for example, that you want to enjoy a certain standard of living when you retire. How much of your income do you need to save to make your dreams a reality? That depends on what the goods and services you plan to buy will cost 30 or 40 years from now. With high and erratic inflation, even guessing what your chosen lifestyle will cost by the time you retire is extremely difficult. You may end up saving too little and having to compromise on your retirement plans; or you may save too much, sacrificing more than you need to during your working years. Either way, inflation will have proved costly.

In summary, inflation damages the economy in a variety of ways. Some of its effects are difficult to quantify and are therefore controversial. But most economists agree that a low and stable inflation rate is instrumental in maintaining a healthy economy.

RECAP	THE TRUE COSTS OF INFLATION

The public sometimes confuses changes in relative prices (such as the price of oil) with inflation, which is a change in the overall level of prices. This confusion can cause problems because the remedies for undesired changes in relative prices and for inflation are different.

There are a number of true costs of inflation, which together tend to reduce economic growth and efficiency. These include

- "Noise" in the price system, which occurs when general inflation makes it difficult for market participants to interpret the information conveyed by prices.
- Distortions of the tax system, for example, when provisions of the tax code are not indexed.
- Shoe-leather costs, or the costs of economizing on cash (for example, by making more frequent trips to the bank or installing a computerized cash management system).
- Unexpected redistributions of wealth, as when higher-than-expected inflation hurts wage earners to the benefit of employers or hurts creditors to the benefit of debtors.
- Interference with long-term planning, arising because people find it difficult to forecast prices over long periods.

HYPERINFLATION

hyperinflation a situation in which the inflation rate is extremely high

Although there is some disagreement about whether an inflation rate of, say, 5 percent per year imposes important costs on an economy, few economists would question the fact that an inflation rate of 500 percent or 1,000 percent per year disrupts economic performance. A situation in which the inflation rate is extremely high is called **hyperinflation.** Although there is no official threshold above which inflation becomes hyperinflation, inflation rates in the range of 500 to 1,000 percent per year would surely qualify. In the past few decades, episodes of hyperinflation have occurred in Israel (400 percent inflation in 1985), several South American countries (including Bolivia, Argentina, and Brazil), Nicaragua (33,000 percent inflation in 1988), Zimbabwe (officially 24,470 percent inflation in 2007, unofficially 150,000 percent), and several countries attempting to make the transition from communism to capitalism, including Russia. Perhaps the most well-known episode occurred in Germany in 1923 when inflation was 102,000,000 percent. In the German hyperinflation, prices rose so rapidly that for a time workers were paid twice each day so their families could buy food before the afternoon price increases, and many people's life savings became worthless. But the most extreme hyperinflation ever recorded was in Hungary in 1945, at the end of the Second World War, when inflation peaked at 3.8×10^{27} percent. The United States has never experienced hyperinflation, although the short-lived Confederate States of America suffered severe inflation during the Civil War. Between 1861 and 1865, prices in the Confederacy rose to 92 times their prewar levels.

Hyperinflation greatly magnifies the costs of inflation. For example, shoe-leather costs—a relatively minor consideration in times of low inflation—become quite important during hyperinflation, when people may visit the bank two or three times per day to hold money for as short a time as possible. With prices changing daily or even hourly, markets work quite poorly, slowing economic growth. Massive redistributions of wealth take place, impoverishing many. Not surprisingly, episodes of hyperinflation rarely last more than a few years; they are so disruptive that they quickly lead to public outcry for relief.

How costly is high inflation?

Economic theory suggests that high inflation rates, especially those associated with hyperinflation, reduce economic efficiency and growth. Most economists believe that the economic costs associated with high inflation outweigh the perceived benefits, yet we continue to see episodes of high inflation throughout the world. In reality, how costly are high inflation rates?

Economists Stanley Fischer, Ratna Sahay, and Carlos A. Végh[4] examined the economic performance of 133 market economies over the period 1960–96 and uncovered 45 episodes of high inflation (12-month inflation rates greater than 100 percent) among 25 different countries. They found that, while uncommon, episodes of high inflation impose significant economic costs on the countries experiencing them. During periods of high inflation, these countries saw real GDP per person fall by an average of 1.6 percent per year, real consumption per person fall by an average of 1.3 percent per year, and real investment per person fall by an average of 3.3 percent per year. During low inflation years, these same countries experienced positive growth in each of these variables. In addition, during periods of high inflation, these countries' trade and government budget deficits were larger than during low inflation years.

Falling output and consumption levels caused by high inflation reduce the economic well-being of households and firms, and have a disproportionate effect on poor workers, who are least likely to have their wages indexed to the inflation rate and thus avoid a real loss in purchasing power. As pointed out in the last section, high inflation rates also distort relative prices in the marketplace, leading to a misallocation of resources that can have long-term economic consequences. Falling investment in new capital caused by high inflation, for example, leads not only to a slowdown in current economic activity but also to reduced growth rates of future output. Because of these adverse economic effects, policymakers have an incentive to keep inflation rates low. ◆

INFLATION AND INTEREST RATES

So far we have focused on the measurement and economic costs of inflation. Another important aspect of inflation is its close relationship to other key macroeconomic variables. For example, economists have long realized that during periods of high inflation, interest rates tend to be high as well. We will close this chapter with a look at the relationship between inflation and interest rates, which will provide a useful background in the chapters to come.

[4]"Modern Hyper- and High Inflations," *Journal of Economic Literature* 11 (September 2002), pp. 837–80.

INFLATION AND THE REAL INTEREST RATE

Earlier in our discussion of the ways in which inflation redistributes wealth, we saw that inflation tends to hurt creditors and help debtors by reducing the value of the dollars with which debts are repaid. The effect of inflation on debtors and creditors can be explained more precisely using an economic concept called the *real interest rate.* An example will illustrate.

Suppose that there are two neighboring countries, Alpha and Beta. In Alpha, whose currency is called the alphan, the inflation rate is zero and is expected to remain at zero. In Beta, where the currency is the betan, the inflation rate is 10 percent and is expected to remain at that level. Bank deposits pay 2 percent annual interest in Alpha and 10 percent annual interest in Beta. In which countries are bank depositors getting a better deal?

You may answer "Beta," since interest rates on deposits are higher in that country. But if you think about the effects of inflation, you will recognize that Alpha, not Beta, offers the better deal to depositors. To see why, think about the change over a year in the real purchasing power of deposits in the two countries. In Alpha, someone who deposits 100 alphans in the bank on January 1 will have 102 alphans on December 31. Because there is no inflation in Alpha, on average prices are the same at the end of the year as they were at the beginning. Thus, the 102 alphans the depositor can withdraw represent a 2 percent increase in buying power.

In Beta, the depositor who deposits 100 betans on January 1 will have 110 betans by the end of the year—10 percent more than she started with. But the prices of goods and services in Beta, we have assumed, also will rise by 10 percent. Thus, the Beta depositor can afford to buy precisely the same amount of goods and services at the end of the year as she could at the beginning; she gets no increase in buying power. So the Alpha depositor has the better deal, after all.

real interest rate the annual percentage increase in the purchasing power of a financial asset; the real interest rate on any asset equals the nominal interest rate on that asset minus the inflation rate

nominal interest rate (or market interest rate) the annual percentage increase in the nominal value of a financial asset

Economists refer to the annual percentage increase in the *real* purchasing power of a financial asset as the **real interest rate,** or the *real rate of return,* on that asset. In our example, the real purchasing power of deposits rises by 2 percent per year in Alpha and by 0 percent per year in Beta. So the real interest rate on deposits is 2 percent in Alpha and 0 percent in Beta. The real interest rate should be distinguished from the more familiar market interest rate, also called the *nominal interest rate.* The **nominal interest rate** is the annual percentage increase in the nominal, or dollar, value of an asset.

As the example of Alpha and Beta illustrates, we can calculate the real interest rate for any financial asset, from a checking account to a government bond, by subtracting the rate of inflation from the market or nominal interest rate on that asset. So in Alpha, the real interest rate on deposits equals the nominal interest rate (2 percent) minus the inflation rate (0 percent), or 2 percent. Likewise in Beta, the real interest rate equals the nominal interest rate (10 percent) minus the inflation rate (10 percent), or 0 percent.

We can write this definition of the real interest rate in mathematical terms:

$$r = i - \pi,$$

where

$$\begin{aligned} r &= \text{the real interest rate,} \\ i &= \text{the nominal, or market, interest rate,} \\ \pi &= \text{the inflation rate.} \end{aligned}$$

Note that the real interest rate is *not* equal to the nominal interest rate divided by the price level. The reason is that the nominal interest rate is a rate of return, measured in percent, not a nominal quantity measured in dollars.

Real interest rates in the 1970s, 1980s, and 1990s

Following are interest rates on government bonds for selected years since 1970. In which of these years did the financial investors who bought government bonds get the best deal? The worst deal?

Year	Interest rate (%)	Inflation rate (%)
1970	6.5	5.7
1975	5.8	9.1
1980	11.5	13.5
1985	7.5	3.6
1990	7.5	5.4
1995	5.5	2.8
2000	5.9	3.4
2005	3.2	3.4

Financial investors and lenders do best when the real (not the nominal) interest rate is high since the real interest rate measures the increase in their purchasing power. We can calculate the real interest rate for each year by subtracting the inflation rate from the nominal interest rate. The results are 0.8 percent for 1970, −3.3 percent for 1975, −2.0 percent for 1980, 3.9 percent for 1985, 2.1 percent for 1990, 2.7 percent for 1995, 2.5 percent for 2000, and −0.2 percent for 2005. For purchasers of government bonds, the best of these years was 1985, when they enjoyed a real return of 3.9 percent. The worst year was 1975, when their real return was actually negative. In other words, despite receiving 5.8 percent nominal interest, financial investors ended up losing buying power in 1975, as the inflation rate exceeded the interest rate earned by their investments.

Figure 13.3 shows the real interest rate in the United States since 1960 as measured by the nominal interest rate paid on the federal government's debt minus the inflation rate. Note that the real interest rate was negative in the 1970s and in 2003–2004 but reached historically high levels in the mid-1980s.

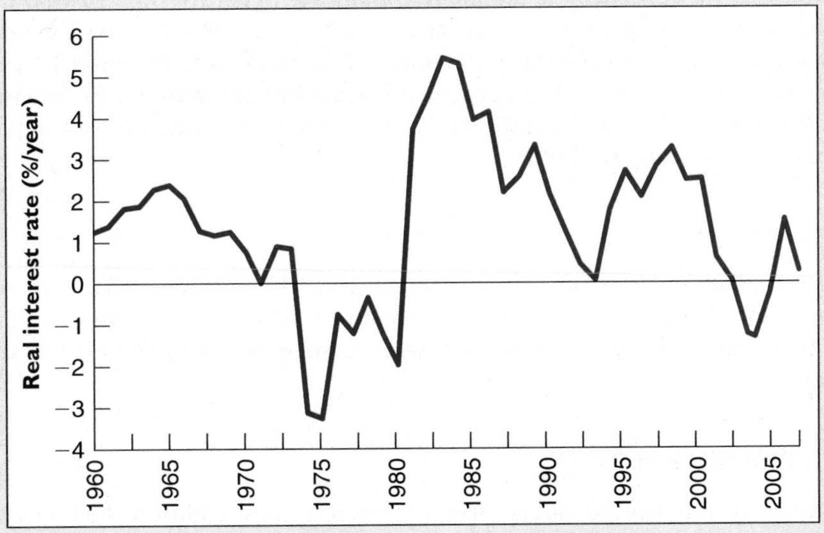

SOURCE: *Economic Report of the President*, February 2008, Tables B-73 and B-64 (http://www.gpoaccess.gov/eop/) and authors' calculations.

FIGURE 13.3

The Real Interest Rate in the United States, 1960–2007.

The real interest rate is the nominal interest rate—here the interest rate on funds borrowed by the federal government for a term of three months—minus the rate of inflation. In the United States, the real interest rate was negative in the 1970s and in 2003–2004 but reached historically high levels in the mid-1980s.

EXERCISE 13.9

You have some funds to invest but are unimpressed with the low interest rates your bank offers. You consult a broker, who suggests a bond issued by the government of a small island nation. The broker points out that these bonds pay 25 percent interest—much more than your bank—and that the island's government has never failed to repay its debts. What should be your next question?

The concept of the real interest rate helps to explain more precisely why an unexpected surge in inflation is bad for lenders and good for borrowers. For any given nominal interest rate that the lender charges the borrower, the higher the inflation rate, the lower the real interest rate the lender actually receives. So unexpectedly high inflation leaves the lender worse off. Borrowers, on the other hand, are better off when inflation is unexpectedly high because their real interest rate is lower than anticipated.

Although unexpectedly high inflation hurts lenders and helps borrowers, a high rate of inflation that is *expected* may not redistribute wealth at all because expected inflation can be built into the nominal interest rate. Suppose, for example, that the lender requires a real interest rate of 2 percent on new loans. If the inflation rate is confidently expected to be zero, the lender can get a 2 percent real interest rate by charging a nominal interest rate of 2 percent. But if the inflation rate is expected to be 10 percent, the lender can still ensure a real interest rate of 2 percent by charging a nominal interest rate of 12 percent. Thus, high inflation, if it is *expected,* need not hurt lenders—as long as the lenders can adjust the nominal interest they charge to reflect the expected inflation rate.

inflation-protected bonds bonds that pay a nominal interest rate each year equal to a fixed real rate plus the actual rate of inflation during that year

In response to people's concerns about unexpected inflation, in 1997 the United States Treasury introduced **inflation-protected bonds,** which pay a fixed real interest rate. People who buy these bonds receive a nominal interest rate each year equal to a fixed real rate plus the actual rate of inflation during that year. Owners of inflation-protected bonds suffer no loss in real wealth even if inflation is unexpectedly high.

EXERCISE 13.10

In May 2008, the annual real rate of return on a 10-year inflation-protected bond was 1.8 percent. The annual nominal rate of return on a 10-year bond without inflation protection was about 4.0 percent. Who made the better financial investment if inflation averages 2 percent over the next 10 years? What if inflation averages 3 percent per year? What inflation rate will make holders of inflation-protected bonds and holders of bonds without inflation protection equally well off?

EXERCISE 13.11

What is the real rate of return to holding cash? (*Hint:* Does cash pay interest?) Does this real rate of return depend on whether the rate of inflation is correctly anticipated? How does your answer relate to the idea of shoe-leather costs?

THE FISHER EFFECT

Earlier we mentioned the observation that interest rates tend to be high when inflation is high and low when inflation is low. This relationship can be seen in Figure 13.4, which shows both the U.S. inflation rate and a nominal interest rate (the rate at which the government borrows for short periods) from 1960 to the

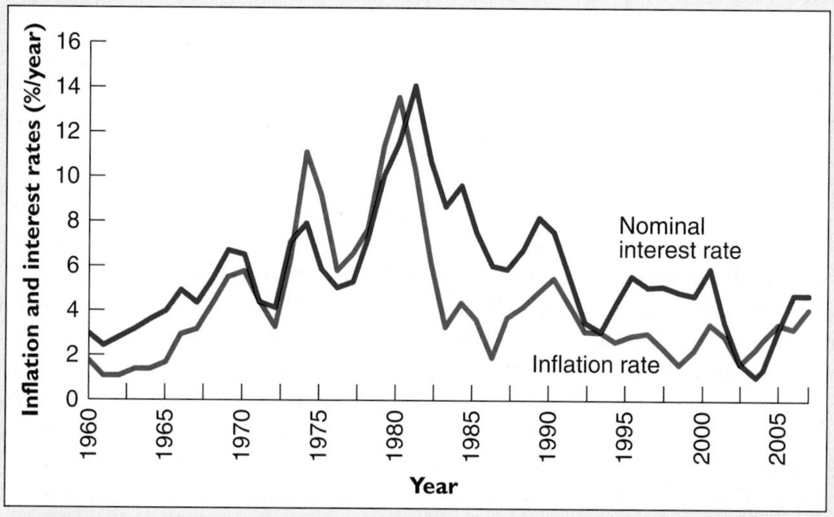

SOURCE: *Economic Report of the President,* February 2008, Tables B-73 and B-64 (http://www.gpoaccess.gov/eop/).

FIGURE 13.4
Inflation and Interest Rates in the United States, 1960–2007.
Nominal interest rates tend to be high when inflation is high and low when inflation is low, a phenomenon called the Fisher effect.

present. Notice that nominal interest rates have tended to be high in periods of high inflation, such as the late 1970s, and relatively low in periods of low inflation, such as the early 1960s and the late 1990s.

Why do interest rates tend to be high when inflation is high? Our discussion of real interest rates provides the answer. Suppose inflation has recently been high, so borrowers and lenders anticipate that it will be high in the near future. We would expect lenders to raise their nominal interest rate so that their real rate of return will be unaffected. For their part, borrowers are willing to pay higher nominal interest rates when inflation is high because they understand that the higher nominal interest rate only serves to compensate the lender for the fact that the loan will be repaid in dollars of reduced real value—in real terms, their cost of borrowing is unaffected by an equal increase in the nominal interest rate and the inflation rate. Conversely, when inflation is low, lenders do not need to charge so high a nominal interest rate to ensure a given real return. Thus, nominal interest rates will be high when inflation is high and low when inflation is low. This tendency for nominal interest rates to follow inflation rates is called the **Fisher effect,** after the early twentieth-century American economist Irving Fisher, who first pointed out the relationship.

Fisher effect the tendency for nominal interest rates to be high when inflation is high and low when inflation is low

SUMMARY

- The basic tool for measuring inflation is the consumer price index, or CPI. The CPI measures the cost of purchasing a fixed basket of goods and services in any period relative to the cost of the same basket of goods and services in a base year. The inflation rate is the annual percentage rate of change in the price level as measured by a price index such as the CPI. **LO1**

- A nominal quantity is a quantity that is measured in terms of its current dollar value. Dividing a nominal quantity such as a family's income or a worker's wage in dollars by a price index such as the CPI expresses that quantity in terms of real purchasing power. This procedure is called deflating the nominal quantity. If nominal quantities from two different years are deflated by a common price index, the purchasing power of the two quantities can be compared. To ensure that a nominal payment such as a Social Security benefit represents a constant level of real purchasing power, the nominal payment should be increased each year by a percentage equal to the inflation rate. This method of adjusting nominal payments to maintain their purchasing power is called indexing. **LO2**

- The official U.S. inflation rate, based on the CPI, may overstate the true inflation rate for two reasons: First, it may not adequately reflect improvements in the quality of goods and services. Second, the method of calculating the CPI ignores the fact that consumers can substitute cheaper goods and services for more expensive ones. **LO3**
- The public sometimes confuses increases in the relative prices for specific goods or services with inflation, which is an increase in the general price level. Since the remedies for a change in relative prices are different from the remedies for inflation, this confusion can cause problems. **LO4**
- Inflation imposes a number of true costs on the economy, including "noise" in the price system; distortions of the tax system; "shoe-leather" costs, which are the real resources that are wasted as people try to economize on cash holdings; unexpected redistributions of wealth; and interference with long-run planning. Because of these costs, most economists agree that sustained economic growth is more likely if inflation is low and stable. Hyperinflation, a situation in which the inflation rate is extremely high, greatly magnifies the costs of inflation and is highly disruptive to the economy. **LO4**
- The real interest rate is the annual percentage increase in the purchasing power of a financial asset. It is equal to the nominal, or market, interest rate minus the inflation rate. When inflation is unexpectedly high, the real interest rate is lower than anticipated, which hurts lenders but benefits borrowers. When inflation is unexpectedly low, lenders benefit and borrowers are hurt. To obtain a given real rate of return, lenders must charge a high nominal interest rate when inflation is high and a low nominal interest rate when inflation is low. The tendency for nominal interest rates to be high when inflation is high and low when inflation is low is called the Fisher effect. **LO5**

■ KEY TERMS ■

consumer price index (CPI) (350)
deflating (a nominal quantity) (354)
deflation (353)
Fisher effect (371)
hyperinflation (366)
indexing (356)
inflation-protected bonds (370)
nominal interest rate (368)
nominal quantity (354)
price index (352)
price level (360)
rate of inflation (352)
real interest rate (368)
real quantity (354)
real wage (355)
relative price (360)

■ REVIEW QUESTIONS ■

1. Explain why changes in the cost of living for any particular individual or family may differ from changes in the official cost-of-living index, the CPI. **LO1**
2. What is the difference between the *price level* and the *rate of inflation* in an economy? **LO1**
3. Why is it important to adjust for inflation when comparing nominal quantities (for example, workers' average wages) at different points in time? What is the basic method for adjusting for inflation? **LO2**
4. Describe how indexation might be used to guarantee that the purchasing power of the wage agreed to in a multiyear labor contract will not be eroded by inflation. **LO2**
5. Give two reasons why the official inflation rate may understate the "true" rate of inflation. Illustrate by examples. **LO3**
6. "It's true that unexpected inflation redistributes wealth, from creditors to debtors, for example. But what one side of the bargain loses, the other side gains. So from the perspective of the society as a whole, there is no real cost." Do you agree? Discuss. **LO4**
7. How does inflation affect the real return on holding cash? **LO5**
8. True or false: If both the potential lender and the potential borrower correctly anticipate the rate of inflation, inflation will not redistribute wealth from the creditor to the debtor. Explain. **LO5**

■ PROBLEMS ■

McGraw-Hill's HOMEWORK MANAGER®

1. Government survey takers determine that typical family expenditures each month in the year designated as the base year are as follows:

   20 pizzas at $10 each
   Rent of apartment, $600 per month
   Gasoline and car maintenance, $100
   Phone service (basic service plus 10 long-distance calls), $50

   In the year following the base year, the survey takers determine that pizzas have risen to $11 each, apartment rent is $640, gasoline and maintenance have risen to $120, and phone service has dropped in price to $40. **LO1**
   a. Find the CPI in the subsequent year and the rate of inflation between the base year and the subsequent year.
   b. The family's nominal income rose by 5 percent between the base year and the subsequent year. Are they worse off or better off in terms of what their income is able to buy?

2. Here are values of the CPI (multiplied by 100) for each year from 1990 to 2000. For each year beginning with 1991, calculate the rate of inflation from the previous year. What happened to inflation rates over the 1990s? **LO1**

1990	130.7
1991	136.2
1992	140.3
1993	144.5
1994	148.2
1995	152.4
1996	156.9
1997	160.5
1998	163.0
1999	166.6
2000	172.2

3. According to the U.S. Census Bureau (http://www.census.gov/), nominal income for the typical family of four in the United States (median income) was $24,332 in 1980, $32,777 in 1985, $41,451 in 1990, and $62,228 in 2000. In purchasing power terms, how did family income compare in each of those four years? You will need to know that the CPI (multiplied by 100, 1982–1984 = 100) was 82.4 in 1980, 107.6 in 1985, 130.7 in 1990, and 172.2 in 2000. In general terms, how would your answer be affected if the Boskin Commission's conclusions about the CPI were confirmed? **LO2, LO3**

4. A report found that the real entry-level wage for college graduates declined by 8 percent between 1990 and 1997. The nominal entry-level wage in 1997 was $13.65 per hour. Assuming that the findings are correct, what was the nominal entry-level wage in 1990? You will need to use data from Problem 2. **LO2**

5. Here is a hypothetical income tax schedule, expressed in nominal terms, for the year 2008:

Family income	Taxes due (percent of income)
≤$20,000	10
$20,001–$30,000	12
$30,001–$50,000	15
$50,001–$80,000	20
> $80,000	25

The legislature wants to ensure that families with a given real income are not pushed up into higher tax brackets by inflation. The CPI (times 100) is 175 in 2008 and 185 in 2010. How should the income tax schedule above be adjusted for the year 2010 to meet the legislature's goal? **LO2**

6. The typical consumer's food basket in the base year 2008 is as follows:

   30 chickens at $3.00 each
   10 hams at $6.00 each
   10 steaks at $8.00 each

   A chicken feed shortage causes the price of chickens to rise to $5.00 each in the year 2009. Hams rise to $7.00 each, and the price of steaks is unchanged. **LO1, LO3**

   a. Calculate the change in the "cost-of-eating" index between 2008 and 2009.
   b. Suppose that consumers are completely indifferent between two chickens and one ham. For this example, how large is the substitution bias in the official "cost-of-eating" index?

7. Here are the actual per-gallon prices for unleaded regular gasoline for June of each year between 1978 and 1986, together with the values of the CPIs for those years. For each year from 1979 to 1986, find the CPI inflation rate and the change in the relative price of gasoline, both from the previous year. Would it be fair to say that most of the changes in gas prices during this period were due to general inflation, or were factors specific to the oil market playing a role as well? **LO1, LO4**

Year	Gasoline price ($/gallon)	CPI (1982–1984 = 1.00)
1978	0.663	0.652
1979	0.901	0.726
1980	1.269	0.824
1981	1.391	0.909
1982	1.309	0.965
1983	1.277	0.996
1984	1.229	1.039
1985	1.241	1.076
1986	0.955	1.136

8. Let's revisit the problem of calculating the shoe-leather costs of inflation at Woodrow's Hardware. Calculate shoe-leather costs (relative to the original situation, in which Woodrow goes to the bank once a week) assuming that **LO4**
   a. Inflation is 5 percent rather than 10 percent.
   b. Inflation is 5 percent and Woodrow's trips to the bank cost $2 each.
   c. Inflation remains at 10 percent and a trip to the bank costs $4, but Woodrow needs $10,000 per day to transact with customers.

9. On January 1, 2009, Albert invested $1,000 at 6 percent interest per year for three years. The CPI on January 1, 2009, stood at 100. On January 1, 2010, the CPI (times 100) was 105; on January 1, 2011, it was 110; and on January 1, 2012, the day Albert's investment matured, the CPI was 118. Find the real rate of interest earned by Albert in each of the three years and his total real return over the three-year period. Assume that interest earnings are reinvested each year and themselves earn interest. **LO5**

10. Frank is lending $1,000 to Sarah for two years. Frank and Sarah agree that Frank should earn a 2 percent real return per year. **LO5**
    a. The CPI (times 100) is 100 at the time that Frank makes the loan. It is expected to be 110 in one year and 121 in two years. What nominal rate of interest should Frank charge Sarah?
    b. Suppose Frank and Sarah are unsure about what the CPI will be in two years. Show how Frank and Sarah could index Sarah's annual repayments to ensure that Frank gets an annual 2 percent real rate of return.

▪ ANSWERS TO IN-CHAPTER EXERCISES ▪

13.1 The cost of the family's basket in 2000 remains at $680, as in Table 13.1. If the rent on their apartment falls to $400 in 2008, the cost of reproducing the 2000 basket of goods and services in 2008 is $620 ($400 for rent + $150 for hamburgers + $70 for movie tickets). The CPI for 2008 is accordingly $620/$680, or 0.912. So in this example, the cost of living fell nearly 9 percent between 2000 and 2008. **LO1**

13.2 To construct your own personal price index, you would need to determine the basket of goods and services that you personally purchased in the base year. Your personal price index in each period would then be defined as the cost of your personal basket in that period relative to its cost in the base year. To the extent that your mix of purchases differs from that of the typical American consumer, your cost-of-living index will differ from the official CPI. For example, if in the base year you spent a higher share of your budget than the typical American on goods and services that have risen relatively rapidly in price, your personal inflation rate will be higher than the CPI inflation rate. **LO1**

13.3 The percentage changes in the CPI in each year from the previous year are as follows:

1930	−2.3% = (0.167 − 0.171)/0.171
1931	−9.0%
1932	−9.9%
1933	−5.1%

Negative inflation is called deflation. The experience of the 1930s, when prices were falling, contrasts sharply with inflation since 2003. **LO1**

13.4 Rodriguez's real earnings, in 1982–1984 dollars, were $22.7 million/2.07, or $10.97 million. In real terms, Rodriguez earned about 89 percent more in 2007 than Bonds did in 2001. **LO2**

13.5 The real minimum wage in 1950 is $0.75/0.241, or $3.11 in 1982–1984 dollars. The real minimum wage in 2007 is $5.85/2.073, or $2.82 in 1982–1984 dollars. So the real minimum wage in 2007 was almost 9 percent less than what it was in 1950. **LO2**

13.6 The increase in the cost of living between 1950 and 2007 is reflected in the ratio of the 2007 CPI to the 1950 CPI, or 2.073/0.241 = 8.60. That is, the cost of living in 2007 was 8.60 times what it was in 1950. If the minimum wage were indexed to preserve its purchasing power, it would have been 8.60 times higher in 2007 than in 1950, or 8.60 × $0.75 = $6.45. **LO2**

13.7 Between April 1991 and April 2008, the price of gasoline increased from $1.08 per gallon to $3.46 per gallon, or by 220.4 percent. During this same period, the CPI increased from 1.35 to 2.15, or by 59.3 percent. Gasoline prices rose more rapidly than the prices of the other goods and services in the CPI. Thus, the relative price of gas rose during this period. **LO4**

13.8 The real average cost of attending a private university in 1980 was $5,013/0.824 = $6084 in 1982–1984 dollars. In 2006, the real average cost was $27,317/2.016 = $13,550. Consequently, the average cost rose relative to other items in the CPI by 122.7 percent between 1980 and 2006. **LO4**

13.9 You should be concerned about the real return on your investment, not your nominal return. To calculate your likely real return, you need to know not only the nominal interest paid on the bonds of the island nation but also the prevailing inflation rate in that country. So your next question should be, "What is the rate of inflation in this country likely to be over the period that I am holding these bonds?" **LO5**

13.10 The owner of the bond with inflation protection earns a 1.8 percent real interest rate regardless of the level of inflation. If inflation averages 2 percent per year over the next decade, the real rate of return on the bond without inflation protection will be 4.0 − 2.0 = 2.0 percent. In this case, the person who bought the bond without inflation protection will be better off. If inflation averages 3 percent per year, the real rate of return on the bond without inflation protection will be 4.0 − 3.0 = 1.0 percent. In this case, the person who bought the inflation-protected bond will be better off. The two bonds will have the same real interest rate (and the two bondholders will be equally well off) if the real interest rate on the bond without inflation protection equals 1.8 percent. This will occur when inflation is 2.2 percent, since 4.0 − 2.2 = 1.8 percent. **LO5**

13.11 The real rate of return to cash, as with any asset, is the nominal interest rate less the inflation rate. But cash pays no interest; that is, the nominal interest rate on cash is zero. Therefore, the real rate of return on cash is just minus the inflation rate. In other words, cash loses buying power at a rate equal to the rate of inflation. This rate of return depends on the actual rate of inflation and does not depend on whether the rate of inflation is correctly anticipated.

If inflation is high so that the real rate of return on cash is very negative, people will take actions to try to reduce their holdings of cash, such as going to the bank more often. The costs associated with trying to reduce holdings of cash are what economists call shoe-leather costs. **LO5**

CHAPTER

14

Wages and Unemployment

LEARNING OBJECTIVES

After reading this chapter, you should be able to:

1. Discuss the five important trends that have characterized labor markets in the United States and Europe since 1960.
2. Use a supply-and-demand model to understand the labor market.
3. Explain how changes in the supply of and the demand for labor explain trends in real wages and employment since 1960.
4. Define and calculate the unemployment rate and the participation rate.
5. Differentiate among the three types of unemployment defined by economists and the costs associated with each.

In 1999, *New York Times* columnist Thomas L. Friedman published a best-selling book about the changing global economy, *The Lexus and the Olive Tree*.[1] The theme of Friedman's book is that one of the most striking features of the modern world is the close juxtaposition of rapid economic and technological change (represented by the Lexus automobile) with traditional values and customs (represented by the olive tree, a tree with deep roots that cannot be easily transplanted). Friedman notes that, in many countries, the conflicting pulls of modernization and traditional ways of life have created enormous social conflicts. Further, the powerful forces of modernization have widened the gap between the "haves" —those who can take advantage of rapid technological and economic change—and the "have-nots"—those who are unable or unwilling to do so.

[1]New York: Farrar, Straus, & Giroux, 1999.

To understand how economic growth and change affect different groups, we must turn to the labor market. Except for retirees and others receiving government support, most people rely almost entirely on wages and salaries to pay their bills and put something away for the future. Hence, it is in the labor market that most people will see the benefits of economic growth. This chapter describes and explains some important trends in the labor markets of industrial countries. We will see that two key factors contributing to recent trends in wages, employment, and unemployment are the *globalization* of the economy, as reflected in the increasing importance of international trade, and ongoing *technological change*. To see this, we focus first on several important trends in real wages and employment and then develop and apply a supply and demand model of the labor market. We then turn to the problem of unemployment and explain how the unemployment rate and some related statistics are defined and measured. We close with a discussion of different types of unemployment and the costs of unemployment, both to the unemployed and to the economy as a whole.

FIVE IMPORTANT LABOR MARKET TRENDS

In recent decades, at least five trends have characterized the labor markets of the industrialized world. We divide these trends into two groups: those affecting real wages and those affecting employment and unemployment.

TRENDS IN REAL WAGES

1. Over the twentieth century, all industrial countries have enjoyed substantial growth in real wages.

In the United States in 2007, the average worker's yearly earnings could command twice as many goods and services as in 1960 and nearly five times as much as in 1929, just prior to the Great Depression. Similar trends have prevailed in other industrialized countries.

2. Since the early 1970s, however, the rate of real wage growth has slowed.

Though the post–World War II period has seen impressive increases in real wages, the fastest rates of increase occurred during the 1960s and early 1970s. In the 13 years between 1960 and 1973, the buying power of workers' incomes rose at a rate of 2.5 percent per year, a strong rate of increase. But from 1973 to 1996, real yearly earnings fell by 1.1 percent per year. The good news is that, from 1996 to 2007, real earnings grew at about 2 percent per year, despite a recession in 2001. Annual earnings growth for the whole 1973 to 2007 period was roughly zero.

3. Furthermore, recent decades have brought a pronounced increase in wage inequality in the United States.

A growing gap in real wages between skilled and unskilled workers has been of particular concern. Although real GDP per capita doubled between 1960 and 2007, the average real weekly earnings among production workers actually fell, and the real wages of the least-skilled, least-educated workers have declined by as much as 25 to 30 percent according to some studies. At the same time, the best-educated, highest-skilled workers have enjoyed continuing gains in real wages. Data for a recent year showed that, in the United States, the typical worker with an advanced degree beyond college earned almost three times the income of a high school graduate, and four times the income of a worker with less than a high school degree. Many observers worry that the United States is developing a "two-tier" labor market: plenty of good jobs at good wages for the well-educated and highly skilled, but less and less opportunity for those without schooling or skills.

Outside the United States, particularly in western Europe, real wages have grown more rapidly and the trend toward wage inequality has been much less pronounced. But, as we will see, employment trends in Europe have not been as encouraging as in the United States. Let's turn now to the trends in employment and unemployment.

TRENDS IN EMPLOYMENT AND UNEMPLOYMENT

4. In the United States, the number of people with jobs has grown substantially in recent decades.

In 1970, about 57 percent of the over-16 population in the United States had jobs. By 2007, total U.S. employment exceeded 146 million people, more than 63 percent of the over-16 population. Between 1980 and 2007, the U.S. economy created 46 million new jobs—an increase in total employment of 46 percent—while the over-16 population grew only 38 percent. Similar job growth has *not* occurred in most other industrialized countries, however. In particular:

5. Western European countries have been suffering high rates of unemployment for almost two decades.

In France, for example, an average of 10 percent of the workforce was unemployed over the period 1990–2007, compared to just 5.5 percent in the United States. Consistent with the high rates of unemployment, rates of job creation in western Europe have been exceptionally weak.

Given the trend toward increasing wage inequality in the United States and the persistence of high unemployment in Europe, a significant fraction of the industrial world's labor force has not been sharing in the recent economic growth and prosperity. Whereas in the United States the problem takes the form of low and falling real wages for unskilled workers, in Europe work is often simply unavailable for the unskilled and sometimes even for the skilled.

What explains these trends in employment and wages? In the next two sections, we will show that a supply and demand analysis of the labor market can help to explain these important developments.

RECAP	FIVE IMPORTANT LABOR MARKET TRENDS

- Over a long period, average real wages have risen substantially both in the United States and in other industrialized countries.
- Despite the long-term upward trend in real wages, real wage growth has slowed significantly in the United States since the early 1970s.
- In the United States, wage inequality has increased dramatically in recent decades. The real wages of most unskilled workers have actually declined, while the real wages of skilled and educated workers have continued to rise.

- Employment has grown substantially—indeed, much faster than the working-age population—in the United States in recent decades.
- Since about 1980, western European nations have experienced very high rates of unemployment and low rates of job creation.

SUPPLY AND DEMAND IN THE LABOR MARKET

In Chapter 3 we saw how supply and demand analysis can be used to determine equilibrium prices and quantities for individual goods and services. The same approach is equally useful for studying labor market conditions. In the market for labor, the "price" is the real wage paid to workers in exchange for their services. The wage is expressed per unit of time, for example, per hour or per year. The "quantity" is the amount of labor firms use, which in this book we will generally measure by number of workers employed. Alternatively, we could state the quantity of labor in terms of the number of hours worked; the choice of units is a matter of convenience.

Who are the demanders and suppliers in the labor market? Firms and other employers demand labor in order to produce goods and services. Virtually all of us supply labor during some phase of our lives. Whenever people work for pay, they are supplying labor services at a price equal to the wage they receive. In this chapter, we will discuss both the supply of and demand for labor, with an emphasis on the demand side of the labor market. Changes in the demand for labor turn out to be key in explaining the aggregate trends in wages and employment described in the preceding section.

The labor market is studied by microeconomists as well as macroeconomists, and both use the tools of supply and demand. However, microeconomists focus on issues such as the determination of wages for specific types of jobs or workers. In this chapter we take the macroeconomic approach and examine factors that affect aggregate, or economywide, trends in employment and wages.

WAGES AND THE DEMAND FOR LABOR

Let's start by thinking about what determines the number of workers employers want to hire at any given wage, that is, the demand for labor. As we will see, the demand for labor depends on both the productivity of labor and the price that the market sets on workers' output. The more productive workers are, or the more valuable the goods and services they produce, the greater the number of workers an employer will want to hire at any given wage.

Table 14.1 shows the relationship between output and the number of workers employed at the Banana Computer Company (BCC), which builds and sells computers. Column 1 of the table shows some different possibilities for the number of technicians BCC could employ in its plant. Column 2 shows how many computers the company can produce each year, depending on the number of workers employed. The more workers, the greater the number of computers BCC can produce. For the sake of simplicity, we will assume that the plant, equipment, and materials the workers use to build computers are fixed quantities.

diminishing returns to labor if the amount of capital and other inputs in use is held constant, then the greater the quantity of labor already employed, the less each additional worker adds to production

Column 3 of Table 14.1 shows the *marginal product* of each worker, the extra production that is gained by adding one more worker. Note that each additional worker adds less to total production than the previous worker did. The tendency for marginal product to decline as more and more workers are added is called **diminishing returns to labor.** Specifically, if the amount of capital and other inputs in use is held constant, then the greater the quantity of labor already employed, the less each additional worker adds to production.

Increasing Opportunity Cost

The economic basis of diminishing returns to labor is the Principle of Increasing Opportunity Cost, also known as the Low-Hanging-Fruit Principle. A firm's managers want to use their available inputs in the most productive way possible. Hence,

TABLE 14.1
Production and Marginal Product for Banana Computers

(1) Number of workers	(2) Computers produced per year	(3) Marginal product	(4) Value of marginal product (at $3,000/computer)
0	0		
		25	$75,000
1	25		
		23	69,000
2	48		
		21	63,000
3	69		
		19	57,000
4	88		
		17	51,000
5	105		
		15	45,000
6	120		
		13	39,000
7	133		
		11	33,000
8	144		

an employer who has one worker will assign that worker to the most productive job. If she hires a second worker, she will assign that worker to the second most productive job. The third worker will be given the third most productive job available, and so on. The greater the number of workers already employed, the lower the marginal product of adding another worker, as shown in Table 14.1.

If BCC computers sell for $3,000 each, then column 4 of Table 14.1 shows the *value of the marginal product* of each worker. The value of a worker's marginal product is the amount of extra revenue that the worker generates for the firm. Specifically, the value of the marginal product of each BCC worker is that worker's marginal product, stated in terms of the number of additional computers produced, multiplied by the price of output, here $3,000 per computer. We now have all the information necessary to find BCC's demand for workers.

BCC's demand for labor

Suppose that the going wage for computer technicians is $60,000 per year. BCC managers know that this is the wage being offered by all their competitors, so they cannot hire qualified workers for less. How many technicians will BCC hire? What would the answer be if the wage were $50,000 per year?

BCC will hire an extra worker if and only if the value of that worker's marginal product (which equals the extra revenue the worker creates for the firm) exceeds the wage BCC must pay. The going wage for computer technicians, which BCC takes as given, is $60,000 per year. Table 14.1 shows that the value of the marginal product of the first, second, and third workers each exceeds $60,000. Hiring these workers will be profitable for BCC because the extra revenue each generates exceeds the wage that BCC must pay. However, the fourth worker's marginal product is worth only $57,000. If BCC's managers hired a fourth worker, they would be paying $60,000 in extra wages for additional output that is worth only $57,000. Since hiring the fourth worker is a money-losing proposition, BCC will hire only three workers. Thus, the quantity of labor BCC demands when the going wage is $60,000 per year is three technicians.

If the market wage for computer technicians were $50,000 per year instead of $60,000, the fourth technician would be worth hiring, since the value of his marginal product, $57,000, would be $7,000 more than his wages. The fifth technician also would be worth hiring, since the fifth worker's marginal product is worth $51,000—$1,000 more than the going wage. The value of the marginal product of a sixth technician, however, is only $45,000, so hiring a sixth worker would not be profitable. When wages are $50,000 per year, then BCC's labor demand is five technicians. ◆

EXERCISE 14.1

How many workers will BCC hire if the going wage for technicians is $35,000 per year?

The lower the wage a firm must pay, the more workers it will hire. Thus, the demand for labor is like the demand for other goods or services in that the quantity demanded rises as the price (in this case, the wage) falls. Figure 14.1 shows a hypothetical labor demand curve for a firm or industry, with the wage on the vertical axis and employment on the horizontal axis. All else being equal, the higher the wage, the fewer workers a firm or industry will demand.

In our example thus far, we have discussed how labor demand depends on the *nominal*, or dollar, wage. As we explained in Chapter 13, it is generally more illuminating to examine the real wage, which is the wage expressed in terms of its purchasing power. We shall temporarily hold the general price level constant so that changes in the nominal wage also reflect changes in the real wage.

FIGURE 14.1
The Demand Curve for Labor.
The demand curve for labor is downward-sloping. The higher the wage, the fewer workers employers will hire.

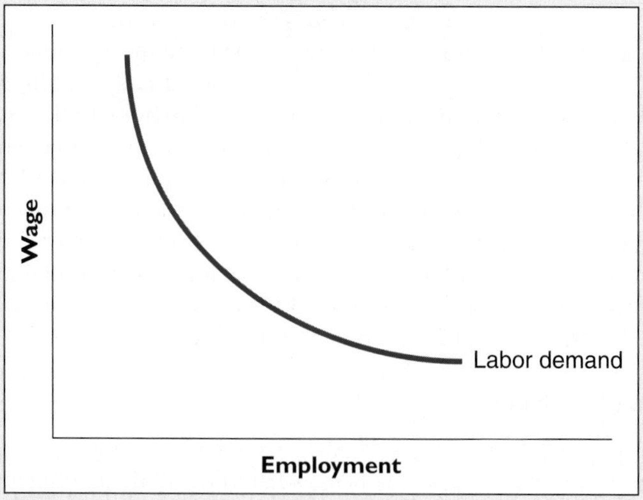

SHIFTS IN THE DEMAND FOR LABOR

The number of workers that BCC will employ at any given real wage depends on the value of their marginal product, as shown in column 4 of Table 14.1. Changes in the economy that increase the value of workers' marginal product will increase the value of extra workers to BCC, and thus BCC's demand for labor at any given real wage. In other words, any factor that raises the value of the marginal product of BCC's workers will shift BCC's labor demand curve to the right.

Two main factors could increase BCC's labor demand: (1) an increase in the price of the company's output (computers) and (2) an increase in the productivity of BCC's workers. The next two examples illustrate both of these possibilities.

The price of computers and BCC's demand for labor

Suppose an increase in the demand for BCC's computers raises the price of its computers to $5,000 each. How many technicians will BCC hire now if the real wage is $60,000 per year? If the real wage is $50,000?

The effect of the increase in computer prices is shown in Table 14.2. Columns 1 to 3 of the table are the same as in Table 14.1. The number of computers a given number of technicians can build (column 2) has not changed; hence, the marginal product of particular technicians (column 3) is the same. But because computers can now be sold for $5,000 each instead of $3,000, the *value* of each worker's marginal product has increased by two-thirds (compare column 4 of Table 14.2 with column 4 of Table 14.1).

TABLE 14.2

Production and Marginal Product for Banana Computers after an Increase in Computer Prices

(1) Number of workers	(2) Computers produced per year	(3) Marginal product	(4) Value of marginal product (at $5,000/computer)
0	0		
		25	$125,000
1	25		
		23	115,000
2	48		
		21	105,000
3	69		
		19	95,000
4	88		
		17	85,000
5	105		
		15	75,000
6	120		
		13	65,000
7	133		
		11	55,000
8	144		

How does the increase in the price of computers affect BCC's demand for labor? Recall from our first example that when the price of computers was $3,000 and the going wage for technicians was $60,000, BCC's demand for labor was three workers. But now, with computers selling for $5,000 each, the value of the marginal product of each of the first seven workers exceeds $60,000 (Table 14.2). So, if the real wage of computer technicians is still $60,000, BCC would increase its demand from three workers to seven.

Suppose instead that the going real wage for technicians is $50,000. In the example above, when the price of computers was $3,000 and the wage was $50,000, BCC demanded five workers. But if computers sell for $5,000, we can see from column 4 of Table 14.2 that the value of the marginal product of even the eighth worker exceeds the wage of $50,000. So if the real wage is $50,000, the increase in computer prices raises BCC's demand for labor from five workers to eight. ◆

EXERCISE 14.2

How many workers will BCC hire if the going wage for technicians is $100,000 per year and the price of computers is $5,000? Compare your answer to the demand for technicians at a wage of $100,000 when the price of computers is $3,000.

The general conclusion to be drawn from this example is that *an increase in the price of workers' output increases the demand for labor,* shifting the labor demand curve to the right, as shown in Figure 14.2. A higher price for workers' output makes workers more valuable, leading employers to demand more workers at any given real wage.

FIGURE 14.2
A Higher Price of Output Increases the Demand for Labor.
An increase in the price of workers' output increases the value of their marginal product, shifting the labor demand curve to the right.

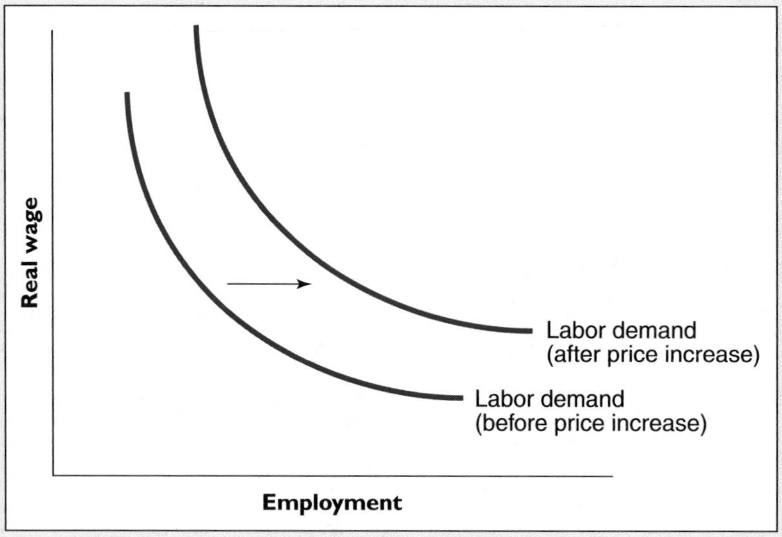

The second factor that affects the demand for labor is worker productivity. Since an increase in productivity increases the value of a worker's marginal product, it also increases the demand for labor, as the next example shows.

Worker productivity and BCC's demand for labor

Suppose BCC adopts a new technology that reduces the number of components to be assembled, permitting each technician to build 50 percent more machines per year. Assume that the price of computers is $3,000 per machine. How many technicians will BCC hire if the real wage is $60,000 per year?

Table 14.3 shows workers' marginal products and the value of their marginal products after the 50 percent increase in productivity, assuming that computers sell for $3,000 each.

TABLE 14.3
Production and Marginal Product for Banana Computers after an Increase in Worker Productivity

(1) Number of workers	(2) Computers produced per year	(3) Marginal product	(4) Value of marginal product ($3,000/computer)
0	0		
		37.5	$112,500
1	37.5		
		34.5	103,500
2	72		
		31.5	94,500
3	103.5		
		28.5	85,500
4	132		
		25.5	76,500
5	157.5		
		22.5	67,500
6	180		
		19.5	58,500
7	199.5		
		16.5	49,500
8	216		

Before the productivity increase, BCC would have demanded three workers at a wage of \$60,000 (see Table 14.1). After the productivity increase, however, the value of the marginal product of the first six workers exceeds \$60,000 (see Table 14.3, column 4). So at a wage of \$60,000, BCC's demand for labor increases from three workers to six. ◆

EXERCISE 14.3

How many workers will BCC hire after the 50 percent increase in productivity if the going wage for technicians is \$50,000 per year? Compare this figure to the demand for workers at a \$50,000 wage before the increase in productivity.

In general, an increase in worker productivity increases the demand for labor, shifting the labor demand curve to the right, as in Figure 14.3.

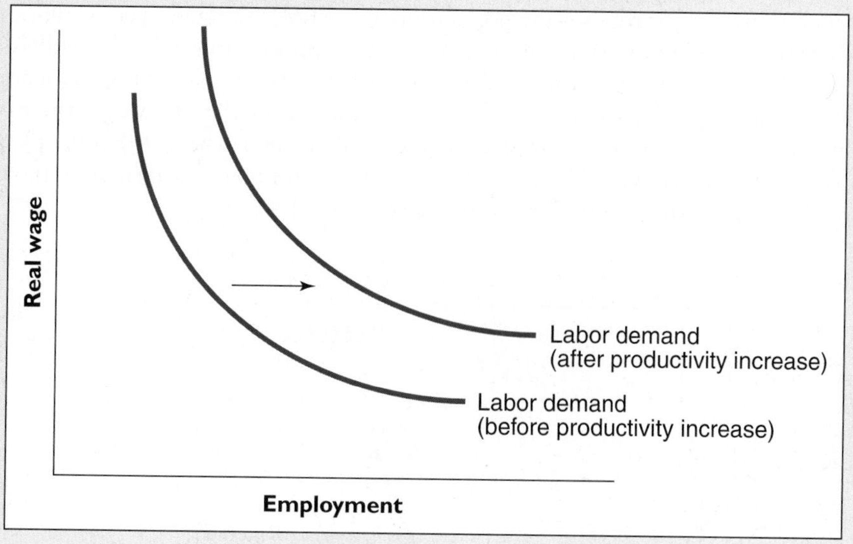

FIGURE 14.3
Higher Productivity Increases the Demand for Labor.
An increase in productivity raises workers' marginal product and—assuming no change in the price of output—the value of their marginal product. Since a productivity increase raises the value of marginal product, employers will hire more workers at any given real wage, shifting the labor demand curve to the right.

THE SUPPLY OF LABOR

We have discussed the demand for labor by employers; to complete the story, we need to consider the supply of labor. The suppliers of labor are workers and potential workers. At any given real wage, potential suppliers of labor must decide if they are willing to work. The total number of people who are willing to work at each real wage is the supply of labor.[2]

Will you clean your neighbor's basement or go to the beach?

You were planning to go to the beach today, but your neighbor asks you to clean out his basement. You like the beach a lot more than fighting cobwebs. Do you take the job?

Unless you are motivated primarily by neighborliness, your answer to this job offer would probably be "It depends on how much my neighbor will pay." You probably would not be willing to take the job for \$10 or \$20, unless you have a severe and immediate need for cash. But if your neighbor were wealthy and eccentric

[2]We are still holding the general price level constant, so any increase in the nominal wage also represents an increase in the real wage.

enough to offer you $500 (to take an extreme example), you would very likely say yes. Somewhere between $20 and the unrealistic figure of $500 is the minimum payment you would be willing to accept to tackle the dirty basement. This minimum payment, the *reservation price* you set for your labor, is the compensation level that leaves you just indifferent between working and not working.

Cost-Benefit

In economic terms, deciding whether to work at any given wage is a straightforward application of the Cost-Benefit Principle. The cost to you of cleaning out the basement is the opportunity cost of your time (you would rather be surfing) plus the cost you place on having to work in unpleasant conditions. You can measure this total cost in dollars simply by asking yourself, "What is the minimum amount of money I would take to clean out the basement instead of going to the beach?" The minimum payment that you would accept is the same as your reservation price. The benefit of taking the job is measured by the pay you receive, which will go toward that new DVD player you want. You should take the job only if the promised pay (the benefit of working) exceeds your reservation price (the cost of working). ◆

In this example, your willingness to supply labor is greater the higher the wage. In general, the same is true for the population as a whole. Certainly people work for many reasons, including personal satisfaction, the opportunity to develop skills and talents, and the chance to socialize with co-workers. Still, for most people, income is one of the principal benefits of working, so the higher the real wage, the more willing they are to sacrifice other possible uses of their time. The fact that people are more willing to work when the wage they are offered is higher is captured in the upward slope of the supply curve of labor (see Figure 14.4).

FIGURE 14.4
The Supply of Labor.
The labor supply curve is upward-sloping because, in general, the higher the wage, the more people are willing to work.

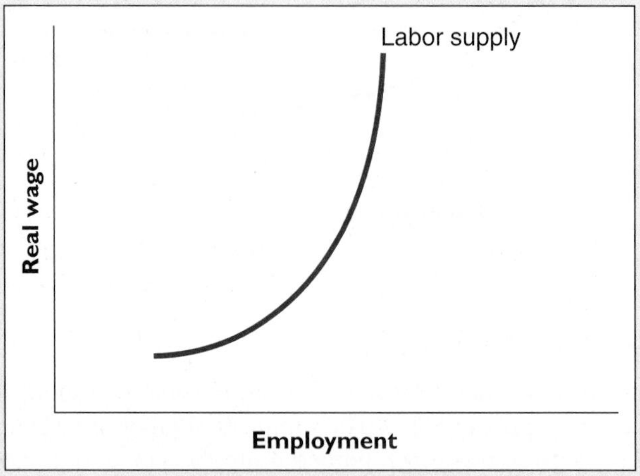

EXERCISE 14.4

You want a career in broadcasting. The local radio station is offering an unpaid summer internship that would give you valuable experience. Your alternative to the internship is to earn $3,000 working in a car wash. How would you decide which job to take? Would a decision to take the internship contradict the conclusion that the labor supply curve is upward-sloping?

SHIFTS IN THE SUPPLY OF LABOR

Any factor that affects the quantity of labor offered at a given real wage will shift the labor supply curve. At the macroeconomic level, the most important factor affecting the supply of labor is the size of the working-age population, which is influenced by factors such as the domestic birthrate, immigration and emigration rates, and the ages at which people normally first enter the workforce and retire. All else being equal, an increase in the working-age population raises the quantity of labor supplied at each real wage, shifting the labor supply curve to the right. Changes in the percentage of people of working age who seek employment—for example, as a result of social changes that encourage women to work outside the home—also can affect the supply of labor.

Now that we have discussed both the demand for and supply of labor, we are ready to apply supply and demand analysis to real-world labor markets. But first, try your hand at using supply and demand analysis to answer the following question.

EXERCISE 14.5

Labor unions typically favor tough restrictions on immigration, while employers tend to favor more liberal rules. Why? (*Hint:* How is an influx of potential workers likely to affect real wages?)

RECAP | SUPPLY AND DEMAND IN THE LABOR MARKET

The demand for labor

The extra production gained by adding one more worker is the *marginal product* of that worker. The *value of the marginal product* of a worker is that worker's marginal product times the price of the firm's output. A firm will employ a worker only if the worker's value of marginal product, which is the same as the extra revenue the worker generates for the firm, exceeds the real wage that the firm must pay. The lower the real wage, the more workers the firm will find it profitable to employ. Thus, the labor demand curve, like most demand curves, is downward-sloping.

For a given real wage, any change that increases the value of workers' marginal products will increase the demand for labor and shift the labor demand curve to the right. Examples of factors that increase labor demand are an increase in the price of workers' output and an increase in productivity.

The supply of labor

An individual is willing to supply labor if the real wage that is offered is greater than the opportunity cost of the individual's time. Generally, the higher the real wage, the more people are willing to work. Thus, the labor supply curve, like most supply curves, is upward-sloping.

For a given real wage, any factor that increases the number of people available and willing to work increases the supply of labor and shifts the labor supply curve to the right. Examples of facts that increase labor supply include an increase in the working-age population or an increase in the share of the working-age population seeking employment.

EXPLAINING THE TRENDS IN REAL WAGES AND EMPLOYMENT

We are now ready to analyze the important trends in real wages and employment discussed earlier in the chapter.

WHY HAVE REAL WAGES INCREASED BY SO MUCH IN THE INDUSTRIALIZED COUNTRIES?

As we discussed, real annual earnings in the United States have quintupled since 1929, and other industrialized countries have experienced similar gains. These increases have greatly improved the standard of living of workers in these countries. Why have real wages increased by so much in the United States and other industrialized countries?

The large increase in real wages results from the sustained growth in productivity experienced by the industrialized countries during the twentieth century. (We discuss the sources of this growth in productivity in the next chapter.) As illustrated by Figure 14.5, increased productivity raises the demand for labor, increasing employment and the real wage.

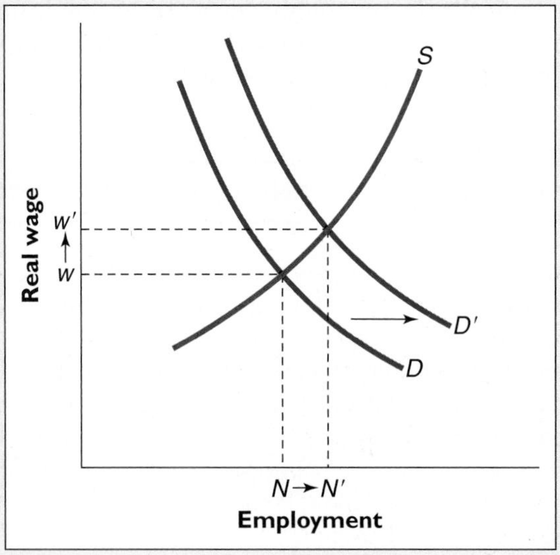

FIGURE 14.5
An Increase in Productivity Raises the Real Wage.
An increase in productivity raises the demand for labor, shifting the labor demand curve from *D* to *D′*. The real wage rises from *w* to *w′* and employment rises from *N* to *N′*.

Of the factors contributing to productivity growth in the industrialized countries, two of the most important were (1) the dramatic technological progress that occurred during the twentieth century and (2) large increases in capital, which provided workers with more and better tools with which to work. Labor supply increased during the century as well, of course (not shown in the diagram). However, the increases in labor demand, driven by rapidly expanding productivity, have been so great as to overwhelm the depressing effect on real wages of increased labor supply.

SINCE THE 1970S, REAL WAGE GROWTH IN THE UNITED STATES HAS SLOWED, WHILE EMPLOYMENT HAS EXPANDED RAPIDLY

With the exception of the period since the late 1990s, rates of real wage growth after 1973 in the United States have been significantly lower than in previous decades. But over much of the recent period, the economy has created new jobs at a record rate. What accounts for these trends?

Let's begin with the slowdown in real wage growth since the early 1970s. Supply and demand analysis tells us that a slowdown in real wage growth must result from slower growth in the demand for labor, more rapid growth in the supply of labor, or both. On the demand side, since the early 1970s the United States and other industrialized nations have experienced a slowdown in productivity growth. Thus, one possible explanation for the slowdown in the growth of real wages since the early 1970s is the decline in the pace of productivity gains.

Some evidence for a relationship between productivity and real wages is given in Table 14.4, which shows the average annual growth rates in labor productivity and real annual earnings for each decade since 1960. You can see that the growth in productivity decade by decade corresponds closely to the growth in real earnings. Particularly striking is the rapid growth of both productivity and wages during the 1960s. Since the 1970s, growth in both productivity and real wages has been significantly slower, although some improvement is apparent after 1990.

While the effects of the slowdown in productivity on the demand for labor are an important reason for declining real wage growth, they can't be the whole story. We know this because, with labor supply held constant, slower growth in labor demand would lead to reduced rates of employment growth, as well as reduced growth in real wages. But job growth in the United States has been rapid in recent decades. Large increases in employment in the face of slow growth of labor demand can be explained only by simultaneous increases in the supply of labor (see the next exercise).

TABLE 14.4
Growth Rates in Productivity and Real Earnings

	Annual Growth Rate (%)	
	Productivity	**Real earnings**
1960–1970	2.74	2.27
1970–1980	1.71	1.23
1980–1990	1.60	0.71
1990–2000	2.04	1.50
2000–2007	2.49	1.27

SOURCE: 1960–2000: *Economic Report of the President,* 2007 (http//www.gpoaccess.gov/eop/index.html); 2000–2007: Bureau of Labor Statistics (http://nmc.bls.gov). Productivity is output per hour in the nonfarm business sector; real earnings equal real compensation per hour in the nonfarm business sector.

Labor supply in the United States does appear to have grown rapidly recently. As we saw in Chapter 12, for example, increased participation in the labor market by women has increased the U.S. supply of labor since the mid-1970s. Other factors, including the coming of age of the baby boomers and high rates of immigration, also help to explain the increase in the supply of labor. The combination of slower growth in labor demand (the result of the productivity slowdown) and accelerated growth in labor supply (the result of increased participation by women in the workforce, together with other factors) helps to explain why real wage growth has been sluggish for many years in the United States, even as employment has grown rapidly.

What about the future? Labor supply growth is likely to slow in the coming decades as the baby boomers retire and the percentage of women in the labor force stabilizes. Productivity has recently grown more quickly, reflecting the benefits of new technologies, among other factors. Especially if the recent productivity trend continues, there seems to be a good chance that workers will see healthy gains in real wages in the years to come.

EXERCISE 14.6

As we just discussed, relatively weak growth in productivity and relatively strong growth in labor supply after about 1973 can explain (1) the slowdown in real wage growth and (2) the more rapid expansion in employment after about 1973. Show this point graphically by drawing two supply and demand diagrams of the labor market, one corresponding to the period 1960–1972 and the other to 1973–2000 (the period ending just before the 2001 recession). Assuming that productivity growth was strong but labor supply growth was modest during 1960–1972, show that we would expect to see rapid real wage growth but only moderate growth in employment in that period. Now apply the same analysis to 1973–2000, assuming that productivity growth is weaker but labor supply growth stronger than in 1960–1972. What do you predict for growth in the real wage and employment in 1973–2000 relative to the earlier period?

INCREASING WAGE INEQUALITY: THE EFFECTS OF GLOBALIZATION

Another important trend in U.S. labor markets is increasing inequality in wages. Specifically, many commentators have blamed the increasing divergence between the wages of skilled and unskilled workers on the phenomenon of "globalization." This popular term refers to the fact that to an increasing extent, the markets for many goods and services are becoming international, rather than national or local in scope. While Americans have long been able to buy products from all over the world, the ease with which goods and services can cross borders is increasing rapidly. In part this trend is the result of international trade agreements such as the North American Free Trade Agreement (NAFTA), which reduced taxes on goods and services traded among Canada, the United States, and Mexico. However, technological advances such as the internet also have promoted globalization.

The main economic benefit of globalization is increased specialization and the efficiency that it brings. Instead of each country trying to produce everything its citizens consume, each can concentrate on producing those goods and services at which it is relatively most efficient. As implied by the Principle of Comparative Advantage (Chapter 2), the result is that consumers of all countries enjoy a greater variety of goods and services, of better quality and at lower prices, than they would without international trade.

Comparative Advantage

The effects of globalization on the *labor* market are mixed, however, which explains why many politicians oppose free trade agreements. Expanded trade means that consumers stop buying certain goods and services from domestic producers and switch to foreign-made products. Consumers would not make this switch unless the foreign products were better, cheaper, or both, so expanded trade clearly makes them better off. But the workers and firm owners in the domestic industries that lose business may well suffer from the increase in foreign competition.

The effects of increasing trade on the labor market can be analyzed using Figure 14.6. The figure contrasts the supply and demand for labor in two different industries: (a) textiles and (b) computer software. Imagine that, initially, there is little or no international trade in these two goods. Without trade, the demand for workers in each industry is indicated by the curves marked D_{textiles} and D_{software}, respectively. Wages and employment in each industry are determined by the intersection of the demand curves and the labor supply curves in each industry. As we have drawn the figure, initially, the real wage is the same in both industries, equal to w. Employment is N_{textiles} in textiles and N_{software} in software.

What will happen when this economy is opened up to trade, perhaps because of a free trade agreement? Under the agreement, countries will begin to produce for

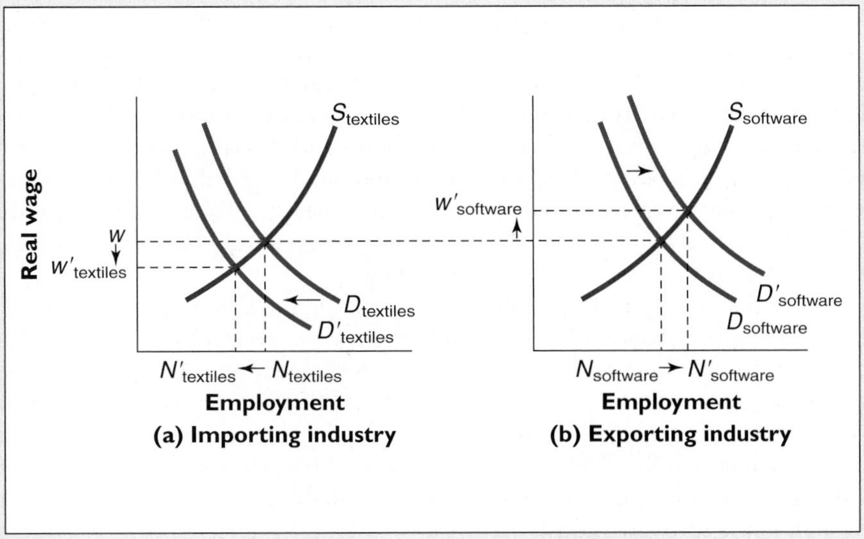

FIGURE 14.6
The Effect of Globalization on the Demand for Workers in Two Industries.
Initially, real wages in the two industries are equal at *w*. After an increase in trade, (a) demand for workers in the importing industry (textiles) declines, lowering real wages and employment, while (b) demand for workers in the exporting industry (software) increases, raising real wages and employment in that industry.

export those goods or services at which they are relatively more efficient and to import goods or services that they are relatively less efficient at producing. Suppose the country in this example is relatively more efficient at producing software than manufacturing textiles. With the opening of trade, the country gains new foreign markets for its software and begins to produce for export as well as for domestic use. Meanwhile, because the country is relatively less efficient at producing textiles, consumers begin to purchase foreign-made textiles, which are cheaper or of higher quality, instead of the domestic product. In short, software becomes an exporting industry and textiles an importing industry.

These changes in the demand for domestic products are translated into changes in the demand for labor. The opening of export markets increases the demand for domestic software, raising its price. The higher price for domestic software, in turn, raises the value of the marginal products of software workers, shifting the labor demand curve in the software industry to the right, from D_{software} to D'_{software} in Figure 14.6(b). Wages in the software industry rise, from w to w'_{software}, and employment in the industry rises as well. In the textile industry the opposite happens. Demand for domestic textiles falls as consumers switch to imports. The price of domestic textiles falls with demand, reducing the value of the marginal product of textile workers and hence the demand for their labor, to D'_{textiles} in Figure 14.6(a). Employment in the textile industry falls, and the real wage falls as well, from w to w'_{textiles}.

In sum, Figure 14.6 shows how globalization can contribute to increasing wage inequality. Initially, we assumed that software workers and textile workers received the same wage. However, the opening up of trade raised the wages of workers in the "winning" industry (software) and lowered the wages of workers in the "losing" industry (textiles), increasing inequality.

EN 14

In practice, the tendency of trade to increase wage inequality may be even worse than depicted in the example because the great majority of the world's workers, particularly those in developing countries, have relatively low skill levels. Thus, when industrialized countries like the United States open up trade with developing countries, the domestic industries that are likely to face the toughest international competition are those that use mostly low-skilled labor. Conversely, the industries that are likely to do the best in international competition are those that employ mostly skilled workers. Thus, increased trade may lower the wages of those workers who are already poorly paid and increase the wages of those who are well paid.

The fact that increasing trade may exacerbate wage inequality explains some of the political resistance to globalization, but in general it does not justify attempts to reverse the trend. Increasing trade and specialization is a major source of improvement in living standards, both in the United States and abroad, so trying to stop the process is counterproductive. Indeed, the economic forces behind globalization—primarily, the desire of consumers for better and cheaper products and of producers for new markets—are so powerful that the process would be hard to stop even if government officials were determined to do so.

Rather than trying to stop globalization, helping the labor market to adjust to the effects of globalization is probably a better course. To a certain extent, indeed, the economy will adjust on its own. Figure 14.6 showed that, following the opening to trade, real wages and employment fall in (a) textiles and rise in (b) software. At that point, wages and job opportunities are much more attractive in the software industry than in textiles. Will this situation persist? Clearly, there is a strong incentive for workers who are able to do so to leave the textile industry and seek employment in the software industry.

worker mobility the movement of workers between jobs, firms, and industries

The movement of workers between jobs, firms, and industries is called **worker mobility.** In our example, worker mobility will tend to reduce labor supply in textiles and increase it in software, as workers move from the contracting industry to the growing one. This process will reverse some of the increase in wage inequality by raising wages in textiles and lowering them in software. It also will shift workers from a less competitive sector to a more competitive sector. To some extent, then, the labor market can adjust on its own to the effects of globalization.

Of course, there are many barriers to a textile worker becoming a software engineer. So there also may be a need for *transition aid* to workers in the affected sectors. Ideally, such aid helps workers train for and find new jobs. If that is not possible or desirable—say, because a worker is nearing retirement—transition aid can take the form of government payments to help the worker maintain his or her standard of living. The Efficiency Principle reminds us that transition aid and similar programs are useful because trade and specialization increase the total economic pie. The "winners" from globalization can afford the taxes necessary to finance aid and still enjoy a net benefit from increased trade.

Efficiency

INCREASING WAGE INEQUALITY: TECHNOLOGICAL CHANGE

A second source of increasing wage inequality is ongoing technological change that favors more highly skilled or educated workers. New scientific knowledge and the technological advances associated with it are a major source of improved productivity and economic growth. Increases in worker productivity are in turn a driving force behind wage increases and higher average living standards. In the long run and on average, technological progress is undoubtedly the worker's friend.

This sweeping statement is not true at all times and in all places, however. Whether a particular technological development is good for a particular worker depends on the effect of that innovation on the worker's value of marginal product and, hence, on his or her wage. For example, at one time the ability to add numbers rapidly and accurately was a valuable skill; a clerk with that skill could expect advancement and higher wages. However, the invention and mass production of the electronic calculator has rendered human calculating skills less valuable, to the detriment of those who have that skill.

History is replete with examples of workers who opposed new technologies out of fear that their skills would become less valuable. In England in the early nineteenth century, rioting workmen destroyed newly introduced labor-saving machinery. The name of the workers' reputed leader, Ned Ludd, has been preserved in the term *Luddite,* meaning a person who is opposed to the introduction of new technologies. The same theme appears in American folk history in the tale of John Henry, the mighty pile-driving man who died in an attempt to show that a human could tunnel into a rock face more quickly than a steam-powered machine.

How do these observations bear on wage inequality? According to some economists, many recent technological advances have taken the form of **skill-biased technological change,** that is, technological change that affects the marginal product of higher-skilled workers differently from that of lower-skilled workers. Specifically, technological developments in recent decades appear to have favored more-skilled and educated workers. Developments in automobile production are a case in point. The advent of mass production techniques in the 1920s provided highly paid work for several generations of relatively low-skilled autoworkers. But in recent years automobile production, like the automobiles themselves, has become considerably more sophisticated. The simplest production jobs have been taken over by robots and computer-controlled machinery, which require skilled operatives who know how to use and maintain the new equipment. Consumer demands for luxury features and customized options also have raised the automakers' demand for highly skilled craftsmen. Thus, in general, the skill requirements for jobs in automobile production have risen. Similarly, few office workers today can escape the need to use computer applications such as word processing and spreadsheets. And in many places, elementary school teachers are expected to know how to set up a web page or use the internet.

skill-biased technological change technological change that affects the marginal products of higher-skilled workers differently from those of lower-skilled workers

Figure 14.7 illustrates the effects of technological change that favors skilled workers. Figure 14.7(a) shows the market for unskilled workers; Figure 14.7(b) shows the market for skilled workers. The demand curves labeled $D_{\text{unskilled}}$ and D_{skilled} show the demand for each type of worker before a skill-biased technological change. Wages and employment for each type of worker are determined by the intersection of the demand and supply curves in each market. Figure 14.7 shows that, even before the technological change, unskilled workers received lower real wages than skilled workers ($w_{\text{unskilled}} < w_{\text{skilled}}$), reflecting the lower marginal products of the unskilled.

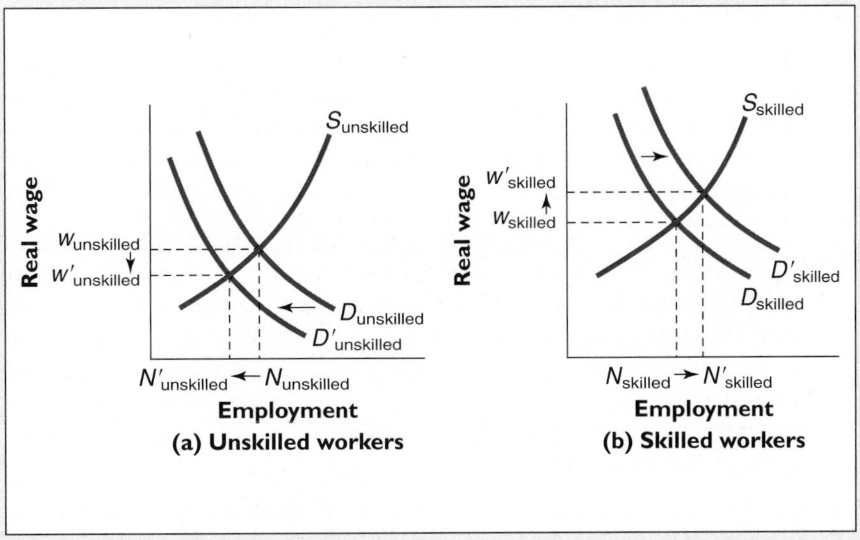

FIGURE 14.7
The Effect of Skill-Biased Technological Change on Wage Inequality.
The figure shows the effects of a skill-biased technological change that increases the marginal product of skilled workers and reduces the marginal product of unskilled workers. The resulting increase in the demand for skilled workers raises their wages (b), while the decline in demand for unskilled workers reduces their wages (a). Wage inequality increases.

Now suppose that a new technology—computer-controlled machinery, for example—is introduced. This technological change is biased toward skilled workers, which means that it raises their marginal productivity relative to unskilled workers.

We will assume in this example that the new technology also lowers the marginal productivity of unskilled workers, perhaps because they are unable to use the new technology, but all that is necessary for our conclusions is that they benefit less than skilled workers. Figure 14.7 shows the effect of this change in marginal products. In part (b) the increase in the marginal productivity of skilled workers raises the demand for those workers; the demand curve shifts rightward to D'_{skilled}. Accordingly, the real wages and employment of skilled workers also rise. In contrast, because they have been made less productive by the technological change, the demand for unskilled workers shifts leftward to $D'_{\text{unskilled}}$ [Figure 14.7(a)]. Lower demand for unskilled workers reduces their real wages and employment.

In summary, this analysis supports the conclusion that technological change that is biased in favor of skilled workers will tend to increase the wage gap between the skilled and unskilled. Empirical studies have confirmed the role of skill-biased technological change in recent increases in wage inequality.

Because new technologies that favor skilled workers increase wage inequality, should government regulators act to block them? As in the case of globalization, most economists would argue against trying to block new technologies since technological advances are necessary for economic growth and improved living standards. If the Luddites had somehow succeeded in preventing the introduction of labor-saving machinery in Great Britain, economic growth and development over the past few centuries might have been greatly reduced.

The remedies for the problem of wage inequalities caused by technological change are similar to those for wage inequalities caused by globalization. First among them is worker mobility. As the pay differential between skilled and unskilled work increases, unskilled workers will have a stronger incentive to acquire education and skills, to everyone's benefit. A second remedy is transition aid. Government policymakers should consider programs that will help workers to retrain if they are able, or provide income support if they are not.

RECAP EXPLAINING THE TRENDS IN REAL WAGES AND EMPLOYMENT

- The long-term increase in real wages enjoyed by workers in industrial countries results primarily from large productivity gains, which have raised the demand for labor. Technological progress and an expanded and modernized capital stock are two important reasons for these long-term increases in productivity.
- The slowdown in real wage growth that began in the 1970s resulted in part from the slowdown in productivity growth (and, hence, the slower growth in labor demand) that occurred at about the same time. Increased labor supply, arising from such factors as the increased participation of women and the coming of age of the baby boom generation, depressed real wages further while also expanding employment. In the latter part of the 1990s, resurgence in productivity growth was accompanied by an increase in real wage growth.
- Both globalization and skill-biased technological change contribute to wage inequality. Globalization raises the wages of workers in exporting industries by raising the demand for those workers, while reducing the wages of workers in importing industries. Technological change that favors more-skilled workers increases the demand for such workers, and hence their wages, relative to the wages of less-skilled workers.

Attempting to block either globalization or technological change is not the best response to the problem of wage inequality. To some extent, worker mobility (movement of workers from low-wage to high-wage industries) will offset the inequality created by these forces. Where mobility is not practical, transition aid—government assistance to workers whose employment prospects have worsened—may be the best solution.

UNEMPLOYMENT AND THE UNEMPLOYMENT RATE

In assessing the level of economic activity in a country, economists look at a variety of statistics. A statistic that receives a great deal of attention, both from economists and from the general public, is the rate of unemployment. The unemployment rate is a sensitive indicator of conditions in the labor market. When the unemployment rate is low, jobs are secure and relatively easier to find. Low unemployment is often associated with improving wages and working conditions as well, as employers compete to attract and retain workers.

MEASURING UNEMPLOYMENT

In the United States, defining and measuring unemployment is the responsibility of the Bureau of Labor Statistics, or BLS. Each month the BLS surveys about 60,000 randomly selected households. Each person in those households who is 16 years or older is placed in one of three categories:

1. *Employed.* A person is employed if he or she worked full-time or part-time (even for a few hours) during the past week or is on vacation or sick leave from a regular job.
2. *Unemployed.* A person is unemployed if he or she did not work during the preceding week but made some effort to find work (for example, by going to a job interview) in the past four weeks.
3. *Out of the labor force.* A person is considered to be out of the labor force if he or she did not work in the past week and did not look for work in the past four weeks. In other words, people who are neither employed nor unemployed (in the sense of looking for work but not being able to find it) are "out of the labor force." Full-time students, unpaid homemakers, retirees, and people unable to work because of disabilities are examples of people who are out of the labor force.

Based on the results of the survey, the BLS estimates how many people in the whole country fit into each of the three categories.

To find the unemployment rate, the BLS must first calculate the size of the *labor force.* The **labor force** is defined as the total number of employed and unemployed people in the economy (the first two categories of respondents to the BLS survey). The **unemployment rate** is then defined as the number of unemployed people divided by the labor force. Notice that people who are out of the labor force (because they are in school, have retired, or are disabled, for example) are not counted as unemployed and thus do not affect the unemployment rate. In general, a high rate of unemployment indicates that the economy is performing poorly.

Another useful statistic is the **participation rate,** or the percentage of the working-age population in the labor force (that is, the percentage that is either employed or looking for work). The participation rate is calculated by dividing the labor force by the working-age (16+) population.

labor force the total number of employed and unemployed people in the economy

unemployment rate the number of unemployed people divided by the labor force

participation rate the percentage of the working-age population in the labor force (that is, the percentage that is either employed or looking for work)

Table 14.5 illustrates the calculation of key labor market statistics, using data based on the BLS survey for January 2008. In that month unemployment was 4.9 percent of the labor force. The participation rate was 66 percent; that is, about two out of every three adults had a job or were looking for work. Figure 14.8 shows the U.S. unemployment rate since 1960. Unemployment rates were exceptionally low—just above 4 percent—in the late 1960s and the late 1990s. By this measure, the latter part of the 1990s was an exceptionally good time for American workers. However, unemployment rose in 2001–2003 following a recession in 2001.

TABLE 14.5
U.S. Employment Data, January 2008 (in millions)

Employed	146.2
Plus:	
Unemployed	7.6
Equals: Labor force	153.8
Plus:	
Not in labor force	78.8
Equals:	
Working-age (over 16) population	232.6
Unemployment rate = unemployed/labor force = 7.6/153.8 = 4.9%	
Participation rate = labor force/working-age population = 153.8/232.6 = 66.1	

SOURCE: Bureau of Labor Statistics (http://stats.bls.gov).

FIGURE 14.8
The U.S. Unemployment Rate, 1960–2007.
The unemployment rate—the fraction of the U.S. labor force that is unemployed—was just above 4 percent in the late 1990s, the lowest recorded rate since the latter part of the 1960s. Unemployment rose above 6 percent in 2003, following a recession.

SOURCE: Bureau of Labor Statistics (http://www.bls.gov).

EXERCISE 14.7

Following are January 2008 BLS U.S. employment data for African Americans.

Employed	16.090 million
Unemployed	1.623 million
Not in the labor force	9.927 million

Find the labor force, the working-age population, the unemployment rate, and the participation rate for African Americans and compare your results to those in Table 14.5.

THE COSTS OF UNEMPLOYMENT

Unemployment imposes *economic, psychological,* and *social* costs on a nation. From an economic perspective, the main cost of unemployment is the output that is lost because the workforce is not fully utilized. Much of the burden of the reduced output is borne by the unemployed themselves, whose incomes fall when they are not working and whose skills may deteriorate from lack of use. However, society at large also bears part of the economic cost of unemployment. For example, workers who become unemployed are liable to stop paying taxes and start receiving government support payments such as unemployment benefits. This net drain on the government's budget is a cost to all taxpayers.

The *psychological* costs of unemployment are felt primarily by unemployed workers and their families. Studies show that lengthy periods of unemployment can lead to a loss of self-esteem, feelings of loss of control over one's life, depression, and even suicidal behavior.[3] The unemployed worker's family is likely to feel increased psychological stress, compounded by the economic difficulties created by the loss of income.

The *social* costs of unemployment are a result of the economic and psychological effects. People who have been unemployed for a while tend not only to face severe financial difficulties but also to feel anger, frustration, and despair. Not surprisingly, increases in unemployment tend to be associated with increases in crime, domestic violence, alcoholism, drug abuse, and other social problems. The costs created by these problems are borne not only by the unemployed but by society in general, as more public resources must be spent to counteract these problems—for example, by hiring more police to control crime or increasing spending on social services.

THE DURATION OF UNEMPLOYMENT

In assessing the impact of unemployment on jobless people, economists must know how long individual workers have been without work. Generally, the longer a person has been out of work, the more severe are the economic and psychological costs that person will face. People who are unemployed for only a few weeks, for example, are not likely to suffer a serious reduction in their standard of living, since for a short period they can draw upon their savings and perhaps on government benefits. Nor would we expect someone who is unemployed for only a short time to experience psychological problems such as depression or loss of self-esteem, at least not to the same extent as someone who has been out of work for months or years.

In its surveys, therefore, the BLS asks respondents how long they have been unemployed. A period during which an individual is continuously unemployed is called an **unemployment spell**; it begins when the worker becomes unemployed and ends when the worker either finds a job or leaves the labor force. (Remember, people outside the labor force are not counted as unemployed.) The length of an unemployment spell is called its **duration.** The duration of unemployment rises during recessions, reflecting the greater difficulty of finding work during those periods.

unemployment spell a period during which an individual is continuously unemployed

duration the length of an unemployment spell

At any given time, a substantial fraction of unemployed workers have been unemployed for six months or more; we will refer to this group as the *long-term unemployed.* Long-term unemployment creates the highest economic, psychological, and social costs, both for the unemployed themselves and for society as a whole.

[3]For a survey of the literature on the psychological effects of unemployment, see William Darity Jr. and Arthur H. Goldsmith, "Social Psychology, Unemployment and Macroeconomics," *Journal of Economic Perspectives* 10 (Winter 1996), pp. 121–40.

Although long-term unemployment is a serious problem, many unemployment spells are quite short. For example, in January 2008, 35 percent of the unemployed had been out of work for just 5 weeks or less, another 32 percent had been unemployed for 5 to 14 weeks, and about 33 percent of the unemployed had been without a job for more than 14 weeks (about three months). These statistics are a bit deceptive, however, because short unemployment spells can arise from two very different patterns of labor-market experience. Some people have short unemployment spells that end in their finding a stable long-term job. For the most part, these workers, whom we will refer to as the *short-term unemployed,* do not bear a high cost of unemployment. But other workers have short unemployment spells that typically end either in their withdrawal from the labor force or in a short-term or temporary job that soon leaves the worker unemployed again. Workers whose unemployment spells are broken up by brief periods of employment or withdrawal from the labor force are referred to as the *chronically unemployed.* In terms of the costs of unemployment, the experience of these workers is similar to that of the long-term unemployed.

THE UNEMPLOYMENT RATE VERSUS "TRUE" UNEMPLOYMENT

Like GDP measurement, unemployment measurement has its critics. Most of them argue that the official unemployment rate understates the true extent of unemployment. They point in particular to two groups of people who are not counted among the unemployed: so-called *discouraged workers* and *involuntary part-time workers.*

discouraged workers people who say they would like to have a job but have not made an effort to find one in the past four weeks

Discouraged workers are people who say they would like to have a job but have not made an effort to find one in the past four weeks. Often, discouraged workers tell the survey takers that they have not searched for work because they have tried without success in the past, or because they are convinced that labor-market conditions are such that they will not be able to find a job. Because they have not sought work in the past four weeks, discouraged workers are counted as being out of the labor force rather than unemployed. Some observers have suggested that treating discouraged workers as unemployed would provide a more accurate picture of the labor market.

Involuntary part-time workers are people who say they would like to work full-time but are able to find only part-time work. Because they do have jobs, involuntary part-time workers are counted as employed rather than unemployed. Some economists have suggested that these workers should be counted as partially unemployed.

In response to these criticisms, in recent years the BLS has released special unemployment rates that include estimates of the number of discouraged workers and involuntary part-time workers. In January 2008, when the official unemployment rate was 4.9 percent (see Table 14.5), the BLS calculated that if both discouraged workers and involuntary part-time workers were counted as unemployed, the unemployment rate would have been 9.0 percent. So the problem of discouraged and underemployed workers appears to be fairly significant.

TYPES OF UNEMPLOYMENT AND THEIR COSTS

Economists have found it useful to think of unemployment as being of three broad types: *frictional* unemployment, *structural* unemployment, and *cyclical* unemployment. Each type of unemployment has different causes and imposes different economic and social costs.

FRICTIONAL UNEMPLOYMENT

The function of the labor market is to match available jobs with available workers. If all jobs and workers were the same, or if the set of jobs and workers were static and unchanging, this matching process would be quick and easy. But the real world is more complicated. In practice, both jobs and workers are highly *heterogeneous*. Jobs differ in their location, in the skills they require, in their working conditions and hours, and in many other ways. Workers differ in their career aspirations, their skills and experience, their preferred working hours, their willingness to travel, and so on.

The real labor market is also *dynamic*, or constantly changing and evolving. On the demand side of the labor market, technological advances, globalization, and changing consumer tastes spur the creation of new products, new firms, and even new industries, while outmoded products, firms, and industries disappear. Thus CD players have replaced record players and word processors have replaced typewriters. As a result of this upheaval, new jobs are constantly being created, while some old jobs cease to be viable. The workforce in a modern economy is equally dynamic. People move, gain new skills, leave the labor force for a time to rear children or go back to school, and even change careers.

Because the labor market is heterogeneous and dynamic, the process of matching jobs with workers often takes time. For example, a software engineer who loses or quits her job in Silicon Valley may take weeks or even months to find an appropriate new job. In her search she will probably consider alternative areas of software development or even totally new challenges. She also may want to think about different regions of the country in which software companies are located, such as North Carolina's Research Triangle or New York City's Silicon Alley. During the period in which she is searching for a new job, she is counted as unemployed.

Short-term unemployment that is associated with the process of matching workers with jobs is called **frictional unemployment**. The *costs* of frictional unemployment are low and may even be negative; that is, frictional unemployment may be economically beneficial. First, frictional unemployment is short-term, so its psychological effects and direct economic losses are minimal. Second, to the extent that the search process leads to a better match between worker and job, a period of frictional unemployment is actually productive, in the sense that it leads to higher output over the long run. Indeed, a certain amount of frictional unemployment seems essential to the smooth functioning of a rapidly changing, dynamic economy.

frictional unemployment the short-term unemployment associated with the process of matching workers with jobs

STRUCTURAL UNEMPLOYMENT

A second major type of unemployment is **structural unemployment**, or the long-term and chronic unemployment that exists even when the economy is producing at a normal rate. Several factors contribute to structural unemployment. First, a *lack of skills, language barriers,* or *discrimination* keeps some workers from finding stable, long-term jobs. Migrant farmworkers and unskilled construction workers who find short-term or temporary jobs from time to time, but never stay in one job for very long, fit the definition of chronically unemployed.

structural unemployment the long-term and chronic unemployment that exists even when the economy is producing at a normal rate

Second, economic changes sometimes create a *long-term mismatch* between the skills some workers have and the available jobs. The U.S. steel industry, for example, has declined over the years, while the computer industry has grown rapidly. Ideally, steelworkers who lose their jobs would be able to find new jobs in computer firms (worker mobility), so their unemployment would only be frictional in nature. In practice, of course, many ex-steelworkers lack the education, ability, or interest necessary to work in the computer industry. Since their skills are no longer in demand, these workers may drift into chronic or long-term unemployment.

Finally, structural unemployment can result from *structural features of the labor market* that act as barriers to employment. Examples of such barriers include unions and minimum wage laws, both of which may keep wages above their market-clearing level, creating unemployment. We will discuss some of these structural features shortly.

"The one single thought that sustains me is that the fundamentals are good."

The *costs* of structural unemployment are much higher than those of frictional unemployment. Because structurally unemployed workers do little productive work over long periods, their idleness causes substantial economic losses both to the unemployed workers and to society. Structurally unemployed workers also lose out on the opportunity to develop new skills on the job, and their existing skills wither from disuse. Long spells of unemployment are also much more difficult for workers to handle psychologically than the relatively brief spells associated with frictional unemployment.

CYCLICAL UNEMPLOYMENT

cyclical unemployment the extra unemployment that occurs during periods of recession

The third type of unemployment occurs during periods of recession (that is, periods of unusually low production) and is called **cyclical unemployment.** The sharp peaks in unemployment shown in Figure 14.8 reflect the cyclical unemployment that occurs during recessions. Increases in cyclical unemployment, although they are relatively short-lived, are associated with significant declines in real GDP and are therefore quite costly economically. We will study cyclical unemployment in more detail later in the chapters dealing with booms and recessions.

In principle, frictional, structural, and cyclical unemployment add up to the total unemployment rate. In practice, sharp distinctions often cannot be made between the different categories, so any breakdown of the total unemployment rate into the three types of unemployment is necessarily subjective and approximate.

IMPEDIMENTS TO FULL EMPLOYMENT

In discussing structural unemployment, we mentioned that structural features of the labor market may contribute to long-term and chronic unemployment. Let's discuss a few of those features.

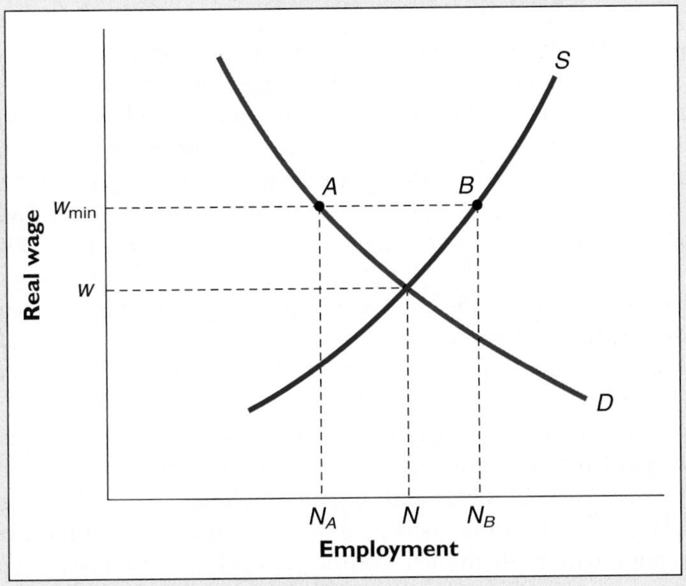

FIGURE 14.9
A Legal Minimum Wage May Create Unemployment.
If the minimum wage w_{min} exceeds the market-clearing wage w for low-skilled workers, it will create unemployment equal to the difference between the number of people who want to work at the minimum wage, N_B, and the number of people that employers are willing to hire, N_A.

MINIMUM WAGE LAWS

The federal government and most states have minimum wage laws, which prescribe the lowest hourly wage that employers may pay to workers. Basic supply and demand analysis shows that if the minimum wage law has any effect at all, it must raise the unemployment rate. Figure 14.9 shows why. The figure shows the demand and supply curves for low-skilled workers, to whom the minimum wage is most relevant. The market-clearing real wage, at which the quantity of labor demanded equals the quantity of labor supplied, is w, and the corresponding level of employment of low-skilled workers is N. Now suppose there is a legal minimum wage w_{min} that exceeds the market-clearing wage w, as shown in Figure 14.9. At the minimum wage, the number of people who want jobs, N_B, exceeds the number of workers that employers are willing to hire, N_A. The result is unemployment in the amount $N_B - N_A$, also equal to the length of the line segment AB in the figure. If there were no minimum wage, this unemployment would not exist, since the labor market would clear at wage w.

If minimum wages create unemployment, why are they politically popular? A minimum wage creates two classes of workers: those who are lucky enough to find jobs at the minimum wage and those who are shut out because the minimum wage exceeds the market-clearing wage. Workers who do find jobs at the minimum wage will earn more than they would have otherwise because the minimum wage is higher than the market-clearing wage. If the minimum wage were put to a vote, the number of workers who benefit from the legislation, and who could thus be expected to support it, might well exceed the number of workers who are hurt by it. In creating groups of "winners" and "losers," minimum wage legislation resembles rent control legislation (see Chapter 3). But like rent controls, minimum wages create economic inefficiency. Thus, other methods of attacking poverty, such as direct grants to the working poor, might prove more effective.

LABOR UNIONS

Labor unions are organizations that negotiate with employers on behalf of workers. Among the issues that unions negotiate, which are embodied in the contracts they draw up with employers, are the wages workers earn, rules for hiring and firing, the duties of different types of workers, working hours and conditions, and procedures for resolving disputes between workers and employers. Unions gain negotiating power by their power to call a strike—that is, to refuse work until a contract agreement has been reached.

Through the threat of a strike, a union can usually get employers to agree to a wage that is higher than the market-clearing wage. Thus, Figure 14.9 could represent conditions in a unionized industry if wmin is interpreted as the union wage instead of the legal minimum wage. As in the case of a minimum wage, a union wage that is higher than the market-clearing wage leads to unemployment, in the amount NB 2 NA in Figure 14.9. Furthermore, a high union wage creates a trade-off similar to the one created by a minimum wage. Those workers who are lucky enough to get jobs as union members will be paid more than they would be otherwise. Unfortunately, their gain comes at the expense of other workers who are unemployed as a result of the artificially high union wage.

Are labor unions good for the economy? That is a controversial, emotionally charged question. Early in the twentieth century, some employers who faced little local competition for workers—coal-mining companies in Appalachia, for example—exploited their advantage by forcing workers to toil long hours in dangerous conditions for low pay. Through bitter and sometimes bloody confrontations with these companies, labor organizations succeeded in eliminating many of the worst abuses. Unions also point with pride to their historic political role in supporting progressive labor legislation, such as laws that banned child labor. Finally, union leaders often claim to increase productivity and promote democracy in the workplace by giving workers some voice in the operations of the firm.

Opponents of unions, while acknowledging that these organizations may have played a positive role in the past, question their value in a modern economy. Today, more and more workers are professionals or semiprofessionals, rather than production workers, so they can move relatively easily from firm to firm. Indeed, many labor markets have become national or even international, so today's workers have numerous potential employers. Thus, the forces of competition—the fact that employers must persuade talented workers to work for them—should provide adequate protection for workers. Indeed, opponents would argue that unions are becoming increasingly self-defeating since firms that must pay artificially high union wages and abide by inflexible work rules will not be able to compete in a global economy. The ultimate effect of such handicaps will be the failure of unionized firms and the loss of union jobs. Indeed, unions are in decline in the United States and now represent 12.5 percent of the workforce—a large fraction of which are government workers such as public school teachers and the police.

UNEMPLOYMENT INSURANCE

Another structural feature of the labor market that may increase the unemployment rate is the availability of *unemployment insurance,* or government transfer payments to unemployed workers. Unemployment insurance provides an important social benefit in that it helps the unemployed to maintain a decent standard of living while they are looking for a job. But because its availability allows the unemployed to search longer or less intensively for a job, it may lengthen the average amount of time the typical unemployed worker is without a job.

Most economists would argue that unemployment insurance should be generous enough to provide basic support to the unemployed but not so generous as to remove the incentive to actively seek work. Thus, unemployment insurance should last for only a limited time, and its benefits should not be as high as the income a worker receives when working.

OTHER GOVERNMENT REGULATIONS

Besides minimum wage legislation, many other government regulations bear on the labor market. They include *health and safety regulations,* which establish the safety standards employers must follow, and rules that prohibit racial or gender-based discrimination in hiring.

Legislators and other policymakers need to keep in mind both the Cost-Benefit Principle and the Efficiency Principle when considering labor-market regulation. Many regulations are beneficial; however, in some cases the costs of complying with them may exceed the benefits they provide. Further, to the extent that regulations increase employer costs and reduce productivity, they depress the demand for labor, lowering real wages and contributing to unemployment and reducing the size of the economic pie.

Cost-Benefit and Efficiency

The points raised in this section can help us to understand one of the important labor market trends discussed earlier in the chapter, namely, the persistence of high unemployment in western Europe.

WHY ARE UNEMPLOYMENT RATES SO HIGH IN WESTERN EUROPE?

For more than two decades, unemployment has been exceptionally high in the major countries of western Europe, as Figure 14.10 shows. In 2007, for example, the unemployment rate was 6.0 percent in Italy, 8.2 percent in France, 8.0 percent in Germany, and 5.3 in the United Kingdom, compared with a U.S. unemployment rate of only 5.5 percent. In the 1950s, 1960s, and 1970s, western Europe consistently enjoyed very low unemployment rates. Why has European unemployment been so stubbornly high for the past two decades?

One explanation for the high unemployment in major western European countries is the existence of structural "rigidities" in their labor markets. Relative to the United States, European labor markets are highly regulated. European governments set rules in matters ranging from the number of weeks of vacation workers must receive to the reasons for which a worker can be dismissed. Minimum wages in Europe are high, and unemployment benefits are much more generous than in the United States. European unions are also far more powerful than those in the United States; their wage agreements are often extended by law to all firms in the industry, whether or not they are unionized. This lack of flexibility in labor markets—which some observers refer to as *Eurosclerosis*—causes higher frictional and structural unemployment.

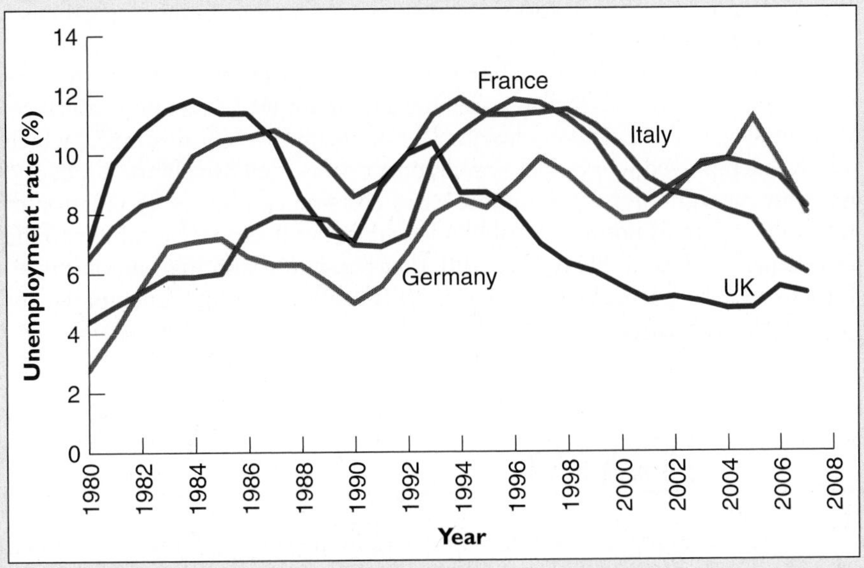

FIGURE 14.10
Unemployment Rates in Western Europe, 1980–2007.
In the major western European countries, unemployment rates have been high for more than two decades.

SOURCE: Standardized unemployment rates, Bureau of Labor Statistics (http://www.stats.bls.gov).

If European labor markets are so dysfunctional, why has serious European unemployment emerged only in the past two decades? One explanation turns on the increasing pace of *globalization* and *skill-biased technological change*. As we saw, these two factors decrease the demand for less-skilled labor relative to the demand for skilled labor. In the United States, falling demand has depressed the wages of the less skilled, increasing wage inequality. But in western Europe, high minimum wages, union contracts, generous unemployment insurance, and other factors may have created a floor for the wage that firms could pay or that workers would accept. As the marginal productivity of the less skilled dropped below that floor, firms no longer found it profitable to employ those workers, swelling the ranks of the unemployed. Thus, the combination of labor market rigidity and the declining marginal productivity of low-skilled workers may be responsible for the European unemployment problem.

Evidence for the idea that inflexible labor markets have contributed to European unemployment comes from the United Kingdom, where the government of Prime Minister Margaret Thatcher instituted a series of reforms beginning in the early 1980s. Britain has since largely deregulated its labor market so that it functions much more like that in the United States. Figure 14.10 shows that unemployment in Britain has gradually declined and is now lower than in other western European countries. Labor market reforms like those in Britain are examples of *structural policies*.

RECAP | UNEMPLOYMENT AND THE UNEMPLOYMENT RATE

Defining and measuring unemployment involves distinguishing among the employed, the unemployed, and those not in the labor force. We can then use these concepts to calculate measures such as the unemployment rate, which is the number of people unemployed divided by the labor force, and the participation rate, which is the labor force divided by the working-age population.

Economists distinguish among three broad types of unemployment. *Frictional unemployment* is the short-term unemployment that is associated with the process of matching workers with jobs. *Structural unemployment* is the long-term or chronic unemployment that occurs even when the economy is producing at a normal rate. *Cyclical unemployment* is the extra unemployment that occurs during periods of recession. Frictional unemployment may be economically beneficial, as improved matching of workers and jobs may increase output in the long run. Structural and cyclical unemployment impose heavy economic costs on workers and society, as well as psychological costs on workers and their families.

Structural features of the labor market may cause structural unemployment. Examples of such features are legal minimum wages or union contracts that set wages above market-clearing levels; unemployment insurance, which allows unemployed workers to search longer or less intensively for a job; and government regulations that impose extra costs on employers. Regulation of the labor market is not necessarily undesirable, but it should be subject to the cost-benefit criterion. Heavy labor market regulation and high unionization rates in western Europe help to explain the persistence of high unemployment rates in those countries.

SUMMARY

- There are five important trends in wages, employment, and unemployment that we focused on in this chapter. First, over a long period, average real wages have risen substantially both in the United States and in other industrialized countries. Second, despite the long-term upward trend in real wages, real wage growth has slowed significantly in the United States since the early 1970s. Third, in the United States, wage inequality has increased dramatically in recent decades. The real wages of most unskilled workers have actually declined, while the real wages of skilled and educated workers have continued to rise. Fourth, employment has grown substantially in the United States in recent decades and has exceeded the growth of the working-age population. Fifth, since about 1980, western European nations have experienced very high rates of unemployment and low rates of job creation. **LO1**

- Trends in real wages and employment can be studied using a supply-and-demand model of the labor market. At a given price level, the productivity of labor and the price of workers' output determine the demand for labor. Employers will hire workers only as long as the value of the marginal product of the last worker hired equals or exceeds the wage the firm must pay. Because of diminishing returns to labor, the more workers a firm employs, the less additional product will be obtained by adding yet another worker. The lower the going wage, the more workers will be hired and thus the demand-for-labor curve slopes downward. Factors that increase the value of labor's marginal product, such as an increase in the price of workers' output or an increase in productivity, shift the labor demand curve to the right. Conversely, changes that reduce the value of labor's marginal product shift the labor demand curve to the left. **LO2**
- The supply curve for labor shows the number of people willing to work at any given real wage. The supply curve slopes downward since more people will generally work at a higher real wage. An increase in the working-age population or a social change that promotes labor market participation (such as the changing role of women in the labor force) will increase labor supply and shift the labor supply curve to the right. **LO2**
- Improvements in productivity, which raise the demand for labor, account for the bulk of the increase in U.S. real wages over the last century. The slowdown in real wage growth that has occurred in recent decades is the result of slower growth in labor demand, which was caused in turn by a slowdown in the rate of productivity improvement, and of more rapid growth in labor supply. Rapid growth in labor supply, caused by such factors as immigration and increased labor force participation by women, also has contributed to the continued expansion of employment. Recently, there has been some improvement in the rate of growth of productivity and real wages. **LO3**
- Two reasons for the increasing wage inequality in the United States are economic globalization and skill-biased technological change. Both have increased the demand for, and hence the real wages of, relatively skilled and educated workers. Attempting to block globalization and technological change is counterproductive, however, since both factors are important in promoting increased productivity. To some extent, the movement of workers from lower-paying to higher-paying jobs or industries will counteract the trend toward wage inequality. A policy of providing transition aid and training for workers with obsolete skills is a more useful response to the problem. **LO3**
- The unemployment rate is based on surveys conducted by the Bureau of Labor Statistics. The surveys classify all respondents over age 16 as employed, unemployed, or not in the labor force. The labor force is the sum of employed and unemployed workers—that is, people who have a job or are looking for one. The unemployment rate is calculated as the number of unemployed workers divided by the labor force. The participation rate is the percentage of the working-age population that is in the labor force. **LO4**
- The costs of unemployment include the economic cost of lost output, the psychological costs borne by unemployed workers and their families, and the social costs associated with problems like increased crime and violence. The greatest costs are imposed by long unemployment spells (periods of unemployment). Critics of the official unemployment rate argue that it understates "true" unemployment by excluding discouraged workers and involuntary part-time workers. **LO5**
- There are three broad types of unemployment: frictional, structural, and cyclical. Frictional unemployment is the short-term unemployment associated with the process of matching workers with jobs in a dynamic, heterogeneous labor market. Structural unemployment is the long-term and chronic unemployment that exists even when the economy is producing at a normal rate. It arises from a variety of factors, including language barriers, discrimination, structural features of the labor market, lack of skills, or long-term mismatches between the skills workers have and the available jobs. Cyclical unemployment is the extra unemployment that occurs during periods of recession. The costs of frictional unemployment are low, as it tends to be brief and to create more productive matches between workers and jobs. Structural unemployment, which is often long term, and cyclical unemployment, which is associated with significant reductions in real GDP, tend to be more costly. **LO5**
- Structural features of the labor market that may contribute to unemployment include minimum wage laws, which discourage firms from hiring low-skilled workers; labor unions, which can set wages above market-clearing levels; unemployment insurance,

which reduces the incentives of the unemployed to find work quickly; and other government regulations, which—although possibly conferring benefits—increase the costs of employing workers. The labor market "rigidity" created by government regulations and union contracts is more of a problem in western Europe than in the United States, which may account for Europe's high unemployment rates. **LO5**

KEY TERMS

cyclical unemployment (400)
diminishing returns to labor (380)
discouraged workers (398)
duration (of an unemployment spell) (397)
frictional unemployment (399)
labor force (395)
participation rate (395)
skill-biased technological change (393)
structural unemployment (399)
unemployment rate (395)
unemployment spell (397)
worker mobility (392)

REVIEW QUESTIONS

1. List and discuss the five important labor market trends given in the first section of the chapter. **LO1**
2. Acme Corporation is considering hiring Jane Smith. Based on her other opportunities in the job market, Jane has told Acme that she will work for them for $40,000 per year. How should Acme determine whether to employ her? **LO2**
3. Why have real wages risen by so much in the United States in the past century? Why did real wage growth slow for 25 years beginning in the early 1970s? What has been happening to real wages recently? **LO3**
4. What are two major factors contributing to increased inequality in wages? Briefly, why do these factors raise wage inequality? Contrast possible policy responses to increasing inequality in terms of their effects on economic efficiency. **LO3**
5. True or false: A high participation rate in an economy implies a low unemployment rate. Explain. **LO4**
6. What are the costs of a high unemployment rate? Do you think providing more generous government benefits to the unemployed would increase these costs, reduce these costs, or leave them unchanged? Discuss. **LO5**
7. List three types of unemployment and their causes. Which of these types is economically and socially the least costly? Explain. **LO5**

PROBLEMS

McGraw-Hill's HOMEWORK MANAGER®

1. Data on the average earnings of people of different education levels are available from the Bureau of the Census (try online at www.census.gov/hhes/www/income/histinc/incpertoc.html). Using these data, prepare a table showing the earnings of college graduates relative to high school graduates and of college graduates relative to those with less than a high school degree. Show the data for the latest year available, for every fifth year going back to the earliest data available. What are the trends in relative earnings? **LO3**
2. Production data for Bob's Bicycle Factory are as follows:

Number of workers	Bikes assembled per day
1	10
2	18
3	24
4	28
5	30

Other than wages, Bob has costs of $100 (for parts and so on) for each bike assembled. **LO2**

a. Bikes sell for \$130 each. Find the marginal product and the value of the marginal product for each worker (don't forget about Bob's cost of parts).
b. Make a table showing Bob's demand curve for labor.
c. Repeat part b for the case in which bikes sell for \$140 each.
d. Repeat part b for the case in which worker productivity increases by 50 percent. Bikes sell for \$130 each.

3. How would each of the following likely affect the real wage and employment of unskilled workers on an automobile plant assembly line? **LO3**
   a. Demand for the type of car made by the plant increases.
   b. A sharp increase in the price of gas causes many commuters to switch to mass transit.
   c. Because of alternative opportunities, people become less willing to do factory work.
   d. The plant management introduces new assembly-line methods that increase the number of cars unskilled workers can produce per hour while reducing defects.
   e. Robots are introduced to do most basic assembly-line tasks.
   f. The workers unionize.
4. How would each of the following factors be likely to affect the economywide supply of labor? **LO2**
   a. The mandatory retirement age is increased.
   b. Increased productivity causes real wages to rise.
   c. War preparations lead to the institution of a national draft, and many young people are called up.
   d. More people decide to have children (consider both short-run and long-run effects).
   e. Social Security benefits are made more generous.
5. Skilled or unskilled workers can be used to produce a small toy. Initially, assume that the wages paid to both types of workers are equal. **LO3**
   a. Suppose that electronic equipment is introduced that increases the marginal product of skilled workers (who can use the equipment to produce more toys per hour worked). The marginal products of unskilled workers are unaffected. Explain, using words and graphs, what happens to the equilibrium wages for the two groups.
   b. Suppose that unskilled workers find it worthwhile to acquire skills when the wage differential between skilled and unskilled workers reaches a certain point. Explain what will happen to the supply of unskilled workers, the supply of skilled workers, and the equilibrium wage for the two groups. In particular, what are equilibrium wages for skilled workers relative to unskilled workers after some unskilled workers acquire training?
6. Here is a report from a not-very-efficient BLS survey taker: "There were 65 people in the houses I visited, 10 of them children under 16 and 10 retired; 25 people had full-time jobs, and 5 had part-time jobs. There ware 5 full-time homemakers, 5 full-time students over age 16, and 2 people who were disabled and cannot work. The remaining people did not have jobs but all said they would like one. One of these people had not looked actively for work for three months, however." Find the labor force, the working-age population, the number of employed workers, and the number of unemployed workers. **LO4**
7. Ellen is downloading labor market data for the most recent month, but her connection is slow and so far this is all she has been able to get:

Unemployment rate	5.0%
Participation rate	62.5%
Not in the labor force	60 million

Find the labor force, the working-age population, the number of employed workers, and the number of unemployed workers. **LO4**

8. For each of the following scenarios, state whether the unemployment is frictional, structural, or cyclical. Justify your answer. **LO5**
   a. Ted lost his job when the steel mill closed down. He lacks the skills to work in another industry and so has been unemployed over a year.
   b. Alice was laid off from her job at the auto plant because the recession reduced the demand for cars. She expects to get her job back when the economy picks up.
   c. Lance is an unskilled worker who works for local moving companies during their busy seasons. The rest of the year he is unemployed.
   d. Gwen had a job as a clerk but quit when her husband was transferred to another state. She looked for a month before finding a new job that she liked.
   e. Tao looked for a job for six weeks after finishing college. He turned down a couple of offers because they didn't let him use the skills he had acquired in college, but now he has a job in the area that he trained for.
   f. Karen, a software engineer, lost her job when the start-up company she was working for went bankrupt. She interviewed at five companies before accepting a new job in another firm in the same industry.

9. The towns of Sawyer and Thatcher each has a labor force of 1,200 people. In Sawyer, 100 people were unemployed for the entire year, while the rest of the labor force was employed continuously. In Thatcher, every member of the labor force was unemployed for 1 month and employed for 11 months. **LO4, LO5**
   a. What is the average unemployment rate over the year in each of the two towns?
   b. What is the average duration of unemployment spells in each of the two towns?
   c. In which town do you think the costs of unemployment are higher? Explain.

10. The *Economic Report of the President* (*ERP*), prepared annually by the President's Council of Economic Advisers, is available in the library or online (www.gpoaccess.gov/eop). *ERP* includes both useful articles on recent economic developments and a statistical section that provides historical data on many macro variables. **LO5**
    a. From the *ERP* or some other source, find data for the nonrecession year 2006 on the percentage of the unemployed who were out of work less than 5 weeks, between 5 and 14 weeks, and over 26 weeks. What do these data suggest about the relative importance of frictional and structural unemployment in the economy when the economy is not in recession?
    b. Compare the data you found for the most recent year to similar data for the recession years 1981–1982, 1990–1991, and 2001. How do recessions change the proportion of unemployment that is short term and long term?

ANSWERS TO IN-CHAPTER EXERCISES

14.1 The value of the marginal product of the seventh worker is \$39,000, and the value of the marginal product of the eighth worker is \$33,000. So the seventh but not the eighth worker is profitable to hire at a wage of \$35,000. **LO2**

14.2 With the computer price at \$5,000, it is profitable to hire three workers at a wage of \$100,000, since the third worker's value of marginal product (\$105,000) exceeds \$100,000, but the fourth worker's value of marginal product (\$95,000) is less than \$100,000. At a computer price of \$3,000, we can refer to Table 14.1 to find that not even the first worker has a value of marginal product as high as \$100,000, so at that computer price, BCC will hire no workers. In short, at a wage of \$100,000, the increase in the computer price raises the demand for technicians from zero to three. **LO2**

14.3 The seventh but not the eighth worker's value of marginal product exceeds \$50,000 (Table 14.3), so it is profitable to hire seven workers if the going wage is \$50,000. From Table 14.1, before the increase in productivity, the first five workers have values of marginal product greater than \$50,000, so the demand for labor at a given wage of \$50,000 is five workers. Thus, the increase in productivity raises the quantity of labor demanded at a wage of \$50,000 from five workers to seven workers. **LO2**

14.4 Even though you are receiving no pay, the valuable experience you gain as an intern is likely to raise the pay you will be able to earn in the future, so it is an investment in human capital. You also find working in the radio station more enjoyable than working in a car wash, presumably. To decide which job to take, you should ask yourself, "Taking into account both the likely increase in my future earnings and my greater enjoyment from working in the radio station, would I be willing to pay \$3,000 to work in the radio station rather than in the car wash?" If the answer is yes, then you should work in the radio station; otherwise, you should go to the car wash.

A decision to work in the radio station does not contradict the idea of an upward-sloping labor supply curve, if we are willing to think of the total compensation for that job as including not just cash wages but such factors as the value of the training that you receive. Your labor supply curve is still upward-sloping in the sense that the greater the value you place on the internship experience, the more likely you are to accept the job. **LO2**

14.5 Immigration to a country raises labor supply—indeed, the search for work is one of the most powerful factors drawing immigrants in the first place. As shown in the accompanying figure, an increase in labor supply will tend to lower the wages that employers have to pay (from w to w'), while raising overall employment (from N to N'). Because of its tendency to reduce real wages, labor unions generally oppose large-scale immigration, while employers support it.

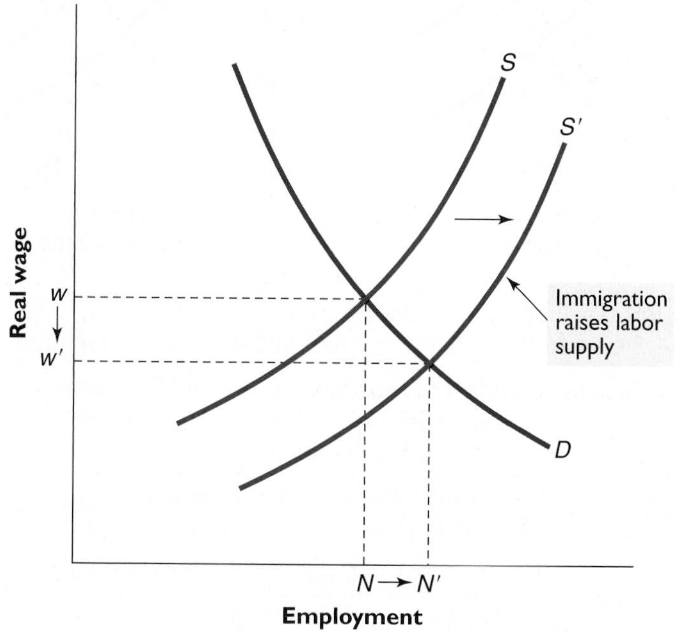

Although the figure shows the overall, or aggregate, supply of labor in the economy, the specific effects of immigration on wages depend on the skills and occupations of the immigrants. Current U.S. immigration policy makes the reunification of families the main reason for admitting immigrants, and for the most part immigrants are not screened by their education or skills. The United States also has a good deal of illegal immigration, made up largely of people looking for economic opportunity. These two factors create a tendency for new immigrants to the United States to be relatively low-skilled. Since immigration tends to increase the supply of unskilled labor by relatively more, it depresses wages of domestic low-skilled workers more than it does the wages of domestic high-skilled workers. Some economists, such as George Borjas of Harvard University, have argued that low-skilled immigration is another important factor reducing the wages of less-skilled workers relative to workers with greater skills and education. Borjas argues that the United States should adopt the approach used by Canada and give preference to potential immigrants with relatively higher levels of skills and education. **LO3**

14.6 Part (a) of the accompanying figure shows the labor market in 1960–1972; part (b) shows the labor market in 1973–2000. For comparability, we set the initial labor supply (*S*) and demand (*D*) curves the same in both parts, implying the same initial values of the real wage (w) and employment (N). In part (a) we show the effects of a large increase in labor demand (from D to D'), the result of rapid productivity growth, and a relatively small increase in labor supply (from S to S'). The real wage rises to w' and employment rises to N'. In part (b) we observe the effects of a somewhat smaller increase in labor demand (from D to D'') and a larger increase in labor supply (from S to S''). Part (b), corresponding to the 1973–2000 period, shows a smaller increase in the real wage and a larger increase in employment than part (a), corresponding to 1960–1972. These results are consistent with actual developments in the U.S. labor market over these two periods. **LO3**

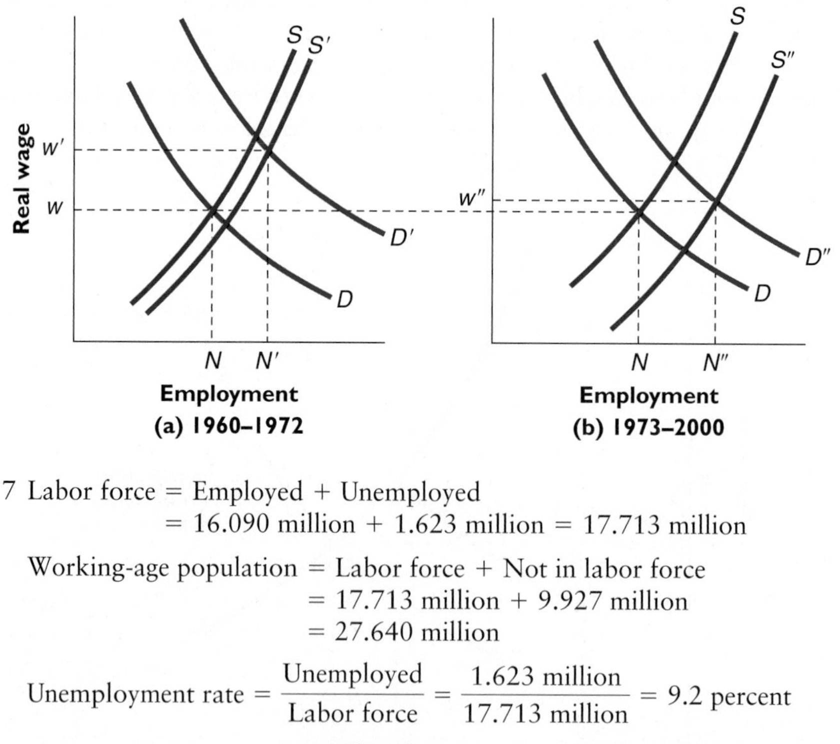

14.7 Labor force = Employed + Unemployed
= 16.090 million + 1.623 million = 17.713 million

Working-age population = Labor force + Not in labor force
= 17.713 million + 9.927 million
= 27.640 million

$$\text{Unemployment rate} = \frac{\text{Unemployed}}{\text{Labor force}} = \frac{1.623 \text{ million}}{17.713 \text{ million}} = 9.2 \text{ percent}$$

$$\text{Participation rate} = \frac{\text{Labor force}}{\text{Working-age population}} = \frac{17.713 \text{ million}}{27.640 \text{ million}}$$
$$= 64.1 \text{ percent}$$

In January 2008, African Americans represented 11.5 percent of the labor force and 11.9 percent of the working-age population. The participation rate for African Americans was slightly lower than that of the population as a whole while the unemployment rate was 88 percent higher than that of the population as a whole. **LO4**

PART

6

THE ECONOMY IN THE LONG RUN

■

For millennia the great majority of the world's inhabitants eked out a spare existence by tilling the soil. Only a small proportion of the population lived above the level of subsistence, learned to read and write, or traveled more than a few miles from their birthplaces. Large cities grew up, serving as imperial capitals and centers of trade, but the great majority of urban populations lived in dire poverty, subject to malnutrition and disease.

Then, about three centuries ago, a fundamental change occurred. Spurred by technological advances and entrepreneurial innovations, a process of economic growth began. Sustained over many years, this growth in the economy's productive capacity has transformed almost every aspect of how we live—from what we eat and wear to how we work and play. What caused this economic growth? And why have some countries enjoyed substantially greater rates of growth than others? As Nobelist Robert E. Lucas Jr. put it in a classic article on economic development, "The consequences for human welfare involved in questions like these are simply staggering: Once one starts to think about them, it is hard to think about anything else." Although most people would attach less significance to these questions than Lucas did, they are undoubtedly of very great importance.

The subject of Part 6 is the behavior of the economy in the long run, including the factors that cause the economy to grow and develop. Chapter 15 begins by tackling directly the causes and consequences of economic growth. A key conclusion of the chapter is that improvements in average labor productivity are the primary source of rising living standards; hence, policies to improve living standards should focus on stimulating productivity. Capital accumulation is an important determinant of economic growth, and Chapters 16 and 17 both touch on this subject. Chapter 16 examines the measurement of national saving, the reasons why people save, and the reasoning behind firms' capital formation decisions, and it develops a supply and demand model of financial markets. Chapter 17 looks more closely at the roles played by banks, bond markets, and stock markets in allocating saving to productive uses, then introduces the concept of money and discusses how the actions of the banking system affect the supply of money. Chapter 17 concludes with an examination of the relationship between the money supply and inflation in the long run.

CHAPTER 15

Economic Growth

LEARNING OBJECTIVES

After reading this chapter, you should be able to:

1. Show how small differences in growth rates can lead to large differences in living standards.
2. Explain why GDP per capita is the product of average labor productivity and the proportion of the population that is employed and use this decomposition to discuss the sources of economic growth.
3. Discuss the determinants of average labor productivity within a particular country and use these concepts to analyze per capita GDP differences across countries.
4. Compare and contrast the benefits of economic growth with its costs.
5. Discuss and evaluate government policies that promote economic growth.
6. Understand the trade-offs between economic growth and environmental quality.

One of us attended a conference on the effects of economic growth and development at which a speaker posed the following question: "Which would you rather be? An ordinary, middle-class American living today, or the richest person in America at the time of George Washington?"

A member of the audience spoke out immediately: "I can answer that question in one word. Dentistry."

The answer drew a laugh, perhaps because it reminded people of George Washington's famous wooden teeth. But it was a good answer. Dentistry in early America—whether the patient was rich or poor—was a primitive affair. Most dentists simply pulled a patient's rotten teeth, with a shot of whiskey for anesthetic.

Other types of medical care were not much better than dentistry. Eighteenth-century doctors had no effective weapons against tuberculosis, typhoid fever, diphtheria, influenza, pneumonia, and other communicable diseases. Such illnesses, now quite treatable, were major killers in Washington's time. Infants and children were particularly susceptible to deadly infectious diseases, especially

Would you rather be a rich person living in the eighteenth century or a middle-class person living in the twenty-first century?

whooping cough and measles. Even a well-to-do family often lost two or three children to these illnesses. Washington, an unusually large and vigorous man, lived to the age of 67, but the average life expectancy during his era was probably not much more than 40 years.

Medical care is not the only aspect of ordinary life that has changed drastically over the past two centuries. Author Stephen Ambrose, in his account of the Lewis and Clark expedition, described the limitations of transportation and communication in early America:

> A critical fact in the world of 1801 was that nothing moved faster than the speed of a horse. No human being, no manufactured item, no bushel of wheat, no side of beef (or any beef on the hoof for that matter), no letter, no information, no idea, order, or instruction of any kind moved faster, and, as far as Jefferson's contemporaries were able to tell, nothing ever would.
>
> And except on a racetrack, no horse moved very fast. Road conditions in the United States ranged from bad to abominable, and there weren't very many of them. The best highway in the country ran from Boston to New York; it took a light stagecoach . . . three full days to make the 175-mile journey. The hundred miles from New York to Philadelphia took two full days.[1]

Today New Yorkers can go to Philadelphia by train in an hour and a half. What would George Washington have thought of that? And how would nineteenth-century pioneers, who crossed the continent by wagon train, have reacted to the idea that their great-grandchildren would be able to have breakfast in New York and lunch the same day in San Francisco?

No doubt you can think of other enormous changes in the way average people live, even over the past few decades. Computer technologies and the internet have changed the ways people work and study in just a few years, for example. Though these changes are due in large part to scientific advances, such discoveries *by themselves* usually have little effect on most people's lives. New scientific knowledge leads to widespread improvements in living standards only when it is commercially applied. Better understanding of the human immune system, for example, has little impact unless it leads to new therapies or drugs. And a new drug will do little to help unless it is affordable to those who need it.

A tragic illustration of this point is the AIDS epidemic in Africa. Although some new drugs will moderate the effects of the virus that causes AIDS, they are so expensive that they are of little practical value in poverty-stricken African nations grappling with the disease. But even if the drugs were affordable, they would have limited benefit without modern hospitals, trained health professionals, and adequate nutrition and sanitation. In short, most improvements in a nation's living standard are the result not just of scientific and technological advances but of an economic system that makes the benefits of those advances available to the average person.

In this chapter we will explore the sources of economic growth and rising living standards in the modern world. We will begin by reviewing the remarkable economic growth in the industrialized countries, as measured by real GDP per person. Since the mid-nineteenth century (and earlier in some countries), a radical transformation in living standards has occurred in these countries. What explains this transformation? The key to rising living standards is a *continuing increase in average labor productivity,* which depends on several factors, from the skills and motivation workers bring to their jobs to the legal and social environment in which they work. We will analyze each of these factors and discuss its implications for government

[1]Stephen E. Ambrose, *Undaunted Courage: Meriwether Lewis, Thomas Jefferson, and the Opening of the American West* (New York: Touchstone [Simon & Schuster], 1996), p. 52.

policies to promote growth. We also will discuss the costs of rapid economic growth and consider whether there may be limits to the amount of economic growth a society can achieve.

THE REMARKABLE RISE IN LIVING STANDARDS: THE RECORD

The advances in health care and transportation mentioned in the beginning of this chapter illustrate only a few of the impressive changes that have taken place in people's material well-being over the past two centuries, particularly in industrialized countries like the United States. To study the factors that affect living standards systematically, however, we must go beyond anecdotes and adopt a specific measure of economic well-being in a particular country and time.

In Chapter 12, we introduced the concept of real GDP as a basic measure of the level of economic activity in a country. Recall that, in essence, real GDP measures the physical volume of goods and services produced within a country's borders during a specific period, such as a quarter or a year. Consequently, real GDP *per person* provides a measure of the quantity of goods and services available to the typical resident of a country at a particular time. Although real GDP per person is certainly not a perfect indicator of economic well-being, as we saw in Chapter 12, it is positively related to a number of pertinent variables, such as life expectancy, infant health, and literacy. Lacking a better alternative, economists have focused on real GDP per person as a key measure of a country's living standard and stage of economic development.

Figure 15.1 shows the remarkable growth in real GDP per person that occurred in the United States between 1929 and 2006. For comparison, Table 15.1 shows real GDP per person in seven countries in selected years from 1870 to 2003. Figure 15.2 displays the same data graphically for five of the eight countries.

The data in Table 15.1 and Figure 15.2 tell a dramatic story. For example, in the United States (which was already a relatively wealthy industrialized country in 1870), real GDP per person grew more than 12-fold between 1870 and 2003. In Japan, real GDP per person grew more than 28 times over the same period. Underlying these statistics is an amazingly rapid process of economic growth and transformation, through which in just a few generations relatively poor agrarian

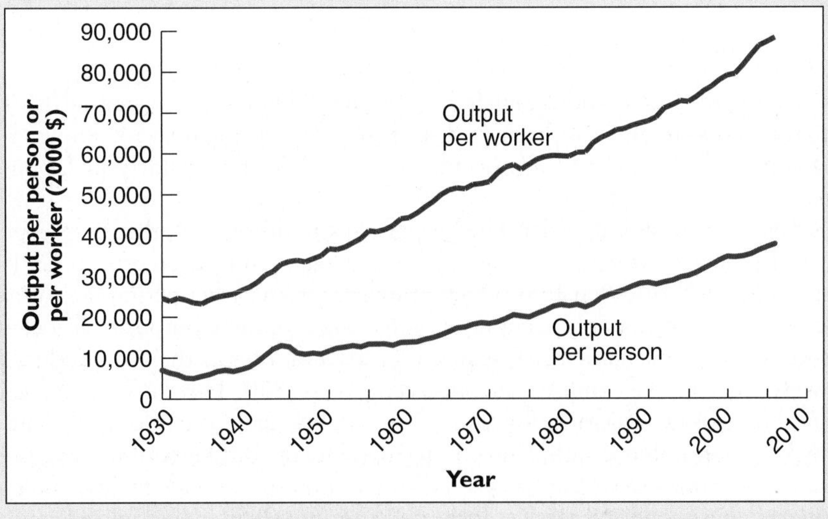

SOURCE: Bureau of Economic Analysis (www.bea.gov).

FIGURE 15.1
Output per Person and per Worker in the U.S. Economy, 1929–2006.
The red line shows the output per worker in the U.S. economy since 1929, and the blue line shows output per person. Both have risen substantially. Relative to 1929, output per person today is five times greater, and output per worker is almost four times greater.

TABLE 15.1
Real GDP per Person in Selected Countries, 1870–2003

Country	1870	1913	1950	1979	2003	Annual % change 1870–2003	Annual % change 1950–2003	Annual % change 1979–2003
United States	2,936	6,366	11,484	22,567	34,875	1.9%	2.1%	1.8%
United Kingdom	3,899	6,014	8,481	16,093	26,046	1.4	2.1	2.0
Germany	2,420	4,800	5,106	18,411	25,188	1.8	3.1	1.3
Japan	835	1,571	2,176	14,912	24,037	2.6	4.6	2.0
Brazil	923	1,050	2,165	6,336	7,205	1.6	2.3	0.5
China	548	571	464	1,076	4,970	1.7	4.6	6.6
Ghana	464	826	1,187	1,281	1,440	0.9	0.4	0.5

SOURCE: Angus Maddison, *The World Economy: A Millennial Perspective* (OECD: 2001), updated tables downloaded from www.ggdc.net/maddison. Rebased to 2000 using Penn World Tables 6.2, http://pwt.econ.upenn.edu/). "Germany" refers to West Germany in 1950 and 1979.

FIGURE 15.2
Real GDP per Person in a Sample of Countries, 1870–2003.
Economic growth has been especially rapid since the 1950s in Japan and since 1979 in China. Other countries have quite low growth rates.

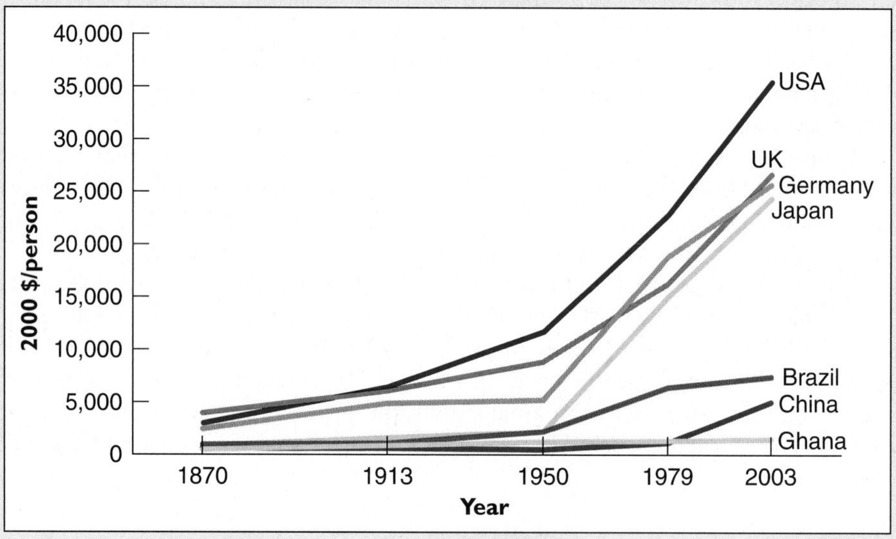

societies became highly industrialized economies—with average standards of living that could scarcely have been imagined in 1870. As Figure 15.2 shows, a significant part of this growth has occurred since 1950, particularly in Japan and China.

A note of caution is in order. The farther back in time we go, the less precise are historical estimates of real GDP. Most governments did not keep official GDP statistics until after World War II; production records from earlier periods are often incomplete or of questionable accuracy. Comparing economic output over a century or more is also problematic because many goods and services that are produced today were unavailable—indeed, inconceivable—in 1870. How many nineteenth-century horse-drawn wagons, for example, would be the economic equivalent of a BMW 328i automobile or a Boeing 757 jet? Despite the difficulty of making precise comparisons, however, we can say with certainty that the variety, quality, and quantity of available goods and services increased enormously in industrialized countries during the nineteenth and twentieth centuries, a fact reflected in the data on real GDP per capita.

WHY "SMALL" DIFFERENCES IN GROWTH RATES MATTER

The last three columns of Table 15.1 show the annual growth rates of real GDP per person, for both the entire 1870–2003 period and two more recent periods. At first glance, these growth rates don't seem to differ much from country to country. For example, for the period 1870–2003, the highest growth rate is 2.6 percent (Japan) and the lowest is 0.9 percent (Ghana). But consider the long-run effect of this seemingly "small" difference in annual growth rates. In 1870, in terms of output per person, Brazil was twice as rich as Ghana. Yet by 2003 Brazil was five times richer than Ghana. This widening of the gap between these two countries is the result of the apparently small difference between a 1.6 percent growth rate and a 0.9 percent growth rate, maintained over 133 years.

The fact that what seem to be small differences in growth rates can have large long-run effects results from what is called the power of compounding, which is often illustrated by *compound interest*.

Compound interest (1)

In 1800 your great-great-grandfather deposited \$10.00 in a checking account at 4 percent interest. Interest is compounded annually (so that interest paid at the end of each year receives interest itself in later years). Great-Great-Grandpa's will specified that the account be turned over to his most direct descendant (you) in the year 2005. When you withdrew the funds in that year, how much was the account worth?

The account was worth \$10.00 in 1800; $\$10.00 \times 1.04 = \$10.40$ in 1801; $\$10.00 \times 1.04 \times 1.04 = \$10.00 \times (1.04)^2 = \$10.82$ in 1802; and so on. Since 205 years elapsed between 1800, when the deposit was made, and the year 2005, when the account was closed, the value of the account in the year 2005 was $\$10.00 \times (1.04)^{205}$, or $\$10.00 \times 1.04$ to the 205th power. Using a calculator, you will find that \$10.00 times 1.04 to the 205th power is \$31,033.77—a good return for a \$10.00 deposit! ◆

Compound interest—an arrangement in which interest is paid not only on the original deposit but on all previously accumulated interest—is distinguished from *simple interest,* in which interest is paid only on the original deposit. If your great-grand-father's account had been deposited at 4 percent simple interest, it would have accumulated only 40 cents each year (4 percent of the original \$10.00 deposit), for a total value of $\$10.00 + 205 \times \$0.40 = \$92.00$ after 205 years. The tremendous growth in the value of his account came from the compounding of the interest—hence the phrase "the power of compound interest."

compound interest the payment of interest not only on the original deposit but on all previously accumulated interest

Compound interest (2)

Continuing with the previous example, what would your great-great-grandfather's \$10.00 deposit have been worth after 205 years if the annual interest rate had been 2 percent? 6 percent?

At 2 percent interest, the account would be worth \$10.00 in 1800; $\$10.00 \times 1.02 = \$10.20$ in 1801; $\$10.00 \times (1.02)^2 = \$10.40$ in 1802; and so on. In the year 2005, the value of the account would be $\$10.00 \times (1.02)^{205}$, or \$579.48. If the interest rate were 6 percent, after 205 years the account would be worth $10.00 × $(1.06)^{205}$, or $1,540,644.29. Let's summarize the results of these two examples:

Interest rate (%)	Value of $10 after 205 years
2	$579.48
4	$31,033.77
6	$1,540,644.29

The power of compound interest is that even at relatively low rates of interest, a small sum, compounded over a long enough period, can greatly increase in value. A more subtle point, illustrated by this example, is that small differences in interest rates matter a lot. The difference between a 2 percent and a 4 percent interest rate doesn't seem tremendous, but over a long period of time it implies large differences in the amount of interest accumulated on an account. Likewise, the effect of switching from a 4 percent to a 6 percent interest rate is enormous, as our calculations show.[2] ◆

Economic growth rates are similar to compound interest rates. Just as the value of a bank deposit grows each year at a rate equal to the interest rate, so the size of a nation's economy expands each year at the rate of economic growth. This analogy suggests that even a relatively modest rate of growth in output per person—say, 1 to 2 percent per year—will produce tremendous increases in average living standard over a long period. And relatively small *differences* in growth rates, as in the case of Brazil and Ghana, will ultimately produce very different living standards. Over the long run, then, the rate of economic growth is an extremely important variable. Hence, government policy changes or other factors that affect the long-term growth rate even by a small amount will have a major economic impact.

EXERCISE 15.1

Suppose that real GDP per capita in the United States had grown at 2.6 percent per year, as Japan's did, instead of the actual 1.9 percent per year, from 1870 to 2003. How much larger would real GDP per person have been in the United States in 2003?

China as Number One?

When your parents were in school in the 1980s, there was a great deal of discussion in the United States about the Japanese economy. Japan's economic growth rate had greatly exceeded that in the United States and Europe since the 1950s. Pundits projected this growth rate into the future and predicted that Japan would have the world's largest output sometime during the twenty-first century and would much sooner become the world's most prosperous economy in terms of output per worker. Books like one entitled *Japan as Number One* were best-sellers.

In the latter part of the 1980s, Japan's torrid growth rate cooled off and Japan entered a lengthy recession from which it has only recently emerged. Now, however, attention has been diverted to its neighbor, China. Not so long ago, China was one of the poorest countries in the world. In recent decades, however, Chinese economic growth has soared. Now China already produces about half of the entire planet's

[2]Economists employ a useful formula for approximating the number of years it will take for an initial amount to double at various growth or interest rates. The formula is 72 divided by the growth or interest rate. Thus, if the interest rate is 2 percent per year, it will take $72/2 = 36$ years for the initial sum to double. If the interest rate is 4 percent, it will take $72/4 = 18$ years. This formula is a good approximation only for small and moderate interest rates.

output of both clothing and cement, and it is also the world's largest producer of coal and steel. It is the world's largest *consumer* of copper, aluminum, and cell phones and the second largest consumer of personal computers.[3] Some observers predict that China will become the world's largest economy sometime during the middle of this century.

Because China also has the world's largest population, its output per person is still much smaller than that in the United States, western Europe, and Japan: China's output per person is only 14 percent as large as that in the United States. In Table 15.2 we list China's share of world population in 2003 as well as its share of world consumption of a variety of items in either 2002 or 2003.

Since China's share of world population is 20.5 percent, its consumption per person exceeds that elsewhere in the world wherever its share of world consumption exceeds 20.5 percent. Thus, for example, China consumes more than twice as much pork per person as the rest of the world, but less than one-fifth as much soda. Even though it consumes less than one-third as many computers per person as the rest of the world, its huge population still makes it the world's second largest consumer of computers.

Will China continue to grow so rapidly? As our compound interest examples showed, small differences in growth rates have tremendous long-run effects. Will China overtake the United States as the world's largest economy? Will it become the world's most prosperous nation in terms of output per worker? Or will it follow the path of Japan and experience smaller growth in the future? Perhaps more importantly, we should examine how China managed to achieve such extraordinary growth and what other less-developed countries can learn from China's experience.

TABLE 15.2
China's Share of World Population and Consumption, 2002–2003*

Population	20.5%
Consumption of	
Pork	51%
Cigarettes	35
Cotton	33
Fish	32
Steel	27
Televisions	23
Ice cream	19
Washing machines	18
Computers	6
Soda	4

*"Inside the New China," *Fortune*, October 4, 2004. Data for fish are for the year 2001.

WHY NATIONS BECOME RICH: THE CRUCIAL ROLE OF AVERAGE LABOR PRODUCTIVITY

What determines a nation's economic growth rate? To get some insight into this vital question, we will find it useful to express real GDP per person as the product of two terms: average labor productivity and the share of the population that is working.

[3]"Inside the New China," *Fortune*, October 4, 2004.

To do this, let Y equal total real output (as measured by real GDP, for example), N equal the number of employed workers, and POP equal the total population. Then real GDP per person can be written as Y/POP; **average labor productivity,** or output per employed worker, equals Y/N; and the share of the population that is working is N/POP. The relationship between these three variables is

average labor productivity output per employed worker

$$\frac{Y}{POP} = \frac{Y}{N} \times \frac{N}{POP},$$

which, as you can see by canceling out N on the right-hand side of the equation, always holds exactly. In words, this basic relationship is

Real GDP per person = Average labor productivity
× Share of population employed.

This expression for real GDP per person tells us something very basic and intuitive: The quantity of goods and services that each person can consume depends on (1) how much each worker can produce and (2) how many people (as a fraction of the total population) are working. Furthermore, because real GDP per person equals average labor productivity times the share of the population that is employed, real GDP per person can *grow* only to the extent that there is *growth* in worker productivity and/or the fraction of the population that is employed.

Figures 15.3 and 15.4 show the U.S. figures for the three key variables in the relationship above for the period 1960–2006. Figure 15.3 shows both real GDP per person and real GDP per worker (average labor productivity). Figure 15.4 shows the portion of the entire U.S. population (not just the working-age population) that was employed during that period. Once again, we see that the expansion in output per person in the United States has been impressive. Between 1960 and 2006, real GDP per person in the United States grew by 172 percent. Thus, in 2006, the average American enjoyed about 2½ times as many goods and services as in 1960. Figures 15.3 and 15.4 show that increases in both labor productivity and the share of the population holding a job contributed to this rise in living standard.

FIGURE 15.3
Real GDP per Person and Average Labor Productivity in the United States, 1960–2006.
Real output per person in the United States grew 172 percent between 1960 and 2006, and real output per worker (average labor productivity) grew by 110 percent.

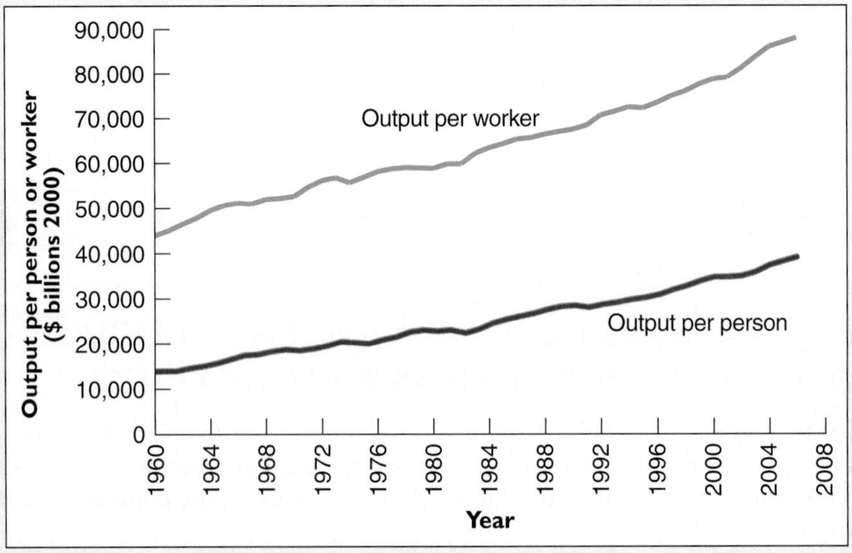

SOURCE: Bureau of Economic Analysis (www.bea.gov).

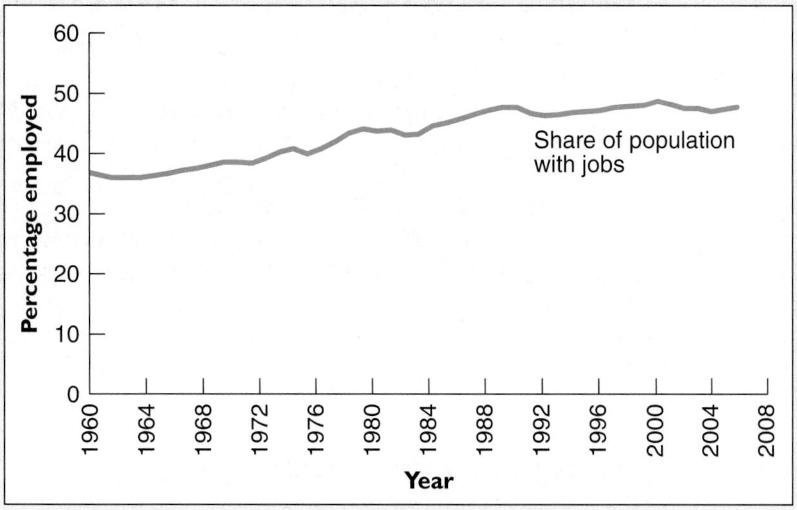

SOURCE: Bureau of Labor Statistics (www.bls.gov).

FIGURE 15.4
Share of the U.S. Population Employed, 1960–2006.
The share of the U.S. population holding a job increased from 36 percent in 1960 to 48 percent in 2007.

Let's look a bit more closely at these two contributing factors, beginning with the share of the population that is employed. As Figure 15.4 shows, between 1960 and 2006, the number of people employed in the United States rose from 36 to 48 percent of the entire population, a remarkable increase. The growing tendency of women to work outside the home was the most important reason for this rise in employment. Another factor leading to higher rates of employment was an increase in the share of the general population that is of working age (ages 16 to 65). The coming of age of the "baby boom" generation, born in the years after World War II, and to a lesser extent the immigration of young workers from other countries, helped cause this growth in the workforce.

Although the rising share of the U.S. population with jobs contributed significantly to the increase in real GDP per person during the past four decades, this trend almost certainly will not continue in the future. Women's participation in the labor force seems unlikely to continue rising at the same rate as in the past four decades. More important, the baby boom generation, now in its prime years of employment, will begin to reach retirement age around the year 2010. As more and more baby boomers retire, the fraction of the population that is employed will begin to drop, probably significantly. In the long run, then, the improvement in living standards brought about by the rising share of Americans with jobs will likely prove transitory.

What about the other factor that determines output per person, average labor productivity? As Figure 15.3 shows, between 1960 and 2006, average labor productivity in the United States increased by 110 percent, accounting for a sizable share of the overall increase in GDP per person. In other periods, the link between average labor productivity and output per person in the United States has often been even stronger, since in most earlier periods the share of the population holding jobs was more stable than it has been recently. (See Figure 15.1 for the behavior of real GDP per person and average labor productivity in the United States over the period 1929–2006.)

This quick look at recent data supports a more general conclusion. *In the long run, increases in output per person arise primarily from increases in average labor productivity.* Furthermore, the more people can produce, the more they can consume. To understand why economies grow, then, we must understand the reasons for increased labor productivity.

RECAP | **ECONOMIC GROWTH AND PRODUCTIVITY**

Real GDP per person, a basic indicator of living standards, has grown dramatically in the industrialized countries. This growth reflects the *power of compound interest:* Even a modest growth rate, if sustained over a long period of time, can lead to large increases in the size of the economy.

Output per person equals average labor productivity times the share of the population that is employed. Since 1960 the share of the U.S. population with jobs has risen significantly, but this variable is likely to decline in coming decades. In the long run, increases in output per person and hence living standards arise primarily from increases in average labor productivity.

THE DETERMINANTS OF AVERAGE LABOR PRODUCTIVITY

What determines the productivity of the average worker in a particular country at a particular time? Popular discussions of this issue often equate worker productivity with the willingness of workers of a given nationality to work hard. Everything else being equal, a culture that promotes hard work certainly tends to increase worker productivity. But intensity of effort alone cannot explain the huge differences in average labor productivity that we observe around the world. For example, average labor productivity in the United States is about 24 times what it is in Indonesia and 100 times what it is in Bangladesh, though there is little doubt that Indonesians and Bangladeshis work very hard.

In this section we will examine six factors that appear to account for the major differences in average labor productivity, both between countries and between generations. Later in the chapter we will discuss how economic policies can influence these factors to spur productivity and growth.

HUMAN CAPITAL

To illustrate the factors that determine average labor productivity, we introduce two prototypical assembly line workers, Lucy and Ethel.

Lucy and Ethel on the assembly line

Lucy and Ethel have jobs wrapping chocolate candies and placing them into boxes. Lucy, a novice wrapper, can wrap only 100 candies per hour. Ethel, who has had on-the-job training, can wrap 300 candies per hour. Lucy and Ethel each works 40 hours per week. What is average labor productivity, in terms of candies wrapped per week and candies wrapped per hour, (a) for Lucy, (b) for Ethel, and (c) for Lucy and Ethel as a team?

How productive are these workers?

We have defined average labor productivity in general terms as output per worker. Note, though, that the measurement of average labor productivity depends on the time period that is specified. For example, the data presented in Figure 15.3 tell us how much the average worker produces *in a year*. In this example we are concerned with how much Lucy and Ethel can produce *per hour* of work or *per week* of work. Any one of these ways of measuring labor productivity is equally valid, as long as we are clear about the time unit we are using.

Lucy and Ethel's hourly productivities are given in the problem: Lucy can wrap 100 candies per hour and Ethel can wrap 300. Lucy's weekly productivity is (40 hours/week) × (100 candies wrapped/hour) = 4,000 wrapped candies per week.

Ethel's weekly productivity is (40 hours/week) × (300 candies wrapped/hour), or 12,000 candies per week.

Together Lucy and Ethel can wrap 16,000 candies per week. As a team, their average weekly productivity is (16,000 candies wrapped)/(2 weeks of work), or 8,000 candies per week. Their average hourly productivity as a team is (16,000 candies wrapped)/(80 hours of work) = 200 candies per hour. Notice that, taken as a team, the two women's productivity lies midway between their individual productivities. ◆

Ethel is more productive than Lucy because she has had on-the-job training, which has allowed her to develop her candy-wrapping skills to a higher level than Lucy's. Because of her training, Ethel can produce more than Lucy can in a given number of hours.

EXERCISE 15.2

Suppose Ethel attends additional classes in candy wrapping and learns how to wrap 500 candies per hour. Find the output per week and output per hour for Lucy and Ethel, both individually and as a team.

Economists would explain the difference in the two women's performance by saying that Ethel has more human capital than Lucy. **Human capital** comprises the talents, education, training, and skills of workers. Workers with a large stock of human capital are more productive than workers with less training. For example, a secretary who knows how to use a word processing program will be able to type more letters than one who doesn't; an auto mechanic who is familiar with computerized diagnostic equipment will be able to fix engine problems that less-well-trained mechanics could not.

human capital an amalgam of factors such as education, training, experience, intelligence, energy, work habits, trustworthiness, initiative, and others that affect the value of a worker's marginal product

Why did West Germany and Japan recover so successfully from the devastation of World War II?

Germany and Japan sustained extensive destruction of their cities and industries during World War II and entered the postwar period impoverished. Yet within 30 years both countries had not only been rebuilt but had become worldwide industrial and economic leaders. What accounts for these "economic miracles"?

Many factors contributed to the economic recovery of West Germany and Japan from World War II, including the substantial aid provided by the United States to Europe under the Marshall Plan and to Japan during the U.S. occupation. Most economists agree, however, that high levels of human capital played a crucial role in both countries.

At the end of the war, Germany's population was exceptionally well educated, with a large number of highly qualified scientists and engineers. The country also had (and still does today) an extensive apprentice system that provided on-the-job training to young workers. As a result, Germany had a skilled industrial workforce. In addition, the area that became West Germany benefited substantially from an influx of skilled workers from East Germany and the rest of Soviet-controlled Europe, including 20,000 trained engineers and technicians. Beginning as early as 1949, this concentration of human capital contributed to a major expansion of Germany's technologically sophisticated, highly productive manufacturing sector. By 1960 West Germany was a leading exporter of high-quality manufactured goods, and its citizens enjoyed one of the highest standards of living in Europe.

Japan, which probably sustained greater physical destruction in the war than Germany, also began the postwar period with a skilled and educated labor force. In addition, occupying American forces restructured the Japanese school system and encouraged all Japanese to obtain a good education. Even more so than the Germans, however, the Japanese emphasized on-the-job training. As part of a lifetime employment system, under which workers were expected to stay with the same company their entire career, Japanese firms invested extensively in worker training. The payoff to these investments in human capital was a steady increase in average labor productivity, particularly in manufacturing. By the 1980s Japanese manufactured goods were among the most advanced in the world and Japan's workers among the most skilled.

Although high levels of human capital were instrumental in the rapid economic growth of West Germany and Japan, human capital alone cannot create a high living standard. A case in point is Soviet-dominated East Germany, which had a level of human capital similar to West Germany's after the war but did not enjoy the same economic growth. For reasons we will discuss later in the chapter, the communist system imposed by the Soviets utilized East Germany's human capital far less effectively than the economic systems of Japan and West Germany. ◆

Human capital is analogous to physical capital (such as machines and factories) in that it is acquired primarily through the investment of time, energy, and money. For example, to learn how to use a word processing program, a secretary might need to attend a technical school at night. The cost of going to school includes not only the tuition paid but also the *opportunity cost* of the secretary's time spent attending class and studying. The benefit of the schooling is the increase in wages the secretary will earn when the course has been completed. We know by the Cost-Benefit Principle that the secretary should learn word processing only if the benefits exceed the costs, including the opportunity costs. In general, then, we would expect to see people acquire additional education and skills when the difference in the wages paid to skilled and unskilled workers is significant.

Cost-Benefit

PHYSICAL CAPITAL

Workers' productivity depends not only on their skills and effort but on the tools they have to work with. Even the most skilled surgeon cannot perform open-heart surgery without sophisticated equipment, and an expert computer programmer is of limited value without a computer. These examples illustrate the importance of *physical capital* such as factories and machines. More and better capital allows workers to produce more efficiently, as the next example shows.

Lucy and Ethel get automated

Continuing with the earlier example, suppose that Lucy and Ethel's boss acquired an electric candy-wrapping machine, which is designed to be operated by one worker. Using this machine, an untrained worker can wrap 500 candies per hour. What are Lucy and Ethel's hourly and weekly outputs now? Will the answer change if the boss gets a second machine? A third?

Suppose for the sake of simplicity that a candy-wrapping machine must be assigned to one worker only. (This assumption rules out sharing arrangements, in which one worker uses the machine on the day shift and another on the night shift.) If the boss buys just one machine, she will assign it to Lucy. (Why? See Exercise 15.3.) Now Lucy will be able to wrap 500 candies per hour, while Ethel can wrap only 300 per hour. Lucy's weekly output will be 20,000 wrapped candies (40 hours × 500 candies wrapped per hour). Ethel's weekly output is still 12,000 wrapped candies (40 hours × 300 candies wrapped per hour). Together they can now wrap 32,000 candies per week, or 16,000 candies per week each. On an hourly basis, average labor productivity for the two women taken together is 32,000 candies wrapped per 80 hours of work, or 400 candies wrapped per hour—twice their average labor productivity before the boss bought the machine.

With two candy-wrapping machines available, both Lucy and Ethel could use a machine. Each could wrap 500 candies per hour, for a total of 40,000 wrapped candies per week. Average labor productivity for both women taken together would be 20,000 wrapped candies per week, or 500 wrapped candies per hour.

What would happen if the boss purchased a third machine? With only two workers, a third machine would be useless: it would add nothing to either total output or average labor productivity. ◆

EXERCISE 15.3

Using the assumptions made in the examples above, explain why the boss should give the single available candy-wrapping machine to Lucy rather than Ethel. (*Hint:* Apply the Principle of Increasing Opportunity Cost.)

Increasing Opportunity Cost

The candy-wrapping machine is an example of a *capital good,* which was defined Chapter 12 as a long-lived good, which is itself produced and used to produce other goods and services. Capital goods include machines and equipment (such as computers, earthmovers, or assembly lines) as well as buildings (such as factories or office buildings).

Capital goods like the candy-wrapping machine enhance workers' productivity. Table 15.3 summarizes the results of our Lucy and Ethel examples. For each number of machines the boss might acquire (column 1), Table 15.3 gives the total weekly output of Lucy and Ethel taken together (column 2), the total number of hours worked by the two women (column 3), and average output per hour (column 4), equal to total weekly output divided by total weekly hours.

Table 15.3 demonstrates two important points about the effect of additional capital on output. First, for a given number of workers, adding more capital generally increases both total output and average labor productivity. For example, adding the first candy-wrapping machine increases weekly output (column 2) by 16,000 candies and average labor productivity (column 4) by 200 candies wrapped per hour.

TABLE 15.3
Capital, Output, and Productivity in the Candy-Wrapping Factory

(1) Number of machines (capital)	(2) Total number of candies wrapped each week (output)	(3) Total hours worked per week	(4) Candies wrapped per hour worked (productivity)
0	16,000	80	200
1	32,000	80	400
2	40,000	80	500
3	40,000	80	500

The second point illustrated by Table 15.3 is that the more capital that is already in place, the smaller the benefits of adding extra capital. Notice that the first machine adds 16,000 candies to total output, but the second machine adds only 8,000. The third machine, which cannot be used since there are only two workers, does not increase output or productivity at all. This result illustrates a general principle of economics, called **diminishing returns to capital:** if the amount of labor and

diminishing returns to capital if the amount of labor and other inputs employed is held constant, then the greater the amount of capital already in use, the less an additional unit of capital adds to production other inputs employed is held constant, then the greater the amount of capital already in use, the less an additional unit of capital adds to production. In the case of the candy-wrapping factory, diminishing returns to capital implies that the first candy-wrapping machine acquired adds more output than the second, which in turn adds more output than the third.

Diminishing returns to capital are a natural consequence of firms' incentive to use each piece of capital as productively as possible. To maximize output, managers will assign the first machine that a firm acquires to the most productive use available, the next machine to the next most productive use, and so on—an illustration of the Principle of Increasing Opportunity Cost, or Low-Hanging-Fruit Principle. When many machines are available, all the highly productive ways of using them already have been exploited. Thus, adding yet another machine will not raise output or productivity by very much. If Lucy and Ethel are already operating two candy-wrapping machines, there is little point to buying a third machine, except perhaps as a replacement or spare.

Increasing Opportunity Cost

The implications of Table 15.3 can be applied to the question of how to stimulate economic growth. First, increasing the amount of capital available to the workforce will tend to increase output and average labor productivity. The more adequately equipped workers are, the more productive they will be. Second, the degree to which productivity can be increased by an expanding stock of capital is limited. Because of diminishing returns to capital, an economy in which the quantity of capital available to each worker is already very high will not benefit much from further expansion of the capital stock.

Is there empirical evidence that giving workers more capital makes them more productive? Figure 15.5 shows the relationship between average labor productivity (real GDP per worker) in 1990 and the amount of capital per worker in 15 countries. The figure shows a strong relationship between the amounts of capital per worker and productivity, consistent with the theory. Note, though, that the relationship between capital and productivity is somewhat weaker for the richest countries. For example, Germany has more capital per worker than the United States, but German workers are less productive than American workers on average. Diminishing returns to capital may help to explain the weakening of the relationship between capital and productivity at high levels of capital. In addition, Figure 15.5 does not account for many other differences among countries, such as differences in economic systems or government policies. Thus, we should not expect to see a perfect relationship between the two variables.

FIGURE 15.5
Average Labor Productivity and Capital per Worker in 15 Countries, 1990.
Countries with large amounts of capital per worker also tend to have high average labor productivity, as measured by real GDP per worker.

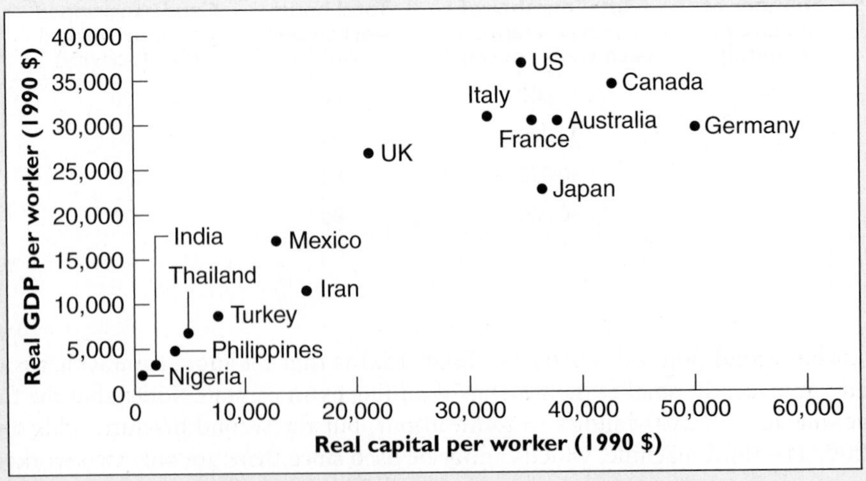

SOURCE: Penn World Tables (www.nber.org).

LAND AND OTHER NATURAL RESOURCES

Besides capital goods, other inputs to production help to make workers more productive, among them land, energy, and raw materials. Fertile land is essential to agriculture, and modern manufacturing processes make intensive use of energy and raw materials.

In general, an abundance of natural resources increases the productivity of the workers who use them. For example, a farmer can produce a much larger crop in a land-rich country like the United States or Australia than in a country where the soil is poor or arable land is limited in supply. With the aid of modern farm machinery and great expanses of land, today's American farmers are so productive that even though they constitute less than 3 percent of the population, they provide enough food not only to feed the country but to export to the rest of the world.

Although there are limits to a country's supply of arable land, many other natural resources, such as petroleum and metals, can be obtained through international markets. Because resources can be obtained through trade, countries need not possess large quantities of natural resources within their own borders to achieve economic growth. Indeed, a number of countries have become rich without substantial natural resources of their own, including Japan, Hong Kong, Singapore, and Switzerland. Just as important as possessing natural resources is the ability to use them productively—for example, by means of advanced technologies.

TECHNOLOGY

Besides human capital, physical capital, and natural resources, a country's ability to develop and apply new, more productive technologies will help to determine its productivity. Consider just one industry, transportation. Two centuries ago, as suggested by the quote from Stephen Ambrose in the beginning of the chapter, the horse and wagon were the primary means of transportation—a slow and costly method indeed. But in the nineteenth century, technological advances such as the steam engine supported the expansion of riverborne transportation and the development of a national rail network. In the twentieth century, the invention of the internal combustion engine and the development of aviation, supported by the construction of an extensive infrastructure of roads and airports, have produced increasingly rapid, cheap, and reliable transport. Technological change has clearly been a driving force in the transportation revolution.

New technologies can improve productivity in industries other than the one in which they are introduced. For instance, in the late 18th century, American farmers could sell their produce only in local and regional markets. Now the availability of rapid shipping and refrigerated transport allows American farmers to sell their products virtually anywhere in the world. With a broader market in which to sell, farmers can specialize in those products best suited to local land and weather conditions. Similarly, factories can obtain their raw materials wherever they are cheapest and most abundant, produce the goods they are most efficient at manufacturing, and sell their products wherever they will fetch the best price. Both these examples illustrate the Principle of Comparative Advantage, that overall productivity increases when producers concentrate on those activities at which they are relatively most efficient.

Comparative Advantage

Numerous other technological developments led to increased productivity, including advances in communication and medicine and the introduction of computer technology. All indications are that the internet will have a major impact on the U.S. economy, not just in retailing but in many other sectors. In fact, *most economists would probably agree that new technologies are the single most important source of productivity improvement,* and hence of economic growth in general.

However, economic growth does not automatically follow from breakthroughs in basic science. To make the best use of new knowledge, an economy needs entrepreneurs who can exploit scientific advances commercially, as well as a legal and political environment that encourages the practical application of new knowledge.

EXERCISE 15.4

A new kind of wrapping paper has been invented that makes candy-wrapping quicker and easier. The use of this paper *increases* the number of candies a person can wrap by hand by 200 per hour, and the number of candies a person can wrap by machine by 300 per hour. Using the data from our Lucy and Ethel examples, construct a table like Table 15.3 that shows how this technological advance affects average labor productivity. Do diminishing returns to capital still hold?

Why has U.S. labor productivity grown so rapidly since 1995?

During the 1950s and 1960s, most industrialized countries experienced rapid growth in real GDP and average labor productivity. Between 1947 and 1973, for example, U.S. labor productivity grew by 2.8 percent per year.[4] Between 1973 and 1995, however, labor productivity growth in the United States fell by half, to 1.4 percent per year. Other countries experienced similar productivity slowdowns, and many articles and books were written trying to uncover the reasons. In recent years, however, there has been a rebound in productivity growth, particularly in the United States. Between 1995 and 2007, U.S. labor productivity growth averaged 3 percent per year. What caused this resurgence in productivity growth? Can it be sustained?

Economists agree that the pickup in productivity growth was the product of rapid technological progress and increased investment in new information and communication technologies (ICT). Research indicates that productivity has grown rapidly in both those industries that *produce* ICT, such as silicon chips and fiber-optics, and those industries that *use* ICT. The application of these advances had ripple effects in areas ranging from automobile production to retail inventory management. The rapid growth of the internet, for example, made it possible for consumers to shop and find information online. But it also helped companies improve their efficiency by improving coordination between manufacturers and their suppliers. On the other hand, there has been no acceleration in labor productivity growth in those industries that neither produce nor use much ICT.[5]

Optimists argue that advances in computers, communications, biotechnology, and other ICT fields will allow productivity growth to continue at this elevated rate. Others are more cautious, arguing that the increases in productivity growth from these developments may be temporary rather than permanent. A great deal is riding on which view will turn out to be correct. ◆

ENTREPRENEURSHIP AND MANAGEMENT

entrepreneurs people who create new economic enterprises

The productivity of workers depends in part on the people who help to decide what to produce and how to produce it: entrepreneurs and managers. **Entrepreneurs** are

[4]Data refer to labor productivity growth in the nonfarm business sector and can be found at www.bls.gov.
[5]Kevin J. Stiroh, "Information Technology and the U.S. Productivity Revival: What Do the Industry Data Say?" *American Economic Review* 92 (December 2002), pp. 1559–76.

people who create new economic enterprises. Because of the new products, services, technological processes, and production methods they introduce, entrepreneurs are critical to a dynamic, healthy economy. In the late nineteenth and early twentieth centuries, individuals like Henry Ford and Alfred Sloan (automobiles), Andrew Carnegie (steel), John D. Rockefeller (oil), and J. P. Morgan (finance) played central roles in the development of American industry—and, not incidentally, amassed huge personal fortunes in the process. These people and others like them (including contemporary entrepreneurs like Bill Gates) have been criticized for some of their business practices, in some cases with justification. Clearly, though, they and dozens of other prominent business leaders of the past century have contributed significantly to the growth of the U.S. economy. Henry Ford, for example, developed the idea of mass production, which lowered costs sufficiently to bring automobiles within reach of the average American family. Ford began his business in his garage, a tradition that has been maintained by thousands of innovators ever since. Larry Page and Sergey Brin, the co-founders of Google, revolutionized the way college students and many professionals conduct research by developing a method to prioritize the list of Web sites obtained in a search of the internet.

Entrepreneurship, like any form of creativity, is difficult to teach, although some of the supporting skills, like financial analysis and marketing, can be learned in college or business school. How, then, does a society encourage entrepreneurship? History suggests that the entrepreneurial spirit will always exist; the challenge to society is to channel entrepreneurial energies in economically productive ways. For example, economic policymakers need to ensure that taxation is not so heavy, and regulation not so inflexible, that small businesses—some of which will eventually become big businesses—cannot get off the ground. Sociological factors may play a role as well. Societies in which business and commerce are considered to be beneath the dignity of refined, educated people are less likely to produce successful entrepreneurs. In the United States, for the most part, business has been viewed as a respectable activity. Overall, a social and economic milieu that allows entrepreneurship to flourish appears to promote economic growth and rising productivity, perhaps especially so in high-technology eras like our own.

Inventing the Personal Computer

In 1975 Steve Jobs and Steve Wozniak were two 20-year-olds who designed computer games for Atari. They had an idea to make a computer that was smaller and cheaper than the closet-sized mainframes that were then in use. To set up shop in Steve Jobs's parents' garage and buy their supplies, they sold their two most valuable possessions, Jobs's used Volkswagen van and Wozniak's Hewlett-Packard scientific calculator, for a total of $1,300. The result was the first personal computer, which they named after their new company (and Jobs's favorite fruit): Apple. The rest is history. Clearly, Jobs's and Wozniak's average labor productivity as the inventors of the personal computer was many times what it was when they designed computer games. Creative entrepreneurship can increase productivity just like additional capital or land. ◆

Example 15.1

THE ECONOMIC NATURALIST

Why did medieval China stagnate economically?

The Sung period in China (A.D. 960–1270) was one of considerable technological sophistication; its inventions included paper, waterwheels, water clocks, gunpowder, and possibly the compass. Yet no significant industrialization occurred, and in subsequent centuries Europe saw more economic growth and technological innovation than China. Why did medieval China stagnate economically?

According to research by economist William Baumol,[6] the main impediment to industrialization during the Sung period was a social system that inhibited entrepreneurship. Commerce and industry were considered low-status activities, not fit for an educated person. In addition, the emperor had the right to seize his subjects' property and to take control of their business enterprises—a right that greatly reduced his subjects' incentives to undertake business ventures. The most direct path to status and riches in medieval China was to go through a system of demanding civil service examinations given by the government every three years. The highest scorers on these national examinations were granted lifetime positions in the imperial bureaucracy, where they wielded much power and often became wealthy, in part through corruption. Not surprisingly, medieval China did not develop a dynamic entrepreneurial class, and consequently its scientific and technological advantages did not translate into sustained economic growth. China's experience shows why scientific advances alone cannot guarantee economic growth; to have economic benefits, scientific knowledge must be commercially applied through new products and new, more efficient means of producing goods and services. ●

Although entrepreneurship may be more glamorous, managers—the people who run businesses on a daily basis—also play an important role in determining average labor productivity. Managerial jobs span a wide range of positions, from the supervisor of the loading dock to the CEO (chief executive officer) at the helm of a *Fortune* 500 company. Managers work to satisfy customers, deal with suppliers, organize production, obtain financing, assign workers to jobs, and motivate them to work hard and effectively. Such activities enhance labor productivity. For example, in the 1970s and 1980s, Japanese managers introduced new production methods that greatly increased the efficiency of Japanese manufacturing plants. Among them was the *just-in-time* inventory system, in which suppliers deliver production components to the factory just when they are needed, eliminating the need for factories to stockpile components. Japanese managers also pioneered the idea of organizing workers into semi-independent production teams, which allowed workers more flexibility and responsibility than the traditional assembly line. Managers in the United States and other countries studied the Japanese managerial techniques closely and adopted many of them.

THE POLITICAL AND LEGAL ENVIRONMENT

So far we have emphasized the role of the private sector in increasing average labor productivity. But government too has a role to play in fostering improved productivity. One of the key contributions government can make is to provide a *political and legal environment* that encourages people to behave in economically productive ways—to work hard, save and invest wisely, acquire useful information and skills, and provide the goods and services that the public demands.

One specific function of government that appears to be crucial to economic success is the establishment of *well-defined property rights*. Property rights are well defined when the law provides clear rules for determining who owns what resources (through a system of deeds and titles, for example) and how those resources can be used. Imagine living in a society in which a dictator, backed by the military and the police, could take whatever he wanted, and regularly did so. In such a country, what incentive would you have to raise a large crop or to produce other valuable goods and services? Very little, since much of what you produced would

[6] "Entrepreneurship: Productive, Unproductive, and Destructive," *Journal of Political Economy*, October 1990, pp. 893–921.

likely be taken away from you. Unfortunately, in many countries of the world today, this situation is far from hypothetical.

Political and legal conditions affect the growth of productivity in other ways, as well. Political scientists and economists have documented the fact that *political instability* can be detrimental to economic growth. This finding is reasonable, since entrepreneurs and savers are unlikely to invest their resources in a country whose government is unstable, particularly if the struggle for power involves civil unrest, terrorism, or guerrilla warfare. On the other hand, a political system that promotes the *free and open exchange of ideas* will speed the development of new technologies and products. For example, some economic historians have suggested that the decline of Spain as an economic power was due in part to the advent of the Spanish Inquisition, which permitted no dissent from religious orthodoxy. Because of the Inquisition's persecution of those whose theories about the natural world contradicted Church doctrine, Spanish science and technology languished, and Spain fell behind more tolerant nations like the Netherlands.

EXERCISE 15.5

A Bangladeshi worker who immigrates to America is likely to find that his average labor productivity is much higher in the United States than it was at home. The worker is, of course, the same person he was when he lived in Bangladesh. How can the simple act of moving to the United States increase the worker's productivity? What does your answer say about the incentive to immigrate?

Why did communism fail?

For more than 70 years, from the Russian revolution in 1917 until the collapse of the Soviet Union in 1991, communism was believed by many to pose a major challenge to market-based economic systems. Yet, by the time of the Soviet Union's breakup, the poor economic record of communism had become apparent. Indeed, low living standards in communist countries, compared to those achieved in the West, were a major reason for the popular discontent that brought down the communist system in Europe. Economically speaking, why did communism fail?

The poor growth records of the Soviet Union and other communist countries did not reflect a lack of resources or economic potential. The Soviet Union had a highly educated workforce; a large capital stock; a vast quantity of natural resources, including land and energy; and access to sophisticated technologies. Yet, at the time of its collapse, output per person in the Soviet Union was probably less than one-seventh what it was in the United States.

Most observers would agree that the political and legal environment that established the structure of the communist economic system was a major cause of its ultimate failure. The economic system of the Soviet Union and other communist countries had two main elements: First, the capital stock and other resources were owned by the government rather than by individuals or private corporations. Second, most decisions regarding production and distribution were made and implemented by a government planning agency rather than by individuals and firms interacting through markets. This system performed poorly, we now understand, for several reasons.

One major problem was *the absence of private property rights*. With no ability to acquire a significant amount of private property, Soviet citizens had little incentive to behave in economically productive ways. The owner of an American or Japanese firm is strongly motivated to cut costs and to produce goods that are highly valued by the public because the owner's income is determined by the firm's profitability. In contrast, the performance of a Soviet firm manager was judged on whether the manager produced the quantities of goods specified by the government's plan—irrespective of the quality of the goods produced or whether consumers wanted them. Soviet managers had little incentive to reduce costs or produce better, more highly valued products, as any extra profits would accrue to the government and not to the manager; nor were there any opportunities for entrepreneurs to start new businesses. Likewise, workers had little reason to work hard or effectively under the communist system, as pay rates were determined by the government planning agency rather than by the economic value of what the workers produced.

A second major weakness of the communist system was the *absence of free markets.* In centrally planned economies, markets are replaced by detailed government plans that specify what should be produced and how. But, as we saw in the example of New York City's food supply (Chapter 3), the coordination of even relatively basic economic activities can be extremely complex and require a great deal of information, much of which is dispersed among many people. In a market system, changes in prices both convey information about the goods and services people want and provide suppliers the incentives to bring these goods and services to market. Indeed, as we know from the Equilibrium Principle, a market in equilibrium leaves individuals with no unexploited opportunities. Central planners in communist countries proved far less able to deal with this complexity than decentralized markets. As a result, under communism consumers suffered constant shortages and shoddy goods.

Equilibrium

After the collapse of communism, many formerly communist countries began the difficult transition to a market-oriented economic system. Changing an entire economic system (the most extreme example of a *structural policy*) is a slow and difficult task, and many countries saw economic conditions worsen at first rather than improve. *Political instability* and the absence of a modern *legal framework,* particularly laws applying to commercial transactions, have often hampered the progress of reforms. However, a number of formerly communist countries, including Poland, the Czech Republic, and the former East Germany, have succeeded in implementing Western-style market systems and have begun to achieve significant economic growth. ◆

RECAP **DETERMINANTS OF AVERAGE LABOR PRODUCTIVITY**

- Key factors determining average labor productivity in a country include
  - The skills and training of workers, called *human capital.*
  - The quantity and quality of *physical capital*—machines, equipment, and buildings.
  - The availability of land and other *natural resources.*
  - The sophistication of the *technologies* applied in production.
  - The effectiveness of *management* and *entrepreneurship.*
  - The broad *social and legal environment.*
- Labor productivity growth slowed throughout the industrialized world in the 1970s and 1980s. Since 1995, it has rebounded (especially in the United States), largely because of advances in information and communication technology.

BOX 15.1: PRODUCTION FUNCTIONS

Economists often use a mathematical expression called a *production function* to describe the relationship between the amounts of inputs and outputs. In its general form, a production function is written as

$$Y = f(K, L, M, A)$$

where

Y = the amount of output or real GDP
K = the amount of physical capital
L = the amount of labor, adjusted for the level of human capital
M = the amount of available land and other natural resources
A = the level of technology and other factors, such as the effectiveness of management and the social and legal environment
$f(\ )$ is some unspecified functional form

In practice, there are a number of specific functional forms that are used to calculate the level of output. One simple but famous one that involves only Y, K, and L is

$$Y = K^{1/2}L^{1/2} = \sqrt{KL}$$

For example, if $K = 25$ and $L = 100$, $Y = \sqrt{25 \times 100} = \sqrt{2{,}500} = 50$. This simple production function has several appealing properties, and a slight variant of it fits the aggregate data reasonably well. First, if all the inputs K and L double, output also will double; that is, if $K = 50$ and $L = 200$, $Y = \sqrt{50 \times 200} = \sqrt{10{,}000} = 100$. Secondly, it exhibits diminishing returns to capital (as well as diminishing returns to labor), so that if we hold the level of labor constant and keep adding more capital, output will rise by smaller and smaller increments. Thus, if L remains equal to 100 and K rises from 25 to 26, output rises from 50 to $\sqrt{26 \times 100} = 50.99$, or by 0.99 unit. If K rises by one more unit to 27, output rises to $\sqrt{27 \times 100} = 51.96$, or by only 0.97 unit.

THE COSTS OF ECONOMIC GROWTH

Both this chapter and Chapter 12 emphasized the positive effects of economic growth on the average person's living standard. But should societies always strive for the highest possible rate of economic growth? The answer is no. Even if we accept for the moment the idea that increased output per person is always desirable, attaining a higher rate of economic growth does impose costs on society.

What are the costs of increasing economic growth? The most straightforward is the cost of creating new capital. We know that by expanding the capital stock we can increase future productivity and output. But, to increase the capital stock, we must divert resources that could otherwise be used to increase the supply of consumer goods. For example, to add more robot-operated assembly lines, a society must employ more of its skilled technicians in building industrial robots and fewer in designing video games. To build new factories, more carpenters and lumber must be assigned to factory construction and less to finishing basements or renovating family rooms. In short, high rates of investment in new capital require people to tighten their belts, consume less, and save more—a real economic cost.

Should a country undertake a high rate of investment in capital goods at the sacrifice of consumer goods? The answer depends on the extent that people are willing and able to sacrifice consumption today to have a bigger economic pie tomorrow. In a country that is very poor, or is experiencing an economic crisis, people may prefer to keep consumption relatively high and savings and investment relatively low. The midst of a thunderstorm is not the time to be putting something aside for a rainy day! But in a society that is relatively well off, people may be more willing to make sacrifices to achieve higher economic growth in the future.

Consumption sacrificed to capital formation is not the only cost of achieving higher growth. In the United States in the nineteenth and early twentieth centuries, periods of rapid economic growth were often times in which many people worked extremely long hours at dangerous and unpleasant jobs. While those workers helped to build the economy that Americans enjoy today, the costs were great in terms of reduced leisure time and, in some cases, workers' health and safety.

Scarcity

Cost-Benefit

Other costs of growth include the cost of the research and development that is required to improve technology and the costs of acquiring training and skill (human capital). The fact that a higher living standard tomorrow must be purchased at the cost of current sacrifices is an example of the Scarcity Principle, that having more of one good thing usually means having less of another. Because achieving higher economic growth imposes real economic costs, we know from the Cost-Benefit Principle that higher growth should be pursued only if the benefits outweigh the costs.

PROMOTING ECONOMIC GROWTH

If a society decides to try to raise its rate of economic growth, what are some of the measures that policymakers might take to achieve this objective? Here is a short list of suggestions, based on our discussion of the factors that contribute to growth in average labor productivity and, hence, output per person.

POLICIES TO INCREASE HUMAN CAPITAL

Because skilled and well-educated workers are more productive than unskilled labor, governments in most countries try to increase the human capital of their citizens by supporting education and training programs. In the United States, government provides public education through high school and grants extensive support to post-secondary schools, including technical schools, colleges, and universities. Publicly funded early intervention programs like Head Start also attempt to build human capital by helping disadvantaged children prepare for school. To a lesser degree than some other countries, the U.S. government also funds job training for unskilled youths and retraining for workers whose skills have become obsolete.

Example 15.2

THE ECONOMIC NATURALIST

Why do almost all countries provide free public education?

All industrial countries provide their citizens free public education through high school, and most subsidize college and other post-secondary schools. Why?

Americans are so used to the idea of free public education that this question may seem odd. But why should the government provide free education when it does not provide even more essential goods and services such as food or medical care for free, except to the most needy? Furthermore, educational services can be, and indeed commonly are, supplied and demanded on the private market, without the aid of the government.

Equilibrium

An important argument for free or at least subsidized education is that the private demand curve for educational services does not include all the social benefits of education. (Recall the Equilibrium Principle, which states in part that a market in equilibrium may not exploit all gains achievable from collective action.) For example, the democratic political system relies on an educated citizenry to operate effectively—a factor that an individual demander of educational services has little reason to consider. From a narrower economic perspective, we might argue that individuals do not capture the full economic returns from their schooling. For example, people with high human capital, and thus high earnings, pay more taxes—funds that can be used to finance government services and aid the less fortunate. Because of income taxation, the private benefit to acquiring human capital is less than the social benefit, and the demand for education on the private market may be less than optimal from society's viewpoint. Similarly, educated people are more likely than others to contribute to technological development, and hence to general productivity growth, which may benefit many other people besides themselves. Finally, another argument for public support of education is that poor people who would like to invest in human capital may not be able to do so because of insufficient income.

Why do almost all countries provide free public education?

The Nobel laureate Milton Friedman, among many economists, suggested that these arguments may justify government grants, called educational *vouchers,* to help citizens purchase educational services in the private sector, but they do *not* justify the government providing education directly, as through the public school system. Defenders of public education, on the other hand, argue that the government should have some direct control over education in order to set standards and monitor quality. What do you think? ●

POLICIES THAT PROMOTE SAVING AND INVESTMENT

EN 15

Average labor productivity increases when workers can utilize a sizable and modern capital stock. To support the creation of new capital, government can encourage high rates of saving and investment in the private sector. Many provisions in the U.S. tax code are designed expressly to stimulate households to save and firms to invest. For example, a household that opens an Individual Retirement Account (IRA) is able to save for retirement without paying taxes on either the funds deposited in the IRA or the interest earned on the account. (However, taxes are due when the funds are withdrawn at retirement.) The intent of IRA legislation is to make saving more financially attractive to American households. Similarly, at various times Congress has instituted an investment tax credit, which reduces the tax bills of firms that invest in new capital. (Private-sector saving and investment are discussed in greater detail in Chapters 16 and 17.)

Government can contribute directly to capital formation through *public investment,* or the creation of government-owned capital. Public investment includes the building of roads, bridges, airports, dams, and, in some countries, energy and communications networks. The construction of the U.S. interstate highway system, begun during the administration of President Eisenhower, is often cited as an example of successful public investment. The interstate system substantially reduced long-haul transportation costs in the United States, improving productivity throughout the economy. Today, the web of computers and communications links we call the internet is having a similar effect. This project, too, received crucial government funding in its early stages. Many research studies have confirmed that government investment in the *infrastructure,* the public capital that supports private-sector economic activities, can be a significant source of growth.

POLICIES THAT SUPPORT RESEARCH AND DEVELOPMENT

Productivity is enhanced by technological progress, which in turn requires investment in research and development (R&D). In many industries, private firms have adequate incentive to conduct research and development activities. There is no need, for example, for the government to finance research for developing a better underarm deodorant. But some types of knowledge, particularly basic scientific knowledge, may have widespread economic benefits that cannot be captured by a single private firm. The developers of the silicon computer chip, for example, were instrumental in creating huge new industries, yet they received only a small portion of the profits flowing from their inventions. Because society in general, rather than the individual inventors, may receive much of the benefit from basic research, government may need to support basic research, as it does through agencies such as the National Science Foundation. The federal government also sponsors a great deal of applied research, particularly in military and space applications. To the extent that national security allows, the government can increase growth by sharing the fruits of such research with the private sector. For example, the Global Positioning System (GPS), which was developed originally for military purposes, is now available in private passenger vehicles, helping drivers find their way.

THE LEGAL AND POLITICAL FRAMEWORK

Although economic growth comes primarily from activities in the private sector, the government plays an essential role in providing the framework within which the private sector can operate productively. We have discussed the importance of secure property rights and a well-functioning legal system, of an economic environment that encourages entrepreneurship, and of political stability and the free and open exchange of ideas. Government policymakers also should consider the potential effects of tax and regulatory policies on activities that increase productivity, such as investment, innovation, and risk taking.

THE POOREST COUNTRIES: A SPECIAL CASE?

Radical disparities in living standards exist between the richest and poorest countries of the world (see Table 12.4 for some data). Achieving economic growth in the poorest countries is thus particularly urgent. Are the policy prescriptions of this section relevant to those countries, or are very different types of measures necessary to spur growth in the poorest nations?

To a significant extent, the same factors and policies that promote growth in richer countries apply to the poorest countries as well. Increasing human capital by supporting education and training, increasing rates of saving and investment, investing in public capital and infrastructure, supporting research and development, and encouraging entrepreneurship are all measures that will enhance economic growth in poor countries.

However, to a much greater degree than in richer countries, most poor countries need to improve the legal and political environment that underpins their economies. For example, many developing countries have poorly developed or corrupt legal systems, which discourage entrepreneurship and investment by creating uncertainty about property rights. Taxation and regulation in developing countries are often heavy-handed and administered by inefficient bureaucracies, to the extent that it may take months or years to obtain the approvals needed to start a small business or expand a factory. In many poor countries, excessive government regulation or government ownership of companies prevents markets from operating efficiently to achieve economic growth. For example, government regulation, rather than the market, may determine the allocation of bank credit or the prices for agricultural products. Structural policies that aim to ameliorate these problems are important preconditions for generating growth in the poorest countries. But probably most important—and most difficult, for some countries—is establishing political stability and the rule of law. Without political stability, domestic and foreign savers will be reluctant to invest in the country, and economic growth will be difficult if not impossible to achieve.

Can rich countries help poor countries to develop? Historically, richer nations have tried to help by providing financial aid through loans or grants from individual countries (foreign aid) or by loans made by international agencies such as the World Bank. Experience has shown, however, that financial aid to countries that do not undertake structural reforms, such as reducing excessive regulation or improving the legal system, is of limited value. To make their foreign aid most effective, rich countries should help poor countries achieve political stability and undertake the necessary reforms to the structure of their economies.

ARE THERE LIMITS TO GROWTH?

Earlier in this chapter, we saw that even relatively low rates of economic growth, if sustained for a long period, will produce huge increases in the size of the economy. This fact raises the question of whether economic growth can continue indefinitely without depleting natural resources and causing massive damage to the global environment. Does the basic truth that we live in a finite world of finite resources imply that, ultimately, economic growth must come to an end?

The concern that economic growth may not be sustainable is not a new one. An influential 1972 book, *The Limits to Growth,*[7] reported the results of computer simulations that suggested that unless population growth and economic expansion were halted, the world would soon be running out of natural resources, drinkable water, and breathable air. This book, and later works in the same vein, raise some fundamental questions that cannot be done full justice here. However, in some ways its conclusions are misleading.

One problem with the "limits to growth" thesis lies in its underlying concept of economic growth. Those who emphasize the environmental limits on growth assume implicitly that economic growth will always take the form of more of what we have now—more smoky factories, more polluting cars, more fast-food restaurants. If that were indeed the case, then surely there would be limits to the growth the planet can sustain. But growth in real GDP does not necessarily take such a form. Increases in real GDP also can arise from new or higher-quality products. For example, not too long ago tennis rackets were relatively simple items made primarily of wood. Today they are made of newly invented synthetic materials and designed for optimum performance using sophisticated computer simulations. Because these new high-tech tennis rackets are more valued by consumers than the old wooden ones, their introduction increased real GDP. Likewise, the introduction of new pharmaceuticals has contributed to economic growth, as have the expanded number of TV channels, digital sound, and internet-based sales. Thus, economic growth need not take the form of more and more of the same old stuff; it can mean newer, better, and perhaps cleaner and more efficient goods and services.

A second problem with the "limits to growth" conclusion is that it overlooks the fact that increased wealth and productivity expand society's capacity to take measures to safeguard the environment. In fact, the most polluted countries in the world are not the richest but those that are in a relatively early stage of industrialization. At this stage countries must devote the bulk of their resources to basic needs—food, shelter, health care—and continued industrial expansion. In these countries, clean air and water may be viewed as a luxury rather than a basic need. In more economically developed countries, where the most basic needs are more easily met, extra resources are available to keep the environment clean. Thus, continuing economic growth may lead to less, not more, pollution.

A third problem with the pessimistic view of economic growth is that it ignores the power of the market and other social mechanisms to deal with scarcity. During the oil-supply disruptions of the 1970s, newspapers were filled with headlines about the energy crisis and the imminent depletion of world oil supplies. Yet 30 years later, the world's known oil reserves are actually *greater* than they were in the 1970s.[8]

[7]Donella H. Meadows, Dennis L. Meadows, Jørgen Randers, and William W. Behrens III, *The Limits to Growth* (New York: New American Library, 1972).
[8]Recent increases in oil prices have again stoked concerns.

Today's energy situation is so much better than was expected 30 years ago because the market went to work. Reduced oil supplies led to an increase in prices that changed the behavior of both demanders and suppliers. Consumers insulated their homes, purchased more energy-efficient cars and appliances, and switched to alternative sources of energy. Suppliers engaged in a massive hunt for new reserves, opening up major new sources in Latin America, China, and the North Sea. In short, market forces helped society respond effectively to the energy crisis.

In general, shortages in any resource will trigger price changes that induce suppliers and demanders to deal with the problem. Simply extrapolating current economic trends into the future ignores the power of the market system to recognize shortages and make the necessary corrections. Government actions spurred by political pressures, such as the allocation of public funds to preserve open space or reduce air pollution, can be expected to supplement market adjustments.

Equilibrium

Despite the shortcomings of the "limits to growth" perspective, most economists would agree that not all the problems created by economic growth can be dealt with effectively through the market or the political process. Probably most important, global environmental problems, such as the possibility of global warming or the ongoing destruction of rain forests, are a particular challenge for existing economic and political institutions. Environmental quality is not bought and sold in markets and thus will not automatically reach its optimal level through market processes (recall the Equilibrium Principle). Nor can local or national governments effectively address problems that are global in scope. Unless international mechanisms are established for dealing with global environmental problems, these problems may become worse as economic growth continues.

Why is the air quality so poor in Mexico City?

Developing countries like Mexico, which are neither fully industrialized nor desperately poor, often have severe environmental problems. Why?

One concern about economic growth is that it will cause ever-increasing levels of environmental pollution. Empirical studies show, however, that the relationship between pollution and real GDP per person is more like an inverted U (see Figure 15.6). In other words, as countries move from very low levels of real GDP per

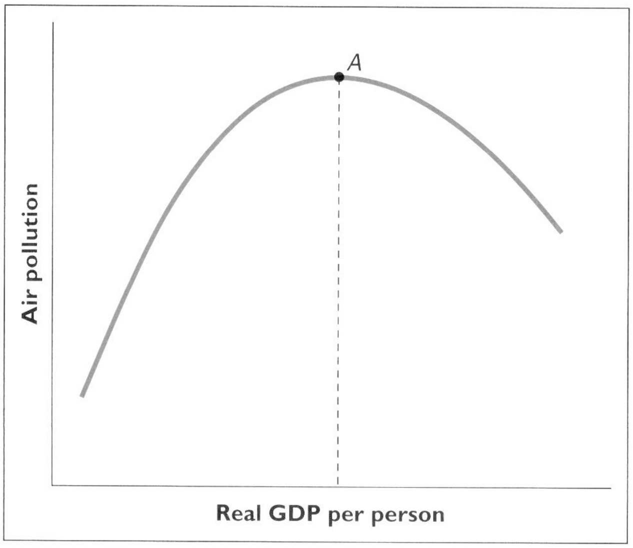

FIGURE 15.6
The Relationship between Air Pollution and Real GDP per Person.
Empirically, air pollution increases with real GDP per person up to a point and then begins to decline. Maximum air pollution (point *A*) occurs at a level of real GDP per person roughly equal to that of Mexico.

person to "middle-income" levels, most measures of pollution tend to worsen, but environmental quality improves as real GDP per person rises even further. One study of the relationship between air quality and real GDP per person found that the level of real GDP per person at which air quality is the worst—indicated by point *A* in Figure 15.6—is roughly equal to the average income level in Mexico.[9] And indeed, the air quality in Mexico City is exceptionally poor, as any visitor to that sprawling metropolis can attest.

That pollution may worsen as a country industrializes is understandable, but why does environmental quality improve when real GDP per person climbs to very high levels? There are a variety of explanations for this phenomenon. Compared to middle-income economies, the richer economies are relatively more concentrated in "clean," high-value services like finance and software production as opposed to pollution-intensive industries like heavy manufacturing. Rich economies are also more likely to have the expertise to develop sophisticated and cost-effective antipollution technologies. But the main reason the richer economies tend to be cleaner is the same reason that the homes of rich people are generally cleaner and in better condition than the homes of the poor. As income rises above the level necessary to fulfill basic needs, more resources remain to dedicate to "luxuries" like a clean environment (the Scarcity Principle). For the rich family, the extra resources will pay for a cleaning service; for the rich country, they will pay for pollution control devices in factories and on automobiles. Indeed, antipollution laws are generally tougher and more strictly enforced in rich countries than in middle-income and poor countries. ◆

Scarcity

RECAP	ECONOMIC GROWTH: DEVELOPMENTS AND ISSUES

- Economic growth has substantial costs, notably the sacrifice of current consumption that is required to free resources for creating new capital and new technologies. Higher rates of growth should be pursued only if the benefits outweigh the costs.
- Policies for promoting economic growth include policies to increase human capital (education and training); policies that promote saving and capital formation; policies that support research and development; and the provision of a legal and political framework within which the private sector can operate productively. Deficiencies in the legal and political framework (for example, official corruption or poorly defined property rights) are a special problem for many developing countries.
- Some have argued that finite resources imply ultimate limits to economic growth. This view overlooks the facts that growth can take the form of better, rather than more, goods and services; that increased wealth frees resources to safeguard the environment; and that political and economic mechanisms exist to address many of the problems associated with growth. However, these mechanisms may not work well when environmental or other problems arising from economic growth are global in scope.

[9]Gene M. Grossman and Alan B. Krueger, "Environmental Impacts of a North American Free Trade Agreement," in Peter Garber, ed., *The Mexico–U.S. Free Trade Agreement* (Cambridge, MA: MIT Press, 1993). See also Grossman and Krueger, "Economic Growth and the Environment," *Quarterly Journal of Economics,* May 1995, pp. 353–78; and World Bank, *World Development Report: Development and the Environment,* 1992.

SUMMARY

- Over the past two centuries, the industrialized nations saw enormous improvements in living standards, as reflected in large increases in real GDP per person. Because of the power of compound interest, relatively small differences in growth rates, if continued over long periods, can produce large differences in real GDP per person and average living standards. Thus, the rate of long-term economic growth is an economic variable of critical importance. **LO1**
- Real GDP per person is the product of average labor productivity (real GDP per employed worker) and the share of the population that is employed. Growth in real GDP per person can occur only through growth in average labor productivity, in the share of the population that is working, or both. In the period since 1960, increases in the share of the U.S. population holding a job contributed significantly to rising real GDP per person. But in the past four decades, as in most periods, the main source of the increase in real GDP per person was rising average labor productivity. **LO2**
- Among the factors that determine labor productivity are the talents, education, training, and skills of workers, or human capital; the quantity and quality of the physical capital that workers use; the availability of land and other natural resources; the application of technology to the production and distribution of goods and services; the effectiveness of entrepreneurs and managers; and the broad social and legal environment. Because of diminishing returns to capital, beyond a certain point expansion of the capital stock is not the most effective way to increase average labor productivity. Economists generally agree that new technologies are the most important single source of improvements in productivity. **LO3**
- In the 1970s and 1980s, the industrial world experienced a slowdown in productivity growth, but productivity growth has rebounded since 1995, largely as a result of advances in information and communication technology. **LO3**
- Economic growth has costs as well as benefits. Prominent among them is the need to sacrifice current consumption to achieve a high rate of investment in new capital goods; other costs of growing more quickly include extra work effort and the costs of research and development. Thus, more economic growth is not necessarily better; whether increased economic growth is desirable depends on whether the benefits of growth outweigh the costs. **LO4**
- Among the ways in which government can stimulate economic growth are by adopting policies that encourage the creation of human capital; that promote saving and investment, including public investment in infrastructure; that support research and development, particularly in the basic sciences; and that provide a legal and political framework that supports private-sector activities. The poorest countries, with poorly developed legal, tax, and regulatory systems, are often in the greatest need of an improved legal and political framework and increased political stability. **LO5**
- Are there limits to growth? Arguments that economic growth must be constrained by environmental problems and the limits of natural resources ignore the fact that economic growth can take the form of increasing quality as well as increasing quantity. Indeed, increases in output can provide additional resources for cleaning up the environment. Finally, the market system, together with political processes, can solve many of the problems associated with economic growth. On the other hand, global environmental problems, which can be handled neither by the market nor by individual national governments, have the potential to constrain economic growth. **LO6**

KEY TERMS

REVIEW QUESTIONS

1. What has happened to real GDP per person over the past century? What implications does this have for the average person? Are the implications different for countries in different regions (e.g., Japan versus Ghana)? **LO1**

2. Why do economists consider growth in average labor productivity to be the key factor in determining long-run living standards? **LO2**
3. What is *human capital*? Why is it economically important? How is new human capital created? **LO3**
4. You have employed five workers of varying physical strength to dig a ditch. Workers without shovels have zero productivity in ditchdigging. How should you assign shovels to workers if you don't have enough shovels to go around? How should you assign any additional shovels that you obtain? Using this example, discuss (a) the relationship between the availability of physical capital and average labor productivity and (b) the concept of diminishing returns to capital. **LO3**
5. What was the cause of the resurgence in U.S. labor productivity growth since 1995? How do we know? **LO3**
6. Discuss how talented entrepreneurs and effective managers can enhance average labor productivity. **LO3**
7. What major contributions can the government make to the goal of increasing average labor productivity? **LO5**
8. Discuss the following statement: "Because the environment is fragile and natural resources are finite, ultimately economic growth must come to an end." **LO6**

PROBLEMS

1. Richland's real GDP per person is $10,000, and Poorland's real GDP per person is $5,000. However, Richland's real GDP per person is growing at 1 percent per year and Poorland's is growing at 3 percent per year. Compare real GDP per person in the two countries after 10 years and after 20 years. Approximately how many years will it take Poorland to catch up to Richland? **LO1**
2. Calculate how much higher U.S. labor productivity will be in the year 2028 (relative to 2008) if **LO1**
   a. productivity continues to grow by 3.1 percent per year.
   b. productivity growth falls to 1.4 percent per year, its average rate during the period 1973–1995. (*Note:* You do not need to know the actual values of average labor productivity in any year to solve this problem.)
3. The "graying of America" will substantially increase the fraction of the population that is retired in the decades to come. To illustrate the implications for U.S. living standards, suppose that over the 46 years following 2006 the share of the population that is working returns to its 1960 level, while average labor productivity increases by as much as it did during 1960–2006. Under this scenario, what would be the net change in real GDP per person between 2006 and 2052? The following data will be useful: **LO2**

	Average labor productivity	Share of population employed
1960	$44,216	36.4%
2006	$88,204	48.1%

4. Here are data for Germany and Japan on the ratio of employment to population in 1979 and 2003:

	1979	2003
Germany	0.33	0.43
Japan	0.48	0.52

   Using data from Table 15.1, find average labor productivity for each country in 1979 and in 2003. How much of the increase in output per person in each country over the 1979–2003 period is due to increased labor productivity? To increased employment relative to population? **LO2**

5. Joanne has just completed high school and is trying to determine whether to go to junior college for two years or go directly to work. Her objective is to maximize the savings she will have in the bank five years from now. If she goes directly to work, she will earn $20,000 per year for each of the next five years. If she goes to junior college, for each of the next two years she will earn nothing—indeed, she will have to borrow $6,000 each year to cover tuition and books. This loan must be repaid in full three years after graduation. If she graduates from junior college, in each of the subsequent three years, her wages will be $38,000 per year. Joanne's total living expenses and taxes, excluding tuition and books, equal $15,000 per year. **LO3**
   a. Suppose, for simplicity, that Joanne can borrow and lend at 0 percent interest. On purely economic grounds, should she go to junior college or work?
   b. Does your answer to part a change if she can earn $23,000 per year with only a high school degree?
   c. Does your answer to part a change if Joanne's tuition and books cost $8,000 per year?
   d.* Suppose that the interest rate at which Joanne can borrow and lend is 10 percent per year, but other data are as in part a. Savings are deposited at the end of the year they are earned and receive (compound) interest at the end of each subsequent year. Similarly, the loans are taken out at the end of the year in which they are needed, and interest does not accrue until the end of the subsequent year. Now that the interest rate has risen, should Joanne go to college or go to work?

6. The Good'n'Fresh Grocery Store has two checkout lanes and four employees. Employees are equally skilled, and all are able to either operate a register (checkers) or bag groceries (baggers). The store owner assigns one checker and one bagger to each lane. A lane with a checker and a bagger can check out 40 customers per hour. A lane with a checker only can check out 25 customers per hour. **LO3**
   a. In terms of customers checked out per hour, what are total output and average labor productivity for the Good'n'Fresh Grocery Store?
   b. The owner adds a third checkout lane and register. Assuming that no employees are added, what is the best way to reallocate the workers to tasks? What are total output and average labor productivity (in terms of customers checked out per hour) now?
   c. Repeat part b for the addition of a fourth checkout lane, and a fifth. Do you observe diminishing returns to capital in this example?

7. Harrison, Carla, and Fred are housepainters. Harrison and Carla can paint 100 square feet per hour using a standard paintbrush, and Fred can paint 80 square feet per hour. Any of the three can paint 200 square feet per hour using a roller. **LO3**
   a. Assume Harrison, Carla, and Fred have only paintbrushes at their disposal. What is the average labor productivity, in terms of square feet per painter-hour, for the three painters taken as a team? Assume that the three painters always work the same number of hours.
   b. Repeat part a for the cases in which the team has one, two, three, or four rollers available. Are there diminishing returns to capital?
   c. An improvement in paint quality increases the area that can be covered per hour (by either brushes or rollers) by 20 percent. How does this technological improvement affect your answers to part b? Are there diminishing returns to

*Problem marked by an asterisk (*) is more difficult.

capital? Does the technological improvement increase or reduce the economic value of an additional roller?

8. Hester's Hatchery raises fish. At the end of the current season she has 1,000 fish in the hatchery. She can harvest any number of fish that she wishes, selling them to restaurants for $5 apiece. Because big fish make little fish, for every fish that she leaves in the hatchery this year, she will have two fish at the end of next year. The price of fish is expected to be $5 each next year as well. Hester relies entirely on income from current fish sales to support herself. **LO3**
   a. How many fish should Hester harvest if she wants to maximize the growth of her stock of fish from this season to next season?
   b. Do you think maximizing the growth of her fish stock is an economically sound strategy for Hester? Why or why not? Relate to the text discussion on the costs of economic growth.
   c. How many fish should Hester harvest if she wants to maximize her current income? Do you think this is a good strategy?
   d. Explain why Hester is unlikely to harvest either all or none of her fish, but instead will harvest some and leave the rest to reproduce.

9. Discuss the following statement, using concrete examples where possible to illustrate your arguments: For advances in basic science to translate into improvements in standards of living, they must be supported by favorable economic conditions. **LO3, LO5**

10. Write a short essay evaluating the U.S. economy in terms of each of the six determinants of average labor productivity discussed in the text. Are there any areas in which the United States is exceptionally strong, relative to other countries? Areas where the United States is less strong than some other countries? Illustrate your arguments with numbers from the *Statistical Abstract of the United States* (available online at www.census.gov/compendia/statab/) and other sources, as appropriate. **LO3, LO5**

ANSWERS TO IN-CHAPTER EXERCISES

15.1 If the United States had grown at the Japanese rate for the period 1870–2003, real GDP per person in 2003 would have been ($2,887) $\times$ $(1.026)^{133}$ = $87,709. Actual GDP per person in the United States in 2003 was $35,488, so at the higher rate of growth, output per person would have been $87,709/$35,488 = 2.47 times higher. **LO1**

15.2 As before, Lucy can wrap 4,000 candies per week, or 100 candies per hour. Ethel can wrap 500 candies per hour, and working 40 hours weekly she can wrap 20,000 candies per week. Together Lucy and Ethel can wrap 24,000 candies per week. Since they work a total of 80 hours between them, their output per hour as a team is 24,000 candies wrapped per 80 hours = 300 candies wrapped per hour, midway between their hourly productivities as individuals. **LO3**

15.3 Because Ethel can wrap 300 candies per hour by hand, the benefit of giving Ethel the machine is 500 − 300 = 200 additional candies wrapped per hour. Because Lucy wraps only 100 candies per hour by hand, the benefit of giving Lucy the machine is 400 additional candies wrapped per hour. So the benefit of giving the machine to Lucy is greater than of giving it to Ethel. Equivalently, if the machine goes to Ethel, then Lucy and Ethel between them can wrap 500 + 100 = 600 candies per hour, but if Lucy uses the machine, the team can wrap 300 + 500 = 800 candies per hour. So output is increased by letting Lucy use the machine. **LO3**

15.4 Now, working by hand, Lucy can wrap 300 candies per hour and Ethel can wrap 500 candies per hour. With a machine, either Lucy or Ethel can wrap 800 candies per hour. As in Exercise 15.3, the benefit of giving a machine to Lucy (500 candies per hour) exceeds the benefit of giving a machine to Ethel (300 candies per hour), so if only one machine is available, Lucy should use it.

The table analogous to Table 15.3 now looks like this:

Relationship of Capital, Output, and Productivity in the Candy-Wrapping Factory

Number of machines (*K*)	Candies wrapped per week (*Y*)	Total hours worked (*N*)	Average hourly labor productivity (*Y*/*N*)
0	32,000	80	400
1	52,000	80	650
2	64,000	80	800
3	64,000	80	800

Comparing this table with Table 15.3, you can see that technological advance has increased labor productivity for any value of K, the number of machines available.

Adding one machine increases output by 20,000 candies wrapped per week, adding the second machine increases output by 12,000 candies wrapped per week, and adding the third machine does not increase output at all (because there is no worker available to use it). So diminishing returns to capital still hold after the technological improvement. **LO3**

15.5 Although the individual worker is the same person he was in Bangladesh, by coming to the United States he gains the benefit of factors that enhance average labor productivity in this country, relative to his homeland. These include more and better capital to work with, more natural resources per person, more advanced technologies, sophisticated entrepreneurs and managers, and a political-legal environment that is conducive to high productivity. It is not guaranteed that the value of the immigrant's human capital will rise (it may not, for example, if he speaks no English and has no skills applicable to the U.S. economy), but normally it will.

Since increased productivity leads to higher wages and living standards, on economic grounds the Bangladeshi worker has a strong incentive to immigrate to the United States if he is able to do so. **LO3**

CHAPTER

16

Saving, Capital Formation, and Financial Markets

LEARNING OBJECTIVES

After reading this chapter, you should be able to:

1. Explain the relationship between saving and wealth.
2. Recognize and work with the components of national saving.
3. Understand the reasons why people save.
4. Discuss the reasons why firms choose to invest in capital rather than in financial assets.
5. Analyze financial markets using the tools of supply and demand.

You've probably heard Aesop's fable of the ant and the grasshopper. All summer the ant worked hard laying up food for the winter. The grasshopper mocked the ant's efforts and contented himself with basking in the sunshine, ignoring the ant's earnest warnings. When winter came the ant was well-fed, while the grasshopper starved. Moral: When times are good, the wise put aside something for the future.

Of course, there is also the modern ending to the fable, in which the grasshopper breaks his leg by tripping over the anthill, sues the ant for negligence, and ends up living comfortably on the ant's savings. (Nobody knows what happened to the ant.) Moral: Saving is risky; live for today.

The pitfalls of modern life notwithstanding, saving is important, both to individuals and to nations. People need to save to provide for their retirement and for other future needs, such as their children's education or a new home. An individual's or a family's savings also can provide a crucial buffer in the event of an economic emergency, such as the loss of a job or unexpected medical bills. At the national level, the production of new capital goods—factories, equipment, and housing—is an important factor promoting economic growth and higher living standards. As we will see in this chapter, the resources necessary to produce new capital come primarily from a nation's collective saving.

Because adequate saving is so important both to ensuring families' financial security and creating new capital goods, many people have expressed concern about the low saving rate of American households. Figure 16.1 shows the U.S. household saving rate (the percentage of after-tax household income that is saved) since 1960. Never very high by international standards, the U.S. household saving rate declined sharply in the mid-1980s and fell again in the mid-1990s, reaching 0.4 percent of household disposable income in 2006.

FIGURE 16.1
Household Saving Rate in the United States, 1960–2006.
The U.S. household saving rate, declining since the mid-1980s, fell to 0.4 percent in 2006.

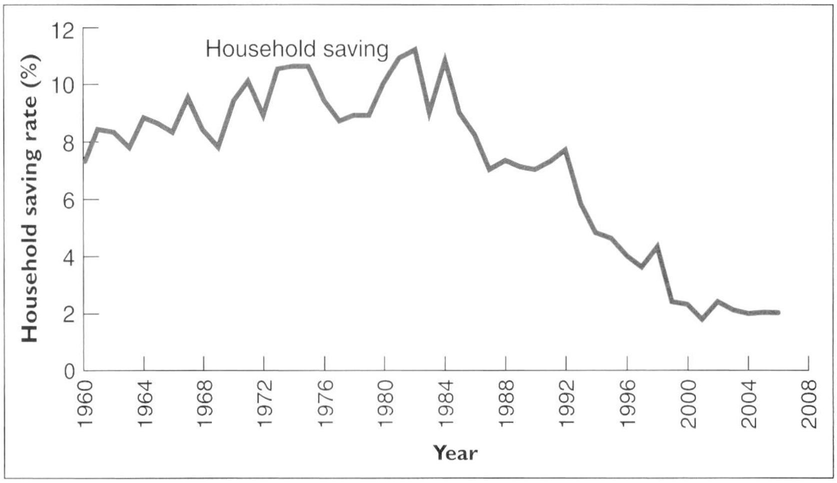

SOURCE: Bureau of Economic Analysis (www.bea.gov/).

What is the significance of this precipitous decline? Alarmists see the data as evidence of "grasshopperish" behavior, and a threat to Americans' future prosperity. The reality, as we will see, is more complex. Many American families do save very little, a choice that is likely to exact a toll on their economic well-being in the long run. On the other hand, household saving is only one part of the total saving of the U.S. economy, as businesses and governments also save. In fact, the total saving of the U.S. economy, called *national saving*, has not declined significantly in recent years. Thus, if the United States is suffering a "savings shortfall," it is much less severe than might be suggested by the figures on household saving only.

In this chapter we will look at saving and its links to the formation of new capital. We begin by defining the concepts of saving and wealth and exploring the connection between them. We then turn to national saving—the collective saving of households, businesses, and government. Because national saving determines the capacity of an economy to create new capital, it is the most important measure of saving from a macroeconomic perspective.

We next discuss the economics of household saving and capital formation by firms. We first consider why people choose to save, rather than spending all their income. Then, we examine capital formation by firms; it turns out that a firm's decision to invest in capital is in many respects analogous to its decision about whether to increase employment. We conclude the chapter by showing how national saving and capital formation are related using a supply and demand approach.

SAVING AND WEALTH

In general, the **saving** of an economic unit—whether a household, a business, a university, or a nation—may be defined as its *current income* minus its *spending on current needs*. For example, if Consuelo earns $300 per week, spends $280 weekly on living expenses such as rent, food, clothes, and entertainment, and deposits the remaining $20 in the bank, her saving is $20 per week. The **saving rate** of any economic unit is its saving divided by its income. Since Consuelo saves $20 of her weekly income of $300, her saving rate is $20/$300, or 6.7 percent.

saving current income minus spending on current needs

saving rate saving divided by income

The saving of an economic unit is closely related to its **wealth,** or the value of its assets minus its liabilities. **Assets** are anything of value that one *owns,* either *financial* or *real.* Examples of financial assets that you or your family might own include cash, a checking account, stocks, and bonds. Examples of real assets include a home or other real estate, jewelry, consumer durables like cars, and valuable collectibles. **Liabilities,** on the other hand, are the debts one *owes*. Examples of liabilities are credit card balances, student loans, and mortgages.

wealth the value of assets minus *liabilities*

assets anything of value that one *owns*

liabilities the debts one *owes*

By comparing an economic unit's assets and liabilities, economists calculate that unit's wealth, also called its *net worth*. This comparison is done using a list of assets and liabilities on a particular date, called a **balance sheet.**

balance sheet a list of an economic unit's assets and liabilities on a specific date

Consuelo constructs her balance sheet

To take stock of her financial position on January 1, 2008, Consuelo lists her assets and liabilities on that date in a balance sheet. The result is shown in Table 16.1. What is Consuelo's wealth?

TABLE 16.1
Consuelo's Balance Sheet on January 1, 2008

Assets		Liabilities	
Cash	$ 80	Student loan	$3,000
Checking account	1,200	Credit card balance	250
Shares of stock	1,000		
Car (market value)	3,500		
Furniture (market value)	500		
Total	**$6,280**		**$3,250**
		Net worth	**$3,030**

Consuelo's financial assets are the cash in her wallet, the balance in her checking account, and the current value of some shares of stock her parents gave her. Together her financial assets are worth $2,280. She also lists $4,000 in real assets, the sum of the market values of her car and her furniture. Consuelo's total assets, both financial and real, come to $6,280. Her liabilities are the student loan she owes the bank and the balance due on her credit card, which total $3,250. Consuelo's wealth, or net worth, on January 1, 2008, is the value of her assets ($6,280) minus the value of her liabilities ($3,250), or $3,030. ◆

EXERCISE 16.1

What would Consuelo's net worth be if her student loan were for $6,500 rather than $3,000? Construct a new balance sheet for her.

Saving and wealth are related because saving contributes to wealth. To understand this relationship better, we must distinguish between *stocks* and *flows*.

STOCKS AND FLOWS

flow a measure that is defined *per unit of time*

stock a measure that is defined *at a point in time*

Saving is an example of a **flow**, a measure that is defined *per unit of time*. For example, Consuelo's saving is $20 *per week*. Wealth, in contrast, is a **stock**, a measure that is defined *at a point in time*. Consuelo's wealth of $3,030, for example, is her wealth on a particular date—January 1, 2008.

To visualize the difference between stocks and flows, think of water running into a bathtub. The amount of water in the bathtub at any specific moment—for example, 40 gallons at 7:15 p.m.—is a stock because it is measured at a specific point in time. The rate at which the water flows into the tub—for example, 2 gallons per minute—is a flow because it is measured per unit of time. In many cases, a flow is the *rate of change* in a stock: If we know that there are 40 gallons of water in the tub at 7:15 p.m., for example, and that water is flowing in at 2 gallons per minute, we can easily determine that the stock of water will be changing at the rate of 2 gallons per minute and will equal 42 gallons at 7:16 p.m., 44 gallons at 7:17 p.m., and so on, until the bathtub overflows.

EXERCISE 16.2

Continuing the example of the bathtub: If there are 40 gallons of water in the tub at 7:15 p.m. and water is being *drained* at the rate of 3 gallons per minute, what will be the stock and flow at 7:16 p.m.? At 7:17 p.m.? Does the flow still equal the rate of change in the stock?

The relationship between saving (a flow) and wealth (a stock) is similar to the relationship between the flow of water into a bathtub and the stock of water in the tub in that the *flow* of saving causes the *stock* of wealth to change at the same rate. Indeed, as the following example illustrates, every dollar that a person saves adds a dollar to his or her wealth.

The link between saving and wealth

Consuelo saves $20 per week. How does this saving affect her wealth on January 8, 2008? Does the change in her wealth depend on whether Consuelo uses her saving to accumulate assets or to pay down her liabilities?

Consuelo could use the $20 she saved during the first week in January to increase her assets—for example, by adding the $20 to her checking account—or to reduce her liabilities—for example, by paying down her credit card balance. Suppose she adds the $20 to her checking account, increasing her assets on January 8, 2008, by $20. Since her liabilities are unchanged, her wealth also increases by $20, to $3,050 (see Table 16.1).

If Consuelo decides to use the $20 she saved during the first week in January to pay down her credit card balance, she reduces it from $250 to $230. That action would reduce her liabilities by $20, leaving her assets unchanged. Since wealth equals assets minus liabilities, reducing her liabilities by $20 increases her wealth by $20, to $3,050. Thus, saving $20 per week raises Consuelo's stock of wealth on January 8, 2008, by $20, regardless of whether she uses her saving to increase her assets or reduce her liabilities. ◆

The close relationship between saving and wealth explains why saving is so important to an economy. Higher rates of saving today lead to faster accumulation of wealth, and the wealthier a nation is, the higher its standard of living. Thus, a high rate of saving today contributes to an improved standard of living in the future.

CAPITAL GAINS AND LOSSES

Though saving increases wealth, it is not the only factor that determines wealth. Wealth also can change because of changes in the values of the real or financial assets one owns. Suppose Consuelo's shares of stock rise in value during January, from $1,000 to $1,500. This increase in the value of Consuelo's stock raises her total assets by $500 without affecting her liabilities. As a result, Consuelo's wealth on February 1, 2008, rises by $500, from $3,030 to $3,530 (see Table 16.2).

TABLE 16.2
Consuelo's Balance Sheet on February 1, 2008, after an Increase in the Value of Her Stocks

Assets		Liabilities	
Cash	$ 80	Student loan	$3,000
Checking account	1,200	Credit card balance	250
Shares of stock	1,500		
Car (market value)	3,500		
Furniture (market value)	500		
Total	**$6,780**		**$3,250**
		Net worth	**$3,530**

Changes in the value of existing assets are called **capital gains** when an asset's value increases and **capital losses** when an asset's value decreases. Just as capital gains increase wealth, capital losses decrease wealth. Capital gains and losses are not counted as part of saving, however. Instead, the change in a person's wealth during any period equals the saving done during the period plus capital gains or minus capital losses during that period. In terms of an equation,

capital gains increases in the value of existing assets

capital losses decreases in the values of existing assets

$$\text{Change in wealth} = \text{Saving} + \text{Capital gains} - \text{Capital losses}.$$

EXERCISE 16.3

How would each of the following actions or events affect Consuelo's *saving* and her *wealth*?

a. Consuelo deposits $20 in the bank at the end of the week as usual. She also charges $50 on her credit card, raising her credit card balance to $300.

b. Consuelo uses $300 from her checking account to pay off her credit card bill.

c. Consuelo's old car is recognized as a classic. Its market value rises from $3,500 to $4,000.

d. Consuelo's furniture is damaged and as a result falls in value from $500 to $200.

Capital gains and losses can have a major effect on one's overall wealth, as our next example illustrates.

The bull market and household wealth

On the whole, Americans felt very prosperous during the 1990s: Measures of household wealth during this period showed enormous gains. Yet, as Figure 16.1

shows, saving by U.S. households was quite low throughout those years. How did American households increase their wealth in the 1990s while saving very little?

During the 1990s an increasing number of Americans acquired stocks, either directly through purchases or indirectly through their pension and retirement funds. At the same time, stock prices rose at record rates (see Figure 16.2). The strongly rising "bull market," which increased the prices of most stocks, enabled many Americans to enjoy significant capital gains and increased wealth without saving much, if anything. Indeed, some economists argued that the low household saving rate of the 1990s is partially *explained* by the bull market; because capital gains increased household wealth by so much, many people saw no need to save.

The stock market peaked in early 2000 and stock prices fell quite sharply over the following two years. It is interesting that U.S. households did not choose to save more in 2000 and in subsequent years (Figure 16.1), despite the decline in their stock market wealth. One explanation is that an even larger component of household wealth—the value of privately owned homes—rose significantly in 2000–2006, partly offsetting the effect of the decline in stock values on household wealth.

FIGURE 16.2
The Bull Market of the 1990s.
Stock prices rose sharply during the 1990s, greatly increasing the wealth of households that held stocks. This figure shows the Standard & Poor's 500 index of stock prices, divided by the CPI to correct for inflation, for the period 1960–2004. Stock prices peaked in 2000, and then fell sharply until reaching a trough in early 2003.

SOURCE: Economic Report of the President (www.gpoaccess.gov/eop/).

RECAP	SAVING AND WEALTH

In general, *saving* is current income minus spending on current needs. *Wealth* is the value of assets—anything of value that one owns—minus liabilities—the debts one owes. Saving is measured per unit of time (for example, dollars per week) and thus is a *flow*. Wealth is measured at a point in time and thus is a *stock*. In the same way the flow of water through the faucet increases the stock of water in a bathtub, the flow of saving increases the stock of wealth.

Wealth also can be increased by *capital gains* (increases in the value of existing assets) or reduced by *capital losses* (decreases in asset values). The capital gains afforded stockholders by the bull market of the 1990s allowed many families to increase their wealth significantly while doing very little saving.

NATIONAL SAVING AND ITS COMPONENTS

Thus far we have been examining the concepts of saving and wealth from the individual's perspective. But macroeconomists are interested primarily in saving and wealth for the country as a whole. In this section we will study *national saving,* or the aggregate saving of the economy. National saving includes the saving of business firms and the government as well as that of households. Later in the chapter we will examine the close link between national saving and the rate of capital formation in an economy.

THE MEASUREMENT OF NATIONAL SAVING

To define the saving rate of a country as a whole, we will start with a basic accounting identity that was introduced in Chapter 12. According to this identity, for the economy as a whole, production (or income) must equal total expenditure. In symbols, the identity is

$$Y = C + I + G + NX,$$

where Y stands for either production or aggregate income (which must be equal), C equals consumption expenditure, I equals investment spending, G equals government purchases of goods and services, and NX equals net exports.

For now, let's assume that net exports (NX) are equal to zero, which would be the case if a country did not trade at all with other countries or if its exports and imports were always balanced. (We discuss the foreign sector in Chapter 22.) With net exports set at zero, the condition that output equals expenditure becomes

$$Y = C + I + G.$$

To determine how much saving is done by the nation as a whole, we can apply the general definition of saving. As for any other economic unit, a nation's saving equals its *current income* less its *spending on current needs.* The current income of the country as a whole is its GDP, or Y, that is, the value of the final goods and services produced within the country's borders during the year.

Identifying the part of total expenditure that corresponds to the nation's spending on current needs is more difficult than identifying the nation's income. The component of aggregate spending that is easiest to classify is investment spending I. We know that investment spending—the acquisition of new factories, equipment, and other capital goods, as well as residential construction—is done to expand the economy's future productive capacity or provide more housing for the future, not to satisfy current needs. So investment spending clearly is *not* part of spending on current needs.

Deciding how much of consumption spending by households, C, and government purchases of goods and services, G, should be counted as spending on current needs is less straightforward. Certainly most consumption spending by households—on food, clothing, utilities, entertainment, and so on—is for current needs. But consumption spending also includes purchases of long-lived *consumer durables* such as cars, furniture, and appliances. Consumer durables are only partially used up during the current year; they may continue to provide service, in fact, for years after their purchase. So household spending on consumer durables is a combination of spending on current needs and spending on future needs.

As with consumption spending, most government purchases of goods and services are intended to provide for current needs. However, like household purchases, a portion of government purchases is devoted to the acquisition or construction of long-lived capital goods such as roads, bridges, schools, government buildings, and military hardware. And like consumer durables, these forms of *public capital* are only partially used up during the current year; most will provide useful services far into the future. So, like consumption spending, government purchases are in fact a mixture of spending on current needs and spending on future needs.

In its official data, the government has begun to distinguish investment in public capital from the rest of government purchases. Nevertheless, this is a relatively small portion of the total, and determining precisely how much of spending is for current needs and how much is for future needs is extremely difficult. For simplicity's sake, in this book we will follow the traditional practice of treating *all* of both consumption expenditures (C) and government purchases (G) as spending on current needs. But keep in mind that because consumption spending and government purchases do in fact include some spending for future rather than current needs, treating all of C and G as spending on current needs will understate the true amount of national saving.

If we treat all consumption spending and government purchases as spending on current needs, then the nation's saving is its income Y less its spending on current needs, $C + G$. So we can define **national saving** S as

national saving the saving of the entire economy, equal to GDP less consumption expenditures and government purchases of goods and services, or $Y - C - G$

$$S = Y - C - G. \quad (16.1)$$

Figure 16.3 shows the U.S. national saving rate (national saving as a percentage of GDP) for the years 1960 through 2006. Since 1960 the U.S. national saving rate has fluctuated between 11 and 18 percent. Like household saving, national saving declined somewhat over time, though by comparing Figures 16.3 and 16.1 you can see that the decline in national saving has been far more modest. Furthermore, unlike household saving, national saving recovered in the latter 1990s. As we will see next, the reason for these differences between the behavior of national saving and household saving is that saving done by business firms and, for a while, by the government has been substantial.

FIGURE 16.3
U.S. National Saving Rate, 1960–2006.
Since 1960, U.S. national saving has fluctuated between 11 and 18 percent of GDP.

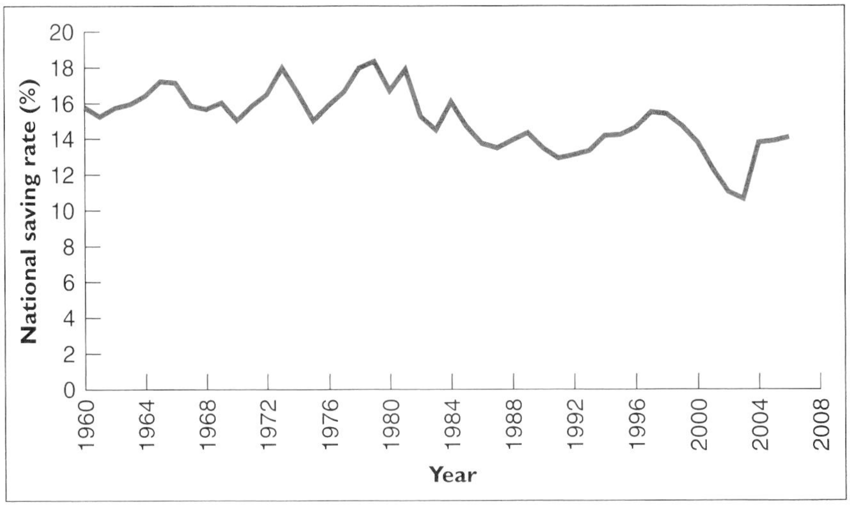

SOURCE: Bureau of Economic Analysis (www.bea.gov/).

PRIVATE AND PUBLIC COMPONENTS OF NATIONAL SAVING

To understand national saving better, let's examine its two major components: private saving and public saving. Private saving is the amount households and businesses save from private-sector income. Public saving is the amount governments save from public-sector income. Although the private sector's total income from the production of goods and services is Y, it must pay taxes from this income and it collects additional amounts from the government in the form of *transfer payments* and *interest* paid to individuals and institutions who hold government bonds. **Transfer payments** are payments the government makes to the public for which it receives no current goods or services in return. Social Security benefits, welfare payments, farm support payments, and pensions to government workers are transfer payments.

transfer payments payments the government makes to the public for which it receives no current goods or services in return

Subtracting transfers and government interest payments from total taxes yields the net amount paid by the private sector to the government—the amount it pays to the government minus the amount it receives from the government. We call this amount *net taxes,* which we label T:

$$T = \text{Total taxes} - \text{Transfer payments} - \text{Government interest payments.}$$

Private saving is the amount of the private sector's after-tax income that is not spent on current consumption expenditures. Private saving S_{private} is therefore equal to total private income from the production of goods and services minus net taxes minus consumption, or

private saving the saving of the private sector of the economy is equal to the after-tax income of the private sector minus consumption expenditures ($Y - T - C$); private saving can be further broken down into household saving and business saving

$$S_{\text{private}} = Y - T - C.$$

Private saving can be further broken down into saving done by households and business firms. *Household saving,* also called *personal saving,* is saving done by families and individuals. Household saving corresponds to the familiar image of families putting aside part of their incomes each month, and it is the focus of much attention in the news media. But businesses are important savers as well—indeed business saving makes up the bulk of private saving in the United States. Businesses use the revenues from their sales to pay workers' salaries and other operating costs, to pay taxes, and to provide dividends to their shareholders. The funds remaining after these payments have been made are equal to *business saving.* A business firm's savings are available for the purchase of new capital equipment or the expansion of its operations. Alternatively, a business can put its savings in the bank for future use.

Public saving is the amount of the public sector's income that is not spent on current needs. The public sector includes state and local governments as well as the federal government. Public sector income is merely net taxes T. Government spending on current needs is equal to government purchases G (remember that, for the sake of simplicity, we are ignoring the investment portion of government purchases). Thus, we calculate public saving S_{public} as

public saving the saving of the government sector is equal to net tax payments minus government purchases ($T - G$)

$$S_{\text{public}} = T - G.$$

If we add public and private saving together, we can derive the expression for total national saving that appears in Equation 16.1 in another way:

$$S_{\text{private}} + S_{\text{public}} = (Y - T - C) + (T - G) = Y - C - G = S \qquad (16.2)$$

This equation confirms that national saving S is the sum of private saving and public saving. Since private saving can be broken down in turn into household and business saving, we see that national saving is made up of the saving of three groups: households, businesses, and the government.

PUBLIC SAVING AND THE GOVERNMENT BUDGET

Although the idea that households and businesses can save is familiar to most people, the fact that the government also can save is less widely understood. Public saving is closely linked to the government's decisions about spending and taxing. Governments finance the bulk of their spending by taxing the private sector. If taxes and spending in a given year are equal, the government is said to have a *balanced*

government budget surplus the excess of government tax collections over government spending ($T - G$); the government budget surplus equals public saving

budget. If in any given year the amount that the government collects in taxes is greater than the amount it spends, the difference is called the **government budget surplus.** When a government has a surplus, it uses the extra funds to pay down its outstanding debt to the public. Algebraically, the government budget surplus may be written as $T - G$, or net tax collections minus government purchases.

If the algebraic expression for the government budget surplus, $T - G$, looks familiar, that is because it is also the definition of public saving. Thus, *public saving is identical to the government budget surplus*. In other words, when the government collects more in taxes than it spends, public saving will be positive. In the year 2000, for example, the federal government had the largest budget surplus in history. The following example illustrates the relationships among public saving, the government budget surplus, and national saving in that year.

Government saving

Following are data on U.S. government revenues and expenditures for 2000, in billions of dollars.

Federal government:	
Receipts	2,053.8
Expenditures	1,864.4
State and local governments:	
Receipts	1,319.5
Expenditures	1,269.5

SOURCE: Economic Report of the President (www.gpoaccess.gov/eop/).

The federal government's receipts minus its expenditures were 2,053.8 − 1,864.4 = 189.4, so the federal government ran a budget surplus of $189.4 billion in 2000. State and local government receipts minus expenditures were 1,319.5 − 1,269.5 = 50.0, so state and local governments ran a collective budget surplus of $50.0 billion. The budget surplus of the entire government sector—that is, the federal surplus plus the state and local surplus—was 189.4 + 50.0 = 239.4, or $239.4 billion. So the contribution of the government sector to U.S. national saving in 2000 was $239.4 billion. ◆

government budget deficit the excess of government spending over tax collections ($G - T$)

If, on the other hand, the government spends more than it collects in taxes, public saving will be negative. In this circumstance, we speak about the **government budget deficit,** which is the amount by which spending exceeds taxes and is calculated by $G - T$.[1] If the government runs a deficit, it must make up the difference by borrowing from the public by issuing new government bonds.

Although the government had a budget surplus of $239.4 billion in the year 2000, it subsequently ran budget deficits. By the year 2006, the budget deficit had grown to $195.4 billion. The box below provides more details.

Federal government:	
Receipts	2,495.8
Expenditures	2,715.8
State and local governments:	
Receipts	1,797.7
Expenditures	1,773.1

SOURCE: Bureau of Economic Analysis (www.bea.gov).

[1]Note that a budget deficit of $100 billion is the same as a budget surplus of −$100 billion.

The federal government's receipts minus expenditures were 2495.8 − 2715.8 = −220 in 2006. Since expenditures were greater than receipts, the federal government ran a budget deficit of −$220 billion. State and local government receipts minus expenditures were 1797.7 − 1773.1 = 24.6, so state and local governments ran a collective budget surplus of $24.6 billion. The entire government sector ran a deficit of $220 billion − $24.6 billion = $195.4 billion. The government sector's contribution to national saving, therefore, was negative and equal to −$195.4 billion.

There were three main reasons for this dramatic turnaround in the government budget. First, government receipts fell because of the recession that began in 2001. During a recession incomes fall. Since many taxes are based on income, during a recession tax receipts also fall or rise more slowly than expected. The second reason was the reduction in tax rates enacted by President Bush and Congress during the president's first term. Finally, government expenditures rose dramatically between 2000 and 2006, in large part as a result of the wars in Iraq and Afghanistan and expenditures by the Department of Homeland Security in response to the terrorist attack on September 11, 2001.[2]

Figure 16.3 showed the U.S. national saving rate since 1960. Figure 16.4 shows the behavior since 1960 of the three components of national saving: household saving, business saving, and public saving, each measured as a percentage of GDP. Note that business saving played a major role in national saving during these years, while the role of household saving was relatively modest. As we saw in Figure 16.1, household saving has been declining since the mid-1980s.

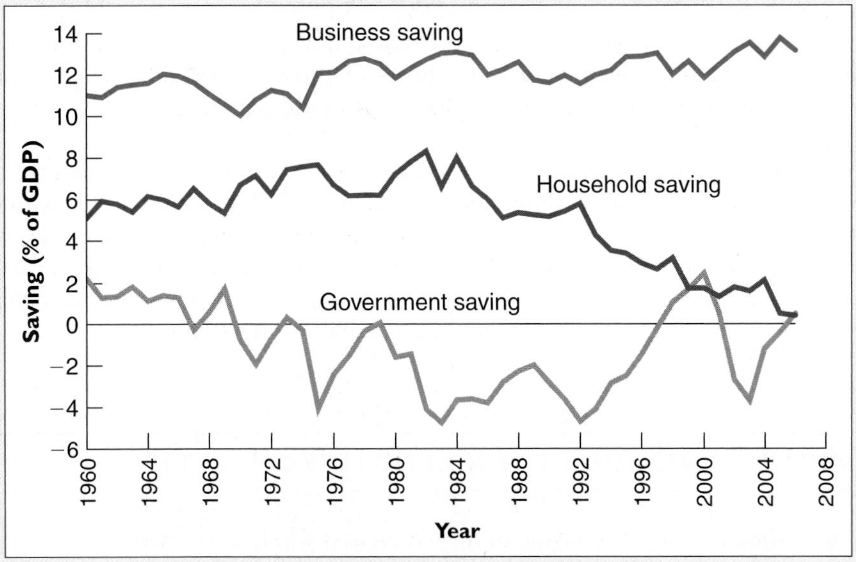

SOURCE: Bureau of Economic Analysis (www.bea.gov/).

FIGURE 16.4
The Three Components of National Saving, 1960–2006.
Of the three components of national saving, business saving is the most important. Household saving has declined since the mid-1980s. Government saving has generally been negative, except in the 1960s and for a brief period in the late 1990s.

The contribution of public saving has varied considerably over time. Until about 1970, the federal, state, and local governments typically ran a combined surplus, making a positive contribution to national saving. But by the late 1970s, public saving had turned negative, reflecting large budget deficits, particularly at the federal level. For the next two decades, the government was a net drain on national saving except for a brief period in the late 1990s.

[2]William G. Gale and Peter R. Orszag, "Bush Administration Tax Policy: Revenue and Budget Effects," *Tax Notes,* October 4, 2004, pp. 105–18.

IS LOW HOUSEHOLD SAVING A PROBLEM?

Figure 16.1 showed that saving by U.S. households, never high by international standards, fell substantially during the 1990s. This decline in the household saving rate received much attention from the news media. Is the United States' low household saving rate as much of a problem as the press suggests?

From a macroeconomic perspective, the problem posed by low household saving has probably been overstated. The key fact often overlooked in media reports is that national saving, not household saving, determines the capacity of an economy to invest in new capital goods and to achieve continued improvement in living standards. Although household saving is low, saving by business firms has been significant. Furthermore, during the 1990s, public saving increased as federal government budgets moved from deficit toward surplus. Until 2002 U.S. national saving had been reasonably stable, despite the sharp decline in the household saving rate shown in Figure 16.1. Indeed, although the U.S. national saving rate has typically been low compared to those of other industrialized countries, it had been sufficient to allow the United States to become one of the world's most productive economies. Since 2002, however, large federal budget deficits (implying negative public saving) have contributed to a decline in the U.S. national saving rate.

From a microeconomic perspective, the low household saving rate does signal a problem, which is the large and growing inequality in wealth among U.S. households. Saving patterns tend to increase this inequality since the economically better-off households tend not only to save more but, as business owners or shareholders, are also the ultimate beneficiaries of the saving done by businesses. In contrast, lower-income families, many of whom save very little and do not own a business or shares in a corporation, have accumulated very little wealth—in many cases, their life savings are less than $5,000. These households have little protection against setbacks such as chronic illness or job loss and must rely almost entirely on government support programs such as Social Security to fund their retirement. For this group, the low household saving rate is definitely a concern.

This inequality has been exacerbated by the run-up in home prices that occurred from 2001 to 2006. Many middle- and upper-income households who do not save a large portion of their income nevertheless accumulated considerable wealth as the values of their homes rose. Unfortunately, the recent declines (in 2007 and 2008) in home prices have reduced, and in some cases wiped out, the capital gains many households accumulated in the first half of the 2000s.

RECAP	NATIONAL SAVING AND ITS COMPONENTS

- *National saving*, the saving of the nation as a whole, is defined by $S = Y - C - G$, where Y is GDP, C is consumption spending, and G is government purchases of goods and services. National saving is the sum of public saving and private saving: $S = S_{\text{private}} + S_{\text{public}}$.
- *Private saving*, the saving of the private sector, is defined by $S_{\text{private}} = Y - T - C$, where T is net tax payments. Private saving can be broken down further into household saving and business saving.
- *Public saving*, the saving of the government, is defined by $S_{\text{public}} = T - G$. Public saving equals the government budget surplus, $T - G$. When the government budget is in surplus, government saving is positive; when the government budget is in deficit, public saving is negative.

WHY DO PEOPLE SAVE?

Why do people save part of their income instead of spending everything they earn? Economists have identified at least three broad reasons for saving. First, people save to meet certain long-term objectives such as a comfortable retirement. By putting away part of their income during their working years, they can live better after retirement than they would if they had to rely solely on Social Security and their company pensions. Other long-term objectives might include college tuition for one's children and the purchase of a new home or car. Since many of these needs occur at fairly predictable stages in one's life, economists call this type of saving **life-cycle saving.**

life-cycle saving saving to meet long-term objectives such as retirement, college attendance, or the purchase of a home

A second reason to save is to protect oneself and family against unexpected setbacks—the loss of a job, for example, or a costly health problem. Personal financial advisors typically suggest that families maintain an emergency reserve (a "rainy-day fund") equal to three to six months' worth of income. Saving for protection against potential emergencies is called **precautionary saving.**

precautionary saving saving for protection against unexpected setbacks such as the loss of a job or a medical emergency

"Fortunately, you have the life savings of a man three times your age."

A third reason to save is to accumulate an estate to leave to one's heirs, usually one's children but possibly a favorite charity or other worthy cause. Saving for the purpose of leaving an inheritance, or bequest, is called **bequest saving.** Bequest saving is done primarily by people at the higher end of the income ladder. But because these people control a large share of the nation's wealth, bequest saving is an important part of overall saving.

bequest saving saving done for the purpose of leaving an inheritance

To be sure, people usually do not mentally separate their saving into these three categories; rather, all three reasons for saving motivate most savers to varying degrees. Our next example shows how the three reasons for saving can explain household saving behavior in Japan.

Household saving in Japan

After World War II Japanese households increased their saving rates to 15–25 percent of their income, an unusually high rate. Although cultural factors often were cited as a reason for the high Japanese propensity to save, saving rates in Japan were much lower before World War II. Moreover, household saving rates in Japan have declined since 1990 (although they remain higher than those in the United States). Why did the Japanese save so much until about 1990, and why have Japanese saving rates declined somewhat since then?

Among the reasons for saving we discussed, *life-cycle* reasons are probably the most important determinants of saving in Japan. The Japanese have long life expectancies, and many retire relatively early. With a long period of retirement to finance, Japanese families must save a great deal during their working years. When the working age population was a high percentage of the total population, the overall saving rate was high. As the baby boom generation reached the age of retirement and the Japanese fertility rate declined, so too has the Japanese saving rate declined.[3]

Other factors also help to explain the changes in Japanese saving rates. Down payment requirements on houses are high in Japan compared to other countries. Before 1990, land and housing prices in Japan were extremely high, so that young people had to save a great deal or borrow their parents' savings to buy their first homes. After the Japanese real estate market crashed at the beginning of the 1990s, however, land and housing prices fell so young people do not need to save as much as before.

Studies also have found that *bequest saving* is important in Japan. Many older people live with their children after retirement. In return for support and attention during their later years, parents feel they must provide substantial inheritances for their children.

Precautionary saving is probably lower in Japan than in some other countries, however. Although Japan's recent economic troubles have reduced the practice of *lifetime employment,* Japanese firms still make extensive use of the system, which essentially guarantees a job for life to workers who join a firm after graduating from college. This type of job security, coupled with Japan's traditionally low unemployment rate, reduces the need for precautionary saving. ◆

Although most people are usually motivated to save for at least one of the three reasons we have discussed, the amount they choose to save may depend on the economic environment. One economic variable that is quite significant in saving decisions is the real interest rate.

SAVING AND THE REAL INTEREST RATE

Most people don't save by putting cash in a mattress. Instead, they make financial investments that they hope will provide a good return on their saving. For example, a checking account may pay interest on the account balance. More sophisticated financial investments such as government bonds or shares of stock in a corporation, which we discuss in the next chapter, also pay returns in the form of interest payments, dividends, or capital gains. High returns are desirable, of course, because the higher the return, the faster one's savings will grow.

The rate of return that is most relevant to saving decisions is the *real interest rate*, denoted r. Recall from Chapter 13 that the real interest rate is the rate at which the real purchasing power of a financial asset increases over time. The real interest rate equals the market, or nominal, interest rate (i) minus the inflation rate (π).

The real interest rate is relevant to savers because it is the "reward" for saving. Suppose you are thinking of increasing your saving by \$1,000 this year, which you can do if you give up your habit of eating out once a week. If the real interest rate is 5 percent, then in a year your extra saving will give you extra purchasing power of \$1,050, measured in today's dollars. But if the real interest rate were 10 percent,

[3]Maiko Koga, "The Decline of the Saving Rate and the Demographic Effects," Bank of Japan Research and Statistics Department, November 2004.

your sacrifice of $1,000 this year would be rewarded by $1,100 in purchasing power next year. Obviously, all else being equal, you would be more willing to save today if you knew the reward next year would be greater. In either case the *cost* of the extra saving—giving up your weekly night out—is the same. But the *benefit* of the extra saving, in terms of increased purchasing power next year, is higher if the real interest rate is 10 percent rather than 5 percent.

Cost-Benefit

By how much does a high savings rate enhance a family's future living standard?

The Spends and the Thrifts are similar families, except that the Spends save 5 percent of their income each year and the Thrifts save 20 percent. The two families began to save in 1980 and plan to continue to save until their respective breadwinners retire in the year 2015. Both families earn $40,000 a year in real terms in the labor market, and both put their savings in a mutual fund that has yielded a real return of 8 percent per year, a return they expect to continue into the future. Compare the amount that the two families consume in each year from 1980 to 2015, and compare the families' wealth at retirement.

In the first year, 1980, the Spends saved $2,000 (5 percent of their $40,000 income) and consumed $38,000 (95 percent of $40,000). The Thrifts saved $8,000 in 1980 (20 percent of $40,000) and hence consumed only $32,000 in that year, $6,000 less than the Spends. In 1981, the Thrifts' income was $40,640, the extra $640 representing the 8 percent return on their $8,000 savings. The Spends saw their income grow by only $160 (8 percent of their savings of $2,000) in 1981. With an income of $40,640, the Thrifts consumed $32,512 in 1981 (80 percent of $40,640) compared to $38,152 (95 percent of $40,160) for the Spends. The consumption gap between the two families, which started out at $6,000, thus fell to $5,640 after one year.

Because of the more rapid increase in the Thrifts' wealth and hence interest income, each year the Thrifts' income grew faster than the Spends'; each year the Thrifts continued to save 20 percent of their higher incomes compared to only 5 percent for the Spends. Figure 16.5 shows the paths followed by the consumption spending of the two families. You can see that the Thrifts' consumption, though starting at a lower level, grows relatively more quickly. By 1995 the Thrifts had overtaken the Spends, and from that point onward, the amount by which the

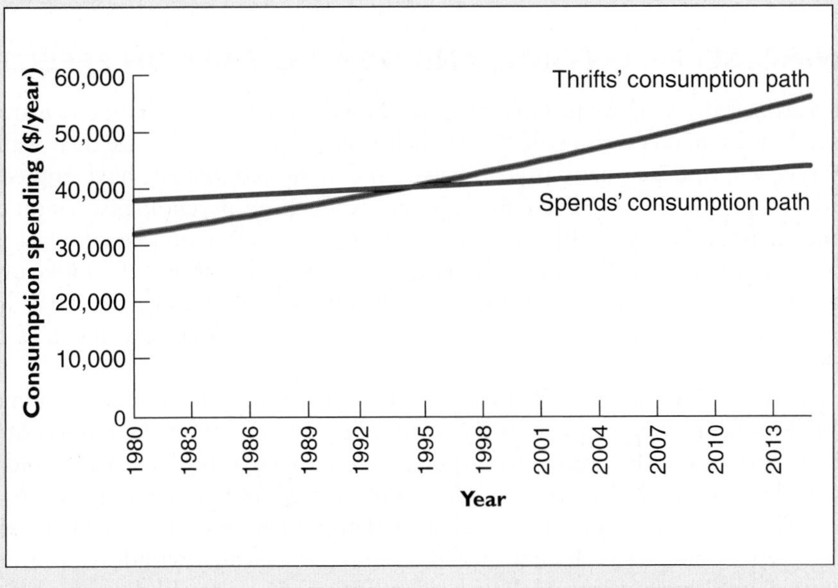

FIGURE 16.5
Consumption Trajectories of the Thrifts and the Spends.
The figure shows consumption spending in each year by two families, the Thrifts and the Spends. Because the Thrifts save more than the Spends, their annual consumption spending rises relatively more quickly. By the time of retirement in the year 2015, the Thrifts are both consuming significantly more each year than the Spends and also have a retirement nest egg that is five times larger.

Thrifts outspent the Spends grew with each passing year. Even though the Spends continued to consume 95 percent of their income each year, their income grew so slowly that by 2000, they were consuming nearly $3,000 a year less than the Thrifts ($41,158 a year versus $43,957). And by the time the two families retire, in 2015, the Thrifts will be consuming more than $12,000 per year more than the Spends ($55,774 versus $43,698). Even more striking is the difference between the retirement nest eggs of the two families. Whereas the Spends will enter retirement with total accumulated savings of just over $77,000, the Thrifts will have more than $385,000, five times as much. ◆

EN 16

These dramatic differences depend in part on the assumption that the real rate of return is 8 percent—lower than the actual return to mutual funds since 1980 but still a relatively high rate of return from a historical perspective. On the other hand, the Spend family in our example actually saves more than typical U.S. households, many of which carry $5,000 or more in credit card debt at high rates of interest and have no significant savings at all. The point of the example, which remains valid under alternative assumptions about the real interest rate and saving rates, is that, because of the power of compound interest, a high rate of saving pays off handsomely in the long run.

While a higher real interest rate increases the reward for saving, which tends to strengthen people's willingness to save, another force counteracts that extra incentive. Recall that a major reason for saving is to attain specific goals: a comfortable retirement, a college education, or a first home. If the goal is a specific amount—say, $25,000 for a down payment on a home—then a higher rate of return means that households can save *less* and still reach their goal because funds that are put aside will grow more quickly. For example, to accumulate $25,000 at the end of five years, at a 5 percent interest rate a person would have to save about $4,309 per year. At a 10 percent interest rate, reaching the $25,000 goal would require saving only about $3,723 per year. To the extent that people are *target savers* who save to reach a specific goal, higher interest rates actually decrease the amount they need to save.

In sum, a higher real interest rate has both positive and negative effects on saving—a positive effect because it increases the reward for saving and a negative effect because it reduces the amount people need to save each year to reach a given target. Empirical evidence suggests that, in practice, higher real interest rates lead to modest increases in saving.

SAVING, SELF-CONTROL, AND DEMONSTRATION EFFECTS

The reasons for saving we just discussed are based on the notion that people are rational decision makers who will choose their saving rates to maximize their welfare over the long run. Yet many psychologists, and some economists, have argued instead that people's saving behavior is based as much on psychological as on economic factors. For example, psychologists stress that many people lack the *self-control* to do what they know is in their own best interest. People smoke or eat greasy food, despite the known long-term health risks. Similarly, they may have good intentions about saving but lack the self-control to put aside as much as they ought to each month.

One way to strengthen self-control is to remove temptations from the immediate environment. A person who is trying to quit smoking will make a point of not having cigarettes in the house, and a person with a weight problem will avoid going to a bakery. Similarly, a person who is not saving enough might arrange to use a payroll savings plan, through which a predetermined amount is deducted from each paycheck and set aside in a special account from which withdrawals are not permitted until retirement. Making saving automatic and withdrawals difficult eliminates the temptation to spend all of current earnings or squander accumulated savings. Payroll savings plans have helped many people to increase the amount that they save for retirement or other purposes.

An implication of the self-control hypothesis is that consumer credit arrangements that make borrowing and spending easier may reduce the amount that people save. For example, in recent years banks have encouraged people to borrow against the *equity* in their homes, that is, the value of the home less the value of the outstanding mortgage. Such financial innovations, by increasing the temptation to spend, may have reduced the household saving rate. The increased availability of credit cards with high borrowing limits is another temptation.

Downward pressure on the saving rate also may occur when additional spending by some consumers stimulates additional spending by others. Such *demonstration effects* arise when people use the spending of others as a yardstick by which to measure the adequacy of their own living standards. For example, a family in an upper-middle-class American suburb in which the average house has 3,000 square feet of living space might regard a 1,500-square-foot house as being uncomfortably small—too cramped, for example, to entertain friends in the manner to which community members have become accustomed. In contrast, a similar family living in a low-income neighborhood might find the very same house luxuriously large.

The implication of demonstration effects for saving is that families who live among others who consume more than they do may be strongly motivated to increase their own consumption spending. When satisfaction depends in part on *relative* living standards, an upward spiral may result in which household spending is higher, and saving lower, than would be best for either the individual families involved or the economy as a whole.

Why do U.S. households save so little?

We began this chapter by looking at household saving, and we observed that the rate of household saving has been falling for the past 20 years. (See Figure 16.1.) Now, we are in a position to answer the question at the heart of this graph: Why do U.S. households save so little?

Economists do not agree on the reasons for low household saving in the United States, although many hypotheses have been suggested.

One possible reason for low saving is the availability of generous government assistance to the elderly. From a *life-cycle* perspective, an important motivation for saving is to provide for retirement. In general, the U.S. government provides a less comprehensive "social safety net" than other industrialized countries; that is, it offers relatively fewer programs to assist people in need. To the extent that the U.S. government does provide income support, however, it is heavily concentrated on the older segment of the population. Together the Social Security and Medicare programs, both of which are designed primarily to assist retired people, constitute a major share of the federal government's expenditures. These programs have been very successful; indeed, they have virtually wiped out poverty among the elderly. To the extent that Americans believe that the government will ensure them an adequate living standard in retirement, however, their incentive to save for the future is reduced.

Another important life-cycle objective is buying a home. We have seen that the Japanese must save a great deal to purchase a home because of high house prices and down payment requirements. The same is true in many other countries. But in the United States, with its highly developed financial system, people can buy homes with down payments of 10 percent or less of the purchase price. The ready availability of mortgages with low or even no down payments reduces the need to save for the purchase of a home.

What about *precautionary saving*? Unlike Japan and Europe, which had to rebuild after World War II, the United States has not known sustained economic hardship since the Great Depression of the 1930s (which fewer and fewer

Americans are alive to remember). Perhaps the nation's prosperous past has led Americans to be more confident about the future and hence less inclined to save for economic emergencies than other people, even though the United States does not offer the level of employment security found in Japan or in Europe.

U.S. household saving is not only low by international standards, it has been declining. The good performance of the stock market in the 1990s along with increases in the prices of family homes probably help to explain this savings decline. As long as Americans enjoy capital gains, they see their wealth increase almost without effort, and their incentive to save is reduced.

Psychological factors also may explain Americans' saving behavior. For example, unlike in most countries, U.S. homeowners can easily borrow against their home equity. This ability, made possible by the highly developed U.S. financial markets, may exacerbate *self-control* problems by increasing the temptation to spend. Finally, *demonstration effects* may have depressed saving in recent decades. Chapter 14 discussed the phenomenon of increasing wage inequality, which has improved the relative position of more skilled and educated workers. Increased spending by households at the top of the earnings scale on houses, cars, and other consumption goods may have led those just below them to spend more as well, and so on. Middle-class families that were once content with medium-priced cars may now feel they need Volvos and BMWs to keep up with community standards. To the extent that demonstration effects lead families to spend beyond their means, they reduce their saving rate. ◆

RECAP | **WHY DO PEOPLE SAVE?**

Motivations for saving include saving to meet long-term objectives such as retirement (*life-cycle saving*), saving for emergencies (*precautionary saving*), and saving to leave an inheritance or bequest (*bequest saving*). The amount that people save also depends on macroeconomic factors such as the real interest rate. A higher real interest rate stimulates saving by increasing the reward for saving, but it also can depress saving by making it easier for savers to reach a specific savings target. On net, a higher real interest rate appears to lead to modest increases in saving.

Psychological factors also may affect saving rates. If people have *self-control* problems, then financial arrangements (such as automatic payroll deductions) that make it more difficult to spend will increase their saving. People's saving decisions also may be influenced by *demonstration effects*, as when people feel compelled to spend at the same rate as their neighbors, even though they may not be able to afford to do so.

INVESTMENT AND CAPITAL FORMATION

From the point of view of the economy as a whole, the importance of national saving is that it provides the funds needed for investment. Investment—the creation of new capital goods and housing—is critical to increasing average labor productivity and improving standards of living.

What factors determine whether and how much firms choose to invest? Firms acquire new capital goods for the same reason they hire new workers: They expect that doing so will be profitable. We saw in Chapter 14 that the profitability of employing an extra worker depends primarily on two factors: the cost of employing the worker and the value of the worker's marginal product. In the same way, firms' willingness to acquire new factories and machines depends on the expected *cost* of using them and the expected *benefit*, equal to the value of the marginal product that they will provide.

Cost-Benefit

Should Larry buy a riding lawn mower?

Larry is thinking of going into the lawn care business. He can buy a $4,000 riding mower by taking out a loan at 6 percent annual interest. With this mower and his own labor, Larry can net $6,000 per summer, after deduction of costs such as gasoline and maintenance. Of the $6,000 net revenues, 20 percent must be paid to the government in taxes. Assume that Larry could earn $4,400 after taxes by working in an alternative job. Assume also that the lawn mower can always be resold for its original purchase price of $4,000. Should Larry buy the lawn mower?

To decide whether to invest in the capital good (the lawn mower), Larry should compare the financial benefits and costs. With the mower he can earn revenue of $6,000, net of gasoline and maintenance costs. However, 20 percent of that, or $1,200, must be paid in taxes, leaving Larry with $4,800. Larry could earn $4,400 after taxes by working at an alternative job, so the financial benefit to Larry of buying the mower is the difference between $4,800 and $4,400, or $400; $400 is the value of the marginal product of the lawn mower.

Since the mower does not lose value over time and since gasoline and maintenance costs have already been deducted, the only remaining cost Larry should take into account is the interest on the loan for the mower. Larry must pay 6 percent interest on $4,000, or $240 per year. Since this financial cost is less than the financial benefit of $400, the value of the mower's marginal product, Larry should buy the mower. ◆

Larry's decision might change if the costs and benefits of his investment in the mower change, as the example below shows.

Should Larry buy a riding lawn mower? (continued)

With all other assumptions the same as in the previous example, decide whether Larry should buy the mower:

a. If the interest rate is 12 percent rather than 6 percent.

b. If the purchase price of the mower is $7,000 rather than $4,000.

c. If the tax rate on Larry's net revenues is 25 percent rather than 20 percent.

d. If the mower is less efficient than Larry originally thought so that his net revenues will be $5,500 rather than $6,000.

In each case, Larry must compare the financial costs and benefits of buying the mower.

a. If the interest rate is 12 percent, then the interest cost will be 12 percent of $4,000, or $480, which exceeds the value of the mower's marginal product ($400). Larry should not buy the mower.

b. If the cost of the mower is $7,000, then Larry must borrow $7,000 instead of $4,000. At 6 percent interest, his interest cost will be $420—too high to justify the purchase since the value of the mower's marginal product is $400.

c. If the tax rate on net revenues is 25 percent, then Larry must pay 25 percent of his $6,000 net revenues, or $1,500, in taxes. After taxes, his revenues from mowing will be $4,500, which is only $100 more than he could make working at an alternative job. Furthermore, the $100 will not cover the $240 in interest that Larry would have to pay. So again, Larry should not buy the mower.

d. If the mower is less efficient than originally expected so that Larry can earn net revenues of only $5,500, Larry will be left with only $4,400 after taxes—the same amount he could earn by working at another job. So in this case, the value of the mower's marginal product is zero. At any interest rate greater than zero, Larry should not buy the mower. ◆

EXERCISE 16.4

Repeat the previous example, but assume that, over the course of the year, wear and tear reduces the resale value of the lawn mower from $4,000 to $3,800. Should Larry buy the mower?

The examples involving Larry and the lawn mower illustrate the main factors firms must consider when deciding whether to invest in new capital goods. On the cost side, two important factors are the *price of capital goods* and the *real interest rate*. Clearly, the more expensive new capital goods are, the more reluctant firms will be to invest in them. Buying the mower was profitable for Larry when its price was $4,000, but not when its price was $7,000.

Why is the real interest rate an important factor in investment decisions? The most straightforward case is when a firm has to borrow (as Larry did) to purchase its new capital. The real interest rate then determines the real cost to the firm of paying back its debt. Since financing costs are a major part of the total cost of owning and operating a piece of capital, much as mortgage payments are a major part of the cost of owning a home, increases in the real interest rate make the purchase of capital goods less attractive to firms, all else being equal.

Increasing Opportunity Cost

Even if a firm does not need to borrow to buy new capital—say, because it has accumulated enough profits to buy the capital outright—the real interest rate remains an important determinant of the desirability of an investment. If a firm does not use its profits to acquire new capital, most likely it will use those profits to acquire financial assets such as bonds, which will earn the firm the real rate of interest. If the firm uses its profits to buy capital rather than to purchase a bond, it forgoes the opportunity to earn the real rate of interest on its funds. Thus, the real rate of interest measures the *opportunity cost* of a capital investment. Since an increase in the real interest rate raises the opportunity cost of investing in new capital, it lowers the willingness of firms to invest, even if they do not literally need to borrow to finance new machines or equipment.

On the benefit side, the key factor in determining business investment is the *value of the marginal product* of the new capital, which should be calculated net of both operating and maintenance expenses and taxes paid on the revenues the capital generates. The value of the marginal product is affected by several factors. For example, a technological advance that allows a piece of capital to produce more goods and services would increase the value of its marginal product, as would lower taxes on the revenues produced by the new capital. An increase in the price of the good or service that the capital is used to produce will also increase the value of the marginal product and, hence, the desirability of the investment. For example, if the going price for lawn-mowing services were to rise, then all else being equal, investing in the mower would become more profitable for Larry.

Example 16.1

THE ECONOMIC NATURALIST

Why has investment in computers increased so much in recent decades?

Since about 1980, investment in new computer systems by U.S. firms has risen sharply (see Figure 16.6). Purchases of new computers and software by firms now exceed 2.5 percent of GDP and amount to about 24 percent of all private nonresidential investment. Why has investment in computers increased so much?

Investment in computers has increased by much more than other types of investment. Hence, the factors that affect all types of investment (such as the real interest rate and the tax rate) are not likely to be responsible for the boom. The two main causes of increased investment in computers appear to be the declining price of computing power and the increase in the value of the marginal product of computers. In recent years, the price of computing power has fallen at a precipitous rate. An industry rule of thumb is that the amount of computing power that is obtainable at a given price doubles every 18 months. As the price of computing power falls, an investment in computers becomes more and more likely to pass the cost-benefit test.

Cost-Benefit

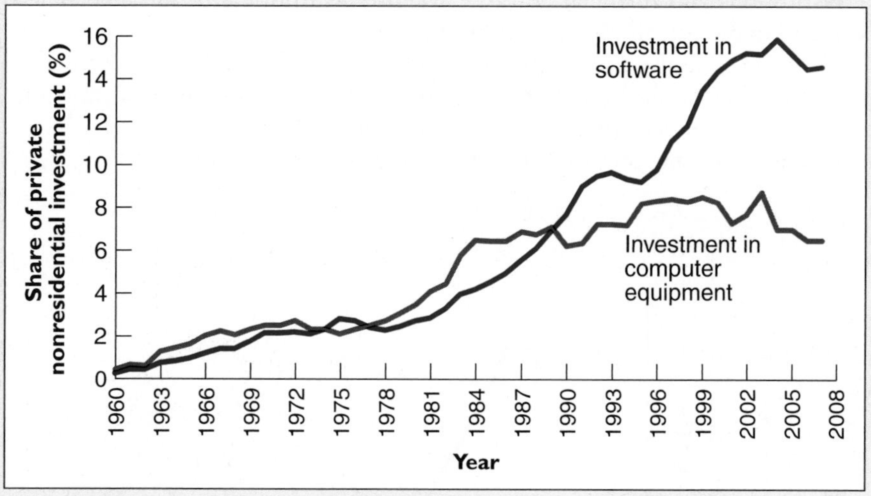

SOURCE: Bureau of Economic Analysis (www.bea.gov/).

FIGURE 16.6
Investment in Computers and Software, 1960–2007.
Investment in computer equipment and software since 1960 shown as a percentage of private nonresidential investment. Computer-related investments by U.S. firms have risen significantly since 1980.

On the benefit side, for some years after the beginning of the computer boom, economists were unable to associate the technology with significant productivity gains. Defenders of investment in computer systems argued that the improvements in goods and services computers create are particularly hard to measure. How does one quantify the value to consumers of 24-hour-a-day access to cash or of the ability to make airline reservations online? Critics responded that the expected benefits of the computer revolution may have proved illusory because of problems such as user-unfriendly software and poor technical training. However, U.S. productivity has increased noticeably in recent years (as we saw in the previous chapter), and many people are now crediting the improvement to investment in computers and computer-related technologies like the internet. As more firms become convinced that computers do add significantly to productivity and profits, the boom in computer investment can be expected to continue. ●

RECAP | INVESTMENT AND CAPITAL FORMATION

Any of the following factors will increase the willingness of firms to invest in new capital:

1. A decline in the price of new capital goods.
2. A decline in the real interest rate.
3. Technological improvement that raises the marginal product of capital.
4. Lower taxes on the revenues generated by capital.
5. A higher relative price for the firm's output.

SAVING, INVESTMENT, AND FINANCIAL MARKETS

In a market economy like that of the United States, savings are allocated by means of a decentralized, market-oriented financial system. The U.S. financial system consists both of financial institutions, like banks, and financial markets such as bond markets and stock markets. Here, we will examine the basic workings of financial markets without regard to the particular assets (bonds or stocks) that are being traded. Rather, we will focus on the role that the real interest rate plays in allocating resources from savers to borrowers. In the next chapter, we will examine financial institutions and financial markets in more institutional detail and relate this discussion to the role of money in a market economy.

Figure 16.7 shows the supply of saving and the demand for investment in a financial market. Quantities of national saving and investment are measured on the horizontal axis; the real interest rate is shown on the vertical axis. As we will see, in the market for saving, the real interest rate functions as the "price."

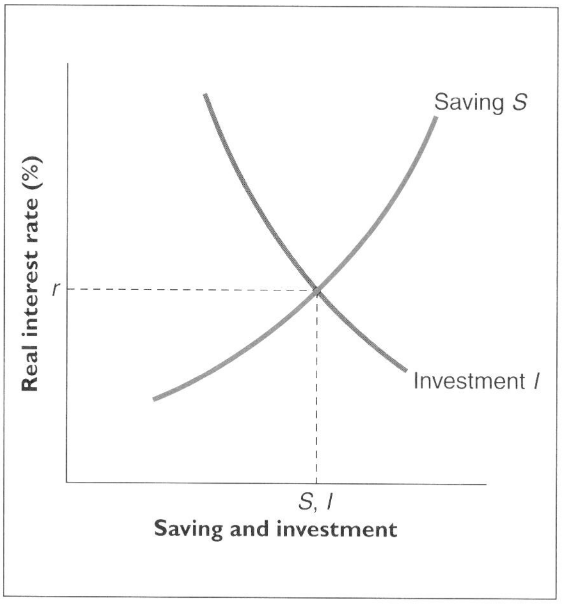

FIGURE 16.7
The Supply of and Demand for Saving. Saving is supplied by households, firms, and the government and demanded by borrowers wishing to invest in new capital goods. The supply of saving (*S*) increases with the real interest rate, and the demand for saving by investors (*I*) decreases with the real interest rate. In financial market equilibrium, the real interest rate takes the value that equates the quantity of saving supplied and demanded.

In the figure the supply of saving is shown by the upward-sloping curve marked *S*. This curve shows the quantity of national saving that households, firms, and the government are willing to supply at each value of the real interest rate. The saving curve is upward-sloping because empirical evidence suggests that increases in the real interest rate stimulate saving. The demand for saving is given by the downward-sloping curve marked *I*. This curve shows the quantity of investment in new capital that firms would choose and hence the amount they would need to borrow in financial markets, at each value of the real interest rate. Because higher real interest rates raise the cost of borrowing and reduce firms' willingness to invest, the demand for saving curve is downward-sloping.

Putting aside the possibility of borrowing from foreigners (which we discuss in Chapter 22), a country can invest only those resources that its savers make available. In equilibrium, then, desired investment (the demand for saving) and desired national saving (the supply of saving) must be equal. As Figure 16.7 suggests, desired saving is equated with desired investment through adjustments in the real interest rate, which functions as the "price" of saving. The movements of the real interest rate clear the market for saving in much the same way that the price of apples clears the market for apples. In Figure 16.7, the real interest rate that clears the market for saving is *r*, the real interest rate that corresponds to the intersection of the supply and demand curves.

The forces that push the real interest rate toward its equilibrium level are similar to the forces that lead to equilibrium in any other supply and demand situation. Suppose, for example, that the real interest rate exceeded *r*. At a higher real interest rate, savers would provide more funds than firms would want to invest. As lenders (savers) competed among themselves to attract borrowers (investors), the real interest rate would be bid down. The real interest rate would fall until it equaled *r*, the only interest rate at which both borrowers and lenders are satisfied, and no opportunities are left unexploited in the financial market. The Equilibrium Principle thus holds in this market as it does in others that we have studied through this book.

Equilibrium

Changes in factors *other than the real interest rate* that affect the supply of or demand for saving will shift the curves, leading to a new equilibrium in the financial market. Changes in the real interest rate cannot shift the supply or demand curves, just as a change in the price of apples cannot shift the supply or demand for apples, because the effects of the real interest rate on saving are already incorporated in the slopes of the curves. A few examples will illustrate the use of the supply and demand model of financial markets.

The effects of new technology

Exciting new technologies have been introduced in recent years, ranging from the internet to new applications of genetics. A number of these technologies appear to have great commercial potential. How does the introduction of new technologies affect saving, investment, and the real interest rate?

The introduction of any new technology with the potential for commercial application creates profit opportunities for those who can bring the fruits of the technology to the public. In economists' language, the technical breakthrough raises the marginal product of new capital. Figure 16.8 shows the effects of a technological breakthrough, with a resulting increase in the marginal product of capital. At any given real interest rate, an increase in the marginal product of capital makes firms more eager to invest. Thus, the advent of the new technology causes the demand for saving to shift upward and to the right, from *I* to *I*′.

At the new equilibrium point *F*, investment and national saving are higher than before, as is the real interest rate, which rises from *r* to *r*′. The rise in the real interest

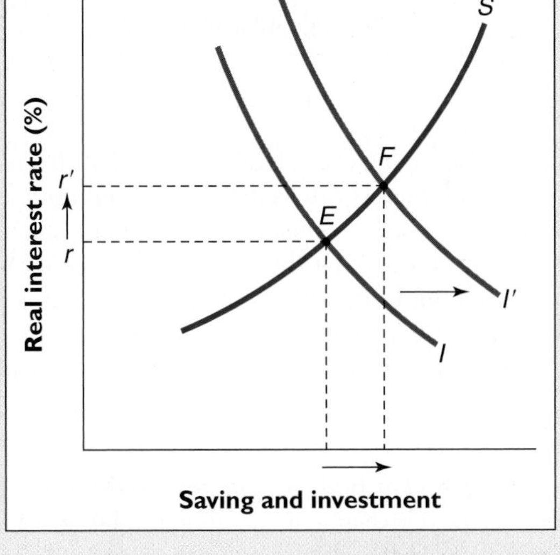

FIGURE 16.8
The Effects of a New Technology on National Saving and Investment.
A technological breakthrough raises the marginal product of new capital goods, increasing desired investment and the demand for saving. The real interest rate rises, as do national saving and investment.

rate reflects the increased demand for funds by investors as they race to apply the new technologies. Because of the incentive of higher real returns, saving increases as well. Indeed, the real interest rate in the United States was relatively high in the late 1990s (Figure 13.3), as was the rate of investment, reflecting the opportunities created by new technologies. ◆

Next, let's examine how a change in the supply of saving affects the financial markets.

An increase in the government budget deficit

Suppose the government increases its spending without raising taxes, thereby increasing its budget deficit (or reducing its budget surplus). How will this decision affect national saving, investment, and the real interest rate?

National saving includes both private saving (saving by households and businesses) and public saving, which is equivalent to the government budget surplus. An increase in the government budget deficit (or a decline in the surplus) reduces public saving. Assuming that private saving does not change, the reduction in public saving will reduce national saving as well.

Figure 16.9 shows the effect of the increased government budget deficit on the market for saving and investment. At any real interest rate, a larger deficit reduces

FIGURE 16.9
The Effects of an Increase in the Government Budget Deficit on National Saving and Investment.
An increase in the government budget deficit reduces the supply of saving, raising the real interest rate and lowering investment. The tendency of increased government deficits to reduce investment in new capital is called *crowding out.*

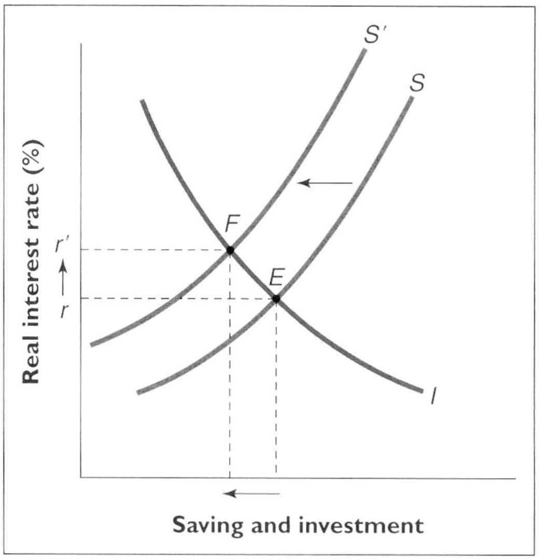

national saving, causing the saving curve to shift to the left, from S to S'. At the new equilibrium point F, the real interest rate is higher at r' and both national saving and investment are lower. In economic terms, the government has dipped further into the pool of private savings to borrow the funds to finance its budget deficit. The government's extra borrowing forces investors to compete for a smaller quantity of available saving, driving up the real interest rate. The higher real interest rate makes investment less attractive, assuring the investment will decrease along with national saving. ◆

crowding out the tendency of increased government deficits to reduce investment spending

The tendency of government budget deficits to reduce investment spending is called **crowding out.** Reduced investment spending implies lower capital formation, and thus lower economic growth, as we saw in the previous chapter. This adverse effect of budget deficits on economic growth is a key reason that economists advise governments to minimize their deficits.

EXERCISE 16.5

Suppose the general public becomes more "grasshopper-like" and less "ant-like" in their saving decisions, becoming less concerned about saving for the future. How will the change in public attitudes affect the country's rate of capital formation and economic growth?

How can we increase national saving?

Most policymakers recognize that the United States would eventually benefit from higher national saving rates. The government could increase public saving by reducing budget deficits, either by decreasing government spending or by increasing taxes. For political reasons, however, a rapid reduction of the government budget deficit may be difficult to achieve.

Alternatively, increasing the incentives for households and firms to save would increase private saving. Some economists, for example, believe that the federal income tax should be scrapped in favor of a federal consumption tax. A consumption tax would be similar to the sales tax collected in most states, wherein people are taxed only when they spend. Taxing the portion of income that is consumed but not the portion that is saved would increase the incentive to save.

Other economists favor further reductions in the tax rates on dividends and capital gains beyond those passed during George W. Bush's first term as president. These tax cuts would increase the after-tax rate of return to saving and thereby promote additional private saving. If private saving rises by more than the immediate loss in tax revenues, national saving also will rise. ◆

At the national level, high saving rates lead to greater investment in new capital goods and thus higher standards of living. At the individual or family level, a high saving rate promotes the accumulation of wealth and the achievement of economic security. In this chapter, we have studied some of the factors that underlie saving and investment decisions. The next chapter will look more closely at how savers hold their wealth and at how the financial system allocates the pool of available saving to the most productive investment projects.

▪ SUMMARY ▪

- In general, saving equals current income minus spending on current needs; the saving rate is the percentage of income that is a saved. Wealth, or net worth, equals the market value of assets (real or financial items of value) minus liabilities (debts). Saving is a flow, being measured in dollars per unit of time; wealth is a stock, measured in dollars at a point in time. As the amount of water in a bathtub changes according to the rate at which water flows in, the stock of wealth increases at the saving rate. Wealth also increases if the value of existing assets rises (capital gains) and decreases if the value of existing assets falls (capital losses). **LO1**
- The saving of an entire country is *national saving S*. National saving is defined by $S = Y - C - G$, where Y represents total output or income, C equals consumption spending, and G equals government purchases of goods and services. National saving can be broken up into private saving, or $Y - T - C$, and public saving, or $T - G$, where T stands for taxes paid to the government less transfer payments and interest paid by the government to the private sector. Private saving can be further broken down into household saving and business saving. In the United States, the bulk of private saving is done by businesses. **LO2**
- Public saving is equivalent to the government budget surplus, $T - G$; if the government runs a budget deficit, then public saving is negative. The U.S. national

saving rate is low relative to other industrialized countries, but it is higher and more stable than U.S. household saving. **LO2**

- Individuals and households save for a variety of reasons, including life-cycle objectives, as saving for retirement or a new home; the need to be prepared for an emergency (precautionary saving); and the desire to leave an inheritance (bequest saving). The amount people save also is affected by the real interest rate, which is the "reward" for saving. Evidence suggests that higher real interest rates lead to modest increases in saving. Saving also can be affected by psychological factors such as the degree of self-control and the desire to consume at the level of one's neighbors (demonstration effects). **LO3**

- Investment is the purchase or construction of new capital goods, including housing. Firms will invest in new capital goods if the benefits of doing so outweigh the costs. Two factors that determine the cost of investment are the price of new capital goods and the real interest rate. The higher the real interest rate, the more expensive it is to borrow, and the less likely firms are to invest. The benefit of investment is the value of the marginal product of new capital, which depends on factors such as the productivity of new capital goods, the taxes levied on the revenues they generate, and the relative price of the firm's output. **LO4**

- In the absence of international borrowing or lending, the supply of and demand for national saving must be equal. The supply of national saving depends on the saving decisions of households and businesses and the fiscal policies of the government (which determine public saving). The demand for saving is the amount business firms want to invest in new capital. The real interest rate, which is the "price" of borrowed funds, changes to equate the supply of and demand for national saving. Factors that affect the supply of or demand for saving will change saving, investment, and the equilibrium real interest rate. For example, an increase in the government budget deficit will reduce national saving and investment and raise the equilibrium real interest rate. The tendency of government budget deficits to reduce investment is called crowding out. **LO5**

KEY TERMS

assets (447)
balance sheet (447)
bequest saving (457)
capital gains (449)
capital losses (449)
crowding out (468)
flow (448)
government budget deficit (454)
government budget surplus (454)
liabilities (447)
life-cycle saving (457)
national saving (452)
precautionary saving (457)
private saving (453)
public saving (453)
saving (447)
saving rate (447)
stock (448)
transfer payments (453)
wealth (447)

REVIEW QUESTIONS

1. Explain the relationship between saving and wealth, using the concepts of flows and stocks. Is saving the only means by which wealth can increase? Explain. **LO1**
2. Give three basic motivations for saving. Illustrate each with an example. What other factors would psychologists cite as being possibly important for saving? LO3
3. Define *national saving*, relating your definition to the general concept of saving. Why does the standard U.S. definition of national saving potentially understate the true amount of saving being done in the economy? **LO2**
4. Household saving rates in the United States are very low. Is this fact a problem for the U.S. economy? Why or why not? **LO2**
5. Why do increases in real interest rates reduce the quantity of saving demanded? (*Hint:* Who are the "demanders" of saving?) **LO3**
6. Name one factor that could increase the supply of saving and one that could increase the demand for saving. Show the effects of each on saving, investment, and the real interest rate. **LO5**

■ PROBLEMS ■

McGraw-Hill's HOMEWORK MANAGER®

1. a. Corey has a mountain bike worth $300, a credit card debt of $150, $200 in cash, a Sandy Koufax baseball card worth $400, $1,200 in a checking account, and an electric bill due for $250. Construct Corey's balance sheet and calculate his net worth. For each remaining part, explain how the event affects Corey's assets, liabilities, and wealth.
   b. Corey goes to a baseball card convention and finds out that his baseball card is a worthless forgery.
   c. Corey uses $150 from his paycheck to pay off his credit card balance. The remainder of his earnings is spent.
   d. Corey writes a $150 check on his checking account to pay off his credit card balance.

   Of the events in the previous three parts, which, if any, corresponds to saving on Corey's part? **LO1**
2. State whether each of the following is a stock or a flow, and explain. **LO1**
   a. The gross domestic product.
   b. National saving.
   c. The value of the U.S. housing stock on January 1, 2005.
   d. The amount of U.S. currency in circulation as of this morning.
   e. The government budget deficit.
   f. The quantity of outstanding government debt on January 1, 2005.
3. Ellie and Vince are a married couple, both with college degrees and jobs. How would you expect each of the following events to affect the amount they save each month? Explain your answers in terms of the basic motivations for saving. **LO3**
   a. Ellie learns she is pregnant.
   b. Vince reads in the paper about possible layoffs in his industry.
   c. Vince had hoped that his parents would lend financial assistance toward the couple's planned purchase of a house, but he learns that they can't afford it.
   d. Ellie announces that she would like to go to law school in the next few years.
   e. A boom in the stock market greatly increases the value of the couple's retirement funds.
   f. Vince and Ellie agree that they would like to leave a substantial amount to local charities in their wills.
4. Individual retirement accounts, or IRAs, were established by the U.S. government to encourage saving. An individual who deposits part of current earnings in an IRA does not have to pay income taxes on the earnings deposited, nor are any income taxes charged on the interest earned by the funds in the IRA. However, when the funds are withdrawn from the IRA, the full amount withdrawn is treated as income and is taxed at the individual's current income tax rate. In contrast, an individual depositing in a non-IRA account has to pay income taxes on the funds deposited and on interest earned in each year but does not have to pay taxes on withdrawals from the account. Another feature of IRAs that is different from a standard savings account is that funds deposited in an IRA cannot be withdrawn prior to retirement, except upon payment of a substantial penalty. **LO3**
   a. Greg, who is five years from retirement, receives a $10,000 bonus at work. He is trying to decide whether to save this extra income in an IRA account or in a regular savings account. Both accounts earn 5 percent nominal interest, and Greg is in the 30 percent tax bracket in every year (including his retirement year). Compare the amounts that Greg will have in five years under each of the two saving strategies, net of all taxes. Is the IRA a good deal for Greg?

b. Would you expect the availability of IRAs to increase the amount that households save? Discuss in light of (1) the response of saving to changes in the real interest rate and (2) psychological theories of saving.

5. In each part that follows, use the economic data given to find national saving, private saving, public saving, and the national saving rate. **LO2**
   a. Household saving = 200 Business saving = 400
   Government purchases of goods and services = 100
   Government transfers and interest payments = 100
   Tax collections = 150 GDP = 2,200
   b. GDP = 6,000 Tax collections = 1,200
   Government transfers and interest payments = 400
   Consumption expenditures = 4,500
   Government budget surplus = 100
   c. Consumption expenditures = 4,000 Investment = 1,000
   Government purchases = 1,000 Net exports = 0
   Tax collections = 1,500
   Government transfers and interest payments = 500

6. Obtain a recent copy of the *Survey of Current Business*, published by the Bureau of Economic Analysis, in the library or online at www.bea.gov. In the national data portion of the *Survey*, find nominal data on GDP, consumption, government purchases of goods and services, total government expenditures, and total government receipts for the most recent complete year available (see Tables 1.1 and 3.1). Calculate national saving, private saving, public saving, and the national saving rate. How does the government's contribution to national saving in the most recent period compare to the data shown in Figure 16.3? **LO2**

7. Ellie and Vince are trying to decide whether to purchase a new home. The house they want is priced at $200,000. Annual expenses such as maintenance, taxes, and insurance equal 4 percent of the home's value. If properly maintained, the house's real value is not expected to change. The real interest rate in the economy is 6 percent, and Ellie and Vince can qualify to borrow the full amount of the purchase price (for simplicity, assume no down payment) at that rate. Ignore the fact that mortgage interest payments are tax-deductible in the United States. **LO4**
   a. Ellie and Vince would be willing to pay $1,500 monthly rent to live in a house of the same quality as the one they are thinking about purchasing. Should they buy the house?
   b. Does the answer to part a change if they are willing to pay $2,000 monthly rent?
   c. Does the answer to part a change if the real interest rate is 4 percent instead of 6 percent?
   d. Does the answer to part a change if the developer offers to sell Ellie and Vince the house for $150,000?
   e. Why do home-building companies dislike high interest rates?

8. The builder of a new movie theater complex is trying to decide how many screens she wants. Below are her estimates of the number of patrons the complex will attract each year, depending on the number of screens available.

Number of screens	Total number of patrons
1	40,000
2	75,000
3	105,000
4	130,000
5	150,000

After paying the movie distributors and meeting all other noninterest expenses, the owner expects to net $2.00 per ticket sold. Construction costs are $1,000,000 per screen. **LO4**

a. Make a table showing the value of marginal product for each screen from the first through the fifth. What property is illustrated by the behavior of marginal products?
b. How many screens will be built if the real interest rate is 5.5 percent?
c. If the real interest rate is 7.5 percent?
d. If the real interest rate is 10 percent?
e. If the real interest rate is 5.5 percent, how far would construction costs have to fall before the builder would be willing to build a five-screen complex?

9. For each of the following scenarios, use supply and demand analysis to predict the resulting changes in the real interest rate, national saving, and investment. Show all your diagrams. **LO5**
   a. The legislature passes a 10 percent investment tax credit. Under this program, for every $100 that a firm spends on new capital equipment, it receives an extra $10 in tax refunds from the government.
   b. A reduction in military spending moves the government's budget from deficit into surplus.
   c. A new generation of computer-controlled machines becomes available. These machines produce manufactured goods much more quickly and with fewer defects.
   d. The government raises its tax on corporate profits. Other tax changes also are made, such that the government's deficit remains unchanged.
   e. Concerns about job security raise precautionary saving.
   f. New environmental regulations increase firms' costs of operating capital.

ANSWERS TO IN-CHAPTER EXERCISES

16.1 If Consuelo's student loan were for $6,500 instead of $3,000, her liabilities would be $6,750 (the student loan plus the credit card balance) instead of $3,250. The value of her assets, $6,280, is unchanged. In this case, Consuelo's wealth is negative, since assets of $6,280 less liabilities of $6,750 equals −$470. Negative wealth or net worth means one owes more than one owns. **LO1**

16.2 If water is being drained from the tub, the flow is negative, equal to −3 gallons per minute. There are 37 gallons in the tub at 7:16 p.m. and 34 gallons at 7:17 p.m. The rate of change of the stock is −3 gallons per minute, which is the same as the flow. **LO1**

16.3 a. Consuelo has set aside her usual $20, but she has also incurred a new liability of $50. So her net saving for the week is *minus* $30. Since her assets (her checking account) have increased by $20 but her liabilities (her credit card balance) have increased by $50, her wealth also has declined by $30. **LO1**

b. In paying off her credit card bill, Consuelo reduces her assets by $300 by drawing down her checking account and reduces her liabilities by the same amount by reducing her credit card balance to zero. Thus, there is no change in her wealth. There is also no change in her saving (note that Consuelo's income and spending on current needs have not changed).

c. The increase in the value of Consuelo's car raises her assets by $500. So her wealth also rises by $500. Changes in the value of existing assets are not treated as part of saving, however, so her saving is unchanged.

d. The decline in the value of Consuelo's furniture is a capital loss of $300. Her assets and wealth fall by $300. Her saving is unchanged.

16.4 The loss of value of \$200 over the year is another financial cost of owning the mower, which Larry should take into account in making his decision. His total cost is now \$240 in interest costs plus \$200 in anticipated loss of value of the mower (known as depreciation), or \$440. This exceeds the value of marginal product, \$400, and so now Larry should not buy the mower. **LO4**

16.5 Household saving is part of national saving. A decline in household saving, and hence national saving, at any given real interest rate shifts the saving supply curve to the left. The results are as in Figure 16.9. The real interest rate rises and the equilibrium values of national saving and investment fall. Lower investment is the same as a lower rate of capital formation, which would be expected to slow economic growth. **LO5**

CHAPTER 17

The Financial System, Money, and Prices

LEARNING OBJECTIVES

After reading this chapter, you should be able to:

1. Describe the role of financial intermediaries such as commercial banks in the financial system.
2. Differentiate between bonds and stocks and show why their prices are inversely related to interest rates.
3. Explain how the financial system improves the allocation of saving to productive uses.
4. Discuss the three functions of money and how the money supply is measured.
5. Analyze how the lending behavior of commercial banks affects the money supply.
6. Understand how a central bank controls the money supply and how control of the money supply is related to inflation in the long run.

We're in the money, come on, my honey,
Let's lend it, spend it, send it rolling along!
"We're in the Money," lyrics by Al Dubin,
music by Harry Warren (from the film *Gold Diggers of 1933*)

When people use the word "money," they often mean something different than what economists mean when they use the word. For an economist, when you get a paycheck, you are receiving income, and any amount that you do not spend is saving. Or think about someone who has done well in the stock market: most people would say that they "made money" in the market. No, an economist would answer, their wealth increased. These terms don't make for a catchy song, but a good economic naturalist must use words like *income*, *saving*, *wealth*, and *money* carefully because each plays a different role in the financial system.

We stated in the previous chapter that the U.S. financial system consists of financial institutions, like banks, and financial markets such as bond markets and stock markets. We then developed a supply and demand model of financial markets that showed how the real interest rate acts to allocate resources from savers to borrowers. In this chapter, we build on this foundation and examine some important institutional details of the financial system. First, we study how institutions such as banks, bond markets, and stock markets actually allocate saving to productive uses. Second, we examine what economists mean by the term "money" and discuss how economists measure its supply and how it is created by the lending behavior of banks. Third, we analyze how central banks, like the Federal Reserve System in the United States, can affect the supply of money and determine the long-run rate of inflation in a market economy. By the end of this chapter, you may not be able to write a classic song, but you'll understand the relationship between "money" in common parlance and money, bonds, stocks, and other financial assets.

THE FINANCIAL SYSTEM AND THE ALLOCATION OF SAVING TO PRODUCTIVE USES

We have emphasized the importance of high rates of saving and capital formation for economic growth and increased productivity. High rates of saving and investment by themselves are not sufficient, however. A successful economy not only saves but also uses its savings wisely by applying these limited funds to the investment projects that seem likely to be the most productive.

The financial system of countries like the United States improves the allocation of savings in at least two distinct ways. First, the financial system provides *information* to savers about which of the many possible uses of their funds are likely to prove most productive and hence pay the highest return. By evaluating the potential productivity of alternative capital investments, the financial system helps to direct savings to its best uses. Second, financial markets help savers to *share the risks* of individual investment projects. Sharing of risks protects individual savers from bearing excessive risk, while at the same time making it possible to direct savings to projects, such as the development of new technologies, which are risky but potentially very productive as well.

In this section, we discuss three key components of the financial system: the banking system, the bond market, and the stock market. In doing so, we elaborate on the role of the financial system as a whole in providing information about investment projects and in helping savers to share the risks of lending.

THE BANKING SYSTEM

financial intermediaries firms that extend credit to borrowers using funds raised from savers

The U.S. banking system consists of thousands of commercial banks that accept deposits from individuals and businesses and use those deposits to make loans. Banks are the most important example of a class of institutions called **financial intermediaries,** firms that extend credit to borrowers using funds raised from savers. Other examples of financial intermediaries are savings and loan associations and credit unions.

Comparative Advantage

Why are financial intermediaries such as banks, which "stand between" savers and investors, necessary? Why don't individual savers just lend directly to borrowers who want to invest in new capital projects? The main reason is that, through specialization, banks and other intermediaries develop a comparative advantage in evaluating the quality of borrowers—the information-gathering function that we referred to a moment ago. Most savers, particularly small savers, do not have the time or the knowledge to determine for themselves which borrowers are likely to use the funds they receive most productively. In contrast, banks and other intermediaries have gained expertise in performing the information-gathering activities necessary for profitable lending, including checking out the borrower's background, determining whether the borrower's business plans make sense, and monitoring the borrower's activities during the life of the loan. Because banks specialize in evaluating potential borrowers, they can perform this function at a much lower cost, and with better results, than individual savers could on their own. Banks also reduce the costs of gathering information about potential borrowers by pooling the savings of many individuals to make large loans. Each large loan needs to be evaluated only once, by the bank, rather than separately by each of the hundreds of individuals whose savings may be pooled to make the loan.

Banks help savers by eliminating their need to gather information about potential borrowers and by directing their savings toward higher-return, more-productive investments. Banks help borrowers as well, by providing access to credit that might otherwise not be available. Unlike a *Fortune* 500 corporation, which typically has many ways to raise funds, a small business that wants to buy a copier or remodel its offices will have few options other than going to a bank. Because the bank's lending officer has developed expertise in evaluating small-business loans, and even may have an ongoing business relationship with the small-business owner, the bank will be able to gather the information it needs to make the loan at a reasonable cost. Likewise, consumers who want to borrow to finish a basement or add a room to a house will find few good alternatives to a bank. In sum, banks' expertise at gathering information about alternative lending opportunities allows them to bring together small savers looking for good uses for their funds and small borrowers with worthwhile investment projects.

"O.K., folks, let's move along. I'm sure you've all seen someone qualify for a loan before."

In addition to being able to earn a return on their savings, a second reason that people hold bank deposits is to make it easier to make payments. Most bank deposits allow the holder to write a check against them or draw on them using a debit card or ATM card. For many transactions, paying by check or debit card is more convenient than using cash. For example, it is safer to send a check through the mail than to send cash, and paying by check gives you a record of the transaction, whereas a cash payment does not.

How did the banking crisis of the 1990s in Japan affect the Japanese economy?

During the 1980s, real estate and stock prices soared in Japan. Japanese banks made many loans to real estate developers, and the banks themselves acquired stock in corporations. (Unlike in the United States, in Japan it is legal for commercial banks to own stock.) However, in the early 1990s, land prices plummeted in Japan, leading many bank borrowers to default on their loans. Stock prices also came down sharply, reducing the value of banks' shareholdings. The net result was that most Japanese banks fell into severe financial trouble, with many large banks near bankruptcy. What was the effect of this crisis, which lasted more than a decade, on the Japanese economy?

Relative to the United States, which has more developed stock and bond markets, Japan has traditionally relied very heavily on banks to allocate its savings. Thus, when the severe financial problems of the banks prevented them from operating normally, many borrowers found it unusually difficult to obtain credit—a situation known as a "credit crunch." Smaller borrowers such as small- and medium-sized businesses had been particularly dependent on banks for credit and thus suffered disproportionately.

The Japanese economy, after many years of robust growth, suffered a severe recession throughout the 1990s. Many factors contributed to this sharp slowdown. However, the virtual breakdown of the banking system certainly did not help the situation, as credit shortages interfered with smaller firms' ability to make capital investments and, in some cases, to purchase raw materials and pay workers. The Japanese government recognized the problem but responded very slowly, in large part out of reluctance to bear the high costs of returning the banks to a healthy financial condition. In recent years, the health of the Japanese banking system appears to have improved significantly, although problems remain and the Japanese economy has not returned to its earlier high rate of growth. ◆

BONDS AND STOCKS

Large and well-established corporations that wish to obtain funds for investment will sometimes go to banks. Unlike the typical small borrower, however, a larger firm usually has alternative ways of raising funds, notably through the corporate bond market and the stock market. We first discuss some of the mechanics of bonds and stocks, then return to the role of bond and stock markets in allocating saving.

bond a legal promise to repay a debt, usually including both the principal amount and regular interest payments

principal amount the amount originally lent

maturation date the date at which the principal will be repaid

coupon payments regular interest payments made to the bondholder

coupon rate the interest rate promised when a bond is issued; the annual coupon payments are equal to the coupon rate times the principal amount of the bond

Bonds A **bond** is a legal promise to repay a debt. These repayments typically consist of two parts. First, the **principal amount,** which is the amount originally lent, is paid at some specific date in the future, called the **maturation date.** Second, the owner of the bond, called the *bondholder,* receives regular interest, or **coupon payments,** until the bond's maturation date. For example, a bond may have a principal amount of $1,000 payable on January 1, 2025, and annual coupon payments of $50. These coupon payments are also equal to the principal amount times the **coupon rate,** where the coupon rate is the interest rate promised when the bond is issued. (The coupon rate therefore is also equal to the annual coupon payment divided by the principal.) In the example above, the principal is $1,000 and the coupon rate is 5 percent, resulting in annual coupon payments of (.05)($1,000), or $50.

Corporations and governments frequently raise funds by issuing bonds and selling them to savers. The coupon rate that a newly issued bond must promise in order to be attractive to savers depends on a number of factors, including the bond's term, its credit risk, and its tax treatment. The *term* of a bond is the length of time until the bond's maturation date, which can range from 30 days to 30 years or more. The annual coupon rates on long-term (30-year) bonds generally exceed those on short-term (1-year) bonds because lenders require higher coupon rates (and, hence, higher annual coupon payments) to lend for a long term. *Credit risk* is the risk that the borrower will go bankrupt and thus not repay the loan. A borrower that is viewed as risky will have to pay a higher coupon rate to compensate lenders for taking the chance of losing all or part of their financial investment. For example, so-called high-yield bonds, less formally known as "junk bonds," are bonds issued by firms judged to be risky by credit-rating agencies; these bonds pay higher coupon rates than bonds issued by companies thought to be less risky.

Bonds also differ in their *tax treatment*. For example, interest paid on bonds issued by local governments, called *municipal bonds,* is exempt from federal taxes, whereas interest on other types of bonds is treated as taxable income. Because of this tax advantage, lenders are willing to accept a lower coupon rate on municipal bonds.

Bond owners are not required to hold their bonds until their maturation dates. They are always free to sell their bonds in the *bond market,* an organized market run by professional bond traders. The market value of a particular bond at any given point in time is called the *price* of the bond. The price of a bond can be greater than, less than, or equal to the principal amount of the bond, depending on how the current or prevailing interest rate in financial markets compares with the interest rate at the time the bond was issued. The close relationship between the price of a bond and the current interest rate is illustrated by the following example.

Bond prices and interest rates

On January 1, 2009, Tanya purchases a newly issued, two-year government bond with a principal amount of $1,000 for a price of $1,000. The coupon rate on the bond is 5 percent, paid annually, reflecting the prevailing interest rates on January 1, 2009. Hence, Tanya, or whoever owns the bond at the time, will receive a coupon payment of $50 (5 percent of $1,000) on January 1, 2010. The owner of the bond will receive another coupon payment of $50 on January 1, 2011, at which time she also will receive repayment of the principal amount of $1,000.

On January 1, 2010, after receiving her first year's coupon payment, Tanya decides to sell her bond to raise the funds to take a vacation. She offers her bond for sale in the bond market. The buyer of the bond will receive $1,050 on January 1, 2011, representing the second coupon payment of $50, plus repayment of the $1,000 principal. How much can Tanya expect to get for her "used" bond? The answer depends on the prevailing interest rate in the bond market when she sells her bond on January 1, 2010.

Suppose first that, on January 1, 2010, when Tanya takes her bond to the bond market, the prevailing interest rate on newly issued one-year bonds has risen to 6 percent. Thus, someone who buys a new one-year bond on January 1, 2010, with a 6 percent coupon rate for $1,000 will receive $1,060 on January 1, 2011 ($1,000 principal repayment plus a $60 coupon payment). Would that person also be willing to pay Tanya the $1,000 Tanya paid for her bond? No. Note that the coupon payment on Tanya's "used" bond does not rise when interest rates rise but remains equal to $50. Consequently, the purchaser of Tanya's "used" bond will receive only $1,050 on January 1, 2011, when the bond matures. In order to sell her "used" bond, Tanya will have to reduce the price below \$1,000. This example illustrates the fact that *bond prices and interest rates are inversely related.* When the interest rate being paid on newly issued bonds rises, the price financial investors are willing to pay for existing bonds falls.

How much would the price for Tanya's "used" bond have to fall? Recall that the person who buys the newly issued one-year bond on January 1, 2010, for \$1,000 will receive \$1,060 on January 1, 2011. This \$60 gain represents a 6 percent return on the price he paid. That person will buy Tanya's "used" bond only if Tanya's bond also will give him a 6 percent return. The price for Tanya's bond that allows the purchaser to earn a 6 percent return must satisfy the equation

$$\text{Bond price} \times 1.06 = \$1{,}050.$$

Solving the equation for the bond price, we find that Tanya's bond will sell for \$1,050/1.06, or just under \$991. To check this result, note that on January 1, 2011, the purchaser of the bond will receive \$1,050, or \$59 more than he paid on January 1, 2010. His rate of return is \$59/\$991, or 6 percent, as expected.

What if the prevailing interest rate had instead fallen to 4 percent? When prevailing interest rates fall, bond prices rise. The price of Tanya's "used" bond would rise until it, too, gave a return of 4 percent. At that point, the price of Tanya's bond would satisfy the relationship

$$\text{Bond price} \times 1.04 = \$1{,}050,$$

implying that the price of her bond would rise to \$1,050/1.04, or almost \$1,010.

Finally, what happens if the interest rate when Tanya wants to sell is 5 percent, the same as it was when she originally bought the bond? You should show that in this case the bond would sell at its original price of \$1,000. ◆

EXERCISE 17.1

Three-year government bonds are issued with a principal amount of \$1,000 and an annual coupon rate of 7 percent. Thus, the owner will receive three coupon payments of (0.07)(\$1,000) = \$70 at the end of each year. One year prior to the maturation date of these bonds, a newspaper headline reads, "Bad Economic News Causes Prices of Bonds to Plunge," and the story reveals that these three-year bonds have fallen in price to \$960. What has happened to prevailing interest rates? What is the one-year interest rate at the time of the newspaper story?

Issuing bonds is one means by which a corporation or a government can obtain funds from savers. Another important way of raising funds, but one restricted to corporations, is by issuing stock to the public.

stock (or equity) a claim to partial ownership of a firm

dividend a regular payment received by stockholders for each share that they own

Stocks A share of **stock** (or *equity*) is a claim to partial ownership of a firm. For example, if a corporation has 1 million shares of stock outstanding, ownership of one share is equivalent to ownership of one-millionth of the company. Stockholders receive returns on their financial investment in two forms. First, stockholders receive a regular payment called a **dividend** for each share of stock they own. Dividends are determined by the firm's management and usually depend on the firm's recent profits. Second, stockholders receive returns in the form of *capital gains* when the price of their stock increases (we discussed capital gains and losses in the previous chapter).

Prices of stocks are determined through trading on a stock exchange such as the New York Stock Exchange. A stock's price rises and falls as the demand for the stock changes. Demand for stocks in turn depends on factors such as news about the prospects of the company. For example, the stock price of a pharmaceutical company that announces the discovery of an important new drug is likely to rise on the announcement, even if actual production and marketing of the drug are some time away, because financial investors expect the company to become more profitable in the future. The next example illustrates numerically some key factors that affect stock prices.

How much should you pay for a share of FortuneCookie.com?

You have the opportunity to buy shares in a new company called FortuneCookie.com, which plans to sell gourmet fortune cookies over the internet. Your stockbroker estimates that the company will pay $1.00 per share in dividends a year from now, and that in a year the market price of the company will be $80.00 per share. Assuming that you accept your broker's estimates as accurate, what is the most that you should be willing to pay today per share of FortuneCookie.com? How does your answer change if you expect a $5.00 dividend? If you expect a $1.00 dividend but an $84.00 stock price in one year?

Based on your broker's estimates, you conclude that in one year each share of FortuneCookie.com you own will be worth $81.00 in your pocket—the $1.00 dividend plus the $80.00 you could get by reselling the stock. Finding the maximum price you would pay for the stock today therefore boils down to asking how much would you invest today to have $81.00 a year from today. Answering this question in turn requires one more piece of information, which is the expected rate of return that you require in order to be willing to buy stock in this company.

How would you determine your required rate of return to hold stock in FortuneCookie.com? For the moment, let's imagine that you are not too worried about the potential riskiness of the stock, either because you think that it is a "sure thing" or because you are a devil-may-care type who is not bothered by risk. In that case, you can apply the Cost-Benefit Principle. Your required rate of return to hold FortuneCookie.com should be about the same as you can get on other financial investments such as government bonds. The available return on other financial investments gives the opportunity cost of your funds. So, for example, if the interest rate currently being offered by government bonds is 6 percent, you should be willing to accept a 6 percent return to hold FortuneCookie.com as well. In that case, the maximum price you would pay today for a share of FortuneCookie.com satisfies the equation

Cost-Benefit

$$\text{Stock price} \times 1.06 = \$81.00.$$

This equation defines the stock price you should be willing to pay if you are willing to accept a 6 percent return over the next year. Solving this equation yields stock price = $81.00/1.06 = $76.42. If you buy FortuneCookie.com for $76.42, then your return over the year will be ($81.00 − $76.42)/$76.42 = $4.58/$71.42 = 6 percent, which is the rate of return you required to buy the stock.

If instead the dividend is expected to be $5.00, then the total benefit of holding the stock in one year, equal to the expected dividend plus the expected price, is $5.00 + $80.00, or $85.00. Assuming again that you are willing to accept a 6 percent return to hold FortuneCookie.com, the price you are willing to pay for the stock today satisfies the relationship stock price × 1.06 = $85.00. Solving this equation for the stock price yields stock price = $85.00/1.06 = $80.19. Comparing this price with that in the previous case, we see that a higher expected dividend in the future increases the value of the stock today. That's why good news about the future prospects of a company—such as the announcement by a pharmaceutical company that it has discovered a useful new drug—affects its stock price immediately.

If the expected future price of the stock is \$84.00, with the dividend at \$1.00, then the value of holding the stock in one year is once again \$85.00, and the calculation is the same as the previous one. Again, the price you should be willing to pay for the stock is \$80.19. ◆

These examples show that an increase in the future dividend or in the future expected stock price raises the stock price today, whereas an increase in the return a saver requires to hold the stock lowers today's stock price. Since we expect required returns in the stock market to be closely tied to market interest rates, this last result implies that increases in interest rates tend to depress stock prices as well as bond prices.

Our examples also took the future stock price as given. But what determines the future stock price? Just as today's stock price depends on the dividend shareholders expect to receive this year and the stock price a year from now, the stock price a year from now depends on the dividend expected for next year and the stock price two years from now, and so on. Ultimately, then, today's stock price is affected not only by the dividend expected this year but future dividends as well. A company's ability to pay dividends depends on its earnings. If a company's earnings are expected to increase rapidly in the future, its future dividends will probably grow too. Thus, as we noted in the example of the pharmaceutical company that announces the discovery of a new drug, news about future earnings—even earnings quite far in the future—is likely to affect a company's stock price immediately.

EXERCISE 17.2

Continuing with the previous example, you expect a share of FortuneCookie.com to be worth \$80.00 per share in one year, and also to pay a dividend of \$1.00 in one year. What should you be willing to pay for the stock today if the prevailing interest rate, equal to your required rate of return, is 4 percent? What if the interest rate is 8 percent? In general, how would you expect stock prices to react if economic news arrives that implies that interest rates will rise in the very near future?

In the examples we have studied, we assumed that you were willing to accept a return of 6 percent to hold FortuneCookie.com, the same return that you could get on a government bond. However, financial investments in the stock market are quite risky in that returns to holding stocks can be highly variable and unpredictable. For example, although you expect a share of FortuneCookie.com to be worth \$80.00 in one year, you also realize that there is a chance it might sell as low as \$50.00 or as high as \$110.00 per share. Most financial investors dislike risk and unpredictability and thus have a higher required rate of return for holding risky assets like stocks than for holding relatively safe assets like government bonds. The difference between the required rate of return to hold risky assets and the rate of return on safe assets, like government bonds, is called the **risk premium.**

risk premium the rate of return that financial investors require to hold risky assets minus the rate of return on safe assets

Riskiness and stock prices

Let's build on our previous examples by introducing risk. Suppose that FortuneCookie.com is expected to pay a \$1.00 dividend and have a market price of \$80.00 per share in one year. The interest rate on government bonds is 6 percent per year. However, to be willing to hold a risky asset like a share of FortuneCookie.com, you require an expected return four percentage points higher than the rate paid by safe assets like government bonds (a risk premium of 4 percent). Hence, you require a 10 percent expected return to hold FortuneCookie.com. What is the most you would be willing to pay for the stock now? What do you conclude about the relationship between perceived riskiness and stock prices?

As a share of FortuneCookie.com is expected to pay \$81.00 in one year and the required return is 10 percent, we have stock price × 1.10 = \$81.00. Solving for the stock price, we find the price to be \$81.00/1.10 [illegible] \$73.64, less than the price of \$76.42 we found when there was no risk premi[illegible]nd the required rate of return was 6 percent. We conclude that financial inve[illegible]islike of risk, and the resulting risk premium, lowers the prices of risky [illegible]tocks. ◆

BOND MARKETS, STOCK MARKETS, AND THE ALLOCATION OF SAVINGS

Like banks, bond markets and stock markets provide a means of channeling funds from savers to borrowers with productive investment opportunities. For example, a corporation that is planning a capital investment but does not want to borrow from a bank has two other options: It can issue new bonds, to be sold to savers in the bond market, or it can issue new shares in itself, which are then sold in the stock market. The proceeds from the sales of new bonds or stocks are then available to the firm to finance its capital investment.

How do stock and bond markets help to ensure that available savings are devoted to the most productive uses? As we mentioned at the beginning of this section, two important functions served by these markets are gathering information about prospective borrowers and helping savers to share the risks of lending. Now that you know the basics of how bonds and stocks are priced, we can look at the role of bond and stock markets.

The informational role of bond and stock markets Savers and their financial advisors know that to get the highest possible returns on their financial investments, they must find the potential borrowers with the most profitable opportunities. This knowledge provides a powerful incentive to scrutinize potential borrowers carefully.

For example, companies considering a new issue of stocks or bonds know that their recent performance and plans for the future will be carefully studied by professional analysts on Wall Street and other financial investors. If the analysts and other potential purchasers have doubts about the future profitability of the firm, they will offer a relatively low price for the newly issued shares or they will demand a high interest rate on newly issued bonds. Knowing this, a company will be reluctant to go to the bond or stock market for financing unless its management is confident that it can convince financial investors that the firm's planned use of the funds will be profitable. Thus, the ongoing search by savers and their financial advisors for high returns leads the bond and stock markets to direct funds to the uses that appear most likely to be productive.

Risk sharing and diversification Many highly promising investment projects are also quite risky. The successful development of a new drug to lower cholesterol could create billions of dollars in profits for a drug company, for example; but if the drug turns out to be less effective than some others on the market, none of the development costs will be recouped. An individual who lent his or her life savings to help finance the development of the anticholesterol drug might enjoy a handsome return but also takes the chance of losing everything. Savers are generally reluctant to take large risks, so without some means of reducing the risk faced by each saver, it might be very hard for the company to find the funds to develop the new drug.

Bond and stock markets help reduce risk by giving savers a means to *diversify* their financial investments. **Diversification** is the practice of spreading one's wealth over a variety of different financial investments to reduce overall risk. The idea of diversification follows from the adage that "you shouldn't put all your eggs in one basket." Rather than putting all of his or her savings in one very risky project, a financial investor will find it much safer to allocate a small amount of savings to each of a large number of stocks and bonds. That way, if some financial assets fall in

diversification the practice of spreading one's wealth over a variety of different financial investments to reduce overall risk value, there is a good chance that others will rise in value, with gains offsetting losses. The following example illustrates the benefits of diversification.

The benefits of diversification

Vikram has $200 to invest and is considering two stocks, the Smith Umbrella Company and the Jones Suntan Lotion Company. Suppose the price of one share of each stock is $100. The umbrella company will turn out to be the better investment if the weather is rainy, but the suntan lotion company will be the better investment if the weather is sunny. In Table 17.1, we illustrate the amounts by which the price of one share of each stock will change and how this depends on the weather.

TABLE 17.1
Changes in the Stock Price of Two Companies

	Increase in Stock Price per Share	
Actual weather	**Smith Umbrella Co.**	**Jones Suntan Lotion Co.**
Rainy	+$10	Unchanged
Sunny	Unchanged	+$10

According to Table 17.1, the price of one share of Smith Umbrella Co. stock will rise by $10 (from $100 to $110) if it rains but will remain unchanged if the weather is sunny. The price of one share of Jones Suntan Co. stock, on the other hand, is expected to rise by $10 (from $100 to $110) if it is sunny but will remain unchanged if there is rain.

Suppose the chance of rain is 50 percent, and the chance of sunshine is 50 percent. How should Vikram invest his $200? If Vikram were to invest all his $200 in Smith Umbrella, he could buy two shares. Half of the time it will rain and each share will rise by $10, for a total gain of $20. Half of the time, however, it will be sunny, in which case the stock price will remain unchanged. Thus, his average gain will be 50 percent (or one-half) times $20 plus 50 percent times $0, which is equal to $10.

If, however, Vikram invested all of his $200 in Jones Suntan Lotion Company, he could again buy two shares for $100 each. Each share would rise by $10 if the weather is sunny (for a total gain of $20) and remain unchanged if the weather is rainy. Since it will be sunny half the time, the average gain will be 50 percent times $20 plus 50 percent times $0, or $10.

Although Vikram can earn an *average* gain of $10 if he puts all of his money into either stock, investing in only one stock is quite risky, since his actual gain varies widely depending on whether there is rain or shine. Can Vikram *guarantee* himself a gain of $10, avoiding the uncertainty and risk? Yes, all he has to do is buy one share of each of the two stocks. If it rains, he will earn $10 on his Smith Umbrella stock and nothing on his Jones Suntan stock. If it's sunny, he will earn nothing on Smith Umbrella but $10 on Jones Suntan. Rain or shine, he is guaranteed to earn $10—without risk. ◆

The existence of bond markets and stock markets makes it easy for savers to diversify by putting a small amount of their savings into each of a wide variety of different financial assets, each of which represents a share of a particular company or investment project. From society's point of view, diversification makes it possible for risky but worthwhile projects to obtain funding, without individual savers having to bear too much risk.

For the typical person, a particularly convenient way to diversify is to buy bonds and stocks indirectly through mutual funds. A **mutual fund** is a financial intermediary that sells shares in itself to the public, then uses the funds raised to buy a wide variety of financial assets. Holding shares in a mutual fund thus amounts to owning a little bit of many different financial assets, which helps to achieve diversification. The advantage of mutual funds is that it is usually less costly and time-consuming to buy shares in one or two mutual funds than to buy many different stocks and bonds directly. Over the past decade, mutual funds have become increasingly popular in the United States.

mutual fund a financial intermediary that sells shares in itself to the public, then uses the funds raised to buy a wide variety of financial assets

Example 17.1

THE ECONOMIC NATURALIST

Why did the U.S. stock market rise sharply in the 1990s, then fall in the new millennium?

Stock prices soared during the 1990s in the United States. The Standard & Poor's 500 index, which summarizes the stock price performance of 500 major companies, rose 60 percent between 1990 and 1995, then more than doubled between 1995 and 2000. However, in the first two years of the new millennium, this index lost nearly half its value. Why did the U.S. stock market boom in the 1990s and bust in the 2000s?

The prices of stocks depend on their purchasers' expectations about future dividends and stock prices and on the rate of return required by potential stockholders. The required rate of return in turn equals the interest rate on safe assets plus the risk premium. In principle, a rise in stock prices could be the result of increased optimism about future dividends, a fall in the required return, or some combination.

Probably both factors contributed to the boom in stock prices in the 1990s. Dividends grew rapidly in the 1990s, reflecting the strong overall performance of the U.S. economy. Encouraged by the promise of new technologies, many financial investors expected future dividends to be even higher.

There is also evidence that the risk premium that people required to hold stocks fell during the 1990s, thereby lowering the total required return and raising stock prices. One possible explanation for a decline in the risk premium in the 1990s is increased diversification. During that decade, the number and variety of mutual funds available increased markedly. Millions of Americans invested in these funds, including many who had never owned stock before or had owned stock in only a few companies. This increase in diversification for the typical stock market investor may have lowered the perceived risk of holding stocks (because she could now own stocks by buying mutual funds), which in turn reduced the risk premium and raised stock prices. An alternative explanation is that investors simply underestimated the riskiness inherent in the economy and, consequently, in the stock market. To the extent that investors underestimated the riskiness of stocks, the risk premium may have fallen to an unrealistically low level.

After 2000 both of these favorable factors reversed. The growth in dividends was disappointing to stockholders, in large part because many high-tech firms did not prove as profitable as had been hoped. An additional blow was a series of corporate accounting scandals in 2002, in which it became known that some large firms had taken illegal or unethical actions to make their profits seem larger than in fact they were. A number of factors, including a recession, a major terrorist attack, and the accounting scandals, also increased stockholders' concerns about the riskiness of stocks, so that the risk premium they required to hold stocks rose from its 1990s lows. The combination of lower expected dividends and a higher premium for risk sent stock prices sharply downward. Only in 2003, when the economy began to grow more rapidly, did stock prices begin to recover. ●

MONEY AND ITS USES

Bonds and stocks are particular types of financial assets. Where does money fit into this scheme? And what exactly is money? To the economist, **money** is any asset that can be used in making purchases. Common examples of money in the modern

money any asset that can be used in making purchases

world are currency and coins. A checking account balance represents another asset that can be used in making payments (as when you write a check to pay for your weekly groceries) and so is also counted as money. In contrast, shares of stock, for example, cannot be used directly in most transactions. Stock must first be sold—that is, converted into cash or a checking account deposit—before further transactions, such as buying your groceries, can be made.

Historically, a wide variety of objects have been used as money, including gold and silver coins, shells, beads, feathers, and, on the Island of Yap, large, immovable boulders. Prior to the use of metallic coins, by far the most common form of money was the cowrie, a type of shell found in the South Pacific. Cowries were used as money in some parts of Africa until very recently, being officially accepted for payment of taxes in Uganda until the beginning of the twentieth century. Today money can be virtually intangible, as in the case of your checking account.

Why do people use money? Money has three principal uses: a *medium of exchange*, a *unit of account*, and a *store of value*.

medium of exchange an asset used in purchasing goods and services

Money serves as a **medium of exchange** when it is used to purchase goods and services, as when you pay cash for a newspaper or write a check to cover your utilities bill. This is perhaps money's most crucial function. Think about how complicated daily life would become if there were no money. Without money, all economic transactions would have to be in the form of **barter,** which is the direct trade of goods or services for other goods or services.

barter the direct trade of goods or services for other goods or services

© Catherine Karnow/CORBIS

In a world without money, she could eat only by finding someone willing to trade food for a musical performance.

Barter is highly inefficient because it requires that each party to a trade has something that the other party wants, a so-called double coincidence of wants. For example, under a barter system, a musician could get her dinner only by finding someone willing to trade food for a musical performance. Finding such a match of needs, where each party happens to want exactly what the other person has to offer, would be difficult to do on a regular basis. In a world with money, the musician's problem is considerably simpler. First, she must find someone who is willing to pay money for her musical performance. Then, with the money received, she can purchase the food and other goods and services that she needs. In a society that uses money, it is not necessary that the person who wants to hear music and the person willing to provide food to the musician be one and the same. In other words, there need not be a double coincidence of wants for trades of goods and services to take place.

Comparative Advantage

By eliminating the problem of having to find a double coincidence of wants in order to trade, the use of money in a society permits individuals to specialize in producing particular goods or services, as opposed to having every family or village produce most of what it needs. Specialization greatly increases economic efficiency and material standards of living, as we discussed in Chapter 2 when we developed the Principle of Comparative Advantage. This usefulness of money in making transactions explains why savers hold money, even though money generally pays a low rate of return. Cash, for example, pays no interest at all, and the balances in checking accounts usually pay a lower rate of interest than could be obtained in alternative financial investments.

unit of account a basic measure of economic value

Money's second function is as a *unit of account*. As a **unit of account,** money is the basic yardstick for measuring economic value. In the United States virtually all prices—including the price of labor (wages) and the prices of financial assets such as shares of stock—are expressed in dollars. Expressing economic values in a common unit of account allows for easy comparisons. For example, grain can be measured in bushels and coal in tons, but to judge whether 20 bushels of grain are economically more or less valuable than a ton of coal, we express both values in dollar terms. The use of money as a unit of account is closely related to its use as a medium of exchange; because money is used to buy and sell things, it makes sense to express prices of all kinds in money terms.

store of value an asset that serves as a means of holding wealth

As a **store of value,** its third function, money is a way of holding wealth. For example, the miser who stuffs cash in his mattress or buries gold coins under the old oak tree at midnight is holding wealth in money form. Likewise, if you regularly keep a balance in your checking account, you are holding part of your wealth in the form of money. Although money is usually the primary medium of exchange or unit of account in an economy, it is not the only store of value. There are numerous other ways of holding wealth, such as owning stocks, bonds, or real estate.

For most people, money is not a particularly good way to hold wealth, apart from its usefulness as a medium of exchange. Unlike government bonds and other types of financial assets, most forms of money pay no interest, and there is always the risk of cash being lost or stolen. However, cash has the advantage of being anonymous and difficult to trace, making it an attractive store of value for smugglers, drug dealers, and others who want their assets to stay out of the view of the Internal Revenue Service.

Private money: Ithaca Hours and LETS

Money is usually issued by the government, not private individuals, but in part this reflects legal restrictions on private money issuance. Where the law allows, private moneys do sometimes emerge.[1] For example, privately issued currencies circulate in more than 30 U.S. communities. In Ithaca, New York, a private currency known as "Ithaca Hours" has circulated since 1991. Instituted by town resident Paul Glover, each Ithaca Hour is equivalent to $10, the average hourly wage of workers in the county. The bills, printed with specially developed inks to prevent counterfeiting, honor local people and the environment. An estimated 1,600 individuals and businesses have earned and spent Hours. Founder Paul Glover argues that the use of Hours, which can't be spent elsewhere, induces people to do more of their shopping in the local economy.

A more high-tech form of private money is associated with computerized trading systems called LETS, for local electronic trading system. These are quite popular in Australia, New Zealand, and Great Britain. Participants in a LETS post a list of goods and services they would like to buy or sell. When transactions are made, the appropriate number of "computer credits" is subtracted from the buyer's account and added to the seller's account. People are allowed to have negative balances in their accounts, so participants have to trust other members not to abuse the system by buying many goods and services and then quitting. LETS credits exist in the computer only and are never in the form of paper or metal. In this respect, LETS may foreshadow the electronic monetary systems of the future.

What do Ithaca Hours and LETS credits have in common? By functioning as a medium of exchange, each facilitates trade within a community. ◆

MEASURING MONEY

How much money, defined as financial assets usable for making purchases, is there in the U.S. economy at any given time? This question is not simple to answer because in practice it is not easy to draw a clear distinction between those assets that should be counted as money and those that should not. Dollar bills are certainly a form of money, and a van Gogh painting certainly is not. However, brokerage firms now offer accounts that allow their owners to combine financial investments in stocks and bonds with check-writing and credit card privileges. Should the balances in these accounts, or some part of them, be counted as money? It is difficult to tell.

Economists skirt the problem of deciding what is and isn't money by using several alternative definitions of money, which vary in how broadly the concept of money is defined. A relatively "narrow" definition of the amount of money in the U.S. economy is called M1. **M1** is the sum of currency outstanding and balances held in checking accounts. A broader measure of money, called **M2,** includes all

M1 sum of currency outstanding and balances held in checking accounts

M2 All the assets in M1 plus some additional assets that are usable in making payments but at greater cost or inconvenience than currency or checks

[1]Barbara A. Good, "Private Money: Everything Old Is New Again," Federal Reserve Bank of Cleveland, *Economic Commentary,* April 1, 1998.

the assets in M1 plus some additional assets that are usable in making payments, but at greater cost or inconvenience than currency or checks. Table 17.2 lists the components of M1 and M2 and also gives the amount of each type of asset outstanding as of January 2008. For most purposes, however, it is sufficient to think of money as the sum of currency outstanding and balances in checking accounts, or M1.

TABLE 17.2
Components of M1 and M2, January 2008

M1		**1,364.7**
Currency	758.1	
Demand deposits	292.5	
Other checkable deposits	307.9	
Travelers' checks	6.2	
M2		**7,498.7**
M1	1,364.7	
Savings deposits	3,903.4	
Small-denomination time deposits	1,224.4	
Money market mutual funds	1,006.1	

NOTES: Billions of dollars, adjusted for seasonal variations. In M1, currency refers to cash and coin. Demand deposits are non-interest-bearing checking accounts, and "other checkable deposits" includes checking accounts that bear interest. M2 includes all the components of M1, balances in savings accounts, "small-denomination" (under $100,000) deposits held at banks for a fixed term, and money market mutual funds (MMMFs). MMMFs are organizations that sell shares, use the proceeds to buy safe assets (like government bonds), and often allow their shareholders some check-writing privileges.

SOURCE: Federal Reserve release H.6 (www.federalreserve.gov/releases/h6/current/).

Note that credit card balances are not included in either M1 or M2 even though people increasingly use credit cards to pay for many of their purchases, including food, clothing, cars, and even college tuition. The main reason credit card balances are not included in the money supply is that they do not represent part of people's wealth. Indeed, a credit card charge of $1,000 represents an obligation to pay someone else $1,000.

RECAP	MONEY AND ITS USES

Money is any asset that can be used in making purchases, such as currency or a checking account. Money serves as a *medium of exchange* when it is used to purchase goods and services. The use of money as a medium of exchange eliminates the need for *barter* and the difficulties of finding a "double coincidence of wants." Money also serves as a *unit of account* and a *store of value*.

In practice, two basic measures of money are M1 and M2. M1, a more narrow measure, is made up primarily of currency and balances held in checking accounts. The broader measure, M2, includes all the assets in M1 plus some additional assets usable in making payments.

COMMERCIAL BANKS AND THE CREATION OF MONEY

What determines the amount of money in the economy? If the economy's supply of money consisted entirely of currency, the answer would be simple: The supply of money would just be equal to the value of the currency created and circulated by the government. However, as we have seen, in modern economies the money supply consists not only of currency but also of deposit balances held by the public in commercial banks.

The determination of the money supply in a modern economy depends in part on the behavior of commercial banks and their depositors. To see how, we will use the example of a fictional country, the Republic of Gorgonzola. Initially, we assume, Gorgonzola has no commercial banking system. To make trading easier and eliminate the need for barter, the government directs the central bank of Gorgonzola to put into circulation a million identical paper notes, called guilders. The central bank prints the guilders and distributes them to the populace. At this point the Gorgonzolan money supply is a million guilders.

However, the citizens of Gorgonzola are unhappy with a money supply made up entirely of paper guilders since the notes may be lost or stolen. In response to the demand for safekeeping of money, some Gorgonzolan entrepreneurs set up a system of commercial banks. At first, these banks are only storage vaults where people can deposit their guilders. When people need to make a payment, they can either physically withdraw their guilders or, more conveniently, write a check on their account. Checks give the banks permission to transfer guilders from the account of the person paying by check to the account of the person to whom the check is made out. With a system of payments based on checks, the paper guilders need never leave the banking system, although they flow from one bank to another as a depositor of one bank makes a payment to a depositor in another bank. Deposits do not pay interest in this economy; indeed, the banks can make a profit only by charging depositors fees in exchange for safeguarding their cash.

Let's suppose for now that people prefer bank deposits to cash and so deposit all of their guilders with the commercial banks. With all guilders in the vaults of banks, the balance sheet of all of Gorgonzola's commercial banks taken together is as shown in Table 17.3.

TABLE 17.3
Consolidated Balance Sheet of Gorgonzolan Commercial Banks (Initial)

Assets		Liabilities	
Currency	1,000,000 guilders	Deposits	1,000,000 guilders

The *assets* of the commercial banking system in Gorgonzola are the paper guilders sitting in the vaults of all the individual banks. The banking system's *liabilities* are the deposits of the banks' customers since checking account balances represent money owed by the banks to the depositors.

bank reserves cash or similar assets held by commercial banks for the purpose of meeting depositor withdrawals and payments

Cash or similar assets held by banks are called **bank reserves.** In this example, bank reserves, for all the banks taken together, equal 1,000,000 guilders—the currency listed on the asset side of the consolidated balance sheet. Banks hold reserves to meet depositors' demands for cash withdrawals or to pay checks drawn on their depositors' accounts. In this example, the bank reserves of 1,000,000 guilders equal 100 percent of banks' deposits, which are also 1,000,000 guilders. A situation in which bank reserves equal 100 percent of bank deposits is called **100 percent reserve banking.**

100 percent reserve banking a situation in which banks' reserves equal 100 percent of their deposits

Bank reserves are held by banks in their vaults, rather than circulated among the public, and thus are *not* counted as part of the money supply. However, bank deposit balances, which can be used in making transactions, *are* counted as money. So, after the introduction of "safekeeper" banks in Gorgonzola, the money supply, equal to the value of bank deposits, is 1,000,000 guilders, which is the same as it was prior to the introduction of banks.

After a while, to continue the story, the commercial bankers of Gorgonzola begin to realize that keeping 100 percent reserves against deposits is not necessary. True, a few guilders flow in and out of the typical bank as depositors receive payments or write checks, but for the most part the stacks of paper guilders just sit there in the vaults, untouched and unused. It occurs to the bankers that they can meet the random inflow and outflow of guilders to their banks with reserves that are less than 100 percent of their deposits. After some observation, the bankers conclude that keeping reserves equal to only 10 percent of deposits is enough to meet the random ebb and flow of withdrawals and payments from their individual banks. The remaining 90 percent of deposits, the bankers realize, can be lent out to borrowers to earn interest.

So the bankers decide to keep reserves equal to 100,000 guilders, or 10 percent of their deposits. The other 900,000 guilders they lend out at interest to Gorgonzolan cheese producers who want to use the money to make improvements to their farms. After the loans are made, the balance sheet of all of Gorgonzola's commercial banks taken together has changed, as shown in Table 17.4.

TABLE 17.4
Consolidated Balance Sheet of Gorgonzolan Commercial Banks after One Round of Loans

Assets		Liabilities	
Currency (= reserves)	100,000 guilders	Deposits	1,000,000 guilders
Loans to farmers	900,000 guilders		

reserve-deposit ratio bank reserves divided by deposits

fractional-reserve banking system a banking system in which bank reserves are less than deposits so that the reserve-deposit ratio is less than 100 percent

After the loans are made, the banks' reserves of 100,000 guilders no longer equal 100 percent of the banks' deposits of 1,000,000 guilders. Instead, the **reserve-deposit ratio,** which is bank reserves divided by deposits, is now equal to 100,000/1,000,000, or 10 percent. A banking system in which banks hold fewer reserves than deposits so that the reserve-deposit ratio is less than 100 percent is called a **fractional-reserve banking system.**

Notice that 900,000 guilders have flowed out of the banking system (as loans to farmers) and are now in the hands of the public. But we have assumed that private citizens prefer bank deposits to cash for making transactions. So ultimately people will redeposit the 900,000 guilders in the banking system. After these deposits are made, the consolidated balance sheet of the commercial banks is as in Table 17.5.

TABLE 17.5
Consolidated Balance Sheet of Gorgonzolan Commercial Banks after Guilders Are Redeposited

Assets		Liabilities	
Currency (= reserves)	1,000,000 guilders	Deposits	1,900,000 guilders
Loans to farmers	900,000 guilders		

Notice that bank deposits, and hence the economy's money supply, now equal 1,900,000 guilders. In effect, the existence of the commercial banking system has permitted the creation of new money. These deposits, which are liabilities of the banks, are balanced by assets of 1,000,000 guilders in reserves and 900,000 guilders in loans owed to the banks.

The story does not end here. On examining their balance sheets, the bankers are surprised to see that they once again have "too many" reserves. With deposits of 1,900,000 guilders and a 10 percent reserve-deposit ratio, they need only 190,000 guilders in reserves. But they have 1,000,000 guilders in reserves—810,000 too many. Since lending out their excess guilders is always more profitable than leaving them in the vault, the bankers proceed to make another 810,000 guilders in loans. Eventually these loaned-out guilders are redeposited in the banking system, after which the consolidated balance sheet of the banks is as shown in Table 17.6.

TABLE 17.6
Consolidated Balance Sheet of Gorgonzolan Commercial Banks after Two Rounds of Loans and Redeposits

Assets		Liabilities	
Currency (= reserves)	1,000,000 guilders	Deposits	2,710,000 guilders
Loans to farmers	1,710,000 guilders		

Now the money supply has increased to 2,710,000 guilders, equal to the value of bank deposits. Despite the expansion of loans and deposits, however, the bankers find that their reserves of 1,000,000 guilders *still* exceed the desired level of 10 percent of deposits, which are 2,710,000 guilders. And so yet another round of lending will take place.

EXERCISE 17.3

Determine what the balance sheet of the banking system of Gorgonzola will look like after a third round of lending to farmers and redeposits of guilders into the commercial banking system. What is the money supply at that point?

The process of expansion of loans and deposits will only end when reserves equal 10 percent of bank deposits because as long as reserves exceed 10 percent of deposits, the banks will find it profitable to lend out the extra reserves. Since reserves at the end of every round equal 1,000,000 guilders, for the reserve-deposit ratio to equal 10 percent, total deposits must equal 10,000,000 guilders. Further, since the balance sheet must balance, with assets equal to liabilities, we know as well that at the end of the process, loans to cheese producers must equal 9,000,000 guilders. If loans equal 9,000,000 guilders, then bank assets, the sum of loans and reserves (1,000,000 guilders), will equal 10,000,000 guilders, which is the same as bank liabilities (bank deposits). The final consolidated balance sheet is as shown in Table 17.7.

TABLE 17.7
Final Consolidated Balance Sheet of Gorgonzolan Commercial Banks

Assets		Liabilities	
Currency (= reserves)	1,000,000 guilders	Deposits	10,000,000 guilders
Loans to farmers	9,000,000 guilders		

The money supply, which is equal to total deposits, is 10,000,000 guilders at the end of the process. We see that the existence of a fractional-reserve banking system has multiplied the money supply by a factor of 10, relative to the economy with no banks or the economy with 100 percent reserve banking. Put another way, with a 10 percent reserve-deposit ratio, each guilder deposited in the banking system can "support" 10 guilders worth of deposits.

To find the money supply in this example more directly, we observe that deposits will expand through additional rounds of lending as long as the ratio of bank reserves to bank deposits exceeds the reserve-deposit ratio desired by banks. When the actual ratio of bank reserves to deposits equals the desired reserve-deposit ratio, the expansion stops. So ultimately, deposits in the banking system satisfy the following relationship:

$$\frac{\text{Bank reserves}}{\text{Bank deposits}} = \text{Desired reserve-deposit ratio.}$$

This equation can be rewritten to solve for bank deposits:

$$\text{Bank deposits} = \frac{\text{Bank reserves}}{\text{Desired reserve-deposit ratio}}. \tag{17.1}$$

In Gorgonzola, since all the currency in the economy flows into the banking system, bank reserves equal 1,000,000 guilders. The reserve-deposit ratio desired by banks is 0.10. Therefore, using Equation 17.1, we find that bank deposits equal (1,000,000 guilders)/0.10, or 10 million guilders, the same answer we found in the consolidated balance sheet of the banks, Table 17.7.

EXERCISE 17.4

Find deposits and the money supply in Gorgonzola if the banks' desired reserve-deposit ratio is 5 percent rather than 10 percent. What if the total amount of currency circulated by the central bank is 2,000,000 guilders and the desired reserve-deposit ratio remains at 10 percent?

THE MONEY SUPPLY WITH BOTH CURRENCY AND DEPOSITS

In the example of Gorgonzola, we assumed that all money is held in the form of deposits in banks. In reality, of course, people keep only part of their money holdings in the form of bank accounts and hold the rest in the form of currency. Fortunately, allowing for the fact that people hold both currency and bank deposits does not greatly complicate the determination of the money supply, as the following example shows.

The money supply with both currency and deposits

Suppose that the citizens of Gorgonzola choose to hold a total of 500,000 guilders in the form of currency and to deposit the rest of their money in banks. Banks keep reserves equal to 10 percent of deposits. What is the money supply in Gorgonzola?

The money supply is the sum of currency in the hands of the public and bank deposits. Currency in the hands of the public is given as 500,000 guilders. What is the quantity of bank deposits? Since 500,000 of the 1,000,000 guilders issued by the central bank are being used by the public in the form of currency, only the remaining 500,000 guilders is available to serve as bank reserves. We know that deposits equal bank reserves divided by the reserve-deposit ratio, so deposits are 500,000 guilders/0.10 = 5,000,000 guilders. The total money supply is the sum of currency in the hands of the public (500,000 guilders) and bank deposits (5,000,000 guilders), or 5,500,000 guilders. ◆

We can write a general relationship that captures the reasoning of this example. First, let's write out the fact that the money supply equals currency plus bank deposits:

$$\text{Money supply} = \text{Currency held by the public} + \text{Bank deposits}.$$

We also know that bank deposits equal bank reserves divided by the reserve-deposit ratio that is desired by commercial banks (Equation 17.1). Using that relationship to substitute for bank deposits in the expression for the money supply, we get

$$\text{Money supply} = \text{Currency held by public} + \frac{\text{Bank reserves}}{\text{Desired reserve-deposit ratio}}. \qquad (17.2)$$

We can use Equation 17.2 to confirm our reasoning in the previous example. In that example, currency held by the public is 500,000 guilders, bank reserves are 500,000 guilders, and the desired reserve-deposit ratio is 0.10. Plugging these values into Equation 17.2, we get that the money supply equals 500,000 + 500,000/0.10 = 5,500,000, the same answer we found before.

The money supply at Christmas

During the Christmas season, people choose to hold unusually large amounts of currency for shopping. With no action by the central bank, how would this change in currency holding affect the national money supply?

To illustrate with a numerical example, suppose that initially bank reserves are 500, the amount of currency held by the public is 500, and the desired reserve-deposit ratio in the banking system is 0.2. Inserting these values into Equation 17.2, we find that the money supply equals 500 + 500/0.2 = 3,000.

Now suppose that because of Christmas shopping needs, the public increases its currency holdings to 600 by withdrawing 100 from commercial banks. These withdrawals reduce bank reserves to 400. Using Equation 17.2, we find now that the money supply is 600 + 400/0.2 = 2,600. So the public's increased holdings of currency have caused the money supply to drop, from 3,000 to 2,600. The reason for the drop is that with a reserve-deposit ratio of 20 percent, every dollar in the vaults of banks can "support" $5 of deposits and hence $5 of money supply. However, the same dollar in the hands of the public becomes $1 of currency, contributing only $1 to the total money supply. So when the public withdraws cash from the banks, the overall money supply declines. (We will see in the next section, however, that in practice the central bank has means to offset the impact of the public's actions on the money supply.) ◆

RECAP	COMMERCIAL BANKS AND THE CREATION OF MONEY

- Part of the money supply consists of deposits in private commercial banks. Hence, the behavior of commercial banks and their depositors helps to determine the money supply.

- Cash or similar assets held by banks are called *bank reserves*. In modern economies, banks' reserves are less than their deposits, a situation called *fractional-reserve banking*. The ratio of bank reserves to deposits is called the *reserve-deposit ratio;* in a fractional-reserve banking system, this ratio is less than 1.
- The portion of deposits not held as reserves can be lent out by the banks to earn interest. Banks will continue to make loans and accept deposits as long as the reserve-deposit ratio exceeds its desired level. This process stops only when the actual and desired reserve-deposit ratios are equal. At that point, total bank deposits equal bank reserves divided by the desired reserve-deposit ratio, and the money supply equals the currency held by the public plus bank deposits.

CENTRAL BANKS, THE MONEY SUPPLY, AND PRICES

Federal Reserve System (or Fed) the central bank of the United States

The **Federal Reserve System** is one of the most important agencies of the federal government. The Fed, as it is referred to in the press, is the central bank of the United States. Central banks in general have two main responsibilities. First, they are responsible for monetary policy, which means that a country's central bank determines how much money circulates in the economy. Second, along with other government agencies, the central bank has important responsibilities for the oversight and regulation of financial markets. In particular, central banks play important roles during periods of crisis in financial markets.

In Chapter 20, we will review the history and structure of the Fed and analyze how the Fed's actions affect the U.S. economy during financial crises and recessions. In this chapter, we will focus on how a central bank can control the money supply and how changes in the money supply affect the price level and the rate of inflation in the long run.

CONTROLLING THE MONEY SUPPLY WITH OPEN-MARKET OPERATIONS

A central bank's primary responsibility is making monetary policy, which involves decisions about the appropriate size of the nation's money supply. As we saw in the previous section, central banks in general, and the Fed in particular, do not control the money supply directly. Nevertheless, they can control the money supply indirectly in several ways. In this chapter we discuss the most important of these, called *open-market operations*. In Chapter 20, we discuss two other methods the Fed can use to change the money supply: lending at the discount window and changing reserve requirements.

Suppose that the Fed wants to increase bank reserves, with the ultimate goal of increasing bank deposits and the money supply. To accomplish this, the Fed buys financial assets, usually government bonds, from the public. To simplify the actual procedure a bit, think of the Fed as buying bonds that the public had originally purchased from the government and paying the public for these bonds with newly printed money.

Assuming that the public is already holding all the currency that it wants, they will deposit the cash they receive as payment for their bonds in commercial banks. Thus, the reserves of the commercial banking system will increase by an amount equal to the value of the bonds purchased by the Fed. The increase in bank reserves will lead in turn, through the process of lending and redeposit of funds described in the previous section, to an expansion of bank deposits and the money supply, as summarized by Equation 17.2. The Fed's purchase of government bonds from the public, with the result that bank reserves and the money supply are increased, is called an **open-market purchase.**

open-market purchase the purchase of government bonds from the public by the Fed for the purpose of increasing the supply of bank reserves and the money supply

To reduce bank reserves and hence the money supply, the Fed reverses the procedure. It sells some of the government bonds that it holds (acquired in previous open-market purchases) to the public. Assume that the public pays for the bonds by writing checks on their accounts in commercial banks. Then, when the Fed presents the checks to the commercial banks for payment, reserves equal in value to the government bonds sold by the Fed are transferred from the commercial banks to the Fed. The Fed retires these reserves from circulation, lowering the supply of bank reserves and, hence, the overall money supply. The sale of government bonds by the Fed to the public for the purpose of reducing bank reserves and hence the money supply is called an **open-market sale.** Open-market purchases and sales together are called **open-market operations.** Open-market operations are the most convenient and flexible tool that the Federal Reserve has for affecting the money supply and are employed on a regular basis.

open-market sale the sale by the Fed of government bonds to the public for the purpose of reducing bank reserves and the money supply

open-market operations open-market purchases and open-market sales

Increasing the money supply by open-market operations

In a particular economy, currency held by the public is 1,000 shekels, bank reserves are 200 shekels, and the desired reserve-deposit ratio is 0.2. What is the money supply? How is the money supply affected if the central bank prints 100 shekels and uses this new currency to buy government bonds from the public? Assume that the public does not wish to change the amount of currency it holds.

As bank reserves are 200 shekels and the reserve-deposit ratio is 0.2, bank deposits must equal 200 shekels/0.2, or 1,000 shekels. The money supply, equal to the sum of currency held by the public and bank deposits, is therefore 2,000 shekels, a result you can confirm using Equation 17.2.

The open-market purchase puts 100 more shekels into the hands of the public. We assume that the public continues to want to hold 1,000 shekels in currency, so they will deposit the additional 100 shekels in the commercial banking system, raising bank reserves from 200 to 300 shekels. As the desired reserve-deposit ratio is 0.2, multiple rounds of lending and redeposit will eventually raise the level of bank deposits to 300 shekels/0.2, or 1,500 shekels. The money supply, equal to 1,000 shekels held by the public plus bank deposits of 1,500 shekels, equals 2,500 shekels. So the open-market purchase of 100 shekels, by raising bank reserves by 100 shekels, has increased the money supply by 500 shekels. Again, you can confirm this result using Equation 17.2. ◆

EXERCISE 17.5

Continuing the above example, suppose that instead of an open-market purchase of 100 shekels, the central bank conducts an open-market sale of 50 shekels' worth of government bonds. What happens to bank reserves, bank deposits, and the money supply?

MONEY AND PRICES

From a macroeconomic perspective, a major reason that control of the supply of money is important is that, *in the long run, the amount of money circulating in an economy and the general level of prices are closely linked.* Indeed, it is virtually unheard of for a country to experience high, sustained inflation without a comparably rapid growth in the amount of money held by its citizens. For instance, the link between money growth and inflation for nine countries in Latin America during the period 1995–2007 is illustrated in Figure 17.1. Although the relationship is somewhat loose, countries with higher rates of money growth clearly tend to have higher rates of inflation, and this relationship has been found in other countries and in other periods. The economist Milton Friedman summarized the inflation–money relationship by saying, "Inflation is always and everywhere a monetary phenomenon." We will see later that, over short periods, inflation can arise from sources other than an increase in the supply of money. But over a longer period, and particularly for more severe inflations, Friedman's dictum is certainly correct: The rate of inflation and the rate of growth of the money supply are closely related.

FIGURE 17.1
Inflation and Money Growth in Latin America, 1995–2007.
Latin American countries with higher rates of growth in their money supplies also tended to have higher rates of inflation between 1995 and 2007.

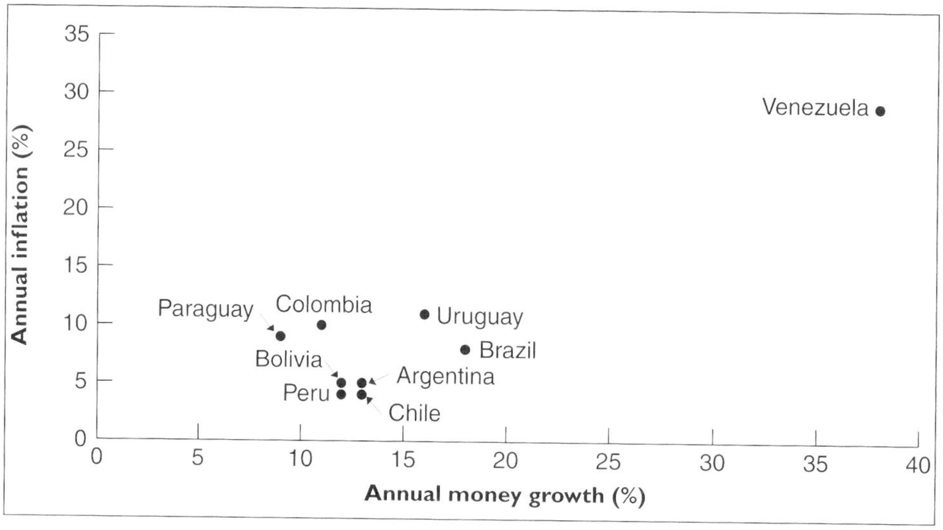

SOURCE: WorldBank, World Development Indicators.

The existence of a close link between money supply and prices should make intuitive sense. Imagine a situation in which the available supply of goods and services is approximately fixed. Then the more cash (say, dollars) that people hold, the more they will be able to bid up the prices of the fixed supply of goods and services. Thus, a large money supply relative to the supply of goods and services (too much money chasing too few goods) tends to result in high prices. Likewise, a rapidly *growing* supply of money will lead to quickly *rising* prices—that is, inflation.

VELOCITY

velocity a measure of the speed at which money changes hands in transactions involving final goods and services, or, equivalently, nominal GDP divided by the stock of money. Numerically, $V = (P \times Y)/M$, where V is velocity, $P \times Y$ is nominal GDP, and M is the money supply whose velocity is being measured

To explore the relationship of money growth and inflation in a bit more detail, it is useful to introduce the concept of *velocity*. In economics, **velocity** is a measure of the speed at which money changes hands in transactions involving final goods and services. For example, a given dollar bill might pass from your hand to the grocer's when you buy a quart of milk. The same dollar may then pass from the grocer to a new car dealer when your grocer buys a car, and then from the car dealer to her doctor in exchange for medical services. The more quickly money circulates from one person to the next, the higher its velocity. More formally, velocity is defined as the number of times per year the typical dollar in the money supply is used to buy final goods or services, according to the following formula:

$$\text{Velocity} = \frac{\text{Nominal GDP}}{\text{Money stock}}.$$

Let V stand for velocity and let M stand for the particular money stock being considered (for example, M1 or M2). Nominal GDP (a measure of the total value of transactions) equals the price level P times real GDP (Y). Using this notation, we can write the definition of velocity as

$$V = \frac{P \times Y}{M}. \tag{17.3}$$

The higher this ratio, the faster the "typical" dollar is circulating.

The velocity of money in the U.S. economy

In the United States in 2007, M1 was \$1,364.2 billion, M2 was \$7,447.1 billion, and nominal GDP was \$13,843.0 billion. We can use these data along with Equation 17.3 to find velocity for both definitions of the money supply. For M1, we have

$$V = \frac{\$13{,}843.0 \text{ billion}}{\$1{,}364.2 \text{ billion}} = 10.15$$

Similarly, velocity for M2 was

$$V = \frac{\$13{,}843.0 \text{ billion}}{\$7{,}447.1 \text{ billion}} = 1.86$$

You can see that the velocity of M1 is higher than that of M2. This makes sense: Because the components of M1, such as cash and checking accounts, are used more frequently for transactions, each dollar of M1 "turns over" more often than the average dollar of M2. ◆

A variety of factors determine velocity. A leading example is advances in payment technologies such as the introduction of credit cards and debit cards or the creation of networks of automatic teller machines (ATMs). These new technologies and payment methods have allowed people to carry out their daily business while holding less cash, and thus have tended to increase velocity over time.

MONEY AND INFLATION IN THE LONG RUN

We can use the definition of velocity to see how money and prices are related in the long run. First, rewrite the definition of velocity, Equation 17.3, by multiplying both sides of the equation by the money stock M. This yields

$$M \times V = P \times Y. \tag{17.4}$$

Equation 17.4 is called, for historical reasons, the *quantity equation*. The **quantity equation** states that money times velocity equals nominal GDP. Because the quantity equation is simply a rewriting of the definition of velocity, Equation 17.3, it always holds exactly.

quantity equation money times velocity equals nominal GDP; $M \times V = P \times Y$

The quantity equation is historically important because late nineteenth and early twentieth-century monetary economists used this relationship to theorize about the relationship between money and prices. We can do the same thing here. To keep things simple, imagine that velocity V is determined by current payment technologies and thus is approximately constant over the period we are considering.

Likewise, suppose that real output Y is approximately constant. If we use a bar over a variable to indicate that the variable is constant, we can rewrite the quantity equation as

$$M \times \overline{V} = P \times \overline{Y}, \tag{17.5}$$

where we are treating $\overline{V}$ and $\overline{Y}$ as fixed numbers.

Now look at Equation 17.5 and imagine that for some reason the Federal Reserve increases the money supply M by 10 percent. Because $\overline{V}$ and $\overline{Y}$ are assumed to be fixed, Equation 17.5 can continue to hold only if the price level P also rises by 10 percent. That is, according to the quantity equation, a 10 percent increase in the money supply M should cause a 10 percent increase in the price level P, that is, an inflation of 10 percent.

The intuition behind this conclusion is the one we mentioned at the beginning of this section. If the quantity of goods and services Y is approximately constant (and assuming that velocity V also is constant), an increase in the supply of money will lead people to bid up the prices of the available goods and services. Thus, high rates of money growth will tend to be associated with high rates of inflation, which is exactly what we observed in Figure 17.1.

EN 17

If high rates of money growth lead to inflation, why do countries allow their money supplies to rise quickly? Usually, rapid rates of money growth are the result of large government budget deficits. Particularly in developing countries or countries suffering from war or political instability, governments sometimes find that they cannot raise sufficient taxes or borrow enough from the public to cover their expenditures. In this situation, the government's only recourse may be to print new money and use this money to pay its bills. If the resulting increase in the amount of money in circulation is large enough, the result will be inflation.

RECAP	CENTRAL BANKS, THE MONEY SUPPLY, AND PRICES

- Central banks control the money supply through open-market operations. Open-market purchases increase the money supply while open-market sales decrease the money supply.
- A high rate of money growth generally leads to inflation. The larger the amount of money in circulation, the higher the public will bid up the prices of available goods and services.
- *Velocity* measures the speed at which money circulates in payments for final goods and services; equivalently it is equal to nominal GDP divided by the stock of money. A numerical value for velocity can be obtained from the equation $V = (P \times Y)/M$, where V is velocity, $P \times Y$ is nominal GDP, and M is the money supply.
- The *quantity equation* states that money times velocity equals nominal GDP, or, in symbols, $M \times V = P \times Y$. The quantity equation is a restatement of the definition of velocity and thus always holds. If velocity and output are approximately constant, the quantity equation implies that a given percentage increase in the money supply leads to the same percentage increase in the price level. In other words, the rate of growth of the money supply equals the rate of inflation.

BOX 17.1: APPROXIMATING THE PERCENTAGE CHANGE OF A PRODUCT

In Equation 17.5, we assumed that V and Y were constant and showed that the percentage change in M would then equal the rate of inflation, which is the percentage change in P. If V and Y are not constant, one can still make some interesting inferences about the connection between changes in the money stock and inflation. According to the quantity equation (Equation 17.4) $M \times V = P \times Y$. Since this relationship is always true by definition, it is an identity. Consequently, any time the left-hand side $M \times V$ changes by a specific amount or by a specific percentage, the right-hand side $P \times Y$ must change by the same amount or by the same percentage. Thus:

$$\% \text{ change in } M \times V = \% \text{ change in } P \times Y. \quad (17.6)$$

Economists often use a simple approximation to disaggregate the percentage changes in Equation 17.6. The percentage change in the product of two (or more) variables is approximately equal to the sum of the percentage changes in each of the variables, as long as those percentage changes are relatively small. Using this approximation, we can rewrite Equation 17.6 as

$$\% \text{ change in } M + \% \text{ change in } V \approx \% \text{ change in } P + \% \text{ change in } Y, \quad (17.7)$$

where the mathematical symbol $\approx$ means "is approximately equal to."

Suppose, for example, the money supply M grows by 4 percent per year, velocity V grows by 1 percent per year, and real GDP Y grows by 3 percent per year. If we insert these values into Equation 17.7, we obtain

$$4\% + 1\% \approx \% \text{ change in } P + 3\%.$$

We can solve this to obtain the approximate rate of inflation:

$$\% \text{ change in } P \approx 4\% + 1\% - 3\% = 2\%.$$

Indeed, whenever any three percentage changes in Equation 17.7 are known, one can use Equation 17.7 to solve for the fourth percentage change. Economists use this "percentage change rule" in a variety of applications.

SUMMARY

- The U.S. banking system consists of thousands of commercial banks that accept deposits from individuals and businesses and use those deposits to make loans. Banks are the most important example of a class of institutions called financial intermediaries. Financial intermediaries develop expertise in evaluating prospective borrowers, making it unnecessary for small savers to do that on their own. **LO1**

- Governments and corporations can also obtain financing by issuing bonds or stocks. A bond is a legal promise to repay a debt, including both the principal amount and regular interest or coupon payments. The prices of existing bonds decline when interest rates rise. A share of stock is a claim to partial ownership of a firm. The price of a stock depends positively on the dividend the stock is expected to pay and on the expected future price of the stock and negatively on the rate of return required by financial investors to hold the stock. The required rate of return in turn is the sum of the return on safe assets and the additional return required to compensate financial investors for the riskiness of stocks, called the risk premium. **LO2**

- The financial system, consisting of banks, bond markets, and stock markets, improves the allocation of saving in two ways. First, it provides information to savers about which of the many possible uses of their funds are likely to prove most productive, and hence pay the highest return. Second, financial markets help savers share the risks of lending by permitting them to diversify their financial investments. **LO3**

- Money is any asset that can be used in making purchases. Money has three main functions: as a medium of exchange, as a unit of account, and as a store of value. In practice, it is difficult to measure the money supply since many assets have some money-like features. A relatively narrow measure of money is M1, which includes currency and checking accounts. A broader measure of money, M2, includes all the assets in M1 plus additional assets that are somewhat less convenient to use in transactions than those included in M1. **LO4**
- Because bank deposits are part of the money supply, the behavior of commercial banks and of bank depositors affects the amount of money in the economy. Specifically, commercial banks create money through multiple rounds of lending and accepting deposits. The money supply equals currency held by the public plus deposits in the banking system. **LO5**
- The central bank of the United States is called the Federal Reserve System, or the Fed for short. The Fed can affect the money supply indirectly in several ways. In the most important of these, called open-market operations, the Fed buys or sells government securities in exchange for currency held by banks or the public. **LO6**
- Control of the money supply is important in the long run because the rate of growth of the money supply and the rate of inflation are closely linked. In particular, the quantity equation can be used to show that under certain conditions, a given percentage increase in the money supply will lead to the same percentage increase in the price level. **LO6**

KEY TERMS

bank reserves (489)
barter (486)
bond (478)
coupon payments (478)
coupon rate (478)
diversification (483)
dividend (480)
Federal Reserve System (the Fed) (494)
financial intermediaries (476)
fractional-reserve banking system (490)
M1 (487)
M2 (487)
maturation date (478)
medium of exchange (486)
money (485)
mutual fund (485)
100 percent reserve banking (489)
open-market operations (495)
open-market purchase (495)
open-market sale (495)
principal amount (478)
quantity equation (497)
reserve-deposit ratio (490)
risk premium (482)
stock (or equity) (480)
store of value (486)
unit of account (486)
velocity (486)

REVIEW QUESTIONS

1. Arjay plans to sell a bond that matures in one year and has a principal value of $1,000. Can he expect to receive $1,000 in the bond market for the bond? Explain. **LO2**
2. Stock prices surge, but the prices of government bonds remain stable. What can you infer from the behavior of bond prices about the possible causes of the increase in stock values? **LO2**
3. Give two ways that the financial system helps to improve the allocation of savings. Illustrate with examples. **LO3**
4. What is money? Why do people hold money even though it pays a lower return than other financial assets? **LO4**
5. Suppose that the public switches from doing most of its shopping with currency to using checks instead. If the Fed takes no action, what will happen to the national money supply? Explain. **LO1, LO5**
6. The Fed wants to reduce the U.S. money supply. Describe what it would do, and explain how this action would accomplish the Fed's objective. **LO6**
7. Use the quantity equation to explain why money growth and inflation tend to be closely linked. **LO6**

■ PROBLEMS ■

McGraw-Hill's HOMEWORK MANAGER®

1. Simon purchases a bond, newly issued by the Amalgamated Corporation, for \$1,000. The bond pays \$60 to its holder at the end of the first and second years and pays \$1,060 upon its maturity at the end of the third year. **LO2**
   a. What are the principal amount, the term, the coupon rate, and the coupon payment for Simon's bond?
   b. After receiving the second coupon payment (at the end of the second year), Simon decides to sell his bond in the bond market. What price can he expect for his bond if the one-year interest rate at that time is 3 percent? 8 percent? 10 percent?
   c. Can you think of a reason that the price of Simon's bond after two years might fall below \$1,000, even though the market interest rate equals the coupon rate?

2. Shares in Brothers Grimm, Inc., manufacturers of gingerbread houses, are expected to pay a dividend of \$5.00 in one year and to sell for \$100 per share at that time. How much should you be willing to pay today per share of Grimm: **LO2**
   a. If the safe rate of interest is 5 percent and you believe that investing in Grimm carries no risk?
   b. If the safe rate of interest is 10 percent and you believe that investing in Grimm carries no risk?
   c. If the safe rate of interest is 5 percent, but your risk premium is 3 percent?
   d. Repeat parts a to c, assuming that Grimm is not expected to pay a dividend, but the expected price is unchanged.

3. Your financial investments consist of U.S. government bonds maturing in 10 years and shares in a start-up company doing research in pharmaceuticals. How would you expect each of the following news items to affect the value of your assets? Explain your reasoning. **LO2**
   a. Interest rates of newly issued government bonds rise.
   b. Inflation is forecasted to be much lower than previously expected (*Hint:* Recall the Fisher effect from Chapter 13.) Assume for simplicity that this information does *not* affect your forecast of the dollar value of the pharmaceutical company's future dividends and stock price.

   In parts c to f, interest rates on newly issued government bonds are assumed to remain unchanged.
   c. Large swings in the stock market increase financial investors' concerns about market risk.
   d. The start-up company whose stock you own announces the development of a valuable new drug. However, the drug will not come to market for at least five years.
   e. The pharmaceutical company announces that it will not pay a dividend next year.
   f. The federal government announces a system of price controls on prescription drugs.

4. You have \$1,000 to invest and are considering buying some combination of the shares of two companies, DonkeyInc and ElephantInc. Shares of DonkeyInc will pay a 10 percent return if the Democrats are elected, an event you believe to have a 40 percent probability; otherwise the shares pay a zero return. Shares of ElephantInc will pay 8 percent if the Republicans are elected (a 60 percent probability), zero otherwise. Either the Democrats or the Republicans will be elected. **LO2, LO3**
   a. If your only concern is maximizing your average expected return, with no regard for risk, how should you invest your \$1,000?

b. What is your expected return if you invest \$500 in each stock? (*Hint:* Consider what your return will be if the Democrats win and if the Republicans win, then weight each outcome by the probability that event occurs.)
c. The strategy of investing \$500 in each stock does *not* give the highest possible average expected return. Why might you choose it anyway?
d. Devise an investment strategy that guarantees at least a 4.4 percent return, no matter which party wins.
e. Devise an investment strategy that is riskless, that is, one in which the return on your \$1,000 does not depend at all on which party wins.

5. During World War II, an Allied soldier named Robert Radford spent several years in a large German prisoner-of-war camp. At times more than 50,000 prisoners were held in the camp, with some freedom to move about within the compound. Radford later wrote an account of his experiences. He described how an economy developed in the camp, in which prisoners traded food, clothing, and other items. Services such as barbering also were exchanged. Lacking paper money, the prisoners began to use cigarettes (provided monthly by the Red Cross) as money. Prices were quoted, and payments made, using cigarettes. **LO4**
   a. In Radford's POW camp, how did cigarettes fulfill the three functions of money?
   b. Why do you think the prisoners used cigarettes as money, as opposed to other items of value such as squares of chocolate or pairs of boots?
   c. Do you think a nonsmoking prisoner would have been willing to accept cigarettes in exchange for a good or service in Radford's camp? Why or why not?

6. Redo the example of Gorgonzola in the text (see Tables 17.3 to 17.7), assuming that (*a*) initially, the Gorgonzolan central bank puts 5,000,000 guilders into circulation and (*b*) commercial banks desire to hold reserves of 20 percent of deposits. As in the text, assume that the public holds no currency. Show the consolidated balance sheets of Gorgonzolan commercial banks after the initial deposits (compare to Table 17.3), after one round of loans (compare to Table 17.4), after the first redeposit of guilders (compare to Table 17.5), and after two rounds of loans and redeposits (compare to Table 17.6). What are the final values of bank reserves, loans, deposits, and the money supply? **LO5**

7. Answer each of the following questions. **LO5**
   a. Bank reserves are 100, the public holds 200 in currency, and the desired reserve-deposit ratio is 0.25. Find deposits and the money supply.
   b. The money supply is 500 and currency held by the public equals bank reserves. The desired reserve-deposit ratio is 0.25. Find currency held by the public and bank reserves.
   c. The money supply is 1,250, of which 250 is currency held by the public. Bank reserves are 100. Find the desired reserve-deposit ratio.

8. When a central bank increases bank reserves by \$1, the money supply rises by more than \$1. The amount of extra money created when the central bank increases bank reserves by \$1 is called the *money multiplier.* **LO6**
   a. Explain why the money multiplier is generally greater than 1. In what special case would it equal 1?
   b. The initial money supply is \$1,000, of which \$500 is currency held by the public. The desired reserve-deposit ratio is 0.2. Find the increase in money supply associated with increases in bank reserves of \$1, \$5, and \$10. What is the money multiplier in this economy?
   c. Find a general rule for calculating the money multiplier.
   d. Suppose the Fed wanted to reduce the money multiplier, perhaps because it believes that change would give it more precise control over the money supply. What action could the Fed take to achieve its goal?

9. Consider a country in which real GDP is \$8 trillion, nominal GDP is \$10 trillion, M1 is \$2 trillion, and M2 is \$5 trillion. **LO6**
   a. Find velocity for M1 and for M2.
   b. Show that the quantity equation holds for both M1 and M2.

10. You are given the following hypothetical data for 2007 and 2008: **LO6**

	2007	2008
Money supply	1,000	1,050
Velocity	8.0	8.0
Real GDP	12,000	12,000

   a. Find the price level for 2007 and 2008. What is the rate of inflation between the two years?
   b. What is the rate of inflation between 2007 and 2008 if the money supply in 2008 is 1,100 instead of 1,050?
   c. What is the rate of inflation between 2007 and 2008 if the money supply in 2008 is 1,100 and output is 2008 is 12,600?

ANSWERS TO IN-CHAPTER EXERCISES

17.1 Since bond prices fell, interest rates must have risen. To find the interest rate, note that bond investors are willing to pay only \$960 today for a bond that will pay back \$1,070 (a coupon payment of \$70 plus the principal amount of \$1,000) in one year. To find the one-year return, divide \$1,070 by \$960 to get 1.115. Thus, the interest rate must have risen to 11.5 percent. **LO2**

17.2 The share of stock will be worth \$81.00 in one year—the sum of its expected future price and the expected dividend. At an interest rate of 4 percent, its value today is \$81.00/1.04 = \$77.88. At an interest rate of 8 percent, the stock's current value is \$81.00/1.08 = 75.00. Recall from the example above that when the interest rate is 6 percent, the value of a share of FortuneCookie.com is \$76.42. Since higher interest rates imply lower stock values, news that interest rates are about to rise should cause the stock market to fall. **LO2**

17.3 Table 17.6 shows the balance sheet of banks after two rounds of lending and redeposits. At that point, deposits are 2,710,000 guilders and reserves are 1,000,000 guilders. Since banks have a desired reserve-deposit ratio of 10 percent, they will keep 271,000 guilders (10 percent of deposits) as reserves and lend out the remaining 729,000 guilders. Loans to farmers are now 2,439,000 guilders. Eventually the 729,000 guilders lent to the farmers will be redeposited into the banks, giving the banks deposits of 3,439,000 guilders and reserves of 1,000,000 guilders. The balance sheet is as shown in the accompanying table.

Assets		Liabilities	
Currency (= reserves)	1,000,000 guilders	Deposits	3,439,000 guilders
Loans to farmers	2,439,000 guilders		

Notice that assets equal liabilities. The money supply equals deposits, or 3,439,000 guilders. Currency held in the banks as reserves does not count in the money supply. **LO5**

17.4 Because the public holds no currency, the money supply equals bank deposits, which in turn equal bank reserves divided by the reserve-deposit ratio (Equation 17.1). If bank reserves are 1,000,000 and the reserve-deposit ratio is 0.05, then deposits equal 20,000,000 guilders, which is also the money supply. If bank reserves are 2,000,000 guilders and the reserve-deposit ratio is 0.10, then the money supply and deposits are again equal to 20,000,000 guilders, or 2,000,000/0.10. **LO5**

17.5 If the central bank sells 50 shekels of government bonds in exchange for currency, the immediate effect is to reduce the amount of currency in the hands of the public by 50 shekels. To restore their currency holding to the desired level of 1,000 shekels, the public will withdraw 50 shekels from commercial banks, reducing bank reserves from 200 shekels to 150 shekels. The desired reserve-deposit ratio is 0.2, so ultimately deposits must equal 150 shekels in reserves divided by 0.2, or 750 shekels. (Note that to reduce their deposits, the commercial banks will have to "call in" loans, reducing their loans outstanding.) The money supply equals 1,000 shekels in currency held by the public plus 750 shekels in deposits, or 1,750 shekels. Thus, the open-market purchase has reduced the money supply from 2,000 to 1,750 shekels. **LO6**

PART 7

THE ECONOMY IN THE SHORT RUN

A sign in Redwood City, California, boasts that the Bay Area town has the world's best climate. Redwood City's mean annual temperature and rainfall are similar to that of many other U.S. cities, so on what basis do Redwood City's boosters make their claim? The weather in Redwood City is attractive to many people because it varies so little over the year, being almost equally comfortable in winter and in summer. A city with the same average yearly temperature as Redwood City, but where the winters are freezing and the summers unbearably hot, would not be nearly so pleasant a place to live.

An analogous idea applies to the performance of the economy. As we saw, over a period of decades or more, the economy's average rate of growth is the crucial determinant of average living standards. But short-term fluctuations of the economy's growth rate around its long-run average matter for economic welfare as well. In particular, periods of slow or negative economic growth, known as *recessions,* may create significant economic hardship and dissatisfaction. In Part 7 we will explore the causes of short-term fluctuations in key economic variables, including output, unemployment, and inflation, and we will discuss the options available to government policymakers for stabilizing the economy.

Chapter 18 provides some necessary background for our study of short-term fluctuations by describing their key characteristics and reviewing the historical record of fluctuations in the U.S. economy. In Chapters 19 through 21, we develop a framework for the analysis of short-term fluctuations and the alternative policy responses. Chapter 19 shows how fluctuations in aggregate spending may lead to short-run fluctuations in output and employment. That chapter also explains how changes in fiscal policy—policies relating to government spending and taxation—can be used to stabilize spending and output. Chapter 20 focuses on monetary policy, a second tool for stabilizing output and employment.

Chapter 21 incorporates inflation into the analysis, discussing both the sources of inflation and the policies that can be used to control it. Chapter 21 also discusses the practices and pitfalls of macroeconomic policymaking in more detail.

CHAPTER

18

Short-Term Economic Fluctuations

LEARNING OBJECTIVES

After reading this chapter, you should be able to:

1. Identify the four phases of the business cycle.
2. Explain the primary characteristics of recessions and expansions.
3. Define potential output, measure the output gap, and use these concepts to analyze an economy's position in the business cycle.
4. Define the natural rate of unemployment and show how it is related to cyclical unemployment.
5. Use Okun's law to analyze the relationship between the output gap and cyclical unemployment.
6. Discuss the basic differences between how the economy operates in the short run versus the long run.

In early 1991, following the defeat of Iraq in the Gulf War by the United States and its allies, polls showed that 90 percent of the American public approved of the job George H. W. Bush was doing as president. The Gulf War victory followed a number of other popular developments in the foreign policy sphere, including the ouster of the corrupt leader General Manuel Noriega from Panama in December 1989; improved relations with China; apparent progress in Middle East peace talks; and the end of apartheid in South Africa. The collapse of the Soviet Union in December 1991—a stunning event that signaled the end of the Cold War—also occurred during Bush's term. Yet despite these political pluses, in the months following the Gulf War, Bush's sky-high approval rating declined sharply. According to one poll, by the time of the Republican national convention in the summer of 1992, only 29 percent of the public approved of Bush's performance. Although the president's ratings improved during the campaign, Bush and his running mate, Dan Quayle, lost the 1992 general election to Bill Clinton and Al Gore, receiving only 39 million of the 104 million votes cast. A third-party candidate, Ross Perot, received nearly 20 million votes.

What caused this turnaround in (the first) President Bush's political fortunes? Despite his high marks from voters in foreign policy, the president's domestic economic policies were widely viewed as ineffective. Bush received much criticism for breaking his campaign pledge not to raise taxes. More important, the economy weakened significantly in 1990–1991, then recovered only slowly. Although inflation was low, by mid-1992 unemployment had reached 7.8 percent of the labor force—2.5 percentage points higher than in the first year of Bush's term, and the highest level since 1984. A sign in Democratic candidate Bill Clinton's campaign headquarters summarized Clinton's strategy for winning the White House: "It's the economy, stupid." Clinton realized the importance of the nation's economic problems and pounded away at the Republican administration's inability to pull the country out of the doldrums. Clinton's focus on the economy was the key to his election.

Clinton's ability to parlay criticism of economic conditions into electoral success is not unusual in U.S. political history. Weakness in the economy played a decisive role in helping Franklin D. Roosevelt to beat Herbert Hoover in 1932, John F. Kennedy to best Richard Nixon in 1960, and Ronald Reagan to defeat Jimmy Carter in 1980. President George W. Bush found the political popularity he enjoyed after ousting the Taliban from Afghanistan in 2001 eroded by an economic downturn and a slow subsequent recovery—although, unlike his father, he succeeded in winning reelection. On the other hand, strong economic conditions often have helped incumbent presidents (or the incumbent's party) to retain office, including Nixon in 1972, Reagan in 1984, and Clinton in 1996. Indeed, a number of empirical studies have suggested that economic performance in the year preceding the election is among the most important determinants of whether an incumbent president is likely to win reelection.

Herbert Hoover © Bettman/CORBIS

Jimmy Carter © Bettman/CORBIS

George Bush © Wally McNamee/CORBIS

Victims of recession.

In the preceding part of the book, we discussed the factors that determine long-run economic growth. Over the broad sweep of history, those factors determine the economic success of a society. Indeed, over a span of 30, 50, or 100 years, relatively small differences in the rate of economic growth can have an enormous effect on the average person's standard of living. But even though the economic "climate" (long-run economic conditions) is the ultimate determinant of living standards, changes in the economic "weather" (short-run fluctuations in economic conditions) are also important. A good long-run growth record is not much consolation to a worker who has lost her job due to a recession. The bearing that short-term macroeconomic performance has on election results is one indicator of the importance the average person attaches to it.

In this part of the book, we study short-term fluctuations in economic activity, commonly known as *recessions* and *expansions*. We will start, in this chapter, with some background on the history and characteristics of these economic ups and downs. However, the main focus of this part is the *causes* of short-term fluctuations, as well as the available *policy responses*. Because the analysis of short-term economic fluctuations can become complex and even controversial, we will proceed in a step-by-step fashion. In this chapter we will introduce a basic—and oversimplified—model of booms and recessions, which we will refer to as the *basic Keynesian model* in honor of its principal originator, the British economist John Maynard Keynes. The basic Keynesian model focuses on the components of aggregate spending, such as consumption spending by households and investment spending by firms, and the effects of changes in spending on total real GDP.

Though this model is a useful starting point, it does not address some key issues. First, and perhaps most important, the basic Keynesian model has little to say about the determinants of inflation. Second, because it focuses on the very short run, this model does not give adequate attention to the economy's own natural tendency to eliminate deviations from full employment over the longer run. Because the basic Keynesian model does not take into account the "self-correcting" tendencies of the economy, it tends to overstate the need for government intervention to offset fluctuations.

RECESSIONS AND EXPANSIONS

As background to the study of short-term economic fluctuations, let's review the historical record of fluctuations in the U.S. economy. Figure 18.1 shows the path of real GDP in the United States since 1929. As you can see, the growth path of real GDP is not always smooth; the bumps and wiggles correspond to short periods of faster or slower growth.

A period in which the economy is growing at a rate significantly below normal is called a **recession** or a *contraction*. An extremely severe or protracted recession is called a **depression.** You should be able to pick out the Great Depression in Figure 18.1, particularly the sharp initial decline between 1929 and 1933. But you also can see that the U.S. economy was volatile in the mid-1970s and the early 1980s, with serious recessions in 1973–1975 and 1981–1982. A moderate recession (but not moderate enough for the first President Bush) occurred in 1990–1991. The next recession did not begin for another 10 years, the longest period without a recession in U.S. history. It, too, was short and relatively mild, beginning in March 2001 and ending eight months later.

recession (or contraction) a period in which the economy is growing at a rate significantly below normal

depression a particularly severe or protracted recession

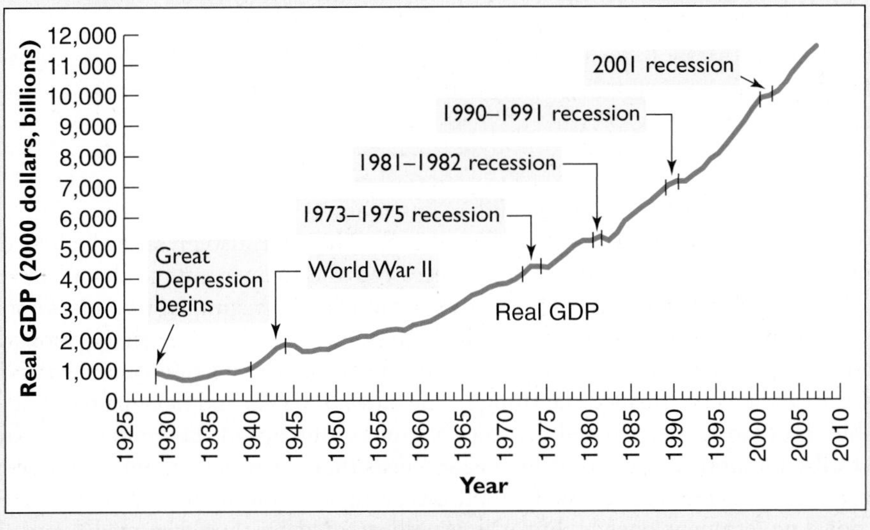

SOURCE: Bureau of Economic Analysis (www.bea.gov).

FIGURE 18.1
Fluctuations in U.S. Real GDP, 1929–2007.
Real GDP does not grow smoothly but has speedups (expansions or booms) and slowdowns (recessions or depressions). Note the contraction from 1929 to 1933 (the first phase of the Great Depression), the boom in 1941–1945 (World War II), and the recessions of 1973–1975, 1981–1982, 1990–1991, and 2001.

An informal definition of a recession, often cited by reporters, is a period during which real GDP falls for at least two consecutive quarters. This definition is not a bad rule of thumb, as real GDP usually does fall during recessions. However, many economists would argue that periods in which real GDP growth is well below normal, though not actually negative, should be counted as recessions. Indeed, real GDP fell in only one quarter during the 2001 recession. Another problem with relying on GDP figures for dating recessions is that GDP data can be substantially revised, sometimes years after the fact. In practice, when trying to determine whether a recession is in progress, economists look at a variety of economic data, not just GDP.

TABLE 18.1
U.S. Recessions since 1929

Peak date (beginning)	Trough date (end)	Duration (months)	Highest unemployment rate (%)	Change in real GDP (%)	Duration of subsequent expansion (months)
Aug. 1929	Mar. 1933	43	24.9	−28.8	50
May 1937	June 1938	13	19.0	−5.5	80
Feb. 1945	Oct. 1945	8	3.9	−8.5	37
Nov. 1948	Oct. 1949	11	5.9	−1.4	45
July 1953	May 1954	10	5.5	−1.2	39
Aug. 1957	Apr. 1958	8	6.8	−1.7	24
Apr. 1960	Feb. 1961	10	6.7	2.3	106
Dec. 1969	Nov. 1970	11	5.9	0.1	36
Nov. 1973	Mar. 1975	16	8.5	−1.1	58
Jan. 1980	July 1980	6	7.6	−0.3	12
July 1981	Nov. 1982	16	9.7	−2.1	92
July 1990	Mar. 1991	8	7.5	−0.9	120
Mar. 2001	Nov. 2001	8	5.8	0.8	

NOTES: Unemployment rate is the annual rate. Peak and trough dates from the National Bureau of Economic Research. Unemployment and real GDP data from *Historical Statistics of the United States* and the *Economic Report of the President*. Unemployment rate is the annual rate for the trough year or the subsequent year, whichever is higher. Change in annual real GDP is measured from the peak year to the trough year, except that the entry for the 1945 recession is the 1945–1946 change in real GDP, the entry for the 1980 recession is the 1979–1980 change, and the entry for 2001 is the 2000–2001 change.

SOURCES: Peak and trough dates, National Bureau of Economic Research; unemployment and real GDP, *Historical Statistics of the United States* and *Economic Report of the President*.

peak the beginning of a recession; the high point of economic activity prior to a downturn

trough the end of a recession; the low point of economic activity prior to a recovery

Table 18.1 lists the beginning and ending dates of U.S. recessions since 1929, as well as the *duration* (length, in months) of each. The table also gives the highest unemployment rate recorded during each recession and the percentage change in real GDP. (Ignore the last column of the table for now.) The beginning of a recession is called the **peak** because it represents the high point of economic activity prior to a downturn. The end of a recession, which marks the low point of economic activity prior to a recovery, is called the **trough.** The dates of peaks and troughs reported in Table 18.1 were determined by the National Bureau of Economic Research (NBER), a nonprofit organization of economists that has been a major source of research on short-term economic fluctuations since its founding in 1920. The NBER is not a government agency, but it is usually treated by the news media and the government as the "official" arbiter of the dates of peaks and troughs.

Table 18.1 shows that since 1929, by far the longest and most severe recession in the United States was the 43-month economic collapse that began in August 1929 and lasted until March 1933, initiating what became known as the Great Depression. Between 1933 and 1937, the economy grew fairly rapidly, so technically the period was not a recession, although unemployment remained very high at close to 20 percent of the workforce. In 1937–1938, the nation was hit by another significant recession. Full economic recovery from the Depression did not come until U.S. entry into World War II at the end of 1941. The economy boomed from 1941 to 1945 (see Figure 18.1), reflecting the enormous wartime production of military equipment and supplies.

In sharp contrast to the 1930s, U.S. recessions since World War II have generally been short—between 6 and 16 months, from peak to trough. As Table 18.1

"Please stand by for a series of tones. The first indicates the official end of the recession, the second indicates prosperity, and the third the return of the recession."

shows, the two most severe postwar recessions, 1973–1975 and 1981–1982, lasted just 16 months. And, though unemployment rates during those two recessions were quite high by today's standards, they were low compared to the Great Depression. Since 1982 the U.S. economy has experienced only two relatively mild recessions: in 1990–1991 and in 2001. Although recent recessions have not been among the worst that Americans have experienced, they warn us to guard against overconfidence. Prosperity and economic stability can never be guaranteed.

The opposite of a recession is an **expansion**—a period in which the economy is growing at a rate that is significantly *above* normal. A particularly strong and protracted expansion is called a **boom.** In the United States, strong expansions occurred during 1933–1937, 1961–1969, 1982–1990, and 1991–2001, with exceptionally strong growth during 1995–2000 (see Figure 18.1). On average, expansions have been much longer than recessions. The final column of Table 18.1 shows the duration, in months, of U.S. expansions since 1929. As you can see in the table, the 1961–1969 expansion lasted 106 months; the 1982–1990 expansion, 92 months. The longest expansion of all began in March 1991, at the trough of the 1990–1991 recession. This expansion lasted 120 months, a full 10 years, until a new recession began in March 2001.

expansion a period in which the economy is growing at a rate significantly above normal

boom a particularly strong and protracted expansion

Calling the 2001 recession

The Business Cycle Dating Committee of the National Bureau of Economic Research determined that a recession, the first in 10 years, began in March 2001. What led the committee to choose that date?

As of the beginning of 2001, there had been no "official" recession in the United States since the one that began in July 1990 and ended in March 1991. As mentioned above, this 10-year period without a recession was the longest expansion in U.S. history. However, the economy weakened considerably during the latter part of 2000 and in the spring and summer of 2001. A further blow was the terrorist attacks of September 11, 2001, which caused the loss of many jobs both in the affected areas and (because people became afraid to travel) in industries such as airlines and hotels. Because of the increased likelihood that a recession had begun, the six economists who form the Business Cycle Dating Committee—the group within the National Bureau of Economic Research that actually determines recession dates—found themselves called upon for the first time in a decade.

The determination of whether and when a recession has begun involves intensive statistical analysis, mixed in with a significant amount of human judgment. The Business Cycle Dating Committee typically relies heavily on a small set of statistical indicators that measure the overall strength of the economy. The committee prefers indicators that are available monthly because they are available quickly and may provide relatively precise information about the timing of peaks and troughs. Four of the most important indicators used by the committee are

- Industrial production, which measures the output of factories and mines.
- Total sales in manufacturing, wholesale trade, and retail trade.
- Nonfarm employment (the number of people at work outside of agriculture).
- Real after-tax income received by households, excluding transfers like Social Security payments.

Each of these indicators measures a different aspect of the economy. Because their movements tend to coincide with the overall movements in the economy, they are called *coincident indicators*.

Normally the coincident indicators move more or less together; during the 2001 recession they did not. Industrial production and sales in the manufacturing sector began to decline as early as September 2000. This early weakness in manufacturing reflected slow sales of information technology (computers, software, communications devices, and the like) following the collapse of the "dot-com bubble" in the stock market during 2000. (The values of high-tech stocks fell by two-thirds or more during the year; see Figure 16.2 for the decline in the S&P 500.) However, the weakness in manufacturing was not immediately reflected in the economy as a whole, as both employment and personal income grew strongly in the fall of 2000. Employment did not start to decline until around March 2001, and real personal income continued to grow into the fall of 2001.

The failure of the coincident indicators to move closely together made the committee's job difficult. The committee ultimately chose the date of the peak, or beginning of the recession, to be March 2001, the month in which nonfarm employment began to decline. A rationale for their choice is that recessions are supposed to reflect declines in the entire economy, not just a few specific sectors. It might be argued that the decline in nonfarm employment in March 2001 (which counts people at work in the entire economy, outside of agriculture) was the first clear indication that the slowdown that had begun in the high-tech sector had spread to the broader economy. ◆

EXERCISE 18.1

Update Table 18.1 using the National Bureau of Economic Research Web site (go to www.nber.org and search under *business cycle dates*). According to the NBER, is the U.S. economy currently in recession or expansion? How much time has elapsed since the last peak or trough?

SOME FACTS ABOUT SHORT-TERM ECONOMIC FLUCTUATIONS

Although Figure 18.1 and Table 18.1 show only twentieth-century data, periods of expansion and recession have been a feature of industrial economies since at least the late eighteenth century. Karl Marx and Friedrich Engels referred to these fluctuations, which they called "commercial crises," in their Communist Manifesto of 1848. In the United States, economists have been studying short-term fluctuations for at least a century. The traditional term for these fluctuations is *business cycles,* and they are still often referred to as *cyclical fluctuations.* Neither term is accurate though; as Figure 18.1 shows, economic fluctuations are not "cyclical" at all in the sense that they recur at predictable intervals, but instead are *irregular in their length and severity.* This irregularity makes the dates of peaks and troughs extremely hard to predict, despite the fact that professional forecasters have devoted a great deal of effort and brainpower to the task.

Expansions and recessions usually are not limited to a few industries or regions but are *felt throughout the economy.* Indeed, the largest fluctuations may have a *global impact.* For instance, the Great Depression of the 1930s affected nearly all the world's economies, and the 1973–1975 and 1981–1982 recessions also were widely felt outside the United States. When East Asia suffered a major slowdown in the late 1990s, the effects of that slowdown spilled over into many other regions (although not so much the United States).

EN 18

Even a relatively moderate recession, like the one that occurred in 2001, can have global effects. Figure 18.2, which shows growth rates of real GDP over the period 1999–2007 for Canada, Germany, Japan, the United Kingdom, and the United States, illustrates this point. You can see that—except for Japan, which has performed poorly since the early 1990s—all the countries experienced relatively strong growth in 1999 and 2000. The 2001 recession lowered growth rates in all of the countries, with recovery beginning in 2002.

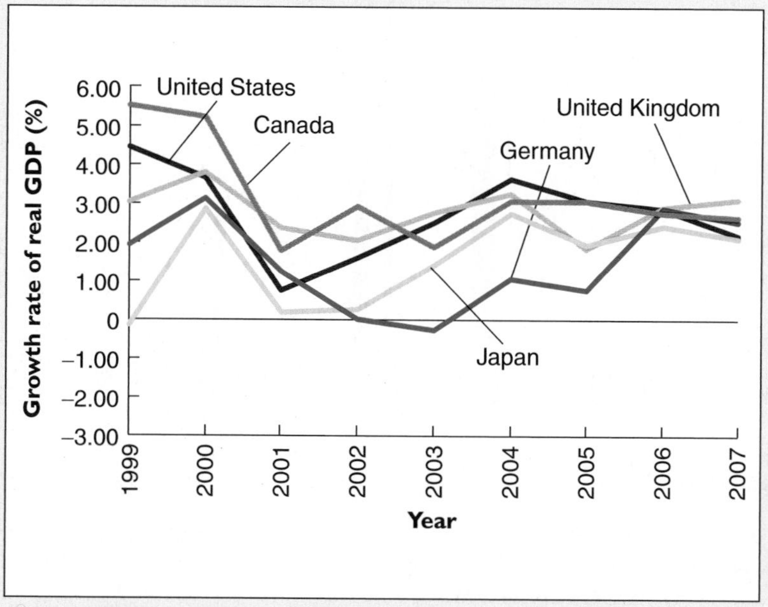

SOURCE: International Monetary Fund World Economic Outlook Database, April 2008.

FIGURE 18.2
Real GDP Growth in Five Major Countries, 1999–2007.
Annual growth rates for five major industrialized countries show that all the countries except Japan enjoyed rapid GDP growth in 1999 and 2000. (Japan has been growing slowly for more than a decade.) The 2001 recession was reflected in falling growth rates in all of the major countries, with recovery beginning in 2002.

Unemployment is a key indicator of short-term economic fluctuations. The unemployment rate typically rises sharply during recessions and recovers (although more slowly) during expansions. Figure 14.8 (in Chapter 14) shows the U.S. unemployment rate since 1960. You should be able to identify the recessions that began in 1960, 1969, 1973, 1981, 1990, and 2001 by noting the sharp peaks in the unemployment rate in those years. Recall from Chapter 14 that the part of unemployment that is associated with recessions is called *cyclical unemployment.* Beyond this increase in unemployment, labor market conditions generally worsen during recessions. For example, during recessions, real wages grow more slowly, workers are

Unemployment among construction workers rises substantially during recessions.

less likely to receive promotions or bonuses, and new entrants to the labor force (such as college graduates) have a much tougher time finding attractive jobs.

Generally, industries that produce *durable goods* such as cars, houses, and capital equipment are more affected than others by recessions and booms. In contrast, industries that provide *services* and *nondurable goods* like food are much less sensitive to short-term fluctuations. Thus, an automobile worker or a construction worker is far more likely to lose his or her job in a recession than is a barber or a baker.

Like unemployment, *inflation* follows a typical pattern in recessions and expansions, though it is not so sharply defined. Figure 18.3 shows the U.S. inflation rate since 1960; in the figure, periods of recession are indicated by shaded vertical bars. As you can see, recessions tend to be followed soon after by a decline in the rate of inflation. For example, the recession of 1981–1982 was followed by a sharp reduction in inflation. Furthermore, many—though not all—postwar recessions have been preceded by increases in inflation, as Figure 18.3 shows. The behavior of inflation during expansions and recessions will be discussed more fully in Chapter 21.

FIGURE 18.3
U.S. Inflation, 1960–2007.
U.S. inflation since 1960 is measured by the change in the CPI, and periods of recession are indicated by the shaded vertical bars. Note that inflation declined following the recessions of 1960–1961, 1969–1970, 1973–1975, 1981–1982, 1990–1991, and 2001, and rose prior to many of those recessions.

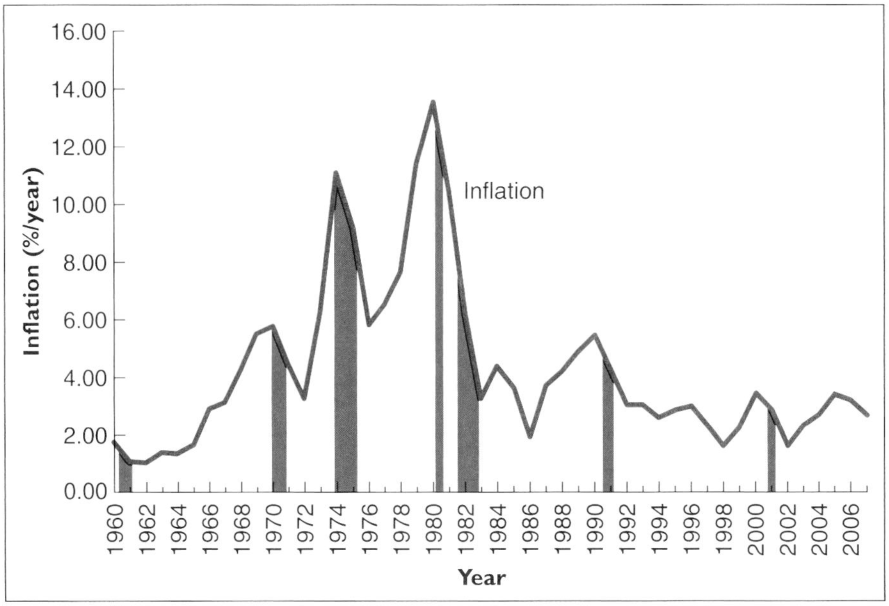

SOURCE: *Economic Report of the President*, February 2008, Table B-64 (www.gpoaccess.gov/eop/).

RECAP	SOME FACTS ABOUT SHORT-TERM ECONOMIC FLUCTUATIONS

- A recession is a period in which output is growing more slowly than normal. An expansion, or boom, is a period in which output is growing more quickly than normal.
- The beginning of a recession is called the peak, and its end (which corresponds to the beginning of the subsequent expansion) is called the trough.
- The sharpest recession in the history of the United States was the initial phase of the Great Depression in 1929–1933. Severe recessions also occurred in 1973–1975 and 1981–1982. Two relatively mild recessions occurred in 1990–1991 and 2001.

- Short-term economic fluctuations (recessions and expansions) are irregular in length and severity, and thus are difficult to predict.
- Expansions and recessions have widespread (and sometimes global) impacts, affecting most regions and industries.
- Unemployment rises sharply during a recession and falls, usually more slowly, during an expansion.
- Durable goods industries are more affected by expansions and recessions than other industries. Services and nondurable goods industries are less sensitive to ups and downs in the economy.
- Recessions tend to be followed by a decline in inflation and are often preceded by an increase in inflation.

OUTPUT GAPS AND CYCLICAL UNEMPLOYMENT

If policymakers are to respond appropriately to recessions and expansions, and if economists are to study them, knowing whether a particular economic fluctuation is "big" or "small" is essential. Intuitively, a "big" recession or expansion is one in which output and the unemployment rate deviate significantly from their normal or trend levels. In this section we will attempt to be more precise about this idea by introducing the concept of the *output gap,* which measures how far output is from its normal level at a particular time. We also will revisit the idea of *cyclical unemployment,* or the deviation of unemployment from its normal level. Finally, we will examine how these two concepts are related.

POTENTIAL OUTPUT AND THE OUTPUT GAP

The concept of potential output is a useful starting point for thinking about the measurement of expansions and recessions. **Potential output,** also called *potential GDP* or *full-employment output,* is the maximum sustainable amount of output (real GDP) that an economy can produce. Note that *potential output* is not simply the maximum amount of output. Because capital and labor can be utilized at greater-than-normal rates for limited periods of time, a country's actual output can temporarily exceed its potential output. These greater-than-normal utilization rates, however, cannot be sustained indefinitely, partly because workers cannot work overtime every week and machinery occasionally must be shut down for maintenance and repairs. Potential output is not a fixed number but grows over time, reflecting increases in both the amounts of available capital and labor and their productivity. We discussed the sources of growth in potential output (the economy's productive capacity) in Chapter 15. We will use the symbol Y^* to signify the economy's potential output at a given point in time.

potential output, Y^* (or potential GDP or full-employment output) the maximum sustainable amount of output (real GDP) that an economy can produce

Why does a nation's output sometimes grow quickly and sometimes slowly, as shown for the United States in Figure 18.1? Logically, there are two possibilities: First, changes in the rate of output growth may reflect *changes in the rate at which the country's potential output is increasing.* For example, unfavorable weather conditions, such as a severe drought, would reduce the rate of potential output growth in an agricultural economy, and a decline in the rate of technological innovation might reduce the rate of potential output growth in an industrial economy. Under the assumption that the country is using its resources at normal rates, so that actual output equals potential output, a significant slowdown in potential output growth would tend to result in recession. Similarly, new technologies, increased capital investment, or a surge in immigration that swells the labor force could produce unusually brisk growth in potential output, and hence an economic boom.

Undoubtedly, changes in the rate of growth of potential output are part of the explanation for expansions and recessions. In the United States, for example, the economic boom of the second half of the 1990s was propelled in part by new information technologies such as the internet. And the severe slowdown in Japan during the decade of the 1990s reflected in part a reduction in the growth of potential output, arising from factors such as slower growth in the Japanese labor force and capital stock. When changes in the rate of GDP growth reflect changes in the growth rate of potential output, the appropriate policy responses are those discussed in Chapter 15. In particular, when a recession results from slowing growth in potential output, the government's best response is to try to promote saving, investment, technological innovation, human capital formation, and other activities that support growth.

A second possible explanation for short-term economic fluctuations is that *actual output does not always equal potential output.* For example, potential output may be growing normally, but for some reason the economy's capital and labor resources may not be fully utilized, so that actual output is significantly below the level of potential output. This low level of output, resulting from underutilization of economic resources, would generally be interpreted as a recession. Alternatively, capital and labor may be working much harder than normal—firms may put workers on overtime, for example—so that actual output expands beyond potential output, creating a boom.

output gap, $Y - Y^*$ the difference between the economy's actual output and its potential output at a point in time

recessionary gap a negative output gap, which occurs when potential output exceeds actual output ($Y < Y^*$)

expansionary gap a positive output gap, which occurs when actual output is higher than potential output ($Y > Y^*$)

At any point in time, the difference between potential output and actual output is called the **output gap.** Recalling that Y^* is the symbol for potential output and that Y stands for actual output (real GDP), we can express the output gap as $Y - Y^*$. A negative output gap—when actual output is below potential and resources are not being fully utilized—is called a **recessionary gap.** A positive output gap—when actual output is above potential and resources are being utilized at above-normal rates—is referred to as an **expansionary gap.**

Policymakers generally view both recessionary gaps and expansionary gaps as problems. It is not difficult to see why a recessionary gap is bad news for the

"Ed, this is Art Simbley over at Hollis, Bingham, Cotter & Krone. What did you get for thirty-four across, 'Persian fairy,' four letters?"

economy: When there is a recessionary gap, capital and labor resources are not being fully utilized, and output and employment are below maximum sustainable levels. This is the sort of situation that poses problems for politicians' reelection prospects, as discussed in this chapter's introduction. In addition to the fact that it is unsustainable, an expansionary gap is considered a problem by policymakers for a more subtle reason: What's wrong, after all, with having higher output and employment, even if it is temporary? A prolonged expansionary gap is problematic because, when faced with a demand for their products that significantly exceeds their sustainable capacity, firms tend to raise prices. Thus, an expansionary gap typically results in increased inflation, which reduces the efficiency of the economy in the longer run. (We discuss the genesis of inflation in more detail in Chapter 21.)

Thus, whenever an output gap exists, whether it is recessionary or expansionary, policymakers have an incentive to try to eliminate the gap by returning actual output to potential. In the next four chapters we will discuss both how output gaps arise and the tools that policymakers have for *stabilizing* the economy—that is, bringing actual output into line with potential output.

THE NATURAL RATE OF UNEMPLOYMENT AND CYCLICAL UNEMPLOYMENT

Whether recessions arise because of slower growth in potential output or because actual output falls below potential, they bring bad times. In either case, output falls (or at least grows more slowly), implying reduced living standards. Recessionary output gaps are particularly frustrating for policymakers, however, because they imply that the economy has the *capacity* to produce more, but for some reason available resources are not being fully utilized. Recessionary gaps violate the Efficiency Principle in that they unnecessarily reduce the total economic pie, making the typical person worse off.

Efficiency

An important indicator of the low utilization of resources during recessions is the unemployment rate. In general, a *high* unemployment rate means that labor resources are not being fully utilized, so that output has fallen below potential (a recessionary gap). By the same logic, an unusually *low* unemployment rate suggests that labor is being utilized at an unsustainably high rate, so that actual output exceeds potential output (an expansionary gap).

To better understand the relationship between the output gap and unemployment, recall from Chapter 14 the three broad types of unemployment: frictional unemployment, structural unemployment, and cyclical unemployment. *Frictional unemployment* is the short-term unemployment that is associated with the matching of workers and jobs. Some amount of frictional unemployment is necessary for the labor market to function efficiently in a dynamic, changing economy. *Structural unemployment* is the long-term and chronic unemployment that occurs even when the economy is producing at its normal rate. Structural unemployment often results when workers' skills are outmoded and do not meet the needs of employers—so, for example, steelworkers may become structurally unemployed as the steel industry goes into a long-term decline, unless those workers can retrain to find jobs in growing industries. Finally, *cyclical unemployment* is the extra unemployment that occurs during periods of recession. Unlike cyclical unemployment, which is present only during recessions, frictional unemployment and structural unemployment are always present in the labor market, even when the economy is operating normally. Economists call the part of the total unemployment rate that is attributable to frictional and structural unemployment the **natural rate of unemployment.** Put another way, the natural rate of unemployment is the unemployment rate that prevails when cyclical unemployment is zero, so that the economy has neither a recessionary

natural rate of unemployment, u^* the part of the total unemployment rate that is attributable to frictional and structural unemployment; equivalently, the unemployment rate that prevails when cyclical unemployment is zero, so that the economy has neither a recessionary nor an expansionary output gap nor an expansionary output gap. We will denote the natural rate of unemployment as u^*.

Cyclical unemployment, which is the difference between the total unemployment rate and the natural rate, can thus be expressed as $u - u^*$, where u is the actual unemployment rate and u^* denotes the natural rate of unemployment. In a recession, the actual unemployment rate u exceeds the natural unemployment rate u^*, so cyclical unemployment, $u - u^*$, is positive. When the economy experiences an expansionary gap, in contrast, the actual unemployment rate is lower than the natural rate, so that cyclical unemployment is negative. Negative cyclical unemployment corresponds to a situation in which labor is being used at an unsustainably high level, so that actual unemployment has dipped below its usual frictional and structural levels.

Why has the natural rate of unemployment in the United States apparently declined?

According to the Congressional Budget Office, which regularly estimates the natural rate of unemployment in the United States, the natural rate has fallen steadily since about 1979, from 6.3 percent of the labor force to about 4.8 percent.[1] Some economists, noting that unemployment remained close to 4 percent for several years around the turn of the millennium, have argued for an even lower natural rate, perhaps as low as 4.5 percent. Why is the U.S. natural rate of unemployment apparently so much lower today than it was 20 years ago?

The natural rate of unemployment may have fallen because of reduced frictional unemployment, reduced structural unemployment, or both. A variety of ideas have been advanced to explain declines in both types of unemployment. One promising suggestion is based on the changing age structure of the U.S. labor force.[2] The average age of U.S. workers is rising, reflecting the aging of the baby boom generation. Indeed, over the past 25 years, the share of the labor force aged 16–24 has fallen from about 25 percent to about 15 percent. Since younger workers are more prone to unemployment than older workers, the aging of the labor force may help to explain the overall decline in unemployment.

Why are young workers more likely to be unemployed? Compared to teenagers and workers in their twenties, older workers are much more likely to hold long-term, stable jobs. In contrast, younger workers tend to hold short-term jobs, perhaps because they are not ready to commit to a particular career, or because their time in the labor market is interrupted by schooling or military service. Because they change jobs more often, younger workers are more prone than others to frictional unemployment. They also have fewer skills, on average, than older workers, so they may experience more structural unemployment. As workers age and gain experience, however, their risk of unemployment declines.

Another possible explanation for the declining natural rate of unemployment is that labor markets have become more efficient at matching workers with jobs, thereby reducing both frictional and structural unemployment. For example, agencies that arrange temporary help have become much more commonplace in the United States in recent years. Although the placements these agencies make are intended to be temporary, they often become permanent when an employer and worker discover that a particularly good match has been made. Online job services, which allow workers to search for jobs nationally and even internationally, also are becoming increasingly important. By reducing the time people must spend in unemployment and by creating more lasting matches between workers and jobs,

[1]Congressional Budget Office, *The Budget and Outlook: Fiscal Years 2008 to 2017*, January 2008, available online at www.cbo.gov/.

[2]See Robert Shimer, "Why Is the U.S. Unemployment Rate So Much Lower?" in B. Bernanke and J. Rotemberg, eds., *NBER Macroeconomics Annual*, 1998.

temporary help agencies, online job services, and similar innovations may have reduced the natural rate of unemployment.[3] ◆

OKUN'S LAW

What is the relationship between the output gap and the amount of cyclical unemployment in the economy? We have already observed that by definition, cyclical unemployment is positive when the economy has a recessionary gap, negative when there is an expansionary gap, and zero when there is no output gap. A more quantitative relationship between cyclical unemployment and the output gap is given by a rule of thumb called *Okun's law,* after Arthur Okun, one of President Kennedy's chief economic advisers. According to **Okun's law,** each extra percentage point of cyclical unemployment is associated with about a 2 percentage point increase in the output gap, measured in relation to potential output.[4] So, for example, if cyclical unemployment increases from 1 percent to 2 percent of the labor force, the recessionary gap will increase from 2 percent to 4 percent of potential GDP. The following example illustrates further.

Okun's law each extra percentage point of cyclical unemployment is associated with about a 2 percentage point increase in the output gap, measured in relation to potential output

Okun's law and the output gap in the U.S. economy

Following are the actual unemployment rate, the natural unemployment rate, and potential GDP (in billions of chained 2000 dollars) for the U.S. economy in four selected years.

Year	u	u^*	Y^*
1982	9.7%	6.1%	5,584
1991	6.8	5.8	7,305
1998	4.5	5.2	8,950
2002	5.8	5.2	10,342

SOURCES: Unemployment rate: www.bls.gov. Natural unemployment rate and potential GDP: Congressional Budget Office (www.cbo.gov/Spreadsheet/6060_Table2-2.xls).

In 1982 cyclical unemployment, $u - u^*$, was 9.7% − 6.1% or 3.6 percent of the labor force. According to Okun's law, the output gap for that year would be −2 times that percentage, or −7.2 percent of potential output. Since potential output was estimated to be $5,584 billion, the value of the output gap for that year was −7.2% × $5,584 billion, or −$402 billion.

In 1991 cyclical unemployment was 6.8% − 5.8%, or 1.0 percent of the labor force. According to Okun's law, the output gap for 1991 would be −2 times 1.0 percent, or −2.0 percent of potential GDP. Since potential GDP in 1991 was $7,305 billion, the output gap in that year should have been −2.0% × $7,305, or −$146 billion.

Both 1982 and 1991 were recession years, so the output gaps were recessionary gaps. In contrast, 1998 was a year of expansion, in which unemployment was below the natural rate and the economy experienced an expansionary gap. Cyclical unemployment in 1998 was 4.5% − 5.2%, or −0.7 percent. The output gap in 1998 therefore should have been about 1.4 percent of the potential GDP of $8,950

[3]For a detailed analysis of factors affecting the natural rate, see Lawrence Katz and Alan Krueger, "The High-Pressure U.S. Labor Market of the 1990s," *Brookings Papers on Economic Activity* 1 (1999), pp. 1–88.

[4]Mathematically, Okun's law can be expressed as $(Y - Y^*)/Y^* = -2(u - u^*)$. This relationship between unemployment and output has weakened over time. When Arthur Okun first formulated his law in the 1960s, he suggested that each extra percentage point of unemployment was associated with about a 3 percentage point increase in the output gap.

billion, or \$125 billion. In other words, in 1998 actual GDP was about \$125 billion greater than potential GDP.

The year 2002 followed a recession year, so the economy was still experiencing a recessionary gap. In 2002 cyclical unemployment was 5.8% − 5.2%, or 0.6 percent of the labor force. According to Okun's law, the output gap for 2002 would be −1.2 percent of the potential GDP of \$10,342, or −\$124 billion. ◆

EXERCISE 18.2

In the first quarter of 2008, the U.S. unemployment rate was 4.9 percent. Assume the natural rate of unemployment was 4.8 percent. By what percentage did actual GDP differ from potential GDP in the first quarter of 2008?

The output losses sustained in recessions, calculated according to Okun's law, can be quite significant. In our earlier example, we found the U.S. output gap in 1982 to be −\$402 billion. The U.S. population in 1982 was about 230 million. Hence, the output loss per person in that year equaled the total output gap of \$402 billion divided by 230 million people, or \$1,748—about \$7,000 for a family of four in 2000 dollars. This calculation implies that output gaps and cyclical unemployment may have significant costs—a conclusion that justifies the concern that the public and policymakers have about recessions.

Why did the Federal Reserve take measures to slow down the economy in 1999 and 2000?

As noted in Chapter 17, monetary policy decisions of the Federal Reserve—actions that change the level of the nation's money supply—affect the performance of the U.S. economy. Why did the Federal Reserve take measures to slow down the economy in 1999 and 2000?

Throughout the 1990s, cyclical unemployment in the United States fell dramatically, becoming negative sometime in 1997, according to Congressional Budget Office estimates. Okun's law indicates that growing negative cyclical unemployment rates signal an increasing expansionary gap, and with it an increased risk of future inflation.

In 1997 and 1998 the Federal Reserve argued that the inflationary pressures typically caused by rapidly expanding output and falling unemployment rates were being offset by productivity gains and international competition, leaving inflation rates lower than expected. Because inflation remained low during this period—despite a small but growing expansionary gap—the Federal Reserve did little to eliminate the gap.

However, as the actual unemployment rate continued to fall throughout 1999 and early 2000, the expansionary gap continued to widen, causing the Federal Reserve to grow increasingly concerned about the growing imbalance between actual and potential GDP and the threat of increasing inflation. In response, the Federal Reserve took actions in 1999 and 2000 to slow the growth of output and bring actual and potential output closer into alignment (we will give more details about how the Fed can do this in Chapter 20). The Fed's actions helped to "promote overall balance in the economy"[5] and restrain inflation throughout 2000. By early 2001, however, the U.S. economy stalled and fell into recession, leading the Federal Reserve to reverse course and take policy measures aimed at eliminating the growing *recessionary* gap. ◆

[5]Testimony of Chairman Alan Greenspan, *The Federal Reserve's semiannual report on the economy and monetary policy*, Committee on Banking and Financial Services, U.S. House of Representatives, February 17, 2000. Available online at www.federalreserve.gov/boarddocs/hh/2000/February/Testimony.htm.

RECAP	OUTPUT GAPS AND CYCLICAL UNEMPLOYMENT

- Potential output is the maximum sustainable amount of output (real GDP) that an economy can produce. The output gap, $Y - Y^*$, is the difference between actual output, Y, and potential output, Y^*. When actual output is below potential, the resulting output gap is called a recessionary gap. When actual output is above potential, the difference is called an expansionary gap. A recessionary gap reflects a waste of resources, while an expansionary gap threatens to ignite inflation; hence, policymakers have an incentive to try to eliminate both types of output gaps.
- The natural rate of unemployment u^* is the sum of the frictional and structural unemployment rates. It is the rate of unemployment that is observed when the economy is operating at a normal level, with no output gap.
- Cyclical unemployment, $u - u^*$, is the difference between the actual unemployment rate u and the natural rate of unemployment u^*. Cyclical unemployment is positive when there is a recessionary gap, negative when there is an expansionary gap, and zero when there is no output gap.
- Okun's law relates cyclical unemployment and the output gap. According to this rule of thumb, each percentage point increase in cyclical unemployment is associated with about a 2 percentage point increase in the output gap, measured in relation to potential output.

WHY DO SHORT-TERM FLUCTUATIONS OCCUR? A PREVIEW AND A PARABLE

What causes periods of recession and expansion? In the preceding section, we discussed two possible reasons for slowdowns and speedups in real GDP growth. First, growth in potential output itself may slow down or speed up, reflecting changes in the growth rates of available capital and labor and in the pace of technological progress. Second, even if potential output is growing normally, actual output may be higher or lower than potential output—that is, expansionary or recessionary output gaps may develop. In Chapter 15, we discussed some of the reasons that growth in potential output can vary, and the options that policymakers have for stimulating growth in potential output. But we have not yet addressed the question of how output gaps can arise or what policymakers should do in response. The causes and cures of output gaps will be a major topic of the next four chapters. Here is a brief preview of the main conclusions of those chapters:

1. In a world in which prices adjusted immediately to balance the quantities supplied and demanded for all goods and services, output gaps would not exist. However, for many goods and services, the assumption that prices will adjust immediately is not realistic. Instead, many firms adjust the prices of their output only periodically. In particular, rather than changing prices with every variation in demand, firms tend to adjust to changes in demand in the short run by varying the quantity of output they produce and sell. This type of behavior is known as "meeting the demand" at a preset price.

2. Because in the short run firms tend to meet the demand for their output at preset prices, changes in the amount that customers decide to spend will affect output. When total spending is low for some reason, output may fall below potential output; conversely, when spending is high, output may rise above potential output. In other words, *changes in economywide spending are the*

primary cause of output gaps. Thus, government policies can help to eliminate output gaps by influencing total spending. For example, the government can affect total spending directly simply by changing its own level of purchases.

3. Although firms tend to meet demand in the short run, they will not be willing to do so indefinitely. If customer demand continues to differ from potential output, firms will eventually adjust their prices to eliminate output gaps. If demand exceeds potential output (an expansionary gap), firms will raise their prices aggressively, spurring inflation. If demand falls below potential output (a recessionary gap), firms will raise their prices less aggressively or even cut prices, reducing inflation.

4. Over the longer run, price changes by firms eliminate any output gap and bring production back into line with the economy's potential output. Thus, the economy is "self-correcting" in the sense that it operates to eliminate output gaps over time. Because of this self-correcting tendency, in the long run actual output equals potential output, so that output is determined by the economy's productive capacity rather than by the rate of spending. In the long run, total spending influences only the rate of inflation.

These ideas will become clearer as we proceed through the next chapters. Before plunging into the details of the analysis, though, let's consider an example that illustrates the links between spending and output in the short and long run.

Al's ice cream store produces gourmet ice cream on the premises and sells it directly to the public. What determines the amount of ice cream that Al produces on a daily basis? The productive capacity, or potential output, of the shop is one important factor. Specifically, Al's potential output of ice cream depends on the amount of capital (number of ice cream makers) and labor (number of workers) that he employs, and on the productivity of that capital and labor. Although Al's potential output usually changes rather slowly, on occasion it can fluctuate significantly—for example, if an ice cream maker breaks down or Al contracts the flu.

The main source of day-to-day variations in Al's ice cream production, however, is not changes in potential output but fluctuations in the demand for ice cream by the public. Some of these fluctuations in spending occur predictably over the course of the day (more demand in the afternoon than in the morning, for example), the week (more demand on weekends), or the year (more demand in the summer). Other changes in demand are less regular—more demand on a hot day than a cool one, or when a parade is passing by the store. Some changes in demand are hard for Al to interpret: For example, a surge in demand for rocky road ice cream on one particular Tuesday could reflect a permanent change in consumer tastes, or it might just be a random, one-time event.

How should Al react to these ebbs and flows in the demand for ice cream? The basic supply-and-demand model that we introduced in Chapter 3, if applied to the market for ice cream, would predict that the price of ice cream should change with every change in the demand for ice cream. For example, prices should rise just after the movie theater next door to Al's shop lets out on Friday night, and they should fall on unusually cold, blustery days, when most people would prefer a hot cider to an ice cream cone. Indeed, taken literally, the supply and demand model of Chapter 3 predicts that ice cream prices should change almost moment to moment. Imagine Al standing in front of his shop like an auctioneer, calling out prices in an effort to determine how many people are willing to buy at each price!

Of course, we do not expect to see this behavior by an ice cream store owner. Price setting by auction does in fact occur in some markets, such as the market for grain or the stock market, but it is not the normal procedure in most retail markets, such as the market for ice cream. Why this difference? The basic reason is that sometimes the economic benefits of hiring an auctioneer and setting up an auction exceed the costs of doing so, and sometimes they do not. In the market for grain, for example, many buyers and sellers gather together in the same place at the same time to trade large volumes of standardized goods (bushels of grain). In that kind of situation, an auction is an efficient way to determine prices and balance the quantities supplied and demanded. In an ice cream store, by contrast, customers come in by twos and threes at random times throughout the day. Some want shakes, some cones, and some sodas. With small numbers of customers and a low sales volume at any given time, the costs involved in selling ice cream by auction are much greater than the benefits of allowing prices to vary with demand.

Cost-Benefit

So how does Al, the ice cream store manager, deal with changes in the demand for ice cream? Observation suggests that he begins by setting prices based on the best information he has about the demand for his product and the costs of production. Perhaps he prints up a menu or makes a sign announcing the prices. Then, over a period of time, he will keep his prices fixed and serve as many customers as want to buy (up to the point where he runs out of ice cream or room in the store at these prices). This behavior is what we call "meeting the demand" at preset prices, and it implies that *in the short run,* the amount of ice cream Al produces and sells is determined by the demand for his products.

However, *in the long run,* the situation is quite different. Suppose, for example, that Al's ice cream earns a citywide reputation for its freshness and flavor. Day after day Al observes long lines in his store. His ice cream maker is overtaxed, as are his employees and his table space. There can no longer be any doubt that at current prices, the quantity of ice cream the public wants to consume exceeds what Al is able and willing to supply on a normal basis (his potential output). Expanding the store is an attractive possibility, but not one (we assume) that is immediately feasible. What will Al do?

Certainly one thing Al can do is raise his prices. At higher prices, Al will earn higher profits. Moreover, raising ice cream prices will bring the quantity of ice cream demanded closer to Al's normal production capacity—his potential output. Indeed, when the price of Al's ice cream finally rises to its equilibrium level, the shop's actual output will equal its potential output. Thus, over the long run, ice cream prices adjust to their equilibrium level, and the amount that is sold is determined by potential output.

This example illustrates in a simple way the links between spending and output—except, of course, that we must think of this story as applying to the whole economy, not to a single business. The key point is that there is an important difference between the short run and the long run. In the short run, producers often choose not to change their prices, but rather to meet the demand at preset prices. Because output is determined by demand, in the short run total spending plays a central role in determining the level of economic activity. Thus, Al's ice cream store enjoys a boom on an unusually hot day, when the demand for ice cream is strong, while an unseasonably cold day brings an ice cream recession. But in the long run, prices adjust to their market-clearing levels, and output equals potential output. Thus, the quantities of inputs and the productivity with which they are used are the primary determinants of economic activity in the long run, as we saw in Chapter 15. Although total spending affects output in the short run, in the long run its main effects are on prices.

Example 18.1

THE ECONOMIC NATURALIST

Why did the Coca-Cola Company test a vending machine that "knows" when the weather is hot?

According to the *New York Times* (October 28, 1999, p. C1), the Coca-Cola Company has quietly tested a soda vending machine that includes a temperature sensor. Why would Coca-Cola want a vending machine that "knows" when the weather is hot?

When the weather is hot, the demand for refreshing soft drinks rises, increasing their market-clearing price. To take advantage of this variation in consumer demand, the vending machines that Coca-Cola tested were equipped with a computer chip that gave them the capability to raise soda prices automatically when the temperature climbs. The company's chairman and chief executive, M. Douglas Ivester, described in an interview how the desire for a cold drink increases during a sports championship final held in the summer heat. "So it is fair that it should be more expensive," Mr. Ivester was quoted as saying. "The machine will simply make this process automatic." Company officials suggested numerous other ways in which vending machine prices could be made dependent on demand. For example, machines could be programmed to reduce prices during off-peak hours or at low-traffic machines.

In traditional vending machines, cold drinks are priced in a way analogous to the way Al prices his ice cream: A price is set, and demand is met at the preset price until the machine runs out of soda. The weather-sensitive vending machine illustrates how technology may change pricing practices in the future. Indeed, increased computing power and access to the internet already have allowed some firms, such as airline companies, to change prices almost continuously in response to variations in demand. Conceivably, the practice of meeting demand at a preset price may someday be obsolete.

On the other hand, Coca-Cola's experiments with "smart" vending machines also illustrate the barriers to fully flexible pricing in practice. First, the new vending machines are more costly than the standard model. In deciding whether to use them, the company must decide whether the extra profits from variable pricing justify the extra cost of the machines. Second, in early tests, many consumers reacted negatively to the new machines, complaining that they take unfair advantage of thirsty customers. In practice, customer complaints and concerns about "fairness" make companies less willing to vary prices sensitively with changing demand. •

SUMMARY

- Real GDP does not grow smoothly. Periods in which the economy is growing at a rate significantly below normal are called recessions; periods in which the economy is growing at a rate significantly above normal are called expansions. A severe or protracted recession, like the long decline that occurred between 1929 and 1933, is called a depression, while a particularly strong expansion is called a boom. **LO1**

- The beginning of a recession is called the peak because it represents the high point of economic activity prior to a downturn. The end of a recession, which marks the low point of economic activity prior to a recovery, is called the trough. Since World War II, U.S. recessions have been much shorter on average than booms, lasting between 6 and 16 months. The longest boom period in U.S. history began with the end of the 1990–1991 recession in March 1991, ending exactly 10 years later in March 2001 when a new recession began. **LO1**

- Short-term economic fluctuations are irregular in length and severity, and are thus hard to forecast. Expansions and recessions are typically felt throughout the economy and may even be global in scope. Unemployment rises sharply during recessions, while inflation tends to fall during or shortly after a recession. Durable goods industries tend to be particularly sensitive to recessions and booms, whereas services and nondurable goods industries are less sensitive. **LO2**

- Potential output, also called potential GDP or full-employment output, is the maximum sustainable amount of output (real GDP) that an economy can produce. The difference between potential output and actual output is the output gap. When output is below potential, the gap is called a recessionary gap; when output is above potential, the difference is called an expansionary gap. Recessions can occur either because potential output is growing unusually slowly or because actual output is below potential. Because recessionary gaps represent wasted resources and expansionary gaps threaten to create inflation, policymakers have an incentive to try to eliminate both types of gap. **LO3**

- The natural rate of unemployment is the part of the total unemployment rate that is attributable to frictional and structural unemployment. Equivalently, the natural rate of unemployment is the rate of unemployment that exists when the output gap is zero. Cyclical unemployment, the part of unemployment that is associated with recessions and expansions, equals the total unemployment rate less the natural unemployment rate. Cyclical unemployment is related to the output gap by Okun's law, which states that each extra percentage point of cyclical unemployment is associated with about a 2 percentage point increase in the output gap, measured in relation to potential output. **LO4, LO5**

- In the next several chapters, our study of recessions and expansions will focus on the role of economy-wide spending. If firms adjust prices only periodically, and in the meantime produce enough output to meet demand, then fluctuations in spending will lead to fluctuations in output over the short run. During that short-run period, government policies that influence aggregate spending may help to eliminate output gaps. In the long run, however, firms' price changes will eliminate output gaps—that is, the economy will "self-correct"—and total spending will influence only the rate of inflation. **LO6**

KEY TERMS

boom (511)
depression (509)
expansion (510)
expansionary gap (516)
natural rate of unemployment, u^* (517)
Okun's law (519)
output gap, $Y - Y^*$ (516)
peak (510)
potential output, Y^* (or potential GDP or full-employment output) (515)
recession (or contraction) (509)
recessionary gap (516)
trough (510)

REVIEW QUESTIONS

1. Define *recession* and *expansion*. What are the beginning and ending points of a recession called? In the postwar United States, which have been longer on average: recessions or expansions? **LO1, LO2**
2. Why is the traditional term *business cycles* a misnomer? How does your answer relate to the ease or difficulty of forecasting peaks and troughs? **LO2**
3. Which firm is likely to see its profits reduced the most in a recession: an automobile producer, a manufacturer of boots and shoes, or a janitorial service? Which is likely to see its profits reduced the least? Explain. **LO2**
4. How is each of the following likely to be affected by a recession: the natural unemployment rate, the cyclical unemployment rate, the inflation rate, the poll ratings of the president? **LO2, LO4**
5. Define *potential output*. Is it possible for an economy to produce an amount greater than potential output? Explain. **LO3**
6. True or false: All recessions are the result of output gaps. Explain. **LO2, LO3**
7. True or false: When output equals potential output, the unemployment rate is zero. Explain. **LO5**
8. If the natural rate of unemployment is 5 percent, what is the total rate of unemployment if output is 2 percent below potential output? What if output is 2 percent above potential output? **LO5**

PROBLEMS

McGraw-Hill's HOMEWORK MANAGER®

1. Using Table 18.1, find the average duration, the minimum duration, and the maximum duration of expansions in the United States since 1929. Are expansions getting longer or shorter on average over time? Is there any tendency for long expansions to be followed by long recessions? **LO1, LO2**
2. From the homepage of the Bureau of Economic Analysis (www.bea.gov) obtain quarterly data for U.S. real GDP from the last three recessions: 1981–1982, 1990–1991, and 2001. **LO1, LO2**
   a. How many quarters of negative real GDP growth occurred in each recession?
   b. Which, if any, of the recessions satisfied the informal criterion that a recession must have two consecutive quarters of negative GDP growth?

3. Given below are data on real GDP and potential GDP for the United States for the years 1999–2007, in billions of 2000 dollars. For each year, calculate the output gap as a percentage of potential GDP and state whether the gap is a recessionary gap or an expansionary gap. Also calculate the year-to-year growth rates of real GDP. Can you identify the recession that occurred during this period? **LO3**

Year	Real GDP	Potential GDP
1999	\$ 9,470	\$ 9,248
2000	\$ 9,817	\$ 9,590
2001	\$ 9,891	\$ 9,927
2002	\$10,049	\$10,227
2003	\$10,301	\$10,501
2004	\$10,676	\$10,777
2005	\$11,003	\$11,068
2006	\$11,319	\$11,372
2007	\$11,567	\$11,687

SOURCE: Potential GDP: Congressional Budget Office; real GDP, www.bea.gov.

4. From the homepage of the Bureau of Labor Statistics (www.bls.gov/), obtain the most recent available data on the unemployment rate for workers aged 16–19 and workers aged 20 or over. How do they differ? What are some of the reasons for the difference? How does this difference relate to the decline in the overall natural rate of unemployment since 1980? **LO4**

5. Using Okun's law, fill in the four pieces of missing data in the table below. The data are hypothetical. **LO5**

Year	Real GDP	Potential GDP	Natural unemployment rate (%)	Actual unemployment rate (%)
2010	7,840	8,000	(a)	6
2011	8,100	(b)	5	5
2012	(c)	8,200	4.5	4
2013	8,415	8,250	5	(d)

ANSWERS TO IN-CHAPTER EXERCISES

18.1 Answers will vary, depending on when the data are obtained. **LO1, LO2**

18.3 The actual unemployment rate in the first quarter of 2008 exceeded the natural rate by 0.1 percent, so by Okun's law actual output fell below potential output by $-2 \times 0.1 = -0.2$ percent of potential output (a recessionary gap). **LO5**

CHAPTER 19

Spending and Output in the Short Run

LEARNING OBJECTIVES

After reading this chapter, you should be able to:

1. Identify the key assumption of the basic Keynesian model and explain how this affects the production decisions made by firms.
2. Discuss the determinants of planned investment and aggregate consumption spending and how these concepts are used to develop a model of planned aggregate expenditure.
3. Analyze, using graphs and numbers, how an economy reaches short-run equilibrium in the basic Keynesian model.
4. Show how a change in planned aggregate expenditure can cause a change in short-run equilibrium output and how this is related to the income-expenditure multiplier.
5. Explain why the basic Keynesian model suggests that fiscal policy is useful as a stabilization policy, and discuss the qualifications that arise in applying fiscal policy in real-world situations.

When one of the authors of this book was a small boy, he used to spend some time every summer with his grandparents, who lived a few hours from his home. A favorite activity of his during these visits was to spend a summer evening on the front porch with his grandmother, listening to her stories.

Grandma had spent the early years of her marriage in New England, during the worst part of the Great Depression. In one of her reminiscences, she remarked that at that time, in the mid-1930s, it had been a satisfaction to her to be able to buy her children a new pair of shoes every year. In the small town where she and her family lived, many children had to wear their shoes until they fell apart, and a few unlucky boys and girls went to school barefoot. Her grandson

thought this was scandalous: "Why didn't their parents just buy them new shoes?" he demanded.

"They couldn't," said Grandma. "They didn't have the money. Most of the fathers had lost their jobs because of the Depression."

"What kind of jobs did they have?"

"They worked in the shoe factories, which had to close down."

"Why did the factories close down?"

"Because," Grandma explained, "nobody had any money to buy shoes."

The grandson was only six or seven years old at the time, but even he could see that there was something badly wrong with Grandma's logic. On the one side were boarded-up shoe factories and shoe workers with no jobs; on the other, children without shoes. Why couldn't the shoe factories just open and produce the shoes the children so badly needed? He made his point quite firmly, but Grandma just shrugged and said it didn't work that way.

The story of the closed-down shoe factories illustrates in a microcosm the cost to society of a recessionary gap. In an economy with a recessionary gap, available resources, which in principle could be used to produce valuable goods and services, are instead allowed to lie fallow. This waste of resources lowers the economy's output and economic welfare, compared to its potential.

Grandma's account also suggests how such an unfortunate situation might come about. Suppose factory owners and other producers, being reluctant to accumulate unsold goods on their shelves, produce just enough output to satisfy the demand for their products. And suppose that, for some reason, the public's willingness or ability to spend declines. If spending declines, factories will respond by

Efficiency

© Bettmann/CORBIS

BOX 19.1: JOHN MAYNARD KEYNES AND THE KEYNESIAN REVOLUTION

John Maynard Keynes (1883–1946), perhaps the most influential economist of the twentieth century, was a remarkable individual who combined a brilliant career as an economic theorist with an active life in diplomacy, finance, journalism, and the arts. Keynes (pronouced "canes") first came to prominence at the end of World War I when he attended the Versailles peace conference as a representative of the British Treasury. He was appalled by the shortsightedness of the diplomats at the conference, particularly their insistence that the defeated Germans make huge compensatory payments (called reparations) to the victorious nations. In his widely read book *The Economic Consequences of the Peace* (1919), Keynes argued that the reparations imposed on Germany were impossibly large, and that attempts to extract the payments would prevent Germany's economic recovery and perhaps lead to another war. Unfortunately for the world, he turned out to be right.

In the period between the two world wars, Keynes held a professorship at Cambridge, where his father had taught economics. Keynes's early writings had been on mathematics and logic, but after his experience in Versailles, he began to work primarily on economics, producing several well-regarded books. He developed an imposing intellectual reputation, editing Great Britain's leading scholarly journal in economics, writing articles for newspapers and magazines, advising the government, and playing a major role in the political and economic debates of the day. On the side, Keynes made fortunes both for himself and for King's College (a part of Cambridge University) by speculating in international currencies and commodities. He was also an active member of the Bloomsbury Group, a circle of leading artists, performers, and writers that included E. M. Forster and Virginia Woolf. In 1925 Keynes married the glamorous Russian ballerina Lydia Lopokova. Theirs was by all cutting their production (because they don't want to produce goods they can't sell) and by laying off workers who are no longer needed. And because the workers who are laid off will lose most of their income—a particularly serious loss in the 1930s, in the days before government-sponsored unemployment insurance was common—they must reduce their own spending. As their spending declines, factories will reduce their production again, laying off more workers, who in turn reduce their spending—and so on, in a vicious circle. In this scenario, the problem is not a lack of productive capacity—the factories have not lost their ability to produce—but rather *insufficient spending* to support the normal level of production.

EN 19

The idea that a decline in aggregate spending may cause output to fall below potential output was one of the key insights of John Maynard Keynes, a highly influential British economist of the first half of the twentieth century. Box 19.1 gives a brief account of Keynes's life and ideas. The goal of this chapter is to present a theory, or model, of how recessions and expansions may arise from fluctuations in aggregate spending, along the lines first suggested by Keynes. This model, which we call the *basic Keynesian model,* is also known as the *Keynesian cross,* after the diagram that is used to illustrate the theory. In the body of the chapter, we will emphasize a numerical and graphical approach to the basic Keynesian model, although an algebraic solution to the simple model is presented in Appendix A, which provides an algebraic analysis to the more general model.

We will begin with a brief discussion of the key assumptions of the basic Keynesian model. We will then turn to the important concept of total, or aggregate, *planned spending* in the economy. We will show how, in the short run, the rate of aggregate spending helps to determine the level of output, which can be greater

accounts a very successful marriage, and Keynes devoted significant energies to managing his wife's career and promoting the arts in Britain.

Like other economists of the time, Keynes struggled to understand the Great Depression that gripped the world in the 1930s. His work on the problem led to the publication in 1936 of *The General Theory of Employment, Interest, and Money.* In *The General Theory,* Keynes tried to explain how economies can remain at low levels of output and employment for protracted periods. He stressed a number of factors, most notably that aggregate spending may be too low to permit full employment during such periods. Keynes recommended increases in government spending as the most effective way to increase aggregate spending and restore full employment.

The General Theory is a difficult book, reflecting Keynes's own struggle to understand the complex causes of the Depression. In retrospect, some of *The General Theory*'s arguments seem unclear or even inconsistent. Yet the book is full of fertile ideas, many of which had a worldwide impact and eventually led to what has been called the *Keynesian revolution.* Over the years, many economists have added to or modified Keynes's conception, to the point that Keynes himself, were he alive today, probably would not recognize much of what is now called *Keynesian economics.* But the ideas that insufficient aggregate spending can lead to recession and that government policies can help to restore full employment are still critical to Keynesian theory.

In 1937 a heart attack curtailed Keynes's activities, but he remained an important figure on the world scene. In 1944 he led the British delegation to the international conference in Bretton Woods, New Hampshire, which established the key elements of the postwar international monetary and financial system, including the International Monetary Fund and the World Bank. Keynes died in 1946.

than or less than potential output. In other words, depending on the level of spending, the economy may develop an output gap. "Too little" spending leads to a recessionary output gap, while "too much" creates an expansionary output gap.

An implication of the basic Keynesian model is that government policies that affect the level of spending can be used to reduce or eliminate output gaps. Policies used in this way are called *stabilization policies*. Keynes himself argued for the active use of fiscal policy—policy relating to government spending and taxes—to eliminate output gaps and stabilize the economy. In the latter part of this chapter, we will show why Keynes thought fiscal policy could help to stabilize the economy, and we will discuss the usefulness of fiscal policy as a stabilization tool.

As we mentioned in the previous chapter, the basic Keynesian model is not a complete or entirely realistic model of the economy, since it applies only to the relatively short period during which firms do not adjust their prices but instead meet the demand forthcoming at preset prices. Nevertheless, this model is an essential building block of leading current theories of short-run economic fluctuations and stabilization policies. In the next two chapters, we will extend the basic Keynesian model to incorporate monetary policy, inflation, and other important features of the economy.

THE KEYNESIAN MODEL'S CRUCIAL ASSUMPTION: FIRMS MEET DEMAND AT PRESET PRICES

The basic Keynesian model is built on a key assumption, highlighted in Box 19.2.

> **BOX 19.2: KEY ASSUMPTION OF THE BASIC KEYNESIAN MODEL**
>
> **In the short run, firms meet the demand for their products at preset prices.**
> Firms do not respond to every change in the demand for their products by changing their prices. Instead, they typically set a price for some period, then *meet the demand* at that price. By "meeting the demand," we mean that firms produce just enough to satisfy their customers at the prices that have been set.[1]

As we will see, the assumption that firms vary their production in order to meet demand at preset prices implies that fluctuations in spending will have powerful effects on the nation's real GDP.

The assumption that, over short periods of time, firms meet the demand for their products at preset prices is generally realistic. Think of the stores where you shop. The price of a pair of jeans does not fluctuate from moment to moment according to the number of customers who enter the store or the latest news about the price of denim. Instead, the store posts a price and sells jeans to any customer who wants to buy at that price, at least until the store runs out of stock. Similarly, the corner pizza restaurant may leave the price of its large pie unchanged for months or longer, allowing its pizza production to be determined by the number of customers who want to buy at the preset price.

menu costs the costs of changing prices

Firms do not normally change their prices frequently because doing so would be costly. Economists refer to the costs of changing prices as **menu costs.** In the case of

[1]Obviously, firms can only meet the forthcoming demand up to the point where they reach the limit of their capacity to produce. For that reason, the Keynesian analysis of this chapter is relevant only when producers have unused capacity.

the pizza restaurant, the menu cost is literally just that—the cost of printing up a new menu when prices change. Similarly, the clothing store faces the cost of remarking all its merchandise if the manager changes prices. But menu costs also may include other kinds of costs—for example, the cost of doing a market survey to determine what price to charge and the cost of informing customers about price changes.

Menu costs will not prevent firms from changing their prices indefinitely. As we saw in the case of Al's ice cream store (in the previous chapter), too great an imbalance between demand and supply, as reflected by a difference between sales and potential output, will eventually lead firms to change their prices. If no one is buying jeans, for example, at some point the clothing store will mark down its jeans prices. Or if the pizza restaurant becomes the local hot spot, with a line of customers stretching out the door, eventually the manager will raise the price of a large pie. Like many other economic decisions, the decision to change prices reflects a cost-benefit comparison: Prices should be changed if the benefit of doing so—the fact that sales will be brought more nearly in line with the firm's normal production capacity—outweighs the menu costs associated with making the change. As we have stressed, the basic Keynesian model developed in this chapter ignores the fact that prices will eventually adjust, and therefore should be interpreted as applying to the short run.

Cost-Benefit

Will new technologies eliminate menu costs?

Keynesian theory is based on the assumption that menu costs are sufficiently large to prevent firms from adjusting prices immediately in response to changing market conditions. However, in many industries, new technologies have eliminated or greatly reduced the direct costs of changing prices. For example, the use of bar codes to identify individual products, together with scanner technologies, allows a grocery store manager to change prices with just a few keystrokes, without having to change the price label on each can of soup or loaf of bread. Airlines use sophisticated computer software to implement complex pricing strategies, under which two travelers on the same flight to Milwaukee may pay very different fares, depending on whether they are business or vacation travelers and on how far in advance their flights were booked. Online retailers such as booksellers have the ability to vary their prices by type of customer and even by individual customer, while other internet-based companies such as eBay and Priceline allow for negotiation over the price of each individual purchase. As we discussed in the previous chapter (Example 18.1), the Coca-Cola company experimented with a vending machine that automatically varied the price of a soft drink according to the outdoor temperature, charging more when the weather is hot.

"You thought we would offer lower fares? How insensitive."

Will these reductions in the direct costs of changing prices make the Keynesian theory, which assumes that firms meet demand at preset prices, less relevant to the real world? This is certainly a possibility that macroeconomists must take into account. However, it is unlikely that new technologies will completely eliminate the costs of changing prices anytime soon. Gathering the information about market conditions needed to set the profit-maximizing price—including the prices charged by competitors, the costs of producing the good or service, and the likely demand for the product—will remain costly for firms. Another cost of changing prices is the use of valuable managerial time and attention needed to make informed pricing decisions. A more subtle cost of changing prices—particularly raising prices—is that doing so may lead regular customers to rethink their choice of suppliers and decide to search for a better deal elsewhere. ◆

PLANNED AGGREGATE EXPENDITURE

In the Keynesian theory discussed in this chapter, output at each point in time is determined by the amount that people throughout the economy want to spend—what we will refer to as *planned aggregate expenditure.* Specifically, **planned aggregate expenditure** ***(PAE)*** is total planned spending on final goods and services.

***planned aggregate expenditure* (PAE)** total planned spending on final goods and services

The four components of spending on final goods and services were introduced in Chapter 12:

1. *Consumption expenditure*, or simply *consumption* (C), is spending by households on final goods and services. Examples of consumption expenditure are spending on food, clothes, and entertainment and on consumer durable goods like automobiles and furniture.
2. *Investment* (I) is spending by domestic firms on new capital goods, such as office buildings, factories, and equipment. Spending on new houses and apartment buildings (residential investment) and increases in inventories (inventory investment) also are included in investment.[2]
3. *Government purchases* (G) are purchases by federal, state, and local governments of final goods and services. Examples of government purchases include new schools and hospitals, military hardware, equipment for the space program, and the services of government employees such as soldiers, police, and government office workers. Recall from Chapter 12 that *transfer payments* such as social security benefits and unemployment insurance and interest on the government debt are *not* included in government purchases.
4. *Net exports* (NX) equal exports minus imports. Exports are sales of domestically produced goods and services to foreigners. Imports are purchases by domestic residents of goods and services produced abroad that have been included in C, I, and G but must now be subtracted because they do not represent domestic production. Net exports therefore represent the net demand for domestic goods and services by foreigners.

Together, these four types of spending—by households, firms, the government, and the rest of the world—sum to total, or aggregate, spending.

PLANNED SPENDING VERSUS ACTUAL SPENDING

In the Keynesian model, output is determined by planned aggregate expenditure, or planned spending, for short. Could *planned* spending ever differ from *actual* spending? The answer is yes. The most important case is that of a firm that sells either less or more of its product than expected. As we noted in Chapter 12, additions to the stocks of goods sitting in a firm's warehouse are treated in official government statistics as inventory investment by the firm. In effect, government statisticians assume that the firm buys its unsold output from itself; they then count those purchases as part of the firm's investment spending.[3]

Suppose, then, that a firm's actual sales are less than expected, so that part of what it had planned to sell remains in the warehouse. In this case, the firm's actual investment, including the unexpected increases in its inventory, is greater than its planned investment, which did not include the added inventory. If this is true for the economy as a whole, we will find that $I > I^p$, where I^p equals the firm's planned investment, including planned inventory investment.

What if firms sell more output than expected? In that case, firms will add less to their inventories than they planned and actual investment will be less than planned investment, that is, $I < I^p$. The following example gives a numerical illustration.

[2] As we discussed earlier, we use "investment" here to mean spending on new capital goods such as factories, housing, and equipment, which is not the same as financial investment. This distinction is important to keep in mind.

[3] For the purposes of measuring GDP, treating unsold output as being purchased by its producer has the advantage of ensuring that actual production and actual expenditure are equal.

Planned versus actual investment

The Fly-by-Night Kite Company produces \$5,000,000 worth of kites during the year. It expects sales of \$4,800,000 for the year, leaving \$200,000 worth of kites to be stored in the warehouse for future sale. During the year, Fly-by-Night adds \$1,000,000 in new production equipment as part of an expansion plan. Fly-by-Night's planned investment, I^p, thus equals its purchases of new production equipment (\$1,000,000) plus its planned additions to inventory (\$200,000), for a total of \$1,200,000 in planned investment. The company's planned investment does not depend on how much it actually sells.

If Fly-by-Night sells only \$4,600,000 worth of kites, it will add \$400,000 in kites to its inventory instead of the \$200,000 worth originally planned. In this case, actual investment equals the \$1,000,000 in new equipment plus the \$400,000 in inventory investment, so $I = \$1{,}400{,}000$. We see that when the firm sells less output than planned, actual investment exceeds planned investment ($I > I^p$).

If Fly-by-Night has \$4,800,000 in sales, then it will add \$200,000 in kites to inventory, just as planned. In this case, actual and planned investment are the same:

$$I = I^p = \$1{,}200{,}000.$$

Finally, if Fly-by-Night sells \$5,000,000 worth of kites, it will have no output to add to inventory. Its inventory investment will be zero, and its total actual investment (including the new equipment) will equal \$1,000,000, which is less than its planned investment of \$1,200,000 ($I < I^p$). ◆

Because firms that are meeting the demand for their product or service at preset prices cannot control how much they sell, their actual investment (including inventory investment) may well differ from their planned investment. On the other hand, for households, the government, and foreign purchasers, we may reasonably assume that actual spending and planned spending are the same. Thus, from now on we will assume that, for consumption, government purchases, and net exports, actual spending equals planned spending.

With these assumptions, we can define planned aggregate expenditure by the following equation:

$$PAE = C + I^p + G + NX. \tag{19.1}$$

Equation 19.1 says that planned aggregate expenditure is the sum of planned spending by households, firms, governments, and foreigners. However, because planned spending equals actual spending for households, the government, and foreigners, we do not need to use superscripts to distinguish between planned versus actual consumption, government purchases, or net exports.

CONSUMER SPENDING AND THE ECONOMY

The largest component of planned aggregate expenditure—nearly two-thirds of total spending—is consumption spending. As already mentioned, consumer spending includes household purchases of goods such as groceries and clothing; services such as health care, concerts, and college tuition; and consumer durables such as cars, furniture, and home computers. Thus, consumers' willingness to spend affects sales and profitability in a wide range of industries. (Households' purchases of new homes are classified as investment, rather than consumption; but home purchases represent another channel through which household decisions affect total spending.)

What factors determine how much people plan to spend on consumer goods and services in a given period? While many factors are relevant, a particularly important determinant is their after-tax, or disposable, income. All else being equal, the higher the private sector's disposable income, the higher will be the level of consumption spending.

Figure 19.1 shows the relationship between real consumption expenditures and real disposable income in the United States for the period 1960–2007. Each point on the graph corresponds to a year between 1960 and 2007 (selected years are indicated in the figure). The position of each point is determined by the combination of relationship between aggregate consumption and disposable income.

FIGURE 19.1
The U.S. Consumption Function, 1960–2007.
Each point on this figure represents a combination of aggregate real consumption and aggregate real disposable income for a specific year between 1960 and 2007. Note the strong positive relationship between consumption and disposable income.

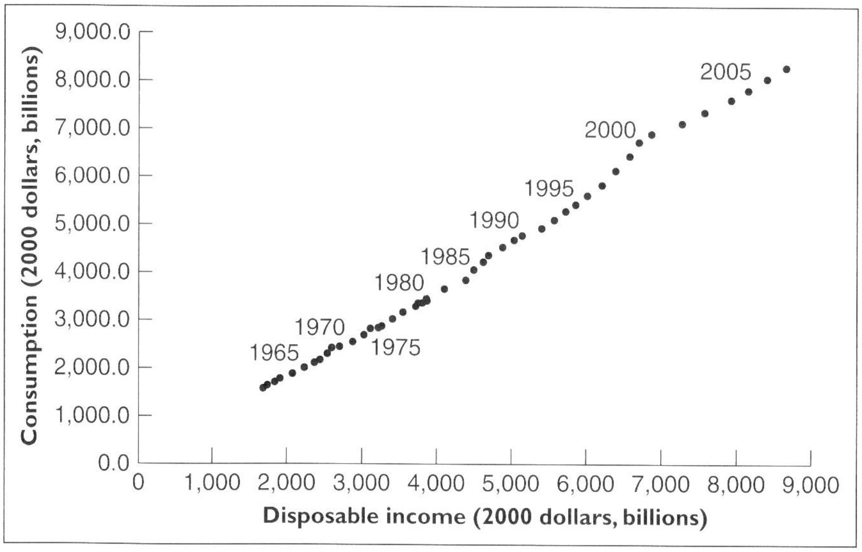

SOURCE: Bureau of Economic Analysis (www.bea.gov).

We can write this relationship between consumption and disposable income as a linear equation:[4]

$$C = \overline{C} + (mpc)(Y - T) \tag{19.2}$$

consumption function the relationship between consumption spending and its determinants, in particular, disposable income

This equation is known as the *consumption function*. The **consumption function** relates consumption spending (C) to disposable income ($Y - T$) and all other factors that might affect household spending.

autonomous consumption consumption spending that is not related to the level of disposable income

Let's look at the consumption function more carefully. The right side of the equation contains two terms, $\overline{C}$ and $(mpc)(Y - T)$. The amount of consumption represented by $\overline{C}$ is called **autonomous consumption** since it is consumption that is not related (i.e., autonomous from) changes in disposable income. For example, suppose consumers became more optimistic about the future, so that they wanted to consume more and save less at any given level of their current disposable income. In this case, $\overline{C}$ will increase and consumption will increase even though disposable income has not changed.

wealth effect the tendency of changes in asset prices to affect households' wealth and thus their consumption spending

We can imagine other factors that could affect autonomous consumption. Suppose, for example, that there is a boom in the stock market or a sharp increase in home prices, making consumers feel wealthier, and hence more inclined to spend, for a given level of current disposable income. This effect could be captured by assuming that $\overline{C}$ increases. Likewise, a fall in home prices or stock prices that made consumers feel poorer and less inclined to spend would be represented by a decrease in $\overline{C}$. Economists refer to the effects of changes in asset prices on consumption via changes in autonomous consumption as the **wealth effect.**

[4]You may want to review the material in the appendix to Chapter 1 if you don't regularly work with linear equations.

Finally, autonomous consumption also takes account of the effects that real interest rates have on consumption. In particular, higher real interest rates will make it more expensive to buy consumer durables on credit and so households may consume less and save more. $\overline{C}$ would thus decrease and consumption will fall even though disposable income has not changed. The opposite is also true: a decline in real interest rates will lower borrowing costs and the opportunity cost of saving, and so households may increase their autonomous consumption and therefore their total consumption spending.

Understanding wealth effects: How did the 2000–2002 decline in U.S. stock market values affect consumption spending?

From March 2000 to October 2002, the U.S. stock market suffered a 49 percent drop in value as measured by the Standard and Poor's 500 stock index, a widely referenced benchmark of U.S. stock performance. According to MIT economist James Poterba, U.S. households owned roughly \$13.3 trillion of corporate stock in 2000.[5] If households' stock market holdings reflect those of the Standard and Poor's stock index, the 49 percent drop in the value of the stock market wiped out approximately \$6.5 trillion of household wealth in two years. According to economic models based on historical experience, a dollar's decrease in household wealth reduces consumer spending by 3 to 7 cents per year, so the reduction in stock market wealth had the potential to reduce overall consumer spending by \$195 billion to \$455 billion, a drop of approximately 3 to 7 percent. Yet, real consumption spending continued to rise from 2000 through 2002. Why did this happen?

Despite the start of a recession in March 2001, overall consumption spending remained strong during 2000–2002 for a variety of reasons. First, consumers' real after-tax income continued to grow into the fall of 2001, helping to maintain strong consumer spending despite the drop in the stock market. Furthermore, throughout 2001 and into early 2002, the Federal Reserve significantly reduced interest rates; we will discuss how the Federal Reserve does this in the next chapter. As we discussed above, a reduction in interest rates helps to promote consumer spending, especially on durable goods such as automobiles, by reducing consumers' borrowing costs. Finally, housing prices rose significantly during this period, increasing consumers' housing wealth and partially offsetting their decline in stock-related wealth. Data on repeat house sales that measure the price of individual houses that are sold and resold over time indicate that housing prices rose by 20.1 percent between the first quarter of 2000 and the third quarter of 2002.[6] The total market value of household real estate was about \$12 trillion in 2000, so house price appreciation added about \$2.4 trillion to household wealth, offsetting about 37 percent of the decline in stock market wealth during this period.[7] ◆

The second term on the right side of Equation 19.2, $(mpc)(Y - T)$, measures the effect of disposable income, $Y - T$, on consumption. The **marginal propensity to consume (*mpc*)**, a fixed number, is the amount by which consumption rises when current disposable income rises by one dollar. The intuition behind the marginal propensity to consume is straightforward: if people receive an extra dollar of income, they will consume part of the dollar and save the rest. That is, their consumption will increase, but by less than the full dollar of extra income. It is therefore realistic to assume that the marginal propensity to consume is greater than 0 (an increase in income leads to an increase in consumption) but less than 1 (the

Marginal propensity to consume (mpc) the amount by which consumption rises when disposable income rises by \$1; we assume that $0 < mpc < 1$

[5]"The Stock Market and the Consumer," Hoover Institution Weekly Essays, November 6, 2000; available at www-hoover.stanford.edu/pubaffairs/we/current/poterba_1100.html.

[6]U.S. Office of Federal Housing Enterprise Oversight (OFHEO), www.ofheo.gov. House prices continued to rise from 2003 through 2006.

[7]Federal Reserve Board, Flow of Funds Accounts of the United States, www.federalreserve.gov.

increase in consumption will be less than the full increase in income). Mathematically, we can summarize these assumptions as $0 < mpc < 1$.

Figure 19.2 shows a hypothetical consumption function, with consumption spending (C) on the vertical axis and disposable income on the horizontal axis.

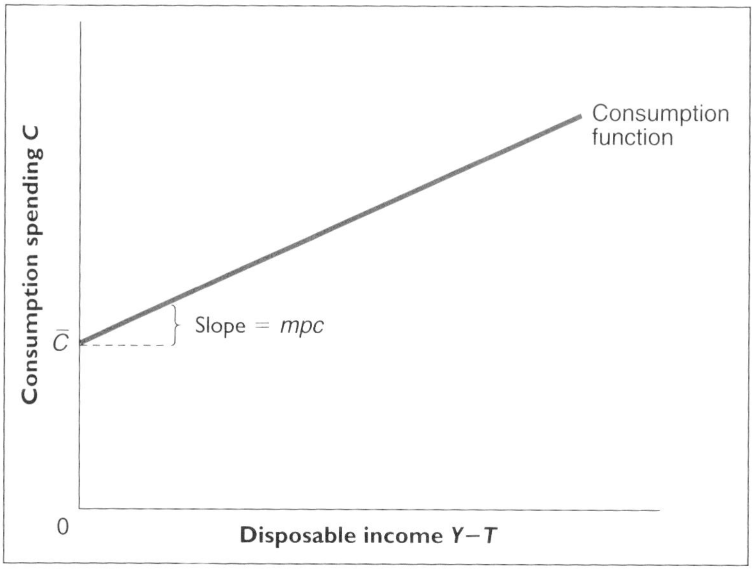

FIGURE 19.2
A Consumption Function.
The consumption function relates consumption spending (C) to disposable income, ($Y - T$). The vertical intercept of the consumption function is autonomous consumption ($\overline{C}$) and the slope of the line equals the marginal propensity to consume (mpc).

The intercept of the consumption function on the vertical axis equals autonomous consumption ($\overline{C}$) and the slope of the consumption function equals the marginal propensity to consume (mpc). To see how this consumption function fits reality, compare Figure 19.2 to Figure 19.1 (which shows the relationship between aggregate real consumption expenditures and real disposable income.) Our theoretical relationship clearly fits with the actual relationship between disposable income and consumption.

PLANNED AGGREGATE EXPENDITURE AND OUTPUT

Thinking back to Grandma's reminiscences, recall that an important element of her story involved the links among production, income, and spending. As the shoe factories in Grandma's town reduced production, the incomes of both factory workers and factory owners fell. Workers' incomes fell as the number of hours of work per week were reduced (a common practice during the Depression), as workers were laid off, or as wages were cut. Factory owners' income fell as profits declined. Reduced incomes, in turn, forced both workers and factory owners to curtail their spending—which led to still lower production and further reductions in income. This vicious circle led the economy further and further into recession.

The logic of Grandma's story has two key elements: (1) declines in production (which imply declines in the income received by producers) lead to reduced spending and (2) reductions in spending lead to declines in production and income. In this section, we look at the first part of the story, the effects of production and income on spending. We return later in this chapter to the effects of spending on production and income.

Why do changes in production and income affect planned aggregate spending? The consumption function, which relates consumption to disposable income, is the basic source of this relationship. Because consumption spending C is a large part of planned aggregate spending, and because consumption depends on output Y, aggregate spending as a whole depends on output.

Let's examine the link between planned aggregate expenditure and output in two ways. We will begin by working with a specific numerical example so that you can see the relationship clearly. Next, we will plot the relationship on a graph so that you can see its general shape and start working with these concepts using graphs.

Linking planned aggregate expenditure to output

In a particular economy, the consumption function is

$$C = 620 + 0.8(Y - T),$$

so that the intercept term in the consumption function $\overline{C}$ equals 620 and the marginal propensity to consume *mpc* equals 0.8. Also, suppose that we are given that planned investment spending $I^p = 220$, government purchases $G = 300$, net exports $NX = 20$, and taxes $T = 250$.

Recall the definition of planned aggregate expenditure, Equation 19.1:

$$PAE = C + I^p + G + NX$$

To find a numerical equation for planned aggregate expenditure, we need to find numerical expressions for each of its four components. The first component of spending, consumption, is defined by the consumption function, $C = 620 + 0.8(Y - T)$. Since $T = 250$, we can substitute for T to write the consumption function as $C = 620 + 0.8(Y - 250)$. Now plug this expression for C into the definition of planned aggregate expenditure above to get

$$PAE = [620 + 0.8(Y - 250)] + I^p + G + NX,$$

Similarly, we can substitute the given numerical values of planned investment I^p, government purchases G, and net exports NX into the definition of planned aggregate expenditure to get

$$PAE = [620 + 0.8(Y - 250)] + 220 + 300 + 20.$$

To simplify this equation, first note that $0.8(Y - 250) = 0.8Y - 200$, then add together all the terms that don't depend on output Y. The result is

$$PAE = (620 - 200 + 220 + 300 + 20) + 0.8Y$$

$$= 960 + 0.8Y.$$

The final expression shows the relationship between planned aggregate expenditure and output in this numerical example. Note that, according to this equation, a \$1 increase in Y leads to an increase in PAE of (0.8)(\$1), or 80 cents. The reason for this is that the marginal propensity to consume, *mpc,* in this example is 0.8. Hence, a \$1 increase in income raises consumption spending by 80 cents. Since consumption is a component of total planned spending, total spending rises by 80 cents as well. ◆

The specific equation we developed illustrates a general point: Planned aggregate expenditure can be divided into two parts, a part that depends on output (Y) and a part that is independent of output. The portion of planned aggregate expenditure that is independent of output is called **autonomous expenditure.** In the equation above, autonomous expenditure is the constant term and is equal to 960. This portion of planned spending, being a fixed number, does not vary when output varies. By contrast, the portion of planned aggregate expenditure that depends on

autonomous expenditure the portion of planned aggregate expenditure that is independent of output

induced expenditure the portion of planned aggregate expenditure that depends on output Y

expenditure line a line showing the relationship between planned aggregate expenditure and output

output (Y) is called **induced expenditure.** In the equation above, induced expenditure equals $0.8Y$, the second term in the expression for planned aggregate expenditure. Note that the numerical value of induced expenditure depends, by definition, on the numerical value taken by output. Autonomous expenditure and induced expenditure together equal planned aggregate expenditure.

Figure 19.3 is a graph of the equation $PAE = 960 + 0.8Y$, which is a straight line with a vertical intercept of 960 and a slope of 0.8. This line, which shows the relationship between planned aggregate expenditure and output graphically, is called the **expenditure line.**

FIGURE 19.3
The Expenditure Line
The line $PAE = 960 + 0.8Y$, referred to as the expenditure line, shows the relationship of planned aggregate expenditure to output.

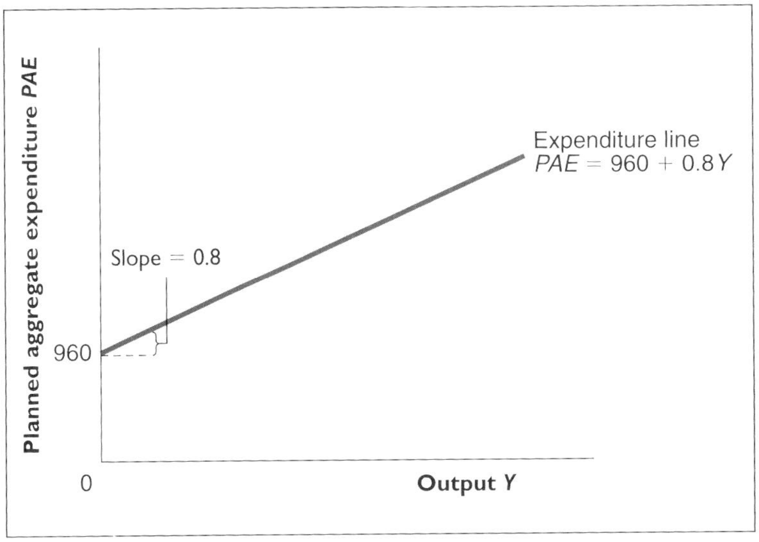

There are three properties of the expenditure line that are important to note. First, the slope of this line is equal to the marginal propensity to consume for our specific numerical example. This point holds in general: the slope of the expenditure line is equal to the marginal propensity to consume. Second, the vertical intercept is equal to autonomous expenditure for our example. This point also holds more generally: the vertical intercept of the expenditure line equals the level of autonomous expenditure. Third, changes in autonomous expenditure will shift the expenditure line: increases in autonomous expenditure will shift the expenditure line up while decreases will shift the line down. We will apply all three of these properties in the rest of the chapter.

RECAP	PLANNED AGGREGATE EXPENDITURE

- Planned aggregate expenditure (PAE) is total planned spending on final goods and services. The four components of planned spending are consumer expenditure (C), planned investment (I^p), government purchases (G), and net exports (NX). Planned investment differs from actual investment when firms' sales are different from what they expected, so that additions to inventory (a component of investment) are different from what firms anticipated.
- The largest component of aggregate expenditure is consumer expenditure, or simply consumption. Consumption depends on disposable, or after-tax, income, according to a relationship known as the consumption function, stated algebraically as $C = \overline{C} + (mpc)(Y - T)$.

- The constant term in the consumption function, $\overline{C}$, captures factors other than disposable income that affect consumer spending. For example, an increase in housing or stock prices that makes households wealthier and thus more willing to spend—an effect called the wealth effect—could be captured by an increase in $\overline{C}$. The slope of the consumption function equals the marginal propensity to consume, *mpc*, where $0 < mpc < 1$. This is the amount by which consumption rises when disposable income rises by one dollar.
- Increases in output Y, which imply equal increases in income, cause consumption to rise. As consumption is part of planned aggregate expenditure, planned spending depends on output as well. The portion of planned aggregate expenditure that depends on output is called induced expenditure. The portion of planned aggregate expenditure that is independent of output is autonomous expenditure.

SHORT-RUN EQUILIBRIUM OUTPUT

Now that we have defined planned aggregate expenditure and seen how it is related to output, the next task is to see how output itself is determined. Recall the assumption of the basic Keynesian model: In the short run, producers leave prices at preset levels and simply meet the demand that is forthcoming at those prices. In other words, during the short-run period in which prices are preset, firms produce an amount that is equal to planned aggregate expenditure. Accordingly, we define **short-run equilibrium output** as the level of output at which output Y equals planned aggregate expenditure *PAE:*

$$Y = PAE. \tag{19.3}$$

Short-run equilibrium output is the level of output that prevails during the period in which prices are predetermined.

short-run equilibrium output the level of output at which output Y equals planned aggregate expenditure *PAE;* short-run equilibrium output is the level of output that prevails during the period in which prices are predetermined

FINDING SHORT-RUN EQUILIBRIUM OUTPUT: NUMERICAL APPROACH

We can find short-run equilibrium output in three ways. First, we can use a table to compute the level of output at which $Y - PAE = 0$. Second, we can use a graph called the *Keynesian cross*. Finally, we can use algebra. Although we focus on the first two methods in this chapter, Appendix A to this chapter uses algebra to solve the model.

First, we use the data in Table 19.1 to find the equilibrium level of output for the economy described in the previous section. Column 2 of Table 19.1 lists the levels of planned aggregate expenditure (*PAE*) for the different levels of output given in column 1. Recall that in our example, planned spending is determined by the equation

$$PAE = 960 + 0.8Y.$$

Thus, for example, when $Y = 4{,}000$, $PAE = 960 + 0.8(4{,}000) = 4{,}160$. Because consumption rises with output, total planned spending (which includes consumption) rises also. But if you compare columns 1 and 2, you will see that when output rises by 200, planned spending rises by only 160. That is because the marginal propensity to consume in this economy is 0.8, so that each dollar in added income raises consumption and planned spending by 80 cents.

TABLE 19.1
Numerical Determination of Short-Run Equilibrium Output

(1) Output Y	(2) Planned aggregate expenditure $PAE = 960 + 0.8Y$	(3) $Y - PAE$	(4) $Y = PAE?$
4,000	4,160	−160	No
4,200	4,320	−120	No
4,400	4,480	−80	No
4,600	4,640	−40	No
4,800	4,800	0	**Yes**
5,000	4,960	40	No
5,200	5,120	80	No

Short-run equilibrium output is the level of output at which $Y = PAE$, or, equivalently, $Y - PAE = 0$. At this level of output, actual investment will equal planned investment and there will be no tendency for output to change. Looking at Table 19.1, we can see there is only one level of output that satisfies that condition, $Y = 4{,}800$. At that level, output and planned aggregate expenditure are precisely equal, so that producers are just meeting the demand for their goods and services.

In this economy, what would happen if output differed from its equilibrium value of 4,800? Suppose, for example, that output were 4,000. Looking at the second column of Table 19.1, you can see that when output is 4,000, planned aggregate expenditure equals 960 + 0.8(4,000), or 4,160. Thus, if output is 4,000, firms are not producing enough to meet the demand. They will find that as sales exceed the amounts they are producing, their inventories of finished goods are being depleted by 160 per year, and that actual investment (including inventory investment) is less than planned investment. Under the assumption that firms are committed to meeting their customers' demand, firms will respond by expanding their production.

Would expanding production to 4,160, the level of planned spending firms faced when output was 4,000, be enough? The answer is no because of induced expenditure. That is, as firms expand their output, aggregate income (wages and profits) rises with it, which in turn leads to higher levels of consumption. Indeed, if output expands to 4,160, planned spending will increase as well, to 960 + 0.8(4,160), or 4,288. So an output level of 4,160 will still be insufficient to meet demand. As Table 19.1 shows, output will not be sufficient to meet planned aggregate expenditure until it expands to its short-run equilibrium value of 4,800.

What if output were initially greater than its equilibrium value—say, 5,000? From Table 19.1, we can see that when output equals 5,000, planned spending equals only 4,960—less than what firms are producing. So at an output level of 5,000, firms will not sell all they produce, and they will find that their merchandise is piling up on store shelves and in warehouses (actual investment, including inventory investment, is greater than planned investment). In response, firms will cut their production runs. As Table 19.1 shows, they will have to reduce production to its equilibrium value of 4,800 before output just matches planned spending.

EXERCISE 19.1

Construct a table like Table 19.1 for an economy like the one we have been working with, assuming that the consumption function is $C = 820 + 0.7(Y - T)$ and that $I^P = 600$, $G = 600$, $NX = 200$, and $T = 600$.

What is short-run equilibrium output in this economy? (*Hint:* Try using values for output above 5,000.)

FINDING SHORT-RUN EQUILIBRIUM OUTPUT: GRAPHICAL APPROACH

Figure 19.4 shows the graphical determination of short-run equilibrium output for the economy we analyzed numerically above. Output (Y) is plotted on the horizontal axis and planned aggregate expenditure (PAE) on the vertical axis. The figure contains two lines. The blue line is the expenditure line, which we discussed earlier. This shows the amount of output people want to purchase at any given level of output. The red dashed line, extending from the origin, shows all of the points at which the variable on the horizontal axis (Y) equals the variable on the vertical axis (PAE). Since an economy is in short-run equilibrium where $Y = PAE$, the short-run equilibrium for our example must be somewhere along this line.

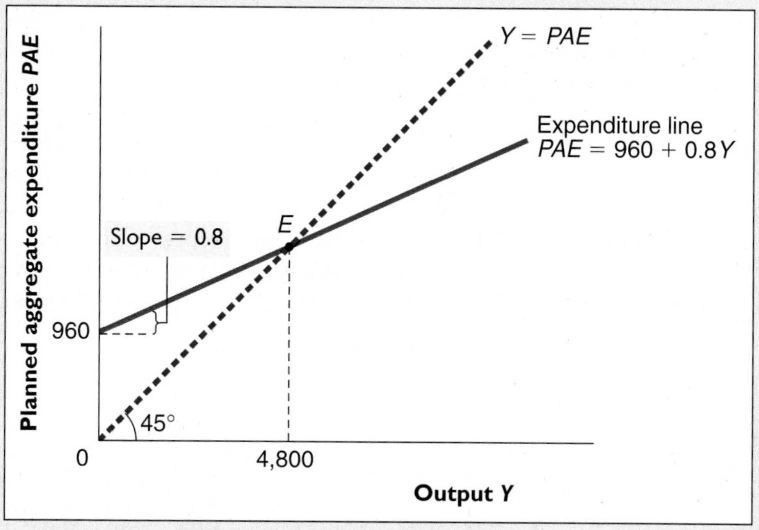

FIGURE 19.4
Determination of Short-Run Equilibrium Output (Keynesian Cross).
Short-run equilibrium output (4,800) is determined at point E the intersection of the expenditure line and the equilibrium condition ($Y = PAE$). This type of diagram is known as a Keynesian cross.

At which particular point on the $Y = PAE$ line will the economy be in short-run equilibrium? Only one point in the figure is on both the $Y = PAE$ line and the expenditure line: point E, where the two lines intersect. At point E, short-run equilibrium output equals 4,800, which is the same value that we obtained using Table 19.1.

What if the economy is above or below point E? At levels of output higher than 4,800, output exceeds planned aggregate expenditure. Hence, firms will be producing more than they can sell, which will lead them to reduce their rate of production. They will continue to reduce their production until output reaches 4,800, where output equals planned aggregate expenditure. By contrast, at levels of output below 4,800, planned aggregate expenditure exceeds output. In that region, firms will not be producing enough to meet demand, and they will tend to increase their production. Only at point E, where output equals 4,800, will firms be producing enough to just satisfy planned spending on goods and services.

The diagram in Figure 19.4 is called the *Keynesian cross,* due to the fact that it is a crosslike, graphical model of Keynes's basic ideas. The Keynesian cross shows graphically how short-run equilibrium output is determined in a world in which producers meet demand at predetermined prices.

EXERCISE 19.2

Use a Keynesian cross diagram to show graphically the determination of short-run equilibrium output for the economy described in Exercise 19.1. What are the intercept and the slope of the expenditure line?

PLANNED SPENDING AND THE OUTPUT GAP

We are now ready to use the basic Keynesian model to show how insufficient spending can lead to a recession. To illustrate the effects of spending changes on output, we will continue to work with the same example we have worked with throughout this chapter. We have shown that in this economy, short-run equilibrium output equals 4,800. Let's now make the additional assumption that potential output in this economy also equals 4,800, or $Y^* = 4{,}800$, so that initially there is no output gap. Starting from this position of full employment, let's analyze how a fall in planned aggregate expenditure can lead to a recession.

A fall in planned spending leads to a recession

Suppose that consumers become more pessimistic about the future, so that they begin to spend less at every level of current disposable income. We can capture this change by assuming that $\overline{C}$, the constant term in the consumption function, falls to a lower level. To be specific, suppose that $\overline{C}$ falls by 10 units, which in turn implies a decline in autonomous expenditure of 10 units.

We can see the effects of the decline in consumer spending on the economy using the Keynesian cross diagram. Figure 19.5 shows the original short-run equilibrium point of the model (E), at the intersection of the 45° line, along which $Y = PAE$, and the original expenditure line, representing the equation $PAE = 960 + 0.8Y$. As before, the initial value of short-run equilibrium output is 4,800, which we have now assumed also corresponds to potential output Y^*.

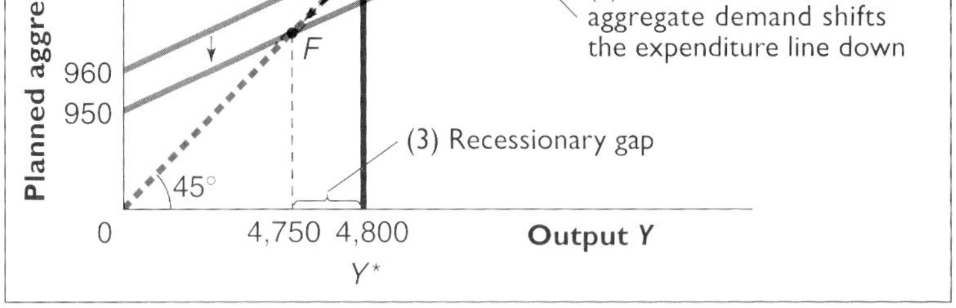

FIGURE 19.5
A Decline in Planned Spending Leads to a Recession.
(1) A decline in consumers' willingness to spend at any given level of output shifts the expenditure line down; (2) the short-run equilibrium point moves from E to F; (3) equilibrium output falls from 4,800 to 4,750; a recessionary gap of 50 is created.

Originally, autonomous expenditure in this economy was 960, so a decline of 10 units causes it to fall to 950. Instead of the economy's planned spending being described by the equation $PAE = 960 + 0.8Y$, as initially, it is now given by $PAE = 950 + 0.8Y$. What does this change imply for the graph in Figure 19.5? Since the intercept of the expenditure line (equal to autonomous expenditure) has decreased from 960 to 950, the effect of the decline in consumer spending will be to shift the expenditure line down in parallel fashion, by 10 units. Figure 19.5 indicates this downward shift in the expenditure line. The new short-run equilibrium point is at point F, where the new, lower expenditure line intersects the $Y = PAE$ line.

Point F is to the left of the original equilibrium point E, so we can see that output and spending have fallen from their initial levels. Since output at point F is lower than potential output, 4,800, we see that the fall in consumer spending has resulted in a recessionary gap in the economy. More generally, starting from a situation of full employment (where output equals potential output), any decline in autonomous expenditure leads to a recession. ◆

Numerically, how large is the recessionary gap in Figure 19.5? To answer this question, we can use Table 19.2, which is in the same form as Table 19.1. The key difference is that in Table 19.2 planned aggregate expenditure is given by $PAE = 950 + 0.8Y$, rather than by $PAE = 960 + 0.8Y$, as in Table 19.1.

TABLE 19.2
Determination of Short-Run Equilibrium Output after a Fall in Spending

(1) Output Y	(2) Planned aggregate expenditure $PAE = 950 + 0.8Y$	(3) $Y - PAE$	(4) $Y = PAE$?
4,600	4,630	−30	No
4,650	4,670	−20	No
4,700	4,710	−10	No
4,750	4,750	0	**Yes**
4,800	4,790	10	No
4,850	4,830	20	No
4,900	4,870	30	No
4,950	4,910	40	No
5,000	4,950	50	No

As in Table 19.1, the first column of the table shows alternative possible values of output Y, and the second column shows the levels of planned aggregate expenditure PAE implied by each value of output in the first column. Notice that 4,800, the value of short-run equilibrium output found in Table 19.1, is no longer an equilibrium; when output is 4,800, planned spending is 4,790, so output and planned spending are not equal. As the table shows, following the decline in planned aggregate expenditure, short-run equilibrium output is 4,750, the only value of output for which $Y = PAE$. Thus, a drop of 10 units in autonomous expenditure has led to a 50-unit decline in short-run equilibrium output. If full-employment output is 4,800, then the recessionary gap shown in Figure 19.5 is $4{,}800 - 4{,}750 = 50$ units.

EXERCISE 19.3

In the economy described above, we found a recessionary gap of 50, relative to potential output of 4,800. Suppose that in this economy, the natural rate of unemployment u^* is 5 percent. What will the actual unemployment rate be after the recessionary gap appears? (*Hint:* Recall Okun's law from the last chapter.)

The example that we just worked through showed that a decline in autonomous expenditure, arising from a decreased willingness of consumers to spend, causes short-run equilibrium output to fall and opens up a recessionary gap. The same conclusion applies to declines in autonomous expenditure arising from other sources. Suppose, for instance, that firms become disillusioned with new technologies and cut back their planned investment in new equipment. In terms of the model, this reluctance of firms to invest can be interpreted as a decline in planned investment spending I^p. Under our assumption that planned investment spending is given and does not depend on output, planned investment is part of autonomous expenditure. So a decline in planned investment spending depresses autonomous expenditure and output, in precisely the same way that a decline in the autonomous part of consumption spending does. Similar conclusions apply to declines in other components of autonomous expenditure, such as government purchases and net exports, as we will see in later applications.

EXERCISE 19.4

Repeat the analysis of the previous example, except assume that consumers become *more* rather than less confident about the future. As a result, $\overline{C}$ rises by 10 units, which in turn raises autonomous expenditure by 10 units. Show graphically that this increase in consumers' willingness to spend leads to an expansionary output gap. Find the numerical value of the expansionary output gap.

"These are hard times for retailers, so we should show them our support in every way we can."

Why was the deep Japanese recession of the 1990s bad news for the rest of East Asia?

During the 1990s, Japan suffered a prolonged economic slump. Japan's economic problems were a major concern not only of the Japanese but of policymakers in other East Asian countries, such as Thailand and Singapore. Why did East Asian policymakers worry about the effects of the Japanese slump on their own economies?

Although the economies of Japan and its East Asian neighbors are intertwined in many ways, one of the most important links is through trade. Much of the economic success of East Asia has been based on the development of export industries, and over the years Japan has been the most important customer for East Asian goods. When the economy slumped in the 1990s, Japanese households and firms reduced their purchases of imported goods sharply. This fall in demand dealt a major blow to the export industries of other East Asian countries.

Not just the owners and workers of export industries were affected, though; as wages and profits in export industries fell, so did domestic spending in the East Asian nations. The declines in domestic spending reduced sales at home as well as abroad, further weakening the East Asian economies. In terms of the model, the decline in exports to Japan reduced net exports *NX*, and thus autonomous expenditure, in East Asian countries. The fall in autonomous expenditure led to a recessionary gap, much like that shown in Figure 19.5.

Japan is not the only country whose economic ups and downs have had a major impact on its trading partners. Because the United States is the most important trading partner of both Canada and Mexico, the U.S. recession that began in 2001 led to declining exports and recessions in Canada and Mexico as well. East Asia, which exports high-tech goods to the United States, also was hurt by the U.S recession, with GDP in countries such as Singapore dropping sharply. Economic growth rebounded throughout most of East Asia after 2001, largely because of increased demand for exports to the United States and China. ◆

What caused the 2001 recession in the United States?

As we discussed in the previous chapter, a recession began in the United States in March 2001—the first U.S. recession in 10 years. What caused the 2001 recession in the United States?

Consumer spending is nearly two-thirds of aggregate expenditure, so it should not be surprising that most recessions involve significant reductions in spending by households. In this respect, the 2001 recession in the United States was quite unusual, as consumer spending remained fairly strong throughout most of the downturn. Instead, this recession can be attributed primarily to a steep drop in investment spending by firms.

Why did investment expenditures fall? The period between 1995 and 2000 had been one of high rates of investment and rapid growth in the U.S. economy, fueled in large part by optimism about new technologies such as the internet, fiber optics, and genetic engineering. However, by mid-2000 it was becoming apparent that some of the new technologies would not be as profitable as had been hoped. The prices of shares in high-tech companies fell sharply during the year and corporations cut back their investments in computers, software, telecommunications equipment, and the like. Although at first the decline was concentrated in the high-tech sector, the slowdown spread to other parts of the economy. Total employment peaked and began to decline in March 2001.

An additional shock occurred on September 11, 2001, when terrorist attacks destroyed the World Trade Center in New York City and inflicted heavy damage on the Pentagon in Washington, D.C. People became afraid to travel, and the demand for air travel, hotel rooms, and tourist services plummeted, worsening the downturn. However, consumers regained confidence surprisingly quickly—for example, spurred by generous rebates, they purchased a record number of automobiles during October. Increased government spending on security and defense also raised planned aggregate expenditure by the end of the year, and the recession ended in November. The economy rebounded in 2002, although employment did not surpass its prerecession peak until 2004.

Neither the decline in investment spending nor the decline in travel were related to changes in income. Thus, these acted as decreases in autonomous expenditure and created a situation like that shown in Figure 19.5. ◆

THE MULTIPLIER

In Table 19.2 and Figure 19.5, we analyzed a case in which the initial decline in autonomous expenditure was only 10 units, and yet short-run equilibrium output fell by 50 units. Why did a relatively modest initial decline in consumer spending lead to a much larger fall in output?

The reason the impact on output was greater than the initial change in spending is the "vicious circle" effect suggested by Grandma's reminiscences about the Great Depression. Specifically, a fall in consumer spending not only reduces the sales of consumer goods directly; it also reduces the incomes of workers and owners in the industries that produce consumer goods. As their incomes fall, these workers and capital owners reduce their spending, which reduces the output and incomes of *other* producers in the economy. And these reductions in income lead to still further cuts in spending. Ultimately, these successive rounds of declines in spending and income may lead to a decrease in planned aggregate expenditure and output that is significantly greater than the change in spending that started the process.

income-expenditure multiplier the effect of a one-unit increase in autonomous expenditure on short-run equilibrium output; for example, a multiplier of 5 means that a 10-unit decrease in autonomous expenditure reduces short-run equilibrium output by 50 units

The effect on short-run equilibrium output of a one-unit increase in autonomous expenditure is called the **income-expenditure multiplier,** or the *multiplier* for short. In our example economy, the multiplier is 5. That is, each 1-unit change in autonomous expenditure leads to a 5-unit change in short-run equilibrium output in the same direction. The idea that a change in spending may lead to a significantly larger change in short-run equilibrium output is a key feature of the basic Keynesian model.

What determines how large the multiplier will be? An important factor is the marginal propensity consume (*mpc*). If the *mpc* is large, then falls in income will cause people to reduce their spending sharply, and the multiplier effect will then also be large. If the marginal propensity to consume is small, then people will not reduce spending so much when income falls, and the multiplier also will be small. Appendix B to this chapter provides more details on the multiplier in the basic Keynesian model, including a formula that allows us to calculate the value of the multiplier under specific assumptions about the economy.

RECAP SHORT-RUN EQUILIBRIUM OUTPUT

- Short-run equilibrium output is the level of output at which output equals planned aggregate expenditure, or, in symbols, $Y = PAE$. For a specific sample economy, short-run equilibrium output can be solved for numerically or graphically.
- The graphical solution is based on a diagram called the Keynesian cross. The Keynesian cross diagram includes two lines: a 45° line that represents the condition $Y = PAE$ and the expenditure line, which shows the relationship of planned aggregate expenditure to output. Short-run equilibrium output is determined at the intersection of the two lines. If short-run equilibrium output differs from potential output, an output gap exists.
- Increases in autonomous expenditure shift the expenditure line upward, increasing short-run equilibrium output; decreases in autonomous expenditure shift the expenditure line downward, leading to declines in short-run equilibrium output. Decreases in autonomous expenditure that drive actual output below potential output are a source of recessions.
- Generally, a one-unit change in autonomous expenditure leads to a larger change in short-run equilibrium output, reflecting the working of the income-expenditure multiplier. The multiplier arises because a given initial increase in spending raises the incomes of producers, which leads them to spend more, raising the incomes and spending of other producers, and so on.

STABILIZING PLANNED SPENDING: THE ROLE OF FISCAL POLICY

According to the basic Keynesian model, inadequate spending is an important cause of recessions. To fight recessions—at least, those caused by insufficient demand rather than slow growth of potential output—policymakers must find ways to stimulate planned spending. Policies that are used to affect planned aggregate expenditure, with the objective of eliminating output gaps, are called **stabilization policies.** Policy actions intended to increase planned spending and output are called **expansionary policies;** expansionary policy actions are normally taken when the economy is in recession. It is also possible, as we have seen, for the economy to be "overheated," with output greater than potential output (an expansionary gap). The risk of an expansionary gap, as we will see in more detail later, is that it may lead to an increase in inflation. To offset an expansionary gap, policymakers will try to reduce spending and output. **Contractionary policies** are policy actions intended to reduce planned spending and output.

stabilization policies government policies that are used to affect planned aggregate expenditure, with the objective of eliminating output gaps

expansionary policies government policy actions intended to increase planned spending and output

contractionary policies government policy actions designed to reduce planned spending and output

The two major tools of stabilization policy are *monetary policy* and *fiscal policy.* Recall that monetary policy refers to decisions about the size of the money supply, whereas fiscal policy refers to decisions about the government's budget—how much the government spends and how much tax revenue it collects. In the remainder of this chapter, we will focus on how fiscal policy can be used to influence spending in the basic Keynesian model. Monetary policy will be discussed in the next two chapters along with some practical issues that arise in formulating macroeconomic policy.

GOVERNMENT PURCHASES AND PLANNED SPENDING

Decisions about government spending represent one of the two main components of fiscal policy, the other being decisions about taxes and transfer payments. As was mentioned earlier (see Box 19.1), Keynes himself felt that changes in government purchases were probably the most effective tool for reducing or eliminating output gaps. His basic argument was straightforward: Government purchases of goods and services, being a component of planned aggregate expenditure, directly affect total spending. If output gaps are caused by too much or too little total spending, then the government can help to guide the economy toward full employment by changing its own level of spending. Keynes's views seemed to be vindicated by the events of the 1930s, notably the fact that the Depression did not finally end until governments greatly increased their military spending in the latter part of the decade.

An increase in the government's purchases eliminates a recessionary gap

In our example economy, we found that a drop of 10 units in consumer spending creates a recessionary gap of 50 units. How can the government eliminate the output gap and restore full employment by changing its purchases of goods and services G?

Planned aggregate expenditure was given by the equation $PAE = 960 + 0.8Y$, so that autonomous expenditure equaled 960. The 10-unit drop in $\overline{C}$ implied a 10-unit drop in autonomous expenditure, to 950. Because the multiplier in that sample economy equaled 5, this 10-unit decline in autonomous expenditure resulted in turn in a 50-unit decline in short-run equilibrium output.

To offset the effects of the consumption decline, the government would have to restore autonomous expenditure to its original value, 960. Under our assumption that government purchases are simply given and do not depend on output, government purchases are part of autonomous expenditure, and changes in government purchases change autonomous expenditure one-for-one. Thus, to increase autonomous expenditure from 950 to 960, the government should simply increase its purchases by 10 units (for example, by increasing spending on military defense or road construction). According to the basic Keynesian model, this increase in government purchases should return autonomous expenditure and, hence, output to their original levels.

The effect of the increase in government purchases is shown graphically in Figure 19.6. After the 10-unit decline in the autonomous component of consumption spending, the economy is at point *F*, with a 50-unit recessionary gap. A 10-unit increase in government purchases raises autonomous expenditure by 10 units, raising the intercept of the expenditure line by 10 units and causing the expenditure line to shift upward in parallel fashion. The economy returns to point *E*, where short-run equilibrium output equals potential output ($Y = Y^* = 4{,}800$) and the output gap has been eliminated.

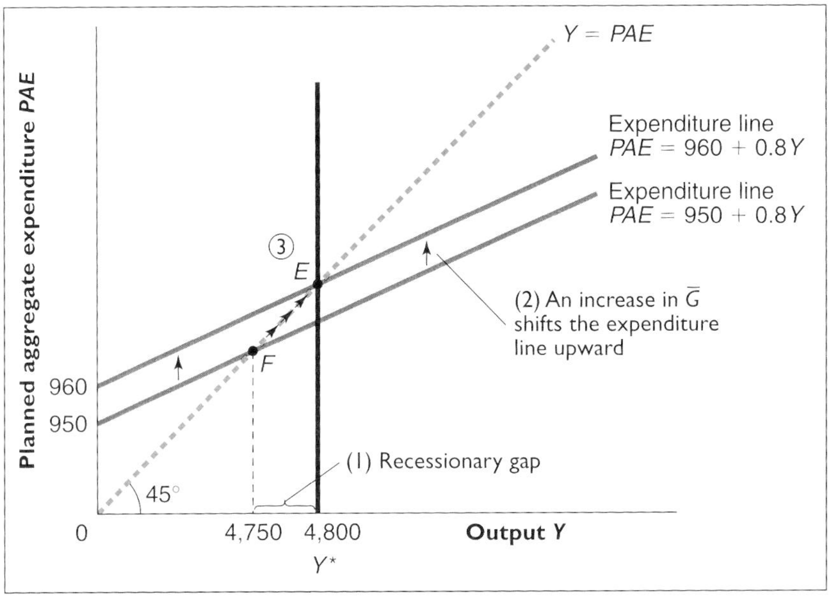

FIGURE 19.6
An Increase in Government Purchases Eliminates a Recessionary Gap.
(1) The economy is initially at point *F*, with a recessionary gap of 50; (2) a 10-unit increase in government purchases raises autonomous expenditure by 10 units, shifting the expenditure line up; (3) the new equilibrium is at point *E*, where output equals potential output. The output gap has been eliminated.

◆

EXERCISE 19.5

In Exercise 19.4, you considered the case in which consumers become more rather than less confident, leading to an expansionary output gap. Discuss how a change in government purchases could be used to eliminate an expansionary gap. Show your analysis graphically.

To this point we have been considering the effect of fiscal policy on a hypothetical economy. Now, let's look at two applications of fiscal policy in real economies.

Example 19.1
THE ECONOMIC NATURALIST

Why did Japan build roads that nobody wanted to use?

A few years ago, Japanese officials decided to build a 160-mile-long toll road on the northern island of Hokkaido. The cost of the road was about $60 million per mile. Very few drivers used the road, largely because an existing highway that runs parallel to the new toll road is free. Officials tried to attract drivers by offering prizes and running promotional contests. Though the campaign succeeded in increasing the average number of cars on the road to 862 per day, the route is still the least-used highway in Japan.[8]

Japan spent the 1990s in a deep slump. In response, the Japanese government periodically initiated large spending programs to try to stimulate the economy. Indeed, during the 1990s, the Japanese government spent more than $1 trillion on public works projects. More than $10 billion was spent on the Tokyo subway system alone, an amount so far over budget that subway tokens will have to cost an estimated $9.50 each if the investment is ever to be recouped. (Even more frustrating to passengers, the subway does not run in a complete circle, requiring them to make inconvenient transfers to traverse the city.) Other examples of government spending programs include the construction of multimillion-dollar concert halls in small towns, elaborate tunnels where simple roads would have been adequate, and the digging up and relaying of cobblestone sidewalks. Despite all this spending, the Japanese slump dragged on.

The basic Keynesian model implies that increases in government spending such as those undertaken in Japan should help to increase output and employment. Japanese public works projects do appear to have stimulated the economy, though not enough to pull Japan out of recession. Why has Japan's fiscal policy proved inadequate to the task? Some critics have argued that the Japanese government was unconscionably slow in initiating the fiscal expansion, and that when spending was finally increased, it was simply not enough, relative to the size of the Japanese economy and the depth of the recession. Another possibility, which lies outside the basic Keynesian model, is that the wasteful nature of much of the government spending demoralized Japanese consumers, who realized that as taxpayers they would at some point be responsible for the costs incurred in building roads nobody wants to use. Reduced consumer confidence implies reduced consumption spending, which, to some extent, may have offset the stimulus from government spending. Very possibly, more productive investments of Japanese public funds would have had a greater impact on aggregate expenditure (by avoiding the fall in consumer confidence); certainly, they would have had a greater long-term benefit in terms of increasing the potential output of the economy. ●

Does military spending stimulate the economy?

An antiwar poster from the 1960s bore the message "War is good business. Invest your son." War itself poses too many economic and human costs to be good business, but military spending could be a different matter. According to the basic Keynesian model, increases in planned aggregate expenditure resulting from stepped-up government purchases may help bring an economy out of a recession or depression. Does military spending stimulate aggregate demand?

Figure 19.7 shows U.S. military spending as a share of GDP from 1940 to 2007. The shaded areas in the figure correspond to periods of recession as shown in Table 18.1. Note the spike that occurred during World War II (1941–1945), when military spending reached nearly 38 percent of U.S. GDP, as well as the surge during the Korean War (1950–1953). Smaller increases in military spending relative to GDP occurred at the peak of the Vietnam War in 1967–1969, during the Reagan military buildup of the 1980s, and during the wars in Afghanistan and Iraq.

Figure 19.7 provides some support for the idea that expanded military spending tends to promote growth in aggregate demand. The clearest case is the World War II era, during which massive military spending helped the U.S. economy to recover from the Great Depression. The U.S. unemployment rate fell from 17.2 percent of the workforce in 1939 (when defense spending was less than 2 percent of GDP) to 1.2 percent in 1944 (when defense spending was greater than 37 percent of GDP). Two brief recessions, in 1945 and 1948–1949, followed the end of the

[8]*New York Times,* November 25, 1999, p. A1.

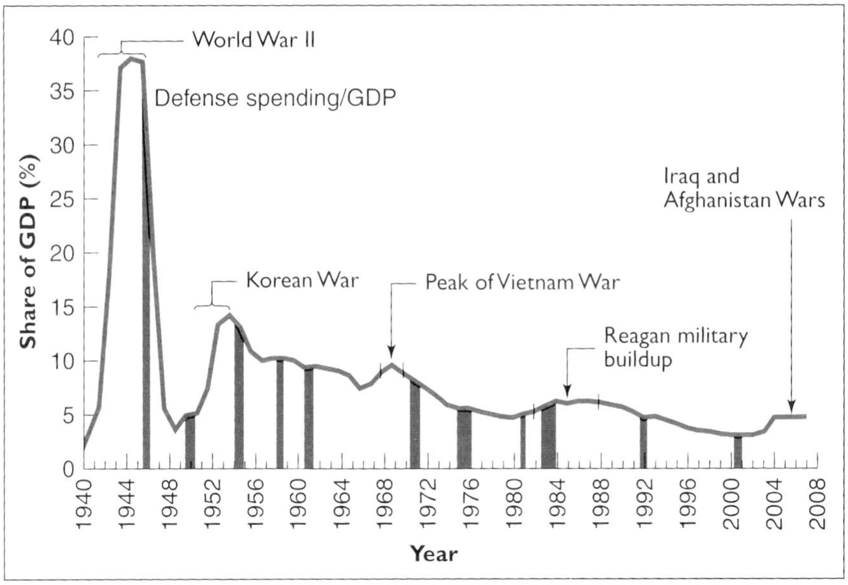

FIGURE 19.7
U.S. Military Expenditures as a Share of GDP, 1940–2007.
Military expenditures as a share of GDP rose during World War II, the Korean War, the Vietnam War, and the Reagan military buildup of the early 1980s. Increased military spending is generally associated with an expanding economy and declining unemployment. The shaded areas indicate periods of recession.

SOURCE: Bureau of Economic Analysis (www.bea.gov).

war and the sharp decline in military spending. At the time, though, many people feared that the war's end would bring a resumption of the Great Depression, so the relative mildness of the two postwar recessions was something of a relief.

Increases in defense spending during the post–World War II period also were associated with economic expansions. The Korean War of 1950–1953 occurred simultaneously with a strong expansion, during which the unemployment rate dropped from 5.9 percent in 1949 to 2.9 percent in 1953. A recession began in 1954, the year after the armistice was signed, though military spending had not yet declined much. Economic expansions also occurred during the Vietnam-era military buildup in the 1960s and the Reagan buildup of the 1980s. Finally, on a smaller scale, increased government spending for homeland security and the wars in Afghanistan and Iraq probably contributed to the relative mildness of the U.S. recession in 2001 and the strength of the subsequent recovery. These episodes support the idea that increases in government purchases—in this case, of weapons, other military supplies, and the services of military personnel—can help to stimulate the economy. ◆

"Your majesty, my voyage will not only forge a new route to the spices of the East but also create over three thousand new jobs."

TAXES, TRANSFERS, AND AGGREGATE SPENDING

Besides making decisions about government purchases of goods and services, fiscal policymakers also determine the level and types of taxes to be collected and transfer payments to be made. (Transfer payments, recall, are payments made by the government to the public, for which no current goods or services are received. Examples of transfer payments are unemployment insurance benefits, Social Security benefits, and income support payments to farmers. Remember: transfer payments are *not* included in government purchases of goods and services.) The basic Keynesian model implies that, like changes in government purchases, changes in the level of taxes or transfers can be used to affect planned aggregate expenditure and thus eliminate output gaps.

Unlike changes in government purchases, however, changes in taxes or transfers do not affect planned spending directly. Instead they work indirectly, by changing disposable income in the private sector. Recall that disposable income is equal to $Y - T$, where T represents *net taxes*. Net taxes, in turn, are equal to taxes minus transfers. Consequently, net taxes will fall by one unit if *either* taxes are cut by one *or* transfers are increased by one. According to the consumption function, when disposable income rises, households should spend more. Thus, a tax cut or increase in transfers should increase planned aggregate expenditure. Likewise, an increase in taxes or a cut in transfers, by lowering households' disposable income, will tend to lower planned spending.

Using a tax cut to close a recessionary gap

In our hypothetical economy, an initial drop in consumer spending of 10 units creates a recessionary gap of 50 units. We showed that this recessionary gap could be eliminated by a 10-unit increase in government purchases. Suppose that, instead of increasing government purchases, fiscal policymakers decided to stimulate consumer spending by changing the level of tax collections. By how much should they change taxes to eliminate the output gap?

A common first guess is that policymakers should cut taxes by 10, but that guess is not correct. Let's see why.

The source of the recessionary gap is the reduction that households made in their consumption spending by 10 units at each level of output Y—that is, the constant term $\overline{C}$ in the consumption function is assumed to have fallen 10 units. To eliminate this recessionary gap, the change in taxes must induce households to increase their consumption spending by 10 units at each output level. However, if taxes T are cut by 10 units, raising disposable income $Y - T$ by 10 units, consumption at each level of output Y will increase by only 8 units.

Why? The reason is that the marginal propensity to consume in our example is 0.8, so that consumption spending increases by only 0.8 times the amount of the tax cut. (The rest of the tax cut is saved.) An increase in autonomous expenditure of eight units is not enough to return output to its full-employment level, in this example.

To raise consumption spending by 10 units at each level of output, fiscal policymakers must instead cut taxes by 12.5 units. This will raise the level of disposable income, $Y - T$, by 12.5 units at each level of output Y. Consequently, consumption will increase by the marginal propensity to consume times the increase in disposable income, or by $0.8(12.5) = 10$. Thus, a tax cut of 12.5 will spur households to increase their consumption by 10 units at each level of output.

These changes are illustrated in Table 19.3. Following the initial 10-unit drop in consumer spending, the equilibrium level of output fell to 4,750. When net taxes are equal to their initial level of 250, column 3 illustrates that disposable income equals $4{,}750 - 250 = 4{,}500$. After the drop in consumer spending, the consumption function becomes $C = 610 + 0.8(Y - T)$. Thus, when $Y = 4{,}750$ and $T = 250$,

TABLE 19.3
Initial Effect of a Reduction in Taxes of 12.5

(1) Output Y	(2) Net taxes T	(3) Disposable income $Y - T$	(4) Consumption $610 + 0.8(Y - T)$
4,750	250	4,500	4,210
4,750	237.5	4,512.5	4,220

consumption will equal 610 + 0.8(4,750 − 250) = 610 + 0.8(4,500) = 4,210, as shown in column 4. If taxes are cut by 12.5 to 237.5, disposable income at that level of output will rise by 12.5 to 4,750 − 237.5 = 4,512.5. Consumption at that level of output will rise by 0.8(12.5) = 10 so that $C = 610 + 0.8(4{,}750 - 237.5) = 4{,}220$. This increase will just offset the initial 10-unit decrease in $\overline{C}$ and will bring the economy back to full employment.

Note that since T refers to *net taxes*, or taxes less transfers, the same result could be obtained by increasing transfer payments by 12.5 units. Because households spend 0.8 times any increase in transfer payments they receive, this policy also would raise consumption spending by 10 units at any level of output.

Graphically, the effect of the tax cut is identical to the effect of the increase in government purchases, shown in Figure 19.6. Because it leads to a 10-unit increase in consumption at any level of output, the tax cut shifts the expenditure line up by 10 units. Equilibrium is attained at point E in Figure 19.6, where output again equals potential output. ◆

EXERCISE 19.6

In a particular economy, a 20-unit increase in planned investment moved the economy from an initial situation with no output gap to a situation with an expansionary gap. Describe two ways in which fiscal policy could be used to offset this expansionary gap. Assume the marginal propensity to consume equals 0.5.

Why did the federal government send out millions of $300 and $600 checks to households in 2001?

On May 25, 2001, Congress passed the Economic Growth and Tax Relief Reconciliation Act (EGTRRA) of 2001, which President George W. Bush signed on June 7. The EGTRRA made significant cuts in income tax rates and also provided for one-time tax rebate checks of up to $300 for individual taxpayers and up to $600 for married taxpayers filing a joint return. Millions of families received these checks in August and September of 2001, with payments totaling about $38 billion.

Although the 2001 recession was not officially "declared" until November 2001 (when the National Bureau of Economic Research announced that the recession had begun in March), there was clear evidence by the spring of 2001 that the economy was slowing. Congress and the president hoped that by sending tax rebate checks to households, they could stimulate spending and perhaps avoid recession. In retrospect, the timing of the tax rebate was quite good, since the economy and consumer confidence were further buffeted by the terrorist attacks on New York City and Washington on September 11, 2001.

Did the tax rebates have their intended effect of stimulating consumer spending? In a recent study, economists found that households spent about two-thirds of their rebates within six months of receiving them.[9] This suggests that the rebate had a substantial effect on consumer spending, which held up remarkably well during the last quarter of 2001 and into 2002. ◆

The weakening of the U.S. economy in late 2007 led Congress and the president to pass the Economic Stimulus Act of 2008. Tax rebate checks of approximately $150 billion were set to be mailed out in mid-2008.

RECAP | FISCAL POLICY AND PLANNED SPENDING

Fiscal policy consists of two tools for affecting total spending and eliminating output gaps: (1) changes in government purchases and (2) changes in taxes or transfer payments. An increase in government purchases increases autonomous expenditure by an equal amount. A reduction in taxes or an increase in transfer payments increases autonomous expenditure by an amount equal to the marginal propensity to consume times the reduction in taxes or increase in transfers. The ultimate effect of a fiscal policy change on short-run equilibrium output equals the change in autonomous expenditure times the multiplier. Accordingly, if the economy is in recession, an increase in government purchases, a cut in taxes, or an increase in transfers can be used to stimulate spending and eliminate the recessionary gap.

FISCAL POLICY AS A STABILIZATION TOOL: THREE QUALIFICATIONS

The basic Keynesian model might lead you to think that precise use of fiscal policy can eliminate output gaps. But as is often the case, the real world is more complicated than economic models suggest. We close the chapter with three qualifications about the use of fiscal policy as a stabilization tool.

FISCAL POLICY AND THE SUPPLY SIDE

We have focused on the use of fiscal policy to affect planned aggregate expenditure. However, most economists would agree that *fiscal policy may affect potential output as well as planned aggregate expenditure.* On the spending side, for example, investments in public capital such as roads, airports, and schools can play a major role in the growth of potential output, as we discussed in Chapter 15. On the other side of the ledger, tax and transfer programs may well affect the incentives, and thus the economic behavior, of households and firms. Some critics of the Keynesian

[9]David S. Johnson, Jonathan A. Parker, and Nicholas S. Souleles, *Household Expenditure and the Income Tax Rebates of 2001,* National Bureau of Economic Research Working Paper 10,784, September 2004.

theory have gone so far as to argue that the *only* effects of fiscal policy that matter are effects on potential output. This was essentially the view of the so-called *supply-siders*, a group of economists and journalists whose influence reached a high point during the first Reagan term (1981–1985). Most economists now agree that fiscal policy affects *both* planned spending *and* potential output.

THE PROBLEM OF DEFICITS

A second consideration for fiscal policymakers thinking about stabilization policies is *the need to avoid large and persistent budget deficits.* Recall from Chapter 16 that the government's budget deficit is the excess of government spending over tax collections. Sustained government deficits can be harmful because they reduce national saving, which in turn reduces investment in new capital goods—an important source of long-run economic growth. The need to keep deficits under control may make increasing spending or cutting taxes to fight a slowdown a less attractive option, both economically and politically. For instance, as we discussed above, Japan substantially increased government spending to fight a recession in the mid-1990s. The Japanese government's budget deficit grew so large that the Japanese prime minister ruled out further use of fiscal policy to stimulate the economy after 1999.

THE RELATIVE INFLEXIBILITY OF FISCAL POLICY

The third qualification about the use of fiscal policy is that *fiscal policy is not always flexible enough to be useful for stabilization.* Our examples have implicitly assumed that the government can change spending or taxes relatively quickly in order to eliminate output gaps. In reality, changes in government spending or taxes must usually go through a lengthy legislative process, which reduces the ability of fiscal policy to respond in a timely way to economic conditions. For example, budget and tax changes proposed by the president must typically be submitted to Congress 18 months or more before they go into effect. Another factor that limits the flexibility of fiscal policy is that fiscal policymakers have many other objectives besides stabilizing aggregate spending, from ensuring an adequate national defense to providing income support to the poor. What happens if, say, the need to strengthen the national defense requires an increase in government spending, but the need to contain planned aggregate expenditure requires a decrease in government spending? Such conflicts can be difficult to resolve through the political process.

This lack of flexibility means that fiscal policy is less useful for stabilizing spending than the basic Keynesian model suggests. Nevertheless, most economists view fiscal policy as an important stabilizing force, for two reasons. The first is the presence of **automatic stabilizers**, provisions in the law that imply *automatic* increases in government spending or decreases in taxes when real output declines. For example, some government spending is earmarked as "recession aid"; it flows to communities automatically when the unemployment rate reaches a certain level. Taxes and transfer payments also respond automatically to output gaps: When GDP declines, income tax collections fall (because households' taxable incomes fall) while unemployment insurance payments and welfare benefits rise—all without any explicit action by Congress. These automatic changes in government spending and tax collections help to increase planned spending during recessions and reduce it during expansions, without the delays inherent in the legislative process.

automatic stabilizers provisions in the law that imply *automatic* increases in government spending or decreases in taxes when real output declines

The second reason that fiscal policy is an important stabilizing force is that although fiscal policy may be difficult to change quickly, it may still be useful for dealing with prolonged episodes of recession. The Great Depression of the 1930s and the Japanese slump of the 1990s are two cases in point. However, because of the relative lack of flexibility of fiscal policy, in modern economies aggregate spending is more usually stabilized through monetary policy. The stabilizing role of monetary policy is the subject of the next chapter.

▪ SUMMARY ▪

- The basic Keynesian model shows how fluctuations in planned aggregate expenditure, or total planned spending, can cause actual output to differ from potential output. Too little spending leads to a recessionary output gap; too much spending creates an expansionary output gap. This model relies on the crucial assumption that firms do not respond to every change in demand by changing prices. Instead, they typically set a price for some period, then meet the demand forthcoming at that price. **LO1**

- Planned aggregate expenditure is total planned spending on final goods and services. The four components of total spending are consumption, investment, government purchases, and net exports. Actual investment may differ from planned investment because firms may sell a greater or lesser amount of their production than they expected. If firms sell less than they expected, for example, they are forced to add more goods to inventory than anticipated. And because additions to inventory are counted as part of investment, in this case actual investment (including inventory investment) is greater than planned investment. **LO2**

- The consumption function summarizes the relationship between disposable income and consumption spending. The amount by which consumption rises when disposable income rises by one dollar is called the marginal propensity to consume (*mpc*). The marginal propensity to consume is always greater than zero but less than one. **LO2**

- An increase in real output raises planned aggregate expenditure, since higher output (and, equivalently, higher income) encourages households to consume more. Planned aggregate expenditure can be broken down into two components: autonomous expenditure and induced expenditure. Autonomous expenditure is the portion of planned spending that is independent of output; induced expenditure is the portion of spending that depends on output. **LO2**

- In the period in which prices are fixed, short-run equilibrium output is the level of output that just equals planned aggregate expenditure. Short-run equilibrium can be determined numerically by a table that compares alternative values of output and the planned spending implied by each level of output. Short-run equilibrium output also can be determined graphically in a Keynesian cross diagram. The diagram contains two lines: an expenditure line, which relates planned aggregate expenditure to output, and a 45° line, which represents the condition that short-run equilibrium output equals planned aggregate expenditure. Short-run equilibrium output is determined at the point at which these two lines intersect. **LO3**

- Changes in autonomous expenditure will lead to changes in short-run equilibrium output. In particular, if the economy is initially at full employment, a fall in autonomous expenditure will create a recessionary gap and a rise in autonomous expenditure will create an expansionary gap. The amount by which a one-unit increase in autonomous expenditure raises short-run equilibrium output is called the multiplier. An increase in autonomous expenditure not only raises spending directly; it also raises the incomes of producers, who in turn increase their spending, and so on. Hence the multiplier is greater than one: a one-dollar increase in autonomous expenditure tends to raise short-run equilibrium output by more than one dollar. **LO4**

- To eliminate output gaps and restore full employment, the government employs stabilization policies. The two major types of stabilization policy are monetary policy and fiscal policy. Stabilization policies work by changing planned aggregate expenditure and, hence, short-run equilibrium output. For example, an increase in government purchases raises autonomous expenditure directly, so it can be used to reduce or eliminate a recessionary gap. Similarly, a cut in taxes or an increase in transfer payments increases the public's disposable income, raising consumption spending at each level of output by an amount equal to the marginal propensity to consume times the cut in taxes or increase in transfers. Higher consumer spending, in turn, raises short-run equilibrium output. **LO5**

- Three qualifications must be made to the use of fiscal policy as a stabilization tool. First, fiscal policy may affect potential output as well as aggregate spending. Second, large and persistent government budget deficits reduce national saving and growth; the need to keep deficits under control may limit the use of expansionary fiscal policies. Finally, because changes in fiscal policy must go through a lengthy legislative process, fiscal policy is not always flexible enough to be useful for short-run stabilization. However, automatic stabilizers—provisions in the law that imply automatic increases in government spending or reductions in taxes when output declines—can overcome the problem of legislative delays to some extent and contribute to economic stability. **LO6**

KEY TERMS

automatic stabilizers (554)
autonomous consumption (534)
autonomous expenditure (537)
consumption function (534)
contractionary policies (547)
expansionary policies (547)
expenditure line (538)
income-expenditure multiplier (546)
induced expenditure (538)
marginal propensity to consume (*mpc*) (535)
menu costs (530)
planned aggregate expenditure (*PAE*) (531)
short-run equilibrium output (539)
stabilization policies (547)
wealth effect (534)

REVIEW QUESTIONS

1. What is the key assumption of the basic Keynesian model? Explain why this assumption is needed if one is to accept the view that aggregate spending is a driving force behind short-term economic fluctuations. **LO1**
2. Give an example of a good or service whose price changes very frequently and one whose price changes relatively infrequently. What accounts for the difference? **LO1**
3. Define *planned aggregate expenditure* and list its components. Why does planned spending change when output changes? **LO2**
4. Explain how planned spending and actual spending can differ. Illustrate with an example. **LO2**
5. Sketch a graph of the consumption function, labeling the axes of the graph. Discuss the economic meaning of (a) a movement from left to right along the graph of the consumption function and (b) a parallel upward shift of the consumption function. Give an example of a factor that could lead to a parallel upward shift of the consumption function. **LO2**
6. Sketch the Keynesian cross diagram. Explain in words the economic significance of the two lines graphed in the diagram. Given only this diagram, how could you determine autonomous expenditure, induced expenditure, the marginal propensity to consume, and short-run equilibrium output? **LO3**
7. Using the Keynesian cross diagram, illustrate the main cause of the 2001 recession discussed throughout the chapter. **LO3, LO4**
8. Define the *multiplier*. In economic terms, why is the multiplier greater than one? **LO4**
9. The government is considering two alternative policies, one involving increased government purchases of 50 units, the other involving a tax cut of 50 units. Which policy will stimulate planned aggregate expenditure by more? Why? **LO4**
10. Discuss three reasons why the use of fiscal policy to stabilize the economy is more complicated than suggested by the basic Keynesian model. **LO5**

PROBLEMS

1. Acme Manufacturing is producing \$4,000,000 worth of goods this year and expects to sell its entire production. It also is planning to purchase \$1,500,000 in new equipment during the year. At the beginning of the year, the company has \$500,000 in inventory in its warehouse. Find actual investment and planned investment if
   a. Acme actually sells \$3,850,000 worth of goods.
   b. Acme actually sells \$4,000,000 worth of goods.
   c. Acme actually sells \$4,200,00 worth of goods.

   Assuming that Acme's situation is similar to that of other firms, in which of these three cases is output equal to short-run equilibrium output? **LO1**
2. Data on before-tax income, taxes paid, and consumption spending for the Simpson family in various years are given below. **LO2**

Before-tax income ($)	Taxes paid ($)	Consumption spending ($)
25,000	3,000	20,000
27,000	3,500	21,350
28,000	3,700	22,070
30,000	4,000	23,600

a. Graph the Simpsons' consumption function and find their household's marginal propensity to consume.
b. How much would you expect the Simpsons to consume if their income was \$32,000 and they paid taxes of \$5,000?
c. Homer Simpson wins a lottery prize. As a result, the Simpson family increases its consumption by \$1,000 at each level of after-tax income. ("Income" does not include the prize money.) How does this change affect the graph of their consumption function? How does it affect their marginal propensity to consume?

3. An economy is described by the following equations: **LO2**

$$C = 1{,}800 + 0.6(Y - T)$$
$$I^p = 900$$
$$G = 1{,}500$$
$$NX = 100$$
$$T = 1{,}500$$
$$Y^* = 9{,}000$$

a. Find a numerical equation linking planned aggregate expenditure to output.
b. Find autonomous expenditure and induced expenditure in this economy.

4. For the economy described in problem 3: **LO3**
a. Construct a table like Table 19.1 to find short-run equilibrium output. Consider possible values for short-run equilibrium output ranging from 8,200 to 9,000.
b. Show the determination of short-run equilibrium output for this economy using the Keynesian cross diagram.
c. What is the output gap for this economy? If the natural rate of unemployment is 4 percent, what is the actual unemployment rate for this economy (use Okun's law)?

5. For the economy described in problems 3 and 4, find the effect on short-run equilibrium output of
a. An increase in government purchases from 1,500 to 1,600.
b. A decrease in tax collections from 1,500 to 1,400 (leaving government purchases at their original value).
c. A decrease in planned investment spending from 900 to 800.

Take as given that the multiplier for this economy is 2.5. If you have studied Appendix B in this chapter, show why this is so. **LO4**

6. An economy is initially at full employment, but a decrease in planned investment spending (a component of autonomous expenditure) pushes the economy into recession. Assume that the *mpc* of this economy is 0.75 and that the multiplier is 4. **LO4**
a. How large is the recessionary gap after the fall in planned investment?
b. By how much would the government have to change its purchases to restore the economy to full employment?

c. Alternatively, by how much would the government have to change taxes?

d.* Suppose that the government's budget is initially in balance, with government spending equal to taxes collected. A balanced-budget law forbids the government from running a deficit. Is there anything that fiscal policymakers could do to restore full employment in this economy, assuming they do not want to violate the balanced-budget law?

7. An economy is described by the following equations:

$$C = 40 + 0.8(Y - T)$$
$$I^p = 70$$
$$G = 120$$
$$NX = 10$$
$$T = 150$$
$$Y^* = 580$$

The multiplier in this economy is 5. **LO4, LO5**

a. Find a numerical equation relating planned aggregate expenditure to output.

b. Construct a table to find the value of short-run equilibrium output. (*Hint:* The economy is fairly close to full employment.)

c. By how much would government purchases have to change in order to eliminate any output gap? By how much would taxes have to change? Show the effects of these fiscal policy changes in a Keynesian cross diagram.

d. Repeat part c assuming that $Y^* = 630$.

e. Show your results for parts b through d on a Keynesian cross diagram.

8.* For the following economy, find autonomous expenditure, the multiplier, short-run equilibrium output, and the output gap. By how much would autonomous expenditure have to change to eliminate the output gap?

$$C = 3{,}000 + 0.5(Y - T)$$
$$I^p = 1{,}500$$
$$G = 2{,}500$$
$$NX = 200$$
$$T = 2{,}000$$
$$Y^* = 12{,}000$$

Illustrate this economy's short-run equilibrium on a Keynesian cross diagram. **LO3, LO4, LO5**

9.* An economy has zero net exports. Otherwise, it is identical to the economy described in problem 7. **LO3, LO4, LO5**

a. Find short-run equilibrium output.

b. Economic recovery abroad increases the demand for the country's exports; as a result, NX rises to 100. What happens to short-run equilibrium output?

c. Repeat part b, but this time assume that foreign economies are slowing, reducing the demand for the country's exports, so that $NX = -100$. (A negative value of net exports means that exports are less than imports.)

d. How do your results help to explain the tendency of recessions and expansions to spread across countries?

10.* This problem illustrates the workings of automatic stabilizers. Suppose that the components of planned spending in an economy are as described in Appendix A:

*Problems marked by an asterisk (*) are more difficult.

$C = \overline{C} + (mpc)(Y - T)$, $I^p = \overline{I}$, $G = \overline{G}$, and $NX = \overline{NX}$. However, suppose that, realistically, taxes are not fixed but depend on income. Specifically, we assume

$$T = tY,$$

where t is the fraction of income paid in taxes (the tax rate). As we will see in this problem, a tax system of this sort serves as an automatic stabilizer because taxes collected automatically fall when incomes fall. **LO3, LO4, LO5**

a. Find an algebraic expression for short-run equilibrium output in this economy.
b. Find an algebraic expression for the multiplier, that is, the amount that output changes when autonomous expenditure changes by one unit. Compare the expression you found to the formula for the multiplier when taxes are fixed. Show that making taxes proportional to income reduces the multiplier.
c. Explain how reducing the size of the multiplier helps to stabilize the economy, holding constant the typical size of fluctuations in the components of autonomous expenditure.
d. Suppose $\overline{C} = 500$, $\overline{I} = 1{,}500$, $\overline{G} = 2{,}000$, $\overline{NX} = 0$, $mpc = 0.8$, and $t = 0.25$. Calculate numerical values for short-run equilibrium output and the multiplier.

ANSWERS TO IN-CHAPTER EXERCISES

19.1 First we need to find an equation that relates planned aggregate expenditure PAE to output Y. We start with the definition of planned aggregate expenditure and then substitute the numerical values given in the problem:

$$\begin{aligned} PAE &= C + I^p + G + NX \\ &= [\overline{C} + (mpc)(Y - T)] + I^p + G + NX \\ &= [820 + 0.7(Y - 600)] + 600 + 600 + 200 \\ &= 1{,}800 + 0.7Y. \end{aligned}$$

Using this relationship, we construct a table analogous to Table 19.1. Some trial and error is necessary to find an appropriate range of guesses for output (column 1).

Determination of Short-Run Equilibrium Output

(1) Output Y	(2) Planned aggregate expenditure $PAE = 1{,}800 + 0.7Y$	(3) $Y - PAE$	(4) $Y = PAE$?
5,000	5,300	−300	No
5,200	5,440	−240	No
5,400	5,580	−180	No
5,600	5,720	−120	No
5,800	5,860	−60	No
6,000	6,000	0	**Yes**
6,200	6,140	60	No
6,400	6,280	120	No
6,600	6,420	180	No

Short-run equilibrium output equals 6,000, as that is the only level of output that satisfies the condition $Y = PAE$. **LO2, LO3**

19.2 The graph shows the determination of short-run equilibrium output, $Y = 6,000$. The intercept of the expenditure line is 1,800 and its slope is 0.7. Notice that the intercept equals autonomous expenditure and the slope equals the marginal propensity to consume. **LO2, LO3**

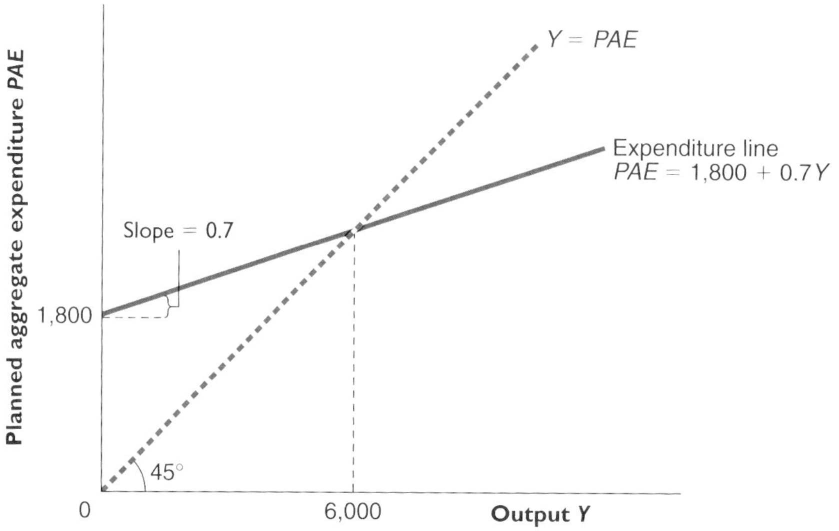

19.3 This problem is an application of Okun's law, introduced in the last chapter. The recessionary gap in this example is −50/4,800, or about −1.04 percent, of potential output. By Okun's law, cyclical unemployment is −1 times one-half the percentage size of the output gap, or 0.52 percent. As the natural rate of unemployment is 5 percent, the total unemployment rate after the recessionary gap appears will be approximately 5.52 percent. **LO3**

19.4 This exercise is just the reverse of the analysis in the text. An increase in $\overline{C}$ of 10 units raises autonomous expenditure and hence the intercept of the expenditure line by 10 units. The expenditure line shifts up, in parallel fashion, by 10 units, leading to an increase in output and an expansionary output gap. As output falls by 50 units in the text, it rises by 50 units, to 4,850, in the case analyzed here. To verify that short-run equilibrium output equals 4,850, note that an increase of 10 units in autonomous expenditure implies that PAE rises from $960 + 0.8Y$ to $970 + 0.8Y$. When $Y = 4,850$, then $PAE = 970 + 0.8(4,850) = 4,850$, so that we have $Y = PAE$. **LO4**

19.5 In Exercise 19.4 we saw that a 10-unit increase in $\overline{C}$ increases autonomous expenditure and hence the intercept of the expenditure line by 10 units. The expenditure line shifts upward, in parallel fashion, by 10 units, leading to an expansionary output gap. To offset this gap, the government should reduce its purchases by 10 units, returning autonomous expenditure to its original level. The expenditure line shifts back down to its original position, restoring output to its initial full-employment level. The graph is just the reverse of Figure 19.6, with the expenditure line being shifted up by the increase in consumption and down by the offsetting reduction in government purchases. **LO4, LO5**

19.6 The 20-unit increase in planned investment is a 20-unit increase in autonomous expenditure, which will lead to an even greater increase in short-run equilibrium output. To offset the 20-unit increase in autonomous expenditure by means of fiscal policy, the government can reduce its purchases by 20 units.

Alternatively, it could raise taxes (or cut transfers) to reduce consumption spending. Since the *mpc* = 0.5, to reduce consumption spending by 20 units at each level of output, the government will need to increase taxes (or reduce transfers) by 40 units. At each level of output, a 40-unit tax increase will reduce disposable income by 40 units and cause consumers to reduce their spending by $0.5 \times 40 = 20$ units, as needed to eliminate the expansionary output gap. **LO4, LO5**

APPENDIX

A

An Algebraic Solution of the Basic Keynesian Model

This chapter has shown how to solve the basic Keynesian model numerically and graphically. In this appendix, we will show how to find a more general algebraic solution for short-run equilibrium output in the basic Keynesian model. This solution has the advantage of showing clearly the links between short-run equilibrium output, the multiplier, and autonomous expenditure. The general method also can be applied when we make changes to the basic Keynesian model, as we will see in following chapters.

The model we will work with is the same one presented in the main part of the chapter. Start with the definition of planned aggregate expenditure, Equation 19.1:

$$PAE = C + I^p + G + NX. \tag{19.1}$$

Equation 19.1 says that planned aggregate expenditure is the sum of the four types of planned spending: consumption spending by households C; planned investment spending by firms I^p; government purchases G; and net exports purchased by foreigners NX.

The first component of planned aggregate expenditure, consumption spending, is determined by the *consumption function,* Equation 19.2:

$$C = \overline{C} + (mpc)(Y - T). \tag{19.2}$$

The consumption function says that consumption spending increases when disposable (after-tax) income $Y - T$ increases. Each dollar increase in disposable income raises consumption spending by mpc dollars, where mpc, known as the *marginal propensity to consume,* is a number between 0 and 1. Other factors affecting consumption spending are captured by the term $\overline{C}$. For example, a boom in the stock market that leads consumers to spend more at each level of disposable income (a *wealth effect*) would be represented as an increase in $\overline{C}$.

As in the body of the chapter, we assume that planned investment, government purchases, net exports, and net tax collections are simply given numbers. A variable whose value is fixed and given from outside the model is called an *exogenous* variable; so, in other words, we are assuming that planned investment, government purchases, net exports, and net tax collections are exogenous variables. Using an overbar to denote the given value of an exogenous variable, we can write this assumption as

$I^p = \overline{I}$	Planned investment,
$G = \overline{G}$	Government purchases,
$NX = \overline{NX}$	Net exports,
$T = \overline{T}$	Net taxes (taxes less transfers).

So, for example, $\overline{I}$ is the given value of planned investment spending, as determined outside the model. In our examples, we will set $\overline{I}$ and the other exogenous variables equal to some particular number.

Our goal is to solve algebraically for *short-run equilibrium output,* the level of output that prevails during the period in which prices are predetermined. The first step is to relate planned aggregate expenditure *PAE* to output *Y*. Starting with the definition of planned aggregate expenditure (Equation 19.1), use the consumption function (Equation 19.2) to substitute for consumption spending *C* and replace I^p, *G*, *NX*, and *T* with their exogenous values. With these substitutions, planned aggregate expenditure can be written as

$$PAE = [\overline{C} - (mpc)(Y - \overline{T})] + \overline{I} + \overline{G} + \overline{NX}.$$

Rearranging this equation to separate the terms that do and do not depend on output *Y*, we get

$$PAE = [\overline{C} - (mpc)\overline{T} + \overline{I} + \overline{G} + \overline{NX}] + (mpc)Y. \qquad (19A.1)$$

Equation 19A.1 is an important equation because it shows the relationship between planned aggregate expenditure *PAE* and output *Y*. The bracketed term on the right side of the equation represents *autonomous expenditure,* the part of planned spending that does not depend on output. The term $(mpc)Y$ represents *induced expenditure,* the part of planned spending that does depend on output. Equation 19A.1 is also the equation that describes the *expenditure line* in the Keynesian cross diagram; it shows that the intercept of the expenditure line equals autonomous expenditure and the slope of the expenditure line equals the marginal propensity to consume.

We can illustrate how Equation 19A.1 works numerically by using the example we studied in the body of the chapter. That example assumed the following numerical values: $\overline{C} = 620$, $\overline{I} = 220$, $\overline{G} = 300$, $\overline{NX} = 20$, $\overline{T} = 250$, and $mpc = 0.8$. Plugging these values into Equation 19A.1 and simplifying, we get

$$PAE = 960 + 0.8Y,$$

which is the same answer we found earlier in the chapter: autonomous expenditure equals 960 and induced expenditure equals $0.8Y$.

The second step in solving for short-run equilibrium output begins with the definition of short-run equilibrium output (Equation 19.3):

$$Y = PAE. \qquad (19.3)$$

Remember that short-run equilibrium output is the value of output at which output equals planned aggregate expenditure. Using Equation 19A.1 to substitute for *PAE* in the definition of short-run equilibrium output, we get

$$Y = [\overline{C} - (mpc)\overline{T} + \overline{I} + \overline{G} + \overline{NX}] + (mpc)Y.$$

The value of Y that solves this equation is the value of short-run equilibrium output. To solve for Y, group all terms involving Y on the left side of the equation:

$$Y - (mpc)Y = [\overline{C} - (mpc)\overline{T} + \overline{I} + \overline{G} + \overline{NX}]$$

or

$$Y(1 - mpc) = [\overline{C} - (mpc)\overline{T} + \overline{I} + \overline{G} + \overline{NX}].$$

Dividing both sides of the equation by $(1 - mpc)$ gives

$$Y = \left(\frac{1}{1 - mpc}\right)[\overline{C} - (mpc)\overline{T} + \overline{I} + \overline{G} + \overline{NX}]. \qquad (19A.2)$$

Equation 19A.2 gives short-run equilibrium output for our model economy in terms of the exogenous values $\overline{C}$, $\overline{I}$, $\overline{G}$, $\overline{NX}$, and $\overline{T}$ and the marginal propensity to consume, *mpc*. We can use this formula to solve for short-run equilibrium output in specific numerical examples. For example, suppose that we once again plug in the numerical values assumed in the body of the chapter: $\overline{C} = 620$, $\overline{I} = 220$, $\overline{G} = 300$, $\overline{NX} = 20$, $\overline{T} = 250$, and $mpc = 0.8$. We get

$$Y = \left(\frac{1}{1 - 0.8}\right)[620 - 0.8(250) + 220 + 300 + 20] = \frac{1}{0.2}(960) = 5(960) = 4{,}800,$$

which is the same answer we found more laboriously using Table 19.1.

EXERCISE 19A.1

Use Equation 19A.2 to find short-run equilibrium output for the economy described in Exercise 19.1 in the text. What are the intercept and the slope of the expenditure line?

Equation 19A.2 shows clearly the relationship between autonomous expenditure and short-run equilibrium output. Autonomous expenditure is the first term on the right side of Equation 19A.1, equal to $\overline{C} - (mpc)\overline{T} + \overline{I} + \overline{G} + \overline{NX}$. The equation shows that a one-unit increase in autonomous expenditure increases short-run equilibrium output by $1/(1 - mpc)$ units. In other words, we can see from Equation 19A.2 that the *multiplier* for this model equals $1/(1 - mpc)$. Further discussion of the multiplier is given in the second appendix to the chapter.

ANSWERS TO IN-APPENDIX EXERCISE

19A.1 The equation describing short-run equilibrium output is

$$Y = \left(\frac{1}{1 - mpc}\right)(\overline{C} - (mpc)\overline{T} + \overline{I} + \overline{G} + \overline{NX}). \qquad (19A.2)$$

Using data from Exercise 19.1, set $\overline{C} = 820$, $mpc = 0.7$, $\overline{I} = 600$, $\overline{G} = 600$, $\overline{NX} = 200$, and $\overline{T} = 600$. Plugging these values into Equation 19A.2, we get

$$Y = \left(\frac{1}{1 - 0.7}\right)[820 - 0.7(600 + 600 + 600 + 200)] = 3.33 \times 1{,}800 = 6{,}000,$$

which is the same result obtained in Exercise 19.1. **LO3**

APPENDIX B

The Multiplier in the Basic Keynesian Model

This appendix builds on the example economy used throughout the chapter to give a more complete explanation of the *income-expenditure multiplier* in the basic Keynesian model. In the chapter, we saw that a drop in autonomous expenditure of 10 units caused a decline in short-run equilibrium output of 50 units, five times as great as the initial change in spending. Hence, the multiplier in this example is 5.

To see why this multiplier effect occurs, note that the initial decrease of 10 in consumer spending (more precisely, in the constant term of the consumption function, $\overline{C}$) has two effects. First, the fall in consumer spending directly reduces planned aggregate expenditure by 10 units. Second, the fall in spending also reduces by 10 units the incomes of producers (workers and firm owners) of consumer goods. Since the marginal propensity to consume is 0.8, the producers of consumer goods will therefore reduce *their* consumption spending by 8, or 0.8 times their income loss of 10. This reduction in spending cuts the income of *other* producers by 8 units, leading them to reduce their spending by 6.4, or 0.8 times their income loss of 8. These income reductions of 6.4 lead still other producers to cut their spending by 5.12, or 0.8 times 6.4, and so on. In principle, this process continues indefinitely, although after many rounds of spending and income reductions, the effects become quite small.

When all these "rounds" of income and spending reductions are added, the *total* effect on planned spending of the initial reduction of 10 in consumer spending is

$$10 + 8 + 6.4 + 5.12 + \cdots.$$

The three dots indicate that the series of reductions continues indefinitely. The total effect of the initial decrease in consumption also can be written as

$$10[1 + 0.8 + (0.8)^2 + (0.8)^3 + \cdots].$$

This expression highlights the fact that the spending that takes place in each round is 0.8 times the spending in the previous round (0.8) because that is the marginal propensity to consume out of the income generated by the previous round of spending.

A useful algebraic relationship, which applies to any number x greater than 0 but less than 1, is

$$1 + x + x^2 + x^3 + \cdots = \frac{1}{1 - x}.$$

If we set $x = 0.8$, this formula implies that the total effect of the decline in consumption spending on aggregate demand and output is

$$10\left(\frac{1}{1 - 0.8}\right) = 10\left(\frac{1}{0.2}\right) = 10 \times 5 = 50.$$

This answer is consistent with our earlier calculation, which showed that short-run equilibrium output fell by 50 units, from 4,800 to 4,750.

By a similar analysis, we also can find a general algebraic expression for the multiplier in the basic Keynesian model. Recalling that mpc is the marginal propensity to consume out of disposable income, we know that a one-unit increase in autonomous expenditure raises spending and income by one unit in the first round; by $mpc \times 1 = mpc$ units in the second round; by $mpc \times mpc = mpc^2$ units in the third round; by $mpc \times mpc^2 = mpc^3$ units in the fouth round; and so on. Thus, the total effect on short-run equilibrium output of a one-unit increase in autonomous expenditure is given by

$$1 + mpc + mpc^2 + mpc^3 + \cdots.$$

Applying the algebraic formula given above, and recalling that $0 < mpc < 1$, we can rewrite this expression as $1/(1 - mpc)$. Thus, in a basic Keynesian model with a marginal propensity to consume of mpc, the multiplier equals $1/(1 - mpc)$, the same result found in Appendix A to this chapter. Note that if $mpc = 0.8$, then $1/(1 - mpc) = 1/(1 - 0.8) = 5$, which is the same value of the multiplier we found numerically above.

CHAPTER 20

Stabilizing the Economy: The Role of the Federal Reserve

LEARNING OBJECTIVES

After reading this chapter, you should be able to:

1. Describe the structure and responsibilities of the Federal Reserve System.
2. Analyze how changes in real interest rates affect planned aggregate expenditures and the short-run equilibrium level of output.
3. Define what a monetary policy rule is and relate this concept to the Fed's role in stabilization policy.
4. Show how the demand for money and the supply of money interact to determine the equilibrium nominal interest rate.
5. Discuss how the Fed uses its ability to control the money supply to influence nominal and real interest rates.

Financial market participants and commentators go to remarkable lengths to try to predict the actions of the Federal Reserve. For a while, the CNBC financial news program *Squawk Box* reported regularly on what the commentators called the Greenspan Briefcase Indicator. The idea was to spot the Fed chairman at that time, Alan Greenspan, on his way to meet with the Federal Open Market Committee, the group that determines U.S. monetary policy. If Greenspan's briefcase was packed full, presumably with macroeconomic data and analyses, the guess was that the Fed planned to change interest rates. A slim briefcase meant no change in rates was likely.

"It was right 17 out of the first 20 times," the program's anchor Mark Haines noted, "but it has a built-in self-destruct mechanism because Greenspan packs his [own] briefcase. He can make it wrong or right. He has never publicly acknowledged the indicator, but we have reason to believe that he knows about it. We have to consider the fact that he wants us to stop doing it because the last two times the briefcase has been wrong, and that's disturbing."[1]

The Briefcase Indicator is but one example of the close public scrutiny that the chairman of the Federal Reserve and other monetary policymakers face. Every speech, every congressional testimony, every interview from a member of the Board of Governors is closely analyzed for clues about the future course of monetary policy. The reason for the intense public interest in the Federal Reserve's decisions about monetary policy—and especially the level of interest rates—is that those decisions have important implications both for financial markets and for the economy in general.

In this chapter, we examine the workings of monetary policy, one of the two major types of *stabilization policy*. (The other type, fiscal policy, was discussed in the last chapter.) As we saw in the last chapter, stabilization policies are government policies that are meant to influence planned aggregate expenditure, with the goal of eliminating output gaps. Both types of stabilization policy, monetary and fiscal, are important and have been useful at various times. However, monetary policy, which can be changed quickly by a decision of the Federal Reserve's Federal Open Market Committee (FOMC), is more flexible and responsive than fiscal policy, which can be changed only by legislative action by Congress. Under normal circumstances, therefore, monetary policy is used more actively in the United States than fiscal policy to help stabilize the economy.

We begin this chapter by studying the Federal Reserve as an institution: how it came to be, how it responded to banking panics early in its history, and how it functions today. Next, we look how monetary policy affects short-run output. Specifically, we first examine how changes in nominal interest rates, which the Fed can influence, affect real interest rates, which affect spending decisions. We then build on our analysis of the basic Keynesian model in the last chapter and show how, in the short run, changes in real interest rates change planned spending and thus short-un equilibrium output. We then look at some of the details of monetary policy by developing a monetary policy rule that describes the Fed's behavior and by examining more closely the relationship between changes in the money supply and changes in nominal interest rates.

THE FEDERAL RESERVE

We first discussed the Federal Reserve in Chapter 17. Recall that the Fed is the central bank of the United States, and that central banks in general have two main responsibilities. First, they are responsible for monetary policy, which means that a country's central bank determines how much money circulates in the economy. We will see in this chapter that this responsibility implies that Federal Reserve actions affect the level of interest rates in the economy as well. Second, along with other government agencies, central banks in general, and the Fed in particular, have important responsibilities for the oversight and regulation of financial markets. In particular, central banks play important roles during periods of crisis in financial markets.

THE HISTORY AND STRUCTURE OF THE FEDERAL RESERVE SYSTEM

Federal Reserve System (the Fed) The central bank of the United States; also called the *Fed*

The **Federal Reserve System** was created by the Federal Reserve Act, passed by Congress in 1913, and began operations in 1914. Like all central banks, the Fed is a government agency. Unlike commercial banks, which are private businesses whose principal objective is making a profit, central banks like the Fed focus on promoting public goals such as economic growth, low inflation, and the smooth operation of financial markets.

[1]Robert H. Frank, "Safety in Numbers," *New York Times Magazine*, November 28, 1999, p. 35.

"I'm sorry, sir, but I don't believe you know us well enough to call us the Fed."

The Federal Reserve Act established a system of 12 regional Federal Reserve banks, each associated with a geographical area called a Federal Reserve district. Congress hoped that the establishment of Federal Reserve banks around the country would ensure that different regions were represented in the national policymaking process. In fact, the regional Feds regularly assess economic conditions in their districts and report this information to policymakers in Washington. Regional Federal Reserve banks also provide various services, such as check-clearing services, to the commercial banks in their district.

EN 20

At the national level, the leadership of the Federal Reserve System is provided by its **Board of Governors.** The Board of Governors, together with a large professional staff, is located in Washington, D.C. The Board consists of seven governors, who are appointed by the president of the United States, subject to confirmation by the Senate, to 14-year terms. The terms are staggered so that one governor comes up for reappointment every other year. The president also appoints one of these Board members to serve as chairman of the Board of Governors for a term of four years. The Fed chairman, along with the secretary of the Treasury, is probably one of the two most powerful economic policymakers in the U.S. government, after the president. Recent chairmen, such as Paul Volcker and Alan Greenspan, have been highly regarded and influential.

Board of Governors the leadership of the Fed, consisting of seven governors appointed by the president to staggered 14-year terms

Decisions about monetary policy are made by a 12-member committee called the **Federal Open Market Committee** (or **FOMC**). The FOMC consists of the seven Fed governors, the president of the Federal Reserve Bank of New York, and four of the presidents of the other regional Federal Reserve banks, who serve on a rotating basis. The FOMC meets approximately eight times a year to review the state of the economy and to determine monetary policy.

Federal Open Market Committee (or FOMC) the committee that makes decisions concerning monetary policy

THE FED'S ROLE IN STABILIZING FINANCIAL MARKETS: BANKING PANICS

The creation of the Fed in 1913 was promoted by a series of financial market crises that disrupted both the markets themselves and the U.S. economy as a whole. The hope of Congress was that the Fed would be able to eliminate or at least control such crises. *Banking panics* were perhaps the most disruptive type of recurrent financial crisis in the United States during the ninetieth and early twentieth centuries. In a **banking panic,** news or rumors of the imminent bankruptcy of one or more banks leads bank depositors to rush to withdraw their funds.

banking panic a situation in which news or rumors of the imminent bankruptcy of one or more banks leads bank depositors to rush to withdraw their funds

Why do banking panics occur? An important factor that makes banking panics possible is the existence of fractional-reserve banking. As we discussed in Chapter 17, in a fractional-reserve banking system, like that of the United States and all other industrialized countries, bank reserves are less than deposits, which means that banks do not keep enough cash on hand to pay off their depositors if they were all to decide to withdraw their deposits. Normally this is not a problem, as only a small percentage of depositors attempt to withdraw their funds on any given day. But if a rumor circulates that one or more banks are in financial trouble and may go bankrupt, depositors may panic, lining up to demand their money. Since bank reserves are less than deposits, a sufficiently severe panic could lead even financially healthy banks to run out of cash, forcing them into bankruptcy and closure. (Think of the scene in the movie *It's a Wonderful Life* when George Bailey tries to convince his depositors not to withdraw all of their deposits and close their accounts.)

The Federal Reserve was established in response to a particularly severe banking panic that occurred in 1907. The Fed was equipped with two principal tools to try to prevent or moderate banking panics. First, the Fed was given the power to supervise and regulate banks. It was hoped that the public would have greater confidence in banks, and thus be less prone to panic, if people knew that the Fed was keeping a close watch on bankers' activities. Second, the Fed was allowed to make loans to banks. The idea was that, during a panic, banks could borrow cash from the Fed with which to pay off depositors, avoiding the need to close.

No banking panics occurred between 1914, when the Fed was established, and 1930. However, between 1930 and 1933, the United States experienced the worst and most protracted series of banking panics in its history. Economic historians agree that much of the blame for this panic should be placed on the Fed, which neither appreciated the severity of the problem nor acted aggressively enough to contain it.

The banking panics of 1930–1933 and the money supply

The worst banking panics ever experienced in the United States occurred during the early stages of the Great Depression, between 1930 and 1933. During this period, approximately one-third of the banks in the United States were forced to close. This near-collapse of the banking system was probably an important reason that the Depression was so severe. With many fewer banks in operation, it was very difficult for small businesses and consumers during the early 1930s to obtain credit. Another important effect of the banking panics was to greatly reduce the nation's money supply.

During a banking panic, people are afraid to keep deposits in a bank because of the risk that the bank will go bankrupt and their money will be lost (this was prior to the introduction of federal deposit insurance, discussed below). During the 1930–1933 period, many bank depositors withdrew their money from banks, holding currency instead. These withdrawals reduced bank reserves. Recall from Chapter 17 that each extra dollar of currency held by the public adds \$1 to the money supply; but each extra dollar of bank reserves translates into several dollars of money supply because in a fractional-reserve banking system each dollar of reserves can "support" several dollars in bank deposits. Thus, the public's withdrawals from banks, which increased currency holdings by the public but reduced bank reserves by an equal amount, led to a net decrease in the total money supply (currency plus deposits).

In addition, fearing banking panics and the associated withdrawals by depositors, banks increased their desired reserve-deposit ratios, which reduced the quantity of deposits that could be supported by any given level of bank reserves. This change in reserve-deposit ratios also tended to reduce the money supply.

Data on currency holdings by the public, the reserve-deposit ratio, bank reserves, and the money supply for selected dates are shown in Table 20.1. Notice the increase over the period in the amount of currency held by the public and in the reserve-deposit ratio, as well as the decline in bank reserves in 1931. The last column shows that the U.S. money supply dropped by about one-third between December 1929 and December 1933.

TABLE 20.1
Key U.S. Monetary Statistics, 1929–1933

	Currency held by public	Reserve-deposit ratio	Bank reserves	Money supply
December 1929	3.85	0.075	3.15	45.9
December 1930	3.79	0.082	3.31	44.1
December 1931	4.59	0.095	3.11	37.3
December 1932	4.82	0.109	3.18	34.0
December 1933	4.85	0.133	3.45	30.8

NOTE: Data on currency, the monetary base, and the money supply are in billions of dollars.

SOURCE: Milton Friedman and Anna J. Schwartz, *A Monetary History of the United States, 1863–1960* (Princeton, NJ: Princeton University Press, 1963), Table A-1.

Using Equation 17.1, we can see that increases in currency holdings by the public and increases in the reserve-deposit ratio both tend to reduce the money supply. These effects were so powerful in 1930–1933 that the nation's money supply, shown in the fourth column of Table 20.1, dropped precipitously, even though currency holdings and bank reserves, taken separately, actually rose during the period. ◆

EXERCISE 20.1

Using the data from Table 20.1, confirm that the relationship between the money supply and its determinants is consistent with Equation 17.2. Would the money supply have fallen in 1931–1933 if the public had stopped withdrawing deposits after December 1930 so that currency held by the public had remained at its December 1930 level?

EXERCISE 20.2

According to Table 20.1, the U.S. money supply fell from $44.1 billion to $37.3 billion over the course of 1931. The Fed did use open-market purchases during 1931 to replenish bank reserves in the face of depositor withdrawals. Find (a) the quantity of reserves that the Fed injected into the economy in 1931 and (b) the quantity of reserves the Fed would have had to add to the economy to keep the money supply unchanged from 1930, assuming that public currency holdings and reserve-deposit ratios for each year remained as reported in the table. Why has the Fed been criticized for being too timid in 1931?

deposit insurance a system under which the government guarantees that depositors will not lose any money even if their bank goes bankrupt

When the Fed failed to stop the banking panics of the 1930s, policymakers decided to look at other strategies for controlling panics. In 1934 Congress instituted a system of deposit insurance. Under a system of **deposit insurance,** the government guarantees depositors—specifically, under current rules, those with deposits of less than $100,000—that they will get their money back even if the bank goes bankrupt. Deposit insurance eliminates the incentive for people to withdraw their deposits when rumors circulate that the bank is in financial trouble, which nips panics in the bud. Indeed, since deposit insurance was instituted, the United States has had no significant banking panics.

Unfortunately, deposit insurance is not a perfect solution to the problem of banking panics. An important drawback is that when deposit insurance is in force, depositors know they are protected no matter what happens to their bank, and they become completely unconcerned about whether their bank is making prudent loans. This situation can lead to reckless behavior by banks or other insured intermediaries. For example, during the 1980s, many savings and loan associations in the United States went bankrupt, in part because of reckless lending and financial investments. Like banks, savings and loans have deposit insurance, so the U.S. government had to pay savings and loan depositors the full value of their deposits. This action ultimately cost U.S. taxpayers hundreds of billions of dollars. To try to prevent such occurrences, the Federal Reserve and other government regulators examine banks to make sure they are lending prudently.

THE EFFECTS OF FEDERAL RESERVE ACTIONS ON THE ECONOMY

We now examine how monetary policy can be used to eliminate output gaps and stabilize the economy. The basic idea is relatively straightforward. As we will see in this section, planned aggregate expenditure is affected by the level of the real interest ate prevailing in the economy. Specifically, a lower real interest rate encourages higher planned spending by households and firms, while a higher real interest rate reduces spending. By adjusting the real interest rate, the Fed can move planned spending in the desired direction. Under the assumption of the basic Keynesian model that firms produce just enough goods and services to meet the demand for their output, the Fed's stabilization of planned spending leads to stabilization of aggregate output and employment as well.

The Fed can control the economy's nominal interest rate through its control of the money supply. We will analyze how it does this later in the chapter; for now, we will look at how control of the nominal interest rate leads to control of the real interest rate in the short run. We will then look at how changes in the real interest rate affect planned spending and equilibrium output.

CAN THE FED CONTROL THE REAL INTEREST RATE?

Through its control of the money supply, the Fed can control the economy's *nominal* interest rate. But many important economic decisions, such as the decisions to save and invest, depend on the *real* interest rate. To affect those decisions, the Fed must exert some control over the real interest rate.

Most economists believe that the Fed can control the real interest rate, at least for some period. To see why, recall the definition of the real interest rate from Chapter 13:

$$r = i - \pi.$$

The real interest rate r equals the nominal interest rate i minus the rate of inflation π. The Fed can control the nominal interest rate quite precisely through its ability to determine the money supply. Furthermore, inflation appears to change relatively slowly in response to changes in policy or economic conditions, for reasons we will discuss in the next chapter. Because inflation tends to adjust slowly, actions by the Fed to change the nominal interest rate generally lead the real interest rate to change by about the same amount.

The idea that the Fed can set the real interest rate appears to contradict our analysis in Chapter 16. There, we concluded that the real interest rate is determined by the condition that national saving must equal investment in new capital goods. *This apparent contradiction is rooted in a difference in the time frame being considered.* Because inflation does not adjust quickly, the Fed can control the real interest rate over the short run. In the long run, however—that is, over periods of several years or more—the inflation rate and other economic variables will adjust, and the balance of saving and investment will determine the real interest rate. Thus, the Fed's ability to influence consumption and investment spending through its control of the real interest rate is strongest in the short run.

The role of the federal funds rate in monetary policy

Although thousands of interest rates and other financial data are easily available, the interest rate that is perhaps most closely watched by the public, politicians, the media, and the financial markets is the *federal funds rate.*

The **federal funds rate** is the interest rate commercial banks charge each other for very short-term (usually overnight) loans. For example, a bank that has insufficient reserves to meet its legal reserve requirements might borrow reserves for a few days from a bank that has extra reserves. Despite its name, the federal funds rate is not an official government interest rate and is not connected to the federal government.

federal funds rate the interest rate that commercial banks charge each other for very short-term (usually overnight) loans; because the Fed frequently sets its policy in terms of the federal funds rate, this rate is closely watched in financial markets

Because the market for loans between commercial banks is tiny compared to some other financial markets, such as the market for government bonds, one might expect the federal funds rate to be of little interest to anyone other than the managers of commercial banks. But enormous attention is paid to this interest rate because, over most of the past 40 years, the Fed has expressed its policies in terms of the federal funds rate. Indeed, at the close of every meeting of the Federal Open Market Committee, the Fed announces whether the federal funds rate will be increased, decreased, or left unchanged. The Fed also may indicate the likely direction of future changes in the federal funds rate. Thus, more than any other financial variable, changes in the federal funds rate indicate the Fed's plans for monetary policy.

Why does the Fed choose to focus on this particular nominal interest rate over all others? As we saw in Chapter 17, in practice the Fed affects the money supply through its control of bank reserves. Because open-market operations directly affect the supply of bank reserves, the Fed's control over the federal funds rate is particularly tight. If, for example, the Fed wants the federal funds rate to fall, it conducts open-market purchases, which increase reserves, until the federal funds rate falls to the new desired level. However, if Fed officials chose to do so, they could probably signal their intended policies just as effectively in terms of another short-term nominal interest rate, such as the rate on short-term government debt.

Figure 20.1 shows the behavior of the federal funds rate from January 1970 through February 2008. As you can see, the Fed has allowed this interest rate to vary considerably in response to economic conditions.

In reality, not just one but many thousands of interest rates are seen in the economy. Because interest rates tend to move together (allowing us to speak of *the* interest rate), an action by the Fed to change the federal funds rate generally causes other interest rates to change in the same direction. However, the tendency of other interest rates (such as the long-term government bond rate or the rate on bonds issued by corporations) to move in the same direction as the federal funds rate is only a tendency, not an exact relationship. In practice, then, the Fed's control of other interest rates may be somewhat less precise than its control of the federal funds rate—a fact that complicates the Fed's policymaking.

FIGURE 20.1
The Federal Funds Rate, 1970–2008.
The federal funds rate is the interest rate commercial banks charge each other for short-term loans. It is closely watched because the Fed expresses its policies in terms of the federal funds rate. The Fed has allowed the federal funds rate to vary considerably in response to economic conditions.

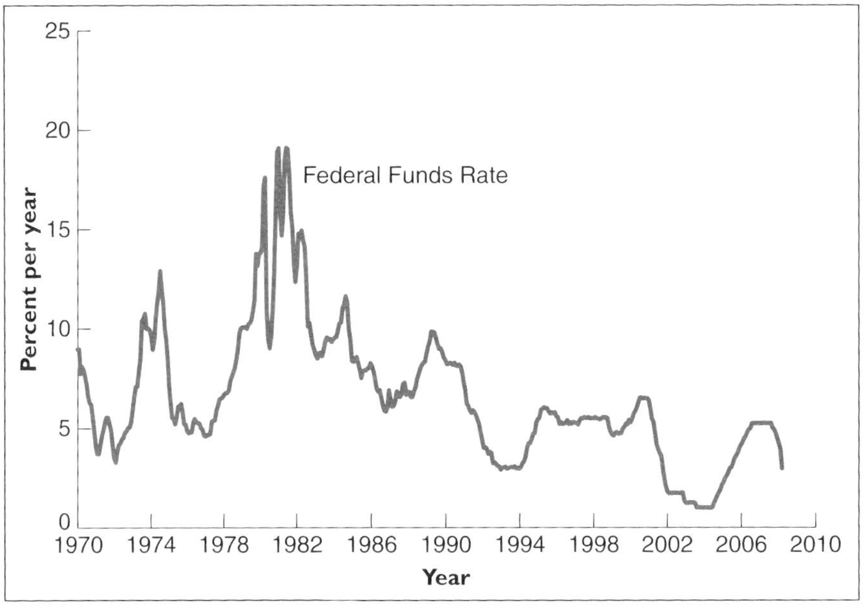

SOURCE: Federal Reserve Bank of St. Louis (http://research.stlouisfed.org/fred2/).

PLANNED AGGREGATE EXPENDITURE AND THE REAL INTEREST RATE

In the last chapter, we saw how planned spending is affected by changes in real output Y. Changes in output affect the private sector's disposable income $(Y - T)$, which in turn influences consumption spending—a relationship captured by the consumption function.

A second variable that has potentially important effects on aggregate expenditure is the real interest rate r. In Chapter 16, we saw that the real interest rate influences both the saving decisions of households and the investment behavior of firms.

For households, the effect of a higher real interest rate is to increase the reward for saving, which leads households to save more.[2] At a given level of income, households can save more only if they consume less. Thus, saying that a higher real interest rate *increases* saving is the same as saying that a higher real interest rate *reduces* consumption spending at each level of income. The idea that higher real interest rates reduce household spending makes intuitive sense. Think, for example, about people's willingness to buy consumer durables such as automobiles or furniture. Purchases of consumer durables, which are part of consumption spending, are often financed by borrowing from a bank, credit union, or finance company. When the real interest rate rises, the monthly finance charges associated with the purchase of a car or a piano are higher, and people become less willing or able to make the purchase. Thus, a higher real interest rate reduces people's willingness to spend on consumer goods, holding constant disposable income and other factors that affect consumption.

Besides reducing consumption spending, a higher real interest rate also discourages firms from making capital investments. As in the case of a consumer thinking

When the real interest rate rises, financing a new car becomes more expensive and fewer cars are purchased.

[2]Because a higher real interest rate also reduces the amount households must put aside to reach a given savings target, a higher real interest rate could theoretically increase or decrease saving. However, empirical evidence suggests that higher real interest rates have a modest positive effect on saving.

of buying a car or a piano, when a rise in the real interest rate increases financing costs, firms may reconsider their plans to invest. For example, upgrading a computer system may be profitable for a manufacturing firm when the cost of the system can be financed by borrowing at a real interest rate of 3 percent. However, if the real interest rate rises to 6 percent, doubling the cost of funds to the firm, the same upgrade may not be profitable and the firm may choose not to invest. We also should remember that residential investment—the building of houses and apartment buildings—is also part of investment spending. Higher interest rates, in the form of higher mortgage rates, certainly discourage this kind of investment spending as well.[3]

The conclusion is that, at any given level of output, *both consumption spending and planned investment spending decline when the real interest rate increases.* Conversely, a fall in the real interest rate tends to stimulate consumption and investment spending by reducing financing costs.

Planned aggregate expenditure and the real interest rate: a numerical example

In a certain economy, the components of planned spending are given by

$$\begin{aligned} C &= 640 + 0.8(Y - T) - 400r, \\ I^P &= 250 - 600r, \\ G &= 300, \\ NX &= 20, \\ T &= 250. \end{aligned}$$

This economy is similar to the one we worked with in the previous chapter except that now the real interest rate r is allowed to affect both consumption and planned investment. For example, the final term in the equation describing consumption, $-400r$, implies that a 1 percentage point (0.01) increase in the real interest rate, from 4 percent to 5 percent—that is, from .04 to .05—reduces consumption spending by $400(0.01) = 4$ units. Similarly, the final term in the equation for planned investment tells us that in this example, a 1 percentage point increase in the real interest rate lowers planned investment by $600(0.01) = 6$ units. Thus, the overall effect of a 1 percentage point increase in the real interest rate is to lower planned aggregate expenditure by 10 units, the sum of the effects on consumption and investment. As in the earlier examples, disposable income $(Y - T)$ is assumed to affect consumption spending through a marginal propensity to consume of 0.8 (see the first equation), and government purchases G, net exports NX, and taxes T are assumed to be fixed numbers.

To find a numerical equation that describes the relationship of planned aggregate expenditure (PAE) to output, we can begin as in the last chapter with the general definition of planned aggregate expenditure:

$$PAE = C + I^P + G + NX.$$

Substituting for the four components of expenditure, using the equations describing each type of spending, we get

$$PAE = [640 + 0.8(Y - 250) - 400r] + [250 - 600r] + 300 + 20.$$

The first term in brackets on the right side of this equation is the expression for consumption, using the fact that taxes $T = 250$; the second bracketed term is planned investment; and the last two terms correspond to the assumed numerical values of government purchases and net exports. If we simplify this equation and group

[3]We discuss the relationship between the real interest rate and investment in Chapter 16.

together the terms that do not depend on output Y and the terms that do depend on output, we get

$$PAE = [(640 - 0.8 \times 250 - 400r) + (250 - 600r) + 300 + 20] + 0.8Y,$$

or, simplifying further,

$$PAE = [1{,}010 - 1{,}000r] + 0.8Y. \qquad (20.1)$$

In Equation 20.1, the term in brackets is *autonomous expenditure*, the portion of planned aggregate expenditure that does not depend on output. *Notice that in this example autonomous expenditure depends on the real interest rate r.* Induced expenditure, the portion of planned aggregate expenditure that does depend on output, equals $0.8Y$ in this example. ◆

The real interest rate and short-run equilibrium output

Now, suppose that the Fed sets the real interest rate at 5 percent. Setting $r = 0.05$ in Equation 20.1 gives

$$PAE = [1{,}010 - 1{,}000 \times (0.05)] + 0.8Y.$$

Simplifying, we get

$$PAE = 960 + 0.8Y.$$

So, when the real interest rate is 5 percent, autonomous expenditure is 960 and induced expenditure is $0.8Y$. Short-run equilibrium output is the level of output that equals planned aggregate spending. To find short-run equilibrium output, we could now apply the tabular method used in the last chapter, comparing alternative values of output with the planned aggregate expenditure at that level of output. Short-run equilibrium output would be determined as the value of output such that output just equals spending, or

$$Y = PAE.$$

However, conveniently, when we compare this example with the example economy in the previous chapter, we see that the equation for planned aggregate expenditure, $PAE = 960 + 0.8Y$, is identical to what we found there. Thus, Table 19.1, applies to this example as well, and we get the same answer for short-run equilibrium output, which is $Y = 4{,}800$.

Short-run equilibrium output also can be found graphically, using the Keynesian cross diagram from the last chapter. Again, since the equation for planned aggregate output is the same as in Chapter 19, Figure 19.4 applies equally well here. ◆

EXERCISE 20.3

For the economy described above, suppose the Fed sets the real interest rate at 3 percent rather than at 5 percent. Find short-run equilibrium output. (*Hint:* Consider values between 4,500 and 5,500.)

THE FED FIGHTS A RECESSION

We have now demonstrated that the following relationship holds between the real interest rate and equilibrium output:

$$\downarrow r \Rightarrow \uparrow \text{planned } C \text{ and planned } I \Rightarrow \uparrow PAE \Rightarrow (\text{via the multiplier}) \uparrow Y$$

A decrease in the real interest rate causes increases in both planned consumption and planned investment, which lead to an increase in planned spending. The increase in planned spending leads, through the multiplier, to an increase in short-run equilibrium output. Similarly,

$$\uparrow r \Rightarrow \downarrow \text{planned } C \text{ and planned } I \Rightarrow \downarrow PAE \Rightarrow \text{(via the multiplier)} \downarrow Y$$

That is, an increase in the real interest rate causes decreases in both planned consumption and planned investment, which lead to a decrease in planned spending. The decrease in planned spending leads, through the multiplier, to a decrease in short-run equilibrium output.

These two relationships are the key to understanding how monetary policy affects short-run economic activity. Let's first analyze how monetary policy can be used to fight a recession; then we will turn to how the Fed can fight inflation.

Suppose the economy faces a recessionary gap—a situation in which real output is below potential output, and planned spending is "too low." To fight a recessionary gap, the Fed should reduce the real interest rate, stimulating consumption and investment spending. According to the theory we have developed, this increase in planned spending will cause output to rise, restoring the economy to full employment.

Let's build on the example we worked through in the previous section. Suppose that potential output Y^* equals 5,000. As before, the Fed has set the real interest rate equal to 5 percent. The multiplier in this economy is 5.

We showed earlier that with the real interest rate at 5 percent, short-run equilibrium output for this economy is 4,800. Potential output is 5,000, so the output gap $(Y - Y^*)$ equals $5{,}000 - 4{,}800 = 200$. Because actual output is below potential, this economy faces a recessionary gap.

To fight the recession, the Fed should lower the real interest rate, raising aggregate expenditure until output reaches 5,000, the full-employment level. That is, the Fed's objective is to increase output by 200. Because the multiplier equals 5, to increase output by 200, the Fed must increase autonomous expenditure by $200/5 = 40$ units. By how much should the Fed reduce the real interest rate to increase autonomous expenditure by 40 units? Autonomous expenditure in this economy is $[1{,}010 - 1{,}000r]$, as you can see from Equation 20.1, so that each percentage point reduction in r increases autonomous expenditure by $1{,}000 \times (0.01) = 10$ units. To increase autonomous expenditure by 40, then, the Fed should lower the real interest rate by 4 percentage points, from 5 percent to 1 percent.

In summary, to eliminate the recessionary gap of 200, the Fed should lower the real interest rate from 5 percent to 1 percent. Notice that the Fed's decrease in the real interest rate increases short-run equilibrium output, as economic logic suggests.

The Fed's recession-fighting policy is shown graphically in Figure 20.2. The reduction in the real interest rate raises planned spending at each level of output, shifting the expenditure line upward. When the real interest rate equals 1 percent, the expenditure line intersects the $Y = PAE$ line at $Y = 5{,}000$, so that output and potential output are equal.

EXERCISE 20.4

Suppose that in the example above potential output is 4,850 rather than 5,000. By how much should the Fed cut the real interest rate to restore full employment? You may take as given that the multiplier is 5.

How did the Fed respond to recession and the terror attacks in 2001?

The U.S. economy began slowing in the fall of 2000, with investment in high-tech equipment falling particularly sharply. According to the National Bureau of Economic

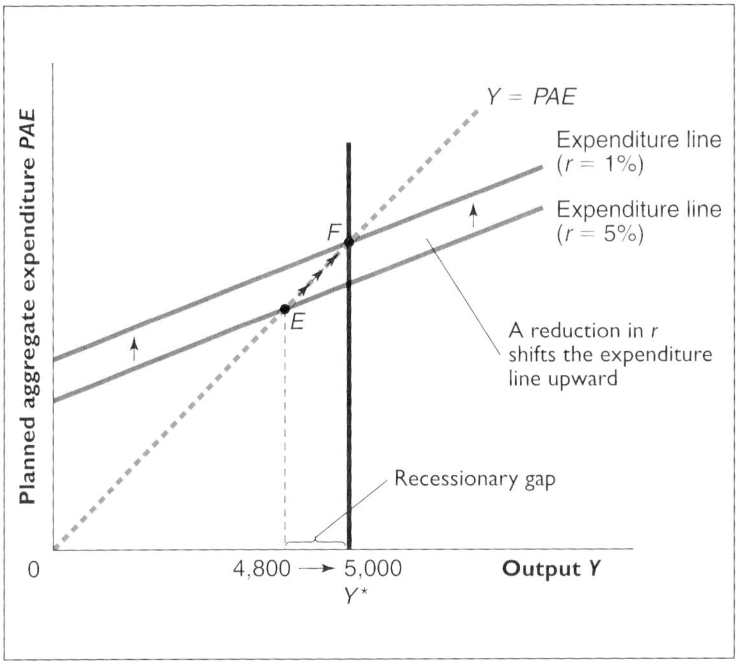

FIGURE 20.2
The Fed Fights a Recession.
(1) When the Fed sets the real interest rate at 5 percent, the economy is in short-run equilibrium at point *E* and output is 4,800; (2) the recessionary gap in equal to 200 since potential output is equal to 5,000; (3) to close the output gap, the Fed reduces the real interest rate, in this case from 5 percent to 1 percent; (4) lowering the real interest rate shifts the expenditure line up and the short-run equilibrium moves from point *E* to point *F*, where output is equal to 5,000.

Research, a recession began in March 2001. To make matters worse, on September 11, 2001, terrorist attacks on New York City and Washington shocked the nation and led to serious problems in the travel and financial industries, among others.

The Fed first began to respond to growing evidence of an economic slowdown at the end of the year 2000. At the time, the federal funds rate stood at about 6.5 percent. (See Figure 20.1.) The Fed's most dramatic move was a surprise cut of 0.5 percentage point in the funds rate in January 2001, between regularly scheduled meetings of the Federal Open Market Committee. Further rate cuts followed, and by July the funds rate was below 4 percent. By summer's end, however, there was still considerable uncertainty about the likely severity of the economic slowdown.

The picture changed suddenly on September 11, 2001, when the terror attacks on the World Trade Center and the Pentagon killed almost 3,000 people. The terrorist attacks imposed great economic as well as human costs. The physical damage in lower Manhattan was in the billions of dollars, and many offices and businesses in the area had to close. The Fed, in its role as supervisor of the financial system, worked hard to assist in the restoration of normal operations in the financial district of New York City. (The Federal Reserve Bank of New York, which actually conducts open-market operations, is only a block from the site of the World Trade Center.) The Fed also tried to ease financial conditions by temporarily lowering the federal funds rate to as low as 1.25 percent in the week following the attack.

In the weeks and months following September 11, the Fed turned its attention from the direct impact of the attack to the possible indirect effects on the U.S. economy. The Fed was worried that consumers, nervous about the future, would severely cut back their spending; together with the ongoing weakness in investment, a fall in consumption spending could sharply worsen the recession. To stimulate spending, the Fed continued to cut the federal funds rate.

By the time the recession officially ended in November 2001, the funds rate was at 2.0 percent, 4.5 percentage points lower than a year earlier. A number of factors made the 2001 recession relatively short and mild, including President Bush's tax cuts and increased government expenditures for homeland security and defense. Nevertheless, most economists agree that the Fed's quick actions helped to moderate the impact of the recession and the September 11 attacks. ◆

THE FED FIGHTS INFLATION

To this point we have focused on the problem of stabilizing output, without considering inflation. In the next chapter, we will see how ongoing inflation can be incorporated into our analysis. For now we will simply note that one important cause of inflation is an expansionary output gap—a situation in which planned spending, and hence actual output, exceeds potential output. When an expansionary gap exists, firms find that the demand for their output exceeds their normal rate of production. Although firms may be content to meet this excess demand at previously determined prices for some time, if the high demand persists, they ultimately will raise their prices, spurring inflation.

Because an expansionary gap tends to lead to inflation, the Fed moves to eliminate expansionary gaps as well as recessionary gaps. The procedure for getting rid of an expansionary gap—a situation in which output is "too high" relative to potential output—is the reverse of that for fighting a recessionary gap, a situation in which output is "too low." As we have seen, the cure for a recessionary gap is to reduce the real interest rate, an action that stimulates planned spending and increases output. The cure for an expansionary gap is to *raise* the real interest rate, which reduces consumption and planned investment by raising the cost of borrowing. The resulting fall in planned spending leads in turn to a decline in output and to a reduction in inflationary pressures.

Using the same example economy we've analyzed above, let's now assume that potential output is 4,600 rather than 5,000. At the initial real interest rate of 5 percent, short-run equilibrium output is 4,800, so this economy has an expansionary gap of 200.

As before, the multiplier in this economy is 5. Hence, to reduce total output by 200, the Fed needs to reduce autonomous expenditure by 200/5 = 40 units. From Equation 20.1, we know that autonomous expenditure in this economy is $[1{,}010 - 1{,}000r]$, so that each percentage point (0.01) increase in the real interest rate lowers autonomous expenditure by 10 units ($1{,}000 \times 0.01$). We conclude that to eliminate the inflationary gap, the Fed should raise the real interest rate by 4 percentage points (0.04), from 5 percent to 9 percent. The higher real interest rate will reduce planned aggregate expenditure and output to the level of potential output, 4,600, eliminating inflationary pressures.

The effects of the Fed's inflation-fighting policy are shown in Figure 20.3. With the real interest rate at 5 percent, the expenditure line intersects the $Y = PAE$ line at point *E* in the figure, where output equals 4,800. To reduce planned spending and output, the Fed raises the real interest rate to 9 percent. The higher real interest rate slows consumption and investment spending, moving the expenditure line downward. At the new equilibrium point *G*, actual output equals potential output at 4,600. The Fed's raising the real interest rate—a contractionary policy action—has thus eliminated the expansionary output gap, and, with it, the threat of inflation.

Why did the Fed raise interest rates in 2004 and 2005?

The Fed began tightening monetary policy in June 2004 when it increased the federal funds rate from 1.0 to 1.25 percent. (See Figure 20.1.) It continued to tighten by raising the federal funds rate by one-quarter percent at each successive meeting of the Federal Open Market Committee. By August 2005, after more than a year of tightening, the federal funds rate was 3.50 percent. Why did the Fed begin increasing the funds rate in 2004?

FIGURE 20.3
The Fed Fights Inflation.
(1) When the Fed sets the real interest rate at 5 percent, the economy is in short-run equilibrium at point *E* and output is 4,800; (2) the expansionary gap is equal to 200 since potential output is equal to 4,600; (3) to close the output gap, the Fed raises the real interest rate, in this case from 5 percent to 9 percent; (4) raising the real interest rate shifts the expenditure line down and the short-run equilibrium moves from point *E* to point *G*, where output is equal to 4,600.

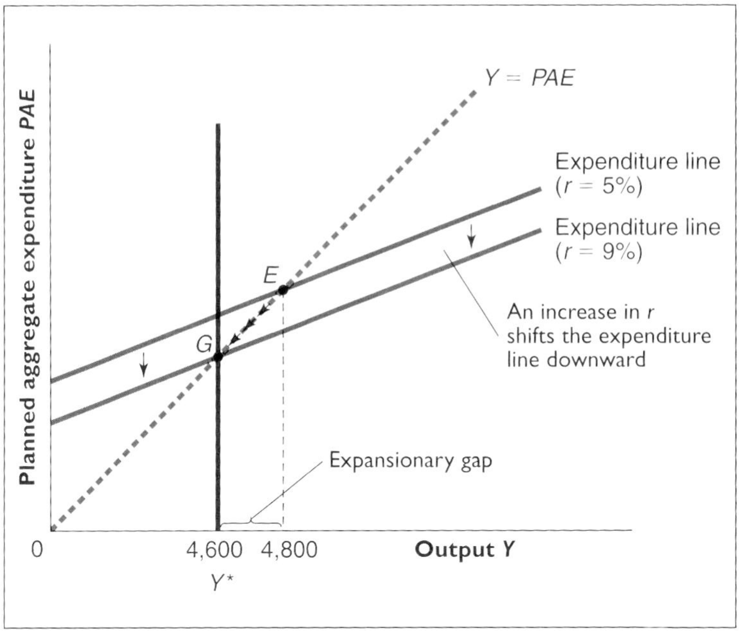

"Personally, I liked this roller coaster a lot better before the Federal Reserve Board got hold of it."

Because the recovery that began in November 2001 was slower than normal and marked by weak job growth, the Fed kept reducing the funds rate until it reached 1.0 percent in June 2003. Once the recovery took hold, however, this very low rate was no longer necessary. While employment had not risen as much during the recovery as it had in previous recoveries, real GDP grew at a rate of nearly 6 percent during the second half of 2003 and by 4.4 percent in 2004. Furthermore, by June 2004 the unemployment rate had fallen to 5.6 percent, not far above most estimates of the natural rate of unemployment. Although inflation began to rise in 2004, most of the increase was due to the sharp run-up in oil prices, and the rate of inflation excluding energy remained low. Nevertheless, the Fed began to raise the federal funds rate in order to prevent the emergence of an expansionary gap, which would result in higher inflation. Thus, the Fed's rate increases could be viewed as a preemptive strike against future inflation. Had the Fed waited until an expansionary gap appeared, a significant inflation problem could have emerged, and the Fed might have had to raise the federal funds rate by even more than it did. ◆

The Fed's interest rate policies affect the economy as a whole, but they have a particularly important effect on financial markets. The introduction to this chapter noted the tremendous lengths financial market participants will go to in an attempt to anticipate Federal Reserve policy changes. Example 20.1 illustrates the type of information financial investors look for, and why it is so important to them.

Example 20.1

THE ECONOMIC NATURALIST

Why does news of inflation hurt the stock market?

Financial market participants watch data on inflation extremely closely. A report that inflation is increasing or is higher than expected often causes stock prices to fall sharply. Why does bad news about inflation hurt the stock market?

Investors in the financial markets worry about inflation because of its likely impact on Federal Reserve policy. Financial investors understand that the Fed, when faced with signs of an expansionary gap, is likely to raise interest rates in an attempt to reduce planned spending and "cool down" the economy. This type of contractionary policy action hurts stock prices in two ways. First, it slows down economic activity, reducing the expected sales and profits of companies whose shares are traded in the stock market. Lower profits, in turn, reduce the dividends those firms are likely to pay their shareholders.

Second, higher real interest rates reduce the value of stocks by increasing the required return for holding stocks. We saw in Chapter 17 that an increase in the return financial investors require in order to hold stocks lowers current stock prices. Intuitively, if interest rates rise, interest-bearing alternatives to stocks such as newly issued government bonds will become more attractive to investors, reducing the demand for, and hence the price of, stocks. ●

Should the Federal Reserve respond to changes in stock prices?

Many credit the Federal Reserve and its chairman at the time, Alan Greenspan, for effective monetary policymaking that set the stage for sustained economic growth and rising asset prices throughout the 1990s, in particular the second half of the decade. Between January 1995 and March 2000, the S&P 500 stock market index rose from a value of 459 to 1,527, a phenomenal 233 percent increase in just over five years, as the U.S. economy enjoyed a record-long business cycle expansion. Indeed, the stock market's strong, sustained rise helped to fuel additional consumer spending, which in turn promoted further economic expansion.

However, as stock prices fell sharply in the two years after their March 2000 peak, some people questioned whether the Federal Reserve should have preemptively raised interest rates to constrain investors' "irrational exuberance."[4] In this view, overly optimistic investor sentiment led to a speculative run-up in stock prices that eventually burst in 2000 as investors began to realize that firms' earnings could not support the stock prices that were being paid. Earlier intervention by the Federal Reserve, critics argued, would have slowed down the dramatic increase in stock prices and therefore could have prevented the resulting stock market "crash" and the resulting loss of consumer wealth. As this chapter makes clear, the Federal Reserve's primary focus is on reducing output gaps and keeping inflation low. Should the Fed also respond to changing stock prices when it makes decisions about monetary policy?

[4]Fed Chairman Alan Greenspan mentioned the possibility of "irrational exuberance" driving investor behavior in a December 5, 1996, speech, which is available online at http://www.federalreserve.gov/boarddocs/speeches/1996/19961205.htm.

At a symposium in August 2002, Alan Greenspan defended the Fed's monetary policymaking performance in the late 1990s, pointing out that it is very difficult to identify asset bubbles—surges in prices of assets to unsustainable levels— "until after the fact—that is, when its bursting confirm(s) its existence."[5] Even if such a speculative bubble could be identified, Greenspan noted, the Federal Reserve could have done little—short of "inducing a substantial contraction in economic activity"—to prevent investors' speculation from driving up stock prices. Indeed, Greenspan claimed, "the notion that a well-timed incremental tightening could have been calibrated to prevent the late 1990s bubble is almost surely an illusion." Rather, the Federal Reserve was focusing as early as 1999 on policies that would "mitigate the fallout when it occurs and, hopefully, ease the transition to the next expansion."[6] ◆

Greenspan's remarks highlight two basic problems with using monetary policy to address "bubbles" in asset markets. First, doing so presupposes that the Federal Reserve is better than financial-market professionals at identifying when asset prices are inappropriately high, relative to the asset's underlying value. In practice, however, the Fed does not have information about the stock market that is not also available to private-sector investors. Second, even if the Fed were sure that a "bubble" existed, monetary policy is not a very good tool for addressing the problem. The Fed could try to lower stock prices by raising the federal funds rate and slowing the economy. But if this policy led to a recession and rising unemployment, the outcome would be precisely the one that the Fed was trying to avoid in the first place. For these reasons, although the Fed monitors conditions in the stock market, when setting monetary policy it focuses on inflation, spending, and output, rather than stock prices themselves. Not all economists agree with the Fed's approach, however, and the debate continues. In particular, the financial market problems caused by the collapse of the subprime mortgage market in 2007 and 2008 rekindled this debate.

THE FED'S MONETARY POLICY RULE

Let's summarize the relationships we developed in the previous section: using symbols, we showed that

$$\downarrow r \Rightarrow \uparrow \text{planned } C \text{ and planned } I \Rightarrow \uparrow PAE \Rightarrow \text{(via the multiplier)} \uparrow Y$$

and

$$\uparrow r \Rightarrow \downarrow \text{planned } C \text{ and planned } I \Rightarrow \downarrow PAE \Rightarrow \text{(via the multiplier)} \downarrow Y$$

Now, we have a sense of *why* the Fed will raise or lower the real interest rate: in order to close either a recessionary gap (in the first case) or an expansionary gap (in the second case). In particular, in the second case we showed that the Fed is reacting to an increase in the inflation rate, π. If we add this to our second relationship, we have

$$\uparrow \pi \Rightarrow \uparrow r \Rightarrow \downarrow \text{planned } C \text{ and planned } I \Rightarrow \downarrow PAE \Rightarrow \text{(via the multiplier)} \downarrow Y$$

Similarly, when there is a recessionary gap, the inflation rate tends to fall. Adding this to our first relationship, we have

$$\downarrow \pi \Rightarrow \uparrow r \Rightarrow \uparrow \text{planned } C \text{ and planned } I \Rightarrow \uparrow PAE \Rightarrow \text{(via the multiplier)} \uparrow Y$$

[5]The text of Greenspan's speech is available online at http://www.federalreserve.gov/boarddocs/speeches/2002/20020830/default.htm.

[6]*The Federal Reserve's Semiannual Report on Monetary Policy*, testimony of Chairman Alan Greenspan before the Committee on Banking and Financial Services, U.S. House of Representatives, July 22, 1999. Available online at http://www.federalreserve.gov/boarddocs/hh/1999/July/Testimony.htm.

These two relationships show that the Fed responds to a change in the inflation rate by changing the real interest rate in the same direction, causing real output to move in the opposite direction.

A *monetary policy rule* is a way of summarizing the relationship between changes in inflation and changes in the real interest rate set by the Fed. More generally, a **monetary policy rule** describes how a central bank takes action in response to changes in the state of the economy. Specifically, the Fed raises or lowers interest rates in response to changes in the rate of inflation.

monetary policy rule describes how a central bank takes action in response to changes in the state of the economy

We can incorporate a monetary policy rule into the simple Keynesian model using graphs, numbers, and equations. We will focus in this section on graphs and numbers while the appendix to this chapter takes an algebraic approach.

Figure 20.4 shows a general monetary policy rule. The Fed has a long-term **target inflation rate** for the economy, shown on the graph as π^*; when inflation is at this target rate, the Fed sets the actual real interest rate at r^*. When actual inflation exceeds the long-run target inflation rate, the Fed sets the actual real interest rate above r^*, and when inflation is below its target rate, the Fed sets the actual real interest rate below r^*.

target inflation rate The Fed's long-run goal for inflation

target real interest rate The Fed's long-run goal for the real interest rate

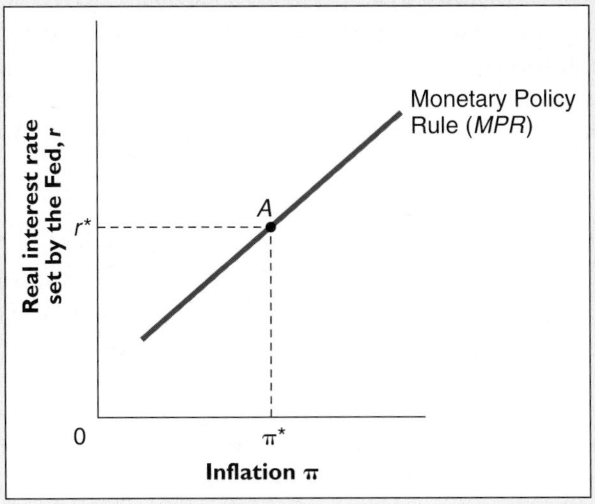

FIGURE 20.4
A General Example of a Monetary Policy Rule.
This is a general version of the Fed's monetary policy rule. The Fed's target real interest rate is r^* and target inflation rate is π^*. When inflation is above π^*, the Fed sets the real interest rate above r^*, and when inflation is below π^*, the Fed sets the real interest rate below r^*.

We refer to r^* and π^* as *long-run* targets because they are generally determined by long-run considerations. As we will discuss further in the next chapter, the Fed generally sets its target for the real interest rate at the level where saving is equal to investment. (Recall from Chapter 16 that this is the level of the real interest rate at which the financial market is in equilibrium.) Likewise, as we will see later, the Fed chooses its target inflation rate at a level that helps to achieve the best long-run economic performance. Although π^* represents the Fed's long-run target for inflation, in the short-run, actual inflation need not equal the target inflation rate. This implies that the actual real interest rate need not equal its target rate, r^*, in the short run either.

Table 20.2 presents a specific example of a monetary policy rule. In this example, suppose that the Fed's target real interest rate is 0.04 (4 percent) and the target inflation rate is 0.02 (2 percent). If actual inflation is equal to its target rate of 2 percent, the Fed sets the real interest rate equal to its real interest rate target of 4 percent, as indicated in the third line of Table 20.2. The other numbers in Table 20.2 show how the Fed changes the real interest rate in response to inflation rising above or falling below the target inflation rate.

TABLE 20.2
A Specific Example of a Monetary Policy Rule

Actual rate of inflation, π	Actual real interest rate set by Fed, r
0.00 (= 0%)	0.02 (= 2%)
0.01	0.03
0.02	0.04
0.03	0.05
0.04	0.06

Let's apply this monetary policy rule to a specific situation. Suppose an expansionary gap begins to "overheat" the economy and push up inflation from its target rate of 2 percent to 3 percent. The table shows that the Fed will increase the actual real interest rate to 5 percent. On the other hand, suppose that a recessionary gap opens up and inflation falls from 2 percent to 1 percent. In this case, the Fed will reduce the actual real interest rate to 3 percent.

Figure 20.5 graphs the monetary policy rule given in Table 20.2. The vertical axis of the graph shows the actual real interest rate chosen by the Fed while the horizontal axis shows the rate of inflation. The upward slope of the monetary policy rule captures the idea that the Fed reacts to increases in inflation by raising the real interest rate.

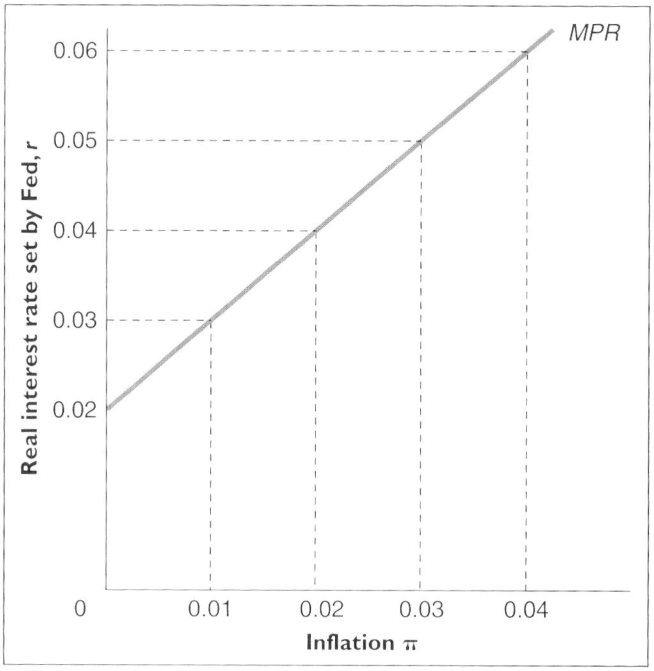

FIGURE 20.5
A Specific Example of a Monetary Policy Rule. This is a graphical version of the rule in Table 20.2 and shows the real interest rate that the Fed will set for any given level of inflation. The line is upward-sloping because the Fed raises the real interest rate in response to higher rates of inflation.

How does the Fed determine its monetary policy rule? In practice the process is a complex one, involving a combination of statistical analysis of the economy and human judgment. One useful insight into the process can be drawn from the simplified policy rule shown in Table 20.2 and Figure 20.5 and the general policy rule shown in Figure 20.4. In particular, the slope of the monetary policy rule contains information about how aggressively the Fed plans to pursue its inflation target.

To illustrate, suppose the Fed's monetary policy rule was very flat. In this case, the Fed changes the real interest rate rather modestly in response to increases or decreases in inflation. We would then conclude that the Fed does not intend to be very aggressive in its attempts to offset movements in inflation away from the target level. In contrast, suppose the monetary policy rule slopes steeply upward; in this second case, a given change in inflation elicits a large adjustment of the real interest rate by the Fed. We would then say that the Fed plans to be quite aggressive in responding to changes in inflation.

In principle, any number of economic variables, from stock prices to the value of the dollar in terms of the Japanese yen, could affect Fed policy and thus appear in the monetary policy rule. In the next chapter, we will adopt the simple policy rule we have worked with here. This simplification does not affect our main results in any significant way. Furthermore, as we will see, this policy rule captures the most important aspect of Fed behavior—namely, its tendency to raise the actual real interest rate when inflation is rising and to reduce it when inflation is falling. Rising inflation usually occurs when the economy is "overheated" and experiencing an expansionary gap. Similarly, falling inflation usually occurs when the economy is sluggish and experiencing a recessionary gap. Consequently, our simple monetary policy rule implicitly includes the size of any output gap (since this will affect actual inflation), even though the gap is not explicitly included as a separate variable.[7]

RECAP | MONETARY POLICY AND THE ECONOMY

- An increase in the real interest rate reduces both consumption spending and planned investment spending. Through its control of the real interest rate, the Fed is able to influence planned spending and short-run equilibrium output. To fight a recession (a recessionary output gap), the Fed lowers the real interest rate, stimulating planned spending and output. Conversely, to fight the threat of inflation (an expansionary output gap), the Fed raises the real interest rate, reducing planned spending and output.
- The Fed's monetary policy rule relates its policy action (specifically, its setting of the real interest rate) to the state of the economy. For the sake of simplicity, we consider a policy rule in which the actual real interest rate set by the Fed depends only on the Fed's real interest rate target and the extent to which the actual rate of inflation differs from the Fed's long-run inflation rate target. In the short run, inflation may be more or less than the Fed's inflation target, implying that in the short run the real interest rate also may be greater or less than the Fed's target for the real interest rate. Because the Fed raises the real interest rate whenever inflation rises above the Fed's inflation target, the Fed's monetary policy rule is upward-sloping. The Fed's policy rule contains information about the central bank's inflation target and real interest rate target, as well as the aggressiveness with which it intends to pursue its inflation target.

[7]An example of a monetary policy rule that includes the output gap is the "Taylor rule," developed by John B. Taylor of Stanford University in the early 1990s. An interview with Taylor that clearly explains the Taylor rule is in the June 2006 issue of *The Region* (published by the Federal Reserve Bank of Minneapolis), http://www.minneapolisfed.org/pubs/region/06-06/taylor.cfm.

THE FEDERAL RESERVE AND INTEREST RATES

When we introduced the Federal Reserve System in Chapter 17, we focused on the Fed's control of the *money supply*, that is, the quantity of currency and checking accounts held by the public. Determining the nation's money supply is the primary task of monetary policymakers. But if you follow the economic news regularly, you may find the idea that the Fed's job is to control the money supply a bit foreign because the news media nearly always focus on the Fed's decisions about *interest rates*. Indeed, the announcement the Fed makes after each meeting of the Federal Open Market Committee nearly always concerns its plan for a particular short-term interest rate, called the *federal funds rate*.

Actually, there is no contradiction between the two ways of looking at monetary policy—as control of the money supply or as the setting of interest rates. As we will see in this section, the Fed changes the money supply to control the nominal interest rate. Thus, controlling the money supply and controlling the nominal interest rate are two sides of the same coin: Any value of the money supply chosen by the Fed implies a specific setting for the nominal interest rate, and vice versa. The reason for this close connection is that the nominal interest rate is effectively the "price" of holding money (or, more accurately, its opportunity cost). So, by controlling the quantity of money supplied to the economy, the Fed also controls the "price" of holding money (the nominal interest rate).

To better understand how the Fed determines interest rates, we will look first at the market for money, beginning with the demand side of that market. We will see that given the demand for money by the public, the Fed can control interest rates by changing the amount of money it supplies.

THE DEMAND FOR MONEY

Recall from Chapter 17, that *money* refers to the set of assets, such as cash and checking accounts, that are usable in transactions. Money is also a store of value, like stocks, bonds, or real estate—in other words, a type of financial asset. As a financial asset, money is a way of holding wealth.

Anyone who has some wealth must determine the *form* in which he or she wishes to hold that wealth. For example, if Larry has wealth of $10,000, he could, if he wished, hold all $10,000 in cash. Or he could hold $5,000 of his wealth in the form of cash and $5,000 in government bonds. Or he could hold $1,000 in cash, $2,000 in a checking account, $2,000 in government bonds, and $5,000 in rare stamps. Indeed, there are thousands of different real and financial assets to choose from, all of which can be held in different amounts and combinations, so Larry's choices are virtually infinite. The decision about the forms in which to hold one's wealth is called the **portfolio allocation decision**.

portfolio allocation decision the decision about the forms in which to hold one's wealth

What determines the particular mix of assets that Larry or another wealth holder will choose? All else being equal, people generally prefer to hold assets that they expect to pay a high *return* and do not carry too much *risk*. They also may try to reduce the overall risk they face through *diversification*—that is, by owning a variety of different assets.[8] Many people own some real assets, such as a car or a home, because they provide services (transportation or shelter) and often a financial return (an increase in value, as when the price of a home rises in a strong real estate market).

Here we do not need to analyze the entire portfolio allocation decision, but only one part of it—namely, the decision about how much of one's wealth to hold in the form of *money* (cash and checking accounts). The amount of wealth an individual chooses to hold in the form of money is that individual's **demand for money**, sometimes called an individual's *liquidity preference*. So if Larry decided to hold his

demand for money the amount of wealth an individual chooses to hold in the form of money

[8]We examined risk, return, and asset diversification in Chapter 17.

entire $10,000 in the form of cash, his demand for money would be $10,000. But if he were to hold $1,000 in cash, $2,000 in a checking account, $2,000 in government bonds, and $5,000 in rare stamps, his demand for money would be only $3,000—that is, $1,000 in cash plus the $2,000 in his checking account.

How much money should an individual (or household) choose to hold? Applying the Cost-Benefit Principle, an individual should increase his or her money holdings only so long as the extra benefit of doing so exceeds the extra cost. As we saw in Chapter 17, the principal *benefit* of holding money is its usefulness in carrying out transactions. Larry's shares of stock, his car, and his furniture are all valuable assets, but he cannot use them to buy groceries or pay his rent. He can make routine payments using cash or his checking account, however. Because of its usefulness in daily transactions, Larry will almost certainly want to hold some of his wealth in the form of money. Furthermore, if Larry is a high-income individual, he will probably choose to hold more money than someone with a lower income would because he is likely to spend more and carry out more transactions than the low-income person.

Cost-Benefit

Larry's benefit from holding money is also affected by the technological and financial sophistication of the society he lives in. For example, in the United States, developments such as credit cards, debit cards, and ATM machines have generally reduced the amount of money people need to carry out routine transactions, decreasing the public's demand for money at given levels of income. In the United States in 1960, for example, money holdings in the form of cash and checking account balances (the monetary aggregate M1) were about 28 percent of GDP. By 2004 that ratio had fallen to about 12 percent of GDP.

Innovations such as ATM machines have reduced the amount of money that people need to hold for routine transactions.

Although money is an extremely useful asset, there is also a cost to holding money—more precisely, an opportunity cost—that arises from the fact that most forms of money pay little or no interest. Cash pays zero interest, and most checking accounts pay either no interest or very low rates. For the sake of simplicity, we will assume that *the nominal interest rate on money is zero*. In contrast, most alternative assets, such as bonds or stocks, pay a positive nominal return. A bond, for example, pays a fixed amount of interest each period to the holder, while stocks pay dividends and also may increase in value (capital gains).

The cost of holding money arises because, in order to hold an extra dollar of wealth in the form of money, a person must reduce by one dollar the amount of wealth held in the form of higher-yielding assets, such as bonds or stocks. The opportunity cost of holding money is measured by the interest rate that could have been earned if the person had chosen to hold interest-bearing assets instead of money. All else being equal, the higher the nominal interest rate, the higher the opportunity cost of holding money, and hence the less money people will choose to hold.

We have been talking about the demand for money by individuals, but businesses also hold money to carry out transactions with customers and to pay workers and suppliers. The same general factors that determine individuals' money demand also affect the demand for money by businesses. That is, in choosing how much money to hold, a business, like an individual, will compare the benefits of holding money for use in transactions with the opportunity cost of holding a non-interest-bearing asset. Although we will not differentiate between the money held by individuals and the money held by businesses in discussing money demand, you should be aware that in the U.S. economy, businesses hold a significant portion—more than half—of the total money stock.

MACROECONOMIC FACTORS THAT AFFECT THE DEMAND FOR MONEY

In any household or business, the demand for money will depend on a variety of individual circumstances. For example, a high-volume retail business that serves thousands of customers each day will probably choose to have more money on hand than a legal firm that bills clients and pays employees monthly. But while individuals and businesses vary considerably in the amount of money they choose to hold, three macroeconomic factors affect the demand for money quite broadly: the nominal interest rate, real output, and the price level.

- *The nominal interest rate (i).* We have seen that the interest rate paid on alternatives to money, such as government bonds, determines the opportunity cost of holding money. The higher the prevailing nominal interest rate, the greater the opportunity cost of holding money, and hence the less money individuals and businesses will demand.

What do we mean by *the* nominal interest rate? As we have discussed, there are thousands of different assets, each with its own interest rate (rate of return). So can we really talk about *the* nominal interest rate? The answer is that, while there are many different assets, each with its own corresponding interest rate, the rates on those assets tend to rise and fall together. This is to be expected because if the interest rates on some assets were to rise sharply while the rates on other assets declined, financial investors would flock to the assets paying high rates and refuse to buy the assets paying low rates. So, although there are many different interest rates in practice, speaking of the general level of interest rates usually does make sense. In this book, when we talk about *the* nominal interest rate, what we have in mind is some average measure of interest rates.

The nominal interest rate is a macroeconomic factor that affects the cost of holding money. A macroeconomic factor that affects the *benefit* of holding money is

- *Real income or output (Y).* An increase in aggregate real income or output—as measured, for example, by real GDP—raises the quantity of goods and services that people and businesses want to buy and sell. When the economy enters a boom, for example, people do more shopping and stores have more customers. To accommodate the increase in transactions, both individuals and businesses need to hold more money. Thus higher real output raises the demand for money.

A second macroeconomic factor affecting the benefit of holding money is

- *The price level (P).* The higher the prices of goods and services, the more dollars (or yen, or euros) are needed to make a given set of transactions. Thus, a higher price level is associated with a higher demand for money.

Today, when a couple of teenagers go out for a movie and snacks on Saturday night, they need probably five times as much cash as their parents did 25 years ago. Because the prices of movie tickets and popcorn have risen steeply over 25 years, more money (that is, more dollars) is needed to pay for a Saturday night date than in the past. By the way, the fact that prices are higher today does *not* imply that people are worse off today than in the past because nominal wages and salaries also have risen substantially. In general, however, higher prices do imply that people need to keep a greater number of dollars available, in cash or in a checking account.

THE MONEY DEMAND CURVE

For the purposes of monetary policymaking, economists are most interested in the aggregate, or economywide, demand for money. The interaction of the aggregate demand for money, determined by the public, and the supply of money, which is set by the Fed, determines the nominal interest rate that prevails in the economy.

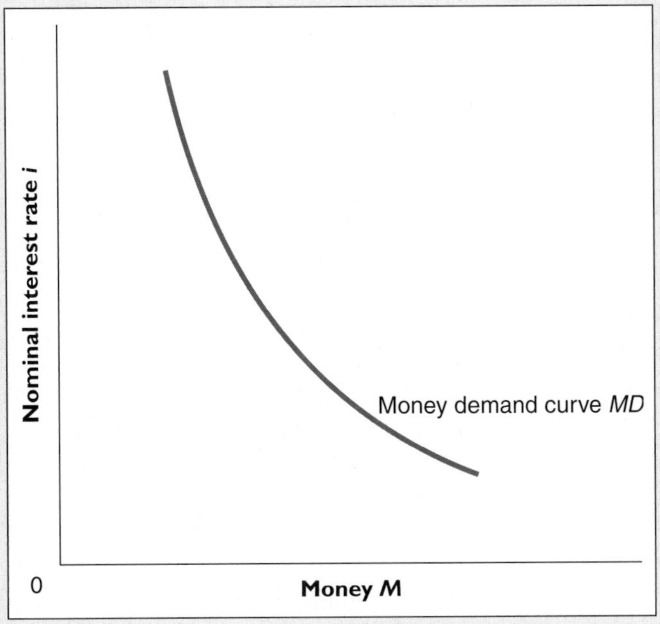

FIGURE 20.6
The Money Demand Curve.
The money demand curve relates the economywide demand for money to the nominal interest rate. Because an increase in the nominal interest rate raises the opportunity cost of holding money, the money demand curve slopes down.

The economywide demand for money can be represented graphically by the *money demand curve* (see Figure 20.6). The **money demand curve** relates the aggregate quantity of money demanded M to the nominal interest rate i. The quantity of money demanded M is a nominal quantity, measured in dollars (or yen, or euros, depending on the country). Because an increase in the nominal interest rate increases the opportunity cost of holding money, which reduces the quantity of money demanded, the money demand curve slopes down.

money demand curve Shows the relationship between the aggregate quantity of money demanded M and the nominal interest rate i; because an increase in the nominal interest rate increases the opportunity cost of holding money, which reduces the quantity of money demanded, the money demand curve slopes down

If we think of the nominal interest rate as the "price" (more precisely, the opportunity cost) of money and the amount of money people want to hold as the "quantity," the money demand curve is analogous to the demand curve for a good or service. As with a standard demand curve, the fact that a higher price of money leads people to demand less of it is captured in the downward slope of the demand curve. Furthermore, as in a standard demand curve, changes in factors other than the price of money (the nominal interest rate) can cause the demand curve for money to shift. For a given nominal interest rate, any change that makes people want to hold more money will shift the money demand curve to the right, and any change that makes people want to hold less money will shift the money demand curve to the left. We have already identified two macroeconomic factors other than the nominal interest rate that affect the economywide demand for money: real output and the price level. Because an increase in either of these variables increases the demand for money, it shifts the money demand curve rightward, as shown in Figure 20.7. Similarly, a fall in real output or the general price level reduces money demand, shifting the money demand curve leftward.

The money demand curve also may shift in response to other changes that affect the cost or benefit of holding money, such as the technological and financial advances we mentioned earlier. For example, the introduction of ATM machines reduced the amount of money people choose to hold and thus shifted the economywide money demand curve to the left. Example 20.2 describes another potential source of shifts in the demand for money, holdings of U.S. dollars by foreigners.

FIGURE 20.7
A Shift in the Money Demand Curve.
At a given nominal interest rate, any change that makes people want to hold more money—such as an increase in the general price level or in real GDP—will shift the money demand curve to the right.

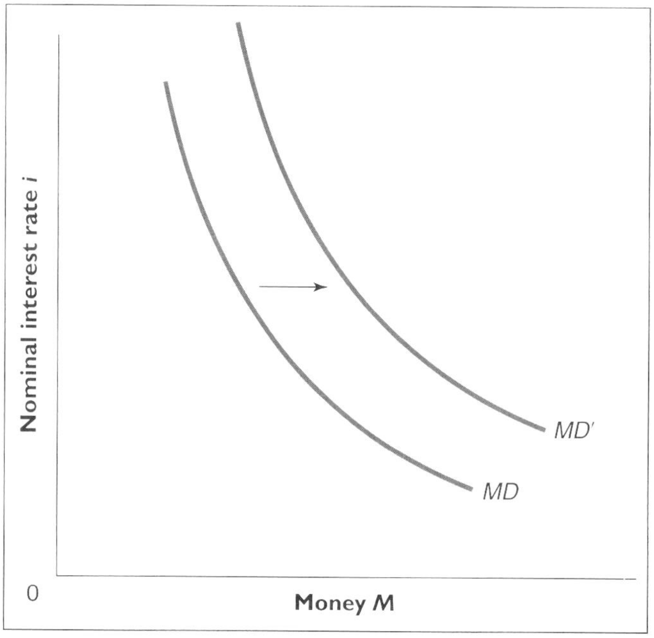

Example 20.2
THE ECONOMIC NATURALIST

Why does the average Argentine hold more U.S. dollars than the average U.S. citizen?

Estimates are that the value of U.S. dollars circulating in Argentina exceeds $1,000 per person, which is higher than the per capita dollar holdings in the United States. A number of other countries, including those that once belonged to the former Soviet Union, also hold large quantities of dollars. In all, as much as $300 billion in U.S. currency—more than half the total amount issued—may be circulating outside the borders of the United States. Why do Argentines and other non-U.S. residents hold so many dollars?

U.S. residents and businesses hold dollars primarily for transaction purposes, rather than as a store of value. As a store of value, interest-bearing bonds and dividend-paying stocks are a better choice for Americans than zero-interest money. But this is not necessarily the case for the citizens of other countries, particularly nations that are economically or politically unstable. Argentina, for example, endured many years of high and erratic inflation in the 1970s and 1980s, which sharply eroded the value of financial investments denominated in Argentine pesos. Lacking better alternatives, many Argentines began saving in the form of U.S. currency, which they correctly believed to be more stable in value than peso-denominated assets.

Argentina's use of dollars became officially recognized in 1990. In that year, the country instituted a new monetary system, called a currency board, under which U.S. dollars and Argentine pesos by law traded freely one for one. Under the currency board system, Argentines became accustomed to carrying U.S. dollars in their wallets for transaction purposes, along with pesos. However, in 2001 Argentina's monetary problems returned with a vengeance, as the currency board system broke down, the peso plummeted in value relative to the dollar, and inflation returned. Consequently, the Argentinian demand for dollars increased during the next few years.

Some countries, including a number formed as a result of the breakup of the Soviet Union, have endured not only high inflation but political instability and uncertainty as well. In a politically volatile environment, citizens face the risk that their savings, including their bank deposits, will be confiscated or heavily taxed by the government. Often they conclude that a hidden cache of U.S. dollars is the safest way to hold wealth. Indeed, an estimated $1 million in 100-dollar bills can be stored in a suitcase. The ability to hold such wealth in a relatively small container is one reason why international criminals, most notably drug dealers, allegedly hold so many 100-dollar bills. Now that the European currency, the euro, which is worth more than $1, can be held in the form of a 500-euro banknote, it has been suggested that drug dealers and other cash-hoarders may switch to holding 500-euro bills in even smaller suitcases. If they do, the demand for dollars would decline. •

RECAP	MONEY DEMAND

- For the economy as a whole, the demand for money is the amount of wealth that individuals, households, and businesses choose to hold in the form of money. The opportunity cost of holding money is measured by the nominal interest rate i, which is the return that could be earned on alternative assets such as bonds. The benefit of holding money is its usefulness in transactions.
- Increases in real GDP (Y) or the price level (P) raise the nominal volume of transactions and thus the economywide demand for money. The demand for money also is affected by technological and financial innovations, such as the introduction of ATM machines, that affect the costs or benefits of holding money.
- The money demand curve relates the economywide demand for money to the nominal interest rate. Because an increase in the nominal interest rate raises the opportunity cost of holding money, the money demand curve slopes downward.
- Changes in factors other than the nominal interest rate that affect the demand for money can shift the money demand curve. For example, increases in real GDP or the price level raise the demand for money, shifting the money demand curve to the right, whereas decreases shift the money demand curve to the left.

THE SUPPLY OF MONEY AND MONEY MARKET EQUILIBRIUM

Where there is demand, can supply be far behind? As we have seen, the *supply* of money is controlled by the central bank—in the United States, the Federal Reserve. As we discussed in Chapter 17, the Fed's primary tool for controlling the money supply is *open-market operations*. For example, to increase the money supply, the Fed can use newly created money to buy government bonds from the public (an open-market purchase), which puts the new money into circulation.

Figure 20.8 shows the demand for and the supply of money in a single diagram. The nominal interest rate is on the vertical axis, and the nominal quantity of money (in dollars) is on the horizontal axis. As we have seen, because a higher nominal interest rate increases the opportunity cost of holding money, the money demand curve slopes downward. And because the Fed fixes the supply of money, we have drawn the *money supply curve* as a vertical line that intercepts the horizontal axis at the quantity of money chosen by the Fed, denoted M.

As in standard supply and demand analysis, equilibrium in the market for money occurs at the intersection of the supply and demand curves, shown as point E in Figure 20.8. The equilibrium amount of money in circulation, M, is simply the amount of money the Fed chooses to supply. The equilibrium nominal interest rate i is the interest rate at which the quantity of money demanded by the public, as determined by the money demand curve, equals the fixed supply of money made available by the Fed.

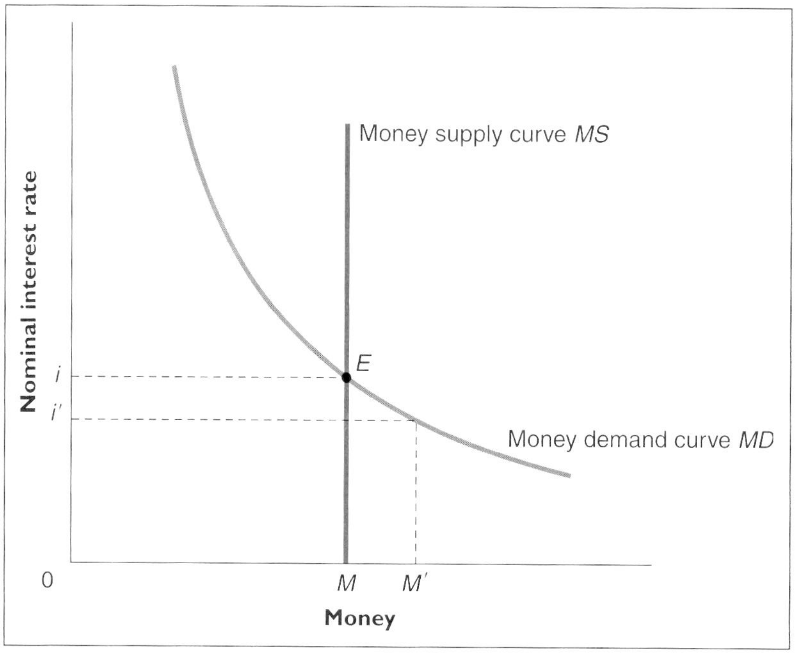

FIGURE 20.8
Equilibrium in the Market for Money.
Equilibrium in the market for money occurs at point *E*, where the demand for money by the public equals the amount of money supplied by the Federal Reserve. The equilibrium nominal interest rate, which equates the supply of and demand for money, is *i*.

To understand how the market for money reaches equilibrium, it is helpful to recall the relationship between interest rates and the market price of bonds that was introduced Chapter 17: the prices of existing bonds are *inversely related* to the current interest rate. Higher interest rates imply lower bond prices, and lower interest rates imply higher bond prices. With this relationship between interest rates and bond prices in mind, let's ask what happens if, say, the nominal interest rate is initially below the equilibrium level in the market for money—for example, at a value such as i' in Figure 20.8. At that interest rate, the public's quantity demanded of money is M', which is greater than the actual amount of money in circulation, equal to M. How will the public—households and firms—react if the amount of money they hold is less than they would like? To increase their holdings of money, people will try to sell some of the interest-bearing assets they hold, such as bonds. But if everyone is trying to sell bonds and there are no willing buyers, then all the attempt to reduce bond holdings will achieve is to drive down the price of bonds, in the same way that a glut of apples will drive down the price of apples.

A fall in the price of bonds, however, is equivalent to an increase in interest rates. Thus, the public's collective attempt to increase its money holdings by selling bonds and other interest-bearing assets, which has the effect of lowering bond prices, also implies higher market interest rates. As interest rates rise, the quantity of money demanded by the public will decline (represented by a right-to-left movement along the money demand curve), as will the desire to sell bonds. Only when the interest rate reaches its equilibrium value, i in Figure 20.8, will people be content to hold the quantities of money and other assets that are actually available in the economy.

EXERCISE 20.5

Describe the adjustment process in the market for money if the nominal interest rate is initially above rather than below its equilibrium value. What happens to the price of bonds as the money market adjusts toward equilibrium?

HOW THE FED CONTROLS THE NOMINAL INTEREST RATE

We began this section by noting that the public and the press usually talk about Fed policy in terms of decisions about the nominal interest rate rather than the money supply. Indeed, Fed policymakers themselves usually describe their plans in terms of a specific value for the interest rate. We now have the necessary background to understand how the Fed translates the ability to determine the economy's money supply into control of the nominal interest rate.

Figure 20.8 showed that the nominal interest rate is determined by equilibrium in the market for money. Let's suppose that for some reason the Fed decides to lower the interest rate. As we will see, to lower the interest rate, the Fed must increase the supply of money, which, as we saw in Chapter 17, is usually accomplished by using newly created money to purchase government bonds from the public (an open-market purchase).

Figure 20.9 shows the effects of such an increase in the money supply by the Fed. If the initial money supply is M, then equilibrium in the money market occurs at point E in the figure, and the equilibrium nominal interest rate is i. Now suppose the Fed, by means of open-market purchases of bonds, increases the money supply to M'. This increase in the money supply shifts the vertical money supply curve to the right, which shifts the equilibrium in the money market from point E to point F. Note that at point F the equilibrium nominal interest rate has declined, from i to i'. The nominal interest rate must decline if the public is to be persuaded to hold the extra money that has been injected into the economy.

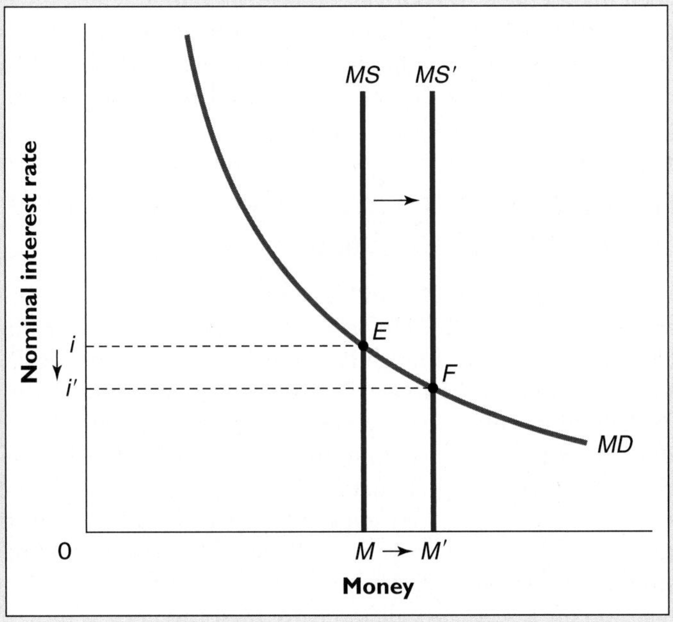

FIGURE 20.9
The Fed Lowers the Nominal Interest Rate.
The Fed can lower the equilibrium nominal interest rate by increasing the supply of money. For the given money demand curve, an increase in the money supply from M to M' shifts the equilibrium point in the money market from E to F, lowering the equilibrium nominal interest rate from i to i'.

To understand what happens in financial markets when the Fed expands the money supply, recall once again the inverse relationship between interest rates and the price of bonds. To increase the money supply, the Fed typically buys government bonds from the public. However, if households and firms are initially satisfied with their asset holdings, they will be willing to sell bonds only at a price that is higher than the initial price. That is, the Fed's bond purchases will drive up the price of bonds in the open market. But we know that higher bond prices imply lower interest rates. Thus, the Fed's bond purchases lower the prevailing nominal interest rate.

A similar scenario unfolds if the Fed decides to raise interest rates. To raise interest rates, the Fed must *reduce* the money supply. Reduction of the money supply may be accomplished by an open-market sale—the sale of government bonds to the public in exchange for money.[9] (The Fed keeps a large inventory of government bonds, acquired through previous open-market purchases, for use in open-market operations.) But in the attempt to sell bonds on the open market, the Fed will drive down the price of bonds. Given the inverse relationship between the price of bonds and the interest rate, the fall in bond prices is equivalent to a rise in the interest rate. In terms of money demand and money supply, the higher interest rate is necessary to persuade the public to hold less money.

As Figures 20.8 and 20.9 illustrate, control of the interest rate is not separate from control of the money supply. If Fed officials choose to set the nominal interest rate at a particular level, they can do so only by setting the money supply at a level consistent with the target interest rate. The Fed *cannot* set the interest rate and the money supply independently, since for any given money demand curve, a particular interest rate implies a particular size of the money supply, and vice versa.

Since monetary policy actions can be expressed in terms of either the interest rate or the money supply, why does the Fed (and almost every other central bank) choose to communicate its policy decisions to the public by referring to the nominal interest rate rather than the money supply? One reason, which we analyzed earlier, is that the main effects of monetary policy on both the economy and financial markets are exerted through interest rates. Consequently, the interest rate is often the best summary of the overall impact of the Fed's actions. Another reason for focusing on interest rates is that they are more familiar to the public than the money supply. Finally, interest rates can be monitored continuously in the financial markets, which makes the effects of Fed policies on interest rates easy to observe. By contrast, measuring the amount of money in the economy requires collecting data on bank deposits, with the consequence that several weeks may pass before policymakers and the public know precisely how Fed actions have affected the money supply.

A SECOND WAY THE FED CONTROLS THE MONEY SUPPLY: DISCOUNT WINDOW LENDING

The Fed controls the money supply, and hence the nominal interest rate, primarily by using open-market operations. However, the Fed can change the money supply with two other tools that it uses much less frequently. One tool is called *discount window lending*. Recall from Chapter 17 that the cash or assets held by a commercial bank for the purpose of meeting depositor withdrawals are called its reserves. Its desired amount of reserves is equal to its deposits multiplied by the desired reserve-deposit ratio, as implied by Equation 17.1. When an individual commercial bank has insufficient reserves, it may choose to borrow reserves from the Fed. For historical reasons, lending of reserves by the Federal Reserve to commercial banks is called **discount window lending.** The interest rate that the Fed charges commercial banks that borrow reserves is called the **discount rate.** Loans of reserves by the Fed directly increase the quantity of reserves in the banking system, leading ultimately to increases in bank deposits and the money supply.

discount window lending the lending of reserves by the Federal Reserve to commercial banks

discount rate *(also known as the primary credit rate)* the interest rate that the Fed charges commercial banks to borrow reserves

Be careful not to confuse the discount rate and the federal funds rate. The discount rate is the interest rate commercial banks pay to the Fed; the federal

[9]The sale of existing government bonds by the Federal Reserve in an open-market sale should not be confused with the sale of newly issued government bonds by the Treasury when it finances government budget deficits. Whereas open-market sales reduce the money supply, Treasury sales of new bonds do not affect the money supply. The difference arises because the Federal Reserve does not put the money it receives in an open-market sale back into circulation, leaving less money for the public to hold. In contrast, the Treasury puts the money it receives from selling newly issued bonds back into circulation as it purchases goods and services.

funds rate is the interest rate commercial banks charge each other for short-term loans.[10]

A THIRD WAY OF CONTROLLING THE MONEY SUPPLY: CHANGING RESERVE REQUIREMENTS

As we showed in Chapter 17 (in particular, Equation 17.2), the economy's money supply depends on three factors: the amount of currency the public chooses to hold, the supply of bank reserves, and the reserve-deposit ratio maintained by commercial banks. The reserve-deposit ratio is equal to total bank reserves divided by total deposits. If banks kept all of their deposits as reserves, the reserve-deposit ratio would be 100 percent, and banks would not make any loans. As banks lend out more of their deposits, the reserve-deposit ratio falls.

Within a certain range, commercial banks are free to set the reserve-deposit ratio they want to maintain. However, Congress granted the Fed the power to set minimum values of the reserve-deposit ratio for commercial banks. The legally required values of the reserve-deposit ratio set by the Fed are called **reserve requirements.**

reserve requirements set by the Fed, the minimum values of the ratio of bank deposits that commercial banks are allowed to maintain

Changes in reserve requirements can be used to affect the money supply, although the Fed does not usually use them in this way. For example, suppose that commercial banks are maintaining a legally mandated minimum 3 percent reserve-deposit ratio. If the Fed wants to expand the money supply, it could reduce required reserves to, say, 2 percent of deposits. This would allow banks to lend a greater portion of their deposits and keep a smaller percentage of deposits as required reserves. If banks wanted to make new loans, these new loans would generate additional deposits, as we saw in Chapter 17. A decline in the economywide reserve-deposit ratio would therefore cause the money supply to rise.

Suppose, on the other hand, the Fed wanted to contract the money supply. If the Fed raised required reserves to, say, 5 percent of deposits, commercial banks would need to raise their reserve-deposit ratio to at least 5 percent. This would lead to a contraction of loans and deposits, which would decrease the money supply.

RECAP	THE FEDERAL RESERVE AND INTEREST RATES

- In the market for money, the money demand curve slopes downward, reflecting the fact that a higher nominal interest rate increases the opportunity cost of holding money and thus reduces the amount of money people want to hold. The money supply curve is vertical at the quantity of money that the Fed chooses to supply. The equilibrium nominal interest rate i is the interest rate at which the quantity of money demanded by the public equals the fixed supply of money made available by the Fed.
- The Federal Reserve controls the nominal interest rate by changing the supply of money. An open-market purchase of government bonds increases the money supply and lowers the equilibrium nominal interest rate. An increase in discount window lending or a reduction in reserve requirements will have the same effect. Conversely, an open-market sale of bonds reduces the money supply and increases the nominal interest rate, as will a decrease in discount window lending or an increase in reserve requirements. The Fed can prevent changes in the demand for money from affecting the nominal interest rate by adjusting the quantity of money supplied appropriately.

[10]The discount rate, also known as the *primary credit rate,* is normally set one percentage point above the federal funds rate.

SUMMARY

- The central bank of the United States is called the Federal Reserve System, or the Fed for short. The Fed's two main responsibilities are making monetary policy, which means determining how much money will circulate in the economy, and overseeing and regulating financial markets, especially banks. Created in 1914, one of the original purposes of the Federal Reserve was to help eliminate or control banking panics. A banking panic is an episode in which depositors, spurred by news or rumors of the imminent bankruptcy of one or more banks, rush to withdraw their deposits from the banking system. Because banks do not keep enough reserves on hand to pay off all depositors, even a financially healthy bank can run out of cash during a panic and be forced to close. **LO1**

- In the short run, the Fed can control the real interest rate as well as the nominal interest rate. Since the real interest rate equals the nominal interest rate minus the inflation rate, and because the inflation rate adjusts relatively slowly, the Fed can change the real interest rate by changing the nominal interest rate. In the long run, the real interest rate is determined by the balance of saving and investment (see Chapter 16). The nominal interest rate that the Fed targets most closely is the federal funds rate, which is the rate commercial banks charge each other for very short-term loans. **LO2, LO5**

- The Federal Reserve's actions affect the economy because changes in the real interest rate affect planned spending. For example, an increase in the real interest rate raises the cost of borrowing, reducing consumption and planned investment. Thus, by increasing the real interest rate, the Fed can reduce planned spending and short-run equilibrium output. Conversely, by reducing the real interest rate, the Fed can stimulate planned aggregate expenditure and thereby raise short-run equilibrium output. The Fed's ultimate objectives are to eliminate output gaps and maintain low inflation. To eliminate a recessionary output gap, the Fed will lower the real interest rate. To eliminate an expansionary output gap, the Fed will raise the real interest rate. **LO2**

- A policy rule describes how the action a policymaker takes depends on the state of the economy. For example, a monetary policy rule for the Fed illustrates how the actual real interest rate set by the Fed depends on its real interest rate target and the extent to which inflation differs from the Fed's target rate of inflation. **LO3**

- The nominal interest rate is determined in the market for money, which has both a demand side and a supply side. The money demand curve relates the aggregate quantity of money demanded to the nominal interest rate. Because an increase in the nominal interest rate increases the opportunity cost of holding money, which reduces the quantity of money demanded, the money demand curve slopes down. Factors other than the nominal interest rate that affect the demand for money (such as the price level of real GDP) will shift the demand curve to the right or left. The supply curve for money is vertical at the value of the money supply set by the Fed. Money market equilibrium occurs at the nominal interest rate at which money demand equals the money supply. The Fed can reduce the nominal interest rate by increasing the money supply (shifting the money supply curve to the right) or increase the nominal interest rate by reducing the money supply (shifting the money supply curve to the left). **LO4, LO5**

- In addition to open-market purchases and sales, the Federal Reserve has two other tools that it can use to change the money supply. The first involves changes in discount window lending, which occur when commercial banks borrow additional reserves from the Fed. The second involves changes in reserve requirements, which are the minimum values of the reserve-deposit ratio that commercial banks are required to maintain. However, the Fed uses these two additional tools infrequently to change the money supply. **LO5**

KEY TERMS

▪ REVIEW QUESTIONS ▪

1. Why does the real interest rate affect planned aggregate expenditure? Give examples. **LO2**
2. The Fed faces a recessionary gap. How would you expect it to respond? Explain step by step how its policy change is likely to affect the economy. **LO2**
3. The Fed decides to take a contractionary policy action. Under what circumstances would this type of policy action be most appropriate? What would you expect to happen to the nominal interest rate, the real interest rate, and the money supply? **LO2, LO4**
4. Sketch a policy rule relating the Fed's setting of the real interest rate to inflation. Explain why it slopes upward. **LO3**
5. Show graphically how the Fed controls the nominal interest rate. Can the Fed control the real interest rate? **LO5**
6. What effect does an open-market purchase of bonds by the Fed have on nominal interest rates? Discuss in terms of (a) the effect of the purchase on bond prices and (b) the effect of the purchase on the supply of money. **LO5**

▪ PROBLEMS ▪

McGraw-Hill's HOMEWORK MANAGER®

1. An economy is described by the following equations:

$$C = 2{,}600 + 0.8(Y - T) - 10{,}000r,$$
$$I^p = 2{,}000 - 10{,}000r,$$
$$G = 1{,}800,$$
$$NX = 0,$$
$$T = 3{,}000.$$

   The real interest rate, expressed as a decimal, is 0.10 (that is, 10 percent). **LO2**
   a. Find a numerical equation relating planned aggregate expenditure to output.
   b. Using a table (or algebra if you have used the appendix to this chapter), solve for short-run equilibrium output.
   c. Show your result graphically using the Keynesian cross diagram.

2. For the economy described in problem 1 above: **LO2**
   a. Suppose that potential output Y^* equals 12,000. What real interest rate should the Fed set to bring the economy to full employment? You may take as given that the multiplier for this economy is 5.
   b. Repeat part a for the case in which potential output Y^* equals 9,000
   c.* Show that the real interest rate you found in part a sets national saving equal to planned investment when the economy is at potential output. This result shows that the real interest rate must be consistent with equilibrium in the market for saving when the economy is at full employment. (*Hint:* Review the material on national saving in Chapter 16).

3.* Here is another set of equations describing an economy: **LO2**

$$C = 14{,}400 + 0.5(Y - T) - 40{,}000r,$$
$$I^p = 8{,}000 - 20{,}000r,$$
$$G = 7{,}800,$$
$$NX = 1{,}800,$$
$$T = 8{,}000,$$
$$Y^* = 40{,}000.$$

*Problems marked with an asterisk (*) are more difficult.

a. Find a numerical equation relating planned aggregate expenditure to output and to the real interest rate.
b. At what value should the Fed set the real interest rate to eliminate any output gap? (*Hint:* Set output Y equal to the value of potential output given above in the equation you found in part a. Then solve for the real interest rate that also sets planned aggregate expenditure equal to potential output.)

4. Suppose that an economy is currently operating above potential output. This has led the inflation rate to rise above the Fed's long-run target for the inflation rate. **LO2, LO3**
   a. Explain, in words, what the Fed's reaction to this situation will be in terms of changes in the real interest rate.
   b. Explain, in words, how the Fed's action in part a will affect planned aggregate expenditure and short-run equilibrium output.
   c. Use a pair of diagrams (the Keynesian cross and the Fed's monetary policy rule) to illustrate the actions you described in parts a and b. Label the graphs so that a reader can match up your verbal descriptions with the graphs.
   d.* Suppose that instead of operating at an output level that is higher than potential output, the economy is at potential output when the inflation rate rises. Do parts a through c for this scenario. What does this tell you about the difficulties the Fed faces in fighting inflation?

5. During the heavy Christmas shopping season, sales of retail stores, online sales firms, and other merchants rise significantly. **LO4**
   a. What would you expect to happen to the money demand curve during the Christmas season? Show graphically.
   b. If the Fed took no action, what would happen to nominal interest rates around Christmas?
   c. In fact, nominal interest rates do not change significantly in the fourth quarter of the year, due to deliberate Fed policy. Explain and show graphically how the Fed can ensure that nominal interest rates remain stable around Christmas.

6. The following table shows Uma's estimated annual benefits of holding different amounts of money: **LO4**

Average money holdings ($)	Total benefit ($)
500	35
600	47
700	57
800	65
900	71
1,000	75
1,100	77
1,200	77

   a. How much money will Uma hold on average if the nominal interest rate is 9 percent? 5 percent? 3 percent? Assume that she wants her money holding to be a multiple of $100. (*Hint:* Make a table comparing the extra benefit of each additional $100 in money holdings with the opportunity cost, in terms of forgone interest, of additional money holdings.)
   b. Graph Uma's money demand curve for interest rates between 1 percent and 12 percent.

*Problems marked with an asterisk (*) are more difficult.

7. How would you expect each of the following to affect the economywide demand for money? Explain. **LO4**
   a. Competition among brokers forces down the commission charge for selling holdings of bonds or stocks.
   b. Grocery stores begin to accept credit cards in payment.
   c. Financial investors become concerned about increasing riskiness of stocks.
   d. Online banking allows customers to check balances and transfer funds between checking and mutual fund investments 24 hours a day.
   e. The economy enters a boom period.
   f. Political instability increases in developing nations.
8. For each of the scenarios described in problem 7, answer the following questions: **LO4, LO5**
   a. What will happen to the nominal interest rate if the Fed does not change the money supply? Explain your reasoning using a supply-and-demand graph of the money market.
   b. What must the Fed do in order to keep the nominal interest rate from changing as you described in part a? Explain your reasoning using a supply-and-demand graph of the money market.
9. By law, the Federal Reserve must report twice each year to Congress about monetary policy and the state of the economy. When the Monetary Policy Report is presented, it is customary for the Fed chairman to testify before Congress, to update legislators on the economic situation. **LO1, LO2, LO5**
   a. Obtain a copy of the most recent Monetary Policy Report from the Fed's Web page, www.federalreserve.gov (click "Monetary policy," then click on "Monetary Policy Report to Congress.")
   b. Read the report and answer the following questions:
      i. In the period covered by the testimony, did monetary policy ease, tighten, or remain neutral?
      ii. What principal developments in the economy led the Fed to take the actions that it did?

ANSWERS TO IN-CHAPTER EXERCISES

20.1 Verify directly for each date in Table 20.1 that

$$\text{Money supply} = \text{Currency} + \frac{\text{Bank reserves}}{\text{Desired reserve} - \text{Deposit ratio}}$$

For example, for December 1929, we can check that 45.9 = 3.85 + 3.15/0.075.

Suppose that the currency held by the public in December 1933 had been 3.79, as in December 1930, rather than 4.85, and that the difference (4.85 − 3.79 = 1.06) had been left in the banks. Then bank reserves in December 1933 would have been 3.45 + 1.06 = 4.51 and the money supply would have been 3.79 + (4.51/0.133) = 37.7. The money supply would still have fallen between 1930 and 1933 if people had not increased their holdings of currency, but only by about half as much. **LO1**

20.2 Over the course of 1931, currency holdings by the public rose by $0.80 billion, but bank reserves fell overall by only $0.20 billion. Thus, the Fed must have replaced $0.60 billion of lost reserves during the year through open-market purchases. Currency holdings at the end of 1931 were $4.59 billion. To have kept the money supply at the December 1930 value of $44.1 billion, the Fed would have had to ensure that bank deposits equaled \$44.1 billion − \$4.59 billion, or \$39.51 billion. As the reserve-deposit ratio in 1931 was 0.095, this would have required bank reserves of 0.095(\$39.51 billion), or \$3.75 billion, compared to the actual value in December 1931 of \$3.11 billion. Thus, to keep the money supply from falling, the Fed would have had to increase bank reserves by \$0.64 billion more than it did. The Fed has been criticized for increasing bank reserves by only about half what was needed to keep the money supply from falling. **LO1**

20.3 If $r = 0.03$, then consumption is $C = 640 + 0.8(Y - 250) - 400(0.03) = 428 + 0.8Y$, and planned investment is $I^P = 250 - 600(0.03) = 232$. Planned aggregate expenditure is given by

$$\begin{aligned} PAE &= C + I^P + G + NX \\ &= (428 + 0.8Y) + 232 + 300 + 20 \\ &= 980 + 0.8Y. \end{aligned}$$

To find short-run equilibrium output, we can construct a table analogous to Table 22.1. As usual, some trial and error is necessary to find an appropriate range of guesses for output (column 1).

Determination of Short-Run Equilibrium Output

(1) Output Y	(2) Planned aggregate expenditure $PAE = 980 + 0.8Y$	(3) $Y - PAE$	(4) $Y = PAE$?
4,500	4,580	−80	No
4,600	4,660	−60	No
4,700	4,740	−40	No
4,800	4,820	−20	No
4,900	4,900	0	**Yes**
5,000	4,980	20	No
5,100	5,060	40	No
5,200	5,140	60	No
5,300	5,220	80	No
5,400	5,300	100	No
5,500	5,380	120	No

Short-run equilibrium output equals 4,900, as that is the only level of output that satisfies the condition $Y = PAE$.

The answer can be obtained more quickly by simply setting $Y = PAE$ and solving for short-run equilibrium output Y. Remembering that $PAE = 980 + 0.8Y$ and substituting for PAE, we get

$$\begin{aligned} Y &= 980 + 0.8Y \\ Y(1 - 0.8) &= 980 \\ Y &= 5 \times 980 = 4{,}900. \end{aligned}$$

So lowering the real interest rate from 5 percent to 3 percent increases short-run equilibrium output from 4,800 to 4,900.

If you have read Appendix B to the preceding chapter on the multiplier, there is yet another way to find the answer. Using that appendix, we can determine that the multiplier in this model is 5, since $1/(1 - mpc) = 1/(1 - 0.8) = 5$.

Each percentage point reduction in the real interest rate increases consumption by 4 units and planned investment by 6 units, for a total impact on planned spending of 10 units per percentage point reduction. Reducing the real interest rate by 2 percentage points, from 5 percent to 3 percent, thus increases autonomous expenditure by 20 units. Because the multiplier is 5, an increase of 20 in autonomous expenditure raises short-run equilibrium output by $20 \times 5 = 100$ units, from the value of 4,800 to the new value of 4,900. **LO2**

20.4 When the real interest rate is 5 percent, output is 4,800. Each percentage point reduction in the real interest rate increases autonomous expenditure by 10 units. Since the multiplier in this model is 5, to raise output by 50 units, the real interest rate should be cut by 1 percentage point, from 5 percent to 4 percent. Increasing output by 50 units, to 4,850, eliminates the output gap. **LO2**

20.5 If the nominal interest rate is above its equilibrium value, then people are holding more money than they would like. To bring their money holdings down, they will use some of their money to buy interest-bearing assets such as bonds. If everyone is trying to buy bonds, however, the price of bonds will be bid up. An increase in bond prices is equivalent to a fall in market interest rates. As interest rates fall, people will be willing to hold more money. Eventually interest rates will fall enough that people are content to hold the amount of money supplied by the Fed, and the money market will be in equilibrium. **LO4, LO5**

APPENDIX

Monetary Policy in the Basic Keynesian Model

This appendix extends the algebraic analysis of the basic Keynesian model (presented in Appendix A to the last chapter) to include the role of monetary policy. The main difference from that appendix is that in this analysis, the real interest rate is allowed to affect planned spending. We will not describe the supply and demand for money algebraically but will simply assume that the Fed can set the real interest rate r at any level it chooses.

The real interest rate affects consumption and planned investment. To capture these effects, we will modify the equations for those two components of spending as follows:

$$C = \overline{C} + (mpc)(Y - T) - ar,$$

$$I^P = \overline{I} - br.$$

The first equation is the consumption function with an additional term, equal to $-ar$. Think of a as a fixed number, greater than zero, that measures the strength of the interest rate effect on consumption. Thus, the term $-ar$ captures the idea that when the real interest rate r rises, consumption declines by a times the increase in the interest rate. Likewise, the second equation adds the term $-br$ to the equation for planned investment spending. The parameter b is a fixed positive number that measures how strongly changes in the real interest rate affect planned investment; for example, if the real interest rate r rises, planned investment is assumed to decline by b times the increase in the real interest rate. We continue to assume that government purchases, taxes, and net exports are exogenous variables, so that $G = \overline{G}$, $T = \overline{T}$, and $NX = \overline{NX}$.

To solve for short-run equilibrium output, we start as usual by finding the relationship of planned aggregate expenditure to output. The definition of planned aggregate expenditure is

$$PAE = C + I^P + G + NX.$$

Substituting the modified equations for consumption and planned investment into this definition, along with the exogenous values of government spending, net exports, and taxes, we get

$$PAE = [\overline{C} + (mpc)(Y - \overline{T}) - ar] + [\overline{I} - br] + \overline{G} + \overline{NX}.$$

The first term in brackets on the right side describes the behavior of consumption, and the second bracketed term describes planned investment. Rearranging this equation in order to group together terms that depend on the real interest rate and terms that depend on output, we find

$$PAE = [\overline{C} - (mpc)\overline{T} + \overline{I} + \overline{G} + \overline{NX}] - (a + b)r + (mpc)Y.$$

This equation is similar to Equation 23A.1, in Appendix A to the last chapter, except that it has an extra term, $-(a + b)r$, on the right side. This extra term captures the idea that an increase in the real interest rate reduces consumption and planned investment, lowering planned spending. Notice that the term $-(a + b)r$ is part of autonomous expenditure since it does not depend on output. Since autonomous expenditure determines the intercept of the expenditure line in the Keynesian cross diagram, changes in the real interest rate will shift the expenditure line up (if the real interest rate decreases) or down (if the real interest rate increases).

To find short-run equilibrium output, we use the definition of short-run equilibrium output to set $Y = PAE$ and solve for Y:

$$\begin{aligned}
Y &= PAE \\
&= [\overline{C} - (mpc)\overline{T} + \overline{I} + \overline{G} + \overline{NX}] - (a + b)r + (mpc)Y \\
Y(1 - mpc) &= [\overline{C} - (mpc)\overline{T} + \overline{I} + \overline{G} + \overline{NX}] - (a + b)r \\
Y &= \left(\frac{1}{1 - mpc}\right)[(\overline{C} - (mpc)\overline{T} + \overline{I} + \overline{G} + \overline{NX}) - (a + b)r]. \quad (20A.1)
\end{aligned}$$

Equation 20A.1 shows that short-run equilibrium output once again equals the multiplier, $1/(1 - mpc)$, times autonomous expenditure, $\overline{C} - (mpc)\overline{T} + \overline{I} + \overline{G} + \overline{NX} - (a + b)r$. Autonomous expenditure in turn depends on the real interest rate r. The equation also shows that the impact of a change in the real interest rate on short-run equilibrium output depends on two factors: (1) the effect of a change in the real interest rate on consumption and planned investment, which depends on the magnitude of $(a + b)$, and (2) the size of the multiplier, $1/(1 - mpc)$, which relates changes in autonomous expenditure to changes in short-run equilibrium output. The larger the effect of the real interest rate on planned spending, and the larger the multiplier, the more powerful will be the effect of a given change in the real interest rate on short-run equilibrium output.

To check Equation 20A.1, we can apply it to the example we worked through numerically and graphically in the chapter. In that example, we are given $\overline{C} = 640$, $\overline{I} = 250$, $\overline{G} = 300$, $\overline{NX} = 20$, $\overline{T} = 250$, $mpc = 0.8$, $a = 400$, and $b = 600$. The real interest rate set by the Fed is 5 percent, or 0.05. Substituting these values into Equation 20A.1 and solving, we obtain

$$\begin{aligned}
Y &= \left(\frac{1}{1 - 0.8}\right)[640 - 0.8 \times 250 + 250 + 300 + 20 - (400 + 600) \times 0.05] \\
&= 5 \times 960 = 4{,}800
\end{aligned}$$

This is the same result we found in the text.

CHAPTER 21

Aggregate Demand, Aggregate Supply, and Macroeconomic Policy

LEARNING OBJECTIVES

After reading this chapter, you should be able to:

1. Define the aggregate demand curve, explain why it slopes downward, and explain why it shifts.
2. Define the aggregate supply curve, explain why it slopes upward, and explain why it shifts.
3. Show how the aggregate demand curve and the aggregate supply curve determine the short-run equilibrium levels of output and inflation, and show how the aggregate demand curve, the aggregate supply curve, and the long-run aggregate supply curve determine the long-run equilibrium levels of output and inflation.
4. Analyze how the economy adjusts to expansionary and recessionary gaps and relate this to the concept of a self-correcting economy.
5. Discuss the policy options available to the Fed in response to aggregate demand and aggregrate supply shocks.
6. Explain the roles played by the core rate of inflation, anchored inflationary expectations, and central bank credibility in keeping inflation low.

During the summer and fall of 1996, the unemployment rate was falling and stood below 5.5 percent, generally considered to be the natural unemployment rate at that time. The rapid pace of economic growth suggested that an expansionary gap would open and an increase in inflation would result. Many economists were urging Federal Reserve chairman Alan

Greenspan to increase the federal funds rate to slow the economy and prevent the possible surge in inflation. Yet Greenspan was unconvinced. He thought he saw evidence of new economic developments that would permit the rapid growth to continue without increased inflation. If he was right, an aggressive increase in interest rates was not only unnecessary but could damage the economy.

In this chapter, we develop and apply the *aggregate demand–aggregate supply model*. This model is designed to help us understand fluctuations in output and inflation and the policy choices faced by policymakers like Alan Greenspan.

We start by building the model in three steps. First, we develop aggregate demand both intuitively and in a way that connects it to the analysis of the previous two chapters on planned aggregate expenditure, output, current inflation, and their relationships with fiscal and monetary policy. Second, we study how current inflation is related to factors such as expectations about future inflation and the output gap and use this analysis to build aggregate supply. Third, we put aggregate demand and aggregate supply together to see how output and inflation are determined simultaneously. We then put the model to work by analyzing the causes of inflation and how monetary policy can respond to changes in inflation and output.

THE AGGREGATE DEMAND–AGGREGATE SUPPLY MODEL: A BRIEF OVERVIEW

The aggregate demand–aggregate supply model, or AD-AS for short, is one of the workhorse models in macroeconomics. Its usefulness is due to the fact that it shows how output and inflation are determined simultaneously in both the short run and the long run. AD-AS thus allows us to show what an economy is doing at a particular point in time and lets us see where the economy is going in the future. This is particularly helpful for analyzing macroeconomic policy since we can use the model to trace out the effects of fiscal and monetary policy on the economy today, in the near future, and in the long run.

Figure 21.1 shows the aggregate demand–aggregate supply (*AS-AD*) diagram, which is a graphical tool we use to apply the AS-AD model to real-world situations. The current inflation rate π is on the vertical axis and the current level of output Y is on the horizontal axis. The aggregate demand (*AD*) curve is downward sloping due to the fact that lower rates of inflation lead to higher levels of spending and output. The aggregate supply (*AS*) curve is upward sloping because the level of output relative to its potential is an important determinant of current inflation. The vertical line labeled **long-run aggregate supply (*LRAS*)** gets its name from the fact that it shows the level of potential output Y^*; in the long run, this is the output level at which the economy will operate. The intersection of the three curves shows the economy in long-run equilibrium: output is equal to potential output Y^* and inflation π_1 is equal to both expected inflation and the Federal Reserve's long-run target for inflation.

long-run aggregate supply* (LRAS) *line a vertical line showing the economy's potential output Y^*

Can any or all of the curves shift? Why are the curves sloped the way that they are? Can the economy be at a point away from long-run equilibrium? If the economy is away from potential output, will it return to its long-run equilibrium? What role can, or should, government policy play in returning the economy to long-run equilibrium? To answer questions like these, and to put this model to work, we need to dig into the details of how aggregate demand and aggregate supply each works. We can then return to the *AD-AS* diagram and use it to answer our questions.

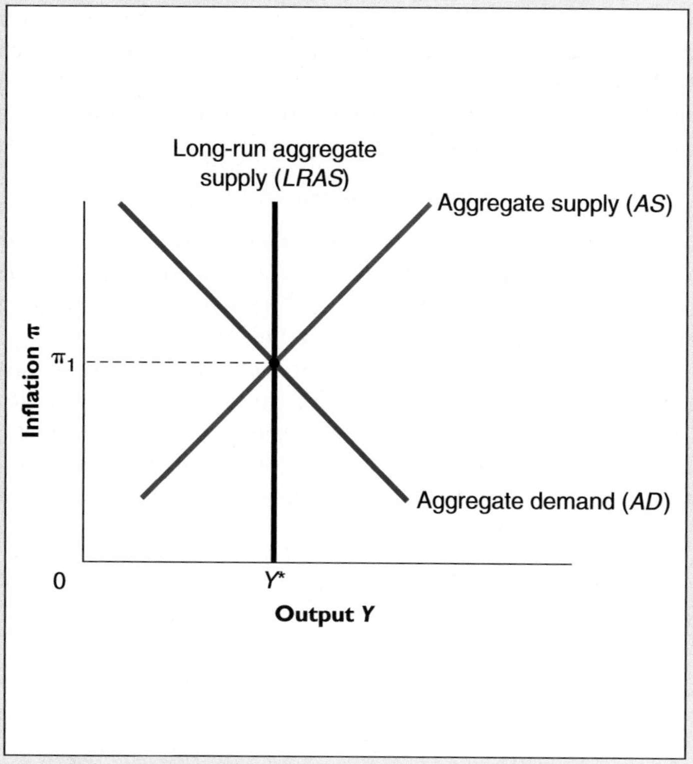

FIGURE 21.1
The Aggregate Demand–Aggregate Supply Diagram.
The aggregate demand (*AD*) curve is downward sloping, due to the fact that lower rates of inflation lead to higher levels of spending and output. The aggregate supply (*AS*) curve is upward sloping because the level of output relative to its potential is an important determinant of current inflation. The vertical line shows the level of potential GDP Y^*. The intersection of the *AD* curve, the *AS* curve, and potential GDP is the economy's long-run equilibrium. At this point, actual inflation π_1 equals expected inflation and the Fed's long-run inflation target.

INFLATION, SPENDING, AND OUTPUT: THE AGGREGATE DEMAND CURVE

In the previous two chapters, we made the assumption that firms are willing to meet the demand for their products at preset prices. When firms simply produce what is demanded, the level of planned aggregate expenditure determines the nation's real GDP. If the resulting level of short-run equilibrium output is lower than potential output, a recessionary output gap develops, and if the resulting level of output exceeds potential output, the economy experiences an expansionary gap.

As we will discuss shortly, output gaps can cause inflation to either increase (if it is an expansionary gap) or decrease (if it is a recessionary gap). Policymakers can eliminate output gaps by taking actions that affect the level of spending through fiscal policy or monetary policy.

INFLATION, THE FED, AND THE *AD* CURVE

One of the primary responsibilities of the Fed is to maintain a low and stable rate of inflation. For example, in recent years, the Fed has tried to keep inflation in the United States in the range of 2 to 3 percent. The Fed can do this by using monetary policy to minimize output gaps; indeed, the Fed's monetary policy rule embodies this idea since it shows that the Fed raises the real interest rate when inflation rises and lowers the real interest rate when inflation falls.

We can connect monetary policy, the inflation rate, and output as follows:[1]

$$\uparrow \pi \Rightarrow \uparrow r \Rightarrow \downarrow \text{planned } C \text{ and planned } I \Rightarrow \downarrow PAE \Rightarrow \downarrow Y.$$

[1]We derived these relationships in Chapters 19 and 20. If you were not assigned these chapters, you can take these relationships as a given.

The link between inflation π and the real interest rate r is the Fed's monetary policy rule: when inflation rises, the Fed increases the nominal interest rate and, since inflation is slow to change, this raises the real interest rate. The increase in the real interest rate decreases planned aggregate expenditure *PAE* by decreasing planned consumption *C* and planned investment *I* and thus decreases short-run equilibrium output *Y* via the multiplier process. The same reasoning applies when inflation falls:

$$\downarrow \pi \Rightarrow \downarrow r \Rightarrow \uparrow \text{planned } C \text{ and planned } I \Rightarrow \uparrow PAE \Rightarrow \uparrow Y.$$

aggregate demand (AD) curve shows the relationship between short-run equilibrium output *Y* and the rate of inflation π, holding all other factors constant; the *AD* curve slopes downward because of the Fed's monetary policy rule: when inflation rises, the Fed raises nominal interest rates, which in turn causes real interest rates to rise, and this causes planned spending and short-run output to fall

The *aggregate demand curve* summarizes these relationships. Specifically, the **aggregate demand (*AD*) curve** shows the relationship between short-run equilibrium output *Y* and the rate of inflation π, holding all other factors constant. Typical *AD* curves are shown in both Figures 21.1 and 21.2.

The name of the curve reflects the fact that short-run equilibrium output equals total planned spending, that is, the *demand* for goods and services on the part of all consumers, businesses, and governments in the economy. The *AD* curve slopes downward because of the Fed's monetary policy rule: when inflation rises, the Fed raises real interest rates and this causes planned spending and short-run output to fall.

We can understand how the *AD* curve works in more detail by deriving it graphically. Figure 21.2 presents three graphs. Let's begin by using the Fed's monetary

Deriving the *AD* Curve Graphically.

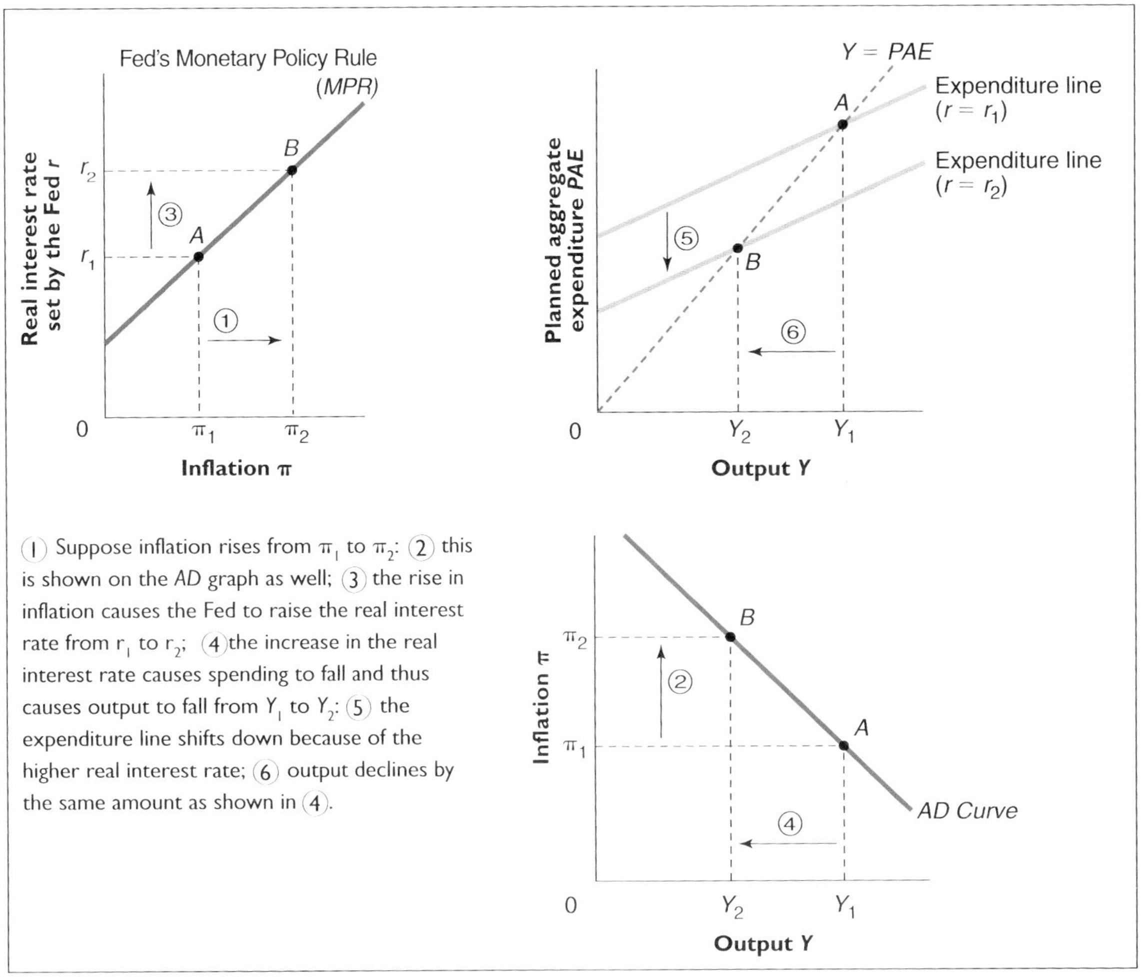

(1) Suppose inflation rises from π_1 to π_2: (2) this is shown on the *AD* graph as well; (3) the rise in inflation causes the Fed to raise the real interest rate from r_1 to r_2; (4) the increase in the real interest rate causes spending to fall and thus causes output to fall from Y_1 to Y_2: (5) the expenditure line shifts down because of the higher real interest rate; (6) output declines by the same amount as shown in (4).

policy rule (shown in the upper-left corner) to derive the *AD* curve (shown in the lower-right corner).

Suppose that the inflation rate rises; this is shown by ① on the monetary policy rule and ② in the *AD* curve. The Fed, following its monetary policy rule, will increase the real interest rate when inflation rises, as shown by ③. Consumers and businesses will decrease their planned spending because of the increase in the real interest rate, and this will reduce the equilibrium level of GDP, as shown by ④ on the *AD* curve.

We can show graphically how the real interest rate affects planned spending, and hence output, by adding a graph of the Keynesian cross (shown in the upper-right corner) to the discussion.[2] When the Fed raises the real interest rate (③ in the monetary policy rule), planned consumption and planned investment decrease, causing the expenditure line to fall as shown by ⑤. Equilibrium output falls as indicated by ⑥. The decrease in output shown by ⑥ is exactly the same amount as shown by arrow ④.

Why does output decline when planned spending falls? Because of the multiplier process: the decline in planned spending causes output to fall, which in turn causes planned spending to fall, and so on until the economy reaches a new, lower equilibrium level of output. The *AD* curve thus embodies everything that you learned in the previous two chapters (the basic Keynesian model, the multiplier process, and the Fed's monetary policy) in one graph.

SHIFTS OF THE *AD* CURVE

The downward slope of the *AD* curve reflects the fact that, if all other factors are held constant, a higher rate of inflation will lead to lower planned spending and thus lower short-run equilibrium output. However, at a *given* inflation rate, other factors can increase or decrease planned spending and short-run equilibrium output. This will cause the *AD* curve to shift to the right or to the left. Specifically, for a given level of inflation, if there is a change in the economy that increases short-run equilibrium output, the *AD* curve will shift to the right. If, on the other hand, the change reduces short-run equilibrium output at each level of inflation, the *AD* curve will shift to the left.

We will focus on two types of changes in the economy that affect planned spending and shift the *AD* curve: (1) exogenous changes in spending and (2) changes in the Fed's monetary policy rule.

Exogenous Changes in Spending

Planned spending is affected by changes in output and the real interest rate. However, many factors other than output or the real interest rate can have an effect on spending. For example, changes in consumer confidence and consumers' wealth affect consumption spending even if there has been no change in output or the real interest rate. Decreased business confidence or new technological opportunities may lead firms to decrease or increase their planned investment. Fiscal policy affects the level of government purchases and taxes collected and thus changes total spending as well. Finally, changes in the willingness of foreigners to purchase domestic goods or of domestic residents to purchase foreign goods will affect net exports.

We will refer to changes in planned spending that are not caused by changes in output or the real interest rate as **exogenous changes in spending.** For instance, at a given inflation rate (and thus for a given real interest rate set by the Fed), an exogenous increase in spending raises short-run equilibrium output. Because output increases at every given level of inflation, an exogenous increase in spending shifts the *AD* curve to the right. This result is illustrated in Figure 21.3.

exogenous changes in spending changes in planned spending that are not caused by changes in output or the real interest rate

[2] If you did not read the last two chapters, then skip ahead to the next section.

FIGURE 21.3
The Effects of Exogenous Changes in Spending on the *AD* curve.
An exogenous increase in spending shifts the *AD* curve to the right, from AD_1 to AD_2. An example of this would be an increase in consumption caused by a stock market boom. The *AD* curve shifts to the left when there is an exogenous decrease in spending.

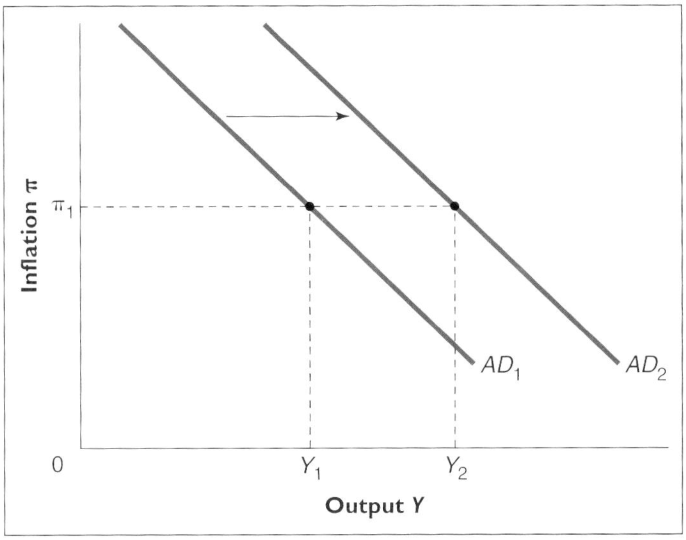

An example of an exogenous increase in spending is an increase in consumer spending caused by a stock market boom. A stock market boom causes consumers' wealth to increase, and thus consumers will be more willing to spend at any given level of output and the real interest rate. If the current inflation rate is π_1, the result of the stock market boom will be that output will rise from Y_1 to Y_2. And, since we chose π_1 arbitrarily, the spending must increase at every level of inflation, resulting in a shift to the right of the *AD* curve from AD_1 to AD_2.

Similarly, at a given inflation rate, an exogenous decline in spending causes short-run equilibrium output to fall. For example, suppose that the government reduces its spending in order to decrease the budget deficit. This will cause spending to decrease at any given inflation rate and thus shifts the *AD* curve to the left.

EXERCISE 21.1

For each of the following events, use a graph and words to show how each event affects the *AD* curve:

a. **Due to widespread concerns about future weakness in the economy, businesses reduce their spending on new capital.**

b. **The federal government reduces income taxes and leaves its spending unchanged.**

Tightening and Easing Monetary Policy

The Fed's monetary policy rule describes how the Fed sets the real interest rate at each level of inflation. Figure 21.4 shows a typical monetary policy rule. The Fed's long-run target for the inflation rate π_1 determines the Fed's long-run target for the real interest rate r_1. The Fed increases the real interest rate above r_1 if inflation rises above its long-run target and lowers the real interest rate below r_1 if inflation falls below its long-run target.

Under normal circumstances, the Fed follows a stable monetary policy rule. This implies that the Fed's normal increases and decreases in the real interest rate move the economy along a stable *AD* curve. However, there are times when

FIGURE 21.4
The Fed's Monetary Policy Rule.
The Fed's monetary policy rule shows the level at which the Fed will set the real interest rate for any given inflation rate. The Fed's long-run target for the inflation rate, π_1, determines the Fed's long-run target for the real interest rate, r_1. The Fed increases the real interest rate above its long-run target if inflation rises above its long-run target and lowers the real interest rate below its long-run target if inflation falls below its long-run target.

the Fed will shift its monetary policy rule in response to economic events and target either a lower or higher long-run rate of inflation; this is known either as tightening monetary policy or easing monetary policy. The Fed is said to be **tightening monetary policy** when it lowers its long-run target for the inflation rate. When the Fed raises its long-run target for the inflation rate, it is **easing monetary policy.**

tightening monetary policy a situation where the Fed lowers its long-run target for the inflation rate

easing monetary policy a situation where the Fed raises its long-run target for the inflation rate

Figure 21.5 shows the effects of tightening and easing monetary policy on the monetary policy rule. Suppose that the current inflation rate is at the Fed's current long-run inflation target π_1. What if the Fed decides that this target is too high? The top graph in Figure 21.5 shows that if the Fed lowers its long-run inflation target from π_1 to π_2, this will shift the monetary policy rule to the left, from MPR_1 to MPR_2. This means that, at the current inflation rate π_1, the Fed must increase the real interest rate from r_1 to r_2 in order to follow its new, tighter monetary policy rule.

Easing monetary policy is shown in the lower graph of Figure 21.5. Again, begin by assuming that the current inflation rate is at the Fed's current long-run inflation target π_1. Now, suppose that the Fed increases its long-run target for the inflation rate from π_1 to π_2. This shifts the monetary policy rule to the right from MPR_1 to MPR_2 and implies that the Fed will lower the real interest rate from r_1 to r_2 at the current inflation rate π_1.

With this analysis in mind, we can now show how tightening and easing monetary policy affect the *AD* curve. Figure 21.6 illustrates the effects of tightening monetary policy. At the current inflation rate, the decrease in the Fed's inflation target causes the Fed to increase the real interest rate (as we showed in Figure 21.5), which in turn reduces spending and output from Y_1 to Y_2. The Fed's monetary policy rule has shifted as well, so the Fed will set the real interest rate at a higher level for *every* inflation rate, thus shifting the entire *AD* curve to the left from AD_1 to AD_2. Correspondingly, easing monetary policy shifts the *AD* curve to the right. That is, the Fed sets a lower real interest rate at every given rate of inflation than it did previously; this causes spending and output to increase at every level of inflation and shifts the *AD* curve rightward.

FIGURE 21.5
A Shift in the Fed's Monetary Policy Rule. Tightening monetary policy: The Fed's monetary policy rule shifts from MPR_1 to MPR_2 when the Fed lowers its long-run target for the inflation rate from π_1 to π_2. This means that if the current inflation rate is π_1 the Fed will raise the real interest rate from r_1 to r_2.
Easing monetary policy: The Fed's monetary policy rule shifts from MPR_1 to MPR_2 when the Fed increases its long-run target for the inflation rate from π_1 to π_2. This means that if the current inflation rate is π_1 the Fed will decrease the real interest rate from r_1 to r_2.

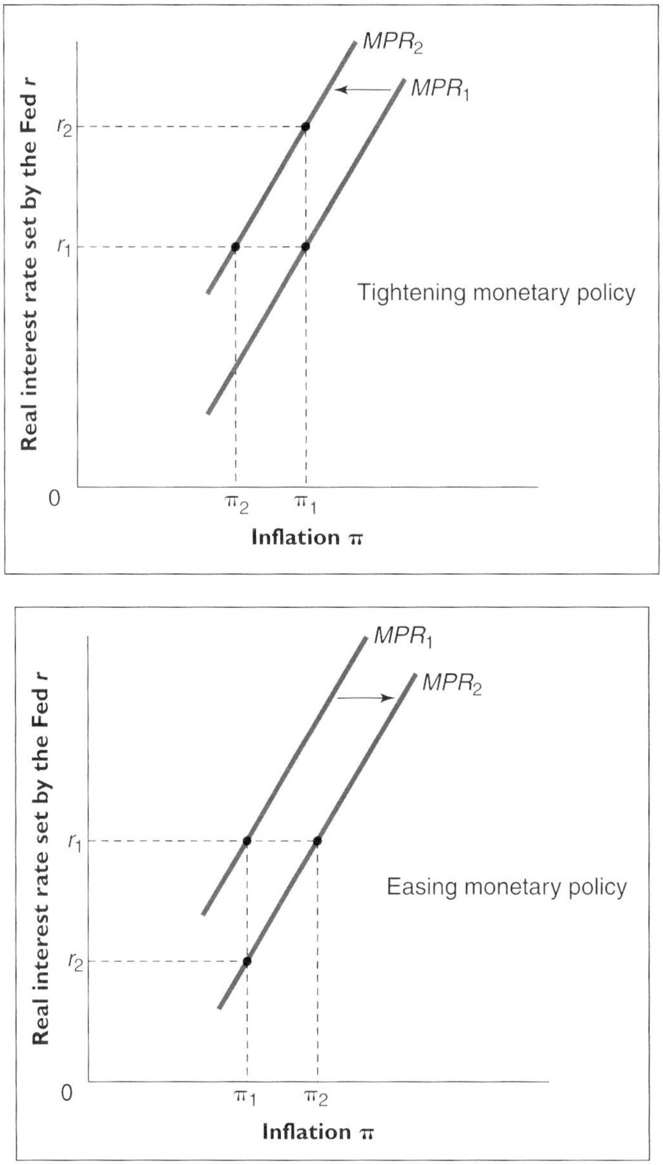

RECAP	THE AGGREGATE DEMAND (*AD*) CURVE

- The *AD* curve shows the relationship between short-run equilibrium output and inflation. The *AD* curve reflects the effects of the Fed's monetary policy rule on spending: higher inflation leads the Fed to raise the real interest rate, which reduces spending and thus short-run equilibrium output. The *AD* curve thus slopes downward.
- An exogenous increase in spending shifts the *AD* curve to the right while an exogenous decrease in spending shifts the *AD* curve to the left. Exogenous changes in spending arise from any change in spending that is not caused by a change in output or the real interest rate.

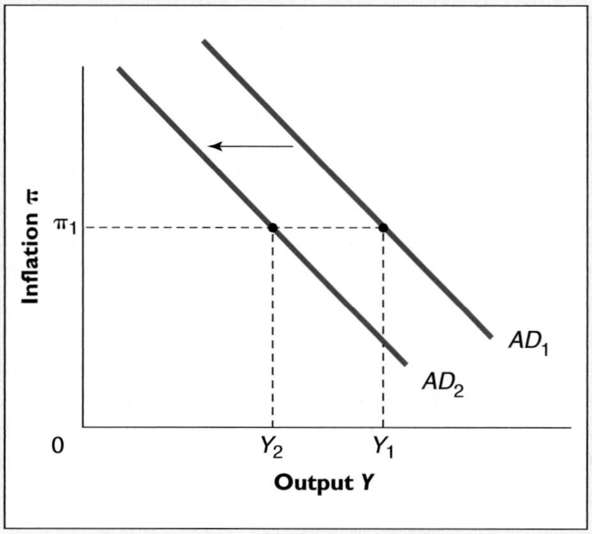

FIGURE 21.6
How Tightening and Easing Monetary Policy Affect the *AD* Curve.
When the Fed tightens monetary policy, it decreases its long-run target for the inflation rate and raises the real interest rate at the current inflation rate π_1. This causes spending and output to fall from Y_1 to Y_2 and shifts the *AD* curve to the left from AD_1 to AD_2. The opposite happens when the Fed eases monetary policy: the *AD* curve shifts to the right.

- Tightening or easing monetary policy shifts the *AD* curve. The Fed tightens monetary policy when it lowers its long-run target for the inflation rate; this causes the *AD* curve to shift to the left since the Fed will raise the real interest rate at any given inflation rate. Easing monetary policy is a situation where the Fed raises its long-run target for the inflation rate, thus lowering real interest rates at every level of inflation and causing the *AD* curve to shift to the right.

INFLATION AND AGGREGATE SUPPLY

So far, we have focused on how changes in inflation affect spending and short-run equilibrium output, a relationship captured by the *AD* curve. Now, we need to examine how changes in output affect the level of inflation; we call this relationship the **aggregate supply (*AS*) curve.** Specifically, the *AS* curve shows the relationship between the inflation rate π and short-run equilibrium output *Y* given current inflation expectations and holding all other factors constant. The *AS* curve slopes upward because actual inflation is related to the gap between actual output and potential output: when output is below potential, actual inflation is below expected inflation and when output is above potential, actual inflation is above expected inflation.

aggregate supply* (AS) *curve shows the relationship between short-run equilibrium output *Y* and inflation given current inflation expectations and holding all other factors constant; the *AS* curve slopes upward because actual inflation is related to the gap between actual output and potential output: when output is below potential, actual inflation is below expected inflation and when output is above potential, actual inflation is above expected inflation

To understand the *AS* curve, we proceed in two steps. First, we examine two factors that affect prices charged by firms: inflation inertia and output gaps. It turns out that these two factors make the *AS* curve slope upward, as shown in Figure 21.1. Second, we examine two other factors that affect the prices charged by firms: changes in inflation expectations and inflation shocks. These last two factors cause the *AS* curve to shift.

INFLATION INERTIA, OUTPUT GAPS, AND THE *AS* CURVE

Inflation Inertia

Physicists have noted that a body will tend to keep moving at a constant speed and direction unless it is acted upon by some outside force—a tendency they refer to as inertia. Applying this concept to economics, many observers have noted that inflation seems to be inertial, in the sense that it tends to remain roughly constant as long as the economy is at potential output and there are no external shocks to the price level.

Economists refer to this phenomenon as *inflation inertia.* If the rate of inflation in one year is 2 percent, it may be 3 percent or even 4 percent in the next year. But unless the nation experiences very unusual economic conditions, inflation is unlikely to rise to 6 percent or 8 percent or fall to −2 percent in the following year. This relatively sluggish behavior contrasts sharply with the behavior of economic variables such as stock prices or commodity prices, which can change rapidly from day to day. For example, oil prices might well rise by 20 percent over the course of a year and then fall 20 percent over the next year. Yet since about 1992, the U.S. inflation rate has generally remained in the rage of 2–4 percent per year.

Why does inflation tend to adjust relatively slowly in modern industrial economies? To answer this question, we must consider two closely related factors that play an important role in determining the inflation rate: the behavior of the public's *inflation expectations* and the existence of *long-term wage and price contracts.*

Inflation Expectations Let's first consider the public's expectations about inflation. In negotiating future wages and prices, both buyers and sellers take into account the rate of inflation they expect to prevail in the next few years. As a result, today's *expectations* of future inflation may help to determine the future inflation rate. Suppose, for example, that office worker Fred and his boss Colleen agree that Fred's performance this past year justifies an increase of 2 percent in his real wage for next year. What *nominal,* or dollar, wage increase should they agree on? If Fred believes that inflation is likely to be 3 percent over the next year, he will ask for a 5 percent increase in his nominal wage to obtain a 2 percent increase in his real wage. If Colleen agrees that inflation is likely to be 3 percent, she should be willing to go along with a 5 percent nominal increase, knowing that it implies only a 2 percent increase in Fred's real wage. Thus, the rate at which Fred and Colleen *expect* prices to rise affects the rate at which at least one price—Fred's nominal wage—*actually* rises.

A similar dynamic affects the contracts for production inputs other than labor. For example, if Colleen is negotiating with her office supply company, the prices she will agree to pay for next year's deliveries of copy paper and staples will depend on what she expects the inflation rate to be. If Colleen anticipates that the price of office supplies will not change relative to the prices of other goods and services, and that the general inflation rate will be 3 percent, then she should be willing to agree to a 3 percent increase in the price of office supplies. On the other hand, if she expects the general inflation rate to be 6 percent, then she will agree to pay 6 percent more for copy paper and staples next year, knowing that a nominal increase of 6 percent implies no change in the price of office supplies relative to other goods and services.

Economywide, then, the higher the expected rate of inflation, the more nominal wages and the cost of other inputs will tend to rise. But if wages and other costs of production grow rapidly in response to expected inflation, firms will have to raise their prices rapidly as well in order to cover their costs. Thus, a high rate of expected inflation tends to lead to a high rate of *actual* inflation. Similarly, if expected inflation is low, leading wages and other costs to rise relatively slowly, actual inflation should be low as well.

EXERCISE 21.2

Assume that employers and workers agree that real wages should rise by 2 percent next year.

a. If inflation is expected to be 2 percent next year, what will happen to nominal wages next year?

b. If inflation is expected to be 4 percent next year, rather than 2 percent, what will happen to nominal wages next year?

c. Use your answers from parts a and b to explain how an increase in expected inflation will affect the following year's actual rate of inflation.

The conclusion that actual inflation is partially determined by expected inflation raises the question of what determines inflation expectations. To a great extent, people's expectations are influenced by their recent experience. If inflation has been low and stable for some time, people are likely to expect it to continue to be low. But if inflation has recently been high, people will expect it to continue to be high. If inflation has been unpredictable, alternating between low and high levels, the public's expectations will likewise tend to be volatile, rising or falling with news or rumors about economic conditions or economic policy.

Figure 21.7 illustrates schematically how low and stable inflation may tend to be self-perpetuating. As the figure shows, if inflation has been low for some time, people will continue to expect low inflation. Increases in nominal wages and other production costs thus will tend to be small. If firms raise prices only enough to cover costs, then actual inflation will be low, as expected. This low actual rate in turn will promote low expected inflation, perpetuating the "virtuous circle."

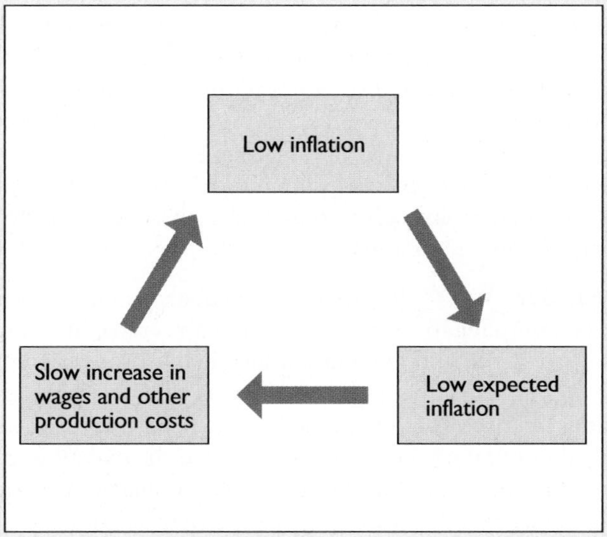

FIGURE 21.7
A Virtuous Circle of Low Inflation and Low Expected Inflation.
Low inflation leads people to expect low inflation in the future. As a result, they agree to accept small increases in wages and in the prices of the goods and services they supply, which keeps inflation—and expected inflation—low. In a similar way, high inflation leads people to expect high inflation, which in turn tends to produce high inflation.

The same logic applies in reverse in an economy with high inflation: A persistently high inflation rate leads the public to expect high inflation, resulting in higher increases in nominal wages and other production costs. As Figure 21.7 demonstrates, this in turn contributes to a high rate of actual inflation, and so on in a vicious circle. This role of inflation expectations in the determination of wage and price increases helps to explain why inflation often seems to adjust slowly.

EN 21A

Long-Term Wage and Price Contracts The role of inflation expectations in inflation inertia is strengthened by a second key element, the existence of long-term wage and price contracts. Union wage contracts, for example, often extend for three years into the future. Likewise, contracts that set the prices manufacturing firms pay for parts and raw materials often cover several years.

Long-term contracts serve to "build in" wage and price increases that depend on inflation expectations at the time the contracts were signed. For example, a union negotiating in a high-inflation environment is much more likely to demand a rapid increase in nominal wages over the life of the contract than would a union in an economy in which prices are stable.

To summarize, in the absence of external shocks, inflation tends to remain relatively stable over time—at least in low-inflation industrial economies like that of the United States. In other words, inflation is inertial (or, as some people put it, "sticky"). Inflation tends to be inertial for two main reasons. The first is the behavior of people's expectations of inflation. A low inflation rate leads people to expect low inflation in the future, which results in reduced pressure for wage and price increases. Similarly, a high inflation rate leads people to expect high inflation in the future, resulting in more rapid increases in wages and prices. The effects of expectations are reinforced by the existence of long-term wage and price contracts, which is the second reason inflation tends to be stable over time. Long-term contracts tend to build in the effects of people's inflation expectations.

EXERCISE 21.3

Using Figure 21.7, discuss why the Federal Reserve has a strong incentive to maintain a low inflation rate in the economy.

Just as a physical object will change speed if it is acted on by outside forces, so various economic forces can change the rate of inflation. An important factor influencing the rate of inflation is the output gap, which we defined in Chapter 18 as the difference between potential output and actual output ($Y - Y^*$). At a particular time, the level of short-run equilibrium output may happen to equal the economy's long-run productive capacity, or potential output. But that is not necessarily the case. Output may exceed potential output, giving rise to an expansionary gap, or it may fall short of potential output, producing a recessionary gap. Let's consider what happens to inflation in each of these three possible cases: no output gap, an expansionary gap, and a recessionary gap.

No Output Gap: $Y = Y^*$ If actual output equals potential output, then by definition there is no output gap. When the output gap is zero, firms are satisfied in the sense that their sales equal their maximum sustainable production rates. As a result, firms have no incentive to either reduce or increase their prices relative to the prices of other goods and services. However, the fact that firms are satisfied with their sales does not imply that inflation—the rate of change in the overall price level—is zero.

To see why, let's go back to the idea of inflation inertia. Suppose that inflation has recently been steady at 3 percent per year, so that the public has come to expect an inflation rate of 3 percent per year. If the public's inflation expectations are reflected in the wage and price increases agreed to in long-term contracts, then firms will find their labor and materials costs are rising at 3 percent per year. To cover their costs, firms will need to raise their prices by 3 percent per year. Note that if all firms are increasing their prices by 3 percent per year, the relative prices of various goods and services in the economy—say, the price of ice cream relative to the price of a taxi ride—will not change. Nevertheless, the economywide rate of inflation equals 3 percent, the same as in previous years. We conclude that, if the output gap is zero, the rate of inflation will tend to remain the same.

Expansionary Gap: $Y > Y^*$ Suppose now that an expansionary gap exists, so that most firms' sales exceed their maximum sustainable production rates. As we might expect in situations in which the quantity demanded exceeds the quantity firms desire to supply, firms will ultimately respond by trying to increase their relative prices. To do so, they will increase their prices by more than the increase in their costs. If all firms behave this way, then the general price level will begin to rise more rapidly than before. Thus, when an expansionary gap exists, the rate of inflation will tend to increase.

Recessionary Gap: $Y < Y^*$ Finally, if a recessionary gap exists, firms will be selling an amount less than their capacity to produce, and they will have an incentive to cut their relative prices so they can sell more. In this case, firms will raise their prices less than needed to cover fully their increases in costs, as determined by the existing inflation rate. As a result, when a recessionary gap exists, the rate of inflation will tend to decrease.

Deriving the *AS* Curve: Graphical Analysis

We can now derive the *AS* curve by combining inflation inertia and the behavior of inflation when there are output gaps. In particular, we can summarize what we have learned in the following equation:

$$\text{Current inflation } (\pi) = \text{expected inflation } (\pi_1) + \text{Change in inflation caused by an output gap}$$

We label the first term on the right-hand side of the equation as expected inflation, rather than inflation inertia, because, as we discussed above, the primary cause of inflation inertia is agents' expectations of future inflation.

Let's begin with the situation where there is no output gap. Then,

$$\text{Current inflation } (\pi_1) = \text{expected inflation } (\pi_1).$$

We show this situation as point *A* in Figure 21.8. Next, suppose that the economy has an expansionary gap. In this situation, the inflation rate will be equal to the amount of inertia in the economy plus some additional amount caused by the economy being above the potential output level, that is,

$$\text{Current inflation } (\pi_2) > \text{expected inflation } (\pi_1).$$

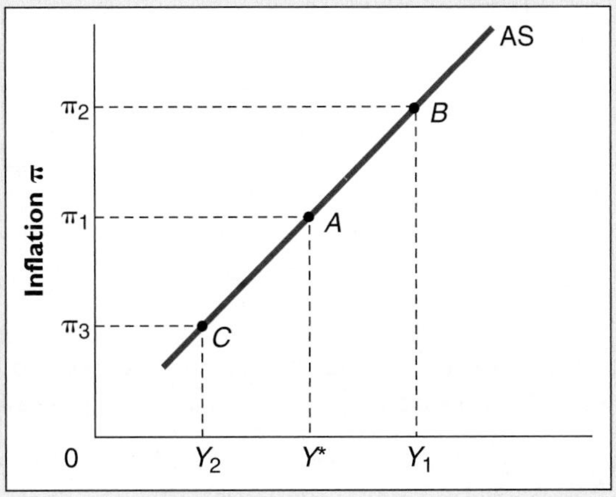

FIGURE 21.8
Deriving the *AS* Curve. At point *A*, output is equal to potential output and so inflation is equal to expected inflation π_1. At point *B*, output is above potential, so inflation π_2 is above its expected level. At point *C*, output is below potential, so inflation π_3 is below its expected level.

This is shown as point *B* in Figure 21.8. Finally, suppose that there is a recessionary gap. In this case,

$$\text{Current inflation } (\pi_3) < \text{expected inflation } (\pi_1).$$

Current inflation is lower than expected inflation because the recessionary gap encourages firms to reduce their prices and thus puts downward pressure on the inflation rate. Points *A*, *B*, and *C* in Figure 21.8 thus trace out the *AS* curve at the expected inflation level of π_1.

SHIFTS OF THE *AS* CURVE

We will focus on two types of changes in the economy that shift the *AS* curve: (1) changes in inflation expectations and (2) inflation shocks.

Changes in Inflation Expectations

We discussed earlier how inflation expectations are formed and how either a virtuous or vicious cycle reinforces these expectations. (See Figure 21.7.) Why might inflation expectations change? What happens to the *AS* curve when inflation expectations change?

Suppose that wages and prices in certain industries begin to rise faster than workers and firms thought they would rise. This will cause the actual rate of inflation to be higher than what was expected and can lead people to revise upward their expected rate of inflation. Figure 21.9 shows what happens to the *AS* curve when expected inflation rises. Originally, AS_1 is the *AS* curve for the economy and expected inflation is at π_1. After inflation expectations rise, expected inflation is at π_2; the entire *AS* curve thus shifts upward because output gaps still have the same effect on actual inflation.

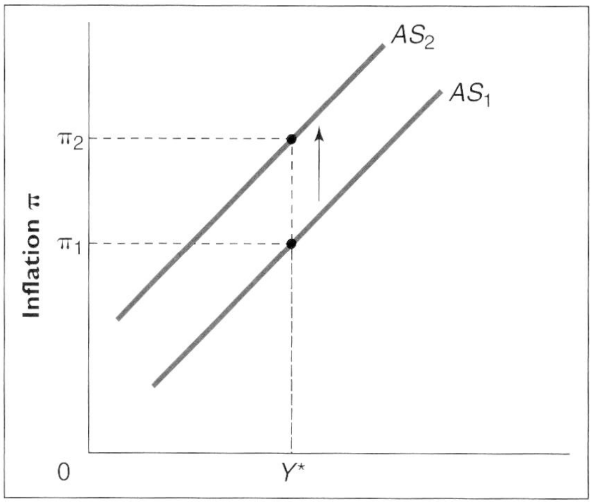

FIGURE 21.9
An Increase in Expected Inflation.
An increase in expected inflation from π_1 to π_2 shifts the *AS* curve upward. Similarly, a decrease in expected inflation would shift the *AS* curve down.

EXERCISE 21.4

Draw an *AS* curve, being sure to label the current level of expected inflation. How will the *AS* curve be affected if inflation expectations fall?

Inflation Shocks

inflation shock a sudden change in the normal behavior of inflation, unrelated to the nation's output gap

The second factor that can affect the inflation rate is a shock that directly affects prices, which we will refer to as an *inflation shock*. An **inflation shock** is a sudden change in the normal behavior of inflation, unrelated to the nation's output gap. A large increase in the price of imported oil, for example, raises the price of gasoline, heating oil, and other fuels, as well as of goods made with oil or services using oil.

A famous example of an inflation shock is the sudden increase in the price of oil that took place in the early 1970s. In late 1973, at the time of the Yom Kippur War between Israel and a coalition of Arab nations, the Organization of Petroleum-Exporting Countries (OPEC) dramatically cut its supplies of crude oil to the industrialized nations, quadrupling world oil prices in a matter of months. The sharp increase in oil prices was quickly transferred to the price of gasoline, heating oil, and goods and services that were heavily dependent on oil, such as air travel. The effects of the oil price increase, together with agricultural shortages that increased the price of food, contributed to a significant rise in the overall U.S. inflation rate in 1974.

An inflation shock that causes an increase in inflation, like the large rise in oil prices in 1973, is called an *adverse* inflation shock and shifts the *AS* curve upward. An inflation shock that reduces inflation, such as the sharp decline in oil prices that occurred in 1986, is called a *favorable* inflation shock and shifts the *AS* curve down.

AGGREGATE DEMAND–AGGREGATE SUPPLY ANALYSIS

We can now put the *AD* curve and the *AS* curve together and analyze how inflation and output are determined simultaneously. Let's return to Figure 21.1: this diagram shows the economy in **long-run equilibrium,** which is the situation where actual output Y_1 is equal to potential output and actual inflation π_1 equals expected inflation and the Fed's inflation target. Graphically, this is shown when the *AD* curve, the *AS* curve, and the *LRAS* curve intersect at a single point.

The economy does not have to be in long-run equilibrium at every point in time. The *AD* curve and the *AS* curve can intersect at levels of output that are above or below potential output; this is called a **short-run equilibrium.** That is, the economy is in a short-run equilibrium when there is either an expansionary gap or a recessionary gap. An economy can be in short-run equilibrium, but it will not remain there. Let's examine both an expansionary gap and a recessionary gap to see why this is the case.

long-run equilibrium situation where actual output is equal to potential output and actual inflation equals expected inflation and the Fed's inflation target graphically, this is where the *AD* curve, the *AS* curve, and the *LRAS* curve intersect at a single point

short-run equilibrium situation when there is either an expansionary gap or a recessionary gap; graphically, this is where the *AD* curve and the *AS* curve intersect at a point either to the left or to the right of the *LRAS* curve

AN EXPANSIONARY GAP

Figure 21.10 illustrates how an economy adjusts over time when it begins with an expansionary gap. The economy is initially in equilibrium with actual output Y_1 and actual inflation π_1. At this point, there is an expansionary gap since actual output Y_1 is greater than potential output Y_2. The *AD* curve will remain at AD_1 as long as there is no change in the Fed's monetary policy rule and there are exogenous changes in spending.

Since the *AD* curve does not move, how will long-run equilibrium be restored? Graphically, the *AS* curve must shift to the left from AS_1 to AS_2 and inflation must rise from π_1 to π_2. But *why* does the *AS* curve shift to the left? What is the economics behind this shift?

As we discussed earlier in the chapter, changes in workers' and firms' expectations about inflation shift the *AS* curve, and this is the mechanism through which the economy adjusts from short-run equilibrium to long-run equilibrium. An expansionary gap causes both the actual and expected rates of inflation to rise as firms respond to high demand by raising their prices more rapidly than their costs are rising. Specifically, suppose that firms see that actual output is above potential output; this means that most firms will be experiencing excess demand for their products and they will respond by raising their prices. This will increase the inflation rate since not just one price relative to another is rising but the *general* level of prices is rising at a faster rate.

This is just the beginning of the story. Go to Figure 21.7 and look at the box marked "low inflation"; if we change this box to "higher inflation" and follow the clockwise arrow to the next box, we will change "low expected inflation" to "higher expected inflation." Higher expected inflation shifts the *AS* curve to the left as wages and production costs begin to rise faster than before; that is, we change the box marked "slow increase in wages and other production costs" to "faster

FIGURE 21.10

Adjustment to an Expansionary Gap.

The economy is initially in equilibrium with output Y_1 and inflation π_1. At this point, there is an expansionary gap (i.e., Y_1 is greater than Y_2). The *AD* curve remains at AD_1 as long as there is no change in the Fed's monetary policy rule. (1) Since the *AD* curve does not move, workers and firms know that the only way to restore long-run equilibrium is for inflation to rise from π_1 to π_2 so they increase the level of expected inflation from π_1 to π_2. This shifts the *AS* curve to the left from AS_1 to AS_2 and causes actual inflation to rise. The Fed follows its monetary policy rule and increases the real interest rate as inflation rises, so spending and output fall as inflation rises and the economy moves along the *AD* curve to long-run equilibrium at output Y_2 and inflation π_2.

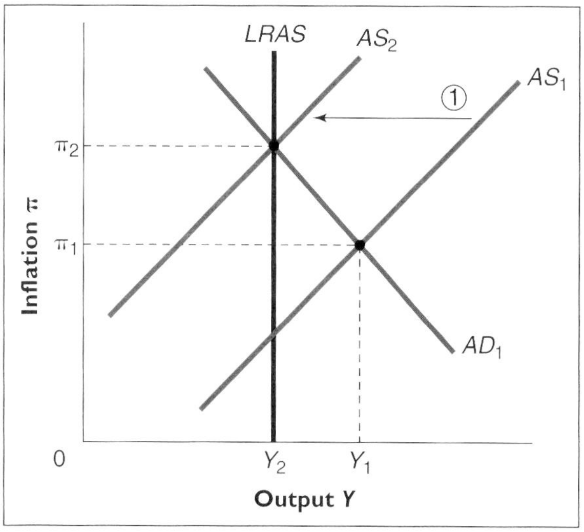

increases in wages and other production costs." The circle is now complete: actual inflation continues to rise, causing expected inflation to rise, causing wages and production costs to increase at a faster rate.

This explains why inflation rises, but why does actual output fall to potential output? Remember the Fed's monetary policy rule: as inflation rises, the Fed increases the real interest rate. So, as inflation rises, the Fed will increase the real interest rate and spending will fall so that the economy moves along the *AD* curve and output falls while inflation is rising. We thus move from short-run equilibrium to long-run equilibrium, with actual output equal to potential output Y_2 and actual inflation equal to expected inflation π_2.

A RECESSIONARY GAP

The economy's adjustment to a recessionary gap is similar to that for an expansionary gap. The adjustment of inflation in response to a recessionary gap is shown graphically in Figure 21.11. Again, the economy is initially in equilibrium with actual output Y_1 and actual inflation π_1. At this point, there is a recessionary gap since actual output Y_1 is less than potential output Y_2. The *AD* curve will remain at AD_1 as long as there is no change in the Fed's monetary policy rule and there are exogenous changes in spending.

As was the case with an expansionary gap, the *AS* curve must shift, in this case to the right from AS_1 to AS_2, to close the gap as long as the *AD* curve is stable. Inflation will fall from π_1 to π_2 as workers' and firms' expectations about inflation fall due to the recessionary gap. (Again, as in the case of an expansionary gap, Figure 21.7 is helpful. In this case, lower inflation causes lower expected inflation and this in turn slows the growth of wages and other production costs.) Actual output will rise from Y_1 to potential output Y_2 because the Fed will follow its monetary

FIGURE 21.11

Adjustment to a Recessionary Gap.

The economy is initially in equilibrium with output Y_1 and inflation π_1. At this point, there is a recessionary gap (i.e., Y_1 is less than Y_2). The *AD* curve remains at AD_1 as long as there is no change in the Fed's monetary policy rule. ① Since the *AD* curve does not move, workers and firms know that the only way to restore long-run equilibrium is for inflation to fall from π_1 to π_2, so they decrease the level of expected inflation from π_1 to π_2. This shifts the *AS* curve to the right from AS_1 to AS_2 and causes actual inflation to fall. The Fed follows its monetary policy rule and decreases the real interest rate as inflation falls, so spending and output rise as inflation falls and the economy moves along the *AD* curve to long-run equilibrium at output Y_2 and inflation π_2.

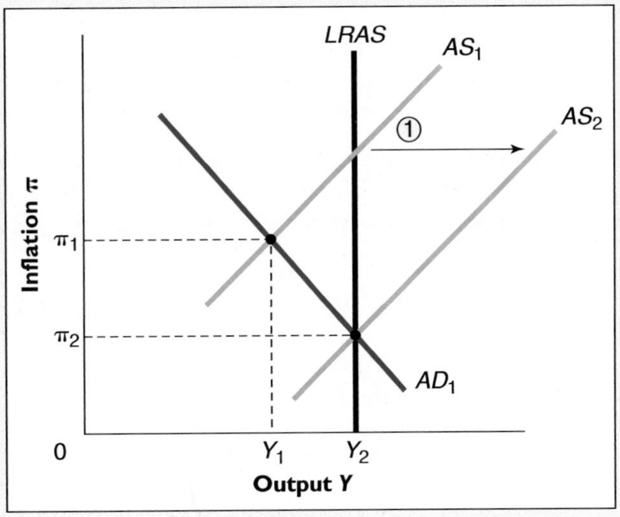

policy rule and lower the real interest rate as inflation falls, stimulating increased levels of consumption and investment spending.

THE SELF-CORRECTING ECONOMY

Our analysis of Figures 21.10 and 21.11 makes an important general point: The economy tends to be *self-correcting* in the long run. In other words, given enough time, output gaps tend to disappear without changes in monetary or fiscal policy (other than the change in the real interest rate embodied in the Fed's policy rule). Expansionary output gaps are eliminated by rising inflation, while recessionary output gaps are eliminated by falling inflation. This result contrasts sharply with the basic Keynesian model, which does not include a self-correcting mechanism. The difference in results is explained by the fact that the basic Keynesian model concentrates on the short-run period, during which prices do not adjust, and does not take into account the changes in prices and inflation that occur over a longer period.

Does the economy's tendency to self-correct imply that aggressive monetary and fiscal policies are not needed to stabilize output? The answer to this question depends crucially on the *speed* with which the self-correction process takes place. If self-correction takes place very slowly, so that actual output differs from potential for protracted periods, then active use of monetary and fiscal policy can help to stabilize output. But if self-correction is rapid, then active stabilization policies are probably not justified in most cases, given the lags and uncertainties that are involved in policymaking in practice. Indeed, if the economy returns to full employment quickly, then attempts by policymakers to stabilize spending and output may end up doing more harm than good, for example, by causing actual output to "overshoot" potential output.

The speed with which a particular economy corrects itself depends on a variety of factors, including the prevalence of long-term contracts and the efficiency and flexibility of product and labor markets. (For a case study, see the comparison of U.S. and European labor markets in Chapter 14.) However, a reasonable conclusion is that the greater the initial output gap, the longer the economy's process of self-correction will take. This observation suggests that stabilization policies should not be used actively to try to eliminate relatively small output gaps, but that they may be quite useful in remedying large gaps—for example, when the unemployment rate is exceptionally high.

RECAP	*AD-AS* AND THE SELF-CORRECTING ECONOMY

- The economy is in short-run equilibrium when there is either an expansionary gap or a recessionary gap. Graphically, this is where the *AD* curve and the *AS* curve intersect at a point either to the left or to the right of the *LRAS* line.
- The economy is in long-run equilibrium when actual output equals potential output (there is no output gap) and the inflation rate is stable. Graphically, long-run equilibrium occurs when the *AD* curve, the *AS* curve, and the *LRAS* line intersect at a common point.
- Inflation adjusts gradually to bring the economy into long-run equilibrium (a phenomenon called the economy's self-correcting tendency). Inflation rises to eliminate an expansionary gap and falls to eliminate a recessionary gap.
- The more rapid the self-correction process, the less need for active stabilization policies to eliminate output gaps. In practice, policymakers' attempts to eliminate output gaps are more likely to be helpful when the output gap is large than when it is small.

MONETARY POLICY AND INFLATION

We have seen that inflation can rise or fall in response to an output gap. But what creates the output gaps that give rise to changes in inflation? And are there factors besides output gaps that can affect the inflation rate? In this section we use the *AD-AS* diagram to explore the ultimate sources of inflation. We first discuss how excessive growth in aggregate spending can spur inflation, then turn to factors operating through the supply side of the economy. In both cases, monetary policy plays an important role in determining the rate of inflation in the long run.

EXCESSIVE AGGREGATE SPENDING

One important source of inflation in practice is excessive aggregate spending—or, in more colloquial terms, "too much spending chasing too few goods."

For example, wars and military buildups are potentially inflationary because increased spending on military hardware raises total demand relative to the economy's productive capacity. In the face of rising sales, firms increase their prices more quickly, raising the inflation rate.

Figure 21.12 illustrates this process. The economy is initially in equilibrium with output Y_1 equal to potential output and inflation π_1 equal to expected inflation and the Fed's long-run inflation target. An increase in military spending, as we discussed

FIGURE 21.12

War and Military Buildup as a Source of Inflation.

The economy is initially in equilibrium with output Y_1 equal to potential output and inflation π_1 equal to expected inflation and the Fed's long-run inflation target. ① An increase in exogenous spending caused by an increase in military spending shifts the AD curve from AD_1 to AD_2. The causes output to increase from Y_1 to Y_2 and opens an expansionary gap, causing the inflation rate to rise from π_1 to π_2. ② If the Fed maintains its current long-run inflation target at π_1 and does not tighten monetary policy, the AD curve will remain at AD_2. Since inflation is now above its expected rate, AS will shift to the left from AS_1 to AS_2, causing inflation to increase. The Fed will raise interest rates as inflation rises from π_2 to π_3, which causes output to return to potential output Y_1.

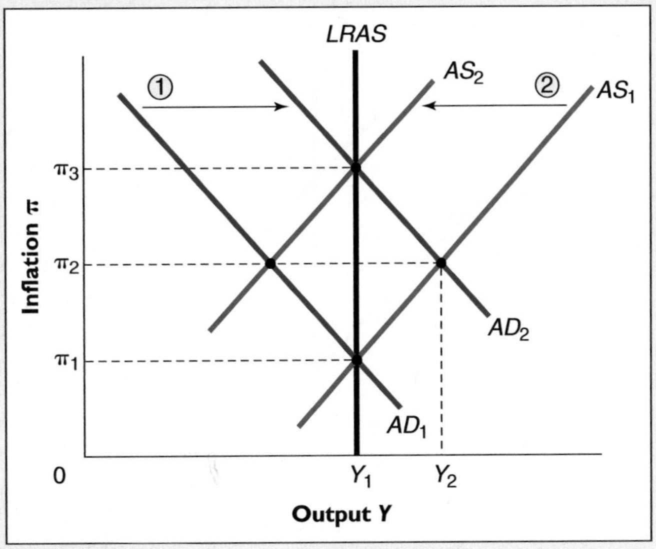

earlier in the chapter, is an exogenous increase in spending and therefore shifts the *AD* curve from AD_1 to AD_2. Output increases from Y_1 to Y_2, opening an expansionary gap that causes the inflation rate to rise from π_1 to π_2.

At this point, the Fed has to choose the type of monetary policy it will pursue. One possibility, shown in Figure 21.12, is to allow the economy's self-correction process to work without interference. This means that the Fed will follow its current monetary policy rule and will keep its long-run inflation target at π_1. Since inflation is now at π_2, the Fed will raise interest rates until the economy reaches potential output at an inflation rate of π_3. The Fed will stop raising the real interest at this point because the expansionary gap has closed and inflation will not rise above π_3 unless there is another shock to *AD* or *AS*.

Economists use the word *accommodating* to describe a policy that allows the effects of a shock to occur. In this example, the Fed's **accommodating policy** is to allow the spending shock to increase output in the short run and inflation in the short run and the long run. There are two important implications of the Fed's accommodating policy. First, in the short run, the economy experiences a period of rapid growth and higher inflation caused by the spending shock followed by a contraction in output with inflation rising even higher. Second, in the long run, the economy returns to potential output, where it began, but now has a higher inflation rate. A short-run boom is paid for with a short-run bust and a higher long-run inflation rate.

accommodating policy a policy that allows the effects of a shock to occur

The other possible policy that the Fed can follow is to drive inflation back to its long-run inflation target. This policy is illustrated in Figure 21.13, where, once again, the economy is initially in equilibrium with output Y_1 equal to potential output and inflation π_1 equal to expected inflation and the Fed's long-run inflation target. An

FIGURE 21.13

Maintaining Low Inflation after a Change in Spending.

The economy is initially in equilibrium with output Y_1 equal to potential output and inflation π_1 equal to expected inflation and the Fed's long-run inflation target. (1) An increase in exogenous spending, caused by an increase in military spending, for instance, shifts the *AD* curve form AD_1 to AD_2. This causes output to increase from Y_1 to Y_2. This opens an expansionary gap and causes the inflation rate to rise from π_1 to π_2. Inflation is above the Fed's long-run inflation target, so the Fed must choose how to respond. (2) The alternative to accommodating the spending shock (see Figure 21.12) is for the Fed to tighten monetary policy. This implies that at every inflation rate, the Fed raises the real interest rate higher than it does when it accommodates the spending shock. This shifts the *AD* curve back from AD_2 to AD_1 and causes output to return to potential output Y_1. *AS* does not shift since the Fed's action prevents any change in inflationary expectations.

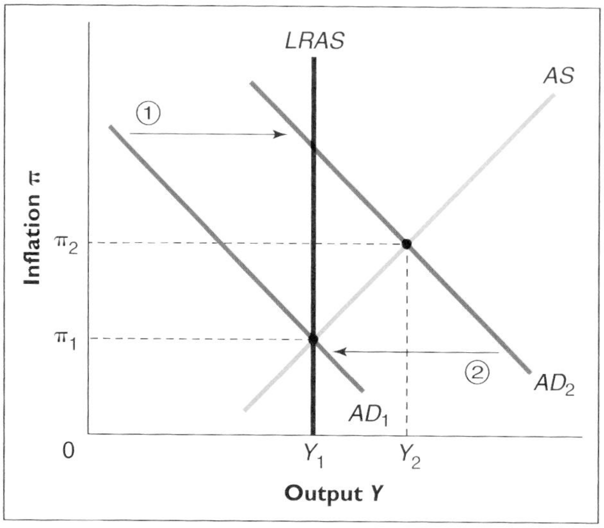

increase in military spending shifts the *AD* curve to the right, from AD_1 to AD_2, causing output to increase from Y_1 to Y_2 and opening an expansionary gap that causes inflation to rise above the Fed's long-run target for inflation, from π_1 to π_2.

Now, suppose that the Fed tightens monetary policy. Recall that a tighter monetary policy implies that the Fed raises the real interest rate at every level of inflation, which reduces planned spending and shifts the *AD* curve to the left. This is shown in Figure 21.13: when the Fed tightens monetary policy, the *AD* curve shifts back from AD_2 to AD_1. Output returns to potential output Y_1 and, since no expansionary gap opens, inflation remains at π_1. The *AS* curve does not shift since the Fed's action prevents any change in inflationary expectations. The Fed's preemptive action thus stabilizes output at potential and keeps inflation at the Fed's long-run target.

Why does the Fed have to increase its target for the real interest rate in order to maintain stable output and inflation? Recall from Chapter 16 that the real interest rate is determined by saving and investment in the long run. An increase in military spending, or any other increase in government spending (or reduction in net taxes) will increase the government budget deficit. As we discussed in Chapter 16, an increase in the federal budget deficit reduces national saving and increases the real interest rate in the long run. In order to avoid long-run inflationary consequences, the Fed must raise its target real interest rate to a level that is compatible with long-run equilibrium in the market for saving and investment.

This model also can be used to analyze a sudden reduction in spending. Starting again at potential output, a reduction in spending will shift the aggregate demand curve to the left. The Fed can eliminate the recessionary gap resulting from this shift by reducing its real interest rate target. Once again, real GDP returns to potential and inflation returns to the Fed's target rate of inflation.

EXERCISE 21.5

Suppose the economy is initially in long-run equilibrium and there is a sudden decrease in spending. Use the aggregate supply–aggregate demand graph to illustrate and explain what happens to output and inflation in the short run and the long run if the Fed accommodates the spending decrease.

Why did the Fed lower interest rates in 2003?

The Fed reduced the federal funds rate from 6.50 percent in January 2001 to 1.75 percent in December 2001 in order to fight the 2001 recession. After the economy began to recover in 2002 and 2003, however, the Fed again reduced the federal funds rate to 1.25 percent in November 2002 and 1.0 percent in June 2003. Why did the Fed continue to reduce the federal funds rate even during the recovery?

There were several reasons for the Fed's policy choices. First, as we mentioned before, economic growth even during the recovery was slower than it had been in previous recoveries. Second, job growth did not keep up with the growth in output, due to the unusual increases in productivity. In addition, there was a major slowdown in investment spending as businesses became more cautious, especially following the decline in the stock market. As a result, the Fed was concerned that aggregate demand might fall and create a recessionary gap. The reduction in investment spending also implied that there might have been a reduction in the long-run real interest rate at which saving equaled investment. In response, the Fed reduced its target real interest rate, which shifted its monetary policy rule down (to the right). (see Figure 21.5.)

The Fed's action prevented the aggregate demand curve from falling further and thereby avoided a recession. This is another illustration of how the Fed can stabilize both inflation and output when there is a shock to aggregate demand. ◆

RESPONDING TO SHOCKS IN AGGREGATE SUPPLY

As we've seen, shocks in aggregate demand do not require the Fed to make a difficult choice between inflation and the stability of output. The Fed can maintain stable inflation and output by adjusting its target real interest rate to the real interest rate at which saving equals investment in the long run.

However, shocks to aggregate supply do create such a dilemma. If the Fed maintains its initial target inflation rate, the economy may experience a protracted recessionary or expansionary gap. If, on the other hand, it wants to hasten the return to potential GDP, it may have to change its inflation target.

We illustrate this dilemma in Figures 21.14 and 21.15. In both figures, the economy is initially in long-run equilibrium with output Y_1 equal to potential output and inflation π_1 equal to expected inflation and the Fed's long-run inflation target. An adverse inflation shock then shifts the *AS* curve from AS_1 to AS_2 in each figure. The Fed responds to the increase in inflation by following its monetary policy rule and increasing the real interest rate; the increase in the real interest rate causes planned spending to decline and output falls from Y_1 to Y_2.

Now, with the economy in a recession at output Y_2 and inflation rate π_2, the Fed faces a choice: accommodate the shock or bring inflation back down to π_1. Figure 21.14 shows the consequences for output and inflation if the Fed loosens monetary policy and accommodates the adverse inflation shock. Specifically, the Fed raises its long-run inflation target to π_3, the level of inflation that workers and firms expect when the economy returns to potential output. The Fed thus lowers the real interest rate at each level of inflation and shifts the *AD* curve to the right, from AD_1 to AD_2. As the *AD* curve shifts to the right, the inflation rate rises towards the Fed's new long-run inflation target, π_3.

The rise in inflation validates the new level of expected inflation π_3: workers and firms expect inflation to continue rising, so they push for faster increases in wages and prices, which drives actual and expected inflation towards π_3. The *AS*

FIGURE 21.14

Accommodating an Aggregate Supply Shock.

The economy is initially in equilibrium with output Y_1 equal to potential output and inflation π_1 equal to expected inflation and the Fed's long-run inflation target. ① An adverse inflation shock shifts the *AS* curve from AS_1 to AS_2. The Fed responds to the increase in inflation by following its monetary policy rule and increasing the real interest rate; this causes output to fall from Y_1 to Y_2. ② The Fed accommodates the aggregate supply shock by loosening monetary policy. Specifically, the Fed raises its long-run inflation target to π_3 since this is the inflation rate that workers and firms expect after the adverse inflation shock. The Fed thus lowers the real interest rate at every inflation rate and shifts the *AD* curve to the right from AD_1 to AD_2 and output returns to potential output Y_1. *AS* does not shift again since the Fed's action ratifies the increase in inflationary expectations.

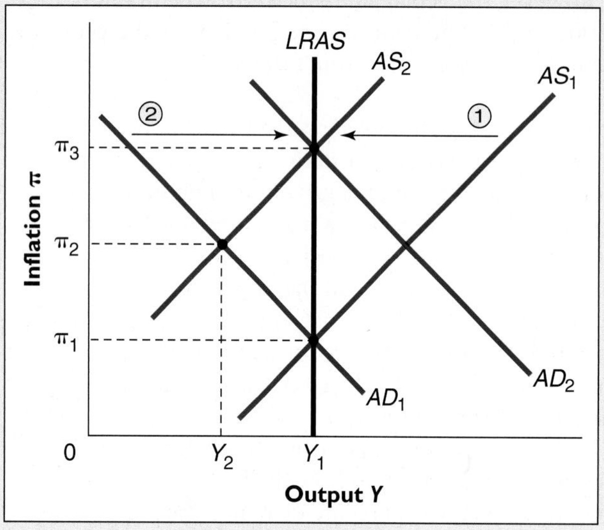

curve thus remains at AS_2 and the economy eventually returns to potential output with the new, higher long-run inflation rate π_3. Consequently, the higher inflation rate caused by the adverse inflation shock will be sustained and, in fact, increased by the Fed's accommodating monetary policy.

The alternative to accommodating the adverse inflation shock is for the Fed to stick to its current long-run inflation target, π_1. To do this, the Fed must keep the real interest rate above its long-run target level and *not* lower it as when it accommodates the adverse inflation shock. Figure 21.15 illustrates this situation. The economy therefore remains at Y_2 for a longer time than when the Fed accommodates the shock, that is, the recession caused by the adverse inflation shock is longer than when the Fed lowers interest rates.

The Fed's willingness to keep interest rates high, and to not close the recessionary gap, will convince workers and firms that inflation will not rise to the level they expected, π_3. Expected inflation therefore starts to fall, and the *AS* curve starts to shift back towards AS_1. Note how the Fed will react: as the *AS* curve shifts to the right, the actual inflation rate will fall and the Fed will follow its monetary policy rule and lower the real interest rate. The lower real interest rate will increase planned spending and output and reduce the recessionary gap and, eventually, the economy will return to potential output and the original level of inflation, π_1.

In deciding which of these two policy alternatives to follow, the Fed might like to know how long it would take for the economy to return to potential if it did not change monetary policy. The answer depends on the speed with which the aggregate supply curve shifts down when an adverse inflation shock creates a recessionary gap. If the *AS* curve shifts down quickly, the Fed is more likely to keep its target inflation rate unchanged at π_1 because any recession will probably be short. If, on

FIGURE 21.15
Maintaining Low Inflation after an Adverse Inflation Shock.
The economy is initially in equilibrium with output Y_1 equal to potential output and inflation π_1 equal to expected inflation and the Fed's long-run inflation target. ① An adverse inflation shock shifts the *AS* curve from AS_1 to AS_2.. The Fed keeps its long-run inflation target at π_1 and raises interest rates in response to the adverse inflation shock. ② Inflation π_2 is lower than what people expect inflation to be after the supply shock (π_3), so workers and firms reduce their inflationary expectations, shifting the *AS* curve to the right. This process continues until long-run equilibrium is restored at the Fed's long-run inflation target of π_1 and inflationary expectations are reduced to π_1 as well.

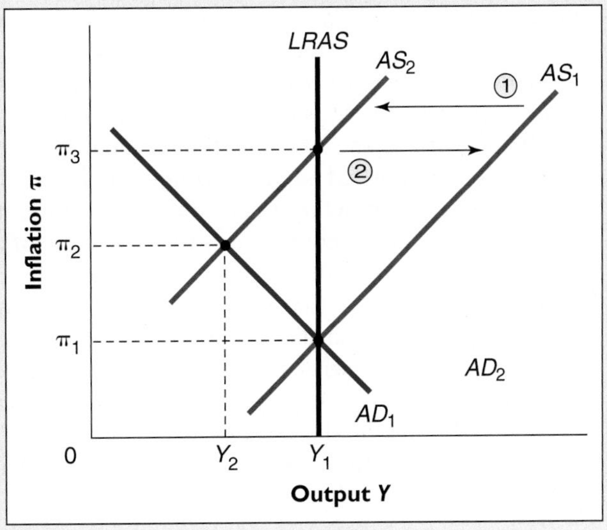

the other hand, the *AS* curve shifts down very slowly, the Fed may be more inclined to increase its target inflation rate to avoid a lengthy recession.

Ironically, the speed with which the aggregate supply curve shifts back down following an adverse inflation shock depends partly on the public's expectation of how the Fed will act. If people are confident that the Fed will maintain its original target inflation rate, their expectations of future inflation will not change even if inflation rises temporarily. If this is the case, we describe people's expectations of inflation as being **anchored.** When an adverse supply shock increases inflation, people with anchored expectations believe that the Fed will act to ensure that inflation quickly falls back to its initial level. Workers will then be less likely to ask for inflationary wage increases and firms will be less likely to raise prices. The second round of inflation will be eliminated, the aggregate supply line will shift back to AS_1 more rapidly, and output will return to potential more quickly. Because any recession will be shorter if inflationary expectations are anchored, the Fed also will be comfortable keeping its target inflation rate unchanged.

anchored inflationary expectations when people's expectations of future inflation do not change even if inflation rises temporarily

If, on the other hand, the Fed has frequently accommodated higher inflation rates in the past, expectations of inflation may not be anchored. If the public believes the Fed will raise its target inflation rate, expectations of future inflation will be higher. Workers will then demand larger wage increases and firms will raise prices more rapidly. In that event, the short-run aggregate supply line will shift down more slowly, and the return to full employment will be prolonged. Thus, the Fed has a stake in convincing the public that it will maintain its original target inflation rate.

THE CORE RATE OF INFLATION

A bulge in inflation is not inevitable when there is an adverse aggregate supply shock such as a sharp increase in energy prices. In principle, the Fed could prevent inflation from rising by adopting such a tight monetary policy that the initial bulge coming from higher energy prices would be offset by declines in nonenergy prices. Yet experience suggests that such a policy is likely to be too costly in terms of lost output as well as unnecessary for keeping inflation under control in the longer term. Instead, some economists suggest that the Fed accept the immediate inflationary effect of an oil price increase but act to minimize any second-round effect that occurs if the shock changes inflationary expectations and thereby affects wages and nonoil prices. If the Fed can prevent energy price increases from changing inflationary expectations, it can prevent inflation from becoming permanently higher.

core rate of inflation the rate of increase of all prices except energy and food

To allow a temporary bulge but keep long-term inflationary expectations from rising, the Fed can focus on the **core rate of inflation,** defined as the rate of increase of all prices *except energy and food,* the two items most frequently responsible for inflation shocks.[3] Because core inflation excludes the sources of the most volatile price changes, it is considered to be a useful short-term measure of the underlying inflation trend. If the core rate of inflation does not change, the initial supply shock probably has not led to any second-round effects. Thus, the Fed may decide to adopt a tighter monetary policy only if the core rate of inflation exceeds its target inflation rate. Note that the Fed's focus on core inflation does not mean that it does not care about overall inflation, which includes oil and food prices. Rather, by focusing on the core rate of inflation, the Fed can prevent the bulge in inflation following an inflation shock from becoming permanent.

Table 21.1 presents the general and core rates of inflation from July 2002 through July 2005. During this period, the general rate of inflation rose significantly, reflecting the sharp increase in oil prices. The core rate of inflation, however, was both lower and increased by less, implying that the Fed successfully mitigated the second-round effects.

TABLE 21.1
U.S. Annualized Inflation Rates, July 2002–July 2005

Period	Annualized CPI inflation (%)	Annualized core inflation (CPI inflation excluding food and energy) (%)
July 2002–July 2003	2.1	1.5
July 2003–July 2004	3.0	1.8
July 2004–July 2005	3.2	2.1

SOURCE: U.S. Bureau of Labor Statistics (http://www.bls.gov/data/).

RECAP MONETARY POLICY AND INFLATION

In response to changes in spending that create shocks in aggregate demand, the Fed can maintain stable inflation and output by adjusting its target real interest rate to the real interest rate at which saving equals investment in the long run. Shocks to aggregate supply (such as inflation shocks), however, force the Fed to choose between maintaining inflation and stabilizing output. If inflationary expectations are anchored, however, the return to potential output following an inflation shock will occur more rapidly. By monitoring the core rate of inflation, the Fed can determine whether an inflation shock has led to any second-round effects on inflation and can act accordingly.

[3]Since energy and food are used as inputs in many other industries, some of the indirect effects of an increase in the prices of energy and food will be included even in the core rate of inflation.

INFLATIONARY EXPECTATIONS AND CREDIBILITY

As we saw in the previous section, macroeconomic performance may be improved if inflationary expectations are anchored. But what determines whether expectations are anchored? Most economists believe that it depends on the **credibility of monetary policy,** which is the degree to which the public believes the central bank's promises to keep inflation low, even if doing so may impose short-run economic costs.

credibility of monetary policy the degree to which the public believes the central bank's promises to keep inflation low, even if doing so may impose short-run economic costs

The importance of credibility was illustrated in our earlier analysis of an adverse inflation shock. In that case, the Fed's credibility as an inflation-fighter preempted the second-round effects of inflation and hastened the return to full employment at the original rate of inflation. Economists have identified several institutional characteristics that may affect the credibility of the central bank's pronouncements to keep inflation low and thus its ability to do so. These include the degree of central bank independence, the announcement of explicit inflation targets, and the establishment of a reputation for fighting inflation.

CENTRAL BANK INDEPENDENCE

The credibility of monetary policy may be enhanced if central bankers are insulated from short-term political considerations, a condition that is sometimes referred to as **central bank independence.** Independent central banks will be better able to take a long-term view of the economy. In particular, they can pursue anti-inflation policy when it is necessary, even if it leads to a temporary recession. Elected politicians, on the other hand, face frequent reelections, and they may be swayed by short-term political considerations to allow the economy to overexpand at the cost of higher inflation in the long run. Because of its enhanced credibility, an independent central bank may find it easier to anchor the public's expectations of inflation, reducing the duration of any inflationary or recessionary gap and promoting overall economic stability.

central bank independence when central bankers are insulated from short-term political considerations and are allowed to take a long-term view of the economy

Various factors contribute to a central bank's independence. Among the many possible factors, we list four:

- The length of appointments to the central bank. Central banks are considered to be more independent if their central bankers are appointed for long terms, especially if the terms are staggered so that a single president or group of legislators cannot replace them all at once.
- Whether the central bank's actions are subject to frequent interference, review, or veto by the legislative branch. Central banks are considered to be more independent if their actions are not subject to frequent interference or review.
- Whether the central bank has the obligation, as it does in some countries, to finance the national deficit by buying newly issued government bonds. The obligation to do so reduces a central bank's independence.
- The degree to which the central bank's budget is controlled by the legislative or executive branch of government. Central banks are considered to be more independent if they are allowed to set and control their own budgets.

The U.S. Federal Reserve is generally considered to be a relatively independent central bank. The seven members of the Federal Reserve are appointed to staggered terms of 14 years, in contrast to the members of the U.S. House of Representatives, the president, and members of the Senate, who must face reelection every two, four, and six years, respectively. Although appointments to the Fed's Board of Governors must be approved by the Senate, and the Federal Reserve is subject to general oversight by the Congress, the daily policy actions of the Fed are not subject to review, approval, or veto by either the executive, legislative, or judicial branches of government. Finally, the Fed is under no obligation to finance the national deficit, and it controls its own budget. On the other hand, the law that created the Fed (the Federal Reserve Act) does not explicitly prohibit interference in monetary policy decisions by the legislative and executive branches of government. This prohibition is explicit in the central banking laws of many other countries.

Empirical evidence supports the proposition that countries should foster the independence of their central banks. Countries whose central banks are more independent have lower rates of inflation. More importantly, the lower inflation does not appear to come at the cost of lower output or higher unemployment, according to most studies. By enhancing a central bank's credibility, greater central bank independence leads to better overall economic outcomes.

ANNOUNCING A NUMERICAL INFLATION TARGET

Some economists believe that expectations are more firmly anchored and the central bank is perceived as more credible in those countries in which the central bank announces an explicit, numerical target for inflation. We have already introduced the idea of a target rate of inflation in our discussion of the monetary policy rule. Generally speaking, central banks must have an idea of the inflation rate they would like to achieve in order to make sensible policy. The more controversial question is whether central banks should announce their target inflation rate to the public. Proponents argue that announcing a numerical target for long-run inflation, and then sticking to it, will increase credibility and better anchor inflation expectations.

Many central banks publicly announce their inflation target. The Bank of Canada, for example, began announcing its inflation target in 1991. Since 1995, that target has been 2 percent. In March 2008, the Bank of England's inflation target was 2 percent, and the Central Bank of Brazil's target was 4.5 percent. Other central banks provide a range for their target rather than, or in addition to, a single number. The Bank of Israel and the Reserve Bank of New Zealand, for example, both had a 1–3 percent target range as of March 2008; in Chile the range was 2–4 percent.

Central banks that announce their targets typically provide additional information to the public. This information may include their forecasts of inflation, real GDP and other variables, as well as some discussion of the specific policies that will be needed to meet their targets. Advocates believe that announcing inflation targets and accompanying them with supporting information enhances the credibility of the central bank and reduces uncertainty among households and firms. This helps to anchor inflationary expectations, keep inflation low, and maintain full employment. Note that it makes sense for a central bank to announce a long-run inflation target, in that the central bank is able to control the rate of inflation in the long run. It would *not* make sense for a central bank to announce a long-run target for real GDP or employment because these variables are determined by a host of factors (such as productivity and the supply of labor) that are not under the control of the central bank.

Once an inflation target is announced, the central bank may choose to adhere to it strictly, or it may be more flexible. A central bank that sets a strict target tries to meet the target all the time without regard for the consequences for output. As we have seen, this policy keeps output at potential when the economy is beset by spending shocks, but it may result in a recession if the central bank acts to eliminate even the initial bulge in inflation following a shock to aggregate supply such as an inflation shock. In practice, virtually all central banks that announce an inflation target are flexible inflation targeters—they try to hit their inflation target in the long run or on average over a long period while responding to short-term shocks to aggregate supply in a way that takes account of both output gaps and inflation. In these cases, the announced inflation targets correspond to the target inflation rate in the monetary policy rule.

Advocates of announcing explicit numerical targets believe that this practice reduces uncertainty in financial markets and among the public. Reduced uncertainty allows people to plan more effectively, save the resources used to protect themselves from unexpected inflation, and improve market functioning. By putting the prestige of the central bank behind its commitment to meet the target, the advocates also believe that explicit inflation targets enhance the central bank's credibility and anchor inflation expectations.

Supporters of inflation targets emphasize that it has been successful in both developing and industrialized countries. They believe that explicit targets in Brazil, Chile, Mexico, and Peru are one important reason why the central banks in nine of the most populous Latin American countries were able to reduce their inflation rates from 160 percent per year in the 1980s and 235 percent during the first half of the 1990s to only 13 percent per year in 1995–1999 and less than 8 percent in the period 2000–2004.[4]

Those central banks, such as the Federal Reserve, that do not announce an explicit target to the public still may have a target or range in mind when making policy. Instead of announcing a specific number to the public, however, these banks typically state that they are interested in keeping inflation low, without defining exactly what that means. Proponents of this approach believe that a system of publicly announced targets is too rigid and may reduce the flexibility of the central bank to deal with unexpected circumstances. They worry that having an explicit inflation target may lead the central bank to pay too much attention to inflation and not enough attention to stabilizing output and maintaining full employment. Finally, opponents of explicit inflation targeting for the United States emphasize that the Fed has achieved good results without having a publicly announced target. They suggest following the adage, "if it ain't broke, don't fix it."

Why shouldn't the inflation target be zero?

Because central banks often state that they are in favor of stable prices, it would seem that the logical long-run target for inflation is 0 percent. However, most economists believe that an inflation target of zero is too low, and central banks that announce an explicit inflation target usually choose values that are low but above zero. Why shouldn't the inflation target be zero?

EN 21B

Several reasons have been offered. First, because hitting the target at all times is impossible in practice, an inflation target of 0 percent increases the risk that the economy will experience periods of deflation (negative inflation). The deflationary experiences of the United States in the 1930s and, more recently, in Japan in the 1990s, illustrate that deflation can be difficult to stop once it starts, and it can lead to painful and persistent declines in real GDP, especially if people expect it to continue. Many policymakers prefer to reduce the risk of deflation by choosing an inflation target above 0 percent.

Second, there are times when the Fed may wish to counteract negative shocks to the economy with a negative real interest rate, but this requires that inflation be greater than zero. Recall that the real interest rate is equal to the nominal interest rate minus the rate of inflation. Thus, a negative real interest rate requires setting a nominal interest rate less than inflation. If inflation is zero (or less than zero), however, a negative real interest rate would require a negative nominal interest rate. But the federal funds rate cannot fall below zero because banks would rather keep their reserves than lend them out at a negative nominal interest rate. Consequently, a negative real interest rate must be accompanied by inflation greater than zero.

Third, as we saw in Chapter 13, some evidence suggests that the conventional measures of inflation tend to overstate the "true" rate of inflation by about one percentage point. Consequently, if the Fed wanted to maintain "true" price stability

[4]Ben Bernanke, "Inflation in Latin America: A New Era?" February 11, 2005, http://www.federalreserve.gov/boarddocs/speeches/2005/20050211/default.htm.

(that is, "true" inflation of 0 percent), this would require conventionally measured rates of inflation of at least 1 percent.

Finally, some economists believe that a small amount of inflation is necessary to "grease" our economic engine. The analysis in Chapter 14 indicated that technological change and shifts in product demand may require real wages in some industries or occupations to fall in an efficiently operating economy, even when real wages in other industries and occupations are rising. If inflation is positive, a worker's real wage will fall whenever her nominal wage rises by less than the rate of inflation. If, for example, her nominal wage rises by 4 percent but prices rise by 5 percent, her real wage (that is, the amount of goods and services she can buy with her earnings) will fall. If, however, inflation is 0 percent and prices are not changing, the only way in which a worker's real wage can fall is if her nominal wage itself falls. Some evidence suggests that workers will strenuously resist cuts in their nominal wages.[5] They seem to be less resistant to having their nominal wages rise by a smaller percent than inflation even though this, too, reduces their real wage. Consequently, inflation can provide the "grease" required to reduce real wages in some industries and achieve economic efficiency.[6] Critics of the "grease" theory, however, argue that workers will become less resistant to nominal wage cuts at very low or zero rates of inflation. In a low inflation environment, nominal wage cuts would, of necessity, be more common and workers would get used to the idea. ◆

Was inflation almost too low in 2002–2003?

By late 2002, some Fed policymakers began to worry that inflation might actually be too low. Minutes of the Federal Reserve's September 24, 2002, Federal Open Market Committee meeting indicate that committee members were concerned that continuing weakness in the U.S. economy was likely to lead to "quite low and perhaps declining inflation" well into 2003.[7] With prices of consumer goods rising only about 1.5 percent from September 2001 to September 2002, members noted that "further sizable disinflation . . . could create problems for the implementation of monetary policy through conventional means in the event of an adverse shock to the economy."

During 2001 and 2002 the Federal Reserve had reduced the federal funds rate to 1.75 percent, the lowest level in four decades, in an attempt to provide economic stimulus to an economy slowly emerging from recession. Why did low inflation and a low federal funds rate create a potential problem for the Fed?

As pointed out in Chapter 19, business and consumer spending respond to real interest rates, not nominal interest rates. With a federal funds rate of 1.75 percent and an inflation rate of 1.5 percent, the resulting real rate of interest—the difference between the nominal interest rate and the inflation rate—was already down to 0.25 percent. If the Fed was forced in the future to stimulate aggregate spending further in response to a negative economywide spending shock, it might need to reduce the real rate of interest below 0 percent, which, as we have learned in our discussion of a 0 percent target for inflation, requires a positive rate of inflation. Thus, if the inflation rate fell to 0 percent, the Fed's ability to conduct expansionary monetary policy to offset a recessionary gap would be limited. Indeed, partly as a preemptive measure to prevent further economic weakening

[5]This does not mean that nominal wages never fall. Many workers in the airline industry, for example, have had to accept lower nominal wages as their employers compete with newer low-cost airlines such as Southwest and Jet Blue.

[6]George A. Akerlof, William T. Dickens, and George L. Perry, "The Macroeconomics of Low Inflation," *Brookings Papers on Economic Activity*, No. 1 (1996), pp. 1–76.

[7]Minutes from the Federal Reserve's September 2002 FOMC meeting are available online at http://www.federalreserve.gov/fomc/minutes/20020924.htm.

and declines in inflation, the Fed acted at its next meeting, in November 2002, to cut the federal funds rate to 1.25 percent, and it was reduced even further, to 1.0 percent, in June 2003.

Even if the federal funds rate were reduced all the way to 0 percent, however, Fed officials at the time also noted that the Fed would still have options available to stimulate aggregate spending. Although the federal funds rate is a very short-term interest rate, large portions of investment and especially mortgage lending are influenced more by long-term interest rates. Long-term rates are typically higher than and may not move in concert with the federal funds rate. If the Fed wanted to spur investment and the federal funds rate was pushed to zero, it could offer to buy large quantities of long-term U.S. Treasury bonds. Recall from Chapter 17 that bond prices and interest rates move in opposite directions. Consequently, if the Fed bought long-term bonds, bond prices would rise and long-term interest rates would fall. Alternatively, a central bank could buy other financial assets. For example, some central banks, although not the Fed, are allowed to buy stocks. Central bank purchases of stocks would increase stock prices and household wealth and might stimulate consumption. When short-term interest rates fell to zero in Japan, for example, the Bank of Japan bought a limited amount of stocks from Japanese banks that were in financial trouble.

Another option might be for the Fed to commit itself to keeping both the current and future federal funds rate very low. This policy, which was actually implemented by the Bank of Japan in its "zero interest rate policy" (called ZIRP), might give some firms the confidence to invest today, which would increase spending and raise output. By using these "nontraditional" monetary policy tools, the Fed could, if necessary, stimulate the economy even if the federal funds rate fell to 0 percent. However, these alternative tools are largely untested and would be difficult to apply with precision. Hence, the Fed and most other central banks try to keep inflation from falling so low that achieving a negative real interest rate is impossible. ◆

CENTRAL BANK REPUTATION

Ultimately, credibility can be won and maintained only by performance, and a central bank's performance will depend partly on its reputation as being an "inflation hawk" or an "inflation dove." An **inflation hawk** is someone who is committed to achieving and maintaining low inflation, even at some short-run cost in reduced output and employment. An **inflation dove** is someone who is not strongly committed to achieving and maintaining low inflation.

inflation hawk someone who is committed to achieving and maintaining low inflation, even at some short-run cost in reduced output and employment

inflation dove someone who is not strongly committed to achieving and maintaining low inflation

Inflation hawks believe that low and stable inflation allows the economy to grow more rapidly in the long run and therefore will be worth the possible short-run cost. Somewhat paradoxically, inflation hawks also may achieve more stable output and employment, even in the short run. Central banks that have acquired reputations as an inflation hawk will find it easier to anchor inflationary expectations. As we have learned, anchored expectations reduce the inflationary impact of an inflation shock by minimizing the second-round effects of that shock. Recall that anchored expectations also increase the speed with which short-run aggregate supply shifts down following an adverse inflation shock or an aggregate demand shock. Consequently, by anchoring expectations, a central bank that is viewed as an inflation hawk may be better able to stabilize output at potential GDP, even in the short run.

But how does a central bank acquire a reputation as an inflation hawk? Some central bankers acquire this reputation only after conducting monetary policy like an inflation hawk. Sometimes, however, the president can select people to serve on the Fed who already have acquired reputations as inflation hawks, based on their professional or academic backgrounds. Jimmy Carter's appointment of Paul Volcker as chair of the Fed is a famous example of a chair coming to the Fed with a well-established reputation as an inflation hawk.

RECAP — INFLATIONARY EXPECTATIONS AND CREDIBILITY

Macroeconomic performance may be improved if expectations of inflation are anchored. Anchored expectations, in turn, depend on the extent to which a central bank's anti-inflation pronouncements are viewed as credible. Several institutional characteristics may help to enhance a central bank's credibility: the extent to which the central bank is independent from the executive and legislative branches of the government, the announcement of a numerical inflation target, and the reputation of the central bank as an "inflation hawk."

- Inflation also may arise from an aggregate supply shock, either an inflation shock or a shock to potential output. An inflation shock is a sudden change in the normal behavior of inflation, unrelated to the nation's output gap. An example of an inflation shock is a run-up in energy and food prices large enough to raise the overall price level. An inflation shock creates stagflation, a combination of recession and higher inflation.
- Stagflation poses a difficult dilemma for policymakers. If they take no action, eventually inflation will subside and output will recover, but in the interim, the economy may suffer a protracted period of recession. If they use monetary or fiscal policy to increase aggregate demand, they will shorten the recession but also may lock in the higher level of inflation.
- A shock to potential output is a sharp change in potential output. Like an adverse inflation shock, an adverse shock to potential output results in both higher inflation and lower output. Because lower potential output implies that productive capacity has fallen, however, output does not recover following a shock to potential output, as it eventually does following an inflation shock.

SUMMARY

- This chapter developed the aggregate demand–aggregate supply (AD-AS) model. This model shows how inflation and output are determined simultaneously and how output and inflation change over time. The *AS-AD* diagram is the graphical tool used to apply the AD-AS model. **LO3**
- The aggregate demand (*AD*) curve shows the relationship between inflation and short-run equilibrium output. The *AD* curve slopes downward because of the Fed's monetary policy rule: when inflation rises, the Fed raises real interest rates and this causes planned spending and short-run output to fall. For any given value of inflation, an exogenous increase in spending raises short-run equilibrium output, shifting the *AD* curve to the right. Likewise, an exogenous decline in spending shifts the *AD* curve to the left. The *AD* curve also can be shifted by a change in the Fed's monetary policy rule. Specifically, if the Fed tightens monetary policy, the *AD* curve will shift to the left and if the Fed loosens monetary policy, the *AD* curve will shift to the right. **LO1**
- The aggregate supply (*AS*) curve shows the relationship between the rate of inflation and short-run equilibrium output given current inflation expectations and holding all other factors constant. In low-inflation industrial economies like the United States today, inflation tends to be inertial, or slow to adjust to changes in the economy. This inertial behavior reflects the fact that inflation depends in part on people's expectations of future inflation, which in turn depend on their recent experience with inflation. Long-term wage and price contracts tend to "build in" the effects of people's expectations for multiyear periods. The *AS* curve slopes upward because actual inflation is related to the gap between actual output and potential output: when output is below potential, actual inflation is below expected inflation and when output is above potential, actual inflation is above expected inflation. **LO2**
- The economy is in short-run equilibrium when there is either an expansionary gap or a recessionary gap; graphically, this is where the *AD* curve and the *AS*

curve intersect at a point either to the left or to the right of the long-run aggregate supply (*LRAS*) curve. The economy is in long-run equilibrium when actual output is equal to potential output and actual inflation equals expected inflation; graphically, this is where the *AD* curve, the *AS* curve, and the *LRAS* curve intersect at a single point. **LO3**

- Inflation adjusts gradually to move the economy from short-run equilibrium to long-run equilibrium (a phenomenon called the economy's self-correcting tendency). Inflation rises to eliminate an expansionary gap and falls to eliminate a recessionary gap. The more rapid the self-correction process, the smaller the need for active stabilization policies to eliminate output gaps. In practice, the larger the output gap, the more useful such policies are. **LO4**
- Changes in exogenous spending shift the aggregate demand curve. In response, the Fed can maintain stable inflation and output by adjusting its target real interest rate to the real interest rate at which saving equals investment in the long run. Supply shocks, such as inflation shocks, however, force the Fed to choose between maintaining inflation and stabilizing output. If inflationary expectations are anchored, the return to potential output following a supply shock will occur more rapidly. **LO5, LO6**
- Changes in the core rate of inflation allow the Fed to determine whether an inflation shock has changed inflationary expectations and led to further changes in wages and nonoil and nonfood prices, which are sometimes called the second-round effects of the inflation shocks. If the core rate of inflation does not change, the effects of the supply shock on inflation are more likely to be temporary. **LO6**
- Anchored inflationary expectations will improve economic performance in the long run and also may reduce the volatility of output and inflation in the short run. Inflationary expectations are more likely to be anchored if the central bank's policies are viewed as credible and the public believes the central bank's promises to keep inflation low. **LO6**

■ KEY TERMS ■

accommodating policy (625)
aggregate demand (*AD*) curve (610)
aggregate supply (*AS*) curve (615)
aggregate supply shock (627)
anchored inflationary expectations (629)
central bank independence (631)
core rate of inflation (630)
credibility of monetary policy (631)
easing monetary policy (613)
exogenous changes in spending (611)
inflation dove (635)
inflation hawk (635)
inflation shock (620)
long-run aggregate supply (*LRAS*) line (608)
long-run equilibrium (621)
short-run equilibrium (621)
tightening monetary policy (613)

■ REVIEW QUESTIONS ■

1. What two variables are related by the aggregate demand (*AD*) curve? Explain how the behavior of the Fed helps to determine the slope of this curve. **LO1**
2. State how each of the following affects the *AD* curve and explain: **LO1**
   a. An increase in government purchases.
   b. A cut in taxes.
   c. A decline in planned investment spending by firms.
   d. A decision by the Fed to increase its target rate of inflation.
3. Why does the overall rate of inflation tend to adjust more slowly than prices of commodities, such as oil or grain? **LO2**
4. Discuss the relationship between output gaps and inflation. How is this relationship captured in the *AS* curve? **LO2**
5. Sketch an *AD-AS* diagram depicting an economy away from long-run equilibrium. Indicate the economy's short-run equilibrium point. Discuss how the economy reaches long-run equilibrium over a period of time. Illustrate the process in your diagram. **LO3**

6. True or false: The economy's self-correcting tendency makes active use of stabilization policy unnecessary. Explain. **LO4**
7. Suppose there is a sudden increase in oil prices. What will be the effect on output and inflation in the short run? What is the "dilemma" faced by the Fed as a result of the adverse inflation shock? **LO5**
8. What are anchored inflationary expectations and how do they reduce the cost of an adverse inflation shock? **LO6**

▪ PROBLEMS ▪

1. For each of the following events, use an *AD-AS* diagram to show the short-run and long-run effects on output and inflation. Assume the economy starts in long-run equilibrium. **LO1, LO2, LO3, LO4**
   a. An increase in consumer confidence leads to higher consumption spending.
   b. The government reduces income taxes.
   c. The Fed loosens monetary policy.
   d. Oil prices drop sharply.
   e. A war increases government purchases.
2. Suppose that the government cuts taxes in response to a recessionary gap, but because of legislative delays the tax cut is not put in place for 18 months. Assuming that the government's objective is to stabilize output and inflation, use an *AD-AS* diagram to illustrate how this policy action might actually prove to be counterproductive. **LO1, LO2, LO3, LO4**
3. Suppose that a permanent increase in oil prices both creates an inflationary shock and reduces potential output. Use an *AD-AS* diagram to show the effects of the oil price increase on output and inflation in the short run and the long run, assuming that there is no policy response. What happens if the Fed responds to the oil price increase by adopting a tighter monetary policy? **LO2, LO3, LO4**
4. An economy is initially in recession. Using an *AD-AS* diagram, show the process of adjustment under each of the following policies. Discuss the costs and benefits of each approach in terms of output loss and inflation. **LO1, LO2, LO3, LO4**
   a. The Fed responds by adopting a looser monetary policy.
   b. The Fed does not change its monetary policy rule.
5. Suppose the economy is initially in long-run equilibrium. Due to a decline in house prices, suppose that consumers reduce their consumption spending. **LO5**
   a. Explain how the decline in consumer spending affects the *AD* curve.
   b. If the Fed does not change its monetary policy rule, how will the Fed react to the decline in consumer spending? Use an *AD-AS* diagram to illustrate and explain your answer.
   c. Now, in addition to the decline in consumer spending, suppose that the economy experiences an adverse inflation shock.
      i. Explain how the adverse inflation shock affects the *AS* curve.
      ii. Discuss, using *AD-AS* diagrams, what choices the Fed now must make regarding monetary policy. (Hint: Think about whether or not they should tighten monetary policy and trace through the effects of tightening versus not tightening policy.)
6. Using the theory presented in this chapter, explain why the adoption of a tighter, more anti-inflationary monetary policy might be politically unpopular. **LO3, LO6**

7. Suppose there is a large increase in oil or food prices. **LO6**
   a. If the core rate of inflation remains unchanged, what might the Fed infer about inflationary expectations and the second-round effects of the inflation shock? How might it respond?
   b. If the core rate of inflation rises substantially, what might the Fed infer about inflationary expectations and the second-round effects of the inflation shock? How might it respond?

8. What are the advantages of having an independent central bank? Describe the institutional features that make a central bank independent. **LO6**

ANSWERS TO IN-CHAPTER EXERCISES

21.1 a. At the current level of inflation, output, and real interest rate, an exogenous reduction in business spending on new capital will reduce planned investment, causing a reduction in short-run equilibrium output. Because output has fallen for a given level of inflation, the decrease in business spending leads to a leftward shift in the *AD* curve.
b. At the current level of inflation, output, and real interest rare, a reduction in federal income taxes increases consumers' disposable income $(Y - T)$, which leads to an exogenous increase in consumption at all income levels and leads to an increase in short-run equilibrium output. Because output has increased for a given level of inflation, the reduction in income taxes leads to a rightward shift in the *AD* curve. **LO2**

21.2 a. If inflation is expected to be 2 percent next year and workers are expecting a 2 percent increase in their real wages, then they will expect, and ask for, a 4 percent increase in their nominal wages.
b. If inflation is expected to be 4 percent next year, rather than 2 percent, workers will expect, and ask for, a 6 percent increase in their nominal wages.
c. If wage costs rise, firms will need to increase the prices of their goods and services to cover their increased costs, leading to an increase in inflation. In part b, when expected inflation was 4 percent, firms will be faced with larger increases in nominal wages than in part a, when expected inflation was only 2 percent. Thus, we can expect firms to raise prices by more when expected inflation is 4 percent than when expected inflation is 2 percent. From this example, we can conclude that increased inflationary expectations lead to higher inflation. **LO2**

21.3 If the inflation rate is high, the economy will tend to stay in this high-inflation state due to expectations of high inflation and the existence of long-term wage and price contracts, while if the inflation rate is low, the economy will likewise tend to stay in this low-inflation state for similar reasons. However, since high inflation rates impose economic costs on society, as pointed out in Chapter 13, the Federal Reserve has an incentive to avoid the high-inflation state by keeping inflation low, which helps to maintain people's expectations of low inflation and leads to lower future inflation rates—perpetuating the "virtuous circle" illustrated in Figure 21.7. **LO1, LO2**

21.4 The graph should look the same as Figure 21.9 except the *AS* curve shifts downward. **LO2**

21.5 The economy is initially in equilibrium with output Y_1 equal to potential output and inflation π_1 equal to expected inflation and the Fed's long-run inflation target. ① A sudden decrease in spending shifts the *AD* curve from AD_1 to AD_2. This causes output to decrease from Y_1 to Y_2. This opens a recessionary gap and causes the inflation rate to fall from π_1 to π_2. ② Since inflation is now below its expected rate, *AS* will shift to the right from AS_1 to AS_2. The Fed will follow its policy rule and lower the real interest rate as inflation falls from π_2 to π_3, which causes output to return to potential output Y_1. **LO2**

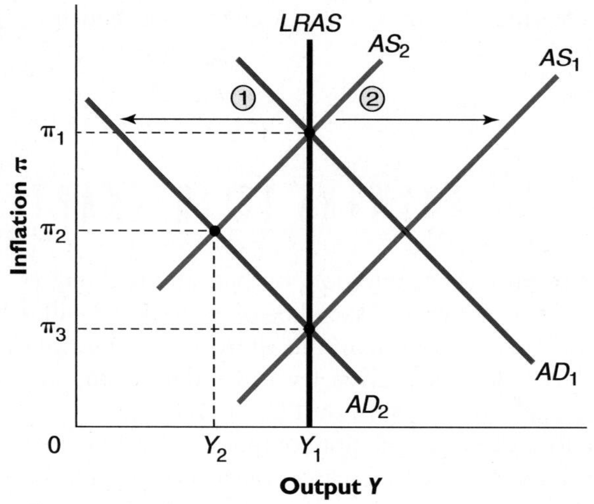

PART 8

THE INTERNATIONAL ECONOMY

One of the defining economic trends of recent decades is the "globalization" of national economies. Since the mid-1980s, the value of international trade has increased at nearly twice the rate of world GDP, and the volume of international financial transactions has expanded at many times that rate. From a long-run perspective, the rapidly increasing integration of national economies we see today is not unprecedented: Before World War I, Great Britain was the center of an international economic system that was in many ways nearly as "globalized" as our own, with extensive international trade and lending. But even the most far-seeing nineteenth-century merchant or banker would be astonished by the sense of *immediacy* that recent revolutionary changes in communications and transportation have imparted to international economic relations. For example, teleconferencing and the internet now permit people on opposite sides of the globe to conduct "face-to-face" business negotiations and transactions.

We introduced international dimensions of the economy at several points in this book already (for example, in our discussion of comparative advantage and trade in Chapter 2 and our analysis of the labor market effects of globalization in Chapter 14). Chapter 22 focuses on two additional topics in international economics. The first topic is the exchange rate; understanding the exchange rate is important since it plays a key role in determining patterns of trade. Furthermore, as we will see, the type of exchange rate system a country adopts has important implications for the effectiveness of its macroeconomic policies. The second topic is the relationship among international trade in goods, international capital flows, and domestic capital formation. We will focus on the determinants of international capital flows and show how a country can augment its domestic capital formation by borrowing from abroad.

CHAPTER

22

Exchange Rates, International Trade, and Capital Flows

LEARNING OBJECTIVES

After reading this chapter, you should be able to:

1. Define the nominal exchange rate and use supply and demand to analyze how the nominal exchange rate is determined in the short run.
2. Distinguish between flexible exchange rates and fixed exchange rates, and discuss the advantages and disadvantages of each system.
3. Define the real exchange rate and show how it is related to the prices of goods across pairs of countries.
4. Understand the law of one price and apply the purchasing power parity theory of exchange rates to long-run exchange rate determination.
5. Analyze the factors that determine international capital flows and how these flows affect domestic saving and the domestic real interest rate.
6. Use the relationship between domestic saving and the trade balance to understand how domestic saving, the trade balance, and net capital inflows are related.

Two Americans visiting London were commiserating over their problems understanding English currency. "Pounds, shillings, tuppence, thrup-pence, bob, and quid, it's driving me crazy," said the first American. "This morning it took me 20 minutes to figure out how much to pay the taxi driver."

The second American was more upbeat. "Actually," he said, "since I adopted my new system, I haven't had any problems at all."

Foreign currency conundrums.

The first American looked interested. "What's your new system?"

"Well," replied the second, "now, whenever I take a taxi, I just give the driver all the English money I have. And would you believe it, I have got the fare exactly right every time!"

Dealing with unfamiliar currencies—and translating the value of foreign money into dollars—is a problem every international traveler faces.[1] The traveler's problem is complicated by the fact that *exchange rates*—the rates at which one country's money trades for another—may change unpredictably. Thus, the number of British pounds, Russian rubles, Japanese yen, or Australian dollars that a U.S. dollar can buy may vary over time, sometimes quite a lot.

The economic consequences of variable exchange rates are much broader than their impact on travel and tourism, however. For example, the competitiveness of U.S. exports depends in part on the prices of U.S. goods in terms of foreign currencies, which in turn depend on the exchange rate between the U.S. dollar and those currencies. Likewise, the prices Americans pay for imported goods depend in part on the value of the dollar relative to the currencies of the countries that produce those goods. Exchange rates also affect the value of financial investments made across national borders. For countries that are heavily dependent on trade and international capital flows—the majority of the world's nations—fluctuations in the exchange rate may have a significant economic impact.

This chapter discusses exchange rates, international trade and international capital flows, and their effects on the broader economy. We will start by introducing the nominal exchange rate—the rate at which one national currency trades for another. Next we will turn to the question of how exchange rates are determined in the short run. Exchange rates may be divided into two broad categories: flexible and fixed. The value of a flexible exchange rate is determined freely in the market for national currencies, known as the foreign exchange market. In contrast, the value of a fixed exchange rate is set by the government at a constant level. Because most large industrial countries, including the United States, have a flexible exchange rate, we will focus on that case first. We show that a country's monetary policy plays a particularly important role in determining the exchange rate. Furthermore, in an open economy with a flexible exchange rate, the exchange rate becomes a tool of monetary policy, in much the same way as the real interest rate.

Although most large industrial countries have a flexible exchange rate, many small and developing economies fix their exchange rates, so we will consider the case of fixed exchange rates as well. We will explain first how a country's government (usually, its central bank) maintains a fixed exchange rate at the officially determined level. We will then discuss the relative merits of fixed and flexible exchange rates. We close our discussion of exchange rates by introducing the real exchange rate—the rate at which one country's goods trade for another's—and discussing how exchange rates are determined in the long run.

Finally, we examine data on U.S. international trade in goods and services, and analyze how trade in goods and services is directly connected with international capital flows. Specifically, we analyze how for many countries, including the United States, foreign saving provides an important supplement to domestic saving as a means of financing capital formation.

EXCHANGE RATES

The economic benefits of trade between nations in goods, services, and assets are similar to the benefits of trade within a nation. In both cases, trade in goods and services permits greater specialization and efficiency, whereas trade in assets allows financial investors to earn higher returns while providing funds for worthwhile

[1]However, British money today is less complicated to understand than suggested by the introductory story. In 1971 the British switched to a decimal monetary system, under which each pound is worth 100 pence. At that time, the traditional British system, under which a pound equaled 20 shillings and each shilling equaled 12 pence, was abandoned.

capital projects. However, there is a difference between the two cases. Trade in goods, services, and assets *within* a nation normally involves a single currency—dollars, yen, pesos, or whatever the country's official form of money happens to be—whereas trade *between* nations usually involves dealing in different currencies. So, for example, if an American resident wants to purchase an automobile manufactured in South Korea, she (or more likely, the automobile dealer) must first trade dollars for the Korean currency, called the won. The Korean car manufacturer is then paid in won. Similarly, an Argentine who wants to purchase shares in a U.S. company (a U.S. financial asset) must first trade his Argentine pesos for dollars and then use the dollars to purchase the shares.

NOMINAL EXCHANGE RATES

Because international transactions generally require that one currency be traded for another, the relative values of different currencies are an important factor in international economic relations. The rate at which two currencies can be traded for each other is called the **nominal exchange rate,** or more simply the *exchange rate,* between the two currencies. For example, if one U.S. dollar can be exchanged for 110 Japanese yen, the nominal exchange rate between the U.S. and Japanese currencies is 110 yen per dollar. Each country has many nominal exchange rates, one corresponding to each currency against which its own currency is traded. Thus, the dollar's value can be quoted in terms of English pounds, Swedish kroner, Israeli shekels, Russian rubles, or dozens of other currencies.

nominal exchange rate the rate at which two currencies can be traded for each other

Table 22.1 gives exchange rates between the dollar and seven other important currencies as of the close of business in New York City on March 20, 2008. As Table 22.1 shows, exchange rates can be expressed either as the amount of foreign currency needed to purchase one U.S. dollar (left column) or as the number of U.S. dollars needed to purchase one unit of the foreign currency (right column). These two ways of expressing the exchange rate are equivalent: each is the reciprocal of the other. For example, on March 20, 2008, the U.S.–Canadian exchange rate could have been expressed either as 1.0265 Canadian dollars per U.S. dollar or as 0.9742 U.S. dollar per Canadian dollar, where 0.9742 = 1/1.0265.

TABLE 22.1
Nominal Exchange Rates for the U.S. Dollar

Country	Foreign currency/U.S. dollar	U.S. dollars/foreign currency
United Kingdom (pound)	0.5045	1.9823
Canada (Canadian dollar)	1.0265	0.9742
Mexico (peso)	10.7230	0.0933
Japan (yen)	98.79	0.0101
Switzerland (Swiss franc)	1.0107	0.9894
South Korea (won)	1009.15	0.0010
European Union (euro)	0.6486	1.5417

Source: Federal Reserve Bank of New York, Rates for March 20, 2008, 12 noon.

We can also use the data in Table 22.1 to find the exchange rate between any pair of countries in the table. For example, suppose that you need to find the exchange rate between the British pound and the Canadian dollar. The table tells us that we can purchase one U.S. dollar for 1.0265 Canadian dollars; it also tells us that we can buy one U.S. dollar for 0.5045 British pound. This implies that

1.0265 Canadian dollars = 0.5045 British pound

Thus, we can find the exchange rate between British pounds and Canadian dollars in two ways. First, we can find out how much one Canadian dollar is worth in terms of British pounds by dividing both sides of the above equation by 1.0265:

$$1 \text{ Canadian dollar} = \frac{0.5045}{1.0265} \text{ British pound} = 0.4915 \text{ British pound}$$

In other words, you could buy 0.4915 British pound for 1 Canadian dollar on March 20, 2008. Alternatively, we can divide both sides of the first equation by 0.5045:

$$1 \text{ British pound} = \frac{1.0265}{0.5045} \text{ Canadian dollars} = 2.035 \text{ Canadian dollars}$$

That is, you could buy 2.035 Canadian dollars for 1 British pound on March 20, 2008.

EXERCISE 22.1

From the business section of a newspaper or an online source (try the Federal Reserve Bank of St. Louis FRED database, http://research.stlouis fed. org/fred2/), find recent quotations of the value of the U.S. dollar against the British pound, the Canadian dollar, and the Japanese yen. Based on these data, find the exchange rate (a) between the pound and the Canadian dollar and (b) between the Canadian dollar and the yen. Express the exchange rates you derive in two ways (e.g., both as pounds per Canadian dollar and as Canadian dollars per pound).

Figure 22.1 shows the nominal exchange rate for the U.S. dollar from 1973 to 2007. Rather than showing the value of the dollar relative to that of an individual foreign currency, such as the Japanese yen or the British pound, the figure expresses the value of the dollar as an average of its values against other major currencies. This average value of the dollar is measured relative to a base value of 100 in 1973. So, for example, a value of 120 for the dollar in a particular year implies that the dollar was 20 percent more valuable in that year, relative to other major currencies, than it was in 1973.

FIGURE 22.1
The U.S. Nominal Exchange Rate, 1973–2007.
This figure shows the value of the dollars as an average of its values against other major currencies, relative to a base value of 100 in 1973.

Source: Federal Reserve Bank of St. Louis, FRED database (http://research.stlouisfed.org/fred2/).

You can see from Figure 22.1 that the dollar's value has fluctuated over time, sometimes increasing (as in the period 1980–1985) and sometimes decreasing (as in 1985–1987 and 2002–2007). An increase in the value of a currency relative to other currencies is known as an **appreciation;** a decline in the value of a currency relative to other currencies is called a **depreciation.** So we can say that the dollar appreciated in 1980–1985 and depreciated in 1985–1987 and 2002–2007.

appreciation an increase in the value of a currency relative to other currencies

depreciation a decrease in the value of a currency relative to other currencies

We will use the symbol *e* to stand for a country's nominal exchange rate. Table 22.1 shows that we can express the exchange rate as either foreign currency units per unit of domestic currency or vice versa. The choice is arbitrary, but it is important because you need to be consistent whenever you are analyzing exchange rates. Thus, we will define *e* as the number of units of foreign currency that each unit of domestic currency will buy. For example, if we treat the United States as the "home" or "domestic" country and Japan as the "foreign" country, *e* will be defined as the number of Japanese yen that one U.S. dollar will buy. Defining the nominal exchange rate this way implies that an *increase* in *e* corresponds to an *appreciation,* or a strengthening, of the home currency since each unit of domestic currency will then buy more units of foreign currency. Similarly, a *decrease* in *e* implies *depreciation,* or weakening, of the home currency since each unit of domestic currency will buy fewer units of foreign currency.

FLEXIBLE VERSUS FIXED EXCHANGE RATES

Figure 22.1 shows that the exchange rate between the U.S. dollar and other currencies isn't constant but varies continually. Indeed, changes in the value of the dollar occur daily, hourly, even minute by minute. Such fluctuations in the value of a currency are normal for countries like the United States, which have a *flexible* or *floating exchange rate.* The value of a **flexible exchange rate** is not officially fixed but varies according to the supply and demand for the currency in the **foreign exchange market**—the market on which currencies of various nations are traded for one another. We will discuss the factors that determine the supply and demand for currencies shortly.

flexible exchange rate an exchange rate whose value is not officially fixed but varies according to the supply and demand for the currency in the foreign exchange market

foreign exchange market the market on which currencies of various nations are traded for one another

Some countries do not allow their currency values to vary with market conditions but instead maintain a *fixed exchange rate.* The value of a **fixed exchange rate** is set by official government policy. (A government that establishes a fixed exchange rate typically determines the exchange rate's value independently, but sometimes exchange rates are set according to an agreement among a number of governments.) Some countries fix their exchange rates in terms of the U.S. dollar (Hong Kong, for example), but there are other possibilities. Many African countries fix the value of their currencies in terms of the euro, the currency of the European Union. Under the gold standard, which many countries used until its collapse during the Great Depression, currency values were fixed in terms of ounces of gold.

fixed exchange rate an exchange rate whose value is set by official government policy

RECAP | NOMINAL EXCHANGE RATES

- The nominal exchange rate between two currencies is the rate at which the currencies can be traded for each other. More precisely, the nominal exchange rate *e* for any given country is the number of units of foreign currency that can be bought for one unit of the domestic currency.
- An appreciation is an increase in the value of a currency relative to other currencies (a rise in *e*); a depreciation is a decline in a currency's value (a fall in *e*).
- An exchange rate can be either flexible—meaning that it varies freely according to supply and demand for the currency in the foreign exchange market—or fixed, meaning that its value is established by official government policy.

THE DETERMINATION OF THE EXCHANGE RATE IN THE SHORT RUN

Countries that have flexible exchange rates, such as the United States, see the international values of their currencies change continually. What determines the value of the nominal exchange rate at any point in time? In this section, we use supply and demand analysis to answer this question for the short run. Our focus for the moment is on flexible exchange rates, whose values are determined by the foreign exchange market. Later in the chapter we discuss the case of fixed exchange rates, the costs and benefits of each type of exchange rate, and the determination of exchange rates in the long run.

A SUPPLY AND DEMAND ANALYSIS

In this section, we analyze the foreign exchange market and discuss the factors that affect the supply of and demand for dollars, and thus the U.S. exchange rate. As we will see, dollars are demanded in the foreign exchange market by foreigners who seek to purchase U.S. goods, services, and assets. Similarly, dollars are supplied by U.S. residents who need foreign currencies to buy foreign goods, services, and assets. The market equilibrium exchange rate is the value of the dollar that equates the number of dollars supplied and demanded in the foreign exchange market.

Before proceeding, we need to be careful about our terminology. In Chapter 20, we analyzed how the supply of money (controlled by the Fed) and the demand for money by the public determine the nominal interest rate. However, the supply of and demand for money in the domestic economy, as presented in that chapter, are *not* equivalent to the supply and demand for dollars in the foreign exchange market. The foreign exchange market is the market in which the currencies of various nations are traded for one another. The supply of dollars to the foreign exchange market is *not* the same as the money supply set by the Fed; rather, it is the number of dollars U.S. households and firms offer to trade for other currencies. Likewise, the demand for dollars in the foreign exchange market is *not* the same as the domestic demand for money, but is the number of dollars holders of foreign currencies seek to buy. To understand the distinction, keep in mind that while the Fed determines the total supply of dollars available in the U.S. economy, a dollar is not supplied to the foreign exchange market until a holder of dollars, such as an American household or firm, offers to trade it for foreign currency.

The Supply of Dollars

Anyone who holds dollars, from an international bank to a Russian citizen whose dollars are buried in the backyard, is a potential supplier of dollars to the foreign exchange market. In practice, however, the principal suppliers of dollars to the foreign exchange market are U.S. households and firms. Why would a U.S. household or firm want to supply dollars in exchange for foreign currency? There are two major reasons. First, a U.S. household or firm may need foreign currency to *purchase foreign goods or services.* For example, a U.S. automobile importer may need yen to purchase Japanese cars, or an American tourist may need yen to make purchases in Tokyo. Second, a U.S. household or firm may need foreign currency *to purchase foreign assets.* For example, an American mutual fund may wish to acquire stocks issued by Japanese companies, or an individual U.S. saver may want to purchase Japanese government bonds. Because Japanese assets are priced in yen, the U.S. household or firm will need to trade dollars for yen to acquire these assets.

The supply of dollars to the foreign exchange market is illustrated by the upward-sloping curve in Figure 22.2. We will focus on the market in which dollars

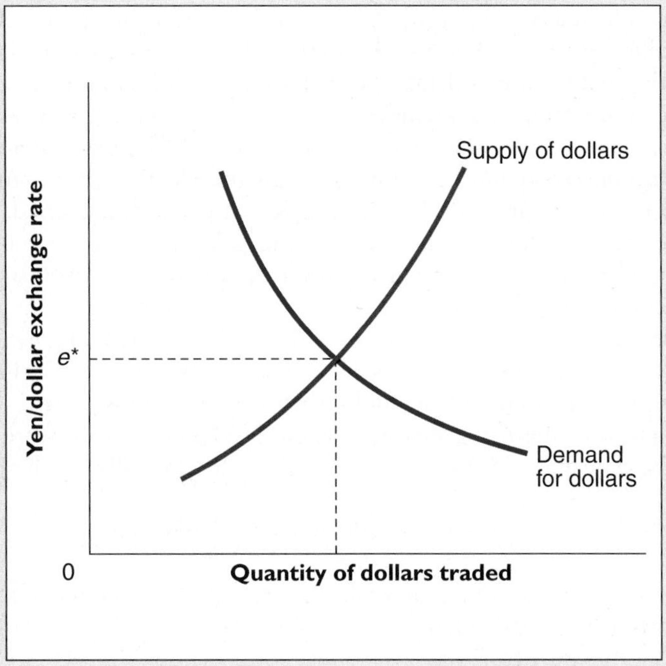

FIGURE 22.2
The Supply and Demand for Dollars in the Yen–Dollar Market.
The supply of dollars to the foreign exchange market is upward-sloping because an increase in the number of yen offered for each dollar makes Japanese goods, services, and assets more attractive to U.S. buyers. Similarly, the demand for dollars is downward-sloping because holders of yen will be less willing to buy dollars the more expensive they are in terms of yen. The *market equilibrium exchange rate* e^* equates the quantities of dollars supplied and demanded.

are traded for Japanese yen, but bear in mind that similar markets exist for every other pair of traded currencies. The vertical axis of the figure shows the U.S.–Japanese exchange rate as measured by the number of yen that can be purchased with each dollar. The horizontal axis shows the number of dollars being traded in the yen–dollar market.

The supply curve for dollars is upward-sloping, indicating that the more yen each dollar can buy, the more dollars people are willing to supply to the foreign exchange market. Why? At given prices for Japanese goods, services, and assets, the more yen a dollar can buy, the cheaper those goods, services, and assets will be in dollar terms.

For example, suppose a video game costs 5,000 yen in Japan and a dollar can buy 100 yen; the dollar price of the video game will be

$$5{,}000 \text{ yen} \times \$1/100 \text{ yen} = \$50.$$[2]

If, however, the yen price of a dollar rises to 200 yen, the dollar price of the same video game that costs 5,000 yen in Japan will then be

$$5{,}000 \text{ yen} \times \$1/200 \text{ yen} = \$25.$$

If lower dollar prices will induce Americans to increase their total dollar expenditures on Japanese goods, services, and assets, a higher yen–dollar exchange rate will increase the supply of dollars to the foreign exchange market. Thus, the supply curve for dollars is upward-sloping.

The Demand for Dollars

In the yen–dollar foreign exchange market, demanders of dollars are those who wish to acquire dollars in exchange for yen. Most demanders of dollars in the

[2]Recall that an exchange rate of one dollar per 100 yen is the same as 100 yen per dollar. We are writing it the first way in this example so that the yen will cancel when we perform the multiplication and we are left with the dollar price.

yen–dollar market are Japanese households and firms, although anyone who happens to hold yen is free to trade them for dollars. Why demand dollars? The reasons for acquiring dollars are analogous to those for acquiring yen. First, households and firms that hold yen will demand dollars *so that they can purchase U.S. goods and services*. For example, a Japanese firm that wants to license U.S.-produced software needs dollars to pay the required fees, and a Japanese student studying in an American university must pay tuition in dollars. The firm or the student can acquire the necessary dollars only by offering yen in exchange. Second, households and firms demand dollars *in order to purchase U.S. assets*. The purchase of Hawaiian real estate by a Japanese company or the acquisition of Microsoft stock by a Japanese pension fund are two examples.

The demand curve for dollars will be downward-sloping, as illustrated in Figure 22.2. The quantity of dollars demanded will be low when dollars are expensive in terms of yen and high when dollars are cheap in terms of yen.

Suppose the licensing fee for a piece of U.S.-produced software is \$30. If it costs a Japanese business 200 yen to buy \$1, the software will cost the Japanese

$$\$30 \times 200 \text{ yen}/\$1 = 6{,}000 \text{ yen.}$$ [3]

If, however, the price of a dollar falls to 100 yen, the yen price of the same software that costs \$30 in the United States will then be

$$\$30 \times 100 \text{ yen}/\$1 = 3{,}000 \text{ yen.}$$

As the yen price per dollar falls, U.S. goods, services, and assets become cheaper and more attractive to the Japanese. They respond by buying more U.S. goods, services, and assets and thereby demanding more dollars.

The Market Equilibrium Value of the Dollar

As mentioned earlier, the United States maintains a flexible, or floating, exchange rate, which means that the value of the dollar is determined by the forces of supply and demand in the foreign exchange market. In Figure 22.2, the equilibrium value of the dollar is e^*, the yen–dollar exchange rate at which the quantity of dollars supplied equals the quantity of dollars demanded. In general, the **market equilibrium value of the exchange rate** is not constant but changes with shifts in the supply of and demand for dollars in the foreign exchange market.

market equilibrium value of the exchange rate the exchange rate that equates the quantities of the currency supplied and demanded in the foreign exchange market

CHANGES IN THE SUPPLY OF DOLLARS

Recall that people supply dollars to the yen–dollar foreign exchange market in order to purchase Japanese goods, services, and assets. Factors that affect the desire of U.S. households and firms to acquire Japanese goods, services, and assets therefore will affect the supply of dollars to the foreign exchange market. Some factors that will *increase* the supply of dollars, shifting the supply curve for dollars to the right, include

- An increased preference for Japanese goods. For example, suppose that Japanese firms produce some popular new consumer electronics. To acquire the yen needed to buy these goods, American importers will increase their supply of dollars to the foreign exchange market.
- An increase in U.S. real GDP. An increase in U.S. real GDP will raise the incomes of Americans, allowing them to consume more goods and services (recall

[3] In this calculation, we use the yen per dollar exchange rate so that the dollars cancel when we perform the multiplication and we are left with the price in yen.

the relationship between consumption and income we discussed in Chapter 19). Some part of this increase in consumption will take the form of goods imported from Japan. To buy more Japanese goods, Americans will supply more dollars to acquire the necessary yen.

- An increase in the real interest rate on Japanese assets or a decrease in the real interest rate on U.S. assets. Recall that U.S. households and firms acquire yen in order to purchase Japanese assets as well as goods and services. Other factors, such as risk, held constant, the higher the real interest rate paid on Japanese assets (or the lower the real interest rate paid on U.S. assets), the more Japanese assets Americans will choose to hold. To purchase additional Japanese assets, U.S. households and firms will supply more dollars to the foreign exchange market.

Supplying dollars, demanding yen.

Conversely, reduced demand for Japanese goods, a lower U.S. GDP, a lower real interest rate on Japanese assets, or a higher real interest rate on U.S. assets will *reduce* the number of yen Americans need, in turn reducing their supply of dollars to the foreign exchange market and shifting the supply curve for dollars to the left.

Suppose, for example, that Japanese firms come to dominate the video game market, with games that are more exciting and realistic than those produced in the United States. All else being equal, how will this change affect the relative value of the yen and the dollar?

The increased quality of Japanese video games will increase the demand for the games in the United States. To acquire the yen necessary to buy more Japanese video games, U.S. importers will supply more dollars to the foreign exchange market. As Figure 22.3 shows, the increased supply of dollars will reduce the value of the dollar. In other words, a dollar will buy fewer yen than it did before. At the same time, the yen will increase in value: A given number of yen will buy more dollars than it did before.

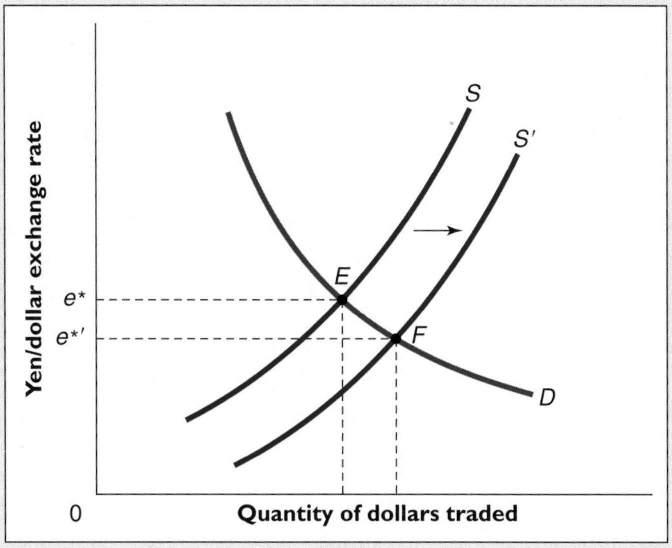

FIGURE 22.3
An Increase in the Supply of Dollars Lowers the Value of the Dollar.
Increased U.S. demand for Japanese video games forces Americans to supply more dollars to the foreign exchange market to acquire the yen they need to buy the games. The supply curve for dollars shifts from S to S', lowering the value of the dollar in terms of yen. The market equilibrium value of the exchange rate falls from e^* to $e^{*\prime}$.

EXERCISE 22.2

The United States goes into a recession, and real GDP falls. All else equal, how is this economic weakness likely to affect the value of the dollar?

CHANGES IN THE DEMAND FOR DOLLARS

The factors that change the demand for dollars in the foreign exchange market, and thus shift the dollar demand curve, are analogous to the factors that affect the supply of dollars. Factors that will *increase* the demand for dollars include

- An increased preference for U.S. goods by foreign customers. For example, Japanese airlines might find that U.S.-built aircraft are superior to others, and decide to expand the number of American-made planes in their fleets. To buy the American planes, Japanese airlines would demand more dollars on the foreign exchange market.
- An increase in real GDP abroad, which implies higher incomes abroad, and thus more demand for imports from the United States.
- An increase in the real interest rate on U.S. assets or a reduction in the real interest rate on Japanese assets would make U.S. assets more attractive to foreign savers. To acquire U.S. assets, Japanese savers would demand more dollars.

Does a Strong Currency Imply a Strong Economy?

Politicians and the public sometimes take pride in the fact that their national currency is "strong," meaning that its value in terms of other currencies is high or rising. Likewise, policymakers sometimes view a depreciating ("weak") currency as a sign of economic failure.

Contrary to popular impression, there is no simple connection between the strength of a country's currency and the strength of its economy. For example, Figure 22.1 shows that the value of the U.S. dollar relative to other major currencies was greater in 1973 than in the year 2007, though U.S. economic performance was considerably better in 2007 than in 1973, a period of deep recession and rising inflation. Indeed, the one period shown in Figure 22.1 during which the dollar rose markedly in value, 1980–1985, was a time of recession and high unemployment in the United States.

One reason a strong currency does not necessarily imply a strong economy is that an appreciating currency (an increase in e) tends to hurt a country's net exports. For example, if the dollar strengthens against the yen (that is, if a dollar buys more yen than before), Japanese goods will become cheaper in terms of dollars. The result may be that Americans prefer to buy Japanese goods rather than goods produced at home. Likewise, a stronger dollar implies that each yen buys fewer dollars, so exported U.S. goods become more expensive to Japanese consumers. As U.S. goods become more expensive in terms of yen, the willingness of Japanese consumers to buy U.S. exports declines. A strong dollar therefore may imply lower sales and profits for U.S. industries that export, as well as for U.S. industries (like automobile manufacturers) that compete with foreign firms for the domestic U.S. market.

MONETARY POLICY AND THE EXCHANGE RATE

Of the many factors that could influence a country's exchange rate, among the most important is the monetary policy of the country's central bank. Monetary policy affects the exchange rate primarily through its effect on the real interest rate.

Suppose the Fed is concerned about inflation and tightens U.S. monetary policy in response. The effects of this policy change on the value of the dollar are shown in Figure 22.4. Before the policy change, the equilibrium value of the exchange rate is e^*, at the intersection of supply curve S and the demand curve D (point E in the figure). The tightening of monetary policy raises the domestic U.S. real interest rate r, making U.S. assets, such as bonds, more attractive to both foreign and American financial investors. The increased willingness of foreign investors to buy U.S.

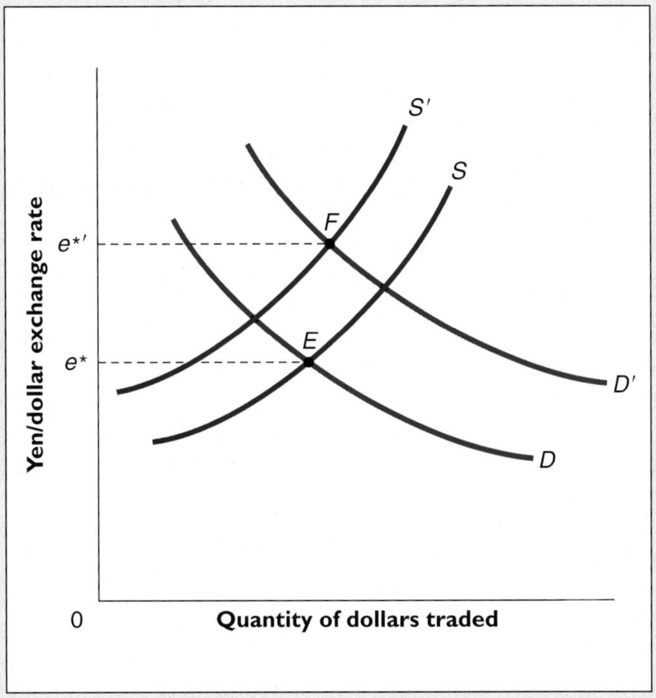

FIGURE 22.4
A Tightening of Monetary Policy Strengthens the Dollar.
Tighter monetary policy in the United States raises the domestic real interest rate, increasing the demand for U.S. assets by foreign and American savers. An increased demand for U.S. assets by foreigners increases the demand for dollars, shifting the demand curve rightward from D to D'. An increased demand for U.S. assets by American savers decreases the supply of dollars, shifting the supply curve to the left. The exchange rate appreciates from e^* to $e^{*\prime}$.

assets increases the demand for dollars, shifting the demand curve rightward from D to D'. The willingness of American investors to buy more U.S. assets (and presumably fewer foreign assets) decreases the supply of dollars and shifts the supply curve leftward from S to S'. The equilibrium moves from point E to point F, and the market equilibrium value of the dollar rises from e^* to $e^{*\prime}$.

In short, a tightening of monetary policy by the Fed raises the demand for dollars and reduces the supply of dollars, causing the dollar to appreciate. By similar logic, an easing of monetary policy, which reduces the real interest rate, would make U.S. assets, such as bonds, less attractive to both Americans and foreigners. This would weaken the demand for dollars but increase the supply of dollars (as Americans buy more foreign assets), causing the dollar to depreciate.

The appreciation of the dollar in the first half of the 1980s and the depreciation of the dollar between 2002 and 2007 were primarily the result of U.S. monetary policy. In particular, the Fed responded to the surge in inflation in the late 1970s by raising the real interest rate sharply in hopes of reducing aggregate demand and inflationary pressures. As a result, the real interest rate in the United States rose from negative values in 1979 and 1980 to more than 7 percent in 1983 and 1984 (see Figure 13.3). Attracted by these high real returns, U.S. and foreign savers rushed to buy U.S. assets, driving the value of the dollar up significantly. The Fed's attempt to bring down inflation was successful. By the middle of the 1980s, the Fed was able to ease U.S. monetary policy. The resulting decline in the real interest rate reduced the demand for U.S. assets, and thus for dollars, at which point the dollar fell back almost to its 1980 level.

Similarly, Figure 22.1 shows that the dollar depreciated substantially starting in early 2002. There are several reasons for this depreciation, but we will focus on two. First, the U.S. economy grew faster during this period than that of most of the countries to which we export (Canada, Mexico, and Japan). Consequently, the supply of dollars (to pay for imports) increased. Second, as we discussed in Chapter 20, the Fed reduced the federal funds rate from 6 percent in early 2001 to 1 percent in June 2003 and kept it at 1 percent until June 2004. Although the steep decline in the federal funds rate was not accompanied by equal declines in long-term nominal and real interest rates, they, too, fell. The decline in U.S. real interest rates reduced the attractiveness of U.S. bonds to both Americans and foreigners. Consequently, the supply of dollars rose and the demand for dollars fell, contributing to the depreciation of the dollar.

THE EXCHANGE RATE AS A TOOL OF MONETARY POLICY

In a closed economy, monetary policy affects aggregate demand solely through the real interest rate. For example, by raising the real interest rate, a tight monetary policy reduces consumption and investment spending. In an open economy with a flexible exchange rate, the exchange rate serves as another channel for monetary policy, one that reinforces the effects of the real interest rate.

To illustrate, suppose that policymakers are concerned about inflation and decide to restrain aggregate demand. To do so, they increase the real interest rate, reducing consumption and investment spending. But, as Figure 22.4 shows, the higher real interest rate also increases the demand for dollars and reduces the supply of dollars, causing the dollar to appreciate. The stronger dollar, in turn, further reduces aggregate demand. Why? As we saw in discussing the exchange rate, a stronger dollar reduces the cost of imported goods, thereby increasing imports. It also makes U.S. exports more costly to foreign buyers, which tends to reduce exports. Recall that net exports—or exports minus imports—is one of the four components of aggregate demand. Thus, by reducing exports and increasing imports, a stronger dollar (more precisely, a higher exchange rate) reduces aggregate demand.[4]

In sum, when the exchange rate is flexible, a tighter monetary policy reduces net exports (through a stronger dollar) as well as consumption and investment spending (through a higher real interest rate). Conversely, an easier monetary policy weakens the dollar and stimulates net exports, reinforcing the effect of the lower real interest rate on consumption and investment spending. Thus, relative to the case of a closed economy we studied earlier, *monetary policy is more effective in an open economy with a flexible exchange rate.*

The tightening of monetary policy under Fed Chairman Volcker in the early 1980s illustrates the effect of monetary policy on net exports. As we discussed above, Volcker's tight-money policies were a major reason for the 50 percent appreciation of the dollar during 1980–1985. In 1980 and 1981, the United States enjoyed a trade surplus, with exports that modestly exceeded imports. Largely in response to a stronger dollar, the U.S. trade balance fell into deficit after 1981. By the end of 1985, the U.S. trade deficit was about 3 percent of GDP, a substantial shift in less than half a decade.

RECAP	DETERMINING THE EXCHANGE RATE IN THE SHORT RUN

- Supply and demand analysis is a useful tool for studying the short-run determination of the exchange rate. U.S. households and firms supply dollars to the foreign exchange market to acquire foreign currencies, which they need to purchase foreign goods, services, and assets. Foreigners demand dollars in the foreign exchange market to purchase U.S. goods, services, and assets. The market equilibrium exchange rate equates the quantities of dollars supplied and demanded in the foreign exchange market.

[4]We are temporarily assuming that the prices of U.S. goods in dollars and the prices of foreign goods in foreign currencies are not changing.

- An increased preference for foreign goods, an increase in U.S. real GDP, an increase in the real interest rate on foreign assets, or a decrease in the real interest rate on U.S. assets will increase the supply of dollars on the foreign exchange market, lowering the value of the dollar. An increased preference for U.S. goods by foreigners, an increase in real GDP abroad, an increase in the real interest rate on U.S. assets, or a decrease in the real interest rate on foreign assets will increase the demand for dollars, raising the value of the dollar.
- A tight monetary policy raises the real interest rate, increasing the demand for dollars, reducing the supply of dollars, and strengthening the dollar. A stronger dollar reinforces the effects of tight monetary policy on aggregate spending by reducing net exports, a component of aggregate demand. Conversely, an easy monetary policy lowers the real interest rate, weakening the dollar.

FIXED EXCHANGE RATES

So far we have focused on the case of flexible exchange rates, the relevant case for most large industrial countries like the United States. However, the alternative approach, fixing the exchange rate, has been quite important historically and is still used in many countries, especially small or developing nations. In this section, we will see how our conclusions change when the nominal exchange rate is fixed rather than flexible. One important difference is that when a country maintains a fixed exchange rate, its ability to use monetary policy as a stabilization tool is greatly reduced.

HOW TO FIX AN EXCHANGE RATE

In contrast to a flexible exchange rate, whose value is determined solely by supply and demand in the foreign exchange market, the value of a fixed exchange rate is determined by the government (in practice, usually the finance ministry or treasury department, with the cooperation of the central bank). Today, the value of a fixed exchange rate is usually set in terms of a major currency such as the U.S. dollar, or relative to a "basket" of currencies, typically those of the country's trading partners. Historically, currency values were often fixed in terms of gold or other precious metals, but in recent years precious metals have rarely if ever been used for that purpose.

Once an exchange rate has been fixed, the government usually attempts to keep it unchanged for some time.[5] However, sometimes economic circumstances force the government to change the value of the exchange rate. A reduction in the official value of a currency is called a **devaluation;** an increase in the official value is called a **revaluation.** The devaluation of a fixed exchange rate is analogous to the depreciation of a flexible exchange rate; both involve a reduction in the currency's value. Conversely, a revaluation is analogous to an appreciation.

devaluation a reduction in the official value of a currency (in a fixed-exchange-rate system)

revaluation an increase in the official value of a currency (in a fixed-exchange-rate system)

The supply and demand diagram we used to study flexible exchange rates can be adapted to analyze fixed exchange rates. Let's consider the case of a country called Latinia, whose currency is called the peso. Figure 22.5 shows the supply and

[5]There are exceptions to this statement. Some countries employ a *crawling peg* system, under which the exchange rate is fixed at a value that changes in a preannounced way over time. For example, the government may announce that the value of the fixed exchange rate will fall 2 percent each year. Other countries use a *target zone* system, in which the exchange rate is allowed to deviate by a small amount from its fixed value. To focus on the key issues, we will assume that the exchange rate is fixed at a single value for a protracted period.

FIGURE 22.5
An Overvalued Exchange Rate.
The peso's official value (0.125 dollar) is shown as greater than its market equilibrium value (0.10 dollar), as determined by supply and demand in the foreign exchange market. Thus, the peso is overvalued. To maintain the fixed value, the government must purchase pesos in the quantity *AB* each period.

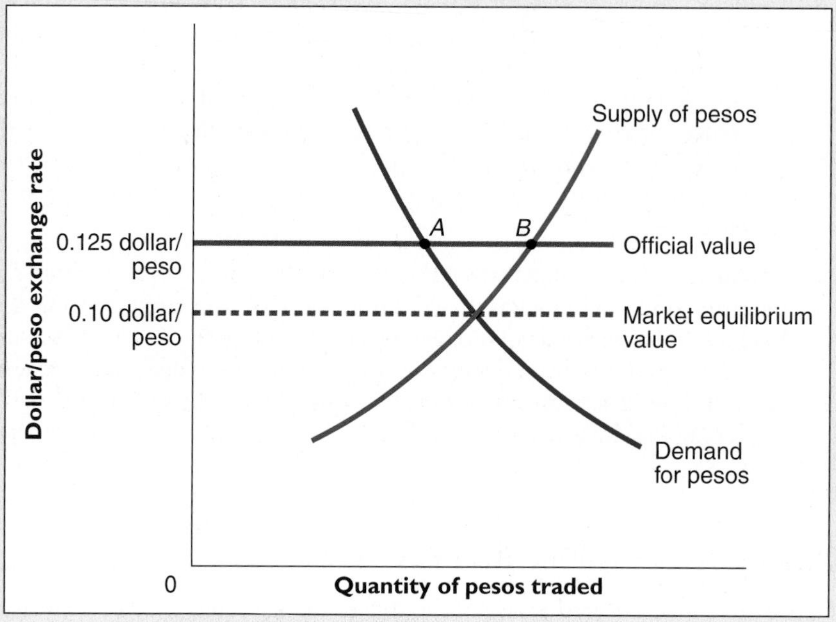

demand for the Latinian peso in the foreign exchange market. Pesos are *supplied* to the foreign exchange market by Latinian households and firms who want to acquire foreign currencies to purchase foreign goods, services, and assets. Pesos are demanded by holders of foreign currencies who need pesos to purchase Latinian goods, services, and assets. The exchange rate on the vertical axis of Figure 22.5 will now be the number of dollars (foreign currency) per peso (domestic currency). Figure 22.5 shows that the quantities of pesos supplied and demanded in the foreign exchange market are equal when a peso equals 0.1 dollar (10 pesos to the dollar). Hence 0.1 dollar per peso is the *market equilibrium value* of the peso. If Latinia had a flexible-exchange-rate system, the market supply and demand for pesos would determine the exchange rate, and the peso would trade at 10 pesos to the dollar in the foreign exchange market.

Instead of flexible exchange rates, suppose that Latinia has decided to fix the exchange rate and that the government has decreed the value of the Latinian peso to be 8 pesos to the dollar, or 0.125 dollar per peso. This official value of the peso, 0.125 dollar, is indicated by the solid horizontal line in Figure 22.5. Notice that it is greater than the market equilibrium value, corresponding to the intersection of the supply and demand curves. When the officially fixed value of an exchange rate is greater than its market equilibrium value, the exchange rate is **overvalued.** The official value of an exchange rate also can be lower than its market equilibrium value, in which case the exchange rate is **undervalued.**

overvalued exchange rate an exchange rate that has an officially fixed value greater than its market equilibrium value

undervalued exchange rate an exchange rate that has an officially fixed value less than its market equilibrium value

In this example, Latinia's commitment to hold the peso at 8 to the dollar is inconsistent with the market equilibrium value of 10 to the dollar, as determined by supply and demand in the foreign exchange market (the Latinian peso is overvalued). How could the Latinian government deal with this inconsistency? There are several possibilities. First, Latinia could simply devalue its currency, from 0.125 dollar per peso to 0.10 dollar per peso, which would bring the peso's official value into line with its market equilibrium value. As we will see, devaluation is often the ultimate result of an overvaluation of a currency. However, a country with a fixed exchange rate will be reluctant to change the official value of its exchange rate every time the market equilibrium value changes. If a country must continuously adjust its exchange rate to market conditions, it might as well switch to a flexible exchange rate.

As a second alternative, Latinia could try to maintain its overvalued exchange rate by restricting international transactions. Imposing quotas on imports and prohibiting domestic households and firms from acquiring foreign assets would effectively reduce the supply of pesos to the foreign exchange market, raising the market equilibrium value of the currency. An even more extreme action would be to prohibit Latinians from exchanging the peso for other currencies without government approval, a policy that would effectively allow the government to determine directly the supply of pesos to the foreign exchange market. Such measures might help to maintain the official value of the peso. However, restrictions on trade and capital flows are extremely costly to the economy because they reduce the gains from specialization and trade and deny domestic households and firms access to foreign capital markets. Thus, a policy of restricting international transactions to maintain a fixed exchange rate is likely to do more harm than good.

The third and most widely used approach to maintaining an overvalued exchange rate is for the government to become a demander of its own currency in the foreign exchange market. Figure 22.5 shows that at the official exchange rate of 0.125 dollar per peso, the private sector quantity of pesos supplied (point *B*) exceeds the private sector quantity of pesos demanded (point *A*). To keep the peso from falling below its official value, in each period the Latinian government could purchase a quantity of pesos in the foreign exchange market equal to the length of the line segment *AB* in Figure 22.5. If the government followed this strategy, then at the official exchange rate of 0.125 dollar per peso, the total quantity of pesos demanded (i.e., the private quantity demanded at point *A* plus the quantity of pesos the government is willing to purchase *AB*) would equal the private quantity of pesos supplied (point *B*). This situation is analogous to government attempts to keep the price of a commodity, like grain or milk, above its market level. To maintain an official price of grain that is above the market-clearing price, the government must stand ready to purchase the excess supply of grain forthcoming at the official price. In the same way, to keep the "price" of its currency above the market-clearing level, the government must buy the excess pesos supplied at the official price.

To be able to purchase its own currency and maintain an overvalued exchange rate, the government (usually the central bank) must hold foreign currency assets, called **international reserves**, or simply *reserves*. For example, the Latinian central bank may hold dollar deposits in U.S. banks or U.S. government debt, which it can trade for pesos in the foreign exchange market as needed. In the situation shown in Figure 22.5, to keep the peso at its official value, in each period the Latinian central bank will have to spend an amount of international reserves equal to the length of the line segment *AB*.

international reserves foreign currency assets held by a government for the purpose of purchasing the domestic currency in the foreign exchange market

Because a country with an overvalued exchange rate must use part of its reserves to support the value of its currency in each period, over time its available reserves will decline. The net decline in a country's stock of international reserves over a year is called its **balance-of-payments deficit.** Conversely, if a country experiences a net increase in its international reserves over the year, the increase is called its **balance-of-payments surplus.**

balance-of-payments deficit the net decline in a country's stock of international reserves over a year

balance-of-payments surplus the net increase in a country's stock of international reserves over a year

Quantifying Latinia's Balance-of-Payments Deficit

Suppose that the demand for and supply of Latinian pesos in the foreign exchange market are

$$\text{Demand} = 25{,}000 - 50{,}000e,$$

$$\text{Supply} = 17{,}600 + 24{,}000e,$$

where the Latinian exchange rate e is measured in dollars per peso. Officially, the value of the peso is 0.125 dollar. We can find the market equilibrium exchange rate of the peso by equating the demand and supply of pesos:

$$25{,}000 - 50{,}000e = 17{,}600 + 24{,}000e.$$

Solving for e, we get

$$7{,}400 = 74{,}000e$$

$$e = 0.10.$$

So the market equilibrium value of the exchange rate is 0.10 dollar per peso, as in Figure 22.5.

At the official exchange rate, 0.125 dollar per peso, the demand for pesos is $25{,}000 - 50{,}000(0.125) = 18{,}750$ and the supply of pesos is $17{,}600 + 24{,}000(0.125) = 20{,}600$. Thus, the quantity of pesos supplied to the foreign exchange market exceeds the quantity of pesos demanded by $20{,}600 - 18{,}750 = 1{,}850$ pesos. To maintain the fixed rate, the Latinian government must purchase 1,850 pesos per period, which is the Latinian balance-of-payments deficit. Since pesos are purchased at the official rate of 8 pesos to the dollar, the balance-of-payments deficit in dollars is 1,850 pesos $\times$ 0.125 dollar/peso = \$1,850/8 = \$231.25.

EXERCISE 22.3

Suppose that, in the example above, the fixed value of the peso is 0.15 dollar per peso. What do you conclude about the relationship between the degree of currency overvaluation and the resulting balance-of-payments deficit?

Although a government can maintain an overvalued exchange rate for a time by offering to buy back its own currency at the official price, there is a limit to this strategy since no government's stock of international reserves is infinite. Eventually the government will run out of reserves, and the fixed exchange rate will collapse.

EXERCISE 22.4

Diagram a case in which a fixed exchange rate is *undervalued* rather than overvalued. Show that, to maintain the fixed exchange rate, the central bank must use domestic currency to purchase foreign currency in the foreign exchange market. With an undervalued exchange rate, is the country's central bank in danger of running out of international reserves? (*Hint:* Keep in mind that a central bank is always free to print more of its own currency.)

MONETARY POLICY AND THE FIXED EXCHANGE RATE

We have seen that there is no really satisfactory way of maintaining a fixed exchange rate above its market equilibrium value for an extended period. A central bank can maintain an overvalued exchange rate for a time by using international reserves to buy up the excess supply of its currency in the foreign exchange market. But a country's international reserves are limited and may eventually be exhausted by the attempt to keep the exchange rate artificially high.

An alternative to trying to maintain an overvalued exchange rate is to take actions that increase the market equilibrium value of the exchange rate. If the exchange rate's market equilibrium value can be raised enough to equal its official value, then the overvaluation problem will be eliminated. The most effective way to change the exchange rate's market equilibrium value is through monetary policy. As we saw earlier in the chapter, a tight monetary policy that raises the real interest rate will increase the demand for the domestic currency, as domestic assets become more attractive to foreign financial investors. Higher real interest rates also will decrease the supply of domestic currency as domestic assets become more attractive to domestic citizens, too. Increased demand and decreased supply of the currency will, in turn, raise its market equilibrium value.

The use of monetary policy to support a fixed exchange rate is shown in Figure 22.6. At first, the demand and supply of the Latinian peso in the foreign exchange market are given by the curves *D* and *S*, so the market equilibrium value of the peso equals 0.10 dollar per peso—less than the official value of 0.125 dollar per peso. Just as before, the peso is overvalued. This time, however, the Latinian central bank uses monetary policy to eliminate the overvaluation problem. To do so, the central bank increases the domestic real interest rate, making Latinian assets more attractive to both foreign and domestic financial investors. This increase in the real interest rate thus will raise the demand for pesos from *D* to *D′* and reduce the supply of pesos from S to *S′*. After the changes in supply and demand, the market equilibrium value of the peso equals the officially fixed value, as can be seen in Figure 22.6. Because the peso is no longer overvalued, it can be maintained at its fixed value without loss of international reserves or fear of speculative attack. Conversely, an easing of monetary policy (a lower real interest rate) could be used to remedy an undervaluation, in which the official exchange rate is below the market equilibrium value.

FIGURE 22.6

A Tightening of Monetary Policy Eliminates an Overvaluation.

With the demand for the peso given by *D* and the supply given by *S*, equilibrium occurs at point *E* and the market equilibrium value of the peso equals 0.10 dollar per peso—below the official value of 0.125 dollar per peso. The overvaluation of the peso can be eliminated by tighter monetary policy, which raises the domestic real interest rate, making domestic assets more attractive to both foreign and domestic financial investors. The demand for pesos will increase from *D* to *D′*, and the supply of pesos will fall from *S* to *S′*. These changes in supply and demand raise the peso's market equilibrium value to 0.125 dollar per peso, the official value. The peso is no longer overvalued.

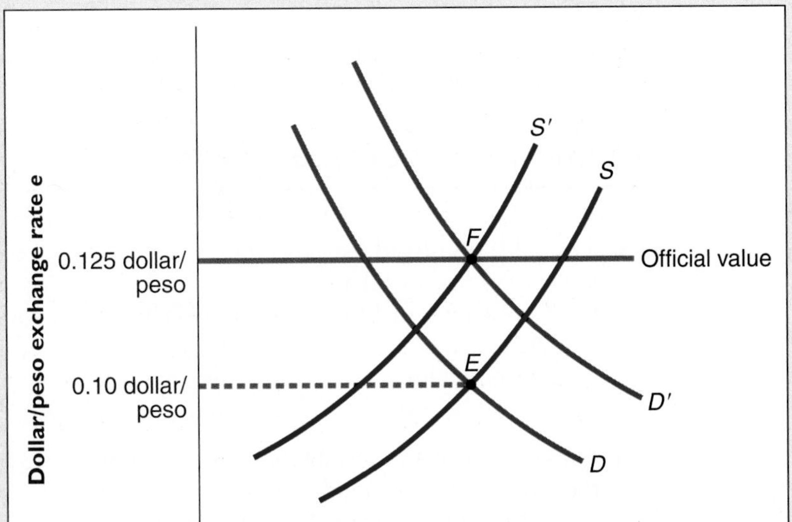

"It's just a flesh wound. I got it defending the dollar."

Although monetary policy can be used to keep the market equilibrium value of the exchange rate equal to the official value, using monetary policy in this way has some drawbacks. In particular, *if monetary policy is used to set the market equilibrium value of the exchange rate equal to the official value, it is no longer available for stabilizing the domestic economy.* Suppose, for example, that the Latinian economy were suffering a recession due to insufficient aggregate demand at the same time that its exchange rate is overvalued. The Latinian central bank could lower the real interest rate to increase spending and output, or it could raise the real interest rate to eliminate overvaluation of the exchange rate, *but it cannot do both.* Hence, if Latinian officials decide to maintain the fixed exchange rate, they must give up any hope of fighting the recession using monetary policy. The fact that a fixed exchange rate limits or eliminates the use of monetary policy for the purpose of stabilizing aggregate demand is one of the most important features of a fixed-exchange-rate system.

RECAP FIXED EXCHANGE RATES

- The value of a fixed exchange rate is set by the government. The official value of a fixed exchange rate may differ from its market equilibrium value, as determined by supply and demand in the foreign exchange market. An exchange rate whose officially fixed value exceeds its market equilibrium value is overvalued; an exchange rate whose officially fixed value is below its market equilibrium value is undervalued.
- For an overvalued exchange rate, the quantity of the currency supplied to the foreign exchange market at the official exchange rate exceeds the quantity demanded. The government can maintain an overvalued exchange rate for a time by using its international reserves (foreign currency assets) to purchase the excess supply of its currency. The net decline in a country's stock of international reserves during the year is its balance-of-payments deficit.

- Because a country's international reserves are limited, it cannot maintain an overvalued exchange rate indefinitely. Moreover, if financial investors fear an impending devaluation of the exchange rate, they may launch a speculative attack, selling domestic currency assets and supplying large amounts of the country's currency to the foreign exchange market—an action that exhausts the country's reserves even more quickly. Because rapid loss of reserves may force a devaluation, financial investors' fear of devaluation may prove a self-fulfilling prophecy.
- A tight monetary policy, which increases the real interest rate, raises the demand for the currency and hence its market equilibrium value. By raising a currency's market equilibrium value to its official value, tight monetary policies can eliminate the problem of overvaluation and stabilize the exchange rate. However, if monetary policy is used to set the market equilibrium value of the exchange rate, it is no longer available for stabilizing the domestic economy.

SHOULD EXCHANGE RATES BE FIXED OR FLEXIBLE?

Should countries adopt fixed or flexible exchange rates? In briefly comparing the two systems, we will focus on two major issues: (1) the effects of the exchange rate system on monetary policy and (2) the effects of the exchange rate system on trade and economic integration.

On the issue of monetary policy, we have seen that the type of exchange rate a country has strongly affects the central bank's ability to use monetary policy to stabilize the economy. A flexible exchange rate actually strengthens the impact of monetary policy on aggregate demand. However, a fixed exchange rate prevents policymakers from using monetary policy to stabilize the economy because they must instead use it to keep the exchange rate's market equilibrium value at its official value (or else risk speculative attacks).

In large economies like that of the United States, giving up the power to stabilize the domestic economy via monetary policy makes little sense. Thus, large economies should nearly always employ a flexible exchange rate. However, in small economies, giving up this power may have some benefits. An interesting case is that of Argentina, which for the period 1991–2001 maintained a one-to-one exchange rate between its peso and the U.S. dollar. Although prior to 1991 Argentina had suffered periods of hyperinflation, while the peso was pegged to the dollar, Argentina's inflation rate essentially equaled that of the United States. By tying its currency to the dollar and giving up the freedom to set its monetary policy, Argentina attempted to commit itself to avoiding the inflationary policies of the past, and instead placed itself under the "umbrella" of the Federal Reserve. Unfortunately, early in 2002, investors' fears that Argentina would not be able to repay its international debts led to a speculative attack on the Argentine peso. The fixed exchange rate collapsed, the peso depreciated, and Argentina experienced an economic crisis from which it has not yet fully recovered. The lesson is that a fixed exchange rate alone cannot stop inflation in a small economy if other policies are not sound as well. Large fiscal deficits, which were financed by foreign borrowing, ultimately pushed Argentina into crisis.

The second important issue is the effect of the exchange rate on trade and economic integration. Proponents of fixed exchange rates argue that fixed rates promote international trade and cross-border economic cooperation by reducing uncertainty about future exchange rates. For example, a firm that is considering building up its export business knows that its potential profits will depend on the future value of its own country's currency relative to the currencies of the countries to which it exports. Under a flexible-exchange-rate regime, the value of the home currency fluctuates with changes in supply and demand and is therefore difficult to predict far in advance. Such uncertainty may make the firm reluctant to expand its export business. Supporters of fixed exchange rates argue that if the exchange rate is officially fixed, uncertainty about the future exchange rate is reduced or eliminated.

One problem with this argument, which has been underscored by episodes like the East Asian crisis and the Argentine crisis, is that fixed exchange rates are not guaranteed to remain fixed forever. Although they do not fluctuate from day to day as flexible rates do, a sustained overvaluation may lead suddenly and unpredictably to a large devaluation. Thus, a firm that is trying to forecast the exchange rate 10 years into the future may face as much uncertainty if the exchange rate is fixed as if it is flexible.

The potential instability of fixed exchange rates has led some countries to try a more radical solution to the problem of uncertainty about exchange rates: the adoption of a common currency.

THE EURO: A COMMON CURRENCY FOR EUROPE

EN 22 A

Since World War II, the nations of western Europe have worked to increase economic cooperation and trade among themselves. European leaders recognized that a unified and integrated European economy would be more productive and perhaps more competitive with the U.S. economy than a fragmented one. As part of this effort, these countries established fixed exchange rates in the 1970s under the auspices of a system called the European Monetary System (EMS). Unfortunately, the EMS did not prove stable. Numerous devaluations of the various currencies occurred, and in 1992 severe problems maintaining their exchange rates forced several nations, including Great Britain, to abandon the fixed-exchange-rate system.

In December 1991, in Maastricht in the Netherlands, the member countries of the European Community (EC) agreed to a pact popularly known as the Maastricht Treaty. One of the major provisions of the treaty, which took effect in November 1993, was the member countries would strive to adopt a common currency. Effective January 1, 1999, 11 western European nations, including France, Germany, and Italy, adopted a common currency, called the euro. In several stages, the euro replaced the French franc, the German mark, the Italian lira, and other national currencies. The process was completed in early 2002, when the old currencies were completely eliminated and replaced by euros.

The advent of the euro means that Europeans no longer have to change currencies when trading with other European countries, much as Americans from different states can trade with each other without worrying that a "New York dollar" will change in value relative to a "California dollar." The euro should help to promote European trade and cooperation while eliminating the necessity of individual countries maintaining fixed exchange rates.

Because western Europe now has a single currency, it also must have a common monetary policy. The EC members agreed that European monetary policy would be put under the control of a new European Central Bank (ECB), a multinational institution located in Frankfurt, Germany. The ECB, in effect, has become "Europe's Fed."

One potential problem with having a single monetary policy for many different countries is that different countries may face different economic conditions, so a single monetary policy cannot respond to all of them. For example, in recent years, some countries in Europe (such as Germany) have grown slowly, suggesting the need for an easier monetary policy, while other countries (such as Ireland) have seen increases in inflation, which implies a need for adopting a tighter monetary policy. Because the ECB can choose only a single monetary policy for all the countries using the euro, conflicts of interest may arise among the member nations of the European Union.

DETERMINATION OF THE EXCHANGE RATE IN THE LONG RUN

In this section, we discuss how exchange rates are determined in the long run. In our short-run analysis, we assumed that both the dollar price of U.S. goods and the foreign currency price of foreign goods (for example, the price of Sony Playstations in yen) did not change. In discussing the long run, we must relax this assumption. The theory we shall use to discuss the long-run determination of the exchange rate is called the theory of *purchasing power parity.* In order to explain this theory, we must first introduce the real exchange rate.

THE REAL EXCHANGE RATE

The nominal exchange rate tells us the price of the domestic currency in terms of a foreign currency. As we will see in this section, the *real exchange rate* is the price of the average domestic *good or service* in terms of the average foreign *good or service.*

To provide background for discussing the real exchange rate, imagine you are in charge of purchasing for a U.S. corporation that is planning to acquire a large number of new computers. The company's computer specialist has identified two models, one Japanese-made and one U.S.-made, that meet the necessary specifications. Since the two models are essentially equivalent, the company will buy the one with the lower price. However, since the computers are priced in the currencies of the countries of manufacture, the price comparison is not so straightforward. Your mission—should you decide to accept it—is to determine which of the two models is cheaper.

To complete your assignment, you will need two pieces of information: the nominal exchange rate between the dollar and the yen and the prices of the two models in terms of the currencies of their countries of manufacture.

Suppose that a U.S.-made computer costs $2,400, and a similar Japanese-made computer costs 242,000 yen. If the nominal exchange rate is 110 yen per dollar, which computer is the better buy? To make this price comparison, we must measure the prices of both computers in terms of the same currency. To make the comparison in dollars, we first convert the Japanese computer's price into dollars. The price in terms of Japanese yen is ¥242,000 (the symbol ¥ means "yen"), and we are told that ¥110 = $1. As we did earlier, we find the dollar price of the Japanese computer by observing that for any good or service,

$$\text{Price in yen} = \text{Price in dollars} \times \text{Value of dollar in terms of yen}.$$

Note that the value of a dollar in terms of yen is just the yen–dollar exchange rate. Making this substitution and solving, we get

$$\text{Price in dollars} = \frac{\text{Price in yen}}{\text{Yen}-\text{dollar exchange rate}}$$

$$= \frac{¥242{,}000}{¥110/\$1} = \$2{,}200.$$

Notice that the yen symbol appears in both the numerator and the denominator of the ratio, so it cancels out. Our conclusion is that the Japanese computer is cheaper than the U.S. computer at $2,200, or $200 less than the price of the U.S. computer, $2,400. The Japanese computer is the better deal.

EXERCISE 22.5

Using the same information, compare the prices of the Japanese and American computers by expressing both prices in terms of yen.

The fact that the Japanese computer was cheaper implied that your firm would choose it over the U.S.-made computer. In general, a country's ability to compete in international markets depends in part on the prices of its goods and services *relative* to the prices of foreign goods and services, when the prices are measured in a common currency. In the hypothetical example of the Japanese and U.S. computers, the price of the domestic (U.S.) good relative to the price of the foreign (Japanese) good is \$2,400/\$2,200, or 1.09. So the U.S. computer is 9 percent more expensive than the Japanese computer, putting the U.S. product at a competitive disadvantage.

More generally, economists ask whether *on average* the goods and services produced by a particular country are expensive relative to the goods and services produced by other countries. This question can be answered by the country's *real exchange rate*. Specifically, a country's **real exchange rate** is the price of the average domestic good or service *relative* to the price of the average foreign good or service, when prices are expressed in terms of a common currency.

real exchange rate the price of the average domestic good or service *relative* to the price of the average foreign good or service, when prices are expressed in terms of a common currency

To obtain a formula for the real exchange rate, recall that e equals the nominal exchange rate (the number of units of foreign currency per dollar) and that P equals the domestic price level, as measured, for example, by the consumer price index. We will use P as a measure of the price of the "average" domestic good or service. Similarly, let P^f equal the foreign price level. We will use P^f as the measure of the price of the "average" foreign good or service.

The real exchange rate equals the price of the average domestic good or service relative to the price of the average foreign good or service. It would not be correct, however, to define the real exchange rate as the ratio P/P^f because the two price levels are expressed in different currencies. As we saw in our example of U.S. versus Japanese computers, to convert foreign prices into dollars, we must divide the foreign price by the exchange rate. By this rule, the price in dollars of the average foreign good or service equals P^f/e. Now we can write the real exchange rate as

$$\text{Real exchange rate} = \frac{\text{Price of domestic good}}{\text{Price of foreign good, in dollars}}$$

$$= \frac{P}{P^f/e}$$

To simplify this expression, multiply the numerator and denominator by e to get

$$\text{Real exchange rate} = \frac{eP}{P^f} \tag{22.1}$$

which is the formula for the real exchange rate.

To check this formula, let's apply it to the computer example. (For this exercise, we imagine that computers are the only good produced by the United States and Japan, so the real exchange rate becomes just the price of U.S. computers relative to Japanese computers.) In that example, the nominal exchange rate e was ¥110/\$1, the domestic price P (of a computer) was \$2,400, and the foreign price P^f was ¥242,000. Applying Equation 22.1, we get

$$\text{Real exchange rate (for computers)} = \frac{(¥110/\$1) \times \$2{,}400}{¥242{,}000}$$

$$= \frac{¥264{,}000}{¥242{,}000}$$

$$= 1.09,$$

which is the same answer we got earlier.

The real exchange rate, an overall measure of the cost of domestic goods relative to foreign goods, is an important economic variable. It incorporates both the nominal exchange rate and the relative prices of goods and services across countries: when the real exchange rate is high, domestic goods are on average more expensive than foreign goods (when priced in the same currency). A high real exchange rate implies that domestic producers will have difficulty exporting to other countries (domestic goods will be "overpriced"), while foreign goods will sell well in the home country (because imported goods are cheap relative to goods produced at home). Since a high real exchange rate tends to reduce exports and increase imports, we conclude that *net exports will tend to be low when the real exchange rate is high*. Conversely, if the real exchange rate is low, then the home country will find it easier to export (because its goods are priced below those of foreign competitors), while domestic residents will buy fewer imports (because imports are expensive relative to domestic goods). *Thus, net exports will tend to be high when the real exchange rate is low.*

In our earlier analysis, we showed how an increase in the nominal exchange rate e will reduce net exports by making exports more expensive to foreigners and by making imports cheaper for Americans. Equation 22.1 shows that an increase in e also will increase the real exchange rate, all other things equal, most notably, the ratio P/P^f. And an increase in the real exchange rate will again reduce net exports.

A SIMPLE THEORY OF EXCHANGE RATES: PURCHASING POWER PARITY (PPP)

The most basic theory of how nominal exchange rates are determined in the long run is called *purchasing power parity*, or PPP. To understand this theory, we must first discuss a market equilibrium economic concept, called *the law of one price*. The **law of one price** states that if transportation costs are relatively small, the price of an internationally traded commodity must be the same in all locations. For example, if transportation costs are not too large, the price of a bushel of wheat ought to be the same in Bombay, India, and Sydney, Australia. Note that this condition implies that the real exchange rate must equal one in the long run. Suppose that were not the case—that the price of wheat in Sydney were only half the price in Bombay. In that case, grain merchants would have a strong incentive to buy wheat in Sydney and ship it to Bombay, where it could be sold at double the price of purchase. As wheat left Sydney, reducing the local supply, the price of wheat in Sydney would rise, while the inflow of wheat into Bombay would reduce the price in Bombay. According to the Equilibrium Principle (Chapter 3), the international market for wheat would return to equilibrium only when unexploited opportunities to profit had been eliminated—specifically, only when the prices of wheat in Sydney and in Bombay became equal or nearly equal (with the difference being less than the cost of transporting wheat from Australia to India).

law of one price if transportation costs are relatively small, the price of an internationally traded commodity must be the same in all locations

Equilibrium

Let's look at a specific example. Suppose that a bushel of grain costs 5 Australian dollars in Sydney and 150 rupees in Bombay. If the law of one price holds for grain, what is the nominal exchange rate between Australia and India? Because the market value of a bushel of grain must be the same in both locations, we know that the Australian price of wheat must equal the Indian price of wheat, so that

$$5 \text{ Australian dollars} = 150 \text{ rupees}.$$

Dividing by 5, we get

$$1 \text{ Australian dollars} = 30 \text{ Indian rupees}.$$

Thus, the nominal exchange rate between Australia and India should be 30 rupees per Australian dollar.

Alternatively, if we use Equation 22.1 and the PPP assumption that the real exchange rate will equal one,

$$1 = \frac{eP}{P^f}$$

and

$$e = P^f/P = 150 \text{ Indian rupees}/5 \text{ Australian dollars}$$
$$= 30 \text{ Indian rupees per 1 Australian dollar.}$$

EXERCISE 22.6

The price of gold is $300 per ounce in New York and 2,500 kronor per ounce in Stockholm, Sweden. If the law of one price holds for gold, what is the nominal exchange rate between the U.S. dollar and the Swedish krona?

purchasing power parity (PPP) the theory that nominal exchange rates are determined as necessary for the law of one price to hold

These examples illustrate the application of the purchasing power parity theory. According to the **purchasing power parity (PPP)** theory, nominal exchange rates are determined as necessary for the law of one price to hold.

A particularly useful prediction of the PPP theory is that in the long run, the *currencies of countries that experience significant inflation will tend to depreciate.* To see why, we will extend our analysis of the price of grain in India and Australia.

Suppose India experiences significant inflation so that the price of a bushel of grain in Bombay rises from 150 to 300 rupees. Australia has no inflation, so the price of grain in Sydney remains unchanged at 5 Australian dollars. If the law of one price holds for grain, what will happen to the nominal exchange rate between Australia and India?

We know that the market value of a bushel of grain must be the same in both locations. Therefore,

$$5 \text{ Australian dollars} = 300 \text{ rupees.}$$

Equivalently,

$$1 \text{ Australian dollar} = 60 \text{ rupees.}$$

The nominal exchange rate is now 60 rupees per Australian dollar. Before India's inflation, the nominal exchange rate was 30 rupees per Australian dollar. So, in this example, inflation has caused the rupee to depreciate against the Australian dollar. Conversely, Australia, with no inflation, has seen its currency appreciate against the rupee.

This link between inflation and depreciation makes economic sense. Inflation implies that a nation's currency is losing purchasing power in the domestic market. Analogously, exchange rate depreciation implies that the nation's currency is losing purchasing power in international markets.

Figure 22.7 shows annual rates of inflation and nominal exchange rate depreciation for the 10 largest South American countries from 1995 to 2004.[6] Inflation is measured as the annual rate of change in the country's consumer price index; depreciation is measured relative to the U.S. dollar. As you can see, inflation varied greatly among South American countries during the period. For example, Chile's inflation rate was within two percentage points of the inflation rate of the United States, while Venezuela's inflation was 33 percent per year.

[6]Since Ecuador, the 10th country, adopted the U.S. dollar as its currency in 2000, the data for Ecuador refer to the period 1995–2000.

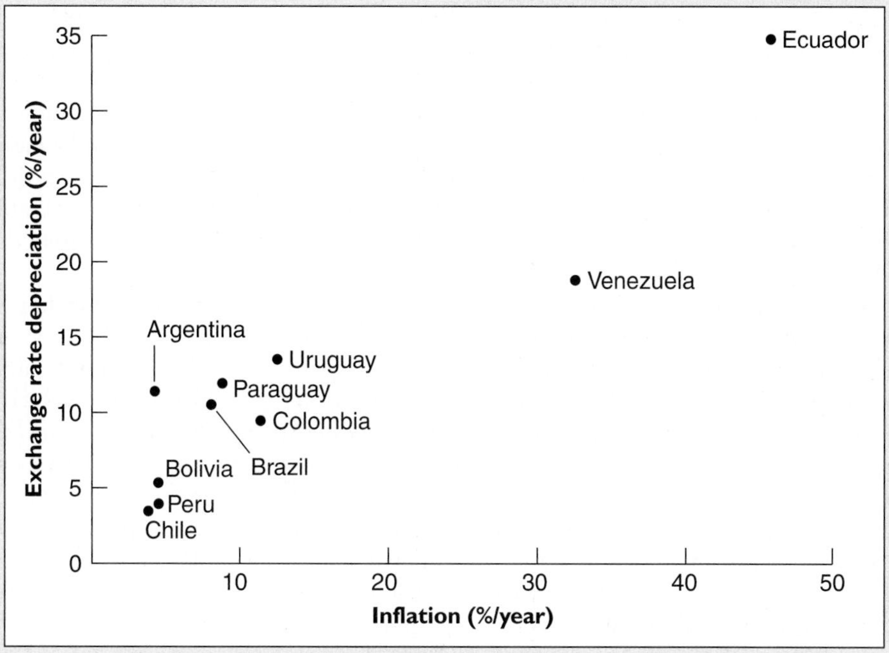

Source: International Monetary Fund, *International Financial Statistics*, and authors' calculations.

FIGURE 22.7
Inflation and Currency Depreciation in South America, 1995–2004.
The annual rates of inflation and nominal exchange-rate depreciation (relative to the U.S. dollar) in the 10 largest South American countries varied considerably during 1995–2004. High inflation was associated with rapid depreciation of the nominal exchange rate. (Data for Ecuador refer to the period 1995–2000.)

Figure 22.7 shows that, as the PPP theory implies, countries with higher inflation during the 1995–2004 period tended to experience the most rapid depreciation of their currencies.

SHORTCOMINGS OF THE PPP THEORY

Empirical studies have found that the PPP theory is useful for predicting changes in nominal exchange rates over the relatively long run. In particular, this theory helps to explain the tendency of countries with high inflation to experience depreciation of their exchange rates, as shown in Figure 22.7. However, the theory is less successful in predicting short-run movements in exchange rates.

A particularly dramatic failure of the PPP theory occurred in the United States in the early 1980s. As Figure 22.1 indicates, between 1980 and 1985, the value of the U.S. dollar rose nearly 50 percent relative to the currencies of U.S. trading partners. This strong appreciation was followed by an even more rapid depreciation during 1986 and 1987. PPP theory could explain this roller-coaster behavior only if inflation were far lower in the United States than in U.S. trading partners from 1980 to 1985, and far higher from 1986 to 1987. In fact, inflation was similar in the United States and its trading partners throughout both periods.

Why does the PPP theory work less well in the short run than the long run? Recall that this theory relies on the law of one price, which says that the price of an internationally traded commodity must be the same in all locations. The law of one price works well for goods such as grain or gold, which are standardized commodities that are traded widely. However, *not all goods and services are traded internationally*, and *not all goods are standardized commodities*.

Many goods and services are not traded internationally because the assumption underlying the law of one price—that transportation costs are relatively small—does not hold. For example, for Indians to export haircuts to Australia, they would need to transport an Indian barber to Australia every time a Sydney resident desired a trim. Because transportation costs prevent haircuts from being traded internationally, the law of one price does not apply to them. Thus, even if the price of haircuts in

Australia were double the price of haircuts in India, market forces would not necessarily force prices toward equality in the short run. (Over the long run, some Indian barbers might emigrate to Australia.) Other examples of nontraded goods and services are agricultural land, buildings, heavy construction materials (whose value is low relative to their transportation costs), and highly perishable foods. In addition, some products use nontraded goods and services as inputs: A McDonald's hamburger served in Moscow has both a tradable component (frozen hamburger patties) and a nontradable component (the labor of counter workers). In general, the greater the share of nontraded goods and services in a nation's output, the less precisely the PPP theory will apply to the country's exchange rate.[7]

The second reason the law of one price and the PPP theory sometimes fail to apply is that not all internationally traded goods and services are perfectly standardized commodities, like grain or gold. For example, U.S.-made automobiles and Japanese-made automobiles are not identical; they differ in styling, horsepower, reliability, and other features. As a result, some people strongly prefer one nation's cars to the other's. Thus, if Japanese cars cost 10 percent more than American cars, U.S. automobile exports will not necessarily flood the Japanese market since many Japanese will still prefer Japanese-made cars even at a 10 percent premium. Of course, there are limits to how far prices can diverge before people will switch to the cheaper product. But the law of one price, and hence the PPP theory, will not apply exactly to nonstandardized goods.

RECAP — DETERMINATION OF THE EXCHANGE RATE IN THE LONG RUN

- The real exchange rate is the price of the average domestic good or service relative to the price of the average foreign good or service, when prices are expressed in terms of a common currency. A useful formula for the real exchange rate is eP/P^f, where e is the nominal exchange rate, P is the domestic price level, and P^f is the foreign price level.
- An increase in the real exchange rate implies that domestic goods are becoming more expensive relative to foreign goods, which tends to reduce exports and stimulate imports. Conversely, a decline in the real exchange rate tends to increase net exports.
- The most basic theory of nominal exchange rate determination in the long run, purchasing power parity (PPP), is based on the law of one price. The law of one price states that if transportation costs are relatively small, the price of an internationally traded commodity must be the same in all locations. According to the PPP theory, the nominal exchange rate between two currencies can be found by setting the price of a traded commodity in one currency equal to the price of the same commodity expressed in the second currency.
- A useful prediction of the PPP theory is that the currencies of countries that experience significant inflation will tend to depreciate over the long run. However, the PPP theory does not work well in the short run. The fact that many goods and services are nontraded, and that not all traded goods are standardized, reduces the applicability of the law of one price, and hence of the PPP theory.

[7]Trade barriers, such as tariffs and quotas, also increase the costs associated with shipping goods from one country to another. Thus, trade barriers reduce the applicability of the law of one price in much the same way that physical transportation costs do.

THE TRADE BALANCE AND NET CAPITAL INFLOWS

In Chapter 12, we introduced the term *net exports (NX),* the value of a country's exports less the value of its imports. An equivalent term for the value of a country's exports less the value of its imports is the **trade balance.** Because exports need not equal imports in each quarter or year, the trade balance (or net exports) need not always equal zero. If the trade balance is positive in a particular period so that the value of exports exceeds the value of imports, a country is said to have a **trade surplus** for that period equal to the value of its exports minus the value of its imports. If the trade balance is negative, with imports greater than exports, the country is said to have a **trade deficit** equal to the value of its imports minus the value of its exports.

trade balance (or net exports) the value of a country's exports less the value of its imports in a particular period (quarter or year)

trade surplus when exports exceed imports, the difference between the value of a country's exports and the value of its imports in a given period

trade deficit when imports exceed exports, the difference between the value of a country's imports and the value of its exports in a given period

Figure 22.8 shows the components of the U.S. trade balance since 1960. The blue line represents U.S. exports as a percentage of GDP; the red line, U.S. imports as a percentage of GDP. When exports exceed imports, the vertical distance between the two lines gives the U.S. trade surplus as a percentage of GDP. When imports exceed exports, the vertical distance between the two lines represents the U.S. trade deficit. Figure 22.8 shows first that international trade has become an increasingly important part of the U.S. economy in the past several decades. In 1960, only 5 percent of U.S. GDP was exported, and the value of imports equaled 4.3 percent of U.S. GDP. In 2007, by comparison, 12 percent of U.S. production was sold abroad and imports amounted to almost 17 percent of U.S. GDP. Second, the figure shows that since the late 1970s, the United States has consistently run trade deficits, frequently equal to 2 percent or more of GDP.

Purchases or sales of real and financial assets across international borders (which are economically equivalent to lending and borrowing across international borders) are known as **international capital flows.** From the perspective of a particular country, say the United States, purchases of domestic (U.S.) assets by foreigners are called **capital inflows;** purchases of foreign assets by domestic (U.S.) households and firms are called **capital outflows.** To remember these terms, it may help to keep in mind that capital inflows represent funds "flowing in" to the country (foreign savers buying domestic assets), while capital outflows are funds "flowing out" of the country (domestic savers buying foreign assets). The difference between the two flows is expressed as **net capital inflows**—capital inflows minus capital outflows—or net capital outflows—capital outflows minus capital inflows.

international capital flows purchases or sales of real and financial assets across international borders

capital inflows purchases of domestic assets by foreign households and firms

capital outflows purchases of foreign assets by domestic households and firms

One can look at net capital flows in either direction; what matters is to choose a perspective and stick with it consistently. For the rest of this chapter, we will focus on net capital inflows, which, once again, are equal to foreign purchases of domestic

net capital inflows capital inflows minus capital outflows

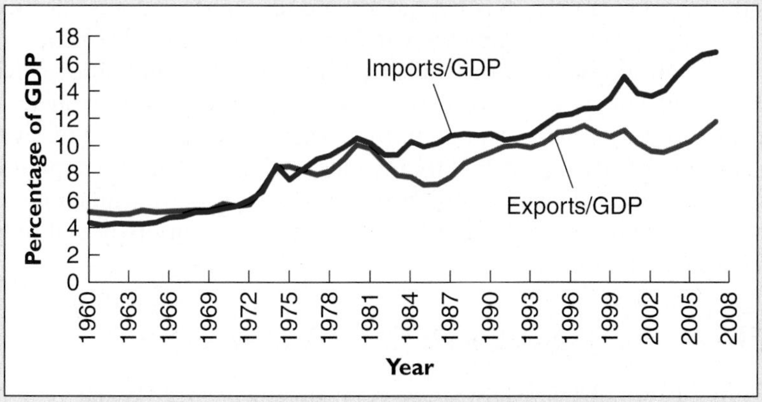

Source: Bureau of Economic Analysis (http://www.bea.gov).

FIGURE 22.8
The U.S. Trade Balance, 1960–2007.
This figure shows U.S. exports and imports as a percentage of GDP. Since the late 1970s, the United States has run a trade deficit, with imports exceeding exports.

assets (which bring funds into the country) minus domestic purchases of foreign assets (which send funds out of the country). Note that capital inflows and outflows are not counted as exports or imports because they refer to the purchase of existing real and financial assets rather than currently produced goods and services.

The trade balance represents the difference between the value of goods and services exported by a country and the value of goods and services imported by the country. Net capital inflows represent the difference between purchases of domestic assets by foreigners and purchases of foreign assets by domestic residents. There is a precise and very important link between these two imbalances: in any given period, the trade balance and net capital inflows sum to zero. It's convenient to write this relationship as an equation:

$$NX + KI = 0, \tag{22.2}$$

where NX is the trade balance (i.e., net exports) and KI stands for net capital inflows. The relationship given by Equation 22.2 is an identity, meaning that it is true by definition.

To see why Equation 22.2 holds, let's think about a specific example. Suppose that a U.S. resident purchases an imported good, say, a Japanese automobile priced at \$20,000. The U.S. buyer pays by check so that the Japanese car manufacturer now holds \$20,000 in an account in a U.S. bank.

What will the Japanese manufacturer do with this \$20,000? Basically, there are two possibilities. First, the Japanese company may use the \$20,000 to buy U.S.-produced goods and services, such as U.S.-manufactured car parts or Hawaiian vacations for its executives. In this case, the United States has \$20,000 in exports to balance the \$20,000 automobile import. Because exports equal imports, the U.S. trade balance is unaffected by these transactions (for these transactions, $NX = 0$). Because no assets are bought or sold, there are no capital inflows or outflows (that is, $KI = 0$). So under this scenario, the condition that the trade balance plus net capital inflows equals zero, as stated in Equation 22.2, is satisfied.

Alternatively, the Japanese car producer might use the \$20,000 to acquire U.S. assets such as a U.S. Treasury bond or some land adjacent to a manufacturing plant it owns in the United States. In this case, the United States compiles a trade deficit of \$20,000 because the \$20,000 car import is not offset by an export (that is, $NX = -\$20{,}000$). And there is a corresponding capital inflow of \$20,000, reflecting the purchase of a U.S. asset by the Japanese company (that is, $KI = \$20{,}000$). Once again, the trade balance and net capital inflows sum to zero and Equation 22.2 is satisfied.

In fact, there is a third possibility, which is that the Japanese car company might swap its dollars to some other party outside the United States. For example, the company might trade its dollars to another Japanese firm or individual in exchange for Japanese yen. However, the acquirer of the dollars would then have the same two options as the car company—to buy U.S. goods and services or acquire U.S. assets—so that the equality of net capital inflows and the trade deficit would continue to hold.

This relationship between the trade balance and net capital inflows makes an important point that policymakers ignore at their peril: A country with a trade deficit also must be receiving capital inflows. That is, Equation 22.2 tells us that if a trade deficit exists (that is, $NX < 0$), then it must be true that net capital inflows are positive (i.e., $KI > 0$). Thus, policies that aim to restrict trade in goods and service, and thus reduce the trade deficit, have a clear cost since they will reduce the flow of international capital.

INTERNATIONAL CAPITAL FLOWS

Like the production of goods and services, saving and investment opportunities are not necessarily restricted by national boundaries. The most productive use of a U.S. citizen's savings might be located far from U.S. soil, in helping to build a factory in

Thailand or starting a small business in Poland. Likewise, the best way for a Brazilian saver to diversify her assets and reduce her risks could be to hold bonds and stocks from a number of different countries. Over time, extensive financial markets have developed to permit cross-border borrowing and lending. Financial markets in which borrowers and lenders are residents of different countries are called *international* financial markets.

International financial markets differ from domestic financial markets in at least one important respect: Unlike a domestic financial transaction, an international financial transaction is subject to the laws and regulations of at least two countries, the country that is home to the lender and the country that is home to the borrower. Thus, the size and vitality of international financial markets depend on the degree of political and economic cooperation among countries. For example, during the relatively peaceful decades of the late nineteenth and early twentieth centuries, international financial markets were remarkably highly developed. Great Britain, at the time the world's dominant economic power, was a major international lender, dispatching its savings for use around the globe. However, during the turbulent years 1914–1945, two world wars and the Great Depression substantially reduced both international finance and international trade in goods and services. The extent of international finance and trade returned to the levels achieved in the late nineteenth century only in the 1980s.

In thinking about international financial markets, it is useful to understand that lending is economically equivalent to acquiring a real or financial asset, and borrowing is economically equivalent to selling a real or financial asset. For example, savers lend to companies by purchasing stocks or bonds, which are financial assets for the lender and financial liabilities for the borrowing firms. Similarly, lending to a government is accomplished in practice by acquiring a government bond—a financial asset for the lender and a financial liability for the borrower, in this case the government. Savers also can provide funds by acquiring real assets such as land; if I purchase a parcel of land from you, though I am not making a loan in the usual sense, I am providing you with funds that you can use for consuming or investing. In lieu of interest or dividends from a bond or a stock, I receive the rental value of the land that I purchased.

From a macroeconomic perspective, international capital flows play two important roles. First, as we discussed earlier in this chapter, they allow countries to run trade imbalances; a trade deficit is matched by net capital inflows and a trade surplus is matched by net capital outflows. (Recall Equation 22.2.) Second, they allow countries whose productive investment opportunities are greater than domestic savings to fill in the gap by borrowing from abroad. The rest of this chapter focuses on this second role.

THE DETERMINANTS OF INTERNATIONAL CAPITAL FLOWS

Capital inflows are purchases of domestic assets by foreigners, while capital outflows are purchases of foreign assets by domestic residents. For example, capital inflows into the United States include foreign purchases of items such as the stocks and bonds of U.S. companies, U.S. government bonds, and real assets such as land or buildings owned by U.S. residents. Why would foreigners want to acquire U.S. assets, and, conversely, why would Americans want to acquire assets abroad?

The basic factors that determine the attractiveness of any asset, either domestic or foreign, are *return* and *risk*. Financial investors seek high real returns; thus, with other factors (such as the degree of risk and the returns available abroad) held constant, a higher real interest rate in the home country promotes capital inflows by making domestic assets more attractive to foreigners. By the same token, a higher real interest rate in the home country reduces capital outflows by inducing domestic residents to invest their savings at home. Thus, all else being equal, a higher real interest rate at home increases net capital inflows. Conversely, a low real interest rate at home tends to reduce net capital inflows (by increasing net capital outflows),

FIGURE 22.9
Net Capital Inflows and the Real Interest Rate.
Holding constant the degree of risk and the real returns available abroad, a high real interest rate in the home country will induce foreigners to buy domestic assets, increasing capital inflows. A high real rate in the home country also reduces the incentive for domestic savers to buy foreign assets, reducing capital outflows. Thus, all else being equal, the higher the domestic real interest rate *r*, the higher will be net capital inflows *KI*.

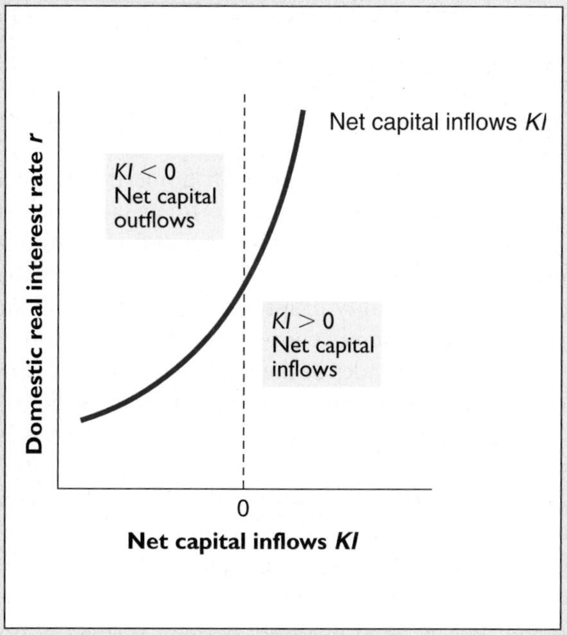

as financial investors look abroad for better opportunities. Figure 22.9 shows the relationship between a country's net capital inflows and the real rate of interest prevailing in that country. When the domestic real interest rate is high, net capital inflows are positive (foreign purchases of domestic assets exceed domestic purchases of foreign assets). But when the real interest rate is low, net capital inflows are negative (that is, the country experiences net capital outflows).

The effect of risk on capital flows is the opposite of the effect of the real interest rate. For a given real interest rate, an increase in the riskiness of domestic assets reduces net capital inflows, as foreigners become less willing to buy the home country's assets, and domestic savers become more inclined to buy foreign assets. For example, political instability, which increases the risk of investing in a country, tends to reduce net capital inflows. Figure 22.10 shows the effect of an increase in risk on capital flows: At each value of the domestic real interest rate, an increase in risk reduces net capital inflows, shifting the capital inflows curve to the left.

FIGURE 22.10
An Increase in Risk Reduces Net Capital Inflows.
An increase in the riskiness of domestic assets, arising, for example, from an increase in political instability, reduces the willingness of foreign and domestic savers to hold domestic assets. The supply of capital inflows declines at each value of the domestic real interest rate, shifting the *KI* curve to the left.

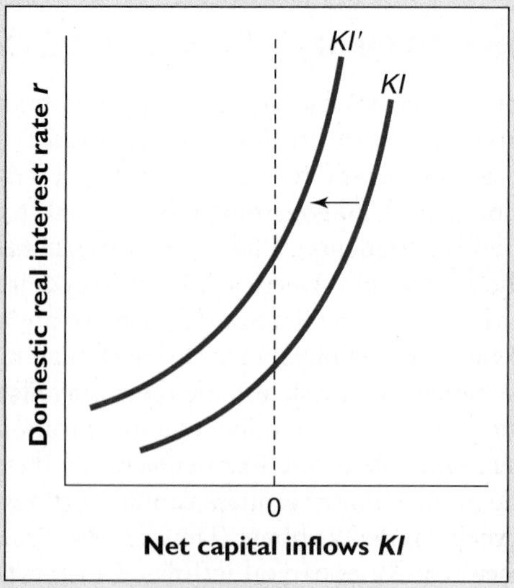

EXERCISE 22.7

For given real interest rate and riskiness in the home country, how would you expect net capital inflows to be affected by an increase in real interest rates abroad? Show your answer graphically.

SAVING, INVESTMENT, AND CAPITAL INFLOWS

International capital flows have a close relationship to domestic saving and investment. As we will see next, capital inflows augment the domestic saving pool, increasing the funds available for investment in physical capital, while capital outflows reduce the amount of saving available for investment. Thus capital inflows can help to promote economic growth within a country, and capital outflows, to restrain it.

To derive the relationship among capital inflows, saving, and investment, recall from Chapter 12 that total output or income Y must always equal the sum of the four components of expenditure: consumption (C), investment (I), government purchases (G), and net exports (NX). Writing out this identity, we have

$$Y = C + I + G + NX.$$

Next, we subtract $C + G + NX$ from both sides of the identity to obtain

$$Y - C - G - NX = I.$$

In Chapter 16 we saw that national saving S is equal to $Y - C - G$. If we make this substitution in the preceding equation, we obtain

$$S - NX = I. \qquad (22.3)$$

Now recall that Equation 22.2 describes the relationship between the trade balance NX and net capital inflows KI. In particular, the trade balance plus capital inflows equals zero, or $NX + KI = 0$. This also can be written as $KI = -NX$. If we make this substitution in the above equation, we find that

$$S + KI = I. \qquad (22.4)$$

Equation 22.4, a key result, says that the sum of national saving S and net capital inflows from abroad KI must equal domestic investment in new capital goods, I. In other words, in an open economy, the pool of saving available for domestic investment includes not only national saving (the saving of the domestic private and public sectors) but funds from savers abroad as well.

In Chapter 16, we introduced the saving-investment diagram, which shows that in a closed economy, the supply of saving must equal the demand for saving. A similar diagram applies to an open economy, except that the supply of saving in an open economy includes net capital inflows as well as domestic saving. Figure 22.11 shows the open-economy version of the saving-investment diagram. The domestic real interest rate is shown on the vertical axis and saving and investment flows on the horizontal axis. As in a closed economy, the downward-sloping curve I shows the demand for funds by firms that want to make capital investments. The curve marked $S + KI$ shows the total supply of saving, including *both* domestic saving S and net capital inflows from abroad KI. Since a higher domestic real interest rate increases both domestic saving and net capital inflows, the $S + KI$ curve is upward-sloping. As Figure 22.11 shows, the equilibrium real interest rate in an open economy, r^*, is the level that sets the total amount of saving supplied (including net capital inflows from abroad) equal to the amount of saving demanded for purposes of domestic capital investment.

FIGURE 22.11
The Saving-Investment Diagram for an Open Economy.
The total supply of saving in an open economy is the sum of national saving S and net capital inflows KI. An increase in the domestic real interest rate will increase both S and KI. The domestic demand for saving for purposes of capital investment is shown by the curve labeled I. The equilibrium real interest rate r^* sets the total supply of saving, including capital inflows, equal to the domestic demand for saving.

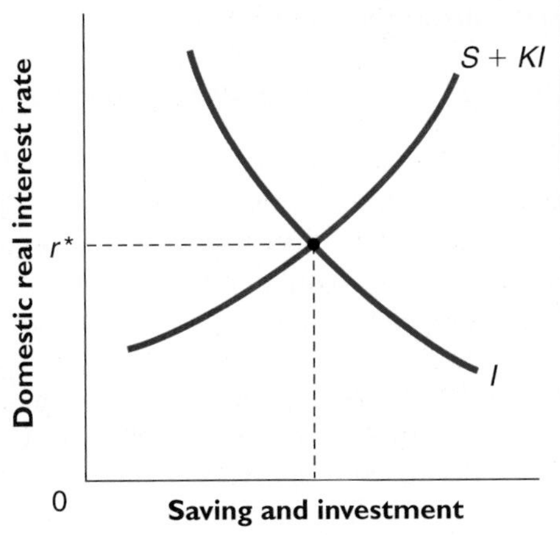

Figure 22.11 also indicates how net capital inflows can benefit an economy. A country that attracts significant amounts of foreign capital flows will have a larger pool of total saving and, hence, both a lower real interest rate and a higher rate of investment in new capital than it otherwise would. The United States and Canada both benefited from large inflows of capital in the early stages of their economic development, as do many developing countries today. Because capital inflows tend to react very sensitively to risk, an implication is that countries that are politically stable and safeguard the rights of foreign investors will attract more foreign capital and thus grow more quickly than countries without those characteristics.

THE SAVING RATE AND THE TRADE DEFICIT

We have seen that a country's exports and imports do not necessarily balance in each period. Indeed, the United States has run a trade deficit, with its imports exceeding exports, for many years. What causes trade deficits? Stories in the media sometimes claim that trade deficits occur because a country produces inferior goods that no one wants to buy or because other countries impose unfair trade restrictions on imports. Despite the popularity of these explanations, however, there is little support for them in either economic theory or evidence. For example, the United States has a large trade deficit with China, but no one would claim U.S. goods are generally inferior to Chinese goods. And many developing countries have significant trade deficits even though they, rather than their trading partners, tend to impose the more stringent restrictions on trade.

Economists argue that, rather than the quality of a country's exports or the existence of unfair trade restrictions, *a low rate of national saving is the primary cause of trade deficits.*

We have already seen the relationship between national saving and the trade balance in Equation 22.3, $S - NX = I$, which we rewrite as

$$S - I = NX. \tag{22.5}$$

According to Equation 22.5, if we hold domestic investment (I) constant, a high rate of national saving S implies a high level of net exports NX, while a low level of national saving implies a low level of net exports. Furthermore, if a country's national saving is less than its investment, or $S < I$, then Equation 22.5 implies that net exports NX will be negative. That is, the country will have a trade deficit. The conclusion from Equation 22.5 is that, holding domestic investment constant, low national saving tends to be associated with a trade deficit ($NX < 0$), and high national saving is associated with a trade surplus ($NX > 0$).

Why does a low rate of national saving tend to be associated with a trade deficit? A country with a low national saving rate is one in which households and the government have high spending rates, relative to domestic income and production. Since part of the spending of households and the government is devoted to imported goods, we would expect a low-saving, high-spending economy to have a high volume of imports. Furthermore, a low-saving economy consumes a large proportion of its domestic production, reducing the quantity of goods and services available for export. With high imports and low exports, a low-saving economy will experience a trade deficit.

A country with a trade deficit also must be receiving capital inflows, as we have seen. (Equation 22.2 tells us that if a trade deficit exists so that $NX < 0$, then it must be true that $KI > 0$—net capital inflows are positive.) Is a low national saving rate also consistent with the existence of net capital inflows? The answer is yes. A country with a low national saving rate will not have sufficient saving of its own to finance domestic investment. Thus, there likely will be many good investment opportunities in the country available to foreign savers, leading to capital inflows. Equivalently, a shortage of domestic saving will tend to drive up the domestic real interest rate, which attracts capital flows from abroad.

Why is the U.S. trade deficit so large?

As shown by Figure 22.8, U.S. trade was more or less in balance until the mid-1970s. Since the late 1970s, however, the United States has run large trade deficits, particularly in the mid-1980s and since the latter part of the 1990s. Indeed, in 2004 the trade deficit equaled 5.2 percent of U.S. GDP. Why is the U.S. trade deficit so large?

Figure 22.12 shows national saving, investment, and the trade balance for the United States from 1960 to 2006 (all measured relative to GDP). Note that the trade balance has been negative since the late 1970s, indicating a trade deficit. Note also that trade deficits correspond to periods in which investment exceeds national saving, as required by Equation 22.5.

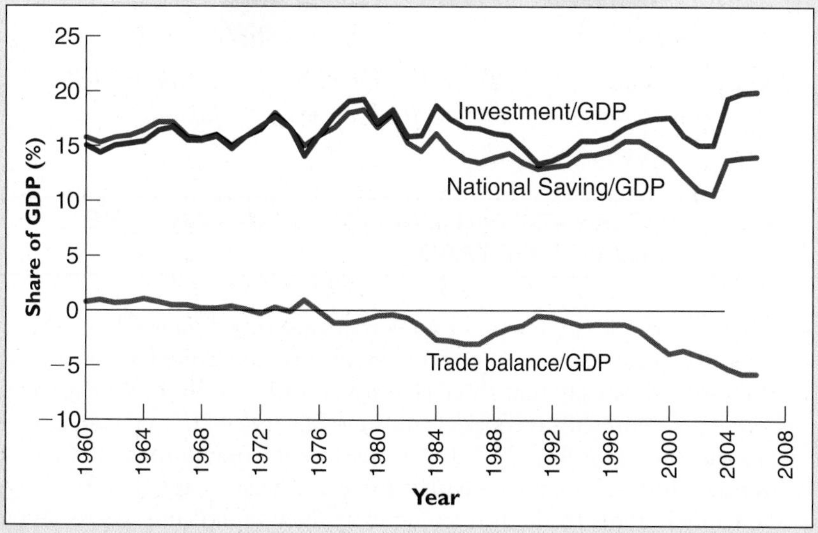

Source: Bureau of Economic Analysis (http://www.bea.gov).

FIGURE 22.12
National Saving, Investment, and the Trade Balance in the United States, 1960–2006.
Since the 1970s, U.S. national saving has fallen below domestic investment, implying a significant trade deficit.

EN 22 B

U.S. national saving and investment were roughly in balance in the 1960s and early 1970s, and, hence, the U.S. trade balance was close to zero during that period. However, U.S. national saving fell sharply during the late 1970s and 1980s. One factor that contributed to the decline in national saving was the large government deficits of the era. Because investment did not decline as much as saving, the U.S. trade deficit ballooned in the 1980s, coming under control only when investment fell during the recession of 1990–1991. Saving and investment both recovered during the 1990s, but in the latter part of the 1990s, national saving dropped again. This time the federal government was not at fault since its budget showed a healthy surplus. Rather, the fall in national saving reflected a decline in private saving, the result of a powerful upsurge in consumption spending. Much of the increase in consumption spending was for imported goods and services, which increased the trade deficit. In 2002, however, the federal government again began to have large budget deficits. This reduced national saving even more and led to a record trade deficit in 2006.

Is the U.S. trade deficit a problem? The trade deficit implies that the United States is relying heavily on foreign saving and net capital inflows to finance its domestic capital formation. These foreign loans must ultimately be repaid with interest. If the foreign savings are well invested and the U.S. economy grows, repayment will not pose a problem. However, if economic growth in the United States slackens, repaying the foreign lenders will impose an economic burden in the future. ◆

"But we're not just talking about buying a car—we're talking about confronting this country's trade deficit with Japan."

RECAP INTERNATIONAL CAPITAL FLOWS AND THE BALANCE OF TRADE

- Purchases or sales of assets across borders are called *international capital flows*. If a person, firm, or government in (say) the United States borrows from abroad, we say that there is a capital inflow into the United States. In this case, foreign savers are acquiring U.S. assets. If a person, firm, or government in the United States lends to someone abroad, thereby acquiring a foreign asset, we say that there has been a capital outflow from the United States to the foreign country. Net capital inflows to a given country equal capital inflows minus outflows.

- If a country imports more goods and services than it exports, it must borrow abroad to cover the difference. Likewise, a country that exports more than it imports will lend the difference to foreigners. Thus, as a matter of accounting, the trade balance *NX* and net capital inflows *KI* must sum to zero in every period.
- The funds available for domestic investment in new capital goods equal the sum of domestic saving and net capital inflows from abroad. The higher the return and the lower the risk of investing in the domestic country, the greater will be the capital inflows from abroad. Capital inflows benefit an economy by providing more funds for capital investment, but they can become a burden if the returns from investing in new capital goods are insufficient to pay back the foreign lenders.
- An important cause of a trade deficit is a low national saving rate. A country that saves little and spends a lot will tend to import a greater quantity of goods and services than it is able to export. At the same time, the country's low saving rate implies a need for more foreign borrowing to finance domestic investment spending.

SUMMARY

- The nominal exchange rate between two currencies is the rate at which the currencies can be traded for each other. A rise in the value of a currency relative to other currencies is called an appreciation; a decline in the value of a currency is called a depreciation. **LO1**
- Supply and demand analysis is a useful tool for studying the determination of exchange rates in the short run. The equilibrium exchange rate, also called the market equilibrium value of the exchange rate, equates the quantities of the currency supplied and demanded in the foreign exchange market. A currency is supplied by domestic residents who wish to acquire foreign currencies to purchase foreign goods, services, and assets. An increased preference for foreign goods, an increase in the domestic GDP, an increase in the real interest rate on foreign assets, or a decrease in the real interest rate on domestic assets all will increase the supply of a currency on the foreign exchange market and thus lower its value. A currency is demanded by foreigners who wish to purchase domestic goods, services, and assets. An increased preference for domestic goods by foreigners, an increase in real GDP abroad, an increase in the domestic real interest rate, or a decrease in the foreign real interest rate all will increase the demand for the currency on the foreign exchange market and thus increase its value. **LO2**
- If the exchange rate is flexible, a tight monetary policy increases the demand for the currency, reduces the supply of currency, and causes it to appreciate. The stronger currency reinforces the effects of the tight monetary policy on aggregate demand by reducing net exports. Conversely, easy monetary policy lowers the real interest rate and weakens the currency, which in turn stimulates net exports. **LO3**
- The value of a fixed exchange rate is officially established by the government. A fixed exchange rate whose official value exceeds its market equilibrium value in the foreign exchange market is said to be overvalued. An exchange rate whose official value is below its market equilibrium value is undervalued. A reduction in the official value of a fixed exchange rate is called a devaluation; an increase in its official value is called a revaluation. **LO3**
- For an overvalued exchange rate, the quantity of the currency supplied at the official exchange rate exceeds the quantity demanded. To maintain the official rate, the country's central bank must use its international reserves (foreign currency assets) to purchase the excess supply of its currency in the foreign exchange market. Because a country's international reserves are limited, it cannot maintain an overvalued exchange rate indefinitely. **LO3**
- A tight monetary policy, by raising the market equilibrium value of the exchange rate, can eliminate the problem of overvaluation. However, if monetary policy is used to set the market equilibrium value of the

exchange rate equal to the official value, it is no longer available for stabilizing the domestic economy. Thus, under fixed exchange rates, monetary policy has little or no power to affect domestic output and employment. **LO3**

- The real exchange rate is the price of the average domestic good or service *relative* to the price of the average foreign good or service, when prices are expressed in terms of a common currency. The real exchange rate incorporates both the nominal exchange rate and the relative levels of prices among countries. An increase in the real exchange rate implies that domestic goods and services are becoming more expensive relative to foreign goods and services, which tends to reduce exports and increase imports. Conversely, a decline in the real exchange rate tends to increase net exports. **LO4**

- A basic theory of nominal exchange rate determination in the long run, the purchasing power parity (PPP) theory, is based on the law of one price. The law of one price states that if transportation costs are relatively small, the price of an internationally traded commodity must be the same in all locations. According to the PPP theory, we can find the nominal exchange rate between two currencies by setting the price of a commodity in one of the currencies equal to the price of the commodity in the second currency. The PPP theory correctly predicts that the currencies of countries that experience significant inflation will tend to depreciate in the long run. However, the fact that many goods and services are not traded internationally, and that not all traded goods are standardized, makes the PPP theory less useful for explaining short-run changes in exchange rates. **LO5**

- The trade balance, or net exports, is the value of a country's exports less the value of its imports in a particular period. Exports need not equal imports in each period. If exports exceed imports, the difference is called a trade surplus, and if imports exceed exports, the difference is called a trade deficit. **LO1**

- The higher the real interest rate in a country, and the lower the risk of investing there, the higher its net capital inflows. The availability of capital inflows expands a country's pool of saving, allowing for more domestic investment and increased growth. A drawback to using capital inflows to finance domestic capital formation is that the returns to capital (interest and dividends) accrue to foreign financial investors rather than domestic residents. **LO5**

- A low rate of national saving is the primary cause of trade deficits. A low-saving, high-spending country is likely to import more than a high-saving country. It also consumes more of its domestic production, leaving less for export. Finally, a low-saving country is likely to have a high real interest rate, which attracts net capital inflows. Because the sum of the trade balance and net capital inflows is zero, a high level of net capital inflows always accompanies a large trade deficit. **LO6**

KEY TERMS

appreciation (647)
balance-of-payments deficit (657)
balance-of-payments surplus (657)
capital inflows (669)
capital outflows (669)
depreciation (647)
devaluation (655)
fixed exchange rate (647)
flexible exchange rate (647)
foreign exchange market (647)
internationl capital flows (669)
international reserves (657)
law of one price (665)
market equilibrium value of the exchange rate (650)
net capital inflows (669)
nominal exchange rate (645)
overvalued exchange rate (656)
purchasing power parity (PPP) (666)
real exchange rate (664)
revaluation (655)
trade balance (669)
trade deficit (669)
trade surplus (669)
undervalued exchange rate (656)

REVIEW QUESTIONS

1. Japanese yen trade at 110 yen per dollar and Mexican pesos trade at 10 pesos per dollar. What is the nominal exchange rate between the yen and the peso? Express in two ways. **LO1**
2. Why do U.S. households and firms supply dollars to the foreign exchange market? Why do foreigners demand dollars in the foreign exchange market? **LO2**

3. Under a flexible exchange rate, how does an easing of monetary policy (a lower real interest rate) affect the value of the exchange rate? Does this change in the exchange rate tend to weaken or strengthen the effect of the monetary ease on output and employment? Explain. **LO3**
4. Contrast fixed and flexible exchange rates in terms of how they affect (a) the ability of monetary policy to stabilize domestic output and (b) the predictability of future exchange rates. **LO3**
5. Define *nominal exchange rate* and *real exchange rate*. How are the two concepts related? **LO1, LO4**
6. Explain with examples why, in any period, a country's net capital inflows equal its trade deficit. **LO1**
7. How are capital inflows or outflows related to domestic investment in new capital goods? **LO2**

▪ PROBLEMS ▪

McGraw-Hill's HOMEWORK MANAGER®

1. Using the data in Table 22.1, find the nominal exchange rate between the Mexican peso and the Japanese yen. Express in two ways. How do your answers change if the peso appreciates by 10 percent against the dollar while the value of the yen against the dollar remains unchanged? **LO1**
2. Suppose a French bottle of champagne costs 20 euros. **LO1, LO2**
   a. If the euro–dollar exchange rate is 0.8 euro per dollar, so that a dollar can buy 0.8 euro, how much will the champagne cost in the United States?
   b. If the euro–dollar exchange rate rises to 1 euro per dollar, how much will the champagne cost in the United States?
   c. If an increase in the euro–dollar exchange rate leads to an increase in Americans' dollar expenditures on French champagne, what will happen to the amount of dollars supplied to the foreign exchange market as the euro–dollar exchange rate rises?
3. Consider an Apple iPod that costs $240. **LO1, LO2**
   a. If the euro–dollar exchange rate is 1 euro per dollar, so that it costs a European 1 euro to buy a dollar, how much will the iPod cost in France?
   b. If the euro–dollar exchange rate falls to 0.8 euro per dollar, how much will the iPod cost in France?
   c. Consequently, what will happen to French purchases of iPods and the amount of dollars demanded in the foreign exchange market as the euro–dollar exchange rate falls?
4. How would each of the following be likely to affect the value of the dollar, all else being equal? Explain. **LO2**
   a. U.S. stocks are perceived as having become much riskier financial investments.
   b. European computer firms switch from U.S.-produced software to software produced in India, Israel, and other nations.
   c. As East Asian economies grow, international financial investors become aware of many new, high-return investment opportunities in the region.
   d. The U.S. government imposes a large tariff on imported automobiles.
   e. The Federal Reserve reports that it is less concerned about inflation and more concerned about an impending recession in the United States.
   f. The European Central Bank becomes less concerned about European inflation and more concerned about an impending recession in Europe.
5. The demand for and supply of shekels in the foreign exchange market are

$$\text{Demand} = 30{,}000 + 8{,}000e,$$

$$\text{Supply} = 25{,}000 + 12{,}000e,$$

where the nominal exchange rate is expressed as U.S. dollars per shekel. **LO2, LO3**

a. What is the market equilibrium value of the shekel?

b. The shekel is fixed at 0.30 U.S. dollar. Is the shekel overvalued, undervalued, or neither? Find the balance-of-payments deficit or surplus in both shekels and dollars. What happens to the country's international reserves over time?

c. Repeat part b for the case in which the shekel is fixed at 0.20 U.S. dollar.

6. The annual demand for and supply of shekels in the foreign exchange market is as given in problem 5. The shekel is fixed at 0.30 dollar per shekel. The country's international reserves are $600. Foreign financial investors hold checking accounts in the country in the amount of 5,000 shekels. **LO2, LO3**
   a. Suppose that foreign financial investors do not fear a devaluation of the shekel, and thus do not convert their shekel checking accounts into dollars. Can the shekel be maintained at its fixed value of 0.30 U.S. dollar for the next year?
   b. Now suppose that foreign financial investors come to expect a possible devaluation of the shekel to 0.25 U.S. dollar. Why should this possibility worry them?
   c. In response to their concern about devaluation, foreign financial investors withdraw all funds from their checking accounts and attempt to convert those shekels into dollars. What happens?
   d. Discuss why the foreign investors' forecast of devaluation can be considered a "self-fulfilling prophecy."

7. A British-made automobile is priced at £20,000 (20,000 British pounds). A comparable U.S.-made car costs $26,000. One pound trades for $1.50 in the foreign exchange market. Find the real exchange rate from the perspective of the United States and from the perspective of Great Britain. Which country's cars are more competitively priced? **LO4**

8. Between last year and this year, the CPI in Blueland rose from 100 to 110 and the CPI in Redland rose from 100 to 105. Blueland's currency unit, the blue, was worth $1 (U.S.) last year and is worth 90 cents (U.S.) this year. Redland's currency unit, the red, was worth 50 cents (U.S.) last year and is worth 45 cents (U.S.) this year.

   Find the percentage change from last year to this year in Blueland's *nominal* exchange rate with Redland and in Blueland's *real* exchange rate with Redland. (Treat Blueland as the home country.) Relative to Redland, do you expect Blueland's exports to be helped or hurt by these changes in exchange rates? **LO1, LO4**

9. How do each of the following transactions affect (1) the trade surplus or deficit and (2) capital inflows or outflows for the United States? Show that in each case the identity that the trade balance plus net capital inflows equals zero applies. **LO1**
   a. A U.S. exporter sells software to Israel. She uses the Israeli shekels received to buy stock in an Israeli company.
   b. A Mexican firm uses proceeds from its sale of oil to the United States to buy U.S. government debt.
   c. A Mexican firm uses proceeds from its sale of oil to the United States to buy oil drilling equipment from a U.S. firm.
   d. A Mexican firm receives U.S. dollars from selling oil to the United States. A French firm accepts the dollars as payment for drilling equipment. The French firm uses the dollars to buy U.S. government debt.
   e. A British financial investor writes a check on his bank account in New York to purchase shares of General Motors stock (GM is a U.S. company).

10. Use a diagram like Figure 22.11 to show the effects of each of the following on the real interest rate and capital investment of a country that is a net borrower from abroad. **LO5**

a. Investment opportunities in the country improve owing to new technologies.
b. The government budget deficit rises.
c. Domestic citizens decide to save more.
d. Foreign investors believe that the riskiness of lending to the country has increased.

ANSWERS TO IN-CHAPTER EXERCISES

22.1 Answers will vary, depending on when the data are obtained. **LO1**

22.2 A decline in U.S. GDP reduces consumer incomes and hence imports. As Americans are purchasing fewer imports, they supply fewer dollars to the foreign exchange market, so the supply curve for dollars shifts to the left. Reduced supply raises the market equilibrium value of the dollar. **LO2**

22.3 At a fixed value for the peso of 0.15 dollar, the demand for the peso equals 25,000 − 50,0000.15 = 17,500. The supply of the peso equals 17,600 + 24,000(0.15) = 21,200. The quantity supplied at the official rate exceeds the quantity demanded by 3,700. Latinia will have to purchase 3,700 pesos each period, so its balance-of-payments deficit will equal 3,700 pesos, or 3,700 × 0.15 = 555 dollars. This balance-of-payments deficit is larger than we found when the exchange rate was 0.125. We conclude that the greater the degree of overvaluation, the larger the country's balance-of-payments deficit is likely to be. **LO2, LO3**

22.4 The figure shows a situation in which the official value of the currency is *below* the market equilibrium value, as determined by the supply of and demand for the currency in the foreign exchange market, so the currency is undervalued. At the official value of the exchange rate, the quantity demanded of the domestic currency (point *B*) exceeds the quantity supplied (point *A*). To maintain the official value, the central bank must supply domestic currency to the foreign exchange market each period in the amount *AB*. In contrast to the case of an overvalued exchange rate, here the central bank is providing its own currency to the foreign exchange market and receiving foreign currencies in return.

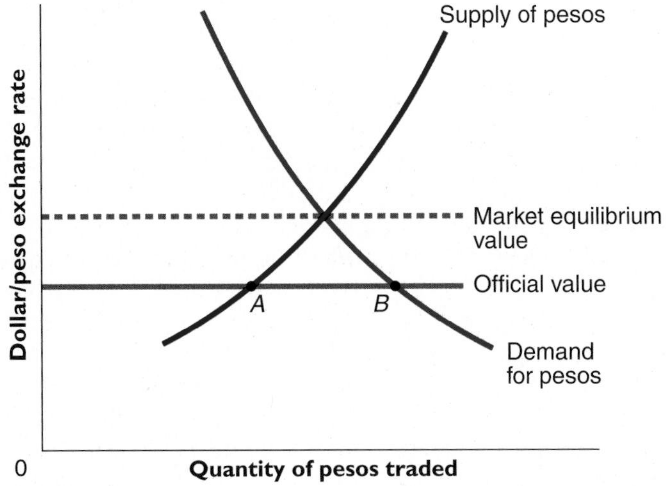

The central bank can print as much of its own currency as it likes, and so with an undervalued currency, there is no danger of running out of international reserves. Indeed, the central bank's stock of international reserves increases in the amount AB each period, as it receives foreign currencies in exchange for the domestic currency it supplies. **LO2, LO3**

22.5 The dollar price of the U.S. computer is \$2,400, and each dollar is equal to 110 yen. Therefore, the yen price of the U.S. computer is (110 yen/dollar) × (\$2,400), or 264,000 yen. The price of the Japanese computer is 242,000 yen. Thus, the conclusion that the Japanese model is cheaper does not depend on the currency in which the comparison is made. **LO4**

22.6 Since the law of one price holds for gold, its price per ounce must be the same in New York and Stockholm:

$$\$300 = 2{,}500 \text{ kronor.}$$

Dividing both sides by 300, we get

$$\$1 = 8.33 \text{ kronor.}$$

So the exchange rate is 8.33 kronor per dollar. **LO5**

22.7 An increase in the real interest rate abroad increases the relative attractiveness of foreign financial investments to both foreign and domestic savers. Net capital inflows to the home country will fall at each level of the domestic real interest rate. The supply curve of net capital inflows shifts left, as in Figure 22.11 **LO5**

GLOSSARY

A

Absolute advantage. One person has an absolute advantage over another if he or she takes fewer hours to perform a task than the other person.

Accommodating policy. A policy that allows the effects of a shock to occur.

Accounting profit. The difference between a firm's total revenue and its explicit costs.

Aggregate demand (*AD*) curve. Shows the relationship between short-run equilibrium output Y and the rate of inflation π, holding all other factors constant; the *AD* curve slopes downward because of the Fed's monetary policy rule: when inflation rises, the Fed raises nominal interest rates, which in turn causes real interest rates to rise, and this causes planned spending and short-run output to fall.

Aggregate supply (*AS*) curve. Shows the relationship between short-run equilibrium output Y and inflation given current inflation expectations and holding all other factors constant; the *AS* curve slopes upward because actual inflation is related to the gap between actual output and potential output: when output is below potential, actual inflation is below expected inflation and when output is above potential, actual inflation is above expected inflation.

Aggregate supply shock. Either an inflation shock or a shock to potential output; adverse aggregate supply shocks of both types reduce output and increase inflation.

Allocative function of price. Changes in prices direct resources away from overcrowded markets and toward markets that are underserved.

Anchored inflationary expectations. When people's expectations of future inflation do not change even if inflation rises temporarily.

Appreciation. An increase in the value of a currency relative to other currencies.

Assets. Anything of value that one owns.

Attainable point. Any combination of goods that can be produced using currently available resources.

Automatic stabilizers. Provisions in the law that imply automatic increases in government spending or decreases in taxes when real output declines.

Autonomous consumption. Consumption spending that is not related to the level of disposable income.

Autonomous expenditure. The portion of planned aggregate expenditure that is independent of output.

Average benefit. Total benefit of undertaking n units of an activity divided by n.

Average cost. Total cost of undertaking n units of an activity divided by n.

Average labor productivity. Output per employed worker.

Average tax rate. Total taxes divided by total before-tax income.

Average total cost (*ATC*). Total cost divided by total output.

Average variable cost (*AVC*). Variable cost divided by total output.

B

Balance-of-payments deficit. The net decline in a country's stock of international reserves over a year.

Balance-of-payments surplus. The net increase in a country's stock of international reserves over a year.

Balance sheet. A list of an economic unit's assets and liabilities on a specific date.

Bank reserves. Cash or similar assets held by commercial banks for the purpose of meeting depositor withdrawals and payments.

Banking panic. A situation in which news or rumors of the imminent bankruptcy of one or more banks leads bank depositors to rush to withdraw their funds.

Barrier to entry. Any force that prevents firms from entering a new market.

Barter. The direct trade of goods or services for other goods or services.

Basic elements of a game. The players, the strategies available to each player, and the payoffs each player receives for each possible combination of strategies.

Bequest saving. Saving done for the purpose of leaving an inheritance.

Board of Governors. The leadership of the Fed, consisting of seven governors appointed by the president to staggered 14-year terms.

Bond. A legal promise to repay a debt, usually including both the principal amount and regular interest, or coupon, payments.

Boom. A particularly strong and protracted expansion.

Buyer's reservation price. The largest dollar amount the buyer would be willing to pay for a good.

Buyer's surplus. The difference between the buyer's reservation price and the price he or she actually pays.

C

Capital gains. Increases in the value of existing assets.

Capital good. A long-lived good that is used in the production of other goods and services.

Capital inflows. Purchases of domestic assets by foreign households and firms.

Capital losses. Decreases in the value of existing assets.

Capital outflows. Purchases of foreign assets by domestic households and firms.

Cartel. A coalition of firms that agree to restrict output for the purpose of earning an economic profit.

Cash on the table. Economic metaphor for unexploited gains from exchange.

Central bank independence. When central bankers are insulated from short-term political considerations and are allowed to take a long-term view of the economy.

Change in demand. A shift of the entire demand curve.

Change in supply. A shift of the entire supply curve.

Change in the quantity demanded. A movement along the demand curve that occurs in response to a change in price.

Change in the quantity supplied. A movement along the supply curve that occurs in response to a change in price.

Coase theorem. If at no cost people can negotiate the purchase and sale of the right to perform activities that cause externalities, they can always arrive at efficient solutions to the problems caused by externalities.

Commitment device. A way of changing incentives so as to make otherwise empty threats or promises credible.

Commitment problem. A situation in which people cannot achieve their goals because of an inability to make credible threats or promises.

Comparative advantage. One person has a comparative advantage over another if his or her opportunity cost of performing a task is lower than the other person's opportunity cost.

Complements. Two goods are complements in consumption if an increase in the price of one causes a leftward shift in the demand curve for the other (or if a decrease causes a rightward shift).

Compound interest. The payment of interest not only on the original deposit but on all previously accumulated interest.

Constant (or parameter). A quantity that is fixed in value.

Constant returns to scale. A production process is said to have constant returns to scale if, when all inputs are changed by a given proportion, output changes by the same proportion.

Consumer price index (CPI). For any period, measures the cost in that period of a standard basket of goods and services relative to the cost of the same basket of goods and services in a fixed year, called the *base year*.

Consumer surplus. The economic surplus gained by the buyers of a product as measured by the cumulative difference between their respective reservation prices and the price they actually paid.

Consumption expenditure. Spending by households on goods and services such as food, clothing, and entertainment.

Consumption function. The relationship between consumption spending and its determinants, in particular, disposable income.

Contraction. *See* **Recession.**

Contractionary policies. Government policy actions designed to reduce planned spending and output.

Core rate of inflation. The rate of increase of all prices except energy and food.

Coupon payments. Regular interest payments made to the bondholder.

Coupon rate. The interest rate promised when a bond is issued; the annual coupon payments are equal to the coupon rate times the principal amount of the bond.

Credibility of monetary policy. The degree to which the public believes the central bank's promises to keep inflation low, even if doing so may impose short-run economic costs.

Credible promise. A promise to take an action that is in the promiser's interest to keep.

Credible threat. A threat to take an action that is in the threatener's interest to carry out.

Cross-price elasticity of demand. The percentage by which the quantity demanded of the first good changes in response to a 1 percent change in the price of the second.

Crowding out. The tendency of increased government deficits to reduce investment spending.

Cyclical unemployment. The extra unemployment that occurs during periods of recession.

D

Decision tree (or game tree). A diagram that describes the possible moves in a game in sequence and lists the payoffs that correspond to each possible combination of moves.

Deflating (a nominal quantity). The process of dividing a nominal quantity by a price index (such as the CPI) to express the quantity in real terms.

Deflation. A situation in which the prices of most goods and services are falling over time so that inflation is negative.

Demand curve. A schedule or graph showing the quantity of a good that buyers wish to buy at each price.

Demand for money. The amount of wealth an individual or firm chooses to hold in the form of money.

Dependent variable. A variable in an equation whose value is determined by the value taken by another variable in the equation.

Deposit insurance. A system under which the government guarantees that depositors will not lose any money even if their bank goes bankrupt.

Depreciation. A decrease in the value of a currency relative to other currencies.

Depression. A particularly severe or protracted recession.

Devaluation. A reduction in the official value of a currency (in a fixed-exchange-rate system).

Diminishing returns to capital. If the amount of labor and other inputs employed is held constant, then the greater the amount of capital already in use, the less an additional unit of capital adds to production.

Diminishing returns to labor. If the amount of capital and other inputs in use is held constant, then the greater the quantity of labor already employed, the less each additional worker adds to production.

Discount rate. The interest rate that the Fed charges commercial banks to borrow reserves.

Discount window lending. The lending of reserves by the Federal Reserve to commercial banks.

Discouraged workers. People who say they would like to have a job but have not made an effort to find one in the past four weeks.

Disinflation. A substantial reduction in the rate of inflation.

Diversification. The practice of spreading one's wealth over a variety of different financial investments to reduce overall risk.

Dividend. A regular payment received by stockholders for each share that they own.

Dominant strategy. One that yields a higher payoff no matter what the other players in a game choose.

Dominated strategy. Any other strategy available to a player who has a dominant strategy.

Duration. The length of an unemployment spell.

E

Earned-income tax credit (EITC). A policy under which low-income workers receive credits on their federal income tax.

Easing monetary policy. A situation where the Fed raises its long-run target for the inflation rate.

Economic efficiency. *See* **Efficiency**.

Economic loss. An economic profit that is less than zero.

Economic profit. The difference between a firm's total revenue and the sum of its explicit and implicit costs; also called *excess profit.*

Economic rent. That part of the payment for a factor of production that exceeds the owner's reservation price, the price below which the owner would not supply the factor.

Economic surplus. The economic surplus from taking any action is the benefit of taking the action minus its cost.

Economics. The study of how people make choices under conditions of scarcity and of the results of those choices for society.

Efficiency (or economic efficiency). Condition that occurs when all goods and services are produced and consumed at their respective socially optimal levels.

Efficient (or Pareto-efficient). A situation is efficient if no change is possible that will help some people without harming others.

Efficient point. Any combination of goods for which currently available resources do not allow an increase in the production of one good without a reduction in the production of the other.

Elastic. The demand for a good is elastic with respect to price if its price elasticity of demand is greater than 1.

Entrepreneurs. People who create new economic enterprises.

Equation. A mathematical expression that describes the relationship between two or more variables.

Equilibrium. A balanced or unchanging situation in which all forces at work within a system are canceled by others.

Equilibrium price and equilibrium quantity. The price and quantity of a good at the intersection of the supply and demand curves for the good.

Excess demand (or shortage). The difference between the quantity supplied and the quantity demanded when the price of a good lies below the equilibrium price; buyers are dissatisfied when there is excess demand.

Excess supply (or surplus). The difference between the quantity supplied and the quantity demanded when the price of a good exceeds the equilibrium price; sellers are dissatisfied when there is excess supply.

Exogenous changes in spending. Changes in planned spending that are not caused by changes in output or the real interest rate.

Expansion. A period in which the economy is growing at a rate significantly above normal.

Expansionary gap. A positive output gap, which occurs when actual output is higher than potential output ($Y > Y^*$).

Expansionary policies. Government policy actions intended to increase planned spending and output.

Expenditure line. A line showing the relationship between planned aggregate expenditure and output.

Explicit costs. The actual payments a firm makes to its factors of production and other suppliers.

External benefit (or positive externality). A benefit of an activity received by people other than those who pursue the activity.

External cost (or negative externality). A cost of an activity that falls on people other than those who pursue the activity.

Externality. An external cost or benefit of an activity.

F

Factor of production. An input used in the production of a good or service.

Federal funds rate. The interest rate that commercial banks charge each other for very short-term (usually overnight) loans; because the Fed frequently sets its policy in terms of the federal funds rate, this rate is closely watched in financial markets.

Federal Open Market Committee (or FOMC). The committee that makes decisions concerning monetary policy.

Federal Reserve System (or Fed). The central bank of the United States.

Final goods or services. Goods or services consumed by the ultimate user; because they are the end products of the production process, they are counted as part of GDP.

Financial intermediaries. Firms that extend credit to borrowers using funds raised from savers.

First-dollar insurance coverage. Insurance that pays all expenses generated by the insured activity.

Fisher effect. The tendency for nominal interest rates to be high when inflation is high and low when inflation is low.

Fixed cost. A cost that does not vary with the level of an activity; the sum of all payments made to the firm's fixed factors of production.

Fixed exchange rate. An exchange rate whose value is set by official government policy.

Fixed factor of production. An input whose quantity cannot be altered in the short run.

Flexible exchange rate. An exchange rate whose value is not officially fixed but varies according to the supply and demand for the currency in the foreign exchange market.

Flow. A measure that is defined per unit of time.

Foreign exchange market. The market on which currencies of various nations are traded for one another.

Fractional-reserve banking system. A banking system in which bank reserves are less than deposits so that the reserve-deposit ratio is less than 100 percent.

Frictional unemployment. The short-term unemployment associated with the process of matching workers with jobs.

G

Game tree. *See* **Decision tree.**

Government budget deficit. The excess of government spending over tax collections ($G - T$).

Government budget surplus. The excess of government tax collections over government spending ($T - G$); the government budget surplus equals public saving.

Government purchases. Purchases by federal, state, and local governments of final goods and services; government purchases do *not* include *transfer payments,* which are payments made by the government in return for which no current goods or services are received, nor do they include interest paid on the government debt.

Gross domestic product (GDP). The market value of the final goods and services produced in a country during a given period.

H

Health maintenance organization (HMO). A group of physicians that provides health services to individuals and families for a fixed annual fee.

Human capital. An amalgam of factors such as education, training, experience, intelligence, energy, work habits, trustworthiness, initiative, and others that affect the value of a worker's marginal product.

Human capital theory. A theory of pay determination that says a worker's wage will be proportional to his or her stock of human capital.

Hurdle method of price discrimination. The practice by which a seller offers a discount to all buyers who overcome some obstacle.

Hyperinflation. A situation in which the inflation rate is extremely high.

I

Imperfectly competitive firm. A firm that has at least some control over the market price of its product.

Implicit costs. The opportunity costs of the resources supplied by the firm's owners.

Income effect. The change in the quantity demanded of a good that results because a change in the price of a good changes the buyer's purchasing power.

Income elasticity of demand. The percentage by which a good's quantity demanded changes in response to a 1 percent change in income.

Income-expenditure multiplier. The effect of a one-unit increase in autonomous expenditure on short-run equilibrium output.

Increasing returns to scale. A production process is said to have increasing returns to scale if, when all inputs are changed by a given proportion, output changes by more than that proportion; also called *economies of scale.*

Independent variable. A variable in an equation whose value determines the value taken by another variable in the equation.

Indexing. The practice of increasing a nominal quantity each period by an amount equal to the percentage increase in a specified price index. Indexing prevents the purchasing power of the nominal quantity from being eroded by inflation.

Induced expenditure. The portion of planned aggregate expenditure that depends on output Y.

Inefficient point. Any combination of goods for which currently available resources enable an increase in the production of one good without a reduction in the production of the other.

Inelastic. The demand for a good is inelastic with respect to price if its price elasticity of demand is less than 1.

Inferior good. A good whose demand curve shifts leftward when the incomes of buyers increase.

Inflation dove. Someone who is not strongly committed to achieving and maintaining low inflation.

Inflation hawk. Someone who is committed to achieving and maintaining low inflation, even at some short-run cost in reduced output and employment.

Inflation-protected bonds. Bonds whose holders receive a nominal interest rate each year equal to the fixed real rate plus the actual rate of inflation during that year.

Inflation shock. A sudden change in the normal behavior of inflation, unrelated to the nation's output gap.

In-kind transfer. A payment made not in the form of cash but in the form of a good or service.

Intermediate goods or services. Goods or services used up in the production of final goods and services and therefore not counted as part of GDP.

International capital flows. Purchases or sales of real and financial assets across international borders.

International reserves. Foreign currency assets held by a government for the purpose of purchasing the domestic currency in the foreign exchange market.

Investment. Spending by firms on final goods and services, primarily capital goods.

Invisible hand theory. Adam Smith's theory stating that the actions of independent, self-interested buyers and sellers will often result in the most efficient allocation of resources.

L

Labor force. The total number of employed and unemployed people in the economy.

Law of demand. People do less of what they want to do as the cost of doing it rises.

Law of diminishing marginal utility. The tendency for the additional utility gained from consuming an additional unit of a good to diminish as consumption increases beyond some point.

Law of diminishing returns. A property of the relationship between the amount of a good or service produced and the amount of a variable factor required to produce it; the law says that when some factors of production are fixed, increased production of the good eventually requires ever larger increases in the variable factor.

Law of one price. If transportation costs are relatively small, the price of an internationally traded commodity must be the same in all locations.

Liabilities. The debts one owes.

Life-cycle saving. Saving to meet long-term objectives such as retirement, college attendance, or the purchase of a home.

Long run. A period of time of sufficient length that all the firm's factors of production are variable.

Long-run aggregate supply (*LRAS*) line. A vertical line showing the economy's potential output Y^*.

Long-run equilibrium. Situation where actual output is equal to potential output and actual inflation equals expected inflation and the Fed's inflation target; graphically, this is where the *AD* curve, the *AS* curve, and the *LRAS* curve intersect at a single point.

M

M1. Sum of currency outstanding and balances held in checking accounts.

M2. All the assets in M1 plus some additional assets that are usable in making payments but at greater cost or inconvenience than currency or checks.

Macroeconomics. The study of the performance of national economies and the policies that governments use to try to improve that performance.

Marginal benefit. The marginal benefit of an activity is the increase in total benefit that results from carrying out one additional unit of the activity.

Marginal cost. The marginal cost of an activity is the increase in total cost that results from carrying out one additional unit of the activity; as output changes from one level to another, the change in total cost divided by the corresponding change in output.

Marginal product of labor (*MP*). The additional output a firm gets by employing one additional unit of labor.

Marginal propensity to consume (*mpc*). The amount by which consumption rises when disposable income rises by $1; we assume that $0 < mpc < 1$.

Marginal revenue. The change in a firm's total revenue that results from a one-unit change in output.

Marginal tax rate. The amount by which taxes rise when before-tax income rises by one dollar.

Marginal utility. The additional utility gained from consuming an additional unit of a good.

Market. The market for any good consists of all buyers or sellers of that good.

Market equilibrium. Occurs when all buyers and sellers are satisfied with their respective quantities at the market price.

Market equilibrium value of the exchange rate. The exchange rate that equates the quantities of the currency supplied and demanded in the foreign exchange market.

Market power. A firm's ability to raise the price of a good without losing all its sales.

Maturation date. The date at which the principal of a bond will be repaid.

Means-tested. A benefit program is means-tested if its benefit level declines as the recipient earns additional income.

Medium of exchange. An asset used in purchasing goods and services.

Menu costs. The costs of changing prices.

Microeconomics. The study of individual choice under scarcity and its implications for the behavior of prices and quantities in individual markets.

Monetary policy. Determination of the nation's money supply.

Monetary policy rule. Describes how a central bank takes action in response to changes in the state of the economy.

Money. Any asset that can be used in making purchases.

Money demand curve. Shows the relationship between the aggregate quantity of money demanded *M* and the nominal interest rate *i*; because an increase in the nominal interest rate increases the opportunity cost of holding money, which reduces the quantity of money demanded, the money demand curve slopes down.

Monopolistic competition. Industry structure in which a large number of firms produce slightly differentiated products that are reasonably close substitutes for one another.

Multiplier. *See* **Income-expenditure multiplier.**

Mutual fund. A financial intermediary that sells shares in itself to the public, then uses the funds raised to buy a wide variety of financial assets.

N

Nash equilibrium. Any combination of strategy choices in which each player's choice is his or her best choice, given the other players' choices.

National saving. The saving of the entire economy, equal to GDP less consumption expenditures and government purchases of goods and services, or $Y - C - G$.

Natural monopoly. A monopoly that results from economies of scale (increasing returns to scale).

Natural rate of unemployment, u^*. The part of the total unemployment rate that is attributable to frictional and structural unemployment; equivalently, the unemployment rate that prevails when cyclical unemployment is zero, so the economy has neither a recessionary nor an expansionary output gap.

Negative externality. *See* **External cost.**

Negative income tax (NIT). A system under which the government would grant every citizen a cash payment each year, financed by an additional tax on earned income.

Net capital inflows. Capital flows that are equal to foreign purchases of domestic assets (which bring funds into the country) minus domestic purchases of foreign assets (which send funds out of the country); that is, capital inflows minus capital outflows.

Net exports. Exports minus imports.

Nominal exchange rate. The rate at which two currencies can be traded for each other.

Nominal GDP. A measure of GDP in which the quantities produced are valued at current-year prices; nominal GDP measures the *current dollar value* of production.

Nominal interest rate. The annual percentage increase in the nominal value of a financial asset; also known as the *market interest rate.*

Nominal price. Absolute price of a good in dollar terms.

Nominal quantity. A quantity that is measured in terms of its current dollar value.

Normal good. A good whose demand curve shifts rightward when the incomes of buyers increase.

Normal profit. The opportunity cost of the resources supplied by the firm's owners; Normal profit = Accounting profit − Economic profit.

Normative economic principle. One that says how people should behave.

O

Okun's law. States that each extra percentage point of cyclical unemployment is associated with about a 2 percentage point increase in the output gap, measured in relation to potential output.

Oligopoly. An industry structure in which a small number of large firms produce products that are either close or perfect substitutes.

100 percent reserve banking. A situation in which banks' reserves equal 100 percent of their deposits.

Open-market operations. Open-market purchases and open-market sales.

Open-market purchase. The purchase of government bonds from the public by the Fed for the purpose of increasing the supply of bank reserves and the money supply.

Open-market sale. The sale by the Fed of government bonds to the public for the purpose of reducing bank reserves and the money supply.

Opportunity cost. The opportunity cost of an activity is the value of what must be forgone to undertake the activity.

Optimal combination of goods. The affordable combination that yields the highest total utility.

Output gap, $Y - Y^*$. The difference between the economy's actual output and its potential output at a point in time.

Outsourcing. A term increasingly used to connote having services performed by low-wage workers overseas.

Overvalued exchange rate. An exchange rate that has an officially fixed value greater than its market equilibrium value.

P

Parameter. *See* **Constant.**

Pareto-efficient. *See* **Efficient.**

Participation rate. The percentage of the working-age population in the labor force (that is, the percentage that is either employed or looking for work).

Payoff matrix. A table that describes the payoffs in a game for each possible combination of strategies.

Peak. The beginning of a recession; the high point of economic activity prior to a downturn.

Perfect hurdle. One that completely segregates buyers whose reservation prices lie above some threshold from others whose reservation prices lie below it, imposing no cost on those who jump the hurdle.

Perfectly competitive market. A market in which no individual supplier has significant influence on the market price of the product.

Perfectly discriminating monopolist. A firm that charges each buyer exactly his or her reservation price.

Perfectly elastic demand. The demand for a good is perfectly elastic with respect to price if its price elasticity of demand is infinite.

Perfectly elastic supply curve. A supply curve whose elasticity with respect to price is infinite.

Perfectly inelastic demand. The demand for a good is perfectly inelastic with respect to price if its price elasticity of demand is zero.

Perfectly inelastic supply curve. A supply curve whose elasticity with respect to price is zero.

Personal Responsibility Act. The 1996 federal law that transferred responsibility for welfare programs from the federal level to the state level and placed a five-year lifetime limit on payment of AFDC benefits to any given recipient.

Planned aggregate expenditure (*PAE*). Total planned spending on final goods and services.

Portfolio allocation decision. The decision about the forms in which to hold one's wealth.

Positional arms control agreement. An agreement in which contestants attempt to limit mutually offsetting investments in performance enhancement.

Positional arms race. A series of mutually offsetting investments in performance enhancement that is stimulated by a positional externality.

Positional externality. Occurs when an increase in one person's performance reduces the expected reward of another's in situations in which reward depends on relative performance.

Positive economic principle. One that predicts how people will behave.

Positive externality. *See* **External benefit.**

Potential output, Y^*. The maximum sustainable amount of output (real GDP) that an economy can produce; also known as *potential GDP* or *full-employment output.*

Poverty threshold. The level of income below which the federal government classifies a family as poor.

Precautionary saving. Saving for protection against unexpected setbacks such as the loss of a job or a medical emergency.

Present value of a perpetual annual payment. For an annual interest rate r, the present value (PV) of a perpetual annual payment (M) is the amount that would have to be deposited today at that interest rate to generate annual interest earnings of M: $PV = M / r$.

Price ceiling. A maximum allowable price, specified by law.

Price discrimination. The practice of charging different buyers different prices for essentially the same good or service.

Price elasticity of demand. The percentage change in the quantity demanded of a good or service that results from a 1 percent change in its price.

Price elasticity of supply. The percentage change in the quantity supplied that will occur in response to a 1 percent change in the price of a good or service.

Price index. A measure of the average price of a given class of goods or services relative to the price of the same goods and services in a base year.

Price level. A measure of the overall level of prices at a particular point in time as measured by a price index such as the CPI.

Price setter. A firm with at least some latitude to set its own price.

Price taker. A firm that has no influence over the price at which it sells its product.

Principal amount. The amount originally lent.

Prisoner's dilemma. A game in which each player has a dominant strategy, and when each plays it, the resulting payoffs are smaller than if each had played a dominated strategy.

Private saving. The saving of the private sector of the economy is equal to the after-tax income of the private sector minus consumption expenditures ($Y - T - C$); private saving can be further broken down into household saving and business saving.

Producer surplus. The economic surplus gained by the sellers of a product as measured by the cumulative difference between the price received and their respective reservation prices.

Production possibilities curve. A graph that describes the maximum amount of one good that can be produced for every possible level of production of the other good.

Profit. The total revenue a firm receives from the sale of its product minus all costs—explicit and implicit—incurred in producing it.

Profit-maximizing firm. A firm whose primary goal is to maximize the difference between its total revenues and total costs.

Profitable firm. A firm whose total revenue exceeds its total cost.

Protectionism. The view that free trade is injurious and should be restricted.

Public saving. The saving of the government sector is equal to net tax payments minus government purchases ($T - G$).

Purchasing power parity (PPP). The theory that nominal exchange rates are determined as necessary for the law of one price to hold.

Pure monopoly. The only supplier of a unique product with no close substitutes.

Q

Quantity equation. Money times velocity equals nominal GDP: $M \times V = P \times Y$.

Quota. A legal limit on the quantity of a good that may be imported.

R

Rate of inflation. The annual percentage rate of change in the price level, as measured, for example, by the CPI.

Rational person. Someone with well-defined goals who tries to fulfill those goals as best he or she can.

Rational spending rule. Spending should be allocated across goods so that the marginal utility per dollar is the same for each good.

Rationing function of price. Changes in prices distribute scarce goods to those consumers who value them most highly.

Real exchange rate. The price of the average domestic good or service *relative* to the price of the average foreign good or service, when prices are expressed in terms of a common currency.

Real GDP. A measure of GDP in which the quantities produced are valued at the prices in a base year rather than at current prices; real GDP measures the actual *physical volume* of production.

Real interest rate. The annual percentage increase in the purchasing power of a financial asset; the real interest rate on any asset equals the nominal interest rate on that asset minus the inflation rate.

Real price. Dollar price of a good relative to the average dollar price of all other goods and services.

Real quantity. A quantity that is measured in physical terms—for example, in terms of quantities of goods and services.

Real wage. The wage paid to workers measured in terms of purchasing power; the real wage for any given period is calculated by dividing the nominal (dollar) wage by the CPI for that period.

Recession (or contraction). A period in which the economy is growing at a rate significantly below normal.

Recessionary gap. A negative output gap, which occurs when potential output exceeds actual output ($Y < Y^*$).

Relative price. The price of a specific good or service *in comparison to* the prices of other goods and services.

Repeated prisoner's dilemma. A standard prisoner's dilemma that confronts the same players repeatedly.

Reserve requirements. Set by the Fed, the minimum values of the ratio of bank reserves to bank deposits that commercial banks are allowed to maintain.

Reserve-deposit ratio. Bank reserves divided by deposits.

Revaluation. An increase in the official value of a currency (in a fixed-exchange-rate system).

Rise. *See* **Slope.**

Risk premium. The rate of return that financial investors require to hold risky assets minus the rate of return on safe assets.

Run. *See* **Slope.**

S

Saving. Current income minus spending on current needs.

Saving rate. Saving divided by income.

Seller's reservation price. The smallest dollar amount for which a seller would be willing to sell an additional unit, generally equal to marginal cost.

Seller's surplus. The difference between the price received by the seller and his or her reservation price.

Short run. A period of time sufficiently short that at least some of the firm's factors of production are fixed.

Short-run equilibrium. Situation when there is either an expansionary gap or a recessionary gap; graphically, this is where the *AD* curve and the *AS* curve intersect at a point either to the left or to the right of the *LRAS* curve.

Short-run equilibrium output. The level of output at which output *Y* equals planned aggregate expenditure *PAE*; the level of output that prevails during the period in which prices are predetermined.

Shortage. *See* **Excess demand.**

Skill-biased technological change. Technological change that affects the marginal products of higher-skilled workers differently from those of lower-skilled workers.

Slope. In a straight line, the ratio of the vertical distance the straight line travels between any two points (*rise*) to the corresponding horizontal distance (*run*).

Socially optimal quantity. The quantity of a good that results in the maximum possible economic surplus from producing and consuming the good.

Stabilization policies. Government policies that are used to affect planned aggregate expenditure, with the objective of eliminating output gaps.

Stock. A measure that is defined at a point in time.

Stock (or equity). A claim to partial ownership of a firm.

Store of value. An asset that serves as a means of holding wealth.

Structural unemployment. The long-term and chronic unemployment that exists even when the economy is producing at a normal rate.

Substitutes. Two goods are substitutes in consumption if an increase in the price of one causes a rightward shift in the demand curve for the other (or if a decrease causes a leftward shift).

Substitution effect. The change in the quantity demanded of a good that results because buyers switch to or from substitutes when the price of the good changes.

Sunk cost. A cost that is beyond recovery at the moment a decision must be made.

Supply curve. A graph or schedule showing the quantity of a good that sellers wish to sell at each price.

Supply-side policy. A policy that affects potential output.

Surplus. *See* **Excess supply.**

T

Target inflation rate. The Fed's long-run goal for inflation.

Target real interest rate. The Fed's long-run goal for the real interest rate.

Tariff. A tax imposed on an imported good.

Tightening monetary policy. A situation where the Fed lowers its long-run target for the inflation rate.

Time value of money. The fact that a given dollar amount today is equivalent to a larger dollar amount in the future because the money can be invested in an interest-bearing account in the meantime.

Tit-for-tat. A strategy for the repeated prisoner's dilemma in which players cooperate on the first move, then mimic their partner's last move on each successive move.

Total cost. The sum of all payments made to the firm's fixed and variable factors of production.

Total expenditure = Total revenue. The dollar amount consumers spend on a product is equal to the dollar amount sellers receive.

Total revenue. *See* **Total expenditure.**

Total surplus. The difference between the buyer's reservation price and the seller's reservation price.

Trade balance (or net exports). The value of a country's exports less the value of its imports in a particular period (quarter or year).

Trade deficit. When imports exceed exports, the difference between the value of a country's imports and the value of its exports in a given period.

Trade surplus. When exports exceed imports, the difference between the value of a country's exports and the value of its imports in a given period.

Tragedy of the commons. The tendency for a resource that has no price to be used until its marginal benefit falls to zero.

Transfer payments. Payments the government makes to the public for which it receives no current goods or services in return.

Trough. The end of a recession; the low point of economic activity prior to a recovery.

U

Unattainable point. Any combination of goods that cannot be produced using currently available resources.

Undervalued exchange rate. An exchange rate that has an officially fixed value less than its market equilibrium value.

Unemployment rate. The number of unemployed people divided by the labor force.

Unemployment spell. A period during which an individual is continuously unemployed.

Unit elastic. The demand for a good is unit elastic with respect to price if its price elasticity of demand is equal to 1.

Unit of account. A basic measure of economic value.

V

Value added. For any firm, the market value of its product or service minus the cost of inputs purchased from other firms.

Value of marginal product of labor (*VMP*). The dollar value of the additional output a firm gets by employing one additional unit of labor.

Variable. A quantity that is free to take a range of different values.

Variable cost. A cost that varies with the level of an activity; the sum of all payments made to the firm's variable factors of production.

Variable factor of production. An input whose quantity can be altered in the short run.

Velocity. A measure of the speed at which money changes hands in transactions involving final goods and services, or, equivalently, nominal GDP divided by the stock of money. Numerically, $V = (P \times Y) / M$, where V is velocity, $P \times Y$ is nominal GDP, and M is the money supply whose velocity is being measured.

Vertical intercept. In a straight line, the value taken by the dependent variable when the independent variable equals zero.

W

Wealth. The value of assets minus liabilities.

Wealth effect. The tendency of changes in asset prices to affect households' wealth and thus their consumption spending.

Worker mobility. The movement of workers between jobs, firms, and industries.

INDEX

Page numbers followed by n indicate material found in notes.

B

E

G

H

P

Q

R

S

T

THINK LIKE AN ECONOMIST

OBSERVE. ANALYZE. UNDERSTAND.

Why do the keypad buttons on drive-up automatic teller machines have Braille dots?

Why do brides spend so much money—often many thousands of dollars—on wedding dresses they will never wear again, while grooms often rent cheap tuxedos, even though they will have many future occasions that would call for one?

Thinking like an economist is looking at your surroundings and seeing that economic principles can help you answer a host of interesting questions from everyday experiences.

Thinking like an economist enables you to first make sense of patterns and trends that surface all around you and then apply your insights to future possibilities in your social and professional world. The ability to provide rational explanations for odd or seemingly irrational situations will develop with practice and application of the principles you will learn in this course.

Are you ready to think like an economist?